# 2017 Valuation Handbook

# International Guide to Cost of Capital

Market Results Through December 2016 and March 2017

Duff & Phelps

WILEY

The *2017 Valuation Handbook – International Guide to Cost of Capital* provides country-level country risk premia (CRPs), Relative Volatility (RV) factors, and equity risk premia (ERPs) which can be used to estimate country-level cost of cost of equity capital globally, for up to 188 countries, and from the perspective of investors based in any one of up to 56 countries.

---

*"Measuring the impact of country risk in determining the international cost of capital is one of the most vexing issues in finance. Any company doing international cost of capital estimation must, at minimum, consult the 2017 Valuation Handbook – International Guide to Cost of Capital".*

**Campbell R. Harvey**, Professor of International Business at the Fuqua School of Business, Duke University

---

# About the Data

The information and data presented in the *2017 Valuation Handbook – International Guide to Cost of Capital* and its associated intra-year update has been obtained with the greatest of care from sources believed to be reliable, but is not guaranteed to be complete, accurate or timely. Duff & Phelps, LLC (www.duffandphelps.com) and/or its data providers expressly disclaim any liability, including incidental or consequential damages, arising from the use of the *2017 Valuation Handbook – International Guide to Cost of Capital* and its associated intra-year update or any errors or omissions that may be contained in the *2017 Valuation Handbook – International Guide to Cost of Capital* and its associated intra-year update, or any other product (existing or to be developed) based upon the methodology and/or data published herein. One of the sources of raw data used to produce the derived data and information herein is Morningstar, Inc. Use of raw data from Morningstar to produce the derived data and information herein does not necessarily constitute agreement by Morningstar, Inc. of any investment philosophy or strategy presented in this publication.

# About Duff & Phelps

Duff & Phelps is the premier global valuation and corporate finance advisor with expertise in complex valuation, disputes and investigations, M&A, real estate, restructuring, and compliance and regulatory consulting. The firm's more than 2,000 employees serve a diverse range of clients from offices around the world. For more information, visit www.duffandphelps.com.

*M&A advisory, capital raising and secondary market advisory services in the United States are provided by Duff & Phelps Securities, LLC. Member FINRA/SIPC. Pagemill Partners is a Division of Duff & Phelps Securities, LLC. M&A advisory and capital raising services in Canada are provided by Duff & Phelps Securities Canada Ltd., a registered Exempt Market Dealer. M&A advisory and capital raising services in the United Kingdom and across Europe are provided by Duff & Phelps Securities Ltd. (DPSL), which is authorized and regulated by the Financial Conduct Authority. In Germany M&A advisory and capital raising services are also provided by Duff & Phelps GmbH, which is a Tied Agent of DPSL. Valuation Advisory Services in India are provided by Duff & Phelps India Private Limited under a category 1 merchant banker license issued by the Securities and Exchange Board of India.*

# Additional Resources

Duff & Phelps authors *five* books that focus on U.S. and international valuation theory, data, and risk premia (e.g., equity risk premia, risk-free rates, size premia, industry risk premia, betas, industry multiples and other statistics, etc.) for use in valuation models. The *Valuation Handbook – International Guide to Cost of Capital* (this book) is one of these five books.

Duff & Phelps produces *one* book that focuses on U.S. capital markets performance data (i.e., the history of returns of the capital markets in the U.S. from 1926 to the present). This resource, the *Stocks, Bonds, Bills, and Inflation*® *(SBBI*®*) Yearbook*, has been published for over 30 years.[i.1] The *SBBI Yearbook* does not provide extensive valuation data or methodology.[i.2]

The six books are:[i.3]

## U.S. and International Valuation Theory and Data

- *Cost of Capital: Applications and Examples (5th edition)*
- *Valuation Handbook – U.S. Guide to Cost of Capital*
- *Valuation Handbook – U.S. Industry Cost of Capital*
- *Valuation Handbook – International Guide to Cost of Capital*
- *Valuation Handbook – International Industry Cost of Capital*

## U.S. Capital Markets Performance Data

- *Stocks, Bonds, Bills, and Inflation (SBBI) Yearbook*

All six Duff & Phelps books are published by John Wiley & Sons (Hoboken, NJ). Each of the six books is summarized in the following sections.

To learn more about cost of capital issues, and to ensure that you are using the most recent Duff & Phelps Recommended ERP, visit www.duffandphelps.com/CostofCapital.

---

[i.1] "Stocks, Bonds, Bills, and Inflation" and "SBBI" are registered trademarks of Morningstar, Inc. All rights reserved. Used with permission.

[i.2] Morningstar previously published two "Ibbotson SBBI" yearbooks: (i) The *SBBI "Classic" Yearbook*, which is now produced by Duff & Phelps and published by John Wiley & Sons as the "SBBI Yearbook" starting in 2016 (the word "Classic" was dropped from the title), and (ii) the *SBBI "Valuation" Yearbook*, which was discontinued by Morningstar in 2013. The former *SBBI Valuation Yearbook* was replaced by the *Valuation Handbook – U.S. Guide to Cost of Capital*, also produced by Duff & Phelps and published by John Wiley & Sons, starting in 2014.

[i.3] In 2014, 2015, and 2016 the four books comprising the Valuation Handbook series were named as follows: *Valuation Handbook – Guide to Cost of Capital, Valuation Handbook – Industry Cost of Capital, International Valuation Handbook – Guide to Cost of Capital*, and *International Valuation Handbook – Industry Cost of Capital*. Starting with the 2017 Valuation Handbook editions, the names of the four books were changed to: *Valuation Handbook – U.S. Guide to Cost of Capital, Valuation Handbook – U.S. Industry Cost of Capital, Valuation Handbook – International Guide to Cost of Capital*, and *Valuation Handbook – International Industry Cost of Capital*, respectively. For simplicity, in all 2017 books, intra-year updates, marketing materials, online tools, etc., the new names are used (even when referring to pre-2017 editions).

***Cost of Capital: Applications and Examples* 5th edition**

The authoritative, comprehensive overview of valuation theory, best practices, and proper use of data. This book puts an emphasis on practical application.

To learn more about the latest theory and practice in cost of capital estimation, see *Cost of Capital: Applications and Examples* 5th edition, by Shannon P. Pratt and Roger J. Grabowski (John Wiley & Sons, Inc., 2014).

The *Cost of Capital: Applications and Examples* 5th edition is a one-stop shop for background and current thinking on the development and uses of rates of return on capital. This book contains expanded materials on estimating the basic building blocks of the cost of equity capital, the risk-free rate, and equity risk premium, plus in-depth discussion of the volatility created by the 2008 financial crisis, the subsequent recession and uncertain recovery, and how those events have fundamentally changed how we need to interpret the inputs to the models we use to develop these estimates.

The *Cost of Capital: Applications and Examples* 5th edition includes case studies providing comprehensive discussion of cost of capital estimates for valuing a business and damages calculations for small and medium-sized businesses, cross-referenced to the chapters covering the theory and data. This book puts an emphasis on practical application. To that end, this updated edition provides readers with exclusive access to a companion website filled with supplementary materials, allowing you to continue to learn in a hands-on fashion long after closing the book.

The *Cost of Capital: Applications and Examples* has been published since 1998, and is updated every three to four years. The 6th edition of this book is scheduled to be available in early 2018.

*"Shannon Pratt and Roger Grabowski have produced a remarkably comprehensive review of the subject...it is a work that valuation practitioners, CFOs, and others will find an invaluable reference".*

**– Professor Richard Brealey**, Emeritus Professor of Finance, London Business School (from the Foreword)

*"Estimating the cost of capital is critical in determining the valuation of assets, in evaluating the capital structure of corporations, and in estimating the long-run expected return of investments. Shannon Pratt and Roger Grabowski have the most thorough text on the subject, not only providing various estimation methods, but also numerous ways to use the cost of capital".*

**– Professor Roger G. Ibbotson**, Professor Emeritus of Finance at the Yale School of Management, Chairman and Chief Investment Officer of Zebra Capital LLC, and former Chairman and founder of Ibbotson Associates, now part of Morningstar, Inc.

### Valuation Handbook – U.S. Guide to Cost of Capital

This annual book includes the U.S. cost of capital data inputs (equity risk premia, size premia, industry risk premia, risk premia over the risk-free rate, risk-free rates) that were previously published in the Morningstar/Ibbotson *Stocks, Bonds, Bills, and Inflation (SBBI) Valuation Yearbook* and the Duff & Phelps *Risk Premium Report*.

The *Valuation Handbook – U.S. Guide to Cost of Capital* can be used to develop cost of equity capital estimates (using both the build-up method and CAPM) for an individual business, business ownership interest, security, or intangible asset. This book includes many examples for using the data properly.

The *Valuation Handbook – U.S. Guide to Cost of Capital* has been published since 2014, and is updated annually with data through December 31 of the previous year (e.g., the *2014 Valuation Handbook – U.S. Guide to Cost of Capital* is "data through" December 31, 2013; the *2015 Valuation Handbook – U.S. Guide to Cost of Capital* is "data through" December 31, 2014, etc.). This book includes three optional intra-year quarterly updates (March, June, and September).

### Valuation Handbook – U.S. Industry Cost of Capital

This annual book provides industry-level cost of capital estimates (cost of equity capital, cost of debt capital, and weighted average cost of capital, or WACC), plus detailed industry-level statistics for sales, market capitalization, capital structure, various levered and unlevered beta estimates (e.g., ordinary-least squares (OLS) beta, sum beta, peer group beta, downside beta, etc.), valuation (trading) multiples, financial and profitability ratios, equity returns, aggregate forward-looking earnings-per share (EPS) growth rates, and more. Over 300 critical industry-level data points are calculated for approximately 180 U.S. industries (depending on data availability). Industries are organized by standard industrial classification (SIC) code.

The *Valuation Handbook – U.S. Industry Cost of Capital* can be used to benchmark, augment, and support the analyst's own custom analysis of the industry in which a subject business, business ownership interest, security, or intangible asset resides.

The *Valuation Handbook – U.S. Industry Cost of Capital* has been published since 2014, and is updated annually with data through March 31 of the current year (e.g., the *2014 Valuation Handbook – U.S. Industry Cost of Capital* is "data through" March 31, 2014; the *2015 Valuation Handbook – U.S. Industry Cost of Capital* is "data through" March 31, 2015, etc.). This book includes three optional intra-year quarterly updates (June, September, and December).

***Valuation Handbook – International Guide to Cost of Capital* (this book)**

This annual book provides country-level equity risk premia (ERPs), relative volatility (RV) factors, and country risk premia (CRPs).

This book can be used to estimate country-level cost of equity capital globally, for up to 188 countries, from the perspective of investors based in any one of up to 56 countries (depending on data availability).

The *Valuation Handbook – International Guide to Cost of Capital* has been published since 2014, and is updated annually with data through December of the previous year and March of the current year (e.g., the *2014 Valuation Handbook – International Guide to Cost of Capital* is "data through" December 31, 2013 and March 31, 2014; the *2015 Valuation Handbook – International Guide to Cost of Capital* is "data through" December 31, 2014 and March 31, 2015, etc.). This book includes one optional semi-annual update with data through June and September.

*"Measuring the impact of country risk in determining the international cost of capital is one of the most vexing issues in finance. Any company doing international cost of capital estimation must, at minimum, consult the Valuation Handbook – International Guide to Cost of Capital".*

– **Campbell R. Harvey**, Professor of International Business at the Fuqua School of Business, Duke University

***Valuation Handbook – International Industry Cost of Capital***

This annual book provides the same type of rigorous industry-level analysis published in the U.S.-centric *Valuation Handbook – U.S. Industry Cost of Capital*, on a global scale.

This book includes industry-level analyses for four global economic areas: (i) the "World", (ii) the European Union, (iii) the Eurozone, and (iv) the United Kingdom.[i.4] Industries in the book are identified by their Global Industry Classification Standard (GICS) code. Each of the four global economic area's industry analyses are presented in three currencies: (i) the euro (€ or EUR), (ii) the British pound (£ or GBP), and (iii) the U.S. Dollar ($ or USD).

This annual book provides industry level cost of capital estimates (cost of equity capital, cost of debt capital, and weighted average cost of capital, or WACC), plus detailed industry-level statistics for sales, market capitalization, capital structure, various levered and unlevered beta estimates (e.g., ordinary-least squares (OLS) beta, sum beta, peer group beta, downside beta, etc.), valuation (trading) multiples, financial and profitability ratios, equity returns, aggregate forward-looking earnings-per share (EPS) growth rates, and more. Over 300 critical industry-level data points are calculated for each industry (depending on data availability). Industries are organized by global industry classification standard (GICS) code.

---

[i.4] In the *Valuation Handbook – International Industry Cost of Capital*, "World" companies are defined as companies that (i) are components of the MSCI ACWI IMI, and (ii) satisfy the rigorous screening requirements that are employed to define the company sets used therein.

The *Valuation Handbook – International Industry Cost of Capital* can be used to benchmark, augment, and support the analyst's own custom analysis of the industry in which a subject business, business ownership interest, security, or intangible asset resides.

The *Valuation Handbook – International Industry Cost of Capital* has been published since 2015, and is updated annually with data through March 31 of the current year (e.g., the *2015 Valuation Handbook – International Industry Cost of Capital* is "data through" March 31, 2015; the *2016 Valuation Handbook – International Industry Cost of Capital* is "data through" March 31, 2016, etc.). This book includes one optional semi-annual update with data through September.

### Stocks, Bonds, Bills, and Inflation (SBBI) Yearbook

This annual book has been the definitive annual resource for historical U.S. capital markets performance data for over 30 years.

Starting with the 2016 edition, the *Stocks, Bonds, Bills, and Inflation (SBBI) Yearbook* is now produced by Duff & Phelps and published by John Wiley & Sons. The *SBBI Yearbook* was previously published by Morningstar, Inc. under the name "Ibbotson *Stocks, Bonds, Bills, and Inflation (SBBI) Classic Yearbook*".[i.5]

This book includes returns, index values, and statistical analyses of U.S. large company stocks, small company stocks, long-term corporate bonds, long-term government bonds, intermediate-term government bonds, U.S. Treasury bills, and inflation from January 1926 to present (monthly).

Anyone serious about investments or investing needs an appreciation of capital market history. Such an appreciation, which can be gained from this book, is equally valuable to the individual and institutional investor, practitioners and scholars in finance, economics, and business; portfolio strategists; and security analysts seeking to benchmark their own investment performance. The *SBBI Yearbook* is a thinking person's guide to using historical data to understand the financial markets and make decisions.

---

[i.5]  The *SBBI Yearbook* was published by Morningstar, Inc. from 2007 through 2015, and by Ibbotson Associates in years prior to 2007.

# Purchasing Information

## U.S. and International Valuation Theory and Data

- *Cost of Capital: Applications and Examples (5th edition)*
- *Valuation Handbook – U.S. Guide to Cost of Capital*
- *Valuation Handbook – U.S. Industry Cost of Capital*
- *Valuation Handbook – International Guide to Cost of Capital*
- *Valuation Handbook – International Industry Cost of Capital*

To order additional copies of the *2017 Valuation Handbook – International Guide to Cost of Capital* (this book), or other Duff & Phelps valuation data resources published by John Wiley & Sons, please visit www.wiley.com/go/ValuationHandbooks, or call: U.S. (800) 762-2974 International (317) 572-3993 or fax (317) 572-4002.

## U.S. Capital Markets Performance Data

- *Stocks, Bonds, Bills, and Inflation (SBBI) Yearbook*

To order copies of the *SBBI Yearbook*, please visit www.wiley.com/go/sbbiyearbook, or call: U.S. (800) 762-2974 International (317) 572-3993 or fax (317) 572-4002.

# Table of Contents

# Acknowledgements

**Authors**

Roger J. Grabowski, FASA
Managing Director, Duff & Phelps

James P. Harrington
Director, Duff & Phelps

Carla Nunes
Managing Director, Duff & Phelps

**Thank you**

The authors give special thanks to Senior Associate Kevin Madden, Vice President Jamie Warner, and Analysts Aaron Russo and Andrew Vey of Duff & Phelps for their assistance in assembling the exhibits presented herein, analysis, editing, and quality control. We thank Executive Assistant Michelle Phillips for production assistance, and Director Kelly Hunter for her coordination of data licensing issues. We give thanks to the following professors: Professors Elroy Dimson, Paul Marsh, and Mike Staunton at the London Business School for providing guidance and data permissions for usage of information from the *Credit Suisse Global Investment Returns Yearbook 2017*; Professor Eric Peek at Rotterdam School of Management, Erasmus University, Netherlands for the ongoing research examining the relationships between firm size and cost of capital in the European equity markets; Professors Javier Estrada and Pablo Fernandez at the University of Navarra IESE Business School for providing data permissions for usage of information from their research and surveys; Dr. Steven Bishop, Director of Education & Management Consulting Services Pty Ltd. and Visiting Fellow at Macquarie University Applied Finance Centre in Sydney, Australia, where he teaches in the Master of Applied Finance program, for his assistance in developing equity risk premium guidance for Australia; Dr. Laurence Booth at Rotman School of Management, University of Toronto, for assisting us in developing the forward-looking ERP and base cost of equity estimates for Canada. Finally, we give special thanks to Professor Campbell R. Harvey of the Duke University Fuqua School of Business for his insights and guidance in regards to international cost of capital, and the Erb-Harvey-Viskanta Country Credit Rating Model.

# Introduction

In 2014, Duff & Phelps introduced the *2014 Valuation Handbook – International Guide to Cost of Capital*. Now in its fourth year of printing, the *2017 Valuation Handbook – International Guide to Cost of Capital* (this book) provides the same type of country-level cost of capital analyses previously published in the (now discontinued) Morningstar/Ibbotson international cost of capital reports.[i.6]

The *2017 Valuation Handbook – International Guide to Cost of Capital* is published with data through (i) December 31, 2016 and (ii) March 31, 2017 (depending on the model being presented). An intra-year Semi-annual Update with data through (i) June 30, 2017 and (ii) September 30, 2017 (depending on the model being presented) is available.[i.7]

The *2017 Valuation Handbook – International Guide to Cost of Capital* provides country-level country risk premia (CRPs), Relative Volatility (RV) factors, and equity risk premia (ERPs) which can be used to estimate country-level cost of equity capital globally, for up to 188 countries, from the perspective of investors based in any one of up to 56 countries.[i.8] The *2017 Valuation Handbook – International Guide to Cost of Capital* contains data which the valuation analyst will find useful in benchmarking, augmenting, and supporting his or her own international cost of capital estimates.

**Who Should Use the *2017 Valuation Handbook – International Guide to Cost of Capital***

The *2017 Valuation Handbook – International Guide to Cost of Capital* is designed to provide useable international valuation data and methodology to:

- **Traditional professional valuation analysts** valuing public and private companies with operations located in multiple countries.

- **Corporate finance officers** when pricing or evaluating proposed cross-border mergers and acquisitions (M&A), raising private or public equity in different jurisdictions, and/or dealing with cross-border stakeholder disputes.

- **Corporate officers** when evaluating investments for capital budgeting decisions in different countries.

- **Investment bankers** when pricing initial (or follow-on) public offerings, proposed M&A transactions, and private equity financing for target entities located in a variety of countries.

---

[i.6] The three discontinued Morningstar/Ibbotson international cost capital reports were (i) the *International Cost of Capital Report*, (ii) the *International Cost of Capital Perspectives Report*, and (iii) the *International Equity Risk Premium Report*. The 2013 versions of these reports, with data primarily through December 31, 2012 (with some models updated through March 2013), were the final versions published by Morningstar.

[i.7] The Semi-annual Update is (i) optional, and (ii) not sold separately.

[i.8] Depending on the estimation model being employed, and data availability. Some models do not include estimates for all countries.

- **Private equity investors** when pricing or evaluating proposed cross-border M&A transactions, making capital budgeting decisions for entities located in different countries, or updating quarterly valuations of portfolio companies with operations located in foreign countries.

- **Portfolio managers** evaluating investments outside of the country where they are based.

- **Real estate investors** when pricing or evaluating proposed real estate investments, or updating valuations of portfolio companies with operations located in foreign countries.

- **CPAs and valuation professionals** dealing with either valuations for financial and tax reporting purposes, or with dispute and bankruptcy valuations issues involving companies with operations located in multiple countries.

- **Transfer pricing economists** dealing with valuation and transfer of intellectual property and other intangible assets across jurisdictions.

- **Judges and attorneys** dealing with valuation issues in M&A, shareholder and partner disputes, damage cases, solvency cases, bankruptcy reorganizations, regulatory rate setting, transfer pricing, and financial reporting involving entities with operations located in multiple jurisdictions.

**New and Notable**

The *Valuation Handbook – International Guide to Cost of Capital* is in its fourth year of publication with the release of the 2017 edition (this book). The inaugural 2014 edition was self-published by Duff & Phelps; starting with the 2015 edition, the *Valuation Handbook – International Guide to Cost of Capital* is published by John Wiley & Sons, marking a significant milestone in the evolution of the book.

Country Credit Ratings (CCRs) are an important input used to produce the country risk premia (CRPs) in Data Exhibit 4, the "Erb-Harvey-Viskanta Country Credit Rating Model". In February 2017, Institutional Investor LLC communicated to Duff & Phelps that it would no longer conduct and publish the results of its semi-annual "Country Credit Survey" from which CCRs were obtained.[i.9] September 2016 was the final publication date of Institutional Investor CCRs.[i.10]

Starting with the *2017 Valuation Handbook – International Guide to Cost of Capital* (this book):

1. The source of *new* country credit ratings (post September 2016) used to produce the CRPs in Data Exhibit 4 is Institutional Investor's parent company, Euromoney Institutional Investor PLC.

---

[i.9] Institutional Investor LLC is a leading business-to-business publisher, focused on international finance. Institutional Investor LLC is a division of Euromoney Institutional Investor PLC. To learn more, visit http://www.institutionalinvestor.com.

[i.10] Institutional Investor CCRs were published from September 1979 through September 2016 on a semi-annual basis (September, March), with one exception: Institutional Investor did not publish March 2010 CCRs.

Specifically, the *previously published* Institutional Investor country credit ratings (through September 2016) will continue to be used in the regression analyses used to produce the CRPs in Data Exhibit 4, and from October 2016 forward Euromoney's country risk scores will be used.[i.11]

**Note:** For simplicity, these inputs (the Institutional Investor country credit ratings and the Euromoney country risk scores) are referred to collectively herein as "country credit ratings", or "CCRs", and the model's name is unchanged and will continue to be referred to as the "Erb Harvey-Viskanta Country Credit Rating Model", or "CCR Model".

2.  The model will now move to a 30-year *rolling* regression, rather than using data back to September 1979. This reflects the trend observed in recent decades by individual countries' economies toward a greater integration with the global economy and global financial markets (i.e., "globalization"); moving this analysis to a 30-year rolling regression ensures that only (relatively) more recent information about the stage of development of each country's economy is impacting the results.

3.  The model will now make the following assumptions:

    a.  If both the "home" country (i.e., the country in which the investor is based) and the "foreign" country (i.e., the investee country; the country in which the investment resides) have an S&P sovereign credit rating of AAA, the concluded country risk premium (CRP) is 0.0%. The United States is treated as a AAA rated country for purposes of implementing this model (see rationale in Chapter 4).

    b.  If the "home" country has an S&P sovereign credit rating of AAA and the "foreign" country has an S&P credit rating *below* AAA (i.e., a worse credit rating), *and* has a calculated CRP of *less* than 0.0% (i.e., a negative implied premium), the CRP assigned is 0.0% (and vice versa).

The first change was out of necessity: a new source of country credit ratings was needed to replace the discontinued series. The source that was identified as being the best fit for a substitute is produced by Institutional Investor's own parent company (Euromoney Institutional Investor PLC).

The second change was a methodological change that was designed with the goal of better reflecting the ongoing change and evolving integration of global markets. These changes may entail significant changes to some countries' relative risk relative to what has been reported in prior years.

The third change (3a) harmonizes the Country Credit Rating Model, the Country Yield Spread Model, and the Relative Volatility Model (this assumption is *already* in place in the latter two models).

---

[i.11]   Euromoney Institutional Investor PLC is an international business-to-business information and events group listed on the London Stock Exchange, with 2,300 employees worldwide and a portfolio of over 50 specialist businesses spanning macroeconomic data, investment research, news and market analysis, industry forums and institutes, financial training and excellence awards. To learn more visit: http://www.euromoneyplc.com/.

The fourth change (3b) is in effect starting with the *2017 Valuation Handbook – International Guide to Cost of Capital* (this book) for (i) the Country Credit Rating Model and (ii) the Country Yield Spread Model, but *not* in the Relative Volatility Model.[i.12]

**About the *Valuation Handbook – International Guide to Cost of Capital***

The *2017 Valuation Handbook – International Guide to Cost of Capital* consists of four primary parts:

**Part 1:** Chapters 1 and 2 include an overview of international cost of capital issues, and a discussion of the strengths and weaknesses of some of the most commonly used models.

**Part 2:** Chapters 3, 4, 5, and 6 include descriptions of the models used to calculate the valuation data presented in the four data exhibits. These chapters also include examples for properly using the data presented in the four data exhibits to estimate cost of equity capital on a global basis.

**Part 3:** Chapter 7 includes a discussion of an academic study sponsored by Duff & Phelps that investigates the "size" effect in Europe. The size effect is based on the empirical observation that companies of smaller size are associated with greater risk and, therefore, have a greater cost of capital.

**Part 4:** Data Exhibits for (i) International ERP, (ii) Country Yield Spread Model, (iii) Relative Volatility Model, (iv) the Erb-Harvey-Viskanta Country Credit Rating Model, and (v) summary statistics from research conducted by Professor Erik Peek (Rotterdam School of Management, Erasmus University) about the size effect in Europe.

Data Exhibits 1 through 4 provide equity risk premia (ERPs), country-level country risk premia (CRPs), and relative volatility (RV) factors that can be used to estimate country-level cost of equity capital for up to 188 countries globally, from the perspective of investors based in any one of up to 56 different countries. Data Exhibits 5A, 5B, and 5C provide "premia over the risk-free rate", "premia over CAPM" (i.e., size premia), and "comparative risk characteristics", respectively, from Professor Peek's research that may aid in the examination of the relationships between firm size and the cost of equity capital in European equity markets.

The risk premia presented herein are calculated as of December 31, 2016 and March 31, 2017 (with the exception of Data Exhibit 1 and Data Exhibit 5, which are as of December 31, 2016 only). The five data exhibits presented herein are described in detail below:

- **Data Exhibit 1 – Historical Equity Risk Premia (ERPs):** The term "equity risk premia" is often interchangeably referred to as the "market risk premium". The ERP represents the extra return (over the expected yield on risk-free securities) that investors expect to receive from an investment in the market portfolio of common stocks, typically represented by a

---

[i.12] Change 3b has *not* been in effect for the Relative Volatility Model in previous editions of the *Valuation Handbook – International Guide to Cost of Capital*, and is *not* in effect in the *2017 Valuation Handbook – International Guide to Cost of Capital* (this book). Change 3b may be instituted in the Relative Volatility Model in future editions, pending further study.

broad-based market index, and is one of the primary building blocks employed in the estimation of cost of capital.

In Data Exhibit 1, "historical" ERP estimates are provided for 16 different countries, in both U.S. Dollars (USD) and "Local" currencies (i.e., the currencies used in each of the 16 countries). Historical (i.e., realized) ERPs are calculated as the average difference in annual equity returns for a given stock market country index, minus the annual returns of a longer-term (and shorter-term) "risk-free" security for the same country.

- **Data Exhibit 2 – Country Yield Spread Model:** This empirical model is a practical adaptation of the capital asset pricing model (CAPM) to an international setting. This model was originally developed in USD in 1993 by researchers at investment bank Goldman Sachs.[i.13] In simple terms, "country" risk was quantified as the spread between the foreign country's government bond yield denominated in U.S. Dollars and the U.S. Treasury bond yield of the same maturity. In the analyses presented herein, the Country Yield Spread Model is used to calculate country risk premia (CRPs).

  The CRP estimates in Data Exhibit 2 (derived by employing the Country Yield Spread Model) can be used to estimate base country-level cost of equity capital estimates for 188 countries, from the perspective of a (i) U.S.-based investor, and (ii) from the perspective of an investor based in Germany.[i.14]

- **Data Exhibit 3 – Relative Volatility Model:** This is an application of the relative volatility (a.k.a. volatility spread) model, originally developed for "segmented" capital markets.[i.15] The volatility in segmented economies' equity markets is often greater than in a more developed, integrated country. In the model version presented herein, the relative volatility of each country's equity market is calculated relative to the U.S. (for the USD-based analysis) and Germany (for the EUR-based analysis). In the analyses presented herein, the Relative Volatility Model is used to calculate relative volatility (RV) factors. The RV factor attempts to isolate the incremental risk premium associated with investing in the foreign country as a function of the relative volatility of the foreign country's equity market and the home country's equity market.

---

[i.13] Jorge O. Mariscal and Rafaelina M. Lee, "The Valuation of Mexican Stocks: An Extension of the Capital Asset Pricing Model", 1993, Goldman Sachs, New York.

[i.14] Note that an investor based in other countries within the Eurozone (e.g., Spain) investing in say, Brazil, could use the same CRP information in Data Exhibit 2, provided that German government securities are being used as the proxy for the risk-free security when estimating the cost of equity for the subject company. This is because the analysis in Data Exhibit 2 is all being conducted in Euros, calculated against German government debt yields.

[i.15] Donald Lessard, "Incorporating country risk in the valuation of offshore projects", *Journal of Applied Corporate Finance* (Fall 1996): 9(3), 52–63.

The RV factor estimates in Data Exhibit 3 (derived by employing the Relative Volatility Model) can be used to estimate base country-level cost of equity capital estimates for 75 countries, from the perspective of a (i) U.S.-based investor, and (ii) from the perspective of an investor based in Germany.[i.16]

- **Data Exhibit 4 – Erb-Harvey-Viskanta Country Credit Rating Model:** The Erb-Harvey-Viskanta Country Credit Rating Model (CCR Model) allows for the calculation of estimated country risk premia (CRPs) for countries that have a country credit rating (published by Euromoney Institutional Investor PLC), even if they do *not* have a developed equity returns history (or even have no data at all).[i.17, i.18] In the analyses presented herein, the CCR Model is used to calculate country risk premia (CRPs). The CRP attempts to isolate the incremental risk premium associated with investing in another market other than the "home" country (i.e., the country in which the investor is based).

  The CRP estimates in Data Exhibit 4 (derived by employing the CCR Model) can be used to estimate base country-level cost of equity capital estimates for 175 countries, from 56 investor perspectives (a U.S.-based investor, plus investors based in any one of 55 additional countries).

- **Data Exhibit 5 – Study of Differences in Returns Between Large and Small Companies in Europe:** Exhibits 5A, 5B, and 5C provide an update through the end of 2016 of research conducted by Professor Erik Peek (Rotterdam School of Management, Erasmus University) about the size effect in Europe.[i.19, i.20]

  Studies of the size effect in countries with longer data availability, such as the United States, show that the size effect fluctuates over time. Given the short period of Professor Peek's original research of European markets (26 years, due to data constraints), a longer-term relationship could not be studied. Over time, adding more years of data to the analysis could help establish a more meaningful size relationship.

---

[i.16] Note that an investor based in other countries within the Eurozone (e.g., Spain) investing in say, Brazil, could use the same RV information in Data Exhibit 3, provided that a German equity risk premium (ERP) is being used as an input when estimating the cost of equity for the subject company. This is because the analysis in Data Exhibit 3 is all being conducted in Euros, calculated against German's equity market volatility.

[i.17] Claude Erb, Campbell Harvey, and Tadas Viskanta, "Expected Returns and Volatility in 135 Countries", *Journal of Portfolio Management* (Spring 1996): 46–58.

[i.18] We utilize Euromoney Country Risk ratings CCRs coupled with MSCI equity index returns to calculate raw cost of equity estimates based on the Erb-Harvey-Viskanta Country Credit Rating (CCR) Model.

[i.19] Professor Peek's original Research Note was commissioned as part of the ongoing research that Duff & Phelps performs and sponsors in the area cost of capital and other valuation issues. We thank Professor Erik Peek for his expertise in exploring this important topic. Professor Peek is at the Rotterdam School of Management, Erasmus University (RSM), Netherlands. The full research note "Differences in Returns Between Large and Small Companies in Europe", is available at http://ssrn.com/abstract=2499205.

[i.20] The original Research Note included analyses through December 2013; in the analyses presented herein the analyses have been updated through December 2016.

The information presented in Exhibits 5A, 5B, and 5C is as follows:

- **Data Exhibit 5A** – "Premia over the risk-free rate" (i.e., excess returns) in terms of the combined effect of *market* risk and *size* risk for 16 portfolios ranked by 6 different measures of size, plus a seventh composite size measure, the latter being a combination of the other 6 different measures of size.

- **Data Exhibit 5B** – "Premia over CAPM" (i.e., size premia) in terms of size risk for 16 portfolios ranked by 6 different measures of size, plus a composite seventh size measure, the latter being a combination of the other 6 different measures of size.

- **Data Exhibit 5C** – "Comparative Risk Characteristics" provides statistics about the companies that were used to form the portfolios in Data Exhibit 5A and 5B.

Overall, the results of Professor Peek's research suggest:

- Over the period 1990–2016, small European stocks earned a statistically and economically significant size premium relative to large stocks, even after controlling for size-related beta differences,

- The "size effect" was observable across a variety of measures of firm size,

- The "size effect" was not observed uniformly across countries or geographic regions within Europe, and

- While the observed "size effect" was statistically significant only for those portfolios comprised of the smallest firms during the 1990–2016 period, this does did not necessarily infer that the size effect is not present for larger companies in Europe.

For a more detailed discussion of Professor Peek's research, see Chapter 7, "Firm Size and the Cost of Equity Capital in Europe".

### ERPs, CRPs, and RVs Are *Different*, and Are Properly Used *Differently*

ERPs, CRPs, and RVs are *all* tools that can be used by analysts to estimate cost of equity capital, but are *different*, and should only be employed within the framework of their prescribed estimation models:

The ERP represents the extra return (over the expected yield on risk-free securities) that investors expect to receive from an investment in the market portfolio of common stocks, represented by a broad-based market index, and is one of the primary building blocks employed in the estimation of cost of capital, and is used in that context within the framework of various cost of capital estimation models (e.g., the CAPM and various build-up methods).

The CRP attempts to isolate the incremental risk premium associated with investing in another market other than the "home" country (i.e., the country in which the investor is based). CRPs are developed in the analyses herein by employing two models: the Country Yield Spread Model, and the CCR Model. The CRP is simply *added* to a cost of equity capital estimate.

The RV factor, on the other hand, attempts to isolate the incremental risk premium associated with investing in the foreign country as a function of the relative volatility of the foreign country's equity market and the home country's equity market. The RV factor is *multiplied* by the "excess return" term (beta x ERP) within the framework of the CAPM.

There is no single international cost of capital estimation model that is perfect (each has strengths, and each has weaknesses). As such, it is suggested that the analyst use the valuation data presented in the *2017 Valuation Handbook – International Guide to Cost of Capital* to develop a *range* of indicated cost of equity capital estimates. The specific facts and circumstances of the subject business, asset, or project being evaluated, coupled with the judgment of the analyst, will determine whether the actual cost of equity capital falls in the upper, middle, or lower part of the indicated range.

**Risk Premia Over the Risk-free Rate and Risk Premia over CAPM (i.e., size premia) Measure *Different* Types of Risks**

The main difference between the "premia over the risk-free rate" in Exhibit 5A and the "premia over CAPM" (i.e., size premia) in Exhibit 5B is the types of risk they are intended to measure, which in turn determines how the associated premia could theoretically be used within the context of various cost of equity capital estimation models.

Exhibit 5A provides "premia over the risk-free rate" which combine the effect of *market* risk and size risk ($RP_{m+s}$). Risk premia over the risk-free rate could theoretically be added to the risk-free rate within the context of a "build-up" model when estimating the cost of equity capital.

Exhibit 5B provides size premia that have been adjusted to remove the portion of excess return that is attributable to beta, leaving the residual as the size effect's contribution to excess return. These "beta-adjusted" size premia could theoretically be added as a "size adjustment" within the context of the capital asset pricing model (CAPM). Size premia are often added to CAPM estimates of the cost of equity capital to adjust for the difference between historical (observed) excess returns over the returns predicted by the textbook form of CAPM. This difference is typically found to be most prevalent in smaller companies, and thus is commonly called a "size premium" or "adjustment for size". For a detailed discussion of the differences in the premia presented in Exhibits 5A and 5B, see Chapter 7, "Firm Size and the Cost of Equity Capital in Europe".

# Chapter 1
# International Cost of Capital – Overview

*Practitioners typically are confronted with this situation: "I know how to value company in the United States, but this one is in Country X, a developing economy. What should I use for a discount rate?"*

**– Shannon P. Pratt and Roger J. Grabowski**, co-authors of *Cost of Capital*, 5th edition[1.1]

*Measuring the impact of country risk is one of most vexing issues in finance, particularly in emerging markets, where political and other country-specific risks can significantly change the dynamics of the project. It is absolutely essential to incorporate these risks into either the expected cash flows or the discount rate. While this point is not controversial, the key is using a reliable method to quantify these extra country risks.*

**– Campbell R. Harvey**, Professor of International Business at the Fuqua School of Business, Duke University

## Cost of Capital Defined

The cost of capital is the expected rate of return that the market requires in order to attract funds to a particular investment.[1.2]

The cost of capital is an opportunity cost, and is one of the most important concepts in finance. For example, if you are a chief finance officer contemplating a possible capital expenditure, you need to know what return you should look to earn from that investment. If you are an investor who needs to plan for future expenditures, you need to ask what return you can expect to earn on your portfolio.[1.3] The opportunity cost of capital is equal to the return that could have been earned on alternative investments at a similar level of risk and liquidity.[1.4]

The cost of capital may be described in simple terms as the expected return appropriate for the expected level of risk.[1.5] The cost of capital is also commonly called the *discount rate*, the *expected return*, or the *required return*.[1.6]

---

[1.1]   Shannon P. Pratt and Roger J. Grabowski, *Cost of Capital: Applications and Examples* 5th ed. (Hoboken, NJ: John Wiley & Sons, 2014).

[1.2]   Ibid.

[1.3]   Richard Brealey, London Business School, as quoted in the *2017 Valuation Handbook – U.S. Guide to Cost of Capital* (John Wiley & Sons, 2017).

[1.4]   Roger Ibbotson, Yale University, as quoted in the *2017 Valuation Handbook – U.S. Guide to Cost of Capital* (John Wiley & Sons, 2017).

[1.5]   Modern portfolio theory and related asset pricing models assume that investors are risk-averse. This means that investors try to maximize expected returns for a given amount of risk, or minimize risk for a given amount of expected returns.

[1.6]   When a business uses a given cost of capital to evaluate a commitment of capital to an investment or project, it often refers to that cost of capital as the "hurdle rate". The hurdle rate is the minimum expected rate of return that the business would be willing to accept to justify making the investment.

There are three broad valuation approaches: (i) the income approach, (ii) the market approach, and (iii) the cost or asset-based approach. The country risk premia (CRPs), equity risk premia (ERPs), and relative volatility (RVs) presented in *2017 Valuation Handbook – International Guide to Cost of Capital* can be used to develop cost of capital estimates for use in income approach-based valuation methods. Of the three aforementioned approaches to estimating value, only the income approach typically requires cost of capital estimates.

The cost of capital is a critical input used in income approaches to equate the *future* economic benefits (typically measured by projected cash flows) of a business, business ownership interest, security, or intangible asset to *present* value. The income approach is most often applied through a discounted cash flow (DCF) model.[1.7, 1.8]

A basic insight of capital market theory, that expected return is a function of risk, still holds when dealing with cost of equity capital in a *global* environment. Estimating a proper cost of capital (i.e., a discount rate) in developed countries, where a relative abundance of market data and comparable companies exist, requires a high degree of expertise. Estimating cost of capital in less-developed (i.e., "emerging") economies can present an even greater challenge, primarily due to lack of data (or poor data quality) and the potential for magnified financial, economic, and political risks. A good understanding of cost of capital concepts is, therefore, essential for executives making global investment decisions.

**Are Country Risks Real?**

Why should there be any incremental challenges when developing cost of capital estimates for a business, business ownership interest, security, or intangible asset based outside the United States? If investors are alike everywhere and markets are integrated, then there is no extra problem. However, if markets are (entirely or partially) isolated (i.e., segmented) from world markets, then we need to address the perceived (and real) risk differences between markets.

"Segmentation" in this context refers to markets (i.e., economies) that are not fully integrated into world markets (i.e., are to some degree isolated from world markets). Markets may be segmented due to a host of issues, such as regulation that restricts foreign investment, taxation differences, legal factors, information, trading costs, and physical barriers, among others. Experts do not agree on the extent or effects of market segmentation, although there can be no doubt that some markets are at least partially segmented.

The most common adjustments made by practitioners aimed at this segmentation problem are addressed by adding ad hoc country-specific risk premia to cost of capital estimates.

---

[1.7] Some common variations of the DCF model include the constant growth dividend discount model (sometimes referred to as Gordon Growth model), and various multi-stage models.

[1.8] The *2017 Valuation Handbook – International Guide to Cost of Capital* focuses on (i) providing *useable* risk premia for estimating cost of capital on a global scale, and (ii) providing guidance for properly using such data. The *2017 Valuation Handbook – International Guide to Cost of Capital*, as such, does *not* include in-depth discussions of valuation theory. Please refer to the *Cost of Capital: Applications and Examples* 5th edition for comprehensive discussions of valuation theory.

However, that does not answer the question of whether there should be an additional risk premium incorporated into the discount rate applied when valuing investments in those segmented markets in the first place. In theory, the only risks that are relevant for purposes of estimating the cost of equity are those that cannot be "diversified away". In a nutshell, the argument is that if there is low correlation across markets, much of the country risk may be considered specific risk that can be diversified away by global investors investing across all markets.

In an increasingly globalized (i.e., integrated) world economy, some researchers argue that country-specific risks have been reduced, and may not be as important as they once might have been. We agree in part – the inherent differences in risk between, say, "developed" countries and "emerging" economies, have likely *diminished* in most recent decades due to the trend toward globalization. However, it would probably be far too ambitious (and possibly ill-advised) to make decisions without considering the very real (albeit likely diminished) differences that continue to exist between countries. Or, as Bekaert and Harvey (2014) succinctly state:

*"Given the dramatic globalization over the past twenty years, does it make sense to segregate global equities into 'developed' and 'emerging' market buckets? We argue that the answer is still yes...emerging market assets still have higher risk than most developed markets – and as a result, continue to command higher expected returns"*.[1.9]

There are, of course, a range of opinions on this point. For example, some argue that the cost of capital for emerging markets may be lower if investing *across* countries is taken into account. The argument is that the low correlation between the risks of individual countries may provide a degree of diversification benefit to an investor who holds a portfolio of assets across many different countries.[1.10] Correlation can be a measure of potential "diversification benefits". Assets that are *highly* correlated offer *less* potential diversification benefit; assets that are *less* correlated offer *more* potential diversification benefits. Diversification in assets that are less correlated may provide a dampening of overall portfolio risk.

While it is true that the imperfect correlation between say, developed countries' and emerging countries' equity market returns implies a degree of risk mitigation due to potential diversification benefits, the correlation of world markets does appear to have significantly *increased* in the most recent decades.

---

[1.9] Geert Bekaert and Campbell Harvey, "Emerging Equity Markets in a Globalizing World", working paper, version: May 20, 2014, www.ssrn.com/abstract=2344817.

[1.10] Correlation can vary from −1 to +1, with a correlation of −1 implying a perfectly *negative* relationship, a correlation of +1 implying a perfectly *positive* relationship, and a correlation of 0 implying *no* relationship (i.e., "random"). If two variables generally move *together* (i.e., they both move up at the same time, or they both move down at the same time), they are *positively* correlated; if the two variables move *opposite* of each other (i.e., when one moves up, the other moves down), they are *negatively* correlated; if the two variables move *randomly* in relation to each other, they have *no* correlation, either positive or negative.

To illustrate, the MSCI "World" equity index (which includes 23 developed countries), and the MSCI "Emerging Market" index (which includes 23 emerging market countries) had a correlation factor of 0.52 over the 120-month period ending December 1998.[1.11, 1.12, 1.13] This correlation increased to 0.82 over the 120-month period ending March 2017, lending support to the notion that the potential diversification benefit to an investor who holds a portfolio of assets across many different countries *decreased* over the December 1998–March 2017 period, due to an *increased* correlation of the asset classes across the globe.

This same pattern exists when the correlations of MSCI's Europe, U.S., and the Far East equity indices are computed against the MSCI Emerging markets equity index (see Exhibit 1.1).[1.14, 1.15]

**Exhibit 1.1:** 120-month Correlation of the Total Returns of the MSCI World, U.S., Europe, and Far East Indices with the MSCI Emerging Markets Equity Index, as of December 1998 and March 2017

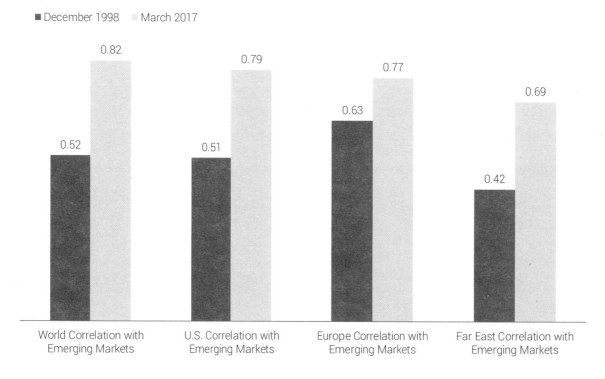

**Source of underlying data:** Morningstar *Direct* database. **Series used:** MSCI World GR LCL and MSCI EM GR LCL series used for "World Correlation with Emerging Markets" correlation; MSCI USA GR USD and MSCI EM GR USD series used for "U.S. Correlation with Emerging Markets" correlation; MSCI Far East GR LCL and MSCI EM GR LCL series used for "Far East Correlation with Emerging Markets" correlation; MSCI Europe GR (in €EUR) and MSCI EM GR (in €EUR) used for "Europe Correlation with Emerging Markets" correlation. All rights reserved, used with permission. For more information about MSCI indices, visit www.msci.com.

[1.11] MSCI is a leading provider of investment decision support tools to clients worldwide. MSCI provides indices, portfolio risk and performance analytics, and ESG data and research. To learn more about MSCI, visit www.msci.com.

[1.12] The MSCI World Index consists of the following 23 *developed* market country indices: Australia, Austria, Belgium, Canada, Denmark, Finland, France, Germany, Hong Kong, Ireland, Israel, Italy, Japan, Netherlands, New Zealand, Norway, Portugal, Singapore, Spain, Sweden, Switzerland, the United Kingdom, and the United States.

[1.13] The MSCI Emerging Market Index consists of the following 23 *emerging* market country indices: Brazil, Chile, China, Colombia, Czech Republic, Egypt, Greece, Hungary, India, Indonesia, Korea, Malaysia, Mexico, Peru, Philippines, Poland, Russia, Qatar, South Africa, Taiwan, Thailand, Turkey, and United Arab Emirates.

[1.14] The MSCI Europe Index consists of the following 15 *developed* market country indices: Austria, Belgium, Denmark, Finland, France, Germany, Ireland, Italy, Netherlands, Norway, Portugal, Spain, Sweden, Switzerland, and the United Kingdom.

[1.15] The MSCI Far East Index consists of the following 3 *developed* market country indices: Hong Kong, Japan, and Singapore.

While this analysis supports the notion that the potential diversification benefit of investors based in developed countries investing in emerging countries *decreased* in recent years, Bekaert and Harvey (2014) caution that "correlations between developed and emerging markets have increased, [but] the process of integration of these markets into world markets is incomplete".[1.16]

We conclude that in today's increasingly integrated economy there may be less theoretical justification for country risk premia than may have been warranted even a few decades ago. However, these risks *still* exist in the real world, and it would likely be unwise to make investment decisions without considering these risks. Furthermore, the ex-ante theoretical expectations that increased global financial market integration would diminish the risk (and therefore, required returns) associated with investing in emerging markets has not fully come to fruition. From a practical perspective, emerging markets are still clearly characterized by substantially more financial, economic, and political turmoil than are mature markets such as the U.S. or Germany. Increased correlation in recent years between developed and emerging markets means that those country-specific risks cannot be completely diversified away and, therefore country risk premia may be priced by investors.

If understood, differences between global economies can be planned for and considered in the structure of an investment well in advance. If not understood, these differences can result in unwise investments being pursued – or turn an otherwise sensible investment into a bad one.

**Risks Typically Associated With International Investment**

The risks associated with international investing can largely be characterized as *financial, economic,* or *political.* Many of these are the types of risks associated with investing in general – the possibility of loan default, the possibility of delayed payments of suppliers' credits, the possibility of inefficiencies brought about by the work of complying with unfamiliar (or burdensome) regulation, unexpected increases in taxes and transaction fees, differences in information availability, and liquidity issues, to name just a few. Some risks, however, are typically associated more with global investing – currency risk, lack of good accounting information, poorly developed legal systems, and even expropriation, government instability, or war.

**Financial Risks**

Financial risks typically entail an issue that is specifically money-centric (e.g., loan default, inability to easily repatriate profits to the home country, etc.). Among these types of risks, currency risk is probably the most familiar. Currency risk is the *financial* risk that exchange rates (the value of one currency versus another) will change unexpectedly.

---

[1.16] Geert Bekaert and Campbell Harvey, "Emerging Equity Markets in a Globalizing World", working paper, version: May 20, 2014, ssrn.com/abstract=2344817.

For example, when a French investor invests in Brazil, he or she must first convert Euros into the local currency, in this case the Brazilian Real (BRL). The returns that the French investor experiences in local currency terms are identical to the returns that a Brazilian investor would experience, but the French investor faces an additional risk in the form of currency risk when returns are "brought home" and must be converted back to Euros.[1.17]

Expected changes in exchange rates can often be hedged. However, even when currency hedging is used, exchange rate risk often remains. To the extent the Euro unexpectedly *increases* in value versus the Real (i.e., the Euro appreciates against the Real), the French investor is able to purchase fewer Euros for each Real he realized in the Brazilian investment when returns from the investment are repatriated, and his return is thus *diminished*.[1.18, 1.19]

Conversely, to the extent the Euro unexpectedly *decreases* in value versus the Real (i.e., the Euro depreciates against the Real), the French investor is able to purchase more Euros for each Real he realized in the Brazilian investment when returns from the investment are repatriated, and his return is thus *enhanced*.

For example, in 2007 Brazilian equities returned an astonishing 50% return in local terms (see Exhibit 1.2). Because the Euro *depreciated* against the Real in 2007, French-based investors in Brazilian stocks experienced an even *higher* return (62%) when they repatriated their returns and converted them to Euros. Similarly, in 2009 the Euro *depreciated* relative to the South African Rand (ZAR), and French-based investors realized higher returns in Euros once again versus the local South African investors. In a more recent example, U.S.-based investors investing in U.S. equities realized an approximate return of just 1.0% in 2015, but French investors making a similar investment in the U.S. realized an approximate 13% return when they repatriated their returns and converted them to Euros (the Euro *depreciated* against the U.S. Dollar in 2015, so the French investors could purchase *more* Euros with their Dollars when they repatriated their returns).

It is important to note that currency conversion effects can also work to *diminish* realized returns. For example, in 2016 U.K. equities returned 19% in local terms. Because the Euro *appreciated* against the British Pound in 2016 (largely due to the Brexit vote), French-based investors in U.K. stocks experienced a much *lower* return (3%) when they repatriated their returns and converted them to Euros.

---

[1.17]  For this example, we assume that the French and local investor are both subject to the same regulations, taxes, and local risks when investing in the same local asset.

[1.18]  We say "unexpectedly" for a reason. If the investor had been able to predict (at the time of investing) the precise exchange rate at which he/she would be repatriating his/her returns, these "expected" changes to the exchange rate would have been reflected in the expected cash flows of the investment at inception.

[1.19]  For example, say the French investor had achieved a 10% return in local (Brazilian) terms on his investment in a given year, but the Euro had unexpectedly appreciated by 3% in value relative to the Real over the same period. When the returns are repatriated, the French investor's overall return is diminished to approximately 6.7% [(1+10%)*(1−3%)−1] in Euro terms. Conversely, had the Euro depreciated in value versus the Real by 3%, the repatriated returns would be enhanced to approximately 13.3% [(1+10%)*(1+3%)−1] in Euro terms.

**Exhibit 1.2:** Currency Conversion Effects

|  |  | Return in Local Terms | Return to French Investors (EUR) | Currency Conversion Effect |
|---|---|---|---|---|
| 2007 | Brazil (BRL) | 50% | 62% | 12% |
| 2009 | South Africa (ZAR) | 26% | 53% | 27% |
| 2015 | Japan (JPY) | 10% | 22% | 12% |
| 2015 | Switzerland (CHF) | 2% | 13% | 11% |
| 2015 | Brazil (BRL) | -12% | -34% | -22% |
| 2015 | Argentina (ARS) | 52% | 11% | -41% |
| 2015 | United States (USD) | 1% | 13% | 12% |
| 2016 | United Kingdom (GBP) | 19% | 3% | -16% |

**Source of underlying data:** Morgan Stanley Capital International (MSCI) Brazil, South Africa, Japan, Switzerland, Brazil, and Argentina, gross return (GR) equity indices. For more information about MSCI, visit www.msci.com. The S&P 500 Index was used as the proxy for the United States equity market. For more information about S&P indices, visit http://us.spindices.com/indices/equity/sp-500. All data accessed through the Morningstar *Direct* database. For more information about Morningstar *Direct*, visit http://corporate.morningstar.com/.

A common misstep we often encounter is companies constructing forward-looking budgets or projection analyses in local currencies, and then converting these projections to the currency of the parent company using the spot rate.

This mistakenly assumes that the exchange rate will not change in the future. Projections, which are inherently forward-looking, need to embody expected currency conversion rates. We are interested in currency risks over the period of the projected net cash flows, not just in the spot market. Even then, these are merely estimates of future currency exchange rates and the actual exchange rate can vary from these estimates.

Does currency risk affect the cost of capital? One team of researchers found that emerging market exchange risks have a significant impact on risk premia and are time varying (for countries in the sample). They found that exchange risks affect risk premia as a separate risk factor and represent more than 50% of total risk premia for investments in emerging market equities. The exchange risk from investments in emerging markets was found to even affect the risk premia for investments in developed market equities.[1.20]

While exchange rate volatility appears to be partly systematic, researchers have found that despite not being constant, the currency risk premium is small and seems to fluctuate around zero.[1.21] A recently-published academic paper set out to study whether corporate managers should include foreign exchange risk premia in cost of equity estimations. The authors empirically estimated the differences between the cost of equity estimates of several risk-return models, including some models that have an explicit currency risk premia and others that do not. They found that adjusting

---

[1.20]   Francesca Carrieri, Vihang Errunza, and Basma Majerbi, "Does Emerging Market Exchange Risk Affect Global Equity Prices?" *Journal of Financial Quantitative Analysis* (September 2006): 511–540.

[1.21]   Piet Sercu, *International Finance: Theory into Practice*, (Princeton, NJ: Princeton University Press, 2009), Chapter 19.

for currency risk makes little difference, on average, in the cost of equity estimates, even for small firms and for firms with extreme currency exposure estimates. The authors concluded that, at a minimum, these results applied to U.S. companies, but future research would still have to be conducted for other countries.[1.22]

Rather than attempting to quantify and add a currency risk premium to the discount rate, using expected or forward exchange rates to translate projected cash flows into the home currency will inherently capture the currency risk, if any, priced by market participants.[1.23]

## Economic Risks

Global investors may also be exposed to *economic* risks associated with international investing. These risks may include the volatility of a country's economy as reflected in the current (and expected) inflation rate, the current account balance as a percentage of goods and services, burdensome regulation, and labor rules, among others. In the current environment, an economic risk that has come to the forefront is the sovereign debt crisis. The recent economic and financial crisis in Greece, for example, has prompted many governments around the world to re-think their own fiscal policies, as it becomes evident that current debt loads are likely unsustainable in many of these countries.

In Exhibit 1.3a, the 20 countries with the *overall* highest estimated government debt-to-GDP ratios are shown (regardless of the size of their economies), as of calendar year 2016. For example, the United States has a debt-to-GDP ratio of 107% (i.e., the United States' government debt is 7% *larger* than the United States' annual GDP), and Egypt has a debt-to-GDP ratio of 97% (i.e., Egypt's government debt is 3% *less* than Egypt's annual GDP)

In Exhibit 1.3b, the estimated government debt-to-GDP ratios for the 20 countries with the *largest* economies (as measured by GDP) are shown, also as of calendar year 2016. The rank of GDP size is shown in parentheses after each country's name. Saudi Arabia (with a ranking of "20") is the smallest GDP, and the United States (with a ranking of "1") is the largest GDP.

---

[1.22] A. Krapl and T. J. O'Brien, (2016), "Estimating Cost of Equity: Do You Need to Adjust for Foreign Exchange Risk?", *Journal of International Financial Management & Accounting*, 27: 5–25.

[1.23] This assumes that the valuation is being conducted in the home currency, by discounting projected cash flows denominated in the home currency, with a discount rate also denominated in home currency. Alternatively, the analyst can conduct the entire valuation in foreign currency terms (projected cash flows and discount rate are both in foreign currency terms), in which case the estimated value would be translated into the home currency using a spot exchange rate.

**Exhibit 1.3a:** 2016 Government Debt-to-GDP (in percent)

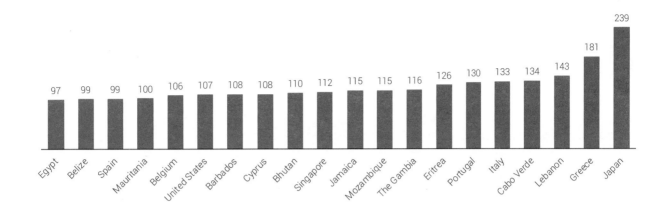

**Exhibit 1.3b:** 2016 Government Debt-to-GDP (in percent), 20 countries with largest GDP

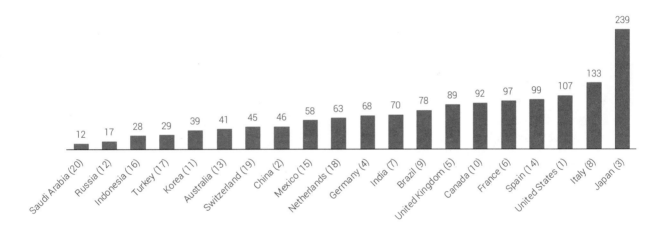

**Source of underlying data for Exhibit 1.3a and Exhibit 1.3b:** World Economic Outlook Database from the International Monetary Fund (IMF). For additional information, please visit: http://www.imf.org/external/pubs/ft/weo/2017/01/weodata/download.aspx.

There are costs that tend to go hand-in-hand with what might be considered unsustainable debt levels by governments. Lenders may demand a higher expected return to compensate them for additional default risk when investing not only in the country's sovereign debt, but also in businesses operating in those countries.

Governments may decide to increase the money supply in an effort to inflate their way out of debt. Ultimately, some governments may decide on outright currency devaluation or even a repudiation of debt (i.e., defaulting on their debt obligations). These risks are not entirely limited to less developed countries, but less developed countries may be more willing to resort to these extreme measures than developed countries.

**Political Risks**

Political risks can include government instability, expropriation, bureaucratic inefficiency, corruption, and even war. A relatively recent example of the effects of political risk is Venezuela's expropriation of various foreign-owned oil, gas, and mining interests. These actions tend to reduce Venezuela's attractiveness to foreign investors, who will likely demand a significantly higher expected return in exchange for future investment in the country – in effect raising their cost of capital estimates for projects located in Venezuela.

Exhibit 1.4 summarizes some of the risks that investors may view as unique or country-specific.

**Exhibit 1.4:** Reasons Typically Cited for Adding a Country Risk Premium Adjustment

**Political Risks**

- Repudiation of contracts by governments
- Expropriation of private investments in total or part through change in taxation
- Economic planning failures
- Political leadership and frequency of change
- External conflict
- Corruption in government
- Military in politics
- Organized religion in politics
- Lack of law-and-order tradition
- Racial and national tensions
- Civil war
- Poor quality of the bureaucracy
- Poorly developed legal system
- Political terrorism

**Financial Risks**

- Currency volatility plus the inability to convert, hedge, or repatriate profits
- Loan default or unfavorable loan restructuring
- Delayed payment of suppliers' credits
- Losses from exchange controls
- Foreign trade collection experience

**Economic Risks**

- Volatility of the economy
- Inflation: current and future expected
- Debt service as a percentage of exports of goods and services
- Current account balance of the country in which the subject company operates as a percentage of goods and services
- Parallel foreign exchange rate market indicators
- Labor issues

## Does the Currency Used to Project Cash Flows Impact the Discount Rate?

According to corporate finance theory, the currency of the projections should *always* be consistent with the currency of the discount rate. In practice, this means that the inputs used to derive a discount rate (the denominator) should be in the same currency used to project cash flows (the numerator). For example, if the projections are denominated in Australian Dollars, then the risk-free rate and equity risk premium inputs should also be denominated in (local) Australian Dollar terms.

There are two basic methods to address foreign currency cash flows in valuations, assuming the analysis is being conducted in *nominal* terms:

- Perform the valuation in the local (foreign) currency, discount the projected cash flows with a local (foreign) currency denominated discount rate (i.e., using foreign currency inputs), and convert the resulting value into the home currency (e.g., USD, EUR) at the spot exchange rate.

- Convert cash flows at a forecasted exchange rate into the home currency (e.g., USD, EUR) and discount the projected cash flows with a home country discount rate (using home currency inputs). In this case, the forecasted exchange rate already includes the risk associated with exchange rate fluctuations.

Notwithstanding the two general approaches outlined above, valuation and finance professionals may find themselves in a position where a local currency discount rate is needed and yet there are no reliable cost of capital inputs in the local (foreign) currency. What should you do in such a situation?

One can go back to one of the central ideas in international finance: the so-called "law of one price". The basic idea is that international investors explore profit arbitrage opportunities across financial markets in different countries, therefore guaranteeing that identical financial assets have similar prices, once adjusted for different currencies. This presumes competitive markets, where market imperfections do not exist.

Five key theoretical economic relationships result from these arbitrage activities:[1.24]

- Purchasing Power Parity

- Fisher Effect

- International Fisher Effect

- Interest Rate Parity

- Forward Rates as Unbiased Predictors of Future Spot Rates

---

[1.24] Alan C. Shapiro, *Multinational Financial Management*, 10th ed. (Hoboken, NJ: John Wiley & Sons, 2013).

It is beyond this publication to discuss these concepts on a detailed level. Several international finance textbooks have been written and published which cover this topic extensively. These theoretical relationships are also central to understanding and forecasting foreign exchange rates, as well as prices of other financial assets denominated in foreign currencies.[1.25]

The International Fisher Effect is formalized in the following equation:

$$Interest\ Rate_{Local\ Currency} = (1 + Interest\ Rate_{Home\ Currency}) * (1 + Inflation_{Local\ Currency}) / (1 + Inflation_{Home\ Currency}) - 1$$

The International Fisher Effect suggests that countries with high inflation rates should expect to see higher interest rates relative to countries with lower inflation rates.

This relationship can be extended from interest rates into discount rates, thereby allowing us to translate a home currency cost of capital estimate into a foreign currency indication.

However, it is crucial to understand that the International Fisher Effect relationship holds only in equilibrium. This presumes that (i) there is no government intervention in capital markets; and (ii) capital can flow freely in international financial markets from one currency to another, such that any potential arbitrage opportunity across countries will be quickly eliminated. In reality, market frictions (e.g., transaction costs, regulations, etc.) and government interventions do exist in practice, which means that using the International Fisher Effect to translate the home currency discount rate into a local currency will result in only an approximation.

Applying the International Fisher Effect to translate the rates of return on equity and debt would result in the following relationships:

$$Cost\ of\ Equity_{Local\ Currency} = (1 + Cost\ of\ Equity_{Home\ Currency}) * (1 + Expected\ Inflation_{Local\ Currency}) / (1 + Expected\ Inflation_{Home\ Currency}) - 1$$

$$Cost\ of\ Debt_{Local\ Currency} = (1 + Cost\ of\ Debt_{Home\ Currency}) * (1 + Expected\ Inflation_{Local\ Currency}) / (1 + Expected\ Inflation_{Home\ Currency}) - 1$$

In practice, these formulas tend to be applied in the context of using a single discount rate to compute the present value of the projected cash flows in both the discrete forecast period and in the terminal (or residual) year. Such application would therefore use long-term expected inflation rates as inputs for both the home and the local (foreign) country.

However, this practical application does not work well when dealing with a country with high inflation for the foreseeable future, but which is expected to decline over time. In such cases, valuation analysts may have to calculate multiple discount rates (one for each year in the projections) to reflect the changing inflation differentials, until a long-term, more sustainable, inflation differential is expected to be reached.

---

[1.25] See for example: 1) Chapters 4 and 19 of Piet Sercu (2009), *International Finance: Theory into Practice*, (Princeton, NJ: Princeton University Press); and 2) Chapter 4 of Alan C. Shapiro (2013), *Multinational Financial Management, 10th ed. (Hoboken, NJ: John Wiley & Sons, 2013).*

Despite these limitations, the International Fisher Effect can be useful in ensuring that inflation assumptions embedded in the projected cash flows are consistent with those implied by the discount rates.[1.26]

## Summary

Cross-border investing creates additional challenges relative to making an investment in domestic (or home) financial markets. Those challenges are exacerbated when contemplating investing in emerging (i.e., less-developed) countries. The latter are often characterized by incremental volatility created by so-called country risk factors.[1.27]

Country risk is generally described as *financial*, *economic*, or *political* in nature. These rules may create incremental complexities when developing cost of capital estimates for a business, business ownership interest, security, or an intangible asset based outside of a mature market such as the United States.

While years ago academics expected that an increase in global integration of financial markets would diminish the reason for expecting a country risk premium for investing in emerging markets (i) there is still a certain degree of market segmentation; and (ii) correlation between developed (mature) and developing (emerging) markets has increased significantly in recent years. This means that the anticipation that country risk could be completely diversified away has not come fully into fruition.

To the extent that country risk is systematic in nature, a related premium may need to be incorporated into discount rate estimates, if not already embedded in the projected cash flows.

---

[1.26] For a discussion and examples of how to apply the methods outlined in this section, refer to the complimentary CFA Institute webinar entitled "Quantifying Country Risk Premiums", presented on December 6, 2016 by James P. Harrington and Carla S. Nunes, CFA. This webcast can be accessed here:
https://www.cfainstitute.org/learning/products/multimedia/Pages/132617.aspx?WPID=BrowseProducts.

[1.27] For additional information on assessing country risk factors, please see Consensus Economics®.
Visit: www.consensuseconomics.com.

# Chapter 2
# Strengths and Weaknesses of Commonly Used Models

The *2017 Valuation Handbook – International Guide to Cost of Capital* data exhibits include (i) equity risk premia (ERPs) for 16 countries in USD and local currencies in Data Exhibit 1, (ii) implied country risk premia (CRPs) calculated using the Country Yield Spread model in Data Exhibit 2, (iii) implied relative volatility (RV) factors calculated using the Relative Volatility Model in Data Exhibit 3, and (iv) base country-level cost of equity capital and implied CRPs calculated using the Erb-Harvey-Viskanta Country Credit Rating Model in Data Exhibit 4.

For completeness, in Chapter 2 we briefly discuss additional international cost of capital models commonly mentioned by academics and/or valuation analysts. This section is largely drawn from Chapter 39 of *Cost of Capital: Applications and Examples* 5th ed.

### World (or Global) CAPM

The World CAPM model has intuitive appeal where markets are integrated and/or when the subject company is a diversified multi-national corporation operating in many countries. This method recognizes cross-border diversification opportunities and prices securities accordingly. The following equation is typically expressed in U.S. Dollars:

$$k_e = R_{f,U.S.} + \left( \beta_w \times RP_w \right)$$

Where:

| | | |
|---|---|---|
| $k_e$ | = | Cost of equity capital |
| $R_{f,U.S.}$ | = | U.S. risk-free rate |
| $\beta_w$ | = | Market risk measured with respect to a world portfolio of stocks (i.e., beta) |
| $RP_w$ | = | Equity risk premium (ERP) (rate of return expressed in terms of U.S. Dollar returns) on a world diversified portfolio |

Because we are estimating expected returns in terms of U.S. Dollars, this discount rate can be used for discounting net cash flows expressed in U.S. Dollars with the currency risk (preferably) treated in either the net cash flows or the discount rate.

The World CAPM model has been shown to work reasonably well for developed markets.[2.1] However, this approach has several potential weaknesses, particularly when dealing with investments located in emerging markets. These potential weaknesses may include:

- Markets are not all fully integrated. In effect, the World CAPM approach assumes away meaningful differences across countries. If the subject company's operations are concentrated in one or two countries, the risks of that business will differ from the risks of nearly identical companies operating in multiple countries. The prior specification is an idealized approximation unless there is complete integration.

- While developed countries' betas may have some ability to discriminate between high and low expected return countries, realized emerging market returns suggest that there is little relation between expected returns and betas measured with respect to the world market portfolio.[2.2]

To illustrate the second point, that there is seemingly little relation between expected returns and betas regressed against the world market portfolio, we present in Exhibit 2.1 the 60-month ordinary least squares (OLS) betas of MSCI developed and frontier market countries, sorted from smallest betas (on the left) to largest betas (on the right), as of December 2016.[2.3]

Countries classified by MSCI as "developed" markets, as the name implies, include the most developed economies (e.g., U.S., Germany, Singapore, etc.), while the MSCI "frontier" markets include the least developed economies (e.g., Bangladesh, Nigeria, Serbia, etc.).[2.4] The betas of the countries classified as "frontier" markets (the solid gray line) are systematically *lower* than the betas of "developed" markets (the solid red line). This would imply that the risk associated with frontier markets is *less* than the risk associated with developed markets (all other things held the same), which investors would reasonably assume to be *incorrect*.

---

[2.1]  See for example, Claude Erb, Campbell Harvey, and Tadas Viskanta, "Expected Returns and Volatility in 135 Countries", *Journal of Portfolio Management* (Spring 1996): 46–58.
[2.2]  Campbell R. Harvey, "12 Ways to Calculate the International Cost of Capital", Duke University, Durham, North Carolina, USA 27708, National Bureau of Economic Research, Cambridge, Massachusetts, USA 02138.
[2.3]  Source of MSCI classifications: www.msci.com.
[2.4]  Countries classified by MSCI as "emerging" market countries are not shown. Emerging market countries have economies *more* developed than *frontier* market countries, but *less* developed than *developed* market countries. Emerging market countries were not used in this analysis because to illustrate the point, the most striking differences are observed between the developed and frontier market classifications.

**Exhibit 2.1:** MSCI Developed and Frontier Markets' OLS Betas as Measured Over the 60-month Period Ending December 31, 2016

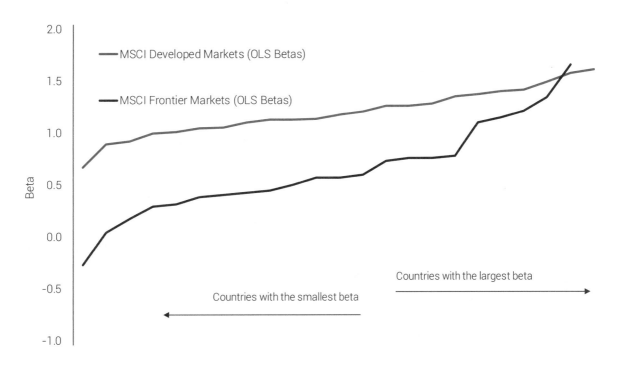

**Source of underlying data:** MSCI: All returns are based on MSCI indices, in U.S. Dollars, and accounting for capital gains/losses and dividends. The classification of developed, emerging, and frontier markets corresponds to the countries in the MSCI indices of developed, emerging, and frontier markets as of January, 2017. MSCI Developed Markets represented in this analysis by: Australia, Austria, Belgium, Canada, Denmark, Finland, France, Germany, Hong Kong, Ireland, Israel, Italy, Japan, the Netherlands, New Zealand, Norway, Portugal, Singapore, Spain, Sweden, Switzerland, United States, and the United Kingdom. MSCI Frontier Markets represented in this analysis by: Argentina, Bahrain, Bangladesh, Croatia, Estonia, Jordan, Kazakhstan, Kenya, Kuwait, Lebanon, Lithuania, Mauritius, Morocco, Nigeria, Oman, Pakistan, Romania, Serbia, Slovenia, Sri Lanka, Tunisia, and Vietnam. The market benchmark used in the calculation of all betas is the MSCI World Index. All rights reserved; used with permission. All calculations by Duff & Phelps, LLC.

## Single-country Version of the CAPM

The single-country version of the CAPM can be expressed as:

$$k_{e,local} = R_{f,local} + \left( \beta_{local} \times RP_{local} \right)$$

Where:

| | | |
|---|---|---|
| $k_{e,local}$ | = | Cost of equity capital in local country |
| $R_{f,local}$ | = | Return on the local country government's (default-risk-free) debt |
| $\beta_{local}$ | = | Market risk of the subject company measured with respect to the local securities market (i.e., beta) |
| $RP_{local}$ | = | Equity risk premium in local country's stock market |

If one estimates all inputs in local currency (e.g., Brazilian Real), then the resulting cost of equity capital estimate can be used to discount expected net cash flows expressed in local currency terms.

If one estimates all expected return in terms of rates of return in U.S. Dollars (or another home currency), then the resulting cost of equity capital is used to discount expected cash flows expressed in U.S. Dollars (or another home currency), with the currency risk treated (preferably) in the expected cash flows or as an adjustment to the discount rate.

This single-country version of the CAPM approach has appeal because local investors provide capital to local firms in the local market. This approach allows more local factors to be incorporated in the measure of local market risks. This type of model works best in developed economies. For example, the analyst could determine betas for U.S. firms relative to the Standard & Poor's (S&P) 500, U.K. firms relative to the FTSE 100, and Japanese firms relative to the Nikkei 225.

Potential weaknesses of the single-country version of the CAPM include:

- The model does not work well in less-developed markets.

- The model generally requires the "local" country to have a history of bond and stock market returns in local currency terms. Data may be poor or non-existent in segmented, developing country settings, especially the type of data required to develop the local beta and ERP.

- Beta estimates using historical returns may be low because the local stock market may be dominated by just a few firms (or industries).

- The local country government's debt is possibly not free of default risk.

## Damodaran's Local Country Risk Exposure Model

The Damodaran model compares the volatility of the local country's stock market returns and bond returns (i.e., a proxy for the relative risk between debt and equity for investors in that country to estimate a country risk premium, or CRP). Damodaran also calls this the Lambda ($\lambda$) approach.[2.5] The Damodaran model can be applied in U.S. Dollars, Euros, or another currency that has a (default free) risk-free rate and is easily accessible. The following equation depicts Damodaran's model expressed in U.S. Dollar terms: [2.6]

$$k_{e,local} = R_{f,U.S.} + \left( \beta_{U.S.} \times RP_{U.S.} \right) + \lambda \times \left( CRP \right)$$

Where:

| | | |
|---|---|---|
| $k_{e,local}$ | = | Discount rate for equity capital in local country |
| $R_{f,U.S.}$ | = | U.S. risk-free rate |
| $\beta_{U.S.} \times RP_{U.S.}$ | = | Risk premium (in U.S. Dollars terms) appropriate for a U.S. company in a similar industry as the subject company in the local country, where $\beta_{U.S.}$ is the beta of the subject company expressed in U.S. Dollars and $RP_{U.S.}$ is the U.S. equity risk premium also expressed in U.S. Dollars |
| $\lambda$ | = | Company's exposure to the local country risk |
| $CRP$ | = | $\left[ \left( R_{local\,euro\,\$\,issue} - R_{f,U.S.} \right) \times \left( \dfrac{\sigma_{stock}}{\sigma_{bond}} \right) \right]$ |
| $(R_{local\,euro\,\$\,issue}$ | = | Yield spread between government bonds issued by the local country in U.S. Dollars versus U.S. government bonds |
| $\sigma_{stock}$ | = | Volatility of returns in local country's stock market |
| $\sigma_{bond}$ | = | Volatility of returns in local country's bond market |

This model is premised on two basic ideas:[2.7]

- A company's exposure to country risk ($\lambda$) comes from where it operates, and not where it is incorporated.

- If the country default spread is estimated through the premium demanded for buying a government bond issued by the subject country relative to a risk-free government bond issued by a developed (mature) market, then the country risk premium used to estimate a cost of equity for that country should be greater, because equities are riskier than bonds.

---

[2.5] Aswath Damodaran, *Investment Valuation*, 2nd ed. (Hoboken, NJ: John Wiley & Sons, 2002): 204–206; Aswath Damodaran, *Damodaran on Valuation*, 2nd ed. (Hoboken, NJ: John Wiley & Sons, 2006): 59–61; and Aswath Damodaran, "Country Risk: Determinants, Measures and Implications –The 2016 Edition", Stern School of Business Working paper, July 2016. Available at http://ssrn.com/abstract=2812261.

[2.6] In previous editions of *the Valuation Handbook – International Guide to Cost of Capital*, we inadvertently showed the lambda term (i.e., λ x CRP) being multiplied by the U.S. Risk Premium (i.e., $\beta_{U.S.}$ x $RP_{U.S.}$). The correct equation should show the lambda term being added to the U.S. Risk Premium.

[2.7] Letter to the Editor, Professor Aswath Damodaran, *Business Valuation Review* 31(2/3) (Summer/Fall 2012): 85–86.

This is accomplished by scaling the equity risk premium by the relative standard deviation of stocks vs. bonds ($\sigma_{stocks} / \sigma_{bonds}$) in the local market, which will generally yield a greater country risk (CRP) than merely using the spread between the respective countries' bonds (sovereigns or corporates).

If we are estimating expected returns in terms of U.S. Dollars, this discount rate can be used for discounting expected net cash flows expressed in U.S. Dollars (with the exchange risk treated preferably in the expected cash flows, or potentially as an adjustment to the discount rate).

For countries without rated debt, you can use country risk ratings to estimate the credit rating and the default spread, which is then used to estimate the country risk premium (CRP).

The company's exposure to the local country risk is measured relative to the average company in the local country. Damodaran indicates that the determinants of such exposure would be influenced by at least three factors (if not more): (i) revenue source from the country in question; (ii) location of production facilities; and (iii) level of usage of risk management products. Using the simplest measure of lambda based entirely on revenues, if the average of local country companies has say 80% revenue from operations in that local country, then you want to measure the subject company's percent of total revenues generated in that country relative to the average company in the local of 80%.

The country exposure measure in the Damodaran model is consistent with a study that measured global, country, and industry effects in firm-level returns between emerging and developed markets.[2.8] The authors found that country effects dominate global and industry effects in emerging markets in contrast to developed markets. The implication of their results is that in applying country risk factors, you should consider the firm level amount of international business in determining the impact of country risk versus global and industry risk. One can incorporate the data published in this book to measure country level risks into the framework of the Damodaran model.

Some analysts are critical of this model, claiming that it does not have a strong theoretical foundation and is not consistent with a CAPM framework.[2.9]

**Alternative Risk Measures (downside risk)**

Is beta a flawed measure of risk in emerging markets? We have already noted that in many local markets, beta measurements may be flawed because "market" returns in some markets are dominated by a few large companies (or industries) and the returns on other "local market" companies may not be correlated with those large companies. Returns of the local market companies may even be highly correlated to one another and experience high variance (risk), but they look like low-risk companies because their betas are low relative to the overall market index.

---

[2.8] Kate Phylaktis and Xia Lichuan, "Sources of Firms' Industry and Country Effects in Emerging Markets", *Journal of International Money and Finance* (April 2006): 459–475.

[2.9] Lutz Kruschwitz, Andreas Löffler, and Gerwald Mandl, "Damodaran's Country Risk Premium: A Serious Critique", *Business Valuation Review* 31(2/3) (Summer/Fall 2012): 75–84.

Mishra and O'Brien studied implied cost of capital estimates for individual stocks from 16 developing (i.e., emerging) economies. They found that total risk (volatility of returns) is the most significant risk factor in explaining implied cost of capital estimates for these stocks.[2.10]

For companies based in those markets, but with global market presence, the global beta does explain, but to a lesser degree, differences in implied cost of capital estimates.

Other researchers have suggested that downside risk measures may result in more accurate risk measures in developing markets. Gendreau and Heckman found returns in emerging markets systematically related to downside risk, measured as the semi-standard deviation of returns compared with a benchmark return.[2.11]

A model that incorporates downside risk as the measure of risk is expressed in the following equation in U.S. Dollars:

$$k_{e,local} = R_{f,U.S.} + \left( \frac{DR_i}{DR_w} \right) \times RP_w$$

Where:

$k_{e,local}$ = Discount rate for equity capital in local country

$R_{f,U.S.}$ = U.S. risk-free rate

$DR_i$ = Downside risk (i.e., semi-deviation with respect to the mean) of returns in the local stock market $i$ (measured in terms of U.S. Dollar returns)

$DR_w$ = Downside risk (i.e., semi-deviation with respect to the mean) of returns in the global ("world") stock market index (measured in terms of U.S. Dollar returns)

$RP_w$ = General market risk premium in global ("world") stock market index

If we are estimating expected returns in terms of U.S. Dollars, this discount rate can be used for discounting expected net cash flows expressed in U.S. Dollars (with the exchange risk treated preferably in the expected cash flows or, alternatively, as an adjustment to the discount rate).

The semi-deviation of returns in the local stock market index (average of squared deviation of downside returns realized in the local market minus the average returns of the local market) is $DR_i$, while $DR_w$ is the semi-deviation of returns in a global stock market index (average of squared deviation of downside returns realized in the global index minus the average returns of the global index).[2.12]

---

[2.10]    Dev R. Mishra and Thomas J. O'Brien, "Risk and Ex Ante Cost of Equity Estimates of Emerging Market Firms", *Emerging Market Review* 6 (2005): 107–120.

[2.11]    Brian Gendreau and Leila Heckman, "Estimating the Equity Premium across Countries", Salomon Smith Barney (2002).

[2.12]    See for example Javier Estrada, "The Cost of Equity in Emerging Markets: A Downside Risk Approach", *Emerging Markets Quarterly*, Fall 2000.

A possible alternative downside risk measure to the preceding formula is using downside betas. This would entail replacing the downside risk ratio ($DR_i/DR_w$) shown in the preceding formula with a downside beta calculated for the subject country relative to the world market portfolio. The downside beta can be calculated in a few different ways, including using the following formula:

$$\beta_i^D = \frac{Cosemivariance\left(R_i, R_w\right)}{Semivariance\left(R_w\right)}$$

Where:

| | | |
|---|---|---|
| $\beta_i^D$ | = | Downside beta for local country $i$ |
| $Cosemivariance(R_i, R_w)$ | = | Cosemivariance of returns (a.k.a. downside covariance) between the local country $i$ and the global ("world") stock market index (all measured in terms of U.S. Dollar returns) |
| $Semivariance(R_w)$ | = | Semivariance of returns (i.e., square of the semi-deviation with respect to the mean) on the global ("world") stock market index (measured in terms of U.S. Dollar returns) |

The advantages of the model are its theoretical foundations and empirical support.[2.13] Downside beta has received some support in the literature. That is, portfolios of company stocks with high downside betas realize greater returns than portfolios of company stocks with low downside betas, consistent with the theory of CAPM.[2.14]

However, from a practical standpoint, this model has gained limited acceptance in part due to limited published data on downside risk measures. In addition, the use of a country downside beta may or may not fully capture the incremental risk of investing in a given emerging market. To test this assertion, we have updated Professor Estrada's calculations of downside betas by country (through December 2016) as fully explained in his 2007 academic paper.[2.15]

As background, Professor Estrada (2007) showed empirical evidence for developed and emerging markets, which supported downside beta as a superior measure of risk relative to CAPM's beta when estimating required returns for emerging markets. Countries were categorized as "developed" or "emerging" based on MSCI's market classification. Professor Estrada found that on average, downside beta generated a higher required return for emerging markets (as a group) than for developed markets (as a group). In contrast, average required returns on equity based on textbook

[2.13] Javier Estrada and Ana Paula Serra, "Risk and Return in Emerging Markets: Family Matters", EFMA Basel Meetings Paper (2004); Javier Estrada, *Finance in a Nutshell* (New York: Financial Times Prentice-Hall, 2005): 96–108.

[2.14] See, for example, Javier Estrada and Ana Paula Serra, "Risk and Return in Emerging Markets: Family Matters", EFMA Basel Meetings Paper (2004); Don Galagedera and Asmah Jaapar, "Modeling Time-Varying Downside Risk", *ICFAI University Journal of Financial Economics* 7(1), March 2009. Available at http://ssrn.com/abstract=1209507. Downside risk measures have been criticized. See Sergei Vasilievich Cheremushkin, "Internal Inconsistency of Downside CAPM Models", January 15, 2012. Available at http://ssrn.com/ abstract=1985372.

[2.15] Javier Estrada, "Mean-Semivariance Behavior: Downside Risk and Capital Asset Pricing". *International Review of Economics and Finance* 16 (2007), 169–185.

CAPM were approximately the same for both groups of countries (i.e., the average OLS beta for developed markets was virtually the same as that for emerging markets).

For the *2017 Valuation Handbook – International Guide to Cost of Capital*, we have updated the same type of analysis as in Estrada (2007) through December 2016, expanding it to include frontier markets. Again, the categorization of developed, emerging, and frontier markets was based on MSCI's classification as of January 2017. Monthly returns data from the MSCI database were used for 23 developed markets, 23 emerging markets, and 22 frontier markets. All returns were measured in U.S. Dollars and accounted for both capital gains and dividends.

Exhibit 2.2 depicts the same 60-month OLS CAPM betas as of December 2016 for developed countries (the solid red line) and frontier markets (the solid gray line) shown in Exhibit 2.1, again sorted from smallest betas (on the left) to largest betas (on the right). In Exhibit 2.2 we have added an additional line: the 60-month downside betas for frontier markets (the dashed gray line) are sorted and presented in a similar fashion. The result of this analysis is shown in Exhibit 2.2.

**Exhibit 2.2:** MSCI Developed Markets' OLS Betas and Frontier Markets' OLS and Downside Betas as Measured over the 60-month period Ending December 31, 2016

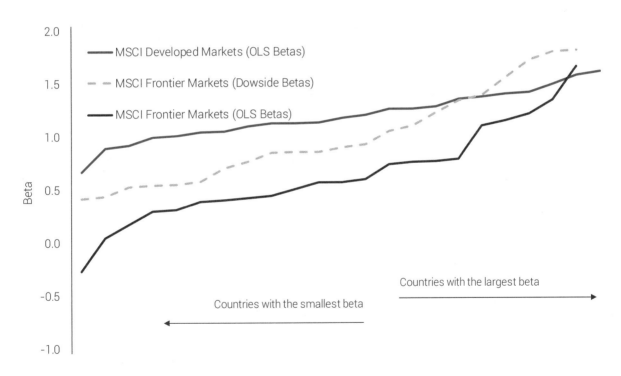

As discussed previously, the OLS betas of the countries classified as "frontier" markets (the solid dark gray line) are systematically lower than the OLS betas of "developed" markets (the solid red line), which we previously concluded runs counter to investors' relative risk perceptions between these two groups of countries. The downside betas of frontier markets (the dashed light gray line), while doing a better job of estimating risk than OLS betas, are still in nearly all the cases below the OLS betas of developed markets.

Either because stock markets located in frontier markets tend to exhibit very low liquidity or due to their low degree of integration with global markets (or both), it appears that expected returns of frontier markets have little relation to expected returns in a world market portfolio, even when risk is measured by downside beta.[2.16]

The observation in Estrada (2007) that the average downside beta of emerging markets was significantly higher than that of developing markets no longer seems to hold in the more recent 2012–2016 period. Contrary to the paper's findings, Exhibit 2.3 shows that on average, downside betas of emerging markets are not materially different from those of developed markets over the period analyzed.[2.17]

**Exhibit 2.3:** Average OLS and Downside Betas for MSCI Developed, Emerging, and Frontier Markets Measured over the 60-Month Period Ending December 31, 2016

|                    | Average CAPM (OLS) Beta | Average Downside Beta |
|--------------------|-------------------------|-----------------------|
| Developed Markets  | 1.19                    | 1.31                  |
| Emerging Markets   | 1.10                    | 1.35                  |
| Frontier Markets   | 0.63                    | 0.99                  |
| World              | 1.00                    | 1.00                  |

**Source of underlying data:** MSCI: All returns are based on MSCI indices, in U.S. Dollars, and accounting for capital gains/losses and dividends. The classification of developed, emerging, and frontier markets corresponds to the countries in the MSCI indices of developed, emerging, and frontier markets as of January, 2017. MSCI Developed Markets represented in this analysis by: Australia, Austria, Belgium, Canada, Denmark, Finland, France, Germany, Hong Kong, Ireland, Israel, Italy, Japan, the Netherlands, New Zealand, Norway, Portugal, Singapore, Spain, Sweden, Switzerland, United States, and the United Kingdom. MSCI Frontier Markets represented in this analysis: Argentina, Bahrain, Bangladesh, Croatia, Estonia, Jordan, Kazakhstan, Kenya, Kuwait, Lebanon, Lithuania, Mauritius, Morocco, Nigeria, Oman, Pakistan, Romania, Serbia, Slovenia, Sri Lanka, Tunisia, and Vietnam. MSCI Emerging Markets represented in this analysis: Brazil, Chile, China, Colombia, Czech Republic, Egypt, Greece, Hungary, India, Indonesia, Korea (South), Malaysia, Mexico, Peru, Philippines, Poland, Qatar, Russia, South Africa, Taiwan, Thailand, Turkey, and United Arab Emirates. The market benchmark used in the calculation of all betas is the MSCI World Index. All rights reserved; used with permission. All calculations by Duff & Phelps, LLC.

Nonetheless, these analyses suggest that downside betas may do a better job at capturing the risk of emerging and frontier markets, when compared to textbook CAPM (OLS) betas. For example, the average downside beta of frontier markets is 57% (0.99/0.63 − 1) higher than its CAPM equivalent. However, based on these recent data, downside betas do not appear to fully distinguish the relative

---

[2.16] There could be other reasons why frontier markets' OLS and downside betas are systematically lower than those of developed markets over the period analyzed, which we do not explore in this publication.

[2.17] In Estrada (2007), the average downside beta of emerging markets was 1.38, relative to that of developed markets of 1.06. Therefore, the emerging markets' downside beta was on average 30% higher than that of developed markets (1.38/1.06 − 1).

riskiness of developed markets vis-à-vis emerging and frontier markets, given that the latter two groupings are typically perceived by investors to be (on average) comprised of riskier countries.

## What Model Should I Use?

There is no consensus among academics and practitioners as to the best model to use in estimating the cost of equity capital in a global environment, particularly with regards to companies operating in emerging economies.

In choosing a model, the goal is to balance several objectives:

- **Acceptance and use:** The model has a degree of acceptance, and the model is actually used by valuation analysts.

- **Data Availability:** Quality data are available for consistent and objective application of the model.

- **Simplicity:** The model's underlying concepts are understandable, and can be explained in plain language.

There are several common approaches to incorporating country factors into a cost of equity capital estimate. None are perfect.

## Economic Integration

A key issue in choosing an international cost of capital estimation model is the degree to which the subject country is integrated into the global economy. An integrated economy has a significant portion of inputs and outputs of its economy that are sourced and sold internationally rather than locally. If all economies were fully integrated, it might be reasonable to expect that *similar* companies or projects located in different countries would have *similar* costs of capital.

However, the economies of developed countries are generally integrated into the global economy to a *greater* degree than are less-developed countries. Choosing the appropriate model(s) for estimating the cost of equity capital for a company or project in a less developed country (i.e., "emerging" and "frontier" countries), where local market volatility may become more important, is indeed an ongoing challenge.

We present a brief overview of models more commonly used for estimating the cost of equity capital in international settings. None of these models is perfect, so it is important to understand the strengths and potential weaknesses of each model in order to make well-informed choices when developing cost of capital estimates for global investments.

Exhibit 2.4 presents a summary of the general strengths and weaknesses of various international cost of equity capital models. In cases where countries lack stock and/or bond market return data, or yields on government debt denominated in "home" (or mature market) currencies, it may be appropriate to correlate the subject country's credit (or risk) rating with ratings of other countries that do have these metrics.[2.18]

**Exhibit 2.4:** A Comparison of International Cost of Capital Models

| International Cost of Capital Model | Strengths | Weaknesses |
|---|---|---|
| World (Global) CAPM Model | Can work well if country is integrated and/or the subject company operates in many countries. | Assumes away meaningful differences across countries. <br><br> Generally requires the "local" country to have a history of bond market and stock market returns. <br><br> Does not work well in emerging markets: generally results in lower betas for companies located in emerging markets, counter to expectations. |
| Single Country CAPM Model | Allows more local factors to be introduced. | Does not work well in emerging markets. <br><br> Generally requires the "local" country to have a history of bond market and stock market returns. |
| Damodaran Model | Introduces a measure of economic integration at the company level. | Complexity. <br><br> Generally requires the "local" country to have a history of bond market and stock market returns. |
| Yield Spread Model | Intuitive / easily implemented. | Requires that the "local" government issues debt denominated in the "home" government's currency. However, this can be overcome by using a regression of observed yield spreads against country risk ratings. <br><br> May double count (or underestimate) *business* cash flow risks, particularly if the default risk of a given country is not a good proxy for the risks faced by the subject company operating locally. |
| Relative Volatility Model | Intuitive / easily implemented. | Does not work well in countries that do not have well-diversified stock markets. <br><br> Requires the "local" country to have a history of stock market returns. <br><br> At times does not work well for even the most developed countries resulting in implied adjustments far in excess of what would be expected. |
| Country Credit Rating Model | Intuitive / it can be applied to a significant number of countries. | Complexity. <br><br> Requires access to quality stock market return data from a large number of countries. |

---

[2.18] Country risk ratings are available from Euromoney's Country Risk Ratings or Political Risk Services' International Country Risk Guide.

# Chapter 3
# International Equity Risk Premia

**Description of Data**

Data Exhibit 1 includes historical equity risk premia (ERPs) estimates for 16 world economies, through December 2016.[3.1]

Both long-horizon and short-horizon historical ERPs are calculated (i) in terms of the U.S. Dollar, and (ii) in terms of each country's "local" currency. In the case of the United States, the "local" currency is the U.S. Dollar, and so the long-horizon and short-horizon are calculated only once, and labeled "in U.S. Dollars", which is also the "local" currency".

The time horizon over which each country's ERPs are calculated is dependent on data availability, and for most countries analyzed herein the time horizon is 1970–2016. However, Canada, the United Kingdom, and the United States' historical ERPs are calculated over the time horizons 1919–2016, 1900–2016, and 1926–2016, respectively. Note that if the analyst wishes to select a long-term ERP measured over the same time horizon as the majority of the other subject countries' long-term historical ERPs are measured in Exhibit 1 (1970–2016 in most cases), that information is *still* provided in the Canada, U.K., and U.S. long-term ERP tables.

The ERPs in Data Exhibit 1:

- Were calculated using the same general *data sources* that were used to calculate the ERPs previously published in the Morningstar/Ibbotson *International Equity Risk Premia Report*.[3.2]

- Were calculated using the same general *methodologies* that were used to calculate the ERPs previously published in the Morningstar/Ibbotson *International Equity Risk Premia Report*.

In estimating historical equity risk premia in the fashion previously reported in the Morningstar/Ibbotson *International Equity Risk Premium Report*, changes in methodology and data were made in an effort to improve the analysis, and to strengthen internal consistency. This was primarily accomplished by:

- Minimizing the number of index "families" used (e.g., MSCI, IMF, DMS) to standardize the analysis and to increase internal consistency.

- Using the same (or similar) time horizons over which ERP estimates were estimated.

---

[3.1]   "Premia" is the plural of premium. A single equity risk premium is denoted "ERP"; the plural equity risk premia is denoted "ERPs".

[3.2]   The Morningstar/Ibbotson *International Equity Risk Premia Report* was discontinued in 2013.

- Eliminating analysis for countries that had data histories which were likely not long enough to provide meaningful historical ERP estimates.[3.3]

A summary of the 16 countries for which historical ERPs are calculated, the currencies in which they are calculated, and the time periods over which they are calculated is presented in Exhibit 3.1.

**Exhibit 3.1:** Countries Covered, Currencies, and Time Periods

| Country | Local Currency | Currency Code | USD | | Local Currency | |
| | | | Long-Horizon Start Date | Short-Horizon Start Date | Long-Horizon Start Date | Short-Horizon Start Date |
|---|---|---|---|---|---|---|
| Australia | Australian Dollar | AUD | 1970 | 1970 | 1970 | 1970 |
| Austria | Euro | EUR | 1972 | 1970 | 1971 | 1970 |
| Belgium | Euro | EUR | 1970 | 1970 | 1970 | 1970 |
| Canada | Canadian Dollar | CAD | 1919 | 1919 | 1919 | 1919 |
| France | Euro | EUR | 1970 | 1970 | 1970 | 1970 |
| Germany | Euro | EUR | 1970 | 1970 | 1970 | 1970 |
| Ireland | Euro | EUR | 1970 | 1970 | 1970 | 1970 |
| Italy | Euro | EUR | 1970 | 1970 | 1970 | 1970 |
| Japan | Yen | JPY | 1970 | 1970 | 1970 | 1970 |
| Netherlands | Euro | EUR | 1970 | 1970 | 1970 | 1970 |
| New Zealand | New Zealand Dollar | NZD | 1970 | 1970 | 1970 | 1970 |
| South Africa | Rand | ZAR | 1971 | 1970 | 1970 | 1970 |
| Spain | Euro | EUR | 1972 | 1970 | 1971 | 1970 |
| Switzerland | Swiss Franc | CHF | 1970 | 1970 | 1970 | 1970 |
| United Kingdom | Pound Sterling | GBP | 1900 | 1900 | 1900 | 1900 |
| United States | U.S. Dollar | USD | 1926 | 1926 | 1926 | 1926 |

---

[3.3] A total of 10 countries' ERP estimates that were previously reported in the Morningstar/Ibbotson *2013 International Equity Risk Report* were eliminated from the analyses presented herein due to insufficient data. The countries eliminated were Czech Republic, Finland, Greece, Hungary, Malaysia, Norway, Poland, Portugal, Singapore, and Thailand.

## Change in Short-term Risk-free Rate Series

In the *2014* and *2015 Valuation Handbook – International Guide to Cost of Capital*, the short-horizon risk-free returns were primarily represented by various International Monetary Fund (IMF) series. Starting in the *2016 Valuation Handbook – International Guide to Cost of Capital*, the data source used to represent short-horizon risk-free returns is the Dimson, Marsh, and Staunton (DMS) short-term risk-free rate series from the *Credit Suisse Global Investment Returns Yearbook 2017*.[3.4] The goals of the change in data source for the short-horizon risk-free return were: (i) to increase the internal consistency of the short-term ERP calculations, and (ii) to enable us to report the short-horizon equity risk premia for three countries that in previous years were not reported (Ireland, the Netherlands, and New Zealand). As such, the calculated value reported for short-term equity risk premia for some countries and over certain time horizon combinations in the analyses herein may be significantly different than reported in prior years.

## U.S. SBBI Long-term Government Bond Series Data Revision (immaterial)

Morningstar reported a data revision in January 2016 for the "SBBI Long-term Government Bond" series, which is an input in the calculation of U.S. long-term ERP estimates herein. The data revisions affected monthly data from June 2011 to December 2015, and were reflected in the Morningstar *Direct* database as of December 31, 2015. These revisions were small, and did not change the long-term U.S. ERP for 2011, 2012, 2013, and 2014 *as reported* in the *2015 Valuation Handbook – International Guide to Cost of Capital* when compared to the long-term U.S. ERP for 2011, 2012, 2013, and 2014 as reported in the *2016 Valuation Handbook – International Guide to Cost of Capital*.[3.5]

---

[3.4] The Dimson, Marsh, Staunton data are summarized in the *Credit Suisse Global Investment Returns Yearbook 2017* (Credit Suisse, 2017) by Elroy Dimson, Paul Marsh, and Mike Staunton. Copyright © Elroy Dimson, Paul Marsh, and Mike Staunton. All rights reserved. Used with Permission. Elroy Dimson is Emeritus Professor of Finance at London Business School. He chairs the Newton Centre for Endowment Asset Management at Cambridge Judge Business School, the Strategy Council for the Norwegian Government Pension Fund, and the Academic Advisory Board and Policy Committee for FTSE Group; Paul Marsh is Emeritus Professor of Finance at London Business School; Mike Staunton is Director of the London Share Price Database, a research resource of London Business School.

[3.5] Historical ERPs are reported at the 1-decimal level in Data Exhibit 1 herein (e.g., 6.9%). At the 1-decimal level, the revisions reported by Morningstar *did not change* the reported values for the long-term U.S. ERP for 2011, 2012, 2013, and 2014, as reported in the 2015 book versus the 2016 book. At the 2-decimal level (not reported herein), the revisions still did *not* change the reported values for the long-term U.S. ERP for 2011, 2012, 2013, but *did* change the 2014 value from 6.99% to 7.00%, a non-meaningful change of 0.01%.

**Methodology**

**The Equity Risk Premium (ERP)**

The ERP (often interchangeably referred to as the *market risk premium*) is defined as the extra return (over the expected yield on risk-free securities) that investors expect to receive from an investment in the market portfolio of common stocks, represented by a broad-based market index (e.g., the S&P 500 Index in the United States). A risk-free rate is the return available, as of the valuation date, on a security that the market generally regards as free of the risk of default (e.g., a U.S. Treasury security in the United States). The risk-free rate and the ERP are interrelated concepts. All ERP estimates are, by definition, developed in relation to the risk-free rate.

**Calculating Historical ERP**

There is no single universally accepted methodology for estimating the ERP. A wide variety of premia are used in practice and recommended by academics and financial professionals. These differences are often due to differences in how ERP is estimated.[3.6] Generally, we can categorize approaches for estimating the ERP as either an *ex post* approach or an *ex ante* approach.

For example, some valuation analysts define expected returns on common stocks in terms of averages of *realized* (historical) single-period returns while others define expected returns on common stocks in terms of realized (i.e., historical) multi-year compound returns. These are *ex post* approaches.

Some valuation analysts estimate the ERP using the returns on the diversified portfolio implied by expected (future) stock prices or expected dividends. These are *ex ante* approaches.

The ERPs herein are all calculated using an *ex post* approach: the examination of the historical relationship between equities (i.e., stocks) and a "risk-free" security.[3.7] For example, the long-term historical average annual return of stocks in Japan as represented by the MSCI Japan equities total return index (in terms of Japanese Yen) over the time period 1970–2016 is 9.7%, and the historical average annual return of a long-horizon risk-free security in Japan (also in terms of Japanese Yen) as represented by a long-horizon risk-free return index for Japan over the same period is 4.2%, implying a long-term ERP of 5.5%:

*"Historical" ERP = Average Annual Return of Stocks – Average Annual Return of Risk-free Security*

*5.5% = 9.7% - 4.2%*

---

[3.6] For a detailed discussion of the equity risk premium, see *Cost of Capital: Applications and Examples* 5th edition, by Shannon P. Pratt and Roger J. Grabowski (John Wiley & Sons, Inc., 2014), Chapter 8 ("Equity Risk Premium"), Appendix 8A ("Deriving ERP Estimates"), and Appendix 8B ("Other Sources of ERP Estimates").

[3.7] No security is truly "risk-free". A risk-free rate is the return available on a security that the market generally regards as free of the risk of default, and thus useable as a *proxy* for a risk-free security. For example, for a valuation denominated in U.S. Dollars (USD), analysts typically use the valuation date yield-to-maturity on a U.S. government security as a proxy for the risk-free rate.

**Equity Returns**

The same "family" of equity indices is used in the analyses presented herein in order to maximize internal consistency. The primary source of equity total returns used in this analysis is MSCI Global Equity Indexes.[3.8, 3.9, 3.10]

The MSCI Total Return Indexes *"measure the price performance of markets with the income from constituent dividend payments. The MSCI Daily Total Return (DTR) Methodology reinvests an index constituent's dividends at the close of trading on the day the security is quoted ex-dividend (the ex-date)"*. In all cases for which an MSCI equity index is available, the MSCI Total Return Indexes (with gross dividends) is used.[3.11]

There are five countries for which MSCI equity data was used, but only in part: Canada, Ireland, New Zealand, South Africa, and the U.K. In these five cases, Dimson, Marsh, Staunton (DMS) equity returns data was used in earlier years (1919–1969 in the case of Canada, 1970–1987 in the case of Ireland and New Zealand; 1970–1992 in the case of South Africa, and 1900–1969 in the case of the U.K.)[3.12] MSCI equity returns data was then used for the respective remainder of the years through 2016, for each of these five countries.

There is one country for which MSCI equity data was *not* used: the United States. For the U.S., equity returns are represented herein by the S&P 500 Index. The reason for this is straightforward: in the *2017 Valuation Handbook – U.S. Guide to Cost of Capital* (and in the former *SBBI Yearbook*), the series used to represent U.S. equities is (and was) the S&P 500 Index (unless otherwise stated). While it would be internally *consistent* to use the MSCI U.S. equity series within the historical equity risk premium analysis presented herein (since all the other countries' equity returns are represented primarily by MSCI indices), doing so would be *inconsistent* with (i) Duff & Phelps' other published valuation data resources, and (ii) what most analysts use to represent U.S. equities (the S&P 500).[3.13, 3.14]

---

[3.8] Calculated since 1969, the MSCI Global Equity Indexes have become integral tools in the investment processes of institutional investors around the world. The indices provide exhaustive equity market coverage for over 80 countries in the Developed, Emerging and Frontier Markets, applying a consistent index construction and maintenance methodology. See http://www.msci.com/.

[3.9] MSCI equity series were also the primary series used in the former Morningstar/Ibbotson *"International Equity Risk Premium Report"*.

[3.10] Source of MSCI Equity Indexes used: Morningstar *Direct* database. To learn more about Morningstar's *Direct* database, visit www.corporate.morningstar.com.

[3.11] Gross total return indices reinvest as much as possible of a company's dividend distributions. The reinvested amount is equal to the total dividend amount distributed to persons residing in the country of the dividend-paying company. Gross total return indices do not, however, include any tax credits. See http://www.msci.com/indexes.

[3.12] The Dimson, Marsh, Staunton data are summarized in the *Credit Suisse Global Investment Returns Yearbook 2017* (Credit Suisse, 2017) by Elroy Dimson, Paul Marsh, and Mike Staunton. Copyright © Elroy Dimson, Paul Marsh, and Mike Staunton. All rights reserved. Used with Permission. Duff & Phelps has a data license to the full DMS dataset through Morningstar *Direct* database.

[3.13] The S&P 500 total return index was also used to represent U.S. equities in the former Morningstar/Ibbotson *"International Equity Risk Premium Report"*. In the *2017 Valuation Handbook – U.S. Guide to Cost of Capital*, the United States long-horizon equity risk premia is also calculated from 1926 to 2016 using the S&P 500 total return index.

[3.14] In any case, a side-by-side analysis of the equity risk premium data over the full time-horizon presented here is calculated using (i) the S&P 500 index and the SBBI U.S. LT Gov't income return index and (ii) MSCI U.S. equity index and IMF U.S. LT Gov't income return index produces very similar results.

Currency translation is used only in cases for which MSCI does not supply a raw series in the appropriate currency. Specifically, the *raw* index data from MSCI is used, if available in the required currency. For example, MSCI creates a total return series for Belgium equities in USD, and so that series is used in the calculations and no additional currency translations are required for this series. When translation does become necessary (i.e., MSCI provides a total return series for the equity data needed, but the series is not denominated in the currency needed), the currencies are translated using the same currency conversion data and methodology that was utilized in the former Morningstar/Ibbotson *International Equity Risk Premium Report*.[3.15, 3.16]

### Risk-free Returns (long-horizon)

The primary data source used in the construction of long-horizon risk-free returns is from the International Monetary Fund (IMF).[3.17, 3.18] Long-horizon government income return series constructed in this fashion are available for all 16 of the countries shown in Exhibit 1.

There is one country for which long-horizon risk-free series based on IMF data were *not* used: the United States. For the U.S., long-horizon risk-free returns are represented by the "SBBI U.S. Long-Term Government Income Return" series.[3.19] The reason for this is straightforward: in the *2017 Valuation Handbook – U.S. Guide to Cost of Capital* (and in the former *SBBI Yearbook*), the series used to represent U.S. long-horizon risk-free returns is (and was) the SBBI U.S. Long-Term Government Income Return series (unless otherwise stated). While it would be internally *consistent* to use the long-horizon risk-free series based on IMF data within the historical equity risk premium analyses presented herein (since all the other countries' long-horizon risk-free returns are represented primarily by these series), doing so would be *inconsistent* with Duff & Phelps' other published valuation data resources.[3.20]

---

[3.15]   Source of currency conversion data: Morningstar *Direct* database. See Appendix A for further information.

[3.16]   MSCI provides a total return equity series in USD for *each* of the 16 countries presented herein, and so for these series no currency translation was required.

[3.17]   The "IMF Long-Term World Government Bond Series" (as they are denoted in the Morningstar *Direct* database) are computed by Morningstar using yields from the IMF. These IMF government bond yields have long-term maturities and vary from country to country. Returns are calculated assuming a single bond is bought at par (i.e., the coupon equals the market yield) at the beginning of each period. The bond is "held" over the period, and "sold" at the end of the period at the then-prevailing market yield. The end-of-period price is calculated as a function of the coupon, yield, and maturity remaining at period-end. The return in excess of yield (capital appreciation) is then derived as the change in price over the period, divided by the beginning-of-period price (i.e., divided by par). The yield is converted to an income return by (dividing it by 12) lagging it one period. Total return is equal to the income return plus the return in excess of yield. Source: Morningstar *Direct* database.

[3.18]   These same series were the primary series used for long-horizon risk-free rates in the former Morningstar/Ibbotson *International Equity Risk Premium Report*.

[3.19]   Source: Morningstar *Direct* database.

[3.20]   The SBBI U.S. Long-Term Government Income Return series was also used to represent the U.S. long-horizon risk-free rate in the former Morningstar/Ibbotson *International Equity Risk Premium Report*.

## Risk-free Returns (short-horizon)

The data source used in the construction of short-horizon risk-free returns are primarily represented herein by the Dimson, Marsh, and Staunton (DMS) short-term risk-free rate series from the *Credit Suisse Global Investment Returns Yearbook 2017* (Credit Suisse, 2017).[3.21]

There is one country for which DMS data based short-horizon risk-free returns were *not* used: the United States. For the U.S., short-horizon risk-free returns are represented by the "SBBI U.S. Treasury Bill Return" series.[3.22] The reason for this is straightforward: in the *2017 Valuation Handbook – U.S. Guide to Cost of Capital* (and in the former *SBBI Yearbook*), the series used to represent U.S. short-horizon risk-free returns is (and was) the SBBI U.S. Treasury Bill Return series (unless otherwise stated). While it would be internally *consistent* to use the IMF data based short-horizon risk-free series within the historical equity risk premium analysis presented here (since all the other countries' short-horizon risk-free returns are represented primarily by these series), doing so would be *inconsistent* with Duff & Phelps' other published valuation data resources.[3.23]

---

[3.21] The Dimson, Marsh, Staunton data are summarized in the *Credit Suisse Global Investment Returns Yearbook 2017* (Credit Suisse, 2017) by Elroy Dimson, Paul Marsh, and Mike Staunton. Copyright © Elroy Dimson, Paul Marsh, and Mike Staunton. All rights reserved. Used with Permission. Elroy Dimson is Emeritus Professor of Finance at London Business School. He chairs the Newton Centre for Endowment Asset Management at Cambridge Judge Business School, the Strategy Council for the Norwegian Government Pension Fund, and the Academic Advisory Board and Policy Committee for FTSE Group; Paul Marsh is Emeritus Professor of Finance at London Business School; Mike Staunton is Director of the London Share Price Database, a research resource of London Business School.

[3.22] Source: Morningstar *Direct* database.

[3.23] The SBBI U.S. Treasury Bill Return series was also used to represent the U.S. short-horizon risk-free rate in the former Morningstar/Ibbotson *"International Equity Risk Premium Report"*.

# Description of Data Series Used[3.24]

## Australia

**Equity Series:** The equity series used is the MSCI Australia Index.[3.25] The MSCI Australia Index is designed to measure the performance of the large and mid-cap segments of the Australia market. With 71 constituents, the index covers approximately 85% of the free float-adjusted market capitalization in Australia.

**Long-Horizon Risk-free Rate:** The long-horizon risk-free series used is the IMF Australia Long-term Government Income Return series. The IMF Australia Long-term Government Income Return series assesses secondary market yields on non-rebate bonds with maturity of 10 years. Yields are calculated before brokerage and on the last business day of the month. The average maturity for the IMF Australia Long-term Government Income Return series is 10 years.

**Short-Horizon Risk-free Rate:** The short-horizon risk-free series used is the DMS Australia short-term risk-free rate series.

## Austria

**Equity Series:** The equity series used is the MSCI Austria Index. The MSCI Austria Index is designed to measure the performance of the large and mid-cap segments of the Austrian market. With 5 constituents, the index covers approximately 85% of the free float-adjusted market capitalization in Austria.

**Long-Horizon Risk-free Rate:** The long-horizon risk-free series used the IMF Austria Long-term Government Income Return series. This series refers to all government bonds issued and not yet redeemed. They are weighted with the share of each bond in the total value of the government bonds in circulation. The data include bonds benefiting from tax privileges under the tax reduction scheme. The average maturity for the IMF Austria Long-term Government Income Return series is 10 years.

**Short-Horizon Risk-free Rate:** The short-horizon risk-free series used is the DMS Australia short-term risk-free rate series.

---

[3.24] The descriptions of the equity series and risk-free series are from the following sources: (i) Morningstar *Direct* database; (ii) MSCI database; (iii) *Credit Suisse Global Investment Returns Yearbook 2017* (Credit Suisse, 2017) by Elroy Dimson, Paul Marsh, Stauton; (iv) International Monetary Fund (IMF) database. All series data was accessed using the Morningstar *Direct* database. To learn more about Morningstar *Direct*, visit www.corporate.morningstar.com.

[3.25] In all cases in this section, the MSCI indices used are "GR" (i.e., gross return) MSCI indices. MSCI "GR" equity indices account for both capital gains and dividends (i.e., "total" returns).

## Belgium

**Equity Series:** The equity series used is the MSCI Belgium Index. The MSCI Belgium Index is designed to measure the performance of the large-, mid-, and small-cap segments of the Belgian market. With 10 constituents, the index covers approximately 85% of the free float-adjusted market capitalization in Belgium.

**Long-Horizon Risk-free Rate:** The long-horizon risk-free series used is the IMF Belgium Long-term Government Income Return series. Prior to 1990, this series was represented by a weighted average yield to maturity of all 5–8 percent bonds issued after December 1962 with more than 5 years to maturity. From 1990 onward, this series was represented by the yield on 10 year government bonds. The average maturity for the IMF Belgium Long-term Government Income Return series is 10 years.

**Short-Horizon Risk-free Rate:** The short-horizon risk-free series used is the DMS Belgium short-term risk-free rate series.

## Canada

**Equity Series:** From 1919 to 1969, the equity series used is Dimson, Marsh, Staunton (DMS) equity returns for Canada.[3.26] The main data source for DMS equity returns for Canada from 1926 forward is Panjer and Tan (2002).[3.27] Prior to 1926, the primary source for DMS equity returns for Canada was the equity returns series produced by Moore (2012).[3.28] From 1970 to present, the equity series used is the MSCI Canada GR Index (total return) series. The MSCI Canada Index is designed to measure the performance of the large and mid-cap segments of the Canada market. With 94 constituents, the index covers approximately 85% of the free float-adjusted market capitalization in Canada.

**Long-Horizon Risk-free Rate:** From 1919 to 1957, long-term government securities data from the Bank of Canada Data and Statistics Office were used.[3.29] From 1958 to present, the long-horizon risk-free series used is the IMF Canada Long-term Government Income Return series, calculated from government bond yield issues with original maturity of 10 years or more. It is calculated based on average yield to maturity.

---

[3.26]  Elroy Dimson, Paul Marsh, and Mike Staunton, *Credit Suisse Global Investment Returns Yearbook 2017* (Credit Suisse, 2017).

[3.27]  Harry Panjer, and Ken Seng Tan, 2002. *Report on Canadian Economic Statistics 1924–2001*, Canadian Institute of Actuaries. [Updated in: *Report on Canadian Economic Statistics 1924–2008*].

[3.28]  Lyndon Moore, 2012, "World Financial Markets, 1900–1925", unpublished manuscript.

[3.29]  Source: Bank of Canada website at: http://www.bankofcanada.ca/rates/interest-rates/selected-historical-interest-rates/. Source document for 1919–1935, 1936–1948, and 1949–1957 long-term government securities data: Government of Canada Marketable Bonds, Average Yield, Over 10 years V122487 Jan. 1919; "selected_historical_v122487.pdf", Bank of Canada, Data and Statistics Office. Rates for 1919 to 1935 are "monthly averages for selected long-term bond issues". Rates from 1936–1948 are "theoretical 15- year bond yields based on middle of the market quotations". Rates from 1949–1957 "refer to direct debt payable in Canadian Dollars, excluding extendible issues and Canada Savings Bonds. Prior to 1975 some extendible issues are included but their inclusion does not materially affect the average yields. The rates shown from 1949 to 1958 are arithmetic averages of yields at month-end".

**Short-Horizon Risk-free Rate:** The short-horizon risk-free series used is the DMS Canada short-term risk-free rate series.

### France

**Equity Series:** The equity series used is the MSCI France Index. The MSCI France Index is designed to measure the performance of the large and mid-cap segments of the French market. With 76 constituents, the index covers approximately 85% of the equity universe in France.

**Long-Horizon Risk-free Rate:** The long-horizon risk-free series used is the IMF France Long-term Government Income Return series. The series uses average yield to maturity on public sector bonds with original maturities of more than 5 years. Monthly yields are based on weighted averages on weekly data. Prior to April 1991, the data are average yields to maturity on bonds with original maturities of 15 to 20 years, issued on behalf of the Treasury by the Consortium of Credit for Public Works. Between April 1991 and December 1998, the data are average yields to maturity on bonds with residual maturities between 9 and 10 years. From January 1999 onward, monthly data are arithmetic averages of daily gross yields to maturity of the fixed coupon 10-year Treasury benchmark bond (last issued bond beginning from the date when it becomes the most-traded issue among government securities with residual maturities between 9 and 10 years), based on prices in the official wholesale market. The average maturity for the IMF France Long-term Government Income Return series is 10 years.

**Short-Horizon Risk-free Rate:** The short-horizon risk-free series used is the DMS France short-term risk-free rate series.

### Germany

**Equity Series:** The equity series used is the MSCI Germany GR Index (total return) series. The MSCI Germany Index is designed to measure the performance of the large and mid-cap segments of the German market. With 58 constituents, the index covers approximately 85% of the equity universe in Germany.

**Long-Horizon Risk-free Rate:** The long-horizon risk-free series used is the IMF Germany Long-term Government Income Return series. From 1970 to 1979, the bonds issued by the federal government, the railways, the portal system, the Lander government, municipalities, specific-purpose public associations, and other public associations established under special legislation are used to compose this series. This series is calculated based upon the average yields on all bonds with remaining maturity of more than 3 years, weighted by the amount of individual bonds in circulation. On January 1980, the series was changed to comprise of yields on listed federal securities that can be traded on the German Financial Futures and Options Exchange (DTB) with a remaining maturity of 9 and 10 years. The average maturity for the IMF Germany Long-term Government Income Return series is 10 years.

**Short-Horizon Risk-free Rate:** The short-horizon risk-free series used is the DMS Germany short-term risk-free rate series.

## Ireland

**Equity Series:** From 1970 to 1987, the equity series used is the DMS Ireland Index. The DMS equity return data for Ireland is comprised of the Irish CSO Price Index of Ordinary Stocks and Shares and Irish Stock Exchange Equity (ISEQ) total return index. From 1988 to present, the equity series used is MSCI Ireland GR Index (total return) series. The MSCI Ireland Index is designed to measure the performance of the large-, mid- and small-cap segments of the Irish market. With 5 constituents, the index covers approximately 85% of the free float-adjusted market capitalization in Ireland.

**Long-Horizon Risk-free Rate:** The long-horizon risk-free series used is the IMF Ireland Long-term Government Income Return series. This series uses secondary market yields of government bonds with a 10-year maturity.

**Short-Horizon Risk-free Rate:** The short-horizon risk-free series used is the DMS Ireland short-term risk-free rate series.

## Italy

**Equity Series:** The equity series used is the MSCI Index. The MSCI Italy Index is designed to measure the performance of the large and mid-cap segments of the Italian market. With 23 constituents, the index covers approximately 85% of the equity universe in Italy.

**Long-Horizon Risk-free Rate:** The long-horizon risk-free series used is the IMF Italy Long-term Government Income Return series. Prior to 1980, the data is derived from average yields to maturity on bonds with original maturities of 15 to 20 years, issued on behalf of the Treasury by the Consortium of Credit for Public Works. Beginning January 1980, average yield to maturity on bonds with residual maturities between 9 and 10 years is used. From January 1999 to present, monthly data are arithmetic averages of daily gross yields to maturity of the fixed coupon 10-year Treasury benchmark bond (last issued bond beginning from the date when it becomes the most traded issue among government securities with residual maturities between 9 and 10 years), based on prices in the official wholesale market. The average maturity for the IMF Italy Long-term Government Income Return is 17.5 years.

**Short-Horizon Risk-free Rate:** The short-horizon risk-free series used is the DMS Italy short-term risk-free rate series.

## Japan

**Equity Series:** The equity series used is the MSCI Japan Index. The MSCI Japan Index is designed to measure the performance of the large and mid-cap segments of the Japanese market. With 319 constituents, the index covers approximately 85% of the free float-adjusted market capitalization in Japan.

**Long-Horizon Risk-free Rate:** The long-horizon risk-free series used is the IMF Japan Long-term Government Income Return series. This series is based on the arithmetic yield on newly issued government bonds with 10-year maturity. The monthly series are compiled from closing (end-of-month) prices quoted on the Tokyo Stock Exchange. The average maturity for the IMF Japan Long-term Government Income Return series is 7 years.

**Short-Horizon Risk-free Rate:** The short-horizon risk-free series used is the DMS Japan short-term risk-free rate series.

### Netherlands

**Equity Series:** The equity series used is the MSCI Netherlands Index. The MSCI Netherlands Index is designed to measure the performance of the large-cap and mid-cap segments of the Netherlands market. With 24 constituents, the index covers approximately 85% of the free float-adjusted market capitalization in Netherlands.

**Long-Horizon Risk-free Rate:** The long-horizon risk-free series used the IMF Netherlands Long-term Government Income Return series. This series is based on the yield of the most recent 10-year government bond. The average maturity for the IMF Netherlands Long-term Government Income Return series is 10 years.

**Short-Horizon Risk-free Rate:** The short-horizon risk-free series used is the DMS Netherlands short-term risk-free rate series.

### New Zealand

**Equity Series:** From 1970 to 1987, the equity series used is the DMS New Zealand Index. The DMS equity return data for New Zealand comprises the Reserve Bank of New Zealand index, the Datex Index, and the New Zealand Stock Exchange gross index. From 1988 to present, the equity series used is the MSCI New Zealand Index. The MSCI New Zealand Index is designed to measure the performance of the large and mid-cap segments of the New Zealand market. With 7 constituents, the index covers approximately 85% of the free float-adjusted market capitalization in New Zealand.

**Long-Horizon Risk-free Rate:** The long-horizon risk-free series used the IMF New Zealand Long-term Government Income Return series. The average maturity for the IMF New Zealand Long-term Government Income Return series is 10 years.

**Short-Horizon Risk-free Rate:** The short-horizon risk-free series used is the DMS New Zealand short-term risk-free rate series.

### South Africa

**Equity Series:** From 1970 to 1992, the equity series used is DMS South Africa Index. The DMS equity return data for South Africa is comprised of the Rand Daily Mail Industrial Index and the Johannesburg Stock Exchange (JSE) Actuaries Equity Index. From 1993 to present, the equity series used is the MSCI South Africa Index. The MSCI South Africa Index is designed to measure the performance of the large and mid-cap segments of the South African market. With 54 constituents, the index covers approximately 85% of the free float-adjusted market capitalization in South Africa.

**Long-Horizon Risk-free Rate:** The long-horizon risk-free series used is the IMF South Africa Long-term Government Income Return series. The average maturity for the IMF South Africa Long-term Government Income Return series is 10 years.

**Short-Horizon Risk-free Rate:** The short-horizon risk-free series used is the DMS South Africa short-term risk-free rate series.

## Spain

**Equity Series:** The equity series used is the MSCI Spain Index series. The MSCI Spain Index is designed to measure the performance of the large and mid-cap segments of the Spanish market. With 25 constituents, the index covers about 85% of the equity universe in Spain.

**Long-Horizon Risk-free Rate:** The long-horizon risk-free series used is the IMF Euro Area Long-term Government Income Return series. This series is based on the Euro Area yield for 10 year government bonds calculated on the basis of harmonized national government bond yields weighted by GDP. The average maturity for the IMF Euro Area Long-term Government Income Return series is 10 years.

**Short-Horizon Risk-free Rate:** The short-horizon risk-free series used is the DMS Spain short-term risk-free rate series.

## Switzerland

**Equity Series:** The equity series used is the MSCI Switzerland GR Index (total return) series. The MSCI Switzerland Index is designed to measure the performance of the large and mid-cap segments of the Swiss market. With 38 constituents, the index covers approximately 85% of the free float-adjusted market capitalization in Switzerland.

**Long-Horizon Risk-free Rate:** The long-horizon risk-free series used is the IMF Switzerland Long-term Government Income Return series. Prior to 1987, the data is derived from yields on 15-year government bonds. Beginning January 1987, the series uses secondary market yields on 10-year bonds. The average maturity for the IMF Switzerland Long-term Government Income Return series is 10 years.

**Short-Horizon Risk-free Rate:** The short-horizon risk-free series used is the DMS Switzerland short-term risk-free rate series.

## United Kingdom

**Equity Series:** From 1900–1969, the equity series used is DMS South Africa Index.[3.30] The main data source for DMS equity returns for the U.K. over the period 1955–1969 is the fully representative record of equity prices maintained by London Business School.[3.31] For earlier periods (specifically, 1900–1954), an index comprised of the largest 100 firms by market capitalization was constructed using share price data collected from the *Financial Times*.[3.32]

From 1970 to present, the equity series used is the MSCI United Kingdom Index. The MSCI United Kingdom Index is designed to measure the performance of the large-cap and mid-cap segments of the U.K. market. With 109 constituents, the index covers approximately 85% of the free float adjusted market capitalization in the U.K.

**Long-Horizon Risk-free Rate:** From 1900–1969, the long-horizon risk-free series is based upon "gilt" redemption yields available from the Bank of England as a proxy for income returns.[3.33, 3.34] From 1970 to present, the long-horizon risk-free series used is the IMF U.K. Long-term Government Income Return series. The average maturity for the IMF U.K. Long-term Government Income Return series is 20 years. These are theoretical gross redemption bond yields.

**Short-Horizon Risk-free Rate:** The short-horizon risk-free series used is the DMS United Kingdom short-term risk-free rate series.

## United States

**Equity Series:** U.S. equities are represented by the Standard & Poor's S&P 500® Index (total return) series. The S&P 500 Index is a readily available, carefully constructed, market-value-weighted benchmark of common stock performance. Market-value-weighted means that the weight of each stock in the index, for a given month, is proportionate to its market capitalization (price times the number of shares outstanding) at the beginning of that month. Currently, this composite index includes 500 of the largest stocks (in terms of stock market value) in the United States; prior to March 1957 it consisted of 90 of the largest stocks.

**Long-Horizon Risk-free Rate:** The long-horizon risk-free series used is the SBBI U.S. Long-term Government Income Return series. The total returns on long-term government bonds from 1977 to present are constructed with data from the *Wall Street Journal*. The data from 1926–1976 are obtained from the Government Bond File at the Center for Research in Security Prices (CRSP) at the

---

[3.30] Elroy Dimson, Paul Marsh, and Mike Staunton, *Credit Suisse Global Investment Returns Yearbook 2017* (Credit Suisse, 2017).

[3.31] As described in Elroy Dimson, and Paul Marsh, 1983, "The stability of UK risk measures and the problem of thin trading", *Journal of Finance*, 38: 753–783.

[3.32] For detailed index construction methodology, see Elroy Dimson, Paul Marsh, and Mike Staunton, *Credit Suisse Global Investment Returns Yearbook 2017* (Credit Suisse, 2017), pages 210–212.

[3.33] "Redemption" yield of a gilt is a measure of the return implicit in its prevailing market price, assuming that the gilt is held to maturity and that all cash flows are reinvested back into the gilt.

[3.34] Historical average conventional gilt yields are provided, these being calculated as the *average* daily close of business yields for the prevailing short, medium, long and ultra-long dated benchmark gilts for each month since April 1998. *Average* daily yields for 2½% Consolidated Stock are available on an annual basis from 1727 to 2016. To learn more, visit: http://www.dmo.gov.uk/index.aspx?page=Gilts/Yields.

University of Chicago Graduate School of Business. To the greatest extent possible, a one-bond portfolio with a term of approximately 20 years and a reasonably current coupon whose returns did not reflect potential tax benefits, impaired negotiability, or special redemption or call privileges was used each year. Where "flower" bonds (tenderable to the Treasury at par in payment of estate taxes) had to be used, the bond with the smallest potential tax benefit was chosen. Where callable bonds had to be used, the term of the bond was assumed to be a simple average of the maturity and first call dates minus the current date.

The bond was "held" for the calendar year and returns were computed. From 1977 to present, the income return is calculated as the change in flat price plus any coupon actually paid from one period to the next, holding the yield constant over the period. As in the total return series, the exact number of days comprising the period is used. From 1926–1976, the income return for a given month is calculated as the total return minus the capital appreciation return.

**Short-Horizon Risk-free Rate:** The risk-free series used is the IA SBBI U.S. 30 Day Treasury bill series. For the U.S. Treasury bill index, data from the *Wall Street Journal* are used from 1977–present; the CRSP U.S. Government Bond File is the source until 1976. Each month a one-bill portfolio containing the shortest-term bill having not less than one month to maturity is constructed. (The bill's original term to maturity is not relevant.) To measure holding period returns for the one-bill portfolio, the bill is priced as of the last trading day of the previous month-end and as of the last trading day of the current month.

**Currency Translation**

Currency translation is used only in cases in which a series *not* in the needed currency (specifically, USD or "local") is available.

**Equities:** MSCI provides a total return equity series in USD for each of the 16 countries presented here, and so for these series no currency translation was required. MSCI provides a total return equity series in local for each of the 16 countries presented here, and so for these series no currency translation was required. Dimson, Marsh, Staunton (DMS) total return equity series were available in USD and local, and so for these series no currency translation was required.

**Risk-free Rates:** Long-term IMF risk-free series in local currency were available, and so for these series no currency translation was required. These series were then translated into USD currency.[3.35] Short-term Dimson, Marsh, Staunton (DMS) risk-free series were available in USD and local, and so for these series no currency translation was required.

Exhibit 3.2 provides a summary of the data series used to calculate the historical ERPs presented in Data Exhibit 1, "2017 International Equity Risk Premia".

---

[3.35] Source of currency conversion data: Morningstar *Direct* database. Exchange rate sources (as reported by Morningstar): 1960–1987 Main Economic Indicators Historical Statistics (Organisation for Economic Co-operation and Development); 1988–present the *Wall Street Journal*.

**Exhibit 3.2:** Data Series Used to Calculate the Equity Risk Premia (ERPs) Presented in Data Exhibit 1

| Country | Long-Horizon ERP Start Date | Short-Horizon ERP Start Date | Equity Series | Long-Horizon Risk-Free Series | Short-Horizon Risk-Free Series |
|---|---|---|---|---|---|
| Australia | 1970 | 1970 | MSCI Australia GR | IMF Australia LT Gvt Inc Ret | DMS Australia Bill TR |
| Austria | 1972 USD 1971 Local | 1970 | MSCI Austria GR | IMF Austria LT Gvt Inc Ret | DMS Austria Bill TR |
| Belgium | 1970 | 1970 | MSCI Belgium GR | IMF Belgium LT Gvt Inc Ret | DMS Belgium Bill TR |
| Canada | 1919 | 1919 | 1919–1969 DMS Canada Equity TR 1970–2016 MSCI Canada GR | 1919–1957 Bank of Canada Yield Data 1958–2016 IMF Canada LT Gvt Inc Ret | DMS Canada Bill TR |
| France | 1970 | 1970 | MSCI France GR | IMF France LT Gvt Inc Ret | DMS France Bill TR |
| Germany | 1970 | 1970 | MSCI Germany GR | IMF Germany LT Gvt Inc Ret | DMS Germany Bill TR |
| Ireland | 1970 | 1970 | 1970–1987 DMS Ireland Equity 1988–2016 MSCI Ireland GR | IMF Ireland LT Gvt Inc Ret | DMS Ireland Bill TR |
| Italy | 1970 | 1970 | MSCI Italy GR | IMF Italy LT Gvt Inc Ret | DMS Italy Bill TR |
| Japan | 1970 | 1970 | MSCI Japan GR | IMF Japan LT Gvt Inc Ret | DMS Japan Bill TR |
| Netherlands | 1970 | 1970 | MSCI Netherlands GR | IMF Netherlands LT Gvt Inc Ret | DMS Netherlands Bill TR |
| New Zealand | 1970 | 1970 | 1970–1987 DMS New Zealand Equity 1988–2016 MSCI New Zealand GR | IMF New Zealand LT Gvt Inc Ret | DMS New Zealand Bill TR |
| South Africa | 1971 USD 1970 Local | 1970 | 1970–1992 DMS South Africa Equity 1993–2016 MSCI South Africa GR | IMF South Africa LT Gvt Inc Ret | DMS South Africa Bill TR |
| Spain | 1972 USD 1971 Local | 1970 | MSCI Spain GR | IMF Euro Area LT Gvt Inc Ret | DMS Spain Bill TR |
| Switzerland | 1970 | 1970 | MSCI Switzerland GR | IMF Switzerland LT Gvt Inc Ret | DMS Switzerland Bill TR |
| United Kingdom | 1900 | 1900 | 1900–1969 DMS United Kingdom Equity 1970–2016 MSCI United Kingdom GR | 1900–1969 Bank of England "Gilt" Redemption Yields 1970–2016 IMF U.K. LT Gvt Inc Ret | DMS UK Bill TR |
| United States | 1926 | 1926 | S&P 500 TR (IA Extended) | IA SBBI U.S. LT Gvt IR | IA SBBI U.S. 30 Day Tbill |

## How to Use the International ERP Tables

The previous Morningstar/Ibbotson *International Equity Risk Premium Report* included large "wedge" tables in which historical ERP estimates were calculated over all possible start-year and end-year combinations (e.g., ERPs calculated over the time horizon 1970–2016, 1984–1995, or 1976–1977). While this presentation was complete, one could argue that ERPs calculated over many of these possible time horizons are extraneous, and not very informative.

For this reason, the historical ERP estimates presented herein include all possible estimates calculated over the (i) longest period available, and then (ii) beginning in years divisible by 5, and finally (iii) the most recent completed calendar year.

For example, Germany has equity return and risk-free rate data available starting in 1970, and so 1970–2016 is the longest period available (see Exhibit 3.3 on the next page). Then, the "starting years divisible by 5" are 1975, 1980, etc. Finally, 2016 is the "most recent completed calendar year".

Like the previous Morningstar/Ibbotson *International Equity Risk Premium Report*, historical ERPs are calculated in USD and "local" currencies.

Using "Germany Long-Horizon Equity Risk Premia In Local Currency" (see Exhibit 3.3 on the next page), in example "A" the long-horizon historical ERP as measured over the period 1970 (the "start date") and 2016 (the "end date") is 5.1%. Alternatively, in example "B" the long-horizon historical ERP as measured over the period 1980 (the "start date") and 1987 (the "end date") is 8.0%.[3.36]

Note that the example shown in Exhibit 3.3 is Germany long-horizon ERP, as calculated in local currency. In the case of Germany, the "local" currency is the Euro, as reported in Exhibit 3.1.

---

[3.36] All values are presented in percent format, rounded to one decimal place.

**Exhibit 3.3:** Using the Tables (examples using an abbreviated version of Data Exhibit 1)

## Germany Long-Horizon Equity Risk Premia

in Local Currency (Euro - EUR)
in Percent

|  | A | | B | | | | |
|---|---|---|---|---|---|---|---|
|  | Start Date | | | | | | |
| End Date | 1970 | 1975 | 1980 | 1985 | 1990 | 1995 | 2000 |
| 1970 | -31.7 | | | | | | |
| 1971 | -14.2 | | | | | | |
| 1972 | -6.7 | | | | | | |
| 1973 | -12.1 | | | | | | |
| 1974 | -10.8 | | | | | | |
| 1975 | -3.6 | 32.4 | | | | | |
| 1976 | -4.8 | 10.2 | | | | | |
| 1977 | -3.5 | 8.6 | | | | | |
| 1978 | -2.8 | 7.1 | | | | | |
| 1979 | -4.1 | 2.5 | | | | | |
| 1980 | -4.3 | 1.0 | -6.4 | | | | |
| 1981 | -4.5 | -0.1 | -6.5 | | | | |
| 1982 | -3.6 | 0.9 | -1.8 | | | | |
| 1983 | -0.9 | 4.6 | 7.1 | | | | |
| 1984 | -0.8 | 4.2 | 6.0 | | | | |
| 1985 | 4.2 | 10.9 | 18.0 | 77.8 | | | |
| 1986 | 4.0 | 10.1 | 15.5 | 39.4 | | | |
| 1987 | 1.3 | 5.9 | 8.0 | 11.5 | | | |
| 1988 | 2.8 | 7.6 | 10.5 | 16.1 | | | |
| // | | | | | | | |
| 2011 | 4.0 | 6.0 | 6.6 | 6.7 | 3.7 | 5.4 | -1.5 |
| 2012 | 4.6 | 6.6 | 7.2 | 7.4 | 4.8 | 6.7 | 0.8 |
| 2013 | 5.0 | 7.1 | 7.7 | 8.1 | 5.7 | 7.7 | 2.6 |
| 2014 | 5.0 | 6.9 | 7.6 | 7.8 | 5.5 | 7.4 | 2.5 |
| 2015 | 5.1 | 7.0 | 7.6 | 7.9 | 5.6 | 7.5 | 2.9 |
| 2016 | 5.1 | 7.0 | 7.6 | 7.8 | 5.7 | 7.4 | 3.1 |

# Appendix 3A
# Additional Sources of International Equity Risk Premium Data

Data Exhibit 1 includes historical equity risk premia (ERPs) estimates for 16 economies around the world, through December 2016.[3A.1] The ERP values in Data Exhibit 1 are calculated using the same general data sources and methodologies that were used to calculate the ERPs previously published in the Morningstar/Ibbotson *International Equity Risk Premia Report*.[3A.2]

For completeness, in Appendix 3A we briefly discuss additional sources of international ERP information.

### Dimson, Marsh, and Staunton Equity Risk Premia Data

Dimson, Marsh, and Staunton (DMS) studied the realized equity returns and equity premia relative to bonds for 21 countries (including the United States) from 1900 to the end of 2016.[3A.3, 3A.4] These authors report the following realized equity risk premia relative to the total return on long-term government bonds (returns for the three geographic regions are expressed in U.S. Dollars, from a global investor perspective):

**Exhibit 3A.1:** Dimson, Marsh, and Staunton Equity Risk Premia Relative to Bonds 1900–2016

|  | Geometric Mean (%) | Arithmetic Mean (%) |
|---|---|---|
| Canada | 3.4 | 5.0 |
| Japan | 5.0 | 9.0 |
| United Kingdom | 3.6 | 4.9 |
| Europe | 3.1 | 4.4 |
| World ex-U.S. | 2.8 | 3.8 |
| World | 3.2 | 4.4 |

---

[3A.1]  "Premia" is the plural of premium. A single equity risk premium is denoted "ERP"; the plural equity risk premia is denoted "ERPs".

[3A.2]  The Morningstar/Ibbotson *International Equity Risk Premia Report* was discontinued in 2013.

[3A.3]  Elroy Dimson, Paul Marsh, and Mike Staunton, *Credit Suisse Global Investment Returns Yearbook 2017* (London: Credit Suisse/London Business School, 2017).

[3A.4]  The *Credit Suisse Global Investment Returns Yearbook 2017* reports equity risk premia relative to (i) bills and (ii) bonds in Table 9 and Table 10 therein, respectively, for 21 countries and the world, the world ex-USA, and Europe. The 21 countries for which ERPs are reported are: Australia, Austria, Belgium, Canada, Denmark, Finland, France, Germany, Ireland, Italy, Japan, the Netherlands, New Zealand, Norway, Portugal, South Africa, Spain, Sweden, Switzerland, United Kingdom, and the United States. Dimson, Marsh, and Staunton's database also includes two additional countries, China and Russia, but these two countries have "discontinuous histories", and are thus not reported in Table 9 or Table 10. China and Russia are, however, included in full in the DMS "World" index.

Dimson, Marsh, and Staunton observe larger equity returns earned in the second half of the twentieth century than in the first half due to (i) corporate cash flows growing faster than investors anticipated (fueled by rapid technological change and unprecedented growth in productivity and efficiency), (ii) transaction and monitoring costs falling over the course of the century, and (iii) required rates of return on equity declining because of diminished business and investment risks.

The authors conclude that:

- The 8.7% annualized real return on the world equity index from 1950 to 1999 (or the 6.9% from 1950–2016) almost certainly exceeded expectations and more than compensated for the poor first half of the 20th century when the annualized real return was only 2.7%;

- Prior to 1950, dividend growth was only positive for three countries (Australia, New Zealand, and the U.S.), in real terms. In contrast, from 1950 to 2016 real dividend growth was positive for 20 of the 21 countries reported (the exception was Italy). However, the healthy real dividend growth on the world index post-1950 relied heavily on the contribution of the U.S. market. The authors argue that the positive 1900–2016 average real dividend growth was partly due to "good luck" observed in the post-1950 years, which far outweighed the "bad luck" seen in the first half of the century, and this trend should not be expected to continue in the future. Alternatively, they argue that the expected dividend yield should be lower than in the past, if one assumes the same (or a higher) real growth rate in dividends. The authors conclude that a dividend yield similar to the 1900–2016 historical average, combined with a real dividend growth rate in excess of 2.0% per year (similar to the post-1950 level) is highly unlikely.

- The observed increase in the overall price-to-dividend ratio during the past century is attributable to the long-term decrease in the required risk premium. Equity risk became more diversifiable as diversified funds and new industries came into existence, while liquidity (accompanied by a decline in transaction costs) and risk management improved. These developments have likely reduced the required equity premium, but the resulting increase in realized equity returns does not signal an increase in the required ERP going forward. In addition, a further increase in stock prices due to declining barriers to diversification is not a repeatable phenomenon and the price-to-dividend ratio re-rating is not likely to continue into the future.

Dimson, Marsh, and Staunton conclude that downward adjustment to real growth in dividends in the future compared to history is likely and the realized risk premia due to the increase in price-to-dividend ratio are warranted.[3A.5] One can estimate a range of likely forward-looking ERP estimates by adjusting the historical data via (i) a reduction in the expected real growth rate in dividends or (ii) by removing the increase in the price-to-dividend ratio, while keeping the same expected real growth rate in dividends.

---

[3A.5]    See discussion in Elroy Dimson, Paul Marsh, and Mike Staunton, *Credit Suisse Global Investment Returns Yearbook 2017*: 32–37.

Applying the guidance in Dimson et al. to remove non-repeatable factors, and using a 50-year average standard deviation in ERP (over the 1967–2016 period) as a proxy for forward-looking volatility, one can estimate an expected world (or global) arithmetic average ERP in early 2017 of 4.0% to 4.5% (2.0% – 2.5% on a geometric basis) relative to *long-term* government bonds, in U.S. Dollar terms. This is consistent with the authors' own estimate of 4.5% to 5.0% arithmetic average ERP (3.0% – 3.5% on a geometric basis) relative to a *short-term* risk-free rate (i.e., government bills). Exhibit 3A.2 displays a possible application of the authors' guidance, which supports these estimates. This forward looking ERP estimate is useful in implementing the World CAPM model.

**Exhibit 3A.2:** Estimated World ERP Based on Dimson, Marsh, and Staunton Analysis 1900–2016 (in USD)

| | | Historical World Data (%)[*] | Conversion to Expectations | |
| --- | --- | --- | --- | --- |
| | | | Low (%) | High (%) |
| | Geometric average dividend yield | 4.05% | 4.05% | 4.05% |
| Plus: | Growth rate in real dividends | 0.51% | 0.00% | 0.51% |
| Plus: | Expansion in the Price-to-Dividend ratio | 0.45% | 0.00%[****] | 0.00%[****] |
| Plus: | Changes in real exchange rate | 0.00% | 0.00% | 0.00% |
| Minus: | Real rate of return on bonds[**] | 1.8% | 1.8% | 1.8% |
| Equals: | Geometric Average Equity Risk Premium in excess of bonds | 3.2% | 2.2% | 2.7% |
| Plus: | Conversion to arithmetic average equivalent[***] | 1.2% | 1.6% | 1.6% |
| Equals: | Arithmetic Average Equity Risk Premium in excess of bonds | 4.4% | 3.8% | 4.3% |

**Source of underlying data:** Elroy Dimson, Paul Marsh, and Mike Staunton, *Credit Suisse Global Investment Returns Yearbook 2017*; calculations by Duff & Phelps, LLC. [*]Decomposition of historical World ERP based on Dimson, Marsh, and Staunton analysis (see Table 11 in *Credit Suisse Global Investment Returns Yearbook 2017*). [**]Real bond returns for the World portfolio, based on Dimson, Marsh, and Staunton analysis (see Table 5 in *Credit Suisse Global Investment Returns Yearbook 2017*). [***]Historical Arithmetic Average ERP equivalent = Geometric Average ERP + (Variance of ERP divided by two). Using the standard deviation of ERP over the 1900–2016 period (see Table 10 in *Credit Suisse Global Investment Returns Yearbook 2017*) results in the incremental premium of 1.2% (rounded). The authors of the *2017 Valuation Handbook – International Guide to Cost of Capital* estimate the conversion to arithmetic average equivalent based on standard deviation over a 50-year period (1967–2016) (17.9%) to be a better proxy for an estimated future volatility. Using the same formula results in an upwards adjustment of 1.6% (rounded). [****]Further expansion in price-to-dividend ratio is not likely for mature markets.

For the *2017 Valuation Handbook – International Guide to Cost of Capital*, we asked Professors Dimson, Marsh, and Staunton for an extended analysis of their database, which would enable us to report information under two different investor perspectives: (i) U.S. investor (in U.S. Dollars, or USD); and (ii) U.K. investor (in British Pounds, or GBP). Using their database, Professor Dimson and his co-authors calculated the 1900–2016 geometric average equity risk premia relative to bonds for the following countries and geographic regions (as defined by Dimson et al.): (i) Canada; (ii) Japan; (iii) United Kingdom; (iv) Europe excluding Russia; (v) World excluding U.S.; and (vi) World. This information is presented in Exhibit 3A.3, under the columns labeled as "Historical" for each of the countries/regions.

Exhibit 3A.3 shows each historical ERP decomposed into its underlying elements (i.e., dividend yield, growth rate of real dividends, expansion of price-to-dividend ratio, and changes in real exchange rate), similar to the information contained in the authors' published work. This historical geometric ERP was then converted into its arithmetic equivalent, using a standard deviation over the same historical period (1900–2016). The top half of Exhibit 3A.3 displays information under a U.S. investor perspective, while the bottom half depicts similar data from a U.K. investor perspective. For example, over the 1900–2016 period, the realized average arithmetic ERP relative to bonds was 5.0% in Canada, from a U.S. investor perspective (in USD terms). Similarly, the realized average arithmetic ERP relative to bonds by a U.K. investor investing in the United Kingdom was 5.1% (in GBP terms).

A similar approach was used to convert historical realized ERPs into a possible forward-looking indication for each of the countries and geographic regions (see the column labeled "Forward" in Exhibit 3A.3).

**Exhibit 3A.3** Historical and Forward-looking ERP Indications Based on Dimson, Marsh, and Staunton Analysis under U.S. and U.K. Investor Perspectives

**United States Investor Perspective (U.S. Dollars – USD)**
1900–2016
in Percent

| | Canada | | Japan | | United Kingdom | | Europe ex-Russia***** | | World ex-U.S. | | World | |
|---|---|---|---|---|---|---|---|---|---|---|---|---|
| | Historical* | Forward | Historical* | Forward | Historical* | Forward | Historical* | Forward | Historical* | Forward | Historical* | Forward |
| Geometric average dividend yield | 4.31 | 4.31 | 5.06 | 5.06 | 4.59 | 4.59 | 4.15 | 4.15 | 4.02 | 4.02 | 4.05 | 4.05 |
| Plus: Growth rate in real dividends | 0.91 | 0.91 | -1.75 | -1.75 | 0.86 | 0.86 | -0.02 | -0.02 | 0.00 | 0.00 | 0.51 | 0.51 |
| Plus: Expansion in the Price-to-Dividend ratio** | 0.45 | 0.00 | 0.91 | 0.00 | -0.01 | 0.00 | 0.13 | 0.00 | 0.30 | 0.00 | 0.45 | 0.00 |
| Plus: Changes in real exchange rate*** | -0.18 | 0.00 | 0.15 | 0.00 | -0.38 | 0.00 | 0.00 | 0.00 | 0.00 | 0.00 | 0.00 | 0.00 |
| Minus: Real rate of return on bonds | 2.0 | 2.0 | 2.0 | 2.0 | 2.0 | 2.0 | 2.0 | 2.0 | 2.0 | 2.0 | 2.0 | 2.0 |
| Equals: Geometric Average Equity Risk Premium in excess of bonds | 3.5 | 3.2 | 2.3 | 1.2 | 3.0 | 3.4 | 2.3 | 2.1 | 2.3 | 2.0 | 3.0 | 2.5 |
| Plus: Conversion to arithmetic average equivalent**** | 1.7 | 1.8 | 5.2 | 3.2 | 1.5 | 2.3 | 1.3 | 1.6 | 1.1 | 1.6 | 1.2 | 1.6 |
| Equals: Arithmetic Average Equity Risk Premium in excess of bonds | 5.2 | 5.0 | 7.5 | 4.4 | 4.5 | 5.8 | 3.5 | 3.7 | 3.4 | 3.6 | 4.2 | 4.1 |

**United Kingdom Investor Perspective (Pound Sterling – GBP)**
1900–2016
in Percent

| | Canada | | Japan | | United Kingdom | | Europe ex-Russia***** | | World ex-U.S. | | World | |
|---|---|---|---|---|---|---|---|---|---|---|---|---|
| | Historical* | Forward | Historical* | Forward | Historical* | Forward | Historical* | Forward | Historical* | Forward | Historical* | Forward |
| Geometric average dividend yield | 4.31 | 4.31 | 5.06 | 5.06 | 4.59 | 4.59 | 4.15 | 4.15 | 4.02 | 4.02 | 4.05 | 4.05 |
| Plus: Growth rate in real dividends | 0.91 | 0.91 | -1.75 | -1.75 | 0.86 | 0.86 | -0.02 | -0.02 | 0.00 | 0.00 | 0.51 | 0.51 |
| Plus: Expansion in the Price-to-Dividend ratio** | 0.45 | 0.00 | 0.91 | 0.00 | -0.01 | 0.00 | 0.13 | 0.00 | 0.30 | 0.00 | 0.45 | 0.00 |
| Plus: Changes in real exchange rate*** | 0.20 | 0.00 | 0.53 | 0.00 | 0.00 | 0.00 | 0.38 | 0.00 | 0.38 | 0.00 | 0.38 | 0.00 |
| Minus: Real rate of return on bonds | 1.8 | 1.8 | 1.8 | 1.8 | 1.8 | 1.8 | 1.8 | 1.8 | 1.8 | 1.8 | 1.8 | 1.8 |
| Equals: Geometric Average Equity Risk Premium in excess of bonds | 4.1 | 3.4 | 2.9 | 1.4 | 3.6 | 3.6 | 2.8 | 2.3 | 2.9 | 2.2 | 3.6 | 2.7 |
| Plus: Conversion to arithmetic average equivalent**** | 1.7 | 1.8 | 5.2 | 3.2 | 1.5 | 2.3 | 1.3 | 1.6 | 1.1 | 1.6 | 1.2 | 1.6 |
| Equals: Arithmetic Average Equity Risk Premium in excess of bonds | 5.7 | 5.1 | 8.1 | 4.6 | 5.1 | 5.9 | 4.1 | 3.9 | 3.9 | 3.8 | 4.8 | 4.3 |

\* Historical data for "geometric average equity premium in excess of bonds", as calculated and provided by Dimson, Marsh, and Staunton.

** Further expansion in P/D ratio is not likely for mature markets in forward-looking estimate.

*** According to the Dimson, Marsh, and Staunton analysis, the long-term consensus forecast for changes in the real (inflation-adjusted) exchange rate is zero.

**** Historical arithmetic average equivalent = geometric average + (std. deviation)$^2$/2, with standard deviation over the 1900–2016 period sourced from Table 10. The authors of the *2017 Valuation Handbook – International Guide to Cost of Capital* estimate the forward conversion to arithmetic average equivalent based on standard deviation over a 50-year (1967–2016) period to be a better proxy for an estimated future volatility.

***** Standard deviation for the "Europe ex-Russia" portfolio, based on "Europe" portfolio as provided by Dimson, Marsh, and Staunton analysis.

An example of how the "forward" (i.e., future) "arithmetic average equity risk premia in excess of bonds" shown in Exhibit 3A.3 are calculated is provided in Exhibit 3A.4. In this example, we use "Japan" in USD (USD results are shown in the *top* panel of Exhibit 3A.3).

**Exhibit 3A.4**: An Example of Calculating the "Forward" (i.e., future) "Arithmetic Average Equity Risk Premia in Excess of Bonds" Shown in Exhibit 3A.3
1900–2016 (in USD)

|  |  | Japan | |
|---|---|---|---|
|  |  | Historical | Forward |
|  | Geometric average dividend yield | 5.06 | 5.06 |
| Plus: | Growth rate in real dividends | -1.75 | -1.75 |
| Plus: | Expansion in the Price-to-Dividend ratio | **0.91** | **0.00** |
| Plus: | Changes in real exchange rate | **0.15** | **0.00** |
| Minus: | Real rate of return on bonds | 2.0 | 2.0 |
| Equals: | Geometric Average Equity Risk Premium in excess of bonds | 2.3 | 1.2 |
| Plus: | Conversion to arithmetic average equivalent | 5.2 | 3.2 |
| Equals: | Arithmetic Average Equity Risk Premium in excess of bonds | 7.5 | 4.4 |

In this analysis, the *historical* (i) geometric average dividend yield (5.06%), (ii) growth rate in real dividends (-1.75%), and (iii) real rate of return on bonds (2.0%) are all assumed to be good proxies for these values going *forward*. The historical "expansion in the price-to-dividend ratio" (0.91%) and "changes in real exchange rate" (0.15%), however, are considered by Dimson, Marsh, and Staunton to be unsustainable (i.e., non-repeatable) going forward, and so the 0.91% and 0.15% are therefore *not* included in the *forward* calculations column.[3A.6]

The "forward" geometric average equity risk premium in excess of bonds is thus calculated as:

(1 + Geometric average dividend yield; 5.06%) x (1 + Growth rate in real dividends; -1.75%) x
(1 + Expansion in the Price-to-Dividend ratio; assumed to be 0.00% going forward) x
(1 + Changes in real exchange rate; assumed to be 0.00% going forward) /
(1 − Real rate of return on bonds; 2.0%) − 1

= 1.20%

Finally, the *geometric* average equity risk premium in excess of bonds (1.2%) is converted to an *arithmetic* equivalent by adding a conversion factor of 3.2%.[3A.7] The forward arithmetic average equity risk premium in excess of bonds is therefore 4.4% (1.2% + 3.2%).

---

[3A.6] All additions and subtractions were performed in geometric terms, with the exception of the conversion from a geometric into an arithmetic average (the last step in each of the columns).

[3A.7] Calculated assuming returns are lognormally distributed over time, and generally follow the relationship: arithmetic average = geometric average + [((standard deviation in ERP relative to long-term government bonds)^2)/2]. In exhibit 3A.3 the 50-year (1967–2016) standard deviation in ERP relative to long-term government bonds was used in this calculation.

## Pablo Fernandez Equity Risk Premia and Risk-free Rate Surveys

Professor Pablo Fernandez and his co-authors survey "finance and economics professors, analysts and managers", asking them what equity risk premium they are using to "calculate the required return to equity in different countries".[3A.8] [3A.9]

In April 2017, Professor Fernandez sent an email to more than 20,000 finance and economics professors, analysts, and managers of companies. By April 2017, he had received over 4,000 responses for ERPs used in 2017.[3A.10] This year's study by Professor Fernandez and his colleagues focused on equity risk premia *and* risk-free rates for 41 countries. Exhibits 3A.5 and 3A.6 in the *Valuation Handbook — International Guide to Cost of Capital* present data on the equity risk premia for the 41 countries presented in the studies by Professor Fernandez and his colleagues.

The average ERP for 30 of the 41 countries presented was higher in this year's survey than in 2016's. In eight countries the average ERP used in 2017 was more than 1% greater than the one used in 2016.

In Exhibit 3A.5, the ERP survey results are compiled for the results of 41 countries from 2013 through 2017.

In Exhibit 3A.6, the ERP results from the 2017 survey are presented for these same 41 countries (average = red diamonds; standard deviation = black vertical lines).

---

[3A.8] Pablo Fernandez is professor in the Department of Financial Management at IESE, the graduate business school of the University of Navarra, Spain.

[3A.9] Pablo Fernandez, Vitaly Pershin, and Isabel Fernández Acín, "Discount Rate (Risk-Free Rate and Market Risk Premium) Used for 41 Countries in 2017: A Survey.

[3A.10] 1,874 emails contained ERPs for more than one country; 37 of the responses were discarded as outliers (unreasonably low or high); 193 respondents reported that they did not use an ERP; countries that had fewer than 25 valid responses were excluded from the results. The total number of countries with at least 25 valid responses was 41; in Exhibit 3A.4 and Exhibit 3A.5 we report the 41 countries that had data available for the most recent 5 years (2013 through 2017).

**Exhibit 3A.5:** Comparison of Equity Risk Premium (ERP) Survey Results for 41 Countries Over Time 2013 through 2017

| | Average Equity Risk Premium (ERP) (%) | | | | | Median Equity Risk Premium (ERP) (%) | | | | | Standard Deviation (%) | | | | |
|---|---|---|---|---|---|---|---|---|---|---|---|---|---|---|---|
| | 2013 | 2014 | 2015 | 2016 | 2017 | 2013 | 2014 | 2015 | 2016 | 2017 | 2013 | 2014 | 2015 | 2016 | 2017 |
| Argentina | 10.6 | 11.8 | 22.9 | 11.8 | 16.3 | 6.8 | 11.5 | 20.1 | 11.0 | 17.5 | 8.1 | 4.2 | 12.3 | 4.4 | 5.5 |
| Australia | 6.8 | 5.9 | 6.0 | 6.0 | 7.3 | 5.8 | 6.0 | 5.1 | 6.0 | 7.6 | 4.9 | 1.6 | 4.0 | 1.6 | 1.2 |
| Austria | 6.0 | 5.5 | 5.7 | 5.4 | 6.4 | 5.8 | 5.5 | 5.6 | 5.3 | 6.6 | 1.9 | 1.5 | 0.3 | 1.4 | 0.9 |
| Belgium | 6.1 | 5.6 | 5.5 | 5.6 | 6.4 | 6.0 | 5.5 | 5.4 | 5.5 | 6.6 | 1.8 | 1.1 | 1.3 | 1.1 | 0.9 |
| Brazil | 6.5 | 7.8 | 7.5 | 8.2 | 9.0 | 6.0 | 7.0 | 7.0 | 7.0 | 9.6 | 2.1 | 4.2 | 2.1 | 4.9 | 2.3 |
| Canada | 5.4 | 5.3 | 5.9 | 5.4 | 6.0 | 5.3 | 5.0 | 6.0 | 5.2 | 6.4 | 1.3 | 1.2 | 1.3 | 1.3 | 1.3 |
| Chile | 5.0 | 6.0 | 6.5 | 6.1 | 6.2 | 5.5 | 5.6 | 6.5 | 6.0 | 6.4 | 2.2 | 1.5 | 0.9 | 1.6 | 0.7 |
| China | 7.7 | 8.1 | 8.1 | 8.3 | 7.5 | 7.0 | 7.0 | 7.0 | 7.0 | 7.8 | 2.3 | 3.5 | 5.6 | 4.4 | 1.3 |
| Colombia | 8.4 | 8.1 | 8.3 | 8.1 | 7.6 | 8.8 | 7.8 | 8.0 | 7.8 | 8.1 | 3.4 | 3.8 | 1.4 | 3.9 | 1.5 |
| Czech Republic | 6.5 | 6.5 | 5.6 | 6.3 | 6.2 | 7.0 | 6.5 | 5.4 | 6.5 | 6.4 | 1.1 | 1.6 | 0.7 | 1.0 | 0.7 |
| Denmark | 6.4 | 5.1 | 5.5 | 5.3 | 6.1 | 5.9 | 5.0 | 5.5 | 5.0 | 6.3 | 0.8 | 1.8 | 1.2 | 1.7 | 0.8 |
| Finland | 6.8 | 5.6 | 5.7 | 5.5 | 5.9 | 6.0 | 5.4 | 5.8 | 5.0 | 6.1 | 1.2 | 1.6 | 1.1 | 1.6 | 0.7 |
| France | 6.1 | 5.8 | 5.6 | 5.8 | 6.5 | 6.0 | 5.9 | 5.5 | 5.5 | 6.7 | 1.6 | 1.5 | 1.4 | 1.6 | 1.1 |
| Germany | 5.5 | 5.4 | 5.3 | 5.3 | 5.7 | 5.0 | 5.0 | 5.1 | 5.0 | 5.9 | 1.7 | 1.7 | 1.5 | 1.7 | 1.3 |
| Greece | 7.3 | 15.0 | 14.3 | 13.0 | 16.2 | 6.0 | 16.5 | 15.0 | 12.4 | 17.6 | 4.1 | 4.7 | 5.8 | 5.2 | 3.8 |
| Hungary | 8.2 | 8.3 | 8.8 | 8.1 | 8.4 | 8.7 | 8.9 | 8.9 | 8.0 | 8.6 | 1.6 | 2.3 | 0.8 | 2.5 | 0.9 |
| India | 8.5 | 8.0 | 8.4 | 8.1 | 8.5 | 8.8 | 8.0 | 8.3 | 8.0 | 9.0 | 2.9 | 2.4 | 2.5 | 2.4 | 2.3 |
| Indonesia | 7.8 | 7.9 | 8.9 | 8.0 | 8.9 | 8.0 | 8.0 | 9.0 | 8.0 | 9.1 | 1.4 | 2.0 | 1.2 | 2.1 | 0.8 |
| Ireland | 6.2 | 6.8 | 5.5 | 6.6 | 6.7 | 7.0 | 6.3 | 5.2 | 5.8 | 6.8 | 3.3 | 2.4 | 1.3 | 2.2 | 0.7 |
| Israel | 6.4 | 5.8 | 5.2 | 5.9 | 6.5 | 7.0 | 5.0 | 5.0 | 6.0 | 6.6 | 1.1 | 2.1 | 1.1 | 2.2 | 0.7 |
| Italy | 5.7 | 5.6 | 5.4 | 5.6 | 6.4 | 5.5 | 5.5 | 5.2 | 5.5 | 6.7 | 1.5 | 1.5 | 1.5 | 1.5 | 1.2 |
| Japan | 6.6 | 5.3 | 5.8 | 5.4 | 6.0 | 6.4 | 5.0 | 6.0 | 5.0 | 6.1 | 2.7 | 2.4 | 2.0 | 2.3 | 1.3 |
| Korea (South) | 7.0 | 6.3 | 6.2 | 6.7 | 6.6 | 6.9 | 6.3 | 6.0 | 7.0 | 6.8 | 1.8 | 1.8 | 1.5 | 1.8 | 0.7 |
| Mexico | 6.7 | 7.4 | 8.0 | 7.4 | 9.3 | 6.3 | 6.7 | 8.0 | 7.0 | 10.1 | 2.4 | 2.4 | 1.5 | 2.3 | 3.1 |
| Netherlands | 6.0 | 5.2 | 5.9 | 5.1 | 6.0 | 5.8 | 5.0 | 6.0 | 5.0 | 6.2 | 1.3 | 1.2 | 0.6 | 1.2 | 0.8 |
| New Zealand | 5.4 | 5.6 | 6.6 | 5.8 | 5.6 | 5.8 | 5.5 | 6.0 | 6.0 | 5.9 | 1.8 | 1.4 | 1.3 | 1.4 | 1.5 |
| Norway | 6.0 | 5.8 | 5.5 | 5.5 | 6.1 | 6.0 | 5.0 | 5.2 | 5.0 | 6.3 | 1.8 | 2.0 | 1.2 | 1.8 | 0.8 |
| Peru | 6.5 | 7.8 | 7.2 | 7.8 | 7.6 | 6.8 | 7.5 | 7.4 | 7.5 | 7.8 | 2.1 | 2.5 | 1.2 | 2.6 | 0.9 |
| Poland | 6.3 | 6.3 | 5.2 | 6.2 | 6.4 | 6.5 | 6.0 | 5.0 | 5.8 | 6.6 | 1.0 | 1.5 | 1.0 | 1.5 | 0.8 |
| Portugal | 6.1 | 8.5 | 5.7 | 7.9 | 7.6 | 5.9 | 8.5 | 5.5 | 8.0 | 8.0 | 2.3 | 2.0 | 1.5 | 2.1 | 1.3 |
| Russia | 7.3 | 7.9 | 9.7 | 7.9 | 7.7 | 7.0 | 7.0 | 10.0 | 7.0 | 8.1 | 4.1 | 3.4 | 2.9 | 3.5 | 1.5 |
| South Africa | 6.8 | 6.3 | 7.7 | 6.3 | 7.5 | 7.0 | 6.0 | 7.3 | 6.0 | 7.8 | 1.4 | 1.4 | 2.3 | 1.5 | 1.1 |
| Spain | 6.0 | 6.2 | 5.9 | 6.2 | 6.6 | 5.5 | 6.0 | 5.5 | 6.0 | 6.8 | 1.7 | 1.6 | 1.6 | 1.4 | 1.7 |
| Sweden | 6.0 | 5.3 | 5.4 | 5.2 | 6.8 | 5.9 | 5.0 | 5.1 | 5.0 | 7.1 | 1.7 | 1.0 | 1.3 | 1.0 | 1.2 |
| Switzerland | 5.6 | 5.2 | 5.4 | 5.1 | 7.1 | 5.5 | 5.0 | 5.0 | 5.0 | 7.5 | 1.5 | 1.1 | 1.2 | 1.1 | 1.2 |
| Thailand | 7.6 | 8.0 | 7.3 | 8.4 | 8.2 | 8.1 | 7.5 | 7.5 | 8.0 | 8.5 | 0.6 | 1.8 | 0.9 | 1.9 | 1.0 |
| Turkey | 8.2 | 7.9 | 9.3 | 8.1 | 8.0 | 9.4 | 7.0 | 9.1 | 8.0 | 8.6 | 2.9 | 3.3 | 2.5 | 3.4 | 1.7 |
| United Kingdom | 5.5 | 5.1 | 5.2 | 5.3 | 5.9 | 5.0 | 5.0 | 5.0 | 5.0 | 6.2 | 1.4 | 1.4 | 1.7 | 1.4 | 1.2 |
| United States | 5.7 | 5.4 | 5.5 | 5.3 | 5.7 | 5.5 | 5.0 | 5.3 | 5.0 | 5.7 | 1.6 | 1.4 | 1.4 | 1.3 | 1.5 |
| Uruguay | n/a | n/a | 7.1 | 8.2 | 8.0 | n/a | n/a | 7.0 | 9.2 | 8.3 | n/a | n/a | 0.9 | 2.1 | 1.1 |
| Venezuela | n/a | n/a | 19.6 | 15.3 | 17.4 | n/a | n/a | 19.3 | 17.8 | 18.2 | n/a | n/a | 3.7 | 6.5 | 3.4 |

2017 Valuation Handbook – International Guide to Cost of Capital

**Exhibit 3A.6:** 2017 Equity Risk Premium (ERP) Survey Results for 41 Countries (+/− 1 standard deviation)

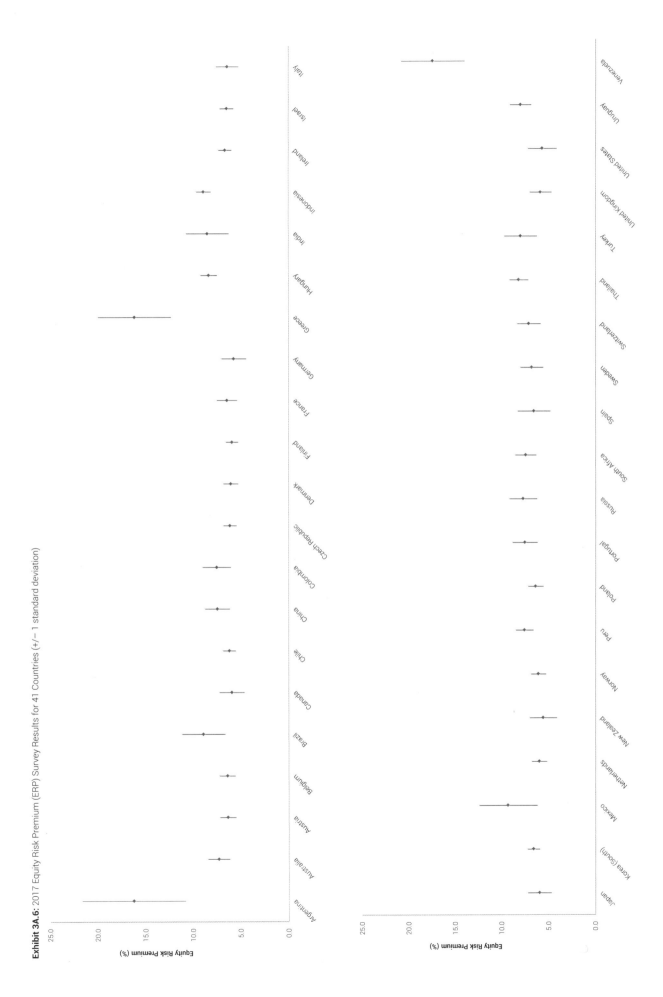

# Appendix 3B
# Additional Sources of Equity Risk Premium Data – Australia

Data Exhibit 1 includes historical equity risk premia (ERPs) estimates for 16 economies around the world, through December 2016.[3B.1] Appendix 3A introduces additional sources of international ERP information, including (i) historical and potential forward-looking adjustments to ERPs based on work by professors Dimson, Marsh, and Staunton; and (ii) survey-based ERPs compiled by professor Pablo Fernandez.

In Appendix 3B of the *2017 Valuation Handbook – International Guide to Cost of Capital*, we provide ERP information specifically focused on Australia. Dr. Steven Bishop, who is renowned in Australia for his ERP research, assists us in developing the ERP estimates included in this Appendix.[3B.2]

**Overview of the Australian Dividend Imputation Tax System**

In 1987, Australia introduced an imputation tax system, with the objective of removing double taxation to shareholders from the receipt of dividend income. In the classical tax system, dividend income is taxed twice: once at the corporation level and once at the shareholder level.

Under the dividend imputation tax system, when a dividend is paid out of Australian earned corporate profits that have been taxed at the statutory corporate tax rate, the shareholder receives a cash dividend plus an imputation tax "credit". This tax credit was changed to a rebate after July 2000 enabling it to be included in tax returns to offset, or in some cases, more than offset individual income tax obligations. Overseas investors are precluded from claiming the imputation tax credits. Therefore, it is often the case that not all of the overall distributed imputation credits can be utilized by a company's shareholders. Accordingly, local resident tax-paying shareholders will value these imputation tax credits, while other investors will not.

Consequently, Australian resident taxpayers earn an additional return over and above capital gains and dividends. This extra return is not captured in published total return (accumulation) indices for the Australian stock market. As a result, traditional historical ERP computations will not capture this incremental return accruing to Australian resident tax-paying shareholders. Additional procedures are needed to estimate an ERP for these investors, so that the incremental return associated with the benefits from the imputation tax credits (a.k.a. franking credits) can be captured. It is beyond the scope of this chapter to fully address how dividend imputation tax systems work in practice or

---

[3B.1] "Premia" is the plural of premium. A single equity risk premium is denoted "ERP"; the plural equity risk premia is denoted "ERPs".

[3B.2] Dr. Steven Bishop is a Director of Education & Management Consulting Services Pty Ltd. His consulting specialties include cost of capital estimation, expert business valuations, implementation of value-based management and strategy consulting. He is an expert witness for regulatory hearings on the cost of capital for valuation compliance. In addition, he teaches in the Master of Applied Finance program for the Macquarie University Applied Finance Centre where he is a Visiting Fellow.

how to place a value on such imputation credits. Several academic papers have been written on the subject, including some focused in the Australian market.[3B.3]

## Australian Equity Risk Premium Under Three Investor Perspectives

The historical ERP in Australia has been estimated from an Australian investor perspective (in AUD) over different periods by a number of researchers and regulatory authorities. It was not our intent to summarize or reconcile that body of work.[3B.4]

Dr. Steve Bishop is one of the researchers working in this area for a number of years. At our request, Dr. Bishop estimated the historical Australian ERP for the period of 1900–2016 under three different investor perspectives: (i) an Australian investor (in Australian Dollars, or AUD) *with* access to (i.e., eligible to receive) imputation tax benefits; (ii) an investor in AUD *without* access to imputation tax benefits; and (iii) a U.S. investor (in U.S. Dollars, or USD) *without* access to imputation tax benefits.

The geometric average and the arithmetic average realized equity risk premia were both calculated relative to Australian long-term government bonds. Exhibit 3B.1 shows each historical ERP decomposed into its underlying elements (i.e., dividend yield, growth rate of real dividends, expansion of price-to-dividend ratio, and changes in real exchange rate), similar to the information contained in Appendix 3A.[3B.5] Both the geometric and the arithmetic average ERP indications were estimated directly from the underlying data.

For example, over the 1900–2016 period, the realized average arithmetic ERP relative to bonds in Australian Dollars was 6.7% for Australian investors with access to imputation tax benefits. Similarly, the realized average arithmetic ERP relative to bonds for a U.S. investor perspective (in USD terms) without access to imputation tax benefits, but subject to exchange rate risk, was 6.8%. The corresponding geometric average ERPs were 5.1% and 4.5%, respectively.

---

[3B.3] See for example Damien Cannavan, Frank Finn, Stephen Gray, "The value of dividend imputation tax credits in Australia", *Journal of Financial Economics* 73, no. 1 (July 2004): 167–197.

[3B.4] For a non-exhaustive list, see for example: (1) T. Brailsford, J. Handley and K. Maheswaran, "The historical equity risk premium in Australia: Post-GFC and 128 Years of Data", *Accounting and Finance*, 2012, 237–247; (2) Dimson, E., P. Marsh, and M. Staunton, *Credit Suisse Global Investment Returns Yearbook 2017*, February 2017; (3) NERA, "Historical Estimates of the Market Risk Premium – A report for Jemena Gas Networks, Jemena Electricity Networks, ActewAGL, Ausgrid, AusNet Services, Australian Gas Networks, CitiPower, Endeavour Energy, Energex, Ergon, Essential Energy, Powercor, SA Power Networks and United Energy", February 2015.

[3B.5] All additions and subtractions were performed in geometric terms, with the exception of the arithmetic average indication (the last step in each of the columns).

**Exhibit 3B.1:** Estimated Australian ERP Under Three Investor Perspectives for the Period Based on Dr. Bishop's Analysis as Measured Over the 1900–2016 Period

|  |  | Australian investor with access to imputation tax benefits (AUD) (%) | Investor in AUD without access to imputation tax benefits (AUD) (%) | US Investor without access to imputation tax benefits (USD) (%) |
|---|---|---|---|---|
|  | Geometric average dividend yield | 5.21 | 4.83 | 4.83 |
| Plus: | Growth rate in real dividends | 1.69 | 1.46 | 1.46 |
| Plus: | Expansion in the Price-to-Dividend ratio | 0.11 | 0.34 | 0.34 |
| Plus: | Changes in real exchange rate | 0.00 | 0.00 | -0.17 |
| Less: | Real rate of return on long-term bonds | 1.92 | 1.92 | 1.92 |
| Equals: | Geometric Average ERP in excess of bonds | 5.09 | 4.71 | 4.53 |
| Equals: | Arithmetic Average ERP in excess of bonds | 6.7 | 6.3 | 6.8 |

**Explanation and Source of underlying data:** Imputation tax benefits were included in the total return to shareholders by adding a yield calculated as dividend yield * (company tax rate) / (1- company tax rate) * % dividends franked * PV factor. For current purposes, the PV factor used was 1. The PV (present value) factor captures the loss in value of $1 of imputation tax benefits distributed but not claimed until personal tax returns are filed. Data from 1900 to 1980 was from Elroy Dimson, Paul Marsh, and Mike Staunton, *Credit Suisse Global Investment Returns and Yearbook 2017*, as was the data underlying the changes in the real exchange rate. Subsequent return data was from the All Ordinaries Accumulation and Price Index series, with the Australian Tax Office being used for the percentage of franked dividend data for the period of 1997 and onward, while an average franking rate was applied to the prior period data (where applicable). Australian long-term government bond return data until 1986 was from Officer, R.R. (1989) "Rates of Return to Shares, Bond Yields and Inflation Rates: An Historical Perspective", in Ball, Brown, Finn, and Officer, "Share Markets and Portfolio Theory: Readings and Australian Evidence", second edition, University of Queensland Press; then Reserve Bank of Australia for the periods thereafter. Inflation data was from the Australian Retail Price Index until December 1948 and the Australian Consumer Price Index thereafter.

The 2008 global financial crisis has had a significant impact on capital markets and ERP indications. ERP is a forward-looking concept and it will change over time to reflect the financial and economic conditions as of a certain valuation date. In a relatively recent research paper, Dr. Bishop and his co-authors proposed a method for adjusting the ERP to reflect unusual risk situations, such as the global financial crisis. Based on this work, the authors would expect the ERP to vary beyond the widely accepted range of 6% to 7% in high and low risk market environments. This would be applicable to all three types of investors in Australia outlined above.[3B.6]

---

[3B.6] Steven Bishop, Michael Fitzsimmons, and Bob Officer, "Adjusting the Market Risk Premium to Reflect the Global Financial Crisis", *JASSA*, no. 1 (2011), 2011: 8–14.

# Appendix 3C
# Additional Sources of Equity Risk Premium Data – Canada

In Appendix 3C of the *2017 Valuation Handbook – International Guide to Cost of Capital*, we introduce a new source of ERP information specifically focused on Canada. We asked Dr. Laurence Booth, who is renowned in Canada for his ERP research, to assist us in developing the forward-looking ERP and base cost of equity estimates for Canada included in this Appendix 3C, which is authored by Professor Booth.[3C.1]

In arriving at his ERP estimates, Professor Booth has also considered the current state of the Canadian government bond market and corresponding impact on the risk-free rate, as documented herein. As a reminder, the risk-free rate and the ERP are interrelated concepts. All ERP estimates are, by definition, developed in relation to the risk-free rate. Specifically, the ERP is the extra return investors expect as compensation for assuming the additional risk associated with an investment in a diversified portfolio of common stocks, compared to the return they would expect from an investment in risk-free securities.

Throughout this appendix, the International Organization for Standardization (ISO) currency codes will be used as a convention: CAD stands for Canadian Dollars, while USD stands for U.S. Dollars.

**The Current State of the Canadian Bond Market, and an Estimate of the Canadian Equity Risk Premium**

Capital has traditionally been in short supply in Canada relative to demand. This shortage was worsened in the 1970s, 1980s, and 1990s when the Government of Canada crowded out private borrowers from the bond market, forcing many, including the Canadian provinces, into the U.S. market (see the middle of Exhibit 3C.1). This crowding-out effect was likely reduced when Canadian government budgets moved from deficits to surpluses in the late 1990s and early to mid-2000s (see the mid-right section of Exhibit 3C.1). Canada returned to federal deficits in the aftermath of the 2008 global financial crisis (see the rightmost section of Exhibit 3C.1).

---

[3C.1] Dr. Laurence Booth is a Professor of Finance and the CIT Chair in Structured Finance at the Rotman School of Management, University of Toronto. His major research interests are in corporate finance and the behavior of regulated industries. He has published extensively in top academic and professional journals, and is the co-author of two major textbooks: *International Business* and *Introduction to Corporate Finance*. Professor Booth is on the editorial board of four academic journals and in 2003 was awarded the Financial Post's Leader in Management Education Award.

**Exhibit 3C.1:** Federal Surplus or Deficit [-] as Percent of Gross Domestic Product (GDP) 1952–2016

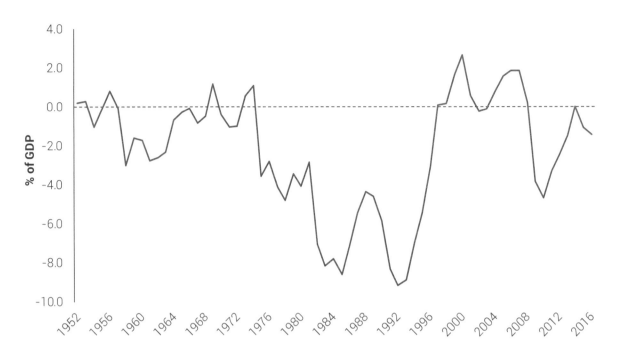

Exhibit 3C.2 depicts U.S. and Canadian long-term government bond yields since 1994 through the present. There are two major insights that can be gleaned from Exhibit 3C.2: (i) the collapse in the level of sovereign yields in both the U.S. and Canada, and (ii) the change in the relationship between yields in Canada versus the U.S.

**Exhibit 3C.2:** Canadian and U.S. Long-term Government Bond Yields

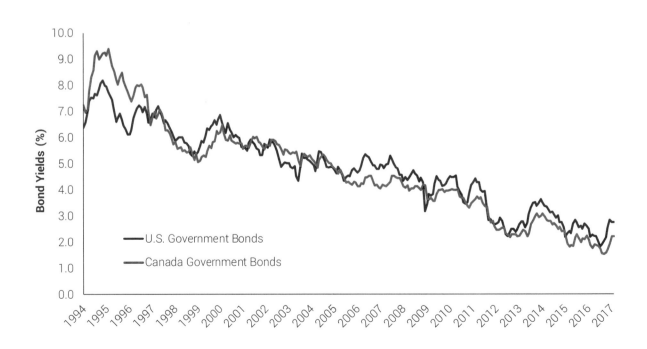

In the mid-1990s Canadian yields averaged 1.25% more than those in the U.S., primarily due to: (i) the budget deficits in Canada, and (ii) the international importance of the U.S. government bond market.

This started to change as Canadian government budgets became balanced and the supply of bonds dropped, and so from 1997 until 2005 Canadian and U.S. government bond yields were approximately the same. Since 2006, Canadian long-term government bond yields have been about 0.50% below those in the U.S. except for periods during the 2008–2009 financial and the 2011 Euro sovereign debt crisis.

Lower long-term Canadian government bond yields have not translated into significantly lower borrowing costs for A-rated corporate debt issuers in Canada, primarily due to the importance of changes in the Government of Canada segment of the Canadian bond market (rather than changes in the overall market). Prior to 2002, A-rated corporate debt spreads were similar in both countries (see Exhibit 3C.3).[3C.2] After 2002, Canadian credit spreads have tended to be *wider* (i.e., larger) than those in the U.S., and, except for the impact of the 2008–2009 financial crisis and the 2011 Euro sovereign debt crises, have been consistently wider.[3C.3] Since 2013, Canadian A-rated corporate bond spreads have averaged 0.55% wider than those in the U.S.[3C.4]

**Exhibit 3C.3:** Canadian and U.S. A-rated Corporate Bond Spreads

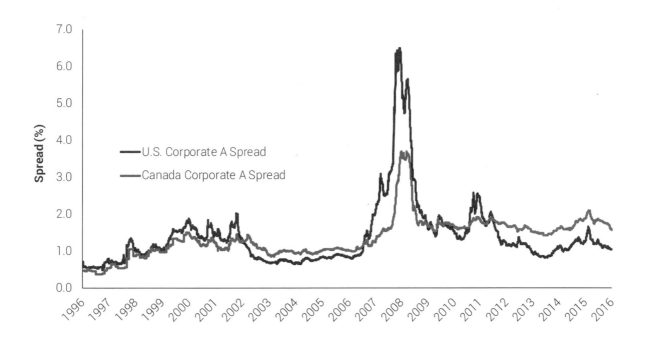

[3C.2]  Sources: The U.S. data from Bank America Merrill Lynch's U.S. A-rated Option-adjusted Spread. The Canadian data is based on the spread between Datastream series SCM1ALG for A-rated issuers and SCMCLNG for government bonds.

[3C.3]  During the 2008–2009 financial crisis and the 2011 Euro sovereign debt crises, Canadian A-rated credit spreads tended to be "narrower" (i.e., smaller) than those in the U.S.

[3C.4]  U.S. banks were far more exposed to these crises than were Canadian banks.

On a global basis, Canada remains one of a very small number of AAA-rated countries, and thus is an attractive location to invest government reserves. The Bank of Canada indicated that in early 2015 almost 30% of the Canadian government bond market was owned by non-residents.[3C.5] In early 2016, this figure increased slightly to just over 30% of the overall market, which represents a nearly 3% rise from the prior year.[3C.6] Given that the market is only about CAD 661 billion (or approximately USD 496 billion),[3C.7] this implies capital inflows of nearly CAD 200 billion (or approximately USD 150 billion) which, while small in relation to the USD 87.7 trillion global bond market,[3C.8] is still large for Canada. As the Bank of Canada states:[3C.9]

*"In the post-crisis period, Canada has experienced sizable foreign portfolio investment flows, particularly in Government of Canada (GoC) bonds, which has resulted in an increase in the share of GoC bonds held by foreigners. These portfolio investment inflows had a significant downward influence on interest rates in Canada".*

Since 2012, Canadian A-rated corporates debt spreads (over Canadian government bonds) have exceeded the equivalent credit spreads observed in the U.S. This suggests that the Canadian corporate bond market may not have been as affected by an increased demand by foreign investors, relative to that seen for Canadian government bonds.

The other major trend is the temporal change in the level of government interest rates in both the U.S. and Canada. For example, at the end of 2016, the yield on Canadian government bonds with maturities greater than 10 years was 2.34%, or only 0.34% over the Bank of Canada's 2% inflation target, which historically is abnormally low. Several academics have suggested that this is part of a global trend towards declining interest rates.[3C.10]

---

[3C.5]  Bank of Canada, *Financial System Review*, June 2015 page 26.
[3C.6]  Department of Finance Canada, *2015–2016 Debt Management Report*, December 2016, pages 22-23. Data reported as of March 31, 2016. Report can be found here: https://www.fin.gc.ca/dtman/2015-2016/dmr-rgd16-eng.asp.
[3C.7]  Bank of Canada's "Government of Canada Treasury Bills and Domestic Marketable Bonds Outstanding", as of March 31, 2017. Data retrieved from http://www.bankofcanada.ca/stats/goc/results/27973. Amounts translated from Canadian into U.S. Dollars using exchange rate as of March 31, 2017, sourced from S&P *Capital IQ*.
[3C.8]  Source: Securities Industry and Financial Markets Association (SIFMA) *2016 Fact Book*.
[3C.9]  Bank of Canada, *Financial System Review*, June 2015 page 25.
[3C.10]  See, for example, Lukasz Rachel and Thomas D Smith, "Secular Drivers of the Global Real Interest Rate", Bank of England Staff Working Paper No. 571, December 2015.

## Monetary Policy's Effect on Rates

Bank of Canada researchers Eric Santor and Lena Suchanek analyzed the impact of "unconventional monetary policy" by the major central banks around the world, where "unconventional" is their euphemism for massive bond-buying programs (i.e., "quantitative easing" or "QE").[3C.11] These researchers estimated that as of the end of 2015:

- The Federal Reserve had bought USD 4.2 trillion in bonds, amounting to 18% of the U.S. Treasury Bond market and 28% of the agency and mortgage-backed security markets,

- The Bank of England had bought 32% of the U.K. government bond market,

- The European Central Bank had bought 21% of the Eurozone government debt market, and

- The Bank of Japan had bought 36% of the Japanese government bond market.[3C.12]

In total, these purchases amount to almost CAD 13 trillion (or USD 10 trillion), depending on the exchange rates used. Since this study was prepared, the share of government bonds held by central banks globally has likely increased.[3C.13] This level of activity has likely had a significant impact on the level of market interest rates.

To assess how much current government bond yields have been distorted by unconventional monetary policy, Professor Booth performed a regression analysis of the real Canadian bond yield against five independent variables, which are further defined below: risk, budget surplus/deficit, indicator variable 1 ("Dum1"), indicator variable 2 ("Dum2"), and indicator variable 3 ("Dum3"). The results of this regression analysis and the impact of each of the five variables on Canadian real long-term yields are shown in Exhibit 3C.4. The real Canada yield is defined here as the average yield on the long Canada bond with a maturity over 10 years minus the average CPI (Consumer Price Index) rate of inflation, calculated as the average of the current, past, and forward-year rates of inflation.[3C.14] The regression model explains a large amount of the variation in real Canada yields, and each of the five explanatory (or independent) variables is statistically significant. Moreover, the overall regression relationship explains approximately 86% of the movements in real rates over the 1936–2016 period.

---

[3C.11] Eric Santor and Lena Suchanek, "A New Era of Central Banking: Unconventional Monetary Policies", *Bank of Canada Review*, Spring 2016.

[3C.12] The Japanese buying alone amounts to 80% of Japanese GDP.

[3C.13] During 2016, new rounds of QE have been implemented by the European Central Bank, the Bank of Japan, and the Bank of England. For a summary discussion on this topic, refer to the *2017 Valuation Handbook – U.S. Guide to Cost of Capital*, Chapter 3, "Basic Building Blocks of the Cost of Equity Capita – Risk-free Rate and Equity Risk Premium".

[3C.14] Before 1991 there was no real return bond in Canada.

**Exhibit 3C.4:** Factors Influencing Canadian Long-Term Real Yields and Their Impact

| Explanatory (Independent) Variable | Impact on Real Rates | Regression Analysis Coefficient |
|---|---|---|
| Risk | Upward | 0.22% |
| Budget Surplus (Deficit) | Downward (Upward) | -0.27% |
| Indicator Variable ("Dum1") | Downward | -5.41% |
| Indicator Variable ("Dum2") | Downward | -3.66% |
| Indicator Variable ("Dum3") | Downward | -2.48% |
| Constant (Regression Intercept) | n/a | 1.47% |

The two main independent variables are:

- **Risk:** Bond market uncertainty (risk), which affects the demand for government bonds. Risk is defined as the standard deviation of the returns on the long-term Canada bond over the preceding ten years.

- **Budget Surplus/Deficit:** Government deficit, which affects supply of government bonds. Budget Surplus/Deficit is defined as the aggregate government lending as percentage of real GDP.

All other things held the same, *more* uncertainty (risk) or *more* supply causes bond values to *fall* and interest rates to *rise*. The coefficient on the bond market risk variable indicates that for every 1% increase in volatility, real Canada yields increased by about 22 basis points. The coefficient on budget surplus/deficit variable indicates that for every 1% increase in the budget surplus (deficit), the real Canada yield has decreased (increased) by 27 basis points. That is, a relative increase in government borrowing has driven up real interest rates.

When these two effects are added together we can explain the huge increase in real yields in the early 1990s. For example, in 1994 real yields were over 7%. Of that, 1.9% (= 7% * 0.27) was attributable to the budget deficit according this model, and 1.5% (= 7% * 0.22) was attributable to uncertainty per this model. This represented 3.4% (1.5% + 1.9%), or about half of the total real yield of 7%.

In addition to the demand and supply variables, there are three "indicator" variables in their analysis that represent three unique periods of intervention in the financial markets.[3C.15] The three indicator variables are summarized as follows:

- **Dum1:** Dum1 captures the years from 1940–1951, which were the "war" years, when interest rates were controlled to finance World War II and the subsequent recovery. The coefficient indicates that government controls *reduced* real Canada yields by over 5.0% below where they would otherwise have been.[3C.16, 3C.17]

- **Dum2:** Dum2 captures the years 1972–1980, which were the oil crisis years, when huge amounts of "petrodollars" were recycled from the suddenly rich Organization of the Petroleum Exporting Countries (OPEC) back to Western capital markets, thereby essentially acting as a tax to depress real yields. The coefficient indicates that this recycling and the oil crisis *reduced* real yields by about 3.7% below where they would otherwise have been.

- **Dum3:** Dum3 captures the recent period of unconventional monetary policy from 2010 through 2016. The coefficient indicates that recent extreme measures taken by central banks in the U.S., U.K., Eurozone, and Japan *reduced* real yields by about 2.5% below where they would otherwise have been.

## Conclusions

There is a wealth of data on rates of return. These estimates are extremely useful in constraining the exercise of judgment, but they also assume that the process is stationary, which implies that estimating over longer time horizons delivers a better estimate of the equity risk premium.[3C.18, 3C.19] However, the historical record also indicates that the average return on the government bond has not been constant and in particular imparts a noticeable bias when we average the data back versus forward, that is, we get a different interpretation based on how we order the data. For this reason, adding more data may not be as useful as understanding what has happened in the bond market.

---

[3C.15] Indicator variables are sometimes referred to as "dummy" variables. The indicator variable in this case inserts a "1" for the years when a unique period of intervention in the financial markets is present, and a "0" for the years when it is not present.

[3C.16] We normally refer to these years of financial repression as periods when governments needed to get their war debt back to normal levels.

[3C.17] This is akin to the "World War II Interest Rate Bias" years in the U.S., as discussed in the *2017 Valuation Handbook – U.S. Guide to Cost of Capital*, Chapter 3, "Basic Building Blocks of the Cost of Equity Capital – Risk-free Rate & Equity Risk Premium". From 1942 through 1951 the U.S. Treasury decreed that interest rates had to be kept at artificially low levels to reduce government financing costs related to World War II.

[3C.18] The historical equity risk premium has not been constant, primarily due to changes in the bond market over time. To some extent the huge cycle in Canadian bond yields increasing from the approximate 4% *average* level of 1957, after markets were liberalized, to the approximate 15% level of 1981, and back down to the approximate 4% level of 2007–2008 completed an adjustment to changes in fiscal versus monetary policy. However, since 2009 long Canada bond yields have dropped to the anomalous 1.8% average for 2016.

[3C.19] For a detailed discussion of the equity risk premium estimation methodologies and changing relationship between equities and the so-called risk-free security, see Chapter 3, "Basic Building Blocks of the Cost of Equity Capital – Risk-free Rate & Equity Risk Premium" in the *2017 Valuation Handbook – U.S. Guide to Cost of Capital*. To order copies of the *2017 Valuation Handbook – U.S. Guide to Cost of Capital*, or other Duff & Phelps valuation data resources published by John Wiley & Sons, please visit www.wiley.com/go/ValuationHandbooks, or call: U.S. (800) 762-2974 International (317) 572-3993 or fax (317) 572-4002.

In standard finance models the equity risk premium reflects the price of risk as investors trade-off the higher expected return from the riskier security against its increased risk.[3C.20] It may be plausible that this price of risk should be relatively constant, since it reflects the aggregate risk aversion of the investing public. However, in such models debt is in zero excess supply and there is no government or monetary policy. Yet the dominant fact since the 1930s has been the growth in the size of government and regulation, and since 2008 the key players in the capital markets have been the central banks.[3C.21] Overall, Professor Booth concludes:

- The historical Canadian equity risk premium as calculated over the time horizon 1926–2016 is approximately 5.0% (based on arithmetic mean returns) and is slightly lower than the approximate 6.0% arithmetic value for the U.S.[3C.22, 3C.23, 3C.24]

- The 5.0–6.0% range of the Canadian historical equity risk premium and the historical U.S. equity risk premium is generally consistent with survey data.[3C.25]

- The drop in Canadian government bond yields (relative to U.S. government bond yields) has not translated into significantly lower borrowing costs for A-rated issuers in Canada relative to their U.S. counterparts. After 2002, except for the impact of the 2008–2009 financial crisis and the 2011 Euro sovereign crises, Canadian spreads have tended to be *wider* (i.e., larger) than those in the U.S.

- Using an indicator variable for the post-2009 years, a simple regression analysis indicates that current long-term Canadian government bond yields would be approximately 2.5% higher. These results suggest that the 1.8% average yield of long-term Canadian Government bonds would have been approximately 4.3% (1.8% + 2.5%) but for the impact of

---

[3C.20] For example, the capital asset pricing model or CAPM.

[3C.21] A simple listing of the key government initiatives in the U.S introduced by President Roosevelt's New Deal that have never been reversed would take several pages.

[3C.22] The Canadian and U.S. equity risk premia reported in this Appendix is calculated as the historical difference between the *total* returns of equities ("stocks") and the *total* returns of the risk-free security ("long-term government bonds"). If one were to use the income returns of the risk-free security, these estimates would be higher.

[3C.23] Duff & Phelps employs a multi-faceted analysis to estimate a "conditional" ERP that considers a broad range of economic information and multiple ERP estimation methodologies to arrive at its recommendation. The Duff & Phelps Recommended U.S. ERP as of December 31, 2016 is 5.5%, developed in relation to a 3.5% "normalized" risk-free rate, implying a 9.0% (3.5% + 5.5%) base cost of equity capital in the U.S. as of the end of 2016. To learn more about cost of capital issues, and to ensure that you are using the most recent Duff & Phelps Recommended ERP, visit www.duffandphelps.com/CostofCapital, and click "View Historical Equity Risk Premium Recommendations".

[3C.24] There is no "perfect" way of estimating the equity risk premium, and Duff & Phelps therefore discusses (and publishes) equity risk premia based upon multiple calculation methodologies, including "historical" equity risk premia (i) for 16 different countries (including the U.S.) in the *2017 Valuation Handbook – International Guide to Cost of Capital* (this book) in Data Exhibit 1, "International Equity Risk Premia (ERPs)", and (ii) for the U.S. in the *2017 Valuation Handbook – U.S. Guide to Cost of Capital* (see Appendix 3, "CRSP Deciles Size Premia Study: Key Variables", of that book). Those equity risk premia are calculated as the historical difference between the *total* returns of equities ("stocks") and the *income* returns (in essence, yields) of the risk-free security ("long-term government bonds"). This methodology is in harmony with the methodology used in all yearly versions of the former Ibbotson/Morningstar *International Equity Risk Premium Report* (2000–2013), and in all yearly versions of the former *Stocks, Bonds, Bills, and Inflation (SBBI) Valuation Yearbook* (1999–2013). Using this method, the equivalent arithmetic-average historical ERP would be 5.6% for Canada and 6.9% for the U.S. .

[3C.25] A good example is Pablo Fernandez, Vitaly Pershin, and Isabel Fernández Acín, "Discount Rate (Risk-Free Rate and Market Risk Premium) Used for 41 Countries in 2017: A Survey". IESE business school, University of Navarra, April 17, 2017. Refer to Appendix 3B, for a summary of the results by country.

---

unconventional monetary policy. Apart from the impact of higher government deficits, this is consistent with average yields from 2005–2008.

- Adding 4.0–4.5% to the historical equity risk premium in Canada of 5.0% implies an estimated base cost of equity capital in Canada of 9.0–9.5%, or (with the Bank of Canada's target inflation rate of 2.0%) a real equity return of 7.0–7.5%. This result is consistent with long-run averages. It is also consistent with recent survey data.[3C.26]

**Final Thoughts: Duff & Phelps Analysis on Methods of Estimating a Normalized Risk-free Rate**

To corroborate Professor Booth's analysis of the Canadian government bond market and his observation that Canadian yields are currently abnormally low, Duff & Phelps conducted a separate analysis – similar to that prepared for the U.S. in a sister publication – on possible methods to normalize the risk-free rate.[3C.27]

Estimating a normalized risk-free rate can be accomplished in a number of ways, including (i) simple averaging, or (ii) various "build-up" methods.

The first method of estimating a normalized risk-free rate entails calculating averages of yields to maturity on long-term government securities over various periods. This method's implied assumption is that government bond yields revert to the mean. In Exhibit 3C.5, the solid red line is the spot yield on long-term (greater than 10-year) Canadian government bonds (December 2007– March 2017), whereas the dashed dark-gray line shows a 3.0% average monthly yield of the long-term (greater than 10-year) Canadian government bond over the previous 10 years ending on March 31, 2017.[3C.28] Canadian government bond spot yields at the end of March 2017 were lower than the monthly average over the last 10 years.

---

[3C.26] Ibid. According to the Fernandez et al. survey, respondents are currently using a base cost of equity for Canada of 9.0% on average, with a median of 8.4%.

[3C.27] See Chapter 3 of the *2017 Valuation Handbook – U.S. Guide to Cost of Capital* for a more complete description of these methods and how they were applied to estimate a normalized risk-free rate for the United States.

[3C.28] CANSIM (database), Bank of Canada (2017).Table 176-0048 – Bank of Canada, money market, and other interest rates, daily percent. Available from: http://www5.statcan.gc.ca/cansim/a26?
lang=eng&retrLang=eng&id=1760048&pattern=Financial+market+statistics&tabMode=dataTable&srchLan=-1&p1=1&p2=-1.

**Exhibit 3C.5:** Spot and Average Yields on Long-Term (Greater than 10-years) Canadian Government Bonds
December 2007–March 2017

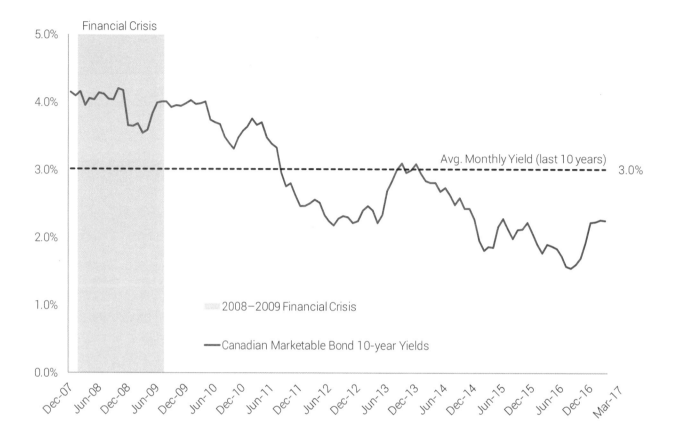

Taking the average over the last 10 years is a simple way of "normalizing" the risk-free rate. An issue with using historical averages, though, is selecting an appropriate comparison period that can be used as a reasonable proxy for the future.

The second method of estimating a normalized risk-free rate entails using a simple build-up method, where the components of the risk-free rate are estimated and then added together. Conceptually, the risk-free rate can be (loosely) illustrated as the return on the following two components:[3C.29]

| Risk-Free Rate | = | Real Rate | + | Expected Inflation |
| --- | --- | --- | --- | --- |

We assembled data from various sources for long-term Canadian government bonds, which are commonly used as inputs to cost of equity estimates, comparing the estimated normalized rates relative to the spot rates as of March 31, 2017. We present the results of this analysis in Exhibit 3C.6.

---

[3C.29] This is a simplified version of the "Fisher equation", named after Irving Fisher. Fisher's *The Theory of Interest* was first published by Macmillan (New York), in 1930.

**Exhibit 3C.6:** Long-Term Spot and Normalized Risk-Free Rates for Canada[3C.30, 3C.31]

| | |
|---|---|
| Estimated Long-term Real Rate | 1.0% to 2.0% |
| Range of Expected Inflation Forecasts | 1.7% to 2.1% |
| **Range of Estimated Long-term Normalized Risk-free Rate** | **2.7% to 4.1%** |
| Midpoint | 3.4% |
| **Concluded (rounded)** | **3.5%** |
| Spot Yield | 2.2% |

Adding the estimated ranges for the "real" risk-free rate and longer-term inflation together produces an estimated normalized risk-free rate range of 2.7% to 4.1%, with a midpoint of 3.4% (or 3.5%, if rounding to the nearest 50 basis points) for Canada.

How should the analyst use this information? One can calculate the cost of equity by either starting with a normalized risk-free rate or a spot rate. However, it's critical to match the second building block, the estimated ERP, to the selected risk-free rate. There must be internal consistency between these two inputs.

Adjustments to the ERP or to the risk-free rate are, in principle, a response to the same underlying concerns and should result in broadly similar costs of capital. Adjusting the risk-free rate in conjunction with the ERP is only one of the alternatives available when estimating the cost of equity capital.

For example, one could use a spot yield for the risk-free rate, but increase the ERP or other adjustment to account for higher (systematic) risk. If the valuation analyst chooses to use the spot yield to estimate the cost of capital during periods when those yields are less than "normal", the valuation analyst must use an estimated ERP that is matched to (or implied by) those below-normal yields. However, we note that the most commonly used data sources for ERP estimates are long-term series measured when interest rates were largely not subject to such market intervention.

Using those data series with an abnormally low spot yield creates a mismatch.

---

[3C.30] Sources for estimated real rate: "The Neutral Rate of Interest in Canada", Bank of Canada (September 30, 2014); "Is Slower Growth The New Normal In Advanced Economies?", Bank of Canada (November 19, 2015); "Monetary Policy in a Low R-star World", Federal Reserve Bank of San Francisco (August 15, 2016); "(S)low for Long and Financial Stability", Bank of Canada (September 14, 2016); "Measuring the Natural Rate of Interest: International Trends and Determinants", Federal Reserve Bank of San Francisco (December 1, 2016); "January 2017 Monetary Policy Report", Bank of Canada (January 18, 2017); "April 2017 Monetary Policy Report", Bank of Canada (April 12, 2017).

[3C.31] Sources for expected long-term inflation: PwC's Global Economic Watch dated April 2017; IMF World Economic Outlook dated April 2017; Oxford Economics: Canada Country Economic Forecast dated March 17, 2017; Consensus Forecasts: Global Outlook dated April 10, 2017; FocusEconomics: Canada Consensus Forecast February 2017; IHS Markit's long-term average CPI inflation forecasts for Canada dated March 15, 2017.

Alternatively, if the valuation analyst chooses to use a normalized risk-free rate in estimating the cost of capital, the valuation analyst must again use an estimated ERP that is matched to those normalized yields. Normalizing the risk-free rate is likely a more direct (and more easily implemented) analysis than adjusting the ERP due to a temporary reduction in the yields on risk-free securities, while longer-term trends may be more appropriately reflected in the ERP.

# Chapter 4
# Country Yield Spread Model

## Introduction

The Country Yield Spread Model is a practical adaptation of the CAPM to an international setting. This model was originally developed in U.S. Dollars (USD) in 1993 by researchers at investment bank Goldman Sachs.[4.1] In order to arrive at a USD-denominated cost of equity capital for each foreign country, a country risk premium (CRP) was added to the cost of equity capital derived for the domestic base country (the "home country").[4.2] In simple terms, the country risk was quantified as the spread between the foreign country's government bond yield denominated in USD and the U.S. government bond yield of the same maturity.[4.3]

The CRP results from the Country Yield Spread Model attempt to isolate the incremental risk premium associated with investing in another market (i.e., "foreign" country) other than the "home" country (i.e., the country in which the investor is based) as a function of the spread between the foreign country's sovereign yields and the home country's sovereign yields (both denominated in the home country currency).

The Country Yield Spread Model as presented herein starts by calculating observed yield spreads, but uses alternative analyses when countries do not issue publicly-traded government debt denominated in either USD or in EUR (see the section entitled "Methodology – Country Yield Spread Model").

---

[4.1]    Jorge O. Mariscal, and Rafaelina M. Lee, "The Valuation of Mexican Stocks: An Extension of the Capital Asset Pricing Model", 1993, Goldman Sachs, New York.

[4.2]    Throughout this book, "investor perspective" (i.e., the "home" country; the country in which the investor is based) is defined by the currency in which the inputs used in each respective model are expressed. The investee country (the country in which the investment resides) is referred to as the "foreign" country.

[4.3]    The Country Yield Spread Model is also referred to as the "Sovereign" Yield Spread Model.

**Brief Background on Euromoney's ECR Score[4.4]**

Euromoney Country Risk (ECR) is an online community of economic and political experts that provide real time scores in 15 categories that relate to economic, structural and political risk. Results are calibrated on a quarterly basis.

The consensus expert scores, combined with data from (i) the IMF and World Bank on debt indicators, (ii) a survey of debt syndicate managers at international banks on access to capital, and (iii) Moody's/Fitch credit ratings are aggregated to create Euromoney's ECR score for 186 individual countries.

ECR evaluates the investment risk of a country, such as risk of default on a bond, risk of losing direct investment, risk to global business relations etc., by taking a qualitative model, which seeks an expert opinion on risk variables within a country (70% weighting) and combining it with three basic quantitative values (30% weighting).

To obtain the overall ECR score, Euromoney assigns a weighting to six categories. The three qualitative expert opinions are political risk (30% weighting), economic performance (30%), and structural assessment (10%). The three quantitative values are debt indicators (10%), credit ratings (10%), and access to bank financing and capital markets (10%).

The ECR score is displayed on a 100 point scale, with 100 being nearly devoid of any risk, and 0 being completely exposed to every risk.

---

[4.4] Euromoney's ECR scores are available through subscription only. This section is based on Euromoney's methodology section found here: http://www.euromoney.com/Article/2773899/Euromoney-Country-Risk-Methodology.html.

**Investor Perspectives**

The CRPs derived from the Country Yield Spread Model are presented in Data Exhibit 2 from two investor perspectives: (i) from the perspective of a U.S.-based investor and (ii) from the perspective of an investor based in Germany, who uses the Euro as their local currency. For CRPs calculated from the perspective of a German investor, the yields on German government debt instruments are used in all cases.[4.5]

Each of the two investor perspective exhibits are 4 pages long, and include 188 investee countries each, with a corresponding CRP listed.[4.6] The CRPs are:

- Presented as of two dates: December 31, 2016 and March 31, 2017[4.7]

- Are different for each investor perspective.

This means that:

- If the valuation analyst's cash flows projections are denominated in U.S. Dollars, the valuation analyst should use the country risk analysis denominated in U.S. Dollars.

- If the valuation analyst's cash flows projections are denominated in Euros, the valuation analyst should use the country risk analysis denominated in Euros, if performing the analysis from a German investor perspective.

For example, a U.S.-based investor (i.e., cash flows projections are denominated in U.S. Dollars) who is valuing a business, business ownership interest, security, or intangible asset that is located in, say, India, would use the country risk premium analysis in Data Exhibit 2 which is denominated in *U.S. Dollars*.

Alternatively, a German-based investor (i.e., cash flows projections are denominated in Euros) who is valuing a business, business ownership interest, security, or intangible asset that is located in, say, Brazil, would use the country risk premium analysis in Data Exhibit 2 which is denominated in *Euros*. Note that an investor based in other countries within the Eurozone (e.g., Spain) investing in say, Brazil, could use the same CRP information in Data Exhibit 2, provided that German government securities are being used as the basis for the risk-free rate when estimating the cost of

---

[4.5] It is not unusual for German securities to be used as proxies in these types of calculations. Germany is the largest economy in Europe, and in the Eurozone, therefore the yields on German government debt instruments are considered by market participants as the 'gold standard' for the risk-free security denominated in Euros.

[4.6] Depending on data availability; some countries may not have adequate data available.

[4.7] The *2017 Valuation Handbook – International Guide to Cost of Capital* (this book) is published with data through (i) December 31, 2016 and (ii) March 31, 2017 (depending on the model being presented). An intra-year Semi-annual Update with data through (i) June 30, 2017 and (ii) September 30, 2017 (depending on the model being presented) will be available. The Country Yield Spread Model (Data Exhibit 2), the Relative Volatility Model (Data Exhibit 3) and the Erb-Harvey-Viskanta Country Credit Rating (CCR) Model (Data Exhibit 4) are updated in the Semi-annual Update; Data Exhibit 1, "International Equity Risk Premia", is not included in the Semi-annual Update because this data is updated at year-end only. The Semi-annual Update is optional, and is not sold separately.

equity for the subject company. This is because the analysis in Data Exhibit 2 is all being conducted in Euros, calculated against German government debt yields.

In the following sections, the Country Yield Spread Model is described in detail.

## Country Yield Spread Model

The Country Yield Spread Model is expressed as follows:

$$k_{e,foreign\ country} = R_{f,home\ country} + \beta_{home\ country} \times ERP_{home\ country} + CRP$$

Where:

| | | |
|---|---|---|
| $k_{e,foreign\ country}$ | = | Cost of equity capital in the foreign country (denominated in the home country currency) |
| $R_{f,home\ country}$ | = | Risk-free rate on government bonds in the home country currency. "Home country" in Data Exhibit 2 (Country Yield Spread Model) means either the (i) United States (if discount rate is being developed in USD) or (ii) Germany (if discount rate is being developed in Euros) |
| $\beta_{home\ country}$ | = | Beta appropriate for a company located in the home country in a similar industry as the foreign country's subject company (i.e., beta is measured using returns expressed in the home currency) |
| $ERP_{home\ country}$ | = | Equity risk premium of home country |
| $CRP$ | = | Country risk premium, in its general form, determined as the difference between the yield-to-maturity on a foreign country government bond issued in the home country's currency and the yield-to-maturity on a home country government bond with a similar maturity |

The Country Yield Spread Model has particular appeal where debt securities denominated in USD (or EUR) issued by the local country government can be observed (i.e., they are publicly traded). In that case, if the government debt instrument (of the foreign country) denominated in, say, U.S. Dollars has a higher yield than the yield observed on U.S. government debt of the same maturity, the yield difference may be looked upon as the market's pricing of country-specific risk of default. This country-specific risk is clearly not included in the U.S.-based risk premium, so it must be added separately.[4.8]

---

[4.8] An alternative way of looking at this is that the analyst would be *double-counting* country risk if the yield on the foreign country's government debt were used in the Country Yield Spread Model equation (instead of the home country's risk-free rate). This is because the "country risk premium" is assumed to be embedded in the foreign country's sovereign yield by the model itself, when that country's debt is not perceived to be risk-free by market participants.

The risk of government default is correlated with, and arguably a proxy for, one type of country risk. Emerging market countries tend to default on their sovereign debt when their economic conditions deteriorate, and bond betas for sovereign debt are a meaningful indicator of their relative risks.[4.9] Exhibit 4.1 shows a sampling of yield spreads as of March 31, 2017.

**Exhibit 4.1:** Sample Country Yield Spreads as of March 31, 2017

|              | USD-Perspective (%) | EUR-Perspective (%) |
|--------------|:-------------------:|:-------------------:|
| Brazil       | 3.2                 | 2.1                 |
| Indonesia    | 1.7                 | 2.6                 |
| Israel       | 1.3                 | 1.6                 |
| Romania      | 1.6                 | 2.6                 |
| South Africa | 2.4                 | 2.9                 |
| Turkey       | 3.1                 | 3.3                 |

There are several potential problems with the Country Yield Spread Model approach:[4.10]

- In some cases, the local *government's* credit quality may be a very poor proxy for risks affecting *business* cash flows.

- This approach may double-count country-level risks that are already incorporated into projections of expected cash flows.

- A method based on spot observed yield is prone to be more volatile from period to period than, for example, a country risk estimated via the Country Credit Rating Model. The point is to be aware of extremes in yields. This may cause the spread method to have extreme indications in some crisis environments.

- Debt is typically less volatile than equity, so by using debt yields as the reference point, this method inherently could underestimate equity risk.

- Depending on facts and circumstances, the yield spread method may, in fact, be less appropriate in industries that are global in nature (integrated oil, chemicals, mining and minerals, other global sectors) where *country* is less important than *sector*.

---

[4.9]  Nicola Borri and Adrien Verdelhan, "Sovereign Risk Premia", AFA 2010 Atlanta Meetings Paper, updated September 2011. Available at http://ssrn.com/abstract=1343746.

[4.10]  Between updates of the *Valuation Handbook – International Guide to Cost of Capital*, an additional adjustment to the provided country risk premium data is warranted for countries whose sovereign debt credit rating is upgraded or downgraded intra-year. Additional analyses may be   necessary, due to the timing of the update versus recent developments in the specific country.

During the financial crisis that began in 2008, yield spreads increased, dramatically so for certain countries. As of September 30, 2009, yield spreads on *higher* credit rating countries' debt had mostly returned to pre-crisis levels, whereas the yield spreads on lower credit rating countries' debt, while subsiding from their crisis peak levels, remained somewhat high. The Euro sovereign debt crisis that started in 2010, reaching its peak in 2012, caused yield spreads in lower-rated countries to go up again.

Exhibit 4.2 shows the changes in yield spreads by debt quality (investment grade versus non-investment grade) at each quarter end from December 2007 to December 2016, on a semi-annual basis, (plus March 2017).

**Exhibit 4.2:** Observed Yield Spreads By S&P Country Credit Rating (Investment Grade versus Non-Investment Grade) from December 2007 through March 2017 (in USD)

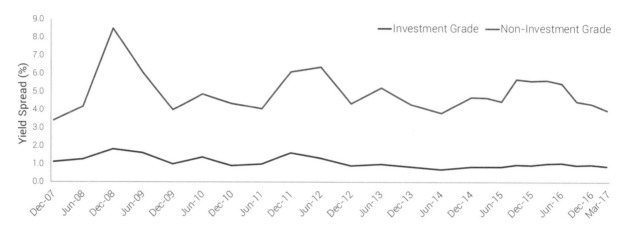

**Methodology – Country Yield Spread Model**

The CRPs presented in Data Exhibit 2 are derived under the Country Yield Spread Model based on a four-tiered algorithm (in the following order of preference):

- **Tier 1 CRPs:** Tier 1 CRPs are, by definition, 0.0%. In all cases in which a foreign country has an S&P credit rating of AAA, the country is assumed to have a CRP of 0.0%. In addition, despite having been downgraded to AA+ by S&P in 2011, our analysis treats the U.S. as if it were a AAA-rated country (see rationale behind this assumption later in this chapter).

- **Tier 2 CRPs:** Tier 2 CRPs are based on observed yield spreads. Tier 2 CRPs can be calculated when the foreign country has sovereign bonds denominated in either USD or EUR (depending on the investor perspective being analyzed). When this is true, the foreign country sovereign bond with the longest maturity is selected.[4.11] The yield of an equivalent U.S. or German government security (depending on the investor perspective being analyzed) of the same (or similar) maturity is then subtracted from the yield of the foreign country sovereign bond to arrive at the CRP.

---

[4.11]   Foreign country bond is screened for the longest maturity USD (or EUR) fixed coupon bullet bond, with no callable features or make-whole provisions, and for which a U.S. or German government security of similar maturity exists.

- **Tier 3 CRPs:** Tier 3 CRPs are based on a regression of S&P sovereign credit ratings and observed yield spreads. This method is employed when the foreign country does *not* have publicly traded sovereign bonds denominated in either USD or EUR (depending on the investor perspective being analyzed), but *does* have an S&P sovereign credit rating. In this method, all observed yield spreads (i.e., Tier 2 CRPs as the *dependent* variable; the variable being predicted) are regressed against a numerical equivalent of each of the respective country's S&P sovereign credit rating (as the *independent* variable; the "predictor" variable). Then, the resulting regression equation is used to estimate a Tier 3 CRP for all foreign countries with an S&P sovereign credit rating, but no observable yields.

- **Tier 4 CRPs:** Tier 4 CRPs are based on a regression of Euromoney country risk (ECR) scores and observed yield spreads. This method is employed when the foreign country does *not* have publicly-traded sovereign bonds denominated in either USD or EUR (depending on the investor perspective being analyzed), and does *not* have an S&P sovereign credit rating.

  In this method, all Tier 2 CRPs (as the *dependent* variable; the variable being predicted) are regressed against Tier 2 CRP countries' ECR score (as the *independent* variable; the "predictor" variable). Then, the resulting regression equation is used to estimate a Tier 4 CRP for all foreign countries with no observable yields and no S&P sovereign credit rating.

Whether the estimated CRPs were categorized as "Tier 1", "Tier 2", "Tier 3", or "Tier 4" CRPs is reported in Data Exhibit 2. In Exhibit 4.3 an extract of Data Exhibit 2 is shown. For example, as of December 2016, Sierra Leone's CRP was derived in Tier 4 calculations, indicating that as of the December 2016 calculations, Sierra Leone did not have an observable yield spread, and also did not have an S&P sovereign credit rating.

Alternatively, as of December 2016 and March 2017, Singapore's CRP was derived in Tier 1 calculations, indicating that as of the December 2016 and March 2017 calculations, Singapore had an S&P sovereign credit rating of "AAA", and thus the CRP is assumed to be 0.0%.

**Exhibit 4.3:** Extract of Data Exhibit 2: Country Yield Spread Model (Investor Perspective: Germany (EUR)

Investor Perspective: Germany
Currency: Euro (EUR)

| Investee Country | Data Updated Through December 2016 | | Data Updated Through March 2017 | |
| --- | --- | --- | --- | --- |
| | December 2016 Country Risk Premium (CRP) (%) | Tier Method* | March 2017 Country Risk Premium (CRP) (%) | Tier Method* |
| Senegal | 4.9 | 3 | 4.8 | 3 |
| Serbia | 4.4 | 2 | 4.2 | 2 |
| Seychelles | 4.0 | 3 | 3.8 | 3 |
| Sierra Leone | 9.2 | 4 ⟵ | 10.0 | 4 |
| Singapore | 0.0 ⟶ | 1 | 0.0 ⟶ | 1 |

## Why Is the United States Being Treated as a 'AAA' Rated Country?

On August 5, 2011, S&P's Ratings Services lowered its long-term sovereign credit rating on the United States to "AA+" from "AAA". S&P indicated that lowering the U.S. rating was prompted by S&P's view on the rising U.S. public debt burden and S&P's perception of greater policymaking uncertainty. On the other hand, S&P stated that their opinion of the U.S. federal government's other economic, external, and monetary credit attributes, which form the basis for the sovereign rating, were broadly unchanged.

This move triggered a number of discussions around the finance community on whether or not the U.S. sovereign debt could still be considered "risk-free". If U.S. government bond yields are no longer deemed risk-free, then issues arise regarding a key input to corporate finance and valuation models. This would also impact the current methodology we use to estimate country risk premia.

We believe that for the short- and medium-term the U.S. government will continue to be perceived by market participants as risk-free. The following are some reasons supporting that belief (this is a non-exhaustive list):

- **S&P's rating opinion differs from that of other rating agencies:** The other two major rating agencies, Moody's and Fitch Ratings, have reaffirmed the United States sovereign rating as AAA. On August 2, 2011, Moody's confirmed the Aaa government bond rating of the United States following the raising of the statutory debt limit on August 2. Similarly, on August 16, 2011, Fitch Ratings confirmed the U.S.'s AAA credit rating after evaluating Congress's agreement to raise the U.S's debt ceiling. These decisions have been reaffirmed since then by both Moody's and Fitch Ratings.

- **Flight-to-quality:** The week following S&P's downgrade, signs of a global economic slowdown resurfaced. Financial markets reacted by moving away from risky securities, such as equities and high yield debt, into U.S. government debt securities, in search for a safe haven. As a result, the yields on U.S. Treasuries (which have an inverse relationship to price) declined significantly, and continued to do so through August 2011. While U.S. government bond yields are now slightly above their record lows reached in 2012, interest rates still remain at what are arguably historically low levels.

- **Lack of alternatives:** U.S. Treasury's market liquidity is unparalleled to any other government security. According to Fitch Ratings, daily trading volumes of U.S. Treasuries ($580 billion) were almost 10 times higher than that of U.K. gilts ($34 billion) and German bunds ($28 billion) combined in 2011. In a report,[4.12] Fitch Ratings indicated that this deep market liquidity enables holders to convert U.S. Treasury securities into Dollars with negligible transaction costs, irrespective of market conditions. Fitch also stated that the size of the U.S. Treasury securities market ($9.3 trillion) was roughly five times the size of French ($1.9 trillion), U.K. ($1.8 trillion), and German ($1.6 trillion) government bond markets.

In the following section, three examples for estimating cost of equity capital are presented using Country Yield Spread Model CRPs:[4.13]

- **Example 4-1:** Estimating base country-level cost of equity capital assuming an investment in the foreign country's "market" *as a whole* (i.e., an assumed beta of 1.0), using *published* values.

- **Example 4-2:** Estimating base country-level cost of equity capital assuming an investment in the foreign country's "market" *as a whole* (i.e., an assumed beta of 1.0), using the valuation analyst's *own* estimate of his/her home country's base country-level cost of equity capital.

- **Example 4-3:** Estimating cost of equity capital for use in evaluating a subject business, asset, or project.

---

[4.12] "U.S. Treasuries Expected to Remain Global Benchmark", Fitch Ratings, July 27, 2011.

[4.13] For additional examples estimating cost of equity capital, please refer to the complimentary CFA Institute webinar entitled "Quantifying Country Risk Premiums", presented on December 6, 2016 by James P. Harrington and Carla S. Nunes, CFA. This webcast can be accessed here:
https://www.cfainstitute.org/learning/products/multimedia/Pages/132617.aspx?WPID=BrowseProducts.

**Using Country Yield Spread Model CRPs to Estimate Base Country-level Cost of Equity Capital**

The CRPs derived from the Country Yield Spread Model (found in Data Exhibit 2) can be used by the analyst to calculate base country-level cost of equity capital estimates for any of the 188 foreign countries listed in Data Exhibit 2 from the perspective of (i) a U.S.-based investor and (ii) an investor based in Germany.[4.14]

By "base country-level cost of equity capital estimate" we mean an estimate of cost of equity capital in foreign Country Y from the perspective of home Country X; this can be thought of as the sum of the risk-free rate plus the equity risk premium in the foreign country, but denominated in the home country's currency.

Note that a base country-level cost of equity capital estimated in this fashion assumes an investment in the "market" of the foreign country *as a whole*, <u>and does not include any adjustment for company/industry risk</u>.

This is equivalent to substituting a beta of 1.0 (i.e., the market's beta) into the Country Yield Spread Model formula:

$$k_{e, foreign\ country} = R_{f, home\ country} + \beta_{home\ country} \times ERP_{home\ country} + CRP$$

$$k_{e, foreign\ country} = R_{f, home\ country} + 1.0 \times ERP_{home\ country} + CRP$$

The analyst can develop a base country-level cost of equity capital estimate for a foreign country derived by (i) using home country base country-level cost of equity capital estimates *published* herein, or (ii) the analyst's *own* custom estimate of the home country base country-level cost of equity capital.

**Example 4-1:** Estimating base country-level cost of equity capital from the perspective of an investor based in Germany investing in Brazil's "market" *as a whole* (i.e., an assumed beta of 1.0), using *published* values, as of March 2017.

Estimating cost of equity in this example is a four-step process:

> **Step 1:** In Data Exhibit 4, locate the 4-page exhibit that reads "Investor Perspective: Germany; Currency: Euro (EUR)"

---

[4.14] Note that an investor based in other countries within the Eurozone (e.g., Spain) investing in say, Brazil, could use the same CRP information in Data Exhibit 2, provided that German government securities are being used as the proxy for the risk-free security when estimating the cost of equity for the subject company. This is because the analysis in Data Exhibit 2 is all being conducted in Euros, calculated against German government debt yields.

**Step 2:** Identify the base country-level cost of equity capital for an investor based in Germany *investing in Germany* as a whole as of March 2017 (as calculated within the context of the Erb-Harvey-Viskanta Country Credit Rating Model in Data Exhibit 4).[4.15] This information is found in the lower right quadrant of page 4 of the 4-page Germany-based investor perspective report (identified in Step 1). As of March 2017, the base country-level cost of equity capital for an investor based in Germany *investing in Germany* as a whole is 7.6%.

**Step 3:** In Data Exhibit 2, identify the Country Yield Spread Model CRP as of March 2017 from the perspective of a German investor, investing in Brazil. As of March 2017, the CRP was 2.1%.

**Step 4:** Add the CRP from Step 3 to the base country-level cost of equity capital for an investor based in Germany investing in the German *market as a whole* identified in Step 2 (7.6% + 2.1%). The result (9.7%) is the base country-level cost of equity capital estimate for an investor based in Germany investing in the Brazilian market *as a whole* as of March 2017.

**Example 4-2:** Calculate the base country-level cost of equity capital estimate for an investor based in the U.S. investing in the Brazilian market *as a whole* (i.e., can assume beta of 1.0), as of March 2017, using the valuation analyst's *own* estimate of his/her home country's base country-level cost of equity capital.

Financial professionals often come to different conclusions as far as cost of capital (and the inputs for its components) is concerned. For example, as of March 31, 2017 Duff & Phelps internal estimate of base country-level cost of equity capital for a U.S. investor investing in the U.S. market *as a whole* is 9.0% (based on a *normalized* risk-free rate of 3.5% and a conditional ERP of 5.5%).[4.16] Using this custom estimate, base country-level cost of equity capital for an investor based in the U.S. investing in Brazil as of March 2017 is a three-step process:

**Step 1:** In this example, the valuation analyst's *own* custom estimate of base country-level cost of equity capital for an investor based in the U.S., *investing in the U.S.*, is 9.0%.

**Step 2:** In Data Exhibit 2, identify the Country Yield Spread Model CRP as of March 2017 from the perspective of an investor based in the U.S., investing in Brazil. As of March 2017, the CRP was 3.2%.

---

[4.15]  Base country-level cost of equity capital estimates are presented in Data Exhibit 4 for *each* of 56 different investor perspectives, based on the Erb-Harvey-Viskanta Country Credit Rating Model. Base country-level cost of equity capital estimates are *not* presented in Data Exhibit 2.

[4.16]  For more information on the equity risk premium, risk-free rates, the size effect, and other valuation issues, visit: www.duffandphelps.com/CostofCapital, and download (free PDF) *Duff & Phelps' U.S. Equity Risk Premium Recommendation reaffirmed at 5.5%, but U.S. Normalized Risk-free Rate Decreased to 3.5%.*

**Step 3:** Add the CRP from Step 2 to the base country-level cost of equity capital for an investor based in the U.S. investing in the U.S. *market as a whole* identified in Step 1 (9.0% + 3.2%). The result (12.2%) is the base country-level cost of equity capital estimate for an investor based in the U.S. investing in the Brazilian *market as a whole* as of March 2017.

Again, the base country-level cost of equity capital estimates in Example 4-1 and Example 4-2 assumes an investment in the foreign country's market *as a whole* (i.e., a beta of 1.0), <u>and do not include any adjustment for company/industry risk</u>.

## Using Country Yield Spread Model CRPs to Estimate Cost of Equity Capital for Use in Evaluating a Subject Business, Asset, or Project

The ability to estimate base country-level cost of equity capital from the perspective of an investor in Country X into Country Y's *market as a whole* (as was done in Examples 4-1 and 4-2) is very valuable information that can be used for *benchmarking* and *support* purposes. Most of the time, however, valuation analysts are developing discount rates for use in evaluating a subject *business, asset*, or *project*.

For example, valuation analysts are often confronted with the following problem: "I know how to value a company in the United States, but this one is in Country ABC, a developing economy. What should I use for a discount rate?" Can the CRP be used as an input in developing cost of equity capital estimates for, say, a company that operates in GICS 3030 (household & personal products) in a different country? Yes, but it is important to understand the assumptions one is making when doing this.

Using the household & personal products company as an example, an analyst typically would develop discount rates for this company *as if it were located in* the "home" country, and then add a CRP to account for the differences in risk between the home country, and the country in which the household & personal products company is *actually* located (i.e., the investee or "foreign" country).

The implied assumption in this analysis is that what it means to be a household & personal products company in the home country means the same thing as being a household & personal products company in the foreign country. Some questions that the analyst may wish to consider:

- Are the risks of being a household & personal products company in the foreign country the *same* as the risks of being a household & personal products company in the home country?

- Does a household & personal products company in the foreign country have the *same* beta ($\beta$) as a household & personal products company in the home country?[4.17]

---

[4.17] Beta ($\beta$) is a measure of systematic risk used as an input in some methods of estimating cost of equity capital (e.g., the CAPM requires a beta).

- Does the household & personal products company in the foreign country operate in a different industry environment from a household & personal products company in the home country?

- Did the analyst apply any additional adjustments when the discount rate was developed for the household & personal products company *as if it were located in* the home country? For example, was a size premium applied? "Large company" and "small company" can mean very different things from country to country. For example, a smaller-sized company in the U.S. or Germany may be a "large" company in Estonia or Norway.

Valuation analysis is an inherently comparative process, so questions like these are no different from the type of questions that are asked in any valuation analysis. For example, a subject company might be compared to a set of companies (i.e., peer group, or comparables) that possess characteristics that are arguably similar to the characteristics of the subject company. To the degree that the subject company and the peer group *do* have differences, further adjustment(s) may be required.

The process for using the information in Data Exhibit 2 for estimating cost of equity capital for a subject *business*, *asset*, or *project*, is quite similar to developing base country-level cost of equity capital (as was done in Examples 4-1 and 4-2). The difference is that *additional* adjustments may be necessary, as outlined earlier.

In the case of our household & personal products company located in the foreign country, the "peer group" is household & personal products companies in the home country, and to the extent that a household & personal products company located in the foreign country is different (other than location), further adjustments may be required. Again, the CRP attempts to isolate the incremental risk premium associated with investing in another market *as a whole*, without regard to differing *industry* risks or other risks that may be particular to that type of business in the foreign country.

**Example 4-3:** Estimate cost of equity capital for a company in Belgium that operates in GICS 3030 (household & personal products ) as of March 2017, from the perspective of an investor based in the U.S.

Estimating cost of equity in this example is a three-step process:

**Step 1:** Calculate a cost of equity capital estimate for a household & personal products company located in the U.S. For the purposes of this example, assume 8.0%.[4.18]

**Step 2:** In Data Exhibit 2, identify the Country Yield Spread Model CRP as of March 2017 from the perspective of an investor based in the U.S., investing in Belgium. As of March 2017, the CRP was 0.3%.

**Step 3:** Add the CRP identified in Step 2 to the cost of equity capital estimate for a household & personal products company in the U.S. estimated in Step 1 (8.0% + 0.3%). The result (8.3%) is the cost of equity capital estimate for an investor based in the U.S. investing in a household & personal products company located in Belgium, _prior_ to any adjustments due to intrinsic differences in the household & personal products industry environment (or other risks) between the U.S. and Belgium.

---

[4.18] An excellent source of international industry statistics (including cost of equity capital estimates and peer group betas for use in CAPM estimates) is the _2016 Valuation Handbook – International Industry Cost of Capital_, with data through March 31, 2016 and includes one optional intra-year Semi-annual Update (data through September 30, 2016). The 2017 edition will be available late summer 2017. This resource includes industry-level analyses for four global economic areas: (i) the "World", (ii) the European Union, (iii) the Eurozone, and (iv) the United Kingdom. Industries in the book are identified by their Global Industry Classification Standard (GICS) code. Each of the four global economic area's industry analyses are presented in three currencies: (i) the Euro (€ or EUR), (ii) the British Pound (£ or GBP), and (iii) the U.S. Dollar ($ or USD).

An excellent source of U.S. industry statistics (including cost of equity capital estimates and peer group betas for use in CAPM estimates) is the _2017 Valuation Handbook – U.S. Industry Cost of Capital_, with data through March 31, 2017 and includes three optional quarterly updates (June, September, and December). This resource provides cost of capital estimates (i.e., equity capital, debt capital, and WACC) for approximately 180 U.S. industries and size groupings (i.e., Large-, Mid-, Low-, and Micro-capitalization companies), plus a host of detailed statistics that can be used for benchmarking purposes (over 300 critical industry-level data points calculated for each industry, depending on data availability). For more information about Duff & Phelps valuation data resources published by John Wiley & Sons, please go to: www.wiley.com/go/ValuationHandbooks or call Wiley's Customer Care Department within the United States at (800) 762-2974, outside the United States at (317) 572-3993, or fax (317) 572 4002.

# Chapter 5
# Relative Volatility Model

**Relative Volatility Model**

In the Relative Volatility Model (originally developed for segmented capital markets), the traditional beta is replaced by a modified beta.[5.1] The modified beta is a result of multiplying the selected subject company beta by the ratio of the volatility of the foreign equity market to the volatility of the home market's benchmark market index. An alternative version, which we present herein (and which produces the same net result), is to adjust the home country's market equity risk premium by this relative volatility (RV) factor.

The RV factor attempts to isolate the incremental risk premium associated with investing in the foreign country as a function of the relative volatility of the foreign country's equity market and the home country's equity market.

The Relative Volatility Model can be expressed as follows:[5.2]

$$k_{e,foreign\ country} = R_{f,home\ country} + \beta_{home\ country} \times ERP_{home\ country} \times Relative\ Volatilty$$

Where:

| | | |
|---|---|---|
| $k_{e,foreign\ country}$ | = | Cost of equity capital in the foreign country (denominated in the home country currency) |
| $R_{f,home\ country}$ | = | Risk-free rate on government bonds in the home country currency. "Home country" in Data Exhibit 3 (Relative Volatility Model) means either the (i) United States (if discount rate is being developed in USD) or (ii) Germany (if discount rate is being developed in Euros) |
| $\beta_{home\ country}$ | = | Beta appropriate for a company located in the home country in a similar industry as the foreign country's subject company (i.e., beta is measured using returns expressed in the home currency) |
| $ERP_{home\ county}$ | = | Equity risk premium of home country |
| Relative Volatility | = | In its general form, determined as the ratio of the annualized monthly standard deviation of the foreign country equity returns (denominated in home country currency) relative to the annualized monthly standard deviation of the home country equity returns (denominated in home country currency) |

---

[5.1] "Segmentation" in this context refers to markets (i.e., economies) that are not fully integrated into world markets (i.e., to some degree isolated from world markets). Markets may be segmented due to a host of issues, such as regulation that restricts foreign investment, taxation differences, legal factors, information, and trading costs, and physical barriers, among others.

[5.2] Versions of this model have been published by MIT professor Donald Lessard (see Donald Lessard, "Incorporating Country Risk in the Valuation of Offshore Projects", *Journal of Applied Corporate Finance* (Fall 1996): 9(3), 52–63) as well as by analysts at Goldman Sachs and Bank of America, Stephen Godfrey and Ramon Espinosa, "A Practical Approach to Calculating Costs of Equity for Investments in Emerging Markets", *Journal of Applied Corporate Finance* (Fall 1996): 80–89.

This approach has appeal in cases where the stock market in the foreign country is relatively diversified. If the foreign country's stock market has greater volatility than the U.S. stock market (or the German stock market, depending on the investor perspective being employed), that greater volatility may be evidence of differences in country-level market risk and, therefore, may indicate that the cost of equity capital estimate should incorporate a country risk premium. The adjustment shown re-scales a home country equity risk premium to foreign country volatility.

This approach has two primary potential problems:

- The observed difference in volatilities may reflect mostly a difference in the composition of the subject country's economy and particular concentration in certain industries (e.g., lots of natural resources but not many service businesses). This is not a country effect but an industry effect. It is incorrect to apply it to other industries.

- This adjustment is troublesome when the investor (e.g., a multi-national firm) clearly has access to global markets.

Again, some countries do not have local stock markets, or their stock markets are so thin (small volumes of trading moves the market up or down with wide swings) that observed variance in returns may not be representative of the true risk from that country. For certain "frontier" countries, the opposite occurs: the local stock markets have very little trading volume, but prices move very little. This means that the equity market volatility is much lower than would be expected for a liquid stock market of a mature market, resulting in a RV factor close to, or even lower than 1.0. In such cases, relying on the Relative Volatility Model would potentially result in a significantly underestimated cost of equity capital.

**Investor Perspectives**

The RV factors derived from Relative Volatility Model are presented in Data Exhibit 3 from two investor perspectives: (i) from the perspective of a U.S.-based investor, wherein the RV factor is calculated as the standard deviation of the equity returns of the foreign country (the "investee" country; the country in which the investment is located) divided by the standard deviation of the equity returns of the U.S., and (ii) from the perspective of a German investor in which EUR is the local currency, wherein the RV factor is calculated as the standard deviation of the equity returns of the foreign country divided by the standard deviation of the equity returns of Germany.[5.3]

---

[5.3] It is not unusual for German securities to be used as proxies in these types of calculations. For example, the yields on German government debt instruments are considered by market participants as the 'gold standard' for the risk-free security denominated in Euros. Germany is the largest economy in Europe.

Each of the two investor perspective exhibits are 2 pages long, and include 75 investee countries each, with a corresponding RV factor listed. The RV factors are:

- Presented as of two dates: December 31, 2016 and March 31, 2017.[5.4]

- Are different for each investor perspective.

This means that:

- If the valuation analyst's cash flow projections are denominated in U.S. Dollars, the valuation analyst should use the country risk analysis denominated in U.S. Dollars.

- If the valuation analyst's cash flow projections are denominated in Euros, the valuation analyst should use the country risk analysis denominated in Euros, if performing the analysis from a German investor perspective.

For example, a U.S.-based investor (i.e., cash flow projections are denominated in U.S. Dollars) who is valuing a business, business ownership interest, security, or intangible asset that is located in, say, India, would use the country risk analysis in Data Exhibit 3 which is denominated in *U.S. Dollars*.

Alternatively, a Germany-based investor (i.e., cash flow projections are denominated in Euros) who is valuing a business, business ownership interest, security, or intangible asset that is located in, say, Brazil, would use the country risk analysis in Data Exhibit 3 which is denominated in *Euros*. Note that an investor based in other countries within the Eurozone (e.g., Spain) investing in say, Brazil, could use the same RV factor information in Data Exhibit 3, provided that a German risk-free rate and equity risk premium (ERP) are being used as inputs when estimating the cost of equity for the subject company. This is because the analysis in Data Exhibit 3 is all being conducted in *Euros*, calculated against Germany's equity market volatility.

---

[5.4] The *2017 Valuation Handbook – International Guide to Cost of Capital* (this book) is published with data through (i) December 31, 2016 and (ii) March 31, 2017 (depending on the model being presented). An intra-year Semi-annual Update with data through (i) June 30, 2017 and (ii) September 30, 2017 (depending on the model being presented) is available. The Country Yield Spread Model (Data Exhibit 2), the Relative Volatility Model (Data Exhibit 3) and the Erb-Harvey-Viskanta Country Credit Rating (CCR) Model (Data Exhibit 4) are updated in the Semi-annual Update; Data Exhibit 1, "International Equity Risk Premia", is not included in the Semi-annual Update because this data is updated at year-end only. The Semi-annual Update is optional, and is not sold separately.

## Methodology – Relative Volatility Model

MSCI Global Equity Indices for a total of 75 countries are used in calculating the Relative Volatility Model.[5.5, 5.6]

In all cases presented herein, annualized monthly standard deviation of equity returns is calculated using the following formula:

$$Annualized\ Monthly\ Standard\ Deviation = \sqrt{\left[\sigma_n^2 + \left(1+\mu_n\right)^2\right]^n - \left(1+\mu_n\right)^{2n}}$$

Where:

| | | |
|---|---|---|
| $\sigma_n$ | = | Standard deviation of $n$-period returns |
| $\mu_n$ | = | Average of $n$-period returns |
| $n$ | = | Number of periods in one year (i.e., monthly returns, $n$ = 12) |

The RV factors are calculated in the following fashion:

- **Step 1:** In all cases in which a foreign country has an S&P credit rating of AAA, the country is assumed to have an RV factor of 1.0. The United States is treated as a AAA-rated country (see rationale in Chapter 4).

- **Step 2:** Trailing 60-months of equity returns (denominated in either USD or EUR, depending on the investor perspective) ending December 2016 and March 2017 (in turn), are used to calculate annualized monthly standard deviations for each of the 75 MSCI equity indices (in turn).

- **Step 3:** The annualized monthly standard deviation result from Step 2 (based upon equity returns denominated in either USD or EUR, depending on the investor perspective) for *each* of the 75 MSCI equity indices is divided (in turn) by the annualized monthly standard deviation from Step 2 for the U.S. or Germany (depending on the investor perspective). The resulting ratio is the RV factor.

For example, the annualized monthly standard deviation of equity returns (in USD) for the 60-month period ending March 2017 for Slovenia was 22.8%, and the annualized monthly standard deviation of equity returns (in USD) for the 60-month period ending March 2017 for the U.S. was 11.6%. The resulting RV factor is 2.0 (22.8% ÷ 11.6%). Similarly, the annualized monthly standard deviation of equity returns (in EUR) for the 60-month period ending March 2017 for Greece was 37.7, and the

---

[5.5] The MSCI series used are GR series (except for Botswana, Ghana, and Jamaica). "GR" indicates that *total return* is calculated reinvesting gross dividends. The MSCI series used for Botswana, Ghana, and Jamaica are based on NR series. "NR" indicates the *net total return* is calculated applying a withholding tax rate on dividends. Use of net returns does not materially impact the RV results.

[5.6] MSCI is a leading provider of investment decision support tools to clients worldwide. MSCI provides indices, portfolio risk and performance analytics, and ESG data and research. To learn more about MSCI, visit www.msci.com.

annualized monthly standard deviation of equity returns (in EUR) for the 60-month period ending March 2017 for Germany was 16.9%. The RV factor is 2.2 (37.7% ÷ 16.9%).

In the following section, two examples for estimating cost of equity capital are presented using Relative Volatility Model RV factors:[5.7]

- **Example 5-1:** Using Relative Volatility Model RV factors to estimate base country-level cost of equity capital assuming an investment in the foreign country's market as a whole (i.e., an assumed beta of 1.0).

- **Example 5-2:** Using Relative Volatility Model RV factors to estimate cost of equity capital for use in evaluating a subject business, asset, or project.

**Using Relative Volatility Model RV Factors to Estimate Base Country-level Cost of Equity Capital**

The RV factors derived from the Relative Volatility Model are presented in Data Exhibit 3 from two investor perspectives: (i) from the perspective of a U.S.-based investor for which USD is the local currency, and (ii) from the perspective of a German investor for which EUR is the local currency. Each of the two investor perspective exhibits is 2 pages long. The RV factors can be used by the analyst to calculate base country-level cost of equity capital estimates for the countries listed in Data Exhibit 3.

By "base country-level cost of equity capital estimate" we mean an estimate of cost of equity capital in foreign Country Y from the perspective of home Country X; base country-level cost of equity in this sense can be thought of as the sum of the risk-free rate plus the equity risk premium in the foreign country (in terms of the home country's currency).

Note that a base country-level cost of equity capital estimated in this fashion assumes an investment in the "market" of a foreign country *as a whole*, <u>and does not include any adjustment for company/industry risk</u>.

Example 5-1: Calculate the base country-level cost of equity capital estimate for an investor based in the U.S. investing in the India market *as a whole*, as of March 2017.

Because we are calculating a base level cost of equity capital estimate for an investment in the Indian market as a whole, this is equivalent to substituting a beta of 1.0 (i.e., the market's beta) into the Relative Volatility Model formula:

$$k_{e,foreign\ country} = R_{f,home\ country} + \beta_{home\ country} \times ERP_{home\ country} \times Relative\ Volatilty$$

$$k_{e,foreign\ country} = R_{f,home\ country} + 1.0 \times ERP_{home\ country} \times Relative\ Volatilty$$

---

[5.7] For additional examples estimating cost of equity capital, please refer to the complimentary CFA Institute webinar entitled "Quantifying Country Risk Premiums", presented on December 6, 2016 by James P. Harrington and Carla S. Nunes, CFA. This webcast can be accessed here:
https://www.cfainstitute.org/learning/products/multimedia/Pages/132617.aspx?WPID=BrowseProducts.

*Three* additional inputs are needed to calculate the base country-level cost of equity capital estimate: (i) the home country's risk-free rate, (ii) the home country's equity risk premium (ERP), and (iii) an RV factor from Data Exhibit 3.

The analyst can select a risk-free rate and ERP of his or her own choosing. Financial professionals often come to *different* conclusions as far as cost of capital and its components (e.g., risk-free rates, betas, equity risk premia) is concerned. There are a number of sources for risk-free rates and ERP estimates.

In the U.S., for example, a long-term government bond yield can be used as a proxy for the long-term risk-free rate. This is typically the practice in other countries as well: a long-term sovereign is selected as a proxy for the long-term risk-free rate.

As far as selection of an appropriate ERP, financial analysts and academics oftentimes have *very* different opinions of what the long-term ERP is at any given time. In the *2017 Valuation Handbook – U.S. Guide to Cost of Capital*,[5.8] for example, several U.S. ERP estimates are reported, including the "historical" ERP (as estimated over the time horizon 1926–2016), the "supply-side" ERP, "implied" ERP estimates, ERP estimates developed by surveying academics and financial professionals, and the Duff & Phelps recommended U.S. ERP.

In the *2017 Valuation Handbook – International Guide to Cost of Capital* (this book), there are several ERP estimates provided. Data Exhibit 1, "International Equity Risk Premia (ERPs)", includes historical ERP estimates for 16 world economies, through December 2016. The ERP data tables in Data Exhibit 1 provide the same type of "historical" ERP calculations as were previously provided in the (now discontinued) Morningstar/Ibbotson *International Equity Risk Premium Report*.[5.9]

For this example, we will use the Duff & Phelps recommended U.S. ERP as of March 31, 2017 (5.5%), coupled with a *normalized* risk-free rate of 3.5%[5.10, 5.11] to calculate a base country-level cost of equity capital estimate for an investor based in the U.S. investing in India as of March 2017.

---

[5.8]   *The 2017 Valuation Handbook – U.S. Guide to Cost of Capital* (John Wiley & Sons, 2017) was published in March 2017, and includes two valuation data sets: (i) the critical data (U.S. ERPs, size premia, industry risk premia) previously published in the (now discontinued) Morningstar/Ibbotson® SBBI® *Valuation Yearbook*, and (ii) the U.S. risk premia and size premia data previously published in the Duff & Phelps *Risk Premium Report*.

[5.9]   Additional sources of international ERP estimates are provided in an appendix to Chapter 3, Appendix 3a, "Additional Sources of International Equity Risk Premium Data".

[5.10]  For more information on the equity risk premium, risk-free rates, the size effect, and other valuation issues, visit: www.duffandphelps.com/CostofCapital, and download (free PDF) *Duff & Phelps' U.S. Equity Risk Premium Recommendation reaffirmed at 5.5%, but U.S. Normalized Risk-Free Rate Decreased to 3.5%*. **Note:** The recommendation in this document is for developing discount rates as of November 15, 2016 and thereafter, until further guidance is issued. Duff & Phelps regularly reviews fluctuations in global economic and financial market conditions that warrant a periodic reassessment of the ERP. To ensure you are always using the most recent recommendation, check www.duffandphelps.com/CostofCapital.

[5.11]  The analyses presented here assume that that the assets being valued are long-lived assets, and therefore a *long-term* risk-free rate and *long-term* ERP are appropriate. In this example, the normalized long-term risk-free rate and long-term ERP estimates are Duff & Phelps' outlook as of March 31, 2017 for the U.S. This implies a base cost of equity capital in the U.S. market as a whole of 9.0% (3.5% + 5.5%).

Estimating cost of equity in this example is a four step process:

**Step 1:** The analyst selects the appropriate long-term risk-free rate ($R_f$) for the home country (the U.S. in this example) as of March 2017. For the purposes of this example, we have assumed a normalized long-term risk-free rate of 3.5%.

**Step 2:** The analyst selects the appropriate long-term equity risk premium (ERP) for the home country (the U.S. in this example) as of March 2017. For the purposes of this example, we have assumed a long-term ERP of 5.5%.

**Step 3:** In Data Exhibit 3, identify the Relative Volatility model's RV factor as of March 2017 from the perspective of an investor based in the U.S., investing in India. As of March 2017, the RV was 1.8.

**Step 4:** Multiply the assumed beta (in this case the assumed beta is 1.0, the beta of the "market"), the ERP identified in Step 2, and the RV factor identified in Step 3 together (1.0 x 5.5% x 1.8); the result is 9.9%. Add this number to the risk-free rate identified in Step 1 (3.5% + 9.9%). The resulting 13.4% is the country-level cost of equity capital estimate for an investor based in the U.S. investing in the Indian *market as a whole* as of March 2017.

**Using Relative Volatility Model RV Factors to Estimate Cost of Equity Capital for Use in Evaluating a Subject Business, Asset, or Project**

The ability to estimate base country-level cost of equity capital from the perspective of an investor in a home country into a foreign country's *market as a whole* (as was done in Example 5-1) is very valuable information that can be used for *benchmarking* and *support* purposes. Most of the time, however, valuation analysts are developing discount rates for use in evaluating a subject *business*, *asset*, or *project*.

For example, valuation analysts are often confronted with the following problem: "I know how to value a company in the United States, but this one is in Country ABC, a developing economy. What should I use for a discount rate?" Can an RV factor be used as an input in developing cost of equity capital estimates for, say, a company that operates in GICS 3030 (household & personal products) in a different country? Yes, but it is important to understand the assumptions one is making when doing this.

Using the aforementioned household & personal products company as an example, an analyst typically would develop discount rates for the household & personal products company *as if it were located in* the "home" country, and then use an RV factor to account for the differences in risk between the "home" country, and the "foreign" country in which the household & personal products company is *actually* located (i.e., the investee country, or "foreign" country).

The implied assumption in this analysis is that what it means to be a household & personal products company in the home country means the same thing as being a household & personal products company in the foreign country. Some questions that the analyst may wish to consider:

- Are the risks of being a household & personal products company in the foreign country the *same* as the risks of being an household & personal products company in the home country?

- Does a household & personal products company in the foreign country have the *same* beta ($\beta$) as a household & personal products company in the home country?[5.12]

- Does the household & personal products company in the foreign country operate in a different industry environment from a household & personal products company in the home country?

- Did the analyst apply any additional adjustments when the discount rate was developed for the household & personal products company *as if it were located in* the home country? For example, was a size premium applied? "Large company" and "small company" can mean very different things from country to country. For example, a smaller-sized company in the U.S. or Germany may be a "large" company in Estonia or Norway.

Valuation analysis is an inherently comparative process, so questions like these are no different from the type of questions that are asked in any valuation analysis. For example, a subject company might be compared to a set of companies (i.e., peer group, or comparables) that possess characteristics that are arguably similar to the characteristics of the subject company. To the extent that the subject company and the peer group *do* have differences, further adjustment(s) may be required.

The process for using the RV factor information in Data Exhibit 3 for estimating cost of equity capital for a subject business, asset, or project, is quite similar to developing base country-level cost of equity capital (see example 5-1). The difference is that *additional* adjustments may be necessary, as outlined earlier.

In the case of our household & personal products company located in the foreign country, the "peer group" is household & personal products companies in the home country, and to the extent that household & personal products companies located in the investee country are different (other than location), further adjustments may be required.

---

[5.12] Beta ($\beta$) is a measure of systematic risk used as an input in some methods of estimating cost of equity capital (e.g., the CAPM requires a beta).

5-8                                        2017 Valuation Handbook – International Guide to Cost of Capital

**Example 5-2:** Estimate cost of equity capital for a company in Bulgaria that operates in GICS 3030 (household & personal products ) as of March 2017, for a investor based in France, taking a German investor perspective (France's local currency is also the Euro).[5.13]

Within the context of the Relative Volatility Model, the only difference in estimating cost of equity capital for use in evaluating a business, asset, or project in a foreign country (as is being done in this example) and estimating cost of equity capital for an investment in a foreign market as a whole (as was done in the previous example) is the beta estimate. In the previous examples, the "market's" beta of 1.0 was used; in this example, the analyst must supply a beta for a household & personal products company located in the home country. In this example we will assume a beta of 1.3:[5.14]

$$k_{e,\ foreign\ country} = R_{f,\ home\ country} + \beta_{home\ country} \times ERP_{home\ country} \times Relative\ Volatility$$

$$k_{e,\ foreign\ country} = R_{f,\ home\ country} + 1.3 \times ERP_{home\ country} \times Relative\ Volatility$$

Three additional inputs are needed to calculate the base country-level cost of equity capital estimate: (i) the home country's risk-free rate, (ii) the home country's ERP, and (iii) an RV factor from Data Exhibit 3.

Estimating cost of equity in this example is a four-step process:

**Step 1:** The analyst selects the appropriate long-term risk-free rate ($R_f$) for the home country (France, in this example, taking a German investor perspective) as of March 2017. For the purposes of this example, we assume a German risk-free rate of 3.0%.[5.15]

---

[5.13]  It is important to understand that all Relative Volatility Model RV factors "from the perspective of an investor based in Germany" are calculated relative to the annualized monthly standard deviation of the German equity market (Germany is the largest economy in Europe). It is not unusual for German benchmarks to be used as inputs in valuation analyses in Europe. For example, the yields on German government debt instruments are often used as the risk-free security (when the analysis cash flows are denominated in Euros).

[5.14]  An excellent source of international industry statistics (including cost of equity capital estimates and peer group betas for use in CAPM estimates) is the *2016 Valuation Handbook – International Industry Cost of Capital*, with data through March 31, 2016 and includes one optional intra-year Semi-annual Update (data through September 30, 2016). The 2017 edition will be available late summer 2017. This resource includes industry-level analyses for four global economic areas: (i) the "World", (ii) the European Union, (iii) the Eurozone, and (iv) the United Kingdom. Industries in the book are identified by their Global Industry Classification Standard (GICS) code. Each of the four global economic area's industry analyses are presented in three currencies: (i) the Euro (€ or EUR), (ii) the British Pound (£ or GBP), and (iii) the U.S. Dollar ($ or USD).

An excellent source of U.S. industry statistics (including cost of equity capital estimates and peer group betas for use in CAPM estimates) is the *2017 Valuation Handbook – U.S. Industry Cost of Capital*, with data through March 31, 2017 and includes three option quarterly updates (June, September, and December). This resource provides cost of capital estimates (i.e., equity capital, debt capital, and WACC) for approximately 180 U.S. industries and size groupings (i.e., Large-, Mid-, Low-, and Micro-capitalization companies), plus a host of detailed statistics that can be used for benchmarking purposes (over 300 critical industry-level data points calculated for each industry, depending on data availability). For more information about Duff & Phelps valuation data resources published by John Wiley & Sons, please go to: www.wiley.com/go/ValuationHandbooks or call Wiley's Customer Care Department within the United States at (800) 762-2974, outside the United States at (317) 572-3993, or fax (317) 572 4002.

[5.15]  In the Eurozone, the yields on German government debt instruments are often used as the risk-free security (when the analysis cash flows are denominated in Euros).

**Step 2:** The analyst selects the appropriate long-term ERP for the home country (France in this example, taking German investor perspective) as of March 2017. For the purposes of this example, we assume a German long-term ERP of 5.0% in Euro terms.

**Step 3:** In Data Exhibit 3, identify the Relative Volatility model's RV factor as of March 2017 from the perspective of a German investor investing in Bulgaria. As of March 2017, the RV factor was 1.6.

**Step 4:** Multiply the assumed beta (1.3), the ERP identified in Step 2, and the RV factor identified in Step 3 together (1.3 x 5.0% x 1.6). The result is (10.4%). Add this number to the risk-free rate identified in Step 1 (3.0% + 10.4%). The result (13.4%) is the cost of equity capital estimate for an investor based in France (taking a German investor perspective) investing in an household & personal products company located in Bulgaria, _prior_ to any adjustments due to intrinsic differences in the household & personal products industry environment (or other risks) between France and Bulgaria.

# Chapter 6
# Erb-Harvey-Viskanta Country Credit Rating Model

The Erb-Harvey-Viskanta Country Credit Rating Model ("CCR Model") is one of the more widely known methods to estimate cost of equity capital in an international setting.[6.1] Whereas the application of a single-country version of the CAPM or a Relative Volatility Model requires that a country have equity returns data, the CCR Model allows for the estimation of cost of equity capital for countries that have a country credit risk rating – even if they do not have a long history of equity returns available (or even if they have no equity returns history at all).

This model is based on the assumption that countries with lower creditworthiness, which is translated into *lower* credit ratings, are associated with *higher* costs of equity capital, and vice versa.

The valuation data calculated using the CCR Model and reported in Data Exhibit 4 of the *2017 Valuation Handbook – International Guide to Cost of Capital* is calculated using:

- The *same* (or similar) data sources that were used to calculate the base country-level cost of equity estimates previously published in the now discontinued Morningstar/Ibbotson *International Cost of Capital Report*, and the *International Cost of Capital Perspectives Report*.

- The *same* (or similar) methodology that was used to calculate the base country-level cost of equity estimates previously published in the now discontinued Morningstar/Ibbotson *International Cost of Capital Report*, and the *International Cost of Capital Perspectives Report*.

---

[6.1] The analysis in Data Exhibit 4, "Erb-Harvey-Viskanta Country Credit Rating (CCR) Model", is based upon the work of Claude Erb, Campbell Harvey, and Tadas Viskanta, "Expected Returns and Volatility in 135 Countries", *Journal of Portfolio Management* (Spring 1996): 46–58. See also Claude Erb, Campbell R. Harvey, and Tadas Viskanta, "Country Credit Risk and Global Portfolio Selection: Country Credit Ratings Have Substantial Predictive Power", *Journal of Portfolio Management*, Winter 1995. We thank Professor Campbell Harvey of the Duke University Fuqua School of Business for his insights and guidance in performing this analysis.

Data Exhibit 4 includes (although on a significantly larger scale) the international cost of capital data that was calculated using the CCR Model previously published in the (now discontinued) Morningstar/Ibbotson *International Cost of Capital Report*, and the *International Cost of Capital Perspectives Report*.

We say "on a significantly larger scale" because the (former) Morningstar/Ibbotson international reports used the CCR Model to estimate base country-level cost of equity capital for 175 countries from the "perspective" of investors (through the lens of the currency changes) based in (i) the U.S. and (ii) six additional countries (Australia, Canada, France, Germany, Japan, and the U.K.).[6.2]

In the CCR model analyses presented in the *2017 Valuation Handbook – International Guide to Cost of Capital*, base country-level cost of equity estimates are calculated for 175 countries and converted into country risk premium indications from the "perspective" of investors (again through the lens of the currency used) based in (i) the U.S. and (ii) 55 additional countries.[6.3, 6.4]

In Data Exhibit 4 the country risk premium indications are calculated as of two dates: (i) December 31, 2016 and (ii) March 31, 2017. The *2017 Valuation Handbook – International Guide to Cost of Capital* includes an optional intra-year Semi-annual Update with data through (i) June 30, 2017 and (ii) September 30, 2017 (depending on the model being presented).[6.5]

**A Notable Difference with Previous Reports: Country Risk Premia (CRPs)**

In the previous Morningstar/Ibbotson international reports, base country-level cost of equity capital estimates were published. In the *2017 Valuation Handbook – International Guide to Cost of Capital*, country risk premia (CRPs) are the primary data presented. Through consultation with various stakeholders using this type of data, it is clear that users are typically more interested in CRP information that they can incorporate into their own custom cost of equity estimates, in lieu of data presenting base country-level cost of equity capital estimates.

The CRP attempts to isolate the *incremental* risk premium associated with investing in a "foreign" country (i.e., the investee country; the country in which the investment is located) other than the "home" country (i.e., the country in which the investor is based).

Calculation of the CRP is straightforward: the base country-level cost of equity capital estimate for a home-country-based investor investing in the home country is subtracted from the base

---

[6.2]   This is done with the reasonable assumption that just as the regression results using returns in USD can be interpreted as being from the "perspective" of a U.S.-based investor, the regression results using returns transformed into currency X can be interpreted as being from the perspective of an investor based in country X.

[6.3]   Source of currency conversion data: Morningstar *Direct* database. Exchange rate sources (as reported by Morningstar): 1960–1987 Main Economic Indicators Historical Statistics (Organization for Economic Cooperation & Development); 1988–present the *Wall Street Journal*.

[6.4]   Investee countries that have expected inflation rates that are very different from the perspective country's expected inflation rates may yield results that significantly under-/over-estimate expected return, and may require additional adjustments (i.e., the base country-level cost of equity capital should exceed the projected inflation, if the analysis is being conducted in nominal terms).

[6.5]   The Country Yield Spread Model (Data Exhibit 2), the Relative Volatility Model (Data Exhibit 3) and the Erb-Harvey-Viskanta Country Credit Rating (CCR) Model (Data Exhibit 4) are updated in the Semi-annual Update; Data Exhibit 1, "International Equity Risk Premia", is not included in the Semi-annual Update because this data is updated at year-end only. The Semi-annual Update is optional, and is not sold separately.

country-level cost of equity capital estimate for a home-country-based investor investing in the foreign country. The difference is the CRP.

## Data Sources

## A Change in 2017

Country Credit Ratings (CCRs) are an important input used to produce the country risk premia (CRPs) in Data Exhibit 4, the "Erb-Harvey-Viskanta Country Credit Rating Model". In February 2017, Institutional Investor LLC communicated to Duff & Phelps that it would no longer conduct and publish the results of its semi-annual "Country Credit Survey" from which CCRs were obtained.[6.6] September 2016 was the final publication date of Institutional Investor CCRs.[6.7]

Starting with the *2017 Valuation Handbook – International Guide to Cost of Capital* (this book):

1.  The source of *new* country credit ratings (post September 2016) used to produce the CRPs in Data Exhibit 4 is Institutional Investor's parent company, Euromoney Institutional Investor PLC.

    Specifically, the *previously published* Institutional Investor country credit ratings (through September 2016) will continue to be used in the regression analyses used to produce the CRPs in Data Exhibit 4, and from October 2016 forward Euromoney's country risk scores will be used.[6.8]

    **Note:** For simplicity, these inputs (the Institutional Investor country credit ratings and the Euromoney country risk scores) are referred to collectively herein as "country credit ratings", or "CCRs", and the model's name is unchanged and will continue to be referred to as the "Erb-Harvey-Viskanta Country Credit Rating Model", or "CCR Model".

2.  The model will now move to a 30-year *rolling* regression, rather than using data back to September 1979. This reflects the trend observed in recent decades by individual countries' economies toward a greater integration with the global economy and global financial markets (i.e., "globalization"); moving this analysis to a 30-year rolling regression ensures that only (relatively) more recent information about the stage of development of each country's economy is impacting the results.

---

[6.6] Institutional Investor LLC is a leading business-to-business publisher, focused on international finance. Institutional Investor LLC is a division of Euromoney Institutional Investor PLC. To learn more, visit http://www.institutionalinvestor.com.

[6.7] Institutional Investor CCRs were published from September 1979 through September 2016 on a semi-annual basis (September, March), with one exception: Institutional Investor did not publish March 2010 CCRs.

[6.8] Euromoney Institutional Investor PLC is an international business-to-business information and events group listed on the London Stock Exchange, with 2,300 employees worldwide and a portfolio of over 50 specialist businesses spanning macroeconomic data, investment research, news and market analysis, industry forums and institutes, financial training, and excellence awards. To learn more visit: http://www.euromoneyplc.com/.

3. The model will now make the following assumptions:

   a. If both the "home" country (i.e., the country in which the investor is based) and the "foreign" country (i.e., the investee country; the country in which the investment resides) have an S&P sovereign credit rating of AAA, the concluded country risk premium (CRP) is 0.0%. The United States is treated as a AAA-rated country for purposes of implementing this model (see rationale in Chapter 4).

   b. If the "home" country has an S&P sovereign credit rating of AAA and the "foreign" country has an S&P credit rating *below* AAA (i.e., a worse credit rating), *and* has a calculated CRP of *less* than 0.0% (i.e., a negative implied premium), the CRP assigned is 0.0% (and vice-versa).

The first change was out of necessity: a new source of country credit ratings was needed to replace the discontinued series. The source that was identified as being the best fit for a substitute is produced by Institutional Investor's own parent company (Euromoney Institutional Investor PLC).

The second change was a methodological change that was designed with the goal of better reflecting the ongoing change and evolving integration of global markets. These changes may entail significant changes to some countries' relative risk relative to what has been reported in prior years.

The third change (3a) harmonizes the Country Credit Rating Model, the Country Yield Spread Model, and the Relative Volatility Model (this assumption is *already* in place in the latter two models).

The fourth change (3b) is in effect starting with the *2017 Valuation Handbook – International Guide to Cost of Capital* (this book) for (i) the Country Credit Rating Model and (ii) the Country Yield Spread Model, but *not* in the Relative Volatility Model.[6.9]

In the following section, a brief overview of Institutional Investor's country credit ratings is first provided, and then a brief overview of Euromoney's country risk scores is provided.

**About Institutional Investor "Country Credit Ratings" and Euromoney "Country Risk Scores"**

To calculate the analyses presented in Data Exhibit 4, "Erb-Harvey-Viskanta Country Credit Rating Model: Country Risk Premia (CRPs)" utilize Institutional Investor's country credit ratings (CCRs) through September 2016, and Euromoney's country risk scores from October 2016 forward.[6.10]

Institutional Investor's CCRs were created based on information confidentially provided by senior economists and sovereign-risk analysts at leading global banks and money management and securities firms. The respondents graded each country on a scale of zero to 100, with 100 representing the least likelihood of default. Participant's responses are then weighted according to

---

[6.9] Change 3b has *not* been in effect for the Relative Volatility Model in previous editions of the *Valuation Handbook – International Guide to Cost of Capital*, and is *not* in effect in the *2017 Valuation Handbook – International Guide to Cost of Capital* (this book). Change 3b may be instituted in the Relative Volatility Model in future editions, pending further study.

[6.10] Country-level credit ratings are available from various sources, including Euromoney's Country Risk scores, Political Risk Services' and International Country Risk Guide.

their institutions' global exposure.[6.11, 6.12] Institutional Investor country credit ratings are on a scale from 1 (lowest, most risky score) to 100 (highest, least risky score).

In the model version presented herein, "monthly" CCR values are calculated with a simple interpolation between each country's semi-annual Institutional Investor CCRs. For example, if the published March 2007 CCR is 76 and the published September 2007 CCR is 70, then one would subtract $(76 - 70) \div 6 = 1$ from each intra-semi-annual period to calculate CCRs for months April through August 2007.[6.13]

Euromoney country risk scores take into account 15 different categories that relate to economic, structural, and political risk.[6.14] Consensus expert scores, combined with data from the IMF/ World Bank on debt indicators, a survey of debt syndicate managers at international banks on access to capital and Moody's/Fitch credit ratings are combined to create the Euromoney country risk score for over 180 individual countries. Euromoney Country Risk Scores are published monthly.

Euromoney evaluates the investment risk of a country, such as risk of default on a bond, risk of losing direct investment, risk to global business relations etc., by taking a qualitative model, which seeks an expert opinion on risk variables within a country (70% weighting) and combining it with three basic quantitative values (30% weighting).

To obtain the overall score, Euromoney assigns a weighting to six categories. The three qualitative expert opinions are political risk (30% weighting), economic performance (30%), and structural assessment (10%). The three quantitative values are debt indicators (10%), credit ratings (10%), and access to bank financing and capital markets (10%). Euromoney country risk ratings are on a scale from 1 (lowest, most risky score) to 100 (highest, least risky score). This is the same scale used by Institutional Investor.

---

[6.11] As paraphrased from Institutional Investor's website country credit ratings "Methodology" page at: http://www.institutionalinvestor.com/Research/6160/Methodology.html#.VzCqClQrKUk.

[6.12] Institutional Investor CCRs were published from September 1979 through September 2016 on a semi-annual basis (September, March), with one exception: Institutional Investor did not publish March 2010 CCRs. For the purposes of the analyses herein, March 2010 CCRs were estimated for each country by taking a simple average of each country's respective September 2009 and September 2010 CCRs.

[6.13] In this example, March, April, May, June, July, August, and September 2007 CCRs would be 76, 75, 74, 73, 72, 71, and 70, respectively.

[6.14] For more information, visit https://www.euromoneycountryrisk.com/Methodology.

## Equity Returns

A total of 72 countries' MSCI Global Equity Indices are used in calculating the CCR Model analyses presented herein, as summarized in Exhibit 6.1.[6.15, 6.16]

**Exhibit 6.1:** MSCI Global Equity Indices Used in Calculating the CCR Model Analyses Presented Herein

| | | |
|---|---|---|
| Argentina | Indonesia | Poland |
| Australia | Ireland | Portugal |
| Austria | Israel | Qatar |
| Bahrain | Italy | Romania |
| Bangladesh | Japan | Russia |
| Belgium | Jordan | Saudi Arabia |
| Brazil | Kazakstan | Serbia |
| Bulgaria | Kenya | Singapore |
| Canada | Korea (South) | Slovenia |
| Chile | Kuwait | South Africa |
| China | Lebanon | Spain |
| Colombia | Lithuania | Sri Lanka |
| Croatia | Malaysia | Sweden |
| Czech Republic | Mauritius | Switzerland |
| Denmark | Mexico | Taiwan |
| Egypt | Morocco | Thailand |
| Estonia | Netherlands | Trinidad & Tobago |
| Finland | New Zealand | Tunisia |
| France | Nigeria | Turkey |
| Germany | Norway | Ukraine |
| Greece | Oman | United Arab Emirates |
| Hong Kong | Pakistan | United Kingdom |
| Hungary | Peru | United States |
| India | Philippines | Vietnam |

---

[6.15] The MSCI series used are GR series. "GR" indicates that *total return* is calculated reinvesting gross dividends.

[6.16] MSCI is a leading provider of investment decision support tools to clients worldwide. MSCI provides indices, portfolio risk and performance analytics, and ESG data and research. To learn more about MSCI, visit www.msci.com.

## The CCR Model

The Erb-Harvey-Viskanta Country Credit Rating Model can be expressed as:

$$k_{e,local} = \alpha + \beta \times Natural\,Log\left(CCR_{local}\right) + \varepsilon$$

Where:

| | | |
|---|---|---|
| $k_{e,local}$ | = | Cost of equity capital in local country |
| $\alpha$ | = | Regression constant |
| $\beta$ | = | Regression coefficient |
| $CCR_{local}$ | = | Country credit rating of local country |
| $\varepsilon$ | = | Regression error term |

This model was originally developed in 1996 by academics Claude Erb, Campbell Harvey, and Tadas Viskanta. The objective of the research was to develop a country risk model that could be used to establish hurdle rates for segmented markets. The research showed that while models such as the World (Global) CAPM worked reasonably well for developed markets, they did a poor job in explaining returns for emerging markets. In subsequent work, Professor Harvey recommended the use of either a CAPM or a multi-factor model in developed, liquid markets. In emerging markets, Professor Harvey indicated that he would often examine the indications of a number of models, including, but not limited to, the Erb-Harvey-Viskanta CCR model and average the corresponding results.[6.17]

The Erb-Harvey-Viskanta Country Credit Rating Model regresses all available CCRs (as of the month of calculation) for all countries in a given period $t$ against all the available (equivalent) equity returns (for all countries that have returns) in the *next* period $t + 1$.

For example, to estimate country-level cost of equity from a U.S. investor's perspective as of March 2017, all available countries' CCRs from March 1987 through February 2017 are matched with each of the 72 countries' respective monthly equity returns (in USD) from April 1987 through March 2017. This results in 19,721 matched pairs of CCRs in period $t$ and returns in period $t + 1$. A regression analysis is then performed, with the natural log of the CCRs as the independent variable (the "predictor" variable), and the equity returns as the dependent variable (what is being "predicted").

Then, the March 2017 CCR for *each* of the 175 countries for which Euromoney Institutional Investor PLC has a rating (as of March 2017, in this example) is then used (in conjunction with the *intercept* and *coefficient* generated by the regression) to predict the *next* 1-month period's return for each of the countries. This result is then multiplied by 12 to annualize the "monthly" estimate.

---

[6.17] Campbell R. Harvey, "12 Ways to Calculate the International Cost of Capital" (Durham, NC: Duke University), National Bureau of Economic Research, Cambridge, MA, USA 02138.

For example, as of March 2017 the CCR for Peru was 58.9 (on a 100-point scale). And, as of March 2017 the intercept and coefficient generated by regressing all available CCRs in time $t$ against all available monthly returns (in USD, for the 72 countries that have returns) in time $t + 1$ are 0.057491 and -0.011641 respectively.[6.18]

The country-level cost of equity estimate for Peru (from the perspective of an investor based in the U.S.) as of March 2017 (12.1%) is therefore calculated as follows:

$$COE_{Peru} = \{Intercept_{U.S.\ March2017} + [Coefficient_{U.S.\ March2017} \times Natural\ Log\ (CCR\ Peru_{March2017})]\} \times 12$$

$$COE_{Peru} = \{0.057491 + [-0.011641 \times Natural\ Log\ (58.9)]\} \times 12 = 0.120530 = 12.1\%$$

**Different Investor Perspectives**

In the previous example, the 72 MSCI equity return indices used in the regressions were expressed in U.S. Dollar (USD) terms, and the results can thus be interpreted as "from the perspective of a U.S. investor" investing in (in this case) Peru. Alternatively, transforming the 72 MSCI equity return indices (as a group) into Canadian Dollar (CAD) terms or Japanese Yen (JPY) terms and then recalculating the regressions would produce results that can be interpreted as "from the perspective" of investors in Canada and Japan, respectively. As such, investor perspective (i.e., the country in which the investor is based) is defined herein by the currency in which the equity returns used in the regression analyses are expressed in.

Unexpected changes in the value of one currency versus another can have significant effects on the "money in pocket" of an investor. For example, in 2004 a local investor in the German stock market would have realized an increase of approximately 8% in his or her equity investments. However, a U.S.-based investor investing in the German stock market would have realized an increase of approximately 17% in his or her investments that year. The reason is simple: the Euro appreciated significantly against the U.S. Dollar in 2004, so the U.S. investor could buy more Dollars per Euro at the end of 2004 when repatriating the Euro investment back home. This change in the value of the two currencies in relation to each other enhanced the U.S.-based investor's return by approximately 9% (17% − 8%).[6.19, 6.20]

In Exhibit 6.2, the 72 MSCI equity return indices used in the analyses herein were translated into (as a group, and in turn) U.S. Dollars (USD), British Pounds (GBP), German Euros (EUR), Brazilian Reals (BRL), and Japanese yen (JPY). CCR Model regression analyses were then performed in each currency (in turn), and a base country-level cost of equity capital estimate for investors based in the U.S., the U.K., Germany, Brazil, and Japan was then developed for each investing in Belgium, China,

---

[6.18]  The negative coefficient implies that as credit ratings *increase* (better credit), country-level cost of equity estimates *decrease*, and vice versa.

[6.19]  Source of underlying data: equity returns: MSCI German Gross Return (GR) Index as published in Morningstar *Direct*; exchange rates: Morningstar *Direct*.

[6.20]  Unexpected changes in the relative value of currencies can work in the opposite direction also: In the following year (2005), the Euro significantly declined in value versus the U.S. Dollar. In this case, the "local" German investor would have realized a return of approximately 27%, whereas the U.S.-based investor would have realized a return of only 11%, that is, his or her Euros would have bought *fewer* Dollars per Euro at the end of 2005 than they could have at the beginning of 2005.

India, Kuwait, Mexico, South Africa, Slovenia, and Uruguay. As can be seen, the effect of currency fluctuations can have significant impact on expected return.

**Exhibit 6.2:** Using the CCR Model to Estimate Cost of Equity Capital from Differing Investor Perspectives (March 2017)

| | U.S.-based Investor | U.K.-based Investor | Germany-based Investor | Brazil-based Investor | Japan-based Investor |
|---|---|---|---|---|---|
| Investing in Belgium | 8.9% | 10.2% | 9.1% | 12.8% | 8.9% |
| Investing in China | 12.3% | 13.5% | 12.7% | 15.6% | 12.5% |
| Investing in India | 13.7% | 14.8% | 14.1% | 16.6% | 14.0% |
| Investing in Kuwait | 10.6% | 11.8% | 10.8% | 14.1% | 10.7% |
| Investing in Mexico | 11.7% | 13.0% | 12.1% | 15.1% | 11.9% |
| Investing in South Africa | 13.9% | 15.1% | 14.4% | 16.8% | 14.2% |
| Investing in Slovenia | 11.3% | 12.5% | 11.6% | 14.7% | 11.4% |
| Investing in Uruguay | 12.5% | 13.7% | 12.8% | 15.7% | 12.7% |

In the CCR Model analyses presented herein, 56 different investor perspectives are presented, as summarized in Exhibit 6.3.[6.21, 6.22]

---

[6.21] Of the 56 investor perspectives, 19 of these investor perspective countries are members of the Eurozone, in which the local currency is the Euro (€). In the (former) Morningstar/Ibbotson *International Cost of Capital Perspectives Report*, the Erb-Harvey-Viskanta Country Credit Rating Model was used to estimate country-level cost of equity capital from the "perspective" of investors based in any one of *six* different countries (Australia, Canada, France, Germany, Japan, and the U.K.). In the analyses presented herein, the number of investor perspectives has been expanded to 56 investor perspectives.

[6.22] Source of local currency and currency code information used in Exhibit 6.3: International Organization for Standardization (ISO), "List one: Currency, fund and precious metal codes", published 2-24-16; http://www.iso.org/iso/currency_codes.

**Exhibit 6.3:** Investor Perspectives Presented Herein (total 56), calculated Using the CCR Model

| Investor Perspective | Currency | Investor Perspective | Currency |
|---|---|---|---|
| Argentina | Argentine Peso (ARS) | Latvia | Euro (EUR) |
| Australia | Australian Dollar (AUD) | Lithuania | Euro (EUR) |
| Austria | Euro (EUR) | Luxembourg | Euro (EUR) |
| Bahrain | Bahraini Dinar (BHD) | Malaysia | Malaysian Ringgit (MYR) |
| Belgium | Euro (EUR) | Malta | Euro (EUR) |
| Brazil | Brazilian Real (BRL) | Morocco | Moroccan Dirham (MAD) |
| Canada | Canadian Dollar (CAD) | Netherlands | Euro (EUR) |
| Chile | Chilean Peso (CLP) | New Zealand | New Zealand Dollar (NZD) |
| China | Yuan Renminbi (CNY) | Norway | Norwegian Krone (NOK) |
| Colombia | Colombian Peso (COP) | Philippines | Philippine Peso (PHP) |
| Cyprus | Euro (EUR) | Poland | Zloty (PLN) |
| Czech Republic | Czech Koruna (CZK) | Portugal | Euro (EUR) |
| Denmark | Danish Krone (DKK) | Qatar | Qatari Rial (QAR) |
| Estonia | Euro (EUR) | Russia | Russian Ruble (RUB) |
| Finland | Euro (EUR) | Saudi Arabia | Saudi Riyal (SAR) |
| France | Euro (EUR) | Singapore | Singapore Dollar (SGD) |
| Germany | Euro (EUR) | Slovakia | Euro (EUR) |
| Greece | Euro (EUR) | Slovenia | Euro (EUR) |
| Hong Kong | Hong Kong Dollar (HKD) | South Africa | Rand (ZAR) |
| Hungary | Forint (HUF) | Spain | Euro (EUR) |
| Iceland | Iceland Krona (ISK) | Sweden | Swedish Krona (SEK) |
| India | Indian Rupee (INR) | Switzerland | Swiss Franc (CHF) |
| Indonesia | Rupiah (IDR) | Taiwan | New Taiwan Dollar (TWD) |
| Ireland | Euro (EUR) | Thailand | Thai Baht (THB) |
| Italy | Euro (EUR) | United Arab Emirates | UAE Dirham (AED) |
| Japan | Yen (JPY) | United Kingdom | Pound Sterling (GBP) |
| Korea (South) | Won (KRW) | United States | U.S. Dollar (USD) |
| Kuwait | Kuwaiti Dinar (KWD) | Uruguay | Peso Uruguayo (UYU) |

## Global Cost of Equity Capital – High-level Comparisons

The CCR Model allows for the comparison of cost of equity capital estimates for any combination of available countries. We now present several examples of base country-level cost of equity capital estimated by (i) level of economic development, (ii) country, (iii) financial crisis impact, (iv) S&P sovereign credit rating, and (v) geographic region.

## Cost of Equity Capital by Level of Economic Development

MSCI classifies the countries for which it has indices into various groupings, including level of economic development. This grouping categorizes countries as (i) developed markets, (ii) emerging markets, and (iii) frontier markets.[6.23]

In Exhibit 6.4, the CCR model is used to calculate a base country-level cost of equity capital from the perspective of a U.K.-based investor investing in (i) the U.K., (ii) developed markets, (iii) emerging markets, and (iv) frontier markets, as of March 2017.[6.24]

**Exhibit 6.4:** Base Country-level Cost of Equity Capital Estimates for the U.K., MSCI Developed Markets, MSCI Emerging Markets, and MSCI Frontier Markets, from the Perspective of a U.K.-based Investor (as of March 2017)

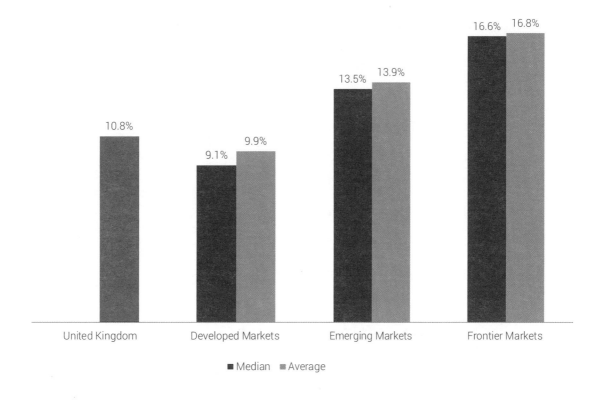

**Source of underlying data:** Institutional Investor's Country Credit Ratings; equity (stock) indices from MSCI Global Equity Indices, as published in Morningstar *Direct*. All estimates are expressed in terms of British Pounds (GBP). All calculations by Duff & Phelps, LLC.

---

[6.23] The MSCI Market Classification Framework consists of the following three criteria: economic development, size and liquidity, and market accessibility. Developed market countries are countries with the most developed economies. Emerging market countries have economies that are less developed than developed market economies, but whose markets have greater liquidity than frontier market economies, while exhibiting significant openness to capital inflows/outflows and openness to foreign ownership. Frontier market countries have economies that are less developed than both developed and emerging market economies, while exhibiting lower market size and liquidity, as well as more restricted market accessibility. To learn more about the MSCI Market Classification Framework, visit: https://www.msci.com/www/product-documentation/msci-market-classification/0164200476.

[6.24] "From the perspective of a U.K.-based investor" means the returns for the 72 MSCI equity returns series used in the regression calculations used to perform this analysis were expressed in British Pounds (GBP).

The relationships between the values are intuitively pleasing: the estimated cost of equity capital *increases* as we move from *more* developed economies to *less* developed economies. This makes sense – less-developed economies tend to have greater financial, economic, and political risks than more-developed economies do.

**Cost of Equity Capital by Country**

In another example, Exhibit 6.5 lists the base country-level cost of equity capital for the largest 10 countries ranked by 2016 gross domestic product (GDP) as calculated using the CCR Model, this time from the perspective of a China-based investor. Canada, which has the tenth-largest economy, has the *lowest* cost of equity capital estimate (8.5%) of the group as of March 2017. Alternatively, Brazil, which has the ninth-largest economy, has the *highest* cost of equity capital estimate (15.7%) in the group.

**Exhibit 6.5:** Cost of Equity Capital Estimates for the 10 Largest Countries by GDP from the Perspective of a China-based Investor (as of March 2017)

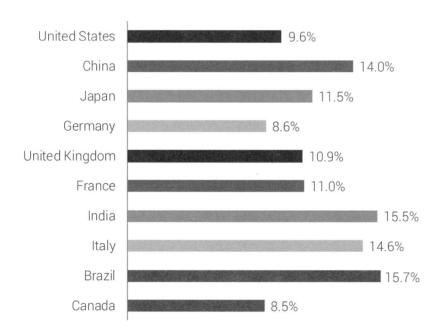

**Source of underlying data:** Institutional Investor's Country Credit Ratings; Euromoney Institutional Investor; equity (stock) indices from MSCI Global Equity Indices, as published in Morningstar *Direct*. GDP estimates are from the World Economic Outlook Database from the International Monetary Fund (IMF). For additional information, please visit: http://www.imf.org/external/pubs/ft/weo/2017/01/weodata/download.aspx. All estimates are expressed in terms of Yuan Renminbi (CNY). All calculations by Duff & Phelps, LLC.

## Cost of Equity Capital by Financial Crisis Impact

Possible weakening of Eurozone economies has been of interest recently, particularly after the 2008 financial crisis and the onset of the Eurozone sovereign debt crisis. The issues are often discussed within the framework of the "healthier" core economies (e.g., Germany, U.K., France) compared to "less healthy" periphery economies (e.g., Greece, Portugal, Spain).

In Exhibit 6.6, the CCR Model is used to calculate a base country-level cost of equity capital (again from the perspective of a U.S.-based investor) for each of the six "healthier" and "less healthy" countries listed earlier. Then, the median value of the two groupings ("healthier" and "less healthy") over the period January 2007–March 2017 was plotted.

The model's output seems reasonable over this time period – the less healthy group is *riskier* than the healthier group over the entire 123-month period, and the gap *widens* after the 2008 financial crisis and the subsequent impact of the Eurozone sovereign debt crisis.

For example, by mid-2011 many analysts expected Greece to default on its government debt, despite the two bailout packages Greece was forced to accept in May 2010 and July 2011. Although not in such precarious conditions as Greece, Portugal was also forced into a bailout package in April 2011. Markets reacted negatively to the second EU-approved Greek bailout of July 2011 and the crisis spread to Spain and Italy, countries considered "too big to fail". In late summer 2012, the European Central Bank (ECB) was forced to reenact its government bonds purchase program and to provide additional liquidity to banks. In September 2012, the ECB also announced a new quantitative easing (QE) program to purchase certain sovereign debt securities in secondary markets, which resulted in peripheral sovereign yields declining significantly.

However, lackluster growth trends, coupled with deflation fears, induced the ECB to cut its benchmark rate to a new record low in early June 2014, while also announcing an unprecedented measure to charge negative interest rates on deposits held at the central bank. The loss in economic momentum, coupled with early third-quarter indicators falling short of expectations, prompted the ECB to again cut its benchmark rate to 0.05% in September 2014. The ECB also confirmed the start of an asset-backed securities purchase program and unveiled a new Euro-denominated covered bond purchase program. The continued threat of deflation led the ECB to announce a larger scale sovereign debt buying program in January 2015, which consists of €60 billion monthly asset purchases starting in March 2015, with a target end date of September 2016. In the midst of these events, a new government in Greece was elected in January 2014, bringing fears of a Greek exit from the Eurozone back to the forefront. These events impacted the CCRs for these countries, which translated into a higher cost of equity as implied by the CCR Model.

**Exhibit 6.6:** Median Calibrated Cost of Equity Capital Estimates for Healthier European Economies (Germany, U.K., France) versus Less Healthy European Economies (Greece, Portugal, Spain) (Monthly, January 2007–March 2017)

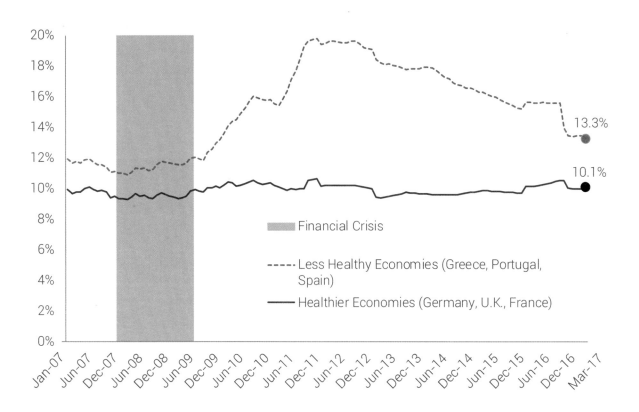

**Source of underlying data:** Institutional Investor's Country Credit Ratings; Euromoney Institutional Investor; equity (stock) indices from MSCI Global Equity Indices, as published in Morningstar *Direct*. CCR-based estimates of cost of equity capital are calibrated in this exhibit to Duff & Phelps published "base" U.S. cost of equity capital estimates. All estimates are expressed in terms of U.S. Dollars. All calculations by Duff & Phelps, LLC.

## Cost of Equity Capital by S&P Sovereign Credit Rating

The CCR Model can also be used to compare the estimated cost of equity capital through the lens of credit rating agencies' debt ratings of countries.

In Exhibit 6.7, the CCR Model is used to estimate base country-level cost of equity capital (this time, from the perspective of a China-based investor) for countries with a Standard & Poor's (S&P) sovereign credit rating of AAA, AA, A, BBB, BB, and B–SD (SD stands for "Selective Default") as of March 2017; the median and average cost of equity capital estimates for countries in each rating group is then calculated. These groupings' median and average are then compared to the model's base country-level cost of equity capital estimate for a China-based investor investing in China. For purposes of this analysis, we have treated the U.S. as if it were rated AAA by S&P (see rationale in Chapter 4).

**Exhibit 6.7:** Median and Average Cost of Equity Capital Estimates from the Perspective of a China-based Investor for Groupings of Countries with Various S&P Credit Ratings; Compared to China's Estimated Cost of Equity Capital (as of March 2017)

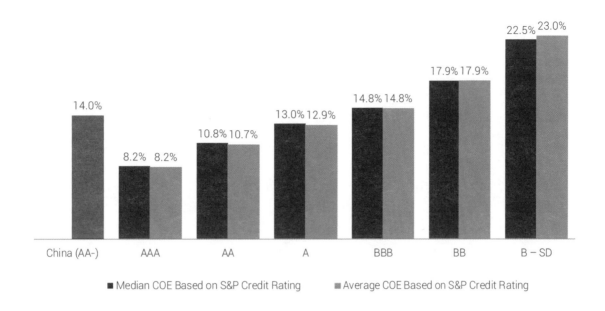

**Source of underlying data:** Institutional Investor's Country Credit Ratings; Euromoney Institutional Investor; equity (stock) indices from MSCI Global Equity Indices, as published in Morningstar *Direct*. S&P credit ratings from Standard & Poor's Global Credit Portal. All estimates are expressed in terms of Yuan Renminbi (CNY). All calculations by Duff & Phelps, LLC.

Again, the relationships between the values make sense — countries with *lower* S&P credit grades tend to have *higher* cost of equity capital.

**Cost of Equity Capital By Geographic Region**

The CCR Model can also be used to compare the estimated cost of equity capital across geographic regions.

In Exhibit 6.8, the model was used to estimate base country-level cost of equity capital as of March 2017, from the perspective of a U.S.-based investor considering an investment in Brazil. This estimate is then compared to the median and average base country-level cost of equity estimate for countries in the Latin America geographic region (as a group).[6.25] The base country-level cost of equity capital for Brazil (13.9%) is significantly *lower* than the median (i.e., typical) and average cost of equity capital for the region.

---

[6.25] Regional classification based on Euromoney's Country Risk definitions. For further information please visit: http://www.euromoneycountryrisk.com.

**Exhibit 6.8:** Cost of Equity Capital for Countries in the Latin America/Caribbean Geographic Region, from the Perspective of a U.S.-based Investor (as of March 2017)

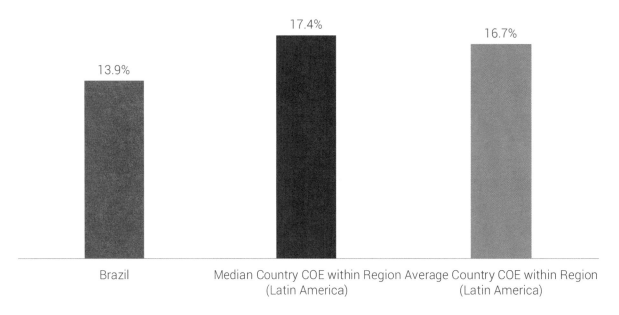

**Source of underlying data:** Regional classification based on Euromoney's Country Risk definitions; equity (stock) indices from MSCI Global Equity Indices, as published in Morningstar *Direct*. All estimates are expressed in terms of U.S. Dollars. All calculations by Duff & Phelps, LLC.

## Presentation of Cost of Capital Data

In the previous Morningstar/Ibbotson international reports, base country-level cost of equity capital estimates were published. In the *2017 Valuation Handbook – International Guide to Cost of Capital*, however, country risk premia (CRPs) are the primary data presented.[6.26]

The CRP data presented in Data Exhibit 4 can be used to estimate base country-level cost of equity capital estimates for 175 countries, from the perspective of 56 investor perspectives (a U.S.-based investor, plus investors based in any one of 55 additional countries).

---

[6.26] "Base country-level cost of equity capital" estimates are also presented from the perspective of an investor based in Country X investing in Country X (e.g., a German-based Euro investor, an Australia-based Australian Dollar investor, etc.). These statistics are found in the lower right quadrant of page 4 of each 4-page investor perspective report in Data Exhibit 4.

## Country Risk Premia (CRP) Defined

The CRP attempts to isolate the incremental risk premium associated with investing in a "foreign" country (i.e., the investee country; the country in which the investment is located) other than the "home" country (i.e., the country in which the investor is based).

The publication of CRPs makes using the information published herein easier to use. Because the CRP is designed to isolate the incremental risks of investing in one country versus investing in another country (all other things held the same), the analyst can simply add the CRP to his or her own cost of equity estimate (see examples later in this section).

Data Exhibit 4 includes 56 exhibits (one for *each* investor perspective; each investor perspective report is 4 pages long). In each of those 56 investor perspective reports, 175 investee countries are listed, with a corresponding CRP. The CRPs are:

- Presented as of two dates: (i) December 2016 and (ii) March 2017[6.27]

- Different for each investor perspective

The CRPs presented in Data Exhibit 4 are designed to be a gauge of the *relative* risks between investing in the "home" country and the "foreign" country, as determined within the framework of the Erb-Harvey-Viskanta Country Credit Rating Model, as calculated herein. This difference in relative risk is assumed to be a linear function, and remains the same regardless of the base country-level cost of equity capital for an investor investing in his or her home country selected by the analyst, whether that selection is (i) the *published* value in Data Exhibit 4, or (ii) a *custom* value calculated by the analyst. Examples for both of these scenarios are provided later in this section.

## How CRPs Are Calculated

Calculation of the CRP is straightforward: the base country-level cost of equity capital estimate for a home-country-based investor investing in the home country is subtracted from the base country-level cost of equity capital estimate for a home-country-based investor investing in the foreign country. The difference is the CRP.

For example, the base country-level cost of equity capital as of March 2017 as estimated in the analyses herein using the CCR Model for a U.K.-based investor investing in the U.K. is 10.8% (in other words, 10.8% is the country-level discount rate for U.K.-based British Pound (GBP) investors).

---

[6.27] The previous Morningstar/Ibbotson international reports included data only for March using the CCR Model.

Alternatively, the base country-level cost of equity capital as of March 2017 for a U.K.-based investor investing in China is 13.5% (in other words, 13.5% is the country-level discount rate for U.K.-based investors in a Chinese-based investment, denominated in GBP).[6.28] The CRP is calculated as follows:

*CRP = (Base country-level cost of equity capital estimate for a home-country-based investor investing in the foreign country) − (Base country-level cost of equity capital estimate for a home-country-based investor investing in the home country)*

*2.7% = 13.5% − 10.8%*

A "base country-level cost of equity capital estimate" is the risk of investing in a country's market *as a whole* (i.e., an assumed beta of 1.0). The CRP therefore represents the *incremental* risk of investing in the foreign country's market *as a whole*, as opposed to investing in the home country's market *as a whole*.

In the following section, three examples for estimating cost of equity capital are presented:

- Using CRPs to Estimate Base Country-level Cost of Equity Capital: Estimating base country-level cost of equity capital assuming an investment in the foreign country's market as a whole (i.e., an assumed beta of 1.0), using *published* values.

- Using CRPs to Estimate Base Country-level Cost of Equity Capital: Estimating base country-level cost of equity capital assuming an investment in the foreign country's market as a whole (i.e., an assumed beta of 1.0), using the valuation analyst's *own* estimate of his/her home country's base country-level cost of equity capital.

- Using CRPs to Estimate Cost of Equity Capital for use in Evaluating a Business, Asset, or Project.

---

[6.28] It is assumed that upon making the investment the investor must translate GBP into CNY, and upon repatriating returns must translate CNY back into GBP. In the implementation of the CCR Model presented herein, it is assumed that returns must ultimately be repatriated.

## Using CCR Model CRPs to Estimate Base Country-level Cost of Equity Capital

In the lower right quadrant of page 4 of each 4-page investor perspective report in Data Exhibit 4, the base country-level cost of equity capital estimate *from the point of an investor based in each respective country (i.e., "home" country), investing in the home country as a whole* is presented.

For example, as calculated within the context of the CCR Model, the base country-level cost of equity capital for Brazil is 16.8% as of March 2017, as reported in the lower right quadrant of page 4 of the Brazilian-based investor perspective report in Data Exhibit 4. This represents the base country-level cost of equity capital for an investor based in Brazil, investing in Brazil. Alternatively, the base country-level cost of equity capital for Germany is 7.6%. This represents the base country-level cost of equity capital for an investor based in Germany, investing in Germany.

Investor "perspective" (i.e., the country in which the investor is based) is defined herein by the currency in which the equity returns used in the regression analyses are expressed in. An investor "based in Brazil" is therefore an investor who is estimating cost of capital with inputs (cash flows, etc.) that are expressed in the "local" currency of Brazil, the Real (BRL). Alternatively, an investor "based in Germany" is therefore an investor who is estimating cost of capital with inputs (cash flows, etc.) that are expressed in the "local" currency of Germany, the Euro (EUR).

Note that the base country-level cost of equity capital estimates reported in the lower right quadrant of page 4 of each 4-page investor perspective report assume an investment in the "market" of the home country *as a whole* (i.e., a beta of 1.0), *and do not include any adjustment for company/industry risk*. These values can be thought of as the sum of the risk-free rate plus the equity risk premium in each perspective country, expressed in the perspective country's local currency, as calculated within the context of the Erb-Harvey-Viskanta CCR model as presented herein. These values do not represent CRPs.

The base country-level cost of equity capital estimates reported in the lower right quadrant of page 4 of each 4-page investor perspective report in Data Exhibit 4 are presented primarily for benchmarking purposes. They can also be used (in conjunction with the CRPs reported herein) to estimate base country-level cost of equity capital estimates from the perspective of an investor (based in any one of the 56 perspective countries) investing in any one of the 175 investee countries markets *as a whole*, as outlined in Examples 6-1 and 6-2.[6.29]

---

[6.29] For additional examples estimating cost of equity capital, please refer to the complimentary CFA Institute webinar entitled "Quantifying Country Risk Premiums", presented on December 6, 2016 by James P. Harrington and Carla S. Nunes, CFA. This webcast can be accessed here:
https://www.cfainstitute.org/learning/products/multimedia/Pages/132617.aspx?WPID=BrowseProducts.

**Example 6-1:** Calculate the base country-level cost of equity capital estimate for an investor based in Brazil, investing in the U.S. market *as a whole,* as of March 2017, using the *published* values.

Estimating the base country-level cost of equity capital estimate for an investor based in Brazil investing in the U.S. *market as a whole* as of March 2017 is a four-step process:

**Step 1:** In Data Exhibit 4, locate the 4-page investor perspective report that reads "Investor Perspective: Brazil; Currency: Brazilian Real (BRL)".

**Step 2:** Identify the base country-level cost of equity capital for an investor based in Brazil, *investing in Brazil.* We have previously determined that this is 16.8% as of March 2017. This information is found in the lower right quadrant of page 4 of the 4-page Brazilian-based investor perspective report identified in Step 1.

**Step 3:** Identify the CRP as of March 2017 for the United States in the Brazilian-based investor perspective report identified in Step 1. This value is −4.4% (which in this case is not a premium, but a discount instead; in *either* case the value is *added* in Step 4).

**Step 4:** Add the CRP identified in Step 3 to the base country-level cost of equity capital for an investor based in Brazil, investing in the Brazil *market as a whole*, as identified in Step 2 (16.8% + (−4.4%)). The result (12.4%) is the base country-level cost of equity capital estimate for an investor based in Brazil investing in the United States market *as a whole* as of March 2017.

**Example 6-2:** Calculate the base country-level cost of equity capital estimate for an investor based in Brazil, investing in the U.S. market *as a whole,* as of March 2017, using the valuation analyst's *own* estimate of Brazil's base country-level cost of equity capital.

Financial professionals often come to *different* conclusions as far as cost of capital (and the inputs used for its components) is concerned. If, for example, the analyst wishes to use a *different* base country-level cost of equity capital as of March 2017 for an investor based in Brazil investing in Brazil, say 15.0% (instead of 16.8%, the *published* value used in the previous example), the *same* process is followed, but with the analyst's own custom estimate (15.0%) substituted:

> **Step 1:** In Data Exhibit 4, locate the 4-page exhibit that reads "Investor Perspective: Brazil; Currency: Brazilian Real (BRL)".

> **Step 2:** In Example 6-1, we first identified the base country-level cost of equity capital estimate for an investor based in Brazil, *investing in Brazil*. We determined that as of March 2017 this estimate is 16.8%. However, in this example, we are using the valuation analyst's *own* estimate of base country-level cost of equity capital for an investor based in Brazil, *investing in Brazil*, which is 15.0%.

> **Step 3:** Identify the CRP as of March 2017 for the United States in the Brazilian-based investor perspective report identified in Step 1. This value is −4.4% (which in this case is not a premium, but a discount instead; in *either* case the value is *added* in Step 4).

> **Step 4:** Add the CRP identified in Step 3 to the base country-level cost of equity capital for an investor based in Brazil, investing in the Brazil *market as a whole*, as identified in Step 2 (15.0% + (−4.4%)). The result (10.6%) is the base country-level cost of equity capital estimate for an investor based in Brazil investing in the United States *market as a whole* as of March 2017.

Again, the base country-level cost of equity capital estimates in Data Exhibit 4 assume an investment in the "market" of the home country as a whole (i.e., a beta of 1.0), <u>and do not include any adjustment for company/industry risk</u>. Adding the appropriate CRP for an investor based in the "home" country investing in the "foreign" country will thus *also* be an estimate of the base cost of equity capital for investing in the foreign country's *market as a whole*, from the perspective of an investor based in the home country.

**Using CCR Model CRPs to Estimate Cost of Equity Capital for Use in Evaluating a Subject Business, Asset, or Project**

The ability to estimate base country-level cost of equity capital from the perspective of an investor in the "home" country into the "foreign" country's *market as a whole* (as was done in Examples 6-1 and 6-2) is very valuable information that can be used for *benchmarking* and *support* purposes. Most of the time, however, valuation analysts are developing discount rates for use in evaluating a subject *business*, *asset*, or *project*.

For example, valuation analysts are often confronted with the following problem: "I know how to value a company in the United States, but this one is in Country ABC, a developing economy. What should I use for a discount rate?" Can the CRP be used as an input in developing cost of equity capital estimates for, say, a company that operates in GICS 3030 (household & personal products) in a different country? Yes, but it is important to understand the assumptions one is making when doing this.

Using the aforementioned household & personal products company as an example, an analyst typically would develop discount rates for this company *as if it were located in* the "home" country, and then add a country risk premium (CRP) to account for the differences in risk between the home country, and the country in which the household & personal products company is *actually* located (i.e., the investee or "foreign" country).

The implied assumption in this analysis is that what it means to be a household & personal products company in the home country means the same thing as being a household & personal products company in the foreign country. Some questions that the analyst may wish to consider:

- Are the risks of being a household & personal products company in the foreign country the *same* as the risks of being a household & personal products company in the home country?

- Does a household & personal products company in the foreign country have the *same* beta (β) as a household & personal products company in the home country?[6.30]

- Does the household & personal products company in the foreign country operate in a different industry environment from a household & personal products company in the home country?

---

[6.30] Beta (β) is a measure of systematic risk used as an input in some methods of estimating cost of equity capital (e.g., the CAPM requires a beta).

- Did the analyst apply any additional adjustments when the discount rate was developed for the household & personal products company *as if it were located in* the home country? For example, was a size premium applied? "Large company" and "small company" can mean very different things from country to country. For example, a smaller-sized company in the U.S. or Germany may be a "large" company in Estonia or Norway.

Valuation analysis is an inherently comparative process, so questions like these are no different from the type of questions that are asked in any valuation analysis. For example, a subject company might be compared to a set of companies (i.e., peer group, or comparables) that possess characteristics that are arguably similar to the characteristics of the subject company. To the degree that the subject company and the peer group *do* have differences, further adjustment(s) may be required.

The process for using the information in Data Exhibit 4 for estimating cost of equity capital for a subject *business*, *asset*, or *project*, is quite similar to developing base country-level cost of equity capital (as was done in the previous examples). The difference is that *additional* adjustments may be necessary, as outlined earlier.

In the case of our household & personal products company located in the foreign country, the "peer group" is household & personal products companies in the home country, and to the extent that a household & personal products company located in the foreign country is different (other than location), further adjustments may be required. Again, the CRP attempts to isolate the incremental risk premium associated with investing in another market *as a whole*, without regard to differing *industry* risks or other risks that may be particular to that type of business in the foreign country.

**Example 6-3:** Estimate cost of equity capital for a company in Belgium that operates in GICS 3030 (household & personal products ) as of March 2017, from the perspective of an investor based in the U.S.

Estimating cost of equity in this example is a four-step process:

> **Step 1:** Calculate cost of equity capital estimate for household & personal products company located in the U.S. For the purposes of this example, assume 8.0%.[6.31]
>
> **Step 2:** In Data Exhibit 4, locate the 4-page exhibit that reads "Investor Perspective: U.S.; Currency: United States Dollar (USD)".
>
> **Step 3:** Identify the country risk premium (CRP) as of March 2017 for Belgium, from the perspective of a U.S.-based investor in the 4-page exhibit identified in Step 2. This value is 0.5%.
>
> **Step 4:** Add the CRP identified in Step 3 to the cost of equity capital estimate for a household & personal products company in the U.S. estimated in Step 1 (8.0% + 0.5%). The result (8.5%) is the cost of equity capital estimate for an investor based in the U.S. investing in a household & personal products company located in Belgium, _prior_ to any adjustments due to intrinsic differences in in the household & personal products industry environment (or other risks) between the U.S. and Belgium.

---

[6.31] An excellent source of international industry statistics (including cost of equity capital estimates and peer group betas for use in CAPM estimates) is the _2016 Valuation Handbook – International Industry Cost of Capital_, with data through March 31, 2016 and includes one optional intra-year Semi-annual Update (data through September 30, 2016). The 2017 edition will be available late summer 2017. This resource includes industry-level analyses for four global economic areas: (i) the "World", (ii) the European Union, (iii) the Eurozone, and (iv) the United Kingdom. Industries in the book are identified by their Global Industry Classification Standard (GICS) code. Each of the four global economic area's industry analyses are presented in three currencies: (i) the Euro (€ or EUR), (ii) the British Pound (£ or GBP), and (iii) the U.S. Dollar ($ or USD).

An excellent source of U.S. industry statistics (including cost of equity capital estimates and peer group betas for use in CAPM estimates) is the _2017 Valuation Handbook – U.S. Industry Cost of Capital_, with data through March 31, 2017 and includes three optional quarterly updates (June, September, and December). This resource provides cost of capital estimates (i.e., equity capital, debt capital, and WACC) for approximately 180 U.S. industries and size groupings (i.e., Large-, Mid-, Low-, and Micro-capitalization companies), plus a host of detailed statistics that can be used for benchmarking purposes (over 300 critical industry-level data points calculated for each industry, depending on data availability). For more information about Duff & Phelps valuation data resources published by John Wiley & Sons, please go to: www.wiley.com/go/ValuationHandbooks or call Wiley's Customer Care Department within the United States at (800) 762-2974, outside the United States at (317) 572-3993 or fax (317) 572 4002.

# Chapter 7
# Firm Size and the Cost of Equity Capital in Europe

Chapter 7 is a brief synopsis of a Research Note (and its subsequent update through December 2016, as presented herein) authored by Professor Erik Peek of the Rotterdam School of Management, Erasmus University (RSM). The Research Note examines the relationships between firm size and the cost of equity capital in European equity markets.[7.1] While a statistically significant "size effect" was detected in Europe, this effect was (i) limited to only the smallest of companies, and (ii) was not uniformly detected in all countries examined.

In the analyses presented herein, Professor Peek updated his analysis through the end of 2016. These results are summarized in Data Exhibit 5A, "Premia over the Risk-free Rate", Data Exhibit 5B, "Premia over CAPM", and Data Exhibit 5C, "Comparative Risk Characteristics".

**Differences in Returns Between Large and Small Companies in Europe**

Numerous studies have examined U.S. equity returns and found that stocks of companies whose market capitalization is small (i.e., "small-cap" stocks) tend to earn greater returns, on average, than stocks of companies whose market capitalization is large (i.e., "large-cap" stocks), suggesting that small firms have a greater cost of equity capital. In fact, these studies show that depending on sample selection procedures, research period, and sorting methodology, the estimated monthly return difference between small-cap and large-cap stocks may range from approximately 0.4% to almost 2.5%.

Researchers have posited many explanations for the size effect, including (i) firm size proxies for differences in liquidity, or for other priced (yet unobservable) risk factors, or (ii) investor preferences or recognition depend on firm size.

To potentially assist investors to estimate the cost of equity in non-U.S. markets, some researchers have investigated the size effect in samples of non-U.S. stocks. Many of these studies, especially those focusing on a single country, may have been inhibited by a lack of data. Another potential issue has been the historic lack of integration among some or all of the stock markets in the sample, particularly with studies examining various groups of countries during the 1970s and 1980s. Moreover, it is entirely conceivable that the risk differences between small- and large-cap stocks in a segregated locality could differ significantly from the risk differences between small- and large-cap stocks in an internationally diversified portfolio. This may occur, for example, if a lack

---

[7.1]   The full Research Note "Differences in Returns Between Large and Small Companies in Europe", is available at http://ssrn.com/abstract=2499205. The Research Note was published as part of the ongoing research that Duff & Phelps performs and sponsors in the area cost of capital and other valuation issues. Professor Erik Peek is at Rotterdam School of Management, Erasmus University (RSM), Netherlands. We thank Professor Peek for his expertise in exploring this important topic.

of diversification opportunities in segregated markets makes investors averse to small-cap stocks' greater idiosyncratic risk.

In Professor Peek's research, the existence of the size effect outside the U.S. is reassessed using a large sample of Western European stocks over the period 1990–2016, a time in which the European economies and stock exchanges were largely and increasingly integrated.[7.2] The size effect is examined in a "pooled" sample in which all European exchanges are treated as a single integrated market, and also examined by splitting the sample into potentially more homogeneous geographic regions.

**Countries Included**

The original Research Note (and the updated analysis herein) focused on a set of 17 Western European countries (and stock exchanges) that have exhibited a large degree of integration during the past two decades. These countries are summarized in Exhibit 7.1.

**Exhibit 7.1:** Countries Included

| | |
|---|---|
| Austria | Luxembourg |
| Belgium | The Netherlands |
| Denmark | Norway |
| Finland | Portugal |
| France | Spain |
| Germany | Sweden |
| Greece | Switzerland |
| Ireland | United Kingdom |
| Italy | |

**Data Sources**

The sample of companies used to perform the analysis presented comes from the intersection of Thomson Reuters *Datastream* database (from which market and return data were gathered) and Thomson Reuters *Worldscope* database (from which fundamental or accounting-based data was gathered).[7.3]

---

[7.2] E. Freimann, "Economic Integration and Country Allocation in Europe", *Financial Analysts Journal* 54, no. 5 (1998): 32–41.

[7.3] Returns are expressed in Euros. For years prior to introduction of the Euro, the returns are expressed in Deutsche Mark. Company types *included*: non-start-up, financially healthy companies the typical company in most investment portfolios (i.e., "Low-Financial-Risk" companies). Company types *excluded*: financial service companies, financially-distressed companies, companies having illiquid stock, companies in the early stages of their life cycle (see the original Research Note for details about the company set selection methodology employed).

## Regional Differences

Prior country-specific studies on the firm size effect have produced mixed evidence, leading some researchers and practitioners to conclude that the effect does not exist in some non-U.S. countries.[7.4]

To shed some light on differences in the significance of the size effect across economic regions and their potential origin, the sample was split into groups of geographically proximate and economically integrated countries and the differences between returns for portfolios comprised of the largest and smallest companies were analyzed, with the data being subdivided into quartiles.[7.5]

Exhibit 7.2 displays the average portfolio return spreads between the bottom quartile portfolio (comprised of the smallest companies as measured by market capitalization) and the top quartile portfolio (comprised of the largest companies as measured by market capitalization) for the following four regions:

- Europe (as defined by the 17 countries listed in Exhibit 7.1)

- Continental Europe (i.e., the countries included in the Europe sample, excluding Ireland and U.K.)

- Ireland and United Kingdom (£ Investor)

- Ireland and United Kingdom (€ Investor)

The regional return spreads are presented in order of significance, measured as the (one-sided) probability that the differential (i.e., the size premium) is positive. While the reader is cautioned to interpret the observed regional differences with care (especially because splitting up the sample unavoidably affects statistical power), the patterns in Exhibit 7.2 provide interesting exploratory evidence on how country factors affect the size premium. Specifically, Exhibit 7.2 suggests that the size premium is positive in every economic region considered.

---

[7.4]  For example, some studies of the German equity market conclude that in recent decades stock returns of small German firms have not significantly exceeded stock returns of large German firms (see e.g., Schulz, 2009). With their view seemingly supported by these findings, the German Institute of Public Auditors ('Institut der Wirtschaftsprüfer') recommends in its (nationally authoritative) Principles for the Performance of Business Valuations not to add size premia to cost of capital estimates.

[7.5]  Firm-size breakpoints were first determined in the full European sample, and then these same breakpoints were used to construct portfolios in the regional samples (thus ensuring that size portfolios are consistently defined across samples).

**Exhibit 7.2:** Average Annual Return Spreads between Top and Bottom Market Capitalization Quartiles by Region (December 2016)

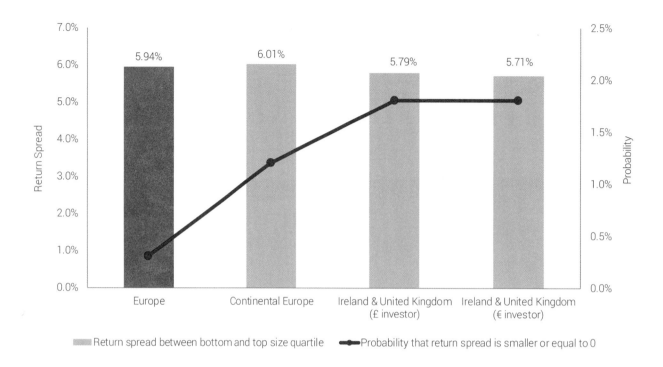

Exhibit 7.3 displays the average portfolio return spreads between the bottom quartile portfolio (comprised of the small countries as measured by size factor) and the top quartile portfolio (comprised of the largest countries as measured by size factor) for the same four regions listed above and in Exhibit 7.2.[7.6]

Similar to Exhibit 7.2, the regional return spreads in Exhibit 7.3 are presented in order of significance, measured as the (one-sided) probability that the differential (i.e., the size premium) is positive. Once again, the reader is cautioned to interpret the observed regional differences with care, since splitting up the sample unavoidably affects statistical power. Exhibit 7.3 suggests that the size premium is positive in every economic region considered; however, the economic and statistical significance of the return spreads varies considerably. Return spreads are economically and statistically significant (at the 2% significance level) in Ireland and United Kingdom, while only marginally significant in Continental Europe. This is consistent with the original Research Note findings that the size effect varies across countries and regions within Europe.

---

[7.6]   The size factor is an aggregation of the other six measures of size analyzed in the Research Note: market capitalization, book equity, market value of invested capital, total assets, sales, and number of employees.

**Exhibit 7.3:** Average Annual Return Spreads between Top and Bottom Size Factor Quartiles by Region (December 2016)

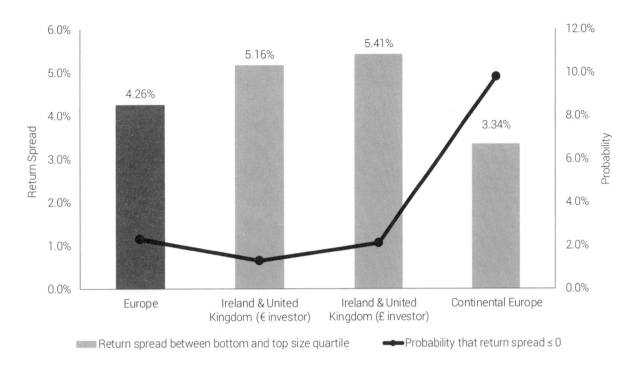

## Two Types of Risk Premia Examined

The data exhibits in Professor Peek's Research Note summarize (and may aid in the examination of) the relationships between firm size and the cost of equity capital in European equity markets. These exhibits present different types of size-related risk premia data, including (i) "risk premia over the risk-free rate", and (ii) "risk premia over CAPM".

The main difference between "risk premia over the risk-free rate" and "risk premia over CAPM" is how size-related risks are being measured, which in turn determines the cost of equity capital models (i.e., build-up method or CAPM) in which they could be used.

The risk premia were developed using six different measures of firm size, plus a seventh size measure that is a combination of the six different measures of size.[7.7]

---

[7.7] The six measures of size analyzed in the Research Note are: market capitalization, book equity, market value of invested capital, total assets, sales, and number of employees. The seventh measure, the aggregation of the other six measures was determined as follows: Size Factor = $(-2.5303) + 0.0801 \times$ Ln(Market capitalization) + $0.0844 \times$ Ln(Market value of invested capital) + $0.0853 \times$ Ln(Book equity) + $0.0855 \times$ Ln(Total assets) + $0.0735 \times$ Ln(Sales) + $0.0790 \times$ Ln(Employees).

## Risk Premia Over the Risk-free Rate

"Risk premia over the risk-free rate" (i.e., excess returns) are a measure of the combined effect of *market* risk and *size* risk. These premia could be used within the context of a build-up method of estimating the cost of equity capital. These premia are simply added to a risk-free rate to determine a cost of equity capital estimate.

For example, a basic build-up model of cost of equity capital estimation could be written as:[7.8]

$$E\left(R_i\right) = R_f + RP_{m+s}$$

Where:

| | | |
|---|---|---|
| $E(R_i)$ | = | Expected rate of return on security $i$ |
| $R_f$ | = | Risk-free rate |
| $RP_{m+s}$ | = | Market risk plus a risk premium for size |

In Exhibit 7.4, the simple average of all arithmetic average "risk premia over the risk-free rate" for all seven measures of firm size from the Research Note are shown, updated through 2016.[7.9] Exhibit 7.4 suggests that "risk premia over the risk-free rate" generally increase as size decreases (and vice versa), albeit *non-monotonically*. This suggests that the firm "size effect" on the cost of equity may be present in the European sample, although it seems to be fairly concentrated in the smallest companies. For further detail on the data of the 16 portfolios in Exhibit 7.4, refer to Data Exhibit 5A: Premia over the Risk-free Rate.

**Exhibit 7.4:** Composite Average of Arithmetic Average "Risk Premium Over the Risk-free Rate" (December 2016)

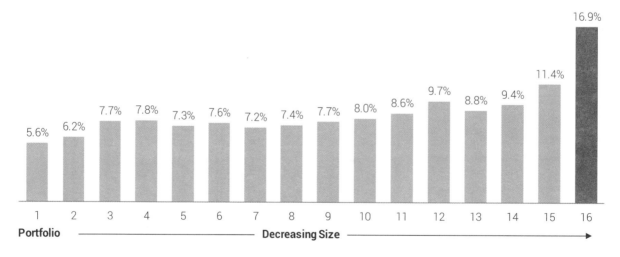

7.8  The simple build-up equation shown represents cost of equity capital *prior* to any additional adjustments attributable to the specific company that the individual analyst may deem appropriate.

7.9  This information is extracted from Exhibits A1 through A7 included in Data Exhibit 5A.

## Premia Over CAPM (Size Premia)

Risk premia over CAPM (i.e., size premia) were also developed for each of the seven different measures of firm size. These premia could be applied when estimating the cost of equity capital using a modified CAPM.[7.10]

The following is an example of the "Modified" CAPM:[7.11, 7.12]

$$E(R_i) = R_f + (\beta \times RP_m) + RP_s$$

Where:

| | | |
|---|---|---|
| $E(R_i)$ | = | Expected rate of return on security $i$ |
| $R_f$ | = | Risk-free rate |
| $\beta$ | = | Beta estimate for security $i$ |
| $RP_m$ | = | Market risk premium, or ERP |
| $RP_s$ | = | Risk premium for size |

In Exhibit 7.5, the simple average of all arithmetic average "risk premia over CAPM" for all seven measures of firm size from the Research Note are shown. Exhibit 7.5 suggests that "risk premia over CAPM" generally increase as size decreases (and vice versa), albeit *non-monotonically*. Again, this suggests that the firm "size effect" on the cost of equity may be present in the European sample, although it seems to be fairly concentrated in the smallest companies. For further detail on the data of the 16 portfolios in Exhibit 7.5, refer to Data Exhibit 5B: Premia over CAPM (i.e., size premia).

---

[7.10] The "textbook" CAPM is defined as $E(R_i) = R_f + (\beta \times RP_m)$. A "modified" CAPM typically entails adding additional risk premium adjustments (in this case, the additional adjustment is for "size"). The individual analyst may conclude that additional risk factors are appropriate.

[7.11] This information is extracted from Exhibits B1 through B7 included in Data Exhibit 5B.

[7.12] The modified CAPM equation shown represents cost of equity capital *prior* to any additional adjustments attributable to the specific company that the individual analyst may deem appropriate.

**Exhibit 7.5:** Composite Average of Arithmetic Average "Risk Premium Over CAPM" (i.e., Size Premia) (December 2016)

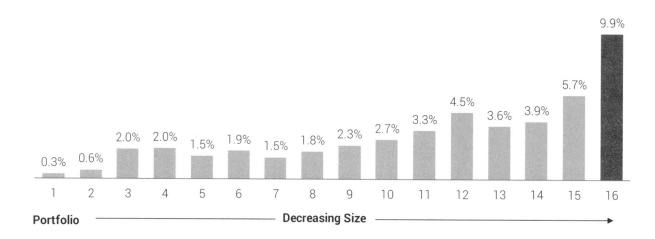

## Effects On Size Premia when Using OLS Betas and Sum Betas

Smaller companies generally trade less frequently and exhibit more of a lagged price reaction (relative to the market) than do larger companies. One of the ways of capturing this lag movement is called "sum" beta.[7.13] Sum betas are designed to compensate for the less frequent trading of smaller company stocks. All of the size premia in the Research Note (and the updated analysis herein) are calculated using sum betas, which appear to correct for the lesser OLS beta estimates of smaller companies.

In Exhibit 7.6, OLS betas and sum betas are calculated for the portfolios comprised of low-financial-risk companies, ranked by their size factor, as examined in the Research Note (updated through 2016).[7.14, 7.15] Sum betas tend to be *larger* than the OLS betas. The OLS betas and sum betas for the portfolios comprised of larger companies are approximately the same. The net result of the *larger* sum betas is *smaller* size premia.

For example, portfolio 1 (comprised of the *largest* companies) has an OLS beta of 0.91, and a sum beta of 0.93. Alternatively, portfolio 10 (comprised of the *smallest* companies) has an OLS beta of 0.70, and a sum beta of 1.23. All things held the same, the *larger* sum beta of decile 10 results in a *smaller* size premia than would be calculated using its OLS beta counterpart.

---

[7.13] See Roger G. Ibbotson, Paul D. Kaplan, and James D. Peterson, "Estimates of Small-Stock Betas Are Much Too Low", *Journal of Portfolio Management* (Summer 1997): 104–111. See also Shannon P. Pratt and Roger J. Grabowski, *Cost of Capital: Applications and Examples* 5th ed. (Hoboken, NJ: Wiley & Sons, 2014), Chapter 11, Beta: "Differing Definitions and Estimates", and Appendix 11A: "Examples of Computing OLS Beta, Sum Beta, and Full-information Beta Estimates".

[7.14] "Low-financial-risk" companies were the primary set of companies examined in the Research Note. A set of companies identified as "high-financial-risk" were also examined separately.

[7.15] The size factor is an aggregation of the other six measures of size analyzed in the Research Note: market capitalization, book equity, market value of invested capital, total assets, sales, and number of employees.

**Exhibit 7.6:** Comparison of OLS Betas and Sum Betas by Equal-Weighted Market Capitalization Portfolio as Calculated Over the Time Horizon 1990−2016

| Size Portfolio | Upper bound in 2016 | N in 2016 | Portfolio OLS Beta | Portfolio Sum Beta | Difference |
|---|---|---|---|---|---|
| 1 (big) | 223,793 | 225 | 0.91 | 0.93 | 0.02 |
| 2 | 6,533 | 213 | 0.92 | 1.03 | 0.12 |
| 3 | 2,136 | 201 | 0.90 | 1.08 | 0.18 |
| 4 | 869 | 188 | 0.84 | 1.04 | 0.20 |
| 5 | 404 | 192 | 0.78 | 1.01 | 0.22 |
| 6 | 206 | 180 | 0.76 | 0.98 | 0.22 |
| 7 | 108 | 158 | 0.73 | 0.94 | 0.20 |
| 8 | 60 | 146 | 0.75 | 1.00 | 0.25 |
| 9 | 28 | 107 | 0.75 | 1.01 | 0.26 |
| 10 (small) | 11 | 59 | 0.70 | 1.23 | 0.53 |
| Mid-Cap 3 - 5 | 2,136 | 581 | 0.79 | 1.01 | 0.22 |
| Low-Cap 6 - 8 | 206 | 484 | 0.75 | 0.98 | 0.24 |
| Micro-Cap 9-10 | 28 | 166 | 0.70 | 1.23 | 0.53 |

One can see in Exhibit 7.7 that using the sum beta method also results in greater betas for smaller companies across regions included in the Research Note (and the updated analysis herein).[7.16]

**Exhibit 7.7:** Comparison of OLS Betas and Sum Betas for Different Regions (December 2016)

| Country | | N in 2016 | Portfolio OLS Beta | Portfolio Sum Beta | Difference |
|---|---|---|---|---|---|
| Europe | All Companies | 1,652 | 0.83 | 1.02 | 0.19 |
| | Over € 1 billion | 606 | 0.91 | 0.98 | 0.07 |
| | Under € 100 million | 438 | 0.74 | 1.01 | 0.27 |
| Continental Europe | All Companies | 1,255 | 0.79 | 0.94 | 0.15 |
| | Over € 1 billion | 450 | 0.91 | 0.96 | 0.05 |
| | Under € 100 million | 338 | 0.65 | 0.87 | 0.21 |
| United Kingdom & Ireland (€ investor) | All Companies | 397 | 0.88 | 1.13 | 0.25 |
| | Over € 1 billion | 156 | 0.90 | 1.00 | 0.10 |
| | Under € 100 million | 100 | 0.86 | 1.20 | 0.34 |
| United Kingdom & Ireland (£ investor) | All Companies | 397 | 0.61 | 1.01 | 0.40 |
| | Over € 1 billion | 134 | 0.68 | 0.89 | 0.21 |
| | Under € 100 million | 115 | 0.53 | 1.03 | 0.50 |

In applying CAPM, one should be internally consistent between how the beta was estimated and how the size premium was calculated. Using a sum beta times the ERP estimate and adding a sum-beta-based size premium would arguably result in a better reflection of the cost of equity faced by a small company.

Having said that, regardless of which type of beta calculation method is ultimately employed (OLS vs. sum beta), one should match the source of the size premium (i.e., how it was computed), with the type of beta estimate chosen for the subject company. In other words, one should use a size premium derived using OLS betas in conjunction with a subject company beta estimated through OLS; similarly, one should use a size premium derived using sum betas when a sum beta was selected for the subject company. Therefore, if one is utilizing this study's results, one should properly estimate beta using the sum beta method.

---

[7.16]   Like Exhibit 7.6, Exhibit 7.7 is also comprised of the "low-financial-risk" set of companies examined in the Research Note.

## Conclusion

This chapter summarizes the findings of Professor Erik Peek's Research Note (and the updated analysis herein), which examines whether the realized share price returns of small European firms have exceeded those of large firms over the period 1990–2016. Using various measures of firm size, the Research Note finds that small company shares have likely outperformed large company shares, on average, suggesting that investors perceive small European firms as riskier, and thus demand a "size" premium to compensate for this additional risk. The evidence also indicates that the relationship between firm size and returns is strongly *non-linear*, and that the size premium is significant only for the *smallest* companies.

While the observed "size effect" is statistically significant only for those portfolios comprised of the *smallest* firms during the 1990–2016 period, this does not necessarily infer that the size effect is not present for larger companies in Europe. Studies of the size effect in countries with longer data availability, such as the United States, show that the size effect fluctuates over time. Given the short period of the current analysis of European markets (27 years, due to data constraints), a longer-term relationship could not be studied.

Breaking the European sample into regional and country subsamples, the Research Note's findings suggest that the relationship between firm size and returns varies across regions. In particular, Professor Peek finds in his original Research Note that the firm size effect may be strongest in the Anglo-Saxon and Nordic countries in the sample.

Again, while the size premium shown in the Research Note (and the updated analysis herein) is *not* significant in some European regions, the reader need not automatically conclude from it that firm size does not matter for cost of capital estimation in some countries. Splitting up the sample unavoidably affects the statistical power of the study's tests and tends to reduce statistical significance in at least some of the subsamples, by default. Leaving aside statistical significance, Professor Peek's research suggest that the average return spread between small and large firms is positive in each of the examined regional subsamples, and that size and liquidity distributions likely differ across regions. As Professor Peek posits, such differences may potentially explain why the size effect appears strong in some regions but weaker in others.

# Data Exhibit 1:
# International Equity Risk Premia (ERPs)

Data Exhibit 1 includes historical equity risk premia (ERP) estimates for 16 world economies. Both long-horizon and short-horizon ERPs are calculated (i) in terms of the United States Dollar, and (ii) in terms of each country's "local" currency. The time horizon over which each of the covered country's ERP is calculated is dependent on data availability (which varies from country to country), but for most countries analyzed here the historical ERP information is available back to "at least" 1970.

The ERPs in Data Exhibit 1:

- Were calculated using the same general data sources that were used to calculate the equity risk premia previously published in the Morningstar/Ibbotson *International Equity Risk Premia Report*.

- Were calculated using the same general methodologies that were used to calculate the equity risk premia previously published in the Morningstar/Ibbotson *International Equity Risk Premia Report*.

**Exhibit 3.1:** Countries Covered, Currencies, and Time Periods[D1.1]

| Country | Local Currency | Currency Code | USD Long-Horizon Start Date | USD Short-Horizon Start Date | Local Currency Long-Horizon Start Date | Local Currency Short-Horizon Start Date |
|---|---|---|---|---|---|---|
| Australia | Australian Dollar | AUD | 1970 | 1970 | 1970 | 1970 |
| Austria | Euro | EUR | 1972 | 1970 | 1971 | 1970 |
| Belgium | Euro | EUR | 1970 | 1970 | 1970 | 1970 |
| Canada | Canadian Dollar | CAD | 1919 | 1919 | 1919 | 1919 |
| France | Euro | EUR | 1970 | 1970 | 1970 | 1970 |
| Germany | Euro | EUR | 1970 | 1970 | 1970 | 1970 |
| Ireland | Euro | EUR | 1970 | 1970 | 1970 | 1970 |
| Italy | Euro | EUR | 1970 | 1970 | 1970 | 1970 |
| Japan | Yen | JPY | 1970 | 1970 | 1970 | 1970 |
| Netherlands | Euro | EUR | 1970 | 1970 | 1970 | 1970 |
| New Zealand | New Zealand Dollar | NZD | 1970 | 1970 | 1970 | 1970 |
| South Africa | Rand | ZAR | 1971 | 1970 | 1970 | 1970 |
| Spain | Euro | EUR | 1972 | 1970 | 1971 | 1970 |
| Switzerland | Swiss Franc | CHF | 1970 | 1970 | 1970 | 1970 |
| United Kingdom | Pound Sterling | GBP | 1900 | 1900 | 1900 | 1900 |
| United States | U.S. Dollar | USD | 1926 | 1926 | 1926 | 1926 |

---

[D1.1] For Reader convenience, Exhibit 3.1 as it appears in Chapter 3, "International Equity Risk Premia", is reproduced here.

**Australia Long-Horizon Equity Risk Premia**

in Local Currency (Australian Dollar – AUD)
in Percent

| End Date | Start Date 1970 | 1975 | 1980 | 1985 | 1990 | 1995 | 2000 | 2005 | 2010 | 2015 | 2016 |
|---|---|---|---|---|---|---|---|---|---|---|---|
| 1970 | -25.4 | | | | | | | | | | |
| 1971 | -19.8 | | | | | | | | | | |
| 1972 | -10.1 | | | | | | | | | | |
| 1973 | -15.8 | | | | | | | | | | |
| 1974 | -19.1 | | | | | | | | | | |
| 1975 | -8.0 | 47.7 | | | | | | | | | |
| 1976 | -7.7 | 20.7 | | | | | | | | | |
| 1977 | -7.2 | 12.6 | | | | | | | | | |
| 1978 | -5.1 | 12.4 | | | | | | | | | |
| 1979 | -0.6 | 18.0 | | | | | | | | | |
| 1980 | 2.6 | 20.8 | 34.7 | | | | | | | | |
| 1981 | -0.3 | 13.1 | 0.9 | | | | | | | | |
| 1982 | -2.3 | 8.2 | -8.0 | | | | | | | | |
| 1983 | 1.9 | 13.6 | 8.0 | | | | | | | | |
| 1984 | 0.5 | 10.4 | 2.8 | | | | | | | | |
| 1985 | 2.6 | 12.5 | 7.8 | 33.1 | | | | | | | |
| 1986 | 4.4 | 14.2 | 11.4 | 33.1 | | | | | | | |
| 1987 | 3.5 | 12.2 | 8.5 | 18.1 | | | | | | | |
| 1988 | 3.5 | 11.6 | 8.0 | 14.6 | | | | | | | |
| 1989 | 3.7 | 11.3 | 7.9 | 13.1 | | | | | | | |
| 1990 | 2.2 | 8.9 | 4.8 | 6.4 | -27.0 | | | | | | |
| 1991 | 3.3 | 9.9 | 6.5 | 9.2 | -0.5 | | | | | | |
| 1992 | 2.7 | 8.8 | 5.3 | 6.8 | -3.6 | | | | | | |
| 1993 | 3.9 | 9.9 | 7.1 | 9.4 | 4.8 | | | | | | |
| 1994 | 3.2 | 8.7 | 5.6 | 7.1 | 1.1 | | | | | | |
| 1995 | 3.3 | 8.7 | 5.8 | 7.1 | 2.1 | 7.4 | | | | | |
| 1996 | 3.3 | 8.4 | 5.5 | 6.7 | 2.1 | 4.8 | | | | | |
| 1997 | 3.3 | 8.1 | 5.4 | 6.4 | 2.2 | 4.2 | | | | | |
| 1998 | 3.4 | 8.1 | 5.5 | 6.5 | 2.9 | 5.1 | | | | | |
| 1999 | 3.5 | 8.0 | 5.6 | 6.5 | 3.2 | 5.3 | | | | | |
| 2000 | 3.4 | 7.7 | 5.3 | 6.1 | 2.9 | 4.5 | 0.5 | | | | |
| 2001 | 3.5 | 7.7 | 5.3 | 6.1 | 3.2 | 4.7 | 3.2 | | | | |
| 2002 | 2.9 | 6.9 | 4.4 | 4.9 | 1.8 | 2.2 | -2.9 | | | | |
| 2003 | 3.1 | 6.9 | 4.6 | 5.1 | 2.2 | 2.8 | -0.3 | | | | |
| 2004 | 3.6 | 7.4 | 5.2 | 5.9 | 3.5 | 4.6 | 4.0 | | | | |
| 2005 | 4.0 | 7.8 | 5.8 | 6.6 | 4.5 | 6.1 | 6.7 | 20.3 | | | |
| 2006 | 4.4 | 8.1 | 6.3 | 7.1 | 5.3 | 7.1 | 8.3 | 19.1 | | | |
| 2007 | 4.6 | 8.2 | 6.4 | 7.2 | 5.6 | 7.3 | 8.6 | 16.3 | | | |
| 2008 | 3.4 | 6.7 | 4.7 | 5.1 | 3.0 | 3.7 | 2.9 | 1.5 | | | |
| 2009 | 4.1 | 7.4 | 5.6 | 6.2 | 4.5 | 5.7 | 5.8 | 7.7 | | | |
| 2010 | 3.9 | 7.1 | 5.3 | 5.8 | 4.1 | 5.0 | 4.9 | 5.6 | -4.8 | | |
| 2011 | 3.4 | 6.4 | 4.6 | 5.0 | 3.1 | 3.8 | 3.1 | 2.5 | -10.4 | | |
| 2012 | 3.7 | 6.7 | 5.0 | 5.4 | 3.8 | 4.5 | 4.2 | 4.3 | -1.2 | | |
| 2013 | 4.0 | 7.0 | 5.4 | 5.8 | 4.3 | 5.2 | 5.2 | 5.8 | 3.5 | | |
| 2014 | 4.0 | 6.9 | 5.3 | 5.7 | 4.2 | 5.0 | 4.9 | 5.4 | 3.2 | | |
| 2015 | 3.9 | 6.7 | 5.1 | 5.5 | 4.0 | 4.7 | 4.6 | 4.8 | 2.4 | -1.3 | |
| 2016 | 4.0 | 6.8 | 5.2 | 5.6 | 4.2 | 5.0 | 4.9 | 5.2 | 3.5 | 4.2 | 9.7 |

in U.S. Dollars (USD)
in Percent

| End Date | Start Date 1970 | 1975 | 1980 | 1985 | 1990 | 1995 | 2000 | 2005 | 2010 | 2015 | 2016 |
|---|---|---|---|---|---|---|---|---|---|---|---|
| 1970 | -25.4 | | | | | | | | | | |
| 1971 | -17.1 | | | | | | | | | | |
| 1972 | -6.5 | | | | | | | | | | |
| 1973 | -9.7 | | | | | | | | | | |
| 1974 | -15.9 | | | | | | | | | | |
| 1975 | -6.3 | 41.9 | | | | | | | | | |
| 1976 | -8.1 | 11.5 | | | | | | | | | |
| 1977 | -6.9 | 8.1 | | | | | | | | | |
| 1978 | -4.8 | 9.2 | | | | | | | | | |
| 1979 | -0.8 | 14.4 | | | | | | | | | |
| 1980 | 3.3 | 19.3 | 43.5 | | | | | | | | |
| 1981 | 0.0 | 11.4 | 3.8 | | | | | | | | |
| 1982 | -2.7 | 5.5 | -9.3 | | | | | | | | |
| 1983 | 0.6 | 9.7 | 3.8 | | | | | | | | |
| 1984 | -1.1 | 6.2 | -1.9 | | | | | | | | |
| 1985 | -0.5 | 6.6 | 0.1 | 10.0 | | | | | | | |
| 1986 | 1.3 | 8.5 | 4.3 | 19.8 | | | | | | | |
| 1987 | 1.0 | 7.5 | 3.2 | 11.8 | | | | | | | |
| 1988 | 2.2 | 8.6 | 5.4 | 14.7 | | | | | | | |
| 1989 | 2.0 | 8.0 | 4.8 | 11.5 | | | | | | | |
| 1990 | 0.6 | 5.7 | 1.8 | 4.8 | -28.7 | | | | | | |
| 1991 | 1.6 | 6.8 | 3.6 | 7.6 | -2.3 | | | | | | |
| 1992 | 0.8 | 5.4 | 1.9 | 4.3 | -7.6 | | | | | | |
| 1993 | 1.9 | 6.6 | 3.8 | 7.0 | 1.3 | | | | | | |
| 1994 | 1.8 | 6.2 | 3.4 | 6.1 | 0.7 | | | | | | |
| 1995 | 1.8 | 6.0 | 3.4 | 5.8 | 1.1 | 3.0 | | | | | |
| 1996 | 2.1 | 6.2 | 3.7 | 6.1 | 2.2 | 6.0 | | | | | |
| 1997 | 1.4 | 5.2 | 2.7 | 4.4 | 0.0 | -1.1 | | | | | |
| 1998 | 1.5 | 5.1 | 2.6 | 4.2 | 0.2 | -0.5 | | | | | |
| 1999 | 1.8 | 5.4 | 3.1 | 4.8 | 1.5 | 2.2 | | | | | |
| 2000 | 1.3 | 4.6 | 2.3 | 3.6 | 0.0 | -0.6 | -14.7 | | | | |
| 2001 | 1.2 | 4.4 | 2.1 | 3.2 | -0.2 | -0.9 | -8.6 | | | | |
| 2002 | 0.9 | 4.0 | 1.7 | 2.7 | -0.7 | -1.6 | -7.9 | | | | |
| 2003 | 2.2 | 5.3 | 3.5 | 4.9 | 2.5 | 3.5 | 5.1 | | | | |
| 2004 | 2.9 | 6.0 | 4.4 | 5.9 | 4.1 | 5.8 | 9.3 | | | | |
| 2005 | 3.2 | 6.2 | 4.7 | 6.3 | 4.6 | 6.4 | 9.8 | 12.6 | | | |
| 2006 | 3.8 | 6.9 | 5.5 | 7.2 | 5.9 | 8.1 | 12.2 | 19.6 | | | |
| 2007 | 4.3 | 7.4 | 6.1 | 7.9 | 6.9 | 9.2 | 13.6 | 20.9 | | | |
| 2008 | 2.8 | 5.6 | 4.0 | 5.3 | 3.6 | 4.7 | 6.0 | 1.9 | | | |
| 2009 | 4.5 | 7.4 | 6.3 | 7.9 | 7.0 | 9.1 | 12.5 | 15.7 | | | |
| 2010 | 4.6 | 7.5 | 6.3 | 7.9 | 7.1 | 9.1 | 12.2 | 14.5 | 8.6 | | |
| 2011 | 4.1 | 6.8 | 5.6 | 7.0 | 6.0 | 7.6 | 9.8 | 10.2 | -3.7 | | |
| 2012 | 4.5 | 7.1 | 6.0 | 7.4 | 6.6 | 8.2 | 10.5 | 11.2 | 3.7 | | |
| 2013 | 4.4 | 7.0 | 5.9 | 7.2 | 6.4 | 7.8 | 9.8 | 10.1 | 3.1 | | |
| 2014 | 4.1 | 6.6 | 5.5 | 6.8 | 5.8 | 7.1 | 8.7 | 8.4 | 1.1 | | |
| 2015 | 3.8 | 6.2 | 5.0 | 6.2 | 5.1 | 6.2 | 7.4 | 6.6 | -1.1 | -12.3 | |
| 2016 | 3.9 | 6.2 | 5.1 | 6.2 | 5.3 | 6.3 | 7.5 | 6.8 | 0.3 | -1.7 | 8.9 |

Source of underlying data: 1.) Morningstar *Direct* database. Used with permission. All rights reserved. All calculations performed by Duff & Phelps LLC.

# Australia Short-Horizon Equity Risk Premia

## in Local Currency (Australian Dollar – AUD)
in Percent

| End Date | 1970 | 1975 | 1980 | 1985 | 1990 | 1995 | 2000 | 2005 | 2010 | 2015 | 2016 |
|---|---|---|---|---|---|---|---|---|---|---|---|
| 1970 | -24.7 | | | | | | | | | | |
| 1971 | -18.9 | | | | | | | | | | |
| 1972 | -8.9 | | | | | | | | | | |
| 1973 | -14.8 | | | | | | | | | | |
| 1974 | -18.5 | | | | | | | | | | |
| 1975 | -7.2 | 49.2 | | | | | | | | | |
| 1976 | -6.8 | 22.6 | | | | | | | | | |
| 1977 | -6.2 | 14.3 | | | | | | | | | |
| 1978 | -4.1 | 13.9 | | | | | | | | | |
| 1979 | 0.3 | 19.1 | | | | | | | | | |
| 1980 | 3.4 | 21.6 | 33.8 | | | | | | | | |
| 1981 | 0.2 | 13.6 | -0.2 | | | | | | | | |
| 1982 | -1.8 | 8.6 | -9.0 | | | | | | | | |
| 1983 | 2.5 | 14.1 | 7.9 | | | | | | | | |
| 1984 | 1.2 | 11.1 | 3.1 | | | | | | | | |
| 1985 | 3.1 | 13.0 | 7.9 | 31.5 | | | | | | | |
| 1986 | 4.8 | 14.5 | 11.1 | 31.1 | | | | | | | |
| 1987 | 3.8 | 12.4 | 8.2 | 16.6 | | | | | | | |
| 1988 | 3.9 | 11.9 | 7.8 | 13.7 | | | | | | | |
| 1989 | 3.8 | 11.2 | 7.3 | 11.5 | | | | | | | |
| 1990 | 2.2 | 8.7 | 3.9 | 4.6 | -30.0 | | | | | | |
| 1991 | 3.3 | 9.7 | 5.8 | 7.7 | -1.6 | | | | | | |
| 1992 | 2.8 | 8.8 | 4.8 | 5.8 | -3.5 | | | | | | |
| 1993 | 4.1 | 10.1 | 6.8 | 8.9 | 5.7 | | | | | | |
| 1994 | 3.5 | 9.0 | 5.6 | 6.8 | 2.1 | | | | | | |
| 1995 | 3.7 | 9.0 | 5.8 | 7.0 | 3.3 | 9.3 | | | | | |
| 1996 | 3.7 | 8.7 | 5.6 | 6.7 | 3.3 | 6.1 | | | | | |
| 1997 | 3.7 | 8.5 | 5.6 | 6.5 | 3.5 | 5.7 | | | | | |
| 1998 | 3.9 | 8.5 | 5.8 | 6.7 | 4.0 | 6.4 | | | | | |
| 1999 | 4.0 | 8.5 | 5.8 | 6.7 | 4.3 | 6.4 | | | | | |
| 2000 | 3.9 | 8.2 | 5.6 | 6.3 | 4.0 | 5.5 | 1.2 | | | | |
| 2001 | 3.9 | 8.1 | 5.6 | 6.3 | 4.2 | 5.6 | 3.7 | | | | |
| 2002 | 3.4 | 7.3 | 4.7 | 5.2 | 2.8 | 3.2 | -2.2 | | | | |
| 2003 | 3.5 | 7.3 | 4.9 | 5.4 | 3.2 | 3.8 | 0.4 | | | | |
| 2004 | 4.1 | 7.8 | 5.6 | 6.2 | 4.4 | 5.5 | 4.6 | | | | |
| 2005 | 4.5 | 8.2 | 6.1 | 6.8 | 5.4 | 6.8 | 7.2 | 20.0 | | | |
| 2006 | 4.8 | 8.5 | 6.5 | 7.3 | 6.1 | 7.7 | 8.7 | 18.7 | | | |
| 2007 | 5.0 | 8.5 | 6.7 | 7.4 | 6.3 | 7.9 | 8.8 | 15.8 | | | |
| 2008 | 3.7 | 7.0 | 4.9 | 5.3 | 3.6 | 4.2 | 2.9 | 0.8 | | | |
| 2009 | 4.5 | 7.8 | 5.9 | 6.4 | 5.1 | 6.1 | 6.0 | 7.4 | | | |
| 2010 | 4.3 | 7.4 | 5.6 | 6.0 | 4.7 | 5.5 | 5.1 | 5.5 | -3.7 | | |
| 2011 | 3.8 | 6.8 | 4.9 | 5.2 | 3.8 | 4.3 | 3.4 | 2.5 | -9.6 | | |
| 2012 | 4.1 | 7.1 | 5.3 | 5.6 | 4.4 | 5.0 | 4.5 | 4.3 | -0.7 | | |
| 2013 | 4.4 | 7.4 | 5.6 | 6.1 | 5.0 | 5.7 | 5.4 | 5.9 | 4.0 | | |
| 2014 | 4.4 | 7.3 | 5.6 | 6.0 | 5.0 | 5.7 | 5.4 | 5.8 | 4.3 | | |
| 2015 | 4.3 | 7.1 | 5.5 | 5.8 | 4.7 | 5.4 | 5.0 | 5.2 | 3.4 | -0.7 | |
| 2016 | 4.5 | 7.2 | 5.6 | 6.0 | 5.0 | 5.6 | 5.4 | 5.7 | 4.4 | 4.9 | 10.4 |

Start Date

## in U.S. Dollars (USD)
in Percent

| End Date | 1970 | 1975 | 1980 | 1985 | 1990 | 1995 | 2000 | 2005 | 2010 | 2015 | 2016 |
|---|---|---|---|---|---|---|---|---|---|---|---|
| 1970 | -24.4 | | | | | | | | | | |
| 1971 | -19.4 | | | | | | | | | | |
| 1972 | -9.8 | | | | | | | | | | |
| 1973 | -16.2 | | | | | | | | | | |
| 1974 | -19.2 | | | | | | | | | | |
| 1975 | -7.9 | 48.4 | | | | | | | | | |
| 1976 | -7.3 | 22.5 | | | | | | | | | |
| 1977 | -6.6 | 14.4 | | | | | | | | | |
| 1978 | -4.5 | 13.9 | | | | | | | | | |
| 1979 | -0.1 | 18.9 | | | | | | | | | |
| 1980 | 3.1 | 21.7 | 35.7 | | | | | | | | |
| 1981 | 0.2 | 13.9 | 1.5 | | | | | | | | |
| 1982 | -1.6 | 9.3 | -6.7 | | | | | | | | |
| 1983 | 2.3 | 14.2 | 8.3 | | | | | | | | |
| 1984 | 1.2 | 11.4 | 3.8 | | | | | | | | |
| 1985 | 2.7 | 12.7 | 7.5 | 26.1 | | | | | | | |
| 1986 | 4.3 | 14.1 | 10.7 | 27.9 | | | | | | | |
| 1987 | 3.3 | 12.0 | 7.7 | 14.1 | | | | | | | |
| 1988 | 3.5 | 11.6 | 7.5 | 12.0 | | | | | | | |
| 1989 | 3.4 | 11.0 | 7.0 | 10.1 | | | | | | | |
| 1990 | 1.9 | 8.4 | 3.7 | 3.6 | -29.3 | | | | | | |
| 1991 | 3.0 | 9.5 | 5.6 | 6.8 | -1.5 | | | | | | |
| 1992 | 2.6 | 8.6 | 4.6 | 5.2 | -3.1 | | | | | | |
| 1993 | 3.8 | 9.9 | 6.6 | 8.2 | 5.8 | | | | | | |
| 1994 | 3.1 | 8.7 | 5.3 | 6.0 | 1.9 | | | | | | |
| 1995 | 3.3 | 8.7 | 5.5 | 6.3 | 3.0 | 8.9 | | | | | |
| 1996 | 3.3 | 8.4 | 5.4 | 6.0 | 3.1 | 6.0 | | | | | |
| 1997 | 3.4 | 8.2 | 5.3 | 5.8 | 3.2 | 5.3 | | | | | |
| 1998 | 3.5 | 8.2 | 5.4 | 6.0 | 3.7 | 6.1 | | | | | |
| 1999 | 3.6 | 8.2 | 5.5 | 6.1 | 4.0 | 6.2 | | | | | |
| 2000 | 3.5 | 7.9 | 5.3 | 5.7 | 3.8 | 5.3 | 1.0 | | | | |
| 2001 | 3.6 | 7.8 | 5.3 | 5.7 | 3.9 | 5.4 | 3.4 | | | | |
| 2002 | 3.0 | 7.0 | 4.4 | 4.6 | 2.4 | 2.8 | -2.9 | | | | |
| 2003 | 3.3 | 7.1 | 4.7 | 4.9 | 3.1 | 3.7 | 0.6 | | | | |
| 2004 | 3.8 | 7.6 | 5.4 | 5.8 | 4.3 | 5.6 | 5.0 | | | | |
| 2005 | 4.2 | 8.0 | 5.9 | 6.4 | 5.2 | 6.8 | 7.2 | 18.7 | | | |
| 2006 | 4.6 | 8.3 | 6.4 | 7.0 | 6.0 | 7.8 | 8.9 | 18.7 | | | |
| 2007 | 4.8 | 8.4 | 6.5 | 7.1 | 6.3 | 8.0 | 9.2 | 16.2 | | | |
| 2008 | 3.8 | 7.1 | 5.1 | 5.4 | 4.1 | 4.9 | 4.2 | 3.3 | | | |
| 2009 | 4.8 | 8.2 | 6.4 | 6.9 | 6.1 | 7.5 | 8.2 | 11.4 | | | |
| 2010 | 4.5 | 7.8 | 6.1 | 6.5 | 5.6 | 6.8 | 7.1 | 8.8 | -4.2 | | |
| 2011 | 4.1 | 7.2 | 5.4 | 5.7 | 4.6 | 5.5 | 5.2 | 5.3 | -9.9 | | |
| 2012 | 4.4 | 7.5 | 5.7 | 6.1 | 5.2 | 6.1 | 6.1 | 6.8 | -0.8 | | |
| 2013 | 4.6 | 7.7 | 6.0 | 6.4 | 5.6 | 6.6 | 6.8 | 7.8 | 3.3 | | |
| 2014 | 4.6 | 7.6 | 5.9 | 6.3 | 5.5 | 6.5 | 6.5 | 7.3 | 3.3 | | |
| 2015 | 4.5 | 7.4 | 5.8 | 6.1 | 5.3 | 6.1 | 6.1 | 6.6 | 2.6 | -0.8 | |
| 2016 | 4.6 | 7.4 | 5.9 | 6.2 | 5.5 | 6.3 | 6.3 | 6.9 | 3.7 | 4.9 | 10.6 |

Start Date

**Austria Long-Horizon Equity Risk Premia**

in Local Currency (Euro – EUR)
in Percent

| End Date | 1971 | 1975 | 1980 | 1985 | 1990 | 1995 | 2000 | 2005 | 2010 | 2015 | 2016 |
|---|---|---|---|---|---|---|---|---|---|---|---|
| 1970 | – | | | | | | | | | | |
| 1971 | -9.1 | | | | | | | | | | |
| 1972 | 8.9 | | | | | | | | | | |
| 1973 | 5.6 | | | | | | | | | | |
| 1974 | 1.8 | | | | | | | | | | |
| 1975 | 0.4 | -4.9 | | | | | | | | | |
| 1976 | -0.4 | -4.7 | | | | | | | | | |
| 1977 | -2.3 | -7.8 | | | | | | | | | |
| 1978 | -2.8 | -7.3 | | | | | | | | | |
| 1979 | -2.1 | -5.2 | | | | | | | | | |
| 1980 | -2.9 | -6.1 | -10.5 | | | | | | | | |
| 1981 | -4.5 | -8.1 | -15.3 | | | | | | | | |
| 1982 | -5.3 | -8.9 | -15.0 | | | | | | | | |
| 1983 | -4.5 | -7.3 | -10.0 | | | | | | | | |
| 1984 | -4.1 | -6.4 | -7.6 | | | | | | | | |
| 1985 | 3.5 | 4.1 | 11.9 | 109.1 | | | | | | | |
| 1986 | 3.2 | 3.7 | 10.0 | 54.1 | | | | | | | |
| 1987 | 1.6 | 1.6 | 5.8 | 28.2 | | | | | | | |
| 1988 | 1.9 | 2.0 | 5.9 | 22.8 | | | | | | | |
| 1989 | 6.5 | 7.7 | 14.2 | 35.9 | | | | | | | |
| 1990 | 5.5 | 6.4 | 11.6 | 27.6 | -13.8 | | | | | | |
| 1991 | 4.3 | 4.9 | 9.1 | 21.0 | -16.5 | | | | | | |
| 1992 | 3.5 | 3.9 | 7.4 | 16.7 | -15.3 | | | | | | |
| 1993 | 4.7 | 5.3 | 9.0 | 18.3 | -3.8 | | | | | | |
| 1994 | 3.6 | 3.9 | 6.9 | 14.2 | -7.5 | | | | | | |
| 1995 | 2.6 | 2.8 | 5.3 | 11.2 | -9.5 | -19.2 | | | | | |
| 1996 | 2.8 | 3.0 | 5.4 | 10.8 | -7.2 | -6.4 | | | | | |
| 1997 | 3.2 | 3.4 | 5.8 | 11.0 | -4.6 | 0.2 | | | | | |
| 1998 | 2.6 | 2.8 | 4.9 | 9.4 | -5.4 | -2.8 | | | | | |
| 1999 | 2.6 | 2.8 | 4.8 | 8.9 | -4.6 | -1.7 | | | | | |
| 2000 | 2.2 | 2.3 | 4.0 | 7.7 | -5.2 | -3.2 | -10.9 | | | | |
| 2001 | 2.0 | 2.0 | 3.6 | 6.9 | -5.2 | -3.5 | -8.0 | | | | |
| 2002 | 1.7 | 1.7 | 3.2 | 6.2 | -5.2 | -3.7 | -7.1 | | | | |
| 2003 | 2.5 | 2.6 | 4.2 | 7.3 | -2.9 | -0.3 | 1.4 | | | | |
| 2004 | 4.1 | 4.4 | 6.3 | 9.7 | 1.0 | 5.3 | 12.2 | | | | |
| 2005 | 5.1 | 5.5 | 7.6 | 11.2 | 3.5 | 8.5 | 17.0 | 40.8 | | | |
| 2006 | 5.5 | 6.0 | 8.0 | 11.6 | 4.4 | 9.4 | 17.3 | 29.9 | | | |
| 2007 | 5.0 | 5.4 | 7.3 | 10.6 | 3.5 | 7.8 | 13.7 | 16.1 | | | |
| 2008 | 3.0 | 3.2 | 4.6 | 7.2 | -0.4 | 2.1 | 4.3 | -5.7 | | | |
| 2009 | 3.9 | 4.1 | 5.7 | 8.3 | 1.4 | 4.4 | 7.5 | 2.7 | | | |
| 2010 | 4.2 | 4.4 | 6.0 | 8.6 | 2.1 | 5.1 | 8.2 | 4.8 | 15.1 | | |
| 2011 | 3.2 | 3.3 | 4.6 | 6.9 | 0.3 | 2.6 | 4.4 | -1.2 | -11.1 | | |
| 2012 | 3.6 | 3.8 | 5.2 | 7.5 | 1.3 | 3.7 | 5.8 | 1.8 | 0.1 | | |
| 2013 | 3.7 | 3.9 | 5.2 | 7.5 | 1.5 | 3.9 | 5.9 | 2.4 | 1.9 | | |
| 2014 | 3.1 | 3.3 | 4.5 | 6.5 | 0.6 | 2.6 | 4.1 | 0.0 | -2.7 | | |
| 2015 | 3.4 | 3.6 | 4.8 | 6.8 | 1.2 | 3.2 | 4.8 | 1.4 | 0.2 | 15.0 | |
| 2016 | 3.7 | 3.8 | 5.0 | 7.0 | 1.7 | 3.8 | 5.4 | 2.5 | 2.3 | 14.9 | 14.8 |

in U.S. Dollars (USD)
in Percent

| End Date | 1972 | 1975 | 1980 | 1985 | 1990 | 1995 | 2000 | 2005 | 2010 | 2015 | 2016 |
|---|---|---|---|---|---|---|---|---|---|---|---|
| 1970 | | | | | | | | | | | |
| 1971 | | | | | | | | | | | |
| 1972 | – | | | | | | | | | | |
| 1973 | 30.1 | | | | | | | | | | |
| 1974 | 23.0 | | | | | | | | | | |
| 1975 | 16.8 | -12.1 | | | | | | | | | |
| 1976 | 9.5 | -3.3 | | | | | | | | | |
| 1977 | 8.7 | -3.5 | | | | | | | | | |
| 1978 | 6.6 | -1.2 | | | | | | | | | |
| 1979 | 6.5 | 1.3 | | | | | | | | | |
| 1980 | 7.1 | -2.3 | -20.2 | | | | | | | | |
| 1981 | 4.0 | -6.2 | -24.8 | | | | | | | | |
| 1982 | 0.7 | -8.2 | -23.9 | | | | | | | | |
| 1983 | -1.4 | -8.2 | -20.1 | | | | | | | | |
| 1984 | -2.0 | -8.6 | -18.4 | | | | | | | | |
| 1985 | -2.7 | 7.4 | 12.6 | 167.2 | | | | | | | |
| 1986 | 9.4 | 8.9 | 14.4 | 96.5 | | | | | | | |
| 1987 | 10.5 | 7.8 | 11.8 | 62.2 | | | | | | | |
| 1988 | 8.6 | 6.9 | 10.0 | 45.4 | | | | | | | |
| 1989 | 13.6 | 12.9 | 18.7 | 55.9 | | | | | | | |
| 1990 | 12.7 | 11.9 | 16.8 | 46.1 | -2.5 | | | | | | |
| 1991 | 11.1 | 10.0 | 13.7 | 36.6 | -11.5 | | | | | | |
| 1992 | 9.7 | 8.5 | 11.3 | 29.8 | -13.7 | | | | | | |
| 1993 | 10.2 | 9.2 | 12.0 | 28.9 | -4.8 | | | | | | |
| 1994 | 9.2 | 8.1 | 10.3 | 24.7 | -6.5 | | | | | | |
| 1995 | 8.3 | 7.1 | 8.9 | 21.3 | -7.5 | -12.5 | | | | | |
| 1996 | 7.9 | 6.7 | 8.3 | 19.4 | -6.6 | -6.8 | | | | | |
| 1997 | 7.5 | 6.3 | 7.7 | 17.7 | -6.1 | -5.5 | | | | | |
| 1998 | 7.1 | 5.8 | 7.0 | 16.1 | -6.0 | -5.3 | | | | | |
| 1999 | 6.4 | 5.1 | 6.1 | 14.2 | -6.6 | -6.7 | | | | | |
| 2000 | 5.6 | 4.3 | 5.0 | 12.3 | -7.5 | -8.4 | -16.6 | | | | |
| 2001 | 5.0 | 3.7 | 4.3 | 11.0 | -7.7 | -8.6 | -13.2 | | | | |
| 2002 | 5.3 | 4.0 | 4.6 | 11.0 | -6.2 | -6.1 | -5.0 | | | | |
| 2003 | 6.7 | 5.7 | 6.6 | 13.2 | -2.0 | 0.4 | 9.4 | | | | |
| 2004 | 8.6 | 7.8 | 9.1 | 15.9 | 2.6 | 7.2 | 21.1 | | | | |
| 2005 | 9.0 | 8.2 | 9.6 | 16.2 | 3.8 | 8.5 | 21.2 | 22.2 | | | |
| 2006 | 9.7 | 9.0 | 10.4 | 17.0 | 5.6 | 10.6 | 22.9 | 27.6 | | | |
| 2007 | 9.4 | 8.7 | 10.0 | 16.2 | 5.1 | 9.6 | 19.8 | 17.8 | | | |
| 2008 | 7.1 | 6.3 | 7.2 | 12.5 | 1.1 | 3.8 | 9.6 | -4.8 | | | |
| 2009 | 8.0 | 7.3 | 8.3 | 13.6 | 3.0 | 6.2 | 12.7 | 4.3 | | | |
| 2010 | 8.0 | 7.3 | 8.3 | 13.4 | 3.3 | 6.3 | 12.2 | 4.9 | 7.6 | | |
| 2011 | 6.8 | 6.0 | 6.8 | 11.4 | 1.3 | 3.6 | 8.0 | -1.4 | -15.8 | | |
| 2012 | 7.3 | 6.5 | 7.3 | 11.9 | 2.3 | 4.8 | 9.2 | 1.8 | -2.4 | | |
| 2013 | 7.4 | 6.7 | 7.5 | 11.9 | 2.7 | 5.2 | 9.4 | 3.0 | 1.3 | | |
| 2014 | 6.5 | 5.7 | 6.4 | 10.5 | 1.4 | 3.4 | 6.7 | -0.4 | -5.2 | | |
| 2015 | 6.4 | 5.7 | 6.3 | 10.2 | 1.5 | 3.4 | 6.5 | -0.1 | -3.8 | 3.2 | |
| 2016 | 6.5 | 5.8 | 6.4 | 10.3 | 1.8 | 3.7 | 6.8 | 0.9 | -1.6 | 7.2 | 11.1 |

Source of underlying data: 1.) Morningstar *Direct* database. Used with permission. All rights reserved. All calculations performed by Duff & Phelps LLC.

## Austria Short-Horizon Equity Risk Premia

### in Local Currency (Euro – EUR) in Percent

| End Date | 1970 | 1975 | 1980 | 1985 | 1990 | 1995 | 2000 | 2005 | 2010 | 2015 | 2016 |
|---|---|---|---|---|---|---|---|---|---|---|---|
| 1970 | 5.0 | | | | | | | | | | |
| 1971 | -1.4 | | | | | | | | | | |
| 1972 | 8.2 | | | | | | | | | | |
| 1973 | 6.2 | | | | | | | | | | |
| 1974 | 3.4 | | | | | | | | | | |
| 1975 | 2.3 | -2.8 | | | | | | | | | |
| 1976 | 1.5 | -3.2 | | | | | | | | | |
| 1977 | -0.4 | -6.7 | | | | | | | | | |
| 1978 | -0.9 | -6.3 | | | | | | | | | |
| 1979 | -0.5 | -4.4 | | | | | | | | | |
| 1980 | -1.4 | -5.4 | -10.3 | | | | | | | | |
| 1981 | -2.9 | -7.4 | -15.0 | | | | | | | | |
| 1982 | -3.8 | -8.3 | -14.9 | | | | | | | | |
| 1983 | -3.2 | -6.9 | -10.1 | | | | | | | | |
| 1984 | -2.9 | -6.1 | -7.8 | | | | | | | | |
| 1985 | 4.1 | 4.4 | 11.7 | 108.8 | | | | | | | |
| 1986 | 3.8 | 3.9 | 9.9 | 54.0 | | | | | | | |
| 1987 | 2.3 | 1.9 | 5.8 | 28.3 | | | | | | | |
| 1988 | 2.6 | 2.3 | 5.9 | 23.1 | | | | | | | |
| 1989 | 6.8 | 8.0 | 14.1 | 36.0 | | | | | | | |
| 1990 | 5.8 | 6.6 | 11.6 | 27.6 | -14.3 | | | | | | |
| 1991 | 4.6 | 5.0 | 8.9 | 20.8 | -17.3 | | | | | | |
| 1992 | 3.8 | 3.9 | 7.1 | 16.4 | -16.4 | | | | | | |
| 1993 | 4.9 | 5.3 | 8.8 | 18.0 | -4.6 | | | | | | |
| 1994 | 3.9 | 4.0 | 6.8 | 14.0 | -7.9 | | | | | | |
| 1995 | 3.1 | 3.0 | 5.3 | 11.3 | -9.3 | -16.4 | | | | | |
| 1996 | 3.3 | 3.3 | 5.6 | 11.1 | -6.7 | -3.4 | | | | | |
| 1997 | 3.8 | 3.8 | 6.1 | 11.5 | -3.9 | 2.9 | | | | | |
| 1998 | 3.3 | 3.3 | 5.3 | 9.9 | -4.6 | -0.4 | | | | | |
| 1999 | 3.3 | 3.3 | 5.2 | 9.5 | -3.7 | 0.5 | | | | | |
| 2000 | 2.9 | 2.8 | 4.5 | 8.3 | -4.3 | -1.2 | -9.7 | | | | |
| 2001 | 2.7 | 2.5 | 4.1 | 7.6 | -4.3 | -1.7 | -7.0 | | | | |
| 2002 | 2.5 | 2.3 | 3.7 | 6.9 | -4.3 | -1.9 | -6.0 | | | | |
| 2003 | 3.2 | 3.2 | 4.8 | 8.1 | -1.9 | 1.5 | 2.7 | | | | |
| 2004 | 4.8 | 5.0 | 6.9 | 10.6 | 2.1 | 7.1 | 13.7 | | | | |
| 2005 | 5.8 | 6.2 | 8.3 | 12.1 | 4.6 | 10.3 | 18.5 | 42.1 | | | |
| 2006 | 6.2 | 6.6 | 8.7 | 12.4 | 5.5 | 11.1 | 18.6 | 30.9 | | | |
| 2007 | 5.7 | 6.1 | 8.0 | 11.4 | 4.5 | 9.3 | 14.9 | 16.7 | | | |
| 2008 | 3.8 | 3.8 | 5.2 | 7.9 | 0.5 | 3.5 | 5.3 | -5.4 | | | |
| 2009 | 4.6 | 4.8 | 6.3 | 9.2 | 2.4 | 5.9 | 8.6 | 3.5 | | | |
| 2010 | 4.9 | 5.2 | 6.7 | 9.5 | 3.2 | 6.6 | 9.4 | 5.8 | 17.7 | | |
| 2011 | 4.0 | 4.1 | 5.4 | 7.8 | 1.4 | 4.2 | 5.7 | 0.0 | -8.7 | | |
| 2012 | 4.5 | 4.6 | 6.0 | 8.4 | 2.4 | 5.3 | 7.1 | 3.0 | 2.3 | | |
| 2013 | 4.6 | 4.7 | 6.1 | 8.4 | 2.7 | 5.5 | 7.3 | 3.7 | 4.0 | | |
| 2014 | 4.0 | 4.1 | 5.3 | 7.5 | 1.8 | 4.2 | 5.5 | 1.3 | -0.8 | | |
| 2015 | 4.3 | 4.4 | 5.6 | 7.8 | 2.3 | 4.8 | 6.1 | 2.6 | 2.0 | 15.7 | |
| 2016 | 4.5 | 4.7 | 5.9 | 8.0 | 2.8 | 5.3 | 6.7 | 3.7 | 3.9 | 15.6 | 15.5 |

### in U.S. Dollars (USD) in Percent

| End Date | 1970 | 1975 | 1980 | 1985 | 1990 | 1995 | 2000 | 2005 | 2010 | 2015 | 2016 |
|---|---|---|---|---|---|---|---|---|---|---|---|
| 1970 | 5.0 | | | | | | | | | | |
| 1971 | -1.7 | | | | | | | | | | |
| 1972 | 8.4 | | | | | | | | | | |
| 1973 | 6.3 | | | | | | | | | | |
| 1974 | 3.3 | | | | | | | | | | |
| 1975 | 2.3 | -2.7 | | | | | | | | | |
| 1976 | 1.4 | -3.3 | | | | | | | | | |
| 1977 | -0.5 | -6.9 | | | | | | | | | |
| 1978 | -1.3 | -7.0 | | | | | | | | | |
| 1979 | -0.7 | -4.7 | | | | | | | | | |
| 1980 | -1.5 | -5.5 | -9.5 | | | | | | | | |
| 1981 | -2.9 | -7.2 | -13.5 | | | | | | | | |
| 1982 | -3.9 | -8.4 | -14.4 | | | | | | | | |
| 1983 | -3.4 | -7.1 | -10.0 | | | | | | | | |
| 1984 | -3.1 | -6.2 | -7.7 | | | | | | | | |
| 1985 | 5.8 | 6.9 | 16.6 | 138.3 | | | | | | | |
| 1986 | 5.4 | 6.2 | 14.1 | 68.5 | | | | | | | |
| 1987 | 3.5 | 3.6 | 8.9 | 36.5 | | | | | | | |
| 1988 | 3.7 | 3.8 | 8.6 | 29.0 | | | | | | | |
| 1989 | 8.1 | 9.7 | 17.0 | 41.7 | | | | | | | |
| 1990 | 7.0 | 8.1 | 13.9 | 32.0 | -16.5 | | | | | | |
| 1991 | 5.7 | 6.5 | 11.1 | 24.6 | -18.1 | | | | | | |
| 1992 | 4.9 | 5.4 | 9.3 | 19.9 | -16.5 | | | | | | |
| 1993 | 5.9 | 6.6 | 10.6 | 20.8 | -5.3 | | | | | | |
| 1994 | 4.7 | 5.1 | 8.3 | 16.3 | -9.0 | | | | | | |
| 1995 | 3.8 | 4.0 | 6.7 | 13.2 | -10.5 | -17.7 | | | | | |
| 1996 | 4.0 | 4.2 | 6.8 | 12.9 | -7.7 | -4.5 | | | | | |
| 1997 | 4.4 | 4.6 | 7.2 | 12.9 | -5.1 | 1.5 | | | | | |
| 1998 | 3.8 | 3.9 | 6.2 | 11.2 | -5.7 | -1.7 | | | | | |
| 1999 | 3.8 | 3.9 | 6.1 | 10.7 | -4.8 | -0.7 | | | | | |
| 2000 | 3.4 | 3.4 | 5.4 | 9.4 | -5.2 | -2.1 | -9.1 | | | | |
| 2001 | 3.2 | 3.1 | 4.9 | 8.6 | -5.1 | -2.4 | -6.6 | | | | |
| 2002 | 2.9 | 2.9 | 4.5 | 7.9 | -5.1 | -2.6 | -5.9 | | | | |
| 2003 | 3.9 | 4.0 | 5.8 | 9.3 | -2.2 | 1.5 | 4.2 | | | | |
| 2004 | 5.5 | 5.9 | 8.0 | 12.0 | 2.1 | 7.6 | 15.8 | | | | |
| 2005 | 6.4 | 6.9 | 9.1 | 13.1 | 4.2 | 10.2 | 19.3 | 36.5 | | | |
| 2006 | 6.8 | 7.4 | 9.6 | 13.5 | 5.3 | 11.2 | 19.7 | 29.3 | | | |
| 2007 | 6.3 | 6.7 | 8.8 | 12.4 | 4.2 | 9.3 | 15.6 | 15.2 | | | |
| 2008 | 4.4 | 4.5 | 6.1 | 9.0 | 0.4 | 3.8 | 6.3 | -5.6 | | | |
| 2009 | 5.3 | 5.6 | 7.3 | 10.3 | 2.4 | 6.2 | 9.7 | 3.5 | | | |
| 2010 | 5.5 | 5.9 | 7.6 | 10.5 | 3.1 | 6.9 | 10.3 | 5.7 | 16.5 | | |
| 2011 | 4.6 | 4.8 | 6.3 | 8.9 | 1.4 | 4.5 | 6.6 | 0.0 | -8.8 | | |
| 2012 | 5.1 | 5.3 | 6.8 | 9.4 | 2.4 | 5.6 | 8.0 | 3.1 | 2.4 | | |
| 2013 | 5.2 | 5.4 | 6.9 | 9.4 | 2.7 | 5.8 | 8.1 | 3.8 | 4.2 | | |
| 2014 | 4.7 | 4.8 | 6.2 | 8.5 | 1.9 | 4.6 | 6.4 | 1.7 | -0.1 | | |
| 2015 | 4.9 | 5.1 | 6.4 | 8.7 | 2.4 | 5.1 | 6.9 | 2.8 | 2.2 | 13.7 | |
| 2016 | 5.1 | 5.3 | 6.7 | 8.9 | 2.8 | 5.5 | 7.4 | 3.8 | 4.1 | 14.6 | 15.5 |

Source of underlying data: 1.) Morningstar *Direct* database. Used with permission. All rights reserved. All calculations performed by Duff & Phelps LLC.

**Belgium Long-Horizon Equity Risk Premia**

in Local Currency (Euro – EUR)
in Percent

| End Date | 1970 | 1975 | 1980 | 1985 | 1990 | 1995 | 2000 | 2005 | 2010 | 2015 | 2016 |
|---|---|---|---|---|---|---|---|---|---|---|---|
| 1970 | -0.5 | | | | | | | | | | |
| 1971 | 0.8 | | | | | | | | | | |
| 1972 | 8.5 | | | | | | | | | | |
| 1973 | 6.2 | | | | | | | | | | |
| 1974 | -1.6 | | | | | | | | | | |
| 1975 | 1.7 | 18.3 | | | | | | | | | |
| 1976 | -0.2 | 3.4 | | | | | | | | | |
| 1977 | -1.3 | -0.7 | | | | | | | | | |
| 1978 | -0.5 | 1.0 | | | | | | | | | |
| 1979 | 0.3 | 2.2 | | | | | | | | | |
| 1980 | -1.8 | -2.0 | -22.6 | | | | | | | | |
| 1981 | -1.6 | -1.6 | -11.0 | | | | | | | | |
| 1982 | -0.6 | 0.0 | -3.6 | | | | | | | | |
| 1983 | 1.9 | 3.9 | 6.1 | | | | | | | | |
| 1984 | 2.8 | 5.0 | 7.8 | | | | | | | | |
| 1985 | 4.6 | 7.4 | 11.7 | 31.1 | | | | | | | |
| 1986 | 6.5 | 9.9 | 15.4 | 34.3 | | | | | | | |
| 1987 | 5.0 | 7.6 | 11.0 | 16.3 | | | | | | | |
| 1988 | 8.3 | 11.8 | 17.2 | 28.9 | | | | | | | |
| 1989 | 8.1 | 11.3 | 15.9 | 24.0 | | | | | | | |
| 1990 | 6.2 | 8.7 | 11.6 | 14.8 | -31.2 | | | | | | |
| 1991 | 6.3 | 8.6 | 11.3 | 13.7 | -12.1 | | | | | | |
| 1992 | 5.9 | 7.9 | 10.2 | 11.6 | -9.1 | | | | | | |
| 1993 | 6.8 | 9.0 | 11.4 | 13.5 | 0.2 | | | | | | |
| 1994 | 6.1 | 8.0 | 10.0 | 11.0 | -1.9 | | | | | | |
| 1995 | 6.2 | 8.1 | 10.0 | 10.9 | 0.0 | 9.8 | | | | | |
| 1996 | 6.6 | 8.4 | 10.3 | 11.3 | 2.2 | 12.6 | | | | | |
| 1997 | 7.3 | 9.3 | 11.3 | 12.6 | 5.4 | 17.6 | | | | | |
| 1998 | 8.8 | 11.0 | 13.4 | 15.3 | 10.5 | 26.1 | | | | | |
| 1999 | 8.4 | 10.5 | 12.5 | 14.1 | 9.1 | 20.2 | | | | | |
| 2000 | 7.6 | 9.4 | 11.2 | 12.2 | 6.8 | 14.1 | -16.1 | | | | |
| 2001 | 7.1 | 8.7 | 10.2 | 10.9 | 5.4 | 10.6 | -13.3 | | | | |
| 2002 | 5.9 | 7.2 | 8.3 | 8.5 | 2.5 | 5.3 | -19.6 | | | | |
| 2003 | 6.0 | 7.3 | 8.4 | 8.5 | 3.0 | 5.7 | -12.3 | | | | |
| 2004 | 6.7 | 8.1 | 9.3 | 9.6 | 4.8 | 8.2 | -3.8 | | | | |
| 2005 | 7.2 | 8.6 | 9.8 | 10.3 | 6.0 | 9.6 | 0.7 | 23.5 | | | |
| 2006 | 7.5 | 8.9 | 10.2 | 10.7 | 6.8 | 10.4 | 3.4 | 21.6 | | | |
| 2007 | 6.9 | 8.2 | 9.2 | 9.6 | 5.5 | 8.4 | 1.1 | 9.2 | | | |
| 2008 | 4.9 | 5.9 | 6.6 | 6.3 | 1.6 | 2.9 | -6.7 | -10.3 | | | |
| 2009 | 6.1 | 7.2 | 8.0 | 8.0 | 4.0 | 6.0 | -1.1 | 1.7 | | | |
| 2010 | 6.0 | 7.1 | 7.9 | 7.9 | 4.0 | 5.9 | -0.6 | 2.0 | 3.7 | | |
| 2011 | 5.6 | 6.6 | 7.3 | 7.2 | 3.3 | 4.9 | -1.5 | 0.1 | -3.7 | | |
| 2012 | 6.3 | 7.3 | 8.1 | 8.2 | 4.7 | 6.6 | 1.3 | 4.5 | 9.2 | | |
| 2013 | 6.6 | 7.7 | 8.5 | 8.6 | 5.4 | 7.3 | 2.7 | 6.3 | 12.1 | | |
| 2014 | 6.9 | 7.9 | 8.7 | 8.9 | 5.9 | 7.8 | 3.7 | 7.5 | 13.2 | | |
| 2015 | 7.3 | 8.3 | 9.2 | 9.4 | 6.6 | 8.6 | 5.0 | 9.0 | 15.2 | 25.0 | |
| 2016 | 7.0 | 8.0 | 8.8 | 9.0 | 6.2 | 8.0 | 4.5 | 7.9 | 12.4 | 10.3 | -4.5 |

in U.S. Dollars (USD)
in Percent

| End Date | 1970 | 1975 | 1980 | 1985 | 1990 | 1995 | 2000 | 2005 | 2010 | 2015 | 2016 |
|---|---|---|---|---|---|---|---|---|---|---|---|
| 1970 | -0.5 | | | | | | | | | | |
| 1971 | 6.8 | | | | | | | | | | |
| 1972 | 12.8 | | | | | | | | | | |
| 1973 | 11.3 | | | | | | | | | | |
| 1974 | 4.4 | | | | | | | | | | |
| 1975 | 4.6 | 5.9 | | | | | | | | | |
| 1976 | 4.0 | 3.0 | | | | | | | | | |
| 1977 | 3.3 | 1.5 | | | | | | | | | |
| 1978 | 5.1 | 5.9 | | | | | | | | | |
| 1979 | 5.4 | 6.3 | | | | | | | | | |
| 1980 | 2.2 | 0.5 | -28.9 | | | | | | | | |
| 1981 | -0.1 | -3.2 | -27.2 | | | | | | | | |
| 1982 | -0.2 | -3.0 | -18.6 | | | | | | | | |
| 1983 | 0.9 | -1.0 | -10.2 | | | | | | | | |
| 1984 | 1.0 | -0.7 | -7.6 | | | | | | | | |
| 1985 | 5.0 | 5.3 | 4.5 | 65.2 | | | | | | | |
| 1986 | 8.8 | 10.6 | 13.7 | 67.0 | | | | | | | |
| 1987 | 8.2 | 9.7 | 11.8 | 44.1 | | | | | | | |
| 1988 | 10.3 | 12.5 | 15.9 | 45.3 | | | | | | | |
| 1989 | 10.3 | 12.3 | 15.3 | 38.2 | | | | | | | |
| 1990 | 8.8 | 10.2 | 12.0 | 28.3 | -20.9 | | | | | | |
| 1991 | 8.7 | 9.9 | 11.5 | 25.1 | -7.6 | | | | | | |
| 1992 | 7.9 | 8.9 | 9.9 | 20.9 | -7.9 | | | | | | |
| 1993 | 8.3 | 9.4 | 10.5 | 20.5 | -1.5 | | | | | | |
| 1994 | 8.1 | 9.0 | 9.9 | 18.6 | -0.9 | | | | | | |
| 1995 | 8.5 | 9.5 | 10.4 | 18.6 | 2.4 | 18.7 | | | | | |
| 1996 | 8.4 | 9.3 | 10.2 | 17.7 | 3.0 | 12.9 | | | | | |
| 1997 | 8.5 | 9.3 | 10.2 | 17.0 | 3.8 | 11.7 | | | | | |
| 1998 | 10.3 | 11.6 | 13.0 | 20.3 | 10.4 | 24.6 | | | | | |
| 1999 | 9.4 | 10.4 | 11.5 | 17.8 | 7.6 | 16.2 | | | | | |
| 2000 | 8.4 | 9.2 | 9.9 | 15.4 | 5.0 | 9.9 | -21.4 | | | | |
| 2001 | 7.7 | 8.3 | 8.8 | 13.6 | 3.3 | 6.3 | -18.3 | | | | |
| 2002 | 6.8 | 7.3 | 7.5 | 11.7 | 1.5 | 3.0 | -18.9 | | | | |
| 2003 | 7.6 | 8.1 | 8.5 | 12.8 | 3.7 | 6.2 | -6.2 | | | | |
| 2004 | 8.5 | 9.2 | 9.8 | 14.1 | 6.1 | 9.6 | 3.1 | | | | |
| 2005 | 8.5 | 9.1 | 9.7 | 13.8 | 6.2 | 9.4 | 3.8 | 7.1 | | | |
| 2006 | 9.2 | 9.9 | 10.6 | 14.7 | 7.8 | 11.4 | 8.0 | 20.4 | | | |
| 2007 | 8.7 | 9.4 | 10.0 | 13.8 | 7.0 | 10.1 | 6.2 | 11.5 | | | |
| 2008 | 6.7 | 7.1 | 7.2 | 10.3 | 2.9 | 4.3 | -2.3 | -9.0 | | | |
| 2009 | 7.9 | 8.4 | 8.8 | 12.1 | 5.5 | 7.7 | 3.4 | 3.7 | | | |
| 2010 | 7.6 | 8.1 | 8.4 | 11.5 | 5.1 | 7.0 | 2.8 | 2.6 | -3.1 | | |
| 2011 | 7.1 | 7.5 | 7.7 | 10.5 | 4.2 | 5.8 | 1.4 | 0.2 | -8.5 | | |
| 2012 | 7.8 | 8.3 | 8.6 | 11.5 | 5.7 | 7.5 | 4.2 | 4.9 | 6.7 | | |
| 2013 | 8.3 | 8.8 | 9.1 | 12.0 | 6.5 | 8.5 | 5.8 | 7.2 | 11.6 | | |
| 2014 | 8.1 | 8.6 | 8.9 | 11.7 | 6.4 | 8.2 | 5.6 | 6.8 | 9.9 | | |
| 2015 | 8.2 | 8.7 | 9.0 | 11.7 | 6.6 | 8.4 | 6.0 | 7.3 | 10.3 | 12.2 | |
| 2016 | 7.9 | 8.3 | 8.6 | 11.1 | 6.1 | 7.7 | 5.2 | 6.1 | 7.8 | 2.3 | -7.6 |

Source of underlying data: 1.) Morningstar *Direct* database. Used with permission. All rights reserved. All calculations performed by Duff & Phelps LLC.

# Belgium Short-Horizon Equity Risk Premia

## in Local Currency (Euro – EUR) in Percent

| End Date | Start Date 1970 | 1975 | 1980 | 1985 | 1990 | 1995 | 2000 | 2005 | 2010 | 2015 | 2016 |
|---|---|---|---|---|---|---|---|---|---|---|---|
| 1970 | -0.1 | | | | | | | | | | |
| 1971 | 1.2 | | | | | | | | | | |
| 1972 | 8.8 | | | | | | | | | | |
| 1973 | 6.4 | | | | | | | | | | |
| 1974 | -1.7 | | | | | | | | | | |
| 1975 | 1.7 | 18.6 | | | | | | | | | |
| 1976 | -0.3 | 3.2 | | | | | | | | | |
| 1977 | -1.4 | -0.9 | | | | | | | | | |
| 1978 | -0.6 | 0.6 | | | | | | | | | |
| 1979 | 0.0 | 1.7 | | | | | | | | | |
| 1980 | -2.1 | -2.5 | -23.8 | | | | | | | | |
| 1981 | -2.0 | -2.3 | -12.3 | | | | | | | | |
| 1982 | -1.0 | -0.6 | -4.6 | | | | | | | | |
| 1983 | 1.6 | 3.5 | 5.6 | | | | | | | | |
| 1984 | 2.5 | 4.6 | 7.4 | | | | | | | | |
| 1985 | 4.4 | 7.1 | 11.7 | 32.8 | | | | | | | |
| 1986 | 6.4 | 9.8 | 15.5 | 35.6 | | | | | | | |
| 1987 | 5.0 | 7.6 | 11.2 | 17.5 | | | | | | | |
| 1988 | 8.3 | 11.9 | 17.5 | 30.2 | | | | | | | |
| 1989 | 8.1 | 11.4 | 16.2 | 24.9 | | | | | | | |
| 1990 | 6.2 | 8.7 | 11.8 | 15.5 | -31.6 | | | | | | |
| 1991 | 6.2 | 8.6 | 11.4 | 14.3 | -12.3 | | | | | | |
| 1992 | 5.8 | 7.9 | 10.3 | 12.0 | -9.5 | | | | | | |
| 1993 | 6.7 | 8.9 | 11.5 | 13.7 | -0.4 | | | | | | |
| 1994 | 6.0 | 8.0 | 10.1 | 11.4 | -2.2 | | | | | | |
| 1995 | 6.3 | 8.2 | 10.2 | 11.5 | 0.3 | 12.9 | | | | | |
| 1996 | 6.8 | 8.7 | 10.7 | 12.1 | 3.0 | 15.9 | | | | | |
| 1997 | 7.6 | 9.6 | 11.8 | 13.5 | 6.4 | 20.6 | | | | | |
| 1998 | 9.2 | 11.4 | 14.0 | 16.3 | 11.5 | 28.6 | | | | | |
| 1999 | 8.8 | 10.9 | 13.2 | 15.1 | 10.2 | 22.5 | | | | | |
| 2000 | 8.0 | 9.9 | 11.8 | 13.2 | 7.9 | 16.3 | -14.8 | | | | |
| 2001 | 7.5 | 9.2 | 10.9 | 11.9 | 6.4 | 12.6 | -12.2 | | | | |
| 2002 | 6.3 | 7.8 | 9.1 | 9.5 | 3.6 | 7.2 | -18.3 | | | | |
| 2003 | 6.5 | 7.9 | 9.2 | 9.6 | 4.2 | 7.7 | -10.8 | | | | |
| 2004 | 7.2 | 8.7 | 10.1 | 10.8 | 6.1 | 10.2 | -2.2 | | | | |
| 2005 | 7.7 | 9.2 | 10.7 | 11.4 | 7.2 | 11.5 | 2.3 | 24.9 | | | |
| 2006 | 8.1 | 9.6 | 11.0 | 11.9 | 8.0 | 12.3 | 4.9 | 22.7 | | | |
| 2007 | 7.4 | 8.8 | 10.1 | 10.7 | 6.7 | 10.1 | 2.4 | 10.0 | | | |
| 2008 | 5.5 | 6.6 | 7.4 | 7.4 | 2.8 | 4.5 | -5.5 | -9.6 | | | |
| 2009 | 6.7 | 7.9 | 8.9 | 9.2 | 5.3 | 7.7 | 0.3 | 2.8 | | | |
| 2010 | 6.7 | 7.8 | 8.8 | 9.1 | 5.3 | 7.7 | 0.9 | 3.5 | 6.8 | | |
| 2011 | 6.3 | 7.4 | 8.3 | 8.5 | 4.7 | 6.8 | 0.2 | 1.9 | -0.6 | | |
| 2012 | 7.1 | 8.2 | 9.2 | 9.5 | 6.2 | 8.5 | 3.1 | 6.4 | 12.4 | | |
| 2013 | 7.4 | 8.6 | 9.6 | 10.0 | 6.9 | 9.3 | 4.6 | 8.3 | 15.1 | | |
| 2014 | 7.7 | 8.9 | 9.9 | 10.3 | 7.4 | 9.8 | 5.5 | 9.4 | 16.0 | | |
| 2015 | 8.1 | 9.3 | 10.4 | 10.8 | 8.1 | 10.6 | 6.8 | 10.9 | 17.6 | 26.0 | |
| 2016 | 7.9 | 9.0 | 10.0 | 10.4 | 7.7 | 9.9 | 6.2 | 9.7 | 14.6 | 11.3 | -3.4 |

## in U.S. Dollars (USD) in Percent

| End Date | Start Date 1970 | 1975 | 1980 | 1985 | 1990 | 1995 | 2000 | 2005 | 2010 | 2015 | 2016 |
|---|---|---|---|---|---|---|---|---|---|---|---|
| 1970 | -0.1 | | | | | | | | | | |
| 1971 | 1.8 | | | | | | | | | | |
| 1972 | 9.0 | | | | | | | | | | |
| 1973 | 6.7 | | | | | | | | | | |
| 1974 | -2.4 | | | | | | | | | | |
| 1975 | 0.5 | 14.8 | | | | | | | | | |
| 1976 | -1.1 | 2.0 | | | | | | | | | |
| 1977 | -2.5 | -2.6 | | | | | | | | | |
| 1978 | -1.6 | -0.6 | | | | | | | | | |
| 1979 | -1.0 | 0.3 | | | | | | | | | |
| 1980 | -2.7 | -2.9 | -18.9 | | | | | | | | |
| 1981 | -3.2 | -3.7 | -13.8 | | | | | | | | |
| 1982 | -1.6 | -1.2 | -3.7 | | | | | | | | |
| 1983 | 0.7 | 2.4 | 5.1 | | | | | | | | |
| 1984 | 1.6 | 3.7 | 7.0 | | | | | | | | |
| 1985 | 4.1 | 7.0 | 12.6 | 40.9 | | | | | | | |
| 1986 | 6.5 | 10.2 | 17.3 | 43.1 | | | | | | | |
| 1987 | 5.0 | 7.8 | 12.5 | 21.7 | | | | | | | |
| 1988 | 7.9 | 11.6 | 17.9 | 31.4 | | | | | | | |
| 1989 | 7.8 | 11.1 | 16.5 | 26.1 | | | | | | | |
| 1990 | 5.7 | 8.2 | 11.7 | 15.7 | -36.4 | | | | | | |
| 1991 | 5.7 | 8.1 | 11.3 | 14.4 | -14.9 | | | | | | |
| 1992 | 5.3 | 7.4 | 10.2 | 12.2 | -11.1 | | | | | | |
| 1993 | 6.1 | 8.4 | 11.2 | 13.6 | -2.1 | | | | | | |
| 1994 | 5.4 | 7.4 | 9.8 | 11.1 | -3.8 | | | | | | |
| 1995 | 5.8 | 7.7 | 10.0 | 11.4 | -0.9 | 13.9 | | | | | |
| 1996 | 6.2 | 8.1 | 10.5 | 11.9 | 1.8 | 15.7 | | | | | |
| 1997 | 6.9 | 8.9 | 11.3 | 13.0 | 4.8 | 19.0 | | | | | |
| 1998 | 8.6 | 10.9 | 13.7 | 16.1 | 10.6 | 28.5 | | | | | |
| 1999 | 8.3 | 10.4 | 12.9 | 14.9 | 9.3 | 22.5 | | | | | |
| 2000 | 7.6 | 9.5 | 11.7 | 13.1 | 7.2 | 16.4 | -13.8 | | | | |
| 2001 | 7.0 | 8.8 | 10.7 | 11.8 | 5.9 | 12.8 | -11.5 | | | | |
| 2002 | 5.7 | 7.2 | 8.7 | 9.2 | 2.7 | 6.7 | -19.6 | | | | |
| 2003 | 6.0 | 7.4 | 8.9 | 9.4 | 3.5 | 7.5 | -11.2 | | | | |
| 2004 | 6.8 | 8.3 | 9.9 | 10.7 | 5.6 | 10.2 | -2.0 | | | | |
| 2005 | 7.2 | 8.8 | 10.4 | 11.2 | 6.6 | 11.3 | 1.9 | 21.6 | | | |
| 2006 | 7.6 | 9.2 | 10.9 | 11.7 | 7.5 | 12.2 | 4.9 | 22.3 | | | |
| 2007 | 7.0 | 8.4 | 9.9 | 10.5 | 6.2 | 10.0 | 2.2 | 9.2 | | | |
| 2008 | 5.1 | 6.3 | 7.3 | 7.3 | 2.4 | 4.6 | -5.3 | -9.4 | | | |
| 2009 | 6.4 | 7.6 | 8.8 | 9.2 | 5.0 | 7.9 | 0.7 | 3.4 | | | |
| 2010 | 6.4 | 7.6 | 8.8 | 9.1 | 5.1 | 7.8 | 1.2 | 3.8 | 6.3 | | |
| 2011 | 6.0 | 7.2 | 8.3 | 8.5 | 4.5 | 6.9 | 0.5 | 2.2 | -0.7 | | |
| 2012 | 6.8 | 8.0 | 9.2 | 9.6 | 6.0 | 8.7 | 3.4 | 6.8 | 12.6 | | |
| 2013 | 7.2 | 8.4 | 9.6 | 10.1 | 6.8 | 9.5 | 4.9 | 8.8 | 15.5 | | |
| 2014 | 7.4 | 8.7 | 9.8 | 10.3 | 7.2 | 9.9 | 5.7 | 9.6 | 15.8 | | |
| 2015 | 7.8 | 9.0 | 10.2 | 10.7 | 7.8 | 10.5 | 6.8 | 10.8 | 17.0 | 22.9 | |
| 2016 | 7.5 | 8.7 | 9.9 | 10.3 | 7.4 | 9.9 | 6.2 | 9.7 | 14.2 | 10.0 | -2.9 |

Data Exhibit 1-6

## Canada Long-Horizon Equity Risk Premia

in Local Currency (Canadian Dollar – CAD)
in Percent

| End Date | Start Date 1919 | 1920 | 1925 | 1930 | 1935 | 1940 | 1945 | 1950 | 1955 | 1960 | 1965 | 1970 | 1975 | 1980 | 1985 | 1990 | 1995 | 2000 | 2005 | 2010 | 2015 | 2016 |
|---|---|---|---|---|---|---|---|---|---|---|---|---|---|---|---|---|---|---|---|---|---|---|
| 1919 | 7.8 | | | | | | | | | | | | | | | | | | | | | |
| 1920 | -2.1 | -12.0 | | | | | | | | | | | | | | | | | | | | |
| 1921 | -3.6 | -9.3 | | | | | | | | | | | | | | | | | | | | |
| 1922 | 2.1 | 0.3 | | | | | | | | | | | | | | | | | | | | |
| 1923 | 2.2 | 0.9 | | | | | | | | | | | | | | | | | | | | |
| 1924 | 2.9 | 2.0 | | | | | | | | | | | | | | | | | | | | |
| 1925 | 4.7 | 4.2 | 15.2 | | | | | | | | | | | | | | | | | | | |
| 1926 | 6.6 | 6.4 | 17.4 | | | | | | | | | | | | | | | | | | | |
| 1927 | 10.3 | 10.6 | 25.0 | | | | | | | | | | | | | | | | | | | |
| 1928 | 12.1 | 12.6 | 25.9 | | | | | | | | | | | | | | | | | | | |
| 1929 | 9.5 | 9.7 | 17.4 | | | | | | | | | | | | | | | | | | | |
| 1930 | 5.7 | 5.6 | 8.6 | -35.6 | | | | | | | | | | | | | | | | | | |
| 1931 | 2.4 | 2.0 | 2.0 | -36.6 | | | | | | | | | | | | | | | | | | |
| 1932 | 1.0 | 0.4 | -0.5 | -30.4 | | | | | | | | | | | | | | | | | | |
| 1933 | 4.0 | 3.8 | 4.7 | -11.1 | | | | | | | | | | | | | | | | | | |
| 1934 | 4.8 | 4.6 | 5.9 | -5.6 | | | | | | | | | | | | | | | | | | |
| 1935 | 6.1 | 6.0 | 7.8 | -0.1 | 27.0 | | | | | | | | | | | | | | | | | |
| 1936 | 7.0 | 7.0 | 9.0 | 3.1 | 24.7 | | | | | | | | | | | | | | | | | |
| 1937 | 5.6 | 5.5 | 6.9 | 0.3 | 10.1 | | | | | | | | | | | | | | | | | |
| 1938 | 5.7 | 5.5 | 6.8 | 0.9 | 9.1 | | | | | | | | | | | | | | | | | |
| 1939 | 5.2 | 5.1 | 6.2 | 0.6 | 6.7 | | | | | | | | | | | | | | | | | |
| 1940 | 4.0 | 3.8 | 4.4 | -1.5 | 1.8 | -22.4 | | | | | | | | | | | | | | | | |
| 1941 | 3.8 | 3.6 | 4.1 | -1.5 | 1.4 | -11.8 | | | | | | | | | | | | | | | | |
| 1942 | 4.1 | 3.9 | 4.4 | -0.5 | 2.6 | -4.2 | | | | | | | | | | | | | | | | |
| 1943 | 4.6 | 4.4 | 5.1 | 0.7 | 4.2 | 1.0 | | | | | | | | | | | | | | | | |
| 1944 | 4.8 | 4.7 | 5.3 | 1.3 | 4.8 | 2.9 | | | | | | | | | | | | | | | | |
| 1945 | 5.8 | 5.8 | 6.7 | 3.3 | 7.4 | 7.9 | 33.1 | | | | | | | | | | | | | | | |
| 1946 | 5.5 | 5.4 | 6.2 | 2.9 | 6.4 | 6.2 | 14.5 | | | | | | | | | | | | | | | |
| 1947 | 5.2 | 5.1 | 5.8 | 2.6 | 5.8 | 5.2 | 8.9 | | | | | | | | | | | | | | | |
| 1948 | 5.4 | 5.3 | 6.0 | 2.9 | 6.0 | 5.6 | 9.0 | | | | | | | | | | | | | | | |
| 1949 | 5.8 | 5.8 | 6.5 | 3.8 | 6.9 | 7.0 | 11.1 | | | | | | | | | | | | | | | |
| 1950 | 7.1 | 7.0 | 8.0 | 5.8 | 9.3 | 10.5 | 16.9 | 45.6 | | | | | | | | | | | | | | |
| 1951 | 7.5 | 7.5 | 8.5 | 6.5 | 10.0 | 11.4 | 17.4 | 33.2 | | | | | | | | | | | | | | |
| 1952 | 7.1 | 7.1 | 8.0 | 6.0 | 9.2 | 10.2 | 14.8 | 20.8 | | | | | | | | | | | | | | |
| 1953 | 6.9 | 6.9 | 7.7 | 5.7 | 8.7 | 9.4 | 13.0 | 15.2 | | | | | | | | | | | | | | |
| 1954 | 7.7 | 7.7 | 8.6 | 6.9 | 10.0 | 11.1 | 15.2 | 19.3 | | | | | | | | | | | | | | |
| 1955 | 8.2 | 8.2 | 9.2 | 7.6 | 10.7 | 12.0 | 16.1 | 20.2 | 24.7 | | | | | | | | | | | | | |
| 1956 | 8.2 | 8.2 | 9.2 | 7.7 | 10.7 | 11.8 | 15.6 | 18.7 | 17.1 | | | | | | | | | | | | | |
| 1957 | 7.3 | 7.3 | 8.2 | 6.5 | 9.1 | 9.8 | 12.5 | 13.3 | 3.2 | | | | | | | | | | | | | |

Source of underlying data: 1.) Morningstar *Direct* database. Used with permission. All rights reserved. All calculations performed by Duff & Phelps LLC.

# Canada Long-Horizon Equity Risk Premia

in Local Currency (Canadian Dollar – CAD)
in Percent

| End Date | 1919 | 1920 | 1925 | 1930 | 1935 | 1940 | 1945 | 1950 | 1955 | 1960 | 1965 | 1970 | 1975 | 1980 | 1985 | 1990 | 1995 | 2000 | 2005 | 2010 | 2015 | 2016 |
|---|---|---|---|---|---|---|---|---|---|---|---|---|---|---|---|---|---|---|---|---|---|---|
| 1958 | 7.8 | 7.8 | 8.7 | 7.2 | 9.9 | 10.7 | 13.5 | 14.8 | 9.2 | | | | | | | | | | | | | |
| 1959 | 7.6 | 7.6 | 8.5 | 7.0 | 9.5 | 10.2 | 12.6 | 13.3 | 7.3 | | | | | | | | | | | | | |
| 1960 | 7.4 | 7.4 | 8.1 | 6.6 | 9.0 | 9.5 | 11.6 | 11.8 | 5.5 | -3.5 | | | | | | | | | | | | |
| 1961 | 7.9 | 7.9 | 8.6 | 7.3 | 9.7 | 10.3 | 12.5 | 13.1 | 8.7 | 12.0 | | | | | | | | | | | | |
| 1962 | 7.4 | 7.4 | 8.1 | 6.7 | 8.9 | 9.4 | 11.2 | 11.2 | 6.1 | 4.0 | | | | | | | | | | | | |
| 1963 | 7.5 | 7.5 | 8.2 | 6.8 | 8.9 | 9.4 | 11.1 | 11.1 | 6.6 | 5.6 | | | | | | | | | | | | |
| 1964 | 7.7 | 7.7 | 8.5 | 7.2 | 9.3 | 9.8 | 11.6 | 11.7 | 7.9 | 8.5 | | | | | | | | | | | | |
| 1965 | 7.6 | 7.6 | 8.3 | 7.0 | 9.1 | 9.5 | 11.1 | 11.1 | 7.3 | 7.4 | 1.6 | | | | | | | | | | | |
| 1966 | 7.2 | 7.2 | 7.8 | 6.5 | 8.4 | 8.7 | 10.0 | 9.7 | 5.7 | 4.5 | -5.5 | | | | | | | | | | | |
| 1967 | 7.3 | 7.3 | 7.9 | 6.7 | 8.5 | 8.8 | 10.1 | 9.8 | 6.2 | 5.5 | 0.4 | | | | | | | | | | | |
| 1968 | 7.5 | 7.5 | 8.1 | 6.9 | 8.7 | 9.1 | 10.4 | 10.2 | 6.9 | 6.6 | 4.3 | | | | | | | | | | | |
| 1969 | 7.2 | 7.2 | 7.7 | 6.5 | 8.2 | 8.5 | 9.6 | 9.2 | 5.9 | 5.2 | 1.8 | | | | | | | | | | | |
| 1970 | 7.0 | 7.0 | 7.6 | 6.4 | 8.0 | 8.2 | 9.3 | 8.8 | 5.5 | 4.7 | 1.5 | 0.1 | | | | | | | | | | |
| 1971 | 7.0 | 7.0 | 7.5 | 6.3 | 8.0 | 8.2 | 9.1 | 8.7 | 5.5 | 4.8 | 2.1 | 3.0 | | | | | | | | | | |
| 1972 | 7.4 | 7.4 | 7.9 | 6.8 | 8.4 | 8.7 | 9.7 | 9.4 | 6.7 | 6.4 | 5.1 | 10.6 | | | | | | | | | | |
| 1973 | 7.0 | 7.0 | 7.5 | 6.4 | 8.0 | 8.1 | 9.0 | 8.6 | 5.8 | 5.2 | 3.4 | 5.4 | | | | | | | | | | |
| 1974 | 6.3 | 6.3 | 6.7 | 5.5 | 6.9 | 6.9 | 7.6 | 6.8 | 3.7 | 2.5 | -0.5 | -2.7 | | | | | | | | | | |
| 1975 | 6.3 | 6.3 | 6.7 | 5.6 | 6.9 | 7.0 | 7.6 | 6.9 | 4.0 | 3.0 | 0.4 | -0.7 | 9.4 | | | | | | | | | |
| 1976 | 6.2 | 6.2 | 6.6 | 5.4 | 6.8 | 6.8 | 7.4 | 6.7 | 3.8 | 2.8 | 0.4 | -0.6 | 4.6 | | | | | | | | | |
| 1977 | 6.1 | 6.0 | 6.4 | 5.3 | 6.6 | 6.5 | 7.1 | 6.4 | 3.5 | 2.5 | 0.2 | -0.9 | 2.3 | | | | | | | | | |
| 1978 | 6.3 | 6.3 | 6.7 | 5.6 | 6.9 | 6.9 | 7.5 | 6.9 | 4.3 | 3.5 | 1.7 | 1.7 | 7.1 | | | | | | | | | |
| 1979 | 6.9 | 6.9 | 7.3 | 6.3 | 7.6 | 7.8 | 8.5 | 8.0 | 5.8 | 5.4 | 4.3 | 5.6 | 13.9 | | | | | | | | | |
| 1980 | 7.0 | 7.0 | 7.4 | 6.4 | 7.8 | 7.9 | 8.6 | 8.2 | 6.0 | 5.7 | 4.8 | 6.2 | 13.6 | 12.4 | | | | | | | | |
| 1981 | 6.5 | 6.5 | 6.9 | 5.9 | 7.1 | 7.1 | 7.7 | 7.2 | 4.9 | 4.4 | 3.1 | 3.7 | 8.3 | -5.7 | | | | | | | | |
| 1982 | 6.3 | 6.3 | 6.9 | 5.6 | 6.8 | 6.8 | 7.3 | 6.7 | 4.4 | 3.8 | 2.5 | 2.7 | 6.2 | -6.7 | | | | | | | | |
| 1983 | 6.5 | 6.5 | 6.9 | 5.9 | 7.1 | 7.1 | 7.6 | 7.1 | 5.0 | 4.6 | 3.5 | 4.1 | 7.9 | 0.5 | | | | | | | | |
| 1984 | 6.2 | 6.2 | 6.5 | 5.5 | 6.7 | 6.6 | 7.1 | 6.5 | 4.4 | 3.8 | 2.7 | 2.9 | 5.8 | -2.3 | | | | | | | | |
| 1985 | 6.3 | 6.3 | 6.6 | 5.6 | 6.7 | 6.8 | 7.2 | 6.7 | 4.6 | 4.1 | 3.1 | 3.5 | 6.3 | 0.0 | 11.5 | | | | | | | |
| 1986 | 6.2 | 6.2 | 6.5 | 5.5 | 6.6 | 6.6 | 7.0 | 6.5 | 4.5 | 4.0 | 2.9 | 3.2 | 5.7 | -0.1 | 5.5 | | | | | | | |
| 1987 | 6.1 | 6.0 | 6.4 | 5.4 | 6.5 | 6.4 | 6.8 | 6.3 | 4.3 | 3.8 | 2.7 | 3.0 | 5.2 | -0.2 | 3.2 | | | | | | | |
| 1988 | 6.0 | 5.9 | 6.2 | 5.3 | 6.3 | 6.3 | 6.6 | 6.1 | 4.1 | 3.6 | 2.5 | 2.7 | 4.7 | -0.4 | 1.9 | | | | | | | |
| 1989 | 6.0 | 6.0 | 6.3 | 5.4 | 6.4 | 6.4 | 6.7 | 6.2 | 4.3 | 3.8 | 2.9 | 3.2 | 5.1 | 0.7 | 3.8 | | | | | | | |
| 1990 | 5.6 | 5.6 | 5.9 | 4.9 | 5.9 | 5.8 | 6.1 | 5.5 | 3.6 | 3.0 | 1.9 | 2.0 | 3.4 | -1.3 | -0.5 | -22.1 | | | | | | |
| 1991 | 5.6 | 5.6 | 5.6 | 4.9 | 5.8 | 5.7 | 6.0 | 5.4 | 3.5 | 2.9 | 1.9 | 1.9 | 3.3 | -1.1 | -0.3 | -10.4 | | | | | | |
| 1992 | 5.4 | 5.3 | 5.6 | 4.6 | 5.5 | 5.4 | 5.7 | 5.0 | 3.1 | 2.5 | 1.4 | 1.3 | 2.5 | -1.9 | -1.7 | -10.8 | | | | | | |
| 1993 | 5.5 | 5.5 | 5.7 | 4.8 | 5.7 | 5.6 | 5.8 | 5.2 | 3.4 | 2.9 | 1.9 | 1.9 | 3.1 | -0.7 | 0.2 | -4.3 | | | | | | |
| 1994 | 5.4 | 5.3 | 5.6 | 4.6 | 5.5 | 5.4 | 5.6 | 5.0 | 3.2 | 2.7 | 1.7 | 1.7 | 2.8 | -0.9 | -0.3 | -4.3 | | | | | | |
| 1995 | 5.4 | 5.3 | 5.6 | 4.7 | 5.5 | 5.7 | 5.7 | 5.1 | 3.3 | 2.8 | 1.9 | 1.9 | 3.0 | -0.4 | 0.4 | -2.4 | 6.9 | | | | | |
| 1996 | 5.6 | 5.6 | 5.8 | 4.9 | 5.8 | 5.7 | 6.0 | 5.4 | 3.8 | 3.3 | 2.5 | 2.6 | 3.9 | 0.9 | 2.2 | 1.1 | 14.7 | | | | | |

## Canada Long-Horizon Equity Risk Premia

in Local Currency (Canadian Dollar – CAD)
in Percent

| End Date | Start Date | | | | | | | | | | | | | | | | | | | | | |
|---|---|---|---|---|---|---|---|---|---|---|---|---|---|---|---|---|---|---|---|---|---|---|
| | 1919 | 1920 | 1925 | 1930 | 1935 | 1940 | 1945 | 1950 | 1955 | 1960 | 1965 | 1970 | 1975 | 1980 | 1985 | 1990 | 1995 | 2000 | 2005 | 2010 | 2015 | 2016 |
| 1997 | 5.7 | 5.6 | 5.9 | 5.0 | 5.9 | 5.8 | 6.1 | 5.6 | 4.0 | 3.5 | 2.8 | 3.0 | 4.2 | 1.5 | 3.0 | 2.5 | 13.7 | | | | | |
| 1998 | 5.5 | 5.5 | 5.8 | 4.9 | 5.7 | 5.6 | 5.9 | 5.4 | 3.8 | 3.3 | 2.6 | 2.7 | 3.8 | 1.2 | 2.4 | 1.7 | 9.2 | | | | | |
| 1999 | 6.0 | 6.0 | 6.2 | 5.4 | 6.3 | 6.2 | 6.5 | 6.1 | 4.6 | 4.3 | 3.6 | 4.0 | 5.3 | 3.2 | 5.0 | 5.6 | 15.4 | | | | | |
| 2000 | 5.9 | 5.9 | 6.2 | 5.4 | 6.2 | 6.2 | 6.5 | 6.0 | 4.6 | 4.2 | 3.6 | 3.9 | 5.2 | 3.2 | 4.9 | 5.4 | 13.4 | 3.3 | | | | |
| 2001 | 5.6 | 5.6 | 5.8 | 5.0 | 5.8 | 5.7 | 6.0 | 5.5 | 4.0 | 3.6 | 3.0 | 3.2 | 4.3 | 2.1 | 3.4 | 3.2 | 8.5 | -8.8 | | | | |
| 2002 | 5.3 | 5.3 | 5.5 | 4.7 | 5.4 | 5.3 | 5.6 | 5.0 | 3.5 | 3.1 | 2.4 | 2.5 | 3.4 | 1.1 | 2.1 | 1.4 | 5.0 | -12.3 | | | | |
| 2003 | 5.5 | 5.5 | 5.7 | 4.9 | 5.7 | 5.6 | 5.8 | 5.3 | 3.9 | 3.5 | 2.9 | 3.0 | 4.0 | 2.0 | 3.1 | 2.9 | 6.9 | -3.8 | | | | |
| 2004 | 5.6 | 5.5 | 5.7 | 5.0 | 5.7 | 5.7 | 5.9 | 5.4 | 4.0 | 3.6 | 3.0 | 3.2 | 4.2 | 2.3 | 3.4 | 3.3 | 7.1 | -1.3 | | | | |
| 2005 | 5.7 | 5.7 | 5.9 | 5.2 | 5.9 | 5.9 | 6.1 | 5.7 | 4.3 | 4.0 | 3.5 | 3.7 | 4.7 | 3.0 | 4.3 | 4.4 | 8.3 | 2.4 | 21.0 | | | |
| 2006 | 5.8 | 5.8 | 6.0 | 5.3 | 6.1 | 6.0 | 6.3 | 5.8 | 4.5 | 4.2 | 3.7 | 4.0 | 5.0 | 3.4 | 4.7 | 4.9 | 8.8 | 4.0 | 17.4 | | | |
| 2007 | 5.8 | 5.8 | 6.0 | 5.3 | 6.1 | 6.0 | 6.3 | 5.8 | 4.6 | 4.3 | 3.8 | 4.0 | 5.1 | 3.5 | 4.7 | 5.0 | 8.6 | 4.3 | 13.6 | | | |
| 2008 | 5.4 | 5.3 | 5.5 | 4.8 | 5.5 | 5.4 | 5.6 | 5.1 | 3.8 | 3.5 | 2.9 | 3.0 | 3.9 | 2.1 | 3.1 | 2.9 | 5.4 | -0.1 | 1.4 | | | |
| 2009 | 5.6 | 5.6 | 5.8 | 5.1 | 5.8 | 5.8 | 6.0 | 5.5 | 4.3 | 4.0 | 3.5 | 3.7 | 4.6 | 3.1 | 4.1 | 4.2 | 7.1 | 2.9 | 7.1 | | | |
| 2010 | 5.7 | 5.7 | 5.9 | 5.2 | 5.9 | 5.8 | 6.1 | 5.6 | 4.4 | 4.1 | 3.6 | 3.9 | 4.8 | 3.3 | 4.4 | 4.6 | 7.3 | 3.6 | 7.7 | 11.1 | | |
| 2011 | 5.5 | 5.5 | 5.7 | 5.0 | 5.6 | 5.6 | 5.8 | 5.3 | 4.1 | 3.8 | 3.3 | 3.5 | 4.3 | 2.8 | 3.8 | 3.7 | 6.1 | 2.2 | 4.7 | -1.1 | | |
| 2012 | 5.5 | 5.5 | 5.7 | 5.0 | 5.6 | 5.6 | 5.8 | 5.3 | 4.1 | 3.8 | 3.3 | 3.5 | 4.3 | 2.9 | 3.8 | 3.8 | 6.1 | 2.4 | 4.8 | 0.9 | | |
| 2013 | 5.5 | 5.6 | 5.7 | 5.0 | 5.7 | 5.6 | 5.8 | 5.4 | 4.2 | 3.9 | 3.5 | 3.7 | 4.5 | 3.1 | 4.1 | 4.1 | 6.3 | 3.1 | 5.5 | 3.5 | | |
| 2014 | 5.6 | 5.6 | 5.8 | 5.1 | 5.7 | 5.7 | 5.9 | 5.5 | 4.3 | 4.0 | 3.6 | 3.8 | 4.6 | 3.3 | 4.2 | 4.3 | 6.4 | 3.4 | 5.8 | 4.5 | | |
| 2015 | 5.4 | 5.4 | 5.6 | 4.9 | 5.5 | 5.5 | 5.6 | 5.2 | 4.1 | 3.8 | 3.3 | 3.5 | 4.2 | 2.9 | 3.7 | 3.7 | 5.6 | 2.6 | 4.3 | 2.0 | -10.4 | |
| 2016 | 5.6 | 5.5 | 5.7 | 5.1 | 5.7 | 5.6 | 5.8 | 5.4 | 4.3 | 4.0 | 3.6 | 3.8 | 4.6 | 3.3 | 4.2 | 4.3 | 6.3 | 3.5 | 5.6 | 4.5 | 4.4 | 19.3 |

Source of underlying data: 1.) Morningstar *Direct* database. Used with permission. All rights reserved. All calculations performed by Duff & Phelps LLC.

## Canada Long-Horizon Equity Risk Premia

in U.S. Dollars (USD)

in Percent

| End Date | Start Date 1919 | 1920 | 1925 | 1930 | 1935 | 1940 | 1945 | 1950 | 1955 | 1960 | 1965 | 1970 | 1975 | 1980 | 1985 | 1990 | 1995 | 2000 | 2005 | 2010 | 2015 | 2016 |
|---|---|---|---|---|---|---|---|---|---|---|---|---|---|---|---|---|---|---|---|---|---|---|
| 1919 | -0.4 | | | | | | | | | | | | | | | | | | | | | |
| 1920 | -8.3 | -16.2 | | | | | | | | | | | | | | | | | | | | |
| 1921 | -4.7 | -6.8 | | | | | | | | | | | | | | | | | | | | |
| 1922 | 2.5 | 3.4 | | | | | | | | | | | | | | | | | | | | |
| 1923 | 2.3 | 3.0 | | | | | | | | | | | | | | | | | | | | |
| 1924 | 3.3 | 4.1 | | | | | | | | | | | | | | | | | | | | |
| 1925 | 5.1 | 6.0 | 15.4 | | | | | | | | | | | | | | | | | | | |
| 1926 | 6.9 | 7.9 | 17.5 | | | | | | | | | | | | | | | | | | | |
| 1927 | 10.6 | 12.0 | 25.1 | | | | | | | | | | | | | | | | | | | |
| 1928 | 12.4 | 13.8 | 25.9 | | | | | | | | | | | | | | | | | | | |
| 1929 | 9.7 | 10.7 | 17.2 | | | | | | | | | | | | | | | | | | | |
| 1930 | 5.9 | 6.5 | 8.5 | -35.0 | | | | | | | | | | | | | | | | | | |
| 1931 | 1.9 | 2.0 | 0.6 | -41.1 | | | | | | | | | | | | | | | | | | |
| 1932 | 0.7 | 0.7 | -1.3 | -32.3 | | | | | | | | | | | | | | | | | | |
| 1933 | 5.1 | 5.5 | 6.3 | -7.5 | | | | | | | | | | | | | | | | | | |
| 1934 | 5.9 | 6.3 | 7.4 | -2.5 | | | | | | | | | | | | | | | | | | |
| 1935 | 7.0 | 7.5 | 9.0 | 2.2 | 25.5 | | | | | | | | | | | | | | | | | |
| 1936 | 7.9 | 8.4 | 10.2 | 5.1 | 24.3 | | | | | | | | | | | | | | | | | |
| 1937 | 6.5 | 6.9 | 7.9 | 2.1 | 9.8 | | | | | | | | | | | | | | | | | |
| 1938 | 6.4 | 6.8 | 7.8 | 2.5 | 8.8 | | | | | | | | | | | | | | | | | |
| 1939 | 5.6 | 5.9 | 6.5 | 1.1 | 4.7 | | | | | | | | | | | | | | | | | |
| 1940 | 4.3 | 4.5 | 4.7 | -1.1 | 0.2 | -22.4 | | | | | | | | | | | | | | | | |
| 1941 | 4.1 | 4.3 | 4.3 | -1.1 | 0.0 | -11.8 | | | | | | | | | | | | | | | | |
| 1942 | 4.4 | 4.6 | 4.7 | -0.1 | 1.3 | -4.2 | | | | | | | | | | | | | | | | |
| 1943 | 4.8 | 5.1 | 5.3 | 1.1 | 3.0 | 1.0 | | | | | | | | | | | | | | | | |
| 1944 | 5.1 | 5.3 | 5.6 | 1.7 | 3.8 | 2.9 | | | | | | | | | | | | | | | | |
| 1945 | 6.1 | 6.4 | 6.9 | 3.7 | 6.5 | 7.9 | 33.1 | | | | | | | | | | | | | | | |
| 1946 | 5.9 | 6.2 | 6.6 | 3.5 | 6.0 | 6.9 | 17.1 | | | | | | | | | | | | | | | |
| 1947 | 5.4 | 5.6 | 5.9 | 2.8 | 4.8 | 4.9 | 8.2 | | | | | | | | | | | | | | | |
| 1948 | 5.7 | 5.9 | 6.3 | 3.4 | 5.5 | 5.9 | 9.7 | | | | | | | | | | | | | | | |
| 1949 | 6.0 | 6.2 | 6.6 | 3.9 | 6.1 | 6.8 | 10.7 | | | | | | | | | | | | | | | |
| 1950 | 7.0 | 7.3 | 7.9 | 5.6 | 8.2 | 9.8 | 15.5 | 39.8 | | | | | | | | | | | | | | |
| 1951 | 8.0 | 8.3 | 9.1 | 7.2 | 10.1 | 12.3 | 19.0 | 39.8 | | | | | | | | | | | | | | |
| 1952 | 7.8 | 8.1 | 8.8 | 6.9 | 9.5 | 11.4 | 16.7 | 26.8 | | | | | | | | | | | | | | |
| 1953 | 7.5 | 7.8 | 8.4 | 6.5 | 8.9 | 10.4 | 14.6 | 19.6 | | | | | | | | | | | | | | |
| 1954 | 8.3 | 8.6 | 9.3 | 7.8 | 10.3 | 12.2 | 16.9 | 23.1 | | | | | | | | | | | | | | |
| 1955 | 8.7 | 8.9 | 9.7 | 8.3 | 10.8 | 12.7 | 17.2 | 22.7 | 20.5 | | | | | | | | | | | | | |
| 1956 | 8.8 | 9.1 | 9.8 | 8.5 | 11.0 | 12.8 | 17.0 | 21.4 | 17.3 | | | | | | | | | | | | | |
| 1957 | 7.9 | 8.1 | 8.7 | 7.2 | 9.3 | 10.6 | 13.6 | 15.4 | 2.7 | | | | | | | | | | | | | |

Data Exhibit 1-10

## Canada Long-Horizon Equity Risk Premia

in U.S. Dollars (USD)
in Percent

| End Date | 1919 | 1920 | 1925 | 1930 | 1935 | 1940 | 1945 | 1950 | 1955 | 1960 | 1965 | 1970 | 1975 | 1980 | 1985 | 1990 | 1995 |
|---|---|---|---|---|---|---|---|---|---|---|---|---|---|---|---|---|---|
| 1958 | 8.5 | 8.7 | 9.4 | 8.0 | 10.2 | 11.6 | 14.8 | 17.0 | 9.5 | | | | | | | | |
| 1959 | 8.3 | 8.5 | 9.1 | 7.8 | 9.8 | 11.1 | 13.9 | 15.4 | 7.8 | | | | | | | | |
| 1960 | 7.9 | 8.1 | 8.7 | 7.3 | 9.2 | 10.2 | 12.5 | 13.3 | 5.2 | -7.8 | | | | | | | |
| 1961 | 8.2 | 8.4 | 9.0 | 7.7 | 9.6 | 10.7 | 13.0 | 14.0 | 7.6 | 7.0 | | | | | | | |
| 1962 | 7.7 | 7.9 | 8.4 | 7.0 | 8.7 | 9.6 | 11.5 | 11.8 | 4.8 | -0.3 | | | | | | | |
| 1963 | 7.8 | 7.9 | 8.4 | 7.1 | 8.8 | 9.7 | 11.4 | 11.7 | 5.4 | 2.3 | | | | | | | |
| 1964 | 8.0 | 8.2 | 8.7 | 7.5 | 9.2 | 10.1 | 11.9 | 12.3 | 6.9 | 6.1 | | | | | | | |
| 1965 | 7.9 | 8.1 | 8.6 | 7.4 | 8.9 | 9.8 | 11.4 | 11.6 | 6.4 | 5.3 | 1.4 | | | | | | |
| 1966 | 7.5 | 7.6 | 8.0 | 6.8 | 8.3 | 8.9 | 10.3 | 10.2 | 4.8 | 2.6 | -5.9 | | | | | | |
| 1967 | 7.6 | 7.7 | 8.1 | 7.0 | 8.4 | 9.0 | 10.4 | 10.3 | 5.4 | 3.9 | 0.2 | | | | | | |
| 1968 | 7.7 | 7.9 | 8.3 | 7.2 | 8.6 | 9.3 | 10.6 | 10.6 | 6.2 | 5.3 | 4.4 | | | | | | |
| 1969 | 7.4 | 7.6 | 8.0 | 6.8 | 8.1 | 8.7 | 9.9 | 9.7 | 5.2 | 4.0 | 1.8 | | | | | | |
| 1970 | 7.4 | 7.6 | 8.0 | 6.8 | 8.1 | 8.7 | 9.8 | 9.6 | 5.4 | 4.2 | 2.7 | 7.2 | | | | | |
| 1971 | 7.4 | 7.6 | 7.9 | 6.8 | 8.1 | 8.6 | 9.7 | 9.5 | 5.5 | 4.5 | 3.4 | 7.1 | | | | | |
| 1972 | 7.8 | 7.9 | 8.3 | 7.3 | 8.6 | 9.2 | 10.3 | 10.2 | 6.6 | 6.2 | 6.2 | 13.5 | | | | | |
| 1973 | 7.4 | 7.6 | 7.9 | 6.9 | 8.1 | 8.6 | 9.6 | 9.3 | 5.7 | 5.0 | 4.4 | 7.5 | | | | | |
| 1974 | 6.7 | 6.8 | 7.1 | 6.0 | 7.0 | 7.3 | 8.1 | 7.6 | 3.7 | 2.3 | 0.5 | -0.9 | | | | | |
| 1975 | 6.7 | 6.8 | 7.1 | 6.0 | 7.0 | 7.3 | 8.0 | 7.5 | 3.8 | 2.6 | 1.0 | 0.3 | 6.6 | | | | |
| 1976 | 6.6 | 6.7 | 6.9 | 5.8 | 6.8 | 7.1 | 7.8 | 7.3 | 3.7 | 2.5 | 1.0 | 0.3 | 3.5 | | | | |
| 1977 | 6.3 | 6.4 | 6.6 | 5.5 | 6.5 | 6.7 | 7.3 | 6.7 | 3.1 | 1.8 | 0.1 | -0.9 | -0.9 | | | | |
| 1978 | 6.4 | 6.5 | 6.7 | 5.7 | 6.6 | 6.8 | 7.4 | 6.9 | 3.5 | 2.3 | 1.0 | 0.5 | 2.4 | | | | |
| 1979 | 7.0 | 7.1 | 7.4 | 6.4 | 7.4 | 7.7 | 8.4 | 8.0 | 5.0 | 4.3 | 3.7 | 4.7 | 10.3 | | | | |
| 1980 | 7.1 | 7.2 | 7.4 | 6.5 | 7.5 | 7.8 | 8.5 | 8.1 | 5.3 | 4.7 | 4.2 | 5.3 | 10.5 | 11.3 | | | |
| 1981 | 6.6 | 6.7 | 6.9 | 5.9 | 6.8 | 7.0 | 7.6 | 7.1 | 4.2 | 3.4 | 2.6 | 2.9 | 5.6 | -6.4 | | | |
| 1982 | 6.3 | 6.4 | 6.6 | 5.6 | 6.4 | 6.6 | 7.1 | 6.5 | 3.6 | 2.7 | 1.7 | 1.7 | 3.4 | -8.3 | | | |
| 1983 | 6.5 | 6.6 | 6.8 | 5.9 | 6.7 | 7.0 | 7.5 | 7.0 | 4.2 | 3.5 | 2.8 | 3.2 | 5.4 | -0.7 | | | |
| 1984 | 6.1 | 6.2 | 6.4 | 5.4 | 6.2 | 6.4 | 6.8 | 6.3 | 3.5 | 2.6 | 1.7 | 1.7 | 3.0 | -4.4 | | | |
| 1985 | 6.1 | 6.2 | 6.4 | 5.4 | 6.2 | 6.3 | 6.8 | 6.2 | 3.5 | 2.7 | 1.9 | 1.9 | 3.2 | -2.8 | 5.2 | | |
| 1986 | 6.0 | 6.1 | 6.3 | 5.3 | 6.1 | 6.2 | 6.6 | 6.1 | 3.4 | 2.6 | 1.8 | 1.8 | 3.0 | -2.3 | 3.0 | | |
| 1987 | 6.0 | 6.1 | 6.3 | 5.3 | 6.1 | 6.2 | 6.6 | 6.0 | 3.5 | 2.7 | 2.0 | 2.0 | 3.1 | -1.4 | 3.5 | | |
| 1988 | 6.0 | 6.1 | 6.3 | 5.3 | 6.1 | 6.2 | 6.6 | 6.1 | 3.6 | 2.8 | 2.2 | 2.2 | 3.4 | -0.5 | 4.4 | | |
| 1989 | 6.1 | 6.2 | 6.4 | 5.5 | 6.2 | 6.4 | 6.8 | 6.3 | 3.9 | 3.2 | 2.7 | 2.9 | 4.1 | 1.0 | 6.4 | | |
| 1990 | 5.7 | 5.8 | 6.0 | 5.0 | 5.7 | 5.8 | 6.1 | 5.6 | 3.2 | 2.4 | 1.7 | 1.7 | 2.5 | -1.1 | 1.7 | -22.2 | |
| 1991 | 5.7 | 5.8 | 5.9 | 5.0 | 5.6 | 5.7 | 6.0 | 5.5 | 3.1 | 2.4 | 1.7 | 1.7 | 2.4 | -0.9 | 1.7 | -10.3 | |
| 1992 | 5.4 | 5.4 | 5.5 | 4.6 | 5.2 | 5.3 | 5.5 | 4.9 | 2.5 | 1.7 | 0.9 | 0.7 | 1.2 | -2.3 | -1.0 | -13.4 | |
| 1993 | 5.4 | 5.5 | 5.6 | 4.7 | 5.3 | 5.4 | 5.6 | 5.0 | 2.7 | 2.0 | 1.3 | 1.2 | 1.7 | -1.4 | 0.3 | -7.4 | |
| 1994 | 5.2 | 5.3 | 5.4 | 4.5 | 5.1 | 5.1 | 5.3 | 4.7 | 2.4 | 1.6 | 0.9 | 0.7 | 1.1 | -1.9 | -0.7 | -7.9 | |
| 1995 | 5.3 | 5.4 | 5.4 | 4.6 | 5.1 | 5.2 | 5.4 | 4.8 | 2.6 | 1.9 | 1.2 | 1.1 | 1.6 | -1.2 | 0.3 | -4.9 | 10.0 |
| 1996 | 5.5 | 5.6 | 5.7 | 4.8 | 5.4 | 5.5 | 5.7 | 5.2 | 3.1 | 2.4 | 1.8 | 1.8 | 2.5 | 0.2 | 2.1 | -1.1 | 15.9 |

Start Date

## Canada Long-Horizon Equity Risk Premia

in U.S. Dollars (USD)
in Percent

| End Date | Start Date 1919 | 1920 | 1925 | 1930 | 1935 | 1940 | 1945 | 1950 | 1955 | 1960 | 1965 | 1970 | 1975 | 1980 | 1985 | 1990 | 1995 | 2000 | 2005 | 2010 | 2015 | 2016 |
|---|---|---|---|---|---|---|---|---|---|---|---|---|---|---|---|---|---|---|---|---|---|---|
| 1997 | 5.5 | 5.6 | 5.7 | 4.8 | 5.4 | 5.5 | 5.7 | 5.2 | 3.1 | 2.5 | 2.0 | 2.0 | 2.7 | 0.5 | 2.4 | -0.1 | 12.9 | | | | | |
| 1998 | 5.3 | 5.4 | 5.5 | 4.6 | 5.2 | 5.2 | 5.4 | 4.9 | 2.8 | 2.2 | 1.6 | 1.6 | 2.1 | -0.1 | 1.5 | -1.3 | 7.0 | | | | | |
| 1999 | 5.8 | 5.9 | 6.0 | 5.2 | 5.8 | 5.9 | 6.2 | 5.8 | 3.8 | 3.4 | 3.0 | 3.2 | 4.0 | 2.4 | 4.6 | 3.7 | 15.3 | | | | | |
| 2000 | 5.8 | 5.8 | 6.0 | 5.2 | 5.8 | 5.8 | 6.1 | 5.7 | 3.8 | 3.3 | 2.9 | 3.0 | 3.8 | 2.3 | 4.3 | 3.4 | 12.7 | -0.2 | | | | |
| 2001 | 5.4 | 5.5 | 5.6 | 4.7 | 5.3 | 5.3 | 5.5 | 5.1 | 3.1 | 2.6 | 2.1 | 2.2 | 2.7 | 1.0 | 2.6 | 1.0 | 7.3 | -12.8 | | | | |
| 2002 | 5.1 | 5.2 | 5.2 | 4.4 | 4.9 | 5.0 | 5.1 | 4.6 | 2.7 | 2.1 | 1.6 | 1.5 | 2.0 | 0.1 | 1.4 | -0.5 | 4.0 | -14.7 | | | | |
| 2003 | 5.6 | 5.7 | 5.8 | 5.0 | 5.6 | 5.6 | 5.9 | 5.4 | 3.6 | 3.2 | 2.8 | 2.9 | 3.6 | 2.2 | 3.9 | 3.0 | 9.0 | 1.2 | | | | |
| 2004 | 5.8 | 5.8 | 5.9 | 5.2 | 5.7 | 5.8 | 6.1 | 5.6 | 3.9 | 3.5 | 3.1 | 3.3 | 4.0 | 2.8 | 4.6 | 3.9 | 9.8 | 4.4 | | | | |
| 2005 | 6.0 | 6.0 | 6.2 | 5.4 | 6.0 | 6.1 | 6.4 | 6.0 | 4.3 | 3.9 | 3.7 | 3.9 | 4.7 | 3.6 | 5.5 | 5.2 | 11.1 | 7.7 | 24.1 | | | |
| 2006 | 6.1 | 6.1 | 6.3 | 5.6 | 6.1 | 6.2 | 6.5 | 6.1 | 4.5 | 4.1 | 3.9 | 4.2 | 5.0 | 4.0 | 5.9 | 5.7 | 11.4 | 8.6 | 19.1 | | | |
| 2007 | 6.3 | 6.4 | 6.5 | 5.8 | 6.4 | 6.5 | 6.8 | 6.4 | 4.9 | 4.6 | 4.4 | 4.7 | 5.6 | 4.8 | 6.7 | 6.8 | 12.5 | 10.7 | 21.2 | | | |
| 2008 | 5.7 | 5.7 | 5.8 | 5.1 | 5.6 | 5.7 | 5.9 | 5.5 | 3.9 | 3.5 | 3.2 | 3.4 | 4.0 | 2.9 | 4.4 | 3.9 | 8.1 | 4.1 | 3.8 | | | |
| 2009 | 6.2 | 6.3 | 6.4 | 5.7 | 6.3 | 6.4 | 6.6 | 6.3 | 4.8 | 4.5 | 4.3 | 4.6 | 5.4 | 4.6 | 6.4 | 6.4 | 11.1 | 9.0 | 13.6 | | | |
| 2010 | 6.3 | 6.4 | 6.5 | 5.9 | 6.4 | 6.5 | 6.8 | 6.5 | 5.0 | 4.7 | 4.6 | 4.9 | 5.7 | 5.0 | 6.8 | 6.9 | 11.5 | 9.7 | 14.2 | 17.2 | | |
| 2011 | 6.1 | 6.1 | 6.3 | 5.6 | 6.1 | 6.2 | 6.5 | 6.1 | 4.6 | 4.3 | 4.2 | 4.4 | 5.2 | 4.4 | 6.0 | 5.9 | 9.9 | 7.6 | 10.0 | 0.9 | | |
| 2012 | 6.1 | 6.2 | 6.3 | 5.6 | 6.1 | 6.2 | 6.5 | 6.2 | 4.7 | 4.4 | 4.2 | 4.5 | 5.2 | 4.4 | 6.0 | 5.9 | 9.8 | 7.6 | 9.7 | 3.1 | | |
| 2013 | 6.1 | 6.1 | 6.3 | 5.6 | 6.1 | 6.2 | 6.5 | 6.1 | 4.7 | 4.4 | 4.2 | 4.5 | 5.2 | 4.4 | 6.0 | 5.9 | 9.5 | 7.4 | 9.0 | 3.3 | | |
| 2014 | 6.0 | 6.1 | 6.2 | 5.5 | 6.0 | 6.1 | 6.4 | 6.0 | 4.6 | 4.3 | 4.1 | 4.4 | 5.1 | 4.3 | 5.7 | 5.6 | 9.0 | 6.9 | 8.1 | 2.6 | | |
| 2015 | 5.7 | 5.7 | 5.8 | 5.2 | 5.6 | 5.7 | 5.9 | 5.5 | 4.1 | 3.8 | 3.6 | 3.7 | 4.3 | 3.5 | 4.7 | 4.4 | 7.3 | 4.9 | 5.1 | -2.1 | -25.3 | |
| 2016 | 5.9 | 5.9 | 6.0 | 5.4 | 5.9 | 5.9 | 6.2 | 5.8 | 4.4 | 4.1 | 3.9 | 4.2 | 4.8 | 4.0 | 5.3 | 5.1 | 8.1 | 5.9 | 6.6 | 1.6 | -1.0 | 23.4 |

Source of underlying data: 1.) Morningstar *Direct* database. Used with permission. All rights reserved. All calculations performed by Duff & Phelps LLC.

## Canada Short-Horizon Equity Risk Premia

in Local Currency (Canadian Dollar – CAD)
in Percent

| End Date | 1919 | 1920 | 1925 | 1930 | 1935 | 1940 | 1945 | 1950 | 1955 |
|---|---|---|---|---|---|---|---|---|---|
| 1919 | 7.8 | | | | | | | | |
| 1920 | -2.9 | -13.6 | | | | | | | |
| 1921 | -4.4 | -10.6 | | | | | | | |
| 1922 | 1.7 | -0.4 | | | | | | | |
| 1923 | 1.9 | 0.4 | | | | | | | |
| 1924 | 2.8 | 1.8 | | | | | | | |
| 1925 | 4.7 | 4.1 | 16.0 | | | | | | |
| 1926 | 6.6 | 6.4 | 18.0 | | | | | | |
| 1927 | 10.4 | 10.7 | 25.6 | | | | | | |
| 1928 | 12.1 | 12.6 | 26.2 | | | | | | |
| 1929 | 9.4 | 9.6 | 17.4 | | | | | | |
| 1930 | 5.8 | 5.6 | 8.8 | -34.7 | | | | | |
| 1931 | 2.6 | 2.1 | 2.4 | -35.1 | | | | | |
| 1932 | 1.3 | 0.8 | 0.1 | -28.7 | | | | | |
| 1933 | 4.5 | 4.3 | 5.7 | -9.0 | | | | | |
| 1934 | 5.5 | 5.3 | 7.1 | -3.3 | | | | | |
| 1935 | 6.9 | 6.8 | 9.1 | 2.2 | 29.5 | | | | |
| 1936 | 7.8 | 7.8 | 10.4 | 5.3 | 27.0 | | | | |
| 1937 | 6.6 | 6.5 | 8.3 | 2.6 | 12.5 | | | | |
| 1938 | 6.7 | 6.6 | 8.3 | 3.3 | 11.5 | | | | |
| 1939 | 6.3 | 6.2 | 7.7 | 2.9 | 9.1 | | | | |
| 1940 | 5.1 | 5.0 | 6.0 | 0.8 | 4.3 | -19.9 | | | |
| 1941 | 5.0 | 4.8 | 5.7 | 0.9 | 3.8 | -9.3 | | | |
| 1942 | 5.3 | 5.2 | 6.2 | 1.8 | 5.0 | -1.7 | | | |
| 1943 | 5.9 | 5.8 | 6.8 | 3.1 | 6.6 | 3.5 | | | |
| 1944 | 6.1 | 6.1 | 7.2 | 3.7 | 7.3 | 5.4 | | | |
| 1945 | 7.2 | 7.2 | 8.5 | 5.7 | 9.8 | 10.5 | 35.7 | | |
| 1946 | 6.9 | 6.9 | 8.0 | 5.3 | 8.9 | 8.7 | 16.9 | | |
| 1947 | 6.7 | 6.6 | 7.7 | 5.0 | 8.2 | 7.6 | 11.2 | | |
| 1948 | 6.8 | 6.8 | 7.9 | 5.3 | 8.4 | 8.1 | 11.4 | | |
| 1949 | 7.3 | 7.3 | 8.4 | 6.2 | 9.3 | 9.5 | 13.5 | | |
| 1950 | 8.6 | 8.6 | 9.9 | 8.2 | 11.8 | 13.0 | 19.2 | 47.9 | |
| 1951 | 9.0 | 9.1 | 10.4 | 8.9 | 12.4 | 13.8 | 19.8 | 35.6 | |
| 1952 | 8.7 | 8.8 | 10.0 | 8.4 | 11.7 | 12.7 | 17.2 | 23.2 | |
| 1953 | 8.5 | 8.5 | 9.7 | 8.1 | 11.1 | 11.8 | 15.3 | 17.5 | |
| 1954 | 9.3 | 9.4 | 10.6 | 9.3 | 12.4 | 13.5 | 17.5 | 21.5 | |
| 1955 | 9.8 | 9.8 | 11.1 | 9.9 | 13.1 | 14.3 | 18.3 | 22.3 | 26.3 |
| 1956 | 9.8 | 9.8 | 11.1 | 9.9 | 12.9 | 14.1 | 17.7 | 20.6 | 18.3 |
| 1957 | 8.9 | 8.9 | 10.0 | 8.7 | 11.3 | 11.9 | 14.4 | 15.0 | 4.1 |

Start Date

# Canada Short-Horizon Equity Risk Premia

in Local Currency (Canadian Dollar – CAD)
in Percent

| End Date | Start Date 1919 | 1920 | 1925 | 1930 | 1935 | 1940 | 1945 | 1950 | 1955 | 1960 | 1965 | 1970 | 1975 | 1980 | 1985 | 1990 | 1995 | 2000 | 2005 | 2010 | 2015 | 2016 |
|---|---|---|---|---|---|---|---|---|---|---|---|---|---|---|---|---|---|---|---|---|---|---|
| 1958 | 9.4 | 9.5 | 10.6 | 9.4 | 12.0 | 12.8 | 15.5 | 16.6 | 10.3 | | | | | | | | | | | | | |
| 1959 | 9.2 | 9.2 | 10.3 | 9.1 | 11.6 | 12.2 | 14.4 | 14.9 | 8.2 | | | | | | | | | | | | | |
| 1960 | 8.9 | 8.9 | 9.9 | 8.7 | 11.0 | 11.5 | 13.4 | 13.4 | 6.6 | -1.7 | | | | | | | | | | | | |
| 1961 | 9.4 | 9.4 | 10.5 | 9.4 | 11.7 | 12.4 | 14.4 | 14.7 | 9.9 | 14.1 | | | | | | | | | | | | |
| 1962 | 8.9 | 9.0 | 9.9 | 8.8 | 10.9 | 11.3 | 13.0 | 12.8 | 7.3 | 5.7 | | | | | | | | | | | | |
| 1963 | 9.0 | 9.0 | 10.0 | 8.9 | 11.0 | 11.4 | 12.9 | 12.7 | 7.8 | 7.2 | | | | | | | | | | | | |
| 1964 | 9.3 | 9.3 | 10.3 | 9.2 | 11.3 | 11.8 | 13.3 | 13.3 | 9.2 | 10.1 | | | | | | | | | | | | |
| 1965 | 9.1 | 9.2 | 10.1 | 9.0 | 11.0 | 11.4 | 12.8 | 12.6 | 8.6 | 8.9 | 2.7 | | | | | | | | | | | |
| 1966 | 8.7 | 8.7 | 9.5 | 8.5 | 10.3 | 10.5 | 11.7 | 11.2 | 6.8 | 5.9 | -4.8 | | | | | | | | | | | |
| 1967 | 8.8 | 8.8 | 9.6 | 8.6 | 10.4 | 10.6 | 11.8 | 11.3 | 7.4 | 6.8 | 1.3 | | | | | | | | | | | |
| 1968 | 8.9 | 9.0 | 9.8 | 8.8 | 10.6 | 10.8 | 12.0 | 11.5 | 8.0 | 7.8 | 5.0 | | | | | | | | | | | |
| 1969 | 8.6 | 8.6 | 9.4 | 8.4 | 10.0 | 10.2 | 11.1 | 10.6 | 6.9 | 6.2 | 2.3 | | | | | | | | | | | |
| 1970 | 8.5 | 8.5 | 9.2 | 8.2 | 9.8 | 9.9 | 10.8 | 10.1 | 6.6 | 5.8 | 2.2 | 1.7 | | | | | | | | | | |
| 1971 | 8.5 | 8.5 | 9.2 | 8.2 | 9.8 | 9.9 | 10.7 | 10.1 | 6.7 | 6.1 | 3.2 | 5.4 | | | | | | | | | | |
| 1972 | 8.9 | 8.9 | 9.6 | 8.7 | 10.3 | 10.5 | 11.4 | 10.9 | 8.0 | 7.8 | 6.4 | 13.3 | | | | | | | | | | |
| 1973 | 8.5 | 8.6 | 9.3 | 8.3 | 9.8 | 9.9 | 10.7 | 10.1 | 7.1 | 6.7 | 4.8 | 7.9 | | | | | | | | | | |
| 1974 | 7.8 | 7.8 | 8.4 | 7.4 | 8.7 | 8.6 | 9.2 | 8.3 | 5.0 | 3.9 | 0.8 | -0.8 | | | | | | | | | | |
| 1975 | 7.8 | 7.8 | 8.4 | 7.4 | 8.7 | 8.7 | 9.2 | 8.4 | 5.2 | 4.3 | 1.7 | 1.1 | 10.7 | | | | | | | | | |
| 1976 | 7.7 | 7.7 | 8.2 | 7.3 | 8.5 | 8.4 | 8.9 | 8.1 | 5.0 | 4.0 | 1.5 | 0.9 | 5.2 | | | | | | | | | |
| 1977 | 7.5 | 7.5 | 8.1 | 7.1 | 8.3 | 8.2 | 8.6 | 7.7 | 4.7 | 3.7 | 1.3 | 0.6 | 2.9 | | | | | | | | | |
| 1978 | 7.8 | 7.8 | 8.3 | 7.4 | 8.6 | 8.5 | 9.0 | 8.2 | 5.4 | 4.7 | 2.7 | 3.0 | 7.6 | | | | | | | | | |
| 1979 | 8.2 | 8.3 | 8.8 | 8.0 | 9.2 | 9.3 | 9.8 | 9.2 | 6.7 | 6.3 | 5.1 | 6.5 | 13.7 | | | | | | | | | |
| 1980 | 8.3 | 8.3 | 8.9 | 8.0 | 9.3 | 9.3 | 9.8 | 9.2 | 6.9 | 6.5 | 5.4 | 6.8 | 13.2 | 10.3 | | | | | | | | |
| 1981 | 7.7 | 7.7 | 8.2 | 7.3 | 8.4 | 8.3 | 8.7 | 8.0 | 5.5 | 4.8 | 3.3 | 3.7 | 6.8 | -10.4 | | | | | | | | |
| 1982 | 7.4 | 7.4 | 7.9 | 7.0 | 8.0 | 7.9 | 8.3 | 7.5 | 4.9 | 4.2 | 2.6 | 2.7 | 4.9 | -9.9 | | | | | | | | |
| 1983 | 7.7 | 7.7 | 8.2 | 7.3 | 8.4 | 8.3 | 8.7 | 7.9 | 5.6 | 5.1 | 3.7 | 4.2 | 7.0 | -1.4 | | | | | | | | |
| 1984 | 7.3 | 7.3 | 7.8 | 6.9 | 7.9 | 7.8 | 8.1 | 7.3 | 5.0 | 4.3 | 2.9 | 3.1 | 5.0 | -3.8 | | | | | | | | |
| 1985 | 7.4 | 7.4 | 7.9 | 7.0 | 8.0 | 7.9 | 8.2 | 7.5 | 5.2 | 4.7 | 3.4 | 3.7 | 5.7 | -1.0 | 13.2 | | | | | | | |
| 1986 | 7.3 | 7.3 | 7.8 | 6.9 | 7.9 | 7.8 | 8.0 | 7.3 | 5.1 | 4.5 | 3.2 | 3.5 | 5.2 | -0.8 | 6.5 | | | | | | | |
| 1987 | 7.2 | 7.2 | 7.6 | 6.8 | 7.7 | 7.6 | 7.8 | 7.1 | 4.9 | 4.3 | 3.1 | 3.3 | 4.8 | -0.8 | 4.3 | | | | | | | |
| 1988 | 7.1 | 7.1 | 7.5 | 6.6 | 7.6 | 7.4 | 7.6 | 6.9 | 4.7 | 4.1 | 2.9 | 3.0 | 4.3 | -0.9 | 2.8 | | | | | | | |
| 1989 | 7.1 | 7.1 | 7.5 | 6.7 | 7.6 | 7.4 | 7.6 | 6.9 | 4.8 | 4.3 | 3.1 | 3.3 | 4.6 | 0.1 | 4.0 | | | | | | | |
| 1990 | 6.6 | 6.6 | 7.0 | 6.1 | 7.0 | 6.8 | 6.9 | 6.1 | 4.0 | 3.3 | 2.0 | 1.9 | 2.7 | -2.3 | -1.0 | -26.0 | | | | | | |
| 1991 | 6.6 | 6.6 | 6.9 | 6.1 | 6.9 | 6.7 | 6.8 | 6.0 | 3.9 | 3.2 | 2.0 | 1.9 | 2.7 | -1.9 | -0.6 | -12.0 | | | | | | |
| 1992 | 6.4 | 6.3 | 6.7 | 5.8 | 6.6 | 6.4 | 6.5 | 5.7 | 3.6 | 2.9 | 1.6 | 1.4 | 2.0 | -2.5 | -1.7 | -11.1 | | | | | | |
| 1993 | 6.5 | 6.5 | 6.8 | 6.0 | 6.8 | 6.6 | 6.7 | 5.9 | 3.9 | 3.3 | 2.1 | 2.1 | 2.9 | -1.0 | 0.5 | -3.8 | | | | | | |
| 1994 | 6.4 | 6.4 | 6.7 | 5.9 | 6.7 | 6.4 | 6.5 | 5.8 | 3.8 | 3.2 | 2.0 | 1.9 | 2.6 | -1.1 | 0.3 | -3.4 | | | | | | |
| 1995 | 6.4 | 6.4 | 6.7 | 5.9 | 6.7 | 6.5 | 6.6 | 5.8 | 3.9 | 3.3 | 2.2 | 2.2 | 2.9 | -0.5 | 1.0 | -1.4 | 8.3 | | | | | |
| 1996 | 6.7 | 6.7 | 7.0 | 6.2 | 7.0 | 6.8 | 6.9 | 6.2 | 4.4 | 3.9 | 2.9 | 3.1 | 3.9 | 1.0 | 3.1 | 2.4 | 16.9 | | | | | |

## Canada Short-Horizon Equity Risk Premia

in Local Currency (Canadian Dollar – CAD)
in Percent

| End Date | Start Date | | | | | | | | | | | | | | | | | | | | | |
|---|---|---|---|---|---|---|---|---|---|---|---|---|---|---|---|---|---|---|---|---|---|---|
| | 1919 | 1920 | 1925 | 1930 | 1935 | 1940 | 1945 | 1950 | 1955 | 1960 | 1965 | 1970 | 1975 | 1980 | 1985 | 1990 | 1995 | 2000 | 2005 | 2010 | 2015 | 2016 |
| 1997 | 6.8 | 6.8 | 7.1 | 6.4 | 7.1 | 7.0 | 7.1 | 6.4 | 4.7 | 4.2 | 3.3 | 3.5 | 4.4 | 1.8 | 4.0 | 4.0 | 16.3 | | | | | |
| 1998 | 6.7 | 6.6 | 7.0 | 6.2 | 7.0 | 6.8 | 6.9 | 6.2 | 4.5 | 4.0 | 3.1 | 3.2 | 4.1 | 1.5 | 3.4 | 3.1 | 11.3 | | | | | |
| 1999 | 7.1 | 7.1 | 7.4 | 6.7 | 7.5 | 7.3 | 7.5 | 6.9 | 5.3 | 4.9 | 4.2 | 4.5 | 5.5 | 3.5 | 5.9 | 6.9 | 17.3 | | | | | |
| 2000 | 7.0 | 7.0 | 7.4 | 6.7 | 7.4 | 7.3 | 7.5 | 6.9 | 5.3 | 4.9 | 4.2 | 4.5 | 5.5 | 3.5 | 5.8 | 6.7 | 15.0 | 3.9 | | | | |
| 2001 | 6.7 | 6.7 | 7.0 | 6.3 | 7.0 | 6.9 | 7.0 | 6.4 | 4.7 | 4.3 | 3.5 | 3.7 | 4.6 | 2.5 | 4.3 | 4.5 | 10.1 | -7.8 | | | | |
| 2002 | 6.4 | 6.4 | 6.7 | 6.0 | 6.7 | 6.5 | 6.6 | 5.9 | 4.3 | 3.8 | 3.0 | 3.1 | 3.8 | 1.7 | 3.2 | 2.9 | 6.8 | -10.6 | | | | |
| 2003 | 6.7 | 6.6 | 7.0 | 6.2 | 6.9 | 6.8 | 6.9 | 6.3 | 4.7 | 4.3 | 3.6 | 3.7 | 4.5 | 2.6 | 4.3 | 4.4 | 8.7 | -1.9 | | | | |
| 2004 | 6.7 | 6.7 | 7.0 | 6.3 | 7.0 | 6.8 | 7.0 | 6.4 | 4.8 | 4.5 | 3.8 | 4.0 | 4.8 | 3.0 | 4.7 | 4.9 | 9.0 | 0.8 | | | | |
| 2005 | 6.9 | 6.9 | 7.2 | 6.5 | 7.2 | 7.1 | 7.2 | 6.7 | 5.2 | 4.9 | 4.2 | 4.5 | 5.3 | 3.7 | 5.5 | 6.0 | 10.3 | 4.5 | 23.0 | | | |
| 2006 | 7.0 | 7.0 | 7.3 | 6.6 | 7.3 | 7.2 | 7.3 | 6.8 | 5.4 | 5.1 | 4.5 | 4.8 | 5.6 | 4.1 | 5.9 | 6.5 | 10.6 | 5.8 | 18.5 | | | |
| 2007 | 7.0 | 7.0 | 7.3 | 6.6 | 7.3 | 7.2 | 7.3 | 6.8 | 5.4 | 5.1 | 4.5 | 4.8 | 5.6 | 4.2 | 5.9 | 6.5 | 10.3 | 5.9 | 14.4 | | | |
| 2008 | 6.5 | 6.5 | 6.8 | 6.1 | 6.7 | 6.6 | 6.7 | 6.1 | 4.7 | 4.3 | 3.6 | 3.8 | 4.5 | 2.9 | 4.3 | 4.3 | 7.1 | 1.5 | 2.3 | | | |
| 2009 | 6.8 | 6.8 | 7.1 | 6.4 | 7.1 | 7.0 | 7.1 | 6.5 | 5.2 | 4.9 | 4.3 | 4.5 | 5.3 | 3.9 | 5.4 | 5.8 | 8.8 | 4.6 | 8.5 | | | |
| 2010 | 6.9 | 6.9 | 7.2 | 6.5 | 7.2 | 7.1 | 7.2 | 6.7 | 5.3 | 5.1 | 4.5 | 4.8 | 5.5 | 4.2 | 5.8 | 6.2 | 9.2 | 5.5 | 9.5 | 14.4 | | |
| 2011 | 6.7 | 6.7 | 7.0 | 6.3 | 7.0 | 6.8 | 6.9 | 6.4 | 5.1 | 4.7 | 4.2 | 4.4 | 5.1 | 3.7 | 5.1 | 5.4 | 8.0 | 4.2 | 6.6 | 1.8 | | |
| 2012 | 6.7 | 6.7 | 7.0 | 6.3 | 7.0 | 6.8 | 6.9 | 6.4 | 5.1 | 4.8 | 4.2 | 4.4 | 5.1 | 3.8 | 5.2 | 5.5 | 7.9 | 4.3 | 6.6 | 3.4 | | |
| 2013 | 6.8 | 6.8 | 7.0 | 6.4 | 7.0 | 6.9 | 7.0 | 6.5 | 5.2 | 4.9 | 4.4 | 4.6 | 5.3 | 4.1 | 5.5 | 5.8 | 8.2 | 4.9 | 7.2 | 5.7 | | |
| 2014 | 6.8 | 6.8 | 7.1 | 6.5 | 7.1 | 6.9 | 7.0 | 6.5 | 5.3 | 5.0 | 4.5 | 4.8 | 5.5 | 4.3 | 5.6 | 6.0 | 8.3 | 5.3 | 7.6 | 6.6 | | |
| 2015 | 6.6 | 6.6 | 6.9 | 6.3 | 6.9 | 6.7 | 6.8 | 6.3 | 5.1 | 4.8 | 4.3 | 4.5 | 5.1 | 3.9 | 5.2 | 5.4 | 7.5 | 4.4 | 6.1 | 4.0 | -9.0 | |
| 2016 | 6.8 | 6.8 | 7.0 | 6.4 | 7.0 | 6.9 | 7.0 | 6.5 | 5.3 | 5.1 | 4.6 | 4.8 | 5.5 | 4.4 | 5.6 | 5.9 | 8.1 | 5.4 | 7.3 | 6.4 | 5.8 | 20.7 |

Source of underlying data: 1.) Morningstar *Direct* database. Used with permission. All rights reserved. All calculations performed by Duff & Phelps LLC.

## Canada Short-Horizon Equity Risk Premia

in U.S. Dollars (USD)
in Percent

| End Date | Start Date 1919 | 1920 | 1925 | 1930 | 1935 | 1940 | 1945 | 1950 | 1955 | 1960 | 1965 | 1970 | 1975 | 1980 | 1985 | 1990 | 1995 | 2000 | 2005 | 2010 | 2015 | 2016 |
|---|---|---|---|---|---|---|---|---|---|---|---|---|---|---|---|---|---|---|---|---|---|---|
| 1919 | 7.2 | | | | | | | | | | | | | | | | | | | | | |
| 1920 | -2.8 | -12.9 | | | | | | | | | | | | | | | | | | | | |
| 1921 | -4.7 | -10.6 | | | | | | | | | | | | | | | | | | | | |
| 1922 | 1.7 | -0.1 | | | | | | | | | | | | | | | | | | | | |
| 1923 | 1.9 | 0.5 | | | | | | | | | | | | | | | | | | | | |
| 1924 | 2.8 | 1.9 | | | | | | | | | | | | | | | | | | | | |
| 1925 | 4.7 | 4.3 | 16.0 | | | | | | | | | | | | | | | | | | | |
| 1926 | 6.6 | 6.5 | 18.0 | | | | | | | | | | | | | | | | | | | |
| 1927 | 10.4 | 10.8 | 25.6 | | | | | | | | | | | | | | | | | | | |
| 1928 | 12.2 | 12.7 | 26.2 | | | | | | | | | | | | | | | | | | | |
| 1929 | 9.5 | 9.7 | 17.5 | | | | | | | | | | | | | | | | | | | |
| 1930 | 5.8 | 5.6 | 8.7 | -35.0 | | | | | | | | | | | | | | | | | | |
| 1931 | 3.0 | 2.7 | 3.2 | -32.5 | | | | | | | | | | | | | | | | | | |
| 1932 | 1.6 | 1.2 | 0.7 | -27.2 | | | | | | | | | | | | | | | | | | |
| 1933 | 5.3 | 5.1 | 6.9 | -6.2 | | | | | | | | | | | | | | | | | | |
| 1934 | 6.2 | 6.1 | 8.2 | -1.0 | | | | | | | | | | | | | | | | | | |
| 1935 | 7.5 | 7.6 | 10.1 | 4.0 | 29.1 | | | | | | | | | | | | | | | | | |
| 1936 | 8.5 | 8.6 | 11.3 | 7.0 | 26.8 | | | | | | | | | | | | | | | | | |
| 1937 | 7.2 | 7.2 | 9.2 | 4.0 | 12.4 | | | | | | | | | | | | | | | | | |
| 1938 | 7.2 | 7.2 | 9.1 | 4.5 | 11.4 | | | | | | | | | | | | | | | | | |
| 1939 | 6.9 | 6.9 | 8.5 | 4.0 | 9.0 | | | | | | | | | | | | | | | | | |
| 1940 | 5.7 | 5.6 | 6.7 | 1.8 | 4.2 | -19.9 | | | | | | | | | | | | | | | | |
| 1941 | 5.5 | 5.4 | 6.4 | 1.8 | 3.8 | -9.3 | | | | | | | | | | | | | | | | |
| 1942 | 5.8 | 5.7 | 6.8 | 2.7 | 5.0 | -1.7 | | | | | | | | | | | | | | | | |
| 1943 | 6.3 | 6.3 | 7.5 | 3.9 | 6.6 | 3.5 | | | | | | | | | | | | | | | | |
| 1944 | 6.6 | 6.6 | 7.7 | 4.5 | 7.2 | 5.4 | | | | | | | | | | | | | | | | |
| 1945 | 7.7 | 7.7 | 9.1 | 6.4 | 9.8 | 10.5 | 35.7 | | | | | | | | | | | | | | | |
| 1946 | 7.3 | 7.3 | 8.6 | 5.9 | 8.8 | 8.7 | 16.8 | | | | | | | | | | | | | | | |
| 1947 | 7.1 | 7.1 | 8.2 | 5.6 | 8.2 | 7.6 | 11.2 | | | | | | | | | | | | | | | |
| 1948 | 7.2 | 7.2 | 8.4 | 6.0 | 8.4 | 8.1 | 11.5 | | | | | | | | | | | | | | | |
| 1949 | 7.7 | 7.7 | 8.9 | 6.7 | 9.3 | 9.4 | 13.4 | | | | | | | | | | | | | | | |
| 1950 | 8.9 | 8.9 | 10.3 | 8.6 | 11.6 | 12.8 | 18.8 | 46.0 | | | | | | | | | | | | | | |
| 1951 | 9.4 | 9.5 | 10.9 | 9.4 | 12.5 | 13.9 | 20.0 | 36.5 | | | | | | | | | | | | | | |
| 1952 | 9.1 | 9.2 | 10.5 | 8.9 | 11.7 | 12.7 | 17.3 | 23.8 | | | | | | | | | | | | | | |
| 1953 | 8.9 | 8.9 | 10.1 | 8.6 | 11.1 | 11.9 | 15.4 | 18.0 | | | | | | | | | | | | | | |
| 1954 | 9.7 | 9.7 | 11.0 | 9.8 | 12.5 | 13.6 | 17.7 | 21.9 | | | | | | | | | | | | | | |
| 1955 | 10.1 | 10.2 | 11.5 | 10.4 | 13.1 | 14.3 | 18.4 | 22.5 | 25.5 | | | | | | | | | | | | | |
| 1956 | 10.1 | 10.2 | 11.5 | 10.4 | 13.0 | 14.1 | 17.8 | 20.8 | 18.1 | | | | | | | | | | | | | |
| 1957 | 9.2 | 9.3 | 10.4 | 9.2 | 11.4 | 12.0 | 14.6 | 15.3 | 4.1 | | | | | | | | | | | | | |

Source of underlying data: 1.) Morningstar *Direct* database. Used with permission. All rights reserved. All calculations performed by Duff & Phelps LLC.

## Canada Short-Horizon Equity Risk Premia

in U.S. Dollars (USD)
in Percent

| End Date | Start Date | | | | | | | | | | | | | | | | | | | | | |
|---|---|---|---|---|---|---|---|---|---|---|---|---|---|---|---|---|---|---|---|---|---|---|
| | 1919 | 1920 | 1925 | 1930 | 1935 | 1940 | 1945 | 1950 | 1955 | 1960 | 1965 | 1970 | 1975 | 1980 | 1985 | 1990 | 1995 | 2000 | 2005 | 2010 | 2015 | 2016 |
| 1958 | 9.8 | 9.8 | 11.0 | 9.9 | 12.1 | 13.0 | 15.6 | 16.9 | 10.5 | | | | | | | | | | | | | |
| 1959 | 9.5 | 9.6 | 10.7 | 9.5 | 11.6 | 12.3 | 14.6 | 15.2 | 8.4 | | | | | | | | | | | | | |
| 1960 | 9.3 | 9.3 | 10.3 | 9.2 | 11.1 | 11.6 | 13.6 | 13.6 | 6.7 | -1.7 | | | | | | | | | | | | |
| 1961 | 9.7 | 9.8 | 10.8 | 9.8 | 11.8 | 12.4 | 14.4 | 14.9 | 9.8 | 13.4 | | | | | | | | | | | | |
| 1962 | 9.2 | 9.3 | 10.2 | 9.2 | 11.0 | 11.4 | 13.0 | 12.9 | 7.2 | 5.3 | | | | | | | | | | | | |
| 1963 | 9.3 | 9.3 | 10.3 | 9.2 | 11.0 | 11.4 | 13.0 | 12.8 | 7.8 | 7.0 | | | | | | | | | | | | |
| 1964 | 9.6 | 9.6 | 10.6 | 9.6 | 11.4 | 11.8 | 13.4 | 13.4 | 9.2 | 9.9 | | | | | | | | | | | | |
| 1965 | 9.4 | 9.5 | 10.4 | 9.4 | 11.1 | 11.5 | 12.9 | 12.8 | 8.6 | 8.7 | 2.7 | | | | | | | | | | | |
| 1966 | 9.0 | 9.0 | 9.8 | 8.8 | 10.4 | 10.6 | 11.8 | 11.3 | 6.8 | 5.8 | -4.7 | | | | | | | | | | | |
| 1967 | 9.1 | 9.1 | 9.9 | 8.9 | 10.4 | 10.7 | 11.8 | 11.4 | 7.4 | 6.7 | 1.4 | | | | | | | | | | | |
| 1968 | 9.2 | 9.2 | 10.1 | 9.1 | 10.6 | 10.9 | 12.0 | 11.7 | 8.0 | 7.8 | 5.0 | | | | | | | | | | | |
| 1969 | 8.9 | 8.9 | 9.7 | 8.7 | 10.1 | 10.3 | 11.2 | 10.7 | 6.9 | 6.2 | 2.4 | | | | | | | | | | | |
| 1970 | 8.7 | 8.8 | 9.5 | 8.5 | 9.9 | 10.0 | 10.9 | 10.3 | 6.6 | 5.8 | 2.4 | 2.6 | | | | | | | | | | |
| 1971 | 8.8 | 8.8 | 9.5 | 8.6 | 9.9 | 10.0 | 10.8 | 10.2 | 6.8 | 6.1 | 3.4 | 6.0 | | | | | | | | | | |
| 1972 | 9.1 | 9.2 | 9.9 | 9.0 | 10.4 | 10.6 | 11.5 | 11.1 | 8.0 | 7.9 | 6.6 | 13.7 | | | | | | | | | | |
| 1973 | 8.8 | 8.8 | 9.5 | 8.6 | 9.9 | 10.0 | 10.8 | 10.2 | 7.2 | 6.7 | 4.9 | 8.1 | | | | | | | | | | |
| 1974 | 8.0 | 8.0 | 8.6 | 7.7 | 8.7 | 8.7 | 9.2 | 8.4 | 5.3 | 3.9 | 0.9 | -0.6 | | | | | | | | | | |
| 1975 | 8.1 | 8.1 | 8.7 | 7.7 | 8.8 | 8.7 | 9.3 | 8.5 | 5.3 | 4.3 | 1.8 | 1.2 | 10.3 | | | | | | | | | |
| 1976 | 7.9 | 7.9 | 8.5 | 7.6 | 8.6 | 8.5 | 9.0 | 8.2 | 5.0 | 4.1 | 1.6 | 1.0 | 5.1 | | | | | | | | | |
| 1977 | 7.8 | 7.8 | 8.3 | 7.4 | 8.3 | 8.2 | 8.7 | 7.8 | 4.8 | 3.7 | 1.4 | 0.7 | 2.9 | | | | | | | | | |
| 1978 | 8.0 | 8.0 | 8.5 | 7.6 | 8.6 | 8.5 | 9.0 | 8.2 | 5.4 | 4.6 | 2.7 | 2.9 | 7.1 | | | | | | | | | |
| 1979 | 8.5 | 8.5 | 9.1 | 8.2 | 9.3 | 9.3 | 9.8 | 9.2 | 6.7 | 6.3 | 5.0 | 6.4 | 13.3 | | | | | | | | | |
| 1980 | 8.5 | 8.5 | 9.1 | 8.3 | 9.3 | 9.3 | 9.9 | 9.3 | 6.9 | 6.5 | 5.4 | 6.8 | 13.0 | 11.3 | | | | | | | | |
| 1981 | 7.9 | 7.9 | 8.4 | 7.5 | 8.4 | 8.4 | 8.7 | 8.0 | 5.4 | 4.8 | 3.2 | 3.6 | 6.6 | -10.3 | | | | | | | | |
| 1982 | 7.6 | 7.6 | 8.1 | 7.2 | 8.1 | 8.0 | 8.3 | 7.5 | 4.9 | 4.2 | 2.6 | 2.7 | 4.7 | -9.7 | | | | | | | | |
| 1983 | 7.9 | 7.9 | 8.4 | 7.5 | 8.4 | 8.3 | 8.7 | 8.0 | 5.6 | 5.0 | 3.7 | 4.2 | 6.9 | -1.1 | | | | | | | | |
| 1984 | 7.5 | 7.6 | 8.0 | 7.2 | 8.0 | 7.9 | 8.2 | 7.4 | 5.0 | 4.3 | 2.9 | 3.1 | 4.9 | -3.5 | | | | | | | | |
| 1985 | 7.6 | 7.6 | 8.1 | 7.3 | 8.1 | 8.0 | 8.3 | 7.6 | 5.2 | 4.6 | 3.4 | 3.7 | 5.6 | -0.9 | 12.3 | | | | | | | |
| 1986 | 7.5 | 7.5 | 8.0 | 7.1 | 7.9 | 7.8 | 8.1 | 7.3 | 5.1 | 4.5 | 3.2 | 3.4 | 5.1 | -0.7 | 6.1 | | | | | | | |
| 1987 | 7.4 | 7.4 | 7.8 | 7.0 | 7.8 | 7.6 | 7.9 | 7.1 | 4.9 | 4.3 | 3.0 | 3.2 | 4.7 | -0.7 | 3.9 | | | | | | | |
| 1988 | 7.3 | 7.3 | 7.7 | 6.8 | 7.6 | 7.4 | 7.6 | 6.9 | 4.7 | 4.1 | 2.8 | 3.0 | 4.2 | -0.8 | 2.5 | | | | | | | |
| 1989 | 7.3 | 7.3 | 7.7 | 6.9 | 7.6 | 7.5 | 7.7 | 7.0 | 4.8 | 4.2 | 3.1 | 3.3 | 4.6 | 0.2 | 3.8 | | | | | | | |
| 1990 | 6.8 | 6.8 | 7.2 | 6.3 | 7.0 | 6.8 | 7.0 | 6.2 | 4.0 | 3.3 | 2.0 | 1.9 | 2.6 | -2.2 | -1.1 | -25.9 | | | | | | |
| 1991 | 6.8 | 6.8 | 7.1 | 6.3 | 6.9 | 6.7 | 6.8 | 6.1 | 3.9 | 3.2 | 2.0 | 1.9 | 2.6 | -1.9 | -0.7 | -12.0 | | | | | | |
| 1992 | 6.6 | 6.6 | 6.9 | 6.1 | 6.7 | 6.4 | 6.5 | 5.7 | 3.6 | 2.9 | 1.6 | 1.5 | 2.0 | -2.3 | -1.6 | -10.6 | | | | | | |
| 1993 | 6.7 | 6.7 | 7.0 | 6.2 | 6.8 | 6.6 | 6.8 | 6.0 | 3.9 | 3.3 | 2.2 | 2.1 | 2.8 | -0.9 | 0.5 | -3.7 | | | | | | |
| 1994 | 6.6 | 6.6 | 6.9 | 6.1 | 6.7 | 6.5 | 6.6 | 5.8 | 3.8 | 3.2 | 2.0 | 1.9 | 2.6 | -1.0 | 0.2 | -3.4 | | | | | | |
| 1995 | 6.6 | 6.6 | 6.9 | 6.1 | 6.7 | 6.5 | 6.6 | 5.9 | 3.9 | 3.3 | 2.2 | 2.2 | 2.9 | -0.4 | 1.0 | -1.4 | 8.6 | | | | | |
| 1996 | 6.9 | 6.8 | 7.2 | 6.4 | 7.0 | 6.8 | 7.0 | 6.3 | 4.4 | 3.9 | 3.0 | 3.1 | 3.9 | 1.1 | 3.0 | 2.4 | 16.9 | | | | | |

Source of underlying data: 1.) Morningstar *Direct* database. Used with permission. All rights reserved. All calculations performed by Duff & Phelps LLC.

**Canada Short-Horizon Equity Risk Premia**

in U.S. Dollars (USD)
in Percent

| End Date | Start Date 1919 | 1920 | 1925 | 1930 | 1935 | 1940 | 1945 | 1950 | 1955 | 1960 | 1965 | 1970 | 1975 | 1980 | 1985 | 1990 | 1995 | 2000 | 2005 | 2010 | 2015 | 2016 |
|---|---|---|---|---|---|---|---|---|---|---|---|---|---|---|---|---|---|---|---|---|---|---|
| 1997 | 6.9 | 6.9 | 7.3 | 6.5 | 7.1 | 7.0 | 7.1 | 6.5 | 4.7 | 4.2 | 3.3 | 3.5 | 4.3 | 1.8 | 3.9 | 3.9 | 16.1 | | | | | |
| 1998 | 6.8 | 6.8 | 7.1 | 6.4 | 7.0 | 6.8 | 6.9 | 6.3 | 4.5 | 4.0 | 3.1 | 3.2 | 4.0 | 1.6 | 3.4 | 3.1 | 11.2 | | | | | |
| 1999 | 7.3 | 7.3 | 7.6 | 6.9 | 7.5 | 7.4 | 7.6 | 7.0 | 5.3 | 5.0 | 4.3 | 4.6 | 5.6 | 3.7 | 6.0 | 7.2 | 17.7 | | | | | |
| 2000 | 7.2 | 7.2 | 7.6 | 6.9 | 7.5 | 7.3 | 7.5 | 6.9 | 5.3 | 4.9 | 4.2 | 4.5 | 5.5 | 3.7 | 5.9 | 6.9 | 15.4 | 3.8 | | | | |
| 2001 | 6.9 | 6.9 | 7.2 | 6.5 | 7.1 | 6.9 | 7.1 | 6.5 | 4.8 | 4.4 | 3.6 | 3.8 | 4.6 | 2.7 | 4.5 | 4.7 | 10.5 | -7.3 | | | | |
| 2002 | 6.6 | 6.6 | 6.9 | 6.2 | 6.7 | 6.6 | 6.7 | 6.0 | 4.4 | 3.9 | 3.1 | 3.2 | 3.9 | 1.8 | 3.3 | 3.1 | 7.2 | -10.3 | | | | |
| 2003 | 6.9 | 6.9 | 7.2 | 6.5 | 7.1 | 6.9 | 7.1 | 6.5 | 4.9 | 4.5 | 3.8 | 4.0 | 4.8 | 3.0 | 4.7 | 5.0 | 9.7 | -0.3 | | | | |
| 2004 | 7.0 | 7.0 | 7.3 | 6.6 | 7.2 | 7.0 | 7.1 | 6.6 | 5.0 | 4.7 | 4.0 | 4.2 | 5.0 | 3.4 | 5.1 | 5.5 | 9.9 | 2.2 | | | | |
| 2005 | 7.2 | 7.2 | 7.5 | 6.8 | 7.4 | 7.3 | 7.4 | 6.9 | 5.4 | 5.1 | 4.5 | 4.8 | 5.6 | 4.2 | 6.0 | 6.6 | 11.2 | 5.8 | 23.6 | | | |
| 2006 | 7.2 | 7.2 | 7.6 | 6.9 | 7.5 | 7.4 | 7.5 | 7.0 | 5.6 | 5.3 | 4.7 | 5.0 | 5.9 | 4.5 | 6.3 | 7.1 | 11.4 | 7.0 | 18.8 | | | |
| 2007 | 7.2 | 7.2 | 7.6 | 6.9 | 7.5 | 7.4 | 7.5 | 7.0 | 5.6 | 5.3 | 4.8 | 5.1 | 5.9 | 4.6 | 6.4 | 7.1 | 11.1 | 7.0 | 15.0 | | | |
| 2008 | 6.9 | 6.9 | 7.2 | 6.5 | 7.0 | 6.9 | 7.0 | 6.4 | 5.0 | 4.6 | 4.0 | 4.3 | 5.0 | 3.5 | 5.0 | 5.3 | 8.4 | 3.2 | 4.4 | | | |
| 2009 | 7.2 | 7.2 | 7.5 | 6.9 | 7.4 | 7.3 | 7.5 | 7.0 | 5.6 | 5.3 | 4.8 | 5.1 | 5.9 | 4.7 | 6.3 | 7.0 | 10.4 | 6.8 | 11.4 | | | |
| 2010 | 7.3 | 7.3 | 7.6 | 7.0 | 7.5 | 7.4 | 7.6 | 7.1 | 5.8 | 5.5 | 5.0 | 5.4 | 6.2 | 5.0 | 6.7 | 7.4 | 10.7 | 7.6 | 12.0 | 15.2 | | |
| 2011 | 7.1 | 7.1 | 7.4 | 6.8 | 7.3 | 7.2 | 7.3 | 6.8 | 5.5 | 5.2 | 4.7 | 5.0 | 5.7 | 4.6 | 6.0 | 6.6 | 9.5 | 6.0 | 8.8 | 2.3 | | |
| 2012 | 7.1 | 7.1 | 7.4 | 6.8 | 7.3 | 7.2 | 7.3 | 6.8 | 5.5 | 5.2 | 4.8 | 5.0 | 5.8 | 4.6 | 6.1 | 6.6 | 9.3 | 6.1 | 8.5 | 3.8 | | |
| 2013 | 7.2 | 7.2 | 7.5 | 6.9 | 7.4 | 7.2 | 7.4 | 6.9 | 5.6 | 5.4 | 4.9 | 5.2 | 5.9 | 4.8 | 6.3 | 6.8 | 9.4 | 6.5 | 8.9 | 5.8 | | |
| 2014 | 7.2 | 7.2 | 7.5 | 6.9 | 7.4 | 7.3 | 7.4 | 6.9 | 5.7 | 5.4 | 5.0 | 5.3 | 6.0 | 5.0 | 6.4 | 6.9 | 9.5 | 6.7 | 9.0 | 6.5 | | |
| 2015 | 7.0 | 7.0 | 7.3 | 6.7 | 7.2 | 7.1 | 7.2 | 6.7 | 5.5 | 5.2 | 4.7 | 5.0 | 5.7 | 4.6 | 5.9 | 6.3 | 8.6 | 5.8 | 7.5 | 4.2 | -7.5 | |
| 2016 | 7.2 | 7.2 | 7.5 | 6.9 | 7.4 | 7.3 | 7.4 | 6.9 | 5.7 | 5.5 | 5.1 | 5.4 | 6.1 | 5.1 | 6.4 | 6.9 | 9.2 | 6.7 | 8.6 | 6.7 | 7.0 | 21.4 |

Source of underlying data: 1.) Morningstar *Direct* database. Used with permission. All rights reserved. All calculations performed by Duff & Phelps LLC.

## France Long-Horizon Equity Risk Premia

in Local Currency (Euro – EUR)
in Percent

| End Date | Start Date | | | | | | | | | | |
|---|---|---|---|---|---|---|---|---|---|---|---|
| | 1970 | 1975 | 1980 | 1985 | 1990 | 1995 | 2000 | 2005 | 2010 | 2015 | 2016 |
| 1970 | -13.2 | | | | | | | | | | |
| 1971 | -12.8 | | | | | | | | | | |
| 1972 | -3.4 | | | | | | | | | | |
| 1973 | -4.8 | | | | | | | | | | |
| 1974 | -11.6 | | | | | | | | | | |
| 1975 | -3.7 | 35.7 | | | | | | | | | |
| 1976 | -6.2 | 7.6 | | | | | | | | | |
| 1977 | -6.6 | 1.8 | | | | | | | | | |
| 1978 | -1.0 | 12.4 | | | | | | | | | |
| 1979 | 0.6 | 12.9 | | | | | | | | | |
| 1980 | 0.4 | 10.5 | -1.4 | | | | | | | | |
| 1981 | -1.6 | 5.6 | -12.8 | | | | | | | | |
| 1982 | -1.7 | 4.5 | -9.5 | | | | | | | | |
| 1983 | 2.0 | 9.6 | 5.4 | | | | | | | | |
| 1984 | 2.4 | 9.4 | 6.0 | | | | | | | | |
| 1985 | 4.3 | 11.5 | 10.3 | 32.0 | | | | | | | |
| 1986 | 6.5 | 14.1 | 15.0 | 37.5 | | | | | | | |
| 1987 | 4.1 | 10.2 | 8.5 | 12.7 | | | | | | | |
| 1988 | 6.4 | 12.8 | 12.8 | 21.3 | | | | | | | |
| 1989 | 7.2 | 13.4 | 13.7 | 21.4 | | | | | | | |
| 1990 | 5.3 | 10.5 | 9.5 | 12.4 | -32.9 | | | | | | |
| 1991 | 5.5 | 10.6 | 9.6 | 12.2 | -10.9 | | | | | | |
| 1992 | 5.3 | 10.1 | 9.0 | 10.8 | -6.9 | | | | | | |
| 1993 | 6.1 | 10.7 | 9.9 | 12.1 | 0.5 | | | | | | |
| 1994 | 5.0 | 9.2 | 7.9 | 8.9 | -3.7 | | | | | | |
| 1995 | 4.7 | 8.6 | 7.3 | 7.8 | -3.5 | -2.7 | | | | | |
| 1996 | 5.4 | 9.3 | 8.2 | 9.1 | 0.3 | 10.1 | | | | | |
| 1997 | 6.1 | 9.9 | 9.1 | 10.3 | 3.3 | 14.9 | | | | | |
| 1998 | 6.8 | 10.6 | 10.0 | 11.5 | 5.9 | 17.9 | | | | | |
| 1999 | 8.1 | 12.1 | 11.9 | 13.9 | 10.1 | 23.9 | | | | | |
| 2000 | 7.8 | 11.5 | 11.2 | 12.8 | 8.9 | 19.4 | -2.9 | | | | |
| 2001 | 6.8 | 10.3 | 9.6 | 10.7 | 6.3 | 13.4 | -12.9 | | | | |
| 2002 | 5.5 | 8.5 | 7.6 | 8.0 | 2.9 | 7.0 | -21.2 | | | | |
| 2003 | 5.7 | 8.7 | 7.8 | 8.3 | 3.6 | 7.7 | -12.6 | | | | |
| 2004 | 5.7 | 8.6 | 7.8 | 8.2 | 3.8 | 7.5 | -8.8 | | | | |
| 2005 | 6.2 | 9.1 | 8.4 | 9.0 | 5.1 | 9.0 | -3.3 | 24.0 | | | |
| 2006 | 6.5 | 9.4 | 8.7 | 9.3 | 5.8 | 9.7 | -0.4 | 20.7 | | | |
| 2007 | 6.3 | 9.1 | 8.4 | 8.9 | 5.4 | 8.9 | -0.5 | 13.4 | | | |
| 2008 | 5.0 | 7.5 | 6.6 | 6.7 | 2.8 | 5.1 | -5.3 | -1.0 | | | |
| 2009 | 5.6 | 8.0 | 7.2 | 7.4 | 3.9 | 6.5 | -2.2 | 4.3 | | | |
| 2010 | 5.4 | 7.8 | 7.0 | 7.2 | 3.8 | 6.1 | -2.0 | 3.6 | 0.3 | | |
| 2011 | 4.9 | 7.1 | 6.2 | 6.3 | 2.8 | 4.8 | -3.2 | 0.8 | -8.1 | | |
| 2012 | 5.2 | 7.4 | 6.6 | 6.7 | 3.5 | 5.5 | -1.6 | 2.9 | 0.6 | | |
| 2013 | 5.5 | 7.7 | 7.0 | 7.2 | 4.2 | 6.3 | 0.0 | 4.8 | 5.5 | | |
| 2014 | 5.5 | 7.6 | 6.8 | 7.0 | 4.1 | 6.0 | 0.1 | 4.5 | 4.7 | | |
| 2015 | 5.6 | 7.7 | 7.0 | 7.1 | 4.4 | 6.3 | 0.8 | 5.2 | 5.9 | 11.4 | |
| 2016 | 5.7 | 7.7 | 7.0 | 7.2 | 4.5 | 6.4 | 1.3 | 5.5 | 6.3 | 10.1 | 8.7 |

in U.S. Dollars (USD)
in Percent

| End Date | Start Date | | | | | | | | | | |
|---|---|---|---|---|---|---|---|---|---|---|---|
| | 1970 | 1975 | 1980 | 1985 | 1990 | 1995 | 2000 | 2005 | 2010 | 2015 | 2016 |
| 1970 | -13.3 | | | | | | | | | | |
| 1971 | -10.0 | | | | | | | | | | |
| 1972 | -0.9 | | | | | | | | | | |
| 1973 | -1.9 | | | | | | | | | | |
| 1974 | -8.0 | | | | | | | | | | |
| 1975 | -0.9 | 34.9 | | | | | | | | | |
| 1976 | -4.8 | 3.2 | | | | | | | | | |
| 1977 | -4.8 | 0.7 | | | | | | | | | |
| 1978 | 2.7 | 16.1 | | | | | | | | | |
| 1979 | 4.4 | 16.7 | | | | | | | | | |
| 1980 | 2.8 | 11.8 | -12.7 | | | | | | | | |
| 1981 | -0.7 | 4.5 | -26.3 | | | | | | | | |
| 1982 | -2.1 | 1.7 | -23.4 | | | | | | | | |
| 1983 | -0.4 | 3.9 | -12.2 | | | | | | | | |
| 1984 | -0.8 | 2.9 | -11.0 | | | | | | | | |
| 1985 | 3.6 | 8.8 | 2.3 | 68.5 | | | | | | | |
| 1986 | 7.3 | 13.7 | 11.6 | 68.1 | | | | | | | |
| 1987 | 5.6 | 10.8 | 7.1 | 37.3 | | | | | | | |
| 1988 | 6.9 | 12.2 | 9.7 | 35.5 | | | | | | | |
| 1989 | 7.9 | 13.2 | 11.5 | 34.0 | | | | | | | |
| 1990 | 6.4 | 10.9 | 8.3 | 24.3 | -24.0 | | | | | | |
| 1991 | 6.5 | 10.8 | 8.3 | 22.1 | -7.5 | | | | | | |
| 1992 | 6.0 | 9.9 | 7.3 | 18.8 | -6.6 | | | | | | |
| 1993 | 6.4 | 10.2 | 7.8 | 18.3 | -1.3 | | | | | | |
| 1994 | 5.7 | 9.1 | 6.5 | 15.3 | -3.4 | | | | | | |
| 1995 | 5.7 | 8.9 | 6.5 | 14.5 | -1.8 | 6.2 | | | | | |
| 1996 | 6.0 | 9.2 | 7.0 | 14.6 | 0.7 | 10.9 | | | | | |
| 1997 | 6.1 | 9.2 | 7.1 | 14.0 | 1.6 | 9.8 | | | | | |
| 1998 | 7.2 | 10.3 | 8.6 | 15.6 | 5.5 | 16.5 | | | | | |
| 1999 | 7.8 | 10.9 | 9.5 | 16.3 | 7.5 | 18.4 | | | | | |
| 2000 | 7.2 | 10.2 | 8.6 | 14.7 | 6.0 | 13.8 | -9.1 | | | | |
| 2001 | 6.2 | 8.8 | 7.0 | 12.3 | 3.3 | 8.0 | -17.9 | | | | |
| 2002 | 5.2 | 7.5 | 5.5 | 10.1 | 1.0 | 3.7 | -20.8 | | | | |
| 2003 | 6.1 | 8.5 | 6.8 | 11.5 | 3.5 | 7.3 | -6.6 | | | | |
| 2004 | 6.3 | 8.7 | 7.1 | 11.7 | 4.2 | 8.0 | -2.4 | | | | |
| 2005 | 6.4 | 8.7 | 7.1 | 11.5 | 4.4 | 8.0 | -0.7 | 7.5 | | | |
| 2006 | 7.0 | 9.4 | 8.0 | 12.4 | 6.0 | 9.9 | 3.9 | 19.5 | | | |
| 2007 | 7.1 | 9.4 | 8.1 | 12.2 | 6.2 | 9.9 | 4.6 | 16.1 | | | |
| 2008 | 5.7 | 7.7 | 6.2 | 9.8 | 3.4 | 5.8 | -1.1 | 0.4 | | | |
| 2009 | 6.3 | 8.4 | 7.0 | 10.6 | 4.7 | 7.4 | 1.9 | 6.2 | | | |
| 2010 | 6.0 | 8.0 | 6.5 | 9.9 | 4.2 | 6.6 | 1.2 | 4.1 | -6.2 | | |
| 2011 | 5.4 | 7.2 | 5.7 | 8.8 | 3.1 | 5.1 | -0.5 | 0.8 | -12.7 | | |
| 2012 | 5.8 | 7.6 | 6.2 | 9.2 | 3.9 | 5.9 | 1.1 | 3.2 | -1.8 | | |
| 2013 | 6.2 | 8.0 | 6.7 | 9.8 | 4.8 | 6.9 | 2.8 | 5.7 | 5.0 | | |
| 2014 | 5.8 | 7.6 | 6.2 | 9.1 | 4.2 | 6.0 | 1.9 | 4.0 | 1.9 | | |
| 2015 | 5.7 | 7.4 | 6.1 | 8.8 | 4.0 | 5.8 | 1.8 | 3.7 | 1.6 | 0.0 | |
| 2016 | 5.7 | 7.3 | 6.1 | 8.7 | 4.0 | 5.7 | 2.0 | 3.8 | 2.1 | 2.6 | 5.2 |

Source of underlying data: 1.) Morningstar *Direct* database. Used with permission. All rights reserved. All calculations performed by Duff & Phelps LLC.

# France Short-Horizon Equity Risk Premia

in Local Currency (Euro – EUR)
in Percent

| End Date | 1970 | 1975 | 1980 | 1985 | 1990 | 1995 | 2000 | 2005 | 2010 | 2015 | 2016 |
|---|---|---|---|---|---|---|---|---|---|---|---|
| 1970 | -9.7 | | | | | | | | | | |
| 1971 | -9.4 | | | | | | | | | | |
| 1972 | -0.5 | | | | | | | | | | |
| 1973 | -2.8 | | | | | | | | | | |
| 1974 | -10.3 | | | | | | | | | | |
| 1975 | -2.4 | 36.8 | | | | | | | | | |
| 1976 | -4.6 | 9.5 | | | | | | | | | |
| 1977 | -4.8 | 4.4 | | | | | | | | | |
| 1978 | 1.1 | 15.4 | | | | | | | | | |
| 1979 | 2.9 | 16.1 | | | | | | | | | |
| 1980 | 3.0 | 14.1 | 4.3 | | | | | | | | |
| 1981 | 1.4 | 9.7 | -6.3 | | | | | | | | |
| 1982 | 1.6 | 9.1 | -2.6 | | | | | | | | |
| 1983 | 5.5 | 14.3 | 12.1 | | | | | | | | |
| 1984 | 6.1 | 14.3 | 12.6 | | | | | | | | |
| 1985 | 8.1 | 16.4 | 16.7 | 37.3 | | | | | | | |
| 1986 | 10.3 | 18.9 | 20.9 | 41.6 | | | | | | | |
| 1987 | 7.7 | 14.6 | 13.7 | 15.7 | | | | | | | |
| 1988 | 9.9 | 17.1 | 17.7 | 24.1 | | | | | | | |
| 1989 | 10.5 | 17.4 | 18.0 | 23.5 | | | | | | | |
| 1990 | 8.4 | 14.2 | 13.3 | 13.9 | -33.8 | | | | | | |
| 1991 | 8.5 | 14.0 | 13.1 | 13.5 | -11.4 | | | | | | |
| 1992 | 8.1 | 13.2 | 12.1 | 11.8 | -7.8 | | | | | | |
| 1993 | 8.6 | 13.6 | 12.7 | 12.7 | -0.7 | | | | | | |
| 1994 | 7.5 | 11.9 | 10.5 | 9.5 | -4.5 | | | | | | |
| 1995 | 7.1 | 11.2 | 9.7 | 8.4 | -4.1 | -1.9 | | | | | |
| 1996 | 7.8 | 11.9 | 10.6 | 9.8 | 0.1 | 11.7 | | | | | |
| 1997 | 8.4 | 12.5 | 11.5 | 11.1 | 3.4 | 16.7 | | | | | |
| 1998 | 9.1 | 13.2 | 12.4 | 12.4 | 6.2 | 19.6 | | | | | |
| 1999 | 10.5 | 14.6 | 14.2 | 14.8 | 10.4 | 25.4 | | | | | |
| 2000 | 10.1 | 14.0 | 13.5 | 13.8 | 9.4 | 20.9 | -1.6 | | | | |
| 2001 | 9.1 | 12.6 | 11.9 | 11.6 | 6.7 | 14.8 | -11.9 | | | | |
| 2002 | 7.7 | 10.9 | 9.8 | 9.0 | 3.4 | 8.4 | -20.0 | | | | |
| 2003 | 7.9 | 11.0 | 10.0 | 9.3 | 4.2 | 9.1 | -11.3 | | | | |
| 2004 | 7.9 | 11.0 | 9.9 | 9.3 | 4.5 | 9.1 | -7.3 | | | | |
| 2005 | 8.4 | 11.4 | 10.5 | 10.0 | 5.8 | 10.5 | -1.8 | 25.4 | | | |
| 2006 | 8.7 | 11.6 | 10.8 | 10.4 | 6.6 | 11.2 | 1.0 | 21.9 | | | |
| 2007 | 8.4 | 11.3 | 10.4 | 9.9 | 6.2 | 10.3 | 0.8 | 14.2 | | | |
| 2008 | 7.1 | 9.6 | 8.5 | 7.7 | 3.5 | 6.4 | -4.2 | -0.2 | | | |
| 2009 | 7.6 | 10.2 | 9.2 | 8.5 | 4.8 | 7.9 | -0.9 | 5.5 | | | |
| 2010 | 7.5 | 10.0 | 9.0 | 8.3 | 4.7 | 7.6 | -0.5 | 5.1 | 3.1 | | |
| 2011 | 7.0 | 9.3 | 8.3 | 7.5 | 3.8 | 6.3 | -1.7 | 2.4 | -5.4 | | |
| 2012 | 7.3 | 9.6 | 8.7 | 8.0 | 4.6 | 7.1 | 0.1 | 4.7 | 3.4 | | |
| 2013 | 7.7 | 10.0 | 9.0 | 8.4 | 5.3 | 7.9 | 1.6 | 6.6 | 8.0 | | |
| 2014 | 7.6 | 9.8 | 8.9 | 8.3 | 5.2 | 7.7 | 1.8 | 6.3 | 7.1 | | |
| 2015 | 7.7 | 9.9 | 9.0 | 8.4 | 5.5 | 7.9 | 2.4 | 6.9 | 8.0 | 12.4 | |
| 2016 | 7.7 | 9.9 | 9.0 | 8.5 | 5.7 | 8.0 | 2.9 | 7.1 | 8.3 | 11.1 | 9.7 |

in U.S. Dollars (USD)
in Percent

| End Date | 1970 | 1975 | 1980 | 1985 | 1990 | 1995 | 2000 | 2005 | 2010 | 2015 | 2016 |
|---|---|---|---|---|---|---|---|---|---|---|---|
| 1970 | -10.4 | | | | | | | | | | |
| 1971 | -9.7 | | | | | | | | | | |
| 1972 | -0.7 | | | | | | | | | | |
| 1973 | -4.2 | | | | | | | | | | |
| 1974 | -11.3 | | | | | | | | | | |
| 1975 | -3.3 | 36.7 | | | | | | | | | |
| 1976 | -5.1 | 10.3 | | | | | | | | | |
| 1977 | -5.2 | 4.9 | | | | | | | | | |
| 1978 | 1.4 | 17.3 | | | | | | | | | |
| 1979 | 3.2 | 17.8 | | | | | | | | | |
| 1980 | 3.3 | 15.4 | 3.7 | | | | | | | | |
| 1981 | 1.9 | 11.3 | -5.0 | | | | | | | | |
| 1982 | 2.0 | 10.4 | -2.0 | | | | | | | | |
| 1983 | 5.2 | 14.3 | 9.9 | | | | | | | | |
| 1984 | 5.7 | 14.1 | 10.5 | | | | | | | | |
| 1985 | 8.2 | 17.1 | 16.5 | 46.7 | | | | | | | |
| 1986 | 10.9 | 20.1 | 21.8 | 50.1 | | | | | | | |
| 1987 | 7.9 | 15.3 | 13.8 | 19.2 | | | | | | | |
| 1988 | 9.8 | 17.3 | 17.1 | 25.3 | | | | | | | |
| 1989 | 10.4 | 17.7 | 17.6 | 24.7 | | | | | | | |
| 1990 | 8.1 | 14.1 | 12.5 | 14.1 | -38.7 | | | | | | |
| 1991 | 8.2 | 13.9 | 12.3 | 13.7 | -14.0 | | | | | | |
| 1992 | 7.8 | 13.1 | 11.4 | 11.9 | -9.4 | | | | | | |
| 1993 | 8.3 | 13.5 | 11.9 | 12.7 | -2.2 | | | | | | |
| 1994 | 7.1 | 11.7 | 9.7 | 9.2 | -6.2 | | | | | | |
| 1995 | 6.7 | 11.0 | 8.9 | 8.2 | -5.5 | -2.1 | | | | | |
| 1996 | 7.4 | 11.6 | 9.8 | 9.5 | -1.3 | 10.8 | | | | | |
| 1997 | 7.9 | 12.1 | 10.5 | 10.6 | 1.7 | 14.9 | | | | | |
| 1998 | 8.7 | 12.9 | 11.6 | 12.0 | 4.9 | 18.8 | | | | | |
| 1999 | 9.8 | 14.0 | 13.1 | 14.0 | 8.6 | 23.4 | | | | | |
| 2000 | 9.4 | 13.4 | 12.4 | 13.0 | 7.7 | 19.2 | -1.5 | | | | |
| 2001 | 8.5 | 12.2 | 10.9 | 11.0 | 5.3 | 13.5 | -11.3 | | | | |
| 2002 | 6.9 | 10.2 | 8.5 | 8.0 | 1.6 | 6.4 | -21.8 | | | | |
| 2003 | 7.3 | 10.5 | 8.9 | 8.5 | 2.8 | 7.7 | -11.8 | | | | |
| 2004 | 7.3 | 10.4 | 9.0 | 8.6 | 3.2 | 7.9 | -7.6 | | | | |
| 2005 | 7.7 | 10.8 | 9.5 | 9.2 | 4.4 | 9.2 | -2.7 | 22.0 | | | |
| 2006 | 8.1 | 11.1 | 9.9 | 9.7 | 5.3 | 10.1 | 0.6 | 21.3 | | | |
| 2007 | 7.8 | 10.7 | 9.5 | 9.3 | 5.0 | 9.3 | 0.4 | 13.8 | | | |
| 2008 | 6.6 | 9.2 | 7.7 | 7.1 | 2.5 | 5.6 | -4.2 | 0.0 | | | |
| 2009 | 7.1 | 9.8 | 8.4 | 8.0 | 3.8 | 7.2 | -0.9 | 5.8 | | | |
| 2010 | 7.0 | 9.6 | 8.3 | 7.8 | 3.8 | 6.9 | -0.5 | 5.3 | 2.9 | | |
| 2011 | 6.5 | 9.0 | 7.6 | 7.0 | 3.0 | 5.7 | -1.6 | 2.6 | -5.3 | | |
| 2012 | 6.9 | 9.3 | 8.0 | 7.5 | 3.8 | 6.6 | 0.1 | 5.0 | 3.5 | | |
| 2013 | 7.3 | 9.6 | 8.4 | 8.1 | 4.6 | 7.5 | 1.8 | 7.0 | 8.4 | | |
| 2014 | 7.2 | 9.5 | 8.3 | 7.9 | 4.6 | 7.2 | 1.9 | 6.6 | 7.4 | | |
| 2015 | 7.2 | 9.5 | 8.3 | 8.0 | 4.8 | 7.4 | 2.4 | 7.0 | 7.9 | 10.7 | |
| 2016 | 7.3 | 9.5 | 8.4 | 8.1 | 5.0 | 7.5 | 2.9 | 7.2 | 8.2 | 10.3 | 9.9 |

Source of underlying data: 1.) Morningstar *Direct* database. Used with permission. All rights reserved. All calculations performed by Duff & Phelps LLC.

**Germany Long-Horizon Equity Risk Premia**

in Local Currency (Euro – EUR)
in Percent

| End Date | \ Start Date 1970 | 1975 | 1980 | 1985 | 1990 | 1995 | 2000 | 2005 | 2010 | 2015 | 2016 |
|---|---|---|---|---|---|---|---|---|---|---|---|
| 1970 | -31.7 | | | | | | | | | | |
| 1971 | -14.2 | | | | | | | | | | |
| 1972 | -6.7 | | | | | | | | | | |
| 1973 | -12.1 | | | | | | | | | | |
| 1974 | -10.8 | | | | | | | | | | |
| 1975 | -3.6 | 32.4 | | | | | | | | | |
| 1976 | -4.8 | 10.2 | | | | | | | | | |
| 1977 | -3.5 | 8.6 | | | | | | | | | |
| 1978 | -2.8 | 7.1 | | | | | | | | | |
| 1979 | -4.1 | 2.5 | | | | | | | | | |
| 1980 | -4.3 | 1.0 | -6.4 | | | | | | | | |
| 1981 | -4.5 | -0.1 | -6.5 | | | | | | | | |
| 1982 | -3.6 | 0.9 | -1.8 | | | | | | | | |
| 1983 | -0.9 | 4.6 | 7.1 | | | | | | | | |
| 1984 | -0.8 | 4.2 | 6.0 | | | | | | | | |
| 1985 | 4.2 | 10.9 | 18.0 | 77.8 | | | | | | | |
| 1986 | 4.0 | 10.1 | 15.5 | 39.4 | | | | | | | |
| 1987 | 1.3 | 5.9 | 8.0 | 11.5 | | | | | | | |
| 1988 | 2.8 | 7.6 | 10.5 | 16.1 | | | | | | | |
| 1989 | 4.3 | 9.4 | 12.8 | 19.6 | | | | | | | |
| 1990 | 2.8 | 7.1 | 9.2 | 11.8 | -27.1 | | | | | | |
| 1991 | 2.8 | 6.8 | 8.5 | 10.4 | -12.7 | | | | | | |
| 1992 | 2.1 | 5.7 | 7.0 | 7.6 | -12.5 | | | | | | |
| 1993 | 3.7 | 7.5 | 9.3 | 11.1 | 0.5 | | | | | | |
| 1994 | 3.0 | 6.5 | 7.8 | 8.7 | -2.1 | | | | | | |
| 1995 | 3.0 | 6.2 | 7.4 | 8.0 | -1.6 | 0.8 | | | | | |
| 1996 | 3.5 | 6.7 | 7.9 | 8.7 | 1.0 | 8.8 | | | | | |
| 1997 | 4.8 | 8.1 | 9.7 | 11.2 | 5.9 | 19.2 | | | | | |
| 1998 | 5.1 | 8.5 | 10.0 | 11.5 | 7.0 | 18.3 | | | | | |
| 1999 | 6.2 | 9.6 | 11.4 | 13.2 | 10.0 | 22.0 | | | | | |
| 2000 | 5.5 | 8.7 | 10.1 | 11.4 | 7.7 | 15.9 | -14.8 | | | | |
| 2001 | 4.6 | 7.5 | 8.6 | 9.4 | 5.2 | 10.4 | -18.7 | | | | |
| 2002 | 3.1 | 5.5 | 6.2 | 6.2 | 1.1 | 3.1 | -28.4 | | | | |
| 2003 | 3.9 | 6.5 | 7.3 | 7.6 | 3.4 | 6.4 | -13.1 | | | | |
| 2004 | 3.9 | 6.4 | 7.2 | 7.5 | 3.4 | 6.2 | -9.6 | | | | |
| 2005 | 4.5 | 7.0 | 7.8 | 8.2 | 4.7 | 7.8 | -4.0 | 23.9 | | | |
| 2006 | 4.9 | 7.3 | 8.2 | 8.7 | 5.5 | 8.7 | -0.8 | 21.3 | | | |
| 2007 | 5.2 | 7.7 | 8.6 | 9.2 | 6.3 | 9.5 | 1.6 | 20.4 | | | |
| 2008 | 3.9 | 6.1 | 6.7 | 6.8 | 3.5 | 5.5 | -3.7 | 3.6 | | | |
| 2009 | 4.3 | 6.4 | 7.1 | 7.3 | 4.3 | 6.4 | -1.4 | 6.8 | | | |
| 2010 | 4.5 | 6.7 | 7.3 | 7.6 | 4.7 | 6.9 | 0.0 | 8.0 | 14.1 | | |
| 2011 | 4.0 | 6.0 | 6.6 | 6.7 | 3.7 | 5.4 | -1.5 | 4.4 | -1.7 | | |
| 2012 | 4.6 | 6.6 | 7.2 | 7.4 | 4.8 | 6.7 | 0.8 | 7.4 | 8.4 | | |
| 2013 | 5.0 | 7.1 | 7.7 | 8.1 | 5.7 | 7.7 | 2.6 | 9.4 | 12.6 | | |
| 2014 | 5.0 | 6.9 | 7.6 | 7.8 | 5.5 | 7.4 | 2.5 | 8.6 | 10.4 | | |
| 2015 | 5.1 | 7.0 | 7.6 | 7.9 | 5.6 | 7.5 | 2.9 | 8.6 | 10.2 | 9.5 | |
| 2016 | 5.1 | 7.0 | 7.6 | 7.8 | 5.7 | 7.4 | 3.1 | 8.5 | 9.7 | 8.0 | 6.5 |

in U.S. Dollars (USD)
in Percent

| End Date | \ Start Date 1970 | 1975 | 1980 | 1985 | 1990 | 1995 | 2000 | 2005 | 2010 | 2015 | 2016 |
|---|---|---|---|---|---|---|---|---|---|---|---|
| 1970 | -31.8 | | | | | | | | | | |
| 1971 | -8.1 | | | | | | | | | | |
| 1972 | -1.9 | | | | | | | | | | |
| 1973 | -5.1 | | | | | | | | | | |
| 1974 | -2.9 | | | | | | | | | | |
| 1975 | 1.2 | 21.5 | | | | | | | | | |
| 1976 | 0.7 | 9.6 | | | | | | | | | |
| 1977 | 2.9 | 12.5 | | | | | | | | | |
| 1978 | 4.7 | 14.1 | | | | | | | | | |
| 1979 | 3.1 | 9.0 | | | | | | | | | |
| 1980 | 1.1 | 4.5 | -18.2 | | | | | | | | |
| 1981 | -0.2 | 1.8 | -16.4 | | | | | | | | |
| 1982 | -0.1 | 1.7 | -10.5 | | | | | | | | |
| 1983 | 1.2 | 3.4 | -3.6 | | | | | | | | |
| 1984 | 0.3 | 1.9 | -5.3 | | | | | | | | |
| 1985 | 8.2 | 13.3 | 16.8 | 127.5 | | | | | | | |
| 1986 | 9.4 | 14.5 | 18.4 | 77.8 | | | | | | | |
| 1987 | 7.1 | 10.9 | 12.2 | 41.3 | | | | | | | |
| 1988 | 7.6 | 11.3 | 12.5 | 34.9 | | | | | | | |
| 1989 | 9.2 | 13.2 | 15.3 | 35.9 | | | | | | | |
| 1990 | 7.9 | 11.3 | 12.3 | 27.0 | -17.7 | | | | | | |
| 1991 | 7.6 | 10.6 | 11.3 | 23.1 | -8.7 | | | | | | |
| 1992 | 6.5 | 9.1 | 9.1 | 18.1 | -11.6 | | | | | | |
| 1993 | 7.4 | 10.2 | 10.6 | 19.4 | -1.2 | | | | | | |
| 1994 | 7.1 | 9.6 | 9.7 | 17.3 | -1.4 | | | | | | |
| 1995 | 7.2 | 9.5 | 9.7 | 16.5 | 0.4 | 9.2 | | | | | |
| 1996 | 7.2 | 9.5 | 9.6 | 15.9 | 1.5 | 8.8 | | | | | |
| 1997 | 7.7 | 10.0 | 10.2 | 16.2 | 3.9 | 12.6 | | | | | |
| 1998 | 8.2 | 10.6 | 11.0 | 16.8 | 6.2 | 15.6 | | | | | |
| 1999 | 8.5 | 10.8 | 11.3 | 16.8 | 7.2 | 15.9 | | | | | |
| 2000 | 7.6 | 9.6 | 9.8 | 14.5 | 4.7 | 9.9 | -20.2 | | | | |
| 2001 | 6.5 | 8.3 | 8.1 | 12.1 | 2.1 | 4.6 | -23.4 | | | | |
| 2002 | 5.2 | 6.6 | 6.1 | 9.3 | -1.0 | -0.7 | -28.4 | | | | |
| 2003 | 6.8 | 8.4 | 8.3 | 11.9 | 3.4 | 6.0 | -6.4 | | | | |
| 2004 | 6.9 | 8.6 | 8.5 | 11.9 | 3.9 | 6.6 | -2.7 | | | | |
| 2005 | 7.0 | 8.5 | 8.4 | 11.7 | 4.2 | 6.7 | -1.0 | 7.5 | | | |
| 2006 | 7.7 | 9.3 | 9.3 | 12.7 | 5.8 | 8.9 | 3.9 | 20.1 | | | |
| 2007 | 8.3 | 10.0 | 10.1 | 13.5 | 7.3 | 10.6 | 7.3 | 23.9 | | | |
| 2008 | 6.8 | 8.2 | 8.1 | 10.9 | 4.3 | 6.3 | 1.0 | 5.6 | | | |
| 2009 | 7.2 | 8.7 | 8.6 | 11.4 | 5.2 | 7.4 | 3.2 | 9.1 | | | |
| 2010 | 7.2 | 8.6 | 8.5 | 11.2 | 5.3 | 7.4 | 3.5 | 8.7 | 6.7 | | |
| 2011 | 6.5 | 7.8 | 7.6 | 10.0 | 4.1 | 5.8 | 1.6 | 4.6 | -6.7 | | |
| 2012 | 7.1 | 8.4 | 8.3 | 10.8 | 5.3 | 7.1 | 3.8 | 7.8 | 5.7 | | |
| 2013 | 7.6 | 9.0 | 9.0 | 11.5 | 6.4 | 8.4 | 5.7 | 10.4 | 12.0 | | |
| 2014 | 7.2 | 8.5 | 8.4 | 10.7 | 5.7 | 7.4 | 4.6 | 8.3 | 7.4 | | |
| 2015 | 7.0 | 8.2 | 8.1 | 10.3 | 5.4 | 7.0 | 4.2 | 7.4 | 5.9 | -1.7 | |
| 2016 | 7.0 | 8.1 | 8.0 | 10.1 | 5.3 | 6.8 | 4.2 | 7.0 | 5.5 | 0.6 | 3.0 |

Source of underlying data: 1.) Morningstar *Direct* database. Used with permission. All rights reserved. All calculations performed by Duff & Phelps LLC.

**Germany Short-Horizon Equity Risk Premia**

in Local Currency (Euro – EUR)
in Percent

| End Date | 1970 | 1975 | 1980 | 1985 | 1990 | 1995 | 2000 | 2005 | 2010 | 2015 | 2016 |
|---|---|---|---|---|---|---|---|---|---|---|---|
| 1970 | -30.5 | | | | | | | | | | |
| 1971 | -11.8 | | | | | | | | | | |
| 1972 | -3.6 | | | | | | | | | | |
| 1973 | -9.1 | | | | | | | | | | |
| 1974 | -7.7 | | | | | | | | | | |
| 1975 | -0.3 | 36.2 | | | | | | | | | |
| 1976 | -1.6 | 13.5 | | | | | | | | | |
| 1977 | -0.4 | 11.6 | | | | | | | | | |
| 1978 | 0.1 | 9.8 | | | | | | | | | |
| 1979 | -1.4 | 4.9 | | | | | | | | | |
| 1980 | -1.8 | 3.0 | -6.4 | | | | | | | | |
| 1981 | -2.4 | 1.4 | -7.3 | | | | | | | | |
| 1982 | -1.6 | 2.3 | -2.1 | | | | | | | | |
| 1983 | 1.1 | 6.0 | 7.5 | | | | | | | | |
| 1984 | 1.3 | 5.8 | 6.7 | | | | | | | | |
| 1985 | 6.2 | 12.5 | 18.9 | 79.7 | | | | | | | |
| 1986 | 6.0 | 11.8 | 16.7 | 41.5 | | | | | | | |
| 1987 | 3.3 | 7.6 | 9.3 | 13.4 | | | | | | | |
| 1988 | 4.9 | 9.3 | 11.8 | 18.1 | | | | | | | |
| 1989 | 6.3 | 10.9 | 13.9 | 21.1 | | | | | | | |
| 1990 | 4.6 | 8.5 | 10.1 | 13.0 | -27.9 | | | | | | |
| 1991 | 4.5 | 8.0 | 9.4 | 11.2 | -13.5 | | | | | | |
| 1992 | 3.7 | 6.8 | 7.6 | 8.1 | -13.6 | | | | | | |
| 1993 | 5.1 | 8.5 | 9.8 | 11.4 | -0.7 | | | | | | |
| 1994 | 4.4 | 7.5 | 8.3 | 9.1 | -2.9 | | | | | | |
| 1995 | 4.4 | 7.3 | 8.0 | 8.6 | -1.9 | 3.3 | | | | | |
| 1996 | 4.9 | 7.8 | 8.7 | 9.5 | 1.2 | 11.3 | | | | | |
| 1997 | 6.3 | 9.3 | 10.6 | 12.0 | 6.3 | 21.8 | | | | | |
| 1998 | 6.7 | 9.6 | 10.9 | 12.4 | 7.5 | 20.5 | | | | | |
| 1999 | 7.7 | 10.8 | 12.3 | 14.1 | 10.6 | 24.0 | | | | | |
| 2000 | 7.0 | 9.8 | 11.0 | 12.3 | 8.4 | 17.7 | -13.8 | | | | |
| 2001 | 6.1 | 8.6 | 9.5 | 10.3 | 5.8 | 12.0 | -18.0 | | | | |
| 2002 | 4.5 | 6.7 | 7.1 | 7.2 | 1.8 | 4.7 | -27.5 | | | | |
| 2003 | 5.4 | 7.6 | 8.2 | 8.6 | 4.1 | 8.0 | -11.9 | | | | |
| 2004 | 5.4 | 7.6 | 8.1 | 8.5 | 4.3 | 7.9 | -8.3 | | | | |
| 2005 | 6.0 | 8.2 | 8.8 | 9.3 | 5.6 | 9.4 | -2.7 | 25.2 | | | |
| 2006 | 6.3 | 8.5 | 9.2 | 9.7 | 6.4 | 10.3 | 0.4 | 22.4 | | | |
| 2007 | 6.7 | 8.8 | 9.5 | 10.1 | 7.1 | 10.9 | 2.7 | 21.2 | | | |
| 2008 | 5.3 | 7.2 | 7.6 | 7.8 | 4.3 | 6.8 | -2.7 | 4.2 | | | |
| 2009 | 5.7 | 7.6 | 8.1 | 8.3 | 5.1 | 7.8 | -0.3 | 7.7 | | | |
| 2010 | 6.0 | 7.9 | 8.3 | 8.7 | 5.7 | 8.4 | 1.2 | 9.2 | 16.6 | | |
| 2011 | 5.5 | 7.2 | 7.6 | 7.8 | 4.7 | 7.0 | -0.1 | 5.7 | 0.7 | | |
| 2012 | 6.0 | 7.8 | 8.3 | 8.6 | 5.8 | 8.3 | 2.2 | 8.8 | 10.5 | | |
| 2013 | 6.5 | 8.3 | 8.8 | 9.2 | 6.7 | 9.2 | 3.9 | 10.8 | 14.5 | | |
| 2014 | 6.4 | 8.2 | 8.7 | 9.0 | 6.5 | 8.9 | 3.9 | 10.0 | 12.2 | | |
| 2015 | 6.5 | 8.2 | 8.7 | 9.0 | 6.7 | 9.0 | 4.3 | 10.0 | 11.8 | 10.2 | |
| 2016 | 6.5 | 8.2 | 8.7 | 9.0 | 6.7 | 8.9 | 4.4 | 9.8 | 11.2 | 8.7 | 7.2 |

in U.S. Dollars (USD)
in Percent

| End Date | 1970 | 1975 | 1980 | 1985 | 1990 | 1995 | 2000 | 2005 | 2010 | 2015 | 2016 |
|---|---|---|---|---|---|---|---|---|---|---|---|
| 1970 | -31.8 | | | | | | | | | | |
| 1971 | -5.7 | | | | | | | | | | |
| 1972 | -3.5 | | | | | | | | | | |
| 1973 | -10.3 | | | | | | | | | | |
| 1974 | -8.6 | | | | | | | | | | |
| 1975 | -1.7 | 33.0 | | | | | | | | | |
| 1976 | -2.9 | 11.4 | | | | | | | | | |
| 1977 | -1.5 | 10.4 | | | | | | | | | |
| 1978 | -0.7 | 9.2 | | | | | | | | | |
| 1979 | -2.2 | 4.2 | | | | | | | | | |
| 1980 | -2.5 | 2.5 | -6.1 | | | | | | | | |
| 1981 | -2.6 | 1.7 | -4.7 | | | | | | | | |
| 1982 | -1.8 | 2.4 | -0.6 | | | | | | | | |
| 1983 | 0.6 | 5.7 | 7.5 | | | | | | | | |
| 1984 | 0.8 | 5.5 | 6.7 | | | | | | | | |
| 1985 | 7.0 | 14.1 | 22.4 | 101.0 | | | | | | | |
| 1986 | 6.8 | 13.3 | 19.7 | 52.3 | | | | | | | |
| 1987 | 3.6 | 8.3 | 10.8 | 17.7 | | | | | | | |
| 1988 | 4.9 | 9.8 | 12.8 | 20.5 | | | | | | | |
| 1989 | 6.4 | 11.4 | 15.0 | 23.4 | | | | | | | |
| 1990 | 4.6 | 8.7 | 10.8 | 14.2 | -31.8 | | | | | | |
| 1991 | 4.4 | 8.3 | 9.9 | 12.3 | -15.5 | | | | | | |
| 1992 | 3.7 | 7.1 | 8.2 | 9.2 | -14.6 | | | | | | |
| 1993 | 5.0 | 8.6 | 10.2 | 12.1 | -2.0 | | | | | | |
| 1994 | 4.3 | 7.5 | 8.6 | 9.6 | -4.3 | | | | | | |
| 1995 | 4.3 | 7.3 | 8.3 | 9.0 | -3.0 | 3.5 | | | | | |
| 1996 | 4.8 | 7.8 | 8.9 | 9.8 | 0.0 | 10.8 | | | | | |
| 1997 | 5.9 | 9.1 | 10.4 | 11.8 | 4.6 | 19.4 | | | | | |
| 1998 | 6.3 | 9.4 | 10.8 | 12.3 | 6.1 | 19.0 | | | | | |
| 1999 | 7.2 | 10.4 | 11.9 | 13.6 | 8.7 | 21.7 | | | | | |
| 2000 | 6.6 | 9.5 | 10.7 | 12.0 | 6.8 | 16.0 | -12.9 | | | | |
| 2001 | 5.7 | 8.3 | 10.0 | 10.0 | 4.5 | 10.7 | -17.0 | | | | |
| 2002 | 3.9 | 6.1 | 6.5 | 6.4 | -0.1 | 2.5 | -29.6 | | | | |
| 2003 | 5.0 | 7.3 | 7.9 | 8.3 | 2.9 | 6.8 | -11.8 | | | | |
| 2004 | 5.0 | 7.3 | 7.9 | 8.2 | 3.1 | 6.8 | -8.1 | | | | |
| 2005 | 5.5 | 7.8 | 8.4 | 8.8 | 4.3 | 8.2 | -3.1 | 21.9 | | | |
| 2006 | 5.9 | 8.2 | 8.9 | 9.4 | 5.3 | 9.3 | 0.5 | 21.9 | | | |
| 2007 | 6.3 | 8.6 | 9.3 | 9.9 | 6.2 | 10.2 | 3.0 | 21.5 | | | |
| 2008 | 5.0 | 7.0 | 7.5 | 7.7 | 3.5 | 6.3 | -2.2 | 5.1 | | | |
| 2009 | 5.5 | 7.5 | 8.0 | 8.3 | 4.5 | 7.4 | 0.2 | 8.6 | | | |
| 2010 | 5.7 | 7.7 | 8.2 | 8.5 | 5.0 | 7.9 | 1.6 | 9.7 | 15.5 | | |
| 2011 | 5.2 | 7.1 | 7.5 | 7.7 | 4.1 | 6.6 | 0.3 | 6.2 | 0.4 | | |
| 2012 | 5.8 | 7.7 | 8.2 | 8.5 | 5.3 | 7.9 | 2.6 | 9.3 | 10.4 | | |
| 2013 | 6.3 | 8.2 | 8.8 | 9.2 | 6.2 | 9.0 | 4.4 | 11.3 | 14.8 | | |
| 2014 | 6.2 | 8.1 | 8.6 | 8.9 | 6.0 | 8.6 | 4.3 | 10.4 | 12.3 | | |
| 2015 | 6.3 | 8.1 | 8.6 | 8.9 | 6.2 | 8.6 | 4.5 | 10.3 | 11.7 | 8.8 | |
| 2016 | 6.3 | 8.1 | 8.6 | 8.9 | 6.2 | 8.6 | 4.7 | 10.0 | 11.1 | 8.1 | 7.5 |

Source of underlying data: 1.) Morningstar *Direct* database. Used with permission. All rights reserved. All calculations performed by Duff & Phelps LLC.

## Ireland Long-Horizon Equity Risk Premia

### in Local Currency (Euro – EUR) in Percent

| End Date | \ Start Date 1970 | 1975 | 1980 | 1985 | 1990 | 1995 | 2000 | 2005 | 2010 | 2015 | 2016 |
|---|---|---|---|---|---|---|---|---|---|---|---|
| 1970 | -16.7 | | | | | | | | | | |
| 1971 | -7.0 | | | | | | | | | | |
| 1972 | 17.1 | | | | | | | | | | |
| 1973 | 6.8 | | | | | | | | | | |
| 1974 | -6.4 | | | | | | | | | | |
| 1975 | 4.7 | 60.0 | | | | | | | | | |
| 1976 | -0.8 | 13.0 | | | | | | | | | |
| 1977 | 7.7 | 31.2 | | | | | | | | | |
| 1978 | 10.5 | 31.7 | | | | | | | | | |
| 1979 | 7.6 | 21.6 | | | | | | | | | |
| 1980 | 7.5 | 19.1 | 6.2 | | | | | | | | |
| 1981 | 5.6 | 14.1 | -4.6 | | | | | | | | |
| 1982 | 3.3 | 9.3 | -11.2 | | | | | | | | |
| 1983 | 8.0 | 15.9 | 8.8 | | | | | | | | |
| 1984 | 6.3 | 12.6 | 3.5 | | | | | | | | |
| 1985 | 8.3 | 14.9 | 9.4 | 38.8 | | | | | | | |
| 1986 | 10.3 | 17.2 | 14.1 | 40.6 | | | | | | | |
| 1987 | 8.8 | 14.7 | 10.3 | 21.8 | | | | | | | |
| 1988 | 9.9 | 15.7 | 12.3 | 23.4 | | | | | | | |
| 1989 | 10.8 | 16.5 | 13.9 | 24.3 | | | | | | | |
| 1990 | 8.5 | 13.2 | 9.3 | 14.2 | -36.7 | | | | | | |
| 1991 | 8.3 | 12.7 | 8.9 | 12.8 | -16.0 | | | | | | |
| 1992 | 6.9 | 10.6 | 6.4 | 8.2 | -18.8 | | | | | | |
| 1993 | 8.9 | 13.0 | 9.9 | 13.4 | -0.2 | | | | | | |
| 1994 | 8.5 | 12.2 | 9.0 | 11.8 | -0.7 | | | | | | |
| 1995 | 8.5 | 12.1 | 9.1 | 11.6 | 1.0 | 9.5 | | | | | |
| 1996 | 8.9 | 12.3 | 9.6 | 12.1 | 3.4 | 13.6 | | | | | |
| 1997 | 9.6 | 13.1 | 10.8 | 13.6 | 6.8 | 19.4 | | | | | |
| 1998 | 10.1 | 13.6 | 11.5 | 14.3 | 8.8 | 20.6 | | | | | |
| 1999 | 9.7 | 13.0 | 10.8 | 13.2 | 7.7 | 16.1 | | | | | |
| 2000 | 9.0 | 12.0 | 9.7 | 11.6 | 5.9 | 11.3 | -12.3 | | | | |
| 2001 | 8.7 | 11.5 | 9.1 | 10.8 | 5.2 | 9.4 | -7.4 | | | | |
| 2002 | 7.1 | 9.5 | 6.9 | 7.9 | 1.5 | 2.9 | -19.1 | | | | |
| 2003 | 7.4 | 9.7 | 7.3 | 8.2 | 2.5 | 4.3 | -10.4 | | | | |
| 2004 | 8.0 | 10.4 | 8.1 | 9.3 | 4.2 | 6.7 | -2.6 | | | | |
| 2005 | 8.0 | 10.3 | 8.2 | 9.3 | 4.6 | 7.0 | -0.6 | 9.4 | | | |
| 2006 | 8.6 | 10.9 | 8.9 | 10.1 | 6.0 | 8.7 | 3.5 | 18.9 | | | |
| 2007 | 7.5 | 9.6 | 7.5 | 8.3 | 3.9 | 5.6 | -0.9 | 2.1 | | | |
| 2008 | 5.4 | 7.1 | 4.6 | 4.9 | -0.3 | -0.1 | -9.1 | -17.1 | | | |
| 2009 | 5.4 | 7.1 | 4.6 | 4.8 | 0.0 | 0.2 | -7.7 | -12.8 | | | |
| 2010 | 4.8 | 6.4 | 3.9 | 4.0 | -0.8 | -0.9 | -8.6 | -13.5 | -17.2 | | |
| 2011 | 4.9 | 6.5 | 4.1 | 4.2 | -0.4 | -0.3 | -7.1 | -10.3 | -3.9 | | |
| 2012 | 4.8 | 6.2 | 3.9 | 3.9 | -0.5 | -0.4 | -6.8 | -9.4 | -3.6 | | |
| 2013 | 5.4 | 6.9 | 4.7 | 4.9 | 0.8 | 1.3 | -4.0 | -4.8 | 5.2 | | |
| 2014 | 5.6 | 7.0 | 5.0 | 5.2 | 1.4 | 1.9 | -2.8 | -2.9 | 7.0 | | |
| 2015 | 6.1 | 7.6 | 5.6 | 6.0 | 2.4 | 3.2 | -0.8 | 0.0 | 10.6 | 29.0 | |
| 2016 | 5.8 | 7.3 | 5.3 | 5.6 | 2.2 | 2.8 | -1.1 | -0.4 | 8.4 | 12.1 | -4.7 |

### in U.S. Dollars (USD) in Percent

| End Date | \ Start Date 1970 | 1975 | 1980 | 1985 | 1990 | 1995 | 2000 | 2005 | 2010 | 2015 | 2016 |
|---|---|---|---|---|---|---|---|---|---|---|---|
| 1970 | -16.9 | | | | | | | | | | |
| 1971 | -3.7 | | | | | | | | | | |
| 1972 | 14.8 | | | | | | | | | | |
| 1973 | 4.9 | | | | | | | | | | |
| 1974 | -7.8 | | | | | | | | | | |
| 1975 | -0.2 | 37.9 | | | | | | | | | |
| 1976 | -6.5 | -3.3 | | | | | | | | | |
| 1977 | 5.5 | 27.5 | | | | | | | | | |
| 1978 | 9.5 | 31.0 | | | | | | | | | |
| 1979 | 7.1 | 21.9 | | | | | | | | | |
| 1980 | 5.9 | 17.2 | -6.0 | | | | | | | | |
| 1981 | 2.9 | 10.6 | -17.6 | | | | | | | | |
| 1982 | 0.1 | 5.1 | -22.9 | | | | | | | | |
| 1983 | 2.8 | 8.7 | -7.7 | | | | | | | | |
| 1984 | 0.7 | 5.0 | -11.9 | | | | | | | | |
| 1985 | 5.4 | 11.4 | 2.6 | 75.2 | | | | | | | |
| 1986 | 8.7 | 15.5 | 11.0 | 68.2 | | | | | | | |
| 1987 | 8.2 | 14.3 | 9.6 | 45.4 | | | | | | | |
| 1988 | 8.6 | 14.4 | 10.3 | 38.1 | | | | | | | |
| 1989 | 9.8 | 15.6 | 12.5 | 36.9 | | | | | | | |
| 1990 | 8.0 | 12.9 | 8.9 | 26.2 | -27.7 | | | | | | |
| 1991 | 7.8 | 12.3 | 8.4 | 22.8 | -12.4 | | | | | | |
| 1992 | 6.1 | 10.0 | 5.4 | 16.3 | -18.2 | | | | | | |
| 1993 | 7.3 | 11.3 | 7.5 | 18.3 | -4.9 | | | | | | |
| 1994 | 7.3 | 11.1 | 7.5 | 17.2 | -2.6 | | | | | | |
| 1995 | 7.6 | 11.2 | 7.9 | 16.8 | 0.1 | 13.6 | | | | | |
| 1996 | 8.2 | 11.8 | 8.8 | 17.5 | 3.6 | 19.0 | | | | | |
| 1997 | 8.3 | 11.7 | 8.9 | 16.9 | 4.4 | 16.1 | | | | | |
| 1998 | 9.0 | 12.5 | 10.0 | 17.9 | 7.3 | 19.5 | | | | | |
| 1999 | 8.2 | 11.3 | 8.7 | 15.6 | 4.9 | 12.4 | | | | | |
| 2000 | 7.3 | 10.2 | 7.4 | 13.5 | 2.8 | 7.3 | -17.9 | | | | |
| 2001 | 6.8 | 9.6 | 6.8 | 12.2 | 2.0 | 5.2 | -12.7 | | | | |
| 2002 | 5.7 | 8.1 | 5.1 | 9.8 | -0.7 | 0.5 | -19.2 | | | | |
| 2003 | 6.6 | 9.1 | 6.5 | 11.3 | 2.2 | 4.8 | -4.7 | | | | |
| 2004 | 7.6 | 10.1 | 7.8 | 12.7 | 4.6 | 8.2 | 4.0 | | | | |
| 2005 | 7.2 | 9.6 | 7.3 | 11.8 | 4.0 | 7.0 | 2.5 | -5.1 | | | |
| 2006 | 8.2 | 10.7 | 8.6 | 13.3 | 6.3 | 10.0 | 8.3 | 19.2 | | | |
| 2007 | 7.3 | 9.6 | 7.4 | 11.6 | 4.6 | 7.4 | 4.3 | 4.8 | | | |
| 2008 | 5.2 | 7.1 | 4.6 | 8.0 | 0.4 | 1.4 | -4.7 | -15.4 | | | |
| 2009 | 5.3 | 7.1 | 4.7 | 8.0 | 0.7 | 1.8 | -3.4 | -10.8 | | | |
| 2010 | 4.6 | 6.3 | 3.8 | 6.8 | -0.4 | 0.3 | -5.1 | -12.7 | -22.5 | | |
| 2011 | 4.6 | 6.3 | 3.8 | 6.8 | -0.1 | 0.6 | -4.2 | -10.1 | -8.4 | | |
| 2012 | 4.5 | 6.1 | 3.7 | 6.5 | -0.1 | 0.5 | -4.0 | -9.0 | -6.0 | | |
| 2013 | 5.2 | 6.9 | 4.7 | 7.5 | 1.4 | 2.5 | -1.1 | -3.8 | 4.8 | | |
| 2014 | 5.1 | 6.7 | 4.6 | 7.3 | 1.4 | 2.4 | -1.0 | -3.4 | 3.9 | | |
| 2015 | 5.3 | 6.9 | 4.9 | 7.6 | 1.9 | 3.0 | 0.1 | -1.7 | 5.9 | 15.8 | |
| 2016 | 5.1 | 6.6 | 4.5 | 7.1 | 1.6 | 2.5 | -0.4 | -2.2 | 3.9 | 3.9 | -7.9 |

Source of underlying data: 1.) Morningstar *Direct* database. Used with permission. All rights reserved. All calculations performed by Duff & Phelps LLC.

## Ireland Short-Horizon Equity Risk Premia

### in Local Currency (Euro – EUR)
in Percent

| End Date | Start Date | | | | | | | | | | |
|---|---|---|---|---|---|---|---|---|---|---|---|
| | 1970 | 1975 | 1980 | 1985 | 1990 | 1995 | 2000 | 2005 | 2010 | 2015 | 2016 |
| 1970 | -14.0 | | | | | | | | | | |
| 1971 | -3.5 | | | | | | | | | | |
| 1972 | 20.9 | | | | | | | | | | |
| 1973 | 10.1 | | | | | | | | | | |
| 1974 | -3.1 | | | | | | | | | | |
| 1975 | 8.9 | 69.0 | | | | | | | | | |
| 1976 | 3.6 | 20.5 | | | | | | | | | |
| 1977 | 12.9 | 39.7 | | | | | | | | | |
| 1978 | 15.6 | 39.0 | | | | | | | | | |
| 1979 | 12.2 | 27.5 | | | | | | | | | |
| 1980 | 11.6 | 23.9 | 6.0 | | | | | | | | |
| 1981 | 9.3 | 18.2 | -4.9 | | | | | | | | |
| 1982 | 6.8 | 12.9 | -11.3 | | | | | | | | |
| 1983 | 11.2 | 19.2 | 8.8 | | | | | | | | |
| 1984 | 9.3 | 15.5 | 3.6 | | | | | | | | |
| 1985 | 11.3 | 17.8 | 9.7 | 40.6 | | | | | | | |
| 1986 | 13.0 | 19.8 | 14.3 | 41.0 | | | | | | | |
| 1987 | 11.5 | 17.1 | 10.6 | 22.4 | | | | | | | |
| 1988 | 12.5 | 18.0 | 12.8 | 24.4 | | | | | | | |
| 1989 | 13.2 | 18.6 | 14.2 | 24.8 | | | | | | | |
| 1990 | 10.7 | 15.0 | 9.4 | 14.2 | -38.6 | | | | | | |
| 1991 | 10.4 | 14.4 | 8.9 | 12.7 | -17.5 | | | | | | |
| 1992 | 8.6 | 11.9 | 5.9 | 7.3 | -21.8 | | | | | | |
| 1993 | 10.5 | 14.1 | 9.4 | 12.6 | -2.7 | | | | | | |
| 1994 | 10.0 | 13.3 | 8.6 | 11.2 | -2.5 | | | | | | |
| 1995 | 10.1 | 13.3 | 8.8 | 11.2 | -0.1 | 11.6 | | | | | |
| 1996 | 10.4 | 13.5 | 9.4 | 11.9 | 2.7 | 15.5 | | | | | |
| 1997 | 11.2 | 14.3 | 10.7 | 13.4 | 6.3 | 20.8 | | | | | |
| 1998 | 11.6 | 14.7 | 11.3 | 14.1 | 8.2 | 21.6 | | | | | |
| 1999 | 11.2 | 14.1 | 10.7 | 13.1 | 7.3 | 17.1 | | | | | |
| 2000 | 10.5 | 13.1 | 9.7 | 11.6 | 5.6 | 12.4 | -11.2 | | | | |
| 2001 | 10.1 | 12.6 | 9.2 | 10.8 | 5.0 | 10.3 | -6.6 | | | | |
| 2002 | 8.6 | 10.6 | 7.0 | 7.9 | 1.5 | 3.9 | -18.1 | | | | |
| 2003 | 8.8 | 10.9 | 7.4 | 8.4 | 2.6 | 5.4 | -9.3 | | | | |
| 2004 | 9.4 | 11.5 | 8.3 | 9.5 | 4.5 | 7.9 | -1.3 | | | | |
| 2005 | 9.5 | 11.5 | 8.4 | 9.6 | 4.8 | 8.2 | 0.7 | 10.6 | | | |
| 2006 | 10.0 | 12.0 | 9.2 | 10.5 | 6.3 | 9.9 | 4.7 | 19.8 | | | |
| 2007 | 8.9 | 10.7 | 7.7 | 8.6 | 4.1 | 6.7 | 0.1 | 2.6 | | | |
| 2008 | 6.7 | 8.2 | 4.8 | 5.1 | -0.1 | 0.8 | -8.3 | -17.1 | | | |
| 2009 | 6.7 | 8.1 | 4.9 | 5.2 | 0.3 | 1.2 | -6.8 | -12.3 | | | |
| 2010 | 6.2 | 7.5 | 4.3 | 4.5 | -0.4 | 0.3 | -7.4 | -12.4 | -13.1 | | |
| 2011 | 6.5 | 7.8 | 4.7 | 4.9 | 0.4 | 1.2 | -5.4 | -8.3 | 1.7 | | |
| 2012 | 6.4 | 7.7 | 4.7 | 4.9 | 0.5 | 1.4 | -4.7 | -6.8 | 2.3 | | |
| 2013 | 7.1 | 8.4 | 5.6 | 5.9 | 2.0 | 3.2 | -1.8 | -2.1 | 10.5 | | |
| 2014 | 7.3 | 8.6 | 5.9 | 6.3 | 2.6 | 3.8 | -0.6 | -0.3 | 11.7 | | |
| 2015 | 7.8 | 9.1 | 6.6 | 7.0 | 3.6 | 5.1 | 1.3 | 2.5 | 14.8 | 30.1 | |
| 2016 | 7.5 | 8.8 | 6.3 | 6.7 | 3.3 | 4.7 | 1.0 | 2.0 | 12.1 | 13.1 | -3.8 |

### in U.S. Dollars (USD)
in Percent

| End Date | Start Date | | | | | | | | | | |
|---|---|---|---|---|---|---|---|---|---|---|---|
| | 1970 | 1975 | 1980 | 1985 | 1990 | 1995 | 2000 | 2005 | 2010 | 2015 | 2016 |
| 1970 | -14.0 | | | | | | | | | | |
| 1971 | -3.2 | | | | | | | | | | |
| 1972 | 19.2 | | | | | | | | | | |
| 1973 | 8.8 | | | | | | | | | | |
| 1974 | -4.2 | | | | | | | | | | |
| 1975 | 6.4 | 59.5 | | | | | | | | | |
| 1976 | 2.1 | 17.9 | | | | | | | | | |
| 1977 | 12.8 | 41.3 | | | | | | | | | |
| 1978 | 15.8 | 40.8 | | | | | | | | | |
| 1979 | 12.3 | 28.7 | | | | | | | | | |
| 1980 | 11.6 | 24.8 | 5.3 | | | | | | | | |
| 1981 | 9.6 | 19.4 | -3.9 | | | | | | | | |
| 1982 | 7.2 | 14.3 | -9.7 | | | | | | | | |
| 1983 | 10.7 | 19.0 | 6.8 | | | | | | | | |
| 1984 | 9.0 | 15.6 | 2.4 | | | | | | | | |
| 1985 | 11.6 | 18.8 | 10.6 | 51.2 | | | | | | | |
| 1986 | 13.7 | 21.1 | 15.7 | 49.0 | | | | | | | |
| 1987 | 12.0 | 18.2 | 11.6 | 26.8 | | | | | | | |
| 1988 | 12.8 | 18.9 | 13.4 | 27.1 | | | | | | | |
| 1989 | 13.5 | 19.4 | 14.8 | 27.2 | | | | | | | |
| 1990 | 10.8 | 15.5 | 9.5 | 15.3 | -44.0 | | | | | | |
| 1991 | 10.4 | 14.7 | 8.9 | 13.6 | -20.4 | | | | | | |
| 1992 | 8.8 | 12.4 | 6.1 | 8.4 | -23.0 | | | | | | |
| 1993 | 10.4 | 14.2 | 9.0 | 12.7 | -5.4 | | | | | | |
| 1994 | 9.9 | 13.4 | 8.3 | 11.3 | -4.6 | | | | | | |
| 1995 | 10.0 | 13.4 | 8.6 | 11.3 | -1.9 | 12.0 | | | | | |
| 1996 | 10.4 | 13.7 | 9.3 | 12.1 | 1.4 | 16.3 | | | | | |
| 1997 | 10.9 | 14.2 | 10.2 | 13.2 | 4.5 | 19.7 | | | | | |
| 1998 | 11.4 | 14.7 | 11.0 | 14.0 | 6.8 | 21.0 | | | | | |
| 1999 | 11.0 | 14.1 | 10.4 | 13.1 | 6.0 | 16.7 | | | | | |
| 2000 | 10.3 | 13.1 | 9.4 | 11.6 | 4.5 | 12.1 | -10.4 | | | | |
| 2001 | 9.9 | 12.6 | 8.9 | 10.8 | 4.0 | 10.1 | -6.2 | | | | |
| 2002 | 8.2 | 10.4 | 6.4 | 7.5 | 0.0 | 2.8 | -20.2 | | | | |
| 2003 | 8.5 | 10.7 | 7.0 | 8.2 | 1.4 | 4.8 | -10.0 | | | | |
| 2004 | 9.2 | 11.5 | 8.0 | 9.4 | 3.5 | 7.6 | -1.4 | | | | |
| 2005 | 9.2 | 11.4 | 8.1 | 9.4 | 3.9 | 7.8 | 0.3 | 9.2 | | | |
| 2006 | 9.9 | 12.1 | 9.0 | 10.5 | 5.6 | 9.8 | 4.9 | 20.8 | | | |
| 2007 | 8.7 | 10.6 | 7.4 | 8.5 | 3.3 | 6.3 | -0.1 | 2.1 | | | |
| 2008 | 6.6 | 8.2 | 4.7 | 5.1 | -0.7 | 0.7 | -8.1 | -16.5 | | | |
| 2009 | 6.6 | 8.2 | 4.7 | 5.2 | -0.3 | 1.2 | -6.6 | -11.8 | | | |
| 2010 | 6.2 | 7.6 | 4.2 | 4.5 | -0.9 | 0.3 | -7.1 | -11.8 | -12.3 | | |
| 2011 | 6.4 | 7.8 | 4.6 | 5.0 | -0.1 | 1.2 | -5.2 | -7.9 | 1.8 | | |
| 2012 | 6.3 | 7.7 | 4.5 | 4.9 | 0.1 | 1.4 | -4.5 | -6.5 | 2.4 | | |
| 2013 | 7.0 | 8.5 | 5.5 | 6.0 | 1.6 | 3.2 | -1.6 | -1.6 | 11.0 | | |
| 2014 | 7.2 | 8.6 | 5.7 | 6.3 | 2.1 | 3.8 | -0.5 | 0.0 | 11.7 | | |
| 2015 | 7.6 | 9.1 | 6.3 | 6.9 | 3.1 | 4.9 | 1.2 | 2.4 | 14.2 | 26.6 | |
| 2016 | 7.4 | 8.8 | 6.1 | 6.6 | 2.8 | 4.5 | 0.9 | 1.9 | 11.7 | 11.7 | -3.3 |

Source of underlying data: 1.) Morningstar Direct database. Used with permission. All rights reserved. All calculations performed by Duff & Phelps LLC.

## Italy Long-Horizon Equity Risk Premia

### in Local Currency (Euro – EUR)
in Percent

| End Date | \ Start Date 1970 | 1975 | 1980 | 1985 | 1990 | 1995 | 2000 | 2005 | 2010 | 2015 | 2016 |
|---|---|---|---|---|---|---|---|---|---|---|---|
| 1970 | -25.3 | | | | | | | | | | |
| 1971 | -25.2 | | | | | | | | | | |
| 1972 | -15.3 | | | | | | | | | | |
| 1973 | -9.2 | | | | | | | | | | |
| 1974 | -14.9 | | | | | | | | | | |
| 1975 | -15.1 | -15.9 | | | | | | | | | |
| 1976 | -15.4 | -16.8 | | | | | | | | | |
| 1977 | -17.6 | -22.2 | | | | | | | | | |
| 1978 | -12.9 | -10.4 | | | | | | | | | |
| 1979 | -11.6 | -8.3 | | | | | | | | | |
| 1980 | -2.0 | 8.8 | 94.2 | | | | | | | | |
| 1981 | -1.8 | 7.5 | 46.9 | | | | | | | | |
| 1982 | -3.9 | 3.0 | 21.8 | | | | | | | | |
| 1983 | -3.2 | 3.4 | 17.9 | | | | | | | | |
| 1984 | -2.3 | 4.0 | 16.3 | | | | | | | | |
| 1985 | 3.4 | 11.7 | 28.4 | 88.9 | | | | | | | |
| 1986 | 6.4 | 15.3 | 32.2 | 72.0 | | | | | | | |
| 1987 | 3.8 | 11.0 | 23.0 | 34.1 | | | | | | | |
| 1988 | 4.4 | 11.3 | 22.1 | 29.4 | | | | | | | |
| 1989 | 4.4 | 10.9 | 20.4 | 24.6 | | | | | | | |
| 1990 | 2.3 | 7.6 | 14.8 | 13.6 | -41.1 | | | | | | |
| 1991 | 1.6 | 6.4 | 12.6 | 9.9 | -26.7 | | | | | | |
| 1992 | 1.0 | 5.4 | 10.7 | 7.2 | -21.8 | | | | | | |
| 1993 | 2.5 | 7.1 | 12.5 | 10.4 | -7.2 | | | | | | |
| 1994 | 2.3 | 6.6 | 11.5 | 9.1 | -6.3 | | | | | | |
| 1995 | 1.7 | 5.6 | 10.0 | 7.1 | -7.4 | -12.8 | | | | | |
| 1996 | 1.6 | 5.3 | 9.3 | 6.4 | -6.7 | -7.5 | | | | | |
| 1997 | 3.3 | 7.3 | 11.6 | 9.8 | 0.6 | 12.1 | | | | | |
| 1998 | 4.5 | 8.5 | 13.0 | 11.8 | 4.7 | 18.4 | | | | | |
| 1999 | 4.8 | 8.7 | 13.0 | 11.9 | 5.5 | 17.4 | | | | | |
| 2000 | 4.6 | 8.4 | 12.4 | 11.2 | 5.1 | 14.6 | 0.4 | | | | |
| 2001 | 3.6 | 7.1 | 10.6 | 8.9 | 2.4 | 8.6 | -13.4 | | | | |
| 2002 | 2.8 | 5.9 | 9.0 | 7.0 | 0.2 | 4.3 | -17.5 | | | | |
| 2003 | 3.0 | 6.1 | 9.1 | 7.2 | 1.0 | 5.1 | -10.3 | | | | |
| 2004 | 3.5 | 6.6 | 9.5 | 7.8 | 2.3 | 6.6 | -4.3 | | | | |
| 2005 | 3.8 | 6.8 | 9.7 | 8.2 | 3.1 | 7.3 | -1.0 | 15.1 | | | |
| 2006 | 4.2 | 7.1 | 10.0 | 8.5 | 3.8 | 8.1 | 1.4 | 15.6 | | | |
| 2007 | 3.8 | 6.7 | 9.4 | 7.8 | 3.2 | 6.9 | 0.3 | 7.9 | | | |
| 2008 | 2.4 | 5.0 | 7.3 | 5.4 | 0.3 | 2.7 | -5.4 | -6.8 | | | |
| 2009 | 2.9 | 5.4 | 7.7 | 6.0 | 1.3 | 3.8 | -2.9 | -1.6 | | | |
| 2010 | 2.5 | 4.9 | 7.0 | 5.3 | 0.7 | 2.9 | -3.7 | -3.3 | -12.1 | | |
| 2011 | 1.9 | 4.1 | 6.1 | 4.2 | -0.5 | 1.2 | -5.5 | -6.3 | -18.3 | | |
| 2012 | 1.9 | 4.2 | 6.0 | 4.2 | -0.2 | 1.5 | -4.6 | -4.9 | -10.4 | | |
| 2013 | 2.2 | 4.3 | 6.2 | 4.5 | 0.3 | 2.0 | -3.5 | -3.0 | -4.9 | | |
| 2014 | 2.1 | 4.2 | 6.0 | 4.3 | 0.3 | 1.9 | -3.2 | -2.7 | -3.9 | | |
| 2015 | 2.3 | 4.5 | 6.2 | 4.6 | 0.8 | 2.4 | -2.2 | -1.3 | -1.1 | 12.9 | |
| 2016 | 2.1 | 4.1 | 5.8 | 4.2 | 0.4 | 2.0 | -2.6 | -1.9 | -2.1 | 2.3 | -8.3 |

### in U.S. Dollars (USD)
in Percent

| End Date | \ Start Date 1970 | 1975 | 1980 | 1985 | 1990 | 1995 | 2000 | 2005 | 2010 | 2015 | 2016 |
|---|---|---|---|---|---|---|---|---|---|---|---|
| 1970 | -25.3 | | | | | | | | | | |
| 1971 | -23.3 | | | | | | | | | | |
| 1972 | -13.3 | | | | | | | | | | |
| 1973 | -9.2 | | | | | | | | | | |
| 1974 | -15.5 | | | | | | | | | | |
| 1975 | -16.3 | -20.1 | | | | | | | | | |
| 1976 | -19.1 | -27.9 | | | | | | | | | |
| 1977 | -20.8 | -29.5 | | | | | | | | | |
| 1978 | -15.0 | -14.3 | | | | | | | | | |
| 1979 | -13.1 | -10.8 | | | | | | | | | |
| 1980 | -5.8 | 2.3 | 67.8 | | | | | | | | |
| 1981 | -7.2 | -1.2 | 22.6 | | | | | | | | |
| 1982 | -9.5 | -5.8 | 2.6 | | | | | | | | |
| 1983 | -9.7 | -6.5 | -1.1 | | | | | | | | |
| 1984 | -9.4 | -6.4 | -2.0 | | | | | | | | |
| 1985 | -1.5 | 4.8 | 17.8 | 117.1 | | | | | | | |
| 1986 | 4.0 | 12.2 | 28.5 | 105.0 | | | | | | | |
| 1987 | 2.0 | 8.7 | 20.9 | 59.1 | | | | | | | |
| 1988 | 2.0 | 8.3 | 18.9 | 45.1 | | | | | | | |
| 1989 | 2.4 | 8.3 | 17.9 | 37.8 | | | | | | | |
| 1990 | 0.6 | 5.7 | 13.2 | 25.9 | -33.9 | | | | | | |
| 1991 | 0.0 | 4.5 | 10.9 | 20.1 | -24.0 | | | | | | |
| 1992 | -1.4 | 2.5 | 7.6 | 13.7 | -26.5 | | | | | | |
| 1993 | -0.6 | 3.3 | 8.4 | 14.2 | -15.4 | | | | | | |
| 1994 | -0.5 | 3.3 | 8.0 | 13.0 | -11.8 | | | | | | |
| 1995 | -0.9 | 2.6 | 6.8 | 10.8 | -11.6 | -10.8 | | | | | |
| 1996 | -0.7 | 2.6 | 6.5 | 10.1 | -9.7 | -4.4 | | | | | |
| 1997 | 0.4 | 3.8 | 7.8 | 11.6 | -4.7 | 7.1 | | | | | |
| 1998 | 2.0 | 5.6 | 9.9 | 14.2 | 1.1 | 17.2 | | | | | |
| 1999 | 1.8 | 5.3 | 9.3 | 13.0 | 0.6 | 13.0 | | | | | |
| 2000 | 1.5 | 4.8 | 8.5 | 11.8 | 0.0 | 9.9 | -5.9 | | | | |
| 2001 | 0.5 | 3.5 | 6.7 | 9.3 | -2.6 | 4.0 | -18.5 | | | | |
| 2002 | 0.1 | 2.9 | 5.9 | 8.1 | -3.3 | 2.0 | -16.4 | | | | |
| 2003 | 1.1 | 4.0 | 7.1 | 9.5 | -0.7 | 5.5 | -3.9 | | | | |
| 2004 | 1.9 | 4.8 | 8.0 | 10.4 | 1.3 | 7.9 | 2.7 | | | | |
| 2005 | 1.9 | 4.7 | 7.6 | 9.9 | 1.2 | 7.2 | 2.3 | -0.1 | | | |
| 2006 | 2.6 | 5.5 | 8.5 | 10.9 | 2.9 | 9.1 | 6.2 | 14.9 | | | |
| 2007 | 2.6 | 5.4 | 8.3 | 10.5 | 2.9 | 8.6 | 5.7 | 10.8 | | | |
| 2008 | 1.2 | 3.6 | 6.1 | 7.8 | -0.1 | 4.1 | -0.8 | -5.3 | | | |
| 2009 | 1.7 | 4.2 | 6.7 | 8.4 | 1.1 | 5.4 | 1.6 | 0.4 | | | |
| 2010 | 1.3 | 3.6 | 5.9 | 7.4 | 0.2 | 4.0 | -0.2 | -2.6 | -17.8 | | |
| 2011 | 0.6 | 2.8 | 4.9 | 6.2 | -1.0 | 2.1 | -2.4 | -6.1 | -22.4 | | |
| 2012 | 0.7 | 2.9 | 4.9 | 6.2 | -0.7 | 2.4 | -1.7 | -4.4 | -12.6 | | |
| 2013 | 1.1 | 3.2 | 5.3 | 6.6 | 0.0 | 3.2 | -0.4 | -2.1 | -5.3 | | |
| 2014 | 0.8 | 2.9 | 4.8 | 5.9 | -0.4 | 2.4 | -1.2 | -3.1 | -6.6 | | |
| 2015 | 0.8 | 2.8 | 4.7 | 5.8 | -0.4 | 2.3 | -1.0 | -2.7 | -5.3 | 1.4 | |
| 2016 | 0.6 | 2.5 | 4.3 | 5.3 | -0.8 | 1.7 | -1.6 | -3.4 | -6.1 | -4.9 | -11.2 |

Source of underlying data: 1.) Morningstar *Direct* database. Used with permission. All rights reserved. All calculations performed by Duff & Phelps LLC.

**Italy Short-Horizon Equity Risk Premia**

in Local Currency (Euro – EUR)
in Percent

| End Date | 1970 | 1975 | 1980 | 1985 | 1990 | 1995 | 2000 | 2005 | 2010 | 2015 | 2016 |
|---|---|---|---|---|---|---|---|---|---|---|---|
| 1970 | -22.3 | | | | | | | | | | |
| 1971 | -21.6 | | | | | | | | | | |
| 1972 | -11.7 | | | | | | | | | | |
| 1973 | -5.9 | | | | | | | | | | |
| 1974 | -12.2 | | | | | | | | | | |
| 1975 | -12.3 | -12.5 | | | | | | | | | |
| 1976 | -13.0 | -15.0 | | | | | | | | | |
| 1977 | -15.4 | -20.6 | | | | | | | | | |
| 1978 | -10.5 | -8.4 | | | | | | | | | |
| 1979 | -9.2 | -6.1 | | | | | | | | | |
| 1980 | 0.4 | 11.0 | 96.5 | | | | | | | | |
| 1981 | 0.5 | 9.6 | 48.9 | | | | | | | | |
| 1982 | -1.3 | 5.5 | 24.9 | | | | | | | | |
| 1983 | -0.4 | 6.1 | 21.4 | | | | | | | | |
| 1984 | 0.5 | 6.9 | 19.9 | | | | | | | | |
| 1985 | 6.2 | 14.6 | 31.8 | 91.3 | | | | | | | |
| 1986 | 9.3 | 18.3 | 35.6 | 75.0 | | | | | | | |
| 1987 | 6.6 | 13.8 | 26.2 | 36.8 | | | | | | | |
| 1988 | 7.2 | 14.1 | 25.4 | 32.2 | | | | | | | |
| 1989 | 7.2 | 13.7 | 23.6 | 27.4 | | | | | | | |
| 1990 | 5.2 | 10.6 | 18.2 | 16.8 | -36.0 | | | | | | |
| 1991 | 4.6 | 9.5 | 16.1 | 13.3 | -21.9 | | | | | | |
| 1992 | 4.0 | 8.5 | 14.1 | 10.5 | -17.6 | | | | | | |
| 1993 | 5.5 | 10.2 | 16.0 | 13.9 | -3.1 | | | | | | |
| 1994 | 5.4 | 9.8 | 15.1 | 12.7 | -2.1 | | | | | | |
| 1995 | 5.0 | 9.1 | 13.8 | 11.0 | -2.6 | -5.1 | | | | | |
| 1996 | 4.9 | 8.9 | 13.2 | 10.5 | -1.6 | -0.5 | | | | | |
| 1997 | 6.7 | 10.9 | 15.6 | 13.9 | 5.5 | 18.1 | | | | | |
| 1998 | 7.9 | 12.1 | 16.9 | 15.8 | 9.4 | 23.7 | | | | | |
| 1999 | 8.1 | 12.2 | 16.8 | 15.7 | 9.9 | 21.8 | | | | | |
| 2000 | 7.9 | 11.8 | 16.0 | 14.8 | 9.1 | 18.5 | 1.7 | | | | |
| 2001 | 6.8 | 10.4 | 14.1 | 12.4 | 6.2 | 12.1 | -12.3 | | | | |
| 2002 | 5.9 | 9.2 | 12.5 | 10.4 | 3.9 | 7.6 | -16.2 | | | | |
| 2003 | 6.1 | 9.3 | 12.5 | 10.6 | 4.5 | 8.2 | -8.8 | | | | |
| 2004 | 6.6 | 9.7 | 12.9 | 11.1 | 5.7 | 9.6 | -2.6 | | | | |
| 2005 | 6.9 | 10.0 | 13.0 | 11.4 | 6.4 | 10.3 | 0.6 | 16.7 | | | |
| 2006 | 7.2 | 10.2 | 13.2 | 11.7 | 7.0 | 10.8 | 3.0 | 16.9 | | | |
| 2007 | 6.8 | 9.7 | 12.5 | 10.8 | 6.3 | 9.5 | 1.7 | 8.9 | | | |
| 2008 | 5.3 | 7.9 | 10.3 | 8.3 | 3.3 | 5.2 | -4.1 | -5.9 | | | |
| 2009 | 5.8 | 8.3 | 10.7 | 8.9 | 4.3 | 6.4 | -1.3 | -0.1 | | | |
| 2010 | 5.4 | 7.8 | 10.1 | 8.2 | 3.6 | 5.4 | -2.0 | -1.5 | -8.7 | | |
| 2011 | 4.8 | 7.1 | 9.1 | 7.1 | 2.5 | 3.9 | -3.6 | -4.4 | -15.1 | | |
| 2012 | 4.9 | 7.1 | 9.1 | 7.2 | 2.8 | 4.2 | -2.6 | -2.6 | -6.7 | | |
| 2013 | 5.1 | 7.4 | 9.3 | 7.5 | 3.4 | 4.8 | -1.3 | -0.6 | -1.1 | | |
| 2014 | 5.1 | 7.3 | 9.2 | 7.4 | 3.4 | 4.7 | -1.0 | -0.2 | -0.2 | | |
| 2015 | 5.3 | 7.4 | 9.3 | 7.6 | 3.8 | 5.2 | 0.0 | 1.2 | 2.3 | 14.7 | |
| 2016 | 5.0 | 7.1 | 8.9 | 7.2 | 3.4 | 4.7 | -0.4 | 0.5 | 1.0 | 4.1 | -6.5 |

in U.S. Dollars (USD)
in Percent

| End Date | 1970 | 1975 | 1980 | 1985 | 1990 | 1995 | 2000 | 2005 | 2010 | 2015 | 2016 |
|---|---|---|---|---|---|---|---|---|---|---|---|
| 1970 | -23.6 | | | | | | | | | | |
| 1971 | -22.3 | | | | | | | | | | |
| 1972 | -12.1 | | | | | | | | | | |
| 1973 | -6.6 | | | | | | | | | | |
| 1974 | -12.3 | | | | | | | | | | |
| 1975 | -12.1 | -11.5 | | | | | | | | | |
| 1976 | -12.4 | -12.6 | | | | | | | | | |
| 1977 | -14.6 | -18.6 | | | | | | | | | |
| 1978 | -9.9 | -7.0 | | | | | | | | | |
| 1979 | -8.6 | -4.9 | | | | | | | | | |
| 1980 | -0.2 | 9.8 | 83.2 | | | | | | | | |
| 1981 | -0.1 | 8.6 | 42.2 | | | | | | | | |
| 1982 | -1.7 | 5.0 | 21.4 | | | | | | | | |
| 1983 | -0.9 | 5.4 | 18.2 | | | | | | | | |
| 1984 | 0.0 | 6.1 | 17.0 | | | | | | | | |
| 1985 | 6.5 | 15.0 | 31.5 | 104.0 | | | | | | | |
| 1986 | 10.4 | 19.8 | 37.4 | 88.3 | | | | | | | |
| 1987 | 7.3 | 14.8 | 27.1 | 43.9 | | | | | | | |
| 1988 | 7.8 | 14.9 | 25.9 | 37.0 | | | | | | | |
| 1989 | 7.8 | 14.5 | 24.2 | 31.4 | | | | | | | |
| 1990 | 5.5 | 11.1 | 18.3 | 19.3 | -40.7 | | | | | | |
| 1991 | 4.9 | 10.0 | 16.1 | 15.5 | -24.3 | | | | | | |
| 1992 | 4.4 | 9.0 | 14.3 | 12.7 | -18.5 | | | | | | |
| 1993 | 5.7 | 10.4 | 15.8 | 15.2 | -5.1 | | | | | | |
| 1994 | 5.5 | 10.0 | 14.9 | 13.9 | -3.6 | | | | | | |
| 1995 | 5.1 | 9.3 | 13.7 | 12.1 | -3.9 | -5.2 | | | | | |
| 1996 | 5.1 | 9.0 | 13.1 | 11.5 | -2.7 | -0.4 | | | | | |
| 1997 | 6.6 | 10.7 | 15.0 | 14.2 | 3.6 | 15.5 | | | | | |
| 1998 | 7.9 | 12.1 | 16.5 | 16.3 | 8.0 | 22.5 | | | | | |
| 1999 | 8.0 | 12.1 | 16.3 | 16.1 | 8.4 | 20.4 | | | | | |
| 2000 | 7.8 | 11.7 | 15.6 | 15.2 | 7.8 | 17.3 | 1.6 | | | | |
| 2001 | 6.8 | 10.3 | 13.8 | 12.8 | 5.1 | 11.3 | -11.7 | | | | |
| 2002 | 5.7 | 8.9 | 11.9 | 10.5 | 2.5 | 6.3 | -17.2 | | | | |
| 2003 | 6.0 | 9.2 | 12.1 | 10.8 | 3.5 | 7.4 | -8.9 | | | | |
| 2004 | 6.5 | 9.7 | 12.6 | 11.5 | 4.8 | 9.1 | -2.3 | | | | |
| 2005 | 6.8 | 9.8 | 12.7 | 11.6 | 5.4 | 9.6 | 0.5 | 14.5 | | | |
| 2006 | 7.1 | 10.1 | 12.9 | 12.0 | 6.2 | 10.4 | 3.2 | 16.8 | | | |
| 2007 | 6.7 | 9.6 | 12.2 | 11.1 | 5.5 | 9.0 | 1.8 | 8.6 | | | |
| 2008 | 5.3 | 7.9 | 10.1 | 8.6 | 2.7 | 4.9 | -3.7 | -5.5 | | | |
| 2009 | 5.8 | 8.3 | 10.5 | 8.9 | 3.7 | 6.2 | -1.0 | 0.3 | | | |
| 2010 | 5.4 | 7.9 | 9.9 | 8.6 | 3.1 | 5.3 | -1.6 | -1.1 | -8.2 | | |
| 2011 | 4.8 | 7.1 | 9.0 | 7.5 | 2.1 | 3.7 | -3.2 | -3.9 | -14.4 | | |
| 2012 | 4.9 | 7.2 | 9.0 | 7.6 | 2.4 | 4.1 | -2.2 | -2.1 | -6.2 | | |
| 2013 | 5.2 | 7.4 | 9.2 | 7.9 | 3.0 | 4.7 | -0.9 | -0.1 | -0.6 | | |
| 2014 | 5.1 | 7.3 | 9.1 | 7.7 | 3.0 | 4.7 | -0.6 | 0.2 | 0.1 | | |
| 2015 | 5.3 | 7.4 | 9.2 | 7.9 | 3.4 | 5.0 | 0.2 | 1.4 | 2.2 | 12.8 | |
| 2016 | 5.1 | 7.1 | 8.7 | 7.5 | 3.0 | 4.5 | -0.1 | 0.8 | 1.1 | 3.4 | -5.9 |

Source of underlying data: 1.) Morningstar *Direct* database. Used with permission. All rights reserved. All calculations performed by Duff & Phelps LLC.

**Japan Long-Horizon Equity Risk Premia**

in Local Currency (Japanese Yen – JPY)
in Percent

| End Date | 1970 | 1975 | 1980 | 1985 | 1990 | 1995 | 2000 | 2005 | 2010 | 2015 | 2016 |
|---|---|---|---|---|---|---|---|---|---|---|---|
| | | | | | | | Start Date | | | | |
| 1970 | -18.5 | | | | | | | | | | |
| 1971 | 4.8 | | | | | | | | | | |
| 1972 | 39.9 | | | | | | | | | | |
| 1973 | 21.8 | | | | | | | | | | |
| 1974 | 13.8 | | | | | | | | | | |
| 1975 | 13.5 | 12.2 | | | | | | | | | |
| 1976 | 13.3 | 12.0 | | | | | | | | | |
| 1977 | 10.0 | 3.6 | | | | | | | | | |
| 1978 | 10.9 | 7.3 | | | | | | | | | |
| 1979 | 10.0 | 6.2 | | | | | | | | | |
| 1980 | 9.2 | 5.5 | 1.9 | | | | | | | | |
| 1981 | 9.8 | 7.0 | 8.9 | | | | | | | | |
| 1982 | 8.9 | 5.9 | 5.4 | | | | | | | | |
| 1983 | 9.4 | 7.0 | 8.0 | | | | | | | | |
| 1984 | 10.1 | 8.3 | 10.4 | | | | | | | | |
| 1985 | 10.0 | 8.3 | 10.0 | 8.3 | | | | | | | |
| 1986 | 12.6 | 12.1 | 16.3 | 31.0 | | | | | | | |
| 1987 | 12.1 | 11.5 | 14.8 | 22.1 | | | | | | | |
| 1988 | 13.3 | 13.2 | 17.1 | 25.4 | | | | | | | |
| 1989 | 13.3 | 13.1 | 16.6 | 22.8 | | | | | | | |
| 1990 | 10.5 | 9.4 | 10.9 | 11.3 | -46.1 | | | | | | |
| 1991 | 9.7 | 8.5 | 9.5 | 8.8 | -26.3 | | | | | | |
| 1992 | 8.1 | 6.5 | 6.7 | 4.4 | -26.4 | | | | | | |
| 1993 | 8.1 | 6.6 | 6.8 | 4.8 | -17.7 | | | | | | |
| 1994 | 8.0 | 6.6 | 6.7 | 4.9 | -13.1 | | | | | | |
| 1995 | 7.8 | 6.3 | 6.4 | 4.6 | -10.7 | 1.4 | | | | | |
| 1996 | 7.2 | 5.7 | 5.6 | 3.6 | -10.1 | -2.8 | | | | | |
| 1997 | 6.4 | 4.8 | 4.4 | 2.1 | -10.9 | -7.3 | | | | | |
| 1998 | 5.8 | 4.2 | 3.6 | 1.2 | -10.8 | -7.9 | | | | | |
| 1999 | 7.1 | 5.8 | 5.7 | 4.2 | -5.2 | 2.7 | | | | | |
| 2000 | 6.2 | 4.8 | 4.4 | 2.6 | -6.7 | -1.3 | -21.5 | | | | |
| 2001 | 5.4 | 3.8 | 3.3 | 1.2 | -7.8 | -4.0 | -20.9 | | | | |
| 2002 | 4.6 | 3.0 | 2.3 | 0.0 | -8.7 | -6.0 | -20.5 | | | | |
| 2003 | 5.1 | 3.6 | 3.1 | 1.2 | -6.5 | -2.9 | -9.9 | | | | |
| 2004 | 5.3 | 3.8 | 3.4 | 1.6 | -5.5 | -1.7 | -6.0 | | | | |
| 2005 | 6.3 | 5.1 | 4.9 | 3.6 | -2.4 | 2.4 | 2.2 | 43.3 | | | |
| 2006 | 6.3 | 5.1 | 4.9 | 3.7 | -1.9 | 2.7 | 2.7 | 24.5 | | | |
| 2007 | 5.8 | 4.6 | 4.3 | 3.0 | -2.5 | 1.6 | 0.9 | 12.4 | | | |
| 2008 | 4.5 | 3.2 | 2.7 | 1.1 | -4.7 | -1.7 | -4.1 | -1.7 | | | |
| 2009 | 4.6 | 3.3 | 2.8 | 1.3 | -4.0 | -1.0 | -2.9 | 0.2 | | | |
| 2010 | 4.5 | 3.2 | 2.7 | 1.3 | -3.9 | -1.0 | -2.7 | 0.1 | -0.5 | | |
| 2011 | 3.9 | 2.6 | 2.0 | 0.5 | -4.6 | -2.1 | -4.1 | -2.7 | -10.1 | | |
| 2012 | 4.3 | 3.1 | 2.6 | 1.2 | -3.5 | -0.8 | -2.2 | 0.2 | 0.2 | | |
| 2013 | 5.5 | 4.4 | 4.1 | 3.0 | -1.1 | 2.1 | 1.8 | 6.2 | 13.7 | | |
| 2014 | 5.5 | 4.5 | 4.3 | 3.2 | -0.7 | 2.4 | 2.3 | 6.5 | 12.8 | | |
| 2015 | 5.6 | 4.6 | 4.4 | 3.5 | -0.3 | 2.8 | 2.8 | 6.8 | 12.3 | 9.9 | |
| 2016 | 5.5 | 4.5 | 4.3 | 3.3 | -0.3 | 2.6 | 2.6 | 6.2 | 10.5 | 4.8 | -0.3 |

in U.S. Dollars (USD)
in Percent

| End Date | 1970 | 1975 | 1980 | 1985 | 1990 | 1995 | 2000 | 2005 | 2010 | 2015 | 2016 |
|---|---|---|---|---|---|---|---|---|---|---|---|
| | | | | | | | Start Date | | | | |
| 1970 | -18.5 | | | | | | | | | | |
| 1971 | 14.1 | | | | | | | | | | |
| 1972 | 49.3 | | | | | | | | | | |
| 1973 | 30.1 | | | | | | | | | | |
| 1974 | 19.3 | | | | | | | | | | |
| 1975 | 17.8 | 10.6 | | | | | | | | | |
| 1976 | 17.6 | 13.6 | | | | | | | | | |
| 1977 | 16.2 | 11.0 | | | | | | | | | |
| 1978 | 19.5 | 19.7 | | | | | | | | | |
| 1979 | 15.8 | 12.3 | | | | | | | | | |
| 1980 | 16.2 | 13.6 | 19.8 | | | | | | | | |
| 1981 | 15.4 | 12.7 | 13.6 | | | | | | | | |
| 1982 | 13.6 | 10.1 | 6.4 | | | | | | | | |
| 1983 | 13.9 | 10.9 | 9.2 | | | | | | | | |
| 1984 | 13.7 | 10.9 | 9.5 | | | | | | | | |
| 1985 | 15.1 | 13.1 | 13.8 | 35.4 | | | | | | | |
| 1986 | 19.6 | 19.8 | 25.1 | 64.2 | | | | | | | |
| 1987 | 20.6 | 21.1 | 26.7 | 55.3 | | | | | | | |
| 1988 | 21.2 | 21.9 | 27.2 | 49.3 | | | | | | | |
| 1989 | 20.0 | 20.3 | 24.2 | 39.0 | | | | | | | |
| 1990 | 17.0 | 16.3 | 18.1 | 25.4 | -42.9 | | | | | | |
| 1991 | 16.3 | 15.5 | 16.8 | 22.0 | -20.6 | | | | | | |
| 1992 | 14.5 | 13.1 | 13.4 | 15.9 | -22.6 | | | | | | |
| 1993 | 14.7 | 13.6 | 14.0 | 16.5 | -11.6 | | | | | | |
| 1994 | 14.9 | 13.8 | 14.3 | 16.6 | -5.7 | | | | | | |
| 1995 | 14.2 | 13.0 | 13.2 | 15.0 | -5.1 | -2.0 | | | | | |
| 1996 | 13.1 | 11.6 | 11.4 | 12.3 | -6.9 | -9.7 | | | | | |
| 1997 | 11.7 | 10.0 | 9.4 | 9.4 | -9.1 | -14.8 | | | | | |
| 1998 | 11.4 | 9.8 | 9.1 | 9.0 | -7.7 | -10.1 | | | | | |
| 1999 | 13.0 | 11.8 | 11.7 | 12.4 | -0.9 | 3.9 | | | | | |
| 2000 | 11.7 | 10.2 | 9.7 | 9.8 | -3.5 | -1.7 | -29.6 | | | | |
| 2001 | 10.3 | 8.7 | 7.9 | 7.4 | -5.8 | -5.8 | -30.0 | | | | |
| 2002 | 9.7 | 8.0 | 7.0 | 6.3 | -6.2 | -6.5 | -23.9 | | | | |
| 2003 | 10.4 | 8.9 | 8.2 | 7.9 | -3.3 | -1.9 | -9.1 | | | | |
| 2004 | 10.5 | 9.1 | 8.4 | 8.2 | -2.1 | -0.3 | -4.4 | | | | |
| 2005 | 10.9 | 9.6 | 9.1 | 9.0 | -0.4 | 2.0 | 0.4 | 24.4 | | | |
| 2006 | 10.8 | 9.4 | 8.9 | 8.8 | -0.1 | 2.2 | 1.0 | 14.6 | | | |
| 2007 | 10.3 | 9.0 | 8.4 | 8.1 | -0.5 | 1.6 | 0.1 | 7.7 | | | |
| 2008 | 9.3 | 7.8 | 7.0 | 6.5 | -2.1 | -0.7 | -3.3 | -1.9 | | | |
| 2009 | 9.2 | 7.7 | 6.9 | 6.4 | -1.7 | -0.4 | -2.5 | -0.5 | | | |
| 2010 | 9.3 | 7.9 | 7.2 | 6.7 | -0.9 | 0.6 | -1.0 | 1.9 | 14.2 | | |
| 2011 | 8.7 | 7.3 | 6.5 | 5.9 | -1.6 | -0.4 | -2.2 | -0.5 | -0.6 | | |
| 2012 | 8.7 | 7.3 | 6.5 | 6.0 | -1.2 | 0.1 | -1.4 | 0.5 | 2.2 | | |
| 2013 | 9.1 | 7.8 | 7.1 | 6.7 | 0.0 | 1.5 | 0.6 | 3.4 | 8.3 | | |
| 2014 | 8.8 | 7.5 | 6.8 | 6.3 | -0.2 | 1.2 | 0.3 | 2.6 | 5.8 | | |
| 2015 | 8.8 | 7.5 | 6.9 | 6.4 | 0.2 | 1.6 | 0.9 | 3.3 | 6.4 | 9.6 | |
| 2016 | 8.7 | 7.4 | 6.7 | 6.3 | 0.3 | 1.6 | 1.0 | 3.2 | 5.8 | 6.0 | 2.4 |

Source of underlying data: 1.) Morningstar *Direct* database. Used with permission. All rights reserved. All calculations performed by Duff & Phelps LLC.

# Japan Short-Horizon Equity Risk Premia

## in Local Currency (Japanese Yen – JPY) in Percent

| End Date | Start Date 1970 | 1975 | 1980 | 1985 | 1990 | 1995 | 2000 | 2005 | 2010 | 2015 | 2016 |
|---|---|---|---|---|---|---|---|---|---|---|---|
| 1970 | -17.4 | | | | | | | | | | |
| 1971 | 6.2 | | | | | | | | | | |
| 1972 | 41.7 | | | | | | | | | | |
| 1973 | 23.5 | | | | | | | | | | |
| 1974 | 15.5 | | | | | | | | | | |
| 1975 | 15.4 | 15.1 | | | | | | | | | |
| 1976 | 15.4 | 15.0 | | | | | | | | | |
| 1977 | 12.2 | 6.7 | | | | | | | | | |
| 1978 | 13.1 | 10.2 | | | | | | | | | |
| 1979 | 12.2 | 9.0 | | | | | | | | | |
| 1980 | 11.5 | 8.1 | 3.9 | | | | | | | | |
| 1981 | 12.1 | 9.7 | 11.6 | | | | | | | | |
| 1982 | 11.3 | 8.6 | 8.0 | | | | | | | | |
| 1983 | 11.7 | 9.6 | 10.4 | | | | | | | | |
| 1984 | 12.4 | 10.9 | 12.7 | | | | | | | | |
| 1985 | 12.2 | 10.7 | 12.2 | 9.6 | | | | | | | |
| 1986 | 14.7 | 14.3 | 18.2 | 31.8 | | | | | | | |
| 1987 | 14.2 | 13.6 | 16.5 | 22.9 | | | | | | | |
| 1988 | 15.3 | 15.2 | 18.7 | 26.1 | | | | | | | |
| 1989 | 15.1 | 15.0 | 18.0 | 23.3 | | | | | | | |
| 1990 | 12.2 | 11.1 | 12.1 | 11.5 | -47.3 | | | | | | |
| 1991 | 11.3 | 10.0 | 10.5 | 8.9 | -27.1 | | | | | | |
| 1992 | 9.7 | 8.1 | 7.7 | 4.6 | -26.6 | | | | | | |
| 1993 | 9.7 | 8.1 | 7.9 | 5.1 | -17.6 | | | | | | |
| 1994 | 9.5 | 8.1 | 7.8 | 5.3 | -12.8 | | | | | | |
| 1995 | 9.3 | 7.8 | 7.4 | 5.0 | -10.2 | 2.6 | | | | | |
| 1996 | 8.7 | 7.2 | 6.7 | 4.2 | -9.5 | -1.4 | | | | | |
| 1997 | 7.9 | 6.2 | 5.5 | 2.7 | -10.2 | -5.9 | | | | | |
| 1998 | 7.3 | 5.6 | 4.7 | 1.8 | -10.2 | -6.9 | | | | | |
| 1999 | 8.6 | 7.2 | 6.8 | 4.8 | -4.5 | 3.8 | | | | | |
| 2000 | 7.7 | 6.2 | 5.5 | 3.2 | -5.9 | -0.2 | -19.9 | | | | |
| 2001 | 6.8 | 5.2 | 4.4 | 1.9 | -7.0 | -2.9 | -19.4 | | | | |
| 2002 | 6.1 | 4.4 | 3.4 | 0.8 | -7.9 | -4.8 | -19.2 | | | | |
| 2003 | 6.6 | 5.0 | 4.2 | 1.9 | -5.7 | -1.8 | -8.6 | | | | |
| 2004 | 6.7 | 5.2 | 4.5 | 2.4 | -4.6 | -0.5 | -4.7 | | | | |
| 2005 | 7.7 | 6.5 | 6.0 | 4.4 | -1.5 | 3.6 | 3.5 | 44.7 | | | |
| 2006 | 7.7 | 6.5 | 6.0 | 4.5 | -1.0 | 3.9 | 4.0 | 25.9 | | | |
| 2007 | 7.2 | 6.0 | 5.4 | 3.9 | -1.5 | 2.8 | 2.2 | 13.7 | | | |
| 2008 | 5.9 | 4.5 | 3.8 | 1.9 | -3.7 | -0.5 | -2.8 | -0.5 | | | |
| 2009 | 6.0 | 4.7 | 4.0 | 2.2 | -3.1 | 0.2 | -1.6 | 1.4 | | | |
| 2010 | 5.9 | 4.6 | 3.8 | 2.1 | -2.9 | 0.2 | -1.4 | 1.3 | 0.6 | | |
| 2011 | 5.3 | 3.9 | 3.1 | 1.4 | -3.6 | -0.9 | -2.9 | -1.6 | -9.1 | | |
| 2012 | 5.7 | 4.4 | 3.7 | 2.1 | -2.5 | 0.3 | -1.0 | 1.3 | 1.2 | | |
| 2013 | 6.8 | 5.7 | 5.2 | 3.9 | -0.1 | 3.2 | 3.0 | 7.3 | 14.6 | | |
| 2014 | 6.9 | 5.8 | 5.3 | 4.1 | 0.3 | 3.5 | 3.4 | 7.5 | 13.6 | | |
| 2015 | 6.9 | 5.9 | 5.5 | 4.3 | 0.6 | 3.8 | 3.9 | 7.8 | 13.1 | 10.3 | |
| 2016 | 6.8 | 5.8 | 5.3 | 4.2 | 0.6 | 3.7 | 3.6 | 7.1 | 11.2 | 5.0 | -0.2 |

## in U.S. Dollars (USD) in Percent

| End Date | Start Date 1970 | 1975 | 1980 | 1985 | 1990 | 1995 | 2000 | 2005 | 2010 | 2015 | 2016 |
|---|---|---|---|---|---|---|---|---|---|---|---|
| 1970 | -17.5 | | | | | | | | | | |
| 1971 | 8.7 | | | | | | | | | | |
| 1972 | 45.1 | | | | | | | | | | |
| 1973 | 25.4 | | | | | | | | | | |
| 1974 | 17.3 | | | | | | | | | | |
| 1975 | 16.9 | 14.9 | | | | | | | | | |
| 1976 | 16.7 | 15.3 | | | | | | | | | |
| 1977 | 13.1 | 6.0 | | | | | | | | | |
| 1978 | 14.5 | 10.9 | | | | | | | | | |
| 1979 | 13.4 | 9.4 | | | | | | | | | |
| 1980 | 12.6 | 8.6 | 4.3 | | | | | | | | |
| 1981 | 13.0 | 9.9 | 11.1 | | | | | | | | |
| 1982 | 12.1 | 8.8 | 7.7 | | | | | | | | |
| 1983 | 12.5 | 9.8 | 10.3 | | | | | | | | |
| 1984 | 13.0 | 10.9 | 12.3 | | | | | | | | |
| 1985 | 12.9 | 10.9 | 12.1 | 11.5 | | | | | | | |
| 1986 | 16.1 | 15.6 | 20.0 | 39.1 | | | | | | | |
| 1987 | 15.6 | 15.0 | 18.5 | 28.8 | | | | | | | |
| 1988 | 16.6 | 16.4 | 20.3 | 30.3 | | | | | | | |
| 1989 | 16.3 | 16.0 | 19.3 | 26.3 | | | | | | | |
| 1990 | 13.2 | 11.9 | 13.0 | 13.6 | -50.2 | | | | | | |
| 1991 | 12.2 | 10.7 | 11.3 | 10.6 | -28.7 | | | | | | |
| 1992 | 10.6 | 8.7 | 8.4 | 6.1 | -27.7 | | | | | | |
| 1993 | 10.6 | 8.8 | 8.6 | 6.6 | -18.1 | | | | | | |
| 1994 | 10.5 | 8.7 | 8.5 | 6.6 | -13.0 | | | | | | |
| 1995 | 10.2 | 8.4 | 8.1 | 6.3 | -10.4 | 2.5 | | | | | |
| 1996 | 9.6 | 7.8 | 7.4 | 5.3 | -9.6 | -1.1 | | | | | |
| 1997 | 8.8 | 6.9 | 6.2 | 3.9 | -10.1 | -5.2 | | | | | |
| 1998 | 8.1 | 6.2 | 5.3 | 2.8 | -10.2 | -6.7 | | | | | |
| 1999 | 9.5 | 8.0 | 7.6 | 6.0 | -4.1 | 4.8 | | | | | |
| 2000 | 8.6 | 7.0 | 6.4 | 4.5 | -5.4 | 1.0 | -17.8 | | | | |
| 2001 | 7.9 | 6.1 | 5.3 | 3.3 | -6.3 | -1.5 | -17.2 | | | | |
| 2002 | 7.0 | 5.1 | 4.2 | 2.0 | -7.4 | -3.8 | -18.3 | | | | |
| 2003 | 7.5 | 5.8 | 5.1 | 3.2 | -5.0 | -0.6 | -7.4 | | | | |
| 2004 | 7.6 | 6.0 | 5.3 | 3.6 | -4.0 | 0.6 | -3.6 | | | | |
| 2005 | 8.5 | 7.1 | 6.6 | 5.3 | -1.3 | 4.1 | 3.4 | 38.8 | | | |
| 2006 | 8.5 | 7.1 | 6.6 | 5.4 | -0.8 | 4.3 | 4.0 | 23.0 | | | |
| 2007 | 7.9 | 6.5 | 6.0 | 4.6 | -1.4 | 3.1 | 2.0 | 11.5 | | | |
| 2008 | 6.4 | 4.8 | 4.0 | 2.2 | -4.1 | -0.9 | -4.1 | -4.6 | | | |
| 2009 | 6.4 | 4.9 | 4.1 | 2.5 | -3.4 | -0.2 | -2.8 | -1.9 | | | |
| 2010 | 6.3 | 4.8 | 4.0 | 2.4 | -3.3 | -0.2 | -2.5 | -1.5 | 0.7 | | |
| 2011 | 5.7 | 4.1 | 3.3 | 1.6 | -4.0 | -1.3 | -3.9 | -4.1 | -9.5 | | |
| 2012 | 6.0 | 4.5 | 3.8 | 2.2 | -3.0 | -0.2 | -2.1 | -1.2 | 0.1 | | |
| 2013 | 6.9 | 5.5 | 5.0 | 3.7 | -1.0 | 2.2 | 1.2 | 3.9 | 11.3 | | |
| 2014 | 6.9 | 5.6 | 5.1 | 3.9 | -0.6 | 2.5 | 1.7 | 4.4 | 10.8 | | |
| 2015 | 7.0 | 5.7 | 5.2 | 4.1 | -0.2 | 2.9 | 2.3 | 5.0 | 10.7 | 10.4 | |
| 2016 | 6.8 | 5.6 | 5.1 | 3.9 | -0.2 | 2.7 | 2.1 | 4.5 | 9.1 | 5.0 | -0.5 |

Source of underlying data: 1.) Morningstar *Direct* database. Used with permission. All rights reserved. All calculations performed by Duff & Phelps LLC.

2017 Valuation Handbook – International Guide to Cost of Capital

Data Exhibit 1-28

## Netherlands Long-Horizon Equity Risk Premia

in Local Currency (Euro – EUR)
in Percent

| End Date | Start Date 1970 | 1975 | 1980 | 1985 | 1990 | 1995 | 2000 | 2005 | 2010 | 2015 | 2016 |
|---|---|---|---|---|---|---|---|---|---|---|---|
| 1970 | -14.6 | | | | | | | | | | |
| 1971 | -15.3 | | | | | | | | | | |
| 1972 | -3.1 | | | | | | | | | | |
| 1973 | -8.4 | | | | | | | | | | |
| 1974 | -13.6 | | | | | | | | | | |
| 1975 | -2.6 | 52.6 | | | | | | | | | |
| 1976 | -2.5 | 25.5 | | | | | | | | | |
| 1977 | -2.2 | 16.8 | | | | | | | | | |
| 1978 | -2.3 | 11.8 | | | | | | | | | |
| 1979 | -1.4 | 10.8 | | | | | | | | | |
| 1980 | 0.3 | 11.9 | 17.7 | | | | | | | | |
| 1981 | -0.6 | 8.7 | 3.3 | | | | | | | | |
| 1982 | 0.5 | 9.3 | 6.8 | | | | | | | | |
| 1983 | 4.2 | 14.1 | 18.2 | | | | | | | | |
| 1984 | 5.3 | 14.8 | 18.8 | | | | | | | | |
| 1985 | 6.1 | 15.1 | 18.7 | 18.3 | | | | | | | |
| 1986 | 6.1 | 14.3 | 16.9 | 12.1 | | | | | | | |
| 1987 | 4.7 | 11.8 | 12.5 | 1.9 | | | | | | | |
| 1988 | 5.7 | 12.7 | 13.7 | 7.4 | | | | | | | |
| 1989 | 6.7 | 13.4 | 14.8 | 10.7 | | | | | | | |
| 1990 | 5.3 | 11.3 | 11.5 | 5.4 | -21.4 | | | | | | |
| 1991 | 5.6 | 11.3 | 11.5 | 6.3 | -4.8 | | | | | | |
| 1992 | 5.4 | 10.7 | 10.7 | 5.7 | -2.7 | | | | | | |
| 1993 | 6.8 | 12.2 | 12.7 | 9.4 | 7.6 | | | | | | |
| 1994 | 6.3 | 11.3 | 11.5 | 7.9 | 5.0 | | | | | | |
| 1995 | 6.5 | 11.3 | 11.5 | 8.2 | 6.1 | 11.7 | | | | | |
| 1996 | 7.5 | 12.3 | 12.8 | 10.3 | 9.9 | 22.1 | | | | | |
| 1997 | 8.7 | 13.5 | 14.3 | 12.6 | 13.7 | 28.2 | | | | | |
| 1998 | 8.7 | 13.4 | 14.0 | 12.4 | 13.3 | 23.6 | | | | | |
| 1999 | 9.1 | 13.7 | 14.4 | 13.0 | 14.1 | 23.2 | | | | | |
| 2000 | 8.8 | 13.1 | 13.6 | 12.0 | 12.6 | 18.9 | -2.5 | | | | |
| 2001 | 7.8 | 11.8 | 12.0 | 10.0 | 9.7 | 13.0 | -12.4 | | | | |
| 2002 | 6.4 | 10.0 | 9.8 | 7.4 | 6.1 | 6.7 | -20.7 | | | | |
| 2003 | 6.3 | 9.8 | 9.6 | 7.2 | 5.9 | 6.4 | -14.7 | | | | |
| 2004 | 6.2 | 9.5 | 9.2 | 6.8 | 5.5 | 5.8 | -11.6 | | | | |
| 2005 | 6.8 | 10.1 | 10.0 | 7.9 | 7.0 | 7.9 | -4.8 | 29.0 | | | |
| 2006 | 7.0 | 10.3 | 10.2 | 8.2 | 7.5 | 8.5 | -2.0 | 21.9 | | | |
| 2007 | 7.0 | 10.1 | 10.0 | 8.1 | 7.3 | 8.2 | -1.1 | 16.3 | | | |
| 2008 | 5.5 | 8.4 | 7.9 | 5.7 | 4.4 | 4.1 | -6.5 | -0.1 | | | |
| 2009 | 6.3 | 9.1 | 8.8 | 6.9 | 5.9 | 6.2 | -2.3 | 6.9 | | | |
| 2010 | 6.3 | 9.0 | 8.8 | 6.8 | 5.9 | 6.2 | -1.6 | 6.8 | 6.1 | | |
| 2011 | 5.8 | 8.5 | 8.1 | 6.1 | 5.1 | 5.1 | -2.4 | 4.1 | -2.8 | | |
| 2012 | 6.1 | 8.7 | 8.4 | 6.5 | 5.6 | 5.8 | -0.9 | 5.8 | 3.9 | | |
| 2013 | 6.5 | 9.1 | 8.9 | 7.1 | 6.4 | 6.8 | 0.9 | 7.8 | 9.0 | | |
| 2014 | 6.6 | 9.1 | 8.8 | 7.2 | 6.5 | 6.9 | 1.4 | 7.9 | 8.9 | | |
| 2015 | 6.7 | 9.2 | 9.0 | 7.4 | 6.7 | 7.1 | 2.1 | 8.3 | 9.5 | 12.7 | |
| 2016 | 6.7 | 9.1 | 8.9 | 7.4 | 6.8 | 7.2 | 2.4 | 8.3 | 9.3 | 10.2 | 7.7 |

in U.S. Dollars (USD)
in Percent

| End Date | Start Date 1970 | 1975 | 1980 | 1985 | 1990 | 1995 | 2000 | 2005 | 2010 | 2015 | 2016 |
|---|---|---|---|---|---|---|---|---|---|---|---|
| 1970 | -14.6 | | | | | | | | | | |
| 1971 | -10.6 | | | | | | | | | | |
| 1972 | 0.4 | | | | | | | | | | |
| 1973 | -3.1 | | | | | | | | | | |
| 1974 | -7.7 | | | | | | | | | | |
| 1975 | 0.6 | 41.9 | | | | | | | | | |
| 1976 | 1.6 | 24.6 | | | | | | | | | |
| 1977 | 2.3 | 18.9 | | | | | | | | | |
| 1978 | 3.3 | 17.1 | | | | | | | | | |
| 1979 | 4.1 | 15.9 | | | | | | | | | |
| 1980 | 4.1 | 14.0 | 4.6 | | | | | | | | |
| 1981 | 1.9 | 8.7 | -9.3 | | | | | | | | |
| 1982 | 2.2 | 8.4 | -4.1 | | | | | | | | |
| 1983 | 4.3 | 10.9 | 4.7 | | | | | | | | |
| 1984 | 4.3 | 10.2 | 4.6 | | | | | | | | |
| 1985 | 7.2 | 14.0 | 12.5 | 51.8 | | | | | | | |
| 1986 | 8.8 | 15.7 | 15.6 | 42.9 | | | | | | | |
| 1987 | 8.3 | 14.5 | 13.7 | 28.7 | | | | | | | |
| 1988 | 8.4 | 14.2 | 13.2 | 24.0 | | | | | | | |
| 1989 | 9.5 | 15.3 | 14.9 | 25.3 | | | | | | | |
| 1990 | 8.5 | 13.6 | 12.6 | 19.2 | -11.3 | | | | | | |
| 1991 | 8.6 | 13.4 | 12.4 | 17.9 | -0.5 | | | | | | |
| 1992 | 8.0 | 12.4 | 11.1 | 15.1 | -1.8 | | | | | | |
| 1993 | 9.0 | 13.3 | 12.4 | 16.8 | 6.1 | | | | | | |
| 1994 | 8.8 | 13.0 | 12.0 | 15.7 | 6.1 | | | | | | |
| 1995 | 9.3 | 13.3 | 12.5 | 16.1 | 8.5 | 21.0 | | | | | |
| 1996 | 9.8 | 13.8 | 13.1 | 16.7 | 10.6 | 21.9 | | | | | |
| 1997 | 10.1 | 14.0 | 13.5 | 16.9 | 11.7 | 21.2 | | | | | |
| 1998 | 10.4 | 14.2 | 13.8 | 17.0 | 12.5 | 20.5 | | | | | |
| 1999 | 10.2 | 13.8 | 13.3 | 16.2 | 11.6 | 17.2 | | | | | |
| 2000 | 9.6 | 12.9 | 12.2 | 14.6 | 9.8 | 12.9 | -8.7 | | | | |
| 2001 | 8.5 | 11.5 | 10.5 | 12.2 | 6.8 | 7.3 | -17.5 | | | | |
| 2002 | 7.4 | 10.1 | 8.9 | 10.1 | 4.2 | 3.1 | -20.3 | | | | |
| 2003 | 7.9 | 10.6 | 9.5 | 10.8 | 5.7 | 5.4 | 3.1 | | | | |
| 2004 | 8.0 | 10.6 | 9.5 | 10.7 | 5.9 | 5.8 | -5.6 | | | | |
| 2005 | 8.1 | 10.6 | 9.6 | 10.8 | 6.2 | 6.3 | -2.7 | 11.9 | | | |
| 2006 | 8.6 | 11.2 | 10.3 | 11.6 | 7.6 | 8.2 | 1.8 | 20.2 | | | |
| 2007 | 8.8 | 11.3 | 10.5 | 11.8 | 8.1 | 8.8 | 3.6 | 19.0 | | | |
| 2008 | 7.3 | 9.5 | 8.4 | 9.1 | 4.9 | 4.5 | -2.6 | 1.2 | | | |
| 2009 | 8.1 | 10.3 | 9.4 | 10.3 | 6.6 | 6.8 | 1.6 | 8.8 | | | |
| 2010 | 7.9 | 10.0 | 9.1 | 9.9 | 6.3 | 6.3 | 1.4 | 7.2 | -0.7 | | |
| 2011 | 7.3 | 9.3 | 8.3 | 9.0 | 5.3 | 5.1 | 0.1 | 4.1 | -7.7 | | |
| 2012 | 7.6 | 9.6 | 8.6 | 9.4 | 5.9 | 5.9 | 1.5 | 6.0 | 1.2 | | |
| 2013 | 8.1 | 10.1 | 9.3 | 10.1 | 6.9 | 7.1 | 3.6 | 8.6 | 8.4 | | |
| 2014 | 7.8 | 9.7 | 8.9 | 9.6 | 6.4 | 6.5 | 3.0 | 7.3 | 5.8 | | |
| 2015 | 7.7 | 9.5 | 8.7 | 9.3 | 6.2 | 6.3 | 2.9 | 6.7 | 5.0 | 1.1 | |
| 2016 | 7.6 | 9.4 | 8.5 | 9.2 | 6.2 | 6.2 | 3.0 | 6.6 | 4.9 | 2.8 | 4.6 |

# Netherlands Short-Horizon Equity Risk Premia

## in Local Currency (Euro – EUR) in Percent

| End Date | Start Date 1970 | 1975 | 1980 | 1985 | 1990 | 1995 | 2000 | 2005 | 2010 | 2015 | 2016 |
|---|---|---|---|---|---|---|---|---|---|---|---|
| 1970 | -12.7 | | | | | | | | | | |
| 1971 | -12.8 | | | | | | | | | | |
| 1972 | 0.3 | | | | | | | | | | |
| 1973 | -5.0 | | | | | | | | | | |
| 1974 | -10.5 | | | | | | | | | | |
| 1975 | 0.7 | 57.1 | | | | | | | | | |
| 1976 | 0.8 | 29.1 | | | | | | | | | |
| 1977 | 1.2 | 20.6 | | | | | | | | | |
| 1978 | 0.9 | 15.3 | | | | | | | | | |
| 1979 | 1.5 | 13.5 | | | | | | | | | |
| 1980 | 2.8 | 13.9 | 16.0 | | | | | | | | |
| 1981 | 1.5 | 10.1 | 1.7 | | | | | | | | |
| 1982 | 2.6 | 10.9 | 6.5 | | | | | | | | |
| 1983 | 6.4 | 15.8 | 18.6 | | | | | | | | |
| 1984 | 7.5 | 16.5 | 19.6 | | | | | | | | |
| 1985 | 8.3 | 16.8 | 19.5 | 19.4 | | | | | | | |
| 1986 | 8.2 | 16.0 | 17.7 | 13.1 | | | | | | | |
| 1987 | 6.7 | 13.4 | 13.3 | 2.8 | | | | | | | |
| 1988 | 7.7 | 14.2 | 14.6 | 8.4 | | | | | | | |
| 1989 | 8.5 | 14.8 | 15.5 | 11.5 | | | | | | | |
| 1990 | 7.1 | 12.5 | 12.1 | 5.9 | -22.1 | | | | | | |
| 1991 | 7.2 | 12.5 | 12.0 | 6.6 | -5.4 | | | | | | |
| 1992 | 6.9 | 11.8 | 11.1 | 5.8 | -3.6 | | | | | | |
| 1993 | 8.2 | 13.2 | 13.0 | 9.4 | 6.9 | | | | | | |
| 1994 | 7.7 | 12.3 | 11.9 | 8.0 | 4.6 | | | | | | |
| 1995 | 8.0 | 12.4 | 12.0 | 8.6 | 6.2 | 14.4 | | | | | |
| 1996 | 9.0 | 13.4 | 13.4 | 10.8 | 10.4 | 24.9 | | | | | |
| 1997 | 10.2 | 14.7 | 15.0 | 13.3 | 14.4 | 30.8 | | | | | |
| 1998 | 10.2 | 14.6 | 14.8 | 13.1 | 14.1 | 25.9 | | | | | |
| 1999 | 10.6 | 14.9 | 15.2 | 13.8 | 14.9 | 25.3 | | | | | |
| 2000 | 10.3 | 14.3 | 14.4 | 12.8 | 13.5 | 20.9 | -1.3 | | | | |
| 2001 | 9.3 | 12.9 | 12.8 | 10.8 | 10.5 | 14.8 | -11.5 | | | | |
| 2002 | 7.9 | 11.2 | 10.7 | 8.2 | 7.0 | 8.5 | -19.5 | | | | |
| 2003 | 7.8 | 11.0 | 10.5 | 8.1 | 6.9 | 8.1 | -13.3 | | | | |
| 2004 | 7.7 | 10.7 | 10.2 | 7.8 | 6.6 | 7.6 | -10.0 | | | | |
| 2005 | 8.3 | 11.4 | 10.9 | 8.9 | 8.1 | 9.7 | -3.3 | 30.4 | | | |
| 2006 | 8.5 | 11.5 | 11.1 | 9.2 | 8.5 | 10.2 | -0.6 | 23.0 | | | |
| 2007 | 8.4 | 11.3 | 10.9 | 9.0 | 8.4 | 9.8 | 0.2 | 17.2 | | | |
| 2008 | 7.0 | 9.5 | 8.9 | 6.6 | 5.3 | 5.6 | -5.3 | 0.6 | | | |
| 2009 | 7.7 | 10.3 | 9.8 | 7.9 | 7.0 | 7.8 | -1.0 | 8.0 | | | |
| 2010 | 7.8 | 10.3 | 9.8 | 7.9 | 7.1 | 7.8 | -0.1 | 8.2 | 8.9 | | |
| 2011 | 7.4 | 9.8 | 9.2 | 7.3 | 6.3 | 6.8 | -0.9 | 5.7 | -0.2 | | |
| 2012 | 7.6 | 10.0 | 9.5 | 7.7 | 6.9 | 7.5 | 0.7 | 7.4 | 6.3 | | |
| 2013 | 8.1 | 10.4 | 10.0 | 8.3 | 7.7 | 8.5 | 2.5 | 9.5 | 11.3 | | |
| 2014 | 8.1 | 10.4 | 10.0 | 8.4 | 7.8 | 8.6 | 3.0 | 9.5 | 11.0 | | |
| 2015 | 8.2 | 10.5 | 10.1 | 8.6 | 8.0 | 8.8 | 3.7 | 9.9 | 11.5 | 13.7 | |
| 2016 | 8.2 | 10.5 | 10.1 | 8.6 | 8.0 | 8.8 | 4.0 | 9.8 | 11.1 | 11.1 | 8.6 |

## in U.S. Dollars (USD) in Percent

| End Date | Start Date 1970 | 1975 | 1980 | 1985 | 1990 | 1995 | 2000 | 2005 | 2010 | 2015 | 2016 |
|---|---|---|---|---|---|---|---|---|---|---|---|
| 1970 | -13.5 | | | | | | | | | | |
| 1971 | -13.7 | | | | | | | | | | |
| 1972 | -0.2 | | | | | | | | | | |
| 1973 | -6.1 | | | | | | | | | | |
| 1974 | -12.2 | | | | | | | | | | |
| 1975 | -1.3 | 52.7 | | | | | | | | | |
| 1976 | -1.0 | 27.0 | | | | | | | | | |
| 1977 | -0.4 | 19.3 | | | | | | | | | |
| 1978 | -0.4 | 14.2 | | | | | | | | | |
| 1979 | 0.3 | 12.8 | | | | | | | | | |
| 1980 | 1.5 | 12.9 | 13.7 | | | | | | | | |
| 1981 | 0.5 | 9.5 | 1.4 | | | | | | | | |
| 1982 | 1.6 | 10.2 | 5.9 | | | | | | | | |
| 1983 | 4.9 | 14.3 | 16.3 | | | | | | | | |
| 1984 | 5.9 | 14.9 | 17.0 | | | | | | | | |
| 1985 | 7.0 | 15.8 | 18.2 | 24.2 | | | | | | | |
| 1986 | 7.2 | 15.2 | 16.9 | 16.7 | | | | | | | |
| 1987 | 5.5 | 12.3 | 12.0 | 3.7 | | | | | | | |
| 1988 | 6.4 | 13.1 | 13.2 | 8.5 | | | | | | | |
| 1989 | 7.4 | 13.9 | 14.4 | 11.7 | | | | | | | |
| 1990 | 5.8 | 11.4 | 10.8 | 5.6 | -25.2 | | | | | | |
| 1991 | 6.0 | 11.4 | 10.8 | 6.3 | -7.2 | | | | | | |
| 1992 | 5.8 | 10.8 | 10.0 | 5.6 | -4.7 | | | | | | |
| 1993 | 7.0 | 12.1 | 11.8 | 9.0 | 5.5 | | | | | | |
| 1994 | 6.5 | 11.2 | 10.7 | 7.5 | 3.3 | | | | | | |
| 1995 | 6.9 | 11.4 | 11.0 | 8.3 | 5.4 | 15.6 | | | | | |
| 1996 | 7.9 | 12.4 | 12.3 | 10.3 | 9.3 | 24.2 | | | | | |
| 1997 | 8.9 | 13.5 | 13.6 | 12.3 | 12.7 | 28.3 | | | | | |
| 1998 | 9.0 | 13.4 | 13.6 | 12.3 | 12.6 | 24.2 | | | | | |
| 1999 | 9.3 | 13.6 | 13.9 | 12.8 | 13.3 | 23.3 | | | | | |
| 2000 | 9.0 | 13.1 | 13.1 | 11.9 | 12.0 | 19.2 | -1.2 | | | | |
| 2001 | 8.1 | 11.8 | 11.6 | 10.0 | 9.3 | 13.5 | -10.9 | | | | |
| 2002 | 6.6 | 9.9 | 9.3 | 7.1 | 5.3 | 6.6 | -21.3 | | | | |
| 2003 | 6.5 | 9.8 | 9.1 | 7.1 | 5.4 | 6.5 | -14.4 | | | | |
| 2004 | 6.5 | 9.6 | 8.9 | 6.9 | 5.3 | 6.2 | -10.8 | | | | |
| 2005 | 7.0 | 10.1 | 9.6 | 7.8 | 6.6 | 8.1 | -4.6 | 26.4 | | | |
| 2006 | 7.3 | 10.3 | 9.9 | 8.3 | 7.2 | 8.9 | -1.5 | 22.0 | | | |
| 2007 | 7.3 | 10.2 | 9.7 | 8.2 | 7.2 | 8.6 | -0.5 | 16.6 | | | |
| 2008 | 5.9 | 8.5 | 7.8 | 5.9 | 4.3 | 4.7 | -5.6 | 0.8 | | | |
| 2009 | 6.7 | 9.4 | 8.8 | 7.2 | 6.1 | 7.0 | -1.2 | 8.4 | | | |
| 2010 | 6.7 | 9.4 | 8.8 | 7.2 | 6.2 | 7.1 | -0.3 | 8.4 | 8.3 | | |
| 2011 | 6.4 | 8.9 | 8.3 | 6.6 | 5.5 | 6.1 | -1.1 | 5.9 | -0.4 | | |
| 2012 | 6.7 | 9.2 | 8.6 | 7.1 | 6.1 | 6.9 | 0.5 | 7.6 | 6.3 | | |
| 2013 | 7.1 | 9.6 | 9.2 | 7.8 | 7.0 | 7.9 | 2.5 | 9.8 | 11.6 | | |
| 2014 | 7.2 | 9.6 | 9.2 | 7.8 | 7.1 | 8.0 | 2.9 | 9.7 | 11.0 | | |
| 2015 | 7.3 | 9.7 | 9.2 | 8.0 | 7.2 | 8.2 | 3.4 | 9.9 | 11.2 | 11.7 | |
| 2016 | 7.3 | 9.6 | 9.2 | 8.0 | 7.3 | 8.2 | 3.8 | 9.9 | 10.9 | 10.5 | 9.2 |

## New Zealand Long-Horizon Equity Risk Premia

in Local Currency (New Zealand Dollar – NZD)
in Percent

| End Date | Start Date | | | | | | | | | | |
|---|---|---|---|---|---|---|---|---|---|---|---|
| | 1970 | 1975 | 1980 | 1985 | 1990 | 1995 | 2000 | 2005 | 2010 | 2015 | 2016 |
| 1970 | -10.6 | | | | | | | | | | |
| 1971 | -7.9 | | | | | | | | | | |
| 1972 | 1.1 | | | | | | | | | | |
| 1973 | -0.5 | | | | | | | | | | |
| 1974 | -5.2 | | | | | | | | | | |
| 1975 | -1.7 | 15.6 | | | | | | | | | |
| 1976 | -1.1 | 9.2 | | | | | | | | | |
| 1977 | -3.0 | 0.7 | | | | | | | | | |
| 1978 | -1.4 | 3.4 | | | | | | | | | |
| 1979 | -0.1 | 5.1 | | | | | | | | | |
| 1980 | 4.0 | 11.7 | 44.7 | | | | | | | | |
| 1981 | 5.4 | 13.1 | 32.9 | | | | | | | | |
| 1982 | 3.4 | 8.9 | 15.1 | | | | | | | | |
| 1983 | 10.8 | 19.7 | 38.0 | | | | | | | | |
| 1984 | 11.2 | 19.3 | 33.6 | | | | | | | | |
| 1985 | 11.5 | 19.1 | 30.7 | 16.7 | | | | | | | |
| 1986 | 15.8 | 24.5 | 38.4 | 50.6 | | | | | | | |
| 1987 | 11.3 | 17.7 | 25.6 | 12.2 | | | | | | | |
| 1988 | 9.5 | 14.8 | 20.2 | 3.5 | | | | | | | |
| 1989 | 9.3 | 14.2 | 18.8 | 3.9 | | | | | | | |
| 1990 | 6.6 | 10.3 | 12.7 | -4.7 | -48.1 | | | | | | |
| 1991 | 7.2 | 10.9 | 13.3 | -1.2 | -14.1 | | | | | | |
| 1992 | 6.8 | 10.1 | 12.0 | -1.4 | -10.4 | | | | | | |
| 1993 | 8.5 | 12.2 | 14.7 | 4.2 | 4.5 | | | | | | |
| 1994 | 7.8 | 11.0 | 13.0 | 2.8 | 1.6 | | | | | | |
| 1995 | 7.9 | 11.1 | 12.9 | 3.5 | 3.2 | 11.4 | | | | | |
| 1996 | 7.7 | 10.7 | 12.3 | 3.4 | 3.1 | 6.8 | | | | | |
| 1997 | 7.4 | 10.1 | 11.5 | 3.1 | 2.5 | 4.1 | | | | | |
| 1998 | 6.4 | 8.9 | 9.8 | 1.4 | -0.1 | -2.1 | | | | | |
| 1999 | 6.6 | 8.9 | 9.9 | 2.0 | 1.0 | 0.4 | | | | | |
| 2000 | 5.4 | 7.5 | 8.1 | 0.1 | -1.7 | -4.4 | -28.0 | | | | |
| 2001 | 5.6 | 7.6 | 8.2 | 0.7 | -0.7 | -2.3 | -8.9 | | | | |
| 2002 | 5.2 | 7.1 | 7.5 | 0.3 | -1.1 | -2.7 | -7.9 | | | | |
| 2003 | 5.7 | 7.6 | 8.1 | 1.4 | 0.4 | -0.2 | -0.9 | | | | |
| 2004 | 6.1 | 7.9 | 8.5 | 2.2 | 1.7 | 1.7 | 3.1 | | | | |
| 2005 | 6.0 | 7.8 | 8.3 | 2.3 | 1.8 | 1.9 | 3.1 | 3.5 | | | |
| 2006 | 6.0 | 7.8 | 8.3 | 2.5 | 2.1 | 2.4 | 3.8 | 5.6 | | | |
| 2007 | 5.7 | 7.4 | 7.8 | 2.2 | 1.7 | 1.7 | 2.6 | 1.8 | | | |
| 2008 | 4.4 | 5.8 | 6.0 | 0.2 | -0.8 | -1.6 | -2.7 | -10.0 | | | |
| 2009 | 4.7 | 6.2 | 6.3 | 0.9 | 0.1 | -0.4 | -0.7 | -4.5 | | | |
| 2010 | 4.5 | 5.9 | 6.0 | 0.7 | 0.0 | -0.5 | -1.0 | -4.3 | -3.3 | | |
| 2011 | 4.5 | 5.8 | 5.9 | 0.8 | 0.1 | -0.4 | -0.7 | -3.4 | -0.6 | | |
| 2012 | 4.8 | 6.2 | 6.3 | 1.5 | 0.9 | 0.8 | 0.9 | -0.5 | 6.3 | | |
| 2013 | 4.9 | 6.2 | 6.4 | 1.7 | 1.3 | 1.2 | 1.5 | 0.6 | 7.0 | | |
| 2014 | 5.1 | 6.3 | 6.5 | 2.0 | 1.6 | 1.6 | 2.0 | 1.5 | 7.6 | | |
| 2015 | 5.0 | 6.3 | 6.5 | 2.1 | 1.7 | 1.8 | 2.2 | 1.8 | 7.1 | 4.8 | |
| 2016 | 5.3 | 6.5 | 6.7 | 2.5 | 2.2 | 2.4 | 3.0 | 2.9 | 8.2 | 9.8 | 14.7 |

in U.S. Dollars (USD)
in Percent

| End Date | Start Date | | | | | | | | | | |
|---|---|---|---|---|---|---|---|---|---|---|---|
| | 1970 | 1975 | 1980 | 1985 | 1990 | 1995 | 2000 | 2005 | 2010 | 2015 | 2016 |
| 1970 | -10.8 | | | | | | | | | | |
| 1971 | -4.9 | | | | | | | | | | |
| 1972 | 3.1 | | | | | | | | | | |
| 1973 | 5.7 | | | | | | | | | | |
| 1974 | -1.4 | | | | | | | | | | |
| 1975 | -2.6 | -8.4 | | | | | | | | | |
| 1976 | -3.1 | -7.4 | | | | | | | | | |
| 1977 | -3.9 | -8.1 | | | | | | | | | |
| 1978 | -1.7 | -2.1 | | | | | | | | | |
| 1979 | -1.2 | -1.1 | | | | | | | | | |
| 1980 | 2.7 | 6.1 | 41.7 | | | | | | | | |
| 1981 | 2.8 | 5.7 | 22.7 | | | | | | | | |
| 1982 | 0.3 | 1.3 | 5.3 | | | | | | | | |
| 1983 | 6.3 | 10.6 | 25.2 | | | | | | | | |
| 1984 | 4.8 | 8.0 | 17.0 | | | | | | | | |
| 1985 | 6.0 | 9.3 | 18.0 | 22.9 | | | | | | | |
| 1986 | 11.2 | 16.5 | 29.1 | 59.3 | | | | | | | |
| 1987 | 7.5 | 10.9 | 18.4 | 20.7 | | | | | | | |
| 1988 | 5.7 | 8.3 | 13.4 | 9.0 | | | | | | | |
| 1989 | 5.4 | 7.7 | 12.1 | 7.3 | | | | | | | |
| 1990 | 2.9 | 4.2 | 6.6 | -2.1 | -48.8 | | | | | | |
| 1991 | 3.2 | 4.6 | 6.9 | -0.3 | -19.3 | | | | | | |
| 1992 | 2.7 | 3.9 | 5.8 | -1.3 | -15.4 | | | | | | |
| 1993 | 5.2 | 6.9 | 9.8 | 5.8 | 4.0 | | | | | | |
| 1994 | 5.1 | 6.7 | 9.3 | 5.5 | 3.8 | | | | | | |
| 1995 | 5.4 | 7.1 | 9.6 | 6.3 | 5.4 | 13.8 | | | | | |
| 1996 | 5.6 | 7.2 | 9.7 | 6.6 | 6.2 | 12.1 | | | | | |
| 1997 | 4.8 | 6.1 | 8.1 | 4.7 | 3.0 | 1.8 | | | | | |
| 1998 | 3.6 | 4.7 | 6.2 | 2.3 | -0.4 | -5.6 | | | | | |
| 1999 | 3.8 | 4.8 | 6.3 | 2.8 | 0.5 | -2.7 | | | | | |
| 2000 | 2.4 | 3.2 | 4.2 | 0.2 | -3.1 | -8.8 | -38.9 | | | | |
| 2001 | 2.5 | 3.2 | 4.2 | 0.4 | -2.5 | -7.0 | -17.6 | | | | |
| 2002 | 2.9 | 3.7 | 4.8 | 1.4 | -0.9 | -3.8 | -5.7 | | | | |
| 2003 | 4.3 | 5.3 | 6.7 | 4.0 | 2.8 | 2.2 | 8.4 | | | | |
| 2004 | 5.1 | 6.2 | 7.6 | 5.3 | 4.7 | 5.1 | 12.9 | | | | |
| 2005 | 4.9 | 5.9 | 7.3 | 4.9 | 4.2 | 4.4 | 10.4 | -2.5 | | | |
| 2006 | 5.1 | 6.1 | 7.4 | 5.2 | 4.6 | 5.0 | 10.6 | 4.6 | | | |
| 2007 | 5.0 | 6.0 | 7.3 | 5.1 | 4.5 | 4.8 | 9.6 | 4.0 | | | |
| 2008 | 3.4 | 4.1 | 5.0 | 2.5 | 1.2 | 0.3 | 2.0 | -11.7 | | | |
| 2009 | 4.5 | 5.3 | 6.4 | 4.2 | 3.5 | 3.4 | 6.4 | -0.1 | | | |
| 2010 | 4.4 | 5.3 | 6.3 | 4.2 | 3.5 | 3.4 | 6.2 | 0.5 | 3.8 | | |
| 2011 | 4.4 | 5.2 | 6.1 | 4.1 | 3.4 | 3.3 | 5.8 | 0.8 | 2.9 | | |
| 2012 | 4.9 | 5.7 | 6.8 | 4.9 | 4.4 | 4.6 | 7.5 | 4.0 | 10.9 | | |
| 2013 | 5.0 | 5.8 | 6.8 | 5.1 | 4.6 | 4.9 | 7.6 | 4.6 | 10.4 | | |
| 2014 | 5.0 | 5.8 | 6.8 | 5.1 | 4.6 | 4.8 | 7.3 | 4.5 | 9.2 | | |
| 2015 | 4.7 | 5.4 | 6.3 | 4.6 | 4.1 | 4.2 | 6.4 | 3.4 | 6.3 | -8.2 | |
| 2016 | 4.9 | 5.7 | 6.6 | 5.0 | 4.6 | 4.7 | 6.9 | 4.4 | 7.7 | 3.9 | 16.1 |

Source of underlying data: 1.) Morningstar *Direct* database. Used with permission. All rights reserved. All calculations performed by Duff & Phelps LLC.

# New Zealand Short-Horizon Equity Risk Premia

## in Local Currency (New Zealand Dollar – NZD) in Percent

| End Date | 1970 | 1975 | 1980 | 1985 | 1990 | 1995 | 2000 | 2005 | 2010 | 2015 | 2016 |
|---|---|---|---|---|---|---|---|---|---|---|---|
| 1970 | -10.1 | | | | | | | | | | |
| 1971 | -7.5 | | | | | | | | | | |
| 1972 | 1.6 | | | | | | | | | | |
| 1973 | 0.2 | | | | | | | | | | |
| 1974 | -4.2 | | | | | | | | | | |
| 1975 | -0.7 | 16.9 | | | | | | | | | |
| 1976 | -0.1 | 10.2 | | | | | | | | | |
| 1977 | -2.2 | 1.3 | | | | | | | | | |
| 1978 | -0.4 | 4.3 | | | | | | | | | |
| 1979 | 0.8 | 5.8 | | | | | | | | | |
| 1980 | 4.9 | 12.5 | 46.0 | | | | | | | | |
| 1981 | 6.3 | 13.9 | 34.2 | | | | | | | | |
| 1982 | 4.3 | 9.7 | 16.3 | | | | | | | | |
| 1983 | 11.8 | 20.6 | 39.2 | | | | | | | | |
| 1984 | 12.2 | 20.4 | 35.1 | | | | | | | | |
| 1985 | 11.9 | 19.3 | 30.5 | 7.7 | | | | | | | |
| 1986 | 16.0 | 24.4 | 37.7 | 44.1 | | | | | | | |
| 1987 | 11.1 | 17.0 | 24.0 | 5.5 | | | | | | | |
| 1988 | 9.2 | 14.0 | 18.6 | -2.0 | | | | | | | |
| 1989 | 9.0 | 13.4 | 17.2 | -0.6 | | | | | | | |
| 1990 | 6.2 | 9.4 | 11.1 | -8.9 | -50.5 | | | | | | |
| 1991 | 6.8 | 10.1 | 11.9 | -4.6 | -14.8 | | | | | | |
| 1992 | 6.5 | 9.4 | 10.9 | -4.3 | -10.4 | | | | | | |
| 1993 | 8.3 | 11.6 | 13.6 | 1.7 | 4.6 | | | | | | |
| 1994 | 7.5 | 10.5 | 12.0 | 0.5 | 1.6 | | | | | | |
| 1995 | 7.6 | 10.5 | 11.9 | 1.4 | 3.1 | 10.5 | | | | | |
| 1996 | 7.4 | 10.0 | 11.2 | 1.3 | 2.6 | 5.3 | | | | | |
| 1997 | 7.0 | 9.5 | 10.5 | 1.0 | 2.1 | 2.8 | | | | | |
| 1998 | 6.0 | 8.2 | 8.8 | -0.6 | -0.5 | -3.2 | | | | | |
| 1999 | 6.2 | 8.3 | 8.9 | 0.2 | 0.6 | -0.4 | | | | | |
| 2000 | 5.1 | 6.9 | 7.2 | -1.5 | -1.9 | -4.9 | -27.4 | | | | |
| 2001 | 5.3 | 7.0 | 7.3 | -0.8 | -0.9 | -2.7 | -8.5 | | | | |
| 2002 | 5.0 | 6.6 | 6.8 | -1.1 | -1.2 | -3.0 | -7.4 | | | | |
| 2003 | 5.4 | 7.1 | 7.3 | 0.1 | 0.3 | -0.4 | -0.5 | | | | |
| 2004 | 5.8 | 7.5 | 7.8 | 1.0 | 1.5 | 1.5 | 3.4 | | | | |
| 2005 | 5.7 | 7.3 | 7.6 | 1.1 | 1.6 | 1.6 | 3.3 | 2.8 | | | |
| 2006 | 5.7 | 7.3 | 7.6 | 1.3 | 1.9 | 2.0 | 3.8 | 4.6 | | | |
| 2007 | 5.4 | 6.9 | 7.1 | 1.0 | 1.4 | 1.3 | 2.4 | 0.7 | | | |
| 2008 | 4.1 | 5.3 | 5.2 | -1.0 | -1.1 | -2.1 | -3.0 | -11.0 | | | |
| 2009 | 4.4 | 5.7 | 5.7 | -0.2 | -0.1 | -0.7 | -0.8 | -5.1 | | | |
| 2010 | 4.3 | 5.5 | 5.5 | -0.2 | -0.2 | -0.7 | -0.8 | -4.4 | -1.0 | | |
| 2011 | 4.3 | 5.5 | 5.4 | -0.1 | 0.0 | -0.4 | -0.5 | -3.2 | 1.4 | | |
| 2012 | 4.7 | 5.9 | 5.9 | 0.7 | 0.9 | 0.7 | 1.2 | -0.2 | 7.9 | | |
| 2013 | 4.8 | 6.0 | 6.0 | 1.0 | 1.3 | 1.2 | 1.8 | 0.9 | 8.4 | | |
| 2014 | 4.9 | 6.1 | 6.1 | 1.3 | 1.7 | 1.7 | 2.4 | 1.9 | 8.9 | | |
| 2015 | 4.9 | 6.1 | 6.1 | 1.4 | 1.8 | 1.9 | 2.6 | 2.2 | 8.2 | 4.9 | |
| 2016 | 5.2 | 6.3 | 6.3 | 1.8 | 2.3 | 2.5 | 3.3 | 3.2 | 9.2 | 10.0 | 15.0 |

## in U.S. Dollars (USD) in Percent

| End Date | 1970 | 1975 | 1980 | 1985 | 1990 | 1995 | 2000 | 2005 | 2010 | 2015 | 2016 |
|---|---|---|---|---|---|---|---|---|---|---|---|
| 1970 | -10.1 | | | | | | | | | | |
| 1971 | -7.6 | | | | | | | | | | |
| 1972 | 1.5 | | | | | | | | | | |
| 1973 | 0.0 | | | | | | | | | | |
| 1974 | -4.1 | | | | | | | | | | |
| 1975 | -1.2 | 13.4 | | | | | | | | | |
| 1976 | -0.5 | 8.3 | | | | | | | | | |
| 1977 | -2.7 | -0.4 | | | | | | | | | |
| 1978 | -0.9 | 3.2 | | | | | | | | | |
| 1979 | 0.3 | 4.7 | | | | | | | | | |
| 1980 | 4.4 | 11.4 | 45.0 | | | | | | | | |
| 1981 | 5.6 | 12.5 | 32.1 | | | | | | | | |
| 1982 | 3.8 | 8.8 | 15.6 | | | | | | | | |
| 1983 | 10.4 | 18.5 | 35.9 | | | | | | | | |
| 1984 | 10.6 | 18.0 | 31.4 | | | | | | | | |
| 1985 | 10.5 | 17.1 | 27.5 | 8.1 | | | | | | | |
| 1986 | 14.9 | 22.8 | 35.7 | 46.7 | | | | | | | |
| 1987 | 9.1 | 14.2 | 20.1 | 1.4 | | | | | | | |
| 1988 | 7.4 | 11.5 | 15.3 | -4.8 | | | | | | | |
| 1989 | 7.3 | 11.1 | 14.3 | -2.8 | | | | | | | |
| 1990 | 4.5 | 7.2 | 8.4 | -10.7 | -50.2 | | | | | | |
| 1991 | 5.2 | 8.0 | 9.3 | -6.4 | -15.4 | | | | | | |
| 1992 | 4.9 | 7.4 | 8.5 | -5.8 | -10.7 | | | | | | |
| 1993 | 7.0 | 9.9 | 11.8 | 0.9 | 5.4 | | | | | | |
| 1994 | 6.2 | 8.8 | 10.2 | -0.4 | 1.9 | | | | | | |
| 1995 | 6.4 | 8.9 | 10.2 | 0.6 | 3.4 | 10.7 | | | | | |
| 1996 | 6.2 | 8.5 | 9.6 | 0.5 | 2.9 | 5.4 | | | | | |
| 1997 | 5.9 | 8.0 | 9.0 | 0.4 | 2.3 | 3.1 | | | | | |
| 1998 | 5.0 | 6.9 | 7.5 | -1.0 | -0.1 | -2.6 | | | | | |
| 1999 | 5.2 | 7.0 | 7.6 | -0.3 | 1.0 | 0.1 | | | | | |
| 2000 | 4.3 | 5.9 | 6.2 | -1.7 | -1.2 | -3.8 | -23.4 | | | | |
| 2001 | 4.4 | 6.0 | 6.3 | -1.0 | -0.3 | -1.9 | -6.7 | | | | |
| 2002 | 4.1 | 5.6 | 5.8 | -1.3 | -0.8 | -2.4 | -6.6 | | | | |
| 2003 | 4.7 | 6.3 | 6.6 | 0.1 | 1.1 | 0.7 | 1.4 | | | | |
| 2004 | 5.2 | 6.8 | 7.2 | 1.1 | 2.4 | 2.7 | 5.3 | | | | |
| 2005 | 5.1 | 6.6 | 7.0 | 1.2 | 2.5 | 2.7 | 4.9 | 2.6 | | | |
| 2006 | 5.2 | 6.6 | 7.0 | 1.5 | 2.7 | 3.0 | 5.1 | 4.6 | | | |
| 2007 | 4.8 | 6.2 | 6.5 | 1.1 | 2.1 | 2.2 | 3.5 | 0.5 | | | |
| 2008 | 3.8 | 5.0 | 5.0 | -0.5 | 0.2 | -0.5 | -0.8 | -8.4 | | | |
| 2009 | 4.3 | 5.5 | 5.6 | 0.5 | 1.3 | 1.1 | 1.6 | -2.1 | | | |
| 2010 | 4.2 | 5.3 | 5.4 | 0.4 | 1.2 | 1.0 | 1.4 | -1.9 | -1.1 | | |
| 2011 | 4.2 | 5.3 | 5.4 | 0.6 | 1.3 | 1.1 | 1.6 | -1.1 | 1.4 | | |
| 2012 | 4.6 | 5.7 | 5.9 | 1.3 | 2.2 | 2.3 | 3.1 | 1.8 | 8.2 | | |
| 2013 | 4.7 | 5.8 | 6.0 | 1.6 | 2.5 | 2.7 | 3.6 | 2.7 | 8.7 | | |
| 2014 | 4.8 | 5.9 | 6.1 | 1.9 | 2.8 | 3.1 | 4.1 | 3.5 | 9.0 | | |
| 2015 | 4.8 | 5.9 | 6.1 | 2.0 | 2.9 | 3.1 | 4.1 | 3.5 | 8.2 | 4.4 | |
| 2016 | 5.0 | 6.1 | 6.3 | 2.4 | 3.4 | 3.7 | 4.7 | 4.5 | 9.2 | 9.8 | 15.2 |

Source of underlying data: 1.) Morningstar *Direct* database. Used with permission. All rights reserved. All calculations performed by Duff & Phelps LLC.

Data Exhibit 1-32

**South Africa Long-Horizon Equity Risk Premia**

in Local Currency (South African Rand – ZAR)
in Percent

| End Date | Start Date 1970 | 1975 | 1980 | 1985 | 1990 | 1995 | 2000 | 2005 | 2010 | 2015 | 2016 |
|---|---|---|---|---|---|---|---|---|---|---|---|
| 1970 | -33.1 | | | | | | | | | | |
| 1971 | -15.7 | | | | | | | | | | |
| 1972 | 7.9 | | | | | | | | | | |
| 1973 | 5.2 | | | | | | | | | | |
| 1974 | 5.5 | | | | | | | | | | |
| 1975 | 0.9 | -22.3 | | | | | | | | | |
| 1976 | -1.1 | -17.6 | | | | | | | | | |
| 1977 | 1.5 | -5.0 | | | | | | | | | |
| 1978 | 4.3 | 2.8 | | | | | | | | | |
| 1979 | 12.3 | 19.1 | | | | | | | | | |
| 1980 | 14.0 | 21.0 | 30.7 | | | | | | | | |
| 1981 | 11.8 | 16.4 | 9.7 | | | | | | | | |
| 1982 | 12.8 | 17.4 | 14.7 | | | | | | | | |
| 1983 | 12.1 | 15.8 | 11.7 | | | | | | | | |
| 1984 | 11.0 | 13.8 | 8.5 | | | | | | | | |
| 1985 | 11.9 | 14.8 | 11.3 | 25.6 | | | | | | | |
| 1986 | 13.5 | 16.8 | 15.2 | 32.2 | | | | | | | |
| 1987 | 11.6 | 14.0 | 10.8 | 14.8 | | | | | | | |
| 1988 | 11.0 | 13.0 | 9.5 | 10.9 | | | | | | | |
| 1989 | 12.4 | 14.7 | 12.5 | 16.5 | | | | | | | |
| 1990 | 10.8 | 12.4 | 9.4 | 10.2 | -21.0 | | | | | | |
| 1991 | 11.0 | 12.6 | 9.9 | 10.9 | -3.0 | | | | | | |
| 1992 | 9.7 | 10.9 | 7.7 | 7.3 | -8.1 | | | | | | |
| 1993 | 10.9 | 12.3 | 9.9 | 10.6 | 3.3 | | | | | | |
| 1994 | 10.9 | 12.3 | 10.0 | 10.8 | 5.1 | | | | | | |
| 1995 | 10.1 | 11.2 | 8.8 | 8.9 | 2.7 | -9.3 | | | | | |
| 1996 | 9.4 | 10.3 | 7.7 | 7.4 | 0.9 | -9.4 | | | | | |
| 1997 | 8.3 | 9.0 | 6.2 | 5.3 | -1.7 | -13.1 | | | | | |
| 1998 | 7.1 | 7.5 | 4.4 | 3.0 | -4.5 | -16.5 | | | | | |
| 1999 | 8.5 | 9.1 | 6.6 | 6.0 | 0.8 | -3.5 | | | | | |
| 2000 | 7.9 | 8.3 | 5.7 | 4.9 | -0.4 | -4.9 | -12.1 | | | | |
| 2001 | 8.2 | 8.7 | 6.3 | 5.7 | 1.2 | -1.5 | 3.3 | | | | |
| 2002 | 7.3 | 7.7 | 5.2 | 4.3 | -0.4 | -3.8 | -4.5 | | | | |
| 2003 | 7.2 | 7.5 | 5.1 | 4.2 | -0.1 | -3.0 | -2.5 | | | | |
| 2004 | 7.4 | 7.7 | 5.4 | 4.7 | 0.7 | -1.4 | 0.6 | | | | |
| 2005 | 8.2 | 8.6 | 6.6 | 6.2 | 2.9 | 2.0 | 6.5 | 36.2 | | | |
| 2006 | 8.7 | 9.2 | 7.3 | 7.1 | 4.3 | 4.0 | 9.4 | 31.2 | | | |
| 2007 | 8.6 | 9.1 | 7.3 | 7.1 | 4.4 | 4.2 | 9.0 | 23.1 | | | |
| 2008 | 7.8 | 8.1 | 6.2 | 5.7 | 2.9 | 2.2 | 5.3 | 11.1 | | | |
| 2009 | 8.0 | 8.4 | 6.6 | 6.2 | 3.7 | 3.2 | 6.5 | 12.4 | | | |
| 2010 | 8.1 | 8.5 | 6.8 | 6.4 | 4.0 | 3.7 | 7.0 | 12.3 | 11.7 | | |
| 2011 | 7.8 | 8.1 | 6.4 | 6.0 | 3.7 | 3.3 | 6.1 | 10.0 | 3.9 | | |
| 2012 | 8.0 | 8.4 | 6.7 | 6.4 | 4.2 | 4.0 | 6.9 | 10.8 | 8.2 | | |
| 2013 | 8.0 | 8.4 | 6.8 | 6.5 | 4.4 | 4.3 | 7.0 | 10.6 | 8.4 | | |
| 2014 | 8.1 | 8.4 | 6.8 | 6.6 | 4.6 | 4.5 | 7.1 | 10.4 | 8.4 | | |
| 2015 | 7.7 | 8.0 | 6.4 | 6.1 | 4.1 | 3.9 | 6.2 | 8.8 | 5.7 | -7.6 | |
| 2016 | 7.4 | 7.7 | 6.1 | 5.8 | 3.8 | 3.5 | 5.6 | 7.6 | 4.2 | -6.2 | -4.7 |

in U.S. Dollars (USD)
in Percent

| End Date | Start Date 1971 | 1975 | 1980 | 1985 | 1990 | 1995 | 2000 | 2005 | 2010 | 2015 | 2016 |
|---|---|---|---|---|---|---|---|---|---|---|---|
| 1970 | — | | | | | | | | | | |
| 1971 | -4.6 | | | | | | | | | | |
| 1972 | 23.6 | | | | | | | | | | |
| 1973 | 20.2 | | | | | | | | | | |
| 1974 | 16.0 | | | | | | | | | | |
| 1975 | 5.2 | -38.3 | | | | | | | | | |
| 1976 | 2.1 | -25.7 | | | | | | | | | |
| 1977 | 4.8 | -10.1 | | | | | | | | | |
| 1978 | 7.5 | -1.1 | | | | | | | | | |
| 1979 | 16.9 | 17.6 | | | | | | | | | |
| 1980 | 19.7 | 22.2 | 45.3 | | | | | | | | |
| 1981 | 15.1 | 14.6 | 7.2 | | | | | | | | |
| 1982 | 14.8 | 14.2 | 8.5 | | | | | | | | |
| 1983 | 12.9 | 11.5 | 3.9 | | | | | | | | |
| 1984 | 9.1 | 6.3 | -5.1 | | | | | | | | |
| 1985 | 6.1 | 2.4 | -10.2 | -35.9 | | | | | | | |
| 1986 | 6.0 | 2.6 | -8.1 | -15.6 | | | | | | | |
| 1987 | 6.9 | 4.1 | -4.3 | -3.1 | | | | | | | |
| 1988 | 5.5 | 2.4 | -6.0 | -7.1 | | | | | | | |
| 1989 | 8.0 | 5.8 | 0.0 | 5.0 | | | | | | | |
| 1990 | 6.7 | 4.4 | -1.6 | 1.3 | -17.3 | | | | | | |
| 1991 | 7.6 | 5.6 | 0.6 | 4.7 | 4.1 | | | | | | |
| 1992 | 5.0 | 2.5 | -3.3 | -2.2 | -14.1 | | | | | | |
| 1993 | 7.4 | 5.5 | 1.2 | 4.7 | 4.4 | | | | | | |
| 1994 | 7.8 | 6.2 | 2.4 | 6.2 | 7.3 | | | | | | |
| 1995 | 7.7 | 6.1 | 2.5 | 5.9 | 6.7 | 3.8 | | | | | |
| 1996 | 6.3 | 4.5 | 0.6 | 3.0 | 1.5 | -12.9 | | | | | |
| 1997 | 5.2 | 3.3 | -0.7 | 1.0 | -1.6 | -16.4 | | | | | |
| 1998 | 3.6 | 1.5 | -2.8 | -1.9 | -5.8 | -22.1 | | | | | |
| 1999 | 4.9 | 3.1 | -0.5 | 1.0 | -1.0 | -9.3 | | | | | |
| 2000 | 3.8 | 1.9 | -1.9 | -0.8 | -3.5 | -12.5 | -28.5 | | | | |
| 2001 | 2.8 | 0.9 | -2.3 | -2.3 | -5.3 | -14.3 | -26.8 | | | | |
| 2002 | 3.1 | 1.3 | -1.5 | -1.5 | -4.0 | -11.0 | -13.9 | | | | |
| 2003 | 4.0 | 2.4 | -0.8 | 0.3 | -1.4 | -6.2 | -2.2 | | | | |
| 2004 | 4.9 | 3.4 | 0.6 | 2.0 | 1.0 | -2.2 | 5.0 | | | | |
| 2005 | 5.4 | 4.0 | 1.4 | 2.9 | 2.2 | -0.1 | 7.7 | 21.0 | | | |
| 2006 | 5.6 | 4.3 | 1.8 | 3.4 | 2.9 | 1.1 | 8.5 | 17.3 | | | |
| 2007 | 5.7 | 4.5 | 2.1 | 3.7 | 3.3 | 1.8 | 8.7 | 14.9 | | | |
| 2008 | 4.4 | 3.0 | 0.5 | 1.7 | 0.8 | -1.5 | 2.8 | 0.1 | | | |
| 2009 | 5.5 | 4.3 | 2.1 | 3.5 | 3.1 | 1.8 | 7.3 | 9.6 | | | |
| 2010 | 6.0 | 4.9 | 2.8 | 4.3 | 4.2 | 3.2 | 8.8 | 12.0 | 24.3 | | |
| 2011 | 5.3 | 4.2 | 2.0 | 3.4 | 3.0 | 1.7 | 6.3 | 7.3 | 1.5 | | |
| 2012 | 5.4 | 4.3 | 2.3 | 3.6 | 3.4 | 2.3 | 6.7 | 7.8 | 4.7 | | |
| 2013 | 5.0 | 3.9 | 1.9 | 3.1 | 2.7 | 1.5 | 5.4 | 5.6 | 0.6 | | |
| 2014 | 4.9 | 3.8 | 1.8 | 2.9 | 2.5 | 1.3 | 4.9 | 4.8 | 0.1 | | |
| 2015 | 4.1 | 2.9 | 0.9 | 1.9 | 1.2 | -0.2 | 2.6 | 1.6 | -5.1 | -31.0 | |
| 2016 | 4.2 | 3.1 | 1.1 | 2.1 | 1.5 | 0.2 | 3.0 | 2.2 | -3.0 | -10.8 | 9.5 |

Source of underlying data: 1.) Morningstar *Direct* database. Used with permission. All rights reserved. All calculations performed by Duff & Phelps LLC.

## South Africa Short-Horizon Equity Risk Premia

### in Local Currency (South African Rand – ZAR)
in Percent

| End Date | Start Date | | | | | | | | | | |
|---|---|---|---|---|---|---|---|---|---|---|---|
|  | 1970 | 1975 | 1980 | 1985 | 1990 | 1995 | 2000 | 2005 | 2010 | 2015 | 2016 |
| 1970 | -33.2 | | | | | | | | | | |
| 1971 | -15.8 | | | | | | | | | | |
| 1972 | 8.3 | | | | | | | | | | |
| 1973 | 6.1 | | | | | | | | | | |
| 1974 | 5.7 | | | | | | | | | | |
| 1975 | 0.9 | -22.7 | | | | | | | | | |
| 1976 | -1.3 | -18.7 | | | | | | | | | |
| 1977 | 1.5 | -5.4 | | | | | | | | | |
| 1978 | 4.5 | 3.0 | | | | | | | | | |
| 1979 | 12.8 | 19.9 | | | | | | | | | |
| 1980 | 14.8 | 22.4 | 35.2 | | | | | | | | |
| 1981 | 12.6 | 17.5 | 11.5 | | | | | | | | |
| 1982 | 13.1 | 17.8 | 14.3 | | | | | | | | |
| 1983 | 12.1 | 15.7 | 10.6 | | | | | | | | |
| 1984 | 10.5 | 12.9 | 6.0 | | | | | | | | |
| 1985 | 11.1 | 13.6 | 8.4 | 20.1 | | | | | | | |
| 1986 | 13.0 | 16.1 | 13.4 | 32.1 | | | | | | | |
| 1987 | 11.5 | 13.8 | 10.0 | 16.6 | | | | | | | |
| 1988 | 11.0 | 12.9 | 9.0 | 12.8 | | | | | | | |
| 1989 | 12.3 | 14.5 | 11.8 | 17.5 | | | | | | | |
| 1990 | 10.4 | 11.9 | 8.3 | 10.3 | -26.1 | | | | | | |
| 1991 | 10.5 | 11.9 | 8.6 | 10.5 | -7.0 | | | | | | |
| 1992 | 9.3 | 10.3 | 6.6 | 7.0 | -10.6 | | | | | | |
| 1993 | 10.5 | 11.8 | 9.0 | 10.6 | 2.0 | | | | | | |
| 1994 | 10.7 | 11.9 | 9.3 | 10.9 | 4.3 | | | | | | |
| 1995 | 10.0 | 11.0 | 8.2 | 9.2 | 2.3 | -7.3 | | | | | |
| 1996 | 9.2 | 10.0 | 7.1 | 7.5 | 0.4 | -9.3 | | | | | |
| 1997 | 8.1 | 8.6 | 5.5 | 5.3 | -2.4 | -13.5 | | | | | |
| 1998 | 6.7 | 7.0 | 3.6 | 2.7 | -5.6 | -17.8 | | | | | |
| 1999 | 8.1 | 8.6 | 5.8 | 5.8 | -0.1 | -4.5 | | | | | |
| 2000 | 7.6 | 8.0 | 5.1 | 4.9 | -0.9 | -5.2 | -8.8 | | | | |
| 2001 | 8.0 | 8.4 | 5.9 | 5.8 | 0.9 | -1.4 | 6.1 | | | | |
| 2002 | 7.2 | 7.4 | 4.7 | 4.4 | -0.7 | -3.7 | -2.5 | | | | |
| 2003 | 7.0 | 7.2 | 4.6 | 4.3 | -0.5 | -3.1 | -1.4 | | | | |
| 2004 | 7.2 | 7.5 | 5.0 | 4.8 | 0.5 | -1.4 | 1.7 | | | | |
| 2005 | 8.1 | 8.4 | 6.3 | 6.3 | 2.8 | 2.2 | 7.7 | 37.3 | | | |
| 2006 | 8.6 | 9.0 | 7.0 | 7.2 | 4.2 | 4.2 | 10.4 | 32.0 | | | |
| 2007 | 8.5 | 8.9 | 7.0 | 7.2 | 4.3 | 4.3 | 9.8 | 23.1 | | | |
| 2008 | 7.6 | 7.8 | 5.8 | 5.7 | 2.6 | 2.0 | 5.7 | 10.5 | | | |
| 2009 | 7.8 | 8.1 | 6.2 | 6.2 | 3.4 | 3.0 | 6.8 | 11.9 | | | |
| 2010 | 7.9 | 8.3 | 6.4 | 6.5 | 3.8 | 3.7 | 7.4 | 12.2 | 13.7 | | |
| 2011 | 7.7 | 8.0 | 6.2 | 6.2 | 3.6 | 3.4 | 6.7 | 10.2 | 6.2 | | |
| 2012 | 8.0 | 8.3 | 6.5 | 6.6 | 4.3 | 4.3 | 7.6 | 11.3 | 10.5 | | |
| 2013 | 8.1 | 8.4 | 6.7 | 6.8 | 4.6 | 4.6 | 7.9 | 11.3 | 10.6 | | |
| 2014 | 8.1 | 8.4 | 6.8 | 6.9 | 4.8 | 4.9 | 8.1 | 11.2 | 10.6 | | |
| 2015 | 7.8 | 8.1 | 6.4 | 6.5 | 4.4 | 4.4 | 7.2 | 9.7 | 7.8 | -6.2 | |
| 2016 | 7.6 | 7.8 | 6.2 | 6.1 | 4.1 | 4.1 | 6.6 | 8.6 | 6.3 | -4.5 | -2.8 |

### in U.S. Dollars (USD)
in Percent

| End Date | Start Date | | | | | | | | | | |
|---|---|---|---|---|---|---|---|---|---|---|---|
|  | 1970 | 1975 | 1980 | 1985 | 1990 | 1995 | 2000 | 2005 | 2010 | 2015 | 2016 |
| 1970 | -33.1 | | | | | | | | | | |
| 1971 | -15.8 | | | | | | | | | | |
| 1972 | 7.9 | | | | | | | | | | |
| 1973 | 5.8 | | | | | | | | | | |
| 1974 | 5.4 | | | | | | | | | | |
| 1975 | 1.5 | -18.0 | | | | | | | | | |
| 1976 | -0.8 | -16.4 | | | | | | | | | |
| 1977 | 2.0 | -3.7 | | | | | | | | | |
| 1978 | 4.8 | 4.2 | | | | | | | | | |
| 1979 | 13.5 | 21.6 | | | | | | | | | |
| 1980 | 15.8 | 24.5 | 39.1 | | | | | | | | |
| 1981 | 13.7 | 19.7 | 14.9 | | | | | | | | |
| 1982 | 14.0 | 19.4 | 15.8 | | | | | | | | |
| 1983 | 13.0 | 17.2 | 11.7 | | | | | | | | |
| 1984 | 11.6 | 14.7 | 7.8 | | | | | | | | |
| 1985 | 11.6 | 14.4 | 8.4 | 10.9 | | | | | | | |
| 1986 | 13.0 | 16.1 | 12.2 | 23.1 | | | | | | | |
| 1987 | 11.1 | 13.3 | 8.1 | 8.4 | | | | | | | |
| 1988 | 10.5 | 12.4 | 7.3 | 6.6 | | | | | | | |
| 1989 | 12.0 | 14.2 | 10.5 | 13.2 | | | | | | | |
| 1990 | 10.1 | 11.6 | 7.1 | 6.5 | -27.1 | | | | | | |
| 1991 | 10.3 | 11.7 | 7.6 | 7.4 | -7.1 | | | | | | |
| 1992 | 9.3 | 10.4 | 6.1 | 5.0 | -8.6 | | | | | | |
| 1993 | 10.8 | 12.3 | 8.9 | 9.5 | 4.9 | | | | | | |
| 1994 | 11.0 | 12.3 | 9.3 | 10.0 | 6.8 | | | | | | |
| 1995 | 10.2 | 11.4 | 8.2 | 8.3 | 4.3 | -8.1 | | | | | |
| 1996 | 9.5 | 10.5 | 7.2 | 6.9 | 2.4 | -8.5 | | | | | |
| 1997 | 8.4 | 9.1 | 5.6 | 4.8 | -0.5 | -12.7 | | | | | |
| 1998 | 7.3 | 7.6 | 4.0 | 2.6 | -3.3 | -15.9 | | | | | |
| 1999 | 8.6 | 9.2 | 6.1 | 5.5 | 1.7 | -3.3 | | | | | |
| 2000 | 8.1 | 8.6 | 5.5 | 4.7 | 0.9 | -4.0 | -7.2 | | | | |
| 2001 | 8.2 | 8.8 | 5.8 | 5.2 | 1.9 | -1.5 | 3.0 | | | | |
| 2002 | 7.1 | 7.5 | 4.4 | 3.4 | -0.3 | -4.8 | -7.2 | | | | |
| 2003 | 7.0 | 7.3 | 4.3 | 3.4 | -0.2 | -4.0 | -4.8 | | | | |
| 2004 | 7.3 | 7.6 | 4.8 | 4.1 | 1.0 | -1.9 | -0.4 | | | | |
| 2005 | 8.0 | 8.4 | 5.9 | 5.4 | 3.0 | 1.3 | 5.2 | 33.1 | | | |
| 2006 | 8.4 | 8.9 | 6.6 | 6.3 | 4.2 | 3.2 | 7.9 | 28.5 | | | |
| 2007 | 8.4 | 8.8 | 6.5 | 6.2 | 4.3 | 3.4 | 7.6 | 20.9 | | | |
| 2008 | 7.6 | 8.0 | 5.6 | 5.2 | 3.0 | 1.7 | 4.5 | 10.6 | | | |
| 2009 | 8.0 | 8.4 | 6.1 | 5.8 | 4.0 | 3.0 | 6.2 | 12.8 | | | |
| 2010 | 8.2 | 8.5 | 6.4 | 6.2 | 4.5 | 3.8 | 7.0 | 13.2 | 15.2 | | |
| 2011 | 7.9 | 8.3 | 6.2 | 5.9 | 4.2 | 3.5 | 6.3 | 11.2 | 7.1 | | |
| 2012 | 8.2 | 8.5 | 6.6 | 6.3 | 4.8 | 4.3 | 7.3 | 12.0 | 10.8 | | |
| 2013 | 8.2 | 8.5 | 6.6 | 6.4 | 5.0 | 4.6 | 7.4 | 11.7 | 10.3 | | |
| 2014 | 8.2 | 8.6 | 6.7 | 6.5 | 5.2 | 4.8 | 7.5 | 11.5 | 10.2 | | |
| 2015 | 8.0 | 8.3 | 6.4 | 6.2 | 4.8 | 4.4 | 6.8 | 10.1 | 7.8 | -4.3 | |
| 2016 | 7.7 | 8.0 | 6.1 | 5.9 | 4.5 | 4.0 | 6.2 | 8.9 | 6.1 | -4.0 | -3.6 |

Source of underlying data: 1.) Morningstar *Direct* database. Used with permission. All rights reserved. All calculations performed by Duff & Phelps LLC.

## Spain Long-Horizon Equity Risk Premia

### in Local Currency (Euro – EUR)
in Percent

| End Date | Start Date 1971 | 1975 | 1980 | 1985 | 1990 | 1995 | 2000 | 2005 | 2010 | 2015 | 2016 |
|---|---|---|---|---|---|---|---|---|---|---|---|
| 1970 | — | | | | | | | | | | |
| 1971 | 10.9 | | | | | | | | | | |
| 1972 | 19.5 | | | | | | | | | | |
| 1973 | 14.6 | | | | | | | | | | |
| 1974 | 6.1 | | | | | | | | | | |
| 1975 | 4.1 | -3.6 | | | | | | | | | |
| 1976 | -2.7 | -20.1 | | | | | | | | | |
| 1977 | -6.9 | -24.2 | | | | | | | | | |
| 1978 | -8.1 | -22.2 | | | | | | | | | |
| 1979 | -8.4 | -19.9 | | | | | | | | | |
| 1980 | -6.2 | -14.4 | 13.4 | | | | | | | | |
| 1981 | -3.4 | -8.8 | 19.0 | | | | | | | | |
| 1982 | -5.1 | -10.7 | 4.7 | | | | | | | | |
| 1983 | -4.3 | -8.9 | 4.8 | | | | | | | | |
| 1984 | -0.9 | -3.6 | 12.7 | | | | | | | | |
| 1985 | 1.1 | -0.7 | 15.2 | 28.1 | | | | | | | |
| 1986 | 6.1 | 6.1 | 24.7 | 55.0 | | | | | | | |
| 1987 | 6.0 | 6.0 | 22.2 | 38.1 | | | | | | | |
| 1988 | 6.3 | 6.3 | 20.9 | 31.2 | | | | | | | |
| 1989 | 5.8 | 5.7 | 18.6 | 24.5 | | | | | | | |
| 1990 | 3.8 | 3.2 | 13.8 | 14.7 | -34.2 | | | | | | |
| 1991 | 4.0 | 3.5 | 13.3 | 13.7 | -13.2 | | | | | | |
| 1992 | 3.1 | 2.4 | 11.0 | 10.0 | -14.2 | | | | | | |
| 1993 | 5.3 | 5.1 | 14.1 | 14.9 | 2.9 | | | | | | |
| 1994 | 4.3 | 3.9 | 11.9 | 11.5 | -1.5 | | | | | | |
| 1995 | 4.6 | 4.3 | 11.9 | 11.5 | 0.8 | 11.9 | | | | | |
| 1996 | 6.1 | 6.1 | 13.8 | 14.2 | 6.9 | 27.9 | | | | | |
| 1997 | 7.4 | 7.7 | 15.3 | 16.3 | 11.3 | 32.5 | | | | | |
| 1998 | 8.4 | 8.8 | 16.4 | 17.7 | 13.9 | 33.1 | | | | | |
| 1999 | 8.8 | 9.2 | 16.5 | 17.8 | 14.4 | 30.3 | | | | | |
| 2000 | 8.0 | 8.3 | 15.0 | 15.7 | 11.7 | 22.7 | -15.2 | | | | |
| 2001 | 7.4 | 7.5 | 13.8 | 14.1 | 9.8 | 17.9 | -13.2 | | | | |
| 2002 | 6.1 | 6.1 | 11.8 | 11.5 | 6.5 | 11.5 | -19.7 | | | | |
| 2003 | 6.8 | 6.9 | 12.4 | 12.4 | 8.1 | 13.4 | -7.7 | | | | |
| 2004 | 7.0 | 7.2 | 12.6 | 12.6 | 8.6 | 13.6 | -3.0 | | | | |
| 2005 | 7.3 | 7.5 | 12.8 | 12.8 | 9.2 | 14.0 | 0.4 | 17.4 | | | |
| 2006 | 8.0 | 8.2 | 13.4 | 13.6 | 10.4 | 15.4 | 4.7 | 24.0 | | | |
| 2007 | 8.0 | 8.2 | 13.3 | 13.4 | 10.3 | 14.8 | 5.2 | 18.8 | | | |
| 2008 | 6.7 | 6.8 | 11.4 | 11.1 | 7.6 | 10.8 | 0.0 | 3.7 | | | |
| 2009 | 7.5 | 7.6 | 12.2 | 12.1 | 9.0 | 12.5 | 3.7 | 10.3 | | | |
| 2010 | 6.8 | 6.9 | 11.2 | 10.9 | 7.7 | 10.5 | 1.6 | 5.4 | -19.4 | | |
| 2011 | 6.3 | 6.3 | 10.5 | 10.0 | 6.8 | 9.2 | 0.4 | 2.8 | -15.9 | | |
| 2012 | 6.2 | 6.2 | 10.1 | 9.7 | 6.5 | 8.7 | 0.3 | 2.4 | -10.7 | | |
| 2013 | 6.6 | 6.6 | 10.5 | 10.2 | 7.2 | 9.5 | 2.0 | 4.8 | -2.1 | | |
| 2014 | 6.6 | 6.6 | 10.4 | 10.0 | 7.1 | 9.3 | 2.3 | 5.0 | -0.4 | | |
| 2015 | 6.3 | 6.3 | 9.9 | 9.5 | 6.6 | 8.5 | 1.7 | 3.9 | -1.5 | -7.1 | |
| 2016 | 6.2 | 6.2 | 9.7 | 9.2 | 6.4 | 8.2 | 1.7 | 3.7 | -1.1 | -2.8 | 1.6 |

### in U.S. Dollars (USD)
in Percent

| End Date | Start Date 1972 | 1975 | 1980 | 1985 | 1990 | 1995 | 2000 | 2005 | 2010 | 2015 | 2016 |
|---|---|---|---|---|---|---|---|---|---|---|---|
| 1970 | | | | | | | | | | | |
| 1971 | — | | | | | | | | | | |
| 1972 | — | | | | | | | | | | |
| 1973 | 33.3 | | | | | | | | | | |
| 1974 | 24.5 | | | | | | | | | | |
| 1975 | 10.0 | -9.2 | | | | | | | | | |
| 1976 | 5.2 | -28.0 | | | | | | | | | |
| 1977 | -5.2 | -33.9 | | | | | | | | | |
| 1978 | -12.0 | -26.4 | | | | | | | | | |
| 1979 | -10.8 | -22.1 | | | | | | | | | |
| 1980 | -10.1 | -19.4 | -6.0 | | | | | | | | |
| 1981 | -9.6 | -16.5 | -2.3 | | | | | | | | |
| 1982 | -8.5 | -19.8 | -15.8 | | | | | | | | |
| 1983 | -11.6 | -19.4 | -16.0 | | | | | | | | |
| 1984 | -12.0 | -14.4 | -6.3 | | | | | | | | |
| 1985 | -8.7 | -9.3 | 1.3 | 41.1 | | | | | | | |
| 1986 | -5.2 | 0.7 | 17.1 | 76.3 | | | | | | | |
| 1987 | 2.6 | 2.8 | 18.3 | 60.0 | | | | | | | |
| 1988 | 4.1 | 3.0 | 17.0 | 46.5 | | | | | | | |
| 1989 | 4.3 | 2.9 | 15.4 | 37.4 | | | | | | | |
| 1990 | 4.1 | 1.2 | 11.7 | 27.1 | -24.8 | | | | | | |
| 1991 | 2.6 | 1.5 | 11.3 | 24.2 | -9.1 | | | | | | |
| 1992 | 2.8 | -0.2 | 8.2 | 17.4 | -16.0 | | | | | | |
| 1993 | 1.2 | 1.0 | 9.2 | 18.0 | -6.3 | | | | | | |
| 1994 | 2.2 | 0.3 | 7.8 | 15.0 | -7.5 | | | | | | |
| 1995 | 1.6 | 1.3 | 8.6 | 15.6 | -2.6 | 21.8 | | | | | |
| 1996 | 2.4 | 2.8 | 10.1 | 17.1 | 2.6 | 27.8 | | | | | |
| 1997 | 3.7 | 3.6 | 10.7 | 17.4 | 4.9 | 25.5 | | | | | |
| 1998 | 4.3 | 5.3 | 12.5 | 19.4 | 9.3 | 30.4 | | | | | |
| 1999 | 5.8 | 5.2 | 12.0 | 18.2 | 8.6 | 24.6 | | | | | |
| 2000 | 5.7 | 4.2 | 10.4 | 15.8 | 5.9 | 17.1 | -20.6 | | | | |
| 2001 | 4.8 | 3.4 | 9.2 | 13.9 | 4.1 | 12.4 | -18.2 | | | | |
| 2002 | 4.1 | 2.6 | 7.9 | 12.0 | 2.2 | 8.3 | -19.1 | | | | |
| 2003 | 3.3 | 4.3 | 9.9 | 14.2 | 5.9 | 13.3 | -0.8 | | | | |
| 2004 | 4.9 | 5.0 | 10.5 | 14.7 | 7.2 | 14.5 | 4.4 | | | | |
| 2005 | 5.5 | 4.9 | 10.1 | 14.1 | 6.8 | 13.4 | 4.0 | 1.9 | | | |
| 2006 | 5.4 | 6.2 | 11.5 | 15.6 | 9.1 | 16.1 | 6.7 | 24.0 | | | |
| 2007 | 6.5 | 6.6 | 11.8 | 15.8 | 9.8 | 16.4 | 6.9 | 22.7 | | | |
| 2008 | 6.9 | 5.1 | 9.8 | 13.3 | 6.9 | 12.1 | 5.5 | 5.9 | | | |
| 2009 | 5.5 | 6.2 | 10.9 | 14.4 | 8.6 | 14.0 | 6.5 | 12.9 | | | |
| 2010 | 6.5 | 5.3 | 9.7 | 12.9 | 7.0 | 11.6 | 5.7 | 6.7 | -24.7 | | |
| 2011 | 5.7 | 4.8 | 8.9 | 11.8 | 6.0 | 10.0 | 5.1 | 3.5 | -20.0 | | |
| 2012 | 5.1 | 4.7 | 8.7 | 11.5 | 5.8 | 9.5 | 5.1 | 3.3 | -12.9 | | |
| 2013 | 5.1 | 5.3 | 9.3 | 12.1 | 6.8 | 10.6 | 5.6 | 6.2 | -2.3 | | |
| 2014 | 5.6 | 5.0 | 8.9 | 11.5 | 6.3 | 9.7 | 5.3 | 4.9 | -3.2 | | |
| 2015 | 5.3 | 4.5 | 8.2 | 10.6 | 5.4 | 8.4 | 4.9 | 2.9 | -5.4 | -16.6 | |
| 2016 | 4.7 | 4.3 | 7.9 | 10.2 | 5.1 | 8.0 | 4.7 | 2.5 | -4.9 | -9.2 | -1.7 |

Source of underlying data: 1) Morningstar Direct database. Used with permission. All rights reserved. All calculations performed by Duff & Phelps LLC.

## Spain Short-Horizon Equity Risk Premia

### in Local Currency (Euro – EUR)
in Percent

| End Date | Start Date 1970 | 1975 | 1980 | 1985 | 1990 | 1995 | 2000 | 2005 | 2010 | 2015 | 2016 |
|---|---|---|---|---|---|---|---|---|---|---|---|
| 1970 | -9.2 | | | | | | | | | | |
| 1971 | 1.6 | | | | | | | | | | |
| 1972 | 11.4 | | | | | | | | | | |
| 1973 | 10.5 | | | | | | | | | | |
| 1974 | 4.3 | | | | | | | | | | |
| 1975 | 3.5 | -0.3 | | | | | | | | | |
| 1976 | -2.4 | -18.9 | | | | | | | | | |
| 1977 | -6.9 | -25.5 | | | | | | | | | |
| 1978 | -9.0 | -25.5 | | | | | | | | | |
| 1979 | -9.9 | -24.0 | | | | | | | | | |
| 1980 | -8.2 | -18.6 | 8.1 | | | | | | | | |
| 1981 | -5.8 | -13.0 | 14.5 | | | | | | | | |
| 1982 | -7.3 | -14.6 | 1.0 | | | | | | | | |
| 1983 | -7.1 | -13.4 | -0.1 | | | | | | | | |
| 1984 | -3.8 | -7.8 | 8.4 | | | | | | | | |
| 1985 | -1.8 | -4.6 | 11.6 | 27.7 | | | | | | | |
| 1986 | 3.2 | 2.7 | 21.8 | 55.1 | | | | | | | |
| 1987 | 3.2 | 2.7 | 19.4 | 37.8 | | | | | | | |
| 1988 | 3.4 | 3.2 | 18.2 | 30.5 | | | | | | | |
| 1989 | 2.9 | 2.5 | 15.7 | 22.9 | | | | | | | |
| 1990 | 0.9 | -0.1 | 10.8 | 12.7 | -38.5 | | | | | | |
| 1991 | 1.1 | 0.2 | 10.3 | 11.6 | -16.6 | | | | | | |
| 1992 | 0.2 | -0.9 | 8.0 | 7.8 | -17.5 | | | | | | |
| 1993 | 2.4 | 1.9 | 11.1 | 12.7 | -0.2 | | | | | | |
| 1994 | 1.5 | 0.8 | 9.1 | 9.4 | -4.1 | | | | | | |
| 1995 | 1.9 | 1.3 | 9.2 | 9.6 | -1.5 | 11.5 | | | | | |
| 1996 | 3.5 | 3.3 | 11.3 | 12.5 | 5.0 | 27.7 | | | | | |
| 1997 | 4.9 | 5.0 | 13.0 | 14.8 | 9.7 | 32.6 | | | | | |
| 1998 | 5.9 | 6.3 | 14.2 | 16.3 | 12.6 | 33.5 | | | | | |
| 1999 | 6.4 | 6.8 | 14.5 | 16.6 | 13.4 | 30.9 | | | | | |
| 2000 | 5.8 | 6.0 | 13.2 | 14.7 | 10.9 | 23.4 | -14.0 | | | | |
| 2001 | 5.2 | 5.4 | 12.1 | 13.2 | 9.1 | 18.6 | -12.2 | | | | |
| 2002 | 4.1 | 4.1 | 10.2 | 10.7 | 6.0 | 12.4 | -18.5 | | | | |
| 2003 | 4.9 | 5.0 | 11.1 | 11.7 | 7.8 | 14.3 | -6.4 | | | | |
| 2004 | 5.3 | 5.5 | 11.3 | 12.1 | 8.5 | 14.7 | -1.4 | | | | |
| 2005 | 5.7 | 5.9 | 11.6 | 12.4 | 9.1 | 15.1 | 1.9 | 18.9 | | | |
| 2006 | 6.4 | 6.7 | 12.4 | 13.3 | 10.4 | 16.5 | 6.2 | 25.2 | | | |
| 2007 | 6.4 | 6.7 | 12.2 | 13.1 | 10.3 | 15.9 | 6.5 | 19.7 | | | |
| 2008 | 5.2 | 5.3 | 10.4 | 10.8 | 7.6 | 11.8 | 1.2 | 4.5 | | | |
| 2009 | 6.1 | 6.3 | 11.4 | 12.0 | 9.2 | 13.7 | 5.1 | 11.6 | | | |
| 2010 | 5.5 | 5.7 | 10.5 | 10.9 | 8.0 | 11.8 | 3.1 | 7.0 | -16.0 | | |
| 2011 | 5.2 | 5.3 | 9.9 | 10.1 | 7.2 | 10.5 | 2.1 | 4.6 | -13.0 | | |
| 2012 | 5.1 | 5.2 | 9.6 | 9.8 | 7.0 | 10.0 | 2.0 | 4.2 | -8.2 | | |
| 2013 | 5.6 | 5.7 | 10.1 | 10.4 | 7.7 | 10.9 | 3.7 | 6.6 | 0.3 | | |
| 2014 | 5.6 | 5.8 | 10.0 | 10.3 | 7.8 | 10.7 | 4.0 | 6.8 | 2.0 | | |
| 2015 | 5.4 | 5.5 | 9.6 | 9.8 | 7.3 | 10.0 | 3.4 | 5.6 | 0.7 | -5.8 | |
| 2016 | 5.3 | 5.4 | 9.4 | 9.6 | 7.1 | 9.6 | 3.4 | 5.4 | 1.0 | -1.5 | 2.8 |

### in U.S. Dollars (USD)
in Percent

| End Date | Start Date 1970 | 1975 | 1980 | 1985 | 1990 | 1995 | 2000 | 2005 | 2010 | 2015 | 2016 |
|---|---|---|---|---|---|---|---|---|---|---|---|
| 1970 | -22.4 | | | | | | | | | | |
| 1971 | -4.2 | | | | | | | | | | |
| 1972 | 7.8 | | | | | | | | | | |
| 1973 | 7.9 | | | | | | | | | | |
| 1974 | 2.2 | | | | | | | | | | |
| 1975 | 1.9 | 0.0 | | | | | | | | | |
| 1976 | -3.1 | -16.4 | | | | | | | | | |
| 1977 | -6.8 | -21.8 | | | | | | | | | |
| 1978 | -9.4 | -23.8 | | | | | | | | | |
| 1979 | -10.3 | -22.8 | | | | | | | | | |
| 1980 | -8.7 | -17.9 | 6.7 | | | | | | | | |
| 1981 | -6.6 | -12.9 | 11.6 | | | | | | | | |
| 1982 | -7.5 | -13.6 | 1.6 | | | | | | | | |
| 1983 | -7.2 | -12.4 | 0.6 | | | | | | | | |
| 1984 | -4.1 | -7.3 | 8.2 | | | | | | | | |
| 1985 | -2.0 | -3.8 | 11.9 | 30.4 | | | | | | | |
| 1986 | 3.8 | 4.5 | 24.0 | 63.4 | | | | | | | |
| 1987 | 3.8 | 4.4 | 21.4 | 43.4 | | | | | | | |
| 1988 | 4.1 | 4.7 | 20.0 | 34.8 | | | | | | | |
| 1989 | 3.5 | 3.9 | 17.2 | 26.3 | | | | | | | |
| 1990 | 1.2 | 0.9 | 11.7 | 14.5 | -44.3 | | | | | | |
| 1991 | 1.4 | 1.2 | 11.1 | 13.2 | -19.4 | | | | | | |
| 1992 | 0.6 | 0.2 | 9.0 | 9.6 | -18.3 | | | | | | |
| 1993 | 2.3 | 2.4 | 11.4 | 13.1 | -3.4 | | | | | | |
| 1994 | 1.4 | 1.2 | 9.2 | 9.7 | -6.9 | | | | | | |
| 1995 | 1.8 | 1.7 | 9.4 | 9.9 | -3.7 | 12.5 | | | | | |
| 1996 | 3.3 | 3.5 | 11.2 | 12.5 | 2.7 | 26.7 | | | | | |
| 1997 | 4.5 | 4.9 | 12.6 | 14.3 | 6.9 | 29.9 | | | | | |
| 1998 | 5.6 | 6.3 | 14.0 | 16.1 | 10.4 | 32.1 | | | | | |
| 1999 | 6.0 | 6.8 | 14.2 | 16.2 | 11.1 | 29.2 | | | | | |
| 2000 | 5.4 | 6.0 | 12.9 | 14.3 | 8.9 | 22.1 | -13.1 | | | | |
| 2001 | 4.9 | 5.4 | 11.8 | 12.9 | 7.3 | 17.6 | -11.5 | | | | |
| 2002 | 3.7 | 3.9 | 9.7 | 10.2 | 4.0 | 10.8 | -19.9 | | | | |
| 2003 | 4.6 | 5.0 | 10.8 | 11.5 | 6.3 | 13.6 | -5.9 | | | | |
| 2004 | 5.1 | 5.5 | 11.2 | 11.9 | 7.2 | 14.2 | -0.8 | | | | |
| 2005 | 5.4 | 5.9 | 11.4 | 12.1 | 7.7 | 14.4 | 2.1 | 16.3 | | | |
| 2006 | 6.2 | 6.8 | 12.3 | 13.2 | 9.3 | 16.1 | 6.8 | 25.8 | | | |
| 2007 | 6.3 | 6.9 | 12.2 | 13.0 | 9.4 | 15.6 | 7.2 | 20.4 | | | |
| 2008 | 5.1 | 5.5 | 10.4 | 10.9 | 6.8 | 11.7 | 2.1 | 5.6 | | | |
| 2009 | 6.0 | 6.6 | 11.4 | 12.1 | 8.5 | 13.7 | 5.9 | 12.7 | | | |
| 2010 | 5.5 | 6.0 | 10.6 | 11.0 | 7.4 | 11.9 | 4.0 | 8.1 | -15.0 | | |
| 2011 | 5.1 | 5.5 | 10.0 | 10.3 | 6.6 | 10.6 | 2.9 | 5.5 | -12.3 | | |
| 2012 | 5.0 | 5.4 | 9.7 | 10.0 | 6.4 | 10.1 | 2.8 | 5.0 | -7.7 | | |
| 2013 | 5.5 | 6.0 | 10.2 | 10.5 | 7.3 | 11.0 | 4.5 | 7.5 | 1.0 | | |
| 2014 | 5.6 | 6.0 | 10.1 | 10.4 | 7.3 | 10.8 | 4.7 | 7.5 | 2.3 | | |
| 2015 | 5.4 | 5.7 | 9.7 | 9.9 | 6.8 | 10.1 | 4.1 | 6.3 | 1.0 | -5.6 | |
| 2016 | 5.3 | 5.7 | 9.5 | 9.7 | 6.7 | 9.7 | 4.0 | 6.0 | 1.3 | -1.2 | 3.2 |

Source of underlying data: 1.) Morningstar *Direct* database. Used with permission. All rights reserved. All calculations performed by Duff & Phelps LLC.

Data Exhibit 1-36

**Switzerland Long-Horizon Equity Risk Premia**

in Local Currency (Swiss Franc – CHF)
in Percent

| End Date | 1970 | 1975 | 1980 | 1985 | 1990 | 1995 | 2000 | 2005 | 2010 | 2015 | 2016 |
|---|---|---|---|---|---|---|---|---|---|---|---|
| 1970 | -18.8 | | | | | | | | | | |
| 1971 | -4.4 | | | | | | | | | | |
| 1972 | 3.4 | | | | | | | | | | |
| 1973 | -3.0 | | | | | | | | | | |
| 1974 | -10.0 | | | | | | | | | | |
| 1975 | -1.8 | 39.0 | | | | | | | | | |
| 1976 | -1.9 | 18.4 | | | | | | | | | |
| 1977 | -1.5 | 12.7 | | | | | | | | | |
| 1978 | -1.9 | 8.3 | | | | | | | | | |
| 1979 | -1.0 | 8.0 | | | | | | | | | |
| 1980 | -1.0 | 6.4 | -1.6 | | | | | | | | |
| 1981 | -2.1 | 3.6 | -7.5 | | | | | | | | |
| 1982 | -1.2 | 4.4 | -1.8 | | | | | | | | |
| 1983 | 0.8 | 6.8 | 5.2 | | | | | | | | |
| 1984 | 0.8 | 6.2 | 4.4 | | | | | | | | |
| 1985 | 4.6 | 11.2 | 13.8 | 60.8 | | | | | | | |
| 1986 | 4.4 | 10.3 | 12.0 | 31.0 | | | | | | | |
| 1987 | 2.3 | 7.0 | 6.4 | 9.8 | | | | | | | |
| 1988 | 3.3 | 8.1 | 8.1 | 12.8 | | | | | | | |
| 1989 | 4.5 | 9.3 | 9.9 | 15.4 | | | | | | | |
| 1990 | 2.9 | 7.0 | 6.5 | 8.2 | -27.6 | | | | | | |
| 1991 | 3.6 | 7.6 | 7.4 | 9.6 | -4.8 | | | | | | |
| 1992 | 4.4 | 8.4 | 8.5 | 11.0 | 3.7 | | | | | | |
| 1993 | 6.0 | 10.2 | 11.0 | 14.6 | 13.7 | | | | | | |
| 1994 | 5.2 | 9.1 | 9.4 | 11.9 | 8.4 | | | | | | |
| 1995 | 5.9 | 9.7 | 10.2 | 12.9 | 10.8 | 22.7 | | | | | |
| 1996 | 6.3 | 10.0 | 10.6 | 13.2 | 11.5 | 19.4 | | | | | |
| 1997 | 8.0 | 11.9 | 13.0 | 16.3 | 16.8 | 30.9 | | | | | |
| 1998 | 8.2 | 12.0 | 13.0 | 16.1 | 16.5 | 26.6 | | | | | |
| 1999 | 8.1 | 11.7 | 12.7 | 15.4 | 15.4 | 22.5 | | | | | |
| 2000 | 8.0 | 11.4 | 12.2 | 14.7 | 14.4 | 19.4 | 3.9 | | | | |
| 2001 | 7.0 | 10.2 | 10.7 | 12.5 | 11.3 | 13.4 | -9.4 | | | | |
| 2002 | 6.0 | 8.8 | 9.0 | 10.2 | 8.3 | 8.2 | -15.7 | | | | |
| 2003 | 6.3 | 9.1 | 9.4 | 10.7 | 9.0 | 9.3 | -7.2 | | | | |
| 2004 | 6.2 | 8.9 | 9.1 | 10.3 | 8.6 | 8.7 | -5.1 | | | | |
| 2005 | 7.0 | 9.7 | 10.1 | 11.4 | 10.2 | 11.0 | 1.4 | 33.6 | | | |
| 2006 | 7.2 | 9.9 | 10.3 | 11.6 | 10.5 | 11.4 | 3.5 | 25.0 | | | |
| 2007 | 6.9 | 9.5 | 9.8 | 10.9 | 9.7 | 10.2 | 2.5 | 15.2 | | | |
| 2008 | 5.8 | 8.1 | 8.2 | 8.9 | 7.2 | 6.8 | -1.9 | 2.1 | | | |
| 2009 | 6.2 | 8.5 | 8.6 | 9.4 | 7.9 | 7.7 | 0.4 | 5.9 | | | |
| 2010 | 6.0 | 8.3 | 8.3 | 9.1 | 7.5 | 7.3 | 0.4 | 4.9 | 0.1 | | |
| 2011 | 5.7 | 7.8 | 7.8 | 8.4 | 6.9 | 6.4 | -0.3 | 3.1 | -3.6 | | |
| 2012 | 6.0 | 8.1 | 8.1 | 8.8 | 7.4 | 7.1 | 1.1 | 5.0 | 3.7 | | |
| 2013 | 6.4 | 8.5 | 8.6 | 9.3 | 8.0 | 7.9 | 2.7 | 7.0 | 8.5 | | |
| 2014 | 6.5 | 8.6 | 8.7 | 9.4 | 8.2 | 8.1 | 3.3 | 7.5 | 9.2 | | |
| 2015 | 6.4 | 8.4 | 8.5 | 9.1 | 7.9 | 7.8 | 3.2 | 7.0 | 8.0 | 2.0 | |
| 2016 | 6.2 | 8.2 | 8.2 | 8.8 | 7.5 | 7.4 | 2.9 | 6.2 | 6.5 | -0.1 | -2.2 |

in U.S. Dollars (USD)
in Percent

| End Date | 1970 | 1975 | 1980 | 1985 | 1990 | 1995 | 2000 | 2005 | 2010 | 2015 | 2016 |
|---|---|---|---|---|---|---|---|---|---|---|---|
| 1970 | -18.8 | | | | | | | | | | |
| 1971 | 1.3 | | | | | | | | | | |
| 1972 | 8.7 | | | | | | | | | | |
| 1973 | 4.0 | | | | | | | | | | |
| 1974 | -1.0 | | | | | | | | | | |
| 1975 | 5.0 | 34.6 | | | | | | | | | |
| 1976 | 4.9 | 19.7 | | | | | | | | | |
| 1977 | 7.3 | 21.0 | | | | | | | | | |
| 1978 | 8.4 | 20.1 | | | | | | | | | |
| 1979 | 8.5 | 17.9 | | | | | | | | | |
| 1980 | 6.7 | 13.0 | -11.3 | | | | | | | | |
| 1981 | 4.9 | 9.1 | -13.0 | | | | | | | | |
| 1982 | 4.4 | 7.8 | -9.1 | | | | | | | | |
| 1983 | 5.2 | 8.6 | -3.0 | | | | | | | | |
| 1984 | 3.8 | 6.3 | -5.4 | | | | | | | | |
| 1985 | 9.9 | 14.9 | 12.4 | 101.5 | | | | | | | |
| 1986 | 11.1 | 16.1 | 14.8 | 65.1 | | | | | | | |
| 1987 | 9.3 | 13.7 | 11.2 | 38.7 | | | | | | | |
| 1988 | 9.3 | 13.0 | 10.3 | 30.0 | | | | | | | |
| 1989 | 10.0 | 13.7 | 11.5 | 28.5 | | | | | | | |
| 1990 | 8.9 | 12.0 | 9.3 | 21.6 | -12.7 | | | | | | |
| 1991 | 9.0 | 11.9 | 9.5 | 20.1 | -1.0 | | | | | | |
| 1992 | 9.1 | 12.0 | 9.7 | 19.1 | 3.4 | | | | | | |
| 1993 | 10.5 | 13.5 | 12.0 | 21.6 | 13.0 | | | | | | |
| 1994 | 10.0 | 12.8 | 11.1 | 19.3 | 10.2 | | | | | | |
| 1995 | 11.2 | 14.1 | 12.9 | 21.2 | 15.1 | 39.5 | | | | | |
| 1996 | 10.6 | 13.4 | 12.1 | 19.4 | 12.9 | 19.5 | | | | | |
| 1997 | 11.8 | 14.6 | 13.7 | 21.1 | 16.5 | 26.9 | | | | | |
| 1998 | 12.2 | 14.9 | 14.1 | 21.1 | 16.9 | 25.4 | | | | | |
| 1999 | 11.4 | 13.9 | 12.9 | 19.1 | 14.3 | 18.5 | | | | | |
| 2000 | 11.2 | 13.5 | 12.5 | 18.0 | 13.3 | 15.8 | 2.6 | | | | |
| 2001 | 10.1 | 12.1 | 11.3 | 15.5 | 10.1 | 10.1 | -10.9 | | | | |
| 2002 | 9.3 | 11.2 | 9.7 | 13.9 | 8.3 | 7.1 | -11.9 | | | | |
| 2003 | 10.0 | 11.9 | 10.6 | 14.8 | 10.0 | 9.9 | -0.9 | | | | |
| 2004 | 10.1 | 11.9 | 10.7 | 14.7 | 10.2 | 10.1 | 1.8 | | | | |
| 2005 | 10.6 | 12.0 | 10.9 | 14.8 | 10.5 | 10.6 | 4.0 | 15.2 | | | |
| 2006 | 10.4 | 12.4 | 11.4 | 15.3 | 11.4 | 11.9 | 7.1 | 20.5 | | | |
| 2007 | 10.4 | 12.2 | 11.1 | 14.7 | 10.9 | 11.2 | 6.6 | 14.7 | | | |
| 2008 | 9.3 | 10.8 | 9.6 | 12.7 | 8.6 | 8.0 | 2.2 | 2.7 | | | |
| 2009 | 9.7 | 11.2 | 10.1 | 13.2 | 9.4 | 9.1 | 4.4 | 7.1 | | | |
| 2010 | 9.7 | 11.2 | 10.1 | 13.1 | 9.5 | 9.2 | 5.0 | 7.7 | 11.0 | | |
| 2011 | 9.3 | 10.7 | 9.6 | 12.3 | 8.7 | 8.2 | 4.0 | 5.5 | 1.7 | | |
| 2012 | 9.6 | 11.0 | 9.9 | 12.6 | 9.2 | 8.9 | 5.3 | 7.4 | 8.1 | | |
| 2013 | 10.0 | 11.4 | 10.4 | 13.1 | 9.9 | 9.9 | 6.8 | 9.6 | 12.7 | | |
| 2014 | 9.7 | 11.1 | 10.1 | 12.7 | 9.5 | 9.4 | 6.3 | 8.6 | 10.2 | | |
| 2015 | 9.6 | 10.8 | 9.9 | 12.3 | 9.2 | 9.0 | 6.0 | 7.9 | 8.7 | 1.2 | |
| 2016 | 9.3 | 10.5 | 9.5 | 11.8 | 8.7 | 8.4 | 5.4 | 6.9 | 6.9 | -1.4 | -4.0 |

## Switzerland Short-Horizon Equity Risk Premia

### in Local Currency (Swiss Franc – CHF)
in Percent

| End Date | 1970 | 1975 | 1980 | 1985 | 1990 | 1995 | 2000 | 2005 | 2010 | 2015 | 2016 |
|---|---|---|---|---|---|---|---|---|---|---|---|
| | | | | | | | Start Date | | | | |
| 1970 | -18.7 | | | | | | | | | | |
| 1971 | -3.2 | | | | | | | | | | |
| 1972 | 5.1 | | | | | | | | | | |
| 1973 | -1.3 | | | | | | | | | | |
| 1974 | -8.6 | | | | | | | | | | |
| 1975 | -0.1 | 42.5 | | | | | | | | | |
| 1976 | 0.2 | 22.3 | | | | | | | | | |
| 1977 | 0.6 | 15.9 | | | | | | | | | |
| 1978 | 0.3 | 11.5 | | | | | | | | | |
| 1979 | 1.2 | 10.9 | | | | | | | | | |
| 1980 | 0.8 | 8.7 | -2.4 | | | | | | | | |
| 1981 | -0.6 | 5.1 | -9.4 | | | | | | | | |
| 1982 | 0.3 | 5.9 | -2.6 | | | | | | | | |
| 1983 | 2.2 | 8.2 | 4.8 | | | | | | | | |
| 1984 | 2.2 | 7.6 | 4.3 | | | | | | | | |
| 1985 | 5.9 | 12.5 | 13.8 | 61.4 | | | | | | | |
| 1986 | 5.7 | 11.6 | 12.1 | 31.6 | | | | | | | |
| 1987 | 3.6 | 8.3 | 6.7 | 10.6 | | | | | | | |
| 1988 | 4.6 | 9.4 | 8.5 | 13.7 | | | | | | | |
| 1989 | 5.6 | 10.3 | 10.0 | 15.7 | | | | | | | |
| 1990 | 3.9 | 7.8 | 6.3 | 8.0 | -30.1 | | | | | | |
| 1991 | 4.4 | 8.3 | 7.2 | 9.2 | -6.9 | | | | | | |
| 1992 | 5.1 | 8.9 | 8.1 | 10.5 | 1.8 | | | | | | |
| 1993 | 6.7 | 10.7 | 10.6 | 14.1 | 12.1 | | | | | | |
| 1994 | 5.9 | 9.5 | 9.1 | 11.5 | 7.3 | | | | | | |
| 1995 | 6.6 | 10.2 | 10.0 | 12.6 | 10.1 | 24.3 | | | | | |
| 1996 | 7.0 | 10.6 | 10.5 | 13.1 | 11.3 | 21.3 | | | | | |
| 1997 | 8.8 | 12.6 | 13.0 | 16.4 | 16.8 | 32.8 | | | | | |
| 1998 | 9.0 | 12.7 | 13.2 | 16.3 | 16.7 | 28.4 | | | | | |
| 1999 | 9.0 | 12.5 | 12.9 | 15.7 | 15.8 | 24.3 | | | | | |
| 2000 | 8.8 | 12.2 | 12.5 | 15.1 | 14.8 | 21.1 | 4.8 | | | | |
| 2001 | 7.9 | 10.9 | 10.9 | 12.9 | 11.7 | 14.9 | -8.6 | | | | |
| 2002 | 6.8 | 9.6 | 9.3 | 10.7 | 8.8 | 9.7 | -14.5 | | | | |
| 2003 | 7.2 | 10.0 | 9.8 | 11.2 | 9.6 | 10.9 | -5.8 | | | | |
| 2004 | 7.2 | 9.8 | 9.6 | 10.9 | 9.4 | 10.4 | -3.4 | | | | |
| 2005 | 8.0 | 10.7 | 10.6 | 12.1 | 11.0 | 12.7 | 3.0 | 35.1 | | | |
| 2006 | 8.2 | 10.9 | 10.9 | 12.3 | 11.4 | 13.1 | 5.0 | 26.3 | | | |
| 2007 | 7.9 | 10.4 | 10.3 | 11.6 | 10.5 | 11.8 | 3.9 | 16.1 | | | |
| 2008 | 6.8 | 9.0 | 8.7 | 9.6 | 8.0 | 8.3 | -0.6 | 2.9 | | | |
| 2009 | 7.2 | 9.4 | 9.2 | 10.1 | 8.7 | 9.2 | 1.7 | 6.8 | | | |
| 2010 | 7.0 | 9.2 | 8.9 | 9.8 | 8.4 | 8.7 | 1.7 | 5.9 | 1.6 | | |
| 2011 | 6.7 | 8.8 | 8.4 | 9.2 | 7.7 | 7.9 | 1.0 | 4.2 | -2.2 | | |
| 2012 | 7.0 | 9.0 | 8.8 | 9.6 | 8.2 | 8.5 | 2.4 | 6.1 | 4.8 | | |
| 2013 | 7.4 | 9.4 | 9.2 | 10.1 | 8.9 | 9.3 | 4.0 | 8.1 | 9.6 | | |
| 2014 | 7.5 | 9.5 | 9.3 | 10.1 | 9.0 | 9.5 | 4.5 | 8.5 | 10.2 | | |
| 2015 | 7.4 | 9.3 | 9.1 | 9.9 | 8.8 | 9.2 | 4.4 | 8.0 | 9.0 | 2.8 | |
| 2016 | 7.2 | 9.1 | 8.8 | 9.9 | 8.4 | 8.7 | 4.1 | 7.2 | 7.5 | 0.6 | -1.6 |

### in U.S. Dollars (USD)
in Percent

| End Date | 1970 | 1975 | 1980 | 1985 | 1990 | 1995 | 2000 | 2005 | 2010 | 2015 | 2016 |
|---|---|---|---|---|---|---|---|---|---|---|---|
| | | | | | | | Start Date | | | | |
| 1970 | -19.0 | | | | | | | | | | |
| 1971 | -2.7 | | | | | | | | | | |
| 1972 | 5.8 | | | | | | | | | | |
| 1973 | -1.8 | | | | | | | | | | |
| 1974 | -11.2 | | | | | | | | | | |
| 1975 | -2.4 | 41.5 | | | | | | | | | |
| 1976 | -1.8 | 21.8 | | | | | | | | | |
| 1977 | -1.2 | 15.6 | | | | | | | | | |
| 1978 | -1.2 | 11.3 | | | | | | | | | |
| 1979 | -0.2 | 10.9 | | | | | | | | | |
| 1980 | -0.3 | 8.8 | -1.7 | | | | | | | | |
| 1981 | -1.7 | 5.2 | -9.1 | | | | | | | | |
| 1982 | -0.7 | 5.8 | -2.7 | | | | | | | | |
| 1983 | 1.1 | 7.9 | 4.1 | | | | | | | | |
| 1984 | 1.1 | 7.3 | 3.7 | | | | | | | | |
| 1985 | 5.8 | 13.5 | 15.7 | 75.8 | | | | | | | |
| 1986 | 5.6 | 12.6 | 13.8 | 38.9 | | | | | | | |
| 1987 | 3.1 | 8.6 | 7.1 | 12.8 | | | | | | | |
| 1988 | 3.9 | 9.4 | 8.5 | 14.5 | | | | | | | |
| 1989 | 4.9 | 10.3 | 10.0 | 16.3 | | | | | | | |
| 1990 | 2.9 | 7.3 | 5.7 | 7.4 | -36.9 | | | | | | |
| 1991 | 3.5 | 7.8 | 6.5 | 8.5 | -10.9 | | | | | | |
| 1992 | 4.1 | 8.4 | 7.4 | 9.7 | -1.2 | | | | | | |
| 1993 | 5.7 | 10.2 | 9.9 | 13.4 | 9.8 | | | | | | |
| 1994 | 4.9 | 9.0 | 8.3 | 10.7 | 5.1 | | | | | | |
| 1995 | 5.8 | 9.9 | 9.6 | 12.2 | 8.8 | 27.7 | | | | | |
| 1996 | 6.2 | 10.1 | 9.9 | 12.5 | 9.8 | 21.6 | | | | | |
| 1997 | 7.8 | 11.9 | 12.2 | 15.5 | 15.0 | 31.6 | | | | | |
| 1998 | 8.1 | 12.1 | 12.4 | 15.5 | 15.1 | 27.7 | | | | | |
| 1999 | 8.0 | 11.9 | 12.1 | 15.0 | 14.3 | 23.5 | | | | | |
| 2000 | 7.9 | 11.6 | 11.8 | 14.3 | 13.4 | 20.4 | 4.8 | | | | |
| 2001 | 7.0 | 10.4 | 10.3 | 12.2 | 10.5 | 14.4 | -8.4 | | | | |
| 2002 | 5.8 | 8.9 | 8.5 | 9.8 | 7.3 | 8.7 | -16.1 | | | | |
| 2003 | 6.3 | 9.4 | 9.1 | 10.5 | 8.4 | 10.2 | -6.4 | | | | |
| 2004 | 6.3 | 9.3 | 9.0 | 10.3 | 8.3 | 9.9 | -3.8 | | | | |
| 2005 | 7.0 | 9.9 | 9.8 | 11.2 | 9.6 | 11.7 | 1.9 | 30.3 | | | |
| 2006 | 7.3 | 10.2 | 10.1 | 11.6 | 10.2 | 12.3 | 4.3 | 24.5 | | | |
| 2007 | 7.0 | 9.8 | 9.6 | 10.9 | 9.4 | 11.0 | 3.2 | 14.9 | | | |
| 2008 | 5.8 | 8.3 | 7.9 | 8.8 | 6.8 | 7.4 | -1.5 | 1.4 | | | |
| 2009 | 6.3 | 8.8 | 8.4 | 9.4 | 7.6 | 8.5 | 1.0 | 5.7 | | | |
| 2010 | 6.2 | 8.6 | 8.2 | 9.1 | 7.3 | 8.1 | 1.0 | 5.1 | 1.7 | | |
| 2011 | 5.9 | 8.2 | 7.8 | 8.5 | 6.7 | 7.2 | 0.4 | 3.5 | -2.1 | | |
| 2012 | 6.2 | 8.5 | 8.1 | 8.9 | 7.3 | 7.9 | 1.9 | 5.5 | 5.0 | | |
| 2013 | 6.6 | 8.9 | 8.6 | 9.4 | 8.0 | 8.8 | 3.5 | 7.6 | 10.0 | | |
| 2014 | 6.7 | 8.9 | 8.7 | 9.5 | 8.1 | 8.9 | 4.0 | 8.0 | 10.2 | | |
| 2015 | 6.6 | 8.8 | 8.5 | 9.2 | 7.9 | 8.6 | 3.9 | 7.4 | 8.8 | 1.7 | |
| 2016 | 6.4 | 8.5 | 8.2 | 8.9 | 7.6 | 8.2 | 3.6 | 6.7 | 7.5 | 0.6 | -0.6 |

Source of underlying data: 1.) Morningstar *Direct* database. Used with permission. All rights reserved. All calculations performed by Duff & Phelps LLC.

2017 Valuation Handbook - International Guide to Cost of Capital

Data Exhibit 1-38

## United Kingdom Long-Horizon Equity Risk Premia

in Local Currency (Pound Sterling – GBP)
in Percent

| End Date | 1900 | 1905 | 1910 | 1915 | 1920 | 1925 | 1930 | 1935 | 1940 | 1945 | 1950 | 1955 | 1960 | 1965 | 1970 | 1975 | 1980 | 1985 | 1990 | 1995 | 2000 | 2005 | 2010 | 2015 | 2016 |
|---|---|---|---|---|---|---|---|---|---|---|---|---|---|---|---|---|---|---|---|---|---|---|---|---|---|
| 1900 | -1.2 | | | | | | | | | | | | | | | | | | | | | | | | |
| 1901 | -3.9 | | | | | | | | | | | | | | | | | | | | | | | | |
| 1902 | -2.4 | | | | | | | | | | | | | | | | | | | | | | | | |
| 1903 | -3.1 | | | | | | | | | | | | | | | | | | | | | | | | |
| 1904 | -0.6 | | | | | | | | | | | | | | | | | | | | | | | | |
| 1905 | 0.1 | 3.5 | | | | | | | | | | | | | | | | | | | | | | | |
| 1906 | 0.1 | 1.9 | | | | | | | | | | | | | | | | | | | | | | | |
| 1907 | -0.4 | 0.0 | | | | | | | | | | | | | | | | | | | | | | | |
| 1908 | -0.3 | 0.0 | | | | | | | | | | | | | | | | | | | | | | | |
| 1909 | 0.2 | 1.1 | | | | | | | | | | | | | | | | | | | | | | | |
| 1910 | 0.5 | 1.5 | 3.5 | | | | | | | | | | | | | | | | | | | | | | |
| 1911 | 0.4 | 1.1 | 1.3 | | | | | | | | | | | | | | | | | | | | | | |
| 1912 | 0.4 | 1.1 | 1.2 | | | | | | | | | | | | | | | | | | | | | | |
| 1913 | 0.3 | 0.7 | 0.3 | | | | | | | | | | | | | | | | | | | | | | |
| 1914 | -0.5 | -0.4 | -1.9 | | | | | | | | | | | | | | | | | | | | | | |
| 1915 | -0.9 | -1.0 | -2.8 | -7.4 | | | | | | | | | | | | | | | | | | | | | |
| 1916 | -0.4 | -0.4 | -1.4 | -0.1 | | | | | | | | | | | | | | | | | | | | | |
| 1917 | 0.0 | 0.3 | -0.2 | 2.5 | | | | | | | | | | | | | | | | | | | | | |
| 1918 | 1.1 | 1.8 | 2.1 | 7.1 | | | | | | | | | | | | | | | | | | | | | |
| 1919 | 2.2 | 3.1 | 4.1 | 10.2 | | | | | | | | | | | | | | | | | | | | | |
| 1920 | 0.9 | 1.4 | 1.6 | 4.5 | -24.0 | | | | | | | | | | | | | | | | | | | | |
| 1921 | 0.6 | 1.0 | 1.0 | 3.0 | -14.8 | | | | | | | | | | | | | | | | | | | | |
| 1922 | 1.8 | 2.5 | 3.1 | 6.2 | -0.5 | | | | | | | | | | | | | | | | | | | | |
| 1923 | 1.8 | 2.5 | 3.0 | 5.7 | 0.1 | | | | | | | | | | | | | | | | | | | | |
| 1924 | 2.3 | 3.0 | 3.6 | 6.4 | 2.6 | | | | | | | | | | | | | | | | | | | | |
| 1925 | 2.4 | 3.1 | 3.8 | 6.4 | 3.2 | 6.2 | | | | | | | | | | | | | | | | | | | |
| 1926 | 2.4 | 3.1 | 3.7 | 6.1 | 3.1 | 4.4 | | | | | | | | | | | | | | | | | | | |
| 1927 | 2.5 | 3.2 | 3.8 | 6.0 | 3.4 | 4.7 | | | | | | | | | | | | | | | | | | | |
| 1928 | 2.8 | 3.5 | 4.2 | 6.4 | 4.3 | 6.3 | | | | | | | | | | | | | | | | | | | |
| 1929 | 2.2 | 2.8 | 3.2 | 4.9 | 2.3 | 2.1 | | | | | | | | | | | | | | | | | | | |
| 1930 | 1.7 | 2.1 | 2.4 | 3.7 | 0.8 | -0.7 | -14.5 | | | | | | | | | | | | | | | | | | |
| 1931 | 0.7 | 1.0 | 1.0 | 1.8 | -1.7 | -4.7 | -21.6 | | | | | | | | | | | | | | | | | | |
| 1932 | 1.6 | 2.0 | 2.2 | 3.4 | 0.8 | -0.4 | -4.4 | | | | | | | | | | | | | | | | | | |
| 1933 | 2.1 | 2.6 | 2.9 | 4.1 | 2.0 | 1.7 | 1.2 | | | | | | | | | | | | | | | | | | |
| 1934 | 2.4 | 2.9 | 3.3 | 4.6 | 2.7 | 2.7 | 3.4 | | | | | | | | | | | | | | | | | | |
| 1935 | 2.6 | 3.1 | 3.5 | 4.8 | 3.2 | 3.4 | 4.6 | 10.5 | | | | | | | | | | | | | | | | | |
| 1936 | 2.9 | 3.5 | 3.9 | 5.2 | 3.8 | 4.3 | 5.9 | 12.2 | | | | | | | | | | | | | | | | | |
| 1937 | 2.5 | 2.9 | 3.3 | 4.4 | 2.8 | 2.9 | 3.4 | 3.3 | | | | | | | | | | | | | | | | | |
| 1938 | 2.2 | 2.6 | 2.9 | 3.8 | 2.2 | 2.0 | 2.0 | 0.2 | | | | | | | | | | | | | | | | | |
| 1939 | 1.9 | 2.3 | 2.5 | 3.3 | 1.6 | 1.3 | 0.9 | -1.6 | | | | | | | | | | | | | | | | | |
| 1940 | 1.6 | 1.9 | 2.0 | 2.7 | 1.0 | 0.5 | -0.3 | -3.3 | -11.9 | | | | | | | | | | | | | | | | |
| 1941 | 1.9 | 2.2 | 2.4 | 3.2 | 1.6 | 1.3 | 1.0 | -0.6 | 1.9 | | | | | | | | | | | | | | | | |
| 1942 | 2.2 | 2.5 | 2.8 | 3.6 | 2.2 | 2.0 | 2.0 | 1.2 | 5.9 | | | | | | | | | | | | | | | | |
| 1943 | 2.4 | 2.7 | 3.0 | 3.8 | 2.5 | 2.5 | 2.6 | 2.2 | 7.0 | | | | | | | | | | | | | | | | |
| 1944 | 2.5 | 2.9 | 3.1 | 4.0 | 2.7 | 2.7 | 3.0 | 2.8 | 7.1 | | | | | | | | | | | | | | | | |
| 1945 | 2.5 | 2.9 | 3.1 | 3.9 | 2.7 | 2.7 | 2.9 | 2.8 | 6.4 | 2.7 | | | | | | | | | | | | | | | |
| 1946 | 2.8 | 3.2 | 3.5 | 4.3 | 3.2 | 3.4 | 3.8 | 3.9 | 7.9 | 9.9 | | | | | | | | | | | | | | | |

# United Kingdom Long-Horizon Equity Risk Premia

in Local Currency (Pound Sterling – GBP)
in Percent

| End Date | 1900 | 1905 | 1910 | 1915 | 1920 | 1925 | 1930 | 1935 | 1940 | 1945 | 1950 | 1955 | 1960 | 1965 | 1970 | 1975 | 1980 | 1985 | 1990 | 1995 | 2000 | 2005 | 2010 | 2015 | 2016 |
|---|---|---|---|---|---|---|---|---|---|---|---|---|---|---|---|---|---|---|---|---|---|---|---|---|---|
| 1947 | 2.7 | 3.1 | 3.3 | 4.1 | 3.0 | 3.1 | 3.4 | 3.5 | 6.6 | 5.8 | | | | | | | | | | | | | | | |
| 1948 | 2.5 | 2.9 | 3.1 | 3.9 | 2.8 | 2.8 | 3.0 | 2.9 | 5.4 | 3.3 | | | | | | | | | | | | | | | |
| 1949 | 2.2 | 2.5 | 2.7 | 3.4 | 2.2 | 2.2 | 2.2 | 1.8 | 3.5 | -0.2 | | | | | | | | | | | | | | | |
| 1950 | 2.3 | 2.6 | 2.8 | 3.5 | 2.4 | 2.3 | 2.4 | 2.1 | 3.8 | 1.0 | 7.1 | | | | | | | | | | | | | | |
| 1951 | 2.4 | 2.7 | 2.9 | 3.5 | 2.5 | 2.5 | 2.5 | 2.3 | 3.9 | 1.6 | 6.2 | | | | | | | | | | | | | | |
| 1952 | 2.3 | 2.6 | 2.7 | 3.3 | 2.3 | 2.3 | 2.3 | 2.0 | 3.4 | 1.1 | 3.2 | | | | | | | | | | | | | | |
| 1953 | 2.6 | 2.9 | 3.1 | 3.8 | 2.8 | 2.9 | 3.0 | 3.0 | 4.6 | 3.2 | 7.4 | | | | | | | | | | | | | | |
| 1954 | 3.4 | 3.8 | 4.1 | 4.9 | 4.1 | 4.4 | 4.9 | 5.2 | 7.5 | 7.7 | 15.6 | | | | | | | | | | | | | | |
| 1955 | 3.5 | 3.9 | 4.2 | 4.9 | 4.2 | 4.5 | 5.0 | 5.3 | 7.5 | 7.7 | 14.2 | 7.2 | | | | | | | | | | | | | |
| 1956 | 3.5 | 3.9 | 4.1 | 4.9 | 4.1 | 4.4 | 4.8 | 5.2 | 7.1 | 7.2 | 12.4 | 4.3 | | | | | | | | | | | | | |
| 1957 | 3.2 | 3.6 | 3.8 | 4.5 | 3.8 | 3.9 | 4.3 | 4.5 | 6.1 | 5.8 | 9.5 | -0.7 | | | | | | | | | | | | | |
| 1958 | 3.8 | 4.2 | 4.5 | 5.2 | 4.6 | 4.9 | 5.3 | 5.7 | 7.7 | 7.9 | 12.4 | 8.3 | | | | | | | | | | | | | |
| 1959 | 4.5 | 4.9 | 5.3 | 6.1 | 5.6 | 6.0 | 6.7 | 7.3 | 9.6 | 10.4 | 15.7 | 15.7 | | | | | | | | | | | | | |
| 1960 | 4.2 | 4.7 | 5.0 | 5.8 | 5.3 | 5.6 | 6.2 | 6.7 | 8.7 | 9.2 | 13.5 | 11.7 | -8.3 | | | | | | | | | | | | |
| 1961 | 4.2 | 4.6 | 5.0 | 5.7 | 5.2 | 5.5 | 6.1 | 6.6 | 8.4 | 8.8 | 12.6 | 10.4 | -2.8 | | | | | | | | | | | | |
| 1962 | 4.2 | 4.6 | 4.9 | 5.7 | 5.1 | 5.5 | 6.0 | 6.4 | 8.2 | 8.5 | 11.8 | 9.5 | -1.0 | | | | | | | | | | | | |
| 1963 | 4.4 | 4.8 | 5.1 | 5.9 | 5.4 | 5.7 | 6.3 | 6.7 | 8.5 | 8.9 | 12.1 | 10.1 | 3.1 | | | | | | | | | | | | |
| 1964 | 4.2 | 4.5 | 4.9 | 5.5 | 5.0 | 5.3 | 5.8 | 6.2 | 7.8 | 7.9 | 10.6 | 8.1 | 0.5 | | | | | | | | | | | | |
| 1965 | 4.2 | 4.6 | 4.9 | 5.5 | 5.0 | 5.3 | 5.8 | 6.2 | 7.7 | 7.8 | 10.3 | 7.9 | 1.3 | 5.5 | | | | | | | | | | | |
| 1966 | 4.0 | 4.3 | 4.6 | 5.3 | 4.7 | 5.0 | 5.4 | 5.7 | 7.1 | 7.0 | 9.2 | 6.5 | -0.1 | -1.6 | | | | | | | | | | | |
| 1967 | 4.4 | 4.8 | 5.1 | 5.8 | 5.3 | 5.6 | 6.1 | 6.5 | 7.9 | 8.1 | 10.4 | 8.4 | 3.8 | 9.3 | | | | | | | | | | | |
| 1968 | 5.0 | 5.5 | 5.9 | 6.6 | 6.2 | 6.6 | 7.2 | 7.8 | 9.4 | 9.8 | 12.5 | 11.4 | 8.9 | 19.5 | | | | | | | | | | | |
| 1969 | 4.6 | 5.0 | 5.3 | 6.0 | 5.6 | 5.9 | 6.4 | 6.8 | 8.2 | 8.5 | 10.6 | 9.0 | 5.6 | 10.7 | | | | | | | | | | | |
| 1970 | 4.3 | 4.7 | 5.0 | 5.6 | 5.2 | 5.5 | 5.9 | 6.2 | 7.5 | 7.6 | 9.4 | 7.5 | 3.7 | 6.4 | -14.9 | | | | | | | | | | |
| 1971 | 4.7 | 5.1 | 5.4 | 6.1 | 5.7 | 6.0 | 6.5 | 6.9 | 8.2 | 8.4 | 10.3 | 8.8 | 5.9 | 9.8 | 7.5 | | | | | | | | | | |
| 1972 | 4.7 | 5.1 | 5.4 | 6.0 | 5.6 | 6.0 | 6.4 | 6.8 | 8.1 | 8.3 | 10.1 | 8.6 | 5.8 | 9.1 | 6.6 | | | | | | | | | | |
| 1973 | 4.2 | 4.5 | 4.8 | 5.3 | 4.9 | 5.1 | 5.5 | 5.7 | 6.8 | 6.8 | 8.2 | 6.3 | 2.9 | 4.2 | -3.8 | | | | | | | | | | |
| 1974 | 3.3 | 3.5 | 3.7 | 4.2 | 3.6 | 3.8 | 3.9 | 4.0 | 4.8 | 4.4 | 5.3 | 2.8 | -1.5 | -2.6 | -15.8 | | | | | | | | | | |
| 1975 | 5.0 | 5.4 | 5.7 | 6.3 | 6.0 | 6.3 | 6.8 | 7.2 | 8.4 | 8.6 | 10.3 | 9.0 | 6.9 | 9.8 | 9.1 | 133.8 | | | | | | | | | |
| 1976 | 4.8 | 5.1 | 5.4 | 6.0 | 5.7 | 6.0 | 6.4 | 6.7 | 7.9 | 8.0 | 9.5 | 8.1 | 5.9 | 8.1 | 6.3 | 61.5 | | | | | | | | | |
| 1977 | 5.0 | 5.4 | 5.8 | 6.4 | 6.0 | 6.4 | 6.8 | 7.2 | 8.4 | 8.5 | 10.1 | 8.9 | 7.0 | 9.5 | 8.8 | 49.8 | | | | | | | | | |
| 1978 | 4.9 | 5.3 | 5.6 | 6.2 | 5.9 | 6.2 | 6.6 | 6.9 | 8.0 | 8.2 | 9.6 | 8.4 | 6.4 | 8.6 | 7.4 | 36.3 | | | | | | | | | |
| 1979 | 4.8 | 5.2 | 5.5 | 6.1 | 5.7 | 6.0 | 6.4 | 6.8 | 7.8 | 7.9 | 9.2 | 8.0 | 6.0 | 7.9 | 6.5 | 28.7 | | | | | | | | | |
| 1980 | 5.0 | 5.4 | 5.7 | 6.2 | 5.9 | 6.2 | 6.6 | 7.0 | 8.0 | 8.2 | 9.5 | 8.3 | 6.6 | 8.5 | 7.5 | 26.8 | 17.3 | | | | | | | | |
| 1981 | 4.9 | 5.3 | 5.6 | 6.1 | 5.8 | 6.1 | 6.5 | 6.8 | 7.8 | 7.9 | 9.2 | 8.0 | 6.2 | 7.9 | 6.7 | 22.8 | 8.0 | | | | | | | | |
| 1982 | 5.0 | 5.4 | 5.7 | 6.2 | 5.9 | 6.2 | 6.6 | 6.9 | 7.9 | 8.0 | 9.3 | 8.2 | 6.5 | 8.2 | 7.2 | 21.6 | 9.8 | | | | | | | | |
| 1983 | 5.2 | 5.6 | 5.9 | 6.4 | 6.1 | 6.4 | 6.8 | 7.2 | 8.2 | 8.3 | 9.6 | 8.6 | 7.1 | 8.8 | 8.1 | 21.4 | 12.2 | | | | | | | | |
| 1984 | 5.4 | 5.8 | 6.1 | 6.6 | 6.4 | 6.7 | 7.1 | 7.5 | 8.5 | 8.7 | 9.9 | 9.0 | 7.6 | 9.4 | 9.0 | 21.4 | 14.1 | | | | | | | | |
| 1985 | 5.5 | 5.8 | 6.2 | 6.7 | 6.5 | 6.8 | 7.2 | 7.6 | 8.6 | 8.8 | 10.0 | 9.1 | 7.8 | 9.6 | 9.2 | 20.6 | 13.7 | 12.1 | | | | | | | |
| 1986 | 5.6 | 5.9 | 6.3 | 6.8 | 6.6 | 6.9 | 7.3 | 7.7 | 8.7 | 8.9 | 10.1 | 9.2 | 8.0 | 9.7 | 9.5 | 20.0 | 13.7 | 12.9 | | | | | | | |
| 1987 | 5.5 | 5.8 | 6.1 | 6.7 | 6.4 | 6.7 | 7.1 | 7.5 | 8.4 | 8.6 | 9.7 | 8.8 | 7.6 | 9.1 | 8.7 | 18.1 | 11.5 | 7.2 | | | | | | | |
| 1988 | 5.4 | 5.7 | 6.0 | 6.6 | 6.3 | 6.6 | 7.0 | 7.3 | 8.2 | 8.4 | 9.5 | 8.6 | 7.3 | 8.7 | 8.2 | 16.8 | 10.2 | 5.4 | | | | | | | |
| 1989 | 5.6 | 6.0 | 6.3 | 6.8 | 6.6 | 6.9 | 7.3 | 7.7 | 8.6 | 8.8 | 9.9 | 9.1 | 8.0 | 9.1 | 9.1 | 17.5 | 11.8 | 9.6 | | | | | | | |
| 1990 | 5.4 | 5.7 | 6.0 | 6.5 | 6.3 | 6.5 | 6.9 | 7.2 | 8.1 | 8.2 | 9.2 | 8.3 | 7.1 | 8.4 | 7.8 | 15.2 | 9.1 | 4.9 | -18.4 | | | | | | |
| 1991 | 5.4 | 5.7 | 6.0 | 6.5 | 6.3 | 6.6 | 6.9 | 7.2 | 8.1 | 8.2 | 9.2 | 8.3 | 7.2 | 8.4 | 7.9 | 14.9 | 9.1 | 5.5 | -4.7 | | | | | | |
| 1992 | 5.4 | 5.8 | 6.1 | 6.6 | 6.3 | 6.6 | 7.0 | 7.3 | 8.1 | 8.2 | 9.2 | 8.4 | 7.2 | 8.4 | 7.9 | 14.5 | 9.1 | 6.0 | -0.1 | | | | | | |
| 1993 | 5.6 | 5.9 | 6.2 | 6.7 | 6.5 | 6.8 | 7.2 | 7.5 | 8.3 | 8.4 | 9.4 | 8.6 | 7.6 | 8.8 | 8.4 | 14.8 | 9.8 | 7.5 | 4.8 | | | | | | |

Start Date

## United Kingdom Long-Horizon Equity Risk Premia

in Local Currency (Pound Sterling – GBP)
in Percent

| End Date | Start Date 1900 | 1905 | 1910 | 1915 | 1920 | 1925 | 1930 | 1935 | 1940 | 1945 | 1950 | 1955 | 1960 | 1965 | 1970 | 1975 | 1980 | 1985 | 1990 | 1995 | 2000 | 2005 | 2010 | 2015 | 2016 |
|---|---|---|---|---|---|---|---|---|---|---|---|---|---|---|---|---|---|---|---|---|---|---|---|---|---|
| 1994 | 5.4 | 5.7 | 6.0 | 6.5 | 6.2 | 6.5 | 6.8 | 7.1 | 7.9 | 8.0 | 8.9 | 8.1 | 7.0 | 8.1 | 7.5 | 13.4 | 8.2 | 5.3 | 1.1 | | | | | | |
| 1995 | 5.5 | 5.8 | 6.1 | 6.6 | 6.3 | 6.6 | 6.9 | 7.2 | 8.0 | 8.1 | 9.0 | 8.2 | 7.2 | 8.2 | 7.8 | 13.4 | 8.6 | 6.1 | 3.2 | 13.7 | | | | | |
| 1996 | 5.5 | 5.8 | 6.1 | 6.6 | 6.4 | 6.6 | 7.0 | 7.2 | 8.0 | 8.1 | 9.0 | 8.2 | 7.2 | 8.2 | 7.8 | 13.1 | 8.6 | 6.3 | 3.9 | 10.9 | | | | | |
| 1997 | 5.6 | 6.0 | 6.3 | 6.8 | 6.5 | 6.8 | 7.2 | 7.5 | 8.2 | 8.3 | 9.2 | 8.5 | 7.5 | 8.6 | 8.2 | 13.4 | 9.2 | 7.3 | 5.9 | 13.9 | | | | | |
| 1998 | 5.7 | 6.0 | 6.3 | 6.8 | 6.6 | 6.9 | 7.2 | 7.5 | 8.3 | 8.4 | 9.3 | 8.5 | 7.6 | 8.6 | 8.3 | 13.3 | 9.3 | 7.5 | 6.4 | 13.0 | | | | | |
| 1999 | 5.8 | 6.1 | 6.4 | 6.8 | 6.6 | 6.9 | 7.3 | 7.6 | 8.3 | 8.4 | 9.3 | 8.6 | 7.7 | 8.7 | 8.4 | 13.2 | 9.4 | 7.8 | 6.9 | 12.7 | | | | | |
| 2000 | 5.6 | 5.9 | 6.2 | 6.7 | 6.4 | 6.7 | 7.0 | 7.3 | 8.0 | 8.1 | 8.9 | 8.2 | 7.3 | 8.2 | 7.8 | 12.3 | 8.4 | 6.7 | 5.4 | 8.9 | -9.9 | | | | |
| 2001 | 5.4 | 5.7 | 5.9 | 6.4 | 6.2 | 6.4 | 6.7 | 6.9 | 7.6 | 7.7 | 8.4 | 7.7 | 6.7 | 7.5 | 7.0 | 11.3 | 7.3 | 5.3 | 3.5 | 5.3 | -13.3 | | | | |
| 2002 | 5.1 | 5.3 | 5.6 | 6.0 | 5.7 | 5.9 | 6.2 | 6.4 | 7.1 | 7.0 | 7.7 | 6.9 | 5.9 | 6.6 | 6.0 | 9.9 | 5.8 | 3.4 | 1.1 | 1.1 | -18.3 | | | | |
| 2003 | 5.1 | 5.4 | 5.7 | 6.1 | 5.8 | 6.0 | 6.3 | 6.5 | 7.2 | 7.2 | 7.9 | 7.1 | 6.1 | 6.8 | 6.2 | 10.0 | 6.1 | 4.0 | 2.0 | 2.5 | -10.2 | | | | |
| 2004 | 5.2 | 5.4 | 5.7 | 6.1 | 5.9 | 6.1 | 6.3 | 6.5 | 7.2 | 7.2 | 7.8 | 7.0 | 6.1 | 6.8 | 6.2 | 9.9 | 6.1 | 4.1 | 2.3 | 2.9 | -6.8 | | | | |
| 2005 | 5.3 | 5.5 | 5.8 | 6.2 | 6.0 | 6.2 | 6.4 | 6.7 | 7.3 | 7.3 | 8.0 | 7.2 | 6.3 | 7.0 | 6.5 | 10.1 | 6.5 | 4.7 | 3.2 | 4.1 | -3.1 | 15.6 | | | |
| 2006 | 5.3 | 5.6 | 5.8 | 6.2 | 6.0 | 6.2 | 6.5 | 6.7 | 7.3 | 7.3 | 8.0 | 7.3 | 6.4 | 7.1 | 6.6 | 10.1 | 6.6 | 4.9 | 3.6 | 4.6 | -1.2 | 12.9 | | | |
| 2007 | 5.3 | 5.6 | 5.8 | 6.2 | 6.0 | 6.2 | 6.4 | 6.6 | 7.2 | 7.3 | 7.9 | 7.2 | 6.3 | 7.0 | 6.5 | 9.8 | 6.5 | 4.8 | 3.5 | 4.4 | -0.8 | 9.2 | | | |
| 2008 | 4.9 | 5.2 | 5.4 | 5.8 | 5.5 | 5.7 | 5.9 | 6.1 | 6.7 | 6.6 | 7.2 | 6.4 | 5.5 | 6.0 | 5.4 | 8.6 | 5.1 | 3.2 | 1.5 | 1.7 | -4.4 | -1.4 | | | |
| 2009 | 5.1 | 5.4 | 5.6 | 6.0 | 5.7 | 5.9 | 6.2 | 6.3 | 6.9 | 6.9 | 7.5 | 6.7 | 5.8 | 6.4 | 5.9 | 9.0 | 5.7 | 4.1 | 2.7 | 3.2 | -1.5 | 3.7 | | | |
| 2010 | 5.1 | 5.4 | 5.6 | 6.0 | 5.8 | 5.9 | 6.2 | 6.4 | 6.9 | 6.9 | 7.5 | 6.8 | 5.9 | 6.5 | 6.0 | 9.0 | 5.8 | 4.2 | 3.0 | 3.5 | -0.6 | 4.5 | 8.5 | | |
| 2011 | 5.0 | 5.3 | 5.5 | 5.9 | 5.6 | 5.8 | 6.0 | 6.2 | 6.8 | 6.7 | 7.3 | 6.6 | 5.7 | 6.2 | 5.7 | 8.6 | 5.5 | 3.9 | 2.6 | 3.0 | -1.0 | 3.1 | 1.6 | | |
| 2012 | 5.1 | 5.3 | 5.5 | 5.9 | 5.7 | 5.8 | 6.1 | 6.2 | 6.8 | 6.8 | 7.3 | 6.6 | 5.7 | 6.3 | 5.8 | 8.6 | 5.6 | 4.0 | 2.8 | 3.3 | -0.3 | 3.8 | 3.8 | | |
| 2013 | 5.2 | 5.4 | 5.6 | 6.0 | 5.8 | 6.0 | 6.2 | 6.4 | 6.9 | 6.9 | 7.5 | 6.8 | 5.9 | 6.5 | 6.0 | 8.8 | 5.9 | 4.5 | 3.4 | 4.0 | 0.9 | 5.2 | 7.0 | | |
| 2014 | 5.1 | 5.3 | 5.6 | 5.9 | 5.7 | 5.9 | 6.1 | 6.3 | 6.8 | 6.8 | 7.3 | 6.6 | 5.8 | 6.3 | 5.8 | 8.5 | 5.6 | 4.2 | 3.2 | 3.7 | 0.7 | 4.4 | 5.1 | | |
| 2015 | 5.0 | 5.3 | 5.5 | 5.8 | 5.6 | 5.8 | 6.0 | 6.1 | 6.6 | 6.6 | 7.1 | 6.4 | 5.6 | 6.1 | 5.6 | 8.2 | 5.4 | 4.0 | 2.9 | 3.3 | 0.4 | 3.7 | 3.6 | -4.1 | |
| 2016 | 5.1 | 5.4 | 5.6 | 5.9 | 5.7 | 5.9 | 6.1 | 6.3 | 6.8 | 6.8 | 7.3 | 6.6 | 5.8 | 6.3 | 5.9 | 8.4 | 5.7 | 4.4 | 3.4 | 4.0 | 1.4 | 4.8 | 5.6 | 6.9 | 17.8 |

Source of underlying data: 1.) Morningstar *Direct* database. Used with permission. All rights reserved. All calculations performed by Duff & Phelps LLC.

**United Kingdom Long-Horizon Equity Risk Premia**

in U.S. Dollars (USD)
in Percent

| End Date | Start Date 1900 | 1905 | 1910 | 1915 | 1920 | 1925 | 1930 | 1935 | 1940 | 1945 | 1950 | 1955 | 1960 | 1965 | 1970 | 1975 | 1980 | 1985 | 1990 | 1995 | 2000 | 2005 | 2010 | 2015 | 2016 |
|---|---|---|---|---|---|---|---|---|---|---|---|---|---|---|---|---|---|---|---|---|---|---|---|---|---|
| 1900 | -1.2 | | | | | | | | | | | | | | | | | | | | | | | | |
| 1901 | -3.7 | | | | | | | | | | | | | | | | | | | | | | | | |
| 1902 | -2.3 | | | | | | | | | | | | | | | | | | | | | | | | |
| 1903 | -3.2 | | | | | | | | | | | | | | | | | | | | | | | | |
| 1904 | -0.5 | | | | | | | | | | | | | | | | | | | | | | | | |
| 1905 | 0.1 | 2.9 | | | | | | | | | | | | | | | | | | | | | | | |
| 1906 | 0.0 | 1.2 | | | | | | | | | | | | | | | | | | | | | | | |
| 1907 | -0.3 | 0.0 | | | | | | | | | | | | | | | | | | | | | | | |
| 1908 | -0.2 | 0.1 | | | | | | | | | | | | | | | | | | | | | | | |
| 1909 | 0.3 | 1.2 | | | | | | | | | | | | | | | | | | | | | | | |
| 1910 | 0.6 | 1.5 | 3.2 | | | | | | | | | | | | | | | | | | | | | | |
| 1911 | 0.5 | 1.2 | 1.3 | | | | | | | | | | | | | | | | | | | | | | |
| 1912 | 0.5 | 1.1 | 1.1 | | | | | | | | | | | | | | | | | | | | | | |
| 1913 | 0.3 | 0.8 | 0.3 | | | | | | | | | | | | | | | | | | | | | | |
| 1914 | -0.4 | -0.4 | -1.9 | | | | | | | | | | | | | | | | | | | | | | |
| 1915 | -1.0 | -1.2 | -3.2 | -9.5 | | | | | | | | | | | | | | | | | | | | | |
| 1916 | -0.5 | -0.5 | -1.7 | -1.0 | | | | | | | | | | | | | | | | | | | | | |
| 1917 | 0.0 | 0.2 | -0.5 | 2.0 | | | | | | | | | | | | | | | | | | | | | |
| 1918 | 1.1 | 1.6 | 1.9 | 6.7 | | | | | | | | | | | | | | | | | | | | | |
| 1919 | 0.9 | 1.3 | 1.4 | 4.7 | | | | | | | | | | | | | | | | | | | | | |
| 1920 | -0.5 | -0.6 | -1.3 | -0.8 | -28.4 | | | | | | | | | | | | | | | | | | | | |
| 1921 | 0.0 | 0.2 | -0.2 | 1.0 | -8.0 | | | | | | | | | | | | | | | | | | | | |
| 1922 | 1.8 | 2.5 | 3.0 | 6.0 | 8.3 | | | | | | | | | | | | | | | | | | | | |
| 1923 | 1.6 | 2.1 | 2.4 | 4.8 | 5.1 | | | | | | | | | | | | | | | | | | | | |
| 1924 | 2.4 | 3.1 | 3.8 | 6.6 | 8.6 | | | | | | | | | | | | | | | | | | | | |
| 1925 | 2.7 | 3.4 | 4.1 | 6.9 | 8.7 | 8.9 | | | | | | | | | | | | | | | | | | | |
| 1926 | 2.7 | 3.4 | 4.0 | 6.5 | 7.8 | 5.7 | | | | | | | | | | | | | | | | | | | |
| 1927 | 2.8 | 3.5 | 4.1 | 6.4 | 7.6 | 5.8 | | | | | | | | | | | | | | | | | | | |
| 1928 | 3.0 | 3.8 | 4.5 | 6.7 | 7.9 | 7.0 | | | | | | | | | | | | | | | | | | | |
| 1929 | 2.5 | 3.0 | 3.5 | 5.3 | 5.7 | 2.7 | | | | | | | | | | | | | | | | | | | |
| 1930 | 1.9 | 2.3 | 2.6 | 4.1 | 3.8 | -0.3 | -14.9 | | | | | | | | | | | | | | | | | | |
| 1931 | 0.3 | 0.4 | 0.2 | 0.9 | -0.7 | -7.4 | -32.6 | | | | | | | | | | | | | | | | | | |
| 1932 | 1.1 | 1.3 | 1.4 | 2.3 | 1.4 | -3.1 | -12.8 | | | | | | | | | | | | | | | | | | |
| 1933 | 3.4 | 4.1 | 4.7 | 6.4 | 7.1 | 6.2 | 10.6 | | | | | | | | | | | | | | | | | | |
| 1934 | 3.6 | 4.3 | 4.9 | 6.6 | 7.2 | 6.5 | 10.4 | | | | | | | | | | | | | | | | | | |
| 1935 | 3.8 | 4.5 | 5.1 | 6.8 | 7.4 | 6.9 | 10.3 | 10.1 | | | | | | | | | | | | | | | | | |
| 1936 | 4.0 | 4.7 | 5.4 | 7.1 | 7.8 | 7.4 | 10.8 | 11.8 | | | | | | | | | | | | | | | | | |
| 1937 | 3.6 | 4.2 | 4.7 | 6.2 | 6.6 | 5.9 | 7.8 | 3.6 | | | | | | | | | | | | | | | | | |
| 1938 | 3.1 | 3.6 | 4.1 | 5.3 | 5.5 | 4.3 | 5.3 | -1.1 | | | | | | | | | | | | | | | | | |
| 1939 | 2.5 | 2.9 | 3.2 | 4.2 | 4.1 | 2.6 | 2.6 | -5.2 | | | | | | | | | | | | | | | | | |
| 1940 | 2.1 | 2.5 | 2.7 | 3.6 | 3.4 | 1.7 | 1.3 | -6.3 | -11.9 | | | | | | | | | | | | | | | | |
| 1941 | 2.5 | 2.9 | 3.1 | 4.1 | 3.9 | 2.5 | 2.5 | -3.2 | 1.9 | | | | | | | | | | | | | | | | |
| 1942 | 2.7 | 3.2 | 3.5 | 4.4 | 4.4 | 3.2 | 3.4 | -1.0 | 5.9 | | | | | | | | | | | | | | | | |
| 1943 | 2.9 | 3.3 | 3.7 | 4.6 | 4.6 | 3.6 | 3.9 | 0.2 | 7.0 | | | | | | | | | | | | | | | | |
| 1944 | 3.0 | 3.4 | 3.8 | 4.7 | 4.7 | 3.8 | 4.1 | 1.0 | 7.1 | | | | | | | | | | | | | | | | |
| 1945 | 3.0 | 3.4 | 3.7 | 4.7 | 4.7 | 3.7 | 4.0 | 1.1 | 6.4 | 2.7 | | | | | | | | | | | | | | | |
| 1946 | 2.7 | 3.0 | 3.3 | 4.1 | 4.0 | 3.0 | 3.0 | 0.0 | 3.6 | -5.1 | | | | | | | | | | | | | | | |

Source of underlying data: 1.) Morningstar *Direct* database. Used with permission. All rights reserved. All calculations performed by Duff & Phelps LLC.

**United Kingdom Long-Horizon Equity Risk Premia**

in U.S. Dollars (USD)
in Percent

| End Date | 1900 | 1905 | 1910 | 1915 | 1920 | 1925 | 1930 | 1935 | 1940 | 1945 | 1950 | 1955 | 1960 | 1965 | 1970 | 1975 | 1980 | 1985 | 1990 | 1995 | 2000 | 2005 | 2010 | 2015 | 2016 |
|---|---|---|---|---|---|---|---|---|---|---|---|---|---|---|---|---|---|---|---|---|---|---|---|---|---|
| 1947 | 2.2 | 2.5 | 2.7 | 3.4 | 3.2 | 2.0 | 1.8 | -1.5 | 0.9 | -9.6 | | | | | | | | | | | | | | | |
| 1948 | 2.5 | 2.8 | 3.1 | 3.8 | 3.6 | 2.6 | 2.6 | -0.2 | 2.5 | -3.2 | | | | | | | | | | | | | | | |
| 1949 | 1.8 | 2.1 | 2.2 | 2.7 | 2.4 | 1.2 | 0.8 | -2.4 | -1.0 | -9.1 | | | | | | | | | | | | | | | |
| 1950 | 2.0 | 2.3 | 2.4 | 3.0 | 2.8 | 1.7 | 1.4 | -1.4 | 0.3 | -5.3 | 13.5 | | | | | | | | | | | | | | |
| 1951 | 2.3 | 2.6 | 2.8 | 3.4 | 3.2 | 2.2 | 2.1 | -0.3 | 1.7 | -2.2 | 14.9 | | | | | | | | | | | | | | |
| 1952 | 2.2 | 2.5 | 2.7 | 3.3 | 3.1 | 2.1 | 1.9 | -0.4 | 1.4 | -2.2 | 9.2 | | | | | | | | | | | | | | |
| 1953 | 2.6 | 2.9 | 3.1 | 3.7 | 3.6 | 2.7 | 2.7 | 0.6 | 2.7 | 0.3 | 12.0 | | | | | | | | | | | | | | |
| 1954 | 3.4 | 3.7 | 4.0 | 4.8 | 4.8 | 4.2 | 4.5 | 3.0 | 5.7 | 5.0 | 19.0 | | | | | | | | | | | | | | |
| 1955 | 3.4 | 3.8 | 4.1 | 4.9 | 4.9 | 4.3 | 4.6 | 3.2 | 5.8 | 5.2 | 17.1 | 7.8 | | | | | | | | | | | | | |
| 1956 | 3.4 | 3.8 | 4.0 | 4.8 | 4.8 | 4.2 | 4.4 | 3.1 | 5.5 | 4.9 | 14.8 | 4.3 | | | | | | | | | | | | | |
| 1957 | 3.2 | 3.5 | 3.8 | 4.4 | 4.4 | 3.7 | 3.9 | 2.5 | 4.7 | 3.7 | 11.7 | -0.4 | | | | | | | | | | | | | |
| 1958 | 3.7 | 4.1 | 4.4 | 5.1 | 5.2 | 4.7 | 5.0 | 3.9 | 6.3 | 6.0 | 14.3 | 8.4 | | | | | | | | | | | | | |
| 1959 | 4.4 | 4.8 | 5.2 | 6.0 | 6.2 | 5.8 | 6.3 | 5.5 | 8.2 | 8.6 | 17.4 | 15.8 | | | | | | | | | | | | | |
| 1960 | 4.2 | 4.6 | 5.0 | 5.7 | 5.8 | 5.4 | 5.9 | 5.0 | 7.4 | 7.5 | 15.1 | 11.8 | -8.2 | | | | | | | | | | | | |
| 1961 | 4.2 | 4.6 | 4.9 | 5.6 | 5.8 | 5.4 | 5.8 | 4.9 | 7.2 | 7.3 | 14.1 | 10.5 | -2.7 | | | | | | | | | | | | |
| 1962 | 4.1 | 4.5 | 4.9 | 5.6 | 5.7 | 5.3 | 5.7 | 4.8 | 7.0 | 7.0 | 13.2 | 9.5 | -0.9 | | | | | | | | | | | | |
| 1963 | 4.3 | 4.7 | 5.1 | 5.8 | 5.9 | 5.5 | 6.0 | 5.2 | 7.4 | 7.4 | 13.3 | 10.1 | 3.0 | | | | | | | | | | | | |
| 1964 | 4.1 | 4.5 | 4.8 | 5.4 | 5.5 | 5.1 | 5.5 | 4.7 | 6.7 | 6.5 | 11.7 | 8.1 | 0.4 | | | | | | | | | | | | |
| 1965 | 4.1 | 4.5 | 4.8 | 5.5 | 5.5 | 5.2 | 5.5 | 4.7 | 6.6 | 6.5 | 11.4 | 7.9 | 1.3 | 6.0 | | | | | | | | | | | |
| 1966 | 3.9 | 4.3 | 4.6 | 5.2 | 5.2 | 4.8 | 5.1 | 4.3 | 6.0 | 5.8 | 10.2 | 6.5 | -0.2 | -1.6 | | | | | | | | | | | |
| 1967 | 4.1 | 4.4 | 4.7 | 5.3 | 5.4 | 5.0 | 5.3 | 4.6 | 6.3 | 6.1 | 10.3 | 7.0 | 1.5 | 3.3 | | | | | | | | | | | |
| 1968 | 4.7 | 5.1 | 5.4 | 6.1 | 6.3 | 6.0 | 6.4 | 5.9 | 7.8 | 7.9 | 12.4 | 10.0 | 6.7 | 14.6 | | | | | | | | | | | |
| 1969 | 4.3 | 4.7 | 5.0 | 5.6 | 5.7 | 5.3 | 5.7 | 5.0 | 6.7 | 6.6 | 10.5 | 7.7 | 3.7 | 6.9 | | | | | | | | | | | |
| 1970 | 4.0 | 4.4 | 4.6 | 5.2 | 5.3 | 4.9 | 5.2 | 4.5 | 6.0 | 5.8 | 9.3 | 6.3 | 2.0 | 3.3 | -14.9 | | | | | | | | | | |
| 1971 | 4.5 | 4.9 | 5.2 | 5.8 | 5.9 | 5.6 | 6.0 | 5.4 | 7.0 | 7.0 | 10.6 | 8.2 | 5.0 | 8.2 | 11.6 | | | | | | | | | | |
| 1972 | 4.4 | 4.7 | 5.0 | 5.6 | 5.7 | 5.4 | 5.7 | 5.1 | 6.7 | 6.6 | 10.0 | 7.5 | 4.3 | 6.8 | 6.5 | | | | | | | | | | |
| 1973 | 3.8 | 4.2 | 4.4 | 4.9 | 5.0 | 4.6 | 4.8 | 4.1 | 5.4 | 5.2 | 8.1 | 5.2 | 1.5 | 2.1 | -4.0 | | | | | | | | | | |
| 1974 | 3.0 | 3.2 | 3.4 | 3.8 | 3.7 | 3.2 | 3.3 | 2.4 | 3.5 | 2.9 | 5.3 | 1.8 | -2.9 | -4.5 | -15.9 | | | | | | | | | | |
| 1975 | 4.2 | 4.6 | 4.8 | 5.4 | 5.5 | 5.1 | 5.4 | 4.8 | 6.2 | 6.0 | 9.0 | 6.6 | 3.7 | 5.1 | 3.7 | 101.4 | | | | | | | | | |
| 1976 | 3.9 | 4.2 | 4.4 | 4.9 | 4.9 | 4.6 | 4.8 | 4.1 | 5.4 | 5.1 | 7.7 | 5.1 | 2.0 | 2.6 | -0.4 | 38.2 | | | | | | | | | |
| 1977 | 4.3 | 4.7 | 4.9 | 5.5 | 5.6 | 5.3 | 5.5 | 5.0 | 6.3 | 6.2 | 8.9 | 6.7 | 4.2 | 5.6 | 4.8 | 39.2 | | | | | | | | | |
| 1978 | 4.3 | 4.6 | 4.9 | 5.4 | 5.5 | 5.2 | 5.5 | 4.9 | 6.2 | 6.1 | 8.7 | 6.5 | 4.1 | 5.4 | 4.5 | 30.1 | | | | | | | | | |
| 1979 | 4.4 | 4.7 | 4.9 | 5.5 | 5.5 | 5.3 | 5.5 | 5.0 | 6.2 | 6.1 | 8.7 | 6.6 | 4.3 | 5.6 | 4.9 | 25.7 | | | | | | | | | |
| 1980 | 4.6 | 5.0 | 5.2 | 5.8 | 5.9 | 5.6 | 5.9 | 5.4 | 6.7 | 6.7 | 9.2 | 7.3 | 5.3 | 6.8 | 6.8 | 25.7 | 25.8 | | | | | | | | |
| 1981 | 4.3 | 4.6 | 4.9 | 5.4 | 5.4 | 5.2 | 5.4 | 4.9 | 6.1 | 5.9 | 8.2 | 6.3 | 4.1 | 5.2 | 4.4 | 18.9 | 2.2 | | | | | | | | |
| 1982 | 4.2 | 4.5 | 4.8 | 5.2 | 5.3 | 5.0 | 5.2 | 4.7 | 5.8 | 5.7 | 7.9 | 5.9 | 3.7 | 4.7 | 3.8 | 16.1 | 0.2 | | | | | | | | |
| 1983 | 4.3 | 4.6 | 4.8 | 5.3 | 5.3 | 5.0 | 5.3 | 4.7 | 5.9 | 5.7 | 7.9 | 5.9 | 3.9 | 4.8 | 4.1 | 15.1 | 2.0 | | | | | | | | |
| 1984 | 4.2 | 4.5 | 4.7 | 5.2 | 5.2 | 4.9 | 5.1 | 4.6 | 5.7 | 5.5 | 7.6 | 5.7 | 3.6 | 4.4 | 3.6 | 13.4 | 1.1 | | | | | | | | |
| 1985 | 4.6 | 4.9 | 5.1 | 5.6 | 5.7 | 5.5 | 5.7 | 5.3 | 6.4 | 6.3 | 8.5 | 6.8 | 5.0 | 6.1 | 5.8 | 15.7 | 7.5 | 39.4 | | | | | | | |
| 1986 | 4.7 | 5.0 | 5.3 | 5.8 | 5.9 | 5.6 | 5.9 | 5.5 | 6.6 | 6.6 | 8.7 | 7.0 | 5.4 | 6.6 | 6.5 | 15.8 | 8.7 | 27.8 | | | | | | | |
| 1987 | 4.9 | 5.2 | 5.5 | 6.0 | 6.1 | 5.9 | 6.2 | 5.8 | 6.9 | 6.9 | 9.0 | 7.5 | 6.0 | 7.2 | 7.3 | 16.2 | 10.3 | 25.6 | | | | | | | |
| 1988 | 4.8 | 5.1 | 5.4 | 5.9 | 6.0 | 5.8 | 6.0 | 5.6 | 6.7 | 6.7 | 8.7 | 7.2 | 5.7 | 6.8 | 6.7 | 14.8 | 8.8 | 18.4 | | | | | | | |
| 1989 | 4.9 | 5.2 | 5.5 | 6.0 | 6.1 | 5.9 | 6.1 | 5.7 | 6.8 | 6.8 | 8.8 | 7.3 | 5.9 | 7.0 | 7.0 | 14.7 | 9.2 | 17.3 | | | | | | | |
| 1990 | 4.8 | 5.1 | 5.4 | 5.9 | 5.9 | 5.7 | 6.0 | 5.6 | 6.7 | 6.6 | 8.5 | 7.1 | 5.6 | 6.6 | 6.6 | 13.6 | 8.1 | 14.0 | -2.5 | | | | | | |
| 1991 | 4.8 | 5.1 | 5.4 | 5.9 | 5.9 | 5.7 | 6.0 | 5.6 | 6.6 | 6.6 | 8.4 | 7.0 | 5.6 | 6.6 | 6.5 | 13.1 | 7.9 | 12.8 | 1.6 | | | | | | |
| 1992 | 4.7 | 4.9 | 5.2 | 5.6 | 5.7 | 5.5 | 5.7 | 5.3 | 6.3 | 6.2 | 8.0 | 6.5 | 5.1 | 6.0 | 5.8 | 11.8 | 6.4 | 9.8 | -2.8 | | | | | | |
| 1993 | 4.8 | 5.1 | 5.3 | 5.8 | 5.8 | 5.6 | 5.7 | 5.5 | 6.5 | 6.4 | 8.2 | 6.8 | 5.5 | 6.3 | 6.2 | 12.0 | 7.1 | 10.5 | 2.1 | | | | | | |

Source of underlying data: 1.) Morningstar *Direct* database. Used with permission. All rights reserved. All calculations performed by Duff & Phelps LLC.

**United Kingdom Long-Horizon Equity Risk Premia**

in U.S. Dollars (USD)
in Percent

| End Date | Start Date 1900 | 1905 | 1910 | 1915 | 1920 | 1925 | 1930 | 1935 | 1940 | 1945 | 1950 | 1955 | 1960 | 1965 | 1970 | 1975 | 1980 | 1985 | 1990 | 1995 | 2000 | 2005 | 2010 | 2015 | 2016 |
|---|---|---|---|---|---|---|---|---|---|---|---|---|---|---|---|---|---|---|---|---|---|---|---|---|---|
| 1994 | 4.6 | 4.9 | 5.1 | 5.6 | 5.7 | 5.4 | 5.6 | 5.3 | 6.2 | 6.1 | 7.8 | 6.4 | 5.0 | 5.8 | 5.6 | 11.0 | 6.1 | 8.6 | -0.1 | | | | | | |
| 1995 | 4.7 | 5.0 | 5.2 | 5.7 | 5.7 | 5.5 | 5.8 | 5.4 | 6.3 | 6.2 | 7.9 | 6.6 | 5.3 | 6.0 | 5.9 | 11.1 | 6.5 | 9.0 | 2.0 | 12.8 | | | | | |
| 1996 | 4.9 | 5.2 | 5.4 | 5.8 | 5.9 | 5.7 | 6.0 | 5.6 | 6.5 | 6.5 | 8.1 | 6.8 | 5.6 | 6.5 | 6.4 | 11.4 | 7.2 | 9.8 | 4.5 | 16.0 | | | | | |
| 1997 | 5.0 | 5.3 | 5.5 | 6.0 | 6.0 | 5.9 | 6.1 | 5.8 | 6.7 | 6.7 | 8.3 | 7.0 | 5.9 | 6.7 | 6.7 | 11.6 | 7.7 | 10.2 | 5.8 | 15.8 | | | | | |
| 1998 | 5.0 | 5.3 | 5.6 | 6.0 | 6.1 | 5.9 | 6.2 | 5.8 | 6.8 | 6.7 | 8.4 | 7.2 | 6.0 | 6.9 | 6.9 | 11.6 | 7.9 | 10.3 | 6.5 | 14.7 | | | | | |
| 1999 | 5.1 | 5.4 | 5.6 | 6.0 | 6.1 | 6.0 | 6.2 | 5.9 | 6.8 | 6.8 | 8.4 | 7.2 | 6.1 | 6.9 | 6.9 | 11.5 | 7.9 | 10.2 | 6.6 | 13.4 | | | | | |
| 2000 | 4.9 | 5.1 | 5.4 | 5.8 | 5.9 | 5.7 | 5.9 | 5.5 | 6.4 | 6.4 | 7.9 | 6.7 | 5.5 | 6.2 | 6.1 | 10.4 | 6.7 | 8.5 | 4.5 | 8.4 | -16.5 | | | | |
| 2001 | 4.6 | 4.9 | 5.1 | 5.5 | 5.6 | 5.4 | 5.5 | 5.2 | 6.0 | 5.9 | 7.4 | 6.1 | 5.0 | 5.6 | 5.4 | 9.3 | 5.6 | 6.9 | 2.6 | 4.5 | -17.7 | | | | |
| 2002 | 4.4 | 4.6 | 4.8 | 5.2 | 5.2 | 5.0 | 5.2 | 4.8 | 5.6 | 5.5 | 6.8 | 5.6 | 4.4 | 4.9 | 4.6 | 8.2 | 4.4 | 5.4 | 0.8 | 1.4 | -18.7 | | | | |
| 2003 | 4.6 | 4.9 | 5.1 | 5.4 | 5.5 | 5.3 | 5.5 | 5.1 | 5.9 | 5.8 | 7.2 | 6.0 | 4.9 | 5.4 | 5.2 | 8.9 | 5.4 | 6.5 | 2.7 | 4.2 | -7.2 | | | | |
| 2004 | 4.7 | 5.0 | 5.2 | 5.5 | 5.6 | 5.4 | 5.6 | 5.2 | 6.1 | 6.0 | 7.3 | 6.2 | 5.1 | 5.7 | 5.5 | 9.1 | 5.7 | 6.9 | 3.4 | 5.2 | -2.9 | | | | |
| 2005 | 4.7 | 4.9 | 5.1 | 5.5 | 5.6 | 5.4 | 5.6 | 5.2 | 6.0 | 5.9 | 7.3 | 6.1 | 5.0 | 5.6 | 5.4 | 8.9 | 5.6 | 6.7 | 3.4 | 5.0 | -1.9 | 3.4 | | | |
| 2006 | 4.9 | 5.1 | 5.3 | 5.7 | 5.8 | 5.6 | 5.8 | 5.5 | 6.3 | 6.2 | 7.6 | 6.5 | 5.5 | 6.1 | 6.0 | 9.4 | 6.4 | 7.6 | 4.8 | 6.8 | 2.1 | 14.6 | | | |
| 2007 | 4.9 | 5.1 | 5.3 | 5.7 | 5.8 | 5.6 | 5.8 | 5.5 | 6.3 | 6.2 | 7.5 | 6.4 | 5.4 | 5.9 | 5.9 | 9.2 | 6.3 | 7.4 | 4.7 | 6.5 | 2.3 | 10.9 | | | |
| 2008 | 4.3 | 4.6 | 4.8 | 5.1 | 5.1 | 4.9 | 5.1 | 4.7 | 5.4 | 5.3 | 6.5 | 5.3 | 4.3 | 4.7 | 4.4 | 7.4 | 4.3 | 5.0 | 1.7 | 2.4 | -3.7 | -4.8 | | | |
| 2009 | 4.7 | 4.9 | 5.1 | 5.5 | 5.5 | 5.3 | 5.5 | 5.2 | 5.9 | 5.8 | 7.1 | 6.0 | 5.0 | 5.5 | 5.3 | 8.3 | 5.5 | 6.3 | 3.6 | 4.8 | 0.6 | 4.1 | | | |
| 2010 | 4.7 | 4.9 | 5.1 | 5.5 | 5.5 | 5.3 | 5.5 | 5.2 | 5.9 | 5.8 | 7.0 | 6.0 | 5.0 | 5.5 | 5.3 | 8.3 | 5.4 | 6.3 | 3.7 | 4.9 | 1.0 | 4.2 | 5.2 | | |
| 2011 | 4.6 | 4.8 | 5.0 | 5.3 | 5.4 | 5.2 | 5.4 | 5.0 | 5.7 | 5.6 | 6.8 | 5.7 | 4.8 | 5.2 | 5.0 | 7.9 | 5.1 | 5.8 | 3.2 | 4.2 | 0.4 | 2.8 | -0.3 | | |
| 2012 | 4.7 | 4.9 | 5.1 | 5.4 | 5.5 | 5.3 | 5.4 | 5.1 | 5.8 | 5.7 | 6.9 | 5.9 | 4.9 | 5.4 | 5.2 | 8.0 | 5.3 | 6.1 | 3.7 | 4.7 | 1.4 | 4.1 | 4.2 | | |
| 2013 | 4.8 | 5.0 | 5.2 | 5.6 | 5.6 | 5.4 | 5.6 | 5.3 | 6.0 | 5.9 | 7.1 | 6.1 | 5.2 | 5.7 | 5.5 | 8.3 | 5.7 | 6.5 | 4.3 | 5.4 | 2.6 | 5.7 | 7.8 | | |
| 2014 | 4.7 | 4.9 | 5.1 | 5.4 | 5.5 | 5.3 | 5.4 | 5.1 | 5.8 | 5.7 | 6.9 | 5.9 | 5.0 | 5.4 | 5.2 | 7.9 | 5.3 | 6.0 | 3.8 | 4.8 | 1.9 | 4.3 | 4.6 | | |
| 2015 | 4.5 | 4.8 | 4.9 | 5.3 | 5.3 | 5.1 | 5.3 | 5.0 | 5.6 | 5.5 | 6.6 | 5.6 | 4.7 | 5.1 | 4.9 | 7.5 | 4.9 | 5.6 | 3.3 | 4.1 | 1.2 | 3.1 | 2.3 | -9.3 | |
| 2016 | 4.5 | 4.7 | 4.9 | 5.2 | 5.2 | 5.1 | 5.2 | 4.9 | 5.5 | 5.4 | 6.5 | 5.5 | 4.6 | 5.0 | 4.8 | 7.2 | 4.8 | 5.3 | 3.1 | 3.8 | 1.0 | 2.7 | 1.7 | -5.5 | -1.6 |

Source of underlying data: 1.) Morningstar *Direct* database. Used with permission. All rights reserved. All calculations performed by Duff & Phelps LLC.

## United Kingdom Short-Horizon Equity Risk Premia

in Local Currency (Pound Sterling – GBP)
in Percent

| End Date | Start Date 1900 | 1905 | 1910 | 1915 | 1920 | 1925 | 1930 | 1935 | 1940 | 1945 | 1950 | 1955 | 1960 | 1965 | 1970 | 1975 | 1980 | 1985 | 1990 | 1995 | 2000 | 2005 | 2010 | 2015 | 2016 |
|---|---|---|---|---|---|---|---|---|---|---|---|---|---|---|---|---|---|---|---|---|---|---|---|---|---|
| 1900 | -2.8 | | | | | | | | | | | | | | | | | | | | | | | | |
| 1901 | -5.0 | | | | | | | | | | | | | | | | | | | | | | | | |
| 1902 | -3.2 | | | | | | | | | | | | | | | | | | | | | | | | |
| 1903 | -4.0 | | | | | | | | | | | | | | | | | | | | | | | | |
| 1904 | -1.3 | | | | | | | | | | | | | | | | | | | | | | | | |
| 1905 | -0.4 | 3.8 | | | | | | | | | | | | | | | | | | | | | | | |
| 1906 | -0.4 | 1.6 | | | | | | | | | | | | | | | | | | | | | | | |
| 1907 | -1.1 | -0.8 | | | | | | | | | | | | | | | | | | | | | | | |
| 1908 | -0.9 | -0.5 | | | | | | | | | | | | | | | | | | | | | | | |
| 1909 | -0.2 | 0.9 | | | | | | | | | | | | | | | | | | | | | | | |
| 1910 | 0.1 | 1.3 | 3.4 | | | | | | | | | | | | | | | | | | | | | | |
| 1911 | 0.1 | 1.0 | 1.3 | | | | | | | | | | | | | | | | | | | | | | |
| 1912 | 0.1 | 1.0 | 1.1 | | | | | | | | | | | | | | | | | | | | | | |
| 1913 | -0.1 | 0.5 | 0.0 | | | | | | | | | | | | | | | | | | | | | | |
| 1914 | -0.8 | -0.6 | -2.1 | | | | | | | | | | | | | | | | | | | | | | |
| 1915 | -1.2 | -1.2 | -2.9 | -7.1 | | | | | | | | | | | | | | | | | | | | | |
| 1916 | -0.8 | -0.6 | -1.6 | -0.4 | | | | | | | | | | | | | | | | | | | | | |
| 1917 | -0.3 | 0.0 | -0.5 | 2.2 | | | | | | | | | | | | | | | | | | | | | |
| 1918 | 0.8 | 1.6 | 2.0 | 7.0 | | | | | | | | | | | | | | | | | | | | | |
| 1919 | 2.0 | 3.0 | 4.1 | 10.3 | | | | | | | | | | | | | | | | | | | | | |
| 1920 | 0.7 | 1.3 | 1.5 | 4.4 | -24.9 | | | | | | | | | | | | | | | | | | | | |
| 1921 | 0.4 | 0.8 | 0.8 | 2.9 | -15.5 | | | | | | | | | | | | | | | | | | | | |
| 1922 | 1.6 | 2.5 | 3.1 | 6.3 | -0.5 | | | | | | | | | | | | | | | | | | | | |
| 1923 | 1.7 | 2.5 | 3.1 | 6.0 | 0.6 | | | | | | | | | | | | | | | | | | | | |
| 1924 | 2.2 | 3.1 | 3.8 | 6.7 | 3.2 | | | | | | | | | | | | | | | | | | | | |
| 1925 | 2.4 | 3.2 | 4.0 | 6.7 | 3.7 | 6.5 | | | | | | | | | | | | | | | | | | | |
| 1926 | 2.4 | 3.2 | 3.9 | 6.4 | 3.5 | 4.5 | | | | | | | | | | | | | | | | | | | |
| 1927 | 2.5 | 3.3 | 4.0 | 6.3 | 3.8 | 4.7 | | | | | | | | | | | | | | | | | | | |
| 1928 | 2.8 | 3.6 | 4.4 | 6.7 | 4.6 | 6.5 | | | | | | | | | | | | | | | | | | | |
| 1929 | 2.2 | 2.9 | 3.3 | 5.2 | 2.6 | 2.0 | | | | | | | | | | | | | | | | | | | |
| 1930 | 1.7 | 2.3 | 2.6 | 4.0 | 1.2 | -0.5 | -12.8 | | | | | | | | | | | | | | | | | | |
| 1931 | 0.8 | 1.2 | 1.2 | 2.2 | -1.2 | -4.3 | -20.0 | | | | | | | | | | | | | | | | | | |
| 1932 | 1.7 | 2.2 | 2.5 | 3.8 | 1.3 | 0.2 | -2.9 | | | | | | | | | | | | | | | | | | |
| 1933 | 2.3 | 2.9 | 3.3 | 4.7 | 2.7 | 2.4 | 3.0 | | | | | | | | | | | | | | | | | | |
| 1934 | 2.6 | 3.3 | 3.7 | 5.2 | 3.5 | 3.6 | 5.2 | | | | | | | | | | | | | | | | | | |
| 1935 | 2.9 | 3.6 | 4.1 | 5.5 | 4.1 | 4.5 | 6.5 | 12.8 | | | | | | | | | | | | | | | | | |
| 1936 | 3.3 | 4.0 | 4.5 | 6.0 | 4.8 | 5.4 | 7.9 | 14.5 | | | | | | | | | | | | | | | | | |
| 1937 | 2.9 | 3.5 | 4.0 | 5.3 | 3.9 | 4.1 | 5.5 | 5.8 | | | | | | | | | | | | | | | | | |
| 1938 | 2.6 | 3.2 | 3.6 | 4.8 | 3.3 | 3.4 | 4.2 | 2.8 | | | | | | | | | | | | | | | | | |
| 1939 | 2.4 | 2.9 | 3.3 | 4.3 | 2.8 | 2.7 | 3.1 | 0.9 | | | | | | | | | | | | | | | | | |
| 1940 | 2.1 | 2.6 | 2.8 | 3.8 | 2.2 | 1.9 | 1.9 | -0.9 | -9.6 | | | | | | | | | | | | | | | | |
| 1941 | 2.5 | 3.0 | 3.3 | 4.3 | 2.9 | 2.9 | 3.2 | 1.8 | 4.1 | | | | | | | | | | | | | | | | |
| 1942 | 2.8 | 3.3 | 3.7 | 4.7 | 3.5 | 3.6 | 4.2 | 3.6 | 8.1 | | | | | | | | | | | | | | | | |
| 1943 | 3.0 | 3.6 | 3.9 | 5.0 | 3.9 | 4.1 | 4.8 | 4.6 | 9.1 | | | | | | | | | | | | | | | | |
| 1944 | 3.2 | 3.7 | 4.1 | 5.1 | 4.1 | 4.3 | 5.1 | 5.1 | 9.3 | | | | | | | | | | | | | | | | |
| 1945 | 3.2 | 3.7 | 4.1 | 5.1 | 4.1 | 4.4 | 5.1 | 5.0 | 8.5 | 4.7 | | | | | | | | | | | | | | | |
| 1946 | 3.5 | 4.1 | 4.5 | 5.6 | 4.7 | 5.0 | 5.9 | 6.2 | 10.0 | 11.9 | | | | | | | | | | | | | | | |

## United Kingdom Short-Horizon Equity Risk Premia

in Local Currency (Pound Sterling – GBP)
in Percent

| End Date \ Start Date | 1900 | 1905 | 1910 | 1915 | 1920 | 1925 | 1930 | 1935 | 1940 | 1945 | 1950 | 1955 | 1960 | 1965 | 1970 | 1975 | 1980 | 1985 | 1990 |
|---|---|---|---|---|---|---|---|---|---|---|---|---|---|---|---|---|---|---|---|
| 1947 | 3.5 | 4.0 | 4.4 | 5.4 | 4.5 | 4.8 | 5.6 | 5.7 | 8.7 | 7.9 | | | | | | | | | |
| 1948 | 3.3 | 3.9 | 4.3 | 5.2 | 4.3 | 4.5 | 5.2 | 5.2 | 7.6 | 5.5 | | | | | | | | | |
| 1949 | 3.1 | 3.5 | 3.9 | 4.7 | 3.8 | 3.9 | 4.4 | 4.1 | 5.7 | 2.2 | | | | | | | | | |
| 1950 | 3.2 | 3.7 | 4.0 | 4.9 | 4.0 | 4.1 | 4.7 | 4.5 | 6.1 | 3.5 | 10.2 | | | | | | | | |
| 1951 | 3.3 | 3.8 | 4.1 | 5.0 | 4.1 | 4.3 | 4.8 | 4.7 | 6.3 | 4.2 | 9.4 | | | | | | | | |
| 1952 | 3.2 | 3.7 | 4.0 | 4.8 | 4.0 | 4.1 | 4.6 | 4.4 | 5.8 | 3.6 | 6.0 | | | | | | | | |
| 1953 | 3.6 | 4.1 | 4.4 | 5.3 | 4.5 | 4.7 | 5.3 | 5.3 | 6.9 | 5.6 | 9.9 | | | | | | | | |
| 1954 | 4.4 | 5.0 | 5.4 | 6.4 | 5.8 | 6.3 | 7.1 | 7.6 | 9.8 | 10.1 | 18.0 | | | | | | | | |
| 1955 | 4.5 | 5.0 | 5.5 | 6.4 | 5.9 | 6.3 | 7.1 | 7.6 | 9.7 | 9.9 | 16.3 | 7.8 | | | | | | | |
| 1956 | 4.4 | 5.0 | 5.4 | 6.3 | 5.7 | 6.2 | 6.9 | 7.3 | 9.2 | 9.2 | 14.2 | 4.5 | | | | | | | |
| 1957 | 4.2 | 4.7 | 5.1 | 5.9 | 5.3 | 5.6 | 6.3 | 6.5 | 8.1 | 7.6 | 11.0 | -0.6 | | | | | | | |
| 1958 | 4.7 | 5.2 | 5.7 | 6.6 | 6.1 | 6.5 | 7.3 | 7.7 | 9.6 | 9.6 | 13.7 | 8.4 | | | | | | | |
| 1959 | 5.4 | 6.0 | 6.5 | 7.5 | 7.1 | 7.7 | 8.6 | 9.3 | 11.4 | 12.1 | 17.1 | 16.1 | | | | | | | |
| 1960 | 5.2 | 5.7 | 6.2 | 7.1 | 6.7 | 7.2 | 8.1 | 8.6 | 10.5 | 10.4 | 14.8 | 12.1 | -7.9 | | | | | | |
| 1961 | 5.1 | 5.7 | 6.2 | 7.1 | 6.7 | 7.1 | 7.9 | 8.4 | 10.2 | 10.4 | 13.9 | 10.9 | -2.1 | | | | | | |
| 1962 | 5.1 | 5.7 | 6.1 | 7.0 | 6.6 | 7.1 | 7.8 | 8.3 | 9.9 | 10.1 | 13.1 | 10.0 | 0.0 | | | | | | |
| 1963 | 5.3 | 5.9 | 6.3 | 7.2 | 6.8 | 7.3 | 8.1 | 8.6 | 10.2 | 10.4 | 13.4 | 10.8 | 4.2 | | | | | | |
| 1964 | 5.1 | 5.6 | 6.1 | 6.9 | 6.5 | 6.9 | 7.6 | 8.0 | 9.5 | 9.5 | 12.0 | 8.9 | 1.8 | | | | | | |
| 1965 | 5.1 | 5.6 | 6.1 | 6.9 | 6.5 | 6.9 | 7.6 | 8.0 | 9.3 | 9.3 | 11.6 | 8.6 | 2.4 | 5.7 | | | | | |
| 1966 | 4.9 | 5.4 | 5.8 | 6.6 | 6.2 | 6.5 | 7.2 | 7.4 | 8.7 | 8.5 | 10.4 | 7.2 | 0.9 | -1.2 | | | | | |
| 1967 | 5.3 | 5.8 | 6.3 | 7.1 | 6.7 | 7.1 | 7.8 | 8.2 | 9.5 | 9.5 | 11.6 | 9.1 | 4.8 | 9.8 | | | | | |
| 1968 | 6.0 | 6.5 | 7.0 | 7.8 | 7.6 | 8.1 | 8.9 | 9.4 | 10.9 | 11.2 | 13.6 | 12.0 | 9.8 | 19.9 | | | | | |
| 1969 | 5.5 | 6.1 | 6.5 | 7.3 | 7.0 | 7.4 | 8.1 | 8.5 | 9.7 | 9.8 | 11.8 | 9.7 | 6.5 | 11.2 | | | | | |
| 1970 | 5.3 | 5.8 | 6.2 | 6.9 | 6.6 | 7.0 | 7.6 | 7.9 | 9.0 | 9.0 | 10.6 | 8.2 | 4.7 | 7.1 | -13.2 | | | | |
| 1971 | 5.7 | 6.2 | 6.6 | 7.4 | 7.1 | 7.5 | 8.2 | 8.6 | 9.8 | 9.9 | 11.6 | 9.7 | 7.1 | 10.8 | 10.0 | | | | |
| 1972 | 5.7 | 6.2 | 6.6 | 7.4 | 7.1 | 7.5 | 8.2 | 8.5 | 9.7 | 9.8 | 11.4 | 9.6 | 7.1 | 10.4 | 9.2 | | | | |
| 1973 | 5.2 | 5.6 | 6.0 | 6.7 | 6.3 | 6.7 | 7.2 | 7.4 | 8.4 | 8.3 | 9.5 | 7.3 | 4.1 | 5.5 | -1.7 | | | | |
| 1974 | 4.2 | 4.6 | 4.9 | 5.5 | 5.1 | 5.3 | 5.6 | 5.7 | 6.3 | 5.9 | 6.6 | 3.7 | -0.4 | -1.4 | -14.1 | | | | |
| 1975 | 6.0 | 6.5 | 7.0 | 7.7 | 7.5 | 7.9 | 8.5 | 8.9 | 10.1 | 10.2 | 11.7 | 10.2 | 8.4 | 11.4 | 11.6 | 140.0 | | | |
| 1976 | 5.8 | 6.3 | 6.7 | 7.5 | 7.2 | 7.6 | 8.2 | 8.5 | 9.6 | 9.6 | 11.0 | 9.4 | 7.5 | 9.8 | 8.9 | 66.3 | | | |
| 1977 | 6.2 | 6.7 | 7.1 | 7.9 | 7.6 | 8.1 | 8.7 | 9.1 | 10.2 | 10.3 | 11.8 | 10.4 | 8.8 | 11.6 | 11.8 | 54.9 | | | |
| 1978 | 6.1 | 6.6 | 7.0 | 7.7 | 7.5 | 7.9 | 8.5 | 8.9 | 9.9 | 10.0 | 11.3 | 9.9 | 8.3 | 10.7 | 10.4 | 41.0 | | | |
| 1979 | 6.0 | 6.5 | 6.9 | 7.6 | 7.3 | 7.7 | 8.3 | 8.6 | 9.6 | 9.6 | 10.9 | 9.5 | 7.8 | 9.8 | 9.2 | 32.4 | | | |
| 1980 | 6.1 | 6.6 | 7.0 | 7.7 | 7.5 | 7.8 | 8.4 | 8.8 | 9.7 | 9.8 | 11.0 | 9.7 | 8.1 | 10.1 | 9.7 | 29.5 | 14.7 | | |
| 1981 | 6.0 | 6.5 | 6.9 | 7.5 | 7.3 | 7.7 | 8.2 | 8.5 | 9.5 | 9.5 | 10.6 | 9.3 | 7.7 | 9.5 | 8.7 | 25.0 | 6.6 | | |
| 1982 | 6.1 | 6.6 | 7.0 | 7.7 | 7.4 | 7.8 | 8.4 | 8.7 | 9.6 | 9.6 | 10.8 | 9.5 | 8.0 | 9.8 | 9.2 | 23.8 | 9.5 | | |
| 1983 | 6.3 | 6.8 | 7.2 | 7.8 | 7.6 | 8.0 | 8.6 | 8.9 | 9.8 | 9.9 | 11.1 | 9.9 | 8.6 | 10.4 | 10.1 | 23.5 | 12.3 | | |
| 1984 | 6.5 | 7.0 | 7.4 | 8.0 | 7.9 | 8.3 | 8.8 | 9.2 | 10.1 | 10.2 | 11.4 | 10.3 | 9.1 | 10.9 | 10.9 | 23.3 | 14.3 | | |
| 1985 | 6.5 | 7.0 | 7.4 | 8.1 | 7.9 | 8.3 | 8.9 | 9.2 | 10.1 | 10.2 | 11.4 | 10.3 | 9.2 | 11.0 | 10.9 | 22.2 | 13.7 | 11.1 | |
| 1986 | 6.6 | 7.1 | 7.5 | 8.2 | 8.0 | 8.4 | 9.0 | 9.3 | 10.2 | 10.3 | 11.4 | 10.4 | 9.3 | 11.1 | 11.0 | 21.5 | 13.7 | 12.2 | |
| 1987 | 6.5 | 7.0 | 7.4 | 8.0 | 7.8 | 8.2 | 8.7 | 9.1 | 9.9 | 10.0 | 11.0 | 10.0 | 8.9 | 10.4 | 10.2 | 19.6 | 11.5 | 6.9 | |
| 1988 | 6.4 | 6.9 | 7.3 | 7.9 | 7.7 | 8.1 | 8.6 | 8.9 | 9.7 | 9.8 | 10.7 | 9.7 | 8.6 | 10.0 | 9.7 | 18.1 | 10.2 | 5.1 | |
| 1989 | 6.6 | 7.1 | 7.5 | 8.1 | 7.9 | 8.3 | 8.8 | 9.1 | 10.0 | 10.0 | 11.0 | 10.0 | 9.0 | 10.5 | 10.3 | 18.4 | 11.4 | 8.6 | |
| 1990 | 6.3 | 6.7 | 7.1 | 7.7 | 7.5 | 7.8 | 8.3 | 8.6 | 9.3 | 9.3 | 10.2 | 9.1 | 8.0 | 9.2 | 8.7 | 15.8 | 8.3 | 3.3 | -23.6 |
| 1991 | 6.3 | 6.7 | 7.1 | 7.7 | 7.5 | 7.8 | 8.3 | 8.5 | 9.3 | 9.3 | 10.1 | 9.1 | 8.0 | 9.1 | 8.7 | 15.3 | 8.2 | 3.9 | -7.9 |
| 1992 | 6.3 | 6.7 | 7.1 | 7.7 | 7.5 | 7.8 | 8.3 | 8.5 | 9.3 | 9.3 | 10.1 | 9.1 | 8.0 | 9.1 | 8.6 | 15.0 | 8.3 | 4.5 | -2.4 |
| 1993 | 6.5 | 6.9 | 7.3 | 7.9 | 7.7 | 8.0 | 8.5 | 8.8 | 9.5 | 9.5 | 10.4 | 9.4 | 8.4 | 9.5 | 9.2 | 15.3 | 9.2 | 6.4 | 3.6 |

Additional column headers (no data): 1995, 2000, 2005, 2010, 2015, 2016

**United Kingdom Short-Horizon Equity Risk Premia**

in Local Currency (Pound Sterling – GBP)
in Percent

| End Date | 1900 | 1905 | 1910 | 1915 | 1920 | 1925 | 1930 | 1935 | 1940 | 1945 | 1950 | 1955 | 1960 | 1965 | 1970 | 1975 | 1980 | 1985 | 1990 | 1995 | 2000 | 2005 | 2010 | 2015 | 2016 |
|---|---|---|---|---|---|---|---|---|---|---|---|---|---|---|---|---|---|---|---|---|---|---|---|---|---|
| 1994 | 6.3 | 6.7 | 7.0 | 7.6 | 7.4 | 7.7 | 8.2 | 8.4 | 9.1 | 9.1 | 9.9 | 8.8 | 7.8 | 8.8 | 8.3 | 13.9 | 7.8 | 4.5 | 0.5 | | | | | | |
| 1995 | 6.4 | 6.8 | 7.1 | 7.7 | 7.5 | 7.8 | 8.3 | 8.5 | 9.2 | 9.2 | 10.0 | 9.0 | 8.0 | 9.0 | 8.6 | 14.0 | 8.3 | 5.5 | 3.0 | 15.6 | | | | | |
| 1996 | 6.4 | 6.8 | 7.2 | 7.7 | 7.6 | 7.9 | 8.3 | 8.6 | 9.2 | 9.2 | 10.0 | 9.0 | 8.1 | 9.1 | 8.7 | 13.8 | 8.4 | 5.9 | 3.9 | 12.6 | | | | | |
| 1997 | 6.6 | 7.0 | 7.3 | 7.9 | 7.7 | 8.0 | 8.5 | 8.8 | 9.4 | 9.4 | 10.2 | 9.3 | 8.4 | 9.4 | 9.1 | 14.1 | 9.1 | 7.0 | 6.1 | 15.4 | | | | | |
| 1998 | 6.6 | 7.0 | 7.3 | 7.9 | 7.8 | 8.1 | 8.5 | 8.8 | 9.4 | 9.4 | 10.2 | 9.3 | 8.4 | 9.4 | 9.1 | 13.9 | 9.1 | 7.2 | 6.4 | 13.8 | | | | | |
| 1999 | 6.6 | 7.0 | 7.4 | 7.9 | 7.8 | 8.1 | 8.5 | 8.8 | 9.4 | 9.5 | 10.2 | 9.3 | 8.5 | 9.4 | 9.2 | 13.8 | 9.1 | 7.4 | 6.8 | 13.2 | | | | | |
| 2000 | 6.5 | 6.9 | 7.2 | 7.7 | 7.6 | 7.9 | 8.3 | 8.5 | 9.1 | 9.1 | 9.8 | 8.9 | 8.0 | 8.9 | 8.5 | 12.9 | 8.2 | 6.3 | 5.3 | 9.3 | -10.5 | | | | |
| 2001 | 6.2 | 6.6 | 6.9 | 7.4 | 7.3 | 7.5 | 7.9 | 8.1 | 8.7 | 8.7 | 9.3 | 8.3 | 7.4 | 8.2 | 7.7 | 11.8 | 7.1 | 4.9 | 3.4 | 5.5 | -13.7 | | | | |
| 2002 | 5.9 | 6.3 | 6.6 | 7.0 | 6.9 | 7.1 | 7.4 | 7.6 | 8.1 | 8.0 | 8.6 | 7.6 | 6.6 | 7.3 | 6.7 | 10.4 | 5.6 | 3.1 | 1.0 | 1.4 | -18.3 | | | | |
| 2003 | 6.0 | 6.4 | 6.6 | 7.1 | 6.9 | 7.2 | 7.5 | 7.7 | 8.2 | 8.0 | 8.7 | 7.8 | 6.8 | 7.5 | 6.9 | 10.5 | 6.0 | 3.8 | 2.1 | 2.9 | -9.9 | | | | |
| 2004 | 6.0 | 6.4 | 6.7 | 7.1 | 6.9 | 7.2 | 7.5 | 7.7 | 8.2 | 8.1 | 8.7 | 7.7 | 6.8 | 7.4 | 6.9 | 10.4 | 6.0 | 3.9 | 2.4 | 3.3 | -6.5 | | | | |
| 2005 | 6.1 | 6.5 | 6.7 | 7.2 | 7.0 | 7.3 | 7.6 | 7.8 | 8.3 | 8.2 | 8.8 | 7.9 | 7.0 | 7.6 | 7.1 | 10.6 | 6.4 | 4.5 | 3.2 | 4.4 | -2.9 | 15.3 | | | |
| 2006 | 6.1 | 6.5 | 6.8 | 7.3 | 7.1 | 7.3 | 7.7 | 7.8 | 8.3 | 8.3 | 8.8 | 7.9 | 7.1 | 7.7 | 7.2 | 10.5 | 6.5 | 4.7 | 3.6 | 4.9 | -1.1 | 12.6 | | | |
| 2007 | 6.1 | 6.4 | 6.7 | 7.2 | 7.0 | 7.2 | 7.6 | 7.7 | 8.2 | 8.2 | 8.7 | 7.8 | 6.9 | 7.5 | 7.1 | 10.3 | 6.3 | 4.6 | 3.4 | 4.6 | -0.8 | 8.7 | | | |
| 2008 | 5.7 | 6.0 | 6.3 | 6.8 | 6.6 | 6.8 | 7.1 | 7.2 | 7.6 | 7.5 | 8.0 | 7.0 | 6.1 | 6.6 | 6.0 | 9.0 | 4.9 | 3.0 | 1.5 | 1.9 | -4.5 | -1.8 | | | |
| 2009 | 5.9 | 6.2 | 6.5 | 6.8 | 6.8 | 7.0 | 7.3 | 7.4 | 7.9 | 7.8 | 8.3 | 7.4 | 6.5 | 7.1 | 6.5 | 9.5 | 5.7 | 3.9 | 2.8 | 3.5 | -1.3 | 3.9 | | | |
| 2010 | 6.0 | 6.3 | 6.6 | 7.0 | 6.8 | 7.0 | 7.4 | 7.5 | 8.0 | 7.9 | 8.3 | 7.5 | 6.6 | 7.2 | 6.7 | 9.5 | 5.9 | 4.2 | 3.2 | 4.0 | -0.1 | 5.2 | 11.7 | | |
| 2011 | 5.9 | 6.2 | 6.5 | 6.9 | 6.7 | 6.9 | 7.2 | 7.4 | 7.8 | 7.7 | 8.2 | 7.3 | 6.5 | 7.0 | 6.5 | 9.2 | 5.6 | 4.0 | 2.9 | 3.7 | -0.3 | 4.1 | 4.7 | | |
| 2012 | 5.9 | 6.3 | 6.5 | 7.0 | 6.8 | 7.0 | 7.3 | 7.4 | 7.9 | 7.7 | 8.2 | 7.3 | 6.5 | 7.0 | 6.5 | 9.2 | 5.7 | 4.2 | 3.2 | 4.0 | 0.5 | 4.9 | 6.4 | | |
| 2013 | 6.0 | 6.4 | 6.6 | 7.1 | 6.9 | 7.1 | 7.4 | 7.5 | 8.0 | 7.9 | 8.3 | 7.5 | 6.7 | 7.2 | 6.8 | 9.5 | 6.1 | 4.7 | 3.9 | 4.8 | 1.7 | 6.3 | 9.4 | | |
| 2014 | 6.0 | 6.3 | 6.6 | 7.0 | 6.8 | 7.0 | 7.3 | 7.4 | 7.9 | 7.8 | 8.2 | 7.4 | 6.6 | 7.1 | 6.6 | 9.2 | 5.9 | 4.5 | 3.7 | 4.5 | 1.6 | 5.7 | 7.5 | | |
| 2015 | 5.9 | 6.2 | 6.5 | 6.9 | 6.7 | 6.9 | 7.2 | 7.3 | 7.7 | 7.6 | 8.1 | 7.2 | 6.5 | 6.9 | 6.4 | 8.9 | 5.7 | 4.3 | 3.5 | 4.2 | 1.4 | 5.0 | 5.8 | -2.6 | |
| 2016 | 6.0 | 6.3 | 6.6 | 7.0 | 6.8 | 7.0 | 7.3 | 7.5 | 7.9 | 7.8 | 8.2 | 7.4 | 6.7 | 7.1 | 6.7 | 9.2 | 6.0 | 4.8 | 4.0 | 4.9 | 2.4 | 6.1 | 7.7 | 8.1 | 18.9 |

Source of underlying data: 1 ) Morningstar *Direct* database. Used with permission. All rights reserved. All calculations performed by Duff & Phelps LLC.

## United Kingdom Short-Horizon Equity Risk Premia

in U.S. Dollars (USD)
in Percent

| End Date | Start Date 1900 | 1905 | 1910 | 1915 | 1920 | 1925 | 1930 | 1935 | 1940 | 1945 |
|---|---|---|---|---|---|---|---|---|---|---|
| 1900 | -2.8 | | | | | | | | | |
| 1901 | -5.0 | | | | | | | | | |
| 1902 | -3.3 | | | | | | | | | |
| 1903 | -4.0 | | | | | | | | | |
| 1904 | -1.2 | | | | | | | | | |
| 1905 | -0.4 | 3.7 | | | | | | | | |
| 1906 | -0.4 | 1.6 | | | | | | | | |
| 1907 | -1.1 | -0.8 | | | | | | | | |
| 1908 | -0.9 | -0.5 | | | | | | | | |
| 1909 | -0.2 | 0.9 | | | | | | | | |
| 1910 | 0.1 | | 3.4 | | | | | | | |
| 1911 | 0.1 | 1.0 | 1.3 | | | | | | | |
| 1912 | 0.1 | 0.9 | 1.1 | | | | | | | |
| 1913 | -0.1 | 0.5 | 0.0 | | | | | | | |
| 1914 | -0.8 | -0.6 | -2.1 | | | | | | | |
| 1915 | -1.2 | -1.2 | -2.9 | -6.9 | | | | | | |
| 1916 | -0.8 | -0.6 | -1.6 | -0.4 | | | | | | |
| 1917 | -0.3 | 0.0 | -0.5 | 2.2 | | | | | | |
| 1918 | 0.8 | 1.6 | 2.0 | 7.1 | | | | | | |
| 1919 | 1.7 | 2.7 | 3.6 | 9.3 | | | | | | |
| 1920 | 0.5 | 1.1 | 1.2 | 3.9 | -23.5 | | | | | |
| 1921 | 0.2 | 0.6 | 0.5 | 2.3 | -15.4 | | | | | |
| 1922 | 1.6 | 2.4 | 2.9 | 6.1 | 0.6 | | | | | |
| 1923 | 1.7 | 2.4 | 3.0 | 5.8 | 1.3 | | | | | |
| 1924 | 2.2 | 3.0 | 3.8 | 6.7 | 4.0 | | | | | |
| 1925 | 2.4 | 3.2 | 3.9 | 6.7 | 4.5 | 6.7 | | | | |
| 1926 | 2.4 | 3.2 | 3.9 | 6.3 | 4.2 | 4.6 | | | | |
| 1927 | 2.5 | 3.3 | 3.9 | 6.3 | 4.3 | 4.8 | | | | |
| 1928 | 2.8 | 3.6 | 4.3 | 6.6 | 5.1 | 6.5 | | | | |
| 1929 | 2.2 | 2.8 | 3.3 | 5.1 | 3.0 | 2.0 | | | | |
| 1930 | 1.7 | 2.2 | 2.6 | 4.0 | 1.6 | -0.5 | -12.7 | | | |
| 1931 | 1.0 | 1.4 | 1.6 | 2.7 | -0.1 | -3.1 | -15.9 | | | |
| 1932 | 1.9 | 2.5 | 2.8 | 4.2 | 2.2 | 1.1 | -0.4 | | | |
| 1933 | 2.8 | 3.5 | 4.0 | 5.6 | 4.3 | 4.5 | 7.6 | | | |
| 1934 | 3.1 | 3.8 | 4.4 | 6.1 | 5.0 | 5.4 | 8.9 | | | |
| 1935 | 3.4 | 4.1 | 4.8 | 6.4 | 5.5 | 6.1 | 9.5 | 12.8 | | |
| 1936 | 3.7 | 4.5 | 5.2 | 6.8 | 6.1 | 6.9 | 10.5 | 14.5 | | |
| 1937 | 3.3 | 4.0 | 4.6 | 6.0 | 5.1 | 5.5 | 7.7 | 5.7 | | |
| 1938 | 3.1 | 3.7 | 4.2 | 5.5 | 4.5 | 4.7 | 6.2 | 2.8 | | |
| 1939 | 2.9 | 3.4 | 3.9 | 5.1 | 4.0 | 4.0 | 5.0 | 1.1 | | |
| 1940 | 2.6 | 3.1 | 3.4 | 4.5 | 3.3 | 3.1 | 3.7 | -0.7 | -9.6 | |
| 1941 | 2.9 | 3.5 | 3.9 | 5.0 | 4.0 | 4.0 | 4.8 | 2.0 | 4.1 | |
| 1942 | 3.2 | 3.8 | 4.3 | 5.4 | 4.5 | 4.7 | 5.7 | 3.7 | 8.1 | |
| 1943 | 3.4 | 4.0 | 4.5 | 5.6 | 4.9 | 5.1 | 6.2 | 4.7 | 9.1 | |
| 1944 | 3.6 | 4.2 | 4.6 | 5.8 | 5.0 | 5.3 | 6.4 | 5.2 | 9.3 | |
| 1945 | 3.6 | 4.2 | 4.6 | 5.7 | 5.0 | 5.3 | 6.3 | 5.1 | 8.5 | 4.7 |
| 1946 | 3.8 | 4.4 | 4.9 | 6.0 | 5.4 | 5.7 | 6.8 | 5.9 | 9.3 | 9.4 |

Additional Start Date column headers shown (no data): 1950, 1955, 1960, 1965, 1970, 1975, 1980, 1985, 1990, 1995, 2000, 2005, 2010, 2015, 2016.

Source of underlying data: 1.) Morningstar *Direct* database. Used with permission. All rights reserved. All calculations performed by Duff & Phelps LLC.

## United Kingdom Short-Horizon Equity Risk Premia

in U.S. Dollars (USD)
in Percent

| End Date | Start Date 1900 | 1905 | 1910 | 1915 | 1920 | 1925 | 1930 | 1935 | 1940 | 1945 | 1950 | 1955 | 1960 | 1965 | 1970 | 1975 | 1980 | 1985 | 1990 |
|---|---|---|---|---|---|---|---|---|---|---|---|---|---|---|---|---|---|---|---|
| 1947 | 3.7 | 4.3 | 4.8 | 5.8 | 5.2 | 5.4 | 6.4 | 5.4 | 8.1 | 6.3 | | | | | | | | | |
| 1948 | 3.6 | 4.2 | 4.6 | 5.6 | 4.9 | 5.1 | 5.9 | 4.9 | 7.0 | 4.2 | | | | | | | | | |
| 1949 | 3.4 | 3.9 | 4.3 | 5.2 | 4.5 | 4.6 | 5.2 | 4.0 | 5.4 | 1.6 | | | | | | | | | |
| 1950 | 3.5 | 4.0 | 4.4 | 5.3 | 4.7 | 4.8 | 5.5 | 4.4 | 5.9 | 3.1 | 10.8 | | | | | | | | |
| 1951 | 3.6 | 4.2 | 4.5 | 5.4 | 4.8 | 5.0 | 5.4 | 4.7 | 6.2 | 4.0 | 10.2 | | | | | | | | |
| 1952 | 3.5 | 4.0 | 4.4 | 5.3 | 4.7 | 4.8 | 5.4 | 4.4 | 5.7 | 3.4 | 6.5 | | | | | | | | |
| 1953 | 3.9 | 4.4 | 4.8 | 5.7 | 5.2 | 5.4 | 6.1 | 5.3 | 6.8 | 5.5 | 10.3 | | | | | | | | |
| 1954 | 4.7 | 5.3 | 5.8 | 6.8 | 6.4 | 6.8 | 7.8 | 7.5 | 9.7 | 9.9 | 18.2 | | | | | | | | |
| 1955 | 4.8 | 5.4 | 5.9 | 6.8 | 6.5 | 6.9 | 7.8 | 7.6 | 9.6 | 9.7 | 16.5 | 7.9 | | | | | | | |
| 1956 | 4.7 | 5.3 | 5.8 | 6.7 | 6.3 | 6.7 | 7.6 | 7.3 | 9.1 | 9.0 | 14.3 | 4.5 | | | | | | | |
| 1957 | 4.4 | 5.0 | 5.4 | 6.3 | 5.9 | 6.2 | 6.9 | 6.5 | 8.0 | 7.5 | 11.2 | -0.6 | | | | | | | |
| 1958 | 5.0 | 5.5 | 6.0 | 6.9 | 6.6 | 7.0 | 7.9 | 7.7 | 9.4 | 9.5 | 13.8 | 8.3 | | | | | | | |
| 1959 | 5.7 | 6.3 | 6.8 | 7.8 | 7.6 | 8.2 | 9.2 | 9.2 | 11.3 | 12.0 | 17.1 | 16.0 | | | | | | | |
| 1960 | 5.4 | 6.0 | 6.5 | 7.5 | 7.3 | 7.7 | 8.6 | 8.6 | 10.4 | 10.7 | 14.9 | 12.0 | -7.9 | | | | | | |
| 1961 | 5.4 | 6.0 | 6.5 | 7.4 | 7.2 | 7.6 | 8.5 | 8.4 | 10.1 | 10.3 | 13.9 | 10.8 | -2.1 | | | | | | |
| 1962 | 5.4 | 6.0 | 6.5 | 7.3 | 7.1 | 7.5 | 8.3 | 8.3 | 9.8 | 10.0 | 13.2 | 10.0 | 0.0 | | | | | | |
| 1963 | 5.6 | 6.2 | 6.6 | 7.5 | 7.3 | 7.8 | 8.6 | 8.6 | 10.1 | 10.3 | 13.5 | 10.8 | 4.2 | | | | | | |
| 1964 | 5.4 | 5.9 | 6.4 | 7.2 | 7.0 | 7.4 | 8.1 | 8.0 | 9.4 | 9.4 | 12.0 | 8.9 | 1.8 | | | | | | |
| 1965 | 5.4 | 5.9 | 6.4 | 7.2 | 7.0 | 7.3 | 7.9 | 7.9 | 9.2 | 9.2 | 11.6 | 8.6 | 2.4 | 5.7 | | | | | |
| 1966 | 5.2 | 5.7 | 6.1 | 6.9 | 6.6 | 6.9 | 7.6 | 7.4 | 8.6 | 8.4 | 10.5 | 7.2 | 0.9 | -1.2 | | | | | |
| 1967 | 5.5 | 6.0 | 6.5 | 7.3 | 7.1 | 7.4 | 8.1 | 8.0 | 9.3 | 9.3 | 11.4 | 8.8 | 4.2 | 8.4 | | | | | |
| 1968 | 6.1 | 6.7 | 7.2 | 8.1 | 7.9 | 8.4 | 9.2 | 9.3 | 10.7 | 11.0 | 13.4 | 11.7 | 9.3 | 18.7 | | | | | |
| 1969 | 5.7 | 6.2 | 6.7 | 7.5 | 7.3 | 7.7 | 8.4 | 8.3 | 9.5 | 9.6 | 11.6 | 9.3 | 6.0 | 10.2 | | | | | |
| 1970 | 5.4 | 6.0 | 6.4 | 7.1 | 6.9 | 7.2 | 7.9 | 7.7 | 8.8 | 8.7 | 10.4 | 7.9 | 4.3 | 6.4 | -12.9 | | | | |
| 1971 | 5.9 | 6.4 | 6.8 | 7.6 | 7.4 | 7.8 | 8.5 | 8.5 | 9.6 | 9.7 | 11.5 | 9.5 | 6.8 | 10.4 | 11.0 | | | | |
| 1972 | 5.9 | 6.4 | 6.8 | 7.6 | 7.4 | 7.8 | 8.5 | 8.4 | 9.5 | 9.6 | 11.3 | 9.4 | 6.8 | 10.0 | 9.7 | | | | |
| 1973 | 5.3 | 5.8 | 6.2 | 6.9 | 6.7 | 6.9 | 7.5 | 7.3 | 8.2 | 8.1 | 9.4 | 7.1 | 3.9 | 5.1 | -1.2 | | | | |
| 1974 | 4.4 | 4.8 | 5.1 | 5.7 | 5.4 | 5.5 | 5.9 | 5.5 | 6.2 | 5.7 | 6.5 | 3.5 | -0.6 | -1.8 | -13.9 | | | | |
| 1975 | 5.9 | 6.4 | 6.9 | 7.6 | 7.4 | 7.8 | 8.4 | 8.3 | 9.4 | 9.4 | 10.9 | 9.1 | 6.9 | 9.3 | 8.5 | 120.5 | | | |
| 1976 | 5.8 | 6.3 | 6.7 | 7.4 | 7.2 | 7.5 | 8.1 | 8.0 | 8.9 | 8.9 | 10.2 | 8.4 | 6.2 | 8.0 | 6.4 | 57.2 | | | |
| 1977 | 6.2 | 6.7 | 7.1 | 7.8 | 7.7 | 8.0 | 8.7 | 8.6 | 9.6 | 9.7 | 11.1 | 9.6 | 7.8 | 10.1 | 10.0 | 49.8 | | | |
| 1978 | 6.1 | 6.6 | 7.0 | 7.7 | 7.5 | 7.9 | 8.5 | 8.4 | 9.4 | 9.4 | 10.7 | 9.2 | 7.3 | 9.3 | 8.9 | 37.3 | | | |
| 1979 | 6.0 | 6.5 | 6.9 | 7.6 | 7.4 | 7.7 | 8.3 | 8.2 | 9.1 | 9.1 | 10.3 | 8.7 | 6.9 | 8.6 | 7.9 | 29.6 | | | |
| 1980 | 6.1 | 6.6 | 7.0 | 7.7 | 7.5 | 7.8 | 8.4 | 8.4 | 9.3 | 9.3 | 10.5 | 9.0 | 7.3 | 9.1 | 8.5 | 27.2 | 15.3 | | |
| 1981 | 6.0 | 6.5 | 6.9 | 7.5 | 7.4 | 7.6 | 8.2 | 8.2 | 9.0 | 9.0 | 10.1 | 8.6 | 6.9 | 8.4 | 7.7 | 23.1 | 6.9 | | |
| 1982 | 6.1 | 6.6 | 7.0 | 7.6 | 7.5 | 7.8 | 8.3 | 8.3 | 9.1 | 9.1 | 10.2 | 8.8 | 7.2 | 8.7 | 8.1 | 21.9 | 9.0 | | |
| 1983 | 6.2 | 6.7 | 7.1 | 7.8 | 7.7 | 8.0 | 8.5 | 8.5 | 9.3 | 9.3 | 10.5 | 9.1 | 7.7 | 9.2 | 8.9 | 21.5 | 11.4 | | |
| 1984 | 6.4 | 6.9 | 7.3 | 7.9 | 7.8 | 8.1 | 8.7 | 8.7 | 9.5 | 9.5 | 10.7 | 9.4 | 8.1 | 9.7 | 9.5 | 21.2 | 12.8 | | |
| 1985 | 6.5 | 6.9 | 7.3 | 8.0 | 7.9 | 8.2 | 8.8 | 8.8 | 9.6 | 9.6 | 10.8 | 9.5 | 8.3 | 9.9 | 9.7 | 20.5 | 12.9 | 13.4 | |
| 1986 | 6.5 | 7.0 | 7.4 | 8.1 | 8.0 | 8.3 | 8.8 | 8.8 | 9.7 | 9.7 | 10.8 | 9.7 | 8.5 | 10.0 | 9.9 | 19.9 | 12.9 | 13.3 | |
| 1987 | 6.4 | 6.9 | 7.3 | 7.9 | 7.8 | 8.1 | 8.6 | 8.6 | 9.4 | 9.4 | 10.4 | 9.2 | 8.0 | 9.4 | 9.1 | 18.0 | 10.7 | 7.3 | |
| 1988 | 6.3 | 6.8 | 7.2 | 7.8 | 7.7 | 8.0 | 8.5 | 8.4 | 9.2 | 9.2 | 10.2 | 9.0 | 7.7 | 9.0 | 8.7 | 16.7 | 9.6 | 5.6 | |
| 1989 | 6.5 | 7.0 | 7.3 | 8.0 | 7.9 | 8.2 | 8.7 | 8.7 | 9.4 | 9.3 | 10.4 | 9.3 | 8.2 | 9.4 | 9.2 | 16.9 | 10.6 | 8.5 | |
| 1990 | 6.1 | 6.5 | 6.9 | 7.5 | 7.4 | 7.6 | 8.1 | 8.0 | 8.7 | 8.6 | 9.5 | 8.2 | 7.0 | 8.0 | 7.5 | 14.1 | 7.1 | 2.4 | -28.3 |
| 1991 | 6.1 | 6.6 | 6.9 | 7.5 | 7.4 | 7.6 | 8.1 | 8.0 | 8.6 | 8.6 | 9.4 | 8.2 | 7.0 | 8.0 | 7.5 | 13.7 | 7.1 | 3.1 | -10.5 |
| 1992 | 6.1 | 6.6 | 6.9 | 7.5 | 7.4 | 7.6 | 8.0 | 8.2 | 8.6 | 8.5 | 9.4 | 8.2 | 7.9 | 7.9 | 7.4 | 13.4 | 7.1 | 3.6 | -4.6 |
| 1993 | 6.3 | 6.7 | 7.1 | 7.7 | 7.5 | 7.8 | 8.2 | 8.2 | 8.8 | 8.8 | 9.6 | 8.5 | 7.4 | 8.4 | 8.0 | 13.8 | 8.1 | 5.5 | 1.9 |

Source of underlying data: 1.) Morningstar *Direct* database. Used with permission. All rights reserved. All calculations performed by Duff & Phelps LLC.

**United Kingdom Short-Horizon Equity Risk Premia**

in U.S. Dollars (USD)
in Percent

| End Date | Start Date | | | | | | | | | | | | | | | | | | | | | | | | |
|---|---|---|---|---|---|---|---|---|---|---|---|---|---|---|---|---|---|---|---|---|---|---|---|---|---|
| | 1900 | 1905 | 1910 | 1915 | 1920 | 1925 | 1930 | 1935 | 1940 | 1945 | 1950 | 1955 | 1960 | 1965 | 1970 | 1975 | 1980 | 1985 | 1990 | 1995 | 2000 | 2005 | 2010 | 2015 | 2016 |
| 1994 | 6.1 | 6.5 | 6.8 | 7.4 | 7.3 | 7.5 | 7.9 | 7.8 | 8.5 | 8.4 | 9.1 | 8.0 | 6.8 | 7.7 | 7.2 | 12.4 | 6.7 | 3.7 | -1.1 | | | | | | |
| 1995 | 6.2 | 6.6 | 6.9 | 7.5 | 7.4 | 7.6 | 8.0 | 8.0 | 8.6 | 8.5 | 9.3 | 8.2 | 7.1 | 7.9 | 7.5 | 12.6 | 7.3 | 4.8 | 1.7 | 15.5 | | | | | |
| 1996 | 6.2 | 6.6 | 7.0 | 7.5 | 7.4 | 7.7 | 8.1 | 8.0 | 8.6 | 8.6 | 9.3 | 8.2 | 7.2 | 8.0 | 7.6 | 12.5 | 7.5 | 5.3 | 2.9 | 13.1 | | | | | |
| 1997 | 6.4 | 6.8 | 7.1 | 7.7 | 7.6 | 7.8 | 8.2 | 8.2 | 8.8 | 8.8 | 9.5 | 8.5 | 7.5 | 8.4 | 8.1 | 12.8 | 8.2 | 6.4 | 5.1 | 15.4 | | | | | |
| 1998 | 6.4 | 6.8 | 7.2 | 7.7 | 7.6 | 7.8 | 8.3 | 8.2 | 8.8 | 8.8 | 9.5 | 8.5 | 7.6 | 8.4 | 8.1 | 12.7 | 8.2 | 6.6 | 5.6 | 13.9 | | | | | |
| 1999 | 6.5 | 6.9 | 7.2 | 7.7 | 7.6 | 7.9 | 8.3 | 8.3 | 8.8 | 8.8 | 9.5 | 8.6 | 7.6 | 8.5 | 8.2 | 12.6 | 8.3 | 6.9 | 6.0 | 13.2 | | | | | |
| 2000 | 6.3 | 6.7 | 7.0 | 7.5 | 7.4 | 7.6 | 8.0 | 8.0 | 8.5 | 8.5 | 9.2 | 8.2 | 7.2 | 8.0 | 7.6 | 11.7 | 7.5 | 5.8 | 4.6 | 9.4 | -9.8 | | | | |
| 2001 | 6.1 | 6.4 | 6.7 | 7.3 | 7.1 | 7.3 | 7.7 | 7.6 | 8.1 | 8.0 | 8.7 | 7.6 | 6.6 | 7.3 | 6.8 | 10.7 | 6.4 | 4.5 | 2.8 | 5.7 | -13.1 | | | | |
| 2002 | 5.7 | 6.1 | 6.4 | 6.8 | 6.7 | 6.8 | 7.2 | 7.1 | 7.5 | 7.4 | 7.9 | 6.9 | 5.8 | 6.3 | 5.7 | 9.2 | 4.8 | 2.6 | 0.3 | 1.2 | -18.8 | | | | |
| 2003 | 5.8 | 6.2 | 6.5 | 6.9 | 6.8 | 7.0 | 7.3 | 7.2 | 7.7 | 7.5 | 8.1 | 7.1 | 6.0 | 6.6 | 6.0 | 9.5 | 5.3 | 3.3 | 1.5 | 2.9 | -9.9 | | | | |
| 2004 | 5.8 | 6.2 | 6.5 | 6.9 | 6.8 | 7.0 | 7.3 | 7.2 | 7.7 | 7.5 | 8.1 | 7.1 | 6.1 | 6.6 | 6.1 | 9.4 | 5.4 | 3.5 | 1.9 | 3.4 | -6.4 | | | | |
| 2005 | 5.9 | 6.3 | 6.5 | 7.0 | 6.9 | 7.1 | 7.4 | 7.3 | 7.8 | 7.6 | 8.2 | 7.2 | 6.2 | 6.8 | 6.3 | 9.6 | 5.7 | 4.0 | 2.6 | 4.3 | -3.1 | 13.7 | | | |
| 2006 | 6.0 | 6.3 | 6.6 | 7.1 | 6.9 | 7.1 | 7.4 | 7.3 | 7.8 | 7.7 | 8.2 | 7.3 | 6.3 | 6.9 | 6.4 | 9.6 | 5.9 | 4.4 | 3.1 | 4.9 | -1.0 | 12.5 | | | |
| 2007 | 5.9 | 6.3 | 6.5 | 7.0 | 6.9 | 7.0 | 7.4 | 7.3 | 7.7 | 7.6 | 8.1 | 7.2 | 6.2 | 6.7 | 6.3 | 9.3 | 5.7 | 4.2 | 3.0 | 4.6 | -0.8 | 8.6 | | | |
| 2008 | 5.6 | 6.0 | 6.2 | 6.7 | 6.5 | 6.7 | 7.0 | 6.8 | 7.3 | 7.1 | 7.6 | 6.6 | 5.6 | 6.0 | 5.5 | 8.4 | 4.7 | 3.0 | 1.6 | 2.5 | -3.4 | 0.4 | | | |
| 2009 | 5.9 | 6.2 | 6.5 | 6.9 | 6.8 | 6.9 | 7.3 | 7.1 | 7.6 | 7.5 | 7.9 | 7.0 | 6.1 | 6.6 | 6.1 | 9.0 | 5.6 | 4.1 | 3.0 | 4.4 | 0.0 | 6.4 | | | |
| 2010 | 5.9 | 6.3 | 6.5 | 7.0 | 6.8 | 7.0 | 7.3 | 7.2 | 7.6 | 7.5 | 8.0 | 7.1 | 6.2 | 6.7 | 6.3 | 9.1 | 5.7 | 4.4 | 3.4 | 4.8 | 1.0 | 7.2 | 11.4 | | |
| 2011 | 5.8 | 6.2 | 6.4 | 6.9 | 6.7 | 6.9 | 7.2 | 7.1 | 7.5 | 7.4 | 7.8 | 6.9 | 6.0 | 6.5 | 6.1 | 8.7 | 5.5 | 4.1 | 3.2 | 4.4 | 0.7 | 5.9 | 4.5 | | |
| 2012 | 5.9 | 6.2 | 6.5 | 6.9 | 6.8 | 6.9 | 7.2 | 7.1 | 7.5 | 7.4 | 7.9 | 7.0 | 6.1 | 6.6 | 6.2 | 8.8 | 5.6 | 4.4 | 3.5 | 4.7 | 1.5 | 6.4 | 6.5 | | |
| 2013 | 6.0 | 6.3 | 6.6 | 7.0 | 6.9 | 7.1 | 7.4 | 7.3 | 7.7 | 7.6 | 8.0 | 7.2 | 6.4 | 6.8 | 6.4 | 9.0 | 6.0 | 4.9 | 4.1 | 5.5 | 2.7 | 7.8 | 9.5 | | |
| 2014 | 5.9 | 6.3 | 6.5 | 7.0 | 6.8 | 7.0 | 7.3 | 7.2 | 7.6 | 7.5 | 7.9 | 7.1 | 6.2 | 6.7 | 6.3 | 8.8 | 5.8 | 4.7 | 3.9 | 5.2 | 2.5 | 7.0 | 7.6 | | |
| 2015 | 5.9 | 6.2 | 6.4 | 6.9 | 6.7 | 6.9 | 7.2 | 7.1 | 7.4 | 7.3 | 7.7 | 6.9 | 6.1 | 6.5 | 6.1 | 8.5 | 5.6 | 4.4 | 3.7 | 4.8 | 2.2 | 6.1 | 5.8 | -3.1 | |
| 2016 | 6.0 | 6.3 | 6.5 | 6.9 | 6.8 | 7.0 | 7.3 | 7.2 | 7.6 | 7.4 | 7.9 | 7.0 | 6.3 | 6.7 | 6.3 | 8.7 | 5.9 | 4.8 | 4.1 | 5.3 | 3.0 | 6.9 | 7.3 | 6.6 | 16.3 |

Source of underlying data: 1.) Morningstar *Direct* database. Used with permission. All rights reserved. All calculations performed by Duff & Phelps LLC.

## United States Long-Horizon Equity Risk Premia

in U.S. Dollars (USD, which is also the "local" currency)
in Percent

| End Date | 1926 | 1930 | 1935 | 1940 | 1945 | 1950 | 1955 | 1960 | 1965 | 1970 | 1975 | 1980 | 1985 | 1990 | 1995 | 2000 | 2005 | 2010 | 2015 | 2016 |
|---|---|---|---|---|---|---|---|---|---|---|---|---|---|---|---|---|---|---|---|---|
| | Start Date | | | | | | | | | | | | | | | | | | | |
| 1926 | 7.9 | | | | | | | | | | | | | | | | | | | |
| 1927 | 21.0 | | | | | | | | | | | | | | | | | | | |
| 1928 | 27.5 | | | | | | | | | | | | | | | | | | | |
| 1929 | 17.6 | | | | | | | | | | | | | | | | | | | |
| 1930 | 8.5 | -28.2 | | | | | | | | | | | | | | | | | | |
| 1931 | -0.7 | -37.4 | | | | | | | | | | | | | | | | | | |
| 1932 | -2.3 | -28.9 | | | | | | | | | | | | | | | | | | |
| 1933 | 4.3 | -9.0 | | | | | | | | | | | | | | | | | | |
| 1934 | 3.3 | -8.1 | | | | | | | | | | | | | | | | | | |
| 1935 | 7.5 | 0.7 | 44.9 | | | | | | | | | | | | | | | | | |
| 1936 | 9.6 | 5.1 | 38.0 | | | | | | | | | | | | | | | | | |
| 1937 | 5.7 | -0.3 | 12.8 | | | | | | | | | | | | | | | | | |
| 1938 | 7.4 | 2.9 | 16.7 | | | | | | | | | | | | | | | | | |
| 1939 | 6.7 | 2.3 | 12.8 | | | | | | | | | | | | | | | | | |
| 1940 | 5.5 | 1.0 | 8.7 | -12.0 | | | | | | | | | | | | | | | | |
| 1941 | 4.3 | -0.2 | 5.5 | -12.8 | | | | | | | | | | | | | | | | |
| 1942 | 5.1 | 1.2 | 7.0 | -2.6 | | | | | | | | | | | | | | | | |
| 1943 | 6.1 | 2.8 | 8.9 | 3.9 | | | | | | | | | | | | | | | | |
| 1944 | 6.7 | 3.8 | 9.7 | 6.6 | | | | | | | | | | | | | | | | |
| 1945 | 8.1 | 5.7 | 11.9 | 11.2 | 34.1 | | | | | | | | | | | | | | | |
| 1946 | 7.2 | 4.7 | 10.1 | 8.2 | 12.0 | | | | | | | | | | | | | | | |
| 1947 | 7.0 | 4.7 | 9.6 | 7.6 | 9.2 | | | | | | | | | | | | | | | |
| 1948 | 6.9 | 4.6 | 9.1 | 7.1 | 7.7 | | | | | | | | | | | | | | | |
| 1949 | 7.3 | 5.2 | 9.6 | 8.0 | 9.4 | | | | | | | | | | | | | | | |
| 1950 | 8.2 | 6.4 | 10.9 | 10.0 | 12.8 | 29.6 | | | | | | | | | | | | | | |
| 1951 | 8.7 | 7.0 | 11.5 | 11.0 | 14.1 | 25.6 | | | | | | | | | | | | | | |
| 1952 | 8.9 | 7.4 | 11.7 | 11.3 | 14.3 | 22.3 | | | | | | | | | | | | | | |
| 1953 | 8.5 | 7.0 | 10.9 | 10.2 | 12.3 | 15.8 | | | | | | | | | | | | | | |
| 1954 | 9.9 | 8.7 | 12.9 | 12.9 | 16.0 | 22.6 | | | | | | | | | | | | | | |
| 1955 | 10.5 | 9.4 | 13.6 | 13.9 | 17.2 | 23.6 | 28.8 | | | | | | | | | | | | | |
| 1956 | 10.3 | 9.2 | 13.2 | 13.3 | 16.0 | 20.8 | 16.2 | | | | | | | | | | | | | |
| 1957 | 9.5 | 8.4 | 12.0 | 11.7 | 13.7 | 16.4 | 6.1 | | | | | | | | | | | | | |
| 1958 | 10.5 | 9.5 | 13.1 | 13.2 | 15.6 | 19.0 | 14.6 | | | | | | | | | | | | | |
| 1959 | 10.4 | 9.4 | 12.9 | 13.0 | 15.1 | 17.9 | 13.2 | | | | | | | | | | | | | |
| 1960 | 10.0 | 9.0 | 12.3 | 12.2 | 13.9 | 15.9 | 10.4 | -3.8 | | | | | | | | | | | | |
| 1961 | 10.4 | 9.4 | 12.7 | 12.7 | 14.4 | 16.5 | 12.2 | 9.6 | | | | | | | | | | | | |
| 1962 | 9.7 | 8.8 | 11.8 | 11.6 | 12.9 | 14.3 | 9.1 | 2.2 | | | | | | | | | | | | |
| 1963 | 10.0 | 9.1 | 12.0 | 11.9 | 13.3 | 14.6 | 10.2 | 6.4 | | | | | | | | | | | | |
| 1964 | 10.0 | 9.2 | 12.0 | 11.9 | 13.2 | 14.5 | 10.4 | 7.6 | | | | | | | | | | | | |
| 1965 | 10.0 | 9.1 | 11.9 | 11.7 | 13.0 | 14.1 | 10.2 | 7.7 | 8.3 | | | | | | | | | | | |
| 1966 | 9.4 | 8.5 | 11.1 | 10.8 | 11.7 | 12.4 | 8.1 | 4.5 | -3.1 | | | | | | | | | | | |
| 1967 | 9.6 | 8.8 | 11.3 | 11.1 | 12.1 | 12.8 | 9.0 | 6.4 | 4.4 | | | | | | | | | | | |
| 1968 | 9.5 | 8.7 | 11.2 | 10.9 | 11.8 | 12.4 | 8.8 | 6.3 | 4.7 | | | | | | | | | | | |
| 1969 | 9.0 | 8.1 | 10.4 | 10.0 | 10.7 | 11.1 | 7.2 | 4.2 | 0.8 | | | | | | | | | | | |
| 1970 | 8.7 | 7.9 | 10.1 | 9.6 | 10.2 | 10.4 | 6.6 | 3.6 | 0.2 | -2.9 | | | | | | | | | | |

* S&P 500 total returns minus long-term U.S. government bond income returns.
Source of underlying data: 1.) Morningstar *Direct* database. Used with permisson. All rights reserved. Calculations by Duff & Phelps.

## United States Long-Horizon Equity Risk Premia

in U.S. Dollars (USD, which is also the "local" currency)
in Percent

| End Date | Start Date 1926 | 1930 | 1935 | 1940 | 1945 | 1950 | 1955 | 1960 | 1965 | 1970 | 1975 | 1980 | 1985 | 1990 | 1995 | 2000 | 2005 | 2010 | 2015 | 2016 |
|---|---|---|---|---|---|---|---|---|---|---|---|---|---|---|---|---|---|---|---|---|
| 1971 | 8.7 | 7.9 | 10.0 | 9.6 | 10.1 | 10.3 | 6.7 | 3.9 | 1.3 | 2.5 | | | | | | | | | | |
| 1972 | 8.8 | 8.0 | 10.1 | 9.7 | 10.2 | 10.4 | 7.0 | 4.6 | 2.8 | 6.1 | | | | | | | | | | |
| 1973 | 8.2 | 7.3 | 9.3 | 8.8 | 9.2 | 9.1 | 5.5 | 2.8 | 0.1 | -0.7 | | | | | | | | | | |
| 1974 | 7.3 | 6.4 | 8.2 | 7.6 | 7.7 | 7.4 | 3.6 | 0.4 | -3.3 | -7.3 | | | | | | | | | | |
| 1975 | 7.8 | 6.9 | 8.7 | 8.2 | 8.4 | 8.2 | 4.8 | 2.2 | -0.3 | -1.2 | 29.2 | | | | | | | | | |
| 1976 | 7.9 | 7.1 | 8.9 | 8.4 | 8.7 | 8.5 | 5.3 | 3.0 | 1.1 | 1.2 | 22.6 | | | | | | | | | |
| 1977 | 7.5 | 6.6 | 8.4 | 7.8 | 8.0 | 7.7 | 4.5 | 2.0 | -0.1 | -0.7 | 10.3 | | | | | | | | | |
| 1978 | 7.3 | 6.5 | 8.1 | 7.5 | 7.7 | 7.4 | 4.2 | 1.8 | -0.2 | -0.8 | 7.4 | | | | | | | | | |
| 1979 | 7.4 | 6.6 | 8.2 | 7.6 | 7.7 | 7.5 | 4.4 | 2.2 | 0.5 | 0.3 | 7.9 | | | | | | | | | |
| 1980 | 7.6 | 6.9 | 8.5 | 8.0 | 8.2 | 7.9 | 5.1 | 3.2 | 1.8 | 2.3 | 10.3 | 22.5 | | | | | | | | |
| 1981 | 7.2 | 6.4 | 8.0 | 7.4 | 7.5 | 7.2 | 4.3 | 2.3 | 0.8 | 0.7 | 6.5 | 3.0 | | | | | | | | |
| 1982 | 7.2 | 6.4 | 8.0 | 7.4 | 7.5 | 7.2 | 4.5 | 2.6 | 1.2 | 1.3 | 6.7 | 4.7 | | | | | | | | |
| 1983 | 7.3 | 6.6 | 8.0 | 7.5 | 7.6 | 7.4 | 4.7 | 3.0 | 1.7 | 2.1 | 7.3 | 6.6 | | | | | | | | |
| 1984 | 7.1 | 6.3 | 7.8 | 7.2 | 7.3 | 7.0 | 4.4 | 2.6 | 1.4 | 1.6 | 6.0 | 4.2 | | | | | | | | |
| 1985 | 7.3 | 6.6 | 8.0 | 7.5 | 7.6 | 7.4 | 4.9 | 3.3 | 2.3 | 2.7 | 7.3 | 6.9 | 20.5 | | | | | | | |
| 1986 | 7.4 | 6.6 | 8.1 | 7.6 | 7.7 | 7.4 | 5.1 | 3.5 | 2.6 | 3.2 | 7.5 | 7.3 | 15.1 | | | | | | | |
| 1987 | 7.2 | 6.5 | 7.9 | 7.3 | 7.4 | 7.2 | 4.8 | 3.3 | 2.4 | 2.8 | 6.7 | 6.0 | 9.2 | | | | | | | |
| 1988 | 7.2 | 6.5 | 7.9 | 7.3 | 7.4 | 7.2 | 4.9 | 3.5 | 2.6 | 3.1 | 6.8 | 6.2 | 8.8 | | | | | | | |
| 1989 | 7.5 | 6.8 | 8.1 | 7.7 | 7.8 | 7.6 | 5.4 | 4.1 | 3.4 | 4.1 | 7.9 | 7.9 | 11.6 | | | | | | | |
| 1990 | 7.2 | 6.5 | 7.8 | 7.3 | 7.4 | 7.1 | 5.0 | 3.6 | 2.9 | 3.3 | 6.7 | 6.1 | 7.8 | -11.3 | | | | | | |
| 1991 | 7.4 | 6.7 | 8.0 | 7.6 | 7.7 | 7.5 | 5.4 | 4.2 | 3.6 | 4.2 | 7.6 | 7.5 | 9.9 | 5.5 | | | | | | |
| 1992 | 7.3 | 6.6 | 7.9 | 7.4 | 7.5 | 7.3 | 5.3 | 4.1 | 3.5 | 4.0 | 7.2 | 6.9 | 8.7 | 3.8 | | | | | | |
| 1993 | 7.2 | 6.6 | 7.8 | 7.4 | 7.4 | 7.2 | 5.2 | 4.1 | 3.4 | 4.0 | 7.0 | 6.6 | 8.0 | 3.6 | | | | | | |
| 1994 | 7.0 | 6.4 | 7.6 | 7.1 | 7.2 | 6.9 | 5.0 | 3.8 | 3.2 | 3.6 | 6.4 | 5.9 | 6.7 | 1.8 | | | | | | |
| 1995 | 7.4 | 6.7 | 8.0 | 7.5 | 7.6 | 7.4 | 5.6 | 4.5 | 4.0 | 4.6 | 7.5 | 7.4 | 8.8 | 6.5 | 30.0 | | | | | |
| 1996 | 7.5 | 6.9 | 8.1 | 7.7 | 7.8 | 7.6 | 5.8 | 4.8 | 4.4 | 5.1 | 7.9 | 7.9 | 9.5 | 8.0 | 23.4 | | | | | |
| 1997 | 7.8 | 7.2 | 8.4 | 8.0 | 8.2 | 8.0 | 6.3 | 5.4 | 5.1 | 5.9 | 8.7 | 9.0 | 10.8 | 10.3 | 24.5 | | | | | |
| 1998 | 8.0 | 7.4 | 8.6 | 8.3 | 8.4 | 8.3 | 6.7 | 5.9 | 5.6 | 6.4 | 9.3 | 9.7 | 11.7 | 11.7 | 24.1 | | | | | |
| 1999 | 8.1 | 7.5 | 8.7 | 8.4 | 8.6 | 8.5 | 6.9 | 6.1 | 5.9 | 6.7 | 9.6 | 10.0 | 11.9 | 12.1 | 22.3 | | | | | |
| 2000 | 7.8 | 7.2 | 8.4 | 8.0 | 8.1 | 8.0 | 6.4 | 5.6 | 5.3 | 6.0 | 8.6 | 8.8 | 10.2 | 9.5 | 16.0 | -15.6 | | | | |
| 2001 | 7.4 | 6.9 | 8.0 | 7.6 | 7.7 | 7.5 | 5.9 | 5.0 | 4.7 | 5.3 | 7.6 | 7.6 | 8.6 | 7.3 | 11.2 | -16.5 | | | | |
| 2002 | 7.0 | 6.4 | 7.5 | 7.0 | 7.1 | 6.8 | 5.2 | 4.3 | 3.8 | 4.3 | 6.4 | 6.0 | 6.6 | 4.6 | 6.4 | -20.2 | | | | |
| 2003 | 7.2 | 6.6 | 7.7 | 7.3 | 7.2 | 7.2 | 5.6 | 4.7 | 4.3 | 4.9 | 7.0 | 6.8 | 7.5 | 6.0 | 8.3 | -9.2 | | | | |
| 2004 | 7.2 | 6.6 | 7.7 | 7.3 | 7.3 | 7.1 | 5.6 | 4.7 | 4.4 | 4.9 | 6.9 | 6.7 | 7.4 | 6.0 | 8.1 | -6.2 | | | | |
| 2005 | 7.1 | 6.5 | 7.6 | 7.2 | 7.2 | 7.0 | 5.5 | 4.6 | 4.3 | 4.8 | 6.7 | 6.5 | 7.0 | 5.6 | 7.4 | -5.1 | 0.2 | | | |
| 2006 | 7.1 | 6.6 | 7.6 | 7.2 | 7.3 | 7.1 | 5.6 | 4.8 | 4.4 | 4.9 | 6.9 | 6.7 | 7.2 | 5.9 | 7.7 | -2.8 | 5.7 | | | |
| 2007 | 7.1 | 6.5 | 7.5 | 7.1 | 7.2 | 7.0 | 5.5 | 4.7 | 4.4 | 4.8 | 6.7 | 6.4 | 6.9 | 5.6 | 7.1 | -2.4 | 4.0 | | | |
| 2008 | 6.5 | 5.9 | 6.9 | 6.4 | 6.4 | 6.2 | 4.6 | 3.7 | 3.3 | 3.6 | 5.2 | 4.8 | 4.9 | 3.2 | 3.7 | -6.7 | -7.4 | | | |
| 2009 | 6.7 | 6.1 | 7.1 | 6.7 | 6.7 | 6.4 | 5.0 | 4.1 | 3.8 | 4.1 | 5.8 | 5.4 | 5.6 | 4.2 | 5.0 | -3.7 | -1.3 | | | |
| 2010 | 6.7 | 6.2 | 7.1 | 6.7 | 6.7 | 6.5 | 5.1 | 4.3 | 3.9 | 4.3 | 5.9 | 5.6 | 5.8 | 4.5 | 5.3 | -2.4 | 0.7 | 10.8 | | |
| 2011 | 6.6 | 6.1 | 7.0 | 6.6 | 6.6 | 6.4 | 4.9 | 4.2 | 3.8 | 4.1 | 5.7 | 5.3 | 5.6 | 4.2 | 4.9 | -2.4 | 0.4 | 4.5 | | |
| 2012 | 6.7 | 6.2 | 7.1 | 6.7 | 6.7 | 6.5 | 5.1 | 4.3 | 4.0 | 4.4 | 5.9 | 5.6 | 5.9 | 4.6 | 5.4 | -1.1 | 2.0 | 7.5 | | |
| 2013 | 7.0 | 6.4 | 7.4 | 7.0 | 7.0 | 6.8 | 5.5 | 4.8 | 4.5 | 4.9 | 6.5 | 6.3 | 6.7 | 5.6 | 6.7 | 1.1 | 5.1 | 13.0 | | |
| 2014 | 7.0 | 6.5 | 7.4 | 7.0 | 7.1 | 6.9 | 5.6 | 4.9 | 4.6 | 5.0 | 6.6 | 6.4 | 6.8 | 5.8 | 6.8 | 1.7 | 5.6 | 12.5 | | |
| 2015 | 6.9 | 6.4 | 7.3 | 6.9 | 7.0 | 6.8 | 5.5 | 4.8 | 4.5 | 4.9 | 6.4 | 6.2 | 6.5 | 5.6 | 6.5 | 1.5 | 5.0 | 10.2 | -1.1 | |
| 2016 | 6.9 | 6.4 | 7.3 | 7.0 | 7.0 | 6.8 | 5.5 | 4.9 | 4.6 | 5.0 | 6.5 | 6.3 | 6.6 | 5.7 | 6.6 | 2.0 | 5.4 | 10.1 | 4.3 | 9.7 |

* S&P 500 total returns minus long-term U.S. government bond income returns.
Source of underlying data: 1.) Morningstar *Direct* database. Used with permisson. All rights reserved. Calculations by Duff & Phelps.

## United States Short-Horizon Equity Risk Premia

in U.S. Dollars (USD, which is also the "local" currency)
in Percent

| End Date | Start Date 1926 | 1930 | 1935 | 1940 | 1945 | 1950 | 1955 | 1960 | 1965 | 1970 | 1975 | 1980 | 1985 | 1990 | 1995 | 2000 | 2005 | 2010 | 2015 | 2016 |
|---|---|---|---|---|---|---|---|---|---|---|---|---|---|---|---|---|---|---|---|---|
| 1926 | 8.4 | | | | | | | | | | | | | | | | | | | |
| 1927 | 21.4 | | | | | | | | | | | | | | | | | | | |
| 1928 | 27.6 | | | | | | | | | | | | | | | | | | | |
| 1929 | 17.4 | | | | | | | | | | | | | | | | | | | |
| 1930 | 8.5 | -27.3 | | | | | | | | | | | | | | | | | | |
| 1931 | -0.4 | -35.9 | | | | | | | | | | | | | | | | | | |
| 1932 | -1.6 | -27.0 | | | | | | | | | | | | | | | | | | |
| 1933 | 5.3 | -6.8 | | | | | | | | | | | | | | | | | | |
| 1934 | 4.5 | -5.8 | | | | | | | | | | | | | | | | | | |
| 1935 | 8.8 | 3.1 | 47.5 | | | | | | | | | | | | | | | | | |
| 1936 | 11.1 | 7.5 | 40.6 | | | | | | | | | | | | | | | | | |
| 1937 | 7.2 | 2.1 | 15.3 | | | | | | | | | | | | | | | | | |
| 1938 | 9.1 | 5.4 | 19.3 | | | | | | | | | | | | | | | | | |
| 1939 | 8.4 | 4.8 | 15.3 | | | | | | | | | | | | | | | | | |
| 1940 | 7.2 | 3.5 | 11.1 | -9.8 | | | | | | | | | | | | | | | | |
| 1941 | 6.0 | 2.2 | 7.9 | -10.7 | | | | | | | | | | | | | | | | |
| 1942 | 6.8 | 3.6 | 9.4 | -0.5 | | | | | | | | | | | | | | | | |
| 1943 | 7.9 | 5.1 | 11.2 | 6.0 | | | | | | | | | | | | | | | | |
| 1944 | 8.5 | 6.1 | 12.0 | 8.7 | | | | | | | | | | | | | | | | |
| 1945 | 9.9 | 8.0 | 14.2 | 13.3 | 36.1 | | | | | | | | | | | | | | | |
| 1946 | 9.0 | 7.0 | 12.3 | 10.2 | 13.8 | | | | | | | | | | | | | | | |
| 1947 | 8.8 | 6.9 | 11.8 | 9.6 | 11.0 | | | | | | | | | | | | | | | |
| 1948 | 8.6 | 6.8 | 11.3 | 9.0 | 9.4 | | | | | | | | | | | | | | | |
| 1949 | 9.0 | 7.3 | 11.7 | 9.9 | 11.1 | | | | | | | | | | | | | | | |
| 1950 | 9.9 | 8.4 | 12.9 | 11.8 | 14.3 | 30.5 | | | | | | | | | | | | | | |
| 1951 | 10.4 | 9.1 | 13.4 | 12.7 | 15.5 | 26.5 | | | | | | | | | | | | | | |
| 1952 | 10.6 | 9.4 | 13.6 | 13.0 | 15.6 | 23.3 | | | | | | | | | | | | | | |
| 1953 | 10.1 | 8.9 | 12.8 | 11.8 | 13.6 | 16.7 | | | | | | | | | | | | | | |
| 1954 | 11.6 | 10.6 | 14.7 | 14.5 | 17.4 | 23.7 | | | | | | | | | | | | | | |
| 1955 | 12.2 | 11.4 | 15.4 | 15.5 | 18.5 | 24.8 | 30.0 | | | | | | | | | | | | | |
| 1956 | 11.9 | 11.1 | 14.9 | 14.8 | 17.3 | 21.8 | 17.0 | | | | | | | | | | | | | |
| 1957 | 11.1 | 10.2 | 13.7 | 13.2 | 14.9 | 17.4 | 6.7 | | | | | | | | | | | | | |
| 1958 | 12.0 | 11.3 | 14.8 | 14.7 | 16.9 | 20.1 | 15.5 | | | | | | | | | | | | | |
| 1959 | 11.9 | 11.2 | 14.6 | 14.4 | 16.3 | 19.0 | 14.2 | | | | | | | | | | | | | |
| 1960 | 11.5 | 10.8 | 14.0 | 13.6 | 15.2 | 17.0 | 11.5 | -2.2 | | | | | | | | | | | | |
| 1961 | 11.9 | 11.2 | 14.4 | 14.1 | 15.7 | 17.7 | 13.4 | 11.3 | | | | | | | | | | | | |
| 1962 | 11.3 | 10.5 | 13.4 | 13.0 | 14.2 | 15.4 | 10.3 | 3.7 | | | | | | | | | | | | |
| 1963 | 11.5 | 10.8 | 13.7 | 13.3 | 14.5 | 15.7 | 11.3 | 7.7 | | | | | | | | | | | | |
| 1964 | 11.5 | 10.9 | 13.6 | 13.3 | 14.4 | 15.6 | 11.5 | 8.7 | | | | | | | | | | | | |
| 1965 | 11.5 | 10.8 | 13.5 | 13.1 | 14.2 | 15.1 | 11.2 | 8.7 | 8.5 | | | | | | | | | | | |
| 1966 | 10.8 | 10.1 | 12.6 | 12.1 | 12.8 | 13.4 | 9.0 | 5.3 | -3.1 | | | | | | | | | | | |
| 1967 | 11.0 | 10.4 | 12.8 | 12.3 | 13.1 | 13.7 | 9.9 | 7.2 | 4.5 | | | | | | | | | | | |
| 1968 | 10.9 | 10.2 | 12.6 | 12.1 | 12.8 | 13.3 | 9.6 | 7.0 | 4.8 | | | | | | | | | | | |
| 1969 | 10.3 | 9.6 | 11.8 | 11.2 | 11.7 | 11.9 | 7.9 | 4.8 | 0.8 | | | | | | | | | | | |
| 1970 | 10.0 | 9.3 | 11.4 | 10.8 | 11.2 | 11.2 | 7.3 | 4.1 | 0.3 | -2.7 | | | | | | | | | | |

* S&P 500 total returns minus 30-day U.S. Treasury bill total returns. For 30-day Treasury bills, the income return and total return are the same.
Source of underlying data: 1.) Morningstar *Direct* database. Used with permisson. All rights reserved. Calculations by Duff & Phelps.

# United States Short-Horizon Equity Risk Premia

in U.S. Dollars (USD, which is also the "local" currency)

in Percent

| End Date | Start Date 1926 | 1930 | 1935 | 1940 | 1945 | 1950 | 1955 | 1960 | 1965 | 1970 | 1975 | 1980 | 1985 | 1990 | 1995 | 2000 | 2005 | 2010 | 2015 | 2016 |
|---|---|---|---|---|---|---|---|---|---|---|---|---|---|---|---|---|---|---|---|---|
| 1971 | 10.0 | 9.3 | 11.4 | 10.7 | 11.1 | 11.1 | 7.4 | 4.6 | 1.6 | 3.6 | | | | | | | | | | |
| 1972 | 10.1 | 9.5 | 11.5 | 10.9 | 11.3 | 11.3 | 7.9 | 5.4 | 3.3 | 7.5 | | | | | | | | | | |
| 1973 | 9.5 | 8.8 | 10.6 | 9.9 | 10.1 | 9.9 | 6.3 | 3.5 | 0.6 | 0.2 | | | | | | | | | | |
| 1974 | 8.6 | 7.8 | 9.5 | 8.7 | 8.6 | 8.2 | 4.3 | 1.0 | -2.9 | -6.7 | | | | | | | | | | |
| 1975 | 9.0 | 8.3 | 10.0 | 9.3 | 9.4 | 9.1 | 5.6 | 2.9 | 0.2 | -0.4 | 31.4 | | | | | | | | | |
| 1976 | 9.2 | 8.5 | 10.2 | 9.5 | 9.7 | 9.4 | 6.2 | 3.8 | 1.7 | 2.4 | 25.1 | | | | | | | | | |
| 1977 | 8.8 | 8.1 | 9.7 | 9.0 | 9.0 | 8.6 | 5.4 | 2.9 | 0.7 | 0.5 | 12.7 | | | | | | | | | |
| 1978 | 8.6 | 7.9 | 9.5 | 8.7 | 8.7 | 8.3 | 5.1 | 2.7 | 0.6 | 0.4 | 9.3 | | | | | | | | | |
| 1979 | 8.6 | 7.9 | 9.4 | 8.7 | 8.7 | 8.3 | 5.2 | 3.0 | 1.1 | 1.2 | 9.1 | | | | | | | | | |
| 1980 | 8.9 | 8.2 | 9.7 | 9.0 | 9.1 | 8.7 | 5.9 | 3.9 | 2.3 | 3.0 | 11.1 | 21.3 | | | | | | | | |
| 1981 | 8.3 | 7.7 | 9.1 | 8.3 | 8.3 | 7.9 | 4.9 | 2.8 | 1.0 | 1.1 | 6.8 | 0.8 | | | | | | | | |
| 1982 | 8.4 | 7.7 | 9.1 | 8.4 | 8.4 | 7.9 | 5.1 | 3.2 | 1.6 | 1.9 | 7.3 | 4.2 | | | | | | | | |
| 1983 | 8.5 | 7.8 | 9.2 | 8.5 | 8.5 | 8.1 | 5.4 | 3.6 | 2.2 | 2.7 | 8.0 | 6.6 | | | | | | | | |
| 1984 | 8.3 | 7.6 | 9.0 | 8.3 | 8.2 | 7.8 | 5.1 | 3.3 | 1.9 | 2.3 | 6.8 | 4.6 | | | | | | | | |
| 1985 | 8.5 | 7.9 | 9.3 | 8.6 | 8.6 | 8.2 | 5.7 | 4.1 | 3.0 | 3.7 | 8.4 | 7.8 | 24.0 | | | | | | | |
| 1986 | 8.6 | 8.0 | 9.3 | 8.7 | 8.7 | 8.3 | 5.9 | 4.4 | 3.4 | 4.2 | 8.7 | 8.5 | 18.3 | | | | | | | |
| 1987 | 8.5 | 7.9 | 9.1 | 8.5 | 8.5 | 8.1 | 5.8 | 4.3 | 3.3 | 3.9 | 8.1 | 7.4 | 12.1 | | | | | | | |
| 1988 | 8.5 | 7.9 | 9.2 | 8.5 | 8.5 | 8.2 | 5.9 | 4.5 | 3.6 | 4.3 | 8.2 | 7.7 | 11.6 | | | | | | | |
| 1989 | 8.7 | 8.1 | 9.4 | 8.8 | 8.8 | 8.6 | 6.4 | 5.1 | 4.4 | 5.2 | 9.2 | 9.3 | 14.0 | | | | | | | |
| 1990 | 8.4 | 7.8 | 9.1 | 8.4 | 8.4 | 8.1 | 5.9 | 4.6 | 3.8 | 4.5 | 8.0 | 7.4 | 9.8 | -10.9 | | | | | | |
| 1991 | 8.7 | 8.1 | 9.3 | 8.8 | 8.8 | 8.5 | 6.4 | 5.2 | 4.5 | 5.4 | 9.0 | 8.9 | 12.0 | 7.0 | | | | | | |
| 1992 | 8.6 | 8.0 | 9.2 | 8.7 | 8.7 | 8.4 | 6.4 | 5.2 | 4.5 | 5.3 | 8.7 | 8.5 | 11.0 | 6.0 | | | | | | |
| 1993 | 8.6 | 8.0 | 9.2 | 8.6 | 8.6 | 8.4 | 6.4 | 5.2 | 4.6 | 5.4 | 8.6 | 8.4 | 10.6 | 6.3 | | | | | | |
| 1994 | 8.4 | 7.9 | 9.0 | 8.4 | 8.4 | 8.1 | 6.2 | 5.0 | 4.4 | 5.1 | 8.0 | 7.7 | 9.3 | 4.5 | | | | | | |
| 1995 | 8.8 | 8.2 | 9.4 | 8.9 | 8.9 | 8.6 | 6.8 | 5.8 | 5.3 | 6.1 | 9.2 | 9.2 | 11.3 | 9.1 | 32.0 | | | | | |
| 1996 | 8.9 | 8.4 | 9.5 | 9.0 | 9.0 | 8.8 | 7.0 | 6.1 | 5.7 | 6.6 | 9.6 | 9.7 | 11.9 | 10.3 | 24.9 | | | | | |
| 1997 | 9.2 | 8.7 | 9.8 | 9.3 | 9.4 | 9.2 | 7.5 | 6.7 | 6.3 | 7.3 | 10.4 | 10.7 | 13.1 | 12.6 | 25.9 | | | | | |
| 1998 | 9.4 | 8.9 | 10.0 | 9.6 | 9.5 | 9.5 | 7.9 | 7.1 | 6.9 | 7.9 | 10.9 | 11.4 | 13.9 | 13.8 | 25.4 | | | | | |
| 1999 | 9.4 | 9.0 | 10.1 | 9.7 | 9.8 | 9.7 | 8.1 | 7.3 | 7.1 | 8.2 | 11.2 | 11.7 | 14.0 | 14.1 | 23.6 | | | | | |
| 2000 | 9.1 | 8.7 | 9.7 | 9.3 | 9.3 | 9.2 | 7.6 | 6.8 | 6.5 | 7.4 | 10.1 | 10.4 | 12.2 | 11.4 | 17.2 | -15.0 | | | | |
| 2001 | 8.8 | 8.3 | 9.4 | 8.9 | 8.9 | 8.7 | 7.1 | 6.2 | 5.9 | 6.7 | 9.2 | 9.2 | 10.6 | 9.2 | 12.5 | -15.4 | | | | |
| 2002 | 8.4 | 7.9 | 8.9 | 8.4 | 8.3 | 8.1 | 6.5 | 5.6 | 5.1 | 5.8 | 8.0 | 7.8 | 8.7 | 6.6 | 7.9 | -18.2 | | | | |
| 2003 | 8.6 | 8.1 | 9.2 | 8.7 | 8.7 | 8.4 | 6.9 | 6.1 | 5.7 | 6.4 | 8.7 | 8.6 | 9.7 | 8.1 | 10.1 | -6.7 | | | | |
| 2004 | 8.6 | 8.2 | 9.2 | 8.7 | 8.7 | 8.5 | 6.9 | 6.1 | 5.8 | 6.5 | 8.7 | 8.6 | 9.7 | 8.2 | 10.1 | -3.4 | | | | |
| 2005 | 8.5 | 8.1 | 9.1 | 8.6 | 8.6 | 8.4 | 6.8 | 6.0 | 5.7 | 6.4 | 8.5 | 8.4 | 9.3 | 7.8 | 9.3 | -2.5 | 1.9 | | | |
| 2006 | 8.6 | 8.1 | 9.1 | 8.6 | 8.6 | 8.4 | 6.9 | 6.1 | 5.8 | 6.5 | 8.6 | 8.5 | 9.4 | 8.0 | 9.5 | -0.6 | 6.5 | | | |
| 2007 | 8.5 | 8.0 | 9.0 | 8.5 | 8.5 | 8.3 | 6.8 | 6.0 | 5.7 | 6.4 | 8.3 | 8.2 | 9.0 | 7.6 | 8.8 | -0.4 | 4.6 | | | |
| 2008 | 7.9 | 7.4 | 8.3 | 7.8 | 7.8 | 7.5 | 6.0 | 5.1 | 4.7 | 5.2 | 7.0 | 6.6 | 7.0 | 5.2 | 5.4 | -4.7 | -6.2 | | | |
| 2009 | 8.1 | 7.7 | 8.6 | 8.1 | 8.0 | 7.8 | 6.3 | 5.6 | 5.2 | 5.7 | 7.5 | 7.3 | 7.8 | 6.3 | 6.8 | -1.6 | 0.3 | | | |
| 2010 | 8.2 | 7.8 | 8.7 | 8.2 | 8.1 | 7.9 | 6.5 | 5.7 | 5.4 | 6.0 | 7.7 | 7.5 | 8.1 | 6.7 | 7.3 | -0.1 | 2.7 | 14.9 | | |
| 2011 | 8.1 | 7.7 | 8.6 | 8.1 | 8.1 | 7.8 | 6.4 | 5.7 | 5.3 | 5.9 | 7.6 | 7.3 | 7.8 | 6.5 | 7.0 | 0.1 | 2.6 | 8.5 | | |
| 2012 | 8.2 | 7.8 | 8.7 | 8.2 | 8.2 | 7.9 | 6.6 | 5.9 | 5.6 | 6.1 | 7.8 | 7.6 | 8.1 | 6.9 | 7.5 | 1.3 | 4.3 | 11.0 | | |
| 2013 | 8.5 | 8.1 | 9.0 | 8.5 | 8.5 | 8.3 | 7.0 | 6.4 | 6.1 | 6.7 | 8.4 | 8.3 | 9.0 | 7.9 | 8.8 | 3.6 | 7.4 | 16.3 | | |
| 2014 | 8.6 | 8.2 | 9.0 | 8.6 | 8.6 | 8.4 | 7.1 | 6.5 | 6.3 | 6.9 | 8.6 | 8.5 | 9.1 | 8.2 | 9.1 | 4.2 | 8.1 | 15.8 | | |
| 2015 | 8.5 | 8.1 | 8.9 | 8.5 | 8.5 | 8.3 | 7.0 | 6.4 | 6.2 | 6.7 | 8.4 | 8.3 | 8.9 | 7.9 | 8.7 | 4.0 | 7.4 | 13.4 | 1.4 | |
| 2016 | 8.5 | 8.1 | 9.0 | 8.5 | 8.5 | 8.3 | 7.1 | 6.5 | 6.3 | 6.8 | 8.5 | 8.4 | 9.0 | 8.0 | 8.8 | 4.5 | 7.8 | 13.2 | 6.6 | 11.8 |

* S&P 500 total returns minus 30-day U.S. Treasury bill total returns. For 30-day Treasury bills, the income return and total return are the same.

Source of underlying data: 1.) Morningstar *Direct* database. Used with permisson. All rights reserved. Calculations by Duff & Phelps.

# Data Exhibit 2:
# Country Yield Spread Model: Country Risk Premia (CRPs)

The country risk premia (CRP) estimates in Data Exhibit 2 are derived using the Country Yield Spread Model. These CRPs can be used to estimate base country-level cost of equity capital estimates for 188 countries, from the perspective of:

- An investor based in the U.S.

- An investor based in Germany[D2.1]

The Country Yield Spread Model is an adaptation of the capital asset pricing model (CAPM) to an international setting. In simple terms, country risk is quantified in this model as the spread between the "foreign" country's government bond yield denominated in the "home" country's currency (in Data Exhibit 2, the home country is either the U.S. or Germany).

For examples of using the CRPs presented in Data Exhibit 2 to estimate (i) base country-level cost of equity capital or (ii) cost of equity capital for use in evaluating a subject business, asset, or project, please refer to Chapter 4, "Country Yield Spread Model".

---

[D2.1] Note that an investor based in other countries within the Eurozone (e.g., Spain) investing in say, Brazil, could use the same CRP information in Data Exhibit 2, provided that German government securities are being used as the proxy for the risk-free security when estimating the cost of equity for the subject company. This is because the analysis in Data Exhibit 2 is all being conducted in Euros, calculated against German government debt yields.

The country risk premium (CRP) is not the cost of equity capital (COE). The CRP is to be added to base COE. See Chapter 4 for proper application.

| Investee Country | Data Updated Through December 2016 | | Data Updated Through March 2017 | | | |
|---|---|---|---|---|---|---|
| | December 2016 Country Risk Premium (CRP) (%) | Tier Method* | March 2017 Country Risk Premium (CRP) (%) | Tier Method* | S&P Sovereign Credit Rating § | MSCI Market Classification † |
| Afghanistan | 8.5 | 4 | 7.7 | 4 | | |
| Albania | 4.5 | 3 | 4.2 | 3 | B+ | |
| Algeria | 4.5 | 4 | 4.2 | 4 | | |
| Angola | 7.6 | 2 | 6.6 | 2 | B | |
| Antigua & Barbuda | 1.7 | 2 | 1.6 | 2 | | |
| Argentina | 4.5 | 2 | 4.4 | 2 | B- | Frontier |
| Armenia | 3.9 | 2 | 3.8 | 2 | B+ | |
| Aruba | 1.6 | 2 | 1.5 | 2 | BBB+ | |
| Australia | 0.0 | 1 | 0.0 | 1 | AAA | Developed |
| Austria | 0.3 | 2 | 0.2 | 2 | AA+ | Developed |
| Azerbaijan | 2.6 | 2 | 2.4 | 2 | BB+ | |
| Bahamas | 3.2 | 2 | 3.8 | 2 | BB+ | |
| Bahrain | 4.4 | 2 | 3.9 | 2 | BB- | Frontier |
| Bangladesh | 3.7 | 3 | 3.4 | 3 | BB- | Frontier |
| Barbados | 6.5 | 2 | 7.0 | 2 | CCC+ | |
| Belarus | 3.9 | 2 | 3.7 | 2 | B- | |
| Belgium | 0.4 | 2 | 0.3 | 2 | AA | Developed |
| Belize | 14.6 | 3 | 6.2 | 3 | B- | |
| Benin | 9.7 | 4 | 9.0 | 4 | | |
| Bermuda | 0.8 | 3 | 0.7 | 3 | A+ | |
| Bhutan | 9.4 | 4 | 8.6 | 4 | | |
| Bolivia | 3.1 | 3 | 2.8 | 3 | BB | |
| Bosnia & Herzegovina | 5.5 | 3 | 5.1 | 3 | B | |
| Botswana | 1.2 | 3 | 1.0 | 3 | A- | |
| Brazil | 3.8 | 2 | 3.2 | 2 | BB | Emerging |
| Brunei | 1.8 | 4 | 1.6 | 4 | | |
| Bulgaria | 2.5 | 3 | 2.3 | 3 | BB+ | |
| Burkina Faso | 6.7 | 3 | 6.2 | 3 | B- | |
| Burundi | 17.4 | 4 | 16.4 | 4 | | |
| Cambodia | 5.5 | 3 | 5.1 | 3 | B | |
| Cameroon | 5.5 | 3 | 5.1 | 3 | B | |
| Canada | 0.0 | 1 | 0.0 | 1 | AAA | Developed |
| Cape Verde | 5.5 | 3 | 5.1 | 3 | B | |
| Central African Republic | 20.2 | 4 | 19.1 | 4 | | |
| Chad | 19.2 | 4 | 18.2 | 4 | | |
| Chile | 0.9 | 2 | 0.7 | 2 | AA- | Emerging |
| China | 1.0 | 2 | 0.9 | 2 | AA- | Emerging |
| Colombia | 2.8 | 2 | 2.4 | 2 | BBB | Emerging |
| Congo Republic | 6.7 | 3 | 6.2 | 3 | B- | |
| Congo, DR | 6.7 | 3 | 6.2 | 3 | B- | |
| Costa Rica | 4.6 | 2 | 3.9 | 2 | BB- | |
| Côte d'Ivoire | 3.6 | 2 | 3.9 | 2 | BB- | |
| Croatia | 2.3 | 2 | 1.9 | 2 | BB | Frontier |
| Cuba | 9.9 | 3 | 9.2 | 3 | CCC | |
| Cyprus | 3.1 | 3 | 2.3 | 3 | BB+ | |
| Czech Republic | 0.6 | 3 | 0.6 | 3 | AA- | Emerging |
| Denmark | 0.0 | 1 | 0.0 | 1 | AAA | Developed |
| Djibouti | 25.4 | 4 | 22.9 | 4 | | |
| Dominica | 6.0 | 4 | 5.5 | 4 | | |
| Dominican Republic | 4.2 | 2 | 3.5 | 2 | BB- | |

* Tier 1: S&P sovereign credit rating = AAA; CRP assumed to be 0.0%; Tier 2: Observed Yield Spread, Tier 3: S&P Regression Yield Spread, Tier 4: Euromoney (ECR) Regression Yield Spread. For purposes of this analysis, the U.S. is being treated as if it were rated AAA by S&P.

§ S&P Credit Rating based on long-term foreign currency issuer rating. See http://www.standardandpoors.com/. Moody's or Fitch sovereign credit rating was used for countries where S&P sovereign credit rating was not available.

† MSCI Market Classification based on MSCI Market Classification Framework. See http://www.msci.com/products/indexes/market_classification.html

The country risk premium (CRP) is not the cost of equity capital (COE). The CRP is to be added to base COE. See Chapter 4 for proper application.

| Investee Country | Data Updated Through December 2016 | | Data Updated Through March 2017 | | | |
|---|---|---|---|---|---|---|
| | December 2016 Country Risk Premium (CRP) (%) | Tier Method* | March 2017 Country Risk Premium (CRP) (%) | Tier Method* | S&P Sovereign Credit Rating § | MSCI Market Classification † |
| Ecuador | 5.6 | 2 | 5.9 | 2 | B | |
| Egypt | 5.1 | 2 | 4.8 | 2 | B- | Emerging |
| El Salvador | 5.5 | 2 | 5.4 | 2 | B- | |
| Equatorial Guinea | 14.4 | 4 | 13.5 | 4 | | |
| Eritrea | 23.1 | 4 | 20.8 | 4 | | |
| Estonia | 0.6 | 3 | 0.6 | 3 | AA- | Frontier |
| Ethiopia | 5.6 | 2 | 5.1 | 2 | B | |
| Fiji | 5.3 | 2 | 4.7 | 2 | B+ | |
| Finland | 0.3 | 2 | 0.2 | 2 | AA+ | Developed |
| France | 0.5 | 3 | 0.5 | 3 | AA | Developed |
| Gabon | 5.5 | 2 | 5.0 | 2 | B+ | |
| Gambia | 7.9 | 4 | 7.2 | 4 | | |
| Georgia | 2.5 | 2 | 2.1 | 2 | BB- | |
| Germany | 0.0 | 1 | 0.0 | 1 | AAA | Developed |
| Ghana | 5.9 | 2 | 6.4 | 2 | B- | |
| Greece | 6.7 | 3 | 6.2 | 3 | B- | Emerging |
| Grenada | 5.2 | 4 | 4.8 | 4 | | |
| Guatemala | 2.7 | 2 | 2.2 | 2 | BB | |
| Guinea | 10.9 | 4 | 10.2 | 4 | | |
| Guinea-Bissau | 5.8 | 4 | 5.3 | 4 | | |
| Guyana | 5.0 | 4 | 4.5 | 4 | | |
| Haiti | 13.4 | 4 | 10.9 | 4 | | |
| Honduras | 3.7 | 2 | 3.7 | 2 | B+ | |
| Hong Kong | 0.0 | 1 | 0.0 | 1 | AAA | Developed |
| Hungary | 1.8 | 2 | 1.6 | 2 | BBB- | Emerging |
| Iceland | 1.1 | 2 | 0.7 | 2 | A | |
| India | 2.1 | 3 | 1.9 | 3 | BBB- | Emerging |
| Indonesia | 2.1 | 2 | 1.7 | 2 | BB+ | Emerging |
| Iran | 6.1 | 4 | 5.8 | 4 | | |
| Iraq | 6.7 | 3 | 6.2 | 3 | B+ | |
| Ireland | 0.8 | 3 | 0.7 | 3 | A+ | Developed |
| Israel | 1.4 | 2 | 1.3 | 2 | A+ | Developed |
| Italy | 2.1 | 2 | 2.1 | 2 | BBB- | Developed |
| Jamaica | 4.0 | 2 | 3.7 | 2 | B | |
| Japan | 0.8 | 3 | 0.7 | 3 | A+ | Developed |
| Jordan | 4.0 | 2 | 3.6 | 2 | BB- | Frontier |
| Kazakhstan | 2.4 | 2 | 2.2 | 2 | BBB- | Frontier |
| Kenya | 5.5 | 2 | 4.7 | 2 | B+ | Frontier |
| Korea (North) | 22.7 | 4 | 21.2 | 4 | | |
| Korea (South) | 0.2 | 2 | 0.2 | 2 | AA | Emerging |
| Kuwait | 0.5 | 3 | 1.0 | 2 | AA | Frontier |
| Kyrgyz Republic | 5.5 | 3 | 5.1 | 3 | B | |
| Laos | 12.3 | 4 | 11.1 | 4 | | |
| Latvia | 0.7 | 2 | 0.6 | 2 | A- | |
| Lebanon | 4.6 | 2 | 4.4 | 2 | B- | Frontier |
| Lesotho | 4.5 | 3 | 4.2 | 3 | B+ | |
| Liberia | 5.3 | 4 | 4.8 | 4 | | |
| Libya | 10.2 | 4 | 9.7 | 4 | | |
| Liechtenstein | 0.0 | 1 | 0.0 | 1 | AAA | |
| Lithuania | 1.1 | 2 | 0.8 | 2 | A- | Frontier |

* Tier 1: S&P sovereign credit rating = AAA, CRP assumed to be 0.0%; Tier 2: Observed Yield Spread, Tier 3: S&P Regression Yield Spread, Tier 4: Euromoney (ECR) Regression Yield Spread. For purposes of this analysis, the U.S. is being treated as if it were rated AAA by S&P.

§ S&P Credit Rating based on long-term foreign currency issuer rating. See http://www.standardandpoors.com/. Moody's or Fitch sovereign credit rating was used for countries where S&P sovereign credit rating was not available.

† MSCI Market Classification based on MSCI Market Classification Framework. See http://www.msci.com/products/indexes/market_classification.html

The country risk premium (CRP) is not the cost of equity capital (COE). The CRP is to be added to base COE. See Chapter 4 for proper application.

| Investee Country | Data Updated Through December 2016 | | Data Updated Through March 2017 | | | |
|---|---|---|---|---|---|---|
| | December 2016 Country Risk Premium (CRP) (%) | Tier Method* | March 2017 Country Risk Premium (CRP) (%) | Tier Method* | S&P Sovereign Credit Rating § | MSCI Market Classification † |
| Luxembourg | 0.0 | 1 | 0.0 | 1 | AAA | |
| Macau | 0.6 | 3 | 0.6 | 3 | AA- | |
| Macedonia | 3.7 | 3 | 3.4 | 3 | BB- | |
| Madagascar | 5.9 | 4 | 5.7 | 4 | | |
| Malawi | 5.7 | 4 | 5.2 | 4 | | |
| Malaysia | 1.2 | 2 | 1.0 | 2 | A- | Emerging |
| Maldives | 5.5 | 3 | 5.1 | 3 | B | |
| Mali | 8.5 | 4 | 7.9 | 4 | | |
| Malta | 1.2 | 3 | 1.0 | 3 | A- | |
| Marshall Islands | 23.2 | 4 | 22.0 | 4 | | |
| Mauritania | 12.0 | 4 | 11.2 | 4 | | |
| Mauritius | 1.4 | 3 | 1.3 | 3 | BBB+ | Frontier |
| Mexico | 2.3 | 2 | 2.0 | 2 | BBB+ | Emerging |
| Micronesia | 28.4 | 4 | 27.2 | 4 | | |
| Moldova | 6.7 | 3 | 6.2 | 3 | B- | |
| Mongolia | 6.0 | 2 | 4.8 | 2 | B- | |
| Montenegro | 4.5 | 3 | 4.2 | 3 | B+ | |
| Morocco | 2.2 | 2 | 2.0 | 2 | BBB- | Frontier |
| Mozambique | 20.6 | 2 | 16.6 | 3 | SD | |
| Myanmar | 7.4 | 4 | 6.8 | 4 | | |
| Namibia | 3.1 | 2 | 2.7 | 2 | BBB- | |
| Nepal | 9.6 | 4 | 8.9 | 4 | | |
| Netherlands | 0.0 | 1 | 0.0 | 1 | AAA | Developed |
| New Caledonia | 27.9 | 4 | 26.7 | 4 | | |
| New Zealand | 0.5 | 3 | 0.5 | 3 | AA | Developed |
| Nicaragua | 4.5 | 3 | 4.2 | 3 | B+ | |
| Niger | 6.2 | 4 | 5.7 | 4 | | |
| Nigeria | 4.7 | 2 | 4.9 | 2 | B | Frontier |
| Norway | 0.0 | 1 | 0.0 | 1 | AAA | Developed |
| Oman | 2.7 | 2 | 3.1 | 2 | BBB- | Frontier |
| Pakistan | 5.4 | 2 | 5.1 | 2 | B | Frontier |
| Panama | 2.6 | 2 | 2.5 | 2 | BBB | |
| Papua New Guinea | 4.5 | 3 | 4.2 | 3 | B+ | |
| Paraguay | 2.9 | 2 | 2.6 | 2 | BB | |
| Peru | 1.9 | 2 | 1.7 | 2 | BBB+ | Emerging |
| Philippines | 1.0 | 2 | 0.8 | 2 | BBB | Emerging |
| Poland | 1.5 | 2 | 1.2 | 2 | BBB+ | Emerging |
| Portugal | 3.1 | 2 | 3.4 | 2 | BB+ | Developed |
| Qatar | 1.5 | 2 | 1.4 | 2 | AA | Emerging |
| Romania | 1.9 | 2 | 1.6 | 2 | BBB- | Frontier |
| Russia | 2.1 | 2 | 1.9 | 2 | BB+ | Emerging |
| Rwanda | 4.5 | 2 | 4.3 | 2 | B | |
| Samoa | 13.6 | 4 | 12.8 | 4 | | |
| São Tomé & Príncipe | 12.1 | 4 | 11.7 | 4 | | |
| Saudi Arabia | 1.7 | 2 | 1.5 | 2 | A- | |
| Senegal | 3.9 | 2 | 3.8 | 2 | B+ | |
| Serbia | 2.5 | 2 | 1.9 | 2 | BB- | Frontier |
| Seychelles | 3.7 | 3 | 3.4 | 3 | BB- | |
| Sierra Leone | 6.8 | 4 | 6.2 | 4 | | |
| Singapore | 0.0 | 1 | 0.0 | 1 | AAA | Developed |

* Tier 1: S&P sovereign credit rating = AAA, CRP assumed to be 0.0%; Tier 2: Observed Yield Spread, Tier 3: S&P Regression Yield Spread, Tier 4: Euromoney (ECR) Regression Yield Spread. For purposes of this analysis, the U.S. is being treated as if it were rated AAA by S&P.

§ S&P Credit Rating based on long-term foreign currency issuer rating. See http://www.standardandpoors.com/. Moody's or Fitch sovereign credit rating was used for countries where S&P sovereign credit rating was not available.

† MSCI Market Classification based on MSCI Market Classification Framework. See http://www.msci.com/products/indexes/market_classification.html

The country risk premium (CRP) is not the cost of equity capital (COE). The CRP is to be added to base COE. See Chapter 4 for proper application.

| | Data Updated Through December 2016 | | Data Updated Through March 2017 | | | |
|---|---|---|---|---|---|---|
| Investee Country | December 2016 Country Risk Premium (CRP) (%) | Tier Method* | March 2017 Country Risk Premium (CRP) (%) | Tier Method* | S&P Sovereign Credit Rating § | MSCI Market Classification † |
| Slovakia | 0.6 | 2 | 0.5 | 2 | A+ | |
| Slovenia | 1.4 | 2 | 1.0 | 2 | A | Frontier |
| Solomon Islands | 6.7 | 3 | 6.2 | 3 | B- | |
| Somalia | 14.4 | 4 | 13.5 | 4 | | |
| South Africa | 2.4 | 2 | 2.4 | 2 | BBB- | Emerging |
| Spain | 2.2 | 2 | 2.2 | 2 | BBB+ | Developed |
| Sri Lanka | 4.6 | 2 | 4.0 | 2 | B+ | Frontier |
| St Lucia | 2.4 | 2 | 2.2 | 2 | | |
| St Vincent & Grenadines | 6.7 | 3 | 6.2 | 3 | B- | |
| Sudan | 10.9 | 4 | 10.1 | 4 | | |
| Suriname | 4.5 | 3 | 4.2 | 3 | B+ | |
| Swaziland | 9.5 | 4 | 9.5 | 4 | | |
| Sweden | 0.0 | 1 | 0.0 | 1 | AAA | Developed |
| Switzerland | 0.0 | 1 | 0.0 | 1 | AAA | Developed |
| Syria | 15.1 | 4 | 14.4 | 4 | | |
| Taiwan | 0.6 | 3 | 0.6 | 3 | AA- | Emerging |
| Tajikistan | 10.5 | 4 | 10.1 | 4 | | |
| Tanzania | 4.6 | 4 | 4.3 | 4 | | |
| Thailand | 1.4 | 3 | 1.3 | 3 | BBB+ | Emerging |
| Togo | 5.6 | 4 | 5.1 | 4 | | |
| Tonga | 17.9 | 4 | 17.0 | 4 | | |
| Trinidad & Tobago | 1.9 | 2 | 2.1 | 2 | A- | |
| Tunisia | 3.7 | 3 | 3.4 | 3 | BB- | Frontier |
| Turkey | 3.5 | 2 | 3.1 | 2 | BB | Emerging |
| Turkmenistan | 8.2 | 4 | 7.7 | 4 | | |
| Uganda | 5.5 | 3 | 5.1 | 3 | B | |
| Ukraine | 6.2 | 2 | 6.5 | 2 | B- | |
| United Arab Emirates | 0.9 | 2 | 0.7 | 2 | AA | Emerging |
| United Kingdom | 0.5 | 3 | 0.5 | 3 | AA | Developed |
| United States* | 0.0 | 1 | 0.0 | 1 | AA+ | Developed |
| Uruguay | 2.8 | 2 | 2.5 | 2 | BBB | |
| Uzbekistan | 7.5 | 4 | 6.5 | 4 | | |
| Vanuatu | 8.9 | 4 | 8.2 | 4 | | |
| Venezuela | 14.0 | 2 | 15.2 | 2 | CCC | |
| Vietnam | 2.6 | 2 | 2.3 | 2 | BB- | Frontier |
| Yemen | 12.4 | 4 | 11.6 | 4 | | |
| Zambia | 6.5 | 2 | 5.7 | 2 | B | |
| Zimbabwe | 13.8 | 4 | 12.9 | 4 | | |

## March 2017 Country Risk Premia (CRP) Summary Statistics:

| S&P Rating | Country Count | Average CRP (%) | Median CRP (%) | Min CRP (%) | Max CRP (%) |
|---|---|---|---|---|---|
| AAA* | 13 | 0.0 | 0.0 | 0.0 | 0.0 |
| AA (AA+, AA, AA-) | 16 | 0.6 | 0.6 | 0.2 | 1.4 |
| A (A+, A, A-) | 14 | 1.0 | 0.9 | 0.5 | 2.1 |
| BBB (BBB+, BBB, BBB-) | 20 | 2.0 | 2.0 | 0.8 | 3.1 |
| BB (BB+, BB, BB-) | 25 | 2.9 | 3.1 | 1.7 | 3.9 |
| B+ − SD | 49 | 5.6 | 5.1 | 3.7 | 16.6 |
| Investment Grade ‡ | 63 | 1.0 | 0.7 | 0.0 | 3.1 |
| Non-Investment Grade ‡ | 74 | 4.7 | 4.3 | 1.7 | 16.6 |
| **MSCI Market Classification** | | | | | |
| Developed Markets | 23 | 0.5 | 0.2 | 0.0 | 3.4 |
| Emerging Markets | 23 | 1.8 | 1.6 | 0.2 | 6.2 |
| Frontier Markets | 22 | 2.8 | 2.7 | 0.6 | 5.1 |

* Tier 1: S&P sovereign credit rating = AAA, CRP assumed to be 0.0%; Tier 2: Observed Yield Spread; Tier 3: S&P Regression Yield Spread; Tier 4: Euromoney (ECR) Regression Yield Spread. For purposes of this analysis, the U.S. is being treated as if it were rated AAA by S&P.

§ S&P Credit Rating based on long-term foreign currency issuer rating. See http://www.standardandpoors.com/. Moody's or Fitch sovereign credit rating was used for countries where S&P sovereign credit rating was not available.

† MSCI Market Classification based on MSCI Market Classification Framework. See http://www.msci.com/products/indexes/market_classification.html

‡ Investment grade based on S&P sovereign credit rating from AAA to BBB-. Non-Investment grade based on S&P sovereign credit rating from BB+ to SD.

The country risk premium (CRP) is not the cost of equity capital (COE). The CRP is to be added to base COE. See Chapter 4 for proper application.

| | Data Updated Through December 2016 | | Data Updated Through March 2017 | | | |
| --- | --- | --- | --- | --- | --- | --- |
| Investee Country | December 2016 Country Risk Premium (CRP) (%) | Tier Method* | March 2017 Country Risk Premium (CRP) (%) | Tier Method* | S&P Sovereign Credit Rating § | MSCI Market Classification † |
| Afghanistan | 12.2 | 4 | 13.0 | 4 | | |
| Albania | 3.6 | 2 | 3.2 | 2 | B+ | |
| Algeria | 5.8 | 4 | 6.0 | 4 | | |
| Angola | 6.2 | 3 | 6.1 | 3 | B | |
| Antigua & Barbuda | 8.9 | 4 | 9.7 | 4 | | |
| Argentina | 6.4 | 2 | 5.5 | 2 | B- | Frontier |
| Armenia | 4.9 | 3 | 4.8 | 3 | B+ | |
| Aruba | 1.3 | 3 | 1.2 | 3 | BBB+ | |
| Australia | 0.0 | 1 | 0.0 | 1 | AAA | Developed |
| Austria | 0.4 | 2 | 0.3 | 2 | AA+ | Developed |
| Azerbaijan | 2.5 | 3 | 2.4 | 3 | BB+ | |
| Bahamas | 2.5 | 3 | 2.4 | 3 | BB+ | |
| Bahrain | 4.0 | 3 | 3.8 | 3 | BB- | Frontier |
| Bangladesh | 4.0 | 3 | 3.8 | 3 | BB- | Frontier |
| Barbados | 7.7 | 3 | 9.7 | 3 | CCC+ | |
| Belarus | 7.7 | 3 | 7.7 | 3 | B- | |
| Belgium | 0.6 | 2 | 0.7 | 2 | AA | Developed |
| Belize | 18.6 | 3 | 7.7 | 3 | B- | |
| Benin | 14.2 | 4 | 15.8 | 4 | | |
| Bermuda | 0.7 | 3 | 0.6 | 3 | A+ | |
| Bhutan | 13.7 | 4 | 15.0 | 4 | | |
| Bolivia | 3.2 | 3 | 3.1 | 3 | BB | |
| Bosnia & Herzegovina | 6.2 | 3 | 6.1 | 3 | B | |
| Botswana | 1.1 | 3 | 1.0 | 3 | A- | |
| Brazil | 2.9 | 2 | 2.1 | 2 | BB | Emerging |
| Brunei | 1.8 | 4 | 1.8 | 4 | | |
| Bulgaria | 2.5 | 2 | 2.2 | 2 | BB+ | |
| Burkina Faso | 7.7 | 3 | 7.7 | 3 | B- | |
| Burundi | 28.6 | 4 | 33.7 | 4 | | |
| Cambodia | 6.2 | 3 | 6.1 | 3 | B | |
| Cameroon | 6.2 | 3 | 6.1 | 3 | B | |
| Canada | 0.0 | 1 | 0.0 | 1 | AAA | Developed |
| Cape Verde | 6.2 | 3 | 6.1 | 3 | B | |
| Central African Republic | 34.1 | 4 | 40.8 | 4 | | |
| Chad | 32.0 | 4 | 38.2 | 4 | | |
| Chile | 1.1 | 2 | 1.0 | 2 | AA- | Emerging |
| China | 0.5 | 3 | 0.5 | 3 | AA- | Emerging |
| Colombia | 1.6 | 3 | 1.5 | 3 | BBB | Emerging |
| Congo Republic | 7.7 | 3 | 7.7 | 3 | B- | |
| Congo, DR | 7.7 | 3 | 7.7 | 3 | B- | |
| Costa Rica | 4.0 | 3 | 3.8 | 3 | BB- | |
| Côte d'Ivoire | 4.0 | 3 | 3.8 | 3 | BB- | |
| Croatia | 2.9 | 2 | 2.8 | 2 | BB | Frontier |
| Cuba | 11.9 | 3 | 12.2 | 3 | CCC | |
| Cyprus | 3.4 | 2 | 3.1 | 2 | BB+ | |
| Czech Republic | 0.6 | 2 | 0.5 | 2 | AA- | Emerging |
| Denmark | 0.0 | 1 | 0.0 | 1 | AAA | Developed |
| Djibouti | 44.8 | 4 | 51.0 | 4 | | |
| Dominica | 8.0 | 4 | 8.6 | 4 | | |
| Dominican Republic | 4.0 | 3 | 3.8 | 3 | BB- | |

* Tier 1: S&P sovereign credit rating = AAA, CRP assumed to be 0.0%; Tier 2: Observed Yield Spread; Tier 3: S&P Regression Yield Spread; Tier 4: Euromoney (ECR) Regression Yield Spread. For purposes of this analysis, the U.S. is being treated as if it were rated AAA by S&P.

§ S&P Credit Rating based on long-term foreign currency issuer rating. See http://www.standardandpoors.com/. Moody's or Fitch sovereign credit rating was used for countries where S&P sovereign credit rating was not available.

† MSCI Market Classification based on MSCI Market Classification Framework. See http://www.msci.com/products/indexes/market_classification.html

The country risk premium (CRP) is not the cost of equity capital (COE).  The CRP is to be added to base COE. See Chapter 4 for proper application.

| Investee Country | Data Updated Through December 2016 | | Data Updated Through March 2017 | | | |
|---|---|---|---|---|---|---|
| | December 2016 Country Risk Premium (CRP) (%) | Tier Method* | March 2017 Country Risk Premium (CRP) (%) | Tier Method* | S&P Sovereign Credit Rating § | MSCI Market Classification † |
| Ecuador | 6.2 | 3 | 6.1 | 3 | B | |
| Egypt | 7.7 | 3 | 7.7 | 3 | B- | Emerging |
| El Salvador | 7.7 | 3 | 7.7 | 3 | B- | |
| Equatorial Guinea | 22.7 | 4 | 26.3 | 4 | | |
| Eritrea | 40.0 | 4 | 45.2 | 4 | | |
| Estonia | 0.5 | 3 | 0.5 | 3 | AA- | Frontier |
| Ethiopia | 6.2 | 3 | 6.1 | 3 | B | |
| Fiji | 4.9 | 3 | 4.8 | 3 | B+ | |
| Finland | 0.2 | 2 | 0.1 | 2 | AA+ | Developed |
| France | 0.7 | 2 | 0.9 | 2 | AA | Developed |
| Gabon | 4.9 | 3 | 4.8 | 3 | B+ | |
| Gambia | 11.0 | 4 | 12.1 | 4 | | |
| Georgia | 4.0 | 3 | 3.8 | 3 | BB- | |
| Germany | 0.0 | 1 | 0.0 | 1 | AAA | Developed |
| Ghana | 7.7 | 3 | 7.7 | 3 | B- | |
| Greece | 6.5 | 2 | 8.0 | 2 | B- | Emerging |
| Grenada | 6.7 | 4 | 7.2 | 4 | | |
| Guatemala | 3.2 | 3 | 3.1 | 3 | BB | |
| Guinea | 16.4 | 4 | 18.6 | 4 | | |
| Guinea-Bissau | 7.7 | 4 | 8.1 | 4 | | |
| Guyana | 6.4 | 4 | 6.7 | 4 | | |
| Haiti | 21.0 | 4 | 20.1 | 4 | | |
| Honduras | 4.9 | 3 | 4.8 | 3 | B+ | |
| Hong Kong | 0.0 | 1 | 0.0 | 1 | AAA | Developed |
| Hungary | 0.9 | 2 | 0.9 | 2 | BBB- | Emerging |
| Iceland | 1.3 | 2 | 0.9 | 2 | A | |
| India | 2.0 | 3 | 1.9 | 3 | BBB- | Emerging |
| Indonesia | 3.2 | 2 | 2.6 | 2 | BB+ | Emerging |
| Iran | 8.2 | 4 | 9.1 | 4 | | |
| Iraq | 7.7 | 3 | 7.7 | 3 | B- | |
| Ireland | 0.8 | 2 | 1.0 | 2 | A+ | Developed |
| Israel | 1.1 | 2 | 1.6 | 2 | A+ | Developed |
| Italy | 2.0 | 2 | 2.2 | 2 | BBB- | Developed |
| Jamaica | 6.2 | 3 | 6.1 | 3 | B | |
| Japan | 0.7 | 3 | 0.6 | 3 | A+ | Developed |
| Jordan | 4.0 | 3 | 3.8 | 3 | BB- | Frontier |
| Kazakhstan | 2.0 | 3 | 1.9 | 3 | BBB- | Frontier |
| Kenya | 4.9 | 3 | 4.8 | 3 | B+ | Frontier |
| Korea (North) | 39.1 | 4 | 46.5 | 4 | | |
| Korea (South) | 0.7 | 2 | 0.8 | 2 | AA | Emerging |
| Kuwait | 0.4 | 3 | 0.4 | 3 | AA | Frontier |
| Kyrgyz Republic | 6.2 | 3 | 6.1 | 3 | B | |
| Laos | 18.9 | 4 | 20.5 | 4 | | |
| Latvia | 0.8 | 2 | 1.1 | 2 | A- | |
| Lebanon | 4.4 | 2 | 3.3 | 2 | B- | Frontier |
| Lesotho | 4.9 | 3 | 4.8 | 3 | B+ | |
| Liberia | 6.9 | 4 | 7.2 | 4 | | |
| Libya | 15.0 | 4 | 17.5 | 4 | | |
| Liechtenstein | 0.0 | 1 | 0.0 | 1 | AAA | |
| Lithuania | 0.8 | 2 | 0.8 | 2 | A- | Frontier |

* Tier 1: S&P sovereign credit rating = AAA, CRP assumed to be 0.0%; Tier 2: Observed Yield Spread, Tier 3: S&P Regression Yield Spread, Tier 4: Euromoney (ECR) Regression Yield Spread. For purposes of this analysis, the U.S. is being treated as if it were rated AAA by S&P.

§ S&P Credit Rating based on long-term foreign currency issuer rating. See http://www.standardandpoors.com/. Moody's or Fitch sovereign credit rating was used for countries where S&P sovereign credit rating was not available.

† MSCI Market Classification based on MSCI Market Classification Framework.  See http://www.msci.com/products/indexes/market_classification.html

The country risk premium (CRP) is not the cost of equity capital (COE). The CRP is to be added to base COE. See Chapter 4 for proper application.

| Investee Country | Data Updated Through December 2016 | | Data Updated Through March 2017 | | | |
| --- | --- | --- | --- | --- | --- | --- |
| | December 2016 Country Risk Premium (CRP) (%) | Tier Method* | March 2017 Country Risk Premium (CRP) (%) | Tier Method* | S&P Sovereign Credit Rating § | MSCI Market Classification † |
| Luxembourg | 0.0 | 1 | 0.0 | 1 | AAA | |
| Macau | 0.5 | 3 | 0.5 | 3 | AA- | |
| Macedonia | 5.3 | 2 | 4.8 | 2 | BB- | |
| Madagascar | 7.8 | 4 | 9.0 | 4 | | |
| Malawi | 7.5 | 4 | 7.9 | 4 | | |
| Malaysia | 1.1 | 3 | 1.0 | 3 | A- | Emerging |
| Maldives | 6.2 | 3 | 6.1 | 3 | B | |
| Mali | 12.2 | 4 | 13.5 | 4 | | |
| Malta | 1.3 | 2 | 1.4 | 2 | A- | |
| Marshall Islands | 40.1 | 4 | 48.7 | 4 | | |
| Mauritania | 18.3 | 4 | 20.9 | 4 | | |
| Mauritius | 1.3 | 3 | 1.2 | 3 | BBB+ | Frontier |
| Mexico | 1.8 | 2 | 1.2 | 2 | BBB+ | Emerging |
| Micronesia | 51.1 | 4 | 63.2 | 4 | | |
| Moldova | 7.7 | 3 | 7.7 | 3 | B- | |
| Mongolia | 7.7 | 3 | 7.7 | 3 | B- | |
| Montenegro | 5.2 | 2 | 4.6 | 2 | B+ | |
| Morocco | 2.8 | 2 | 2.3 | 2 | BBB- | Frontier |
| Mozambique | 18.6 | 3 | 24.3 | 3 | SD | |
| Myanmar | 10.3 | 4 | 11.1 | 4 | | |
| Namibia | 2.0 | 3 | 1.9 | 3 | BBB- | |
| Nepal | 14.1 | 4 | 15.7 | 4 | | |
| Netherlands | 0.0 | 1 | 0.0 | 1 | AAA | Developed |
| New Caledonia | 50.1 | 4 | 61.8 | 4 | | |
| New Zealand | 0.4 | 3 | 0.4 | 3 | AA | Developed |
| Nicaragua | 4.9 | 3 | 4.8 | 3 | B+ | |
| Niger | 8.3 | 4 | 8.9 | 4 | | |
| Nigeria | 6.2 | 3 | 6.1 | 3 | B | Frontier |
| Norway | 0.0 | 1 | 0.0 | 1 | AAA | Developed |
| Oman | 2.0 | 3 | 1.9 | 3 | BBB- | Frontier |
| Pakistan | 6.2 | 3 | 6.1 | 3 | B | Frontier |
| Panama | 1.6 | 3 | 1.5 | 3 | BBB | |
| Papua New Guinea | 4.9 | 3 | 4.8 | 3 | B+ | |
| Paraguay | 3.2 | 3 | 3.1 | 3 | BB | |
| Peru | 2.2 | 2 | 1.9 | 2 | BBB+ | Emerging |
| Philippines | 1.6 | 3 | 1.5 | 3 | BBB | Emerging |
| Poland | 1.4 | 2 | 1.2 | 2 | BBB+ | Emerging |
| Portugal | 3.7 | 2 | 3.5 | 2 | BB+ | Developed |
| Qatar | 0.4 | 3 | 0.4 | 3 | AA | Emerging |
| Romania | 2.8 | 2 | 2.6 | 2 | BBB- | Frontier |
| Russia | 1.2 | 2 | 1.0 | 2 | BB+ | Emerging |
| Rwanda | 6.2 | 3 | 6.1 | 3 | B | |
| Samoa | 21.3 | 4 | 24.6 | 4 | | |
| São Tomé & Príncipe | 18.5 | 4 | 22.0 | 4 | | |
| Saudi Arabia | 1.1 | 3 | 1.0 | 3 | A- | |
| Senegal | 4.9 | 3 | 4.8 | 3 | B+ | |
| Serbia | 4.4 | 2 | 4.2 | 2 | BB- | Frontier |
| Seychelles | 4.0 | 3 | 3.8 | 3 | BB- | |
| Sierra Leone | 9.2 | 4 | 10.0 | 4 | | |
| Singapore | 0.0 | 1 | 0.0 | 1 | AAA | Developed |

* Tier 1: S&P sovereign credit rating = AAA, CRP assumed to be 0.0%; Tier 2: Observed Yield Spread; Tier 3: S&P Regression Yield Spread; Tier 4: Euromoney (ECR) Regression Yield Spread. For purposes of this analysis, the U.S. is being treated as if it were rated AAA by S&P.

§ S&P Credit Rating based on long-term foreign currency issuer rating. See http://www.standardandpoors.com/. Moody's or Fitch sovereign credit rating was used for countries where S&P sovereign credit rating was not available.

† MSCI Market Classification based on MSCI Market Classification Framework. See http://www.msci.com/products/indexes/market_classification.html

The country risk premium (CRP) is not the cost of equity capital (COE). The CRP is to be added to base COE. See Chapter 4 for proper application.

| Investee Country | Data Updated Through December 2016 | | Data Updated Through March 2017 | | | |
|---|---|---|---|---|---|---|
| | December 2016 Country Risk Premium (CRP) (%) | Tier Method* | March 2017 Country Risk Premium (CRP) (%) | Tier Method* | S&P Sovereign Credit Rating § | MSCI Market Classification † |
| Slovakia | 0.3 | 2 | 1.0 | 2 | A+ | |
| Slovenia | 1.0 | 2 | 1.3 | 2 | A | Frontier |
| Solomon Islands | 7.7 | 3 | 7.7 | 3 | B- | |
| Somalia | 22.8 | 4 | 26.4 | 4 | | |
| South Africa | 3.2 | 2 | 2.9 | 2 | BBB- | Emerging |
| Spain | 1.7 | 2 | 1.8 | 2 | BBB+ | Developed |
| Sri Lanka | 4.9 | 3 | 4.8 | 3 | B+ | Frontier |
| St Lucia | 6.0 | 4 | 6.5 | 4 | | |
| St Vincent & Grenadines | 7.7 | 3 | 7.7 | 3 | B- | |
| Sudan | 16.3 | 4 | 18.3 | 4 | | |
| Suriname | 4.9 | 3 | 4.8 | 3 | B+ | |
| Swaziland | 13.8 | 4 | 17.1 | 4 | | |
| Sweden | 0.0 | 1 | 0.0 | 1 | AAA | Developed |
| Switzerland | 0.0 | 1 | 0.0 | 1 | AAA | Developed |
| Syria | 24.0 | 4 | 28.5 | 4 | | |
| Taiwan | 0.5 | 3 | 0.5 | 3 | AA- | Emerging |
| Tajikistan | 15.7 | 4 | 18.3 | 4 | | |
| Tanzania | 5.8 | 4 | 6.2 | 4 | | |
| Thailand | 1.3 | 3 | 1.2 | 3 | BBB+ | Emerging |
| Togo | 7.4 | 4 | 7.9 | 4 | | |
| Tonga | 29.6 | 4 | 35.1 | 4 | | |
| Trinidad & Tobago | 1.1 | 3 | 1.0 | 3 | A- | |
| Tunisia | 4.0 | 3 | 3.8 | 3 | BB- | Frontier |
| Turkey | 3.8 | 2 | 3.3 | 2 | BB | Emerging |
| Turkmenistan | 11.6 | 4 | 13.2 | 4 | | |
| Uganda | 6.2 | 3 | 6.1 | 3 | B | |
| Ukraine | 7.7 | 3 | 7.7 | 3 | B- | |
| United Arab Emirates | 0.4 | 3 | 0.4 | 3 | AA | Emerging |
| United Kingdom | 0.4 | 3 | 0.4 | 3 | AA | Developed |
| United States* | 0.0 | 1 | 0.0 | 1 | AA+ | Developed |
| Uruguay | 1.8 | 2 | 1.7 | 2 | BBB | |
| Uzbekistan | 10.5 | 4 | 10.6 | 4 | | |
| Vanuatu | 12.7 | 4 | 14.1 | 4 | | |
| Venezuela | 11.9 | 3 | 12.2 | 3 | CCC | |
| Vietnam | 4.0 | 3 | 3.8 | 3 | BB- | Frontier |
| Yemen | 19.0 | 4 | 21.9 | 4 | | |
| Zambia | 6.2 | 3 | 6.1 | 3 | B | |
| Zimbabwe | 21.6 | 4 | 24.8 | 4 | | |

## March 2017 Country Risk Premia (CRP) Summary Statistics:

| S&P Rating | Country Count | Average CRP (%) | Median CRP (%) | Min CRP (%) | Max CRP (%) |
|---|---|---|---|---|---|
| AAA* | 13 | 0.0 | 0.0 | 0.0 | 0.0 |
| AA (AA+, AA, AA-) | 16 | 0.5 | 0.5 | 0.1 | 1.0 |
| A (A+, A, A-) | 14 | 1.0 | 1.0 | 0.6 | 1.6 |
| BBB (BBB+, BBB, BBB-) | 20 | 1.7 | 1.8 | 0.9 | 2.9 |
| BB (BB+, BB, BB-) | 25 | 3.3 | 3.5 | 1.0 | 4.8 |
| B+ − SD | 49 | 6.8 | 6.1 | 3.2 | 24.3 |
| Investment Grade ‡ | 63 | 0.9 | 0.9 | 0.0 | 2.9 |
| Non-Investment Grade ‡ | 74 | 5.6 | 4.8 | 1.0 | 24.3 |
| **MSCI Market Classification** | | | | | |
| Developed Markets | 23 | 0.6 | 0.1 | 0.0 | 3.5 |
| Emerging Markets | 23 | 1.9 | 1.2 | 0.4 | 8.0 |
| Frontier Markets | 22 | 3.2 | 3.6 | 0.4 | 6.1 |

* Tier 1: S&P sovereign credit rating = AAA, CRP assumed to be 0.0%; Tier 2: Observed Yield Spread; Tier 3: S&P Regression Yield Spread; Tier 4: Euromoney (ECR) Regression Yield Spread. For purposes of this analysis, the U.S. is being treated as if it were rated AAA by S&P.

§ S&P Credit Rating based on long-term foreign currency issuer rating. See http://www.standardandpoors.com/. Moody's or Fitch sovereign credit rating was used for countries where S&P sovereign credit rating was not available.

† MSCI Market Classification based on MSCI Market Classification Framework. See http://www.msci.com/products/indexes/market_classification.html

‡ Investment grade based on S&P sovereign credit rating from AAA to BBB-. Non-Investment grade based on S&P sovereign credit rating from BB+ to SD.

# Data Exhibit 3:
# Relative Volatility Model: Relative Volatility (RV) Factors

The relative volatility (RV) factor estimates in Data Exhibit 3 are derived using the Relative Volatility Model. These RVs can be used to estimate base country-level cost of equity capital estimates for 75 countries, from the perspective of:

- An investor based in the U.S.

- An investor based in Germany[D3.1]

In the Relative Volatility Model (originally developed for segmented capital markets), the traditional beta is replaced by a modified beta.[D3.2] The modified beta is a result of, multiplying the selected subject company beta by the ratio of the volatility of the foreign market to the volatility of the home market's benchmark market index. An alternative version, which we present herein (and which produces the same net result), is to adjust the home country's market equity risk premium by this relative volatility (RV) factor.

For examples of using the RVs presented in Data Exhibit 3 to estimate (i) base country-level cost of equity capital or (ii) cost of equity capital for use in evaluating a subject business, asset, or project, please refer to Chapter 5, "Relative Volatility Model".

---

[D3.1]  Note that an investor based in other countries within the Eurozone (e.g., Spain) investing in say, Brazil, could use the same RV information in Data Exhibit 3, provided that a German equity risk premium (ERP) is being used as an input when estimating the cost of equity for the subject company. This is because the analysis in Data Exhibit 3 is all being conducted in Euros, calculated against Germany's equity market volatility.

[D3.2]  Versions of this model have been published by MIT professor Donald Lessard (see Donald Lessard, "Incorporating Country Risk in the Valuation of Offshore Projects", *Journal of Applied Corporate Finance* (Fall 1996): 9(3), 52–63) as well as by analysts at Goldman Sachs and Bank of America, Stephen Godfrey and Ramon Espinosa, "A Practical Approach to Calculating Costs of Equity for Investments in Emerging Markets", *Journal of Applied Corporate Finance* (Fall 1996): 80–89.

The RV Factor is to be multiplied to the ERP. See Chapter 5 for proper application.

## Data Updated Through March 2017

| Investee Country | December 2016 Relative Volatility Factor (RV)* | March 2017 Relative Volatility Factor (RV)* | S&P Sovereign Credit Rating § | MSCI Market Classification † |
|---|---|---|---|---|
| Argentina | 4.3 | 4.7 | B- | Frontier |
| Australia | 1.0 | 1.0 | AAA | Developed |
| Austria | 2.0 | 2.0 | AA+ | Developed |
| Bahrain | 1.2 | 1.3 | BB- | Frontier |
| Bangladesh | 2.1 | 1.8 | BB- | Frontier |
| Belgium | 1.5 | 1.5 | AA | Developed |
| Botswana | 1.8 | 1.9 | A- | |
| Brazil | 2.8 | 2.8 | BB | Emerging |
| Bulgaria | 2.4 | 2.5 | BB+ | |
| Canada | 1.0 | 1.0 | AAA | Developed |
| Chile | 1.4 | 1.5 | AA- | Emerging |
| China | 1.8 | 1.8 | AA- | Emerging |
| Colombia | 2.2 | 2.1 | BBB | Emerging |
| Croatia | 1.3 | 1.4 | BB | Frontier |
| Czech Republic | 1.8 | 1.8 | AA- | Emerging |
| Denmark | 1.0 | 1.0 | AAA | Developed |
| Egypt | 3.2 | 2.8 | B- | Emerging |
| Estonia | 1.7 | 1.7 | AA- | Frontier |
| Finland | 1.7 | 1.7 | AA+ | Developed |
| France | 1.5 | 1.5 | AA | Developed |
| Germany | 1.0 | 1.0 | AAA | Developed |
| Ghana | 2.5 | 2.6 | B- | |
| Greece | 3.6 | 3.4 | B- | Emerging |
| Hong Kong | 1.0 | 1.0 | AAA | Developed |
| Hungary | 2.7 | 2.5 | BBB- | Emerging |
| India | 2.0 | 1.8 | BBB- | Emerging |
| Indonesia | 1.9 | 1.9 | BB+ | Emerging |
| Ireland | 1.8 | 1.8 | A+ | Developed |
| Israel | 1.4 | 1.4 | A+ | Developed |
| Italy | 2.1 | 2.1 | BBB- | Developed |
| Jamaica | 1.7 | 1.9 | B | |
| Japan | 1.3 | 1.3 | A+ | Developed |
| Jordan | 1.5 | 1.4 | BB- | Frontier |
| Kazakhstan | 2.3 | 2.3 | BBB- | Frontier |
| Kenya | 1.9 | 1.9 | B+ | Frontier |
| Korea (South) | 1.5 | 1.5 | AA | Emerging |
| Kuwait | 1.1 | 1.3 | AA | Frontier |
| Lebanon | 1.2 | 1.2 | B- | Frontier |
| Lithuania | 1.1 | 1.1 | A- | Frontier |
| Malaysia | 1.2 | 1.3 | A- | Emerging |
| Mauritius | 0.9 | 1.0 | BBB+ | Frontier |
| Mexico | 1.5 | 1.5 | BBB+ | Emerging |
| Morocco | 1.2 | 1.3 | BBB- | Frontier |
| Netherlands | 1.0 | 1.0 | AAA | Developed |
| New Zealand | 2.0 | 2.0 | AA | Developed |
| Nigeria | 2.4 | 2.5 | B | Frontier |
| Norway | 1.0 | 1.0 | AAA | Developed |
| Oman | 1.1 | 1.2 | BBB- | Frontier |
| Pakistan | 2.0 | 1.9 | B | Frontier |
| Peru | 1.9 | 1.9 | BBB+ | Emerging |

* S&P sovereign credit rating = AAA, RV assumed to be 1.0. For purposes of this analysis, the U.S. is being treated as if it were rated AAA by S&P.

§ S&P Credit Rating based on long-term foreign currency issuer rating. See http://www.standardandpoors.com/. Moody's or Fitch sovereign credit rating was used for countries where S&P sovereign credit rating was not available.

† MSCI Market Classification based on MSCI Market Classification Framework. See http://www.msci.com/products/indexes/market_classification.html

The RV Factor is to be multiplied to the ERP. See Chapter 5 for proper application.

## Data Updated Through March 2017

| Investee Country | December 2016 Relative Volatility Factor (RV)* | March 2017 Relative Volatility Factor (RV)* | S&P Sovereign Credit Rating § | MSCI Market Classification † |
|---|---|---|---|---|
| Philippines | 1.6 | 1.6 | BBB | Emerging |
| Poland | 2.0 | 2.0 | BBB+ | Emerging |
| Portugal | 1.9 | 2.0 | BB+ | Developed |
| Qatar | 1.8 | 1.8 | AA | Emerging |
| Romania | 2.1 | 2.1 | BBB- | Frontier |
| Russia | 2.5 | 2.4 | BB+ | Emerging |
| Saudi Arabia | 1.9 | 1.8 | A- | |
| Serbia | 2.1 | 2.1 | BB- | Frontier |
| Singapore | 1.0 | 1.0 | AAA | Developed |
| Slovenia | 1.9 | 2.0 | A | Frontier |
| South Africa | 1.9 | 1.8 | BBB- | Emerging |
| Spain | 2.2 | 2.3 | BBB+ | Developed |
| Sri Lanka | 1.8 | 1.9 | B+ | Frontier |
| Sweden | 1.0 | 1.0 | AAA | Developed |
| Switzerland | 1.0 | 1.0 | AAA | Developed |
| Taiwan | 1.3 | 1.2 | AA- | Emerging |
| Thailand | 1.7 | 1.6 | BBB+ | Emerging |
| Trinidad & Tobago | 0.9 | 0.9 | A- | |
| Tunisia | 1.0 | 1.1 | BB- | Frontier |
| Turkey | 2.6 | 2.4 | BB | Emerging |
| Ukraine | 2.6 | 3.0 | B- | |
| United Arab Emirates | 2.9 | 2.8 | AA | Emerging |
| United Kingdom | 1.2 | 1.2 | AA | Developed |
| United States | 1.0 | 1.0 | AA+ | Developed |
| Vietnam | 1.9 | 1.8 | BB- | Frontier |

## March 2017 Relative Volatility (RV) Factor Summary Statistics:

| S&P Rating | Country Count | Average RV | Median RV | Min RV / Max RV |
|---|---|---|---|---|
| AAA * | 11 | 1.0 | 1.0 | 1.0 / 1.0 |
| AA (AA+, AA, AA-) | 15 | 1.7 | 1.7 | 1.2 / 2.8 |
| A (A+, A, A-) | 9 | 1.5 | 1.4 | 0.9 / 2.0 |
| BBB (BBB+, BBB, BBB-) | 16 | 1.8 | 1.9 | 1.0 / 2.5 |
| BB (BB+, BB, BB-) | 13 | 1.9 | 1.9 | 1.1 / 2.8 |
| B+ – SD | 11 | 2.5 | 2.5 | 1.2 / 4.7 |
| Investment Grade ‡ | 51 | 1.5 | 1.5 | 0.9 / 2.8 |
| Non-Investment Grade ‡ | 24 | 2.2 | 2.0 | 1.1 / 4.7 |
| **MSCI Market Classification** | | | | |
| Developed Markets | 23 | 1.4 | 1.2 | 1.0 / 2.3 |
| Emerging Markets | 23 | 2.0 | 1.8 | 1.2 / 3.4 |
| Frontier Markets | 22 | 1.8 | 1.8 | 1.0 / 4.7 |

* S&P sovereign credit rating = AAA, RV assumed to be 1.0. For purposes of this analysis, the U.S. is being treated as if it were rated AAA by S&P.

§ S&P Credit Rating based on long-term foreign currency issuer rating. See http://www.standardandpoors.com/. Moody's or Fitch sovereign credit rating was used for countries where S&P sovereign credit rating was not available.

† MSCI Market Classification based on MSCI Market Classification Framework. See http://www.msci.com/products/indexes/market_classification.html

‡ Investment grade based on S&P sovereign credit rating from AAA to BBB-. Non-Investment grade based on S&P sovereign credit rating from BB+ to SD.

The RV Factor is to be multiplied to the ERP. See Chapter 5 for proper application.

## Data Updated Through March 2017

| Investee Country | December 2016 Relative Volatility Factor (RV)* | March 2017 Relative Volatility Factor (RV)* | S&P Sovereign Credit Rating § | MSCI Market Classification † |
|---|---|---|---|---|
| Argentina | 2.9 | 3.2 | B- | Frontier |
| Australia | 1.0 | 1.0 | AAA | Developed |
| Austria | 1.2 | 1.2 | AA+ | Developed |
| Bahrain | 0.8 | 0.9 | BB- | Frontier |
| Bangladesh | 1.6 | 1.5 | BB- | Frontier |
| Belgium | 1.0 | 1.0 | AA | Developed |
| Botswana | 1.2 | 1.3 | A- | |
| Brazil | 1.7 | 1.8 | BB | Emerging |
| Bulgaria | 1.5 | 1.6 | BB+ | |
| Canada | 1.0 | 1.0 | AAA | Developed |
| Chile | 0.9 | 0.9 | AA- | Emerging |
| China | 1.1 | 1.2 | AA- | Emerging |
| Colombia | 1.3 | 1.3 | BBB | Emerging |
| Croatia | 0.7 | 0.8 | BB | Frontier |
| Czech Republic | 1.1 | 1.1 | AA- | Emerging |
| Denmark | 1.0 | 1.0 | AAA | Developed |
| Egypt | 2.1 | 2.0 | B- | Emerging |
| Estonia | 1.0 | 1.0 | AA- | Frontier |
| Finland | 1.0 | 1.1 | AA+ | Developed |
| France | 0.9 | 0.9 | AA | Developed |
| Germany | 1.0 | 1.0 | AAA | Developed |
| Ghana | 1.8 | 1.9 | B- | |
| Greece | 2.3 | 2.2 | B- | Emerging |
| Hong Kong | 1.0 | 1.0 | AAA | Developed |
| Hungary | 1.6 | 1.6 | BBB- | Emerging |
| India | 1.3 | 1.2 | BBB- | Emerging |
| Indonesia | 1.4 | 1.4 | BB+ | Emerging |
| Ireland | 1.1 | 1.2 | A+ | Developed |
| Israel | 1.1 | 1.1 | A+ | Developed |
| Italy | 1.2 | 1.3 | BBB- | Developed |
| Jamaica | 1.3 | 1.5 | B | |
| Japan | 0.8 | 0.9 | A+ | Developed |
| Jordan | 1.1 | 1.1 | BB- | Frontier |
| Kazakhstan | 1.6 | 1.7 | BBB- | Frontier |
| Kenya | 1.3 | 1.4 | B+ | Frontier |
| Korea (South) | 1.0 | 1.0 | AA | Emerging |
| Kuwait | 0.8 | 0.9 | AA | Frontier |
| Lebanon | 0.9 | 1.0 | B- | Frontier |
| Lithuania | 0.6 | 0.6 | A- | Frontier |
| Malaysia | 0.8 | 0.9 | A- | Emerging |
| Mauritius | 0.7 | 0.7 | BBB+ | Frontier |
| Mexico | 0.9 | 1.0 | BBB+ | Emerging |
| Morocco | 0.8 | 0.9 | BBB- | Frontier |
| Netherlands | 1.0 | 1.0 | AAA | Developed |
| New Zealand | 1.2 | 1.2 | AA | Developed |
| Nigeria | 1.7 | 1.8 | B | Frontier |
| Norway | 1.0 | 1.0 | AAA | Developed |
| Oman | 0.9 | 0.9 | BBB- | Frontier |
| Pakistan | 1.4 | 1.4 | B | Frontier |
| Peru | 1.2 | 1.2 | BBB+ | Emerging |

* S&P sovereign credit rating = AAA, RV assumed to be 1.0. For purposes of this analysis, the U.S. is being treated as if it were rated AAA by S&P.

§ S&P Credit Rating based on long-term foreign currency issuer rating. See http://www.standardandpoors.com/. Moody's or Fitch sovereign credit rating was used for countries where S&P sovereign credit rating was not available.

† MSCI Market Classification based on MSCI Market Classification Framework. See http://www.msci.com/products/indexes/market_classification.html

Investor Perspective: Germany
Currency: Euro (EUR)

Relative Volatility Model:
Relative Volatility RV Factors

The RV Factor is to be multiplied to the ERP. See Chapter 5 for proper application.

## Data Updated Through March 2017

| Investee Country | December 2016 Relative Volatility Factor (RV)* | March 2017 Relative Volatility Factor (RV)* | S&P Sovereign Credit Rating § | MSCI Market Classification † |
|---|---|---|---|---|
| Philippines | 1.1 | 1.2 | BBB | Emerging |
| Poland | 1.1 | 1.2 | BBB+ | Emerging |
| Portugal | 1.0 | 1.1 | BB+ | Developed |
| Qatar | 1.2 | 1.3 | AA | Emerging |
| Romania | 1.2 | 1.2 | BBB- | Frontier |
| Russia | 1.6 | 1.5 | BB+ | Emerging |
| Saudi Arabia | 1.4 | 1.4 | A- | |
| Serbia | 1.2 | 1.2 | BB- | Frontier |
| Singapore | 1.0 | 1.0 | AAA | Developed |
| Slovenia | 1.0 | 1.1 | A | Frontier |
| South Africa | 1.1 | 1.2 | BBB- | Emerging |
| Spain | 1.2 | 1.4 | BBB+ | Developed |
| Sri Lanka | 1.3 | 1.4 | B+ | Frontier |
| Sweden | 1.0 | 1.0 | AAA | Developed |
| Switzerland | 1.0 | 1.0 | AAA | Developed |
| Taiwan | 0.8 | 0.9 | AA- | Emerging |
| Thailand | 1.1 | 1.1 | BBB+ | Emerging |
| Trinidad & Tobago | 0.8 | 0.9 | A- | |
| Tunisia | 0.7 | 0.7 | BB- | Frontier |
| Turkey | 1.6 | 1.6 | BB | Emerging |
| Ukraine | 1.8 | 2.1 | B- | |
| United Arab Emirates | 1.8 | 1.9 | AA | Emerging |
| United Kingdom | 0.7 | 0.7 | AA | Developed |
| United States | 1.0 | 1.0 | AA+ | Developed |
| Vietnam | 1.3 | 1.3 | BB- | Frontier |

## March 2017 Relative Volatility (RV) Factor Summary Statistics:

| S&P Rating | Country Count | Average RV | Median RV | Min RV / Max RV |
|---|---|---|---|---|
| AAA * | 11 | 1.0 | 1.0 | 1.0 / 1.0 |
| AA (AA+, AA, AA-) | 15 | 1.1 | 1.0 | 0.7 / 1.9 |
| A (A+, A, A-) | 9 | 1.0 | 1.1 | 0.6 / 1.4 |
| BBB (BBB+, BBB, BBB-) | 16 | 1.2 | 1.2 | 0.7 / 1.7 |
| BB (BB+, BB, BB-) | 13 | 1.3 | 1.3 | 0.7 / 1.8 |
| B+ − SD | 11 | 1.8 | 1.8 | 1.0 / 3.2 |
| Investment Grade ‡ | 51 | 1.1 | 1.0 | 0.6 / 1.9 |
| Non-Investment Grade ‡ | 24 | 1.5 | 1.5 | 0.7 / 3.2 |
| **MSCI Market Classification** | | | | |
| Developed Markets | 23 | 1.0 | 1.0 | 0.7 / 1.4 |
| Emerging Markets | 23 | 1.3 | 1.2 | 0.9 / 2.2 |
| Frontier Markets | 22 | 1.2 | 1.1 | 0.6 / 3.2 |

* S&P sovereign credit rating = AAA, RV assumed to be 1.0. For purposes of this analysis, the U.S. is being treated as if it were rated AAA by S&P.
§ S&P Credit Rating based on long-term foreign currency issuer rating. See http://www.standardandpoors.com/. Moody's or Fitch sovereign credit rating was used for countries where S&P sovereign credit rating was not available.
† MSCI Market Classification based on MSCI Market Classification Framework. See http://www.msci.com/products/indexes/market_classification.html
‡ Investment grade based on S&P sovereign credit rating from AAA to BBB-. Non-Investment grade based on S&P sovereign credit rating from BB+ to SD.

# Data Exhibit 4:
# Erb-Harvey-Viskanta Country Credit Rating Model: Country Risk Premia (CRPs)[D4.1]

The country risk premia (CRP) estimates in Data Exhibit 4 are derived using the Erb-Harvey-Viskanta Country Credit Rating Model. These CRPs can be used to estimate base country-level cost of equity capital estimates for 175 countries, from the perspective of investors based in a 56 countries:

- The U.S., and

- 55 additional countries[D4.2]

The Erb-Harvey-Viskanta Country Credit Rating Model ("CCR Model") is one the more widely known methods to estimate cost of equity capital in an international setting.[D4.3] This model is based on the assumption that countries with lower creditworthiness, which is translated into *lower* credit ratings, are associated with *higher* costs of equity capital, and vice versa.

For examples of using the CRPs presented in Data Exhibit 4 to estimate (i) base country-level cost of equity capital or (ii) cost of equity capital for use in evaluating a subject business, asset, or project, please refer to Chapter 6, "Erb-Harvey-Viskanta Country Credit Rating Model".

---

[D4.1] On each of the 4-page "investor perspective" exhibits (total 56 investor perspectives) in Data Exhibit 4, we present (i) the world ranking and (ii) the regional ranking. The world ranking is based on ascending order in which '1' equals the smallest country risk premium (CRP) and '175' equals the largest CRP. Regional rankings are based on ascending order in which '1' equals the smallest CRP for each region. A CRP of 0.0% is assumed in the following cases: (i) when the investor country (i.e., the "home" country where the investor is based) and the investee country (i.e., the "foreign" country where the investment is located) *both* have an S&P sovereign credit rating of AAA; or (ii) when the investor's "home" country has an S&P credit rating of AAA, and the "foreign" country has a sovereign credit rating below AAA (i.e., lower credit worthiness), but has a calculated CRP less than 0.0% (which would imply lower risk than a country rated AAA); or (iii) when the investor's "home" country has an S&P credit rating below AAA, and the "foreign" country has a sovereign credit rating of AAA (i.e., higher credit worthiness), but has a calculated CRP greater than 0.0% (which would imply greater risk than a country rated below AAA). The United States is treated as an AAA-rated country (see rationale in Chapter 4). These assumptions can cause various countries in the world and regional rankings to have the same rankings ("ties"). To break ranking ties, the raw country credit rating scores are used (rather than the CRP).

[D4.2] For a complete list of the 56 (total) investor "perspectives" presented in Data Exhibit 4, see Exhibit 6.3 in Chapter 6, "Erb-Harvey-Viskanta Country Credit Rating Model".

[D4.3] The analyses presented in Data Exhibit 4 is based upon the work of Claude Erb, Campbell Harvey, and Tadas Viskanta, "Expected Returns and Volatility in 135 Countries", *Journal of Portfolio Management* (Spring 1996): 46–58. See also Claude Erb, Campbell R. Harvey, and Tadas Viskanta. "Country Credit Risk and Global Portfolio Selection: Country credit ratings have substantial predictive Power", *Journal of Portfolio Management*, Winter 1995.

---

The country risk premium (CRP) is not the cost of equity capital (COE). The CRP is to be added to base COE. See Chapter 6 for proper application.

## Data Updated Through March 2017

| Investee Country | December 2016 Country Risk Premium (CRP) (%) | March 2017 Country Risk Premium (CRP) (%) | S&P Sovereign Credit Rating § | World Rank Out of 175* | MSCI Market Classification † | Euromoney Region ‡ | Regional Rank ‡ |
|---|---|---|---|---|---|---|---|
| Afghanistan | 3.6 | 3.5 | | 139 | | Asia | 23 out of 29 |
| Albania | -0.4 | -0.1 | B+ | 93 | | Central and Eastern Europe | 18 out of 25 |
| Algeria | -0.4 | -0.2 | | 91 | | Africa | 10 out of 51 |
| Angola | 1.3 | 1.5 | B | 121 | | Africa | 26 out of 51 |
| Argentina | 0.0 | 0.0 | B- | 96 | Frontier | Latin America | 13 out of 20 |
| Armenia | -2.2 | -1.8 | | 77 | | Asia | 15 out of 29 |
| Australia | -8.8 | -8.5 | AAA | 12 | Developed | Australasia | 2 out of 7 |
| Austria | -8.7 | -8.3 | AA+ | 13 | Developed | Western Europe | 9 out of 19 |
| Azerbaijan | -1.3 | -0.9 | BB+ | 85 | | Asia | 17 out of 29 |
| Bahamas | -3.3 | -3.2 | BB+ | 65 | | Caribbean | 3 out of 9 |
| Bahrain | -3.3 | -3.2 | BB- | 64 | Frontier | Middle East | 7 out of 13 |
| Bangladesh | 1.7 | 1.7 | BB- | 126 | Frontier | Asia | 20 out of 29 |
| Barbados | -2.1 | -1.1 | CCC+ | 82 | | Caribbean | 4 out of 9 |
| Belarus | 3.4 | 3.8 | B- | 143 | | Central and Eastern Europe | 23 out of 25 |
| Belgium | -7.7 | -7.5 | AA | 17 | Developed | Western Europe | 10 out of 19 |
| Belize | 0.3 | 0.6 | B- | 106 | | Latin America | 17 out of 20 |
| Benin | 4.6 | 4.7 | | 150 | | Africa | 37 out of 51 |
| Bermuda | -5.0 | -4.8 | A+ | 44 | | Caribbean | 1 out of 9 |
| Bhutan | 4.4 | 4.4 | | 148 | | Asia | 25 out of 29 |
| Bolivia | -0.8 | -0.4 | BB | 88 | | Latin America | 12 out of 20 |
| Bosnia & Herzegovina | 3.7 | 3.9 | B | 144 | | Central and Eastern Europe | 24 out of 25 |
| Botswana | -5.0 | -4.8 | A- | 48 | | Africa | 1 out of 51 |
| Brazil | -3.9 | -3.7 | BB | 59 | Emerging | Latin America | 7 out of 20 |
| Bulgaria | -4.0 | -3.6 | BB+ | 61 | | Central and Eastern Europe | 12 out of 25 |
| Burkina Faso | 2.5 | 2.6 | B- | 133 | | Africa | 33 out of 51 |
| Burundi | 11.3 | 11.2 | | 169 | | Africa | 47 out of 51 |
| Cambodia | 5.0 | 4.9 | | 151 | | Asia | 27 out of 29 |
| Cameroon | 1.5 | 1.6 | B | 124 | | Africa | 28 out of 51 |
| Canada | -9.0 | -8.7 | AAA | 9 | Developed | North America | 1 out of 2 |
| Cape Verde | -0.3 | -0.1 | B | 94 | | Africa | 12 out of 51 |
| Central African Republic | 13.9 | 13.8 | | 172 | | Africa | 49 out of 51 |
| Chad | 12.9 | 12.8 | | 171 | | Africa | 48 out of 51 |
| Chile | -8.1 | -7.6 | AA- | 16 | Emerging | Latin America | 1 out of 20 |
| China | -5.2 | -4.9 | AA- | 42 | Emerging | Asia | 7 out of 29 |
| Colombia | -5.2 | -4.9 | BBB | 41 | Emerging | Latin America | 4 out of 20 |
| Congo Republic | 1.2 | 1.2 | B- | 117 | | Africa | 24 out of 51 |
| Congo, DR | 2.1 | 2.2 | B- | 131 | | Africa | 32 out of 51 |
| Costa Rica | -3.0 | -2.6 | BB- | 71 | | Latin America | 8 out of 20 |
| Côte d'Ivoire | -0.4 | -0.2 | | 92 | | Africa | 11 out of 51 |
| Croatia | -3.6 | -3.5 | BB | 63 | Frontier | Central and Eastern Europe | 13 out of 25 |
| Cuba | 6.7 | 6.9 | | 160 | | Caribbean | 9 out of 9 |
| Cyprus | -5.4 | -5.0 | BB+ | 40 | | Central and Eastern Europe | 7 out of 25 |
| Czech Republic | -7.2 | -6.9 | AA- | 23 | Emerging | Central and Eastern Europe | 1 out of 25 |
| Denmark | -9.4 | -9.1 | AAA | 4 | Developed | Western Europe | 3 out of 19 |
| Djibouti | 19.8 | 17.9 | | 175 | | Africa | 51 out of 51 |
| Dominican Republic | -0.5 | -0.2 | BB- | 90 | | Caribbean | 5 out of 9 |
| Ecuador | 0.7 | 0.7 | B | 109 | | Latin America | 18 out of 20 |
| Egypt | 1.0 | 1.1 | B- | 116 | Emerging | Africa | 23 out of 51 |
| El Salvador | -1.2 | -1.1 | B- | 81 | | Latin America | 10 out of 20 |
| Equatorial Guinea | 8.6 | 8.6 | | 165 | | Africa | 45 out of 51 |

§ S&P Credit Rating based on long-term foreign currency issuer rating. See http://www.standardandpoors.com/.

* World rank based on 175 countries covered by Euromoney. Ranking based on ascending order in which '1' equals the smallest country risk premium (CRP) and '175' equals the largest country risk premium (CRP).

† MSCI Market Classification based on MSCI Market Classification Framework. See http://www.msci.com/products/indexes/market_classification.html

‡ Regional classification based on Euromoney. Regional rankings based on ascending order in which '1' equals the smallest country risk premium (CRP) for each region.

Note: A CRP of 0.0% is assumed in the following cases: (i) when the investor country and the investee country both have an S&P sovereign credit rating of AAA; or (ii) when the investor country has an S&P credit rating of AAA, and the investee country has a sovereign credit rating below AAA, but has a calculated CRP below 0.0% (which would imply lower risk than a country rated AAA); or (iii) when the investor country has an S&P credit rating below AAA, and the investee country has a sovereign credit rating of AAA, but has a calculated CRP above 0.0% (which would imply greater risk than a country rated below AAA). For purposes of this analysis, the U.S. is treated as having a sovereign credit rating equivalent to AAA.

The country risk premium (CRP) is not the cost of equity capital (COE). The CRP is to be added to base COE. See Chapter 6 for proper application.

## Data Updated Through March 2017

| Investee Country | December 2016 Country Risk Premium (CRP) (%) | March 2017 Country Risk Premium (CRP) (%) | S&P Sovereign Credit Rating § | World Rank Out of 175∗ | MSCI Market Classification † | Euromoney Region ‡ | Regional Rank ‡ |
|---|---|---|---|---|---|---|---|
| Eritrea | 16.9 | 15.5 | | 173 | | Africa | 50 out of 51 |
| Estonia | -6.7 | -6.2 | AA- | 32 | Frontier | Central and Eastern Europe | 4 out of 25 |
| Ethiopia | 0.1 | 0.4 | B | 101 | | Africa | 16 out of 51 |
| Fiji | 4.1 | 4.1 | B+ | 147 | | Australasia | 5 out of 7 |
| Finland | -8.9 | -8.5 | AA+ | 11 | Developed | Western Europe | 8 out of 19 |
| France | -7.1 | -6.9 | AA | 22 | Developed | Western Europe | 12 out of 19 |
| Gabon | -1.5 | -1.0 | | 83 | | Africa | 7 out of 51 |
| Gambia | 3.0 | 3.1 | | 138 | | Africa | 34 out of 51 |
| Georgia | -2.4 | -2.0 | BB- | 74 | | Central and Eastern Europe | 15 out of 25 |
| Germany | -8.9 | -8.6 | AAA | 10 | Developed | Western Europe | 7 out of 19 |
| Ghana | -0.2 | -0.3 | B- | 89 | | Africa | 9 out of 51 |
| Greece | 0.6 | 0.6 | B- | 108 | Emerging | Western Europe | 19 out of 19 |
| Grenada | 0.3 | 0.6 | | 105 | | Caribbean | 7 out of 9 |
| Guatemala | -1.2 | -1.0 | BB | 84 | | Latin America | 11 out of 20 |
| Guinea | 5.7 | 5.8 | | 156 | | Africa | 41 out of 51 |
| Guinea-Bissau | 1.0 | 1.1 | | 115 | | Africa | 22 out of 51 |
| Guyana | 0.1 | 0.3 | | 100 | | Latin America | 15 out of 20 |
| Haiti | 7.8 | 6.4 | | 157 | | Caribbean | 8 out of 9 |
| Honduras | -0.1 | 0.1 | B+ | 98 | | Latin America | 14 out of 20 |
| Hong Kong | -8.4 | -8.1 | AAA | 14 | Developed | Asia | 2 out of 29 |
| Hungary | -4.2 | -3.8 | BBB- | 57 | Emerging | Central and Eastern Europe | 10 out of 25 |
| Iceland | -6.4 | -6.3 | A | 30 | | Western Europe | 15 out of 19 |
| India | -4.4 | -3.9 | BBB- | 55 | Emerging | Asia | 10 out of 29 |
| Indonesia | -3.8 | -3.5 | BB+ | 62 | Emerging | Asia | 11 out of 29 |
| Iran | 1.3 | 1.7 | | 125 | | Middle East | 10 out of 13 |
| Iraq | 2.7 | 2.8 | B- | 136 | | Middle East | 11 out of 13 |
| Ireland | -6.8 | -6.5 | A+ | 27 | Developed | Western Europe | 14 out of 19 |
| Israel | -6.8 | -6.5 | A+ | 28 | Developed | Middle East | 2 out of 13 |
| Italy | -4.7 | -4.5 | BBB- | 50 | Developed | Western Europe | 18 out of 19 |
| Jamaica | -0.1 | 0.5 | B | 104 | | Caribbean | 6 out of 9 |
| Japan | -6.9 | -6.6 | A+ | 25 | Developed | Asia | 5 out of 29 |
| Jordan | -2.2 | -1.9 | BB- | 76 | Frontier | Middle East | 8 out of 13 |
| Kazakhstan | -2.6 | -2.6 | BBB- | 70 | Frontier | Asia | 13 out of 29 |
| Kenya | -0.1 | 0.2 | B+ | 99 | Frontier | Africa | 15 out of 51 |
| Korea (North) | 16.5 | 16.0 | | 174 | | Asia | 29 out of 29 |
| Korea (South) | -7.5 | -7.1 | AA | 19 | Emerging | Asia | 4 out of 29 |
| Kuwait | -6.7 | -6.3 | AA | 31 | Frontier | Middle East | 3 out of 13 |
| Kyrgyz Republic | 3.7 | 3.7 | | 142 | | Central and Eastern Europe | 22 out of 25 |
| Laos | 6.9 | 6.5 | | 158 | | Asia | 28 out of 29 |
| Latvia | -5.2 | -4.8 | A- | 43 | | Central and Eastern Europe | 8 out of 25 |
| Lebanon | 1.2 | 0.9 | B- | 112 | Frontier | Middle East | 9 out of 13 |
| Lesotho | 3.9 | 4.0 | | 146 | | Africa | 36 out of 51 |
| Liberia | 0.4 | 0.6 | | 107 | | Africa | 17 out of 51 |
| Libya | 5.0 | 5.4 | | 153 | | Africa | 39 out of 51 |
| Lithuania | -5.8 | -5.4 | A- | 36 | Frontier | Central and Eastern Europe | 6 out of 25 |
| Luxembourg | -9.2 | -8.9 | AAA | 5 | | Western Europe | 4 out of 19 |
| Macedonia | -0.8 | -0.4 | BB- | 87 | | Central and Eastern Europe | 17 out of 25 |
| Madagascar | 1.0 | 1.6 | | 123 | | Africa | 27 out of 51 |
| Malawi | 0.8 | 1.0 | | 114 | | Africa | 21 out of 51 |
| Malaysia | -5.6 | -5.4 | A- | 35 | Emerging | Asia | 6 out of 29 |

§ S&P Credit Rating based on long-term foreign currency issuer rating. See http://www.standardandpoors.com/.

∗ World rank based on 175 countries covered by Euromoney. Ranking based on ascending order in which '1' equals the smallest country risk premium (CRP) and '175' equals the largest country risk premium (CRP).

† MSCI Market Classification based on MSCI Market Classification Framework. See http://www.msci.com/products/indexes/market_classification.html

‡ Regional classification based on Euromoney. Regional rankings based on ascending order in which '1' equals the smallest country risk premium (CRP) for each region.

Note: A CRP of 0.0% is assumed in the following cases: (i) when the investor country and the investee country both have an S&P sovereign credit rating of AAA; or (ii) when the investor country has an S&P credit rating of AAA, and the investee country has a sovereign credit rating below AAA, but has a calculated CRP below 0.0% (which would imply lower risk than a country rated AAA); or (iii) when the investor country has an S&P credit rating below AAA, and the investee country has a sovereign credit rating of AAA, but has a calculated CRP above 0.0% (which would imply greater risk than a country rated below AAA). For purposes of this analysis, the U.S. is treated as having a sovereign credit rating equivalent to AAA.

The country risk premium (CRP) is not the cost of equity capital (COE). The CRP is to be added to base COE. See Chapter 6 for proper application.

### Data Updated Through March 2017

| Investee Country | December 2016 Country Risk Premium (CRP) (%) | March 2017 Country Risk Premium (CRP) (%) | S&P Sovereign Credit Rating § | World Rank Out of 175∗ | MSCI Market Classification † | Euromoney Region ‡ | Regional Rank ‡ |
|---|---|---|---|---|---|---|---|
| Mali | 3.6 | 3.7 | | 141 | | Africa | 35 out of 51 |
| Malta | -6.9 | -6.5 | A- | 26 | | Western Europe | 13 out of 19 |
| Mauritania | 6.6 | 6.7 | | 159 | | Africa | 42 out of 51 |
| Mauritius | -3.1 | -2.9 | | 67 | Frontier | Asia | 12 out of 29 |
| Mexico | -5.7 | -5.4 | BBB+ | 37 | Emerging | Latin America | 2 out of 20 |
| Moldova | 2.4 | 2.9 | | 137 | | Central and Eastern Europe | 21 out of 25 |
| Mongolia | 1.1 | 1.5 | B- | 119 | | Asia | 18 out of 29 |
| Montenegro | 0.5 | 0.5 | B+ | 103 | | Central and Eastern Europe | 19 out of 25 |
| Morocco | -3.1 | -2.7 | BBB- | 69 | Frontier | Africa | 4 out of 51 |
| Mozambique | 1.9 | 1.9 | SD | 128 | | Africa | 29 out of 51 |
| Myanmar | 2.6 | 2.6 | | 134 | | Asia | 22 out of 29 |
| Namibia | -3.4 | -3.0 | | 66 | | Africa | 3 out of 51 |
| Nepal | 4.6 | 4.7 | | 149 | | Asia | 26 out of 29 |
| Netherlands | -9.2 | -8.8 | AAA | 6 | Developed | Western Europe | 5 out of 19 |
| New Zealand | -9.1 | -8.7 | AA | 8 | Developed | Australasia | 1 out of 7 |
| Nicaragua | 1.7 | 1.8 | B+ | 127 | | Latin America | 19 out of 20 |
| Niger | 1.4 | 1.5 | | 120 | | Africa | 25 out of 51 |
| Nigeria | -0.1 | 0.1 | B | 97 | Frontier | Africa | 14 out of 51 |
| Norway | -9.7 | -9.3 | AAA | 3 | Developed | Western Europe | 2 out of 19 |
| Oman | -5.1 | -4.8 | BBB- | 46 | Frontier | Middle East | 5 out of 13 |
| Pakistan | 1.4 | 1.5 | B | 122 | Frontier | Asia | 19 out of 29 |
| Panama | -4.6 | -4.3 | BBB | 52 | | Latin America | 6 out of 20 |
| Papua New Guinea | 1.1 | 1.3 | B+ | 118 | | Australasia | 3 out of 7 |
| Paraguay | -1.9 | -1.6 | BB | 80 | | Latin America | 9 out of 20 |
| Peru | -5.5 | -5.1 | BBB+ | 39 | Emerging | Latin America | 3 out of 20 |
| Philippines | -4.3 | -4.1 | BBB | 53 | Emerging | Asia | 9 out of 29 |
| Poland | -6.5 | -6.3 | BBB+ | 29 | Emerging | Central and Eastern Europe | 3 out of 25 |
| Portugal | -4.8 | -4.6 | BB+ | 49 | Developed | Western Europe | 17 out of 19 |
| Qatar | -7.4 | -7.0 | AA | 21 | Emerging | Middle East | 1 out of 13 |
| Romania | -4.2 | -3.9 | BBB- | 56 | Frontier | Central and Eastern Europe | 9 out of 25 |
| Russia | -2.5 | -2.7 | BB+ | 68 | Emerging | Central and Eastern Europe | 14 out of 25 |
| Rwanda | 1.9 | 2.1 | B | 130 | | Africa | 31 out of 51 |
| São Tomé & Príncipe | 6.7 | 7.1 | | 163 | | Africa | 43 out of 51 |
| Saudi Arabia | -4.8 | -4.8 | A- | 47 | | Middle East | 6 out of 13 |
| Senegal | -0.6 | -0.4 | B+ | 86 | | Africa | 8 out of 51 |
| Serbia | -2.0 | -2.0 | BB- | 75 | Frontier | Central and Eastern Europe | 16 out of 25 |
| Seychelles | -2.4 | -2.2 | | 73 | | Africa | 5 out of 51 |
| Sierra Leone | 1.9 | 2.1 | | 129 | | Africa | 30 out of 51 |
| Singapore | -9.8 | -9.4 | AAA | 1 | Developed | Asia | 1 out of 29 |
| Slovakia | -7.1 | -6.7 | A+ | 24 | | Central and Eastern Europe | 2 out of 25 |
| Slovenia | -6.0 | -5.7 | A | 34 | Frontier | Central and Eastern Europe | 5 out of 25 |
| Solomon Islands | 9.9 | 9.9 | | 168 | | Australasia | 6 out of 7 |
| Somalia | 8.6 | 8.7 | | 166 | | Africa | 46 out of 51 |
| South Africa | -4.1 | -3.7 | BBB- | 60 | Emerging | Africa | 2 out of 51 |
| Spain | -5.4 | -5.1 | BBB+ | 38 | Developed | Western Europe | 16 out of 19 |
| Sri Lanka | -2.5 | -2.4 | B+ | 72 | Frontier | Asia | 14 out of 29 |
| Sudan | 5.7 | 5.7 | | 154 | | Africa | 40 out of 51 |
| Suriname | 0.1 | 0.4 | B+ | 102 | | Latin America | 16 out of 20 |
| Swaziland | 4.4 | 5.2 | | 152 | | Africa | 38 out of 51 |
| Sweden | -9.1 | -8.8 | AAA | 7 | Developed | Western Europe | 6 out of 19 |

§ S&P Credit Rating based on long-term foreign currency issuer rating. See http://www.standardandpoors.com/.

∗ World rank based on 175 countries covered by Euromoney. Ranking based on ascending order in which '1' equals the smallest country risk premium (CRP) and '175' equals the largest country risk premium (CRP).

† MSCI Market Classification based on MSCI Market Classification Framework. See http://www.msci.com/products/indexes/market_classification.html

‡ Regional classification based on Euromoney. Regional rankings based on ascending order in which '1' equals the smallest country risk premium (CRP) for each region.

Note: A CRP of 0.0% is assumed in the following cases: (i) when the investor country and the investee country both have an S&P sovereign credit rating of AAA; or (ii) when the investor country has an S&P credit rating of AAA, and the investee country has a sovereign credit rating below AAA, but has a calculated CRP below 0.0% (which would imply lower risk than a country rated AAA); or (iii) when the investor country has an S&P credit rating below AAA, and the investee country has a sovereign credit rating of AAA, but has a calculated CRP above 0.0% (which would imply greater risk than a country rated below AAA). For purposes of this analysis, the U.S. is treated as having a sovereign credit rating equivalent to AAA.

The country risk premium (CRP) is not the cost of equity capital (COE). The CRP is to be added to base COE. See Chapter 6 for proper application.

### Data Updated Through March 2017

| Investee Country | December 2016 Country Risk Premium (CRP) (%) | March 2017 Country Risk Premium (CRP) (%) | S&P Sovereign Credit Rating § | World Rank Out of 175* | MSCI Market Classification † | Euromoney Region ‡ | Regional Rank ‡ |
|---|---|---|---|---|---|---|---|
| Switzerland | -9.6 | -9.4 | AAA | 2 | Developed | Western Europe | 1 out of 19 |
| Syria | 9.2 | 9.4 | | 167 | | Middle East | 13 out of 13 |
| Taiwan | -7.7 | -7.3 | AA- | 18 | Emerging | Asia | 3 out of 29 |
| Tajikistan | 5.4 | 5.7 | | 155 | | Central and Eastern Europe | 25 out of 25 |
| Tanzania | -0.4 | 0.0 | | 95 | | Africa | 13 out of 51 |
| Thailand | -4.5 | -4.4 | BBB+ | 51 | Emerging | Asia | 8 out of 29 |
| Togo | 0.8 | 1.0 | | 113 | | Africa | 20 out of 51 |
| Tonga | 11.7 | 11.7 | | 170 | | Australasia | 7 out of 7 |
| Trinidad & Tobago | -4.3 | -4.0 | A- | 54 | | Caribbean | 2 out of 9 |
| Tunisia | -2.2 | -1.7 | | 79 | Frontier | Africa | 6 out of 51 |
| Turkey | -4.0 | -3.8 | BB | 58 | Emerging | Central and Eastern Europe | 11 out of 25 |
| Turkmenistan | 3.3 | 3.6 | | 140 | | Asia | 24 out of 29 |
| Uganda | 0.4 | 0.8 | B | 110 | | Africa | 18 out of 51 |
| Ukraine | 2.5 | 2.7 | B- | 135 | | Central and Eastern Europe | 20 out of 25 |
| United Arab Emirates | -6.3 | -6.0 | AA | 33 | Emerging | Middle East | 4 out of 13 |
| United Kingdom | -7.5 | -7.0 | AA | 20 | Developed | Western Europe | 11 out of 19 |
| United States | -8.2 | -7.9 | AA+ | 15 | Developed | North America | 2 out of 2 |
| Uruguay | -5.0 | -4.8 | BBB | 45 | | Latin America | 5 out of 20 |
| Uzbekistan | 2.7 | 2.4 | | 132 | | Asia | 21 out of 29 |
| Vanuatu | 3.9 | 4.0 | | 145 | | Australasia | 4 out of 7 |
| Venezuela | 6.7 | 7.1 | CCC | 162 | | Latin America | 20 out of 20 |
| Vietnam | -1.8 | -1.7 | BB- | 78 | Frontier | Asia | 16 out of 29 |
| Yemen | 6.9 | 7.0 | | 161 | | Middle East | 12 out of 13 |
| Zambia | 0.7 | 0.9 | B | 111 | | Africa | 19 out of 51 |
| Zimbabwe | 8.1 | 8.1 | | 164 | | Africa | 44 out of 51 |

### March 2017 Country Risk Premium (CRP) Summary Statistics:

| S&P Rating | Country Count | Average CRP (%) | Median CRP (%) | Min CRP (%) | Max CRP (%) |
|---|---|---|---|---|---|
| AAA ** | 12 | -8.8 | -8.8 | -9.4 | -7.9 |
| AA (AA+, AA, AA-) | 15 | -7.1 | -7.0 | -8.7 | -4.9 |
| A (A+, A, A-) | 14 | -5.6 | -5.6 | -6.7 | -4.0 |
| BBB (BBB+, BBB, BBB-) | 17 | -4.4 | -4.4 | -6.3 | -2.6 |
| BB (BB+, BB, BB-) | 22 | -2.3 | -2.3 | -5.0 | 1.7 |
| B+ – SD | 39 | 1.2 | 0.9 | -2.4 | 7.1 |
| Investment Grade ** | 58 | -6.3 | -6.3 | -9.4 | -2.6 |
| Non-Investment Grade ** | 61 | -0.1 | 0.1 | -5.0 | 7.1 |
| **MSCI Market Classification** | | | | | |
| Developed Markets | 23 | -7.7 | -8.3 | -9.4 | -4.5 |
| Emerging Markets | 23 | -4.6 | -4.9 | -7.6 | 1.1 |
| Frontier Markets | 22 | -2.4 | -2.5 | -6.3 | 1.7 |
| **Euromoney Region ‡** | | | | | |
| Africa | 51 | 3.0 | 1.5 | -4.8 | 17.9 |
| Asia | 29 | -0.8 | -1.8 | -9.4 | 16.0 |
| Australasia | 7 | 2.0 | 4.0 | -8.7 | 11.7 |
| Caribbean | 9 | 0.1 | -0.2 | -4.8 | 6.9 |
| Central and Eastern Europe | 25 | -2.0 | -3.5 | -6.9 | 5.7 |
| Latin America | 20 | -1.6 | -1.1 | -7.6 | 7.1 |
| Middle East | 13 | -1.4 | -3.2 | -7.0 | 9.4 |
| North America | 2 | -8.3 | -8.3 | -8.7 | -7.9 |
| Western Europe | 19 | -7.1 | -7.5 | -9.4 | 0.6 |

### CCR Base Cost of Equity Capital:

| Argentina | COE (%) |
|---|---|
| March 2017 | 29.0 |
| December 2016 | 29.4 |

CCR base country-level COE for an Argentina-based investor investing in Argentina.

§ S&P Credit Rating based on long-term foreign currency issuer rating. See http://www.standardandpoors.com/.

* World rank based on 175 countries covered by Euromoney. Ranking based on ascending order in which '1' equals the smallest country risk premium (CRP) and '175' equals the largest country risk premium (CRP).

† MSCI Market Classification based on MSCI Market Classification Framework. See http://www.msci.com/products/indexes/market_classification.html

‡ Regional classification based on Euromoney. Regional rankings based on ascending order in which '1' equals the smallest country risk premium (CRP) for each region.

** Investment grade based on S&P sovereign credit rating from AAA to BBB-. Non-Investment grade based on S&P sovereign credit rating from BB+ to SD. For purposes of this analysis, the U.S. is being treated as if it were rated AAA by S&P.

Note: A CRP of 0.0% is assumed in the following cases: (i) when the investor country and the investee country both have an S&P sovereign credit rating of AAA; or (ii) when the investor country has an S&P credit rating of AAA, and the investee country has a sovereign credit rating below AAA, but has a calculated CRP below 0.0% (which would imply lower risk than a country rated AAA); or (iii) when the investor country has an S&P credit rating below AAA, and the investee country has a sovereign credit rating of AAA, but has a calculated CRP above 0.0% (which would imply greater risk than a country rated below AAA). For purposes of this analysis, the U.S. is treated as having a sovereign credit rating equivalent to AAA.

The country risk premium (CRP) is not the cost of equity capital (COE). The CRP is to be added to base COE. See Chapter 6 for proper application.

## Data Updated Through March 2017

| Investee Country | December 2016 Country Risk Premium (CRP) (%) | March 2017 Country Risk Premium (CRP) (%) | S&P Sovereign Credit Rating § | World Rank Out of 175* | MSCI Market Classification † | Euromoney Region ‡ | Regional Rank ‡ |
|---|---|---|---|---|---|---|---|
| Afghanistan | 15.9 | 15.7 | | 139 | | Asia | 23 out of 29 |
| Albania | 10.7 | 10.9 | B+ | 93 | | Central and Eastern Europe | 18 out of 25 |
| Algeria | 10.8 | 10.9 | | 91 | | Africa | 10 out of 51 |
| Angola | 13.0 | 13.1 | B | 121 | | Africa | 26 out of 51 |
| Argentina | 11.3 | 11.1 | B- | 96 | Frontier | Latin America | 13 out of 20 |
| Armenia | 8.5 | 8.7 | | 77 | | Asia | 15 out of 29 |
| Australia | 0.0 | 0.0 | AAA | 12 | Developed | Australasia | 2 out of 7 |
| Austria | 0.2 | 0.2 | AA+ | 13 | Developed | Western Europe | 9 out of 19 |
| Azerbaijan | 9.6 | 10.0 | BB+ | 85 | | Asia | 17 out of 29 |
| Bahamas | 7.1 | 6.9 | BB+ | 65 | | Caribbean | 3 out of 9 |
| Bahrain | 7.0 | 6.9 | BB- | 64 | Frontier | Middle East | 7 out of 13 |
| Bangladesh | 13.5 | 13.3 | BB- | 126 | Frontier | Asia | 20 out of 29 |
| Barbados | 8.7 | 9.7 | CCC+ | 82 | | Caribbean | 4 out of 9 |
| Belarus | 15.6 | 16.0 | B- | 143 | | Central and Eastern Europe | 23 out of 25 |
| Belgium | 1.4 | 1.3 | AA | 17 | Developed | Western Europe | 10 out of 19 |
| Belize | 11.7 | 11.9 | B- | 106 | | Latin America | 17 out of 20 |
| Benin | 17.2 | 17.2 | | 150 | | Africa | 37 out of 51 |
| Bermuda | 4.8 | 4.8 | A+ | 44 | | Caribbean | 1 out of 9 |
| Bhutan | 16.9 | 16.8 | | 148 | | Asia | 25 out of 29 |
| Bolivia | 10.3 | 10.6 | BB | 88 | | Latin America | 12 out of 20 |
| Bosnia & Herzegovina | 16.0 | 16.2 | B | 144 | | Central and Eastern Europe | 24 out of 25 |
| Botswana | 4.8 | 4.9 | A- | 48 | | Africa | 1 out of 51 |
| Brazil | 6.3 | 6.2 | BB | 59 | Emerging | Latin America | 7 out of 20 |
| Bulgaria | 6.1 | 6.3 | BB+ | 61 | | Central and Eastern Europe | 12 out of 25 |
| Burkina Faso | 14.5 | 14.5 | B- | 133 | | Africa | 33 out of 51 |
| Burundi | 25.7 | 25.7 | | 169 | | Africa | 47 out of 51 |
| Cambodia | 17.7 | 17.4 | | 151 | | Asia | 27 out of 29 |
| Cameroon | 13.2 | 13.2 | B | 124 | | Africa | 28 out of 51 |
| Canada | 0.0 | 0.0 | AAA | 9 | Developed | North America | 1 out of 2 |
| Cape Verde | 11.0 | 11.0 | B | 94 | | Africa | 12 out of 51 |
| Central African Republic | 29.1 | 29.1 | | 172 | | Africa | 49 out of 51 |
| Chad | 27.8 | 27.8 | | 171 | | Africa | 48 out of 51 |
| Chile | 0.9 | 1.2 | AA- | 16 | Emerging | Latin America | 1 out of 20 |
| China | 4.6 | 4.7 | AA- | 42 | Emerging | Asia | 7 out of 29 |
| Colombia | 4.6 | 4.7 | BBB | 41 | Emerging | Latin America | 4 out of 20 |
| Congo Republic | 12.8 | 12.7 | B- | 117 | | Africa | 24 out of 51 |
| Congo, DR | 14.0 | 14.0 | B- | 131 | | Africa | 32 out of 51 |
| Costa Rica | 7.5 | 7.7 | BB- | 71 | | Latin America | 8 out of 20 |
| Côte d'Ivoire | 10.8 | 10.9 | | 92 | | Africa | 11 out of 51 |
| Croatia | 6.6 | 6.6 | BB | 63 | Frontier | Central and Eastern Europe | 13 out of 25 |
| Cuba | 19.9 | 20.0 | | 160 | | Caribbean | 9 out of 9 |
| Cyprus | 4.4 | 4.5 | BB+ | 40 | | Central and Eastern Europe | 7 out of 25 |
| Czech Republic | 2.1 | 2.2 | AA- | 23 | Emerging | Central and Eastern Europe | 1 out of 25 |
| Denmark | 0.0 | 0.0 | AAA | 4 | Developed | Western Europe | 3 out of 19 |
| Djibouti | 36.6 | 34.4 | | 175 | | Africa | 51 out of 51 |
| Dominican Republic | 10.7 | 10.8 | BB- | 90 | | Caribbean | 5 out of 9 |
| Ecuador | 12.2 | 12.0 | B | 109 | | Latin America | 18 out of 20 |
| Egypt | 12.6 | 12.6 | B- | 116 | Emerging | Africa | 23 out of 51 |
| El Salvador | 9.7 | 9.6 | B- | 81 | | Latin America | 10 out of 20 |
| Equatorial Guinea | 22.3 | 22.3 | | 165 | | Africa | 45 out of 51 |

§ S&P Credit Rating based on long-term foreign currency issuer rating. See http://www.standardandpoors.com/.

* World rank based on 175 countries covered by Euromoney. Ranking based on ascending order in which '1' equals the smallest country risk premium (CRP) and '175' equals the largest country risk premium (CRP).

† MSCI Market Classification based on MSCI Market Classification Framework. See http://www.msci.com/products/indexes/market_classification.html

‡ Regional classification based on Euromoney. Regional rankings based on ascending order in which '1' equals the smallest country risk premium (CRP) for each region.

Note: A CRP of 0.0% is assumed in the following cases: (i) when the investor country and the investee country both have an S&P sovereign credit rating of AAA; or (ii) when the investor country has an S&P credit rating of AAA, and the investee country has a sovereign credit rating below AAA, but has a calculated CRP below 0.0% (which would imply lower risk than a country rated AAA); or (iii) when the investor country has an S&P credit rating below AAA, and the investee country has a sovereign credit rating of AAA, but has a calculated CRP above 0.0% (which would imply greater risk than a country rated below AAA). For purposes of this analysis, the U.S. is treated as having a sovereign credit rating equivalent to AAA.

The country risk premium (CRP) is not the cost of equity capital (COE). The CRP is to be added to base COE. See Chapter 6 for proper application.

### Data Updated Through March 2017

| Investee Country | December 2016 Country Risk Premium (CRP) (%) | March 2017 Country Risk Premium (CRP) (%) | S&P Sovereign Credit Rating § | World Rank Out of 175∗ | MSCI Market Classification † | Euromoney Region ‡ | Regional Rank ‡ |
|---|---|---|---|---|---|---|---|
| Eritrea | 33.0 | 31.3 | | 173 | | Africa | 50 out of 51 |
| Estonia | 2.7 | 3.0 | AA- | 32 | Frontier | Central and Eastern Europe | 4 out of 25 |
| Ethiopia | 11.5 | 11.6 | B | 101 | | Africa | 16 out of 51 |
| Fiji | 16.6 | 16.5 | B+ | 147 | | Australasia | 5 out of 7 |
| Finland | 0.0 | 0.0 | AA+ | 11 | Developed | Western Europe | 8 out of 19 |
| France | 2.1 | 2.0 | AA | 22 | Developed | Western Europe | 12 out of 19 |
| Gabon | 9.4 | 9.7 | | 83 | | Africa | 7 out of 51 |
| Gambia | 15.1 | 15.2 | | 138 | | Africa | 34 out of 51 |
| Georgia | 8.2 | 8.5 | BB- | 74 | | Central and Eastern Europe | 15 out of 25 |
| Germany | 0.0 | 0.0 | AAA | 10 | Developed | Western Europe | 7 out of 19 |
| Ghana | 11.0 | 10.7 | B- | 89 | | Africa | 9 out of 51 |
| Greece | 12.1 | 11.9 | B- | 108 | Emerging | Western Europe | 19 out of 19 |
| Grenada | 11.7 | 11.8 | | 105 | | Caribbean | 7 out of 9 |
| Guatemala | 9.8 | 9.8 | BB | 84 | | Latin America | 11 out of 20 |
| Guinea | 18.6 | 18.6 | | 156 | | Africa | 41 out of 51 |
| Guinea-Bissau | 12.5 | 12.6 | | 115 | | Africa | 22 out of 51 |
| Guyana | 11.4 | 11.5 | | 100 | | Latin America | 15 out of 20 |
| Haiti | 21.3 | 19.4 | | 157 | | Caribbean | 8 out of 9 |
| Honduras | 11.1 | 11.2 | B+ | 98 | | Latin America | 14 out of 20 |
| Hong Kong | 0.0 | 0.0 | AAA | 14 | Developed | Asia | 2 out of 29 |
| Hungary | 5.9 | 6.1 | BBB- | 57 | Emerging | Central and Eastern Europe | 10 out of 25 |
| Iceland | 3.1 | 2.9 | A | 30 | | Western Europe | 15 out of 19 |
| India | 5.7 | 6.0 | BBB- | 55 | Emerging | Asia | 10 out of 29 |
| Indonesia | 6.4 | 6.5 | BB+ | 62 | Emerging | Asia | 11 out of 29 |
| Iran | 13.0 | 13.3 | | 125 | | Middle East | 10 out of 13 |
| Iraq | 14.7 | 14.8 | B- | 136 | | Middle East | 11 out of 13 |
| Ireland | 2.6 | 2.6 | A+ | 27 | Developed | Western Europe | 14 out of 19 |
| Israel | 2.6 | 2.6 | A+ | 28 | Developed | Middle East | 2 out of 13 |
| Italy | 5.3 | 5.2 | BBB- | 50 | Developed | Western Europe | 18 out of 19 |
| Jamaica | 11.2 | 11.8 | B | 104 | | Caribbean | 6 out of 9 |
| Japan | 2.5 | 2.5 | A+ | 25 | Developed | Asia | 5 out of 29 |
| Jordan | 8.4 | 8.7 | BB- | 76 | Frontier | Middle East | 8 out of 13 |
| Kazakhstan | 7.9 | 7.7 | BBB- | 70 | Frontier | Asia | 13 out of 29 |
| Kenya | 11.2 | 11.3 | B+ | 99 | Frontier | Africa | 15 out of 51 |
| Korea (North) | 32.4 | 31.9 | | 174 | | Asia | 29 out of 29 |
| Korea (South) | 1.7 | 1.8 | AA | 19 | Emerging | Asia | 4 out of 29 |
| Kuwait | 2.7 | 2.9 | AA | 31 | Frontier | Middle East | 3 out of 13 |
| Kyrgyz Republic | 16.1 | 16.0 | | 142 | | Central and Eastern Europe | 22 out of 25 |
| Laos | 20.1 | 19.6 | | 158 | | Asia | 28 out of 29 |
| Latvia | 4.7 | 4.8 | A- | 43 | | Central and Eastern Europe | 8 out of 25 |
| Lebanon | 12.9 | 12.3 | B- | 112 | Frontier | Middle East | 9 out of 13 |
| Lesotho | 16.3 | 16.3 | | 146 | | Africa | 36 out of 51 |
| Liberia | 11.8 | 11.9 | | 107 | | Africa | 17 out of 51 |
| Libya | 17.7 | 18.1 | | 153 | | Africa | 39 out of 51 |
| Lithuania | 3.9 | 4.0 | A- | 36 | Frontier | Central and Eastern Europe | 6 out of 25 |
| Luxembourg | 0.0 | 0.0 | AAA | 5 | | Western Europe | 4 out of 19 |
| Macedonia | 10.3 | 10.6 | BB- | 87 | | Central and Eastern Europe | 17 out of 25 |
| Madagascar | 12.6 | 13.2 | | 123 | | Africa | 27 out of 51 |
| Malawi | 12.4 | 12.4 | | 114 | | Africa | 21 out of 51 |
| Malaysia | 4.1 | 4.0 | A- | 35 | Emerging | Asia | 6 out of 29 |

§ S&P Credit Rating based on long-term foreign currency issuer rating. See http://www.standardandpoors.com/.

∗ World rank based on 175 countries covered by Euromoney. Ranking based on ascending order in which '1' equals the smallest country risk premium (CRP) and '175' equals the largest country risk premium (CRP).

† MSCI Market Classification based on MSCI Market Classification Framework. See http://www.msci.com/products/indexes/market_classification.html.

‡ Regional classification based on Euromoney. Regional rankings based on ascending order in which '1' equals the smallest country risk premium (CRP) for each region.

Note: A CRP of 0.0% is assumed in the following cases: (i) when the investor country and the investee country both have an S&P sovereign credit rating of AAA; or (ii) when the investor country has an S&P credit rating of AAA, and the investee country has a sovereign credit rating below AAA, but has a calculated CRP below 0.0% (which would imply lower risk than a country rated AAA); or (iii) when the investor country has an S&P credit rating below AAA, and the investee country has a sovereign credit rating of AAA, but has a calculated CRP above 0.0% (which would imply greater risk than a country rated below AAA). For purposes of this analysis, the U.S. is treated as having a sovereign credit rating equivalent to AAA.

The country risk premium (CRP) is not the cost of equity capital (COE). The CRP is to be added to base COE. See Chapter 6 for proper application.

### Data Updated Through March 2017

| Investee Country | December 2016 Country Risk Premium (CRP) (%) | March 2017 Country Risk Premium (CRP) (%) | S&P Sovereign Credit Rating § | World Rank Out of 175* | MSCI Market Classification † | Euromoney Region ‡ | Regional Rank ‡ |
|---|---|---|---|---|---|---|---|
| Mali | 15.9 | 16.0 | | 141 | | Africa | 35 out of 51 |
| Malta | 2.5 | 2.6 | A- | 26 | | Western Europe | 13 out of 19 |
| Mauritania | 19.8 | 19.8 | | 159 | | Africa | 42 out of 51 |
| Mauritius | 7.3 | 7.3 | | 67 | Frontier | Asia | 12 out of 29 |
| Mexico | 4.0 | 4.1 | BBB+ | 37 | Emerging | Latin America | 2 out of 20 |
| Moldova | 14.4 | 14.8 | | 137 | | Central and Eastern Europe | 21 out of 25 |
| Mongolia | 12.7 | 13.1 | B- | 119 | | Asia | 18 out of 29 |
| Montenegro | 11.9 | 11.8 | B+ | 103 | | Central and Eastern Europe | 19 out of 25 |
| Morocco | 7.3 | 7.6 | BBB- | 69 | Frontier | Africa | 4 out of 51 |
| Mozambique | 13.7 | 13.6 | SD | 128 | | Africa | 29 out of 51 |
| Myanmar | 14.6 | 14.5 | | 134 | | Asia | 22 out of 29 |
| Namibia | 7.0 | 7.2 | | 66 | | Africa | 3 out of 51 |
| Nepal | 17.2 | 17.2 | | 149 | | Asia | 26 out of 29 |
| Netherlands | 0.0 | 0.0 | AAA | 6 | Developed | Western Europe | 5 out of 19 |
| New Zealand | 0.0 | 0.0 | AA | 8 | Developed | Australasia | 1 out of 7 |
| Nicaragua | 13.4 | 13.5 | B+ | 127 | | Latin America | 19 out of 20 |
| Niger | 13.0 | 13.1 | | 120 | | Africa | 25 out of 51 |
| Nigeria | 11.2 | 11.2 | B | 97 | Frontier | Africa | 14 out of 51 |
| Norway | 0.0 | 0.0 | AAA | 3 | Developed | Western Europe | 2 out of 19 |
| Oman | 4.8 | 4.9 | BBB- | 46 | Frontier | Middle East | 5 out of 13 |
| Pakistan | 13.1 | 13.1 | B | 122 | Frontier | Asia | 19 out of 29 |
| Panama | 5.5 | 5.5 | BBB | 52 | | Latin America | 6 out of 20 |
| Papua New Guinea | 12.7 | 12.8 | B+ | 118 | | Australasia | 3 out of 7 |
| Paraguay | 8.8 | 9.0 | BB | 80 | | Latin America | 9 out of 20 |
| Peru | 4.2 | 4.4 | BBB+ | 39 | Emerging | Latin America | 3 out of 20 |
| Philippines | 5.8 | 5.8 | BBB | 53 | Emerging | Asia | 9 out of 29 |
| Poland | 2.9 | 2.8 | BBB+ | 29 | Emerging | Central and Eastern Europe | 3 out of 25 |
| Portugal | 5.2 | 5.1 | BB+ | 49 | Developed | Western Europe | 17 out of 19 |
| Qatar | 1.8 | 2.0 | AA | 21 | Emerging | Middle East | 1 out of 13 |
| Romania | 5.9 | 6.0 | BBB- | 56 | Frontier | Central and Eastern Europe | 9 out of 25 |
| Russia | 8.1 | 7.5 | BB+ | 68 | Emerging | Central and Eastern Europe | 14 out of 25 |
| Rwanda | 13.8 | 13.8 | B | 130 | | Africa | 31 out of 51 |
| São Tomé & Príncipe | 19.9 | 20.3 | | 163 | | Africa | 43 out of 51 |
| Saudi Arabia | 5.1 | 4.9 | A- | 47 | | Middle East | 6 out of 13 |
| Senegal | 10.5 | 10.5 | B+ | 86 | | Africa | 8 out of 51 |
| Serbia | 8.7 | 8.5 | BB- | 75 | Frontier | Central and Eastern Europe | 16 out of 25 |
| Seychelles | 8.2 | 8.3 | | 73 | | Africa | 5 out of 51 |
| Sierra Leone | 13.8 | 13.8 | | 129 | | Africa | 30 out of 51 |
| Singapore | 0.0 | 0.0 | AAA | 1 | Developed | Asia | 1 out of 29 |
| Slovakia | 2.2 | 2.3 | A+ | 24 | | Central and Eastern Europe | 2 out of 25 |
| Slovenia | 3.6 | 3.6 | A | 34 | Frontier | Central and Eastern Europe | 5 out of 25 |
| Solomon Islands | 24.0 | 24.0 | | 168 | | Australasia | 6 out of 7 |
| Somalia | 22.4 | 22.4 | | 166 | | Africa | 46 out of 51 |
| South Africa | 6.0 | 6.3 | BBB- | 60 | Emerging | Africa | 2 out of 51 |
| Spain | 4.3 | 4.4 | BBB+ | 38 | Developed | Western Europe | 16 out of 19 |
| Sri Lanka | 8.2 | 7.9 | B+ | 72 | Frontier | Asia | 14 out of 29 |
| Sudan | 18.6 | 18.5 | | 154 | | Africa | 40 out of 51 |
| Suriname | 11.4 | 11.6 | B+ | 102 | | Latin America | 16 out of 20 |
| Swaziland | 17.0 | 17.9 | | 152 | | Africa | 38 out of 51 |
| Sweden | 0.0 | 0.0 | AAA | 7 | Developed | Western Europe | 6 out of 19 |

§ S&P Credit Rating based on long-term foreign currency issuer rating. See http://www.standardandpoors.com/.
• World rank based on 175 countries covered by Euromoney. Ranking based on ascending order in which '1' equals the smallest country risk premium (CRP) and '175' equals the largest country risk premium (CRP).
† MSCI Market Classification based on MSCI Market Classification Framework. See http://www.msci.com/products/indexes/market_classification.html.
‡ Regional classification based on Euromoney. Regional rankings based on ascending order in which '1' equals the smallest country risk premium (CRP) for each region.
Note: A CRP of 0.0% is assumed in the following cases: (i) when the investor country and the investee country both have an S&P sovereign credit rating of AAA; or (ii) when the investor country has an S&P credit rating of AAA, and the investee country has a sovereign credit rating below AAA, but has a calculated CRP below 0.0% (which would imply lower risk than a country rated AAA); or (iii) when the investor country has an S&P credit rating below AAA, and the investee country has a sovereign credit rating of AAA, but has a calculated CRP above 0.0% (which would imply greater risk than a country rated below AAA). For purposes of this analysis, the U.S. is treated as having a sovereign credit rating equivalent to AAA.

The country risk premium (CRP) is not the cost of equity capital (COE). The CRP is to be added to base COE. See Chapter 6 for proper application.

## Data Updated Through March 2017

| Investee Country | December 2016 Country Risk Premium (CRP) (%) | March 2017 Country Risk Premium (CRP) (%) | S&P Sovereign Credit Rating § | World Rank Out of 175* | MSCI Market Classification † | Euromoney Region ‡ | Regional Rank ‡ |
|---|---|---|---|---|---|---|---|
| Switzerland | 0.0 | 0.0 | AAA | 2 | Developed | Western Europe | 1 out of 19 |
| Syria | 23.1 | 23.3 | | 167 | | Middle East | 13 out of 13 |
| Taiwan | 1.5 | 1.5 | AA- | 18 | Emerging | Asia | 3 out of 29 |
| Tajikistan | 18.2 | 18.5 | | 155 | | Central and Eastern Europe | 25 out of 25 |
| Tanzania | 10.8 | 11.1 | | 95 | | Africa | 13 out of 51 |
| Thailand | 5.5 | 5.4 | BBB+ | 51 | Emerging | Asia | 8 out of 29 |
| Togo | 12.3 | 12.4 | | 113 | | Africa | 20 out of 51 |
| Tonga | 26.3 | 26.4 | | 170 | | Australasia | 7 out of 7 |
| Trinidad & Tobago | 5.8 | 5.9 | A- | 54 | | Caribbean | 2 out of 9 |
| Tunisia | 8.5 | 8.9 | | 79 | Frontier | Africa | 6 out of 51 |
| Turkey | 6.1 | 6.1 | BB | 58 | Emerging | Central and Eastern Europe | 11 out of 25 |
| Turkmenistan | 15.5 | 15.8 | | 140 | | Asia | 24 out of 29 |
| Uganda | 11.8 | 12.2 | B | 110 | | Africa | 18 out of 51 |
| Ukraine | 14.6 | 14.7 | B- | 135 | | Central and Eastern Europe | 20 out of 25 |
| United Arab Emirates | 3.2 | 3.3 | AA | 33 | Emerging | Middle East | 4 out of 13 |
| United Kingdom | 1.7 | 1.9 | AA | 20 | Developed | Western Europe | 11 out of 19 |
| United States | 0.0 | 0.0 | AA+ | 15 | Developed | North America | 2 out of 2 |
| Uruguay | 4.9 | 4.8 | BBB | 45 | | Latin America | 5 out of 20 |
| Uzbekistan | 14.7 | 14.2 | | 132 | | Asia | 21 out of 29 |
| Vanuatu | 16.3 | 16.3 | | 145 | | Australasia | 4 out of 7 |
| Venezuela | 19.9 | 20.3 | CCC | 162 | | Latin America | 20 out of 20 |
| Vietnam | 9.0 | 8.8 | BB- | 78 | Frontier | Asia | 16 out of 29 |
| Yemen | 20.2 | 20.3 | | 161 | | Middle East | 12 out of 13 |
| Zambia | 12.2 | 12.3 | B | 111 | | Africa | 19 out of 51 |
| Zimbabwe | 21.7 | 21.7 | | 164 | | Africa | 44 out of 51 |

### March 2017 Country Risk Premium (CRP) Summary Statistics:

| S&P Rating | Country Count | Average CRP (%) | Median CRP (%) | Min CRP (%) | Max CRP (%) |
|---|---|---|---|---|---|
| AAA ** | 12 | 0.0 | 0.0 | 0.0 | 0.0 |
| AA (AA+, AA, AA-) | 15 | 1.9 | 1.9 | 0.0 | 4.7 |
| A (A+, A, A-) | 14 | 3.7 | 3.8 | 2.3 | 5.9 |
| BBB (BBB+, BBB, BBB-) | 17 | 5.4 | 5.4 | 2.8 | 7.7 |
| BB (BB+, BB, BB-) | 22 | 8.1 | 8.1 | 4.5 | 13.3 |
| B+ − SD | 39 | 12.6 | 12.3 | 7.9 | 20.3 |
| Investment Grade ** | 58 | 3.0 | 2.9 | 0.0 | 7.7 |
| Non-Investment Grade ** | 61 | 11.0 | 11.2 | 4.5 | 20.3 |
| **MSCI Market Classification** | | | | | |
| Developed Markets | 23 | 1.2 | 0.0 | 0.0 | 5.2 |
| Emerging Markets | 23 | 5.1 | 4.7 | 1.2 | 12.6 |
| Frontier Markets | 22 | 8.0 | 7.8 | 2.9 | 13.3 |
| **Euromoney Region ‡** | | | | | |
| Africa | 51 | 15.0 | 13.1 | 4.9 | 34.4 |
| Asia | 29 | 10.0 | 8.7 | 0.0 | 31.9 |
| Australasia | 7 | 13.7 | 16.3 | 0.0 | 26.4 |
| Caribbean | 9 | 11.2 | 10.8 | 4.8 | 20.0 |
| Central and Eastern Europe | 25 | 8.5 | 6.6 | 2.2 | 18.5 |
| Latin America | 20 | 9.0 | 9.7 | 1.2 | 20.3 |
| Middle East | 13 | 9.2 | 6.9 | 2.0 | 23.3 |
| North America | 2 | 0.0 | 0.0 | 0.0 | 0.0 |
| Western Europe | 19 | 2.1 | 1.3 | 0.0 | 11.9 |

### CCR Base Cost of Equity Capital:

| Australia | COE (%) |
|---|---|
| March 2017 | 6.7 |
| December 2016 | 6.9 |

CCR base country-level COE for an Australia-based investor investing in Australia.

§ S&P Credit Rating based on long-term foreign currency issuer rating. See http://www.standardandpoors.com/.

* World rank based on 175 countries covered by Euromoney. Ranking based on ascending order in which '1' equals the smallest country risk premium (CRP) and '175' equals the largest country risk premium (CRP).

† MSCI Market Classification based on MSCI Market Classification Framework. See http://www.msci.com/products/indexes/market_classification.html

‡ Regional classification based on Euromoney. Regional rankings based on ascending order in which '1' equals the smallest country risk premium (CRP) for each region.

** Investment grade based on S&P sovereign credit rating from AAA to BBB-. Non-Investment grade based on S&P sovereign credit rating from BB+ to SD. For purposes of this analysis, the U.S. is being treated as if it were rated AAA by S&P.

Note: A CRP of 0.0% is assumed in the following cases: (i) when the investor country and the investee country both have an S&P sovereign credit rating of AAA; or (ii) when the investor country has an S&P credit rating of AAA, and the investee country has a sovereign credit rating below AAA, but has a calculated CRP below 0.0% (which would imply lower risk than a country rated AAA); or (iii) when the investor country has an S&P credit rating below AAA, and the investee country has a sovereign credit rating of AAA, but has a calculated CRP above 0.0% (which would imply greater risk than a country rated below AAA). For purposes of this analysis, the U.S. is treated as having a sovereign credit rating equivalent to AAA.

The country risk premium (CRP) is not the cost of equity capital (COE). The CRP is to be added to base COE. See Chapter 6 for proper application.

## Data Updated Through March 2017

| Investee Country | December 2016 Country Risk Premium (CRP) (%) | March 2017 Country Risk Premium (CRP) (%) | S&P Sovereign Credit Rating § | World Rank Out of 175* | MSCI Market Classification † | Euromoney Region ‡ | Regional Rank ‡ |
|---|---|---|---|---|---|---|---|
| Afghanistan | 16.7 | 16.5 | | 139 | | Asia | 23 out of 29 |
| Albania | 11.3 | 11.5 | B+ | 93 | | Central and Eastern Europe | 18 out of 25 |
| Algeria | 11.3 | 11.4 | | 91 | | Africa | 10 out of 51 |
| Angola | 13.7 | 13.8 | B | 121 | | Africa | 26 out of 51 |
| Argentina | 11.9 | 11.6 | B- | 96 | Frontier | Latin America | 13 out of 20 |
| Armenia | 8.9 | 9.1 | | 77 | | Asia | 15 out of 29 |
| Australia | -0.2 | -0.2 | AAA | 12 | Developed | Australasia | 2 out of 7 |
| Austria | 0.0 | 0.0 | AA+ | 13 | Developed | Western Europe | 9 out of 19 |
| Azerbaijan | 10.1 | 10.4 | BB+ | 85 | | Asia | 17 out of 29 |
| Bahamas | 7.4 | 7.1 | BB+ | 65 | | Caribbean | 3 out of 9 |
| Bahrain | 7.3 | 7.1 | BB- | 64 | Frontier | Middle East | 7 out of 13 |
| Bangladesh | 14.2 | 14.0 | BB- | 126 | Frontier | Asia | 20 out of 29 |
| Barbados | 9.1 | 10.2 | CCC+ | 82 | | Caribbean | 4 out of 9 |
| Belarus | 16.4 | 16.9 | B- | 143 | | Central and Eastern Europe | 23 out of 25 |
| Belgium | 1.3 | 1.2 | AA | 17 | Developed | Western Europe | 10 out of 19 |
| Belize | 12.3 | 12.5 | B- | 106 | | Latin America | 17 out of 20 |
| Benin | 18.1 | 18.2 | | 150 | | Africa | 37 out of 51 |
| Bermuda | 5.0 | 4.9 | A+ | 44 | | Caribbean | 1 out of 9 |
| Bhutan | 17.8 | 17.7 | | 148 | | Asia | 25 out of 29 |
| Bolivia | 10.8 | 11.1 | BB | 88 | | Latin America | 12 out of 20 |
| Bosnia & Herzegovina | 16.9 | 17.1 | B | 144 | | Central and Eastern Europe | 24 out of 25 |
| Botswana | 5.0 | 5.0 | A- | 48 | | Africa | 1 out of 51 |
| Brazil | 6.5 | 6.4 | BB | 59 | Emerging | Latin America | 7 out of 20 |
| Bulgaria | 6.4 | 6.6 | BB+ | 61 | | Central and Eastern Europe | 12 out of 25 |
| Burkina Faso | 15.3 | 15.3 | B- | 133 | | Africa | 33 out of 51 |
| Burundi | 27.2 | 27.3 | | 169 | | Africa | 47 out of 51 |
| Cambodia | 18.7 | 18.4 | | 151 | | Asia | 27 out of 29 |
| Cameroon | 13.9 | 13.9 | B | 124 | | Africa | 28 out of 51 |
| Canada | -0.4 | -0.4 | AAA | 9 | Developed | North America | 1 out of 2 |
| Cape Verde | 11.5 | 11.5 | B | 94 | | Africa | 12 out of 51 |
| Central African Republic | 30.8 | 30.9 | | 172 | | Africa | 49 out of 51 |
| Chad | 29.4 | 29.5 | | 171 | | Africa | 48 out of 51 |
| Chile | 0.8 | 1.0 | AA- | 16 | Emerging | Latin America | 1 out of 20 |
| China | 4.8 | 4.8 | AA- | 42 | Emerging | Asia | 7 out of 29 |
| Colombia | 4.7 | 4.8 | BBB | 41 | Emerging | Latin America | 4 out of 20 |
| Congo Republic | 13.5 | 13.4 | B- | 117 | | Africa | 24 out of 51 |
| Congo, DR | 14.8 | 14.7 | B- | 131 | | Africa | 32 out of 51 |
| Costa Rica | 7.8 | 8.1 | BB- | 71 | | Latin America | 8 out of 20 |
| Côte d'Ivoire | 11.4 | 11.4 | | 92 | | Africa | 11 out of 51 |
| Croatia | 6.9 | 6.8 | BB | 63 | Frontier | Central and Eastern Europe | 13 out of 25 |
| Cuba | 21.1 | 21.2 | | 160 | | Caribbean | 9 out of 9 |
| Cyprus | 4.5 | 4.6 | BB+ | 40 | | Central and Eastern Europe | 7 out of 25 |
| Czech Republic | 2.1 | 2.1 | AA- | 23 | Emerging | Central and Eastern Europe | 1 out of 25 |
| Denmark | -1.0 | -1.0 | AAA | 4 | Developed | Western Europe | 3 out of 19 |
| Djibouti | 38.8 | 36.6 | | 175 | | Africa | 51 out of 51 |
| Dominican Republic | 11.2 | 11.3 | BB- | 90 | | Caribbean | 5 out of 9 |
| Ecuador | 12.8 | 12.7 | B | 109 | | Latin America | 18 out of 20 |
| Egypt | 13.2 | 13.2 | B- | 116 | Emerging | Africa | 23 out of 51 |
| El Salvador | 10.2 | 10.1 | B- | 81 | | Latin America | 10 out of 20 |
| Equatorial Guinea | 23.6 | 23.7 | | 165 | | Africa | 45 out of 51 |

The country risk premium (CRP) is not the cost of equity capital (COE).  The CRP is to be added to base COE. See Chapter 6 for proper application.

## Data Updated Through March 2017

| Investee Country | December 2016 Country Risk Premium (CRP) (%) | March 2017 Country Risk Premium (CRP) (%) | S&P Sovereign Credit Rating § | World Rank Out of 175* | MSCI Market Classification † | Euromoney Region ‡ | Regional Rank ‡ |
|---|---|---|---|---|---|---|---|
| Eritrea | 35.0 | 33.2 | | 173 | | Africa | 50 out of 51 |
| Estonia | 2.7 | 3.0 | AA- | 32 | Frontier | Central and Eastern Europe | 4 out of 25 |
| Ethiopia | 12.0 | 12.1 | B | 101 | | Africa | 16 out of 51 |
| Fiji | 17.5 | 17.4 | B+ | 147 | | Australasia | 5 out of 7 |
| Finland | -0.3 | -0.3 | AA+ | 11 | Developed | Western Europe | 8 out of 19 |
| France | 2.1 | 2.0 | AA | 22 | Developed | Western Europe | 12 out of 19 |
| Gabon | 9.8 | 10.2 | | 83 | | Africa | 7 out of 51 |
| Gambia | 15.9 | 16.0 | | 138 | | Africa | 34 out of 51 |
| Georgia | 8.6 | 8.8 | BB- | 74 | | Central and Eastern Europe | 15 out of 25 |
| Germany | -0.3 | -0.3 | AAA | 10 | Developed | Western Europe | 7 out of 19 |
| Ghana | 11.6 | 11.2 | B- | 89 | | Africa | 9 out of 51 |
| Greece | 12.7 | 12.5 | B- | 108 | Emerging | Western Europe | 19 out of 19 |
| Grenada | 12.3 | 12.4 | | 105 | | Caribbean | 7 out of 9 |
| Guatemala | 10.2 | 10.3 | BB | 84 | | Latin America | 11 out of 20 |
| Guinea | 19.7 | 19.7 | | 156 | | Africa | 41 out of 51 |
| Guinea-Bissau | 13.2 | 13.2 | | 115 | | Africa | 22 out of 51 |
| Guyana | 12.0 | 12.0 | | 100 | | Latin America | 15 out of 20 |
| Haiti | 22.5 | 20.5 | | 157 | | Caribbean | 8 out of 9 |
| Honduras | 11.7 | 11.8 | B+ | 98 | | Latin America | 14 out of 20 |
| Hong Kong | 0.0 | 0.0 | AAA | 14 | Developed | Asia | 2 out of 29 |
| Hungary | 6.1 | 6.3 | BBB- | 57 | Emerging | Central and Eastern Europe | 10 out of 25 |
| Iceland | 3.1 | 2.9 | A | 30 | | Western Europe | 15 out of 19 |
| India | 5.9 | 6.2 | BBB- | 55 | Emerging | Asia | 10 out of 29 |
| Indonesia | 6.7 | 6.7 | BB+ | 62 | Emerging | Asia | 11 out of 29 |
| Iran | 13.7 | 14.0 | | 125 | | Middle East | 10 out of 13 |
| Iraq | 15.5 | 15.6 | B- | 136 | | Middle East | 11 out of 13 |
| Ireland | 2.6 | 2.6 | A+ | 27 | Developed | Western Europe | 14 out of 19 |
| Israel | 2.6 | 2.6 | A+ | 28 | Developed | Middle East | 2 out of 13 |
| Italy | 5.5 | 5.4 | BBB- | 50 | Developed | Western Europe | 18 out of 19 |
| Jamaica | 11.7 | 12.4 | B | 104 | | Caribbean | 6 out of 9 |
| Japan | 2.4 | 2.5 | A+ | 25 | Developed | Asia | 5 out of 29 |
| Jordan | 8.8 | 9.0 | BB- | 76 | Frontier | Middle East | 8 out of 13 |
| Kazakhstan | 8.3 | 8.0 | BBB- | 70 | Frontier | Asia | 13 out of 29 |
| Kenya | 11.8 | 11.9 | B+ | 99 | Frontier | Africa | 15 out of 51 |
| Korea (North) | 34.3 | 33.9 | | 174 | | Asia | 29 out of 29 |
| Korea (South) | 1.7 | 1.7 | AA | 19 | Emerging | Asia | 4 out of 29 |
| Kuwait | 2.8 | 2.9 | AA | 31 | Frontier | Middle East | 3 out of 13 |
| Kyrgyz Republic | 17.0 | 16.9 | | 142 | | Central and Eastern Europe | 22 out of 25 |
| Laos | 21.3 | 20.8 | | 158 | | Asia | 28 out of 29 |
| Latvia | 4.8 | 4.9 | A- | 43 | | Central and Eastern Europe | 8 out of 25 |
| Lebanon | 13.5 | 12.9 | B- | 112 | Frontier | Middle East | 9 out of 13 |
| Lesotho | 17.2 | 17.3 | | 146 | | Africa | 36 out of 51 |
| Liberia | 12.4 | 12.5 | | 107 | | Africa | 17 out of 51 |
| Libya | 18.7 | 19.1 | | 153 | | Africa | 39 out of 51 |
| Lithuania | 4.0 | 4.1 | A- | 36 | Frontier | Central and Eastern Europe | 6 out of 25 |
| Luxembourg | -0.7 | -0.7 | AAA | 5 | | Western Europe | 4 out of 19 |
| Macedonia | 10.8 | 11.1 | BB- | 87 | | Central and Eastern Europe | 17 out of 25 |
| Madagascar | 13.3 | 13.9 | | 123 | | Africa | 27 out of 51 |
| Malawi | 13.0 | 13.1 | | 114 | | Africa | 21 out of 51 |
| Malaysia | 4.2 | 4.0 | A- | 35 | Emerging | Asia | 6 out of 29 |

§ S&P Credit Rating based on long-term foreign currency issuer rating. See http://www.standardandpoors.com/.

* World rank based on 175 countries covered by Euromoney. Ranking based on ascending order in which '1' equals the smallest country risk premium (CRP) and '175' equals the largest country risk premium (CRP).

† MSCI Market Classification based on MSCI Market Classification Framework.  See http://www.msci.com/products/indexes/market_classification.html.

‡ Regional classification based on Euromoney. Regional rankings based on ascending order in which '1' equals the smallest country risk premium (CRP) for each region.

Note: A CRP of 0.0% is assumed in the following cases: (i) when the investor country and the investee country both have an S&P sovereign credit rating of AAA; or (ii) when the investor country has an S&P credit rating of AAA, and the investee country has a sovereign credit rating below AAA, but has a calculated CRP below 0.0% (which would imply lower risk than a country rated AAA); or (iii) when the investor country has an S&P credit rating below AAA, and the investee country has a sovereign credit rating of AAA, but has a calculated CRP above 0.0% (which would imply greater risk than a country rated below AAA). For purposes of this analysis, the U.S. is treated as having a sovereign credit rating equivalent to AAA.

The country risk premium (CRP) is not the cost of equity capital (COE). The CRP is to be added to base COE. See Chapter 6 for proper application.

Data Updated Through March 2017

| Investee Country | December 2016 Country Risk Premium (CRP) (%) | March 2017 Country Risk Premium (CRP) (%) | S&P Sovereign Credit Rating § | World Rank Out of 175* | MSCI Market Classification † | Euromoney Region ‡ | Regional Rank ‡ |
|---|---|---|---|---|---|---|---|
| Mali | 16.8 | 16.9 | | 141 | | Africa | 35 out of 51 |
| Malta | 2.4 | 2.5 | A- | 26 | | Western Europe | 13 out of 19 |
| Mauritania | 20.9 | 20.9 | | 159 | | Africa | 42 out of 51 |
| Mauritius | 7.6 | 7.6 | | 67 | Frontier | Asia | 12 out of 29 |
| Mexico | 4.0 | 4.2 | BBB+ | 37 | Emerging | Latin America | 2 out of 20 |
| Moldova | 15.2 | 15.7 | | 137 | | Central and Eastern Europe | 21 out of 25 |
| Mongolia | 13.3 | 13.7 | B- | 119 | | Asia | 18 out of 29 |
| Montenegro | 12.5 | 12.4 | B+ | 103 | | Central and Eastern Europe | 19 out of 25 |
| Morocco | 7.6 | 7.9 | BBB- | 69 | Frontier | Africa | 4 out of 51 |
| Mozambique | 14.4 | 14.3 | SD | 128 | | Africa | 29 out of 51 |
| Myanmar | 15.4 | 15.3 | | 134 | | Asia | 22 out of 29 |
| Namibia | 7.3 | 7.5 | | 66 | | Africa | 3 out of 51 |
| Nepal | 18.1 | 18.2 | | 149 | | Asia | 26 out of 29 |
| Netherlands | -0.7 | -0.7 | AAA | 6 | Developed | Western Europe | 5 out of 19 |
| New Zealand | -0.5 | -0.5 | AA | 8 | Developed | Australasia | 1 out of 7 |
| Nicaragua | 14.1 | 14.2 | B+ | 127 | | Latin America | 19 out of 20 |
| Niger | 13.7 | 13.8 | | 120 | | Africa | 25 out of 51 |
| Nigeria | 11.7 | 11.7 | B | 97 | Frontier | Africa | 14 out of 51 |
| Norway | -1.3 | -1.4 | AAA | 3 | Developed | Western Europe | 2 out of 19 |
| Oman | 4.9 | 5.0 | BBB- | 46 | Frontier | Middle East | 5 out of 13 |
| Pakistan | 13.8 | 13.8 | B | 122 | Frontier | Asia | 19 out of 29 |
| Panama | 5.6 | 5.7 | BBB | 52 | | Latin America | 6 out of 20 |
| Papua New Guinea | 13.3 | 13.5 | B+ | 118 | | Australasia | 3 out of 7 |
| Paraguay | 9.2 | 9.4 | BB | 80 | | Latin America | 9 out of 20 |
| Peru | 4.3 | 4.5 | BBB+ | 39 | Emerging | Latin America | 3 out of 20 |
| Philippines | 6.0 | 6.0 | BBB | 53 | Emerging | Asia | 9 out of 29 |
| Poland | 2.9 | 2.8 | BBB+ | 29 | Emerging | Central and Eastern Europe | 3 out of 25 |
| Portugal | 5.4 | 5.2 | BB+ | 49 | Developed | Western Europe | 17 out of 19 |
| Qatar | 1.8 | 1.9 | AA | 21 | Emerging | Middle East | 1 out of 13 |
| Romania | 6.2 | 6.2 | BBB- | 56 | Frontier | Central and Eastern Europe | 9 out of 25 |
| Russia | 8.4 | 7.8 | BB+ | 68 | Emerging | Central and Eastern Europe | 14 out of 25 |
| Rwanda | 14.5 | 14.6 | B | 130 | | Africa | 31 out of 51 |
| São Tomé & Príncipe | 21.0 | 21.5 | | 163 | | Africa | 43 out of 51 |
| Saudi Arabia | 5.3 | 5.0 | A- | 47 | | Middle East | 6 out of 13 |
| Senegal | 11.0 | 11.1 | B+ | 86 | | Africa | 8 out of 51 |
| Serbia | 9.1 | 8.9 | BB- | 75 | Frontier | Central and Eastern Europe | 16 out of 25 |
| Seychelles | 8.6 | 8.6 | | 73 | | Africa | 5 out of 51 |
| Sierra Leone | 14.5 | 14.6 | | 129 | | Africa | 30 out of 51 |
| Singapore | -1.5 | -1.5 | AAA | 1 | Developed | Asia | 1 out of 29 |
| Slovakia | 2.2 | 2.3 | A+ | 24 | | Central and Eastern Europe | 2 out of 25 |
| Slovenia | 3.6 | 3.7 | A | 34 | Frontier | Central and Eastern Europe | 5 out of 25 |
| Solomon Islands | 25.4 | 25.5 | | 168 | | Australasia | 6 out of 7 |
| Somalia | 23.6 | 23.7 | | 166 | | Africa | 46 out of 51 |
| South Africa | 6.2 | 6.5 | BBB- | 60 | Emerging | Africa | 2 out of 51 |
| Spain | 4.4 | 4.5 | BBB+ | 38 | Developed | Western Europe | 16 out of 19 |
| Sri Lanka | 8.5 | 8.3 | B+ | 72 | Frontier | Asia | 14 out of 29 |
| Sudan | 19.6 | 19.6 | | 154 | | Africa | 40 out of 51 |
| Suriname | 12.0 | 12.2 | B+ | 102 | | Latin America | 16 out of 20 |
| Swaziland | 17.9 | 18.9 | | 152 | | Africa | 38 out of 51 |
| Sweden | -0.6 | -0.7 | AAA | 7 | Developed | Western Europe | 6 out of 19 |

§ S&P Credit Rating based on long-term foreign currency issuer rating. See http://www.standardandpoors.com/.

* World rank based on 175 countries covered by Euromoney. Ranking based on ascending order in which '1' equals the smallest country risk premium (CRP) and '175' equals the largest country risk premium (CRP).

† MSCI Market Classification based on MSCI Market Classification Framework. See http://www.msci.com/products/indexes/market_classification.html

‡ Regional classification based on Euromoney. Regional rankings based on ascending order in which '1' equals the smallest country risk premium (CRP) for each region.

Note: A CRP of 0.0% is assumed in the following cases: (i) when the investor country and the investee country both have an S&P sovereign credit rating of AAA; or (ii) when the investor country has an S&P credit rating of AAA, and the investee country has a sovereign credit rating below AAA, but has a calculated CRP below 0.0% (which would imply lower risk than a country rated AAA); or (iii) when the investor country has an S&P credit rating below AAA, and the investee country has a sovereign credit rating of AAA, but has a calculated CRP above 0.0% (which would imply greater risk than a country rated below AAA). For purposes of this analysis, the U.S. is treated as having a sovereign credit rating equivalent to AAA.

The country risk premium (CRP) is not the cost of equity capital (COE). The CRP is to be added to base COE. See Chapter 6 for proper application.

## Data Updated Through March 2017

| Investee Country | December 2016 Country Risk Premium (CRP) (%) | March 2017 Country Risk Premium (CRP) (%) | S&P Sovereign Credit Rating § | World Rank Out of 175* | MSCI Market Classification † | Euromoney Region ‡ | Regional Rank ‡ |
|---|---|---|---|---|---|---|---|
| Switzerland | -1.3 | -1.4 | AAA | 2 | Developed | Western Europe | 1 out of 19 |
| Syria | 24.4 | 24.7 | | 167 | | Middle East | 13 out of 13 |
| Taiwan | 1.4 | 1.4 | AA- | 18 | Emerging | Asia | 3 out of 29 |
| Tajikistan | 19.2 | 19.6 | | 155 | | Central and Eastern Europe | 25 out of 25 |
| Tanzania | 11.4 | 11.6 | | 95 | | Africa | 13 out of 51 |
| Thailand | 5.7 | 5.5 | BBB+ | 51 | Emerging | Asia | 8 out of 29 |
| Togo | 13.0 | 13.0 | | 113 | | Africa | 20 out of 51 |
| Tonga | 27.9 | 28.0 | | 170 | | Australasia | 7 out of 7 |
| Trinidad & Tobago | 6.0 | 6.0 | A- | 54 | | Caribbean | 2 out of 9 |
| Tunisia | 8.9 | 9.3 | | 79 | Frontier | Africa | 6 out of 51 |
| Turkey | 6.4 | 6.3 | BB | 58 | Emerging | Central and Eastern Europe | 11 out of 25 |
| Turkmenistan | 16.3 | 16.7 | | 140 | | Asia | 24 out of 29 |
| Uganda | 12.4 | 12.8 | B | 110 | | Africa | 18 out of 51 |
| Ukraine | 15.3 | 15.5 | B- | 135 | | Central and Eastern Europe | 20 out of 25 |
| United Arab Emirates | 3.2 | 3.3 | AA | 33 | Emerging | Middle East | 4 out of 13 |
| United Kingdom | 1.7 | 1.8 | AA | 20 | Developed | Western Europe | 11 out of 19 |
| United States | 0.0 | 0.0 | AA+ | 15 | Developed | North America | 2 out of 2 |
| Uruguay | 5.0 | 4.9 | BBB | 45 | | Latin America | 5 out of 20 |
| Uzbekistan | 15.5 | 15.0 | | 132 | | Asia | 21 out of 29 |
| Vanuatu | 17.2 | 17.2 | | 145 | | Australasia | 4 out of 7 |
| Venezuela | 21.0 | 21.5 | CCC | 162 | | Latin America | 20 out of 20 |
| Vietnam | 9.5 | 9.2 | BB- | 78 | Frontier | Asia | 16 out of 29 |
| Yemen | 21.3 | 21.5 | | 161 | | Middle East | 12 out of 13 |
| Zambia | 12.8 | 12.9 | B | 111 | | Africa | 19 out of 51 |
| Zimbabwe | 22.9 | 22.9 | | 164 | | Africa | 44 out of 51 |

## March 2017 Country Risk Premium (CRP) Summary Statistics:

| S&P Rating | Country Count | Average CRP (%) | Median CRP (%) | Min CRP (%) | Max CRP (%) |
|---|---|---|---|---|---|
| AAA ** | 12 | -0.7 | -0.7 | -1.5 | 0.0 |
| AA (AA+, AA, AA-) | 15 | 1.8 | 1.8 | -0.5 | 4.8 |
| A (A+, A, A-) | 14 | 3.8 | 3.9 | 2.3 | 6.0 |
| BBB (BBB+, BBB, BBB-) | 17 | 5.5 | 5.5 | 2.8 | 8.0 |
| BB (BB+, BB, BB-) | 22 | 8.5 | 8.5 | 4.6 | 14.0 |
| B+ − SD | 39 | 13.3 | 12.9 | 8.3 | 21.5 |
| Investment Grade ** | 58 | 2.9 | 2.9 | -1.5 | 8.0 |
| Non-Investment Grade ** | 61 | 11.6 | 11.8 | 4.6 | 21.5 |
| **MSCI Market Classification** | | | | | |
| Developed Markets | 23 | 0.8 | 0.0 | -1.5 | 5.4 |
| Emerging Markets | 23 | 5.2 | 4.8 | 1.0 | 13.2 |
| Frontier Markets | 22 | 8.3 | 8.1 | 2.9 | 14.0 |
| **Euromoney Region ‡** | | | | | |
| Africa | 51 | 15.8 | 13.8 | 5.0 | 36.6 |
| Asia | 29 | 10.5 | 9.1 | -1.5 | 33.9 |
| Australasia | 7 | 14.4 | 17.2 | -0.5 | 28.0 |
| Caribbean | 9 | 11.8 | 11.3 | 4.9 | 21.2 |
| Central and Eastern Europe | 25 | 8.9 | 6.8 | 2.1 | 19.6 |
| Latin America | 20 | 9.5 | 10.2 | 1.0 | 21.5 |
| Middle East | 13 | 9.7 | 7.1 | 1.9 | 24.7 |
| North America | 2 | -0.2 | -0.2 | -0.4 | 0.0 |
| Western Europe | 19 | 1.8 | 1.2 | -1.4 | 12.5 |

## CCR Base Cost of Equity Capital:

| Austria | COE (%) |
|---|---|
| March 2017 | 7.9 |
| December 2016 | 7.8 |

CCR base country-level COE for an Austria-based investor investing in Austria.

§ S&P Credit Rating based on long-term foreign currency issuer rating. See http://www.standardandpoors.com/.

* World rank based on 175 countries covered by Euromoney. Ranking based on ascending order in which '1' equals the smallest country risk premium (CRP) and '175' equals the largest country risk premium (CRP).

† MSCI Market Classification based on MSCI Market Classification Framework. See http://www.msci.com/products/indexes/market_classification.html

‡ Regional classification based on Euromoney. Regional rankings based on ascending order in which '1' equals the smallest country risk premium (CRP) for each region.

** Investment grade based on S&P sovereign credit rating from AAA to BBB-. Non-Investment grade based on S&P sovereign credit rating from BB+ to SD. For purposes of this analysis, the U.S. is being treated as if it were rated AAA by S&P.

Note: A CRP of 0.0% is assumed in the following cases: (i) when the investor country and the investee country both have an S&P sovereign credit rating of AAA; or (ii) when the investor country has an S&P credit rating of AAA, and the investee country has a sovereign credit rating below AAA, but has a calculated CRP below 0.0% (which would imply lower risk than a country rated AAA); or (iii) when the investor country has an S&P credit rating below AAA, and the investee country has a sovereign credit rating below AAA, but has a calculated CRP above 0.0% (which would imply greater risk than a country rated below AAA). For purposes of this analysis, the U.S. is treated as having a sovereign credit rating equivalent to AAA.

The country risk premium (CRP) is not the cost of equity capital (COE). The CRP is to be added to base COE. See Chapter 6 for proper application.

### Data Updated Through March 2017

| Investee Country | December 2016 Country Risk Premium (CRP) (%) | March 2017 Country Risk Premium (CRP) (%) | S&P Sovereign Credit Rating § | World Rank Out of 175* | MSCI Market Classification † | Euromoney Region ‡ | Regional Rank ‡ |
|---|---|---|---|---|---|---|---|
| Afghanistan | 8.7 | 8.9 | | 139 | | Asia | 23 out of 29 |
| Albania | 3.7 | 4.1 | B+ | 93 | | Central and Eastern Europe | 18 out of 25 |
| Algeria | 3.7 | 4.0 | | 91 | | Africa | 10 out of 51 |
| Angola | 5.9 | 6.3 | B | 121 | | Africa | 26 out of 51 |
| Argentina | 4.2 | 4.3 | B- | 96 | Frontier | Latin America | 13 out of 20 |
| Armenia | 1.4 | 1.8 | | 77 | | Asia | 15 out of 29 |
| Australia | -6.9 | -6.9 | AAA | 12 | Developed | Australasia | 2 out of 7 |
| Austria | -6.8 | -6.7 | AA+ | 13 | Developed | Western Europe | 9 out of 19 |
| Azerbaijan | 2.6 | 3.1 | BB+ | 85 | | Asia | 17 out of 29 |
| Bahamas | 0.1 | 0.0 | BB+ | 65 | | Caribbean | 3 out of 9 |
| Bahrain | 0.0 | 0.0 | BB- | 64 | Frontier | Middle East | 7 out of 13 |
| Bangladesh | 6.4 | 6.5 | BB- | 126 | Frontier | Asia | 20 out of 29 |
| Barbados | 1.6 | 2.8 | CCC+ | 82 | | Caribbean | 4 out of 9 |
| Belarus | 8.4 | 9.2 | B- | 143 | | Central and Eastern Europe | 23 out of 25 |
| Belgium | -5.6 | -5.6 | AA | 17 | Developed | Western Europe | 10 out of 19 |
| Belize | 4.6 | 5.0 | B- | 106 | | Latin America | 17 out of 20 |
| Benin | 10.0 | 10.4 | | 150 | | Africa | 37 out of 51 |
| Bermuda | -2.2 | -2.1 | A+ | 44 | | Caribbean | 1 out of 9 |
| Bhutan | 9.7 | 10.0 | | 148 | | Asia | 25 out of 29 |
| Bolivia | 3.3 | 3.8 | BB | 88 | | Latin America | 12 out of 20 |
| Bosnia & Herzegovina | 8.9 | 9.4 | B | 144 | | Central and Eastern Europe | 24 out of 25 |
| Botswana | -2.1 | -2.0 | A- | 48 | | Africa | 1 out of 51 |
| Brazil | -0.7 | -0.7 | BB | 59 | Emerging | Latin America | 7 out of 20 |
| Bulgaria | -0.9 | -0.5 | BB+ | 61 | | Central and Eastern Europe | 12 out of 25 |
| Burkina Faso | 7.3 | 7.7 | B- | 133 | | Africa | 33 out of 51 |
| Burundi | 18.4 | 19.0 | | 169 | | Africa | 47 out of 51 |
| Cambodia | 10.6 | 10.7 | | 151 | | Asia | 27 out of 29 |
| Cameroon | 6.1 | 6.4 | B | 124 | | Africa | 28 out of 51 |
| Canada | -7.1 | -7.1 | AAA | 9 | Developed | North America | 1 out of 2 |
| Cape Verde | 3.9 | 4.2 | B | 94 | | Africa | 12 out of 51 |
| Central African Republic | 21.7 | 22.4 | | 172 | | Africa | 49 out of 51 |
| Chad | 20.5 | 21.1 | | 171 | | Africa | 48 out of 51 |
| Chile | -6.0 | -5.8 | AA- | 16 | Emerging | Latin America | 1 out of 20 |
| China | -2.3 | -2.2 | AA- | 42 | Emerging | Asia | 7 out of 29 |
| Colombia | -2.4 | -2.2 | BBB | 41 | Emerging | Latin America | 4 out of 20 |
| Congo Republic | 5.7 | 5.9 | B- | 117 | | Africa | 24 out of 51 |
| Congo, DR | 6.9 | 7.2 | B- | 131 | | Africa | 32 out of 51 |
| Costa Rica | 0.5 | 0.9 | BB- | 71 | | Latin America | 8 out of 20 |
| Côte d'Ivoire | 3.7 | 4.0 | | 92 | | Africa | 11 out of 51 |
| Croatia | -0.4 | -0.3 | BB | 63 | Frontier | Central and Eastern Europe | 13 out of 25 |
| Cuba | 12.7 | 13.3 | | 160 | | Caribbean | 9 out of 9 |
| Cyprus | -2.6 | -2.4 | BB+ | 40 | | Central and Eastern Europe | 7 out of 25 |
| Czech Republic | -4.9 | -4.8 | AA- | 23 | Emerging | Central and Eastern Europe | 1 out of 25 |
| Denmark | -7.7 | -7.7 | AAA | 4 | Developed | Western Europe | 3 out of 19 |
| Djibouti | 29.2 | 27.8 | | 175 | | Africa | 51 out of 51 |
| Dominican Republic | 3.6 | 3.9 | BB- | 90 | | Caribbean | 5 out of 9 |
| Ecuador | 5.1 | 5.2 | B | 109 | | Latin America | 18 out of 20 |
| Egypt | 5.5 | 5.7 | B- | 116 | Emerging | Africa | 23 out of 51 |
| El Salvador | 2.7 | 2.7 | B- | 81 | | Latin America | 10 out of 20 |
| Equatorial Guinea | 15.1 | 15.6 | | 165 | | Africa | 45 out of 51 |

§ S&P Credit Rating based on long-term foreign currency issuer rating. See http://www.standardandpoors.com/.

* World rank based on 175 countries covered by Euromoney. Ranking based on ascending order in which '1' equals the smallest country risk premium (CRP) and '175' equals the largest country risk premium (CRP).

† MSCI Market Classification based on MSCI Market Classification Framework. See http://www.msci.com/products/indexes/market_classification.html

‡ Regional classification based on Euromoney. Regional rankings based on ascending order in which '1' equals the smallest country risk premium (CRP) for each region.

Note: A CRP of 0.0% is assumed in the following cases: (i) when the investor country and the investee country both have an S&P sovereign credit rating of AAA; or (ii) when the investor country has an S&P credit rating of AAA, and the investee country has a sovereign credit rating below AAA, but has a calculated CRP below 0.0% (which would imply lower risk than a country rated AAA); or (iii) when the investor country has an S&P credit rating below AAA, and the investee country has a sovereign credit rating of AAA, but has a calculated CRP above 0.0% (which would imply greater risk than a country rated below AAA). For purposes of this analysis, the U.S. is treated as having a sovereign credit rating equivalent to AAA.

The country risk premium (CRP) is not the cost of equity capital (COE). The CRP is to be added to base COE. See Chapter 6 for proper application.

## Data Updated Through March 2017

| Investee Country | December 2016 Country Risk Premium (CRP) (%) | March 2017 Country Risk Premium (CRP) (%) | S&P Sovereign Credit Rating § | World Rank Out of 175* | MSCI Market Classification † | Euromoney Region ‡ | Regional Rank ‡ |
|---|---|---|---|---|---|---|---|
| Eritrea | 25.6 | 24.6 | | 173 | | Africa | 50 out of 51 |
| Estonia | -4.3 | -3.9 | AA- | 32 | Frontier | Central and Eastern Europe | 4 out of 25 |
| Ethiopia | 4.4 | 4.7 | B | 101 | | Africa | 16 out of 51 |
| Fiji | 9.4 | 9.7 | B+ | 147 | | Australasia | 5 out of 7 |
| Finland | -7.0 | -7.0 | AA+ | 11 | Developed | Western Europe | 8 out of 19 |
| France | -4.8 | -4.9 | AA | 22 | Developed | Western Europe | 12 out of 19 |
| Gabon | 2.3 | 2.9 | | 83 | | Africa | 7 out of 51 |
| Gambia | 8.0 | 8.3 | | 138 | | Africa | 34 out of 51 |
| Georgia | 1.1 | 1.6 | BB- | 74 | | Central and Eastern Europe | 15 out of 25 |
| Germany | -7.0 | -7.0 | AAA | 10 | Developed | Western Europe | 7 out of 19 |
| Ghana | 3.9 | 3.9 | B- | 89 | | Africa | 9 out of 51 |
| Greece | 5.0 | 5.1 | B- | 108 | Emerging | Western Europe | 19 out of 19 |
| Grenada | 4.6 | 5.0 | | 105 | | Caribbean | 7 out of 9 |
| Guatemala | 2.7 | 3.0 | BB | 84 | | Latin America | 11 out of 20 |
| Guinea | 11.4 | 11.9 | | 156 | | Africa | 41 out of 51 |
| Guinea-Bissau | 5.4 | 5.7 | | 115 | | Africa | 22 out of 51 |
| Guyana | 4.3 | 4.6 | | 100 | | Latin America | 15 out of 20 |
| Haiti | 14.1 | 12.6 | | 157 | | Caribbean | 8 out of 9 |
| Honduras | 4.0 | 4.3 | B+ | 98 | | Latin America | 14 out of 20 |
| Hong Kong | -6.5 | -6.4 | AAA | 14 | Developed | Asia | 2 out of 29 |
| Hungary | -1.1 | -0.8 | BBB- | 57 | Emerging | Central and Eastern Europe | 10 out of 25 |
| Iceland | -3.9 | -4.0 | A | 30 | | Western Europe | 15 out of 19 |
| India | -1.3 | -0.9 | BBB- | 55 | Emerging | Asia | 10 out of 29 |
| Indonesia | -0.6 | -0.4 | BB+ | 62 | Emerging | Asia | 11 out of 29 |
| Iran | 5.9 | 6.4 | | 125 | | Middle East | 10 out of 13 |
| Iraq | 7.6 | 8.0 | B- | 136 | | Middle East | 11 out of 13 |
| Ireland | -4.4 | -4.3 | A+ | 27 | Developed | Western Europe | 14 out of 19 |
| Israel | -4.4 | -4.3 | A+ | 28 | Developed | Middle East | 2 out of 13 |
| Italy | -1.7 | -1.7 | BBB- | 50 | Developed | Western Europe | 18 out of 19 |
| Jamaica | 4.1 | 4.9 | B | 104 | | Caribbean | 6 out of 9 |
| Japan | -4.5 | -4.4 | A+ | 25 | Developed | Asia | 5 out of 29 |
| Jordan | 1.4 | 1.8 | BB- | 76 | Frontier | Middle East | 8 out of 13 |
| Kazakhstan | 0.9 | 0.8 | BBB- | 70 | Frontier | Asia | 13 out of 29 |
| Kenya | 4.1 | 4.5 | B+ | 99 | Frontier | Africa | 15 out of 51 |
| Korea (North) | 25.0 | 25.3 | | 174 | | Asia | 29 out of 29 |
| Korea (South) | -5.2 | -5.1 | AA | 19 | Emerging | Asia | 4 out of 29 |
| Kuwait | -4.2 | -4.0 | AA | 31 | Frontier | Middle East | 3 out of 13 |
| Kyrgyz Republic | 8.9 | 9.2 | | 142 | | Central and Eastern Europe | 22 out of 25 |
| Laos | 12.9 | 12.9 | | 158 | | Asia | 28 out of 29 |
| Latvia | -2.3 | -2.1 | A- | 43 | | Central and Eastern Europe | 8 out of 25 |
| Lebanon | 5.8 | 5.5 | B- | 112 | Frontier | Middle East | 9 out of 13 |
| Lesotho | 9.1 | 9.5 | | 146 | | Africa | 36 out of 51 |
| Liberia | 4.7 | 5.0 | | 107 | | Africa | 17 out of 51 |
| Libya | 10.6 | 11.3 | | 153 | | Africa | 39 out of 51 |
| Lithuania | -3.1 | -2.9 | A- | 36 | Frontier | Central and Eastern Europe | 6 out of 25 |
| Luxembourg | -7.4 | -7.4 | AAA | 5 | | Western Europe | 4 out of 19 |
| Macedonia | 3.3 | 3.7 | BB- | 87 | | Central and Eastern Europe | 17 out of 25 |
| Madagascar | 5.5 | 6.3 | | 123 | | Africa | 27 out of 51 |
| Malawi | 5.3 | 5.6 | | 114 | | Africa | 21 out of 51 |
| Malaysia | -2.9 | -2.9 | A- | 35 | Emerging | Asia | 6 out of 29 |

§ S&P Credit Rating based on long-term foreign currency issuer rating. See http://www.standardandpoors.com/.

* World rank based on 175 countries covered by Euromoney. Ranking based on ascending order in which '1' equals the smallest country risk premium (CRP) and '175' equals the largest country risk premium (CRP).

† MSCI Market Classification based on MSCI Market Classification Framework. See http://www.msci.com/products/indexes/market_classification.html

‡ Regional classification based on Euromoney. Regional rankings based on ascending order in which '1' equals the smallest country risk premium (CRP) for each region.

Note: A CRP of 0.0% is assumed in the following cases: (i) when the investor country and the investee country both have an S&P sovereign credit rating of AAA; or (ii) when the investor country has an S&P credit rating of AAA, and the investee country has a sovereign credit rating below AAA, but has a calculated CRP below 0.0% (which would imply lower risk than a country rated AAA); or (iii) when the investor country has an S&P credit rating below AAA, and the investee country has a sovereign credit rating of AAA, but has a calculated CRP above 0.0% (which would imply greater risk than a country rated below AAA). For purposes of this analysis, the U.S. is treated as having a sovereign credit rating equivalent to AAA.

The country risk premium (CRP) is not the cost of equity capital (COE). The CRP is to be added to base COE. See Chapter 6 for proper application.

## Data Updated Through March 2017

| Investee Country | December 2016 Country Risk Premium (CRP) (%) | March 2017 Country Risk Premium (CRP) (%) | S&P Sovereign Credit Rating § | World Rank Out of 175* | MSCI Market Classification † | Euromoney Region ‡ | Regional Rank ‡ |
|---|---|---|---|---|---|---|---|
| Mali | 8.8 | 9.2 | | 141 | | Africa | 35 out of 51 |
| Malta | -4.5 | -4.3 | A- | 26 | | Western Europe | 13 out of 19 |
| Mauritania | 12.6 | 13.0 | | 159 | | Africa | 42 out of 51 |
| Mauritius | 0.3 | 0.4 | | 67 | Frontier | Asia | 12 out of 29 |
| Mexico | -3.0 | -2.8 | BBB+ | 37 | Emerging | Latin America | 2 out of 20 |
| Moldova | 7.3 | 8.0 | | 137 | | Central and Eastern Europe | 21 out of 25 |
| Mongolia | 5.6 | 6.2 | B- | 119 | | Asia | 18 out of 29 |
| Montenegro | 4.8 | 4.9 | B+ | 103 | | Central and Eastern Europe | 19 out of 25 |
| Morocco | 0.3 | 0.7 | BBB- | 69 | Frontier | Africa | 4 out of 51 |
| Mozambique | 6.6 | 6.8 | SD | 128 | | Africa | 29 out of 51 |
| Myanmar | 7.5 | 7.7 | | 134 | | Asia | 22 out of 29 |
| Namibia | -0.1 | 0.3 | | 66 | | Africa | 3 out of 51 |
| Nepal | 10.0 | 10.4 | | 149 | | Asia | 26 out of 29 |
| Netherlands | -7.4 | -7.4 | AAA | 6 | Developed | Western Europe | 5 out of 19 |
| New Zealand | -7.2 | -7.2 | AA | 8 | Developed | Australasia | 1 out of 7 |
| Nicaragua | 6.3 | 6.6 | B+ | 127 | | Latin America | 19 out of 20 |
| Niger | 5.9 | 6.3 | | 120 | | Africa | 25 out of 51 |
| Nigeria | 4.1 | 4.3 | B | 97 | Frontier | Africa | 14 out of 51 |
| Norway | -8.0 | -8.0 | AAA | 3 | Developed | Western Europe | 2 out of 19 |
| Oman | -2.2 | -2.0 | BBB- | 46 | Frontier | Middle East | 5 out of 13 |
| Pakistan | 6.0 | 6.3 | B | 122 | Frontier | Asia | 19 out of 29 |
| Panama | -1.5 | -1.3 | BBB | 52 | | Latin America | 6 out of 20 |
| Papua New Guinea | 5.6 | 6.0 | B+ | 118 | | Australasia | 3 out of 7 |
| Paraguay | 1.8 | 2.2 | BB | 80 | | Latin America | 9 out of 20 |
| Peru | -2.8 | -2.5 | BBB+ | 39 | Emerging | Latin America | 3 out of 20 |
| Philippines | -1.2 | -1.1 | BBB | 53 | Emerging | Asia | 9 out of 29 |
| Poland | -4.1 | -4.1 | BBB+ | 29 | Emerging | Central and Eastern Europe | 3 out of 25 |
| Portugal | -1.8 | -1.8 | BB+ | 49 | Developed | Western Europe | 17 out of 19 |
| Qatar | -5.1 | -5.0 | AA | 21 | Emerging | Middle East | 1 out of 13 |
| Romania | -1.1 | -0.8 | BBB- | 56 | Frontier | Central and Eastern Europe | 9 out of 25 |
| Russia | 1.0 | 0.7 | BB+ | 68 | Emerging | Central and Eastern Europe | 14 out of 25 |
| Rwanda | 6.7 | 7.0 | B | 130 | | Africa | 31 out of 51 |
| São Tomé & Príncipe | 12.7 | 13.6 | | 163 | | Africa | 43 out of 51 |
| Saudi Arabia | -1.9 | -2.0 | A- | 47 | | Middle East | 6 out of 13 |
| Senegal | 3.4 | 3.7 | B+ | 86 | | Africa | 8 out of 51 |
| Serbia | 1.7 | 1.6 | BB- | 75 | Frontier | Central and Eastern Europe | 16 out of 25 |
| Seychelles | 1.2 | 1.4 | | 73 | | Africa | 5 out of 51 |
| Sierra Leone | 6.7 | 7.0 | | 129 | | Africa | 30 out of 51 |
| Singapore | -8.2 | -8.2 | AAA | 1 | Developed | Asia | 1 out of 29 |
| Slovakia | -4.7 | -4.6 | A+ | 24 | | Central and Eastern Europe | 2 out of 25 |
| Slovenia | -3.4 | -3.3 | A | 34 | Frontier | Central and Eastern Europe | 5 out of 25 |
| Solomon Islands | 16.7 | 17.3 | | 168 | | Australasia | 6 out of 7 |
| Somalia | 15.1 | 15.6 | | 166 | | Africa | 46 out of 51 |
| South Africa | -1.0 | -0.6 | BBB- | 60 | Emerging | Africa | 2 out of 51 |
| Spain | -2.7 | -2.5 | BBB+ | 38 | Developed | Western Europe | 16 out of 19 |
| Sri Lanka | 1.1 | 1.1 | B+ | 72 | Frontier | Asia | 14 out of 29 |
| Sudan | 11.4 | 11.7 | | 154 | | Africa | 40 out of 51 |
| Suriname | 4.3 | 4.8 | B+ | 102 | | Latin America | 16 out of 20 |
| Swaziland | 9.8 | 11.1 | | 152 | | Africa | 38 out of 51 |
| Sweden | -7.3 | -7.4 | AAA | 7 | Developed | Western Europe | 6 out of 19 |

§ S&P Credit Rating based on long-term foreign currency issuer rating. See http://www.standardandpoors.com/.

* World rank based on 175 countries covered by Euromoney. Ranking based on ascending order in which '1' equals the smallest country risk premium (CRP) and '175' equals the largest country risk premium (CRP).

† MSCI Market Classification based on MSCI Market Classification Framework. See http://www.msci.com/products/indexes/market_classification.html.

‡ Regional classification based on Euromoney. Regional rankings based on ascending order in which '1' equals the smallest country risk premium (CRP) for each region.

Note: A CRP of 0.0% is assumed in the following cases: (i) when the investor country and the investee country both have an S&P sovereign credit rating of AAA; or (ii) when the investor country has an S&P credit rating of AAA, and the investee country has a sovereign credit rating below AAA, but has a calculated CRP below 0.0% (which would imply lower risk than a country rated AAA); or (iii) when the investor country has an S&P credit rating below AAA, and the investee country has a sovereign credit rating of AAA, but has a calculated CRP above 0.0% (which would imply greater risk than a country rated below AAA). For purposes of this analysis, the U.S. is treated as having a sovereign credit rating equivalent to AAA.

The country risk premium (CRP) is not the cost of equity capital (COE).  The CRP is to be added to base COE. See Chapter 6 for proper application.

## Data Updated Through March 2017

| Investee Country | December 2016 Country Risk Premium (CRP) (%) | March 2017 Country Risk Premium (CRP) (%) | S&P Sovereign Credit Rating § | World Rank Out of 175* | MSCI Market Classification † | Euromoney Region ‡ | Regional Rank ‡ |
|---|---|---|---|---|---|---|---|
| Switzerland | -8.0 | -8.1 | AAA | 2 | Developed | Western Europe | 1 out of 19 |
| Syria | 15.8 | 16.6 | | 167 | | Middle East | 13 out of 13 |
| Taiwan | -5.5 | -5.4 | AA- | 18 | Emerging | Asia | 3 out of 29 |
| Tajikistan | 11.0 | 11.7 | | 155 | | Central and Eastern Europe | 25 out of 25 |
| Tanzania | 3.7 | 4.2 | | 95 | | Africa | 13 out of 51 |
| Thailand | -1.5 | -1.5 | BBB+ | 51 | Emerging | Asia | 8 out of 29 |
| Togo | 5.2 | 5.5 | | 113 | | Africa | 20 out of 51 |
| Tonga | 19.0 | 19.6 | | 170 | | Australasia | 7 out of 7 |
| Trinidad & Tobago | -1.2 | -1.0 | A- | 54 | | Caribbean | 2 out of 9 |
| Tunisia | 1.5 | 2.0 | | 79 | Frontier | Africa | 6 out of 51 |
| Turkey | -0.9 | -0.8 | BB | 58 | Emerging | Central and Eastern Europe | 11 out of 25 |
| Turkmenistan | 8.3 | 9.0 | | 140 | | Asia | 24 out of 29 |
| Uganda | 4.8 | 5.4 | B | 110 | | Africa | 18 out of 51 |
| Ukraine | 7.4 | 7.8 | B- | 135 | | Central and Eastern Europe | 20 out of 25 |
| United Arab Emirates | -3.8 | -3.6 | AA | 33 | Emerging | Middle East | 4 out of 13 |
| United Kingdom | -5.2 | -5.0 | AA | 20 | Developed | Western Europe | 11 out of 19 |
| United States | -6.2 | -6.1 | AA+ | 15 | Developed | North America | 2 out of 2 |
| Uruguay | -2.1 | -2.1 | BBB | 45 | | Latin America | 5 out of 20 |
| Uzbekistan | 7.6 | 7.4 | | 132 | | Asia | 21 out of 29 |
| Vanuatu | 9.1 | 9.5 | | 145 | | Australasia | 4 out of 7 |
| Venezuela | 12.7 | 13.6 | CCC | 162 | | Latin America | 20 out of 20 |
| Vietnam | 2.0 | 2.0 | BB- | 78 | Frontier | Asia | 16 out of 29 |
| Yemen | 12.9 | 13.5 | | 161 | | Middle East | 12 out of 13 |
| Zambia | 5.1 | 5.4 | B | 111 | | Africa | 19 out of 51 |
| Zimbabwe | 14.5 | 14.9 | | 164 | | Africa | 44 out of 51 |

## March 2017 Country Risk Premium (CRP) Summary Statistics:

| S&P Rating | Country Count | Average CRP (%) | Median CRP (%) | Min CRP (%) | Max CRP (%) |
|---|---|---|---|---|---|
| AAA ** | 12 | -7.3 | -7.4 | -8.2 | -6.1 |
| AA (AA+, AA, AA-) | 15 | -5.1 | -5.0 | -7.2 | -2.2 |
| A (A+, A, A-) | 14 | -3.2 | -3.1 | -4.6 | -1.0 |
| BBB (BBB+, BBB, BBB-) | 17 | -1.5 | -1.5 | -4.1 | 0.8 |
| BB (BB+, BB, BB-) | 22 | 1.3 | 1.2 | -2.4 | 6.5 |
| B+ – SD | 39 | 5.8 | 5.4 | 1.1 | 13.6 |
| Investment Grade ** | 58 | -4.0 | -4.0 | -8.2 | 0.8 |
| Non-Investment Grade ** | 61 | 4.2 | 4.3 | -2.4 | 13.6 |
| **MSCI Market Classification** | | | | | |
| Developed Markets | 23 | -5.9 | -6.7 | -8.2 | -1.7 |
| Emerging Markets | 23 | -1.8 | -2.2 | -5.8 | 5.7 |
| Frontier Markets | 22 | 1.1 | 0.9 | -4.0 | 6.5 |
| **Euromoney Region ‡** | | | | | |
| Africa | 51 | 8.2 | 6.3 | -2.0 | 27.8 |
| Asia | 29 | 3.2 | 1.8 | -8.2 | 25.3 |
| Australasia | 7 | 6.9 | 9.5 | -7.2 | 19.6 |
| Caribbean | 9 | 4.4 | 3.9 | -2.1 | 13.3 |
| Central and Eastern Europe | 25 | 1.6 | -0.3 | -4.8 | 11.7 |
| Latin America | 20 | 2.2 | 2.9 | -5.8 | 13.6 |
| Middle East | 13 | 2.4 | 0.0 | -5.0 | 16.6 |
| North America | 2 | -6.6 | -6.6 | -7.1 | -6.1 |
| Western Europe | 19 | -5.0 | -5.6 | -8.1 | 5.1 |

## CCR Base Cost of Equity Capital:

| Bahrain | COE (%) |
|---|---|
| March 2017 | 14.6 |
| December 2016 | 14.7 |

CCR base country-level COE for a Bahrain-based investor investing in Bahrain.

§ S&P Credit Rating based on long-term foreign currency issuer rating. See http://www.standardandpoors.com/.

* World rank based on 175 countries covered by Euromoney. Ranking based on ascending order in which '1' equals the smallest country risk premium (CRP) and '175' equals the largest country risk premium (CRP).

† MSCI Market Classification based on MSCI Market Classification Framework.  See http://www.msci.com/products/indexes/market_classification.html.

‡ Regional classification based on Euromoney. Regional rankings based on ascending order in which '1' equals the smallest country risk premium (CRP) for each region.

** Investment grade based on S&P sovereign credit rating from AAA to BBB-. Non-Investment grade based on S&P sovereign credit rating from BB+ to SD. For purposes of this analysis, the U.S. is being treated as if it were rated AAA by S&P.

Note: A CRP of 0.0% is assumed in the following cases: (i) when the investor country and the investee country both have an S&P sovereign credit rating of AAA; or (ii) when the investor country has an S&P sovereign credit rating of AAA, and the investee country has a sovereign credit rating below AAA, but has a calculated CRP below 0.0% (which would imply lower risk than a country rated AAA); or (iii) when the investor country has an S&P credit rating below AAA, and the investee country has a sovereign credit rating of AAA, but has a calculated CRP above 0.0% (which would imply greater risk than a country rated below AAA). For purposes of this analysis, the U.S. is treated as having a sovereign credit rating equivalent to AAA.

The country risk premium (CRP) is not the cost of equity capital (COE). The CRP is to be added to base COE. See Chapter 6 for proper application.

## Data Updated Through March 2017

| Investee Country | December 2016 Country Risk Premium (CRP) (%) | March 2017 Country Risk Premium (CRP) (%) | S&P Sovereign Credit Rating § | World Rank Out of 175* | MSCI Market Classification † | Euromoney Region ‡ | Regional Rank ‡ |
|---|---|---|---|---|---|---|---|
| Afghanistan | 15.5 | 15.3 | | 139 | | Asia | 23 out of 29 |
| Albania | 10.0 | 10.3 | B+ | 93 | | Central and Eastern Europe | 18 out of 25 |
| Algeria | 10.0 | 10.2 | | 91 | | Africa | 10 out of 51 |
| Angola | 12.4 | 12.6 | B | 121 | | Africa | 26 out of 51 |
| Argentina | 10.6 | 10.4 | B- | 96 | Frontier | Latin America | 13 out of 20 |
| Armenia | 7.6 | 7.9 | | 77 | | Asia | 15 out of 29 |
| Australia | -1.5 | -1.4 | AAA | 12 | Developed | Australasia | 2 out of 7 |
| Austria | -1.3 | -1.2 | AA+ | 13 | Developed | Western Europe | 9 out of 19 |
| Azerbaijan | 8.8 | 9.2 | BB+ | 85 | | Asia | 17 out of 29 |
| Bahamas | 6.1 | 5.9 | BB+ | 65 | | Caribbean | 3 out of 9 |
| Bahrain | 6.0 | 5.9 | BB- | 64 | Frontier | Middle East | 7 out of 13 |
| Bangladesh | 12.9 | 12.8 | BB- | 126 | Frontier | Asia | 20 out of 29 |
| Barbados | 7.8 | 9.0 | CCC+ | 82 | | Caribbean | 4 out of 9 |
| Belarus | 15.1 | 15.7 | B- | 143 | | Central and Eastern Europe | 23 out of 25 |
| Belgium | 0.0 | 0.0 | AA | 17 | Developed | Western Europe | 10 out of 19 |
| Belize | 11.0 | 11.3 | B- | 106 | | Latin America | 17 out of 20 |
| Benin | 16.9 | 17.0 | | 150 | | Africa | 37 out of 51 |
| Bermuda | 3.7 | 3.7 | A+ | 44 | | Caribbean | 1 out of 9 |
| Bhutan | 16.5 | 16.5 | | 148 | | Asia | 25 out of 29 |
| Bolivia | 9.5 | 9.9 | BB | 88 | | Latin America | 12 out of 20 |
| Bosnia & Herzegovina | 15.6 | 15.9 | B | 144 | | Central and Eastern Europe | 24 out of 25 |
| Botswana | 3.7 | 3.8 | A- | 48 | | Africa | 1 out of 51 |
| Brazil | 5.2 | 5.2 | BB | 59 | Emerging | Latin America | 7 out of 20 |
| Bulgaria | 5.1 | 5.4 | BB+ | 61 | | Central and Eastern Europe | 12 out of 25 |
| Burkina Faso | 14.0 | 14.1 | B- | 133 | | Africa | 33 out of 51 |
| Burundi | 25.9 | 26.1 | | 169 | | Africa | 47 out of 51 |
| Cambodia | 17.4 | 17.2 | | 151 | | Asia | 27 out of 29 |
| Cameroon | 12.6 | 12.7 | B | 124 | | Africa | 28 out of 51 |
| Canada | -1.7 | -1.7 | AAA | 9 | Developed | North America | 1 out of 2 |
| Cape Verde | 10.2 | 10.3 | B | 94 | | Africa | 12 out of 51 |
| Central African Republic | 29.5 | 29.7 | | 172 | | Africa | 49 out of 51 |
| Chad | 28.2 | 28.3 | | 171 | | Africa | 48 out of 51 |
| Chile | -0.5 | -0.2 | AA- | 16 | Emerging | Latin America | 1 out of 20 |
| China | 3.5 | 3.6 | AA- | 42 | Emerging | Asia | 7 out of 29 |
| Colombia | 3.4 | 3.5 | BBB | 41 | Emerging | Latin America | 4 out of 20 |
| Congo Republic | 12.2 | 12.1 | B- | 117 | | Africa | 24 out of 51 |
| Congo, DR | 13.5 | 13.5 | B- | 131 | | Africa | 32 out of 51 |
| Costa Rica | 6.5 | 6.8 | BB- | 71 | | Latin America | 8 out of 20 |
| Côte d'Ivoire | 10.1 | 10.2 | | 92 | | Africa | 11 out of 51 |
| Croatia | 5.6 | 5.6 | BB | 63 | Frontier | Central and Eastern Europe | 13 out of 25 |
| Cuba | 19.8 | 20.0 | | 160 | | Caribbean | 9 out of 9 |
| Cyprus | 3.2 | 3.4 | BB+ | 40 | | Central and Eastern Europe | 7 out of 25 |
| Czech Republic | 0.8 | 0.9 | AA- | 23 | Emerging | Central and Eastern Europe | 1 out of 25 |
| Denmark | -2.3 | -2.2 | AAA | 4 | Developed | Western Europe | 3 out of 19 |
| Djibouti | 37.5 | 35.4 | | 175 | | Africa | 51 out of 51 |
| Dominican Republic | 9.9 | 10.1 | BB- | 90 | | Caribbean | 5 out of 9 |
| Ecuador | 11.5 | 11.4 | B | 109 | | Latin America | 18 out of 20 |
| Egypt | 11.9 | 12.0 | B- | 116 | Emerging | Africa | 23 out of 51 |
| El Salvador | 8.9 | 8.8 | B- | 81 | | Latin America | 10 out of 20 |
| Equatorial Guinea | 22.3 | 22.5 | | 165 | | Africa | 45 out of 51 |

§ S&P Credit Rating based on long-term foreign currency issuer rating. See http://www.standardandpoors.com/.

* World rank based on 175 countries covered by Euromoney. Ranking based on ascending order in which '1' equals the smallest country risk premium (CRP) and '175' equals the largest country risk premium (CRP).

† MSCI Market Classification based on MSCI Market Classification Framework. See http://www.msci.com/products/indexes/market_classification.html.

‡ Regional classification based on Euromoney. Regional rankings based on ascending order in which '1' equals the smallest country risk premium (CRP) for each region.

Note: A CRP of 0.0% is assumed in the following cases: (i) when the investor country and the investee country both have an S&P sovereign credit rating of AAA; or (ii) when the investor country has an S&P credit rating of AAA, and the investee country has a sovereign credit rating below AAA, but has a calculated CRP below 0.0% (which would imply lower risk than a country rated AAA); or (iii) when the investor country has an S&P credit rating below AAA, and the investee country has a sovereign credit rating of AAA, but has a calculated CRP above 0.0% (which would imply greater risk than a country rated below AAA). For purposes of this analysis, the U.S. is treated as having a sovereign credit rating equivalent to AAA.

The country risk premium (CRP) is not the cost of equity capital (COE). The CRP is to be added to base COE. See Chapter 6 for proper application.

## Data Updated Through March 2017

| Investee Country | December 2016 Country Risk Premium (CRP) (%) | March 2017 Country Risk Premium (CRP) (%) | S&P Sovereign Credit Rating § | World Rank Out of 175• | MSCI Market Classification † | Euromoney Region ‡ | Regional Rank ‡ |
|---|---|---|---|---|---|---|---|
| Eritrea | 33.7 | 32.0 | | 173 | | Africa | 50 out of 51 |
| Estonia | 1.4 | 1.7 | AA- | 32 | Frontier | Central and Eastern Europe | 4 out of 25 |
| Ethiopia | 10.8 | 10.9 | B | 101 | | Africa | 16 out of 51 |
| Fiji | 16.2 | 16.2 | B+ | 147 | | Australasia | 5 out of 7 |
| Finland | -1.5 | -1.5 | AA+ | 11 | Developed | Western Europe | 8 out of 19 |
| France | 0.8 | 0.7 | AA | 22 | Developed | Western Europe | 12 out of 19 |
| Gabon | 8.5 | 9.0 | | 83 | | Africa | 7 out of 51 |
| Gambia | 14.6 | 14.8 | | 138 | | Africa | 34 out of 51 |
| Georgia | 7.3 | 7.6 | BB- | 74 | | Central and Eastern Europe | 15 out of 25 |
| Germany | -1.5 | -1.5 | AAA | 10 | Developed | Western Europe | 7 out of 19 |
| Ghana | 10.3 | 10.0 | B- | 89 | | Africa | 9 out of 51 |
| Greece | 11.4 | 11.3 | B- | 108 | Emerging | Western Europe | 19 out of 19 |
| Grenada | 11.0 | 11.2 | | 105 | | Caribbean | 7 out of 9 |
| Guatemala | 8.9 | 9.1 | BB | 84 | | Latin America | 11 out of 20 |
| Guinea | 18.4 | 18.5 | | 156 | | Africa | 41 out of 51 |
| Guinea-Bissau | 11.9 | 12.0 | | 115 | | Africa | 22 out of 51 |
| Guyana | 10.7 | 10.8 | | 100 | | Latin America | 15 out of 20 |
| Haiti | 21.2 | 19.3 | | 157 | | Caribbean | 8 out of 9 |
| Honduras | 10.4 | 10.5 | B+ | 98 | | Latin America | 14 out of 20 |
| Hong Kong | -1.0 | -0.9 | AAA | 14 | Developed | Asia | 2 out of 29 |
| Hungary | 4.8 | 5.1 | BBB- | 57 | Emerging | Central and Eastern Europe | 10 out of 25 |
| Iceland | 1.8 | 1.7 | A | 30 | | Western Europe | 15 out of 19 |
| India | 4.6 | 5.0 | BBB- | 55 | Emerging | Asia | 10 out of 29 |
| Indonesia | 5.4 | 5.5 | BB+ | 62 | Emerging | Asia | 11 out of 29 |
| Iran | 12.4 | 12.7 | | 125 | | Middle East | 10 out of 13 |
| Iraq | 14.2 | 14.4 | B- | 136 | | Middle East | 11 out of 13 |
| Ireland | 1.3 | 1.3 | A+ | 27 | Developed | Western Europe | 14 out of 19 |
| Israel | 1.3 | 1.4 | A+ | 28 | Developed | Middle East | 2 out of 13 |
| Italy | 4.2 | 4.1 | BBB- | 50 | Developed | Western Europe | 18 out of 19 |
| Jamaica | 10.4 | 11.2 | B | 104 | | Caribbean | 6 out of 9 |
| Japan | 1.2 | 1.3 | A+ | 25 | Developed | Asia | 5 out of 29 |
| Jordan | 7.5 | 7.8 | BB- | 76 | Frontier | Middle East | 8 out of 13 |
| Kazakhstan | 7.0 | 6.8 | BBB- | 70 | Frontier | Asia | 13 out of 29 |
| Kenya | 10.5 | 10.7 | B+ | 99 | Frontier | Africa | 15 out of 51 |
| Korea (North) | 33.0 | 32.7 | | 174 | | Asia | 29 out of 29 |
| Korea (South) | 0.4 | 0.5 | AA | 19 | Emerging | Asia | 4 out of 29 |
| Kuwait | 1.5 | 1.7 | AA | 31 | Frontier | Middle East | 3 out of 13 |
| Kyrgyz Republic | 15.7 | 15.7 | | 142 | | Central and Eastern Europe | 22 out of 25 |
| Laos | 20.0 | 19.6 | | 158 | | Asia | 28 out of 29 |
| Latvia | 3.5 | 3.7 | A- | 43 | | Central and Eastern Europe | 8 out of 25 |
| Lebanon | 12.3 | 11.7 | B- | 112 | Frontier | Middle East | 9 out of 13 |
| Lesotho | 15.9 | 16.0 | | 146 | | Africa | 36 out of 51 |
| Liberia | 11.1 | 11.3 | | 107 | | Africa | 17 out of 51 |
| Libya | 17.4 | 17.9 | | 153 | | Africa | 39 out of 51 |
| Lithuania | 2.7 | 2.9 | A- | 36 | Frontier | Central and Eastern Europe | 6 out of 25 |
| Luxembourg | -2.0 | -1.9 | AAA | 5 | | Western Europe | 4 out of 19 |
| Macedonia | 9.5 | 9.9 | BB- | 87 | | Central and Eastern Europe | 17 out of 25 |
| Madagascar | 12.0 | 12.6 | | 123 | | Africa | 27 out of 51 |
| Malawi | 11.7 | 11.8 | | 114 | | Africa | 21 out of 51 |
| Malaysia | 2.9 | 2.8 | A- | 35 | Emerging | Asia | 6 out of 29 |

§ S&P Credit Rating based on long-term foreign currency issuer rating. See http://www.standardandpoors.com/.

• World rank based on 175 countries covered by Euromoney. Ranking based on ascending order in which '1' equals the smallest country risk premium (CRP) and '175' equals the largest country risk premium (CRP).

† MSCI Market Classification based on MSCI Market Classification Framework. See http://www.msci.com/products/indexes/market_classification.html.

‡ Regional classification based on Euromoney. Regional rankings based on ascending order in which '1' equals the smallest country risk premium (CRP) for each region.

Note: A CRP of 0.0% is assumed in the following cases: (i) when the investor country and the investee country both have an S&P sovereign credit rating of AAA; or (ii) when the investor country has an S&P credit rating of AAA, and the investee country has a sovereign credit rating below AAA, but has a calculated CRP below 0.0% (which would imply lower risk than a country rated AAA); or (iii) when the investor country has an S&P credit rating below AAA, and the investee country has a sovereign credit rating of AAA, but has a calculated CRP above 0.0% (which would imply greater risk than a country rated below AAA). For purposes of this analysis, the U.S. is treated as having a sovereign credit rating equivalent to AAA.

The country risk premium (CRP) is not the cost of equity capital (COE). The CRP is to be added to base COE. See Chapter 6 for proper application.

### Data Updated Through March 2017

| Investee Country | December 2016 Country Risk Premium (CRP) (%) | March 2017 Country Risk Premium (CRP) (%) | S&P Sovereign Credit Rating § | World Rank Out of 175* | MSCI Market Classification † | Euromoney Region ‡ | Regional Rank ‡ |
|---|---|---|---|---|---|---|---|
| Mali | 15.5 | 15.6 | | 141 | | Africa | 35 out of 51 |
| Malta | 1.2 | 1.3 | A- | 26 | | Western Europe | 13 out of 19 |
| Mauritania | 19.6 | 19.7 | | 159 | | Africa | 42 out of 51 |
| Mauritius | 6.3 | 6.4 | | 67 | Frontier | Asia | 12 out of 29 |
| Mexico | 2.8 | 3.0 | BBB+ | 37 | Emerging | Latin America | 2 out of 20 |
| Moldova | 13.9 | 14.5 | | 137 | | Central and Eastern Europe | 21 out of 25 |
| Mongolia | 12.1 | 12.5 | B- | 119 | | Asia | 18 out of 29 |
| Montenegro | 11.3 | 11.2 | B+ | 103 | | Central and Eastern Europe | 19 out of 25 |
| Morocco | 6.4 | 6.7 | BBB- | 69 | Frontier | Africa | 4 out of 51 |
| Mozambique | 13.2 | 13.1 | SD | 128 | | Africa | 29 out of 51 |
| Myanmar | 14.1 | 14.1 | | 134 | | Asia | 22 out of 29 |
| Namibia | 6.0 | 6.2 | | 66 | | Africa | 3 out of 51 |
| Nepal | 16.8 | 17.0 | | 149 | | Asia | 26 out of 29 |
| Netherlands | -1.9 | -1.9 | AAA | 6 | Developed | Western Europe | 5 out of 19 |
| New Zealand | -1.8 | -1.7 | AA | 8 | Developed | Australasia | 1 out of 7 |
| Nicaragua | 12.8 | 13.0 | B+ | 127 | | Latin America | 19 out of 20 |
| Niger | 12.4 | 12.6 | | 120 | | Africa | 25 out of 51 |
| Nigeria | 10.4 | 10.5 | B | 97 | Frontier | Africa | 14 out of 51 |
| Norway | -2.6 | -2.6 | AAA | 3 | Developed | Western Europe | 2 out of 19 |
| Oman | 3.6 | 3.8 | BBB- | 46 | Frontier | Middle East | 5 out of 13 |
| Pakistan | 12.5 | 12.6 | B | 122 | Frontier | Asia | 19 out of 29 |
| Panama | 4.4 | 4.5 | BBB | 52 | | Latin America | 6 out of 20 |
| Papua New Guinea | 12.0 | 12.2 | B+ | 118 | | Australasia | 3 out of 7 |
| Paraguay | 7.9 | 8.2 | BB | 80 | | Latin America | 9 out of 20 |
| Peru | 3.0 | 3.3 | BBB+ | 39 | Emerging | Latin America | 3 out of 20 |
| Philippines | 4.7 | 4.8 | BBB | 53 | Emerging | Asia | 9 out of 29 |
| Poland | 1.6 | 1.6 | BBB+ | 29 | Emerging | Central and Eastern Europe | 3 out of 25 |
| Portugal | 4.1 | 4.0 | BB+ | 49 | Developed | Western Europe | 17 out of 19 |
| Qatar | 0.5 | 0.7 | AA | 21 | Emerging | Middle East | 1 out of 13 |
| Romania | 4.9 | 5.0 | BBB- | 56 | Frontier | Central and Eastern Europe | 9 out of 25 |
| Russia | 7.1 | 6.6 | BB+ | 68 | Emerging | Central and Eastern Europe | 14 out of 25 |
| Rwanda | 13.2 | 13.4 | B | 130 | | Africa | 31 out of 51 |
| São Tomé & Príncipe | 19.7 | 20.3 | | 163 | | Africa | 43 out of 51 |
| Saudi Arabia | 4.0 | 3.8 | A- | 47 | | Middle East | 6 out of 13 |
| Senegal | 9.7 | 9.8 | B+ | 86 | | Africa | 8 out of 51 |
| Serbia | 7.8 | 7.7 | BB- | 75 | Frontier | Central and Eastern Europe | 16 out of 25 |
| Seychelles | 7.3 | 7.4 | | 73 | | Africa | 5 out of 51 |
| Sierra Leone | 13.2 | 13.4 | | 129 | | Africa | 30 out of 51 |
| Singapore | -2.8 | -2.7 | AAA | 1 | Developed | Asia | 1 out of 29 |
| Slovakia | 0.9 | 1.1 | A+ | 24 | | Central and Eastern Europe | 2 out of 25 |
| Slovenia | 2.3 | 2.4 | A | 34 | Frontier | Central and Eastern Europe | 5 out of 25 |
| Solomon Islands | 24.1 | 24.3 | | 168 | | Australasia | 6 out of 7 |
| Somalia | 22.4 | 22.5 | | 166 | | Africa | 46 out of 51 |
| South Africa | 4.9 | 5.3 | BBB- | 60 | Emerging | Africa | 2 out of 51 |
| Spain | 3.2 | 3.3 | BBB+ | 38 | Developed | Western Europe | 16 out of 19 |
| Sri Lanka | 7.2 | 7.0 | B+ | 72 | Frontier | Asia | 14 out of 29 |
| Sudan | 18.3 | 18.4 | | 154 | | Africa | 40 out of 51 |
| Suriname | 10.7 | 11.0 | B+ | 102 | | Latin America | 16 out of 20 |
| Swaziland | 16.6 | 17.7 | | 152 | | Africa | 38 out of 51 |
| Sweden | -1.9 | -1.9 | AAA | 7 | Developed | Western Europe | 6 out of 19 |

§ S&P Credit Rating based on long-term foreign currency issuer rating. See http://www.standardandpoors.com/.

* World rank based on 175 countries covered by Euromoney. Ranking based on ascending order in which '1' equals the smallest country risk premium (CRP) and '175' equals the largest country risk premium (CRP).

† MSCI Market Classification based on MSCI Market Classification Framework. See http://www.msci.com/products/indexes/market_classification.html.

‡ Regional classification based on Euromoney. Regional rankings based on ascending order in which '1' equals the smallest country risk premium (CRP) for each region.

Note: A CRP of 0.0% is assumed in the following cases: (i) when the investor country and the investee country both have an S&P sovereign credit rating of AAA; or (ii) when the investor country has an S&P credit rating of AAA, and the investee country has a sovereign credit rating below AAA, but has a calculated CRP below 0.0% (which would imply lower risk than a country rated AAA); or (iii) when the investor country has an S&P credit rating below AAA, and the investee country has a sovereign credit rating of AAA, but has a calculated CRP above 0.0% (which would imply greater risk than a country rated below AAA). For purposes of this analysis, the U.S. is treated as having a sovereign credit rating equivalent to AAA.

The country risk premium (CRP) is not the cost of equity capital (COE). The CRP is to be added to base COE. See Chapter 6 for proper application.

## Data Updated Through March 2017

| Investee Country | December 2016 Country Risk Premium (CRP) (%) | March 2017 Country Risk Premium (CRP) (%) | S&P Sovereign Credit Rating § | World Rank Out of 175∗ | MSCI Market Classification † | Euromoney Region ‡ | Regional Rank ‡ |
|---|---|---|---|---|---|---|---|
| Switzerland | -2.6 | -2.6 | AAA | 2 | Developed | Western Europe | 1 out of 19 |
| Syria | 23.1 | 23.5 | | 167 | | Middle East | 13 out of 13 |
| Taiwan | 0.1 | 0.2 | AA- | 18 | Emerging | Asia | 3 out of 29 |
| Tajikistan | 17.9 | 18.4 | | 155 | | Central and Eastern Europe | 25 out of 25 |
| Tanzania | 10.1 | 10.4 | | 95 | | Africa | 13 out of 51 |
| Thailand | 4.4 | 4.3 | BBB+ | 51 | Emerging | Asia | 8 out of 29 |
| Togo | 11.7 | 11.8 | | 113 | | Africa | 20 out of 51 |
| Tonga | 26.6 | 26.8 | | 170 | | Australasia | 7 out of 7 |
| Trinidad & Tobago | 4.7 | 4.8 | A- | 54 | | Caribbean | 2 out of 9 |
| Tunisia | 7.6 | 8.1 | | 79 | Frontier | Africa | 6 out of 51 |
| Turkey | 5.1 | 5.1 | BB | 58 | Emerging | Central and Eastern Europe | 11 out of 25 |
| Turkmenistan | 15.0 | 15.4 | | 140 | | Asia | 24 out of 29 |
| Uganda | 11.2 | 11.6 | B | 110 | | Africa | 18 out of 51 |
| Ukraine | 14.0 | 14.3 | B- | 135 | | Central and Eastern Europe | 20 out of 25 |
| United Arab Emirates | 1.9 | 2.1 | AA | 33 | Emerging | Middle East | 4 out of 13 |
| United Kingdom | 0.4 | 0.6 | AA | 20 | Developed | Western Europe | 11 out of 19 |
| United States | -0.7 | -0.6 | AA+ | 15 | Developed | North America | 2 out of 2 |
| Uruguay | 3.7 | 3.7 | BBB | 45 | | Latin America | 5 out of 20 |
| Uzbekistan | 14.2 | 13.8 | | 132 | | Asia | 21 out of 29 |
| Vanuatu | 15.9 | 16.0 | | 145 | | Australasia | 4 out of 7 |
| Venezuela | 19.7 | 20.3 | CCC | 162 | | Latin America | 20 out of 20 |
| Vietnam | 8.2 | 8.0 | BB- | 78 | Frontier | Asia | 16 out of 29 |
| Yemen | 20.0 | 20.2 | | 161 | | Middle East | 12 out of 13 |
| Zambia | 11.5 | 11.7 | B | 111 | | Africa | 19 out of 51 |
| Zimbabwe | 21.6 | 21.7 | | 164 | | Africa | 44 out of 51 |

## March 2017 Country Risk Premium (CRP) Summary Statistics:

| S&P Rating | Country Count | Average CRP (%) | Median CRP (%) | Min CRP (%) | Max CRP (%) |
|---|---|---|---|---|---|
| AAA ∗∗ | 12 | -1.8 | -1.9 | -2.7 | -0.6 |
| AA (AA+, AA, AA-) | 15 | 0.6 | 0.6 | -1.7 | 3.6 |
| A (A+, A, A-) | 14 | 2.6 | 2.6 | 1.1 | 4.8 |
| BBB (BBB+, BBB, BBB-) | 17 | 4.3 | 4.3 | 1.6 | 6.8 |
| BB (BB+, BB, BB-) | 22 | 7.3 | 7.2 | 3.4 | 12.8 |
| B+ − SD | 39 | 12.1 | 11.7 | 7.0 | 20.3 |
| Investment Grade ∗∗ | 58 | 1.7 | 1.7 | -2.7 | 6.8 |
| Non-Investment Grade ∗∗ | 61 | 10.3 | 10.5 | 3.4 | 20.3 |
| **MSCI Market Classification** | | | | | |
| Developed Markets | 23 | -0.3 | -1.2 | -2.7 | 4.1 |
| Emerging Markets | 23 | 4.0 | 3.6 | -0.2 | 12.0 |
| Frontier Markets | 22 | 7.1 | 6.9 | 1.7 | 12.8 |
| **Euromoney Region ‡** | | | | | |
| Africa | 51 | 14.6 | 12.6 | 3.8 | 35.4 |
| Asia | 29 | 9.3 | 7.9 | -2.7 | 32.7 |
| Australasia | 7 | 13.2 | 16.0 | -1.7 | 26.8 |
| Caribbean | 9 | 10.6 | 10.1 | 3.7 | 20.0 |
| Central and Eastern Europe | 25 | 7.7 | 5.6 | 0.9 | 18.4 |
| Latin America | 20 | 8.2 | 9.0 | -0.2 | 20.3 |
| Middle East | 13 | 8.4 | 5.9 | 0.7 | 23.5 |
| North America | 2 | -1.1 | -1.1 | -1.7 | -0.6 |
| Western Europe | 19 | 0.6 | 0.0 | -2.6 | 11.3 |

## CCR Base Cost of Equity Capital:

| Belgium | COE (%) |
|---|---|
| March 2017 | 9.1 |
| December 2016 | 9.1 |

CCR base country-level COE for a Belgium-based investor investing in Belgium.

§ S&P Credit Rating based on long-term foreign currency issuer rating. See http://www.standardandpoors.com/.

∗ World rank based on 175 countries covered by Euromoney. Ranking based on ascending order in which '1' equals the smallest country risk premium (CRP) and '175' equals the largest country risk premium (CRP).

† MSCI Market Classification based on MSCI Market Classification Framework. See http://www.msci.com/products/indexes/market_classification.html

‡ Regional classification based on Euromoney. Regional rankings based on ascending order in which '1' equals the smallest country risk premium (CRP) for each region.

∗∗ Investment grade based on S&P sovereign credit rating from AAA to BBB-. Non-Investment grade based on S&P sovereign credit rating from BB+ to SD. For purposes of this analysis, the U.S. is being treated as if it were rated AAA by S&P.

Note: A CRP of 0.0% is assumed in the following cases: (i) when the investor country and the investee country both have an S&P sovereign credit rating of AAA; or (ii) when the investor country has an S&P credit rating of AAA, and the investee country has a sovereign credit rating below AAA, but has a calculated CRP below 0.0% (which would imply lower risk than a country rated AAA); or (iii) when the investor country has an S&P credit rating below AAA, and the investee country has a sovereign credit rating of AAA, but has a calculated CRP above 0.0% (which would imply greater risk than a country rated below AAA). For purposes of this analysis, the U.S. is treated as having a sovereign credit rating equivalent to AAA.

The country risk premium (CRP) is not the cost of equity capital (COE).  The CRP is to be added to base COE. See Chapter 6 for proper application.

## Data Updated Through March 2017

| Investee Country | December 2016 Country Risk Premium (CRP) (%) | March 2017 Country Risk Premium (CRP) (%) | S&P Sovereign Credit Rating § | World Rank Out of 175* | MSCI Market Classification † | Euromoney Region ‡ | Regional Rank ‡ |
|---|---|---|---|---|---|---|---|
| Afghanistan | 7.9 | 7.7 | | 139 | | Asia | 23 out of 29 |
| Albania | 3.7 | 3.8 | B+ | 93 | | Central and Eastern Europe | 18 out of 25 |
| Algeria | 3.7 | 3.8 | | 91 | | Africa | 10 out of 51 |
| Angola | 5.5 | 5.6 | B | 121 | | Africa | 26 out of 51 |
| Argentina | 4.1 | 4.0 | B- | 96 | Frontier | Latin America | 13 out of 20 |
| Armenia | 1.8 | 2.0 | | 77 | | Asia | 15 out of 29 |
| Australia | -5.2 | -5.1 | AAA | 12 | Developed | Australasia | 2 out of 7 |
| Austria | -5.0 | -4.9 | AA+ | 13 | Developed | Western Europe | 9 out of 19 |
| Azerbaijan | 2.7 | 3.0 | BB+ | 85 | | Asia | 17 out of 29 |
| Bahamas | 0.7 | 0.5 | BB+ | 65 | | Caribbean | 3 out of 9 |
| Bahrain | 0.6 | 0.5 | BB- | 64 | Frontier | Middle East | 7 out of 13 |
| Bangladesh | 5.9 | 5.8 | BB- | 126 | Frontier | Asia | 20 out of 29 |
| Barbados | 1.9 | 2.8 | CCC+ | 82 | | Caribbean | 4 out of 9 |
| Belarus | 7.6 | 8.0 | B- | 143 | | Central and Eastern Europe | 23 out of 25 |
| Belgium | -4.0 | -4.0 | AA | 17 | Developed | Western Europe | 10 out of 19 |
| Belize | 4.5 | 4.6 | B- | 106 | | Latin America | 17 out of 20 |
| Benin | 9.0 | 8.9 | | 150 | | Africa | 37 out of 51 |
| Bermuda | -1.2 | -1.1 | A+ | 44 | | Caribbean | 1 out of 9 |
| Bhutan | 8.7 | 8.6 | | 148 | | Asia | 25 out of 29 |
| Bolivia | 3.3 | 3.6 | BB | 88 | | Latin America | 12 out of 20 |
| Bosnia & Herzegovina | 8.0 | 8.1 | B | 144 | | Central and Eastern Europe | 24 out of 25 |
| Botswana | -1.2 | -1.1 | A- | 48 | | Africa | 1 out of 51 |
| Brazil | 0.0 | 0.0 | BB | 59 | Emerging | Latin America | 7 out of 20 |
| Bulgaria | -0.1 | 0.1 | BB+ | 61 | | Central and Eastern Europe | 12 out of 25 |
| Burkina Faso | 6.7 | 6.7 | B- | 133 | | Africa | 33 out of 51 |
| Burundi | 16.0 | 15.8 | | 169 | | Africa | 47 out of 51 |
| Cambodia | 9.4 | 9.1 | | 151 | | Asia | 27 out of 29 |
| Cameroon | 5.7 | 5.7 | B | 124 | | Africa | 28 out of 51 |
| Canada | -5.3 | -5.2 | AAA | 9 | Developed | North America | 1 out of 2 |
| Cape Verde | 3.8 | 3.9 | B | 94 | | Africa | 12 out of 51 |
| Central African Republic | 18.7 | 18.6 | | 172 | | Africa | 49 out of 51 |
| Chad | 17.7 | 17.5 | | 171 | | Africa | 48 out of 51 |
| Chile | -4.4 | -4.1 | AA- | 16 | Emerging | Latin America | 1 out of 20 |
| China | -1.4 | -1.2 | AA- | 42 | Emerging | Asia | 7 out of 29 |
| Colombia | -1.4 | -1.3 | BBB | 41 | Emerging | Latin America | 4 out of 20 |
| Congo Republic | 5.4 | 5.3 | B- | 117 | | Africa | 24 out of 51 |
| Congo, DR | 6.4 | 6.3 | B- | 131 | | Africa | 32 out of 51 |
| Costa Rica | 1.0 | 1.2 | BB- | 71 | | Latin America | 8 out of 20 |
| Côte d'Ivoire | 3.7 | 3.8 | | 92 | | Africa | 11 out of 51 |
| Croatia | 0.3 | 0.3 | BB | 63 | Frontier | Central and Eastern Europe | 13 out of 25 |
| Cuba | 11.2 | 11.2 | | 160 | | Caribbean | 9 out of 9 |
| Cyprus | -1.6 | -1.4 | BB+ | 40 | | Central and Eastern Europe | 7 out of 25 |
| Czech Republic | -3.4 | -3.3 | AA- | 23 | Emerging | Central and Eastern Europe | 1 out of 25 |
| Denmark | -5.8 | -5.7 | AAA | 4 | Developed | Western Europe | 3 out of 19 |
| Djibouti | 24.9 | 22.9 | | 175 | | Africa | 51 out of 51 |
| Dominican Republic | 3.6 | 3.7 | BB- | 90 | | Caribbean | 5 out of 9 |
| Ecuador | 4.8 | 4.7 | B | 109 | | Latin America | 18 out of 20 |
| Egypt | 5.2 | 5.2 | B- | 116 | Emerging | Africa | 23 out of 51 |
| El Salvador | 2.8 | 2.7 | B- | 81 | | Latin America | 10 out of 20 |
| Equatorial Guinea | 13.2 | 13.1 | | 165 | | Africa | 45 out of 51 |

§ S&P Credit Rating based on long-term foreign currency issuer rating. See http://www.standardandpoors.com/.

* World rank based on 175 countries covered by Euromoney. Ranking based on ascending order in which '1' equals the smallest country risk premium (CRP) and '175' equals the largest country risk premium (CRP).

† MSCI Market Classification based on MSCI Market Classification Framework.  See http://www.msci.com/products/indexes/market_classification.html

‡ Regional classification based on Euromoney. Regional rankings based on ascending order in which '1' equals the smallest country risk premium (CRP) for each region.

Note: A CRP of 0.0% is assumed in the following cases: (i) when the investor country and the investee country both have an S&P sovereign credit rating of AAA; or (ii) when the investor country has an S&P credit rating of AAA, and the investee country has a sovereign credit rating below AAA, but has a calculated CRP below 0.0% (which would imply lower risk than a country rated AAA); or (iii) when the investor country has an S&P credit rating below AAA, and the investee country has a sovereign credit rating of AAA, but has a calculated CRP above 0.0% (which would imply greater risk than a country rated below AAA). For purposes of this analysis, the U.S. is treated as having a sovereign credit rating equivalent to AAA.

The country risk premium (CRP) is not the cost of equity capital (COE). The CRP is to be added to base COE. See Chapter 6 for proper application.

## Data Updated Through March 2017

| Investee Country | December 2016 Country Risk Premium (CRP) (%) | March 2017 Country Risk Premium (CRP) (%) | S&P Sovereign Credit Rating § | World Rank Out of 175* | MSCI Market Classification † | Euromoney Region ‡ | Regional Rank ‡ |
|---|---|---|---|---|---|---|---|
| Eritrea | 22.0 | 20.3 | | 173 | | Africa | 50 out of 51 |
| Estonia | -3.0 | -2.6 | AA- | 32 | Frontier | Central and Eastern Europe | 4 out of 25 |
| Ethiopia | 4.3 | 4.3 | B | 101 | | Africa | 16 out of 51 |
| Fiji | 8.5 | 8.3 | B+ | 147 | | Australasia | 5 out of 7 |
| Finland | -5.2 | -5.1 | AA+ | 11 | Developed | Western Europe | 8 out of 19 |
| France | -3.4 | -3.4 | AA | 22 | Developed | Western Europe | 12 out of 19 |
| Gabon | 2.5 | 2.9 | | 83 | | Africa | 7 out of 51 |
| Gambia | 7.2 | 7.3 | | 138 | | Africa | 34 out of 51 |
| Georgia | 1.6 | 1.8 | BB- | 74 | | Central and Eastern Europe | 15 out of 25 |
| Germany | -5.2 | -5.1 | AAA | 10 | Developed | Western Europe | 7 out of 19 |
| Ghana | 3.9 | 3.6 | B- | 89 | | Africa | 9 out of 51 |
| Greece | 4.8 | 4.6 | B- | 108 | Emerging | Western Europe | 19 out of 19 |
| Grenada | 4.5 | 4.6 | | 105 | | Caribbean | 7 out of 9 |
| Guatemala | 2.9 | 2.9 | BB | 84 | | Latin America | 11 out of 20 |
| Guinea | 10.1 | 10.1 | | 156 | | Africa | 41 out of 51 |
| Guinea-Bissau | 5.1 | 5.2 | | 115 | | Africa | 22 out of 51 |
| Guyana | 4.2 | 4.3 | | 100 | | Latin America | 15 out of 20 |
| Haiti | 12.4 | 10.7 | | 157 | | Caribbean | 8 out of 9 |
| Honduras | 4.0 | 4.0 | B+ | 98 | | Latin America | 14 out of 20 |
| Hong Kong | -4.8 | -4.6 | AAA | 14 | Developed | Asia | 2 out of 29 |
| Hungary | -0.3 | -0.1 | BBB- | 57 | Emerging | Central and Eastern Europe | 10 out of 25 |
| Iceland | -2.7 | -2.7 | A | 30 | | Western Europe | 15 out of 19 |
| India | -0.5 | -0.2 | BBB- | 55 | Emerging | Asia | 10 out of 29 |
| Indonesia | 0.1 | 0.2 | BB+ | 62 | Emerging | Asia | 11 out of 29 |
| Iran | 5.5 | 5.7 | | 125 | | Middle East | 10 out of 13 |
| Iraq | 6.9 | 7.0 | B- | 136 | | Middle East | 11 out of 13 |
| Ireland | -3.0 | -2.9 | A+ | 27 | Developed | Western Europe | 14 out of 19 |
| Israel | -3.1 | -2.9 | A+ | 28 | Developed | Middle East | 2 out of 13 |
| Italy | -0.8 | -0.8 | BBB- | 50 | Developed | Western Europe | 18 out of 19 |
| Jamaica | 4.0 | 4.5 | B | 104 | | Caribbean | 6 out of 9 |
| Japan | -3.2 | -3.0 | A+ | 25 | Developed | Asia | 5 out of 29 |
| Jordan | 1.8 | 2.0 | BB- | 76 | Frontier | Middle East | 8 out of 13 |
| Kazakhstan | 1.4 | 1.2 | BBB- | 70 | Frontier | Asia | 13 out of 29 |
| Kenya | 4.0 | 4.1 | B+ | 99 | Frontier | Africa | 15 out of 51 |
| Korea (North) | 21.4 | 20.9 | | 174 | | Asia | 29 out of 29 |
| Korea (South) | -3.8 | -3.6 | AA | 19 | Emerging | Asia | 4 out of 29 |
| Kuwait | -2.9 | -2.7 | AA | 31 | Frontier | Middle East | 3 out of 13 |
| Kyrgyz Republic | 8.0 | 7.9 | | 142 | | Central and Eastern Europe | 22 out of 25 |
| Laos | 11.4 | 10.9 | | 158 | | Asia | 28 out of 29 |
| Latvia | -1.3 | -1.1 | A- | 43 | | Central and Eastern Europe | 8 out of 25 |
| Lebanon | 5.4 | 4.9 | B- | 112 | Frontier | Middle East | 9 out of 13 |
| Lesotho | 8.2 | 8.2 | | 146 | | Africa | 36 out of 51 |
| Liberia | 4.5 | 4.6 | | 107 | | Africa | 17 out of 51 |
| Libya | 9.4 | 9.7 | | 153 | | Africa | 39 out of 51 |
| Lithuania | -2.0 | -1.8 | A- | 36 | Frontier | Central and Eastern Europe | 6 out of 25 |
| Luxembourg | -5.6 | -5.4 | AAA | 5 | | Western Europe | 4 out of 19 |
| Macedonia | 3.3 | 3.5 | BB- | 87 | | Central and Eastern Europe | 17 out of 25 |
| Madagascar | 5.2 | 5.6 | | 123 | | Africa | 27 out of 51 |
| Malawi | 5.0 | 5.0 | | 114 | | Africa | 21 out of 51 |
| Malaysia | -1.8 | -1.8 | A- | 35 | Emerging | Asia | 6 out of 29 |

§ S&P Credit Rating based on long-term foreign currency issuer rating. See http://www.standardandpoors.com/.

* World rank based on 175 countries covered by Euromoney. Ranking based on ascending order in which '1' equals the smallest country risk premium (CRP) and '175' equals the largest country risk premium (CRP).

† MSCI Market Classification based on MSCI Market Classification Framework. See http://www.msci.com/products/indexes/market_classification.html.

‡ Regional classification based on Euromoney. Regional rankings based on ascending order in which '1' equals the smallest country risk premium (CRP) for each region.

Note: A CRP of 0.0% is assumed in the following cases: (i) when the investor country and the investee country both have an S&P sovereign credit rating of AAA; or (ii) when the investor country has an S&P credit rating of AAA, and the investee country has a sovereign credit rating below AAA, but has a calculated CRP below 0.0% (which would imply lower risk than a country rated AAA); or (iii) when the investor country has an S&P credit rating below AAA, and the investee country has a sovereign credit rating of AAA, but has a calculated CRP above 0.0% (which would imply greater risk than a country rated below AAA). For purposes of this analysis, the U.S. is treated as having a sovereign credit rating equivalent to AAA.

The country risk premium (CRP) is not the cost of equity capital (COE).  The CRP is to be added to base COE. See Chapter 6 for proper application.

## Data Updated Through March 2017

| Investee Country | December 2016 Country Risk Premium (CRP) (%) | March 2017 Country Risk Premium (CRP) (%) | S&P Sovereign Credit Rating § | World Rank Out of 175∗ | MSCI Market Classification † | Euromoney Region ‡ | Regional Rank ‡ |
|---|---|---|---|---|---|---|---|
| Mali | 7.9 | 7.9 | | 141 | | Africa | 35 out of 51 |
| Malta | -3.2 | -3.0 | A- | 26 | | Western Europe | 13 out of 19 |
| Mauritania | 11.1 | 11.0 | | 159 | | Africa | 42 out of 51 |
| Mauritius | 0.8 | 0.9 | | 67 | Frontier | Asia | 12 out of 29 |
| Mexico | -1.9 | -1.7 | BBB+ | 37 | Emerging | Latin America | 2 out of 20 |
| Moldova | 6.7 | 7.0 | | 137 | | Central and Eastern Europe | 21 out of 25 |
| Mongolia | 5.3 | 5.6 | B- | 119 | | Asia | 18 out of 29 |
| Montenegro | 4.6 | 4.5 | B+ | 103 | | Central and Eastern Europe | 19 out of 25 |
| Morocco | 0.9 | 1.1 | BBB- | 69 | Frontier | Africa | 4 out of 51 |
| Mozambique | 6.1 | 6.0 | SD | 128 | | Africa | 29 out of 51 |
| Myanmar | 6.8 | 6.8 | | 134 | | Asia | 22 out of 29 |
| Namibia | 0.6 | 0.8 | | 66 | | Africa | 3 out of 51 |
| Nepal | 8.9 | 8.9 | | 149 | | Asia | 26 out of 29 |
| Netherlands | -5.5 | -5.4 | AAA | 6 | Developed | Western Europe | 5 out of 19 |
| New Zealand | -5.4 | -5.2 | AA | 8 | Developed | Australasia | 1 out of 7 |
| Nicaragua | 5.9 | 5.9 | B+ | 127 | | Latin America | 19 out of 20 |
| Niger | 5.5 | 5.6 | | 120 | | Africa | 25 out of 51 |
| Nigeria | 4.0 | 4.0 | B | 97 | Frontier | Africa | 14 out of 51 |
| Norway | -6.1 | -5.9 | AAA | 3 | Developed | Western Europe | 2 out of 19 |
| Oman | -1.2 | -1.1 | BBB- | 46 | Frontier | Middle East | 5 out of 13 |
| Pakistan | 5.6 | 5.6 | B | 122 | Frontier | Asia | 19 out of 29 |
| Panama | -0.7 | -0.5 | BBB | 52 | | Latin America | 6 out of 20 |
| Papua New Guinea | 5.2 | 5.3 | B+ | 118 | | Australasia | 3 out of 7 |
| Paraguay | 2.1 | 2.3 | BB | 80 | | Latin America | 9 out of 20 |
| Peru | -1.7 | -1.5 | BBB+ | 39 | Emerging | Latin America | 3 out of 20 |
| Philippines | -0.4 | -0.3 | BBB | 53 | Emerging | Asia | 9 out of 29 |
| Poland | -2.8 | -2.7 | BBB+ | 29 | Emerging | Central and Eastern Europe | 3 out of 25 |
| Portugal | -0.9 | -0.9 | BB+ | 49 | Developed | Western Europe | 17 out of 19 |
| Qatar | -3.7 | -3.5 | AA | 21 | Emerging | Middle East | 1 out of 13 |
| Romania | -0.3 | -0.1 | BBB- | 56 | Frontier | Central and Eastern Europe | 9 out of 25 |
| Russia | 1.5 | 1.1 | BB+ | 68 | Emerging | Central and Eastern Europe | 14 out of 25 |
| Rwanda | 6.2 | 6.2 | B | 130 | | Africa | 31 out of 51 |
| São Tomé & Príncipe | 11.2 | 11.5 | | 163 | | Africa | 43 out of 51 |
| Saudi Arabia | -1.0 | -1.1 | A- | 47 | | Middle East | 6 out of 13 |
| Senegal | 3.5 | 3.5 | B+ | 86 | | Africa | 8 out of 51 |
| Serbia | 2.0 | 1.8 | BB- | 75 | Frontier | Central and Eastern Europe | 16 out of 25 |
| Seychelles | 1.6 | 1.7 | | 73 | | Africa | 5 out of 51 |
| Sierra Leone | 6.2 | 6.2 | | 129 | | Africa | 30 out of 51 |
| Singapore | -6.2 | -6.0 | AAA | 1 | Developed | Asia | 1 out of 29 |
| Slovakia | -3.4 | -3.2 | A+ | 24 | | Central and Eastern Europe | 2 out of 25 |
| Slovenia | -2.2 | -2.1 | A | 34 | Frontier | Central and Eastern Europe | 5 out of 25 |
| Solomon Islands | 14.6 | 14.5 | | 168 | | Australasia | 6 out of 7 |
| Somalia | 13.2 | 13.1 | | 166 | | Africa | 46 out of 51 |
| South Africa | -0.2 | 0.0 | BBB- | 60 | Emerging | Africa | 2 out of 51 |
| Spain | -1.6 | -1.5 | BBB+ | 38 | Developed | Western Europe | 16 out of 19 |
| Sri Lanka | 1.5 | 1.4 | B+ | 72 | Frontier | Asia | 14 out of 29 |
| Sudan | 10.1 | 10.0 | | 154 | | Africa | 40 out of 51 |
| Suriname | 4.2 | 4.4 | B+ | 102 | | Latin America | 16 out of 20 |
| Swaziland | 8.8 | 9.5 | | 152 | | Africa | 38 out of 51 |
| Sweden | -5.5 | -5.4 | AAA | 7 | Developed | Western Europe | 6 out of 19 |

§ S&P Credit Rating based on long-term foreign currency issuer rating. See http://www.standardandpoors.com/.

∗ World rank based on 175 countries covered by Euromoney. Ranking based on ascending order in which '1' equals the smallest country risk premium (CRP) and '175' equals the largest country risk premium (CRP).

† MSCI Market Classification based on MSCI Market Classification Framework.  See http://www.msci.com/products/indexes/market_classification.html.

‡ Regional classification based on Euromoney. Regional rankings based on ascending order in which '1' equals the smallest country risk premium (CRP) for each region.

Note: A CRP of 0.0% is assumed in the following cases: (i) when the investor country and the investee country both have an S&P sovereign credit rating of AAA; or (ii) when the investor country has an S&P credit rating of AAA, and the investee country has a sovereign credit rating below AAA, but has a calculated CRP below 0.0% (which would imply lower risk than a country rated AAA); or (iii) when the investor country has an S&P credit rating below AAA, and the investee country has a sovereign credit rating of AAA, but has a calculated CRP above 0.0% (which would imply greater risk than a country rated below AAA). For purposes of this analysis, the U.S. is treated as having a sovereign credit rating equivalent to AAA.

The country risk premium (CRP) is not the cost of equity capital (COE). The CRP is to be added to base COE. See Chapter 6 for proper application.

## Data Updated Through March 2017

| Investee Country | December 2016 Country Risk Premium (CRP) (%) | March 2017 Country Risk Premium (CRP) (%) | S&P Sovereign Credit Rating § | World Rank Out of 175* | MSCI Market Classification † | Euromoney Region ‡ | Regional Rank ‡ |
|---|---|---|---|---|---|---|---|
| Switzerland | -6.0 | -5.9 | AAA | 2 | Developed | Western Europe | 1 out of 19 |
| Syria | 13.8 | 13.9 | | 167 | | Middle East | 13 out of 13 |
| Taiwan | -4.0 | -3.8 | AA- | 18 | Emerging | Asia | 3 out of 29 |
| Tajikistan | 9.8 | 10.0 | | 155 | | Central and Eastern Europe | 25 out of 25 |
| Tanzania | 3.7 | 3.9 | | 95 | | Africa | 13 out of 51 |
| Thailand | -0.7 | -0.7 | BBB+ | 51 | Emerging | Asia | 8 out of 29 |
| Togo | 5.0 | 5.0 | | 113 | | Africa | 20 out of 51 |
| Tonga | 16.5 | 16.4 | | 170 | | Australasia | 7 out of 7 |
| Trinidad & Tobago | -0.4 | -0.3 | A- | 54 | | Caribbean | 2 out of 9 |
| Tunisia | 1.8 | 2.2 | | 79 | Frontier | Africa | 6 out of 51 |
| Turkey | -0.1 | -0.1 | BB | 58 | Emerging | Central and Eastern Europe | 11 out of 25 |
| Turkmenistan | 7.5 | 7.8 | | 140 | | Asia | 24 out of 29 |
| Uganda | 4.6 | 4.8 | B | 110 | | Africa | 18 out of 51 |
| Ukraine | 6.8 | 6.9 | B- | 135 | | Central and Eastern Europe | 20 out of 25 |
| United Arab Emirates | -2.6 | -2.4 | AA | 33 | Emerging | Middle East | 4 out of 13 |
| United Kingdom | -3.8 | -3.5 | AA | 20 | Developed | Western Europe | 11 out of 19 |
| United States | -4.6 | -4.4 | AA+ | 15 | Developed | North America | 2 out of 2 |
| Uruguay | -1.2 | -1.1 | BBB | 45 | | Latin America | 5 out of 20 |
| Uzbekistan | 6.9 | 6.5 | | 132 | | Asia | 21 out of 29 |
| Vanuatu | 8.2 | 8.2 | | 145 | | Australasia | 4 out of 7 |
| Venezuela | 11.1 | 11.5 | CCC | 162 | | Latin America | 20 out of 20 |
| Vietnam | 2.3 | 2.1 | BB- | 78 | Frontier | Asia | 16 out of 29 |
| Yemen | 11.4 | 11.4 | | 161 | | Middle East | 12 out of 13 |
| Zambia | 4.8 | 4.9 | B | 111 | | Africa | 19 out of 51 |
| Zimbabwe | 12.7 | 12.5 | | 164 | | Africa | 44 out of 51 |

## March 2017 Country Risk Premium (CRP) Summary Statistics:

| S&P Rating | Country Count | Average CRP (%) | Median CRP (%) | Min CRP (%) | Max CRP (%) |
|---|---|---|---|---|---|
| AAA ** | 12 | -5.4 | -5.4 | -6.0 | -4.4 |
| AA (AA+, AA, AA-) | 15 | -3.5 | -3.5 | -5.2 | -1.2 |
| A (A+, A, A-) | 14 | -2.0 | -2.0 | -3.2 | -0.3 |
| BBB (BBB+, BBB, BBB-) | 17 | -0.7 | -0.7 | -2.7 | 1.2 |
| BB (BB+, BB, BB-) | 22 | 1.6 | 1.5 | -1.4 | 5.8 |
| B+ − SD | 39 | 5.2 | 4.9 | 1.4 | 11.5 |
| Investment Grade ** | 58 | -2.7 | -2.7 | -6.0 | 1.2 |
| Non-Investment Grade ** | 61 | 3.9 | 4.0 | -1.4 | 11.5 |
| **MSCI Market Classification** | | | | | |
| Developed Markets | 23 | -4.2 | -4.9 | -6.0 | -0.8 |
| Emerging Markets | 23 | -0.9 | -1.2 | -4.1 | 5.2 |
| Frontier Markets | 22 | 1.4 | 1.3 | -2.7 | 5.8 |
| **Euromoney Region ‡** | | | | | |
| Africa | 51 | 7.1 | 5.6 | -1.1 | 22.9 |
| Asia | 29 | 3.1 | 2.0 | -6.0 | 20.9 |
| Australasia | 7 | 6.1 | 8.2 | -5.2 | 16.4 |
| Caribbean | 9 | 4.1 | 3.7 | -1.1 | 11.2 |
| Central and Eastern Europe | 25 | 1.9 | 0.3 | -3.3 | 10.0 |
| Latin America | 20 | 2.3 | 2.8 | -4.1 | 11.5 |
| Middle East | 13 | 2.4 | 0.5 | -3.5 | 13.9 |
| North America | 2 | -4.8 | -4.8 | -5.2 | -4.4 |
| Western Europe | 19 | -3.5 | -4.0 | -5.9 | 4.6 |

## CCR Base Cost of Equity Capital:

| Brazil | COE (%) |
|---|---|
| March 2017 | 16.8 |
| December 2016 | 16.9 |

CCR base country-level COE for a Brazil-based investor investing in Brazil.

§ S&P Credit Rating based on long-term foreign currency issuer rating. See http://www.standardandpoors.com/.

* World rank based on 175 countries covered by Euromoney. Ranking based on ascending order in which '1' equals the smallest country risk premium (CRP) and '175' equals the largest country risk premium (CRP).

† MSCI Market Classification based on MSCI Market Classification Framework. See http://www.msci.com/products/indexes/market_classification.html

‡ Regional classification based on Euromoney. Regional rankings based on ascending order in which '1' equals the smallest country risk premium (CRP) for each region.

** Investment grade based on S&P sovereign credit rating from AAA to BBB-. Non-Investment grade based on S&P sovereign credit rating from BB+ to SD. For purposes of this analysis, the U.S. is being treated as if it were rated AAA by S&P.

Note: A CRP of 0.0% is assumed in the following cases: (i) when the investor country and the investee country both have an S&P sovereign credit rating of AAA; or (ii) when the investor country has an S&P credit rating of AAA, and the investee country has a sovereign credit rating below AAA, but has a calculated CRP below 0.0% (which would imply lower risk than a country rated AAA); or (iii) when the investor country has an S&P credit rating below AAA, and the investee country has a sovereign credit rating of AAA, but has a calculated CRP above 0.0% (which would imply greater risk than a country rated below AAA). For purposes of this analysis, the U.S. is treated as having a sovereign credit rating equivalent to AAA.

The country risk premium (CRP) is not the cost of equity capital (COE). The CRP is to be added to base COE. See Chapter 6 for proper application.

### Data Updated Through March 2017

| Investee Country | December 2016 Country Risk Premium (CRP) (%) | March 2017 Country Risk Premium (CRP) (%) | S&P Sovereign Credit Rating § | World Rank Out of 175∗ | MSCI Market Classification † | Euromoney Region ‡ | Regional Rank ‡ |
|---|---|---|---|---|---|---|---|
| Afghanistan | 16.3 | 16.2 | | 139 | | Asia | 23 out of 29 |
| Albania | 11.1 | 11.4 | B+ | 93 | | Central and Eastern Europe | 18 out of 25 |
| Algeria | 11.1 | 11.3 | | 91 | | Africa | 10 out of 51 |
| Angola | 13.4 | 13.6 | B | 121 | | Africa | 26 out of 51 |
| Argentina | 11.6 | 11.5 | B- | 96 | Frontier | Latin America | 13 out of 20 |
| Armenia | 8.8 | 9.1 | | 77 | | Asia | 15 out of 29 |
| Australia | 0.0 | 0.0 | AAA | 12 | Developed | Australasia | 2 out of 7 |
| Austria | 0.4 | 0.4 | AA+ | 13 | Developed | Western Europe | 9 out of 19 |
| Azerbaijan | 9.9 | 10.4 | BB+ | 85 | | Asia | 17 out of 29 |
| Bahamas | 7.4 | 7.2 | BB+ | 65 | | Caribbean | 3 out of 9 |
| Bahrain | 7.3 | 7.2 | BB- | 64 | Frontier | Middle East | 7 out of 13 |
| Bangladesh | 13.8 | 13.8 | BB- | 126 | Frontier | Asia | 20 out of 29 |
| Barbados | 8.9 | 10.1 | CCC+ | 82 | | Caribbean | 4 out of 9 |
| Belarus | 16.0 | 16.5 | B- | 143 | | Central and Eastern Europe | 23 out of 25 |
| Belgium | 1.6 | 1.6 | AA | 17 | Developed | Western Europe | 10 out of 19 |
| Belize | 12.1 | 12.3 | B- | 106 | | Latin America | 17 out of 20 |
| Benin | 17.6 | 17.8 | | 150 | | Africa | 37 out of 51 |
| Bermuda | 5.1 | 5.1 | A+ | 44 | | Caribbean | 1 out of 9 |
| Bhutan | 17.3 | 17.3 | | 148 | | Asia | 25 out of 29 |
| Bolivia | 10.6 | 11.0 | BB | 88 | | Latin America | 12 out of 20 |
| Bosnia & Herzegovina | 16.4 | 16.7 | B | 144 | | Central and Eastern Europe | 24 out of 25 |
| Botswana | 5.1 | 5.2 | A- | 48 | | Africa | 1 out of 51 |
| Brazil | 6.6 | 6.5 | BB | 59 | Emerging | Latin America | 7 out of 20 |
| Bulgaria | 6.4 | 6.7 | BB+ | 61 | | Central and Eastern Europe | 12 out of 25 |
| Burkina Faso | 14.8 | 15.0 | B- | 133 | | Africa | 33 out of 51 |
| Burundi | 26.2 | 26.4 | | 169 | | Africa | 47 out of 51 |
| Cambodia | 18.1 | 18.0 | | 151 | | Asia | 27 out of 29 |
| Cameroon | 13.5 | 13.7 | B | 124 | | Africa | 28 out of 51 |
| Canada | 0.0 | 0.0 | AAA | 9 | Developed | North America | 1 out of 2 |
| Cape Verde | 11.3 | 11.4 | B | 94 | | Africa | 12 out of 51 |
| Central African Republic | 29.6 | 29.8 | | 172 | | Africa | 49 out of 51 |
| Chad | 28.3 | 28.6 | | 171 | | Africa | 48 out of 51 |
| Chile | 1.1 | 1.4 | AA- | 16 | Emerging | Latin America | 1 out of 20 |
| China | 4.9 | 5.0 | AA- | 42 | Emerging | Asia | 7 out of 29 |
| Colombia | 4.9 | 5.0 | BBB | 41 | Emerging | Latin America | 4 out of 20 |
| Congo Republic | 13.1 | 13.1 | B- | 117 | | Africa | 24 out of 51 |
| Congo, DR | 14.4 | 14.4 | B- | 131 | | Africa | 32 out of 51 |
| Costa Rica | 7.8 | 8.1 | BB- | 71 | | Latin America | 8 out of 20 |
| Côte d'Ivoire | 11.1 | 11.3 | | 92 | | Africa | 11 out of 51 |
| Croatia | 6.9 | 6.9 | BB | 63 | Frontier | Central and Eastern Europe | 13 out of 25 |
| Cuba | 20.3 | 20.6 | | 160 | | Caribbean | 9 out of 9 |
| Cyprus | 4.6 | 4.8 | BB+ | 40 | | Central and Eastern Europe | 7 out of 25 |
| Czech Republic | 2.3 | 2.4 | AA- | 23 | Emerging | Central and Eastern Europe | 1 out of 25 |
| Denmark | 0.0 | 0.0 | AAA | 4 | Developed | Western Europe | 3 out of 19 |
| Djibouti | 37.2 | 35.3 | | 175 | | Africa | 51 out of 51 |
| Dominican Republic | 11.0 | 11.2 | BB- | 90 | | Caribbean | 5 out of 9 |
| Ecuador | 12.5 | 12.5 | B | 109 | | Latin America | 18 out of 20 |
| Egypt | 12.9 | 13.0 | B- | 116 | Emerging | Africa | 23 out of 51 |
| El Salvador | 10.0 | 10.0 | B- | 81 | | Latin America | 10 out of 20 |
| Equatorial Guinea | 22.8 | 23.0 | | 165 | | Africa | 45 out of 51 |

§ S&P Credit Rating based on long-term foreign currency issuer rating. See http://www.standardandpoors.com/.
∗ World rank based on 175 countries covered by Euromoney. Ranking based on ascending order in which '1' equals the smallest country risk premium (CRP) and '175' equals the largest country risk premium (CRP).
† MSCI Market Classification based on MSCI Market Classification Framework. See http://www.msci.com/products/indexes/market_classification.html.
‡ Regional classification based on Euromoney. Regional rankings based on ascending order in which '1' equals the smallest country risk premium (CRP) for each region.
Note: A CRP of 0.0% is assumed in the following cases: (i) when the investor country and the investee country both have an S&P sovereign credit rating of AAA; or (ii) when the investor country has an S&P credit rating of AAA, and the investee country has a sovereign credit rating below AAA, but has a calculated CRP below 0.0% (which would imply lower risk than a country rated AAA); or (iii) when the investor country has an S&P credit rating below AAA, and the investee country has a sovereign credit rating of AAA, but has a calculated CRP above 0.0% (which would imply greater risk than a country rated below AAA). For purposes of this analysis, the U.S. is treated as having a sovereign credit rating equivalent to AAA.

The country risk premium (CRP) is not the cost of equity capital (COE). The CRP is to be added to base COE. See Chapter 6 for proper application.

### Data Updated Through March 2017

| Investee Country | December 2016 Country Risk Premium (CRP) (%) | March 2017 Country Risk Premium (CRP) (%) | S&P Sovereign Credit Rating § | World Rank Out of 175• | MSCI Market Classification † | Euromoney Region ‡ | Regional Rank ‡ |
|---|---|---|---|---|---|---|---|
| Eritrea | 33.6 | 32.1 | | 173 | | Africa | 50 out of 51 |
| Estonia | 2.9 | 3.2 | AA- | 32 | Frontier | Central and Eastern Europe | 4 out of 25 |
| Ethiopia | 11.8 | 12.0 | B | 101 | | Africa | 16 out of 51 |
| Fiji | 17.0 | 17.0 | B+ | 147 | | Australasia | 5 out of 7 |
| Finland | 0.1 | 0.2 | AA+ | 11 | Developed | Western Europe | 8 out of 19 |
| France | 2.4 | 2.3 | AA | 22 | Developed | Western Europe | 12 out of 19 |
| Gabon | 9.7 | 10.1 | | 83 | | Africa | 7 out of 51 |
| Gambia | 15.5 | 15.6 | | 138 | | Africa | 34 out of 51 |
| Georgia | 8.5 | 8.8 | BB- | 74 | | Central and Eastern Europe | 15 out of 25 |
| Germany | 0.0 | 0.0 | AAA | 10 | Developed | Western Europe | 7 out of 19 |
| Ghana | 11.3 | 11.1 | B- | 89 | | Africa | 9 out of 51 |
| Greece | 12.4 | 12.3 | B- | 108 | Emerging | Western Europe | 19 out of 19 |
| Grenada | 12.0 | 12.3 | | 105 | | Caribbean | 7 out of 9 |
| Guatemala | 10.1 | 10.2 | BB | 84 | | Latin America | 11 out of 20 |
| Guinea | 19.0 | 19.2 | | 156 | | Africa | 41 out of 51 |
| Guinea-Bissau | 12.8 | 13.0 | | 115 | | Africa | 22 out of 51 |
| Guyana | 11.7 | 11.9 | | 100 | | Latin America | 15 out of 20 |
| Haiti | 21.7 | 20.0 | | 157 | | Caribbean | 8 out of 9 |
| Honduras | 11.4 | 11.6 | B+ | 98 | | Latin America | 14 out of 20 |
| Hong Kong | 0.0 | 0.0 | AAA | 14 | Developed | Asia | 2 out of 29 |
| Hungary | 6.2 | 6.4 | BBB- | 57 | Emerging | Central and Eastern Europe | 10 out of 25 |
| Iceland | 3.3 | 3.2 | A | 30 | | Western Europe | 15 out of 19 |
| India | 5.9 | 6.3 | BBB- | 55 | Emerging | Asia | 10 out of 29 |
| Indonesia | 6.7 | 6.8 | BB+ | 62 | Emerging | Asia | 11 out of 29 |
| Iran | 13.3 | 13.7 | | 125 | | Middle East | 10 out of 13 |
| Iraq | 15.1 | 15.3 | B- | 136 | | Middle East | 11 out of 13 |
| Ireland | 2.8 | 2.9 | A+ | 27 | Developed | Western Europe | 14 out of 19 |
| Israel | 2.8 | 2.9 | A+ | 28 | Developed | Middle East | 2 out of 13 |
| Italy | 5.6 | 5.5 | BBB- | 50 | Developed | Western Europe | 18 out of 19 |
| Jamaica | 11.5 | 12.2 | B | 104 | | Caribbean | 6 out of 9 |
| Japan | 2.7 | 2.8 | A+ | 25 | Developed | Asia | 5 out of 29 |
| Jordan | 8.7 | 9.0 | BB- | 76 | Frontier | Middle East | 8 out of 13 |
| Kazakhstan | 8.2 | 8.0 | BBB- | 70 | Frontier | Asia | 13 out of 29 |
| Kenya | 11.5 | 11.7 | B+ | 99 | Frontier | Africa | 15 out of 51 |
| Korea (North) | 32.9 | 32.7 | | 174 | | Asia | 29 out of 29 |
| Korea (South) | 1.9 | 2.1 | AA | 19 | Emerging | Asia | 4 out of 29 |
| Kuwait | 3.0 | 3.2 | AA | 31 | Frontier | Middle East | 3 out of 13 |
| Kyrgyz Republic | 16.4 | 16.5 | | 142 | | Central and Eastern Europe | 22 out of 25 |
| Laos | 20.5 | 20.2 | | 158 | | Asia | 28 out of 29 |
| Latvia | 4.9 | 5.1 | A- | 43 | | Central and Eastern Europe | 8 out of 25 |
| Lebanon | 13.2 | 12.8 | B- | 112 | Frontier | Middle East | 9 out of 13 |
| Lesotho | 16.6 | 16.9 | | 146 | | Africa | 36 out of 51 |
| Liberia | 12.1 | 12.3 | | 107 | | Africa | 17 out of 51 |
| Libya | 18.1 | 18.7 | | 153 | | Africa | 39 out of 51 |
| Lithuania | 4.1 | 4.3 | A- | 36 | Frontier | Central and Eastern Europe | 6 out of 25 |
| Luxembourg | 0.0 | 0.0 | AAA | 5 | | Western Europe | 4 out of 19 |
| Macedonia | 10.6 | 11.0 | BB- | 87 | | Central and Eastern Europe | 17 out of 25 |
| Madagascar | 13.0 | 13.6 | | 123 | | Africa | 27 out of 51 |
| Malawi | 12.7 | 12.9 | | 114 | | Africa | 21 out of 51 |
| Malaysia | 4.3 | 4.3 | A- | 35 | Emerging | Asia | 6 out of 29 |

§ S&P Credit Rating based on long-term foreign currency issuer rating. See http://www.standardandpoors.com/.

• World rank based on 175 countries covered by Euromoney. Ranking based on ascending order in which '1' equals the smallest country risk premium (CRP) and '175' equals the largest country risk premium (CRP).

† MSCI Market Classification based on MSCI Market Classification Framework. See http://www.msci.com/products/indexes/market_classification.html

‡ Regional classification based on Euromoney. Regional rankings based on ascending order in which '1' equals the smallest country risk premium (CRP) for each region.

Note: A CRP of 0.0% is assumed in the following cases: (i) when the investor country and the investee country both have an S&P sovereign credit rating of AAA; or (ii) when the investor country has an S&P credit rating of AAA, and the investee country has a sovereign credit rating below AAA, but has a calculated CRP below 0.0% (which would imply lower risk than a country rated AAA); or (iii) when the investor country has an S&P credit rating below AAA, and the investee country has a sovereign credit rating of AAA, but has a calculated CRP above 0.0% (which would imply greater risk than a country rated below AAA). For purposes of this analysis, the U.S. is treated as having a sovereign credit rating equivalent to AAA.

The country risk premium (CRP) is not the cost of equity capital (COE).  The CRP is to be added to base COE. See Chapter 6 for proper application.

## Data Updated Through March 2017

| Investee Country | December 2016 Country Risk Premium (CRP) (%) | March 2017 Country Risk Premium (CRP) (%) | S&P Sovereign Credit Rating § | World Rank Out of 175* | MSCI Market Classification † | Euromoney Region ‡ | Regional Rank ‡ |
|---|---|---|---|---|---|---|---|
| Mali | 16.3 | 16.5 | | 141 | | Africa | 35 out of 51 |
| Malta | 2.7 | 2.8 | A- | 26 | | Western Europe | 13 out of 19 |
| Mauritania | 20.2 | 20.4 | | 159 | | Africa | 42 out of 51 |
| Mauritius | 7.6 | 7.7 | | 67 | Frontier | Asia | 12 out of 29 |
| Mexico | 4.2 | 4.4 | BBB+ | 37 | Emerging | Latin America | 2 out of 20 |
| Moldova | 14.8 | 15.3 | | 137 | | Central and Eastern Europe | 21 out of 25 |
| Mongolia | 13.0 | 13.5 | B- | 119 | | Asia | 18 out of 29 |
| Montenegro | 12.3 | 12.2 | B+ | 103 | | Central and Eastern Europe | 19 out of 25 |
| Morocco | 7.6 | 7.9 | BBB- | 69 | Frontier | Africa | 4 out of 51 |
| Mozambique | 14.1 | 14.1 | SD | 128 | | Africa | 29 out of 51 |
| Myanmar | 15.0 | 15.0 | | 134 | | Asia | 22 out of 29 |
| Namibia | 7.2 | 7.5 | | 66 | | Africa | 3 out of 51 |
| Nepal | 17.5 | 17.7 | | 149 | | Asia | 26 out of 29 |
| Netherlands | 0.0 | 0.0 | AAA | 6 | Developed | Western Europe | 5 out of 19 |
| New Zealand | 0.0 | 0.0 | AA | 8 | Developed | Australasia | 1 out of 7 |
| Nicaragua | 13.8 | 13.9 | B+ | 127 | | Latin America | 19 out of 20 |
| Niger | 13.4 | 13.5 | | 120 | | Africa | 25 out of 51 |
| Nigeria | 11.5 | 11.6 | B | 97 | Frontier | Africa | 14 out of 51 |
| Norway | 0.0 | 0.0 | AAA | 3 | Developed | Western Europe | 2 out of 19 |
| Oman | 5.0 | 5.2 | BBB- | 46 | Frontier | Middle East | 5 out of 13 |
| Pakistan | 13.5 | 13.6 | B | 122 | Frontier | Asia | 19 out of 29 |
| Panama | 5.7 | 5.9 | BBB | 52 | | Latin America | 6 out of 20 |
| Papua New Guinea | 13.0 | 13.2 | B+ | 118 | | Australasia | 3 out of 7 |
| Paraguay | 9.1 | 9.4 | BB | 80 | | Latin America | 9 out of 20 |
| Peru | 4.5 | 4.7 | BBB+ | 39 | Emerging | Latin America | 3 out of 20 |
| Philippines | 6.1 | 6.1 | BBB | 53 | Emerging | Asia | 9 out of 29 |
| Poland | 3.1 | 3.1 | BBB+ | 29 | Emerging | Central and Eastern Europe | 3 out of 25 |
| Portugal | 5.4 | 5.4 | BB+ | 49 | Developed | Western Europe | 17 out of 19 |
| Qatar | 2.1 | 2.2 | AA | 21 | Emerging | Middle East | 1 out of 13 |
| Romania | 6.2 | 6.4 | BBB- | 56 | Frontier | Central and Eastern Europe | 9 out of 25 |
| Russia | 8.4 | 7.9 | BB+ | 68 | Emerging | Central and Eastern Europe | 14 out of 25 |
| Rwanda | 14.1 | 14.3 | B | 130 | | Africa | 31 out of 51 |
| São Tomé & Príncipe | 20.3 | 20.9 | | 163 | | Africa | 43 out of 51 |
| Saudi Arabia | 5.4 | 5.2 | A- | 47 | | Middle East | 6 out of 13 |
| Senegal | 10.8 | 11.0 | B+ | 86 | | Africa | 8 out of 51 |
| Serbia | 9.0 | 8.9 | BB- | 75 | Frontier | Central and Eastern Europe | 16 out of 25 |
| Seychelles | 8.5 | 8.6 | | 73 | | Africa | 5 out of 51 |
| Sierra Leone | 14.1 | 14.3 | | 129 | | Africa | 30 out of 51 |
| Singapore | 0.0 | 0.0 | AAA | 1 | Developed | Asia | 1 out of 29 |
| Slovakia | 2.4 | 2.6 | A+ | 24 | | Central and Eastern Europe | 2 out of 25 |
| Slovenia | 3.8 | 3.9 | A | 34 | Frontier | Central and Eastern Europe | 5 out of 25 |
| Solomon Islands | 24.5 | 24.7 | | 168 | | Australasia | 6 out of 7 |
| Somalia | 22.8 | 23.0 | | 166 | | Africa | 46 out of 51 |
| South Africa | 6.3 | 6.6 | BBB- | 60 | Emerging | Africa | 2 out of 51 |
| Spain | 4.6 | 4.7 | BBB+ | 38 | Developed | Western Europe | 16 out of 19 |
| Sri Lanka | 8.4 | 8.3 | B+ | 72 | Frontier | Asia | 14 out of 29 |
| Sudan | 19.0 | 19.1 | | 154 | | Africa | 40 out of 51 |
| Suriname | 11.7 | 12.0 | B+ | 102 | | Latin America | 16 out of 20 |
| Swaziland | 17.3 | 18.4 | | 152 | | Africa | 38 out of 51 |
| Sweden | 0.0 | 0.0 | AAA | 7 | Developed | Western Europe | 6 out of 19 |

§ S&P Credit Rating based on long-term foreign currency issuer rating. See http://www.standardandpoors.com/.

* World rank based on 175 countries covered by Euromoney. Ranking based on ascending order in which '1' equals the smallest country risk premium (CRP) and '175' equals the largest country risk premium (CRP).

† MSCI Market Classification based on MSCI Market Classification Framework.  See http://www.msci.com/products/indexes/market_classification.html

‡ Regional classification based on Euromoney. Regional rankings based on ascending order in which '1' equals the smallest country risk premium (CRP) for each region.

Note: A CRP of 0.0% is assumed in the following cases: (i) when the investor country and the investee country both have an S&P sovereign credit rating of AAA; or (ii) when the investor country has an S&P credit rating of AAA, and the investee country has a sovereign credit rating below AAA, but has a calculated CRP below 0.0% (which would imply lower risk than a country rated AAA); or (iii) when the investor country has an S&P credit rating below AAA, and the investee country has a sovereign credit rating of AAA, but has a calculated CRP above 0.0% (which would imply greater risk than a country rated below AAA). For purposes of this analysis, the U.S. is treated as having a sovereign credit rating equivalent to AAA.

The country risk premium (CRP) is not the cost of equity capital (COE). The CRP is to be added to base COE. See Chapter 6 for proper application.

### Data Updated Through March 2017

| Investee Country | December 2016 Country Risk Premium (CRP) (%) | March 2017 Country Risk Premium (CRP) (%) | S&P Sovereign Credit Rating § | World Rank Out of 175* | MSCI Market Classification † | Euromoney Region ‡ | Regional Rank ‡ |
|---|---|---|---|---|---|---|---|
| Switzerland | 0.0 | 0.0 | AAA | 2 | Developed | Western Europe | 1 out of 19 |
| Syria | 23.5 | 24.0 | | 167 | | Middle East | 13 out of 13 |
| Taiwan | 1.7 | 1.8 | AA- | 18 | Emerging | Asia | 3 out of 29 |
| Tajikistan | 18.6 | 19.1 | | 155 | | Central and Eastern Europe | 25 out of 25 |
| Tanzania | 11.1 | 11.5 | | 95 | | Africa | 13 out of 51 |
| Thailand | 5.7 | 5.7 | BBB+ | 51 | Emerging | Asia | 8 out of 29 |
| Togo | 12.6 | 12.8 | | 113 | | Africa | 20 out of 51 |
| Tonga | 26.8 | 27.1 | | 170 | | Australasia | 7 out of 7 |
| Trinidad & Tobago | 6.1 | 6.2 | A- | 54 | | Caribbean | 2 out of 9 |
| Tunisia | 8.8 | 9.3 | | 79 | Frontier | Africa | 6 out of 51 |
| Turkey | 6.4 | 6.4 | BB | 58 | Emerging | Central and Eastern Europe | 11 out of 25 |
| Turkmenistan | 15.8 | 16.3 | | 140 | | Asia | 24 out of 29 |
| Uganda | 12.2 | 12.6 | B | 110 | | Africa | 18 out of 51 |
| Ukraine | 14.9 | 15.2 | B- | 135 | | Central and Eastern Europe | 20 out of 25 |
| United Arab Emirates | 3.4 | 3.6 | AA | 33 | Emerging | Middle East | 4 out of 13 |
| United Kingdom | 1.9 | 2.2 | AA | 20 | Developed | Western Europe | 11 out of 19 |
| United States | 0.0 | 0.0 | AA+ | 15 | Developed | North America | 2 out of 2 |
| Uruguay | 5.1 | 5.1 | BBB | 45 | | Latin America | 5 out of 20 |
| Uzbekistan | 15.1 | 14.7 | | 132 | | Asia | 21 out of 29 |
| Vanuatu | 16.6 | 16.8 | | 145 | | Australasia | 4 out of 7 |
| Venezuela | 20.3 | 20.9 | CCC | 162 | | Latin America | 20 out of 20 |
| Vietnam | 9.3 | 9.2 | BB- | 78 | Frontier | Asia | 16 out of 29 |
| Yemen | 20.6 | 20.9 | | 161 | | Middle East | 12 out of 13 |
| Zambia | 12.5 | 12.7 | B | 111 | | Africa | 19 out of 51 |
| Zimbabwe | 22.1 | 22.3 | | 164 | | Africa | 44 out of 51 |

### March 2017 Country Risk Premium (CRP) Summary Statistics:

| S&P Rating | Country Count | Average CRP (%) | Median CRP (%) | Min CRP (%) | Max CRP (%) |
|---|---|---|---|---|---|
| AAA ** | 12 | 0.0 | 0.0 | 0.0 | 0.0 |
| AA (AA+, AA, AA-) | 15 | 2.1 | 2.2 | 0.0 | 5.0 |
| A (A+, A, A-) | 14 | 4.0 | 4.1 | 2.6 | 6.2 |
| BBB (BBB+, BBB, BBB-) | 17 | 5.7 | 5.7 | 3.1 | 8.0 |
| BB (BB+, BB, BB-) | 22 | 8.5 | 8.5 | 4.8 | 13.8 |
| B+ − SD | 39 | 13.1 | 12.7 | 8.3 | 20.9 |
| Investment Grade ** | 58 | 3.2 | 3.1 | 0.0 | 8.0 |
| Non-Investment Grade ** | 61 | 11.4 | 11.6 | 4.8 | 20.9 |
| **MSCI Market Classification** | | | | | |
| Developed Markets | 23 | 1.3 | 0.0 | 0.0 | 5.5 |
| Emerging Markets | 23 | 5.4 | 5.0 | 1.4 | 13.0 |
| Frontier Markets | 22 | 8.3 | 8.1 | 3.2 | 13.8 |
| **Euromoney Region ‡** | | | | | |
| Africa | 51 | 15.5 | 13.6 | 5.2 | 35.3 |
| Asia | 29 | 10.4 | 9.1 | 0.0 | 32.7 |
| Australasia | 7 | 14.1 | 16.8 | 0.0 | 27.1 |
| Caribbean | 9 | 11.7 | 11.2 | 5.1 | 20.6 |
| Central and Eastern Europe | 25 | 8.9 | 6.9 | 2.4 | 19.1 |
| Latin America | 20 | 9.4 | 10.1 | 1.4 | 20.9 |
| Middle East | 13 | 9.6 | 7.2 | 2.2 | 24.0 |
| North America | 2 | 0.0 | 0.0 | 0.0 | 0.0 |
| Western Europe | 19 | 2.3 | 1.6 | 0.0 | 12.3 |

### CCR Base Cost of Equity Capital:

| Canada | COE (%) |
|---|---|
| March 2017 | 6.9 |
| December 2016 | 7.0 |

CCR base country-level COE for a Canada-based investor investing in Canada.

§ S&P Credit Rating based on long-term foreign currency issuer rating. See http://www.standardandpoors.com/.

* World rank based on 175 countries covered by Euromoney. Ranking based on ascending order in which '1' equals the smallest country risk premium (CRP) and '175' equals the largest country risk premium (CRP).

† MSCI Market Classification based on MSCI Market Classification Framework. See http://www.msci.com/products/indexes/market_classification.html

‡ Regional classification based on Euromoney. Regional rankings based on ascending order in which '1' equals the smallest country risk premium (CRP) for each region.

** Investment grade based on S&P sovereign credit rating from AAA to BBB-. Non-Investment grade based on S&P sovereign credit rating from BB+ to SD. For purposes of this analysis, the U.S. is being treated as if it were rated AAA by S&P.

Note: A CRP of 0.0% is assumed in the following cases: (i) when the investor country and the investee country both have an S&P sovereign credit rating of AAA; or (ii) when the investor country has an S&P credit rating of AAA, and the investee country has a sovereign credit rating below AAA, but has a calculated CRP below 0.0% (which would imply lower risk than a country rated AAA); or (iii) when the investor country has an S&P credit rating below AAA, and the investee country has a sovereign credit rating of AAA, but has a calculated CRP above 0.0% (which would imply greater risk than a country rated below AAA). For purposes of this analysis, the U.S. is treated as having a sovereign credit rating equivalent to AAA.

The country risk premium (CRP) is not the cost of equity capital (COE).  The CRP is to be added to base COE. See Chapter 6 for proper application.

### Data Updated Through March 2017

| Investee Country | December 2016 Country Risk Premium (CRP) (%) | March 2017 Country Risk Premium (CRP) (%) | S&P Sovereign Credit Rating § | World Rank Out of 175* | MSCI Market Classification † | Euromoney Region ‡ | Regional Rank ‡ |
|---|---|---|---|---|---|---|---|
| Afghanistan | 15.0 | 14.9 | | 139 | | Asia | 23 out of 29 |
| Albania | 9.9 | 10.0 | B+ | 93 | | Central and Eastern Europe | 18 out of 25 |
| Algeria | 9.9 | 10.0 | | 91 | | Africa | 10 out of 51 |
| Angola | 12.1 | 12.3 | B | 121 | | Africa | 26 out of 51 |
| Argentina | 10.4 | 10.2 | B- | 96 | Frontier | Latin America | 13 out of 20 |
| Armenia | 7.6 | 7.7 | | 77 | | Asia | 15 out of 29 |
| Australia | -0.9 | -1.2 | AAA | 12 | Developed | Australasia | 2 out of 7 |
| Austria | -0.8 | -1.0 | AA+ | 13 | Developed | Western Europe | 9 out of 19 |
| Azerbaijan | 8.7 | 9.0 | BB+ | 85 | | Asia | 17 out of 29 |
| Bahamas | 6.2 | 5.9 | BB+ | 65 | | Caribbean | 3 out of 9 |
| Bahrain | 6.1 | 5.9 | BB- | 64 | Frontier | Middle East | 7 out of 13 |
| Bangladesh | 12.6 | 12.5 | BB- | 126 | Frontier | Asia | 20 out of 29 |
| Barbados | 7.8 | 8.8 | CCC+ | 82 | | Caribbean | 4 out of 9 |
| Belarus | 14.7 | 15.3 | B- | 143 | | Central and Eastern Europe | 23 out of 25 |
| Belgium | 0.4 | 0.2 | AA | 17 | Developed | Western Europe | 10 out of 19 |
| Belize | 10.9 | 11.0 | B- | 106 | | Latin America | 17 out of 20 |
| Benin | 16.3 | 16.5 | | 150 | | Africa | 37 out of 51 |
| Bermuda | 3.9 | 3.7 | A+ | 44 | | Caribbean | 1 out of 9 |
| Bhutan | 16.0 | 16.0 | | 148 | | Asia | 25 out of 29 |
| Bolivia | 9.4 | 9.7 | BB | 88 | | Latin America | 12 out of 20 |
| Bosnia & Herzegovina | 15.2 | 15.4 | B | 144 | | Central and Eastern Europe | 24 out of 25 |
| Botswana | 3.9 | 3.8 | A- | 48 | | Africa | 1 out of 51 |
| Brazil | 5.4 | 5.2 | BB | 59 | Emerging | Latin America | 7 out of 20 |
| Bulgaria | 5.2 | 5.3 | BB+ | 61 | | Central and Eastern Europe | 12 out of 25 |
| Burkina Faso | 13.6 | 13.7 | B- | 133 | | Africa | 33 out of 51 |
| Burundi | 24.9 | 25.3 | | 169 | | Africa | 47 out of 51 |
| Cambodia | 16.9 | 16.7 | | 151 | | Asia | 27 out of 29 |
| Cameroon | 12.3 | 12.4 | B | 124 | | Africa | 28 out of 51 |
| Canada | -1.1 | -1.4 | AAA | 9 | Developed | North America | 1 out of 2 |
| Cape Verde | 10.1 | 10.1 | B | 94 | | Africa | 12 out of 51 |
| Central African Republic | 28.3 | 28.7 | | 172 | | Africa | 49 out of 51 |
| Chad | 27.0 | 27.4 | | 171 | | Africa | 48 out of 51 |
| Chile | 0.0 | 0.0 | AA- | 16 | Emerging | Latin America | 1 out of 20 |
| China | 3.7 | 3.6 | AA- | 42 | Emerging | Asia | 7 out of 29 |
| Colombia | 3.7 | 3.6 | BBB | 41 | Emerging | Latin America | 4 out of 20 |
| Congo Republic | 11.9 | 11.8 | B- | 117 | | Africa | 24 out of 51 |
| Congo, DR | 13.1 | 13.2 | B- | 131 | | Africa | 32 out of 51 |
| Costa Rica | 6.6 | 6.8 | BB- | 71 | | Latin America | 8 out of 20 |
| Côte d'Ivoire | 9.9 | 10.0 | | 92 | | Africa | 11 out of 51 |
| Croatia | 5.7 | 5.5 | BB | 63 | Frontier | Central and Eastern Europe | 13 out of 25 |
| Cuba | 19.1 | 19.4 | | 160 | | Caribbean | 9 out of 9 |
| Cyprus | 3.5 | 3.4 | BB+ | 40 | | Central and Eastern Europe | 7 out of 25 |
| Czech Republic | 1.2 | 1.0 | AA- | 23 | Emerging | Central and Eastern Europe | 1 out of 25 |
| Denmark | -1.7 | -2.0 | AAA | 4 | Developed | Western Europe | 3 out of 19 |
| Djibouti | 35.9 | 34.2 | | 175 | | Africa | 51 out of 51 |
| Dominican Republic | 9.8 | 9.9 | BB- | 90 | | Caribbean | 5 out of 9 |
| Ecuador | 11.3 | 11.2 | B | 109 | | Latin America | 18 out of 20 |
| Egypt | 11.7 | 11.7 | B- | 116 | Emerging | Africa | 23 out of 51 |
| El Salvador | 8.8 | 8.7 | B- | 81 | | Latin America | 10 out of 20 |
| Equatorial Guinea | 21.5 | 21.8 | | 165 | | Africa | 45 out of 51 |

§ S&P Credit Rating based on long-term foreign currency issuer rating. See http://www.standardandpoors.com/.

* World rank based on 175 countries covered by Euromoney. Ranking based on ascending order in which '1' equals the smallest country risk premium (CRP) and '175' equals the largest country risk premium (CRP).

† MSCI Market Classification based on MSCI Market Classification Framework.  See http://www.msci.com/products/indexes/market_classification.html

‡ Regional classification based on Euromoney. Regional rankings based on ascending order in which '1' equals the smallest country risk premium (CRP) for each region.

Note: A CRP of 0.0% is assumed in the following cases: (i) when the investor country and the investee country both have an S&P sovereign credit rating of AAA; or (ii) when the investor country has an S&P credit rating of AAA, and the investee country has a sovereign credit rating below AAA, but has a calculated CRP below 0.0% (which would imply lower risk than a country rated AAA); or (iii) when the investor country has an S&P credit rating below AAA, and the investee country has a sovereign credit rating of AAA, but has a calculated CRP above 0.0% (which would imply greater risk than a country rated below AAA). For purposes of this analysis, the U.S. is treated as having a sovereign credit rating equivalent to AAA.

The country risk premium (CRP) is not the cost of equity capital (COE). The CRP is to be added to base COE. See Chapter 6 for proper application.

## Data Updated Through March 2017

| Investee Country | December 2016 Country Risk Premium (CRP) (%) | March 2017 Country Risk Premium (CRP) (%) | S&P Sovereign Credit Rating § | World Rank Out of 175∗ | MSCI Market Classification † | Euromoney Region ‡ | Regional Rank ‡ |
|---|---|---|---|---|---|---|---|
| Eritrea | 32.2 | 31.0 | | 173 | | Africa | 50 out of 51 |
| Estonia | 1.8 | 1.8 | AA- | 32 | Frontier | Central and Eastern Europe | 4 out of 25 |
| Ethiopia | 10.6 | 10.7 | B | 101 | | Africa | 16 out of 51 |
| Fiji | 15.7 | 15.7 | B+ | 147 | | Australasia | 5 out of 7 |
| Finland | -1.0 | -1.2 | AA+ | 11 | Developed | Western Europe | 8 out of 19 |
| France | 1.2 | 0.9 | AA | 22 | Developed | Western Europe | 12 out of 19 |
| Gabon | 8.5 | 8.8 | | 83 | | Africa | 7 out of 51 |
| Gambia | 14.2 | 14.4 | | 138 | | Africa | 34 out of 51 |
| Georgia | 7.3 | 7.5 | BB- | 74 | | Central and Eastern Europe | 15 out of 25 |
| Germany | -1.0 | -1.3 | AAA | 10 | Developed | Western Europe | 7 out of 19 |
| Ghana | 10.1 | 9.8 | B- | 89 | | Africa | 9 out of 51 |
| Greece | 11.2 | 11.0 | B- | 108 | Emerging | Western Europe | 19 out of 19 |
| Grenada | 10.8 | 11.0 | | 105 | | Caribbean | 7 out of 9 |
| Guatemala | 8.9 | 8.9 | BB | 84 | | Latin America | 11 out of 20 |
| Guinea | 17.8 | 18.0 | | 156 | | Africa | 41 out of 51 |
| Guinea-Bissau | 11.6 | 11.7 | | 115 | | Africa | 22 out of 51 |
| Guyana | 10.5 | 10.6 | | 100 | | Latin America | 15 out of 20 |
| Haiti | 20.5 | 18.8 | | 157 | | Caribbean | 8 out of 9 |
| Honduras | 10.2 | 10.3 | B+ | 98 | | Latin America | 14 out of 20 |
| Hong Kong | -0.5 | -0.7 | AAA | 14 | Developed | Asia | 2 out of 29 |
| Hungary | 5.0 | 5.1 | BBB- | 57 | Emerging | Central and Eastern Europe | 10 out of 25 |
| Iceland | 2.1 | 1.8 | A | 30 | | Western Europe | 15 out of 19 |
| India | 4.8 | 5.0 | BBB- | 55 | Emerging | Asia | 10 out of 29 |
| Indonesia | 5.5 | 5.5 | BB+ | 62 | Emerging | Asia | 11 out of 29 |
| Iran | 12.1 | 12.4 | | 125 | | Middle East | 10 out of 13 |
| Iraq | 13.9 | 14.0 | B- | 136 | | Middle East | 11 out of 13 |
| Ireland | 1.7 | 1.5 | A+ | 27 | Developed | Western Europe | 14 out of 19 |
| Israel | 1.6 | 1.5 | A+ | 28 | Developed | Middle East | 2 out of 13 |
| Italy | 4.4 | 4.2 | BBB- | 50 | Developed | Western Europe | 18 out of 19 |
| Jamaica | 10.3 | 10.9 | B | 104 | | Caribbean | 6 out of 9 |
| Japan | 1.5 | 1.4 | A+ | 25 | Developed | Asia | 5 out of 29 |
| Jordan | 7.5 | 7.7 | BB- | 76 | Frontier | Middle East | 8 out of 13 |
| Kazakhstan | 7.0 | 6.7 | BBB- | 70 | Frontier | Asia | 13 out of 29 |
| Kenya | 10.3 | 10.4 | B+ | 99 | Frontier | Africa | 15 out of 51 |
| Korea (North) | 31.6 | 31.6 | | 174 | | Asia | 29 out of 29 |
| Korea (South) | 0.8 | 0.7 | AA | 19 | Emerging | Asia | 4 out of 29 |
| Kuwait | 1.8 | 1.8 | AA | 31 | Frontier | Middle East | 3 out of 13 |
| Kyrgyz Republic | 15.2 | 15.2 | | 142 | | Central and Eastern Europe | 22 out of 25 |
| Laos | 19.3 | 19.0 | | 158 | | Asia | 28 out of 29 |
| Latvia | 3.7 | 3.7 | A- | 43 | | Central and Eastern Europe | 8 out of 25 |
| Lebanon | 12.0 | 11.5 | B- | 112 | Frontier | Middle East | 9 out of 13 |
| Lesotho | 15.4 | 15.6 | | 146 | | Africa | 36 out of 51 |
| Liberia | 10.9 | 11.0 | | 107 | | Africa | 17 out of 51 |
| Libya | 16.9 | 17.4 | | 153 | | Africa | 39 out of 51 |
| Lithuania | 3.0 | 3.0 | A- | 36 | Frontier | Central and Eastern Europe | 6 out of 25 |
| Luxembourg | -1.4 | -1.7 | AAA | 5 | | Western Europe | 4 out of 19 |
| Macedonia | 9.4 | 9.7 | BB- | 87 | | Central and Eastern Europe | 17 out of 25 |
| Madagascar | 11.8 | 12.3 | | 123 | | Africa | 27 out of 51 |
| Malawi | 11.5 | 11.6 | | 114 | | Africa | 21 out of 51 |
| Malaysia | 3.2 | 2.9 | A- | 35 | Emerging | Asia | 6 out of 29 |

§ S&P Credit Rating based on long-term foreign currency issuer rating. See http://www.standardandpoors.com/.

∗ World rank based on 175 countries covered by Euromoney. Ranking based on ascending order in which '1' equals the smallest country risk premium (CRP) and '175' equals the largest country risk premium (CRP).

† MSCI Market Classification based on MSCI Market Classification Framework. See http://www.msci.com/products/indexes/market_classification.html.

‡ Regional classification based on Euromoney. Regional rankings based on ascending order in which '1' equals the smallest country risk premium (CRP) for each region.

Note: A CRP of 0.0% is assumed in the following cases: (i) when the investor country and the investee country both have an S&P sovereign credit rating of AAA; or (ii) when the investor country has an S&P credit rating of AAA, and the investee country has a sovereign credit rating below AAA, but has a calculated CRP below 0.0% (which would imply lower risk than a country rated AAA); or (iii) when the investor country has an S&P credit rating below AAA, and the investee country has a sovereign credit rating of AAA, but has a calculated CRP above 0.0% (which would imply greater risk than a country rated below AAA). For purposes of this analysis, the U.S. is treated as having a sovereign credit rating equivalent to AAA.

The country risk premium (CRP) is not the cost of equity capital (COE).  The CRP is to be added to base COE. See Chapter 6 for proper application.

## Data Updated Through March 2017

| Investee Country | December 2016 Country Risk Premium (CRP) (%) | March 2017 Country Risk Premium (CRP) (%) | S&P Sovereign Credit Rating § | World Rank Out of 175* | MSCI Market Classification † | Euromoney Region ‡ | Regional Rank ‡ |
|---|---|---|---|---|---|---|---|
| Mali | 15.1 | 15.2 | | 141 | | Africa | 35 out of 51 |
| Malta | 1.5 | 1.4 | A- | 26 | | Western Europe | 13 out of 19 |
| Mauritania | 18.9 | 19.1 | | 159 | | Africa | 42 out of 51 |
| Mauritius | 6.4 | 6.3 | | 67 | Frontier | Asia | 12 out of 29 |
| Mexico | 3.0 | 3.0 | BBB+ | 37 | Emerging | Latin America | 2 out of 20 |
| Moldova | 13.6 | 14.1 | | 137 | | Central and Eastern Europe | 21 out of 25 |
| Mongolia | 11.8 | 12.2 | B- | 119 | | Asia | 18 out of 29 |
| Montenegro | 11.1 | 10.9 | B+ | 103 | | Central and Eastern Europe | 19 out of 25 |
| Morocco | 6.4 | 6.6 | BBB- | 69 | Frontier | Africa | 4 out of 51 |
| Mozambique | 12.8 | 12.8 | SD | 128 | | Africa | 29 out of 51 |
| Myanmar | 13.7 | 13.8 | | 134 | | Asia | 22 out of 29 |
| Namibia | 6.1 | 6.2 | | 66 | | Africa | 3 out of 51 |
| Nepal | 16.3 | 16.5 | | 149 | | Asia | 26 out of 29 |
| Netherlands | -1.4 | -1.7 | AAA | 6 | Developed | Western Europe | 5 out of 19 |
| New Zealand | -1.3 | -1.4 | AA | 8 | Developed | Australasia | 1 out of 7 |
| Nicaragua | 12.6 | 12.6 | B+ | 127 | | Latin America | 19 out of 20 |
| Niger | 12.2 | 12.2 | | 120 | | Africa | 25 out of 51 |
| Nigeria | 10.3 | 10.3 | B | 97 | Frontier | Africa | 14 out of 51 |
| Norway | -2.0 | -2.3 | AAA | 3 | Developed | Western Europe | 2 out of 19 |
| Oman | 3.9 | 3.8 | BBB- | 46 | Frontier | Middle East | 5 out of 13 |
| Pakistan | 12.2 | 12.3 | B | 122 | Frontier | Asia | 19 out of 29 |
| Panama | 4.5 | 4.5 | BBB | 52 | | Latin America | 6 out of 20 |
| Papua New Guinea | 11.8 | 11.9 | B+ | 118 | | Australasia | 3 out of 7 |
| Paraguay | 7.9 | 8.1 | BB | 80 | | Latin America | 9 out of 20 |
| Peru | 3.3 | 3.3 | BBB+ | 39 | Emerging | Latin America | 3 out of 20 |
| Philippines | 4.9 | 4.8 | BBB | 53 | Emerging | Asia | 9 out of 29 |
| Poland | 2.0 | 1.7 | BBB+ | 29 | Emerging | Central and Eastern Europe | 3 out of 25 |
| Portugal | 4.3 | 4.0 | BB+ | 49 | Developed | Western Europe | 17 out of 19 |
| Qatar | 0.9 | 0.8 | AA | 21 | Emerging | Middle East | 1 out of 13 |
| Romania | 5.0 | 5.0 | BBB- | 56 | Frontier | Central and Eastern Europe | 9 out of 25 |
| Russia | 7.2 | 6.5 | BB+ | 68 | Emerging | Central and Eastern Europe | 14 out of 25 |
| Rwanda | 12.9 | 13.0 | B | 130 | | Africa | 31 out of 51 |
| São Tomé & Príncipe | 19.0 | 19.7 | | 163 | | Africa | 43 out of 51 |
| Saudi Arabia | 4.2 | 3.8 | A- | 47 | | Middle East | 6 out of 13 |
| Senegal | 9.6 | 9.6 | B+ | 86 | | Africa | 8 out of 51 |
| Serbia | 7.8 | 7.5 | BB- | 75 | Frontier | Central and Eastern Europe | 16 out of 25 |
| Seychelles | 7.3 | 7.3 | | 73 | | Africa | 5 out of 51 |
| Sierra Leone | 12.9 | 13.0 | | 129 | | Africa | 30 out of 51 |
| Singapore | -2.2 | -2.5 | AAA | 1 | Developed | Asia | 1 out of 29 |
| Slovakia | 1.3 | 1.2 | A+ | 24 | | Central and Eastern Europe | 2 out of 25 |
| Slovenia | 2.6 | 2.5 | A | 34 | Frontier | Central and Eastern Europe | 5 out of 25 |
| Solomon Islands | 23.2 | 23.5 | | 168 | | Australasia | 6 out of 7 |
| Somalia | 21.5 | 21.8 | | 166 | | Africa | 46 out of 51 |
| South Africa | 5.1 | 5.2 | BBB- | 60 | Emerging | Africa | 2 out of 51 |
| Spain | 3.4 | 3.3 | BBB+ | 38 | Developed | Western Europe | 16 out of 19 |
| Sri Lanka | 7.2 | 6.9 | B+ | 72 | Frontier | Asia | 14 out of 29 |
| Sudan | 17.7 | 17.8 | | 154 | | Africa | 40 out of 51 |
| Suriname | 10.5 | 10.7 | B+ | 102 | | Latin America | 16 out of 20 |
| Swaziland | 16.1 | 17.2 | | 152 | | Africa | 38 out of 51 |
| Sweden | -1.3 | -1.6 | AAA | 7 | Developed | Western Europe | 6 out of 19 |

§ S&P Credit Rating based on long-term foreign currency issuer rating. See http://www.standardandpoors.com/.

* World rank based on 175 countries covered by Euromoney. Ranking based on ascending order in which '1' equals the smallest country risk premium (CRP) and '175' equals the largest country risk premium (CRP).

† MSCI Market Classification based on MSCI Market Classification Framework.  See http://www.msci.com/products/indexes/market_classification.html.

‡ Regional classification based on Euromoney. Regional rankings based on ascending order in which '1' equals the smallest country risk premium (CRP) for each region.

Note: A CRP of 0.0% is assumed in the following cases: (i) when the investor country and the investee country both have an S&P sovereign credit rating of AAA; or (ii) when the investor country has an S&P credit rating of AAA, and the investee country has a sovereign credit rating below AAA, but has a calculated CRP below 0.0% (which would imply lower risk than a country rated AAA), or (iii) when the investor country has an S&P credit rating below AAA, and the investee country has a sovereign credit rating of AAA, but has a calculated CRP above 0.0% (which would imply greater risk than a country rated below AAA). For purposes of this analysis, the U.S. is treated as having a sovereign credit rating equivalent to AAA.

The country risk premium (CRP) is not the cost of equity capital (COE). The CRP is to be added to base COE. See Chapter 6 for proper application.

## Data Updated Through March 2017

| Investee Country | December 2016 Country Risk Premium (CRP) (%) | March 2017 Country Risk Premium (CRP) (%) | S&P Sovereign Credit Rating § | World Rank Out of 175∗ | MSCI Market Classification † | Euromoney Region ‡ | Regional Rank ‡ |
|---|---|---|---|---|---|---|---|
| Switzerland | -2.0 | -2.4 | AAA | 2 | Developed | Western Europe | 1 out of 19 |
| Syria | 22.3 | 22.8 | | 167 | | Middle East | 13 out of 13 |
| Taiwan | 0.5 | 0.4 | AA- | 18 | Emerging | Asia | 3 out of 29 |
| Tajikistan | 17.3 | 17.8 | | 155 | | Central and Eastern Europe | 25 out of 25 |
| Tanzania | 9.9 | 10.2 | | 95 | | Africa | 13 out of 51 |
| Thailand | 4.6 | 4.3 | BBB+ | 51 | Emerging | Asia | 8 out of 29 |
| Togo | 11.4 | 11.5 | | 113 | | Africa | 20 out of 51 |
| Tonga | 25.5 | 25.9 | | 170 | | Australasia | 7 out of 7 |
| Trinidad & Tobago | 4.9 | 4.8 | A- | 54 | | Caribbean | 2 out of 9 |
| Tunisia | 7.6 | 8.0 | | 79 | Frontier | Africa | 6 out of 51 |
| Turkey | 5.2 | 5.1 | BB | 58 | Emerging | Central and Eastern Europe | 11 out of 25 |
| Turkmenistan | 14.6 | 15.0 | | 140 | | Asia | 24 out of 29 |
| Uganda | 11.0 | 11.3 | B | 110 | | Africa | 18 out of 51 |
| Ukraine | 13.7 | 13.9 | B- | 135 | | Central and Eastern Europe | 20 out of 25 |
| United Arab Emirates | 2.2 | 2.2 | AA | 33 | Emerging | Middle East | 4 out of 13 |
| United Kingdom | 0.8 | 0.8 | AA | 20 | Developed | Western Europe | 11 out of 19 |
| United States | -0.2 | -0.4 | AA+ | 15 | Developed | North America | 2 out of 2 |
| Uruguay | 4.0 | 3.7 | BBB | 45 | | Latin America | 5 out of 20 |
| Uzbekistan | 13.8 | 13.4 | | 132 | | Asia | 21 out of 29 |
| Vanuatu | 15.4 | 15.6 | | 145 | | Australasia | 4 out of 7 |
| Venezuela | 19.0 | 19.7 | CCC | 162 | | Latin America | 20 out of 20 |
| Vietnam | 8.2 | 7.9 | BB- | 78 | Frontier | Asia | 16 out of 29 |
| Yemen | 19.3 | 19.6 | | 161 | | Middle East | 12 out of 13 |
| Zambia | 11.3 | 11.4 | B | 111 | | Africa | 19 out of 51 |
| Zimbabwe | 20.9 | 21.1 | | 164 | | Africa | 44 out of 51 |

## March 2017 Country Risk Premium (CRP) Summary Statistics:

| S&P Rating | Country Count | Average CRP (%) | Median CRP (%) | Min CRP (%) | Max CRP (%) |
|---|---|---|---|---|---|
| AAA ∗∗ | 12 | -1.6 | -1.6 | -2.5 | -0.4 |
| AA (AA+, AA, AA-) | 15 | 0.7 | 0.8 | -1.4 | 3.6 |
| A (A+, A, A-) | 14 | 2.6 | 2.7 | 1.2 | 4.8 |
| BBB (BBB+, BBB, BBB-) | 17 | 4.3 | 4.3 | 1.7 | 6.7 |
| BB (BB+, BB, BB-) | 22 | 7.2 | 7.1 | 3.4 | 12.5 |
| B+ − SD | 39 | 11.8 | 11.4 | 6.9 | 19.7 |
| Investment Grade ∗∗ | 58 | 1.8 | 1.8 | -2.5 | 6.7 |
| Non-Investment Grade ∗∗ | 61 | 10.1 | 10.3 | 3.4 | 19.7 |
| **MSCI Market Classification** | | | | | |
| Developed Markets | 23 | -0.2 | -1.0 | -2.5 | 4.2 |
| Emerging Markets | 23 | 4.0 | 3.6 | 0.0 | 11.7 |
| Frontier Markets | 22 | 7.0 | 6.8 | 1.8 | 12.5 |
| **Euromoney Region ‡** | | | | | |
| Africa | 51 | 14.2 | 12.3 | 3.8 | 34.2 |
| Asia | 29 | 9.1 | 7.7 | -2.5 | 31.6 |
| Australasia | 7 | 12.9 | 15.6 | -1.4 | 25.9 |
| Caribbean | 9 | 10.3 | 9.9 | 3.7 | 19.4 |
| Central and Eastern Europe | 25 | 7.5 | 5.5 | 1.0 | 17.8 |
| Latin America | 20 | 8.1 | 8.8 | 0.0 | 19.7 |
| Middle East | 13 | 8.3 | 5.9 | 0.8 | 22.8 |
| North America | 2 | -0.9 | -0.9 | -1.4 | -0.4 |
| Western Europe | 19 | 0.7 | 0.2 | -2.4 | 11.0 |

## CCR Base Cost of Equity Capital:

| Chile | COE (%) |
|---|---|
| March 2017 | 11.4 |
| December 2016 | 11.4 |

CCR base country-level COE for a Chile-based investor investing in Chile.

§ S&P Credit Rating based on long-term foreign currency issuer rating. See http://www.standardandpoors.com/.

∗ World rank based on 175 countries covered by Euromoney. Ranking based on ascending order in which '1' equals the smallest country risk premium (CRP) and '175' equals the largest country risk premium (CRP).

† MSCI Market Classification based on MSCI Market Classification Framework. See http://www.msci.com/products/indexes/market_classification.html.

‡ Regional classification based on Euromoney. Regional rankings based on ascending order in which '1' equals the smallest country risk premium (CRP) for each region.

∗∗ Investment grade based on S&P sovereign credit rating from AAA to BBB-. Non-Investment grade based on S&P sovereign credit rating from BB+ to SD. For purposes of this analysis, the U.S. is being treated as if it were rated AAA by S&P.

Note: A CRP of 0.0% is assumed in the following cases: (i) when the investor country and the investee country both have an S&P sovereign credit rating of AAA; or (ii) when the investor country has an S&P credit rating of AAA, and the investee country has a sovereign credit rating below AAA, but has a calculated CRP below 0.0% (which would imply lower risk than a country rated AAA); or (iii) when the investor country has an S&P credit rating below AAA, and the investee country has a sovereign credit rating of AAA, but has a calculated CRP above 0.0% (which would imply greater risk than a country rated below AAA). For purposes of this analysis, the U.S. is treated as having a sovereign credit rating equivalent to AAA.

The country risk premium (CRP) is not the cost of equity capital (COE).  The CRP is to be added to base COE. See Chapter 6 for proper application.

## Data Updated Through March 2017

| Investee Country | December 2016 Country Risk Premium (CRP) (%) | March 2017 Country Risk Premium (CRP) (%) | S&P Sovereign Credit Rating § | World Rank Out of 175∗ | MSCI Market Classification † | Euromoney Region ‡ | Regional Rank ‡ |
|---|---|---|---|---|---|---|---|
| Afghanistan | 12.6 | 12.4 | | 139 | | Asia | 23 out of 29 |
| Albania | 6.9 | 7.1 | B+ | 93 | | Central and Eastern Europe | 18 out of 25 |
| Algeria | 6.9 | 7.0 | | 91 | | Africa | 10 out of 51 |
| Angola | 9.4 | 9.5 | B | 121 | | Africa | 26 out of 51 |
| Argentina | 7.5 | 7.2 | B- | 96 | Frontier | Latin America | 13 out of 20 |
| Armenia | 4.3 | 4.5 | | 77 | | Asia | 15 out of 29 |
| Australia | -5.2 | -5.3 | AAA | 12 | Developed | Australasia | 2 out of 7 |
| Austria | -5.0 | -5.1 | AA+ | 13 | Developed | Western Europe | 9 out of 19 |
| Azerbaijan | 5.6 | 6.0 | BB+ | 85 | | Asia | 17 out of 29 |
| Bahamas | 2.8 | 2.5 | BB+ | 65 | | Caribbean | 3 out of 9 |
| Bahrain | 2.7 | 2.5 | BB- | 64 | Frontier | Middle East | 7 out of 13 |
| Bangladesh | 9.9 | 9.7 | BB- | 126 | Frontier | Asia | 20 out of 29 |
| Barbados | 4.5 | 5.7 | CCC+ | 82 | | Caribbean | 4 out of 9 |
| Belarus | 12.3 | 12.8 | B- | 143 | | Central and Eastern Europe | 23 out of 25 |
| Belgium | -3.7 | -3.8 | AA | 17 | Developed | Western Europe | 10 out of 19 |
| Belize | 8.0 | 8.1 | B- | 106 | | Latin America | 17 out of 20 |
| Benin | 14.1 | 14.2 | | 150 | | Africa | 37 out of 51 |
| Bermuda | 0.2 | 0.1 | A+ | 44 | | Caribbean | 1 out of 9 |
| Bhutan | 13.7 | 13.6 | | 148 | | Asia | 25 out of 29 |
| Bolivia | 6.4 | 6.7 | BB | 88 | | Latin America | 12 out of 20 |
| Bosnia & Herzegovina | 12.8 | 13.0 | B | 144 | | Central and Eastern Europe | 24 out of 25 |
| Botswana | 0.2 | 0.2 | A- | 48 | | Africa | 1 out of 51 |
| Brazil | 1.8 | 1.7 | BB | 59 | Emerging | Latin America | 7 out of 20 |
| Bulgaria | 1.7 | 1.9 | BB+ | 61 | | Central and Eastern Europe | 12 out of 25 |
| Burkina Faso | 11.0 | 11.1 | B- | 133 | | Africa | 33 out of 51 |
| Burundi | 23.7 | 23.8 | | 169 | | Africa | 47 out of 51 |
| Cambodia | 14.7 | 14.4 | | 151 | | Asia | 27 out of 29 |
| Cameroon | 9.6 | 9.6 | B | 124 | | Africa | 28 out of 51 |
| Canada | -5.4 | -5.5 | AAA | 9 | Developed | North America | 1 out of 2 |
| Cape Verde | 7.1 | 7.1 | B | 94 | | Africa | 12 out of 51 |
| Central African Republic | 27.4 | 27.5 | | 172 | | Africa | 49 out of 51 |
| Chad | 26.0 | 26.1 | | 171 | | Africa | 48 out of 51 |
| Chile | -4.2 | -4.0 | AA- | 16 | Emerging | Latin America | 1 out of 20 |
| China | 0.0 | 0.0 | AA- | 42 | Emerging | Asia | 7 out of 29 |
| Colombia | 0.0 | 0.0 | BBB | 41 | Emerging | Latin America | 4 out of 20 |
| Congo Republic | 9.2 | 9.0 | B- | 117 | | Africa | 24 out of 51 |
| Congo, DR | 10.5 | 10.5 | B- | 131 | | Africa | 32 out of 51 |
| Costa Rica | 3.2 | 3.4 | BB- | 71 | | Latin America | 8 out of 20 |
| Côte d'Ivoire | 6.9 | 7.0 | | 92 | | Africa | 11 out of 51 |
| Croatia | 2.2 | 2.1 | BB | 63 | Frontier | Central and Eastern Europe | 13 out of 25 |
| Cuba | 17.2 | 17.3 | | 160 | | Caribbean | 9 out of 9 |
| Cyprus | -0.3 | -0.2 | BB+ | 40 | | Central and Eastern Europe | 7 out of 25 |
| Czech Republic | -2.9 | -2.9 | AA- | 23 | Emerging | Central and Eastern Europe | 1 out of 25 |
| Denmark | -6.1 | -6.2 | AAA | 4 | Developed | Western Europe | 3 out of 19 |
| Djibouti | 35.9 | 33.6 | | 175 | | Africa | 51 out of 51 |
| Dominican Republic | 6.7 | 6.9 | BB- | 90 | | Caribbean | 5 out of 9 |
| Ecuador | 8.4 | 8.3 | B | 109 | | Latin America | 18 out of 20 |
| Egypt | 8.9 | 8.9 | B- | 116 | Emerging | Africa | 23 out of 51 |
| El Salvador | 5.7 | 5.5 | B- | 81 | | Latin America | 10 out of 20 |
| Equatorial Guinea | 19.8 | 19.9 | | 165 | | Africa | 45 out of 51 |

§ S&P Credit Rating based on long-term foreign currency issuer rating. See http://www.standardandpoors.com/.

∗ World rank based on 175 countries covered by Euromoney. Ranking based on ascending order in which '1' equals the smallest country risk premium (CRP) and '175' equals the largest country risk premium (CRP).

† MSCI Market Classification based on MSCI Market Classification Framework.  See http://www.msci.com/products/indexes/market_classification.html

‡ Regional classification based on Euromoney. Regional rankings based on ascending order in which '1' equals the smallest country risk premium (CRP) for each region.

Note: A CRP of 0.0% is assumed in the following cases: (i) when the investor country and the investee country both have an S&P sovereign credit rating of AAA; or (ii) when the investor country has an S&P credit rating of AAA, and the investee country has a sovereign credit rating below AAA, but has a calculated CRP below 0.0% (which would imply lower risk than a country rated AAA); or (iii) when the investor country has an S&P credit rating below AAA, and the investee country has a sovereign credit rating of AAA, but has a calculated CRP above 0.0% (which would imply greater risk than a country rated below AAA). For purposes of this analysis, the U.S. is treated as having a sovereign credit rating equivalent to AAA.

The country risk premium (CRP) is not the cost of equity capital (COE). The CRP is to be added to base COE. See Chapter 6 for proper application.

## Data Updated Through March 2017

| Investee Country | December 2016 Country Risk Premium (CRP) (%) | March 2017 Country Risk Premium (CRP) (%) | S&P Sovereign Credit Rating § | World Rank Out of 175* | MSCI Market Classification † | Euromoney Region ‡ | Regional Rank ‡ |
|---|---|---|---|---|---|---|---|
| Eritrea | 31.9 | 30.0 | | 173 | | Africa | 50 out of 51 |
| Estonia | -2.2 | -1.9 | AA- | 32 | Frontier | Central and Eastern Europe | 4 out of 25 |
| Ethiopia | 7.7 | 7.8 | B | 101 | | Africa | 16 out of 51 |
| Fiji | 13.4 | 13.3 | B+ | 147 | | Australasia | 5 out of 7 |
| Finland | -5.3 | -5.3 | AA+ | 11 | Developed | Western Europe | 8 out of 19 |
| France | -2.8 | -3.0 | AA | 22 | Developed | Western Europe | 12 out of 19 |
| Gabon | 5.3 | 5.7 | | 83 | | Africa | 7 out of 51 |
| Gambia | 11.8 | 11.8 | | 138 | | Africa | 34 out of 51 |
| Georgia | 4.0 | 4.3 | BB- | 74 | | Central and Eastern Europe | 15 out of 25 |
| Germany | -5.3 | -5.4 | AAA | 10 | Developed | Western Europe | 7 out of 19 |
| Ghana | 7.2 | 6.8 | B- | 89 | | Africa | 9 out of 51 |
| Greece | 8.4 | 8.2 | B- | 108 | Emerging | Western Europe | 19 out of 19 |
| Grenada | 7.9 | 8.1 | | 105 | | Caribbean | 7 out of 9 |
| Guatemala | 5.7 | 5.8 | BB | 84 | | Latin America | 11 out of 20 |
| Guinea | 15.7 | 15.8 | | 156 | | Africa | 41 out of 51 |
| Guinea-Bissau | 8.8 | 8.9 | | 115 | | Africa | 22 out of 51 |
| Guyana | 7.6 | 7.6 | | 100 | | Latin America | 15 out of 20 |
| Haiti | 18.7 | 16.6 | | 157 | | Caribbean | 8 out of 9 |
| Honduras | 7.3 | 7.3 | B+ | 98 | | Latin America | 14 out of 20 |
| Hong Kong | -4.7 | -4.7 | AAA | 14 | Developed | Asia | 2 out of 29 |
| Hungary | 1.4 | 1.6 | BBB- | 57 | Emerging | Central and Eastern Europe | 10 out of 25 |
| Iceland | -1.8 | -2.0 | A | 30 | | Western Europe | 15 out of 19 |
| India | 1.2 | 1.5 | BBB- | 55 | Emerging | Asia | 10 out of 29 |
| Indonesia | 2.0 | 2.0 | BB+ | 62 | Emerging | Asia | 11 out of 29 |
| Iran | 9.4 | 9.7 | | 125 | | Middle East | 10 out of 13 |
| Iraq | 11.3 | 11.4 | B- | 136 | | Middle East | 11 out of 13 |
| Ireland | -2.3 | -2.4 | A+ | 27 | Developed | Western Europe | 14 out of 19 |
| Israel | -2.3 | -2.4 | A+ | 28 | Developed | Middle East | 2 out of 13 |
| Italy | 0.8 | 0.6 | BBB- | 50 | Developed | Western Europe | 18 out of 19 |
| Jamaica | 7.3 | 8.0 | B | 104 | | Caribbean | 6 out of 9 |
| Japan | -2.5 | -2.5 | A+ | 25 | Developed | Asia | 5 out of 29 |
| Jordan | 4.2 | 4.5 | BB- | 76 | Frontier | Middle East | 8 out of 13 |
| Kazakhstan | 3.7 | 3.3 | BBB- | 70 | Frontier | Asia | 13 out of 29 |
| Kenya | 7.4 | 7.5 | B+ | 99 | Frontier | Africa | 15 out of 51 |
| Korea (North) | 31.2 | 30.8 | | 174 | | Asia | 29 out of 29 |
| Korea (South) | -3.3 | -3.3 | AA | 19 | Emerging | Asia | 4 out of 29 |
| Kuwait | -2.1 | -2.0 | AA | 31 | Frontier | Middle East | 3 out of 13 |
| Kyrgyz Republic | 12.8 | 12.7 | | 142 | | Central and Eastern Europe | 22 out of 25 |
| Laos | 17.4 | 16.9 | | 158 | | Asia | 28 out of 29 |
| Latvia | 0.0 | 0.1 | A- | 43 | | Central and Eastern Europe | 8 out of 25 |
| Lebanon | 9.2 | 8.6 | B- | 112 | Frontier | Middle East | 9 out of 13 |
| Lesotho | 13.1 | 13.1 | | 146 | | Africa | 36 out of 51 |
| Liberia | 8.1 | 8.1 | | 107 | | Africa | 17 out of 51 |
| Libya | 14.7 | 15.1 | | 153 | | Africa | 39 out of 51 |
| Lithuania | -0.8 | -0.7 | A- | 36 | Frontier | Central and Eastern Europe | 6 out of 25 |
| Luxembourg | -5.8 | -5.8 | AAA | 5 | | Western Europe | 4 out of 19 |
| Macedonia | 6.4 | 6.6 | BB- | 87 | | Central and Eastern Europe | 17 out of 25 |
| Madagascar | 9.0 | 9.6 | | 123 | | Africa | 27 out of 51 |
| Malawi | 8.7 | 8.7 | | 114 | | Africa | 21 out of 51 |
| Malaysia | -0.6 | -0.8 | A- | 35 | Emerging | Asia | 6 out of 29 |

§ S&P Credit Rating based on long-term foreign currency issuer rating. See http://www.standardandpoors.com/.

* World rank based on 175 countries covered by Euromoney. Ranking based on ascending order in which '1' equals the smallest country risk premium (CRP) and '175' equals the largest country risk premium (CRP).

† MSCI Market Classification based on MSCI Market Classification Framework. See http://www.msci.com/products/indexes/market_classification.html

‡ Regional classification based on Euromoney. Regional rankings based on ascending order in which '1' equals the smallest country risk premium (CRP) for each region.

Note: A CRP of 0.0% is assumed in the following cases: (i) when the investor country and the investee country both have an S&P sovereign credit rating of AAA; or (ii) when the investor country has an S&P credit rating of AAA, and the investee country has a sovereign credit rating below AAA, but has a calculated CRP below 0.0% (which would imply lower risk than a country rated AAA); or (iii) when the investor country has an S&P credit rating below AAA, and the investee country has a sovereign credit rating of AAA, but has a calculated CRP above 0.0% (which would imply greater risk than a country rated below AAA). For purposes of this analysis, the U.S. is treated as having a sovereign credit rating equivalent to AAA.

The country risk premium (CRP) is not the cost of equity capital (COE). The CRP is to be added to base COE. See Chapter 6 for proper application.

Data Updated Through March 2017

| Investee Country | December 2016 Country Risk Premium (CRP) (%) | March 2017 Country Risk Premium (CRP) (%) | S&P Sovereign Credit Rating § | World Rank Out of 175∗ | MSCI Market Classification † | Euromoney Region ‡ | Regional Rank ‡ |
|---|---|---|---|---|---|---|---|
| Mali | 12.7 | 12.7 | | 141 | | Africa | 35 out of 51 |
| Malta | -2.5 | -2.4 | A- | 26 | | Western Europe | 13 out of 19 |
| Mauritania | 17.0 | 17.0 | | 159 | | Africa | 42 out of 51 |
| Mauritius | 3.0 | 3.0 | | 67 | Frontier | Asia | 12 out of 29 |
| Mexico | -0.8 | -0.7 | BBB+ | 37 | Emerging | Latin America | 2 out of 20 |
| Moldova | 11.0 | 11.5 | | 137 | | Central and Eastern Europe | 21 out of 25 |
| Mongolia | 9.0 | 9.4 | B- | 119 | | Asia | 18 out of 29 |
| Montenegro | 8.2 | 8.0 | B+ | 103 | | Central and Eastern Europe | 19 out of 25 |
| Morocco | 3.0 | 3.3 | BBB- | 69 | Frontier | Africa | 4 out of 51 |
| Mozambique | 10.2 | 10.1 | SD | 128 | | Africa | 29 out of 51 |
| Myanmar | 11.2 | 11.1 | | 134 | | Asia | 22 out of 29 |
| Namibia | 2.6 | 2.8 | | 66 | | Africa | 3 out of 51 |
| Nepal | 14.0 | 14.1 | | 149 | | Asia | 26 out of 29 |
| Netherlands | -5.7 | -5.8 | AAA | 6 | Developed | Western Europe | 5 out of 19 |
| New Zealand | -5.6 | -5.6 | AA | 8 | Developed | Australasia | 1 out of 7 |
| Nicaragua | 9.9 | 9.9 | B+ | 127 | | Latin America | 19 out of 20 |
| Niger | 9.4 | 9.5 | | 120 | | Africa | 25 out of 51 |
| Nigeria | 7.3 | 7.3 | B | 97 | Frontier | Africa | 14 out of 51 |
| Norway | -6.4 | -6.5 | AAA | 3 | Developed | Western Europe | 2 out of 19 |
| Oman | 0.2 | 0.2 | BBB- | 46 | Frontier | Middle East | 5 out of 13 |
| Pakistan | 9.5 | 9.5 | B | 122 | Frontier | Asia | 19 out of 29 |
| Panama | 0.9 | 1.0 | BBB | 52 | | Latin America | 6 out of 20 |
| Papua New Guinea | 9.0 | 9.1 | B+ | 118 | | Australasia | 3 out of 7 |
| Paraguay | 4.7 | 4.9 | BB | 80 | | Latin America | 9 out of 20 |
| Peru | -0.5 | -0.3 | BBB+ | 39 | Emerging | Latin America | 3 out of 20 |
| Philippines | 1.3 | 1.3 | BBB | 53 | Emerging | Asia | 9 out of 29 |
| Poland | -2.0 | -2.1 | BBB+ | 29 | Emerging | Central and Eastern Europe | 3 out of 25 |
| Portugal | 0.6 | 0.4 | BB+ | 49 | Developed | Western Europe | 17 out of 19 |
| Qatar | -3.2 | -3.1 | AA | 21 | Emerging | Middle East | 1 out of 13 |
| Romania | 1.4 | 1.5 | BBB- | 56 | Frontier | Central and Eastern Europe | 9 out of 25 |
| Russia | 3.9 | 3.2 | BB+ | 68 | Emerging | Central and Eastern Europe | 14 out of 25 |
| Rwanda | 10.3 | 10.3 | B | 130 | | Africa | 31 out of 51 |
| São Tomé & Príncipe | 17.1 | 17.7 | | 163 | | Africa | 43 out of 51 |
| Saudi Arabia | 0.5 | 0.2 | A- | 47 | | Middle East | 6 out of 13 |
| Senegal | 6.6 | 6.6 | B+ | 86 | | Africa | 8 out of 51 |
| Serbia | 4.6 | 4.3 | BB- | 75 | Frontier | Central and Eastern Europe | 16 out of 25 |
| Seychelles | 4.0 | 4.0 | | 73 | | Africa | 5 out of 51 |
| Sierra Leone | 10.3 | 10.3 | | 129 | | Africa | 30 out of 51 |
| Singapore | -6.6 | -6.7 | AAA | 1 | Developed | Asia | 1 out of 29 |
| Slovakia | -2.7 | -2.7 | A+ | 24 | | Central and Eastern Europe | 2 out of 25 |
| Slovenia | -1.2 | -1.2 | A | 34 | Frontier | Central and Eastern Europe | 5 out of 25 |
| Solomon Islands | 21.8 | 21.9 | | 168 | | Australasia | 6 out of 7 |
| Somalia | 19.9 | 20.0 | | 166 | | Africa | 46 out of 51 |
| South Africa | 1.5 | 1.8 | BBB- | 60 | Emerging | Africa | 2 out of 51 |
| Spain | -0.4 | -0.3 | BBB+ | 38 | Developed | Western Europe | 16 out of 19 |
| Sri Lanka | 3.9 | 3.6 | B+ | 72 | Frontier | Asia | 14 out of 29 |
| Sudan | 15.6 | 15.6 | | 154 | | Africa | 40 out of 51 |
| Suriname | 7.6 | 7.8 | B+ | 102 | | Latin America | 16 out of 20 |
| Swaziland | 13.8 | 14.9 | | 152 | | Africa | 38 out of 51 |
| Sweden | -5.7 | -5.8 | AAA | 7 | Developed | Western Europe | 6 out of 19 |

§ S&P Credit Rating based on long-term foreign currency issuer rating. See http://www.standardandpoors.com/.

∗ World rank based on 175 countries covered by Euromoney. Ranking based on ascending order in which '1' equals the smallest country risk premium (CRP) and '175' equals the largest country risk premium (CRP).

† MSCI Market Classification based on MSCI Market Classification Framework. See http://www.msci.com/products/indexes/market_classification.html

‡ Regional classification based on Euromoney. Regional rankings based on ascending order in which '1' equals the smallest country risk premium (CRP) for each region.

Note: A CRP of 0.0% is assumed in the following cases: (i) when the investor country and the investee country both have an S&P sovereign credit rating of AAA; or (ii) when the investor country has an S&P credit rating of AAA, and the investee country has a sovereign credit rating below AAA, but has a calculated CRP below 0.0% (which would imply lower risk than a country rated AAA); or (iii) when the investor country has an S&P credit rating below AAA, and the investee country has a sovereign credit rating of AAA, but has a calculated CRP above 0.0% (which would imply greater risk than a country rated below AAA). For purposes of this analysis, the U.S. is treated as having a sovereign credit rating equivalent to AAA.

The country risk premium (CRP) is not the cost of equity capital (COE). The CRP is to be added to base COE. See Chapter 6 for proper application.

## Data Updated Through March 2017

| Investee Country | December 2016 Country Risk Premium (CRP) (%) | March 2017 Country Risk Premium (CRP) (%) | S&P Sovereign Credit Rating § | World Rank Out of 175* | MSCI Market Classification † | Euromoney Region ‡ | Regional Rank ‡ |
|---|---|---|---|---|---|---|---|
| Switzerland | -6.4 | -6.6 | AAA | 2 | Developed | Western Europe | 1 out of 19 |
| Syria | 20.7 | 21.0 | | 167 | | Middle East | 13 out of 13 |
| Taiwan | -3.6 | -3.6 | AA- | 18 | Emerging | Asia | 3 out of 29 |
| Tajikistan | 15.2 | 15.6 | | 155 | | Central and Eastern Europe | 25 out of 25 |
| Tanzania | 6.9 | 7.2 | | 95 | | Africa | 13 out of 51 |
| Thailand | 0.9 | 0.8 | BBB+ | 51 | Emerging | Asia | 8 out of 29 |
| Togo | 8.6 | 8.7 | | 113 | | Africa | 20 out of 51 |
| Tonga | 24.4 | 24.5 | | 170 | | Australasia | 7 out of 7 |
| Trinidad & Tobago | 1.3 | 1.3 | A- | 54 | | Caribbean | 2 out of 9 |
| Tunisia | 4.4 | 4.8 | | 79 | Frontier | Africa | 6 out of 51 |
| Turkey | 1.7 | 1.6 | BB | 58 | Emerging | Central and Eastern Europe | 11 out of 25 |
| Turkmenistan | 12.2 | 12.5 | | 140 | | Asia | 24 out of 29 |
| Uganda | 8.1 | 8.5 | B | 110 | | Africa | 18 out of 51 |
| Ukraine | 11.1 | 11.3 | B- | 135 | | Central and Eastern Europe | 20 out of 25 |
| United Arab Emirates | -1.7 | -1.6 | AA | 33 | Emerging | Middle East | 4 out of 13 |
| United Kingdom | -3.3 | -3.1 | AA | 20 | Developed | Western Europe | 11 out of 19 |
| United States | -4.4 | -4.4 | AA+ | 15 | Developed | North America | 2 out of 2 |
| Uruguay | 0.3 | 0.1 | BBB | 45 | | Latin America | 5 out of 20 |
| Uzbekistan | 11.3 | 10.8 | | 132 | | Asia | 21 out of 29 |
| Vanuatu | 13.1 | 13.1 | | 145 | | Australasia | 4 out of 7 |
| Venezuela | 17.1 | 17.6 | CCC | 162 | | Latin America | 20 out of 20 |
| Vietnam | 4.9 | 4.7 | BB- | 78 | Frontier | Asia | 16 out of 29 |
| Yemen | 17.4 | 17.6 | | 161 | | Middle East | 12 out of 13 |
| Zambia | 8.5 | 8.5 | B | 111 | | Africa | 19 out of 51 |
| Zimbabwe | 19.1 | 19.2 | | 164 | | Africa | 44 out of 51 |

## March 2017 Country Risk Premium (CRP) Summary Statistics:

| S&P Rating | Country Count | Average CRP (%) | Median CRP (%) | Min CRP (%) | Max CRP (%) |
|---|---|---|---|---|---|
| AAA ** | 12 | -5.7 | -5.8 | -6.7 | -4.4 |
| AA (AA+, AA, AA-) | 15 | -3.2 | -3.1 | -5.6 | 0.0 |
| A (A+, A, A-) | 14 | -1.1 | -1.0 | -2.7 | 1.3 |
| BBB (BBB+, BBB, BBB-) | 17 | 0.8 | 0.8 | -2.1 | 3.3 |
| BB (BB+, BB, BB-) | 22 | 3.9 | 3.9 | -0.2 | 9.7 |
| B+ – SD | 39 | 9.0 | 8.5 | 3.6 | 17.6 |
| Investment Grade ** | 58 | -2.0 | -2.0 | -6.7 | 3.3 |
| Non-Investment Grade ** | 61 | 7.1 | 7.3 | -0.2 | 17.6 |
| **MSCI Market Classification** | | | | | |
| Developed Markets | 23 | -4.1 | -5.1 | -6.7 | 0.6 |
| Emerging Markets | 23 | 0.4 | 0.0 | -4.0 | 8.9 |
| Frontier Markets | 22 | 3.7 | 3.5 | -2.0 | 9.7 |
| **Euromoney Region ‡** | | | | | |
| Africa | 51 | 11.7 | 9.5 | 0.2 | 33.6 |
| Asia | 29 | 6.0 | 4.5 | -6.7 | 30.8 |
| Australasia | 7 | 10.1 | 13.1 | -5.6 | 24.5 |
| Caribbean | 9 | 7.4 | 6.9 | 0.1 | 17.3 |
| Central and Eastern Europe | 25 | 4.3 | 2.1 | -2.9 | 15.6 |
| Latin America | 20 | 4.9 | 5.7 | -4.0 | 17.6 |
| Middle East | 13 | 5.1 | 2.5 | -3.1 | 21.0 |
| North America | 2 | -5.0 | -5.0 | -5.5 | -4.4 |
| Western Europe | 19 | -3.2 | -3.8 | -6.6 | 8.2 |

## CCR Base Cost of Equity Capital:

| China | COE (%) |
|---|---|
| March 2017 | 14.0 |
| December 2016 | 14.0 |

CCR base country-level COE for a China-based investor investing in China.

§ S&P Credit Rating based on long-term foreign currency issuer rating. See http://www.standardandpoors.com/.

* World rank based on 175 countries covered by Euromoney. Ranking based on ascending order in which '1' equals the smallest country risk premium (CRP) and '175' equals the largest country risk premium (CRP).

† MSCI Market Classification based on MSCI Market Classification Framework. See http://www.msci.com/products/indexes/market_classification.html.

‡ Regional classification based on Euromoney. Regional rankings based on ascending order in which '1' equals the smallest country risk premium (CRP) for each region.

** Investment grade based on S&P sovereign credit rating from AAA to BBB-. Non-Investment grade based on S&P sovereign credit rating from BB+ to SD. For purposes of this analysis, the U.S. is being treated as if it were rated AAA by S&P.

Note: A CRP of 0.0% is assumed in the following cases: (i) when the investor country and the investee country both have an S&P sovereign credit rating of AAA; or (ii) when the investor country has an S&P credit rating of AAA, and the investee country has a sovereign credit rating below AAA, but has a calculated CRP below 0.0% (which would imply lower risk than a country rated AAA); or (iii) when the investor country has an S&P credit rating below AAA, and the investee country has a sovereign credit rating of AAA, but has a calculated CRP above 0.0% (which would imply greater risk than a country rated below AAA). For purposes of this analysis, the U.S. is treated as having a sovereign credit rating equivalent to AAA.

The country risk premium (CRP) is not the cost of equity capital (COE).  The CRP is to be added to base COE. See Chapter 6 for proper application.

### Data Updated Through March 2017

| Investee Country | December 2016 Country Risk Premium (CRP) (%) | March 2017 Country Risk Premium (CRP) (%) | S&P Sovereign Credit Rating § | World Rank Out of 175* | MSCI Market Classification † | Euromoney Region ‡ | Regional Rank ‡ |
|---|---|---|---|---|---|---|---|
| Afghanistan | 12.3 | 12.1 | | 139 | | Asia | 23 out of 29 |
| Albania | 6.7 | 6.9 | B+ | 93 | | Central and Eastern Europe | 18 out of 25 |
| Algeria | 6.7 | 6.9 | | 91 | | Africa | 10 out of 51 |
| Angola | 9.1 | 9.3 | B | 121 | | Africa | 26 out of 51 |
| Argentina | 7.3 | 7.1 | B- | 96 | Frontier | Latin America | 13 out of 20 |
| Armenia | 4.2 | 4.4 | | 77 | | Asia | 15 out of 29 |
| Australia | -5.0 | -5.1 | AAA | 12 | Developed | Australasia | 2 out of 7 |
| Austria | -4.8 | -4.9 | AA+ | 13 | Developed | Western Europe | 9 out of 19 |
| Azerbaijan | 5.4 | 5.9 | BB+ | 85 | | Asia | 17 out of 29 |
| Bahamas | 2.7 | 2.5 | BB+ | 65 | | Caribbean | 3 out of 9 |
| Bahrain | 2.6 | 2.5 | BB- | 64 | Frontier | Middle East | 7 out of 13 |
| Bangladesh | 9.7 | 9.5 | BB- | 126 | Frontier | Asia | 20 out of 29 |
| Barbados | 4.4 | 5.6 | CCC+ | 82 | | Caribbean | 4 out of 9 |
| Belarus | 11.9 | 12.5 | B- | 143 | | Central and Eastern Europe | 23 out of 25 |
| Belgium | -3.5 | -3.7 | AA | 17 | Developed | Western Europe | 10 out of 19 |
| Belize | 7.7 | 7.9 | B- | 106 | | Latin America | 17 out of 20 |
| Benin | 13.7 | 13.9 | | 150 | | Africa | 37 out of 51 |
| Bermuda | 0.3 | 0.2 | A+ | 44 | | Caribbean | 1 out of 9 |
| Bhutan | 13.3 | 13.4 | | 148 | | Asia | 25 out of 29 |
| Bolivia | 6.2 | 6.6 | BB | 88 | | Latin America | 12 out of 20 |
| Bosnia & Herzegovina | 12.4 | 12.7 | B | 144 | | Central and Eastern Europe | 24 out of 25 |
| Botswana | 0.3 | 0.3 | A- | 48 | | Africa | 1 out of 51 |
| Brazil | 1.8 | 1.7 | BB | 59 | Emerging | Latin America | 7 out of 20 |
| Bulgaria | 1.7 | 1.9 | BB+ | 61 | | Central and Eastern Europe | 12 out of 25 |
| Burkina Faso | 10.7 | 10.9 | B- | 133 | | Africa | 33 out of 51 |
| Burundi | 23.0 | 23.2 | | 169 | | Africa | 47 out of 51 |
| Cambodia | 14.3 | 14.1 | | 151 | | Asia | 27 out of 29 |
| Cameroon | 9.3 | 9.4 | B | 124 | | Africa | 28 out of 51 |
| Canada | -5.2 | -5.4 | AAA | 9 | Developed | North America | 1 out of 2 |
| Cape Verde | 6.9 | 7.0 | B | 94 | | Africa | 12 out of 51 |
| Central African Republic | 26.6 | 26.9 | | 172 | | Africa | 49 out of 51 |
| Chad | 25.2 | 25.5 | | 171 | | Africa | 48 out of 51 |
| Chile | -4.0 | -3.8 | AA- | 16 | Emerging | Latin America | 1 out of 20 |
| China | 0.0 | 0.0 | AA- | 42 | Emerging | Asia | 7 out of 29 |
| Colombia | 0.0 | 0.0 | BBB | 41 | Emerging | Latin America | 4 out of 20 |
| Congo Republic | 8.9 | 8.9 | B- | 117 | | Africa | 24 out of 51 |
| Congo, DR | 10.2 | 10.3 | B- | 131 | | Africa | 32 out of 51 |
| Costa Rica | 3.1 | 3.4 | BB- | 71 | | Latin America | 8 out of 20 |
| Côte d'Ivoire | 6.8 | 6.9 | | 92 | | Africa | 11 out of 51 |
| Croatia | 2.2 | 2.1 | BB | 63 | Frontier | Central and Eastern Europe | 13 out of 25 |
| Cuba | 16.7 | 17.0 | | 160 | | Caribbean | 9 out of 9 |
| Cyprus | -0.3 | -0.2 | BB+ | 40 | | Central and Eastern Europe | 7 out of 25 |
| Czech Republic | -2.7 | -2.7 | AA- | 23 | Emerging | Central and Eastern Europe | 1 out of 25 |
| Denmark | -5.9 | -6.0 | AAA | 4 | Developed | Western Europe | 3 out of 19 |
| Djibouti | 34.8 | 32.8 | | 175 | | Africa | 51 out of 51 |
| Dominican Republic | 6.6 | 6.8 | BB- | 90 | | Caribbean | 5 out of 9 |
| Ecuador | 8.2 | 8.1 | B | 109 | | Latin America | 18 out of 20 |
| Egypt | 8.7 | 8.7 | B- | 116 | Emerging | Africa | 23 out of 51 |
| El Salvador | 5.6 | 5.5 | B- | 81 | | Latin America | 10 out of 20 |
| Equatorial Guinea | 19.2 | 19.5 | | 165 | | Africa | 45 out of 51 |

§ S&P Credit Rating based on long-term foreign currency issuer rating. See http://www.standardandpoors.com/.

* World rank based on 175 countries covered by Euromoney. Ranking based on ascending order in which '1' equals the smallest country risk premium (CRP) and '175' equals the largest country risk premium (CRP).

† MSCI Market Classification based on MSCI Market Classification Framework.  See http://www.msci.com/products/indexes/market_classification.html

‡ Regional classification based on Euromoney. Regional rankings based on ascending order in which '1' equals the smallest country risk premium (CRP) for each region.

Note: A CRP of 0.0% is assumed in the following cases: (i) when the investor country and the investee country both have an S&P sovereign credit rating of AAA; or (ii) when the investor country has an S&P credit rating of AAA, and the investee country has a sovereign credit rating below AAA, but has a calculated CRP below 0.0% (which would imply lower risk than a country rated AAA); or (iii) when the investor country has an S&P credit rating below AAA, and the investee country has a sovereign credit rating of AAA, but has a calculated CRP above 0.0% (which would imply greater risk than a country rated below AAA). For purposes of this analysis, the U.S. is treated as having a sovereign credit rating equivalent to AAA.

The country risk premium (CRP) is not the cost of equity capital (COE).  The CRP is to be added to base COE. See Chapter 6 for proper application.

Data Updated Through March 2017

| Investee Country | December 2016 Country Risk Premium (CRP) (%) | March 2017 Country Risk Premium (CRP) (%) | S&P Sovereign Credit Rating § | World Rank Out of 175* | MSCI Market Classification † | Euromoney Region ‡ | Regional Rank ‡ |
|---|---|---|---|---|---|---|---|
| Eritrea | 30.9 | 29.3 | | 173 | | Africa | 50 out of 51 |
| Estonia | -2.1 | -1.9 | AA- | 32 | Frontier | Central and Eastern Europe | 4 out of 25 |
| Ethiopia | 7.5 | 7.6 | B | 101 | | Africa | 16 out of 51 |
| Fiji | 13.0 | 13.0 | B+ | 147 | | Australasia | 5 out of 7 |
| Finland | -5.1 | -5.2 | AA+ | 11 | Developed | Western Europe | 8 out of 19 |
| France | -2.7 | -2.9 | AA | 22 | Developed | Western Europe | 12 out of 19 |
| Gabon | 5.2 | 5.6 | | 83 | | Africa | 7 out of 51 |
| Gambia | 11.4 | 11.6 | | 138 | | Africa | 34 out of 51 |
| Georgia | 3.9 | 4.2 | BB- | 74 | | Central and Eastern Europe | 15 out of 25 |
| Germany | -5.1 | -5.2 | AAA | 10 | Developed | Western Europe | 7 out of 19 |
| Ghana | 7.0 | 6.7 | B- | 89 | | Africa | 9 out of 51 |
| Greece | 8.2 | 8.0 | B- | 108 | Emerging | Western Europe | 19 out of 19 |
| Grenada | 7.7 | 7.9 | | 105 | | Caribbean | 7 out of 9 |
| Guatemala | 5.6 | 5.7 | BB | 84 | | Latin America | 11 out of 20 |
| Guinea | 15.2 | 15.4 | | 156 | | Africa | 41 out of 51 |
| Guinea-Bissau | 8.6 | 8.7 | | 115 | | Africa | 22 out of 51 |
| Guyana | 7.4 | 7.5 | | 100 | | Latin America | 15 out of 20 |
| Haiti | 18.2 | 16.3 | | 157 | | Caribbean | 8 out of 9 |
| Honduras | 7.1 | 7.2 | B+ | 98 | | Latin America | 14 out of 20 |
| Hong Kong | -4.5 | -4.6 | AAA | 14 | Developed | Asia | 2 out of 29 |
| Hungary | 1.4 | 1.6 | BBB- | 57 | Emerging | Central and Eastern Europe | 10 out of 25 |
| Iceland | -1.7 | -1.9 | A | 30 | | Western Europe | 15 out of 19 |
| India | 1.2 | 1.5 | BBB- | 55 | Emerging | Asia | 10 out of 29 |
| Indonesia | 2.0 | 2.0 | BB+ | 62 | Emerging | Asia | 11 out of 29 |
| Iran | 9.1 | 9.5 | | 125 | | Middle East | 10 out of 13 |
| Iraq | 11.0 | 11.2 | B- | 136 | | Middle East | 11 out of 13 |
| Ireland | -2.2 | -2.3 | A+ | 27 | Developed | Western Europe | 14 out of 19 |
| Israel | -2.2 | -2.2 | A+ | 28 | Developed | Middle East | 2 out of 13 |
| Italy | 0.8 | 0.6 | BBB- | 50 | Developed | Western Europe | 18 out of 19 |
| Jamaica | 7.1 | 7.9 | B | 104 | | Caribbean | 6 out of 9 |
| Japan | -2.3 | -2.4 | A+ | 25 | Developed | Asia | 5 out of 29 |
| Jordan | 4.1 | 4.4 | BB- | 76 | Frontier | Middle East | 8 out of 13 |
| Kazakhstan | 3.6 | 3.3 | BBB- | 70 | Frontier | Asia | 13 out of 29 |
| Kenya | 7.2 | 7.3 | B+ | 99 | Frontier | Africa | 15 out of 51 |
| Korea (North) | 30.2 | 30.0 | | 174 | | Asia | 29 out of 29 |
| Korea (South) | -3.1 | -3.1 | AA | 19 | Emerging | Asia | 4 out of 29 |
| Kuwait | -2.0 | -1.9 | AA | 31 | Frontier | Middle East | 3 out of 13 |
| Kyrgyz Republic | 12.5 | 12.5 | | 142 | | Central and Eastern Europe | 22 out of 25 |
| Laos | 16.9 | 16.5 | | 158 | | Asia | 28 out of 29 |
| Latvia | 0.0 | 0.2 | A- | 43 | | Central and Eastern Europe | 8 out of 25 |
| Lebanon | 9.0 | 8.4 | B- | 112 | Frontier | Middle East | 9 out of 13 |
| Lesotho | 12.7 | 12.9 | | 146 | | Africa | 36 out of 51 |
| Liberia | 7.8 | 7.9 | | 107 | | Africa | 17 out of 51 |
| Libya | 14.3 | 14.8 | | 153 | | Africa | 39 out of 51 |
| Lithuania | -0.8 | -0.7 | A- | 36 | Frontier | Central and Eastern Europe | 6 out of 25 |
| Luxembourg | -5.5 | -5.7 | AAA | 5 | | Western Europe | 4 out of 19 |
| Macedonia | 6.2 | 6.5 | BB- | 87 | | Central and Eastern Europe | 17 out of 25 |
| Madagascar | 8.7 | 9.4 | | 123 | | Africa | 27 out of 51 |
| Malawi | 8.4 | 8.6 | | 114 | | Africa | 21 out of 51 |
| Malaysia | -0.6 | -0.7 | A- | 35 | Emerging | Asia | 6 out of 29 |

§ S&P Credit Rating based on long-term foreign currency issuer rating. See http://www.standardandpoors.com/.

* World rank based on 175 countries covered by Euromoney. Ranking based on ascending order in which '1' equals the smallest country risk premium (CRP) and '175' equals the largest country risk premium (CRP).

† MSCI Market Classification based on MSCI Market Classification Framework.  See http://www.msci.com/products/indexes/market_classification.html

‡ Regional classification based on Euromoney. Regional rankings based on ascending order in which '1' equals the smallest country risk premium (CRP) for each region.

Note: A CRP of 0.0% is assumed in the following cases: (i) when the investor country and the investee country both have an S&P sovereign credit rating of AAA; or (ii) when the investor country has an S&P credit rating of AAA, and the investee country has a sovereign credit rating below AAA, but has a calculated CRP below 0.0% (which would imply lower risk than a country rated AAA); or (iii) when the investor country has an S&P credit rating below AAA, and the investee country has a sovereign credit rating of AAA, but has a calculated CRP above 0.0% (which would imply greater risk than a country rated below AAA). For purposes of this analysis, the U.S. is treated as having a sovereign credit rating equivalent to AAA.

The country risk premium (CRP) is not the cost of equity capital (COE). The CRP is to be added to base COE. See Chapter 6 for proper application.

## Data Updated Through March 2017

| Investee Country | December 2016 Country Risk Premium (CRP) (%) | March 2017 Country Risk Premium (CRP) (%) | S&P Sovereign Credit Rating § | World Rank Out of 175* | MSCI Market Classification † | Euromoney Region ‡ | Regional Rank ‡ |
|---|---|---|---|---|---|---|---|
| Mali | 12.3 | 12.5 | | 141 | | Africa | 35 out of 51 |
| Malta | -2.3 | -2.3 | A- | 26 | | Western Europe | 13 out of 19 |
| Mauritania | 16.5 | 16.7 | | 159 | | Africa | 42 out of 51 |
| Mauritius | 2.9 | 2.9 | | 67 | Frontier | Asia | 12 out of 29 |
| Mexico | -0.7 | -0.6 | BBB+ | 37 | Emerging | Latin America | 2 out of 20 |
| Moldova | 10.7 | 11.2 | | 137 | | Central and Eastern Europe | 21 out of 25 |
| Mongolia | 8.8 | 9.3 | B- | 119 | | Asia | 18 out of 29 |
| Montenegro | 8.0 | 7.8 | B+ | 103 | | Central and Eastern Europe | 19 out of 25 |
| Morocco | 3.0 | 3.2 | BBB- | 69 | Frontier | Africa | 4 out of 51 |
| Mozambique | 9.9 | 9.9 | SD | 128 | | Africa | 29 out of 51 |
| Myanmar | 10.9 | 10.9 | | 134 | | Asia | 22 out of 29 |
| Namibia | 2.6 | 2.8 | | 66 | | Africa | 3 out of 51 |
| Nepal | 13.6 | 13.8 | | 149 | | Asia | 26 out of 29 |
| Netherlands | -5.5 | -5.6 | AAA | 6 | Developed | Western Europe | 5 out of 19 |
| New Zealand | -5.4 | -5.4 | AA | 8 | Developed | Australasia | 1 out of 7 |
| Nicaragua | 9.6 | 9.7 | B+ | 127 | | Latin America | 19 out of 20 |
| Niger | 9.2 | 9.3 | | 120 | | Africa | 25 out of 51 |
| Nigeria | 7.1 | 7.2 | B | 97 | Frontier | Africa | 14 out of 51 |
| Norway | -6.2 | -6.3 | AAA | 3 | Developed | Western Europe | 2 out of 19 |
| Oman | 0.2 | 0.2 | BBB- | 46 | Frontier | Middle East | 5 out of 13 |
| Pakistan | 9.3 | 9.3 | B | 122 | Frontier | Asia | 19 out of 29 |
| Panama | 0.9 | 1.0 | BBB | 52 | | Latin America | 6 out of 20 |
| Papua New Guinea | 8.8 | 9.0 | B+ | 118 | | Australasia | 3 out of 7 |
| Paraguay | 4.6 | 4.8 | BB | 80 | | Latin America | 9 out of 20 |
| Peru | -0.4 | -0.3 | BBB+ | 39 | Emerging | Latin America | 3 out of 20 |
| Philippines | 1.3 | 1.3 | BBB | 53 | Emerging | Asia | 9 out of 29 |
| Poland | -1.8 | -2.0 | BBB+ | 29 | Emerging | Central and Eastern Europe | 3 out of 25 |
| Portugal | 0.6 | 0.4 | BB+ | 49 | Developed | Western Europe | 17 out of 19 |
| Qatar | -3.0 | -3.0 | AA | 21 | Emerging | Middle East | 1 out of 13 |
| Romania | 1.4 | 1.5 | BBB- | 56 | Frontier | Central and Eastern Europe | 9 out of 25 |
| Russia | 3.8 | 3.2 | BB+ | 68 | Emerging | Central and Eastern Europe | 14 out of 25 |
| Rwanda | 10.0 | 10.1 | B | 130 | | Africa | 31 out of 51 |
| São Tomé & Príncipe | 16.6 | 17.3 | | 163 | | Africa | 43 out of 51 |
| Saudi Arabia | 0.6 | 0.2 | A- | 47 | | Middle East | 6 out of 13 |
| Senegal | 6.4 | 6.5 | B+ | 86 | | Africa | 8 out of 51 |
| Serbia | 4.5 | 4.2 | BB- | 75 | Frontier | Central and Eastern Europe | 16 out of 25 |
| Seychelles | 3.9 | 4.0 | | 73 | | Africa | 5 out of 51 |
| Sierra Leone | 10.0 | 10.1 | | 129 | | Africa | 30 out of 51 |
| Singapore | -6.4 | -6.5 | AAA | 1 | Developed | Asia | 1 out of 29 |
| Slovakia | -2.6 | -2.6 | A+ | 24 | | Central and Eastern Europe | 2 out of 25 |
| Slovenia | -1.1 | -1.1 | A | 34 | Frontier | Central and Eastern Europe | 5 out of 25 |
| Solomon Islands | 21.1 | 21.4 | | 168 | | Australasia | 6 out of 7 |
| Somalia | 19.3 | 19.5 | | 166 | | Africa | 46 out of 51 |
| South Africa | 1.5 | 1.8 | BBB- | 60 | Emerging | Africa | 2 out of 51 |
| Spain | -0.3 | -0.3 | BBB+ | 38 | Developed | Western Europe | 16 out of 19 |
| Sri Lanka | 3.8 | 3.6 | B+ | 72 | Frontier | Asia | 14 out of 29 |
| Sudan | 15.2 | 15.3 | | 154 | | Africa | 40 out of 51 |
| Suriname | 7.4 | 7.7 | B+ | 102 | | Latin America | 16 out of 20 |
| Swaziland | 13.4 | 14.6 | | 152 | | Africa | 38 out of 51 |
| Sweden | -5.4 | -5.6 | AAA | 7 | Developed | Western Europe | 6 out of 19 |

§ S&P Credit Rating based on long-term foreign currency issuer rating. See http://www.standardandpoors.com/.

* World rank based on 175 countries covered by Euromoney. Ranking based on ascending order in which '1' equals the smallest country risk premium (CRP) and '175' equals the largest country risk premium (CRP).

† MSCI Market Classification based on MSCI Market Classification Framework. See http://www.msci.com/products/indexes/market_classification.html

‡ Regional classification based on Euromoney. Regional rankings based on ascending order in which '1' equals the smallest country risk premium (CRP) for each region.

Note: A CRP of 0.0% is assumed in the following cases: (i) when the investor country and the investee country both have an S&P sovereign credit rating of AAA; or (ii) when the investor country has an S&P credit rating of AAA, and the investee country has a sovereign credit rating below AAA, but has a calculated CRP below 0.0% (which would imply lower risk than a country rated AAA); or (iii) when the investor country has an S&P credit rating below AAA, and the investee country has a sovereign credit rating of AAA, but has a calculated CRP above 0.0% (which would imply greater risk than a country rated below AAA). For purposes of this analysis, the U.S. is treated as having a sovereign credit rating equivalent to AAA.

The country risk premium (CRP) is not the cost of equity capital (COE). The CRP is to be added to base COE. See Chapter 6 for proper application.

## Data Updated Through March 2017

| Investee Country | December 2016 Country Risk Premium (CRP) (%) | March 2017 Country Risk Premium (CRP) (%) | S&P Sovereign Credit Rating § | World Rank Out of 175* | MSCI Market Classification † | Euromoney Region ‡ | Regional Rank ‡ |
|---|---|---|---|---|---|---|---|
| Switzerland | -6.1 | -6.3 | AAA | 2 | Developed | Western Europe | 1 out of 19 |
| Syria | 20.1 | 20.6 | | 167 | | Middle East | 13 out of 13 |
| Taiwan | -3.4 | -3.4 | AA- | 18 | Emerging | Asia | 3 out of 29 |
| Tajikistan | 14.7 | 15.3 | | 155 | | Central and Eastern Europe | 25 out of 25 |
| Tanzania | 6.8 | 7.1 | | 95 | | Africa | 13 out of 51 |
| Thailand | 0.9 | 0.8 | BBB+ | 51 | Emerging | Asia | 8 out of 29 |
| Togo | 8.4 | 8.5 | | 113 | | Africa | 20 out of 51 |
| Tonga | 23.6 | 23.9 | | 170 | | Australasia | 7 out of 7 |
| Trinidad & Tobago | 1.3 | 1.3 | A- | 54 | | Caribbean | 2 out of 9 |
| Tunisia | 4.3 | 4.7 | | 79 | Frontier | Africa | 6 out of 51 |
| Turkey | 1.7 | 1.6 | BB | 58 | Emerging | Central and Eastern Europe | 11 out of 25 |
| Turkmenistan | 11.8 | 12.3 | | 140 | | Asia | 24 out of 29 |
| Uganda | 7.9 | 8.3 | B | 110 | | Africa | 18 out of 51 |
| Ukraine | 10.8 | 11.0 | B- | 135 | | Central and Eastern Europe | 20 out of 25 |
| United Arab Emirates | -1.6 | -1.5 | AA | 33 | Emerging | Middle East | 4 out of 13 |
| United Kingdom | -3.1 | -3.0 | AA | 20 | Developed | Western Europe | 11 out of 19 |
| United States | -4.2 | -4.2 | AA+ | 15 | Developed | North America | 2 out of 2 |
| Uruguay | 0.3 | 0.2 | BBB | 45 | | Latin America | 5 out of 20 |
| Uzbekistan | 11.0 | 10.5 | | 132 | | Asia | 21 out of 29 |
| Vanuatu | 12.7 | 12.8 | | 145 | | Australasia | 4 out of 7 |
| Venezuela | 16.6 | 17.3 | CCC | 162 | | Latin America | 20 out of 20 |
| Vietnam | 4.8 | 4.6 | BB- | 78 | Frontier | Asia | 16 out of 29 |
| Yemen | 16.9 | 17.2 | | 161 | | Middle East | 12 out of 13 |
| Zambia | 8.2 | 8.4 | B | 111 | | Africa | 19 out of 51 |
| Zimbabwe | 18.6 | 18.7 | | 164 | | Africa | 44 out of 51 |

## March 2017 Country Risk Premium (CRP) Summary Statistics:

| S&P Rating | Country Count | Average CRP (%) | Median CRP (%) | Min CRP (%) | Max CRP (%) |
|---|---|---|---|---|---|
| AAA ** | 12 | -5.5 | -5.6 | -6.5 | -4.2 |
| AA (AA+, AA, AA-) | 15 | -3.1 | -3.0 | -5.4 | 0.0 |
| A (A+, A, A-) | 14 | -1.0 | -0.9 | -2.6 | 1.3 |
| BBB (BBB+, BBB, BBB-) | 17 | 0.8 | 0.8 | -2.0 | 3.3 |
| BB (BB+, BB, BB-) | 22 | 3.8 | 3.8 | -0.2 | 9.5 |
| B+ − SD | 39 | 8.8 | 8.4 | 3.6 | 17.3 |
| Investment Grade ** | 58 | -1.9 | -1.9 | -6.5 | 3.3 |
| Non-Investment Grade ** | 61 | 7.0 | 7.2 | -0.2 | 17.3 |
| **MSCI Market Classification** | | | | | |
| Developed Markets | 23 | -4.0 | -4.9 | -6.5 | 0.6 |
| Emerging Markets | 23 | 0.5 | 0.0 | -3.8 | 8.7 |
| Frontier Markets | 22 | 3.7 | 3.5 | -1.9 | 9.5 |
| **Euromoney Region ‡** | | | | | |
| Africa | 51 | 11.4 | 9.3 | 0.3 | 32.8 |
| Asia | 29 | 5.9 | 4.4 | -6.5 | 30.0 |
| Australasia | 7 | 9.9 | 12.8 | -5.4 | 23.9 |
| Caribbean | 9 | 7.3 | 6.8 | 0.2 | 17.0 |
| Central and Eastern Europe | 25 | 4.2 | 2.1 | -2.7 | 15.3 |
| Latin America | 20 | 4.8 | 5.6 | -3.8 | 17.3 |
| Middle East | 13 | 5.0 | 2.5 | -3.0 | 20.6 |
| North America | 2 | -4.8 | -4.8 | -5.4 | -4.2 |
| Western Europe | 19 | -3.1 | -3.7 | -6.3 | 8.0 |

## CCR Base Cost of Equity Capital:

| Colombia | COE (%) |
|---|---|
| March 2017 | 19.0 |
| December 2016 | 19.3 |

CCR base country-level COE for a Colombia-based investor investing in Colombia.

§ S&P Credit Rating based on long-term foreign currency issuer rating. See http://www.standardandpoors.com/.

* World rank based on 175 countries covered by Euromoney. Ranking based on ascending order in which '1' equals the smallest country risk premium (CRP) and '175' equals the largest country risk premium (CRP).

† MSCI Market Classification based on MSCI Market Classification Framework. See http://www.msci.com/products/indexes/market_classification.html

‡ Regional classification based on Euromoney. Regional rankings based on ascending order in which '1' equals the smallest country risk premium (CRP) for each region.

** Investment grade based on S&P sovereign credit rating from AAA to BBB-. Non-Investment grade based on S&P sovereign credit rating from BB+ to SD. For purposes of this analysis, the U.S. is being treated as if it were rated AAA by S&P.

Note: A CRP of 0.0% is assumed in the following cases: (i) when the investor country and the investee country both have an S&P sovereign credit rating of AAA; or (ii) when the investor country has an S&P credit rating of AAA, and the investee country has a sovereign credit rating below AAA, but has a calculated CRP below 0.0% (which would imply lower risk than a country rated AAA); or (iii) when the investor country has an S&P credit rating below AAA, and the investee country has a sovereign credit rating of AAA, but has a calculated CRP above 0.0% (which would imply greater risk than a country rated below AAA). For purposes of this analysis, the U.S. is treated as having a sovereign credit rating equivalent to AAA.

The country risk premium (CRP) is not the cost of equity capital (COE). The CRP is to be added to base COE. See Chapter 6 for proper application.

## Data Updated Through March 2017

| Investee Country | December 2016 Country Risk Premium (CRP) (%) | March 2017 Country Risk Premium (CRP) (%) | S&P Sovereign Credit Rating § | World Rank Out of 175* | MSCI Market Classification † | Euromoney Region ‡ | Regional Rank ‡ |
|---|---|---|---|---|---|---|---|
| Afghanistan | 12.3 | 11.9 | | 139 | | Asia | 23 out of 29 |
| Albania | 6.8 | 6.9 | B+ | 93 | | Central and Eastern Europe | 18 out of 25 |
| Algeria | 6.8 | 6.8 | | 91 | | Africa | 10 out of 51 |
| Angola | 9.2 | 9.2 | B | 121 | | Africa | 26 out of 51 |
| Argentina | 7.4 | 7.0 | B- | 96 | Frontier | Latin America | 13 out of 20 |
| Armenia | 4.4 | 4.5 | | 77 | | Asia | 15 out of 29 |
| Australia | -4.7 | -4.8 | AAA | 12 | Developed | Australasia | 2 out of 7 |
| Austria | -4.5 | -4.6 | AA+ | 13 | Developed | Western Europe | 9 out of 19 |
| Azerbaijan | 5.6 | 5.8 | BB+ | 85 | | Asia | 17 out of 29 |
| Bahamas | 2.9 | 2.5 | BB+ | 65 | | Caribbean | 3 out of 9 |
| Bahrain | 2.8 | 2.5 | BB- | 64 | Frontier | Middle East | 7 out of 13 |
| Bangladesh | 9.7 | 9.4 | BB- | 126 | Frontier | Asia | 20 out of 29 |
| Barbados | 4.6 | 5.6 | CCC+ | 82 | | Caribbean | 4 out of 9 |
| Belarus | 12.0 | 12.3 | B- | 143 | | Central and Eastern Europe | 23 out of 25 |
| Belgium | -3.2 | -3.4 | AA | 17 | Developed | Western Europe | 10 out of 19 |
| Belize | 7.8 | 7.9 | B- | 106 | | Latin America | 17 out of 20 |
| Benin | 13.7 | 13.6 | | 150 | | Africa | 37 out of 51 |
| Bermuda | 0.5 | 0.3 | A+ | 44 | | Caribbean | 1 out of 9 |
| Bhutan | 13.3 | 13.1 | | 148 | | Asia | 25 out of 29 |
| Bolivia | 6.4 | 6.5 | BB | 88 | | Latin America | 12 out of 20 |
| Bosnia & Herzegovina | 12.4 | 12.5 | B | 144 | | Central and Eastern Europe | 24 out of 25 |
| Botswana | 0.5 | 0.4 | A- | 48 | | Africa | 1 out of 51 |
| Brazil | 2.0 | 1.8 | BB | 59 | Emerging | Latin America | 7 out of 20 |
| Bulgaria | 1.9 | 2.0 | BB+ | 61 | | Central and Eastern Europe | 12 out of 25 |
| Burkina Faso | 10.8 | 10.7 | B- | 133 | | Africa | 33 out of 51 |
| Burundi | 22.8 | 22.7 | | 169 | | Africa | 47 out of 51 |
| Cambodia | 14.2 | 13.8 | | 151 | | Asia | 27 out of 29 |
| Cameroon | 9.4 | 9.3 | B | 124 | | Africa | 28 out of 51 |
| Canada | -4.9 | -5.0 | AAA | 9 | Developed | North America | 1 out of 2 |
| Cape Verde | 7.0 | 6.9 | B | 94 | | Africa | 12 out of 51 |
| Central African Republic | 26.3 | 26.3 | | 172 | | Africa | 49 out of 51 |
| Chad | 25.0 | 24.9 | | 171 | | Africa | 48 out of 51 |
| Chile | -3.7 | -3.6 | AA- | 16 | Emerging | Latin America | 1 out of 20 |
| China | 0.3 | 0.2 | AA- | 42 | Emerging | Asia | 7 out of 29 |
| Colombia | 0.3 | 0.2 | BBB | 41 | Emerging | Latin America | 4 out of 20 |
| Congo Republic | 9.0 | 8.7 | B- | 117 | | Africa | 24 out of 51 |
| Congo, DR | 10.3 | 10.1 | B- | 131 | | Africa | 32 out of 51 |
| Costa Rica | 3.3 | 3.5 | BB- | 71 | | Latin America | 8 out of 20 |
| Côte d'Ivoire | 6.9 | 6.8 | | 92 | | Africa | 11 out of 51 |
| Croatia | 2.4 | 2.2 | BB | 63 | Frontier | Central and Eastern Europe | 13 out of 25 |
| Cuba | 16.6 | 16.6 | | 160 | | Caribbean | 9 out of 9 |
| Cyprus | 0.0 | 0.0 | BB+ | 40 | | Central and Eastern Europe | 7 out of 25 |
| Czech Republic | -2.4 | -2.5 | AA- | 23 | Emerging | Central and Eastern Europe | 1 out of 25 |
| Denmark | -5.5 | -5.6 | AAA | 4 | Developed | Western Europe | 3 out of 19 |
| Djibouti | 34.3 | 32.0 | | 175 | | Africa | 51 out of 51 |
| Dominican Republic | 6.7 | 6.7 | BB- | 90 | | Caribbean | 5 out of 9 |
| Ecuador | 8.3 | 8.1 | B | 109 | | Latin America | 18 out of 20 |
| Egypt | 8.8 | 8.6 | B- | 116 | Emerging | Africa | 23 out of 51 |
| El Salvador | 5.7 | 5.4 | B- | 81 | | Latin America | 10 out of 20 |
| Equatorial Guinea | 19.1 | 19.1 | | 165 | | Africa | 45 out of 51 |

§ S&P Credit Rating based on long-term foreign currency issuer rating. See http://www.standardandpoors.com/.

* World rank based on 175 countries covered by Euromoney. Ranking based on ascending order in which '1' equals the smallest country risk premium (CRP) and '175' equals the largest country risk premium (CRP).

† MSCI Market Classification based on MSCI Market Classification Framework. See http://www.msci.com/products/indexes/market_classification.html

‡ Regional classification based on Euromoney. Regional rankings based on ascending order in which '1' equals the smallest country risk premium (CRP) for each region.

Note: A CRP of 0.0% is assumed in the following cases: (i) when the investor country and the investee country both have an S&P sovereign credit rating of AAA; or (ii) when the investor country has an S&P credit rating of AAA, and the investee country has a sovereign credit rating below AAA, but has a calculated CRP below 0.0% (which would imply lower risk than a country rated AAA); or (iii) when the investor country has an S&P credit rating below AAA, and the investee country has a sovereign credit rating of AAA, but has a calculated CRP above 0.0% (which would imply greater risk than a country rated below AAA). For purposes of this analysis, the U.S. is treated as having a sovereign credit rating equivalent to AAA.

The country risk premium (CRP) is not the cost of equity capital (COE). The CRP is to be added to base COE. See Chapter 6 for proper application.

### Data Updated Through March 2017

| Investee Country | December 2016 Country Risk Premium (CRP) (%) | March 2017 Country Risk Premium (CRP) (%) | S&P Sovereign Credit Rating § | World Rank Out of 175* | MSCI Market Classification † | Euromoney Region ‡ | Regional Rank ‡ |
|---|---|---|---|---|---|---|---|
| Eritrea | 30.5 | 28.6 | | 173 | | Africa | 50 out of 51 |
| Estonia | -1.8 | -1.6 | AA- | 32 | Frontier | Central and Eastern Europe | 4 out of 25 |
| Ethiopia | 7.6 | 7.5 | B | 101 | | Africa | 16 out of 51 |
| Fiji | 13.0 | 12.8 | B+ | 147 | | Australasia | 5 out of 7 |
| Finland | -4.7 | -4.9 | AA+ | 11 | Developed | Western Europe | 8 out of 19 |
| France | -2.4 | -2.6 | AA | 22 | Developed | Western Europe | 12 out of 19 |
| Gabon | 5.3 | 5.6 | | 83 | | Africa | 7 out of 51 |
| Gambia | 11.4 | 11.4 | | 138 | | Africa | 34 out of 51 |
| Georgia | 4.1 | 4.2 | BB- | 74 | | Central and Eastern Europe | 15 out of 25 |
| Germany | -4.7 | -4.9 | AAA | 10 | Developed | Western Europe | 7 out of 19 |
| Ghana | 7.1 | 6.6 | B- | 89 | | Africa | 9 out of 51 |
| Greece | 8.2 | 7.9 | B- | 108 | Emerging | Western Europe | 19 out of 19 |
| Grenada | 7.8 | 7.8 | | 105 | | Caribbean | 7 out of 9 |
| Guatemala | 5.7 | 5.7 | BB | 84 | | Latin America | 11 out of 20 |
| Guinea | 15.2 | 15.1 | | 156 | | Africa | 41 out of 51 |
| Guinea-Bissau | 8.7 | 8.6 | | 115 | | Africa | 22 out of 51 |
| Guyana | 7.5 | 7.4 | | 100 | | Latin America | 15 out of 20 |
| Haiti | 18.1 | 15.9 | | 157 | | Caribbean | 8 out of 9 |
| Honduras | 7.2 | 7.1 | B+ | 98 | | Latin America | 14 out of 20 |
| Hong Kong | -4.2 | -4.3 | AAA | 14 | Developed | Asia | 2 out of 29 |
| Hungary | 1.6 | 1.7 | BBB- | 57 | Emerging | Central and Eastern Europe | 10 out of 25 |
| Iceland | -1.4 | -1.7 | A | 30 | | Western Europe | 15 out of 19 |
| India | 1.4 | 1.6 | BBB- | 55 | Emerging | Asia | 10 out of 29 |
| Indonesia | 2.2 | 2.1 | BB+ | 62 | Emerging | Asia | 11 out of 29 |
| Iran | 9.2 | 9.4 | | 125 | | Middle East | 10 out of 13 |
| Iraq | 11.0 | 11.0 | B- | 136 | | Middle East | 11 out of 13 |
| Ireland | -1.9 | -2.1 | A+ | 27 | Developed | Western Europe | 14 out of 19 |
| Israel | -1.9 | -2.0 | A+ | 28 | Developed | Middle East | 2 out of 13 |
| Italy | 1.0 | 0.8 | BBB- | 50 | Developed | Western Europe | 18 out of 19 |
| Jamaica | 7.3 | 7.8 | B | 104 | | Caribbean | 6 out of 9 |
| Japan | -2.0 | -2.1 | A+ | 25 | Developed | Asia | 5 out of 29 |
| Jordan | 4.3 | 4.4 | BB- | 76 | Frontier | Middle East | 8 out of 13 |
| Kazakhstan | 3.8 | 3.4 | BBB- | 70 | Frontier | Asia | 13 out of 29 |
| Kenya | 7.3 | 7.3 | B+ | 99 | Frontier | Africa | 15 out of 51 |
| Korea (North) | 29.8 | 29.3 | | 174 | | Asia | 29 out of 29 |
| Korea (South) | -2.8 | -2.9 | AA | 19 | Emerging | Asia | 4 out of 29 |
| Kuwait | -1.7 | -1.7 | AA | 31 | Frontier | Middle East | 3 out of 13 |
| Kyrgyz Republic | 12.5 | 12.3 | | 142 | | Central and Eastern Europe | 22 out of 25 |
| Laos | 16.8 | 16.2 | | 158 | | Asia | 28 out of 29 |
| Latvia | 0.3 | 0.3 | A- | 43 | | Central and Eastern Europe | 8 out of 25 |
| Lebanon | 9.1 | 8.3 | B- | 112 | Frontier | Middle East | 9 out of 13 |
| Lesotho | 12.7 | 12.7 | | 146 | | Africa | 36 out of 51 |
| Liberia | 7.9 | 7.9 | | 107 | | Africa | 17 out of 51 |
| Libya | 14.2 | 14.5 | | 153 | | Africa | 39 out of 51 |
| Lithuania | -0.5 | -0.5 | A- | 36 | Frontier | Central and Eastern Europe | 6 out of 25 |
| Luxembourg | -5.2 | -5.3 | AAA | 5 | | Western Europe | 4 out of 19 |
| Macedonia | 6.4 | 6.5 | BB- | 87 | | Central and Eastern Europe | 17 out of 25 |
| Madagascar | 8.8 | 9.3 | | 123 | | Africa | 27 out of 51 |
| Malawi | 8.5 | 8.5 | | 114 | | Africa | 21 out of 51 |
| Malaysia | -0.3 | -0.6 | A- | 35 | Emerging | Asia | 6 out of 29 |

§ S&P Credit Rating based on long-term foreign currency issuer rating. See http://www.standardandpoors.com/.

* World rank based on 175 countries covered by Euromoney. Ranking based on ascending order in which '1' equals the smallest country risk premium (CRP) and '175' equals the largest country risk premium (CRP).

† MSCI Market Classification based on MSCI Market Classification Framework. See http://www.msci.com/products/indexes/market_classification.html

‡ Regional classification based on Euromoney. Regional rankings based on ascending order in which '1' equals the smallest country risk premium (CRP) for each region.

Note: A CRP of 0.0% is assumed in the following cases: (i) when the investor country and the investee country both have an S&P sovereign credit rating of AAA; or (ii) when the investor country has an S&P credit rating of AAA, and the investee country has a sovereign credit rating below AAA, but has a calculated CRP below 0.0% (which would imply lower risk than a country rated AAA); or (iii) when the investor country has an S&P credit rating below AAA, and the investee country has a sovereign credit rating of AAA, but has a calculated CRP above 0.0% (which would imply greater risk than a country rated below AAA). For purposes of this analysis, the U.S. is treated as having a sovereign credit rating equivalent to AAA.

The country risk premium (CRP) is not the cost of equity capital (COE). The CRP is to be added to base COE. See Chapter 6 for proper application.

### Data Updated Through March 2017

| Investee Country | December 2016 Country Risk Premium (CRP) (%) | March 2017 Country Risk Premium (CRP) (%) | S&P Sovereign Credit Rating § | World Rank Out of 175* | MSCI Market Classification † | Euromoney Region ‡ | Regional Rank ‡ |
|---|---|---|---|---|---|---|---|
| Mali | 12.3 | 12.2 | | 141 | | Africa | 35 out of 51 |
| Malta | -2.0 | -2.1 | A- | 26 | | Western Europe | 13 out of 19 |
| Mauritania | 16.4 | 16.3 | | 159 | | Africa | 42 out of 51 |
| Mauritius | 3.1 | 3.0 | | 67 | Frontier | Asia | 12 out of 29 |
| Mexico | -0.4 | -0.4 | BBB+ | 37 | Emerging | Latin America | 2 out of 20 |
| Moldova | 10.7 | 11.1 | | 137 | | Central and Eastern Europe | 21 out of 25 |
| Mongolia | 8.9 | 9.1 | B- | 119 | | Asia | 18 out of 29 |
| Montenegro | 8.1 | 7.8 | B+ | 103 | | Central and Eastern Europe | 19 out of 25 |
| Morocco | 3.2 | 3.3 | BBB- | 69 | Frontier | Africa | 4 out of 51 |
| Mozambique | 10.0 | 9.7 | SD | 128 | | Africa | 29 out of 51 |
| Myanmar | 10.9 | 10.7 | | 134 | | Asia | 22 out of 29 |
| Namibia | 2.8 | 2.9 | | 66 | | Africa | 3 out of 51 |
| Nepal | 13.6 | 13.6 | | 149 | | Asia | 26 out of 29 |
| Netherlands | -5.1 | -5.3 | AAA | 6 | Developed | Western Europe | 5 out of 19 |
| New Zealand | -5.0 | -5.1 | AA | 8 | Developed | Australasia | 1 out of 7 |
| Nicaragua | 9.7 | 9.6 | B+ | 127 | | Latin America | 19 out of 20 |
| Niger | 9.2 | 9.2 | | 120 | | Africa | 25 out of 51 |
| Nigeria | 7.2 | 7.1 | B | 97 | Frontier | Africa | 14 out of 51 |
| Norway | -5.8 | -6.0 | AAA | 3 | Developed | Western Europe | 2 out of 19 |
| Oman | 0.4 | 0.4 | BBB- | 46 | Frontier | Middle East | 5 out of 13 |
| Pakistan | 9.3 | 9.2 | B | 122 | Frontier | Asia | 19 out of 29 |
| Panama | 1.2 | 1.1 | BBB | 52 | | Latin America | 6 out of 20 |
| Papua New Guinea | 8.8 | 8.9 | B+ | 118 | | Australasia | 3 out of 7 |
| Paraguay | 4.7 | 4.8 | BB | 80 | | Latin America | 9 out of 20 |
| Peru | -0.1 | -0.1 | BBB+ | 39 | Emerging | Latin America | 3 out of 20 |
| Philippines | 1.5 | 1.4 | BBB | 53 | Emerging | Asia | 9 out of 29 |
| Poland | -1.6 | -1.8 | BBB+ | 29 | Emerging | Central and Eastern Europe | 3 out of 25 |
| Portugal | 0.9 | 0.6 | BB+ | 49 | Developed | Western Europe | 17 out of 19 |
| Qatar | -2.7 | -2.7 | AA | 21 | Emerging | Middle East | 1 out of 13 |
| Romania | 1.7 | 1.6 | BBB- | 56 | Frontier | Central and Eastern Europe | 9 out of 25 |
| Russia | 4.0 | 3.2 | BB+ | 68 | Emerging | Central and Eastern Europe | 14 out of 25 |
| Rwanda | 10.0 | 10.0 | B | 130 | | Africa | 31 out of 51 |
| São Tomé & Príncipe | 16.5 | 16.9 | | 163 | | Africa | 43 out of 51 |
| Saudi Arabia | 0.8 | 0.4 | A- | 47 | | Middle East | 6 out of 13 |
| Senegal | 6.5 | 6.5 | B+ | 86 | | Africa | 8 out of 51 |
| Serbia | 4.6 | 4.3 | BB- | 75 | Frontier | Central and Eastern Europe | 16 out of 25 |
| Seychelles | 4.1 | 4.0 | | 73 | | Africa | 5 out of 51 |
| Sierra Leone | 10.0 | 10.0 | | 129 | | Africa | 30 out of 51 |
| Singapore | -6.0 | -6.1 | AAA | 1 | Developed | Asia | 1 out of 29 |
| Slovakia | -2.3 | -2.3 | A+ | 24 | | Central and Eastern Europe | 2 out of 25 |
| Slovenia | -0.9 | -0.9 | A | 34 | Frontier | Central and Eastern Europe | 5 out of 25 |
| Solomon Islands | 20.9 | 20.9 | | 168 | | Australasia | 6 out of 7 |
| Somalia | 19.2 | 19.1 | | 166 | | Africa | 46 out of 51 |
| South Africa | 1.7 | 1.9 | BBB- | 60 | Emerging | Africa | 2 out of 51 |
| Spain | 0.0 | -0.1 | BBB+ | 38 | Developed | Western Europe | 16 out of 19 |
| Sri Lanka | 4.0 | 3.7 | B+ | 72 | Frontier | Asia | 14 out of 29 |
| Sudan | 15.1 | 15.0 | | 154 | | Africa | 40 out of 51 |
| Suriname | 7.5 | 7.6 | B+ | 102 | | Latin America | 16 out of 20 |
| Swaziland | 13.4 | 14.3 | | 152 | | Africa | 38 out of 51 |
| Sweden | -5.1 | -5.3 | AAA | 7 | Developed | Western Europe | 6 out of 19 |

§ S&P Credit Rating based on long-term foreign currency issuer rating. See http://www.standardandpoors.com/.

* World rank based on 175 countries covered by Euromoney. Ranking based on ascending order in which '1' equals the smallest country risk premium (CRP) and '175' equals the largest country risk premium (CRP).

† MSCI Market Classification based on MSCI Market Classification Framework. See http://www.msci.com/products/indexes/market_classification.html

‡ Regional classification based on Euromoney. Regional rankings based on ascending order in which '1' equals the smallest country risk premium (CRP) for each region.

Note: A CRP of 0.0% is assumed in the following cases: (i) when the investor country and the investee country both have an S&P sovereign credit rating of AAA; or (ii) when the investor country has an S&P credit rating of AAA, and the investee country has a sovereign credit rating below AAA, but has a calculated CRP below 0.0% (which would imply lower risk than a country rated AAA); or (iii) when the investor country has an S&P credit rating below AAA, and the investee country has a sovereign credit rating of AAA, but has a calculated CRP above 0.0% (which would imply greater risk than a country rated below AAA). For purposes of this analysis, the U.S. is treated as having a sovereign credit rating equivalent to AAA.

The country risk premium (CRP) is not the cost of equity capital (COE). The CRP is to be added to base COE. See Chapter 6 for proper application.

## Data Updated Through March 2017

| Investee Country | December 2016 Country Risk Premium (CRP) (%) | March 2017 Country Risk Premium (CRP) (%) | S&P Sovereign Credit Rating § | World Rank Out of 175* | MSCI Market Classification † | Euromoney Region ‡ | Regional Rank ‡ |
|---|---|---|---|---|---|---|---|
| Switzerland | -5.8 | -6.0 | AAA | 2 | Developed | Western Europe | 1 out of 19 |
| Syria | 19.9 | 20.1 | | 167 | | Middle East | 13 out of 13 |
| Taiwan | -3.1 | -3.2 | AA- | 18 | Emerging | Asia | 3 out of 29 |
| Tajikistan | 14.7 | 15.0 | | 155 | | Central and Eastern Europe | 25 out of 25 |
| Tanzania | 6.9 | 7.0 | | 95 | | Africa | 13 out of 51 |
| Thailand | 1.2 | 0.9 | BBB+ | 51 | Emerging | Asia | 8 out of 29 |
| Togo | 8.5 | 8.4 | | 113 | | Africa | 20 out of 51 |
| Tonga | 23.4 | 23.4 | | 170 | | Australasia | 7 out of 7 |
| Trinidad & Tobago | 1.5 | 1.4 | A- | 54 | | Caribbean | 2 out of 9 |
| Tunisia | 4.4 | 4.7 | | 79 | Frontier | Africa | 6 out of 51 |
| Turkey | 1.9 | 1.7 | BB | 58 | Emerging | Central and Eastern Europe | 11 out of 25 |
| Turkmenistan | 11.8 | 12.1 | | 140 | | Asia | 24 out of 29 |
| Uganda | 8.0 | 8.2 | B | 110 | | Africa | 18 out of 51 |
| Ukraine | 10.8 | 10.9 | B- | 135 | | Central and Eastern Europe | 20 out of 25 |
| United Arab Emirates | -1.3 | -1.3 | AA | 33 | Emerging | Middle East | 4 out of 13 |
| United Kingdom | -2.8 | -2.8 | AA | 20 | Developed | Western Europe | 11 out of 19 |
| United States | -3.9 | -4.0 | AA+ | 15 | Developed | North America | 2 out of 2 |
| Uruguay | 0.5 | 0.3 | BBB | 45 | | Latin America | 5 out of 20 |
| Uzbekistan | 11.0 | 10.4 | | 132 | | Asia | 21 out of 29 |
| Vanuatu | 12.7 | 12.6 | | 145 | | Australasia | 4 out of 7 |
| Venezuela | 16.5 | 16.9 | CCC | 162 | | Latin America | 20 out of 20 |
| Vietnam | 5.0 | 4.6 | BB- | 78 | Frontier | Asia | 16 out of 29 |
| Yemen | 16.8 | 16.8 | | 161 | | Middle East | 12 out of 13 |
| Zambia | 8.3 | 8.3 | B | 111 | | Africa | 19 out of 51 |
| Zimbabwe | 18.5 | 18.3 | | 164 | | Africa | 44 out of 51 |

## March 2017 Country Risk Premium (CRP) Summary Statistics:

| S&P Rating | Country Count | Average CRP (%) | Median CRP (%) | Min CRP (%) | Max CRP (%) |
|---|---|---|---|---|---|
| AAA ** | 12 | -5.2 | -5.3 | -6.1 | -4.0 |
| AA (AA+, AA, AA-) | 15 | -2.8 | -2.8 | -5.1 | 0.2 |
| A (A+, A, A-) | 14 | -0.8 | -0.8 | -2.3 | 1.4 |
| BBB (BBB+, BBB, BBB-) | 17 | 0.9 | 0.9 | -1.8 | 3.4 |
| BB (BB+, BB, BB-) | 22 | 3.9 | 3.8 | 0.0 | 9.4 |
| B+ − SD | 39 | 8.7 | 8.3 | 3.7 | 16.9 |
| Investment Grade ** | 58 | -1.7 | -1.7 | -6.1 | 3.4 |
| Non-Investment Grade ** | 61 | 7.0 | 7.1 | 0.0 | 16.9 |
| **MSCI Market Classification** | | | | | |
| Developed Markets | 23 | -3.7 | -4.6 | -6.1 | 0.8 |
| Emerging Markets | 23 | 0.6 | 0.2 | -3.6 | 8.6 |
| Frontier Markets | 22 | 3.7 | 3.5 | -1.7 | 9.4 |
| **Euromoney Region ‡** | | | | | |
| Africa | 51 | 11.2 | 9.2 | 0.4 | 32.0 |
| Asia | 29 | 5.9 | 4.5 | -6.1 | 29.3 |
| Australasia | 7 | 9.8 | 12.6 | -5.1 | 23.4 |
| Caribbean | 9 | 7.2 | 6.7 | 0.3 | 16.6 |
| Central and Eastern Europe | 25 | 4.3 | 2.2 | -2.5 | 15.0 |
| Latin America | 20 | 4.8 | 5.6 | -3.6 | 16.9 |
| Middle East | 13 | 5.1 | 2.5 | -2.7 | 20.1 |
| North America | 2 | -4.5 | -4.5 | -5.0 | -4.0 |
| Western Europe | 19 | -2.8 | -3.4 | -6.0 | 7.9 |

## CCR Base Cost of Equity Capital:

| Cyprus | COE (%) |
|---|---|
| March 2017 | 12.5 |
| December 2016 | 12.3 |

CCR base country-level COE for a Cyprus-based investor investing in Cyprus.

§ S&P Credit Rating based on long-term foreign currency issuer rating. See http://www.standardandpoors.com/.

* World rank based on 175 countries covered by Euromoney. Ranking based on ascending order in which '1' equals the smallest country risk premium (CRP) and '175' equals the largest country risk premium (CRP).

† MSCI Market Classification based on MSCI Market Classification Framework. See http://www.msci.com/products/indexes/market_classification.html

‡ Regional classification based on Euromoney. Regional rankings based on ascending order in which '1' equals the smallest country risk premium (CRP) for each region.

** Investment grade based on S&P sovereign credit rating from AAA to BBB-. Non-Investment grade based on S&P sovereign credit rating from BB+ to SD. For purposes of this analysis, the U.S. is being treated as if it were rated AAA by S&P.

Note: A CRP of 0.0% is assumed in the following cases: (i) when the investor country and the investee country both have an S&P sovereign credit rating of AAA; or (ii) when the investor country has an S&P credit rating of AAA, and the investee country has a sovereign credit rating below AAA, but has a calculated CRP below 0.0% (which would imply lower risk than a country rated AAA); or (iii) when the investor country has an S&P credit rating below AAA, and the investee country has a sovereign credit rating of AAA, but has a calculated CRP above 0.0% (which would imply greater risk than a country rated below AAA). For purposes of this analysis, the U.S. is treated as having a sovereign credit rating equivalent to AAA.

The country risk premium (CRP) is not the cost of equity capital (COE).  The CRP is to be added to base COE. See Chapter 6 for proper application.

## Data Updated Through March 2017

| Investee Country | December 2016 Country Risk Premium (CRP) (%) | March 2017 Country Risk Premium (CRP) (%) | S&P Sovereign Credit Rating § | World Rank Out of 175∗ | MSCI Market Classification † | Euromoney Region ‡ | Regional Rank ‡ |
|---|---|---|---|---|---|---|---|
| Afghanistan | 11.8 | 11.5 | | 139 | | Asia | 23 out of 29 |
| Albania | 7.4 | 7.5 | B+ | 93 | | Central and Eastern Europe | 18 out of 25 |
| Algeria | 7.4 | 7.4 | | 91 | | Africa | 10 out of 51 |
| Angola | 9.3 | 9.3 | B | 121 | | Africa | 26 out of 51 |
| Argentina | 7.8 | 7.6 | B- | 96 | Frontier | Latin America | 13 out of 20 |
| Armenia | 5.4 | 5.5 | | 77 | | Asia | 15 out of 29 |
| Australia | -1.8 | -1.8 | AAA | 12 | Developed | Australasia | 2 out of 7 |
| Austria | -1.7 | -1.7 | AA+ | 13 | Developed | Western Europe | 9 out of 19 |
| Azerbaijan | 6.4 | 6.6 | BB+ | 85 | | Asia | 17 out of 29 |
| Bahamas | 4.3 | 4.0 | BB+ | 65 | | Caribbean | 3 out of 9 |
| Bahrain | 4.2 | 4.0 | BB- | 64 | Frontier | Middle East | 7 out of 13 |
| Bangladesh | 9.7 | 9.5 | BB- | 126 | Frontier | Asia | 20 out of 29 |
| Barbados | 5.6 | 6.4 | CCC+ | 82 | | Caribbean | 4 out of 9 |
| Belarus | 11.5 | 11.8 | B- | 143 | | Central and Eastern Europe | 23 out of 25 |
| Belgium | -0.6 | -0.7 | AA | 17 | Developed | Western Europe | 10 out of 19 |
| Belize | 8.2 | 8.2 | B- | 106 | | Latin America | 17 out of 20 |
| Benin | 12.9 | 12.8 | | 150 | | Africa | 37 out of 51 |
| Bermuda | 2.3 | 2.2 | A+ | 44 | | Caribbean | 1 out of 9 |
| Bhutan | 12.6 | 12.4 | | 148 | | Asia | 25 out of 29 |
| Bolivia | 7.0 | 7.2 | BB | 88 | | Latin America | 12 out of 20 |
| Bosnia & Herzegovina | 11.9 | 11.9 | B | 144 | | Central and Eastern Europe | 24 out of 25 |
| Botswana | 2.3 | 2.3 | A- | 48 | | Africa | 1 out of 51 |
| Brazil | 3.6 | 3.4 | BB | 59 | Emerging | Latin America | 7 out of 20 |
| Bulgaria | 3.4 | 3.6 | BB+ | 61 | | Central and Eastern Europe | 12 out of 25 |
| Burkina Faso | 10.6 | 10.5 | B- | 133 | | Africa | 33 out of 51 |
| Burundi | 20.2 | 20.0 | | 169 | | Africa | 47 out of 51 |
| Cambodia | 13.4 | 13.0 | | 151 | | Asia | 27 out of 29 |
| Cameroon | 9.5 | 9.4 | B | 124 | | Africa | 28 out of 51 |
| Canada | -2.0 | -2.0 | AAA | 9 | Developed | North America | 1 out of 2 |
| Cape Verde | 7.6 | 7.5 | B | 94 | | Africa | 12 out of 51 |
| Central African Republic | 23.0 | 22.9 | | 172 | | Africa | 49 out of 51 |
| Chad | 21.9 | 21.8 | | 171 | | Africa | 48 out of 51 |
| Chile | -1.0 | -0.8 | AA- | 16 | Emerging | Latin America | 1 out of 20 |
| China | 2.2 | 2.2 | AA- | 42 | Emerging | Asia | 7 out of 29 |
| Colombia | 2.1 | 2.1 | BBB | 41 | Emerging | Latin America | 4 out of 20 |
| Congo Republic | 9.1 | 8.9 | B- | 117 | | Africa | 24 out of 51 |
| Congo, DR | 10.2 | 10.0 | B- | 131 | | Africa | 32 out of 51 |
| Costa Rica | 4.6 | 4.7 | BB- | 71 | | Latin America | 8 out of 20 |
| Côte d'Ivoire | 7.4 | 7.4 | | 92 | | Africa | 11 out of 51 |
| Croatia | 3.9 | 3.7 | BB | 63 | Frontier | Central and Eastern Europe | 13 out of 25 |
| Cuba | 15.2 | 15.2 | | 160 | | Caribbean | 9 out of 9 |
| Cyprus | 1.9 | 2.0 | BB+ | 40 | | Central and Eastern Europe | 7 out of 25 |
| Czech Republic | 0.0 | 0.0 | AA- | 23 | Emerging | Central and Eastern Europe | 1 out of 25 |
| Denmark | -2.5 | -2.5 | AAA | 4 | Developed | Western Europe | 3 out of 19 |
| Djibouti | 29.5 | 27.4 | | 175 | | Africa | 51 out of 51 |
| Dominican Republic | 7.3 | 7.3 | BB- | 90 | | Caribbean | 5 out of 9 |
| Ecuador | 8.6 | 8.4 | B | 109 | | Latin America | 18 out of 20 |
| Egypt | 9.0 | 8.8 | B- | 116 | Emerging | Africa | 23 out of 51 |
| El Salvador | 6.5 | 6.3 | B- | 81 | | Latin America | 10 out of 20 |
| Equatorial Guinea | 17.3 | 17.2 | | 165 | | Africa | 45 out of 51 |

§ S&P Credit Rating based on long-term foreign currency issuer rating. Seehttp://www.standardandpoors.com/.

∗ World rank based on 175 countries covered by Euromoney. Ranking based on ascending order in which '1' equals the smallest country risk premium (CRP) and '175' equals the largest country risk premium (CRP).

† MSCI Market Classification based on MSCI Market Classification Framework.  See http://www.msci.com/products/indexes/market_classification.html

‡ Regional classification based on Euromoney. Regional rankings based on ascending order in which '1' equals the smallest country risk premium (CRP) for each region.

Note: A CRP of 0.0% is assumed in the following cases: (i) when the investor country and the investee country both have an S&P sovereign credit rating of AAA; or (ii) when the investor country has an S&P credit rating of AAA, and the investee country has a sovereign credit rating below AAA, but has a calculated CRP below 0.0% (which would imply lower risk than a country rated AAA); or (iii) when the investor country has an S&P credit rating below AAA, and the investee country has a sovereign credit rating of AAA, but has a calculated CRP above 0.0% (which would imply greater risk than a country rated below AAA). For purposes of this analysis, the U.S. is treated as having a sovereign credit rating equivalent to AAA.

2017 Valuation Handbook – International Guide to Cost of Capital               Data Exhibit 4               Investor Perspective: Czech Republic (CZK); Page 1 of 4

The country risk premium (CRP) is not the cost of equity capital (COE). The CRP is to be added to base COE. See Chapter 6 for proper application.

## Data Updated Through March 2017

| Investee Country | December 2016 Country Risk Premium (CRP) (%) | March 2017 Country Risk Premium (CRP) (%) | S&P Sovereign Credit Rating § | World Rank Out of 175∗ | MSCI Market Classification † | Euromoney Region ‡ | Regional Rank ‡ |
|---|---|---|---|---|---|---|---|
| Eritrea | 26.4 | 24.7 | | 173 | | Africa | 50 out of 51 |
| Estonia | 0.5 | 0.7 | AA- | 32 | Frontier | Central and Eastern Europe | 4 out of 25 |
| Ethiopia | 8.0 | 8.0 | B | 101 | | Africa | 16 out of 51 |
| Fiji | 12.4 | 12.2 | B+ | 147 | | Australasia | 5 out of 7 |
| Finland | -1.9 | -1.9 | AA+ | 11 | Developed | Western Europe | 8 out of 19 |
| France | 0.0 | -0.1 | AA | 22 | Developed | Western Europe | 12 out of 19 |
| Gabon | 6.2 | 6.4 | | 83 | | Africa | 7 out of 51 |
| Gambia | 11.1 | 11.0 | | 138 | | Africa | 34 out of 51 |
| Georgia | 5.2 | 5.4 | BB- | 74 | | Central and Eastern Europe | 15 out of 25 |
| Germany | -1.9 | -1.9 | AAA | 10 | Developed | Western Europe | 7 out of 19 |
| Ghana | 7.6 | 7.3 | B- | 89 | | Africa | 9 out of 51 |
| Greece | 8.5 | 8.3 | B- | 108 | Emerging | Western Europe | 19 out of 19 |
| Grenada | 8.2 | 8.2 | | 105 | | Caribbean | 7 out of 9 |
| Guatemala | 6.5 | 6.5 | BB | 84 | | Latin America | 11 out of 20 |
| Guinea | 14.1 | 14.0 | | 156 | | Africa | 41 out of 51 |
| Guinea-Bissau | 8.9 | 8.8 | | 115 | | Africa | 22 out of 51 |
| Guyana | 8.0 | 7.9 | | 100 | | Latin America | 15 out of 20 |
| Haiti | 16.4 | 14.7 | | 157 | | Caribbean | 8 out of 9 |
| Honduras | 7.7 | 7.7 | B+ | 98 | | Latin America | 14 out of 20 |
| Hong Kong | -1.4 | -1.4 | AAA | 14 | Developed | Asia | 2 out of 29 |
| Hungary | 3.2 | 3.3 | BBB- | 57 | Emerging | Central and Eastern Europe | 10 out of 25 |
| Iceland | 0.8 | 0.6 | A | 30 | | Western Europe | 15 out of 19 |
| India | 3.1 | 3.3 | BBB- | 55 | Emerging | Asia | 10 out of 29 |
| Indonesia | 3.7 | 3.7 | BB+ | 62 | Emerging | Asia | 11 out of 29 |
| Iran | 9.3 | 9.4 | | 125 | | Middle East | 10 out of 13 |
| Iraq | 10.8 | 10.7 | B- | 136 | | Middle East | 11 out of 13 |
| Ireland | 0.4 | 0.4 | A+ | 27 | Developed | Western Europe | 14 out of 19 |
| Israel | 0.4 | 0.4 | A+ | 28 | Developed | Middle East | 2 out of 13 |
| Italy | 2.8 | 2.6 | BBB- | 50 | Developed | Western Europe | 18 out of 19 |
| Jamaica | 7.7 | 8.2 | B | 104 | | Caribbean | 6 out of 9 |
| Japan | 0.3 | 0.3 | A+ | 25 | Developed | Asia | 5 out of 29 |
| Jordan | 5.4 | 5.5 | BB- | 76 | Frontier | Middle East | 8 out of 13 |
| Kazakhstan | 5.0 | 4.7 | BBB- | 70 | Frontier | Asia | 13 out of 29 |
| Kenya | 7.8 | 7.8 | B+ | 99 | Frontier | Africa | 15 out of 51 |
| Korea (North) | 25.9 | 25.3 | | 174 | | Asia | 29 out of 29 |
| Korea (South) | -0.3 | -0.3 | AA | 19 | Emerging | Asia | 4 out of 29 |
| Kuwait | 0.5 | 0.7 | AA | 31 | Frontier | Middle East | 3 out of 13 |
| Kyrgyz Republic | 11.9 | 11.7 | | 142 | | Central and Eastern Europe | 22 out of 25 |
| Laos | 15.4 | 14.8 | | 158 | | Asia | 28 out of 29 |
| Latvia | 2.2 | 2.2 | A- | 43 | | Central and Eastern Europe | 8 out of 25 |
| Lebanon | 9.2 | 8.6 | B- | 112 | Frontier | Middle East | 9 out of 13 |
| Lesotho | 12.1 | 12.0 | | 146 | | Africa | 36 out of 51 |
| Liberia | 8.3 | 8.2 | | 107 | | Africa | 17 out of 51 |
| Libya | 13.4 | 13.5 | | 153 | | Africa | 39 out of 51 |
| Lithuania | 1.5 | 1.6 | A- | 36 | Frontier | Central and Eastern Europe | 6 out of 25 |
| Luxembourg | -2.2 | -2.2 | AAA | 5 | | Western Europe | 4 out of 19 |
| Macedonia | 7.0 | 7.2 | BB- | 87 | | Central and Eastern Europe | 17 out of 25 |
| Madagascar | 9.0 | 9.3 | | 123 | | Africa | 27 out of 51 |
| Malawi | 8.8 | 8.7 | | 114 | | Africa | 21 out of 51 |
| Malaysia | 1.7 | 1.6 | A- | 35 | Emerging | Asia | 6 out of 29 |

§ S&P Credit Rating based on long-term foreign currency issuer rating. See http://www.standardandpoors.com/.

∗ World rank based on 175 countries covered by Euromoney. Ranking based on ascending order in which '1' equals the smallest country risk premium (CRP) and '175' equals the largest country risk premium (CRP).

† MSCI Market Classification based on MSCI Market Classification Framework. See http://www.msci.com/products/indexes/market_classification.html.

‡ Regional classification based on Euromoney. Regional rankings based on ascending order in which '1' equals the smallest country risk premium (CRP) for each region.

Note: A CRP of 0.0% is assumed in the following cases: (i) when the investor country and the investee country both have an S&P sovereign credit rating of AAA; or (ii) when the investor country has an S&P credit rating of AAA, and the investee country has a sovereign credit rating below AAA, but has a calculated CRP below 0.0% (which would imply lower risk than a country rated AAA); or (iii) when the investor country has an S&P credit rating below AAA, and the investee country has a sovereign credit rating of AAA, but has a calculated CRP above 0.0% (which would imply greater risk than a country rated below AAA). For purposes of this analysis, the U.S. is treated as having a sovereign credit rating equivalent to AAA.

The country risk premium (CRP) is not the cost of equity capital (COE). The CRP is to be added to base COE. See Chapter 6 for proper application.

## Data Updated Through March 2017

| Investee Country | December 2016 Country Risk Premium (CRP) (%) | March 2017 Country Risk Premium (CRP) (%) | S&P Sovereign Credit Rating § | World Rank Out of 175∗ | MSCI Market Classification † | Euromoney Region ‡ | Regional Rank ‡ |
|---|---|---|---|---|---|---|---|
| Mali | 11.8 | 11.7 | | 141 | | Africa | 35 out of 51 |
| Malta | 0.3 | 0.3 | A- | 26 | | Western Europe | 13 out of 19 |
| Mauritania | 15.1 | 15.0 | | 159 | | Africa | 42 out of 51 |
| Mauritius | 4.4 | 4.4 | | 67 | Frontier | Asia | 12 out of 29 |
| Mexico | 1.6 | 1.7 | BBB+ | 37 | Emerging | Latin America | 2 out of 20 |
| Moldova | 10.5 | 10.8 | | 137 | | Central and Eastern Europe | 21 out of 25 |
| Mongolia | 9.0 | 9.3 | B- | 119 | | Asia | 18 out of 29 |
| Montenegro | 8.4 | 8.2 | B+ | 103 | | Central and Eastern Europe | 19 out of 25 |
| Morocco | 4.5 | 4.6 | BBB- | 69 | Frontier | Africa | 4 out of 51 |
| Mozambique | 9.9 | 9.7 | SD | 128 | | Africa | 29 out of 51 |
| Myanmar | 10.7 | 10.5 | | 134 | | Asia | 22 out of 29 |
| Namibia | 4.2 | 4.3 | | 66 | | Africa | 3 out of 51 |
| Nepal | 12.9 | 12.8 | | 149 | | Asia | 26 out of 29 |
| Netherlands | -2.2 | -2.2 | AAA | 6 | Developed | Western Europe | 5 out of 19 |
| New Zealand | -2.1 | -2.0 | AA | 8 | Developed | Australasia | 1 out of 7 |
| Nicaragua | 9.7 | 9.6 | B+ | 127 | | Latin America | 19 out of 20 |
| Niger | 9.3 | 9.3 | | 120 | | Africa | 25 out of 51 |
| Nigeria | 7.7 | 7.7 | B | 97 | Frontier | Africa | 14 out of 51 |
| Norway | -2.7 | -2.8 | AAA | 3 | Developed | Western Europe | 2 out of 19 |
| Oman | 2.3 | 2.3 | BBB- | 46 | Frontier | Middle East | 5 out of 13 |
| Pakistan | 9.4 | 9.3 | B | 122 | Frontier | Asia | 19 out of 29 |
| Panama | 2.9 | 2.9 | BBB | 52 | | Latin America | 6 out of 20 |
| Papua New Guinea | 9.0 | 9.0 | B+ | 118 | | Australasia | 3 out of 7 |
| Paraguay | 5.7 | 5.8 | BB | 80 | | Latin America | 9 out of 20 |
| Peru | 1.8 | 1.9 | BBB+ | 39 | Emerging | Latin America | 3 out of 20 |
| Philippines | 3.2 | 3.1 | BBB | 53 | Emerging | Asia | 9 out of 29 |
| Poland | 0.7 | 0.6 | BBB+ | 29 | Emerging | Central and Eastern Europe | 3 out of 25 |
| Portugal | 2.6 | 2.5 | BB+ | 49 | Developed | Western Europe | 17 out of 19 |
| Qatar | -0.2 | -0.2 | AA | 21 | Emerging | Middle East | 1 out of 13 |
| Romania | 3.3 | 3.3 | BBB- | 56 | Frontier | Central and Eastern Europe | 9 out of 25 |
| Russia | 5.1 | 4.6 | BB+ | 68 | Emerging | Central and Eastern Europe | 14 out of 25 |
| Rwanda | 10.0 | 9.9 | B | 130 | | Africa | 31 out of 51 |
| São Tomé & Príncipe | 15.2 | 15.4 | | 163 | | Africa | 43 out of 51 |
| Saudi Arabia | 2.6 | 2.3 | A- | 47 | | Middle East | 6 out of 13 |
| Senegal | 7.2 | 7.1 | B+ | 86 | | Africa | 8 out of 51 |
| Serbia | 5.6 | 5.4 | BB- | 75 | Frontier | Central and Eastern Europe | 16 out of 25 |
| Seychelles | 5.2 | 5.2 | | 73 | | Africa | 5 out of 51 |
| Sierra Leone | 10.0 | 9.9 | | 129 | | Africa | 30 out of 51 |
| Singapore | -2.9 | -2.9 | AAA | 1 | Developed | Asia | 1 out of 29 |
| Slovakia | 0.1 | 0.1 | A+ | 24 | | Central and Eastern Europe | 2 out of 25 |
| Slovenia | 1.2 | 1.2 | A | 34 | Frontier | Central and Eastern Europe | 5 out of 25 |
| Solomon Islands | 18.7 | 18.6 | | 168 | | Australasia | 6 out of 7 |
| Somalia | 17.3 | 17.2 | | 166 | | Africa | 46 out of 51 |
| South Africa | 3.3 | 3.5 | BBB- | 60 | Emerging | Africa | 2 out of 51 |
| Spain | 1.9 | 1.9 | BBB+ | 38 | Developed | Western Europe | 16 out of 19 |
| Sri Lanka | 5.2 | 4.9 | B+ | 72 | Frontier | Asia | 14 out of 29 |
| Sudan | 14.1 | 13.9 | | 154 | | Africa | 40 out of 51 |
| Suriname | 7.9 | 8.0 | B+ | 102 | | Latin America | 16 out of 20 |
| Swaziland | 12.7 | 13.4 | | 152 | | Africa | 38 out of 51 |
| Sweden | -2.1 | -2.2 | AAA | 7 | Developed | Western Europe | 6 out of 19 |

§ S&P Credit Rating based on long-term foreign currency issuer rating. See http://www.standardandpoors.com/.

∗ World rank based on 175 countries covered by Euromoney. Ranking based on ascending order in which '1' equals the smallest country risk premium (CRP) and '175' equals the largest country risk premium (CRP).

† MSCI Market Classification based on MSCI Market Classification Framework. See http://www.msci.com/products/indexes/market_classification.html

‡ Regional classification based on Euromoney. Regional rankings based on ascending order in which '1' equals the smallest country risk premium (CRP) for each region.

Note: A CRP of 0.0% is assumed in the following cases: (i) when the investor country and the investee country both have an S&P sovereign credit rating of AAA; or (ii) when the investor country has an S&P credit rating of AAA, and the investee country has a sovereign credit rating below AAA, but has a calculated CRP below 0.0% (which would imply lower risk than a country rated AAA); or (iii) when the investor country has an S&P credit rating below AAA, and the investee country has a sovereign credit rating of AAA, but has a calculated CRP above 0.0% (which would imply greater risk than a country rated below AAA). For purposes of this analysis, the U.S. is treated as having a sovereign credit rating equivalent to AAA.

The country risk premium (CRP) is not the cost of equity capital (COE). The CRP is to be added to base COE. See Chapter 6 for proper application.

## Data Updated Through March 2017

| Investee Country | December 2016 Country Risk Premium (CRP) (%) | March 2017 Country Risk Premium (CRP) (%) | S&P Sovereign Credit Rating § | World Rank Out of 175* | MSCI Market Classification † | Euromoney Region ‡ | Regional Rank ‡ |
|---|---|---|---|---|---|---|---|
| Switzerland | -2.7 | -2.8 | AAA | 2 | Developed | Western Europe | 1 out of 19 |
| Syria | 17.9 | 18.0 | | 167 | | Middle East | 13 out of 13 |
| Taiwan | -0.5 | -0.5 | AA- | 18 | Emerging | Asia | 3 out of 29 |
| Tajikistan | 13.7 | 13.9 | | 155 | | Central and Eastern Europe | 25 out of 25 |
| Tanzania | 7.4 | 7.6 | | 95 | | Africa | 13 out of 51 |
| Thailand | 2.9 | 2.7 | BBB+ | 51 | Emerging | Asia | 8 out of 29 |
| Togo | 8.7 | 8.7 | | 113 | | Africa | 20 out of 51 |
| Tonga | 20.7 | 20.6 | | 170 | | Australasia | 7 out of 7 |
| Trinidad & Tobago | 3.2 | 3.1 | A- | 54 | | Caribbean | 2 out of 9 |
| Tunisia | 5.5 | 5.7 | | 79 | Frontier | Africa | 6 out of 51 |
| Turkey | 3.4 | 3.3 | BB | 58 | Emerging | Central and Eastern Europe | 11 out of 25 |
| Turkmenistan | 11.4 | 11.6 | | 140 | | Asia | 24 out of 29 |
| Uganda | 8.3 | 8.5 | B | 110 | | Africa | 18 out of 51 |
| Ukraine | 10.6 | 10.6 | B- | 135 | | Central and Eastern Europe | 20 out of 25 |
| United Arab Emirates | 0.9 | 1.0 | AA | 33 | Emerging | Middle East | 4 out of 13 |
| United Kingdom | -0.3 | -0.2 | AA | 20 | Developed | Western Europe | 11 out of 19 |
| United States | -1.2 | -1.1 | AA+ | 15 | Developed | North America | 2 out of 2 |
| Uruguay | 2.4 | 2.3 | BBB | 45 | | Latin America | 5 out of 20 |
| Uzbekistan | 10.8 | 10.2 | | 132 | | Asia | 21 out of 29 |
| Vanuatu | 12.1 | 12.0 | | 145 | | Australasia | 4 out of 7 |
| Venezuela | 15.2 | 15.4 | CCC | 162 | | Latin America | 20 out of 20 |
| Vietnam | 5.9 | 5.7 | BB- | 78 | Frontier | Asia | 16 out of 29 |
| Yemen | 15.4 | 15.4 | | 161 | | Middle East | 12 out of 13 |
| Zambia | 8.6 | 8.6 | B | 111 | | Africa | 19 out of 51 |
| Zimbabwe | 16.7 | 16.6 | | 164 | | Africa | 44 out of 51 |

## March 2017 Country Risk Premium (CRP) Summary Statistics:

| S&P Rating | Country Count | Average CRP (%) | Median CRP (%) | Min CRP (%) | Max CRP (%) |
|---|---|---|---|---|---|
| AAA ** | 12 | -2.2 | -2.2 | -2.9 | -1.1 |
| AA (AA+, AA, AA-) | 15 | -0.3 | -0.2 | -2.0 | 2.2 |
| A (A+, A, A-) | 14 | 1.3 | 1.4 | 0.1 | 3.1 |
| BBB (BBB+, BBB, BBB-) | 17 | 2.7 | 2.7 | 0.6 | 4.7 |
| BB (BB+, BB, BB-) | 22 | 5.1 | 5.1 | 2.0 | 9.5 |
| B+ − SD | 39 | 8.9 | 8.6 | 4.9 | 15.4 |
| Investment Grade ** | 58 | 0.6 | 0.6 | -2.9 | 4.7 |
| Non-Investment Grade ** | 61 | 7.5 | 7.7 | 2.0 | 15.4 |
| **MSCI Market Classification** | | | | | |
| Developed Markets | 23 | -1.0 | -1.7 | -2.9 | 2.6 |
| Emerging Markets | 23 | 2.5 | 2.2 | -0.8 | 8.8 |
| Frontier Markets | 22 | 4.9 | 4.8 | 0.7 | 9.5 |
| **Euromoney Region ‡** | | | | | |
| Africa | 51 | 10.9 | 9.3 | 2.3 | 27.4 |
| Asia | 29 | 6.7 | 5.5 | -2.9 | 25.3 |
| Australasia | 7 | 9.8 | 12.0 | -2.0 | 20.6 |
| Caribbean | 9 | 7.7 | 7.3 | 2.2 | 15.2 |
| Central and Eastern Europe | 25 | 5.4 | 3.7 | 0.0 | 13.9 |
| Latin America | 20 | 5.8 | 6.4 | -0.8 | 15.4 |
| Middle East | 13 | 6.0 | 4.0 | -0.2 | 18.0 |
| North America | 2 | -1.6 | -1.6 | -2.0 | -1.1 |
| Western Europe | 19 | -0.2 | -0.7 | -2.8 | 8.3 |

## CCR Base Cost of Equity Capital:

| Czech Republic | COE (%) |
|---|---|
| March 2017 | 8.4 |
| December 2016 | 8.3 |

CCR base country-level COE for a Czech Republic-based investor investing in the Czech Republic.

§ S&P Credit Rating based on long-term foreign currency issuer rating. See http://www.standardandpoors.com/.

• World rank based on 175 countries covered by Euromoney. Ranking based on ascending order in which '1' equals the smallest country risk premium (CRP) and '175' equals the largest country risk premium (CRP).

† MSCI Market Classification based on MSCI Market Classification Framework. See http://www.msci.com/products/indexes/market_classification.html

‡ Regional classification based on Euromoney. Regional rankings based on ascending order in which '1' equals the smallest country risk premium (CRP) for each region.

** Investment grade based on S&P sovereign credit rating from AAA to BBB-. Non-Investment grade based on S&P sovereign credit rating from BB+ to SD. For purposes of this analysis, the U.S. is being treated as if it were rated AAA by S&P.

Note: A CRP of 0.0% is assumed in the following cases: (i) when the investor country and the investee country both have an S&P sovereign credit rating of AAA; or (ii) when the investor country has an S&P credit rating of AAA, and the investee country has a sovereign credit rating below AAA, but has a calculated CRP below 0.0% (which would imply lower risk than a country rated AAA); or (iii) when the investor country has an S&P credit rating below AAA, and the investee country has a sovereign credit rating of AAA, but has a calculated CRP above 0.0% (which would imply greater risk than a country rated below AAA). For purposes of this analysis, the U.S. is treated as having a sovereign credit rating equivalent to AAA.

The country risk premium (CRP) is not the cost of equity capital (COE). The CRP is to be added to base COE. See Chapter 6 for proper application.

## Data Updated Through March 2017

| Investee Country | December 2016 Country Risk Premium (CRP) (%) | March 2017 Country Risk Premium (CRP) (%) | S&P Sovereign Credit Rating § | World Rank Out of 175∗ | MSCI Market Classification † | Euromoney Region ‡ | Regional Rank ‡ |
|---|---|---|---|---|---|---|---|
| Afghanistan | 17.7 | 17.5 | | 139 | | Asia | 23 out of 29 |
| Albania | 12.2 | 12.4 | B+ | 93 | | Central and Eastern Europe | 18 out of 25 |
| Algeria | 12.3 | 12.4 | | 91 | | Africa | 10 out of 51 |
| Angola | 14.6 | 14.8 | B | 121 | | Africa | 26 out of 51 |
| Argentina | 12.8 | 12.6 | B- | 96 | Frontier | Latin America | 13 out of 20 |
| Armenia | 9.8 | 10.0 | | 77 | | Asia | 15 out of 29 |
| Australia | 0.0 | 0.0 | AAA | 12 | Developed | Australasia | 2 out of 7 |
| Austria | 1.0 | 1.0 | AA+ | 13 | Developed | Western Europe | 9 out of 19 |
| Azerbaijan | 11.0 | 11.4 | BB+ | 85 | | Asia | 17 out of 29 |
| Bahamas | 8.4 | 8.1 | BB+ | 65 | | Caribbean | 3 out of 9 |
| Bahrain | 8.3 | 8.1 | BB- | 64 | Frontier | Middle East | 7 out of 13 |
| Bangladesh | 15.1 | 15.0 | BB- | 126 | Frontier | Asia | 20 out of 29 |
| Barbados | 10.0 | 11.1 | CCC+ | 82 | | Caribbean | 4 out of 9 |
| Belarus | 17.4 | 17.8 | B- | 143 | | Central and Eastern Europe | 23 out of 25 |
| Belgium | 2.3 | 2.2 | AA | 17 | Developed | Western Europe | 10 out of 19 |
| Belize | 13.3 | 13.4 | B- | 106 | | Latin America | 17 out of 20 |
| Benin | 19.1 | 19.1 | | 150 | | Africa | 37 out of 51 |
| Bermuda | 6.0 | 5.9 | A+ | 44 | | Caribbean | 1 out of 9 |
| Bhutan | 18.7 | 18.7 | | 148 | | Asia | 25 out of 29 |
| Bolivia | 11.8 | 12.1 | BB | 88 | | Latin America | 12 out of 20 |
| Bosnia & Herzegovina | 17.8 | 18.0 | B | 144 | | Central and Eastern Europe | 24 out of 25 |
| Botswana | 6.0 | 6.0 | A- | 48 | | Africa | 1 out of 51 |
| Brazil | 7.5 | 7.4 | BB | 59 | Emerging | Latin America | 7 out of 20 |
| Bulgaria | 7.3 | 7.6 | BB+ | 61 | | Central and Eastern Europe | 12 out of 25 |
| Burkina Faso | 16.2 | 16.3 | B- | 133 | | Africa | 33 out of 51 |
| Burundi | 28.1 | 28.2 | | 169 | | Africa | 47 out of 51 |
| Cambodia | 19.6 | 19.4 | | 151 | | Asia | 27 out of 29 |
| Cameroon | 14.8 | 14.9 | B | 124 | | Africa | 28 out of 51 |
| Canada | 0.0 | 0.0 | AAA | 9 | Developed | North America | 1 out of 2 |
| Cape Verde | 12.4 | 12.5 | B | 94 | | Africa | 12 out of 51 |
| Central African Republic | 31.6 | 31.7 | | 172 | | Africa | 49 out of 51 |
| Chad | 30.3 | 30.4 | | 171 | | Africa | 48 out of 51 |
| Chile | 1.8 | 2.1 | AA- | 16 | Emerging | Latin America | 1 out of 20 |
| China | 5.8 | 5.8 | AA- | 42 | Emerging | Asia | 7 out of 29 |
| Colombia | 5.7 | 5.8 | BBB | 41 | Emerging | Latin America | 4 out of 20 |
| Congo Republic | 14.4 | 14.3 | B- | 117 | | Africa | 24 out of 51 |
| Congo, DR | 15.7 | 15.7 | B- | 131 | | Africa | 32 out of 51 |
| Costa Rica | 8.8 | 9.0 | BB- | 71 | | Latin America | 8 out of 20 |
| Côte d'Ivoire | 12.3 | 12.4 | | 92 | | Africa | 11 out of 51 |
| Croatia | 7.9 | 7.8 | BB | 63 | Frontier | Central and Eastern Europe | 13 out of 25 |
| Cuba | 21.9 | 22.1 | | 160 | | Caribbean | 9 out of 9 |
| Cyprus | 5.5 | 5.6 | BB+ | 40 | | Central and Eastern Europe | 7 out of 25 |
| Czech Republic | 3.1 | 3.1 | AA- | 23 | Emerging | Central and Eastern Europe | 1 out of 25 |
| Denmark | 0.0 | 0.0 | AAA | 4 | Developed | Western Europe | 3 out of 19 |
| Djibouti | 39.6 | 37.4 | | 175 | | Africa | 51 out of 51 |
| Dominican Republic | 12.1 | 12.3 | BB- | 90 | | Caribbean | 5 out of 9 |
| Ecuador | 13.7 | 13.6 | B | 109 | | Latin America | 18 out of 20 |
| Egypt | 14.2 | 14.2 | B- | 116 | Emerging | Africa | 23 out of 51 |
| El Salvador | 11.2 | 11.0 | B- | 81 | | Latin America | 10 out of 20 |
| Equatorial Guinea | 24.5 | 24.6 | | 165 | | Africa | 45 out of 51 |

§ S&P Credit Rating based on long-term foreign currency issuer rating. See http://www.standardandpoors.com/.

∗ World rank based on 175 countries covered by Euromoney. Ranking based on ascending order in which '1' equals the smallest country risk premium (CRP) and '175' equals the largest country risk premium (CRP).

† MSCI Market Classification based on MSCI Market Classification Framework. See http://www.msci.com/products/indexes/market_classification.html.

‡ Regional classification based on Euromoney. Regional rankings based on ascending order in which '1' equals the smallest country risk premium (CRP) for each region.

Note: A CRP of 0.0% is assumed in the following cases: (i) when the investor country and the investee country both have an S&P sovereign credit rating of AAA; or (ii) when the investor country has an S&P sovereign credit rating of AAA, and the investee country has a sovereign credit rating below AAA, but has a calculated CRP below 0.0% (which would imply lower risk than a country rated AAA); or (iii) when the investor country has an S&P credit rating below AAA, and the investee country has a sovereign credit rating of AAA, but has a calculated CRP above 0.0% (which would imply greater risk than a country rated below AAA). For purposes of this analysis, the U.S. is treated as having a sovereign credit rating equivalent to AAA.

The country risk premium (CRP) is not the cost of equity capital (COE). The CRP is to be added to base COE. See Chapter 6 for proper application.

### Data Updated Through March 2017

| Investee Country | December 2016 Country Risk Premium (CRP) (%) | March 2017 Country Risk Premium (CRP) (%) | S&P Sovereign Credit Rating § | World Rank Out of 175∗ | MSCI Market Classification † | Euromoney Region ‡ | Regional Rank ‡ |
|---|---|---|---|---|---|---|---|
| Eritrea | 35.8 | 34.1 | | 173 | | Africa | 50 out of 51 |
| Estonia | 3.7 | 4.0 | AA- | 32 | Frontier | Central and Eastern Europe | 4 out of 25 |
| Ethiopia | 13.0 | 13.1 | B | 101 | | Africa | 16 out of 51 |
| Fiji | 18.4 | 18.3 | B+ | 147 | | Australasia | 5 out of 7 |
| Finland | 0.8 | 0.8 | AA+ | 11 | Developed | Western Europe | 8 out of 19 |
| France | 3.1 | 3.0 | AA | 22 | Developed | Western Europe | 12 out of 19 |
| Gabon | 10.8 | 11.2 | | 83 | | Africa | 7 out of 51 |
| Gambia | 16.8 | 16.9 | | 138 | | Africa | 34 out of 51 |
| Georgia | 9.5 | 9.8 | BB- | 74 | | Central and Eastern Europe | 15 out of 25 |
| Germany | 0.0 | 0.0 | AAA | 10 | Developed | Western Europe | 7 out of 19 |
| Ghana | 12.5 | 12.2 | B- | 89 | | Africa | 9 out of 51 |
| Greece | 13.7 | 13.5 | B- | 108 | Emerging | Western Europe | 19 out of 19 |
| Grenada | 13.3 | 13.4 | | 105 | | Caribbean | 7 out of 9 |
| Guatemala | 11.2 | 11.3 | BB | 84 | | Latin America | 11 out of 20 |
| Guinea | 20.6 | 20.6 | | 156 | | Africa | 41 out of 51 |
| Guinea-Bissau | 14.1 | 14.2 | | 115 | | Africa | 22 out of 51 |
| Guyana | 12.9 | 13.0 | | 100 | | Latin America | 15 out of 20 |
| Haiti | 23.4 | 21.5 | | 157 | | Caribbean | 8 out of 9 |
| Honduras | 12.6 | 12.7 | B+ | 98 | | Latin America | 14 out of 20 |
| Hong Kong | 0.0 | 0.0 | AAA | 14 | Developed | Asia | 2 out of 29 |
| Hungary | 7.1 | 7.3 | BBB- | 57 | Emerging | Central and Eastern Europe | 10 out of 25 |
| Iceland | 4.1 | 3.9 | A | 30 | | Western Europe | 15 out of 19 |
| India | 6.9 | 7.2 | BBB- | 55 | Emerging | Asia | 10 out of 29 |
| Indonesia | 7.6 | 7.7 | BB+ | 62 | Emerging | Asia | 11 out of 29 |
| Iran | 14.6 | 14.9 | | 125 | | Middle East | 10 out of 13 |
| Iraq | 16.4 | 16.5 | B- | 136 | | Middle East | 11 out of 13 |
| Ireland | 3.6 | 3.6 | A+ | 27 | Developed | Western Europe | 14 out of 19 |
| Israel | 3.6 | 3.6 | A+ | 28 | Developed | Middle East | 2 out of 13 |
| Italy | 6.5 | 6.4 | BBB- | 50 | Developed | Western Europe | 18 out of 19 |
| Jamaica | 12.7 | 13.3 | B | 104 | | Caribbean | 6 out of 9 |
| Japan | 3.4 | 3.5 | A+ | 25 | Developed | Asia | 5 out of 29 |
| Jordan | 9.8 | 10.0 | BB- | 76 | Frontier | Middle East | 8 out of 13 |
| Kazakhstan | 9.2 | 9.0 | BBB- | 70 | Frontier | Asia | 13 out of 29 |
| Kenya | 12.7 | 12.8 | B+ | 99 | Frontier | Africa | 15 out of 51 |
| Korea (North) | 35.1 | 34.8 | | 174 | | Asia | 29 out of 29 |
| Korea (South) | 2.7 | 2.7 | AA | 19 | Emerging | Asia | 4 out of 29 |
| Kuwait | 3.7 | 3.9 | AA | 31 | Frontier | Middle East | 3 out of 13 |
| Kyrgyz Republic | 17.9 | 17.8 | | 142 | | Central and Eastern Europe | 22 out of 25 |
| Laos | 22.2 | 21.7 | | 158 | | Asia | 28 out of 29 |
| Latvia | 5.8 | 5.9 | A- | 43 | | Central and Eastern Europe | 8 out of 25 |
| Lebanon | 14.5 | 13.9 | B- | 112 | Frontier | Middle East | 9 out of 13 |
| Lesotho | 18.1 | 18.2 | | 146 | | Africa | 36 out of 51 |
| Liberia | 13.4 | 13.4 | | 107 | | Africa | 17 out of 51 |
| Libya | 19.6 | 20.1 | | 153 | | Africa | 39 out of 51 |
| Lithuania | 5.0 | 5.1 | A- | 36 | Frontier | Central and Eastern Europe | 6 out of 25 |
| Luxembourg | 0.0 | 0.0 | AAA | 5 | | Western Europe | 4 out of 19 |
| Macedonia | 11.8 | 12.1 | BB- | 87 | | Central and Eastern Europe | 17 out of 25 |
| Madagascar | 14.2 | 14.8 | | 123 | | Africa | 27 out of 51 |
| Malawi | 13.9 | 14.0 | | 114 | | Africa | 21 out of 51 |
| Malaysia | 5.2 | 5.1 | A- | 35 | Emerging | Asia | 6 out of 29 |

§ S&P Credit Rating based on long-term foreign currency issuer rating. See http://www.standardandpoors.com/.

∗ World rank based on 175 countries covered by Euromoney. Ranking based on ascending order in which '1' equals the smallest country risk premium (CRP) and '175' equals the largest country risk premium (CRP).

† MSCI Market Classification based on MSCI Market Classification Framework. See http://www.msci.com/products/indexes/market_classification.html.

‡ Regional classification based on Euromoney. Regional rankings based on ascending order in which '1' equals the smallest country risk premium (CRP) for each region.

Note: A CRP of 0.0% is assumed in the following cases: (i) when the investor country and the investee country both have an S&P sovereign credit rating of AAA; or (ii) when the investor country has an S&P credit rating of AAA, and the investee country has a sovereign credit rating below AAA, but has a calculated CRP below 0.0% (which would imply lower risk than a country rated AAA); or (iii) when the investor country has an S&P sovereign credit rating below AAA, and the investee country has a sovereign credit rating of AAA, but has a calculated CRP above 0.0% (which would imply greater risk than a country rated below AAA). For purposes of this analysis, the U.S. is treated as having a sovereign credit rating equivalent to AAA.

The country risk premium (CRP) is not the cost of equity capital (COE). The CRP is to be added to base COE. See Chapter 6 for proper application.

## Data Updated Through March 2017

| Investee Country | December 2016 Country Risk Premium (CRP) (%) | March 2017 Country Risk Premium (CRP) (%) | S&P Sovereign Credit Rating § | World Rank Out of 175* | MSCI Market Classification † | Euromoney Region ‡ | Regional Rank ‡ |
|---|---|---|---|---|---|---|---|
| Mali | 17.7 | 17.8 | | 141 | | Africa | 35 out of 51 |
| Malta | 3.4 | 3.5 | A- | 26 | | Western Europe | 13 out of 19 |
| Mauritania | 21.8 | 21.9 | | 159 | | Africa | 42 out of 51 |
| Mauritius | 8.6 | 8.6 | | 67 | Frontier | Asia | 12 out of 29 |
| Mexico | 5.0 | 5.2 | BBB+ | 37 | Emerging | Latin America | 2 out of 20 |
| Moldova | 16.1 | 16.6 | | 137 | | Central and Eastern Europe | 21 out of 25 |
| Mongolia | 14.3 | 14.7 | B- | 119 | | Asia | 18 out of 29 |
| Montenegro | 13.5 | 13.3 | B+ | 103 | | Central and Eastern Europe | 19 out of 25 |
| Morocco | 8.6 | 8.9 | BBB- | 69 | Frontier | Africa | 4 out of 51 |
| Mozambique | 15.4 | 15.3 | SD | 128 | | Africa | 29 out of 51 |
| Myanmar | 16.3 | 16.3 | | 134 | | Asia | 22 out of 29 |
| Namibia | 8.2 | 8.4 | | 66 | | Africa | 3 out of 51 |
| Nepal | 19.0 | 19.1 | | 149 | | Asia | 26 out of 29 |
| Netherlands | 0.0 | 0.0 | AAA | 6 | Developed | Western Europe | 5 out of 19 |
| New Zealand | 0.5 | 0.6 | AA | 8 | Developed | Australasia | 1 out of 7 |
| Nicaragua | 15.1 | 15.1 | B+ | 127 | | Latin America | 19 out of 20 |
| Niger | 14.6 | 14.7 | | 120 | | Africa | 25 out of 51 |
| Nigeria | 12.6 | 12.7 | B | 97 | Frontier | Africa | 14 out of 51 |
| Norway | 0.0 | 0.0 | AAA | 3 | Developed | Western Europe | 2 out of 19 |
| Oman | 5.9 | 6.0 | BBB- | 46 | Frontier | Middle East | 5 out of 13 |
| Pakistan | 14.7 | 14.8 | B | 122 | Frontier | Asia | 19 out of 29 |
| Panama | 6.6 | 6.7 | BBB | 52 | | Latin America | 6 out of 20 |
| Papua New Guinea | 14.2 | 14.4 | B+ | 118 | | Australasia | 3 out of 7 |
| Paraguay | 10.2 | 10.4 | BB | 80 | | Latin America | 9 out of 20 |
| Peru | 5.3 | 5.5 | BBB+ | 39 | Emerging | Latin America | 3 out of 20 |
| Philippines | 7.0 | 7.0 | BBB | 53 | Emerging | Asia | 9 out of 29 |
| Poland | 3.9 | 3.8 | BBB+ | 29 | Emerging | Central and Eastern Europe | 3 out of 25 |
| Portugal | 6.3 | 6.2 | BB+ | 49 | Developed | Western Europe | 17 out of 19 |
| Qatar | 2.8 | 2.9 | AA | 21 | Emerging | Middle East | 1 out of 13 |
| Romania | 7.1 | 7.2 | BBB- | 56 | Frontier | Central and Eastern Europe | 9 out of 25 |
| Russia | 9.4 | 8.8 | BB+ | 68 | Emerging | Central and Eastern Europe | 14 out of 25 |
| Rwanda | 15.4 | 15.5 | B | 130 | | Africa | 31 out of 51 |
| São Tomé & Príncipe | 21.9 | 22.4 | | 163 | | Africa | 43 out of 51 |
| Saudi Arabia | 6.3 | 6.0 | A- | 47 | | Middle East | 6 out of 13 |
| Senegal | 12.0 | 12.0 | B+ | 86 | | Africa | 8 out of 51 |
| Serbia | 10.1 | 9.8 | BB- | 75 | Frontier | Central and Eastern Europe | 16 out of 25 |
| Seychelles | 9.5 | 9.6 | | 73 | | Africa | 5 out of 51 |
| Sierra Leone | 15.4 | 15.5 | | 129 | | Africa | 30 out of 51 |
| Singapore | 0.0 | 0.0 | AAA | 1 | Developed | Asia | 1 out of 29 |
| Slovakia | 3.2 | 3.3 | A+ | 24 | | Central and Eastern Europe | 2 out of 25 |
| Slovenia | 4.6 | 4.7 | A | 34 | Frontier | Central and Eastern Europe | 5 out of 25 |
| Solomon Islands | 26.3 | 26.4 | | 168 | | Australasia | 6 out of 7 |
| Somalia | 24.5 | 24.6 | | 166 | | Africa | 46 out of 51 |
| South Africa | 7.2 | 7.5 | BBB- | 60 | Emerging | Africa | 2 out of 51 |
| Spain | 5.4 | 5.5 | BBB+ | 38 | Developed | Western Europe | 16 out of 19 |
| Sri Lanka | 9.5 | 9.2 | B+ | 72 | Frontier | Asia | 14 out of 29 |
| Sudan | 20.5 | 20.5 | | 154 | | Africa | 40 out of 51 |
| Suriname | 12.9 | 13.1 | B+ | 102 | | Latin America | 16 out of 20 |
| Swaziland | 18.8 | 19.8 | | 152 | | Africa | 38 out of 51 |
| Sweden | 0.0 | 0.0 | AAA | 7 | Developed | Western Europe | 6 out of 19 |

§ S&P Credit Rating based on long-term foreign currency issuer rating. See http://www.standardandpoors.com/.

* World rank based on 175 countries covered by Euromoney. Ranking based on ascending order in which '1' equals the smallest country risk premium (CRP) and '175' equals the largest country risk premium (CRP).

† MSCI Market Classification based on MSCI Market Classification Framework. See http://www.msci.com/products/indexes/market_classification.html

‡ Regional classification based on Euromoney. Regional rankings based on ascending order in which '1' equals the smallest country risk premium (CRP) for each region.

Note: A CRP of 0.0% is assumed in the following cases: (i) when the investor country and the investee country both have an S&P sovereign credit rating of AAA; or (ii) when the investor country has an S&P credit rating of AAA, and the investee country has a sovereign credit rating below AAA, but has a calculated CRP below 0.0% (which would imply lower risk than a country rated AAA); or (iii) when the investor country has an S&P credit rating below AAA, and the investee country has a sovereign credit rating of AAA, but has a calculated CRP above 0.0% (which would imply greater risk than a country rated below AAA). For purposes of this analysis, the U.S. is treated as having a sovereign credit rating equivalent to AAA.

The country risk premium (CRP) is not the cost of equity capital (COE). The CRP is to be added to base COE. See Chapter 6 for proper application.

### Data Updated Through March 2017

| Investee Country | December 2016 Country Risk Premium (CRP) (%) | March 2017 Country Risk Premium (CRP) (%) | S&P Sovereign Credit Rating § | World Rank Out of 175* | MSCI Market Classification † | Euromoney Region ‡ | Regional Rank ‡ |
|---|---|---|---|---|---|---|---|
| Switzerland | 0.0 | 0.0 | AAA | 2 | Developed | Western Europe | 1 out of 19 |
| Syria | 25.3 | 25.6 | | 167 | | Middle East | 13 out of 13 |
| Taiwan | 2.4 | 2.5 | AA- | 18 | Emerging | Asia | 3 out of 29 |
| Tajikistan | 20.1 | 20.5 | | 155 | | Central and Eastern Europe | 25 out of 25 |
| Tanzania | 12.3 | 12.6 | | 95 | | Africa | 13 out of 51 |
| Thailand | 6.6 | 6.5 | BBB+ | 51 | Emerging | Asia | 8 out of 29 |
| Togo | 13.9 | 14.0 | | 113 | | Africa | 20 out of 51 |
| Tonga | 28.7 | 28.8 | | 170 | | Australasia | 7 out of 7 |
| Trinidad & Tobago | 7.0 | 7.0 | A- | 54 | | Caribbean | 2 out of 9 |
| Tunisia | 9.9 | 10.3 | | 79 | Frontier | Africa | 6 out of 51 |
| Turkey | 7.3 | 7.3 | BB | 58 | Emerging | Central and Eastern Europe | 11 out of 25 |
| Turkmenistan | 17.2 | 17.6 | | 140 | | Asia | 24 out of 29 |
| Uganda | 13.4 | 13.8 | B | 110 | | Africa | 18 out of 51 |
| Ukraine | 16.2 | 16.4 | B- | 135 | | Central and Eastern Europe | 20 out of 25 |
| United Arab Emirates | 4.2 | 4.3 | AA | 33 | Emerging | Middle East | 4 out of 13 |
| United Kingdom | 2.7 | 2.8 | AA | 20 | Developed | Western Europe | 11 out of 19 |
| United States | 0.0 | 0.0 | AA+ | 15 | Developed | North America | 2 out of 2 |
| Uruguay | 6.0 | 5.9 | BBB | 45 | | Latin America | 5 out of 20 |
| Uzbekistan | 16.4 | 15.9 | | 132 | | Asia | 21 out of 29 |
| Vanuatu | 18.1 | 18.2 | | 145 | | Australasia | 4 out of 7 |
| Venezuela | 21.9 | 22.4 | CCC | 162 | | Latin America | 20 out of 20 |
| Vietnam | 10.4 | 10.2 | BB- | 78 | Frontier | Asia | 16 out of 29 |
| Yemen | 22.2 | 22.4 | | 161 | | Middle East | 12 out of 13 |
| Zambia | 13.7 | 13.8 | B | 111 | | Africa | 19 out of 51 |
| Zimbabwe | 23.8 | 23.8 | | 164 | | Africa | 44 out of 51 |

### March 2017 Country Risk Premium (CRP) Summary Statistics:

| S&P Rating | Country Count | Average CRP (%) | Median CRP (%) | Min CRP (%) | Max CRP (%) |
|---|---|---|---|---|---|
| AAA ** | 12 | 0.0 | 0.0 | 0.0 | 0.0 |
| AA (AA+, AA, AA-) | 15 | 2.8 | 2.8 | 0.6 | 5.8 |
| A (A+, A, A-) | 14 | 4.8 | 4.9 | 3.3 | 7.0 |
| BBB (BBB+, BBB, BBB-) | 17 | 6.5 | 6.5 | 3.8 | 9.0 |
| BB (BB+, BB, BB-) | 22 | 9.5 | 9.4 | 5.6 | 15.0 |
| B+ − SD | 39 | 14.3 | 13.8 | 9.2 | 22.4 |
| Investment Grade ** | 58 | 3.8 | 3.9 | 0.0 | 9.0 |
| Non-Investment Grade ** | 61 | 12.5 | 12.7 | 5.6 | 22.4 |
| **MSCI Market Classification** | | | | | |
| Developed Markets | 23 | 1.7 | 0.6 | 0.0 | 6.4 |
| Emerging Markets | 23 | 6.2 | 5.8 | 2.1 | 14.2 |
| Frontier Markets | 22 | 9.3 | 9.1 | 3.9 | 15.0 |
| **Euromoney Region ‡** | | | | | |
| Africa | 51 | 16.8 | 14.8 | 6.0 | 37.4 |
| Asia | 29 | 11.4 | 10.0 | 0.0 | 34.8 |
| Australasia | 7 | 15.2 | 18.2 | 0.0 | 28.8 |
| Caribbean | 9 | 12.8 | 12.3 | 5.9 | 22.1 |
| Central and Eastern Europe | 25 | 9.8 | 7.8 | 3.1 | 20.5 |
| Latin America | 20 | 10.4 | 11.2 | 2.1 | 22.4 |
| Middle East | 13 | 10.6 | 8.1 | 2.9 | 25.6 |
| North America | 2 | 0.0 | 0.0 | 0.0 | 0.0 |
| Western Europe | 19 | 2.8 | 2.2 | 0.0 | 13.5 |

### CCR Base Cost of Equity Capital:

| Denmark | COE (%) |
|---|---|
| March 2017 | 6.8 |
| December 2016 | 6.8 |

CCR base country-level COE for a Denmark-based investor investing in Denmark.

§ S&P Credit Rating based on long-term foreign currency issuer rating. See http://www.standardandpoors.com/.

• World rank based on 175 countries covered by Euromoney. Ranking based on ascending order in which '1' equals the smallest country risk premium (CRP) and '175' equals the largest country risk premium (CRP).

† MSCI Market Classification based on MSCI Market Classification Framework. See http://www.msci.com/products/indexes/market_classification.html

‡ Regional classification based on Euromoney. Regional rankings based on ascending order in which '1' equals the smallest country risk premium (CRP) for each region.

** Investment grade based on S&P sovereign credit rating from AAA to BBB-. Non-Investment grade based on S&P sovereign credit rating from BB+ to SD. For purposes of this analysis, the U.S. is being treated as if it were rated AAA by S&P.

Note: A CRP of 0.0% is assumed in the following cases: (i) when the investor country and the investee country both have an S&P sovereign credit rating of AAA; or (ii) when the investor country has an S&P credit rating of AAA, and the investee country has a sovereign credit rating below AAA, but has a calculated CRP below 0.0% (which would imply lower risk than a country rated AAA); or (iii) when the investor country has an S&P credit rating below AAA, and the investee country has a sovereign credit rating of AAA, but has a calculated CRP above 0.0% (which would imply greater risk than a country rated below AAA). For purposes of this analysis, the U.S. is treated as having a sovereign credit rating equivalent to AAA.

The country risk premium (CRP) is not the cost of equity capital (COE). The CRP is to be added to base COE. See Chapter 6 for proper application.

### Data Updated Through March 2017

| Investee Country | December 2016 Country Risk Premium (CRP) (%) | March 2017 Country Risk Premium (CRP) (%) | S&P Sovereign Credit Rating § | World Rank Out of 175∙ | MSCI Market Classification † | Euromoney Region ‡ | Regional Rank ‡ |
|---|---|---|---|---|---|---|---|
| Afghanistan | 14.1 | 13.6 | | 139 | | Asia | 23 out of 29 |
| Albania | 8.6 | 8.5 | B+ | 93 | | Central and Eastern Europe | 18 out of 25 |
| Algeria | 8.6 | 8.5 | | 91 | | Africa | 10 out of 51 |
| Angola | 11.0 | 10.8 | B | 121 | | Africa | 26 out of 51 |
| Argentina | 9.2 | 8.7 | B- | 96 | Frontier | Latin America | 13 out of 20 |
| Armenia | 6.2 | 6.1 | | 77 | | Asia | 15 out of 29 |
| Australia | -2.9 | -3.2 | AAA | 12 | Developed | Australasia | 2 out of 7 |
| Austria | -2.7 | -3.0 | AA+ | 13 | Developed | Western Europe | 9 out of 19 |
| Azerbaijan | 7.4 | 7.5 | BB+ | 85 | | Asia | 17 out of 29 |
| Bahamas | 4.7 | 4.2 | BB+ | 65 | | Caribbean | 3 out of 9 |
| Bahrain | 4.6 | 4.2 | BB- | 64 | Frontier | Middle East | 7 out of 13 |
| Bangladesh | 11.5 | 11.1 | BB- | 126 | Frontier | Asia | 20 out of 29 |
| Barbados | 6.4 | 7.2 | CCC+ | 82 | | Caribbean | 4 out of 9 |
| Belarus | 13.7 | 14.0 | B- | 143 | | Central and Eastern Europe | 23 out of 25 |
| Belgium | -1.4 | -1.7 | AA | 17 | Developed | Western Europe | 10 out of 19 |
| Belize | 9.6 | 9.5 | B- | 106 | | Latin America | 17 out of 20 |
| Benin | 15.4 | 15.3 | | 150 | | Africa | 37 out of 51 |
| Bermuda | 2.3 | 2.0 | A+ | 44 | | Caribbean | 1 out of 9 |
| Bhutan | 15.1 | 14.8 | | 148 | | Asia | 25 out of 29 |
| Bolivia | 8.1 | 8.2 | BB | 88 | | Latin America | 12 out of 20 |
| Bosnia & Herzegovina | 14.2 | 14.1 | B | 144 | | Central and Eastern Europe | 24 out of 25 |
| Botswana | 2.3 | 2.0 | A- | 48 | | Africa | 1 out of 51 |
| Brazil | 3.8 | 3.5 | BB | 59 | Emerging | Latin America | 7 out of 20 |
| Bulgaria | 3.7 | 3.6 | BB+ | 61 | | Central and Eastern Europe | 12 out of 25 |
| Burkina Faso | 12.6 | 12.4 | B- | 133 | | Africa | 33 out of 51 |
| Burundi | 24.5 | 24.3 | | 169 | | Africa | 47 out of 51 |
| Cambodia | 16.0 | 15.5 | | 151 | | Asia | 27 out of 29 |
| Cameroon | 11.2 | 11.0 | B | 124 | | Africa | 28 out of 51 |
| Canada | -3.1 | -3.4 | AAA | 9 | Developed | North America | 1 out of 2 |
| Cape Verde | 8.8 | 8.6 | B | 94 | | Africa | 12 out of 51 |
| Central African Republic | 28.1 | 27.9 | | 172 | | Africa | 49 out of 51 |
| Chad | 26.7 | 26.6 | | 171 | | Africa | 48 out of 51 |
| Chile | -1.9 | -1.9 | AA- | 16 | Emerging | Latin America | 1 out of 20 |
| China | 2.1 | 1.8 | AA- | 42 | Emerging | Asia | 7 out of 29 |
| Colombia | 2.0 | 1.8 | BBB | 41 | Emerging | Latin America | 4 out of 20 |
| Congo Republic | 10.8 | 10.4 | B- | 117 | | Africa | 24 out of 51 |
| Congo, DR | 12.1 | 11.8 | B- | 131 | | Africa | 32 out of 51 |
| Costa Rica | 5.1 | 5.1 | BB- | 71 | | Latin America | 8 out of 20 |
| Côte d'Ivoire | 8.7 | 8.5 | | 92 | | Africa | 11 out of 51 |
| Croatia | 4.2 | 3.8 | BB | 63 | Frontier | Central and Eastern Europe | 13 out of 25 |
| Cuba | 18.4 | 18.3 | | 160 | | Caribbean | 9 out of 9 |
| Cyprus | 1.8 | 1.6 | BB+ | 40 | | Central and Eastern Europe | 7 out of 25 |
| Czech Republic | -0.6 | -0.9 | AA- | 23 | Emerging | Central and Eastern Europe | 1 out of 25 |
| Denmark | -3.7 | -4.0 | AAA | 4 | Developed | Western Europe | 3 out of 19 |
| Djibouti | 36.1 | 33.6 | | 175 | | Africa | 51 out of 51 |
| Dominican Republic | 8.5 | 8.4 | BB- | 90 | | Caribbean | 5 out of 9 |
| Ecuador | 10.1 | 9.7 | B | 109 | | Latin America | 18 out of 20 |
| Egypt | 10.5 | 10.3 | B- | 116 | Emerging | Africa | 23 out of 51 |
| El Salvador | 7.5 | 7.1 | B- | 81 | | Latin America | 10 out of 20 |
| Equatorial Guinea | 20.9 | 20.7 | | 165 | | Africa | 45 out of 51 |

§ S&P Credit Rating based on long-term foreign currency issuer rating. See http://www.standardandpoors.com/.

∙ World rank based on 175 countries covered by Euromoney. Ranking based on ascending order in which '1' equals the smallest country risk premium (CRP) and '175' equals the largest country risk premium (CRP).

† MSCI Market Classification based on MSCI Market Classification Framework. See http://www.msci.com/products/indexes/market_classification.html

‡ Regional classification based on Euromoney. Regional rankings based on ascending order in which '1' equals the smallest country risk premium (CRP) for each region.

Note: A CRP of 0.0% is assumed in the following cases: (i) when the investor country and the investee country both have an S&P sovereign credit rating of AAA; or (ii) when the investor country has an S&P credit rating of AAA, and the investee country has a sovereign credit rating below AAA, but has a calculated CRP below 0.0% (which would imply lower risk than a country rated AAA); or (iii) when the investor country has an S&P credit rating below AAA, and the investee country has a sovereign credit rating of AAA, but has a calculated CRP above 0.0% (which would imply greater risk than a country rated below AAA). For purposes of this analysis, the U.S. is treated as having a sovereign credit rating equivalent to AAA.

The country risk premium (CRP) is not the cost of equity capital (COE). The CRP is to be added to base COE. See Chapter 6 for proper application.

## Data Updated Through March 2017

| Investee Country | December 2016 Country Risk Premium (CRP) (%) | March 2017 Country Risk Premium (CRP) (%) | S&P Sovereign Credit Rating § | World Rank Out of 175∗ | MSCI Market Classification † | Euromoney Region ‡ | Regional Rank ‡ |
|---|---|---|---|---|---|---|---|
| Eritrea | 32.3 | 30.3 | | 173 | | Africa | 50 out of 51 |
| Estonia | 0.0 | 0.0 | AA- | 32 | Frontier | Central and Eastern Europe | 4 out of 25 |
| Ethiopia | 9.3 | 9.2 | B | 101 | | Africa | 16 out of 51 |
| Fiji | 14.8 | 14.4 | B+ | 147 | | Australasia | 5 out of 7 |
| Finland | -3.0 | -3.2 | AA+ | 11 | Developed | Western Europe | 8 out of 19 |
| France | -0.6 | -1.0 | AA | 22 | Developed | Western Europe | 12 out of 19 |
| Gabon | 7.1 | 7.2 | | 83 | | Africa | 7 out of 51 |
| Gambia | 13.2 | 13.0 | | 138 | | Africa | 34 out of 51 |
| Georgia | 5.9 | 5.9 | BB- | 74 | | Central and Eastern Europe | 15 out of 25 |
| Germany | -3.0 | -3.3 | AAA | 10 | Developed | Western Europe | 7 out of 19 |
| Ghana | 8.9 | 8.3 | B- | 89 | | Africa | 9 out of 51 |
| Greece | 10.0 | 9.6 | B- | 108 | Emerging | Western Europe | 19 out of 19 |
| Grenada | 9.6 | 9.5 | | 105 | | Caribbean | 7 out of 9 |
| Guatemala | 7.5 | 7.4 | BB | 84 | | Latin America | 11 out of 20 |
| Guinea | 17.0 | 16.8 | | 156 | | Africa | 41 out of 51 |
| Guinea-Bissau | 10.5 | 10.3 | | 115 | | Africa | 22 out of 51 |
| Guyana | 9.3 | 9.1 | | 100 | | Latin America | 15 out of 20 |
| Haiti | 19.8 | 17.6 | | 157 | | Caribbean | 8 out of 9 |
| Honduras | 9.0 | 8.8 | B+ | 98 | | Latin America | 14 out of 20 |
| Hong Kong | -2.4 | -2.6 | AAA | 14 | Developed | Asia | 2 out of 29 |
| Hungary | 3.4 | 3.3 | BBB- | 57 | Emerging | Central and Eastern Europe | 10 out of 25 |
| Iceland | 0.4 | -0.1 | A | 30 | | Western Europe | 15 out of 19 |
| India | 3.2 | 3.3 | BBB- | 55 | Emerging | Asia | 10 out of 29 |
| Indonesia | 4.0 | 3.8 | BB+ | 62 | Emerging | Asia | 11 out of 29 |
| Iran | 11.0 | 11.0 | | 125 | | Middle East | 10 out of 13 |
| Iraq | 12.8 | 12.6 | B- | 136 | | Middle East | 11 out of 13 |
| Ireland | -0.1 | -0.4 | A+ | 27 | Developed | Western Europe | 14 out of 19 |
| Israel | -0.1 | -0.4 | A+ | 28 | Developed | Middle East | 2 out of 13 |
| Italy | 2.8 | 2.4 | BBB- | 50 | Developed | Western Europe | 18 out of 19 |
| Jamaica | 9.0 | 9.4 | B | 104 | | Caribbean | 6 out of 9 |
| Japan | -0.3 | -0.5 | A+ | 25 | Developed | Asia | 5 out of 29 |
| Jordan | 6.1 | 6.1 | BB- | 76 | Frontier | Middle East | 8 out of 13 |
| Kazakhstan | 5.6 | 5.0 | BBB- | 70 | Frontier | Asia | 13 out of 29 |
| Kenya | 9.1 | 8.9 | B+ | 99 | Frontier | Africa | 15 out of 51 |
| Korea (North) | 31.6 | 31.0 | | 174 | | Asia | 29 out of 29 |
| Korea (South) | -1.0 | -1.2 | AA | 19 | Emerging | Asia | 4 out of 29 |
| Kuwait | 0.1 | 0.0 | AA | 31 | Frontier | Middle East | 3 out of 13 |
| Kyrgyz Republic | 14.3 | 13.9 | | 142 | | Central and Eastern Europe | 22 out of 25 |
| Laos | 18.6 | 17.8 | | 158 | | Asia | 28 out of 29 |
| Latvia | 2.1 | 2.0 | A- | 43 | | Central and Eastern Europe | 8 out of 25 |
| Lebanon | 10.8 | 10.0 | B- | 112 | Frontier | Middle East | 9 out of 13 |
| Lesotho | 14.5 | 14.3 | | 146 | | Africa | 36 out of 51 |
| Liberia | 9.7 | 9.5 | | 107 | | Africa | 17 out of 51 |
| Libya | 16.0 | 16.2 | | 153 | | Africa | 39 out of 51 |
| Lithuania | 1.3 | 1.2 | A- | 36 | Frontier | Central and Eastern Europe | 6 out of 25 |
| Luxembourg | -3.4 | -3.7 | AAA | 5 | | Western Europe | 4 out of 19 |
| Macedonia | 8.1 | 8.1 | BB- | 87 | | Central and Eastern Europe | 17 out of 25 |
| Madagascar | 10.6 | 10.9 | | 123 | | Africa | 27 out of 51 |
| Malawi | 10.3 | 10.1 | | 114 | | Africa | 21 out of 51 |
| Malaysia | 1.5 | 1.1 | A- | 35 | Emerging | Asia | 6 out of 29 |

The country risk premium (CRP) is not the cost of equity capital (COE). The CRP is to be added to base COE. See Chapter 6 for proper application.

## Data Updated Through March 2017

| Investee Country | December 2016 Country Risk Premium (CRP) (%) | March 2017 Country Risk Premium (CRP) (%) | S&P Sovereign Credit Rating § | World Rank Out of 175∗ | MSCI Market Classification † | Euromoney Region ‡ | Regional Rank ‡ |
|---|---|---|---|---|---|---|---|
| Mali | 14.1 | 13.9 | | 141 | | Africa | 35 out of 51 |
| Malta | -0.3 | -0.4 | A- | 26 | | Western Europe | 13 out of 19 |
| Mauritania | 18.2 | 18.0 | | 159 | | Africa | 42 out of 51 |
| Mauritius | 4.9 | 4.7 | | 67 | Frontier | Asia | 12 out of 29 |
| Mexico | 1.3 | 1.2 | BBB+ | 37 | Emerging | Latin America | 2 out of 20 |
| Moldova | 12.5 | 12.7 | | 137 | | Central and Eastern Europe | 21 out of 25 |
| Mongolia | 10.7 | 10.8 | B- | 119 | | Asia | 18 out of 29 |
| Montenegro | 9.9 | 9.4 | B+ | 103 | | Central and Eastern Europe | 19 out of 25 |
| Morocco | 4.9 | 4.9 | BBB- | 69 | Frontier | Africa | 4 out of 51 |
| Mozambique | 11.7 | 11.4 | SD | 128 | | Africa | 29 out of 51 |
| Myanmar | 12.7 | 12.4 | | 134 | | Asia | 22 out of 29 |
| Namibia | 4.6 | 4.5 | | 66 | | Africa | 3 out of 51 |
| Nepal | 15.4 | 15.2 | | 149 | | Asia | 26 out of 29 |
| Netherlands | -3.4 | -3.6 | AAA | 6 | Developed | Western Europe | 5 out of 19 |
| New Zealand | -3.2 | -3.4 | AA | 8 | Developed | Australasia | 1 out of 7 |
| Nicaragua | 11.4 | 11.2 | B+ | 127 | | Latin America | 19 out of 20 |
| Niger | 11.0 | 10.8 | | 120 | | Africa | 25 out of 51 |
| Nigeria | 9.0 | 8.8 | B | 97 | Frontier | Africa | 14 out of 51 |
| Norway | -4.0 | -4.3 | AAA | 3 | Developed | Western Europe | 2 out of 19 |
| Oman | 2.2 | 2.0 | BBB- | 46 | Frontier | Middle East | 5 out of 13 |
| Pakistan | 11.1 | 10.8 | B | 122 | Frontier | Asia | 19 out of 29 |
| Panama | 2.9 | 2.8 | BBB | 52 | | Latin America | 6 out of 20 |
| Papua New Guinea | 10.6 | 10.5 | B+ | 118 | | Australasia | 3 out of 7 |
| Paraguay | 6.5 | 6.5 | BB | 80 | | Latin America | 9 out of 20 |
| Peru | 1.6 | 1.5 | BBB+ | 39 | Emerging | Latin America | 3 out of 20 |
| Philippines | 3.3 | 3.0 | BBB | 53 | Emerging | Asia | 9 out of 29 |
| Poland | 0.2 | -0.1 | BBB+ | 29 | Emerging | Central and Eastern Europe | 3 out of 25 |
| Portugal | 2.7 | 2.2 | BB+ | 49 | Developed | Western Europe | 17 out of 19 |
| Qatar | -0.9 | -1.1 | AA | 21 | Emerging | Middle East | 1 out of 13 |
| Romania | 3.5 | 3.3 | BBB- | 56 | Frontier | Central and Eastern Europe | 9 out of 25 |
| Russia | 5.7 | 4.9 | BB+ | 68 | Emerging | Central and Eastern Europe | 14 out of 25 |
| Rwanda | 11.8 | 11.6 | B | 130 | | Africa | 31 out of 51 |
| São Tomé & Príncipe | 18.3 | 18.6 | | 163 | | Africa | 43 out of 51 |
| Saudi Arabia | 2.6 | 2.0 | A- | 47 | | Middle East | 6 out of 13 |
| Senegal | 8.3 | 8.1 | B+ | 86 | | Africa | 8 out of 51 |
| Serbia | 6.4 | 5.9 | BB- | 75 | Frontier | Central and Eastern Europe | 16 out of 25 |
| Seychelles | 5.9 | 5.7 | | 73 | | Africa | 5 out of 51 |
| Sierra Leone | 11.8 | 11.6 | | 129 | | Africa | 30 out of 51 |
| Singapore | -4.2 | -4.5 | AAA | 1 | Developed | Asia | 1 out of 29 |
| Slovakia | -0.5 | -0.7 | A+ | 24 | | Central and Eastern Europe | 2 out of 25 |
| Slovenia | 0.9 | 0.7 | A | 34 | Frontier | Central and Eastern Europe | 5 out of 25 |
| Solomon Islands | 22.7 | 22.5 | | 168 | | Australasia | 6 out of 7 |
| Somalia | 21.0 | 20.8 | | 166 | | Africa | 46 out of 51 |
| South Africa | 3.5 | 3.5 | BBB- | 60 | Emerging | Africa | 2 out of 51 |
| Spain | 1.7 | 1.5 | BBB+ | 38 | Developed | Western Europe | 16 out of 19 |
| Sri Lanka | 5.8 | 5.3 | B+ | 72 | Frontier | Asia | 14 out of 29 |
| Sudan | 16.9 | 16.6 | | 154 | | Africa | 40 out of 51 |
| Suriname | 9.3 | 9.2 | B+ | 102 | | Latin America | 16 out of 20 |
| Swaziland | 15.2 | 16.0 | | 152 | | Africa | 38 out of 51 |
| Sweden | -3.3 | -3.6 | AAA | 7 | Developed | Western Europe | 6 out of 19 |

§ S&P Credit Rating based on long-term foreign currency issuer rating. See http://www.standardandpoors.com/.

∗ World rank based on 175 countries covered by Euromoney. Ranking based on ascending order in which '1' equals the smallest country risk premium (CRP) and '175' equals the largest country risk premium (CRP).

† MSCI Market Classification based on MSCI Market Classification Framework. See http://www.msci.com/products/indexes/market_classification.html

‡ Regional classification based on Euromoney. Regional rankings based on ascending order in which '1' equals the smallest country risk premium (CRP) for each region.

Note: A CRP of 0.0% is assumed in the following cases: (i) when the investor country and the investee country both have an S&P sovereign credit rating of AAA; or (ii) when the investor country has an S&P credit rating of AAA, and the investee country has a sovereign credit rating below AAA, but has a calculated CRP below 0.0% (which would imply lower risk than a country rated AAA); or (iii) when the investor country has an S&P credit rating below AAA, and the investee country has a sovereign credit rating of AAA, but has a calculated CRP above 0.0% (which would imply greater risk than a country rated below AAA). For purposes of this analysis, the U.S. is treated as having a sovereign credit rating equivalent to AAA.

The country risk premium (CRP) is not the cost of equity capital (COE).  The CRP is to be added to base COE. See Chapter 6 for proper application.

## Data Updated Through March 2017

| Investee Country | December 2016 Country Risk Premium (CRP) (%) | March 2017 Country Risk Premium (CRP) (%) | S&P Sovereign Credit Rating § | World Rank Out of 175∗ | MSCI Market Classification † | Euromoney Region ‡ | Regional Rank ‡ |
|---|---|---|---|---|---|---|---|
| Switzerland | -4.0 | -4.4 | AAA | 2 | Developed | Western Europe | 1 out of 19 |
| Syria | 21.7 | 21.8 | | 167 | | Middle East | 13 out of 13 |
| Taiwan | -1.3 | -1.5 | AA- | 18 | Emerging | Asia | 3 out of 29 |
| Tajikistan | 16.5 | 16.6 | | 155 | | Central and Eastern Europe | 25 out of 25 |
| Tanzania | 8.7 | 8.6 | | 95 | | Africa | 13 out of 51 |
| Thailand | 3.0 | 2.6 | BBB+ | 51 | Emerging | Asia | 8 out of 29 |
| Togo | 10.3 | 10.0 | | 113 | | Africa | 20 out of 51 |
| Tonga | 25.2 | 25.0 | | 170 | | Australasia | 7 out of 7 |
| Trinidad & Tobago | 3.3 | 3.1 | A- | 54 | | Caribbean | 2 out of 9 |
| Tunisia | 6.2 | 6.4 | | 79 | Frontier | Africa | 6 out of 51 |
| Turkey | 3.7 | 3.3 | BB | 58 | Emerging | Central and Eastern Europe | 11 out of 25 |
| Turkmenistan | 13.6 | 13.7 | | 140 | | Asia | 24 out of 29 |
| Uganda | 9.7 | 9.9 | B | 110 | | Africa | 18 out of 51 |
| Ukraine | 12.6 | 12.5 | B- | 135 | | Central and Eastern Europe | 20 out of 25 |
| United Arab Emirates | 0.5 | 0.3 | AA | 33 | Emerging | Middle East | 4 out of 13 |
| United Kingdom | -1.0 | -1.1 | AA | 20 | Developed | Western Europe | 11 out of 19 |
| United States | -2.1 | -2.3 | AA+ | 15 | Developed | North America | 2 out of 2 |
| Uruguay | 2.3 | 2.0 | BBB | 45 | | Latin America | 5 out of 20 |
| Uzbekistan | 12.8 | 12.0 | | 132 | | Asia | 21 out of 29 |
| Vanuatu | 14.5 | 14.3 | | 145 | | Australasia | 4 out of 7 |
| Venezuela | 18.3 | 18.6 | CCC | 162 | | Latin America | 20 out of 20 |
| Vietnam | 6.8 | 6.3 | BB- | 78 | Frontier | Asia | 16 out of 29 |
| Yemen | 18.6 | 18.5 | | 161 | | Middle East | 12 out of 13 |
| Zambia | 10.1 | 9.9 | B | 111 | | Africa | 19 out of 51 |
| Zimbabwe | 20.2 | 20.0 | | 164 | | Africa | 44 out of 51 |

## March 2017 Country Risk Premium (CRP) Summary Statistics:

| S&P Rating | Country Count | Average CRP (%) | Median CRP (%) | Min CRP (%) | Max CRP (%) |
|---|---|---|---|---|---|
| AAA ∗∗ | 12 | -3.6 | -3.6 | -4.5 | -2.3 |
| AA (AA+, AA, AA-) | 15 | -1.2 | -1.1 | -3.4 | 1.8 |
| A (A+, A, A-) | 14 | 0.8 | 0.9 | -0.7 | 3.1 |
| BBB (BBB+, BBB, BBB-) | 17 | 2.6 | 2.6 | -0.1 | 5.0 |
| BB (BB+, BB, BB-) | 22 | 5.5 | 5.5 | 1.6 | 11.1 |
| B+ − SD | 39 | 10.3 | 9.9 | 5.3 | 18.6 |
| Investment Grade ∗∗ | 58 | -0.1 | -0.1 | -4.5 | 5.0 |
| Non-Investment Grade ∗∗ | 61 | 8.6 | 8.8 | 1.6 | 18.6 |
| **MSCI Market Classification** | | | | | |
| Developed Markets | 23 | -2.1 | -3.0 | -4.5 | 2.4 |
| Emerging Markets | 23 | 2.3 | 1.8 | -1.9 | 10.3 |
| Frontier Markets | 22 | 5.4 | 5.2 | 0.0 | 11.1 |
| **Euromoney Region ‡** | | | | | |
| Africa | 51 | 12.9 | 10.8 | 2.0 | 33.6 |
| Asia | 29 | 7.5 | 6.1 | -4.5 | 31.0 |
| Australasia | 7 | 11.5 | 14.3 | -3.4 | 25.0 |
| Caribbean | 9 | 8.8 | 8.4 | 2.0 | 18.3 |
| Central and Eastern Europe | 25 | 5.9 | 3.8 | -0.9 | 16.6 |
| Latin America | 20 | 6.5 | 7.2 | -1.9 | 18.6 |
| Middle East | 13 | 6.7 | 4.2 | -1.1 | 21.8 |
| North America | 2 | -2.9 | -2.9 | -3.4 | -2.3 |
| Western Europe | 19 | -1.2 | -1.7 | -4.4 | 9.6 |

## CCR Base Cost of Equity Capital:

| Estonia | COE (%) |
|---|---|
| March 2017 | 10.8 |
| December 2016 | 10.5 |

CCR base country-level COE for an Estonia-based investor investing in Estonia.

§ S&P Credit Rating based on long-term foreign currency issuer rating. See http://www.standardandpoors.com/.

∗ World rank based on 175 countries covered by Euromoney. Ranking based on ascending order in which '1' equals the smallest country risk premium (CRP) and '175' equals the largest country risk premium (CRP).

† MSCI Market Classification based on MSCI Market Classification Framework.  See http://www.msci.com/products/indexes/market_classification.html.

‡ Regional classification based on Euromoney. Regional rankings based on ascending order in which '1' equals the smallest country risk premium (CRP) for each region.

∗∗ Investment grade based on S&P sovereign credit rating from AAA to BBB-. Non-Investment grade based on S&P sovereign credit rating from BB+ to SD. For purposes of this analysis, the U.S. is being treated as if it were rated AAA by S&P.

Note: A CRP of 0.0% is assumed in the following cases: (i) when the investor country and the investee country both have an S&P sovereign credit rating of AAA; or (ii) when the investor country has an S&P credit rating of AAA, and the investee country has a sovereign credit rating below AAA, but has a calculated CRP below 0.0% (which would imply lower risk than a country rated AAA); or (iii) when the investor country has an S&P sovereign credit rating below AAA, and the investee country has a sovereign credit rating of AAA, but has a calculated CRP above 0.0% (which would imply greater risk than a country rated below AAA). For purposes of this analysis, the U.S. is treated as having a sovereign credit rating equivalent to AAA.

The country risk premium (CRP) is not the cost of equity capital (COE). The CRP is to be added to base COE. See Chapter 6 for proper application.

## Data Updated Through March 2017

| Investee Country | December 2016 Country Risk Premium (CRP) (%) | March 2017 Country Risk Premium (CRP) (%) | S&P Sovereign Credit Rating § | World Rank Out of 175* | MSCI Market Classification † | Euromoney Region ‡ | Regional Rank ‡ |
|---|---|---|---|---|---|---|---|
| Afghanistan | 17.0 | 16.8 | | 139 | | Asia | 23 out of 29 |
| Albania | 11.5 | 11.7 | B+ | 93 | | Central and Eastern Europe | 18 out of 25 |
| Algeria | 11.6 | 11.7 | | 91 | | Africa | 10 out of 51 |
| Angola | 13.9 | 14.1 | B | 121 | | Africa | 26 out of 51 |
| Argentina | 12.1 | 11.9 | B- | 96 | Frontier | Latin America | 13 out of 20 |
| Armenia | 9.1 | 9.3 | | 77 | | Asia | 15 out of 29 |
| Australia | 0.0 | 0.0 | AAA | 12 | Developed | Australasia | 2 out of 7 |
| Austria | 0.3 | 0.3 | AA+ | 13 | Developed | Western Europe | 9 out of 19 |
| Azerbaijan | 10.3 | 10.7 | BB+ | 85 | | Asia | 17 out of 29 |
| Bahamas | 7.7 | 7.4 | BB+ | 65 | | Caribbean | 3 out of 9 |
| Bahrain | 7.6 | 7.4 | BB- | 64 | Frontier | Middle East | 7 out of 13 |
| Bangladesh | 14.4 | 14.3 | BB- | 126 | Frontier | Asia | 20 out of 29 |
| Barbados | 9.3 | 10.4 | CCC+ | 82 | | Caribbean | 4 out of 9 |
| Belarus | 16.7 | 17.2 | B- | 143 | | Central and Eastern Europe | 23 out of 25 |
| Belgium | 1.5 | 1.5 | AA | 17 | Developed | Western Europe | 10 out of 19 |
| Belize | 12.6 | 12.7 | B- | 106 | | Latin America | 17 out of 20 |
| Benin | 18.4 | 18.5 | | 150 | | Africa | 37 out of 51 |
| Bermuda | 5.2 | 5.2 | A+ | 44 | | Caribbean | 1 out of 9 |
| Bhutan | 18.1 | 18.0 | | 148 | | Asia | 25 out of 29 |
| Bolivia | 11.1 | 11.4 | BB | 88 | | Latin America | 12 out of 20 |
| Bosnia & Herzegovina | 17.2 | 17.3 | B | 144 | | Central and Eastern Europe | 24 out of 25 |
| Botswana | 5.2 | 5.3 | A- | 48 | | Africa | 1 out of 51 |
| Brazil | 6.8 | 6.7 | BB | 59 | Emerging | Latin America | 7 out of 20 |
| Bulgaria | 6.6 | 6.8 | BB+ | 61 | | Central and Eastern Europe | 12 out of 25 |
| Burkina Faso | 15.5 | 15.6 | B- | 133 | | Africa | 33 out of 51 |
| Burundi | 27.5 | 27.6 | | 169 | | Africa | 47 out of 51 |
| Cambodia | 19.0 | 18.7 | | 151 | | Asia | 27 out of 29 |
| Cameroon | 14.1 | 14.2 | B | 124 | | Africa | 28 out of 51 |
| Canada | -0.1 | -0.2 | AAA | 9 | Developed | North America | 1 out of 2 |
| Cape Verde | 11.7 | 11.8 | B | 94 | | Africa | 12 out of 51 |
| Central African Republic | 31.0 | 31.1 | | 172 | | Africa | 49 out of 51 |
| Chad | 29.7 | 29.8 | | 171 | | Africa | 48 out of 51 |
| Chile | 1.1 | 1.3 | AA- | 16 | Emerging | Latin America | 1 out of 20 |
| China | 5.0 | 5.1 | AA- | 42 | Emerging | Asia | 7 out of 29 |
| Colombia | 5.0 | 5.0 | BBB | 41 | Emerging | Latin America | 4 out of 20 |
| Congo Republic | 13.7 | 13.6 | B- | 117 | | Africa | 24 out of 51 |
| Congo, DR | 15.0 | 15.0 | B- | 131 | | Africa | 32 out of 51 |
| Costa Rica | 8.1 | 8.3 | BB- | 71 | | Latin America | 8 out of 20 |
| Côte d'Ivoire | 11.6 | 11.7 | | 92 | | Africa | 11 out of 51 |
| Croatia | 7.2 | 7.0 | BB | 63 | Frontier | Central and Eastern Europe | 13 out of 25 |
| Cuba | 21.3 | 21.5 | | 160 | | Caribbean | 9 out of 9 |
| Cyprus | 4.7 | 4.9 | BB+ | 40 | | Central and Eastern Europe | 7 out of 25 |
| Czech Republic | 2.3 | 2.3 | AA- | 23 | Emerging | Central and Eastern Europe | 1 out of 25 |
| Denmark | -0.8 | -0.8 | AAA | 4 | Developed | Western Europe | 3 out of 19 |
| Djibouti | 39.1 | 36.8 | | 175 | | Africa | 51 out of 51 |
| Dominican Republic | 11.4 | 11.6 | BB- | 90 | | Caribbean | 5 out of 9 |
| Ecuador | 13.0 | 12.9 | B | 109 | | Latin America | 18 out of 20 |
| Egypt | 13.5 | 13.5 | B- | 116 | Emerging | Africa | 23 out of 51 |
| El Salvador | 10.5 | 10.3 | B- | 81 | | Latin America | 10 out of 20 |
| Equatorial Guinea | 23.8 | 23.9 | | 165 | | Africa | 45 out of 51 |

§ S&P Credit Rating based on long-term foreign currency issuer rating. See http://www.standardandpoors.com/.

* World rank based on 175 countries covered by Euromoney. Ranking based on ascending order in which '1' equals the smallest country risk premium (CRP) and '175' equals the largest country risk premium (CRP).

† MSCI Market Classification based on MSCI Market Classification Framework. See http://www.msci.com/products/indexes/market_classification.html

‡ Regional classification based on Euromoney. Regional rankings based on ascending order in which '1' equals the smallest country risk premium (CRP) for each region.

Note: A CRP of 0.0% is assumed in the following cases: (i) when the investor country and the investee country both have an S&P sovereign credit rating of AAA; or (ii) when the investor country has an S&P credit rating of AAA, and the investee country has a sovereign credit rating below AAA, but has a calculated CRP below 0.0% (which would imply lower risk than a country rated AAA); or (iii) when the investor country has an S&P credit rating below AAA, and the investee country has a sovereign credit rating of AAA, but has a calculated CRP above 0.0% (which would imply greater risk than a country rated below AAA). For purposes of this analysis, the U.S. is treated as having a sovereign credit rating equivalent to AAA.

The country risk premium (CRP) is not the cost of equity capital (COE). The CRP is to be added to base COE. See Chapter 6 for proper application.

### Data Updated Through March 2017

| Investee Country | December 2016 Country Risk Premium (CRP) (%) | March 2017 Country Risk Premium (CRP) (%) | S&P Sovereign Credit Rating § | World Rank Out of 175∗ | MSCI Market Classification † | Euromoney Region ‡ | Regional Rank ‡ |
|---|---|---|---|---|---|---|---|
| Eritrea | 35.2 | 33.5 | | 173 | | Africa | 50 out of 51 |
| Estonia | 3.0 | 3.2 | AA- | 32 | Frontier | Central and Eastern Europe | 4 out of 25 |
| Ethiopia | 12.3 | 12.4 | B | 101 | | Africa | 16 out of 51 |
| Fiji | 17.7 | 17.7 | B+ | 147 | | Australasia | 5 out of 7 |
| Finland | 0.0 | 0.0 | AA+ | 11 | Developed | Western Europe | 8 out of 19 |
| France | 2.4 | 2.2 | AA | 22 | Developed | Western Europe | 12 out of 19 |
| Gabon | 10.1 | 10.5 | | 83 | | Africa | 7 out of 51 |
| Gambia | 16.2 | 16.2 | | 138 | | Africa | 34 out of 51 |
| Georgia | 8.8 | 9.1 | BB- | 74 | | Central and Eastern Europe | 15 out of 25 |
| Germany | 0.0 | 0.0 | AAA | 10 | Developed | Western Europe | 7 out of 19 |
| Ghana | 11.8 | 11.5 | B- | 89 | | Africa | 9 out of 51 |
| Greece | 13.0 | 12.8 | B- | 108 | Emerging | Western Europe | 19 out of 19 |
| Grenada | 12.6 | 12.7 | | 105 | | Caribbean | 7 out of 9 |
| Guatemala | 10.5 | 10.6 | BB | 84 | | Latin America | 11 out of 20 |
| Guinea | 19.9 | 20.0 | | 156 | | Africa | 41 out of 51 |
| Guinea-Bissau | 13.4 | 13.5 | | 115 | | Africa | 22 out of 51 |
| Guyana | 12.2 | 12.3 | | 100 | | Latin America | 15 out of 20 |
| Haiti | 22.8 | 20.8 | | 157 | | Caribbean | 8 out of 9 |
| Honduras | 11.9 | 12.0 | B+ | 98 | | Latin America | 14 out of 20 |
| Hong Kong | 0.0 | 0.0 | AAA | 14 | Developed | Asia | 2 out of 29 |
| Hungary | 6.4 | 6.6 | BBB- | 57 | Emerging | Central and Eastern Europe | 10 out of 25 |
| Iceland | 3.3 | 3.2 | A | 30 | | Western Europe | 15 out of 19 |
| India | 6.1 | 6.5 | BBB- | 55 | Emerging | Asia | 10 out of 29 |
| Indonesia | 6.9 | 7.0 | BB+ | 62 | Emerging | Asia | 11 out of 29 |
| Iran | 13.9 | 14.2 | | 125 | | Middle East | 10 out of 13 |
| Iraq | 15.8 | 15.9 | B- | 136 | | Middle East | 11 out of 13 |
| Ireland | 2.9 | 2.8 | A+ | 27 | Developed | Western Europe | 14 out of 19 |
| Israel | 2.8 | 2.8 | A+ | 28 | Developed | Middle East | 2 out of 13 |
| Italy | 5.8 | 5.6 | BBB- | 50 | Developed | Western Europe | 18 out of 19 |
| Jamaica | 12.0 | 12.6 | B | 104 | | Caribbean | 6 out of 9 |
| Japan | 2.7 | 2.7 | A+ | 25 | Developed | Asia | 5 out of 29 |
| Jordan | 9.1 | 9.3 | BB- | 76 | Frontier | Middle East | 8 out of 13 |
| Kazakhstan | 8.5 | 8.2 | BBB- | 70 | Frontier | Asia | 13 out of 29 |
| Kenya | 12.0 | 12.1 | B+ | 99 | Frontier | Africa | 15 out of 51 |
| Korea (North) | 34.6 | 34.2 | | 174 | | Asia | 29 out of 29 |
| Korea (South) | 1.9 | 2.0 | AA | 19 | Emerging | Asia | 4 out of 29 |
| Kuwait | 3.0 | 3.2 | AA | 31 | Frontier | Middle East | 3 out of 13 |
| Kyrgyz Republic | 17.2 | 17.1 | | 142 | | Central and Eastern Europe | 22 out of 25 |
| Laos | 21.5 | 21.0 | | 158 | | Asia | 28 out of 29 |
| Latvia | 5.0 | 5.2 | A- | 43 | | Central and Eastern Europe | 8 out of 25 |
| Lebanon | 13.8 | 13.2 | B- | 112 | Frontier | Middle East | 9 out of 13 |
| Lesotho | 17.4 | 17.5 | | 146 | | Africa | 36 out of 51 |
| Liberia | 12.7 | 12.7 | | 107 | | Africa | 17 out of 51 |
| Libya | 19.0 | 19.4 | | 153 | | Africa | 39 out of 51 |
| Lithuania | 4.2 | 4.4 | A- | 36 | Frontier | Central and Eastern Europe | 6 out of 25 |
| Luxembourg | -0.4 | -0.5 | AAA | 5 | | Western Europe | 4 out of 19 |
| Macedonia | 11.1 | 11.4 | BB- | 87 | | Central and Eastern Europe | 17 out of 25 |
| Madagascar | 13.5 | 14.1 | | 123 | | Africa | 27 out of 51 |
| Malawi | 13.3 | 13.3 | | 114 | | Africa | 21 out of 51 |
| Malaysia | 4.4 | 4.3 | A- | 35 | Emerging | Asia | 6 out of 29 |

§ S&P Credit Rating based on long-term foreign currency issuer rating. See http://www.standardandpoors.com/.

∗ World rank based on 175 countries covered by Euromoney. Ranking based on ascending order in which '1' equals the smallest country risk premium (CRP) and '175' equals the largest country risk premium (CRP).

† MSCI Market Classification based on MSCI Market Classification Framework. See http://www.msci.com/products/indexes/market_classification.html.

‡ Regional classification based on Euromoney. Regional rankings based on ascending order in which '1' equals the smallest country risk premium (CRP) for each region.

Note: A CRP of 0.0% is assumed in the following cases: (i) when the investor country and the investee country both have an S&P sovereign credit rating of AAA; or (ii) when the investor country has an S&P credit rating of AAA, and the investee country has a sovereign credit rating below AAA, but has a calculated CRP below 0.0% (which would imply lower risk than a country rated AAA); or (iii) when the investor country has an S&P credit rating below AAA, and the investee country has a sovereign credit rating of AAA, but has a calculated CRP above 0.0% (which would imply greater risk than a country rated below AAA). For purposes of this analysis, the U.S. is treated as having a sovereign credit rating equivalent to AAA.

The country risk premium (CRP) is not the cost of equity capital (COE).  The CRP is to be added to base COE. See Chapter 6 for proper application.

### Data Updated Through March 2017

| Investee Country | December 2016 Country Risk Premium (CRP) (%) | March 2017 Country Risk Premium (CRP) (%) | S&P Sovereign Credit Rating § | World Rank Out of 175* | MSCI Market Classification † | Euromoney Region ‡ | Regional Rank ‡ |
|---|---|---|---|---|---|---|---|
| Mali | 17.0 | 17.1 | | 141 | | Africa | 35 out of 51 |
| Malta | 2.7 | 2.8 | A- | 26 | | Western Europe | 13 out of 19 |
| Mauritania | 21.1 | 21.2 | | 159 | | Africa | 42 out of 51 |
| Mauritius | 7.8 | 7.9 | | 67 | Frontier | Asia | 12 out of 29 |
| Mexico | 4.3 | 4.4 | BBB+ | 37 | Emerging | Latin America | 2 out of 20 |
| Moldova | 15.4 | 15.9 | | 137 | | Central and Eastern Europe | 21 out of 25 |
| Mongolia | 13.6 | 14.0 | B- | 119 | | Asia | 18 out of 29 |
| Montenegro | 12.8 | 12.6 | B+ | 103 | | Central and Eastern Europe | 19 out of 25 |
| Morocco | 7.9 | 8.1 | BBB- | 69 | Frontier | Africa | 4 out of 51 |
| Mozambique | 14.7 | 14.6 | SD | 128 | | Africa | 29 out of 51 |
| Myanmar | 15.6 | 15.6 | | 134 | | Asia | 22 out of 29 |
| Namibia | 7.5 | 7.7 | | 66 | | Africa | 3 out of 51 |
| Nepal | 18.4 | 18.4 | | 149 | | Asia | 26 out of 29 |
| Netherlands | -0.4 | -0.4 | AAA | 6 | Developed | Western Europe | 5 out of 19 |
| New Zealand | -0.3 | -0.2 | AA | 8 | Developed | Australasia | 1 out of 7 |
| Nicaragua | 14.4 | 14.4 | B+ | 127 | | Latin America | 19 out of 20 |
| Niger | 14.0 | 14.0 | | 120 | | Africa | 25 out of 51 |
| Nigeria | 12.0 | 12.0 | B | 97 | Frontier | Africa | 14 out of 51 |
| Norway | -1.1 | -1.1 | AAA | 3 | Developed | Western Europe | 2 out of 19 |
| Oman | 5.2 | 5.3 | BBB- | 46 | Frontier | Middle East | 5 out of 13 |
| Pakistan | 14.1 | 14.1 | B | 122 | Frontier | Asia | 19 out of 29 |
| Panama | 5.9 | 6.0 | BBB | 52 | | Latin America | 6 out of 20 |
| Papua New Guinea | 13.6 | 13.7 | B+ | 118 | | Australasia | 3 out of 7 |
| Paraguay | 9.5 | 9.7 | BB | 80 | | Latin America | 9 out of 20 |
| Peru | 4.6 | 4.8 | BBB+ | 39 | Emerging | Latin America | 3 out of 20 |
| Philippines | 6.3 | 6.2 | BBB | 53 | Emerging | Asia | 9 out of 29 |
| Poland | 3.2 | 3.1 | BBB+ | 29 | Emerging | Central and Eastern Europe | 3 out of 25 |
| Portugal | 5.6 | 5.4 | BB+ | 49 | Developed | Western Europe | 17 out of 19 |
| Qatar | 2.0 | 2.1 | AA | 21 | Emerging | Middle East | 1 out of 13 |
| Romania | 6.4 | 6.5 | BBB- | 56 | Frontier | Central and Eastern Europe | 9 out of 25 |
| Russia | 8.7 | 8.1 | BB+ | 68 | Emerging | Central and Eastern Europe | 14 out of 25 |
| Rwanda | 14.8 | 14.8 | B | 130 | | Africa | 31 out of 51 |
| São Tomé & Príncipe | 21.2 | 21.8 | | 163 | | Africa | 43 out of 51 |
| Saudi Arabia | 5.5 | 5.3 | A- | 47 | | Middle East | 6 out of 13 |
| Senegal | 11.3 | 11.3 | B+ | 86 | | Africa | 8 out of 51 |
| Serbia | 9.4 | 9.1 | BB- | 75 | Frontier | Central and Eastern Europe | 16 out of 25 |
| Seychelles | 8.8 | 8.9 | | 73 | | Africa | 5 out of 51 |
| Sierra Leone | 14.8 | 14.8 | | 129 | | Africa | 30 out of 51 |
| Singapore | -1.3 | -1.3 | AAA | 1 | Developed | Asia | 1 out of 29 |
| Slovakia | 2.4 | 2.5 | A+ | 24 | | Central and Eastern Europe | 2 out of 25 |
| Slovenia | 3.9 | 3.9 | A | 34 | Frontier | Central and Eastern Europe | 5 out of 25 |
| Solomon Islands | 25.7 | 25.8 | | 168 | | Australasia | 6 out of 7 |
| Somalia | 23.9 | 24.0 | | 166 | | Africa | 46 out of 51 |
| South Africa | 6.5 | 6.7 | BBB- | 60 | Emerging | Africa | 2 out of 51 |
| Spain | 4.7 | 4.7 | BBB+ | 38 | Developed | Western Europe | 16 out of 19 |
| Sri Lanka | 8.8 | 8.5 | B+ | 72 | Frontier | Asia | 14 out of 29 |
| Sudan | 19.8 | 19.9 | | 154 | | Africa | 40 out of 51 |
| Suriname | 12.2 | 12.4 | B+ | 102 | | Latin America | 16 out of 20 |
| Swaziland | 18.1 | 19.2 | | 152 | | Africa | 38 out of 51 |
| Sweden | -0.3 | -0.4 | AAA | 7 | Developed | Western Europe | 6 out of 19 |

§ S&P Credit Rating based on long-term foreign currency issuer rating. See http://www.standardandpoors.com/.

* World rank based on 175 countries covered by Euromoney. Ranking based on ascending order in which '1' equals the smallest country risk premium (CRP) and '175' equals the largest country risk premium (CRP).

† MSCI Market Classification based on MSCI Market Classification Framework.  See http://www.msci.com/products/indexes/market_classification.html

‡ Regional classification based on Euromoney. Regional rankings based on ascending order in which '1' equals the smallest country risk premium (CRP) for each region.

Note: A CRP of 0.0% is assumed in the following cases: (i) when the investor country and the investee country both have an S&P sovereign credit rating of AAA; or (ii) when the investor country has an S&P credit rating of AAA, and the investee country has a sovereign credit rating below AAA, but has a calculated CRP below 0.0% (which would imply lower risk than a country rated AAA); or (iii) when the investor country has an S&P credit rating below AAA, and the investee country has a sovereign credit rating of AAA, but has a calculated CRP above 0.0% (which would imply greater risk than a country rated below AAA). For purposes of this analysis, the U.S. is treated as having a sovereign credit rating equivalent to AAA.

The country risk premium (CRP) is not the cost of equity capital (COE). The CRP is to be added to base COE. See Chapter 6 for proper application.

## Data Updated Through March 2017

| Investee Country | December 2016 Country Risk Premium (CRP) (%) | March 2017 Country Risk Premium (CRP) (%) | S&P Sovereign Credit Rating § | World Rank Out of 175∗ | MSCI Market Classification † | Euromoney Region ‡ | Regional Rank ‡ |
|---|---|---|---|---|---|---|---|
| Switzerland | -1.0 | -1.1 | AAA | 2 | Developed | Western Europe | 1 out of 19 |
| Syria | 24.7 | 25.0 | | 167 | | Middle East | 13 out of 13 |
| Taiwan | 1.7 | 1.7 | AA- | 18 | Emerging | Asia | 3 out of 29 |
| Tajikistan | 19.4 | 19.9 | | 155 | | Central and Eastern Europe | 25 out of 25 |
| Tanzania | 11.6 | 11.9 | | 95 | | Africa | 13 out of 51 |
| Thailand | 5.9 | 5.8 | BBB+ | 51 | Emerging | Asia | 8 out of 29 |
| Togo | 13.2 | 13.3 | | 113 | | Africa | 20 out of 51 |
| Tonga | 28.1 | 28.2 | | 170 | | Australasia | 7 out of 7 |
| Trinidad & Tobago | 6.3 | 6.3 | A- | 54 | | Caribbean | 2 out of 9 |
| Tunisia | 9.2 | 9.6 | | 79 | Frontier | Africa | 6 out of 51 |
| Turkey | 6.6 | 6.6 | BB | 58 | Emerging | Central and Eastern Europe | 11 out of 25 |
| Turkmenistan | 16.6 | 16.9 | | 140 | | Asia | 24 out of 29 |
| Uganda | 12.7 | 13.1 | B | 110 | | Africa | 18 out of 51 |
| Ukraine | 15.6 | 15.7 | B- | 135 | | Central and Eastern Europe | 20 out of 25 |
| United Arab Emirates | 3.4 | 3.6 | AA | 33 | Emerging | Middle East | 4 out of 13 |
| United Kingdom | 1.9 | 2.1 | AA | 20 | Developed | Western Europe | 11 out of 19 |
| United States | 0.0 | 0.0 | AA+ | 15 | Developed | North America | 2 out of 2 |
| Uruguay | 5.3 | 5.2 | BBB | 45 | | Latin America | 5 out of 20 |
| Uzbekistan | 15.7 | 15.3 | | 132 | | Asia | 21 out of 29 |
| Vanuatu | 17.4 | 17.5 | | 145 | | Australasia | 4 out of 7 |
| Venezuela | 21.2 | 21.8 | CCC | 162 | | Latin America | 20 out of 20 |
| Vietnam | 9.7 | 9.5 | BB- | 78 | Frontier | Asia | 16 out of 29 |
| Yemen | 21.5 | 21.7 | | 161 | | Middle East | 12 out of 13 |
| Zambia | 13.1 | 13.1 | B | 111 | | Africa | 19 out of 51 |
| Zimbabwe | 23.2 | 23.2 | | 164 | | Africa | 44 out of 51 |

## March 2017 Country Risk Premium (CRP) Summary Statistics:

| S&P Rating | Country Count | Average CRP (%) | Median CRP (%) | Min CRP (%) | Max CRP (%) |
|---|---|---|---|---|---|
| AAA ∗∗ | 12 | -0.5 | -0.4 | -1.3 | 0.0 |
| AA (AA+, AA, AA-) | 15 | 2.0 | 2.1 | -0.2 | 5.1 |
| A (A+, A, A-) | 14 | 4.0 | 4.1 | 2.5 | 6.3 |
| BBB (BBB+, BBB, BBB-) | 17 | 5.8 | 5.8 | 3.1 | 8.2 |
| BB (BB+, BB, BB-) | 22 | 8.7 | 8.7 | 4.9 | 14.3 |
| B+ − SD | 39 | 13.6 | 13.1 | 8.5 | 21.8 |
| Investment Grade ∗∗ | 58 | 3.1 | 3.1 | -1.3 | 8.2 |
| Non-Investment Grade ∗∗ | 61 | 11.8 | 12.0 | 4.9 | 21.8 |
| **MSCI Market Classification** | | | | | |
| Developed Markets | 23 | 1.1 | 0.0 | -1.3 | 5.6 |
| Emerging Markets | 23 | 5.5 | 5.1 | 1.3 | 13.5 |
| Frontier Markets | 22 | 8.6 | 8.4 | 3.2 | 14.3 |
| **Euromoney Region ‡** | | | | | |
| Africa | 51 | 16.1 | 14.1 | 5.3 | 36.8 |
| Asia | 29 | 10.7 | 9.3 | -1.3 | 34.2 |
| Australasia | 7 | 14.7 | 17.5 | -0.2 | 28.2 |
| Caribbean | 9 | 12.1 | 11.6 | 5.2 | 21.5 |
| Central and Eastern Europe | 25 | 9.1 | 7.0 | 2.3 | 19.9 |
| Latin America | 20 | 9.7 | 10.4 | 1.3 | 21.8 |
| Middle East | 13 | 9.9 | 7.4 | 2.1 | 25.0 |
| North America | 2 | -0.1 | -0.1 | -0.2 | 0.0 |
| Western Europe | 19 | 2.1 | 1.5 | -1.1 | 12.8 |

### CCR Base Cost of Equity Capital:

| Finland | COE (%) |
|---|---|
| March 2017 | 7.6 |
| December 2016 | 7.6 |

CCR base country-level COE for a Finland-based investor investing in Finland.

§ S&P Credit Rating based on long-term foreign currency issuer rating. See http://www.standardandpoors.com/.

∗ World rank based on 175 countries covered by Euromoney. Ranking based on ascending order in which '1' equals the smallest country risk premium (CRP) and '175' equals the largest country risk premium (CRP).

† MSCI Market Classification based on MSCI Market Classification Framework. See http://www.msci.com/products/indexes/market_classification.html

‡ Regional classification based on Euromoney. Regional rankings based on ascending order in which '1' equals the smallest country risk premium (CRP) for each region.

∗∗ Investment grade based on S&P sovereign credit rating from AAA to BBB-. Non-Investment grade based on S&P sovereign credit rating from BB+ to SD. For purposes of this analysis, the U.S. is being treated as if it were rated AAA by S&P.

Note: A CRP of 0.0% is assumed in the following cases: (i) when the investor country and the investee country both have an S&P sovereign credit rating of AAA; or (ii) when the investor country has an S&P credit rating of AAA, and the investee country has a sovereign credit rating below AAA (which would imply lower risk than a country rated AAA); or (iii) when the investor country has an S&P credit rating below AAA, and the investee country has a sovereign credit rating of AAA, but has a calculated CRP below 0.0% (which would imply greater risk than a country rated below AAA). For purposes of this analysis, the U.S. is treated as having a sovereign credit rating equivalent to AAA.

The country risk premium (CRP) is not the cost of equity capital (COE). The CRP is to be added to base COE. See Chapter 6 for proper application.

### Data Updated Through March 2017

| Investee Country | December 2016 Country Risk Premium (CRP) (%) | March 2017 Country Risk Premium (CRP) (%) | S&P Sovereign Credit Rating § | World Rank Out of 175* | MSCI Market Classification † | Euromoney Region ‡ | Regional Rank ‡ |
|---|---|---|---|---|---|---|---|
| Afghanistan | 14.6 | 14.6 | | 139 | | Asia | 23 out of 29 |
| Albania | 9.2 | 9.5 | B+ | 93 | | Central and Eastern Europe | 18 out of 25 |
| Algeria | 9.2 | 9.5 | | 91 | | Africa | 10 out of 51 |
| Angola | 11.6 | 11.8 | B | 121 | | Africa | 26 out of 51 |
| Argentina | 9.7 | 9.7 | B- | 96 | Frontier | Latin America | 13 out of 20 |
| Armenia | 6.7 | 7.1 | | 77 | | Asia | 15 out of 29 |
| Australia | -2.3 | -2.2 | AAA | 12 | Developed | Australasia | 2 out of 7 |
| Austria | -2.1 | -2.0 | AA+ | 13 | Developed | Western Europe | 9 out of 19 |
| Azerbaijan | 8.0 | 8.5 | BB+ | 85 | | Asia | 17 out of 29 |
| Bahamas | 5.3 | 5.2 | BB+ | 65 | | Caribbean | 3 out of 9 |
| Bahrain | 5.2 | 5.2 | BB- | 64 | Frontier | Middle East | 7 out of 13 |
| Bangladesh | 12.1 | 12.1 | BB- | 126 | Frontier | Asia | 20 out of 29 |
| Barbados | 6.9 | 8.2 | CCC+ | 82 | | Caribbean | 4 out of 9 |
| Belarus | 14.3 | 14.9 | B- | 143 | | Central and Eastern Europe | 23 out of 25 |
| Belgium | -0.8 | -0.7 | AA | 17 | Developed | Western Europe | 10 out of 19 |
| Belize | 10.2 | 10.5 | B- | 106 | | Latin America | 17 out of 20 |
| Benin | 16.0 | 16.3 | | 150 | | Africa | 37 out of 51 |
| Bermuda | 2.9 | 3.0 | A+ | 44 | | Caribbean | 1 out of 9 |
| Bhutan | 15.7 | 15.8 | | 148 | | Asia | 25 out of 29 |
| Bolivia | 8.7 | 9.2 | BB | 88 | | Latin America | 12 out of 20 |
| Bosnia & Herzegovina | 14.8 | 15.1 | B | 144 | | Central and Eastern Europe | 24 out of 25 |
| Botswana | 2.9 | 3.0 | A- | 48 | | Africa | 1 out of 51 |
| Brazil | 4.4 | 4.5 | BB | 59 | Emerging | Latin America | 7 out of 20 |
| Bulgaria | 4.3 | 4.6 | BB+ | 61 | | Central and Eastern Europe | 12 out of 25 |
| Burkina Faso | 13.1 | 13.4 | B- | 133 | | Africa | 33 out of 51 |
| Burundi | 25.1 | 25.3 | | 169 | | Africa | 47 out of 51 |
| Cambodia | 16.6 | 16.5 | | 151 | | Asia | 27 out of 29 |
| Cameroon | 11.8 | 12.0 | B | 124 | | Africa | 28 out of 51 |
| Canada | -2.5 | -2.4 | AAA | 9 | Developed | North America | 1 out of 2 |
| Cape Verde | 9.4 | 9.6 | B | 94 | | Africa | 12 out of 51 |
| Central African Republic | 28.7 | 28.9 | | 172 | | Africa | 49 out of 51 |
| Chad | 27.3 | 27.6 | | 171 | | Africa | 48 out of 51 |
| Chile | -1.3 | -0.9 | AA- | 16 | Emerging | Latin America | 1 out of 20 |
| China | 2.7 | 2.8 | AA- | 42 | Emerging | Asia | 7 out of 29 |
| Colombia | 2.6 | 2.8 | BBB | 41 | Emerging | Latin America | 4 out of 20 |
| Congo Republic | 11.4 | 11.4 | B- | 117 | | Africa | 24 out of 51 |
| Congo, DR | 12.6 | 12.8 | B- | 131 | | Africa | 32 out of 51 |
| Costa Rica | 5.7 | 6.1 | BB- | 71 | | Latin America | 8 out of 20 |
| Côte d'Ivoire | 9.2 | 9.5 | | 92 | | Africa | 11 out of 51 |
| Croatia | 4.8 | 4.8 | BB | 63 | Frontier | Central and Eastern Europe | 13 out of 25 |
| Cuba | 18.9 | 19.3 | | 160 | | Caribbean | 9 out of 9 |
| Cyprus | 2.4 | 2.6 | BB+ | 40 | | Central and Eastern Europe | 7 out of 25 |
| Czech Republic | 0.0 | 0.1 | AA- | 23 | Emerging | Central and Eastern Europe | 1 out of 25 |
| Denmark | -3.1 | -3.0 | AAA | 4 | Developed | Western Europe | 3 out of 19 |
| Djibouti | 36.7 | 34.6 | | 175 | | Africa | 51 out of 51 |
| Dominican Republic | 9.1 | 9.4 | BB- | 90 | | Caribbean | 5 out of 9 |
| Ecuador | 10.7 | 10.7 | B | 109 | | Latin America | 18 out of 20 |
| Egypt | 11.1 | 11.3 | B- | 116 | Emerging | Africa | 23 out of 51 |
| El Salvador | 8.1 | 8.1 | B- | 81 | | Latin America | 10 out of 20 |
| Equatorial Guinea | 21.5 | 21.7 | | 165 | | Africa | 45 out of 51 |

§ S&P Credit Rating based on long-term foreign currency issuer rating. See http://www.standardandpoors.com/.

* World rank based on 175 countries covered by Euromoney. Ranking based on ascending order in which '1' equals the smallest country risk premium (CRP) and '175' equals the largest country risk premium (CRP).

† MSCI Market Classification based on MSCI Market Classification Framework. See http://www.msci.com/products/indexes/market_classification.html

‡ Regional classification based on Euromoney. Regional rankings based on ascending order in which '1' equals the smallest country risk premium (CRP) for each region.

Note: A CRP of 0.0% is assumed in the following cases: (i) when the investor country and the investee country both have an S&P sovereign credit rating of AAA; or (ii) when the investor country has an S&P credit rating of AAA, and the investee country has a sovereign credit rating below AAA, but has a calculated CRP below 0.0% (which would imply lower risk than a country rated AAA); or (iii) when the investor country has an S&P credit rating below AAA, and the investee country has a sovereign credit rating of AAA, but has a calculated CRP above 0.0% (which would imply greater risk than a country rated below AAA). For purposes of this analysis, the U.S. is treated as having a sovereign credit rating equivalent to AAA.

The country risk premium (CRP) is not the cost of equity capital (COE). The CRP is to be added to base COE. See Chapter 6 for proper application.

## Data Updated Through March 2017

| Investee Country | December 2016 Country Risk Premium (CRP) (%) | March 2017 Country Risk Premium (CRP) (%) | S&P Sovereign Credit Rating § | World Rank Out of 175∗ | MSCI Market Classification † | Euromoney Region ‡ | Regional Rank ‡ |
|---|---|---|---|---|---|---|---|
| Eritrea | 32.9 | 31.3 | | 173 | | Africa | 50 out of 51 |
| Estonia | 0.6 | 1.0 | AA- | 32 | Frontier | Central and Eastern Europe | 4 out of 25 |
| Ethiopia | 9.9 | 10.2 | B | 101 | | Africa | 16 out of 51 |
| Fiji | 15.4 | 15.4 | B+ | 147 | | Australasia | 5 out of 7 |
| Finland | -2.4 | -2.2 | AA+ | 11 | Developed | Western Europe | 8 out of 19 |
| France | 0.0 | 0.0 | AA | 22 | Developed | Western Europe | 12 out of 19 |
| Gabon | 7.7 | 8.2 | | 83 | | Africa | 7 out of 51 |
| Gambia | 13.8 | 14.0 | | 138 | | Africa | 34 out of 51 |
| Georgia | 6.4 | 6.9 | BB- | 74 | | Central and Eastern Europe | 15 out of 25 |
| Germany | -2.4 | -2.3 | AAA | 10 | Developed | Western Europe | 7 out of 19 |
| Ghana | 9.5 | 9.3 | B- | 89 | | Africa | 9 out of 51 |
| Greece | 10.6 | 10.6 | B- | 108 | Emerging | Western Europe | 19 out of 19 |
| Grenada | 10.2 | 10.5 | | 105 | | Caribbean | 7 out of 9 |
| Guatemala | 8.1 | 8.4 | BB | 84 | | Latin America | 11 out of 20 |
| Guinea | 17.5 | 17.8 | | 156 | | Africa | 41 out of 51 |
| Guinea-Bissau | 11.0 | 11.3 | | 115 | | Africa | 22 out of 51 |
| Guyana | 9.9 | 10.1 | | 100 | | Latin America | 15 out of 20 |
| Haiti | 20.4 | 18.6 | | 157 | | Caribbean | 8 out of 9 |
| Honduras | 9.5 | 9.8 | B+ | 98 | | Latin America | 14 out of 20 |
| Hong Kong | -1.8 | -1.6 | AAA | 14 | Developed | Asia | 2 out of 29 |
| Hungary | 4.0 | 4.3 | BBB- | 57 | Emerging | Central and Eastern Europe | 10 out of 25 |
| Iceland | 1.0 | 0.9 | A | 30 | | Western Europe | 15 out of 19 |
| India | 3.8 | 4.3 | BBB- | 55 | Emerging | Asia | 10 out of 29 |
| Indonesia | 4.5 | 4.8 | BB+ | 62 | Emerging | Asia | 11 out of 29 |
| Iran | 11.6 | 12.0 | | 125 | | Middle East | 10 out of 13 |
| Iraq | 13.4 | 13.6 | B- | 136 | | Middle East | 11 out of 13 |
| Ireland | 0.5 | 0.6 | A+ | 27 | Developed | Western Europe | 14 out of 19 |
| Israel | 0.4 | 0.6 | A+ | 28 | Developed | Middle East | 2 out of 13 |
| Italy | 3.4 | 3.4 | BBB- | 50 | Developed | Western Europe | 18 out of 19 |
| Jamaica | 9.6 | 10.4 | B | 104 | | Caribbean | 6 out of 9 |
| Japan | 0.3 | 0.5 | A+ | 25 | Developed | Asia | 5 out of 29 |
| Jordan | 6.7 | 7.1 | BB- | 76 | Frontier | Middle East | 8 out of 13 |
| Kazakhstan | 6.2 | 6.0 | BBB- | 70 | Frontier | Asia | 13 out of 29 |
| Kenya | 9.7 | 9.9 | B+ | 99 | Frontier | Africa | 15 out of 51 |
| Korea (North) | 32.2 | 32.0 | | 174 | | Asia | 29 out of 29 |
| Korea (South) | -0.5 | -0.2 | AA | 19 | Emerging | Asia | 4 out of 29 |
| Kuwait | 0.6 | 1.0 | AA | 31 | Frontier | Middle East | 3 out of 13 |
| Kyrgyz Republic | 14.8 | 14.9 | | 142 | | Central and Eastern Europe | 22 out of 25 |
| Laos | 19.2 | 18.8 | | 158 | | Asia | 28 out of 29 |
| Latvia | 2.7 | 3.0 | A- | 43 | | Central and Eastern Europe | 8 out of 25 |
| Lebanon | 11.4 | 11.0 | B- | 112 | Frontier | Middle East | 9 out of 13 |
| Lesotho | 15.0 | 15.3 | | 146 | | Africa | 36 out of 51 |
| Liberia | 10.3 | 10.5 | | 107 | | Africa | 17 out of 51 |
| Libya | 16.6 | 17.2 | | 153 | | Africa | 39 out of 51 |
| Lithuania | 1.9 | 2.1 | A- | 36 | Frontier | Central and Eastern Europe | 6 out of 25 |
| Luxembourg | -2.8 | -2.7 | AAA | 5 | | Western Europe | 4 out of 19 |
| Macedonia | 8.7 | 9.1 | BB- | 87 | | Central and Eastern Europe | 17 out of 25 |
| Madagascar | 11.2 | 11.9 | | 123 | | Africa | 27 out of 51 |
| Malawi | 10.9 | 11.1 | | 114 | | Africa | 21 out of 51 |
| Malaysia | 2.1 | 2.1 | A- | 35 | Emerging | Asia | 6 out of 29 |

§ S&P Credit Rating based on long-term foreign currency issuer rating. See http://www.standardandpoors.com/.
∗ World rank based on 175 countries covered by Euromoney. Ranking based on ascending order in which '1' equals the smallest country risk premium (CRP) and '175' equals the largest country risk premium (CRP).
† MSCI Market Classification based on MSCI Market Classification Framework. See http://www.msci.com/products/indexes/market_classification.html.
‡ Regional classification based on Euromoney. Regional rankings based on ascending order in which '1' equals the smallest country risk premium (CRP) for each region.
Note: A CRP of 0.0% is assumed in the following cases: (i) when the investor country and the investee country both have an S&P sovereign credit rating of AAA; or (ii) when the investor country has an S&P credit rating of AAA, and the investee country has a sovereign credit rating below AAA, but has a calculated CRP below 0.0% (which would imply lower risk than a country rated AAA); or (iii) when the investor country has an S&P credit rating below AAA, and the investee country has a sovereign credit rating of AAA, but has a calculated CRP above 0.0% (which would imply greater risk than a country rated below AAA). For purposes of this analysis, the U.S. is treated as having a sovereign credit rating equivalent to AAA.

The country risk premium (CRP) is not the cost of equity capital (COE). The CRP is to be added to base COE. See Chapter 6 for proper application.

## Data Updated Through March 2017

| Investee Country | December 2016 Country Risk Premium (CRP) (%) | March 2017 Country Risk Premium (CRP) (%) | S&P Sovereign Credit Rating § | World Rank Out of 175* | MSCI Market Classification † | Euromoney Region ‡ | Regional Rank ‡ |
|---|---|---|---|---|---|---|---|
| Mali | 14.7 | 14.9 | | 141 | | Africa | 35 out of 51 |
| Malta | 0.3 | 0.6 | A- | 26 | | Western Europe | 13 out of 19 |
| Mauritania | 18.8 | 19.0 | | 159 | | Africa | 42 out of 51 |
| Mauritius | 5.5 | 5.7 | | 67 | Frontier | Asia | 12 out of 29 |
| Mexico | 1.9 | 2.2 | BBB+ | 37 | Emerging | Latin America | 2 out of 20 |
| Moldova | 13.1 | 13.7 | | 137 | | Central and Eastern Europe | 21 out of 25 |
| Mongolia | 11.2 | 11.8 | B- | 119 | | Asia | 18 out of 29 |
| Montenegro | 10.4 | 10.4 | B+ | 103 | | Central and Eastern Europe | 19 out of 25 |
| Morocco | 5.5 | 5.9 | BBB- | 69 | Frontier | Africa | 4 out of 51 |
| Mozambique | 12.3 | 12.4 | SD | 128 | | Africa | 29 out of 51 |
| Myanmar | 13.3 | 13.4 | | 134 | | Asia | 22 out of 29 |
| Namibia | 5.1 | 5.5 | | 66 | | Africa | 3 out of 51 |
| Nepal | 16.0 | 16.2 | | 149 | | Asia | 26 out of 29 |
| Netherlands | -2.8 | -2.6 | AAA | 6 | Developed | Western Europe | 5 out of 19 |
| New Zealand | -2.6 | -2.4 | AA | 8 | Developed | Australasia | 1 out of 7 |
| Nicaragua | 12.0 | 12.2 | B+ | 127 | | Latin America | 19 out of 20 |
| Niger | 11.6 | 11.8 | | 120 | | Africa | 25 out of 51 |
| Nigeria | 9.6 | 9.8 | B | 97 | Frontier | Africa | 14 out of 51 |
| Norway | -3.4 | -3.3 | AAA | 3 | Developed | Western Europe | 2 out of 19 |
| Oman | 2.8 | 3.0 | BBB- | 46 | Frontier | Middle East | 5 out of 13 |
| Pakistan | 11.7 | 11.8 | B | 122 | Frontier | Asia | 19 out of 29 |
| Panama | 3.5 | 3.8 | BBB | 52 | | Latin America | 6 out of 20 |
| Papua New Guinea | 11.2 | 11.5 | B+ | 118 | | Australasia | 3 out of 7 |
| Paraguay | 7.1 | 7.5 | BB | 80 | | Latin America | 9 out of 20 |
| Peru | 2.2 | 2.5 | BBB+ | 39 | Emerging | Latin America | 3 out of 20 |
| Philippines | 3.9 | 4.0 | BBB | 53 | Emerging | Asia | 9 out of 29 |
| Poland | 0.8 | 0.9 | BBB+ | 29 | Emerging | Central and Eastern Europe | 3 out of 25 |
| Portugal | 3.2 | 3.2 | BB+ | 49 | Developed | Western Europe | 17 out of 19 |
| Qatar | -0.3 | -0.1 | AA | 21 | Emerging | Middle East | 1 out of 13 |
| Romania | 4.0 | 4.3 | BBB- | 56 | Frontier | Central and Eastern Europe | 9 out of 25 |
| Russia | 6.3 | 5.9 | BB+ | 68 | Emerging | Central and Eastern Europe | 14 out of 25 |
| Rwanda | 12.4 | 12.6 | B | 130 | | Africa | 31 out of 51 |
| São Tomé & Príncipe | 18.9 | 19.6 | | 163 | | Africa | 43 out of 51 |
| Saudi Arabia | 3.2 | 3.0 | A- | 47 | | Middle East | 6 out of 13 |
| Senegal | 8.9 | 9.1 | B+ | 86 | | Africa | 8 out of 51 |
| Serbia | 7.0 | 6.9 | BB- | 75 | Frontier | Central and Eastern Europe | 16 out of 25 |
| Seychelles | 6.5 | 6.7 | | 73 | | Africa | 5 out of 51 |
| Sierra Leone | 12.4 | 12.6 | | 129 | | Africa | 30 out of 51 |
| Singapore | -3.6 | -3.5 | AAA | 1 | Developed | Asia | 1 out of 29 |
| Slovakia | 0.1 | 0.3 | A+ | 24 | | Central and Eastern Europe | 2 out of 25 |
| Slovenia | 1.5 | 1.7 | A | 34 | Frontier | Central and Eastern Europe | 5 out of 25 |
| Solomon Islands | 23.3 | 23.5 | | 168 | | Australasia | 6 out of 7 |
| Somalia | 21.5 | 21.8 | | 166 | | Africa | 46 out of 51 |
| South Africa | 4.1 | 4.5 | BBB- | 60 | Emerging | Africa | 2 out of 51 |
| Spain | 2.3 | 2.5 | BBB+ | 38 | Developed | Western Europe | 16 out of 19 |
| Sri Lanka | 6.4 | 6.3 | B+ | 72 | Frontier | Asia | 14 out of 29 |
| Sudan | 17.5 | 17.6 | | 154 | | Africa | 40 out of 51 |
| Suriname | 9.8 | 10.2 | B+ | 102 | | Latin America | 16 out of 20 |
| Swaziland | 15.8 | 17.0 | | 152 | | Africa | 38 out of 51 |
| Sweden | -2.7 | -2.6 | AAA | 7 | Developed | Western Europe | 6 out of 19 |

§ S&P Credit Rating based on long-term foreign currency issuer rating. See http://www.standardandpoors.com/.

* World rank based on 175 countries covered by Euromoney. Ranking based on ascending order in which '1' equals the smallest country risk premium (CRP) and '175' equals the largest country risk premium (CRP).

† MSCI Market Classification based on MSCI Market Classification Framework. See http://www.msci.com/products/indexes/market_classification.html.

‡ Regional classification based on Euromoney. Regional rankings based on ascending order in which '1' equals the smallest country risk premium (CRP) for each region.

Note: A CRP of 0.0% is assumed in the following cases: (i) when the investor country and the investee country both have an S&P sovereign credit rating of AAA; or (ii) when the investor country has an S&P credit rating of AAA, and the investee country has a sovereign credit rating below AAA, but has a calculated CRP below 0.0% (which would imply lower risk than a country rated AAA); or (iii) when the investor country has an S&P credit rating below AAA, and the investee country has a sovereign credit rating of AAA, but has a calculated CRP above 0.0% (which would imply greater risk than a country rated below AAA). For purposes of this analysis, the U.S. is treated as having a sovereign credit rating equivalent to AAA.

The country risk premium (CRP) is not the cost of equity capital (COE).  The CRP is to be added to base COE. See Chapter 6 for proper application.

## Data Updated Through March 2017

| Investee Country | December 2016 Country Risk Premium (CRP) (%) | March 2017 Country Risk Premium (CRP) (%) | S&P Sovereign Credit Rating § | World Rank Out of 175∗∗ | MSCI Market Classification † | Euromoney Region ‡ | Regional Rank ‡ |
|---|---|---|---|---|---|---|---|
| Switzerland | -3.4 | -3.4 | AAA | 2 | Developed | Western Europe | 1 out of 19 |
| Syria | 22.3 | 22.8 | | 167 | | Middle East | 13 out of 13 |
| Taiwan | -0.7 | -0.5 | AA- | 18 | Emerging | Asia | 3 out of 29 |
| Tajikistan | 17.1 | 17.6 | | 155 | | Central and Eastern Europe | 25 out of 25 |
| Tanzania | 9.2 | 9.6 | | 95 | | Africa | 13 out of 51 |
| Thailand | 3.5 | 3.6 | BBB+ | 51 | Emerging | Asia | 8 out of 29 |
| Togo | 10.8 | 11.0 | | 113 | | Africa | 20 out of 51 |
| Tonga | 25.8 | 26.0 | | 170 | | Australasia | 7 out of 7 |
| Trinidad & Tobago | 3.9 | 4.1 | A- | 54 | | Caribbean | 2 out of 9 |
| Tunisia | 6.8 | 7.3 | | 79 | Frontier | Africa | 6 out of 51 |
| Turkey | 4.3 | 4.3 | BB | 58 | Emerging | Central and Eastern Europe | 11 out of 25 |
| Turkmenistan | 14.2 | 14.7 | | 140 | | Asia | 24 out of 29 |
| Uganda | 10.3 | 10.9 | B | 110 | | Africa | 18 out of 51 |
| Ukraine | 13.2 | 13.5 | B- | 135 | | Central and Eastern Europe | 20 out of 25 |
| United Arab Emirates | 1.1 | 1.3 | AA | 33 | Emerging | Middle East | 4 out of 13 |
| United Kingdom | -0.4 | -0.1 | AA | 20 | Developed | Western Europe | 11 out of 19 |
| United States | -1.5 | -1.3 | AA+ | 15 | Developed | North America | 2 out of 2 |
| Uruguay | 2.9 | 3.0 | BBB | 45 | | Latin America | 5 out of 20 |
| Uzbekistan | 13.4 | 13.0 | | 132 | | Asia | 21 out of 29 |
| Vanuatu | 15.0 | 15.3 | | 145 | | Australasia | 4 out of 7 |
| Venezuela | 18.9 | 19.6 | CCC | 162 | | Latin America | 20 out of 20 |
| Vietnam | 7.4 | 7.3 | BB- | 78 | Frontier | Asia | 16 out of 29 |
| Yemen | 19.2 | 19.5 | | 161 | | Middle East | 12 out of 13 |
| Zambia | 10.7 | 10.9 | B | 111 | | Africa | 19 out of 51 |
| Zimbabwe | 20.8 | 21.0 | | 164 | | Africa | 44 out of 51 |

## March 2017 Country Risk Premium (CRP) Summary Statistics:

| S&P Rating | Country Count | Average CRP (%) | Median CRP (%) | Min CRP (%) | Max CRP (%) |
|---|---|---|---|---|---|
| AAA ∗∗ | 12 | -2.6 | -2.6 | -3.5 | -1.3 |
| AA (AA+, AA, AA-) | 15 | -0.2 | -0.1 | -2.4 | 2.8 |
| A (A+, A, A-) | 14 | 1.8 | 1.9 | 0.3 | 4.1 |
| BBB (BBB+, BBB, BBB-) | 17 | 3.6 | 3.6 | 0.9 | 6.0 |
| BB (BB+, BB, BB-) | 22 | 6.5 | 6.5 | 2.6 | 12.1 |
| B+ − SD | 39 | 11.3 | 10.9 | 6.3 | 19.6 |
| Investment Grade ∗∗ | 58 | 0.9 | 0.9 | -3.5 | 6.0 |
| Non-Investment Grade ∗∗ | 61 | 9.6 | 9.8 | 2.6 | 19.6 |
| **MSCI Market Classification** | | | | | |
| Developed Markets | 23 | -1.1 | -2.0 | -3.5 | 3.4 |
| Emerging Markets | 23 | 3.3 | 2.8 | -0.9 | 11.3 |
| Frontier Markets | 22 | 6.4 | 6.2 | 1.0 | 12.1 |
| **Euromoney Region ‡** | | | | | |
| Africa | 51 | 13.9 | 11.8 | 3.0 | 34.6 |
| Asia | 29 | 8.5 | 7.1 | -3.5 | 32.0 |
| Australasia | 7 | 12.5 | 15.3 | -2.4 | 26.0 |
| Caribbean | 9 | 9.8 | 9.4 | 3.0 | 19.3 |
| Central and Eastern Europe | 25 | 6.9 | 4.8 | 0.1 | 17.6 |
| Latin America | 20 | 7.5 | 8.2 | -0.9 | 19.6 |
| Middle East | 13 | 7.7 | 5.2 | -0.1 | 22.8 |
| North America | 2 | -1.9 | -1.9 | -2.4 | -1.3 |
| Western Europe | 19 | -0.2 | -0.7 | -3.4 | 10.6 |

## CCR Base Cost of Equity Capital:

| France | COE (%) |
|---|---|
| March 2017 | 9.8 |
| December 2016 | 10.0 |

CCR base country-level COE for a France-based investor investing in France.

§ S&P Credit Rating based on long-term foreign currency issuer rating. See http://www.standardandpoors.com/.
∗ World rank based on 175 countries covered by Euromoney. Ranking based on ascending order in which '1' equals the smallest country risk premium (CRP) and '175' equals the largest country risk premium (CRP).
† MSCI Market Classification based on MSCI Market Classification Framework.  See http://www.msci.com/products/indexes/market_classification.html
‡ Regional classification based on Euromoney. Regional rankings based on ascending order in which '1' equals the smallest country risk premium (CRP) for each region.
∗∗ Investment grade based on S&P sovereign credit rating from AAA to BBB-. Non-Investment grade based on S&P sovereign credit rating from BB+ to SD. For purposes of this analysis, the U.S. is being treated as if it were rated AAA by S&P.
Note: A CRP of 0.0% is assumed in the following cases: (i) when the investor country and the investee country both have an S&P sovereign credit rating of AAA; or (ii) when the investor country has an S&P credit rating of AAA, and the investee country has a sovereign credit rating below AAA, but has a calculated CRP below 0.0% (which would imply lower risk than a country rated AAA); or (iii) when the investor country has an S&P credit rating below AAA, and the investee country has a sovereign credit rating of AAA, but has a calculated CRP above 0.0% (which would imply greater risk than a country rated below AAA). For purposes of this analysis, the U.S. is treated as having a sovereign credit rating equivalent to AAA.

The country risk premium (CRP) is not the cost of equity capital (COE). The CRP is to be added to base COE. See Chapter 6 for proper application.

### Data Updated Through March 2017

| Investee Country | December 2016 Country Risk Premium (CRP) (%) | March 2017 Country Risk Premium (CRP) (%) | S&P Sovereign Credit Rating § | World Rank Out of 175* | MSCI Market Classification † | Euromoney Region ‡ | Regional Rank ‡ |
|---|---|---|---|---|---|---|---|
| Afghanistan | 17.0 | 16.8 | | 139 | | Asia | 23 out of 29 |
| Albania | 11.5 | 11.8 | B+ | 93 | | Central and Eastern Europe | 18 out of 25 |
| Algeria | 11.6 | 11.7 | | 91 | | Africa | 10 out of 51 |
| Angola | 13.9 | 14.1 | B | 121 | | Africa | 26 out of 51 |
| Argentina | 12.1 | 12.0 | B- | 96 | Frontier | Latin America | 13 out of 20 |
| Armenia | 9.1 | 9.4 | | 77 | | Asia | 15 out of 29 |
| Australia | 0.0 | 0.0 | AAA | 12 | Developed | Australasia | 2 out of 7 |
| Austria | 0.3 | 0.3 | AA+ | 13 | Developed | Western Europe | 9 out of 19 |
| Azerbaijan | 10.3 | 10.7 | BB+ | 85 | | Asia | 17 out of 29 |
| Bahamas | 7.7 | 7.4 | BB+ | 65 | | Caribbean | 3 out of 9 |
| Bahrain | 7.6 | 7.4 | BB- | 64 | Frontier | Middle East | 7 out of 13 |
| Bangladesh | 14.4 | 14.3 | BB- | 126 | Frontier | Asia | 20 out of 29 |
| Barbados | 9.3 | 10.5 | CCC+ | 82 | | Caribbean | 4 out of 9 |
| Belarus | 16.7 | 17.2 | B- | 143 | | Central and Eastern Europe | 23 out of 25 |
| Belgium | 1.5 | 1.5 | AA | 17 | Developed | Western Europe | 10 out of 19 |
| Belize | 12.6 | 12.8 | B- | 106 | | Latin America | 17 out of 20 |
| Benin | 18.4 | 18.5 | | 150 | | Africa | 37 out of 51 |
| Bermuda | 5.2 | 5.2 | A+ | 44 | | Caribbean | 1 out of 9 |
| Bhutan | 18.1 | 18.0 | | 148 | | Asia | 25 out of 29 |
| Bolivia | 11.1 | 11.4 | BB | 88 | | Latin America | 12 out of 20 |
| Bosnia & Herzegovina | 17.2 | 17.4 | B | 144 | | Central and Eastern Europe | 24 out of 25 |
| Botswana | 5.2 | 5.3 | A- | 48 | | Africa | 1 out of 51 |
| Brazil | 6.8 | 6.7 | BB | 59 | Emerging | Latin America | 7 out of 20 |
| Bulgaria | 6.6 | 6.9 | BB+ | 61 | | Central and Eastern Europe | 12 out of 25 |
| Burkina Faso | 15.5 | 15.6 | B- | 133 | | Africa | 33 out of 51 |
| Burundi | 27.5 | 27.6 | | 169 | | Africa | 47 out of 51 |
| Cambodia | 19.0 | 18.7 | | 151 | | Asia | 27 out of 29 |
| Cameroon | 14.1 | 14.2 | B | 124 | | Africa | 28 out of 51 |
| Canada | 0.0 | 0.0 | AAA | 9 | Developed | North America | 1 out of 2 |
| Cape Verde | 11.7 | 11.8 | B | 94 | | Africa | 12 out of 51 |
| Central African Republic | 31.0 | 31.2 | | 172 | | Africa | 49 out of 51 |
| Chad | 29.7 | 29.8 | | 171 | | Africa | 48 out of 51 |
| Chile | 1.1 | 1.3 | AA- | 16 | Emerging | Latin America | 1 out of 20 |
| China | 5.0 | 5.1 | AA- | 42 | Emerging | Asia | 7 out of 29 |
| Colombia | 5.0 | 5.1 | BBB | 41 | Emerging | Latin America | 4 out of 20 |
| Congo Republic | 13.7 | 13.7 | B- | 117 | | Africa | 24 out of 51 |
| Congo, DR | 15.0 | 15.0 | B- | 131 | | Africa | 32 out of 51 |
| Costa Rica | 8.1 | 8.4 | BB- | 71 | | Latin America | 8 out of 20 |
| Côte d'Ivoire | 11.6 | 11.7 | | 92 | | Africa | 11 out of 51 |
| Croatia | 7.2 | 7.1 | BB | 63 | Frontier | Central and Eastern Europe | 13 out of 25 |
| Cuba | 21.3 | 21.5 | | 160 | | Caribbean | 9 out of 9 |
| Cyprus | 4.7 | 4.9 | BB+ | 40 | | Central and Eastern Europe | 7 out of 25 |
| Czech Republic | 2.3 | 2.4 | AA- | 23 | Emerging | Central and Eastern Europe | 1 out of 25 |
| Denmark | 0.0 | 0.0 | AAA | 4 | Developed | Western Europe | 3 out of 19 |
| Djibouti | 39.1 | 36.9 | | 175 | | Africa | 51 out of 51 |
| Dominican Republic | 11.4 | 11.6 | BB- | 90 | | Caribbean | 5 out of 9 |
| Ecuador | 13.0 | 13.0 | B | 109 | | Latin America | 18 out of 20 |
| Egypt | 13.5 | 13.5 | B- | 116 | Emerging | Africa | 23 out of 51 |
| El Salvador | 10.5 | 10.4 | B- | 81 | | Latin America | 10 out of 20 |
| Equatorial Guinea | 23.9 | 24.0 | | 165 | | Africa | 45 out of 51 |

§ S&P Credit Rating based on long-term foreign currency issuer rating. See http://www.standardandpoors.com/.

* World rank based on 175 countries covered by Euromoney. Ranking based on ascending order in which '1' equals the smallest country risk premium (CRP) and '175' equals the largest country risk premium (CRP).

† MSCI Market Classification based on MSCI Market Classification Framework. See http://www.msci.com/products/indexes/market_classification.html

‡ Regional classification based on Euromoney. Regional rankings based on ascending order in which '1' equals the smallest country risk premium (CRP) for each region.

Note: A CRP of 0.0% is assumed in the following cases: (i) when the investor country and the investee country both have an S&P sovereign credit rating of AAA; or (ii) when the investor country has an S&P credit rating of AAA, and the investee country has a sovereign credit rating below AAA, but has a calculated CRP below 0.0% (which would imply lower risk than a country rated AAA); or (iii) when the investor country has an S&P credit rating below AAA, and the investee country has a sovereign credit rating of AAA, but has a calculated CRP above 0.0% (which would imply greater risk than a country rated below AAA). For purposes of this analysis, the U.S. is treated as having a sovereign credit rating equivalent to AAA.

The country risk premium (CRP) is not the cost of equity capital (COE). The CRP is to be added to base COE. See Chapter 6 for proper application.

### Data Updated Through March 2017

| Investee Country | December 2016 Country Risk Premium (CRP) (%) | March 2017 Country Risk Premium (CRP) (%) | S&P Sovereign Credit Rating § | World Rank Out of 175∗ | MSCI Market Classification † | Euromoney Region ‡ | Regional Rank ‡ |
|---|---|---|---|---|---|---|---|
| Eritrea | 35.2 | 33.5 | | 173 | | Africa | 50 out of 51 |
| Estonia | 3.0 | 3.3 | AA- | 32 | Frontier | Central and Eastern Europe | 4 out of 25 |
| Ethiopia | 12.3 | 12.4 | B | 101 | | Africa | 16 out of 51 |
| Fiji | 17.7 | 17.7 | B+ | 147 | | Australasia | 5 out of 7 |
| Finland | 0.0 | 0.0 | AA+ | 11 | Developed | Western Europe | 8 out of 19 |
| France | 2.4 | 2.3 | AA | 22 | Developed | Western Europe | 12 out of 19 |
| Gabon | 10.1 | 10.5 | | 83 | | Africa | 7 out of 51 |
| Gambia | 16.2 | 16.3 | | 138 | | Africa | 34 out of 51 |
| Georgia | 8.8 | 9.1 | BB- | 74 | | Central and Eastern Europe | 15 out of 25 |
| Germany | 0.0 | 0.0 | AAA | 10 | Developed | Western Europe | 7 out of 19 |
| Ghana | 11.8 | 11.5 | B- | 89 | | Africa | 9 out of 51 |
| Greece | 13.0 | 12.8 | B- | 108 | Emerging | Western Europe | 19 out of 19 |
| Grenada | 12.6 | 12.7 | | 105 | | Caribbean | 7 out of 9 |
| Guatemala | 10.5 | 10.6 | BB | 84 | | Latin America | 11 out of 20 |
| Guinea | 19.9 | 20.0 | | 156 | | Africa | 41 out of 51 |
| Guinea-Bissau | 13.4 | 13.5 | | 115 | | Africa | 22 out of 51 |
| Guyana | 12.2 | 12.3 | | 100 | | Latin America | 15 out of 20 |
| Haiti | 22.8 | 20.9 | | 157 | | Caribbean | 8 out of 9 |
| Honduras | 11.9 | 12.1 | B+ | 98 | | Latin America | 14 out of 20 |
| Hong Kong | 0.0 | 0.0 | AAA | 14 | Developed | Asia | 2 out of 29 |
| Hungary | 6.4 | 6.6 | BBB- | 57 | Emerging | Central and Eastern Europe | 10 out of 25 |
| Iceland | 3.3 | 3.2 | A | 30 | | Western Europe | 15 out of 19 |
| India | 6.1 | 6.5 | BBB- | 55 | Emerging | Asia | 10 out of 29 |
| Indonesia | 6.9 | 7.0 | BB+ | 62 | Emerging | Asia | 11 out of 29 |
| Iran | 13.9 | 14.3 | | 125 | | Middle East | 10 out of 13 |
| Iraq | 15.8 | 15.9 | B- | 136 | | Middle East | 11 out of 13 |
| Ireland | 2.9 | 2.9 | A+ | 27 | Developed | Western Europe | 14 out of 19 |
| Israel | 2.8 | 2.9 | A+ | 28 | Developed | Middle East | 2 out of 13 |
| Italy | 5.8 | 5.7 | BBB- | 50 | Developed | Western Europe | 18 out of 19 |
| Jamaica | 12.0 | 12.7 | B | 104 | | Caribbean | 6 out of 9 |
| Japan | 2.7 | 2.8 | A+ | 25 | Developed | Asia | 5 out of 29 |
| Jordan | 9.1 | 9.3 | BB- | 76 | Frontier | Middle East | 8 out of 13 |
| Kazakhstan | 8.5 | 8.3 | BBB- | 70 | Frontier | Asia | 13 out of 29 |
| Kenya | 12.0 | 12.2 | B+ | 99 | Frontier | Africa | 15 out of 51 |
| Korea (North) | 34.6 | 34.2 | | 174 | | Asia | 29 out of 29 |
| Korea (South) | 1.9 | 2.0 | AA | 19 | Emerging | Asia | 4 out of 29 |
| Kuwait | 3.0 | 3.2 | AA | 31 | Frontier | Middle East | 3 out of 13 |
| Kyrgyz Republic | 17.2 | 17.2 | | 142 | | Central and Eastern Europe | 22 out of 25 |
| Laos | 21.5 | 21.1 | | 158 | | Asia | 28 out of 29 |
| Latvia | 5.0 | 5.2 | A- | 43 | | Central and Eastern Europe | 8 out of 25 |
| Lebanon | 13.8 | 13.3 | B- | 112 | Frontier | Middle East | 9 out of 13 |
| Lesotho | 17.4 | 17.6 | | 146 | | Africa | 36 out of 51 |
| Liberia | 12.7 | 12.8 | | 107 | | Africa | 17 out of 51 |
| Libya | 19.0 | 19.4 | | 153 | | Africa | 39 out of 51 |
| Lithuania | 4.2 | 4.4 | A- | 36 | Frontier | Central and Eastern Europe | 6 out of 25 |
| Luxembourg | 0.0 | 0.0 | AAA | 5 | | Western Europe | 4 out of 19 |
| Macedonia | 11.1 | 11.4 | BB- | 87 | | Central and Eastern Europe | 17 out of 25 |
| Madagascar | 13.5 | 14.2 | | 123 | | Africa | 27 out of 51 |
| Malawi | 13.3 | 13.4 | | 114 | | Africa | 21 out of 51 |
| Malaysia | 4.4 | 4.3 | A- | 35 | Emerging | Asia | 6 out of 29 |

§ S&P Credit Rating based on long-term foreign currency issuer rating. See http://www.standardandpoors.com/.
∗ World rank based on 175 countries covered by Euromoney. Ranking based on ascending order in which '1' equals the smallest country risk premium (CRP) and '175' equals the largest country risk premium (CRP).
† MSCI Market Classification based on MSCI Market Classification Framework. See http://www.msci.com/products/indexes/market_classification.html
‡ Regional classification based on Euromoney. Regional rankings based on ascending order in which '1' equals the smallest country risk premium (CRP) for each region.
Note: A CRP of 0.0% is assumed in the following cases: (i) when the investor country and the investee country both have an S&P sovereign credit rating of AAA; or (ii) when the investor country has an S&P credit rating of AAA, and the investee country has a sovereign credit rating below AAA, but has a calculated CRP below 0.0% (which would imply lower risk than a country rated AAA); or (iii) when the investor country has an S&P credit rating below AAA, and the investee country has a sovereign credit rating of AAA, but has a calculated CRP above 0.0% (which would imply greater risk than a country rated below AAA). For purposes of this analysis, the U.S. is treated as having a sovereign credit rating equivalent to AAA.

The country risk premium (CRP) is not the cost of equity capital (COE). The CRP is to be added to base COE. See Chapter 6 for proper application.

## Data Updated Through March 2017

| Investee Country | December 2016 Country Risk Premium (CRP) (%) | March 2017 Country Risk Premium (CRP) (%) | S&P Sovereign Credit Rating § | World Rank Out of 175* | MSCI Market Classification † | Euromoney Region ‡ | Regional Rank ‡ |
|---|---|---|---|---|---|---|---|
| Mali | 17.0 | 17.2 | | 141 | | Africa | 35 out of 51 |
| Malta | 2.7 | 2.8 | A- | 26 | | Western Europe | 13 out of 19 |
| Mauritania | 21.1 | 21.3 | | 159 | | Africa | 42 out of 51 |
| Mauritius | 7.8 | 7.9 | | 67 | Frontier | Asia | 12 out of 29 |
| Mexico | 4.3 | 4.5 | BBB+ | 37 | Emerging | Latin America | 2 out of 20 |
| Moldova | 15.4 | 16.0 | | 137 | | Central and Eastern Europe | 21 out of 25 |
| Mongolia | 13.6 | 14.0 | B- | 119 | | Asia | 18 out of 29 |
| Montenegro | 12.8 | 12.7 | B+ | 103 | | Central and Eastern Europe | 19 out of 25 |
| Morocco | 7.9 | 8.2 | BBB- | 69 | Frontier | Africa | 4 out of 51 |
| Mozambique | 14.7 | 14.6 | SD | 128 | | Africa | 29 out of 51 |
| Myanmar | 15.6 | 15.6 | | 134 | | Asia | 22 out of 29 |
| Namibia | 7.5 | 7.8 | | 66 | | Africa | 3 out of 51 |
| Nepal | 18.4 | 18.5 | | 149 | | Asia | 26 out of 29 |
| Netherlands | 0.0 | 0.0 | AAA | 6 | Developed | Western Europe | 5 out of 19 |
| New Zealand | 0.0 | 0.0 | AA | 8 | Developed | Australasia | 1 out of 7 |
| Nicaragua | 14.4 | 14.5 | B+ | 127 | | Latin America | 19 out of 20 |
| Niger | 14.0 | 14.1 | | 120 | | Africa | 25 out of 51 |
| Nigeria | 12.0 | 12.0 | B | 97 | Frontier | Africa | 14 out of 51 |
| Norway | 0.0 | 0.0 | AAA | 3 | Developed | Western Europe | 2 out of 19 |
| Oman | 5.2 | 5.3 | BBB- | 46 | Frontier | Middle East | 5 out of 13 |
| Pakistan | 14.1 | 14.1 | B | 122 | Frontier | Asia | 19 out of 29 |
| Panama | 5.9 | 6.0 | BBB | 52 | | Latin America | 6 out of 20 |
| Papua New Guinea | 13.6 | 13.8 | B+ | 118 | | Australasia | 3 out of 7 |
| Paraguay | 9.5 | 9.7 | BB | 80 | | Latin America | 9 out of 20 |
| Peru | 4.6 | 4.8 | BBB+ | 39 | Emerging | Latin America | 3 out of 20 |
| Philippines | 6.3 | 6.3 | BBB | 53 | Emerging | Asia | 9 out of 29 |
| Poland | 3.2 | 3.1 | BBB+ | 29 | Emerging | Central and Eastern Europe | 3 out of 25 |
| Portugal | 5.6 | 5.5 | BB+ | 49 | Developed | Western Europe | 17 out of 19 |
| Qatar | 2.0 | 2.2 | AA | 21 | Emerging | Middle East | 1 out of 13 |
| Romania | 6.4 | 6.5 | BBB- | 56 | Frontier | Central and Eastern Europe | 9 out of 25 |
| Russia | 8.7 | 8.1 | BB+ | 68 | Emerging | Central and Eastern Europe | 14 out of 25 |
| Rwanda | 14.8 | 14.9 | B | 130 | | Africa | 31 out of 51 |
| São Tomé & Príncipe | 21.2 | 21.8 | | 163 | | Africa | 43 out of 51 |
| Saudi Arabia | 5.5 | 5.3 | A- | 47 | | Middle East | 6 out of 13 |
| Senegal | 11.3 | 11.4 | B+ | 86 | | Africa | 8 out of 51 |
| Serbia | 9.4 | 9.2 | BB- | 75 | Frontier | Central and Eastern Europe | 16 out of 25 |
| Seychelles | 8.8 | 8.9 | | 73 | | Africa | 5 out of 51 |
| Sierra Leone | 14.8 | 14.9 | | 129 | | Africa | 30 out of 51 |
| Singapore | 0.0 | 0.0 | AAA | 1 | Developed | Asia | 1 out of 29 |
| Slovakia | 2.4 | 2.6 | A+ | 24 | | Central and Eastern Europe | 2 out of 25 |
| Slovenia | 3.9 | 4.0 | A | 34 | Frontier | Central and Eastern Europe | 5 out of 25 |
| Solomon Islands | 25.7 | 25.8 | | 168 | | Australasia | 6 out of 7 |
| Somalia | 23.9 | 24.0 | | 166 | | Africa | 46 out of 51 |
| South Africa | 6.5 | 6.8 | BBB- | 60 | Emerging | Africa | 2 out of 51 |
| Spain | 4.7 | 4.8 | BBB+ | 38 | Developed | Western Europe | 16 out of 19 |
| Sri Lanka | 8.8 | 8.6 | B+ | 72 | Frontier | Asia | 14 out of 29 |
| Sudan | 19.9 | 19.9 | | 154 | | Africa | 40 out of 51 |
| Suriname | 12.2 | 12.5 | B+ | 102 | | Latin America | 16 out of 20 |
| Swaziland | 18.1 | 19.2 | | 152 | | Africa | 38 out of 51 |
| Sweden | 0.0 | 0.0 | AAA | 7 | Developed | Western Europe | 6 out of 19 |

§ S&P Credit Rating based on long-term foreign currency issuer rating. See http://www.standardandpoors.com/.

* World rank based on 175 countries covered by Euromoney. Ranking based on ascending order in which '1' equals the smallest country risk premium (CRP) and '175' equals the largest country risk premium (CRP).

† MSCI Market Classification based on MSCI Market Classification Framework. See http://www.msci.com/products/indexes/market_classification.html

‡ Regional classification based on Euromoney. Regional rankings based on ascending order in which '1' equals the smallest country risk premium (CRP) for each region.

Note: A CRP of 0.0% is assumed in the following cases: (i) when the investor country and the investee country both have an S&P sovereign credit rating of AAA; or (ii) when the investor country has an S&P credit rating of AAA, and the investee country has a sovereign credit rating below AAA, but has a calculated CRP below 0.0% (which would imply lower risk than a country rated AAA); or (iii) when the investor country has an S&P credit rating below AAA, and the investee country has a sovereign credit rating of AAA, but has a calculated CRP above 0.0% (which would imply greater risk than a country rated below AAA). For purposes of this analysis, the U.S. is treated as having a sovereign credit rating equivalent to AAA.

The country risk premium (CRP) is not the cost of equity capital (COE). The CRP is to be added to base COE. See Chapter 6 for proper application.

## Data Updated Through March 2017

| Investee Country | December 2016 Country Risk Premium (CRP) (%) | March 2017 Country Risk Premium (CRP) (%) | S&P Sovereign Credit Rating § | World Rank Out of 175* | MSCI Market Classification † | Euromoney Region ‡ | Regional Rank ‡ |
|---|---|---|---|---|---|---|---|
| Switzerland | 0.0 | 0.0 | AAA | 2 | Developed | Western Europe | 1 out of 19 |
| Syria | 24.7 | 25.0 | | 167 | | Middle East | 13 out of 13 |
| Taiwan | 1.7 | 1.7 | AA- | 18 | Emerging | Asia | 3 out of 29 |
| Tajikistan | 19.4 | 19.9 | | 155 | | Central and Eastern Europe | 25 out of 25 |
| Tanzania | 11.6 | 11.9 | | 95 | | Africa | 13 out of 51 |
| Thailand | 5.9 | 5.8 | BBB+ | 51 | Emerging | Asia | 8 out of 29 |
| Togo | 13.2 | 13.3 | | 113 | | Africa | 20 out of 51 |
| Tonga | 28.1 | 28.3 | | 170 | | Australasia | 7 out of 7 |
| Trinidad & Tobago | 6.3 | 6.3 | A- | 54 | | Caribbean | 2 out of 9 |
| Tunisia | 9.2 | 9.6 | | 79 | Frontier | Africa | 6 out of 51 |
| Turkey | 6.6 | 6.6 | BB | 58 | Emerging | Central and Eastern Europe | 11 out of 25 |
| Turkmenistan | 16.6 | 17.0 | | 140 | | Asia | 24 out of 29 |
| Uganda | 12.7 | 13.1 | B | 110 | | Africa | 18 out of 51 |
| Ukraine | 15.6 | 15.8 | B- | 135 | | Central and Eastern Europe | 20 out of 25 |
| United Arab Emirates | 3.5 | 3.6 | AA | 33 | Emerging | Middle East | 4 out of 13 |
| United Kingdom | 1.9 | 2.1 | AA | 20 | Developed | Western Europe | 11 out of 19 |
| United States | 0.0 | 0.0 | AA+ | 15 | Developed | North America | 2 out of 2 |
| Uruguay | 5.3 | 5.2 | BBB | 45 | | Latin America | 5 out of 20 |
| Uzbekistan | 15.7 | 15.3 | | 132 | | Asia | 21 out of 29 |
| Vanuatu | 17.4 | 17.5 | | 145 | | Australasia | 4 out of 7 |
| Venezuela | 21.2 | 21.8 | CCC | 162 | | Latin America | 20 out of 20 |
| Vietnam | 9.7 | 9.5 | BB- | 78 | Frontier | Asia | 16 out of 29 |
| Yemen | 21.5 | 21.8 | | 161 | | Middle East | 12 out of 13 |
| Zambia | 13.1 | 13.2 | B | 111 | | Africa | 19 out of 51 |
| Zimbabwe | 23.2 | 23.2 | | 164 | | Africa | 44 out of 51 |

## March 2017 Country Risk Premium (CRP) Summary Statistics:

| S&P Rating | Country Count | Average CRP (%) | Median CRP (%) | Min CRP (%) | Max CRP (%) |
|---|---|---|---|---|---|
| AAA ** | 12 | 0.0 | 0.0 | 0.0 | 0.0 |
| AA (AA+, AA, AA-) | 15 | 2.1 | 2.1 | 0.0 | 5.1 |
| A (A+, A, A-) | 14 | 4.1 | 4.2 | 2.6 | 6.3 |
| BBB (BBB+, BBB, BBB-) | 17 | 5.9 | 5.8 | 3.1 | 8.3 |
| BB (BB+, BB, BB-) | 22 | 8.8 | 8.8 | 4.9 | 14.3 |
| B+ − SD | 39 | 13.6 | 13.2 | 8.6 | 21.8 |
| Investment Grade ** | 58 | 3.2 | 3.2 | 0.0 | 8.3 |
| Non-Investment Grade ** | 61 | 11.9 | 12.1 | 4.9 | 21.8 |
| **MSCI Market Classification** | | | | | |
| Developed Markets | 23 | 1.3 | 0.0 | 0.0 | 5.7 |
| Emerging Markets | 23 | 5.5 | 5.1 | 1.3 | 13.5 |
| Frontier Markets | 22 | 8.6 | 8.4 | 3.2 | 14.3 |
| **Euromoney Region ‡** | | | | | |
| Africa | 51 | 16.1 | 14.1 | 5.3 | 36.9 |
| Asia | 29 | 10.8 | 9.4 | 0.0 | 34.2 |
| Australasia | 7 | 14.7 | 17.5 | 0.0 | 28.3 |
| Caribbean | 9 | 12.1 | 11.6 | 5.2 | 21.5 |
| Central and Eastern Europe | 25 | 9.2 | 7.1 | 2.4 | 19.9 |
| Latin America | 20 | 9.8 | 10.5 | 1.3 | 21.8 |
| Middle East | 13 | 10.0 | 7.4 | 2.2 | 25.0 |
| North America | 2 | 0.0 | 0.0 | 0.0 | 0.0 |
| Western Europe | 19 | 2.3 | 1.5 | 0.0 | 12.8 |

## CCR Base Cost of Equity Capital:

| Germany | COE (%) |
|---|---|
| March 2017 | 7.6 |
| December 2016 | 7.6 |

CCR base country-level COE for a Germany-based investor investing in Germany.

§ S&P Credit Rating based on long-term foreign currency issuer rating. See http://www.standardandpoors.com/.

* World rank based on 175 countries covered by Euromoney. Ranking based on ascending order in which '1' equals the smallest country risk premium (CRP) and '175' equals the largest country risk premium (CRP).

† MSCI Market Classification based on MSCI Market Classification Framework. See http://www.msci.com/products/indexes/market_classification.html.

‡ Regional classification based on Euromoney. Regional rankings based on ascending order in which '1' equals the smallest country risk premium (CRP) for each region.

** Investment grade based on S&P sovereign credit rating from AAA to BBB-. Non-Investment grade based on S&P sovereign credit rating from BB+ to SD. For purposes of this analysis, the U.S. is being treated as if it were rated AAA by S&P.

Note: A CRP of 0.0% is assumed in the following cases: (i) when the investor country and the investee country both have an S&P sovereign credit rating of AAA; or (ii) when the investor country has an S&P credit rating of AAA, and the investee country has a sovereign credit rating below AAA, but has a calculated CRP below 0.0% (which would imply lower risk than a country rated AAA); or (iii) when the investor country has an S&P credit rating below AAA, and the investee country has a sovereign credit rating of AAA, but has a calculated CRP above 0.0% (which would imply greater risk than a country rated below AAA). For purposes of this analysis, the U.S. is treated as having a sovereign credit rating equivalent to AAA.

The country risk premium (CRP) is not the cost of equity capital (COE). The CRP is to be added to base COE. See Chapter 6 for proper application.

## Data Updated Through March 2017

| Investee Country | December 2016 Country Risk Premium (CRP) (%) | March 2017 Country Risk Premium (CRP) (%) | S&P Sovereign Credit Rating § | World Rank Out of 175• | MSCI Market Classification † | Euromoney Region ‡ | Regional Rank ‡ |
|---|---|---|---|---|---|---|---|
| Afghanistan | 4.0 | 4.0 | | 139 | | Asia | 23 out of 29 |
| Albania | -1.4 | -1.0 | B+ | 93 | | Central and Eastern Europe | 18 out of 25 |
| Algeria | -1.4 | -1.1 | | 91 | | Africa | 10 out of 51 |
| Angola | 1.0 | 1.3 | B | 121 | | Africa | 26 out of 51 |
| Argentina | -0.9 | -0.9 | B- | 96 | Frontier | Latin America | 13 out of 20 |
| Armenia | -3.9 | -3.5 | | 77 | | Asia | 15 out of 29 |
| Australia | -12.9 | -12.7 | AAA | 12 | Developed | Australasia | 2 out of 7 |
| Austria | -12.7 | -12.5 | AA+ | 13 | Developed | Western Europe | 9 out of 19 |
| Azerbaijan | -2.7 | -2.1 | BB+ | 85 | | Asia | 17 out of 29 |
| Bahamas | -5.3 | -5.4 | BB+ | 65 | | Caribbean | 3 out of 9 |
| Bahrain | -5.4 | -5.4 | BB- | 64 | Frontier | Middle East | 7 out of 13 |
| Bangladesh | 1.5 | 1.5 | BB- | 126 | Frontier | Asia | 20 out of 29 |
| Barbados | -3.7 | -2.4 | CCC+ | 82 | | Caribbean | 4 out of 9 |
| Belarus | 3.7 | 4.4 | B- | 143 | | Central and Eastern Europe | 23 out of 25 |
| Belgium | -11.4 | -11.3 | AA | 17 | Developed | Western Europe | 10 out of 19 |
| Belize | -0.4 | -0.1 | B- | 106 | | Latin America | 17 out of 20 |
| Benin | 5.4 | 5.7 | | 150 | | Africa | 37 out of 51 |
| Bermuda | -7.7 | -7.6 | A+ | 44 | | Caribbean | 1 out of 9 |
| Bhutan | 5.1 | 5.2 | | 148 | | Asia | 25 out of 29 |
| Bolivia | -1.9 | -1.4 | BB | 88 | | Latin America | 12 out of 20 |
| Bosnia & Herzegovina | 4.2 | 4.6 | B | 144 | | Central and Eastern Europe | 24 out of 25 |
| Botswana | -7.7 | -7.5 | A- | 48 | | Africa | 1 out of 51 |
| Brazil | -6.2 | -6.1 | BB | 59 | Emerging | Latin America | 7 out of 20 |
| Bulgaria | -6.4 | -6.0 | BB+ | 61 | | Central and Eastern Europe | 12 out of 25 |
| Burkina Faso | 2.5 | 2.8 | B- | 133 | | Africa | 33 out of 51 |
| Burundi | 14.5 | 14.8 | | 169 | | Africa | 47 out of 51 |
| Cambodia | 6.0 | 5.9 | | 151 | | Asia | 27 out of 29 |
| Cameroon | 1.2 | 1.4 | B | 124 | | Africa | 28 out of 51 |
| Canada | -13.1 | -13.0 | AAA | 9 | Developed | North America | 1 out of 2 |
| Cape Verde | -1.2 | -1.0 | B | 94 | | Africa | 12 out of 51 |
| Central African Republic | 18.1 | 18.4 | | 172 | | Africa | 49 out of 51 |
| Chad | 16.7 | 17.0 | | 171 | | Africa | 48 out of 51 |
| Chile | -11.9 | -11.5 | AA- | 16 | Emerging | Latin America | 1 out of 20 |
| China | -7.9 | -7.7 | AA- | 42 | Emerging | Asia | 7 out of 29 |
| Colombia | -8.0 | -7.8 | BBB | 41 | Emerging | Latin America | 4 out of 20 |
| Congo Republic | 0.8 | 0.8 | B- | 117 | | Africa | 24 out of 51 |
| Congo, DR | 2.0 | 2.2 | B- | 131 | | Africa | 32 out of 51 |
| Costa Rica | -4.9 | -4.5 | BB- | 71 | | Latin America | 8 out of 20 |
| Côte d'Ivoire | -1.4 | -1.1 | | 92 | | Africa | 11 out of 51 |
| Croatia | -5.8 | -5.7 | BB | 63 | Frontier | Central and Eastern Europe | 13 out of 25 |
| Cuba | 8.3 | 8.7 | | 160 | | Caribbean | 9 out of 9 |
| Cyprus | -8.2 | -7.9 | BB+ | 40 | | Central and Eastern Europe | 7 out of 25 |
| Czech Republic | -10.6 | -10.4 | AA- | 23 | Emerging | Central and Eastern Europe | 1 out of 25 |
| Denmark | -13.7 | -13.6 | AAA | 4 | Developed | Western Europe | 3 out of 19 |
| Djibouti | 26.1 | 24.1 | | 175 | | Africa | 51 out of 51 |
| Dominican Republic | -1.5 | -1.2 | BB- | 90 | | Caribbean | 5 out of 9 |
| Ecuador | 0.1 | 0.1 | B | 109 | | Latin America | 18 out of 20 |
| Egypt | 0.5 | 0.7 | B- | 116 | Emerging | Africa | 23 out of 51 |
| El Salvador | -2.5 | -2.5 | B- | 81 | | Latin America | 10 out of 20 |
| Equatorial Guinea | 10.9 | 11.2 | | 165 | | Africa | 45 out of 51 |

§ S&P Credit Rating based on long-term foreign currency issuer rating. See http://www.standardandpoors.com/.

• World rank based on 175 countries covered by Euromoney. Ranking based on ascending order in which '1' equals the smallest country risk premium (CRP) and '175' equals the largest country risk premium (CRP).

† MSCI Market Classification based on MSCI Market Classification Framework. See http://www.msci.com/products/indexes/market_classification.html

‡ Regional classification based on Euromoney. Regional rankings based on ascending order in which '1' equals the smallest country risk premium (CRP) for each region.

Note: A CRP of 0.0% is assumed in the following cases: (i) when the investor country and the investee country both have an S&P sovereign credit rating of AAA; or (ii) when the investor country has an S&P credit rating of AAA, and the investee country has a sovereign credit rating below AAA, but has a calculated CRP below 0.0% (which would imply lower risk than a country rated AAA); or (iii) when the investor country has an S&P credit rating below AAA, and the investee country has a sovereign credit rating of AAA, but has a calculated CRP above 0.0% (which would imply greater risk than a country rated below AAA). For purposes of this analysis, the U.S. is treated as having a sovereign credit rating equivalent to AAA.

The country risk premium (CRP) is not the cost of equity capital (COE). The CRP is to be added to base COE. See Chapter 6 for proper application.

## Data Updated Through March 2017

| Investee Country | December 2016 Country Risk Premium (CRP) (%) | March 2017 Country Risk Premium (CRP) (%) | S&P Sovereign Credit Rating § | World Rank Out of 175* | MSCI Market Classification † | Euromoney Region ‡ | Regional Rank ‡ |
|---|---|---|---|---|---|---|---|
| Eritrea | 22.3 | 20.7 | | 173 | | Africa | 50 out of 51 |
| Estonia | -10.0 | -9.6 | AA- | 32 | Frontier | Central and Eastern Europe | 4 out of 25 |
| Ethiopia | -0.7 | -0.4 | B | 101 | | Africa | 16 out of 51 |
| Fiji | 4.8 | 4.9 | B+ | 147 | | Australasia | 5 out of 7 |
| Finland | -13.0 | -12.8 | AA+ | 11 | Developed | Western Europe | 8 out of 19 |
| France | -10.6 | -10.6 | AA | 22 | Developed | Western Europe | 12 out of 19 |
| Gabon | -2.9 | -2.3 | | 83 | | Africa | 7 out of 51 |
| Gambia | 3.2 | 3.5 | | 138 | | Africa | 34 out of 51 |
| Georgia | -4.2 | -3.7 | BB- | 74 | | Central and Eastern Europe | 15 out of 25 |
| Germany | -13.0 | -12.8 | AAA | 10 | Developed | Western Europe | 7 out of 19 |
| Ghana | -1.2 | -1.3 | B- | 89 | | Africa | 9 out of 51 |
| Greece | 0.0 | 0.0 | B- | 108 | Emerging | Western Europe | 19 out of 19 |
| Grenada | -0.4 | -0.1 | | 105 | | Caribbean | 7 out of 9 |
| Guatemala | -2.5 | -2.2 | BB | 84 | | Latin America | 11 out of 20 |
| Guinea | 6.9 | 7.2 | | 156 | | Africa | 41 out of 51 |
| Guinea-Bissau | 0.4 | 0.7 | | 115 | | Africa | 22 out of 51 |
| Guyana | -0.7 | -0.5 | | 100 | | Latin America | 15 out of 20 |
| Haiti | 9.8 | 8.0 | | 157 | | Caribbean | 8 out of 9 |
| Honduras | -1.1 | -0.8 | B+ | 98 | | Latin America | 14 out of 20 |
| Hong Kong | -12.4 | -12.2 | AAA | 14 | Developed | Asia | 2 out of 29 |
| Hungary | -6.6 | -6.2 | BBB- | 57 | Emerging | Central and Eastern Europe | 10 out of 25 |
| Iceland | -9.6 | -9.6 | A | 30 | | Western Europe | 15 out of 19 |
| India | -6.8 | -6.3 | BBB- | 55 | Emerging | Asia | 10 out of 29 |
| Indonesia | -6.1 | -5.8 | BB+ | 62 | Emerging | Asia | 11 out of 29 |
| Iran | 0.9 | 1.4 | | 125 | | Middle East | 10 out of 13 |
| Iraq | 2.8 | 3.1 | B- | 136 | | Middle East | 11 out of 13 |
| Ireland | -10.1 | -10.0 | A+ | 27 | Developed | Western Europe | 14 out of 19 |
| Israel | -10.2 | -9.9 | A+ | 28 | Developed | Middle East | 2 out of 13 |
| Italy | -7.2 | -7.2 | BBB- | 50 | Developed | Western Europe | 18 out of 19 |
| Jamaica | -1.0 | -0.1 | B | 104 | | Caribbean | 6 out of 9 |
| Japan | -10.3 | -10.1 | A+ | 25 | Developed | Asia | 5 out of 29 |
| Jordan | -3.9 | -3.5 | BB- | 76 | Frontier | Middle East | 8 out of 13 |
| Kazakhstan | -4.4 | -4.6 | BBB- | 70 | Frontier | Asia | 13 out of 29 |
| Kenya | -1.0 | -0.6 | B+ | 99 | Frontier | Africa | 15 out of 51 |
| Korea (North) | 21.6 | 21.4 | | 174 | | Asia | 29 out of 29 |
| Korea (South) | -11.1 | -10.8 | AA | 19 | Emerging | Asia | 4 out of 29 |
| Kuwait | -10.0 | -9.6 | AA | 31 | Frontier | Middle East | 3 out of 13 |
| Kyrgyz Republic | 4.2 | 4.4 | | 142 | | Central and Eastern Europe | 22 out of 25 |
| Laos | 8.5 | 8.3 | | 158 | | Asia | 28 out of 29 |
| Latvia | -7.9 | -7.6 | A- | 43 | | Central and Eastern Europe | 8 out of 25 |
| Lebanon | 0.8 | 0.4 | B- | 112 | Frontier | Middle East | 9 out of 13 |
| Lesotho | 4.4 | 4.7 | | 146 | | Africa | 36 out of 51 |
| Liberia | -0.3 | 0.0 | | 107 | | Africa | 17 out of 51 |
| Libya | 6.0 | 6.6 | | 153 | | Africa | 39 out of 51 |
| Lithuania | -8.7 | -8.4 | A- | 36 | Frontier | Central and Eastern Europe | 6 out of 25 |
| Luxembourg | -13.4 | -13.3 | AAA | 5 | | Western Europe | 4 out of 19 |
| Macedonia | -1.9 | -1.4 | BB- | 87 | | Central and Eastern Europe | 17 out of 25 |
| Madagascar | 0.6 | 1.3 | | 123 | | Africa | 27 out of 51 |
| Malawi | 0.3 | 0.5 | | 114 | | Africa | 21 out of 51 |
| Malaysia | -8.6 | -8.5 | A- | 35 | Emerging | Asia | 6 out of 29 |

§ S&P Credit Rating based on long-term foreign currency issuer rating. See http://www.standardandpoors.com/.

* World rank based on 175 countries covered by Euromoney. Ranking based on ascending order in which '1' equals the smallest country risk premium (CRP) and '175' equals the largest country risk premium (CRP).

† MSCI Market Classification based on MSCI Market Classification Framework. See http://www.msci.com/products/indexes/market_classification.html

‡ Regional classification based on Euromoney. Regional rankings based on ascending order in which '1' equals the smallest country risk premium (CRP) for each region.

Note: A CRP of 0.0% is assumed in the following cases: (i) when the investor country and the investee country both have an S&P sovereign credit rating of AAA; or (ii) when the investor country has an S&P credit rating of AAA, and the investee country has a sovereign credit rating below AAA, but has a calculated CRP below 0.0% (which would imply lower risk than a country rated AAA); or (iii) when the investor country has an S&P credit rating below AAA, and the investee country has a sovereign credit rating of AAA, but has a calculated CRP above 0.0% (which would imply greater risk than a country rated below AAA). For purposes of this analysis, the U.S. is treated as having a sovereign credit rating equivalent to AAA.

The country risk premium (CRP) is not the cost of equity capital (COE). The CRP is to be added to base COE. See Chapter 6 for proper application.

## Data Updated Through March 2017

| Investee Country | December 2016 Country Risk Premium (CRP) (%) | March 2017 Country Risk Premium (CRP) (%) | S&P Sovereign Credit Rating § | World Rank Out of 175* | MSCI Market Classification † | Euromoney Region ‡ | Regional Rank ‡ |
|---|---|---|---|---|---|---|---|
| Mali | 4.1 | 4.3 | | 141 | | Africa | 35 out of 51 |
| Malta | -10.3 | -10.0 | A- | 26 | | Western Europe | 13 out of 19 |
| Mauritania | 8.1 | 8.4 | | 159 | | Africa | 42 out of 51 |
| Mauritius | -5.1 | -4.9 | | 67 | Frontier | Asia | 12 out of 29 |
| Mexico | -8.7 | -8.3 | BBB+ | 37 | Emerging | Latin America | 2 out of 20 |
| Moldova | 2.5 | 3.1 | | 137 | | Central and Eastern Europe | 21 out of 25 |
| Mongolia | 0.6 | 1.2 | B- | 119 | | Asia | 18 out of 29 |
| Montenegro | -0.2 | -0.1 | B+ | 103 | | Central and Eastern Europe | 19 out of 25 |
| Morocco | -5.1 | -4.6 | BBB- | 69 | Frontier | Africa | 4 out of 51 |
| Mozambique | 1.7 | 1.8 | SD | 128 | | Africa | 29 out of 51 |
| Myanmar | 2.7 | 2.8 | | 134 | | Asia | 22 out of 29 |
| Namibia | -5.5 | -5.1 | | 66 | | Africa | 3 out of 51 |
| Nepal | 5.4 | 5.6 | | 149 | | Asia | 26 out of 29 |
| Netherlands | -13.4 | -13.2 | AAA | 6 | Developed | Western Europe | 5 out of 19 |
| New Zealand | -13.2 | -13.0 | AA | 8 | Developed | Australasia | 1 out of 7 |
| Nicaragua | 1.4 | 1.7 | B+ | 127 | | Latin America | 19 out of 20 |
| Niger | 1.0 | 1.3 | | 120 | | Africa | 25 out of 51 |
| Nigeria | -1.0 | -0.8 | B | 97 | Frontier | Africa | 14 out of 51 |
| Norway | -14.0 | -13.9 | AAA | 3 | Developed | Western Europe | 2 out of 19 |
| Oman | -7.8 | -7.5 | BBB- | 46 | Frontier | Middle East | 5 out of 13 |
| Pakistan | 1.1 | 1.3 | B | 122 | Frontier | Asia | 19 out of 29 |
| Panama | -7.1 | -6.8 | BBB | 52 | | Latin America | 6 out of 20 |
| Papua New Guinea | 0.6 | 0.9 | B+ | 118 | | Australasia | 3 out of 7 |
| Paraguay | -3.5 | -3.1 | BB | 80 | | Latin America | 9 out of 20 |
| Peru | -8.4 | -8.0 | BBB+ | 39 | Emerging | Latin America | 3 out of 20 |
| Philippines | -6.7 | -6.5 | BBB | 53 | Emerging | Asia | 9 out of 29 |
| Poland | -9.8 | -9.7 | BBB+ | 29 | Emerging | Central and Eastern Europe | 3 out of 25 |
| Portugal | -7.4 | -7.3 | BB+ | 49 | Developed | Western Europe | 17 out of 19 |
| Qatar | -10.9 | -10.6 | AA | 21 | Emerging | Middle East | 1 out of 13 |
| Romania | -6.6 | -6.3 | BBB- | 56 | Frontier | Central and Eastern Europe | 9 out of 25 |
| Russia | -4.3 | -4.7 | BB+ | 68 | Emerging | Central and Eastern Europe | 14 out of 25 |
| Rwanda | 1.8 | 2.1 | B | 130 | | Africa | 31 out of 51 |
| São Tomé & Príncipe | 8.3 | 9.0 | | 163 | | Africa | 43 out of 51 |
| Saudi Arabia | -7.4 | -7.5 | A- | 47 | | Middle East | 6 out of 13 |
| Senegal | -1.7 | -1.5 | B+ | 86 | | Africa | 8 out of 51 |
| Serbia | -3.6 | -3.7 | BB- | 75 | Frontier | Central and Eastern Europe | 16 out of 25 |
| Seychelles | -4.1 | -3.9 | | 73 | | Africa | 5 out of 51 |
| Sierra Leone | 1.8 | 2.0 | | 129 | | Africa | 30 out of 51 |
| Singapore | -14.2 | -14.0 | AAA | 1 | Developed | Asia | 1 out of 29 |
| Slovakia | -10.5 | -10.2 | A+ | 24 | | Central and Eastern Europe | 2 out of 25 |
| Slovenia | -9.1 | -8.9 | A | 34 | Frontier | Central and Eastern Europe | 5 out of 25 |
| Solomon Islands | 12.7 | 13.0 | | 168 | | Australasia | 6 out of 7 |
| Somalia | 10.9 | 11.2 | | 166 | | Africa | 46 out of 51 |
| South Africa | -6.5 | -6.0 | BBB- | 60 | Emerging | Africa | 2 out of 51 |
| Spain | -8.3 | -8.0 | BBB+ | 38 | Developed | Western Europe | 16 out of 19 |
| Sri Lanka | -4.2 | -4.3 | B+ | 72 | Frontier | Asia | 14 out of 29 |
| Sudan | 6.9 | 7.1 | | 154 | | Africa | 40 out of 51 |
| Suriname | -0.8 | -0.3 | B+ | 102 | | Latin America | 16 out of 20 |
| Swaziland | 5.2 | 6.4 | | 152 | | Africa | 38 out of 51 |
| Sweden | -13.3 | -13.2 | AAA | 7 | Developed | Western Europe | 6 out of 19 |

§ S&P Credit Rating based on long-term foreign currency issuer rating. See http://www.standardandpoors.com/.

* World rank based on 175 countries covered by Euromoney. Ranking based on ascending order in which '1' equals the smallest country risk premium (CRP) and '175' equals the largest country risk premium (CRP).

† MSCI Market Classification based on MSCI Market Classification Framework. See http://www.msci.com/products/indexes/market_classification.html.

‡ Regional classification based on Euromoney. Regional rankings based on ascending order in which '1' equals the smallest country risk premium (CRP) for each region.

Note: A CRP of 0.0% is assumed in the following cases: (i) when the investor country and the investee country both have an S&P sovereign credit rating of AAA; or (ii) when the investor country has an S&P credit rating of AAA, and the investee country has a sovereign credit rating below AAA, but has a calculated CRP below 0.0% (which would imply lower risk than a country rated AAA); or (iii) when the investor country has an S&P credit rating below AAA, and the investee country has a sovereign credit rating of AAA, but has a calculated CRP above 0.0% (which would imply greater risk than a country rated below AAA). For purposes of this analysis, the U.S. is treated as having a sovereign credit rating equivalent to AAA.

The country risk premium (CRP) is not the cost of equity capital (COE). The CRP is to be added to base COE. See Chapter 6 for proper application.

## Data Updated Through March 2017

| Investee Country | December 2016 Country Risk Premium (CRP) (%) | March 2017 Country Risk Premium (CRP) (%) | S&P Sovereign Credit Rating § | World Rank Out of 175∗ | MSCI Market Classification † | Euromoney Region ‡ | Regional Rank ‡ |
|---|---|---|---|---|---|---|---|
| Switzerland | -14.0 | -13.9 | AAA | 2 | Developed | Western Europe | 1 out of 19 |
| Syria | 11.7 | 12.2 | | 167 | | Middle East | 13 out of 13 |
| Taiwan | -11.3 | -11.1 | AA- | 18 | Emerging | Asia | 3 out of 29 |
| Tajikistan | 6.5 | 7.1 | | 155 | | Central and Eastern Europe | 25 out of 25 |
| Tanzania | -1.4 | -0.9 | | 95 | | Africa | 13 out of 51 |
| Thailand | -7.1 | -7.0 | BBB+ | 51 | Emerging | Asia | 8 out of 29 |
| Togo | 0.2 | 0.5 | | 113 | | Africa | 20 out of 51 |
| Tonga | 15.2 | 15.5 | | 170 | | Australasia | 7 out of 7 |
| Trinidad & Tobago | -6.7 | -6.5 | A- | 54 | | Caribbean | 2 out of 9 |
| Tunisia | -3.8 | -3.2 | | 79 | Frontier | Africa | 6 out of 51 |
| Turkey | -6.3 | -6.2 | BB | 58 | Emerging | Central and Eastern Europe | 11 out of 25 |
| Turkmenistan | 3.6 | 4.1 | | 140 | | Asia | 24 out of 29 |
| Uganda | -0.3 | 0.3 | B | 110 | | Africa | 18 out of 51 |
| Ukraine | 2.6 | 2.9 | B- | 135 | | Central and Eastern Europe | 20 out of 25 |
| United Arab Emirates | -9.5 | -9.2 | AA | 33 | Emerging | Middle East | 4 out of 13 |
| United Kingdom | -11.1 | -10.7 | AA | 20 | Developed | Western Europe | 11 out of 19 |
| United States | -12.1 | -11.9 | AA+ | 15 | Developed | North America | 2 out of 2 |
| Uruguay | -7.7 | -7.6 | BBB | 45 | | Latin America | 5 out of 20 |
| Uzbekistan | 2.8 | 2.5 | | 132 | | Asia | 21 out of 29 |
| Vanuatu | 4.4 | 4.7 | | 145 | | Australasia | 4 out of 7 |
| Venezuela | 8.3 | 9.0 | CCC | 162 | | Latin America | 20 out of 20 |
| Vietnam | -3.3 | -3.3 | BB- | 78 | Frontier | Asia | 16 out of 29 |
| Yemen | 8.6 | 8.9 | | 161 | | Middle East | 12 out of 13 |
| Zambia | 0.1 | 0.4 | B | 111 | | Africa | 19 out of 51 |
| Zimbabwe | 10.2 | 10.4 | | 164 | | Africa | 44 out of 51 |

## March 2017 Country Risk Premium (CRP) Summary Statistics:

| S&P Rating | Country Count | Average CRP (%) | Median CRP (%) | Min CRP (%) | Max CRP (%) |
|---|---|---|---|---|---|
| AAA ∗∗ | 12 | -13.1 | -13.2 | -14.0 | -11.9 |
| AA (AA+, AA, AA-) | 15 | -10.8 | -10.7 | -13.0 | -7.7 |
| A (A+, A, A-) | 14 | -8.7 | -8.7 | -10.2 | -6.5 |
| BBB (BBB+, BBB, BBB-) | 17 | -7.0 | -7.0 | -9.7 | -4.6 |
| BB (BB+, BB, BB-) | 22 | -4.0 | -4.1 | -7.9 | 1.5 |
| B+ − SD | 39 | 0.8 | 0.4 | -4.3 | 9.0 |
| Investment Grade ∗∗ | 58 | -9.7 | -9.7 | -14.0 | -4.6 |
| Non-Investment Grade ∗∗ | 61 | -1.0 | -0.8 | -7.9 | 9.0 |
| **MSCI Market Classification** | | | | | |
| Developed Markets | 23 | -11.6 | -12.5 | -14.0 | -7.2 |
| Emerging Markets | 23 | -7.3 | -7.7 | -11.5 | 0.7 |
| Frontier Markets | 22 | -4.2 | -4.4 | -9.6 | 1.5 |
| **Euromoney Region ‡** | | | | | |
| Africa | 51 | 3.3 | 1.3 | -7.5 | 24.1 |
| Asia | 29 | -2.0 | -3.5 | -14.0 | 21.4 |
| Australasia | 7 | 1.9 | 4.7 | -13.0 | 15.5 |
| Caribbean | 9 | -0.7 | -1.2 | -7.6 | 8.7 |
| Central and Eastern Europe | 25 | -3.7 | -5.7 | -10.4 | 7.1 |
| Latin America | 20 | -3.1 | -2.3 | -11.5 | 9.0 |
| Middle East | 13 | -2.9 | -5.4 | -10.6 | 12.2 |
| North America | 2 | -12.4 | -12.4 | -13.0 | -11.9 |
| Western Europe | 19 | -10.7 | -11.3 | -13.9 | 0.0 |

## CCR Base Cost of Equity Capital:

| Greece | COE (%) |
|---|---|
| March 2017 | 20.4 |
| December 2016 | 20.6 |

CCR base country-level COE for a Greece-based investor investing in Greece.

§ S&P Credit Rating based on long-term foreign currency issuer rating. See http://www.standardandpoors.com/.

∗ World rank based on 175 countries covered by Euromoney. Ranking based on ascending order in which '1' equals the smallest country risk premium (CRP) and '175' equals the largest country risk premium (CRP).

† MSCI Market Classification based on MSCI Market Classification Framework. See http://www.msci.com/products/indexes/market_classification.html.

‡ Regional classification based on Euromoney. Regional rankings based on ascending order in which '1' equals the smallest country risk premium (CRP) for each region.

∗∗ Investment grade based on S&P sovereign credit rating from AAA to BBB-. Non-Investment grade based on S&P sovereign credit rating from BB+ to SD. For purposes of this analysis, the U.S. is being treated as if it were rated AAA by S&P.

Note: A CRP of 0.0% is assumed in the following cases: (i) when the investor country and the investee country both have an S&P sovereign credit rating of AAA; or (ii) when the investor country has an S&P credit rating of AAA, and the investee country has a sovereign credit rating below AAA, but has a calculated CRP below 0.0% (which would imply lower risk than a country rated AAA); or (iii) when the investor country has an S&P credit rating below AAA, and the investee country has a sovereign credit rating of AAA, but has a calculated CRP above 0.0% (which would imply greater risk than a country rated below AAA). For purposes of this analysis, the U.S. is treated as having a sovereign credit rating equivalent to AAA.

The country risk premium (CRP) is not the cost of equity capital (COE).  The CRP is to be added to base COE. See Chapter 6 for proper application.

## Data Updated Through March 2017

| Investee Country | December 2016 Country Risk Premium (CRP) (%) | March 2017 Country Risk Premium (CRP) (%) | S&P Sovereign Credit Rating § | World Rank Out of 175* | MSCI Market Classification † | Euromoney Region ‡ | Regional Rank ‡ |
|---|---|---|---|---|---|---|---|
| Afghanistan | 15.3 | 15.3 | | 139 | | Asia | 23 out of 29 |
| Albania | 10.2 | 10.6 | B+ | 93 | | Central and Eastern Europe | 18 out of 25 |
| Algeria | 10.3 | 10.5 | | 91 | | Africa | 10 out of 51 |
| Angola | 12.5 | 12.8 | B | 121 | | Africa | 26 out of 51 |
| Argentina | 10.8 | 10.7 | B- | 96 | Frontier | Latin America | 13 out of 20 |
| Armenia | 8.0 | 8.3 | | 77 | | Asia | 15 out of 29 |
| Australia | 0.0 | 0.0 | AAA | 12 | Developed | Australasia | 2 out of 7 |
| Austria | 0.0 | 0.0 | AA+ | 13 | Developed | Western Europe | 9 out of 19 |
| Azerbaijan | 9.1 | 9.6 | BB+ | 85 | | Asia | 17 out of 29 |
| Bahamas | 6.6 | 6.5 | BB+ | 65 | | Caribbean | 3 out of 9 |
| Bahrain | 6.5 | 6.4 | BB- | 64 | Frontier | Middle East | 7 out of 13 |
| Bangladesh | 12.9 | 13.0 | BB- | 126 | Frontier | Asia | 20 out of 29 |
| Barbados | 8.1 | 9.3 | CCC+ | 82 | | Caribbean | 4 out of 9 |
| Belarus | 15.0 | 15.7 | B- | 143 | | Central and Eastern Europe | 23 out of 25 |
| Belgium | 0.9 | 0.8 | AA | 17 | Developed | Western Europe | 10 out of 19 |
| Belize | 11.2 | 11.5 | B- | 106 | | Latin America | 17 out of 20 |
| Benin | 16.6 | 16.9 | | 150 | | Africa | 37 out of 51 |
| Bermuda | 4.3 | 4.4 | A+ | 44 | | Caribbean | 1 out of 9 |
| Bhutan | 16.3 | 16.5 | | 148 | | Asia | 25 out of 29 |
| Bolivia | 9.8 | 10.2 | BB | 88 | | Latin America | 12 out of 20 |
| Bosnia & Herzegovina | 15.5 | 15.9 | B | 144 | | Central and Eastern Europe | 24 out of 25 |
| Botswana | 4.4 | 4.4 | A- | 48 | | Africa | 1 out of 51 |
| Brazil | 5.8 | 5.8 | BB | 59 | Emerging | Latin America | 7 out of 20 |
| Bulgaria | 5.6 | 5.9 | BB+ | 61 | | Central and Eastern Europe | 12 out of 25 |
| Burkina Faso | 13.9 | 14.2 | B- | 133 | | Africa | 33 out of 51 |
| Burundi | 25.1 | 25.5 | | 169 | | Africa | 47 out of 51 |
| Cambodia | 17.2 | 17.1 | | 151 | | Asia | 27 out of 29 |
| Cameroon | 12.7 | 12.9 | B | 124 | | Africa | 28 out of 51 |
| Canada | 0.0 | 0.0 | AAA | 9 | Developed | North America | 1 out of 2 |
| Cape Verde | 10.4 | 10.6 | B | 94 | | Africa | 12 out of 51 |
| Central African Republic | 28.4 | 28.9 | | 172 | | Africa | 49 out of 51 |
| Chad | 27.2 | 27.7 | | 171 | | Africa | 48 out of 51 |
| Chile | 0.5 | 0.7 | AA- | 16 | Emerging | Latin America | 1 out of 20 |
| China | 4.2 | 4.2 | AA- | 42 | Emerging | Asia | 7 out of 29 |
| Colombia | 4.1 | 4.2 | BBB | 41 | Emerging | Latin America | 4 out of 20 |
| Congo Republic | 12.3 | 12.3 | B- | 117 | | Africa | 24 out of 51 |
| Congo, DR | 13.5 | 13.6 | B- | 131 | | Africa | 32 out of 51 |
| Costa Rica | 7.0 | 7.3 | BB- | 71 | | Latin America | 8 out of 20 |
| Côte d'Ivoire | 10.3 | 10.5 | | 92 | | Africa | 11 out of 51 |
| Croatia | 6.1 | 6.1 | BB | 63 | Frontier | Central and Eastern Europe | 13 out of 25 |
| Cuba | 19.4 | 19.8 | | 160 | | Caribbean | 9 out of 9 |
| Cyprus | 3.9 | 4.0 | BB+ | 40 | | Central and Eastern Europe | 7 out of 25 |
| Czech Republic | 1.6 | 1.7 | AA- | 23 | Emerging | Central and Eastern Europe | 1 out of 25 |
| Denmark | 0.0 | 0.0 | AAA | 4 | Developed | Western Europe | 3 out of 19 |
| Djibouti | 35.9 | 34.3 | | 175 | | Africa | 51 out of 51 |
| Dominican Republic | 10.1 | 10.4 | BB- | 90 | | Caribbean | 5 out of 9 |
| Ecuador | 11.6 | 11.7 | B | 109 | | Latin America | 18 out of 20 |
| Egypt | 12.1 | 12.2 | B- | 116 | Emerging | Africa | 23 out of 51 |
| El Salvador | 9.2 | 9.2 | B- | 81 | | Latin America | 10 out of 20 |
| Equatorial Guinea | 21.7 | 22.1 | | 165 | | Africa | 45 out of 51 |

§ S&P Credit Rating based on long-term foreign currency issuer rating. See http://www.standardandpoors.com/.

* World rank based on 175 countries covered by Euromoney. Ranking based on ascending order in which '1' equals the smallest country risk premium (CRP) and '175' equals the largest country risk premium (CRP).

† MSCI Market Classification based on MSCI Market Classification Framework.  See http://www.msci.com/products/indexes/market_classification.html.

‡ Regional classification based on Euromoney. Regional rankings based on ascending order in which '1' equals the smallest country risk premium (CRP) for each region.

Note: A CRP of 0.0% is assumed in the following cases: (i) when the investor country and the investee country both have an S&P sovereign credit rating of AAA; or (ii) when the investor country has an S&P credit rating of AAA, and the investee country has a sovereign credit rating below AAA, but has a calculated CRP below 0.0% (which would imply lower risk than a country rated AAA); or (iii) when the investor country has an S&P credit rating below AAA, and the investee country has a sovereign credit rating of AAA, but has a calculated CRP above 0.0% (which would imply greater risk than a country rated below AAA). For purposes of this analysis, the U.S. is treated as having a sovereign credit rating equivalent to AAA.

The country risk premium (CRP) is not the cost of equity capital (COE). The CRP is to be added to base COE. See Chapter 6 for proper application.

## Data Updated Through March 2017

| Investee Country | December 2016 Country Risk Premium (CRP) (%) | March 2017 Country Risk Premium (CRP) (%) | S&P Sovereign Credit Rating § | World Rank Out of 175* | MSCI Market Classification † | Euromoney Region ‡ | Regional Rank ‡ |
|---|---|---|---|---|---|---|---|
| Eritrea | 32.4 | 31.1 | | 173 | | Africa | 50 out of 51 |
| Estonia | 2.2 | 2.5 | AA- | 32 | Frontier | Central and Eastern Europe | 4 out of 25 |
| Ethiopia | 10.9 | 11.2 | B | 101 | | Africa | 16 out of 51 |
| Fiji | 16.0 | 16.2 | B+ | 147 | | Australasia | 5 out of 7 |
| Finland | 0.0 | 0.0 | AA+ | 11 | Developed | Western Europe | 8 out of 19 |
| France | 1.7 | 1.5 | AA | 22 | Developed | Western Europe | 12 out of 19 |
| Gabon | 8.9 | 9.4 | | 83 | | Africa | 7 out of 51 |
| Gambia | 14.6 | 14.8 | | 138 | | Africa | 34 out of 51 |
| Georgia | 7.7 | 8.1 | BB- | 74 | | Central and Eastern Europe | 15 out of 25 |
| Germany | 0.0 | 0.0 | AAA | 10 | Developed | Western Europe | 7 out of 19 |
| Ghana | 10.5 | 10.3 | B- | 89 | | Africa | 9 out of 51 |
| Greece | 11.6 | 11.5 | B- | 108 | Emerging | Western Europe | 19 out of 19 |
| Grenada | 11.2 | 11.5 | | 105 | | Caribbean | 7 out of 9 |
| Guatemala | 9.2 | 9.5 | BB | 84 | | Latin America | 11 out of 20 |
| Guinea | 18.0 | 18.4 | | 156 | | Africa | 41 out of 51 |
| Guinea-Bissau | 12.0 | 12.2 | | 115 | | Africa | 22 out of 51 |
| Guyana | 10.9 | 11.1 | | 100 | | Latin America | 15 out of 20 |
| Haiti | 20.7 | 19.1 | | 157 | | Caribbean | 8 out of 9 |
| Honduras | 10.6 | 10.8 | B+ | 98 | | Latin America | 14 out of 20 |
| Hong Kong | 0.0 | 0.0 | AAA | 14 | Developed | Asia | 2 out of 29 |
| Hungary | 5.4 | 5.6 | BBB- | 57 | Emerging | Central and Eastern Europe | 10 out of 25 |
| Iceland | 2.6 | 2.4 | A | 30 | | Western Europe | 15 out of 19 |
| India | 5.2 | 5.6 | BBB- | 55 | Emerging | Asia | 10 out of 29 |
| Indonesia | 5.9 | 6.0 | BB+ | 62 | Emerging | Asia | 11 out of 29 |
| Iran | 12.5 | 12.9 | | 125 | | Middle East | 10 out of 13 |
| Iraq | 14.2 | 14.5 | B- | 136 | | Middle East | 11 out of 13 |
| Ireland | 2.1 | 2.1 | A+ | 27 | Developed | Western Europe | 14 out of 19 |
| Israel | 2.1 | 2.1 | A+ | 28 | Developed | Middle East | 2 out of 13 |
| Italy | 4.8 | 4.8 | BBB- | 50 | Developed | Western Europe | 18 out of 19 |
| Jamaica | 10.6 | 11.4 | B | 104 | | Caribbean | 6 out of 9 |
| Japan | 2.0 | 2.0 | A+ | 25 | Developed | Asia | 5 out of 29 |
| Jordan | 7.9 | 8.2 | BB- | 76 | Frontier | Middle East | 8 out of 13 |
| Kazakhstan | 7.4 | 7.2 | BBB- | 70 | Frontier | Asia | 13 out of 29 |
| Kenya | 10.7 | 10.9 | B+ | 99 | Frontier | Africa | 15 out of 51 |
| Korea (North) | 31.7 | 31.8 | | 174 | | Asia | 29 out of 29 |
| Korea (South) | 1.2 | 1.3 | AA | 19 | Emerging | Asia | 4 out of 29 |
| Kuwait | 2.3 | 2.5 | AA | 31 | Frontier | Middle East | 3 out of 13 |
| Kyrgyz Republic | 15.5 | 15.7 | | 142 | | Central and Eastern Europe | 22 out of 25 |
| Laos | 19.6 | 19.4 | | 158 | | Asia | 28 out of 29 |
| Latvia | 4.2 | 4.4 | A- | 43 | | Central and Eastern Europe | 8 out of 25 |
| Lebanon | 12.3 | 11.9 | B- | 112 | Frontier | Middle East | 9 out of 13 |
| Lesotho | 15.7 | 16.0 | | 146 | | Africa | 36 out of 51 |
| Liberia | 11.3 | 11.5 | | 107 | | Africa | 17 out of 51 |
| Libya | 17.2 | 17.8 | | 153 | | Africa | 39 out of 51 |
| Lithuania | 3.4 | 3.6 | A- | 36 | Frontier | Central and Eastern Europe | 6 out of 25 |
| Luxembourg | 0.0 | 0.0 | AAA | 5 | | Western Europe | 4 out of 19 |
| Macedonia | 9.8 | 10.2 | BB- | 87 | | Central and Eastern Europe | 17 out of 25 |
| Madagascar | 12.1 | 12.8 | | 123 | | Africa | 27 out of 51 |
| Malawi | 11.8 | 12.1 | | 114 | | Africa | 21 out of 51 |
| Malaysia | 3.6 | 3.5 | A- | 35 | Emerging | Asia | 6 out of 29 |

§ S&P Credit Rating based on long-term foreign currency issuer rating. See http://www.standardandpoors.com/.

* World rank based on 175 countries covered by Euromoney. Ranking based on ascending order in which '1' equals the smallest country risk premium (CRP) and '175' equals the largest country risk premium (CRP).

† MSCI Market Classification based on MSCI Market Classification Framework. See http://www.msci.com/products/indexes/market_classification.html

‡ Regional classification based on Euromoney. Regional rankings based on ascending order in which '1' equals the smallest country risk premium (CRP) for each region.

Note: A CRP of 0.0% is assumed in the following cases: (i) when the investor country and the investee country both have an S&P sovereign credit rating of AAA; or (ii) when the investor country has an S&P credit rating of AAA, and the investee country has a sovereign credit rating below AAA, but has a calculated CRP below 0.0% (which would imply lower risk than a country rated AAA); or (iii) when the investor country has an S&P credit rating below AAA, and the investee country has a sovereign credit rating of AAA, but has a calculated CRP above 0.0% (which would imply greater risk than a country rated below AAA). For purposes of this analysis, the U.S. is treated as having a sovereign credit rating equivalent to AAA.

The country risk premium (CRP) is not the cost of equity capital (COE).  The CRP is to be added to base COE. See Chapter 6 for proper application.

### Data Updated Through March 2017

| Investee Country | December 2016 Country Risk Premium (CRP) (%) | March 2017 Country Risk Premium (CRP) (%) | S&P Sovereign Credit Rating § | World Rank Out of 175∗ | MSCI Market Classification † | Euromoney Region ‡ | Regional Rank ‡ |
|---|---|---|---|---|---|---|---|
| Mali | 15.4 | 15.6 | | 141 | | Africa | 35 out of 51 |
| Malta | 2.0 | 2.1 | A- | 26 | | Western Europe | 13 out of 19 |
| Mauritania | 19.2 | 19.5 | | 159 | | Africa | 42 out of 51 |
| Mauritius | 6.8 | 6.9 | | 67 | Frontier | Asia | 12 out of 29 |
| Mexico | 3.5 | 3.6 | BBB+ | 37 | Emerging | Latin America | 2 out of 20 |
| Moldova | 13.9 | 14.5 | | 137 | | Central and Eastern Europe | 21 out of 25 |
| Mongolia | 12.2 | 12.7 | B- | 119 | | Asia | 18 out of 29 |
| Montenegro | 11.4 | 11.4 | B+ | 103 | | Central and Eastern Europe | 19 out of 25 |
| Morocco | 6.8 | 7.1 | BBB- | 69 | Frontier | Africa | 4 out of 51 |
| Mozambique | 13.2 | 13.3 | SD | 128 | | Africa | 29 out of 51 |
| Myanmar | 14.1 | 14.2 | | 134 | | Asia | 22 out of 29 |
| Namibia | 6.5 | 6.7 | | 66 | | Africa | 3 out of 51 |
| Nepal | 16.6 | 16.9 | | 149 | | Asia | 26 out of 29 |
| Netherlands | 0.0 | 0.0 | AAA | 6 | Developed | Western Europe | 5 out of 19 |
| New Zealand | 0.0 | 0.0 | AA | 8 | Developed | Australasia | 1 out of 7 |
| Nicaragua | 12.9 | 13.1 | B+ | 127 | | Latin America | 19 out of 20 |
| Niger | 12.5 | 12.7 | | 120 | | Africa | 25 out of 51 |
| Nigeria | 10.6 | 10.8 | B | 97 | Frontier | Africa | 14 out of 51 |
| Norway | 0.0 | 0.0 | AAA | 3 | Developed | Western Europe | 2 out of 19 |
| Oman | 4.3 | 4.4 | BBB- | 46 | Frontier | Middle East | 5 out of 13 |
| Pakistan | 12.6 | 12.8 | B | 122 | Frontier | Asia | 19 out of 29 |
| Panama | 5.0 | 5.1 | BBB | 52 | | Latin America | 6 out of 20 |
| Papua New Guinea | 12.1 | 12.4 | B+ | 118 | | Australasia | 3 out of 7 |
| Paraguay | 8.3 | 8.6 | BB | 80 | | Latin America | 9 out of 20 |
| Peru | 3.7 | 4.0 | BBB+ | 39 | Emerging | Latin America | 3 out of 20 |
| Philippines | 5.3 | 5.4 | BBB | 53 | Emerging | Asia | 9 out of 29 |
| Poland | 2.4 | 2.4 | BBB+ | 29 | Emerging | Central and Eastern Europe | 3 out of 25 |
| Portugal | 4.7 | 4.6 | BB+ | 49 | Developed | Western Europe | 17 out of 19 |
| Qatar | 1.4 | 1.5 | AA | 21 | Emerging | Middle East | 1 out of 13 |
| Romania | 5.4 | 5.6 | BBB- | 56 | Frontier | Central and Eastern Europe | 9 out of 25 |
| Russia | 7.6 | 7.1 | BB+ | 68 | Emerging | Central and Eastern Europe | 14 out of 25 |
| Rwanda | 13.2 | 13.5 | B | 130 | | Africa | 31 out of 51 |
| São Tomé & Príncipe | 19.3 | 20.1 | | 163 | | Africa | 43 out of 51 |
| Saudi Arabia | 4.6 | 4.4 | A- | 47 | | Middle East | 6 out of 13 |
| Senegal | 10.0 | 10.2 | B+ | 86 | | Africa | 8 out of 51 |
| Serbia | 8.2 | 8.1 | BB- | 75 | Frontier | Central and Eastern Europe | 16 out of 25 |
| Seychelles | 7.7 | 7.9 | | 73 | | Africa | 5 out of 51 |
| Sierra Leone | 13.2 | 13.5 | | 129 | | Africa | 30 out of 51 |
| Singapore | 0.0 | 0.0 | AAA | 1 | Developed | Asia | 1 out of 29 |
| Slovakia | 1.7 | 1.8 | A+ | 24 | | Central and Eastern Europe | 2 out of 25 |
| Slovenia | 3.1 | 3.2 | A | 34 | Frontier | Central and Eastern Europe | 5 out of 25 |
| Solomon Islands | 23.4 | 23.8 | | 168 | | Australasia | 6 out of 7 |
| Somalia | 21.8 | 22.2 | | 166 | | Africa | 46 out of 51 |
| South Africa | 5.5 | 5.8 | BBB- | 60 | Emerging | Africa | 2 out of 51 |
| Spain | 3.8 | 3.9 | BBB+ | 38 | Developed | Western Europe | 16 out of 19 |
| Sri Lanka | 7.6 | 7.5 | B+ | 72 | Frontier | Asia | 14 out of 29 |
| Sudan | 18.0 | 18.2 | | 154 | | Africa | 40 out of 51 |
| Suriname | 10.9 | 11.2 | B+ | 102 | | Latin America | 16 out of 20 |
| Swaziland | 16.4 | 17.6 | | 152 | | Africa | 38 out of 51 |
| Sweden | 0.0 | 0.0 | AAA | 7 | Developed | Western Europe | 6 out of 19 |

§ S&P Credit Rating based on long-term foreign currency issuer rating. See http://www.standardandpoors.com/.

∗ World rank based on 175 countries covered by Euromoney. Ranking based on ascending order in which '1' equals the smallest country risk premium (CRP) and '175' equals the largest country risk premium (CRP).

† MSCI Market Classification based on MSCI Market Classification Framework.  See http://www.msci.com/products/indexes/market_classification.html.

‡ Regional classification based on Euromoney. Regional rankings based on ascending order in which '1' equals the smallest country risk premium (CRP) for each region.

Note: A CRP of 0.0% is assumed in the following cases: (i) when the investor country and the investee country both have an S&P sovereign credit rating of AAA; or (ii) when the investor country has an S&P credit rating of AAA, and the investee country has a sovereign credit rating below AAA, but has a calculated CRP below 0.0% (which would imply lower risk than a country rated AAA); or (iii) when the investor country has an S&P credit rating below AAA, and the investee country has a sovereign credit rating of AAA, but has a calculated CRP above 0.0% (which would imply greater risk than a country rated below AAA). For purposes of this analysis, the U.S. is treated as having a sovereign credit rating equivalent to AAA.

The country risk premium (CRP) is not the cost of equity capital (COE). The CRP is to be added to base COE. See Chapter 6 for proper application.

## Data Updated Through March 2017

| Investee Country | December 2016 Country Risk Premium (CRP) (%) | March 2017 Country Risk Premium (CRP) (%) | S&P Sovereign Credit Rating § | World Rank Out of 175∗ | MSCI Market Classification † | Euromoney Region ‡ | Regional Rank ‡ |
|---|---|---|---|---|---|---|---|
| Switzerland | 0.0 | 0.0 | AAA | 2 | Developed | Western Europe | 1 out of 19 |
| Syria | 22.5 | 23.1 | | 167 | | Middle East | 13 out of 13 |
| Taiwan | 1.0 | 1.0 | AA- | 18 | Emerging | Asia | 3 out of 29 |
| Tajikistan | 17.6 | 18.2 | | 155 | | Central and Eastern Europe | 25 out of 25 |
| Tanzania | 10.3 | 10.7 | | 95 | | Africa | 13 out of 51 |
| Thailand | 5.0 | 4.9 | BBB+ | 51 | Emerging | Asia | 8 out of 29 |
| Togo | 11.8 | 12.0 | | 113 | | Africa | 20 out of 51 |
| Tonga | 25.7 | 26.2 | | 170 | | Australasia | 7 out of 7 |
| Trinidad & Tobago | 5.3 | 5.4 | A- | 54 | | Caribbean | 2 out of 9 |
| Tunisia | 8.0 | 8.5 | | 79 | Frontier | Africa | 6 out of 51 |
| Turkey | 5.6 | 5.7 | BB | 58 | Emerging | Central and Eastern Europe | 11 out of 25 |
| Turkmenistan | 14.9 | 15.5 | | 140 | | Asia | 24 out of 29 |
| Uganda | 11.3 | 11.8 | B | 110 | | Africa | 18 out of 51 |
| Ukraine | 14.0 | 14.3 | B- | 135 | | Central and Eastern Europe | 20 out of 25 |
| United Arab Emirates | 2.7 | 2.8 | AA | 33 | Emerging | Middle East | 4 out of 13 |
| United Kingdom | 1.3 | 1.4 | AA | 20 | Developed | Western Europe | 11 out of 19 |
| United States | 0.0 | 0.0 | AA+ | 15 | Developed | North America | 2 out of 2 |
| Uruguay | 4.4 | 4.4 | BBB | 45 | | Latin America | 5 out of 20 |
| Uzbekistan | 14.2 | 13.9 | | 132 | | Asia | 21 out of 29 |
| Vanuatu | 15.7 | 16.0 | | 145 | | Australasia | 4 out of 7 |
| Venezuela | 19.3 | 20.1 | CCC | 162 | | Latin America | 20 out of 20 |
| Vietnam | 8.5 | 8.4 | BB- | 78 | Frontier | Asia | 16 out of 29 |
| Yemen | 19.6 | 20.0 | | 161 | | Middle East | 12 out of 13 |
| Zambia | 11.7 | 11.9 | B | 111 | | Africa | 19 out of 51 |
| Zimbabwe | 21.1 | 21.4 | | 164 | | Africa | 44 out of 51 |

## March 2017 Country Risk Premium (CRP) Summary Statistics:

| S&P Rating | Country Count | Average CRP (%) | Median CRP (%) | Min CRP (%) | Max CRP (%) |
|---|---|---|---|---|---|
| AAA ∗∗ | 12 | 0.0 | 0.0 | 0.0 | 0.0 |
| AA (AA+, AA, AA-) | 15 | 1.5 | 1.4 | 0.0 | 4.2 |
| A (A+, A, A-) | 14 | 3.3 | 3.3 | 1.8 | 5.4 |
| BBB (BBB+, BBB, BBB-) | 17 | 4.9 | 4.9 | 2.4 | 7.2 |
| BB (BB+, BB, BB-) | 22 | 7.7 | 7.7 | 4.0 | 13.0 |
| B+ – SD | 39 | 12.3 | 11.9 | 7.5 | 20.1 |
| Investment Grade ∗∗ | 58 | 2.6 | 2.4 | 0.0 | 7.2 |
| Non-Investment Grade ∗∗ | 61 | 10.6 | 10.8 | 4.0 | 20.1 |
| **MSCI Market Classification** | | | | | |
| Developed Markets | 23 | 1.0 | 0.0 | 0.0 | 4.8 |
| Emerging Markets | 23 | 4.6 | 4.2 | 0.7 | 12.2 |
| Frontier Markets | 22 | 7.6 | 7.4 | 2.5 | 13.0 |
| **Euromoney Region ‡** | | | | | |
| Africa | 51 | 14.7 | 12.8 | 4.4 | 34.3 |
| Asia | 29 | 9.7 | 8.3 | 0.0 | 31.8 |
| Australasia | 7 | 13.5 | 16.0 | 0.0 | 26.2 |
| Caribbean | 9 | 10.9 | 10.4 | 4.4 | 19.8 |
| Central and Eastern Europe | 25 | 8.1 | 6.1 | 1.7 | 18.2 |
| Latin America | 20 | 8.6 | 9.3 | 0.7 | 20.1 |
| Middle East | 13 | 8.8 | 6.4 | 1.5 | 23.1 |
| North America | 2 | 0.0 | 0.0 | 0.0 | 0.0 |
| Western Europe | 19 | 1.9 | 0.8 | 0.0 | 11.5 |

## CCR Base Cost of Equity Capital:

| Hong Kong | COE (%) |
|---|---|
| March 2017 | 8.1 |
| December 2016 | 8.1 |

CCR base country-level COE for a Hong Kong-based investor investing in Hong Kong.

§ S&P Credit Rating based on long-term foreign currency issuer rating. See http://www.standardandpoors.com/.

∗ World rank based on 175 countries covered by Euromoney. Ranking based on ascending order in which '1' equals the smallest country risk premium (CRP) and '175' equals the largest country risk premium (CRP).

† MSCI Market Classification based on MSCI Market Classification Framework. See http://www.msci.com/products/indexes/market_classification.html

‡ Regional classification based on Euromoney. Regional rankings based on ascending order in which '1' equals the smallest country risk premium (CRP) for each region.

∗∗ Investment grade based on S&P sovereign credit rating from AAA to BBB-. Non-Investment grade based on S&P sovereign credit rating from BB+ to SD. For purposes of this analysis, the U.S. is being treated as if it were rated AAA by S&P.

Note: A CRP of 0.0% is assumed in the following cases: (i) when the investor country and the investee country both have an S&P sovereign credit rating of AAA; or (ii) when the investor country has an S&P credit rating of AAA, and the investee country has a sovereign credit rating below AAA, but has a calculated CRP below 0.0% (which would imply lower risk than a country rated AAA); or (iii) when the investor country has an S&P credit rating below AAA, and the investee country has a sovereign credit rating of AAA, but has a calculated CRP above 0.0% (which would imply greater risk than a country rated below AAA). For purposes of this analysis, the U.S. is treated as having a sovereign credit rating equivalent to AAA.

The country risk premium (CRP) is not the cost of equity capital (COE). The CRP is to be added to base COE. See Chapter 6 for proper application.

## Data Updated Through March 2017

| Investee Country | December 2016 Country Risk Premium (CRP) (%) | March 2017 Country Risk Premium (CRP) (%) | S&P Sovereign Credit Rating § | World Rank Out of 175∗ | MSCI Market Classification † | Euromoney Region ‡ | Regional Rank ‡ |
|---|---|---|---|---|---|---|---|
| Afghanistan | 10.7 | 10.2 | | 139 | | Asia | 23 out of 29 |
| Albania | 5.2 | 5.1 | B+ | 93 | | Central and Eastern Europe | 18 out of 25 |
| Algeria | 5.2 | 5.1 | | 91 | | Africa | 10 out of 51 |
| Angola | 7.6 | 7.4 | B | 121 | | Africa | 26 out of 51 |
| Argentina | 5.8 | 5.3 | B- | 96 | Frontier | Latin America | 13 out of 20 |
| Armenia | 2.7 | 2.8 | | 77 | | Asia | 15 out of 29 |
| Australia | -6.3 | -6.5 | AAA | 12 | Developed | Australasia | 2 out of 7 |
| Austria | -6.1 | -6.2 | AA+ | 13 | Developed | Western Europe | 9 out of 19 |
| Azerbaijan | 4.0 | 4.1 | BB+ | 85 | | Asia | 17 out of 29 |
| Bahamas | 1.3 | 0.8 | BB+ | 65 | | Caribbean | 3 out of 9 |
| Bahrain | 1.2 | 0.8 | BB- | 64 | Frontier | Middle East | 7 out of 13 |
| Bangladesh | 8.1 | 7.7 | BB- | 126 | Frontier | Asia | 20 out of 29 |
| Barbados | 2.9 | 3.8 | CCC+ | 82 | | Caribbean | 4 out of 9 |
| Belarus | 10.3 | 10.5 | B- | 143 | | Central and Eastern Europe | 23 out of 25 |
| Belgium | -4.9 | -5.0 | AA | 17 | Developed | Western Europe | 10 out of 19 |
| Belize | 6.2 | 6.1 | B- | 106 | | Latin America | 17 out of 20 |
| Benin | 12.1 | 11.8 | | 150 | | Africa | 37 out of 51 |
| Bermuda | -1.1 | -1.4 | A+ | 44 | | Caribbean | 1 out of 9 |
| Bhutan | 11.7 | 11.3 | | 148 | | Asia | 25 out of 29 |
| Bolivia | 4.7 | 4.8 | BB | 88 | | Latin America | 12 out of 20 |
| Bosnia & Herzegovina | 10.8 | 10.7 | B | 144 | | Central and Eastern Europe | 24 out of 25 |
| Botswana | -1.1 | -1.3 | A- | 48 | | Africa | 1 out of 51 |
| Brazil | 0.4 | 0.1 | BB | 59 | Emerging | Latin America | 7 out of 20 |
| Bulgaria | 0.2 | 0.3 | BB+ | 61 | | Central and Eastern Europe | 12 out of 25 |
| Burkina Faso | 9.2 | 8.9 | B- | 133 | | Africa | 33 out of 51 |
| Burundi | 21.2 | 20.8 | | 169 | | Africa | 47 out of 51 |
| Cambodia | 12.6 | 12.0 | | 151 | | Asia | 27 out of 29 |
| Cameroon | 7.8 | 7.6 | B | 124 | | Africa | 28 out of 51 |
| Canada | -6.5 | -6.7 | AAA | 9 | Developed | North America | 1 out of 2 |
| Cape Verde | 5.4 | 5.2 | B | 94 | | Africa | 12 out of 51 |
| Central African Republic | 24.7 | 24.4 | | 172 | | Africa | 49 out of 51 |
| Chad | 23.4 | 23.1 | | 171 | | Africa | 48 out of 51 |
| Chile | -5.3 | -5.2 | AA- | 16 | Emerging | Latin America | 1 out of 20 |
| China | -1.3 | -1.5 | AA- | 42 | Emerging | Asia | 7 out of 29 |
| Colombia | -1.4 | -1.5 | BBB | 41 | Emerging | Latin America | 4 out of 20 |
| Congo Republic | 7.4 | 7.0 | B- | 117 | | Africa | 24 out of 51 |
| Congo, DR | 8.7 | 8.4 | B- | 131 | | Africa | 32 out of 51 |
| Costa Rica | 1.7 | 1.8 | BB- | 71 | | Latin America | 8 out of 20 |
| Côte d'Ivoire | 5.2 | 5.1 | | 92 | | Africa | 11 out of 51 |
| Croatia | 0.8 | 0.5 | BB | 63 | Frontier | Central and Eastern Europe | 13 out of 25 |
| Cuba | 15.0 | 14.8 | | 160 | | Caribbean | 9 out of 9 |
| Cyprus | -1.6 | -1.7 | BB+ | 40 | | Central and Eastern Europe | 7 out of 25 |
| Czech Republic | -4.1 | -4.2 | AA- | 23 | Emerging | Central and Eastern Europe | 1 out of 25 |
| Denmark | -7.2 | -7.3 | AAA | 4 | Developed | Western Europe | 3 out of 19 |
| Djibouti | 32.8 | 30.0 | | 175 | | Africa | 51 out of 51 |
| Dominican Republic | 5.1 | 5.0 | BB- | 90 | | Caribbean | 5 out of 9 |
| Ecuador | 6.7 | 6.3 | B | 109 | | Latin America | 18 out of 20 |
| Egypt | 7.1 | 6.9 | B- | 116 | Emerging | Africa | 23 out of 51 |
| El Salvador | 4.1 | 3.7 | B- | 81 | | Latin America | 10 out of 20 |
| Equatorial Guinea | 17.5 | 17.2 | | 165 | | Africa | 45 out of 51 |

§ S&P Credit Rating based on long-term foreign currency issuer rating. See http://www.standardandpoors.com/.

∗ World rank based on 175 countries covered by Euromoney. Ranking based on ascending order in which '1' equals the smallest country risk premium (CRP) and '175' equals the largest country risk premium (CRP).

† MSCI Market Classification based on MSCI Market Classification Framework. See http://www.msci.com/products/indexes/market_classification.html.

‡ Regional classification based on Euromoney. Regional rankings based on ascending order in which '1' equals the smallest country risk premium (CRP) for each region.

Note: A CRP of 0.0% is assumed in the following cases: (i) when the investor country and the investee country both have an S&P sovereign credit rating of AAA; or (ii) when the investor country has an S&P credit rating of AAA, and the investee country has a sovereign credit rating below AAA, but has a calculated CRP below 0.0% (which would imply lower risk than a country rated AAA); or (iii) when the investor country has an S&P credit rating below AAA, and the investee country has a sovereign credit rating of AAA, but has a calculated CRP above 0.0% (which would imply greater risk than a country rated below AAA). For purposes of this analysis, the U.S. is treated as having a sovereign credit rating equivalent to AAA.

The country risk premium (CRP) is not the cost of equity capital (COE). The CRP is to be added to base COE. See Chapter 6 for proper application.

## Data Updated Through March 2017

| Investee Country | December 2016 Country Risk Premium (CRP) (%) | March 2017 Country Risk Premium (CRP) (%) | S&P Sovereign Credit Rating § | World Rank Out of 175* | MSCI Market Classification † | Euromoney Region ‡ | Regional Rank ‡ |
|---|---|---|---|---|---|---|---|
| Eritrea | 29.0 | 26.7 | | 173 | | Africa | 50 out of 51 |
| Estonia | -3.4 | -3.3 | AA- | 32 | Frontier | Central and Eastern Europe | 4 out of 25 |
| Ethiopia | 5.9 | 5.8 | B | 101 | | Africa | 16 out of 51 |
| Fiji | 11.4 | 11.0 | B+ | 147 | | Australasia | 5 out of 7 |
| Finland | -6.4 | -6.5 | AA+ | 11 | Developed | Western Europe | 8 out of 19 |
| France | -4.0 | -4.3 | AA | 22 | Developed | Western Europe | 12 out of 19 |
| Gabon | 3.7 | 3.9 | | 83 | | Africa | 7 out of 51 |
| Gambia | 9.8 | 9.6 | | 138 | | Africa | 34 out of 51 |
| Georgia | 2.4 | 2.5 | BB- | 74 | | Central and Eastern Europe | 15 out of 25 |
| Germany | -6.4 | -6.5 | AAA | 10 | Developed | Western Europe | 7 out of 19 |
| Ghana | 5.5 | 4.9 | B- | 89 | | Africa | 9 out of 51 |
| Greece | 6.6 | 6.2 | B- | 108 | Emerging | Western Europe | 19 out of 19 |
| Grenada | 6.2 | 6.1 | | 105 | | Caribbean | 7 out of 9 |
| Guatemala | 4.1 | 4.0 | BB | 84 | | Latin America | 11 out of 20 |
| Guinea | 13.6 | 13.3 | | 156 | | Africa | 41 out of 51 |
| Guinea-Bissau | 7.1 | 6.9 | | 115 | | Africa | 22 out of 51 |
| Guyana | 5.9 | 5.7 | | 100 | | Latin America | 15 out of 20 |
| Haiti | 16.5 | 14.1 | | 157 | | Caribbean | 8 out of 9 |
| Honduras | 5.6 | 5.4 | B+ | 98 | | Latin America | 14 out of 20 |
| Hong Kong | -5.8 | -5.9 | AAA | 14 | Developed | Asia | 2 out of 29 |
| Hungary | 0.0 | 0.0 | BBB- | 57 | Emerging | Central and Eastern Europe | 10 out of 25 |
| Iceland | -3.0 | -3.4 | A | 30 | | Western Europe | 15 out of 19 |
| India | -0.2 | -0.1 | BBB- | 55 | Emerging | Asia | 10 out of 29 |
| Indonesia | 0.5 | 0.4 | BB+ | 62 | Emerging | Asia | 11 out of 29 |
| Iran | 7.6 | 7.6 | | 125 | | Middle East | 10 out of 13 |
| Iraq | 9.4 | 9.2 | B- | 136 | | Middle East | 11 out of 13 |
| Ireland | -3.5 | -3.7 | A+ | 27 | Developed | Western Europe | 14 out of 19 |
| Israel | -3.6 | -3.7 | A+ | 28 | Developed | Middle East | 2 out of 13 |
| Italy | -0.6 | -0.9 | BBB- | 50 | Developed | Western Europe | 18 out of 19 |
| Jamaica | 5.6 | 6.0 | B | 104 | | Caribbean | 6 out of 9 |
| Japan | -3.7 | -3.8 | A+ | 25 | Developed | Asia | 5 out of 29 |
| Jordan | 2.7 | 2.7 | BB- | 76 | Frontier | Middle East | 8 out of 13 |
| Kazakhstan | 2.2 | 1.7 | BBB- | 70 | Frontier | Asia | 13 out of 29 |
| Kenya | 5.7 | 5.5 | B+ | 99 | Frontier | Africa | 15 out of 51 |
| Korea (North) | 28.3 | 27.4 | | 174 | | Asia | 29 out of 29 |
| Korea (South) | -4.5 | -4.5 | AA | 19 | Emerging | Asia | 4 out of 29 |
| Kuwait | -3.4 | -3.3 | AA | 31 | Frontier | Middle East | 3 out of 13 |
| Kyrgyz Republic | 10.9 | 10.5 | | 142 | | Central and Eastern Europe | 22 out of 25 |
| Laos | 15.2 | 14.4 | | 158 | | Asia | 28 out of 29 |
| Latvia | -1.3 | -1.4 | A- | 43 | | Central and Eastern Europe | 8 out of 25 |
| Lebanon | 7.4 | 6.6 | B- | 112 | Frontier | Middle East | 9 out of 13 |
| Lesotho | 11.1 | 10.9 | | 146 | | Africa | 36 out of 51 |
| Liberia | 6.3 | 6.1 | | 107 | | Africa | 17 out of 51 |
| Libya | 12.6 | 12.7 | | 153 | | Africa | 39 out of 51 |
| Lithuania | -2.1 | -2.2 | A- | 36 | Frontier | Central and Eastern Europe | 6 out of 25 |
| Luxembourg | -6.8 | -7.0 | AAA | 5 | | Western Europe | 4 out of 19 |
| Macedonia | 4.7 | 4.8 | BB- | 87 | | Central and Eastern Europe | 17 out of 25 |
| Madagascar | 7.2 | 7.5 | | 123 | | Africa | 27 out of 51 |
| Malawi | 6.9 | 6.7 | | 114 | | Africa | 21 out of 51 |
| Malaysia | -2.0 | -2.2 | A- | 35 | Emerging | Asia | 6 out of 29 |

§ S&P Credit Rating based on long-term foreign currency issuer rating. See http://www.standardandpoors.com/.

* World rank based on 175 countries covered by Euromoney. Ranking based on ascending order in which '1' equals the smallest country risk premium (CRP) and '175' equals the largest country risk premium (CRP).

† MSCI Market Classification based on MSCI Market Classification Framework. See http://www.msci.com/products/indexes/market_classification.html.

‡ Regional classification based on Euromoney. Regional rankings based on ascending order in which '1' equals the smallest country risk premium (CRP) for each region.

Note: A CRP of 0.0% is assumed in the following cases: (i) when the investor country and the investee country both have an S&P sovereign credit rating of AAA; or (ii) when the investor country has an S&P credit rating of AAA, and the investee country has a sovereign credit rating below AAA, but has a calculated CRP below 0.0% (which would imply lower risk than a country rated AAA); or (iii) when the investor country has an S&P credit rating below AAA, and the investee country has a sovereign credit rating of AAA, but has a calculated CRP above 0.0% (which would imply greater risk than a country rated below AAA). For purposes of this analysis, the U.S. is treated as having a sovereign credit rating equivalent to AAA.

The country risk premium (CRP) is not the cost of equity capital (COE). The CRP is to be added to base COE. See Chapter 6 for proper application.

## Data Updated Through March 2017

| Investee Country | December 2016 Country Risk Premium (CRP) (%) | March 2017 Country Risk Premium (CRP) (%) | S&P Sovereign Credit Rating § | World Rank Out of 175* | MSCI Market Classification † | Euromoney Region ‡ | Regional Rank ‡ |
|---|---|---|---|---|---|---|---|
| Mali | 10.7 | 10.5 | | 141 | | Africa | 35 out of 51 |
| Malta | -3.7 | -3.7 | A- | 26 | | Western Europe | 13 out of 19 |
| Mauritania | 14.8 | 14.5 | | 159 | | Africa | 42 out of 51 |
| Mauritius | 1.5 | 1.3 | | 67 | Frontier | Asia | 12 out of 29 |
| Mexico | -2.1 | -2.1 | BBB+ | 37 | Emerging | Latin America | 2 out of 20 |
| Moldova | 9.1 | 9.3 | | 137 | | Central and Eastern Europe | 21 out of 25 |
| Mongolia | 7.3 | 7.4 | B- | 119 | | Asia | 18 out of 29 |
| Montenegro | 6.4 | 6.0 | B+ | 103 | | Central and Eastern Europe | 19 out of 25 |
| Morocco | 1.5 | 1.6 | BBB- | 69 | Frontier | Africa | 4 out of 51 |
| Mozambique | 8.3 | 8.0 | SD | 128 | | Africa | 29 out of 51 |
| Myanmar | 9.3 | 9.0 | | 134 | | Asia | 22 out of 29 |
| Namibia | 1.1 | 1.2 | | 66 | | Africa | 3 out of 51 |
| Nepal | 12.0 | 11.8 | | 149 | | Asia | 26 out of 29 |
| Netherlands | -6.8 | -6.9 | AAA | 6 | Developed | Western Europe | 5 out of 19 |
| New Zealand | -6.7 | -6.7 | AA | 8 | Developed | Australasia | 1 out of 7 |
| Nicaragua | 8.0 | 7.8 | B+ | 127 | | Latin America | 19 out of 20 |
| Niger | 7.6 | 7.4 | | 120 | | Africa | 25 out of 51 |
| Nigeria | 5.6 | 5.4 | B | 97 | Frontier | Africa | 14 out of 51 |
| Norway | -7.5 | -7.6 | AAA | 3 | Developed | Western Europe | 2 out of 19 |
| Oman | -1.2 | -1.3 | BBB- | 46 | Frontier | Middle East | 5 out of 13 |
| Pakistan | 7.7 | 7.4 | B | 122 | Frontier | Asia | 19 out of 29 |
| Panama | -0.5 | -0.6 | BBB | 52 | | Latin America | 6 out of 20 |
| Papua New Guinea | 7.2 | 7.1 | B+ | 118 | | Australasia | 3 out of 7 |
| Paraguay | 3.1 | 3.1 | BB | 80 | | Latin America | 9 out of 20 |
| Peru | -1.8 | -1.8 | BBB+ | 39 | Emerging | Latin America | 3 out of 20 |
| Philippines | -0.1 | -0.3 | BBB | 53 | Emerging | Asia | 9 out of 29 |
| Poland | -3.2 | -3.4 | BBB+ | 29 | Emerging | Central and Eastern Europe | 3 out of 25 |
| Portugal | -0.8 | -1.1 | BB+ | 49 | Developed | Western Europe | 17 out of 19 |
| Qatar | -4.3 | -4.4 | AA | 21 | Emerging | Middle East | 1 out of 13 |
| Romania | 0.0 | -0.1 | BBB- | 56 | Frontier | Central and Eastern Europe | 9 out of 25 |
| Russia | 2.3 | 1.5 | BB+ | 68 | Emerging | Central and Eastern Europe | 14 out of 25 |
| Rwanda | 8.4 | 8.2 | B | 130 | | Africa | 31 out of 51 |
| São Tomé & Príncipe | 14.9 | 15.1 | | 163 | | Africa | 43 out of 51 |
| Saudi Arabia | -0.8 | -1.3 | A- | 47 | | Middle East | 6 out of 13 |
| Senegal | 4.9 | 4.7 | B+ | 86 | | Africa | 8 out of 51 |
| Serbia | 3.0 | 2.5 | BB- | 75 | Frontier | Central and Eastern Europe | 16 out of 25 |
| Seychelles | 2.5 | 2.3 | | 73 | | Africa | 5 out of 51 |
| Sierra Leone | 8.4 | 8.2 | | 129 | | Africa | 30 out of 51 |
| Singapore | -7.7 | -7.7 | AAA | 1 | Developed | Asia | 1 out of 29 |
| Slovakia | -3.9 | -4.0 | A+ | 24 | | Central and Eastern Europe | 2 out of 25 |
| Slovenia | -2.5 | -2.6 | A | 34 | Frontier | Central and Eastern Europe | 5 out of 25 |
| Solomon Islands | 19.3 | 19.0 | | 168 | | Australasia | 6 out of 7 |
| Somalia | 17.6 | 17.3 | | 166 | | Africa | 46 out of 51 |
| South Africa | 0.1 | 0.2 | BBB- | 60 | Emerging | Africa | 2 out of 51 |
| Spain | -1.7 | -1.8 | BBB+ | 38 | Developed | Western Europe | 16 out of 19 |
| Sri Lanka | 2.4 | 1.9 | B+ | 72 | Frontier | Asia | 14 out of 29 |
| Sudan | 13.5 | 13.2 | | 154 | | Africa | 40 out of 51 |
| Suriname | 5.9 | 5.8 | B+ | 102 | | Latin America | 16 out of 20 |
| Swaziland | 11.8 | 12.5 | | 152 | | Africa | 38 out of 51 |
| Sweden | -6.7 | -6.9 | AAA | 7 | Developed | Western Europe | 6 out of 19 |

§ S&P Credit Rating based on long-term foreign currency issuer rating. See http://www.standardandpoors.com/.

* World rank based on 175 countries covered by Euromoney. Ranking based on ascending order in which '1' equals the smallest country risk premium (CRP) and '175' equals the largest country risk premium (CRP).

† MSCI Market Classification based on MSCI Market Classification Framework. See http://www.msci.com/products/indexes/market_classification.html.

‡ Regional classification based on Euromoney. Regional rankings based on ascending order in which '1' equals the smallest country risk premium (CRP) for each region.

Note: A CRP of 0.0% is assumed in the following cases: (i) when the investor country and the investee country both have an S&P sovereign credit rating of AAA; or (ii) when the investor country has an S&P sovereign credit rating of AAA, and the investee country has a sovereign credit rating below AAA, but has a calculated CRP below 0.0% (which would imply lower risk than a country rated AAA); or (iii) when the investor country has an S&P credit rating below AAA, and the investee country has a sovereign credit rating of AAA, but has a calculated CRP above 0.0% (which would imply greater risk than a country rated below AAA). For purposes of this analysis, the U.S. is treated as having a sovereign credit rating equivalent to AAA.

The country risk premium (CRP) is not the cost of equity capital (COE). The CRP is to be added to base COE. See Chapter 6 for proper application.

## Data Updated Through March 2017

| Investee Country | December 2016 Country Risk Premium (CRP) (%) | March 2017 Country Risk Premium (CRP) (%) | S&P Sovereign Credit Rating § | World Rank Out of 175* | MSCI Market Classification † | Euromoney Region ‡ | Regional Rank ‡ |
|---|---|---|---|---|---|---|---|
| Switzerland | -7.4 | -7.6 | AAA | 2 | Developed | Western Europe | 1 out of 19 |
| Syria | 18.4 | 18.3 | | 167 | | Middle East | 13 out of 13 |
| Taiwan | -4.7 | -4.8 | AA- | 18 | Emerging | Asia | 3 out of 29 |
| Tajikistan | 13.1 | 13.2 | | 155 | | Central and Eastern Europe | 25 out of 25 |
| Tanzania | 5.2 | 5.3 | | 95 | | Africa | 13 out of 51 |
| Thailand | -0.5 | -0.8 | BBB+ | 51 | Emerging | Asia | 8 out of 29 |
| Togo | 6.9 | 6.7 | | 113 | | Africa | 20 out of 51 |
| Tonga | 21.8 | 21.5 | | 170 | | Australasia | 7 out of 7 |
| Trinidad & Tobago | -0.1 | -0.3 | A- | 54 | | Caribbean | 2 out of 9 |
| Tunisia | 2.8 | 3.0 | | 79 | Frontier | Africa | 6 out of 51 |
| Turkey | 0.3 | 0.0 | BB | 58 | Emerging | Central and Eastern Europe | 11 out of 25 |
| Turkmenistan | 10.2 | 10.3 | | 140 | | Asia | 24 out of 29 |
| Uganda | 6.3 | 6.5 | B | 110 | | Africa | 18 out of 51 |
| Ukraine | 9.2 | 9.1 | B- | 135 | | Central and Eastern Europe | 20 out of 25 |
| United Arab Emirates | -2.9 | -3.0 | AA | 33 | Emerging | Middle East | 4 out of 13 |
| United Kingdom | -4.5 | -4.4 | AA | 20 | Developed | Western Europe | 11 out of 19 |
| United States | -5.5 | -5.6 | AA+ | 15 | Developed | North America | 2 out of 2 |
| Uruguay | -1.1 | -1.3 | BBB | 45 | | Latin America | 5 out of 20 |
| Uzbekistan | 9.4 | 8.6 | | 132 | | Asia | 21 out of 29 |
| Vanuatu | 11.1 | 10.8 | | 145 | | Australasia | 4 out of 7 |
| Venezuela | 14.9 | 15.1 | CCC | 162 | | Latin America | 20 out of 20 |
| Vietnam | 3.4 | 2.9 | BB- | 78 | Frontier | Asia | 16 out of 29 |
| Yemen | 15.2 | 15.0 | | 161 | | Middle East | 12 out of 13 |
| Zambia | 6.7 | 6.5 | B | 111 | | Africa | 19 out of 51 |
| Zimbabwe | 16.9 | 16.5 | | 164 | | Africa | 44 out of 51 |

## March 2017 Country Risk Premium (CRP) Summary Statistics:

| S&P Rating | Country Count | Average CRP (%) | Median CRP (%) | Min CRP (%) | Max CRP (%) |
|---|---|---|---|---|---|
| AAA ** | 12 | -6.9 | -6.9 | -7.7 | -5.6 |
| AA (AA+, AA, AA-) | 15 | -4.5 | -4.4 | -6.7 | -1.5 |
| A (A+, A, A-) | 14 | -2.5 | -2.4 | -4.0 | -0.3 |
| BBB (BBB+, BBB, BBB-) | 17 | -0.7 | -0.8 | -3.4 | 1.7 |
| BB (BB+, BB, BB-) | 22 | 2.2 | 2.1 | -1.7 | 7.7 |
| B+ – SD | 39 | 6.9 | 6.5 | 1.9 | 15.1 |
| Investment Grade ** | 58 | -3.4 | -3.4 | -7.7 | 1.7 |
| Non-Investment Grade ** | 61 | 5.2 | 5.4 | -1.7 | 15.1 |
| **MSCI Market Classification** | | | | | |
| Developed Markets | 23 | -5.4 | -6.2 | -7.7 | -0.9 |
| Emerging Markets | 23 | -1.1 | -1.5 | -5.2 | 6.9 |
| Frontier Markets | 22 | 2.0 | 1.8 | -3.3 | 7.7 |
| **Euromoney Region ‡** | | | | | |
| Africa | 51 | 9.5 | 7.4 | -1.3 | 30.0 |
| Asia | 29 | 4.2 | 2.8 | -7.7 | 27.4 |
| Australasia | 7 | 8.1 | 10.8 | -6.7 | 21.5 |
| Caribbean | 9 | 5.5 | 5.0 | -1.4 | 14.8 |
| Central and Eastern Europe | 25 | 2.6 | 0.5 | -4.2 | 13.2 |
| Latin America | 20 | 3.1 | 3.9 | -5.2 | 15.1 |
| Middle East | 13 | 3.3 | 0.8 | -4.4 | 18.3 |
| North America | 2 | -6.1 | -6.1 | -6.7 | -5.6 |
| Western Europe | 19 | -4.5 | -5.0 | -7.6 | 6.2 |

## CCR Base Cost of Equity Capital:

| Hungary | COE (%) |
|---|---|
| March 2017 | 17.9 |
| December 2016 | 17.7 |

CCR base country-level COE for a Hungary-based investor investing in Hungary.

§ S&P Credit Rating based on long-term foreign currency issuer rating. See http://www.standardandpoors.com/.

• World rank based on 175 countries covered by Euromoney. Ranking based on ascending order in which '1' equals the smallest country risk premium (CRP) and '175' equals the largest country risk premium (CRP).

† MSCI Market Classification based on MSCI Market Classification Framework. See http://www.msci.com/products/indexes/market_classification.html.

‡ Regional classification based on Euromoney. Regional rankings based on ascending order in which '1' equals the smallest country risk premium (CRP) for each region.

** Investment grade based on S&P sovereign credit rating from AAA to BBB-. Non-Investment grade based on S&P sovereign credit rating from BB+ to SD. For purposes of this analysis, the U.S. is being treated as if it were rated AAA by S&P.

Note: A CRP of 0.0% is assumed in the following cases: (i) when the investor country and the investee country both have an S&P sovereign credit rating of AAA; or (ii) when the investor country has an S&P sovereign credit rating of AAA, and the investee country has a sovereign credit rating below AAA, but has a calculated CRP below 0.0% (which would imply lower risk than a country rated AAA); or (iii) when the investor country has an S&P credit rating below AAA, and the investee country has a sovereign credit rating of AAA, but has a calculated CRP above 0.0% (which would imply greater risk than a country rated below AAA). For purposes of this analysis, the U.S. is treated as having a sovereign credit rating equivalent to AAA.

The country risk premium (CRP) is not the cost of equity capital (COE).  The CRP is to be added to base COE. See Chapter 6 for proper application.

## Data Updated Through March 2017

| Investee Country | December 2016 Country Risk Premium (CRP) (%) | March 2017 Country Risk Premium (CRP) (%) | S&P Sovereign Credit Rating § | World Rank Out of 175* | MSCI Market Classification † | Euromoney Region ‡ | Regional Rank ‡ |
|---|---|---|---|---|---|---|---|
| Afghanistan | 11.3 | 11.4 | | 139 | | Asia | 23 out of 29 |
| Albania | 6.8 | 7.2 | B+ | 93 | | Central and Eastern Europe | 18 out of 25 |
| Algeria | 6.8 | 7.1 | | 91 | | Africa | 10 out of 51 |
| Angola | 8.8 | 9.2 | B | 121 | | Africa | 26 out of 51 |
| Argentina | 7.3 | 7.3 | B- | 96 | Frontier | Latin America | 13 out of 20 |
| Armenia | 4.8 | 5.2 | | 77 | | Asia | 15 out of 29 |
| Australia | -2.7 | -2.6 | AAA | 12 | Developed | Australasia | 2 out of 7 |
| Austria | -2.6 | -2.4 | AA+ | 13 | Developed | Western Europe | 9 out of 19 |
| Azerbaijan | 5.8 | 6.3 | BB+ | 85 | | Asia | 17 out of 29 |
| Bahamas | 3.6 | 3.6 | BB+ | 65 | | Caribbean | 3 out of 9 |
| Bahrain | 3.5 | 3.6 | BB- | 64 | Frontier | Middle East | 7 out of 13 |
| Bangladesh | 9.2 | 9.3 | BB- | 126 | Frontier | Asia | 20 out of 29 |
| Barbados | 4.9 | 6.1 | CCC+ | 82 | | Caribbean | 4 out of 9 |
| Belarus | 11.1 | 11.8 | B- | 143 | | Central and Eastern Europe | 23 out of 25 |
| Belgium | -1.5 | -1.4 | AA | 17 | Developed | Western Europe | 10 out of 19 |
| Belize | 7.7 | 8.0 | B- | 106 | | Latin America | 17 out of 20 |
| Benin | 12.5 | 12.9 | | 150 | | Africa | 37 out of 51 |
| Bermuda | 1.6 | 1.7 | A+ | 44 | | Caribbean | 1 out of 9 |
| Bhutan | 12.2 | 12.4 | | 148 | | Asia | 25 out of 29 |
| Bolivia | 6.4 | 6.9 | BB | 88 | | Latin America | 12 out of 20 |
| Bosnia & Herzegovina | 11.5 | 11.9 | B | 144 | | Central and Eastern Europe | 24 out of 25 |
| Botswana | 1.6 | 1.8 | A- | 48 | | Africa | 1 out of 51 |
| Brazil | 2.9 | 3.0 | BB | 59 | Emerging | Latin America | 7 out of 20 |
| Bulgaria | 2.7 | 3.1 | BB+ | 61 | | Central and Eastern Europe | 12 out of 25 |
| Burkina Faso | 10.1 | 10.4 | B- | 133 | | Africa | 33 out of 51 |
| Burundi | 20.0 | 20.5 | | 169 | | Africa | 47 out of 51 |
| Cambodia | 13.0 | 13.0 | | 151 | | Asia | 27 out of 29 |
| Cameroon | 9.0 | 9.2 | B | 124 | | Africa | 28 out of 51 |
| Canada | -2.9 | -2.8 | AAA | 9 | Developed | North America | 1 out of 2 |
| Cape Verde | 7.0 | 7.3 | B | 94 | | Africa | 12 out of 51 |
| Central African Republic | 23.0 | 23.5 | | 172 | | Africa | 49 out of 51 |
| Chad | 21.9 | 22.4 | | 171 | | Africa | 48 out of 51 |
| Chile | -1.9 | -1.6 | AA- | 16 | Emerging | Latin America | 1 out of 20 |
| China | 1.4 | 1.6 | AA- | 42 | Emerging | Asia | 7 out of 29 |
| Colombia | 1.4 | 1.6 | BBB | 41 | Emerging | Latin America | 4 out of 20 |
| Congo Republic | 8.6 | 8.8 | B- | 117 | | Africa | 24 out of 51 |
| Congo, DR | 9.7 | 9.9 | B- | 131 | | Africa | 32 out of 51 |
| Costa Rica | 3.9 | 4.3 | BB- | 71 | | Latin America | 8 out of 20 |
| Côte d'Ivoire | 6.9 | 7.2 | | 92 | | Africa | 11 out of 51 |
| Croatia | 3.2 | 3.3 | BB | 63 | Frontier | Central and Eastern Europe | 13 out of 25 |
| Cuba | 14.9 | 15.4 | | 160 | | Caribbean | 9 out of 9 |
| Cyprus | 1.2 | 1.4 | BB+ | 40 | | Central and Eastern Europe | 7 out of 25 |
| Czech Republic | -0.8 | -0.7 | AA- | 23 | Emerging | Central and Eastern Europe | 1 out of 25 |
| Denmark | -3.4 | -3.3 | AAA | 4 | Developed | Western Europe | 3 out of 19 |
| Djibouti | 29.7 | 28.3 | | 175 | | Africa | 51 out of 51 |
| Dominican Republic | 6.7 | 7.1 | BB- | 90 | | Caribbean | 5 out of 9 |
| Ecuador | 8.1 | 8.2 | B | 109 | | Latin America | 18 out of 20 |
| Egypt | 8.4 | 8.7 | B- | 116 | Emerging | Africa | 23 out of 51 |
| El Salvador | 5.9 | 6.0 | B- | 81 | | Latin America | 10 out of 20 |
| Equatorial Guinea | 17.0 | 17.4 | | 165 | | Africa | 45 out of 51 |

§ S&P Credit Rating based on long-term foreign currency issuer rating. See http://www.standardandpoors.com/.

* World rank based on 175 countries covered by Euromoney. Ranking based on ascending order in which '1' equals the smallest country risk premium (CRP) and '175' equals the largest country risk premium (CRP).

† MSCI Market Classification based on MSCI Market Classification Framework.  See http://www.msci.com/products/indexes/market_classification.html

‡ Regional classification based on Euromoney. Regional rankings based on ascending order in which '1' equals the smallest country risk premium (CRP) for each region.

Note: A CRP of 0.0% is assumed in the following cases: (i) when the investor country and the investee country both have an S&P sovereign credit rating of AAA; or (ii) when the investor country has an S&P sovereign credit rating of AAA, and the investee country has a sovereign credit rating below AAA, but has a calculated CRP below 0.0% (which would imply lower risk than a country rated AAA); or (iii) when the investor country has an S&P credit rating below AAA, and the investee country has a sovereign credit rating of AAA, but has a calculated CRP above 0.0% (which would imply greater risk than a country rated below AAA). For purposes of this analysis, the U.S. is treated as having a sovereign credit rating equivalent to AAA.

The country risk premium (CRP) is not the cost of equity capital (COE).  The CRP is to be added to base COE. See Chapter 6 for proper application.

## Data Updated Through March 2017

| Investee Country | December 2016 Country Risk Premium (CRP) (%) | March 2017 Country Risk Premium (CRP) (%) | S&P Sovereign Credit Rating § | World Rank Out of 175• | MSCI Market Classification † | Euromoney Region ‡ | Regional Rank ‡ |
|---|---|---|---|---|---|---|---|
| Eritrea | 26.5 | 25.5 | | 173 | | Africa | 50 out of 51 |
| Estonia | -0.3 | 0.0 | AA- | 32 | Frontier | Central and Eastern Europe | 4 out of 25 |
| Ethiopia | 7.4 | 7.8 | B | 101 | | Africa | 16 out of 51 |
| Fiji | 11.9 | 12.2 | B+ | 147 | | Australasia | 5 out of 7 |
| Finland | -2.8 | -2.7 | AA+ | 11 | Developed | Western Europe | 8 out of 19 |
| France | -0.8 | -0.8 | AA | 22 | Developed | Western Europe | 12 out of 19 |
| Gabon | 5.6 | 6.1 | | 83 | | Africa | 7 out of 51 |
| Gambia | 10.7 | 11.0 | | 138 | | Africa | 34 out of 51 |
| Georgia | 4.5 | 5.0 | BB- | 74 | | Central and Eastern Europe | 15 out of 25 |
| Germany | -2.8 | -2.7 | AAA | 10 | Developed | Western Europe | 7 out of 19 |
| Ghana | 7.0 | 7.0 | B- | 89 | | Africa | 9 out of 51 |
| Greece | 8.0 | 8.1 | B- | 108 | Emerging | Western Europe | 19 out of 19 |
| Grenada | 7.7 | 8.0 | | 105 | | Caribbean | 7 out of 9 |
| Guatemala | 5.9 | 6.2 | BB | 84 | | Latin America | 11 out of 20 |
| Guinea | 13.7 | 14.1 | | 156 | | Africa | 41 out of 51 |
| Guinea-Bissau | 8.4 | 8.7 | | 115 | | Africa | 22 out of 51 |
| Guyana | 7.4 | 7.7 | | 100 | | Latin America | 15 out of 20 |
| Haiti | 16.1 | 14.8 | | 157 | | Caribbean | 8 out of 9 |
| Honduras | 7.1 | 7.4 | B+ | 98 | | Latin America | 14 out of 20 |
| Hong Kong | -2.3 | -2.2 | AAA | 14 | Developed | Asia | 2 out of 29 |
| Hungary | 2.5 | 2.8 | BBB- | 57 | Emerging | Central and Eastern Europe | 10 out of 25 |
| Iceland | 0.0 | 0.0 | A | 30 | | Western Europe | 15 out of 19 |
| India | 2.3 | 2.8 | BBB- | 55 | Emerging | Asia | 10 out of 29 |
| Indonesia | 3.0 | 3.2 | BB+ | 62 | Emerging | Asia | 11 out of 29 |
| Iran | 8.8 | 9.3 | | 125 | | Middle East | 10 out of 13 |
| Iraq | 10.3 | 10.7 | B- | 136 | | Middle East | 11 out of 13 |
| Ireland | -0.4 | -0.3 | A+ | 27 | Developed | Western Europe | 14 out of 19 |
| Israel | -0.4 | -0.3 | A+ | 28 | Developed | Middle East | 2 out of 13 |
| Italy | 2.0 | 2.1 | BBB- | 50 | Developed | Western Europe | 18 out of 19 |
| Jamaica | 7.2 | 8.0 | B | 104 | | Caribbean | 6 out of 9 |
| Japan | -0.5 | -0.4 | A+ | 25 | Developed | Asia | 5 out of 29 |
| Jordan | 4.7 | 5.1 | BB- | 76 | Frontier | Middle East | 8 out of 13 |
| Kazakhstan | 4.3 | 4.3 | BBB- | 70 | Frontier | Asia | 13 out of 29 |
| Kenya | 7.2 | 7.5 | B+ | 99 | Frontier | Africa | 15 out of 51 |
| Korea (North) | 25.9 | 26.0 | | 174 | | Asia | 29 out of 29 |
| Korea (South) | -1.2 | -1.0 | AA | 19 | Emerging | Asia | 4 out of 29 |
| Kuwait | -0.3 | 0.0 | AA | 31 | Frontier | Middle East | 3 out of 13 |
| Kyrgyz Republic | 11.5 | 11.7 | | 142 | | Central and Eastern Europe | 22 out of 25 |
| Laos | 15.1 | 15.0 | | 158 | | Asia | 28 out of 29 |
| Latvia | 1.4 | 1.7 | A- | 43 | | Central and Eastern Europe | 8 out of 25 |
| Lebanon | 8.7 | 8.4 | B- | 112 | Frontier | Middle East | 9 out of 13 |
| Lesotho | 11.7 | 12.0 | | 146 | | Africa | 36 out of 51 |
| Liberia | 7.7 | 8.0 | | 107 | | Africa | 17 out of 51 |
| Libya | 13.0 | 13.6 | | 153 | | Africa | 39 out of 51 |
| Lithuania | 0.7 | 1.0 | A- | 36 | Frontier | Central and Eastern Europe | 6 out of 25 |
| Luxembourg | -3.1 | -3.1 | AAA | 5 | | Western Europe | 4 out of 19 |
| Macedonia | 6.4 | 6.9 | BB- | 87 | | Central and Eastern Europe | 17 out of 25 |
| Madagascar | 8.5 | 9.2 | | 123 | | Africa | 27 out of 51 |
| Malawi | 8.2 | 8.5 | | 114 | | Africa | 21 out of 51 |
| Malaysia | 0.9 | 1.0 | A- | 35 | Emerging | Asia | 6 out of 29 |

§ S&P Credit Rating based on long-term foreign currency issuer rating. See http://www.standardandpoors.com/.

• World rank based on 175 countries covered by Euromoney. Ranking based on ascending order in which '1' equals the smallest country risk premium (CRP) and '175' equals the largest country risk premium (CRP).

† MSCI Market Classification based on MSCI Market Classification Framework.  See http://www.msci.com/products/indexes/market_classification.html.

‡ Regional classification based on Euromoney. Regional rankings based on ascending order in which '1' equals the smallest country risk premium (CRP) for each region.

Note: A CRP of 0.0% is assumed in the following cases: (i) when the investor country and the investee country both have an S&P sovereign credit rating of AAA; or (ii) when the investor country has an S&P credit rating of AAA, and the investee country has a sovereign credit rating below AAA, but has a calculated CRP below 0.0% (which would imply lower risk than a country rated AAA); or (iii) when the investor country has an S&P credit rating below AAA, and the investee country has a sovereign credit rating of AAA, but has a calculated CRP above 0.0% (which would imply greater risk than a country rated below AAA). For purposes of this analysis, the U.S. is treated as having a sovereign credit rating equivalent to AAA.

The country risk premium (CRP) is not the cost of equity capital (COE). The CRP is to be added to base COE. See Chapter 6 for proper application.

## Data Updated Through March 2017

| Investee Country | December 2016 Country Risk Premium (CRP) (%) | March 2017 Country Risk Premium (CRP) (%) | S&P Sovereign Credit Rating § | World Rank Out of 175∗ | MSCI Market Classification † | Euromoney Region ‡ | Regional Rank ‡ |
|---|---|---|---|---|---|---|---|
| Mali | 11.4 | 11.7 | | 141 | | Africa | 35 out of 51 |
| Malta | -0.5 | -0.3 | A- | 26 | | Western Europe | 13 out of 19 |
| Mauritania | 14.8 | 15.1 | | 159 | | Africa | 42 out of 51 |
| Mauritius | 3.7 | 4.0 | | 67 | Frontier | Asia | 12 out of 29 |
| Mexico | 0.8 | 1.1 | BBB+ | 37 | Emerging | Latin America | 2 out of 20 |
| Moldova | 10.0 | 10.7 | | 137 | | Central and Eastern Europe | 21 out of 25 |
| Mongolia | 8.5 | 9.1 | B- | 119 | | Asia | 18 out of 29 |
| Montenegro | 7.9 | 8.0 | B+ | 103 | | Central and Eastern Europe | 19 out of 25 |
| Morocco | 3.8 | 4.2 | BBB- | 69 | Frontier | Africa | 4 out of 51 |
| Mozambique | 9.4 | 9.6 | SD | 128 | | Africa | 29 out of 51 |
| Myanmar | 10.2 | 10.4 | | 134 | | Asia | 22 out of 29 |
| Namibia | 3.5 | 3.8 | | 66 | | Africa | 3 out of 51 |
| Nepal | 12.5 | 12.8 | | 149 | | Asia | 26 out of 29 |
| Netherlands | -3.1 | -3.0 | AAA | 6 | Developed | Western Europe | 5 out of 19 |
| New Zealand | -3.0 | -2.8 | AA | 8 | Developed | Australasia | 1 out of 7 |
| Nicaragua | 9.2 | 9.5 | B+ | 127 | | Latin America | 19 out of 20 |
| Niger | 8.8 | 9.1 | | 120 | | Africa | 25 out of 51 |
| Nigeria | 7.2 | 7.4 | B | 97 | Frontier | Africa | 14 out of 51 |
| Norway | -3.7 | -3.6 | AAA | 3 | Developed | Western Europe | 2 out of 19 |
| Oman | 1.5 | 1.8 | BBB- | 46 | Frontier | Middle East | 5 out of 13 |
| Pakistan | 8.9 | 9.2 | B | 122 | Frontier | Asia | 19 out of 29 |
| Panama | 2.1 | 2.4 | BBB | 52 | | Latin America | 6 out of 20 |
| Papua New Guinea | 8.5 | 8.9 | B+ | 118 | | Australasia | 3 out of 7 |
| Paraguay | 5.1 | 5.5 | BB | 80 | | Latin America | 9 out of 20 |
| Peru | 1.0 | 1.3 | BBB+ | 39 | Emerging | Latin America | 3 out of 20 |
| Philippines | 2.4 | 2.6 | BBB | 53 | Emerging | Asia | 9 out of 29 |
| Poland | -0.1 | -0.1 | BBB+ | 29 | Emerging | Central and Eastern Europe | 3 out of 25 |
| Portugal | 1.9 | 1.9 | BB+ | 49 | Developed | Western Europe | 17 out of 19 |
| Qatar | -1.1 | -0.9 | AA | 21 | Emerging | Middle East | 1 out of 13 |
| Romania | 2.5 | 2.8 | BBB- | 56 | Frontier | Central and Eastern Europe | 9 out of 25 |
| Russia | 4.4 | 4.1 | BB+ | 68 | Emerging | Central and Eastern Europe | 14 out of 25 |
| Rwanda | 9.5 | 9.8 | B | 130 | | Africa | 31 out of 51 |
| São Tomé & Príncipe | 14.9 | 15.6 | | 163 | | Africa | 43 out of 51 |
| Saudi Arabia | 1.8 | 1.8 | A- | 47 | | Middle East | 6 out of 13 |
| Senegal | 6.6 | 6.8 | B+ | 86 | | Africa | 8 out of 51 |
| Serbia | 5.0 | 5.0 | BB- | 75 | Frontier | Central and Eastern Europe | 16 out of 25 |
| Seychelles | 4.6 | 4.8 | | 73 | | Africa | 5 out of 51 |
| Sierra Leone | 9.5 | 9.8 | | 129 | | Africa | 30 out of 51 |
| Singapore | -3.8 | -3.7 | AAA | 1 | Developed | Asia | 1 out of 29 |
| Slovakia | -0.7 | -0.5 | A+ | 24 | | Central and Eastern Europe | 2 out of 25 |
| Slovenia | 0.4 | 0.6 | A | 34 | Frontier | Central and Eastern Europe | 5 out of 25 |
| Solomon Islands | 18.5 | 19.0 | | 168 | | Australasia | 6 out of 7 |
| Somalia | 17.1 | 17.5 | | 166 | | Africa | 46 out of 51 |
| South Africa | 2.6 | 3.0 | BBB- | 60 | Emerging | Africa | 2 out of 51 |
| Spain | 1.1 | 1.3 | BBB+ | 38 | Developed | Western Europe | 16 out of 19 |
| Sri Lanka | 4.5 | 4.5 | B+ | 72 | Frontier | Asia | 14 out of 29 |
| Sudan | 13.7 | 14.0 | | 154 | | Africa | 40 out of 51 |
| Suriname | 7.4 | 7.8 | B+ | 102 | | Latin America | 16 out of 20 |
| Swaziland | 12.3 | 13.4 | | 152 | | Africa | 38 out of 51 |
| Sweden | -3.1 | -3.0 | AAA | 7 | Developed | Western Europe | 6 out of 19 |

§ S&P Credit Rating based on long-term foreign currency issuer rating. See http://www.standardandpoors.com/.

∗ World rank based on 175 countries covered by Euromoney. Ranking based on ascending order in which '1' equals the smallest country risk premium (CRP) and '175' equals the largest country risk premium (CRP).

† MSCI Market Classification based on MSCI Market Classification Framework. See http://www.msci.com/products/indexes/market_classification.html.

‡ Regional classification based on Euromoney. Regional rankings based on ascending order in which '1' equals the smallest country risk premium (CRP) for each region.

Note: A CRP of 0.0% is assumed in the following cases: (i) when the investor country and the investee country both have an S&P sovereign credit rating of AAA; or (ii) when the investor country has an S&P credit rating of AAA, and the investee country has a sovereign credit rating below AAA, but has a calculated CRP below 0.0% (which would imply lower risk than a country rated AAA); or (iii) when the investor country has an S&P credit rating below AAA, and the investee country has a sovereign credit rating of AAA, but has a calculated CRP above 0.0% (which would imply greater risk than a country rated below AAA). For purposes of this analysis, the U.S. is treated as having a sovereign credit rating equivalent to AAA.

The country risk premium (CRP) is not the cost of equity capital (COE). The CRP is to be added to base COE. See Chapter 6 for proper application.

## Data Updated Through March 2017

| Investee Country | December 2016 Country Risk Premium (CRP) (%) | March 2017 Country Risk Premium (CRP) (%) | S&P Sovereign Credit Rating § | World Rank Out of 175∗ | MSCI Market Classification † | Euromoney Region ‡ | Regional Rank ‡ |
|---|---|---|---|---|---|---|---|
| Switzerland | -3.6 | -3.6 | AAA | 2 | Developed | Western Europe | 1 out of 19 |
| Syria | 17.7 | 18.3 | | 167 | | Middle East | 13 out of 13 |
| Taiwan | -1.4 | -1.2 | AA- | 18 | Emerging | Asia | 3 out of 29 |
| Tajikistan | 13.4 | 14.0 | | 155 | | Central and Eastern Europe | 25 out of 25 |
| Tanzania | 6.9 | 7.3 | | 95 | | Africa | 13 out of 51 |
| Thailand | 2.1 | 2.2 | BBB+ | 51 | Emerging | Asia | 8 out of 29 |
| Togo | 8.2 | 8.5 | | 113 | | Africa | 20 out of 51 |
| Tonga | 20.6 | 21.1 | | 170 | | Australasia | 7 out of 7 |
| Trinidad & Tobago | 2.4 | 2.6 | A- | 54 | | Caribbean | 2 out of 9 |
| Tunisia | 4.8 | 5.4 | | 79 | Frontier | Africa | 6 out of 51 |
| Turkey | 2.7 | 2.9 | BB | 58 | Emerging | Central and Eastern Europe | 11 out of 25 |
| Turkmenistan | 11.0 | 11.5 | | 140 | | Asia | 24 out of 29 |
| Uganda | 7.8 | 8.3 | B | 110 | | Africa | 18 out of 51 |
| Ukraine | 10.2 | 10.5 | B- | 135 | | Central and Eastern Europe | 20 out of 25 |
| United Arab Emirates | 0.1 | 0.3 | AA | 33 | Emerging | Middle East | 4 out of 13 |
| United Kingdom | -1.2 | -0.9 | AA | 20 | Developed | Western Europe | 11 out of 19 |
| United States | -2.1 | -1.9 | AA+ | 15 | Developed | North America | 2 out of 2 |
| Uruguay | 1.6 | 1.7 | BBB | 45 | | Latin America | 5 out of 20 |
| Uzbekistan | 10.3 | 10.1 | | 132 | | Asia | 21 out of 29 |
| Vanuatu | 11.7 | 12.0 | | 145 | | Australasia | 4 out of 7 |
| Venezuela | 14.8 | 15.6 | CCC | 162 | | Latin America | 20 out of 20 |
| Vietnam | 5.3 | 5.3 | BB- | 78 | Frontier | Asia | 16 out of 29 |
| Yemen | 15.1 | 15.6 | | 161 | | Middle East | 12 out of 13 |
| Zambia | 8.1 | 8.4 | B | 111 | | Africa | 19 out of 51 |
| Zimbabwe | 16.5 | 16.8 | | 164 | | Africa | 44 out of 51 |

## March 2017 Country Risk Premium (CRP) Summary Statistics:

| S&P Rating | Country Count | Average CRP (%) | Median CRP (%) | Min CRP (%) | Max CRP (%) |
|---|---|---|---|---|---|
| AAA ∗∗ | 12 | -3.0 | -3.0 | -3.7 | -1.9 |
| AA (AA+, AA, AA-) | 15 | -1.0 | -0.9 | -2.8 | 1.6 |
| A (A+, A, A-) | 14 | 0.7 | 0.8 | -0.5 | 2.6 |
| BBB (BBB+, BBB, BBB-) | 17 | 2.2 | 2.2 | -0.1 | 4.3 |
| BB (BB+, BB, BB-) | 22 | 4.7 | 4.7 | 1.4 | 9.3 |
| B+ − SD | 39 | 8.7 | 8.4 | 4.5 | 15.6 |
| Investment Grade ∗∗ | 58 | 0.0 | 0.0 | -3.7 | 4.3 |
| Non-Investment Grade ∗∗ | 61 | 7.3 | 7.4 | 1.4 | 15.6 |
| **MSCI Market Classification** | | | | | |
| Developed Markets | 23 | -1.7 | -2.4 | -3.7 | 2.1 |
| Emerging Markets | 23 | 1.9 | 1.6 | -1.6 | 8.7 |
| Frontier Markets | 22 | 4.5 | 4.4 | 0.0 | 9.3 |
| **Euromoney Region ‡** | | | | | |
| Africa | 51 | 10.9 | 9.2 | 1.8 | 28.3 |
| Asia | 29 | 6.4 | 5.2 | -3.7 | 26.0 |
| Australasia | 7 | 9.7 | 12.0 | -2.8 | 21.1 |
| Caribbean | 9 | 7.5 | 7.1 | 1.7 | 15.4 |
| Central and Eastern Europe | 25 | 5.0 | 3.3 | -0.7 | 14.0 |
| Latin America | 20 | 5.5 | 6.1 | -1.6 | 15.6 |
| Middle East | 13 | 5.7 | 3.6 | -0.9 | 18.3 |
| North America | 2 | -2.4 | -2.4 | -2.8 | -1.9 |
| Western Europe | 19 | -0.9 | -1.4 | -3.6 | 8.1 |

## CCR Base Cost of Equity Capital:

| Iceland | COE (%) |
|---|---|
| March 2017 | 14.1 |
| December 2016 | 14.3 |

CCR base country-level COE for an Iceland-based investor investing in Iceland.

§ S&P Credit Rating based on long-term foreign currency issuer rating. See http://www.standardandpoors.com/.

∗ World rank based on 175 countries covered by Euromoney. Ranking based on ascending order in which '1' equals the smallest country risk premium (CRP) and '175' equals the largest country risk premium (CRP).

† MSCI Market Classification based on MSCI Market Classification Framework. See http://www.msci.com/products/indexes/market_classification.html

‡ Regional classification based on Euromoney. Regional rankings based on ascending order in which '1' equals the smallest country risk premium (CRP) for each region.

∗∗ Investment grade based on S&P sovereign credit rating from AAA to BBB-. Non-Investment grade based on S&P sovereign credit rating from BB+ to SD. For purposes of this analysis, the U.S. is being treated as if it were rated AAA by S&P.

Note: A CRP of 0.0% is assumed in the following cases: (i) when the investor country and the investee country both have an S&P sovereign credit rating of AAA; or (ii) when the investor country has an S&P credit rating of AAA, and the investee country has a sovereign credit rating below AAA, but has a calculated CRP below 0.0% (which would imply lower risk than a country rated AAA); or (iii) when the investor country has an S&P credit rating below AAA, and the investee country has a sovereign credit rating of AAA, but has a calculated CRP above 0.0% (which would imply greater risk than a country rated below AAA). For purposes of this analysis, the U.S. is treated as having a sovereign credit rating equivalent to AAA.

The country risk premium (CRP) is not the cost of equity capital (COE). The CRP is to be added to base COE. See Chapter 6 for proper application.

## Data Updated Through March 2017

| Investee Country | December 2016 Country Risk Premium (CRP) (%) | March 2017 Country Risk Premium (CRP) (%) | S&P Sovereign Credit Rating § | World Rank Out of 175• | MSCI Market Classification † | Euromoney Region ‡ | Regional Rank ‡ |
|---|---|---|---|---|---|---|---|
| Afghanistan | 10.4 | 9.9 | | 139 | | Asia | 23 out of 29 |
| Albania | 5.2 | 5.1 | B+ | 93 | | Central and Eastern Europe | 18 out of 25 |
| Algeria | 5.2 | 5.0 | | 91 | | Africa | 10 out of 51 |
| Angola | 7.5 | 7.3 | B | 121 | | Africa | 26 out of 51 |
| Argentina | 5.7 | 5.2 | B- | 96 | Frontier | Latin America | 13 out of 20 |
| Armenia | 2.8 | 2.7 | | 77 | | Asia | 15 out of 29 |
| Australia | -5.8 | -6.2 | AAA | 12 | Developed | Australasia | 2 out of 7 |
| Austria | -5.6 | -6.0 | AA+ | 13 | Developed | Western Europe | 9 out of 19 |
| Azerbaijan | 4.0 | 4.1 | BB+ | 85 | | Asia | 17 out of 29 |
| Bahamas | 1.5 | 0.9 | BB+ | 65 | | Caribbean | 3 out of 9 |
| Bahrain | 1.4 | 0.9 | BB- | 64 | Frontier | Middle East | 7 out of 13 |
| Bangladesh | 8.0 | 7.5 | BB- | 126 | Frontier | Asia | 20 out of 29 |
| Barbados | 3.0 | 3.8 | CCC+ | 82 | | Caribbean | 4 out of 9 |
| Belarus | 10.1 | 10.3 | B- | 143 | | Central and Eastern Europe | 23 out of 25 |
| Belgium | -4.4 | -4.8 | AA | 17 | Developed | Western Europe | 10 out of 19 |
| Belize | 6.2 | 6.0 | B- | 106 | | Latin America | 17 out of 20 |
| Benin | 11.8 | 11.5 | | 150 | | Africa | 37 out of 51 |
| Bermuda | -0.9 | -1.2 | A+ | 44 | | Caribbean | 1 out of 9 |
| Bhutan | 11.4 | 11.0 | | 148 | | Asia | 25 out of 29 |
| Bolivia | 4.7 | 4.7 | BB | 88 | | Latin America | 12 out of 20 |
| Bosnia & Herzegovina | 10.6 | 10.4 | B | 144 | | Central and Eastern Europe | 24 out of 25 |
| Botswana | -0.8 | -1.2 | A- | 48 | | Africa | 1 out of 51 |
| Brazil | 0.6 | 0.2 | BB | 59 | Emerging | Latin America | 7 out of 20 |
| Bulgaria | 0.5 | 0.3 | BB+ | 61 | | Central and Eastern Europe | 12 out of 25 |
| Burkina Faso | 9.0 | 8.7 | B- | 133 | | Africa | 33 out of 51 |
| Burundi | 20.4 | 20.2 | | 169 | | Africa | 47 out of 51 |
| Cambodia | 12.3 | 11.7 | | 151 | | Asia | 27 out of 29 |
| Cameroon | 7.7 | 7.4 | B | 124 | | Africa | 28 out of 51 |
| Canada | -6.0 | -6.4 | AAA | 9 | Developed | North America | 1 out of 2 |
| Cape Verde | 5.4 | 5.1 | B | 94 | | Africa | 12 out of 51 |
| Central African Republic | 23.8 | 23.7 | | 172 | | Africa | 49 out of 51 |
| Chad | 22.6 | 22.4 | | 171 | | Africa | 48 out of 51 |
| Chile | -4.8 | -5.0 | AA- | 16 | Emerging | Latin America | 1 out of 20 |
| China | -1.1 | -1.4 | AA- | 42 | Emerging | Asia | 7 out of 29 |
| Colombia | -1.1 | -1.4 | BBB | 41 | Emerging | Latin America | 4 out of 20 |
| Congo Republic | 7.3 | 6.8 | B- | 117 | | Africa | 24 out of 51 |
| Congo, DR | 8.5 | 8.2 | B- | 131 | | Africa | 32 out of 51 |
| Costa Rica | 1.9 | 1.8 | BB- | 71 | | Latin America | 8 out of 20 |
| Côte d'Ivoire | 5.2 | 5.0 | | 92 | | Africa | 11 out of 51 |
| Croatia | 1.0 | 0.6 | BB | 63 | Frontier | Central and Eastern Europe | 13 out of 25 |
| Cuba | 14.5 | 14.4 | | 160 | | Caribbean | 9 out of 9 |
| Cyprus | -1.3 | -1.5 | BB+ | 40 | | Central and Eastern Europe | 7 out of 25 |
| Czech Republic | -3.6 | -3.9 | AA- | 23 | Emerging | Central and Eastern Europe | 1 out of 25 |
| Denmark | -6.6 | -6.9 | AAA | 4 | Developed | Western Europe | 3 out of 19 |
| Djibouti | 31.6 | 29.1 | | 175 | | Africa | 51 out of 51 |
| Dominican Republic | 5.1 | 4.9 | BB- | 90 | | Caribbean | 5 out of 9 |
| Ecuador | 6.6 | 6.2 | B | 109 | | Latin America | 18 out of 20 |
| Egypt | 7.0 | 6.7 | B- | 116 | Emerging | Africa | 23 out of 51 |
| El Salvador | 4.1 | 3.7 | B- | 81 | | Latin America | 10 out of 20 |
| Equatorial Guinea | 17.0 | 16.8 | | 165 | | Africa | 45 out of 51 |

The country risk premium (CRP) is not the cost of equity capital (COE). The CRP is to be added to base COE. See Chapter 6 for proper application.

## Data Updated Through March 2017

| Investee Country | December 2016 Country Risk Premium (CRP) (%) | March 2017 Country Risk Premium (CRP) (%) | S&P Sovereign Credit Rating § | World Rank Out of 175* | MSCI Market Classification † | Euromoney Region ‡ | Regional Rank ‡ |
|---|---|---|---|---|---|---|---|
| Eritrea | 27.9 | 25.9 | | 173 | | Africa | 50 out of 51 |
| Estonia | -3.0 | -3.1 | AA- | 32 | Frontier | Central and Eastern Europe | 4 out of 25 |
| Ethiopia | 5.9 | 5.7 | B | 101 | | Africa | 16 out of 51 |
| Fiji | 11.1 | 10.7 | B+ | 147 | | Australasia | 5 out of 7 |
| Finland | -5.9 | -6.2 | AA+ | 11 | Developed | Western Europe | 8 out of 19 |
| France | -3.6 | -4.1 | AA | 22 | Developed | Western Europe | 12 out of 19 |
| Gabon | 3.8 | 3.8 | | 83 | | Africa | 7 out of 51 |
| Gambia | 9.6 | 9.4 | | 138 | | Africa | 34 out of 51 |
| Georgia | 2.6 | 2.5 | BB- | 74 | | Central and Eastern Europe | 15 out of 25 |
| Germany | -5.9 | -6.2 | AAA | 10 | Developed | Western Europe | 7 out of 19 |
| Ghana | 5.4 | 4.8 | B- | 89 | | Africa | 9 out of 51 |
| Greece | 6.6 | 6.1 | B- | 108 | Emerging | Western Europe | 19 out of 19 |
| Grenada | 6.2 | 6.0 | | 105 | | Caribbean | 7 out of 9 |
| Guatemala | 4.2 | 3.9 | BB | 84 | | Latin America | 11 out of 20 |
| Guinea | 13.2 | 13.0 | | 156 | | Africa | 41 out of 51 |
| Guinea-Bissau | 7.0 | 6.7 | | 115 | | Africa | 22 out of 51 |
| Guyana | 5.9 | 5.6 | | 100 | | Latin America | 15 out of 20 |
| Haiti | 16.0 | 13.7 | | 157 | | Caribbean | 8 out of 9 |
| Honduras | 5.5 | 5.3 | B+ | 98 | | Latin America | 14 out of 20 |
| Hong Kong | -5.3 | -5.6 | AAA | 14 | Developed | Asia | 2 out of 29 |
| Hungary | 0.2 | 0.1 | BBB- | 57 | Emerging | Central and Eastern Europe | 10 out of 25 |
| Iceland | -2.7 | -3.2 | A | 30 | | Western Europe | 15 out of 19 |
| India | 0.0 | 0.0 | BBB- | 55 | Emerging | Asia | 10 out of 29 |
| Indonesia | 0.7 | 0.5 | BB+ | 62 | Emerging | Asia | 11 out of 29 |
| Iran | 7.5 | 7.4 | | 125 | | Middle East | 10 out of 13 |
| Iraq | 9.2 | 9.0 | B- | 136 | | Middle East | 11 out of 13 |
| Ireland | -3.1 | -3.5 | A+ | 27 | Developed | Western Europe | 14 out of 19 |
| Israel | -3.2 | -3.5 | A+ | 28 | Developed | Middle East | 2 out of 13 |
| Italy | -0.4 | -0.8 | BBB- | 50 | Developed | Western Europe | 18 out of 19 |
| Jamaica | 5.6 | 5.9 | B | 104 | | Caribbean | 6 out of 9 |
| Japan | -3.3 | -3.6 | A+ | 25 | Developed | Asia | 5 out of 29 |
| Jordan | 2.8 | 2.7 | BB- | 76 | Frontier | Middle East | 8 out of 13 |
| Kazakhstan | 2.3 | 1.7 | BBB- | 70 | Frontier | Asia | 13 out of 29 |
| Kenya | 5.6 | 5.4 | B+ | 99 | Frontier | Africa | 15 out of 51 |
| Korea (North) | 27.2 | 26.6 | | 174 | | Asia | 29 out of 29 |
| Korea (South) | -4.0 | -4.3 | AA | 19 | Emerging | Asia | 4 out of 29 |
| Kuwait | -3.0 | -3.2 | AA | 31 | Frontier | Middle East | 3 out of 13 |
| Kyrgyz Republic | 10.6 | 10.2 | | 142 | | Central and Eastern Europe | 22 out of 25 |
| Laos | 14.7 | 14.0 | | 158 | | Asia | 28 out of 29 |
| Latvia | -1.0 | -1.2 | A- | 43 | | Central and Eastern Europe | 8 out of 25 |
| Lebanon | 7.3 | 6.5 | B- | 112 | Frontier | Middle East | 9 out of 13 |
| Lesotho | 10.8 | 10.6 | | 146 | | Africa | 36 out of 51 |
| Liberia | 6.3 | 6.0 | | 107 | | Africa | 17 out of 51 |
| Libya | 12.3 | 12.4 | | 153 | | Africa | 39 out of 51 |
| Lithuania | -1.8 | -2.0 | A- | 36 | Frontier | Central and Eastern Europe | 6 out of 25 |
| Luxembourg | -6.3 | -6.7 | AAA | 5 | | Western Europe | 4 out of 19 |
| Macedonia | 4.7 | 4.7 | BB- | 87 | | Central and Eastern Europe | 17 out of 25 |
| Madagascar | 7.1 | 7.3 | | 123 | | Africa | 27 out of 51 |
| Malawi | 6.8 | 6.6 | | 114 | | Africa | 21 out of 51 |
| Malaysia | -1.6 | -2.1 | A- | 35 | Emerging | Asia | 6 out of 29 |

§ S&P Credit Rating based on long-term foreign currency issuer rating. See http://www.standardandpoors.com/.

* World rank based on 175 countries covered by Euromoney. Ranking based on ascending order in which '1' equals the smallest country risk premium (CRP) and '175' equals the largest country risk premium (CRP).

† MSCI Market Classification based on MSCI Market Classification Framework. See http://www.msci.com/products/indexes/market_classification.html.

‡ Regional classification based on Euromoney. Regional rankings based on ascending order in which '1' equals the smallest country risk premium (CRP) for each region.

Note: A CRP of 0.0% is assumed in the following cases: (i) when the investor country and the investee country both have an S&P sovereign credit rating of AAA; or (ii) when the investor country has an S&P credit rating of AAA, and the investee country has a sovereign credit rating below AAA, but has a calculated CRP below 0.0% (which would imply lower risk than a country rated AAA); or (iii) when the investor country has an S&P credit rating below AAA, and the investee country has a sovereign credit rating of AAA, but has a calculated CRP above 0.0% (which would imply greater risk than a country rated below AAA). For purposes of this analysis, the U.S. is treated as having a sovereign credit rating equivalent to AAA.

The country risk premium (CRP) is not the cost of equity capital (COE). The CRP is to be added to base COE. See Chapter 6 for proper application.

### Data Updated Through March 2017

| Investee Country | December 2016 Country Risk Premium (CRP) (%) | March 2017 Country Risk Premium (CRP) (%) | S&P Sovereign Credit Rating § | World Rank Out of 175* | MSCI Market Classification † | Euromoney Region ‡ | Regional Rank ‡ |
|---|---|---|---|---|---|---|---|
| Mali | 10.4 | 10.2 | | 141 | | Africa | 35 out of 51 |
| Malta | -3.3 | -3.5 | A- | 26 | | Western Europe | 13 out of 19 |
| Mauritania | 14.4 | 14.1 | | 159 | | Africa | 42 out of 51 |
| Mauritius | 1.6 | 1.3 | | 67 | Frontier | Asia | 12 out of 29 |
| Mexico | -1.8 | -1.9 | BBB+ | 37 | Emerging | Latin America | 2 out of 20 |
| Moldova | 8.9 | 9.1 | | 137 | | Central and Eastern Europe | 21 out of 25 |
| Mongolia | 7.2 | 7.2 | B- | 119 | | Asia | 18 out of 29 |
| Montenegro | 6.4 | 5.9 | B+ | 103 | | Central and Eastern Europe | 19 out of 25 |
| Morocco | 1.7 | 1.6 | BBB- | 69 | Frontier | Africa | 4 out of 51 |
| Mozambique | 8.2 | 7.8 | SD | 128 | | Africa | 29 out of 51 |
| Myanmar | 9.1 | 8.8 | | 134 | | Asia | 22 out of 29 |
| Namibia | 1.3 | 1.2 | | 66 | | Africa | 3 out of 51 |
| Nepal | 11.7 | 11.5 | | 149 | | Asia | 26 out of 29 |
| Netherlands | -6.3 | -6.6 | AAA | 6 | Developed | Western Europe | 5 out of 19 |
| New Zealand | -6.1 | -6.4 | AA | 8 | Developed | Australasia | 1 out of 7 |
| Nicaragua | 7.9 | 7.7 | B+ | 127 | | Latin America | 19 out of 20 |
| Niger | 7.5 | 7.2 | | 120 | | Africa | 25 out of 51 |
| Nigeria | 5.6 | 5.3 | B | 97 | Frontier | Africa | 14 out of 51 |
| Norway | -6.9 | -7.3 | AAA | 3 | Developed | Western Europe | 2 out of 19 |
| Oman | -0.9 | -1.2 | BBB- | 46 | Frontier | Middle East | 5 out of 13 |
| Pakistan | 7.6 | 7.3 | B | 122 | Frontier | Asia | 19 out of 29 |
| Panama | -0.2 | -0.5 | BBB | 52 | | Latin America | 6 out of 20 |
| Papua New Guinea | 7.1 | 7.0 | B+ | 118 | | Australasia | 3 out of 7 |
| Paraguay | 3.2 | 3.1 | BB | 80 | | Latin America | 9 out of 20 |
| Peru | -1.5 | -1.6 | BBB+ | 39 | Emerging | Latin America | 3 out of 20 |
| Philippines | 0.1 | -0.2 | BBB | 53 | Emerging | Asia | 9 out of 29 |
| Poland | -2.8 | -3.2 | BBB+ | 29 | Emerging | Central and Eastern Europe | 3 out of 25 |
| Portugal | -0.5 | -1.0 | BB+ | 49 | Developed | Western Europe | 17 out of 19 |
| Qatar | -3.9 | -4.1 | AA | 21 | Emerging | Middle East | 1 out of 13 |
| Romania | 0.3 | 0.0 | BBB- | 56 | Frontier | Central and Eastern Europe | 9 out of 25 |
| Russia | 2.4 | 1.6 | BB+ | 68 | Emerging | Central and Eastern Europe | 14 out of 25 |
| Rwanda | 8.3 | 8.0 | B | 130 | | Africa | 31 out of 51 |
| São Tomé & Príncipe | 14.5 | 14.7 | | 163 | | Africa | 43 out of 51 |
| Saudi Arabia | -0.6 | -1.2 | A- | 47 | | Middle East | 6 out of 13 |
| Senegal | 4.9 | 4.6 | B+ | 86 | | Africa | 8 out of 51 |
| Serbia | 3.1 | 2.5 | BB- | 75 | Frontier | Central and Eastern Europe | 16 out of 25 |
| Seychelles | 2.6 | 2.3 | | 73 | | Africa | 5 out of 51 |
| Sierra Leone | 8.3 | 8.0 | | 129 | | Africa | 30 out of 51 |
| Singapore | -7.1 | -7.4 | AAA | 1 | Developed | Asia | 1 out of 29 |
| Slovakia | -3.5 | -3.8 | A+ | 24 | | Central and Eastern Europe | 2 out of 25 |
| Slovenia | -2.2 | -2.4 | A | 34 | Frontier | Central and Eastern Europe | 5 out of 25 |
| Solomon Islands | 18.7 | 18.5 | | 168 | | Australasia | 6 out of 7 |
| Somalia | 17.0 | 16.8 | | 166 | | Africa | 46 out of 51 |
| South Africa | 0.3 | 0.3 | BBB- | 60 | Emerging | Africa | 2 out of 51 |
| Spain | -1.4 | -1.7 | BBB+ | 38 | Developed | Western Europe | 16 out of 19 |
| Sri Lanka | 2.5 | 2.0 | B+ | 72 | Frontier | Asia | 14 out of 29 |
| Sudan | 13.1 | 12.8 | | 154 | | Africa | 40 out of 51 |
| Suriname | 5.8 | 5.7 | B+ | 102 | | Latin America | 16 out of 20 |
| Swaziland | 11.5 | 12.2 | | 152 | | Africa | 38 out of 51 |
| Sweden | -6.2 | -6.6 | AAA | 7 | Developed | Western Europe | 6 out of 19 |

§ S&P Credit Rating based on long-term foreign currency issuer rating. See http://www.standardandpoors.com/.

* World rank based on 175 countries covered by Euromoney. Ranking based on ascending order in which '1' equals the smallest country risk premium (CRP) and '175' equals the largest country risk premium (CRP).

† MSCI Market Classification based on MSCI Market Classification Framework. See http://www.msci.com/products/indexes/market_classification.html.

‡ Regional classification based on Euromoney. Regional rankings based on ascending order in which '1' equals the smallest country risk premium (CRP) for each region.

Note: A CRP of 0.0% is assumed in the following cases: (i) when the investor country and the investee country both have an S&P sovereign credit rating of AAA; or (ii) when the investor country has an S&P credit rating of AAA, and the investee country has a sovereign credit rating below AAA, but has a calculated CRP below 0.0% (which would imply lower risk than a country rated AAA); or (iii) when the investor country has an S&P rating below AAA, and the investee country has a sovereign credit rating of AAA, but has a calculated CRP above 0.0% (which would imply greater risk than a country rated below AAA). For purposes of this analysis, the U.S. is treated as having a sovereign credit rating equivalent to AAA.

The country risk premium (CRP) is not the cost of equity capital (COE). The CRP is to be added to base COE. See Chapter 6 for proper application.

## Data Updated Through March 2017

| Investee Country | December 2016 Country Risk Premium (CRP) (%) | March 2017 Country Risk Premium (CRP) (%) | S&P Sovereign Credit Rating § | World Rank Out of 175* | MSCI Market Classification † | Euromoney Region ‡ | Regional Rank ‡ |
|---|---|---|---|---|---|---|---|
| Switzerland | -6.9 | -7.3 | AAA | 2 | Developed | Western Europe | 1 out of 19 |
| Syria | 17.8 | 17.8 | | 167 | | Middle East | 13 out of 13 |
| Taiwan | -4.3 | -4.6 | AA- | 18 | Emerging | Asia | 3 out of 29 |
| Tajikistan | 12.7 | 12.8 | | 155 | | Central and Eastern Europe | 25 out of 25 |
| Tanzania | 5.2 | 5.2 | | 95 | | Africa | 13 out of 51 |
| Thailand | -0.2 | -0.7 | BBB+ | 51 | Emerging | Asia | 8 out of 29 |
| Togo | 6.8 | 6.5 | | 113 | | Africa | 20 out of 51 |
| Tonga | 21.1 | 20.9 | | 170 | | Australasia | 7 out of 7 |
| Trinidad & Tobago | 0.1 | -0.2 | A- | 54 | | Caribbean | 2 out of 9 |
| Tunisia | 2.9 | 3.0 | | 79 | Frontier | Africa | 6 out of 51 |
| Turkey | 0.5 | 0.1 | BB | 58 | Emerging | Central and Eastern Europe | 11 out of 25 |
| Turkmenistan | 10.0 | 10.0 | | 140 | | Asia | 24 out of 29 |
| Uganda | 6.3 | 6.3 | B | 110 | | Africa | 18 out of 51 |
| Ukraine | 9.0 | 8.9 | B- | 135 | | Central and Eastern Europe | 20 out of 25 |
| United Arab Emirates | -2.6 | -2.8 | AA | 33 | Emerging | Middle East | 4 out of 13 |
| United Kingdom | -4.0 | -4.2 | AA | 20 | Developed | Western Europe | 11 out of 19 |
| United States | -5.0 | -5.3 | AA+ | 15 | Developed | North America | 2 out of 2 |
| Uruguay | -0.8 | -1.2 | BBB | 45 | | Latin America | 5 out of 20 |
| Uzbekistan | 9.2 | 8.4 | | 132 | | Asia | 21 out of 29 |
| Vanuatu | 10.8 | 10.6 | | 145 | | Australasia | 4 out of 7 |
| Venezuela | 14.5 | 14.7 | CCC | 162 | | Latin America | 20 out of 20 |
| Vietnam | 3.4 | 2.9 | BB- | 78 | Frontier | Asia | 16 out of 29 |
| Yemen | 14.8 | 14.6 | | 161 | | Middle East | 12 out of 13 |
| Zambia | 6.6 | 6.4 | B | 111 | | Africa | 19 out of 51 |
| Zimbabwe | 16.3 | 16.0 | | 164 | | Africa | 44 out of 51 |

## March 2017 Country Risk Premium (CRP) Summary Statistics:

| S&P Rating | Country Count | Average CRP (%) | Median CRP (%) | Min CRP (%) | Max CRP (%) |
|---|---|---|---|---|---|
| AAA ** | 12 | -6.5 | -6.6 | -7.4 | -5.3 |
| AA (AA+, AA, AA-) | 15 | -4.3 | -4.2 | -6.4 | -1.4 |
| A (A+, A, A-) | 14 | -2.3 | -2.3 | -3.8 | -0.2 |
| BBB (BBB+, BBB, BBB-) | 17 | -0.6 | -0.7 | -3.2 | 1.7 |
| BB (BB+, BB, BB-) | 22 | 2.2 | 2.1 | -1.5 | 7.5 |
| B+ − SD | 39 | 6.8 | 6.4 | 2.0 | 14.7 |
| Investment Grade ** | 58 | -3.2 | -3.2 | -7.4 | 1.7 |
| Non-Investment Grade ** | 61 | 5.1 | 5.3 | -1.5 | 14.7 |
| **MSCI Market Classification** | | | | | |
| Developed Markets | 23 | -5.1 | -6.0 | -7.4 | -0.8 |
| Emerging Markets | 23 | -0.9 | -1.4 | -5.0 | 6.7 |
| Frontier Markets | 22 | 2.0 | 1.8 | -3.2 | 7.5 |
| **Euromoney Region ‡** | | | | | |
| Africa | 51 | 9.2 | 7.3 | -1.2 | 29.1 |
| Asia | 29 | 4.1 | 2.7 | -7.4 | 26.6 |
| Australasia | 7 | 7.9 | 10.6 | -6.4 | 20.9 |
| Caribbean | 9 | 5.4 | 4.9 | -1.2 | 14.4 |
| Central and Eastern Europe | 25 | 2.5 | 0.6 | -3.9 | 12.8 |
| Latin America | 20 | 3.1 | 3.8 | -5.0 | 14.7 |
| Middle East | 13 | 3.3 | 0.9 | -4.1 | 17.8 |
| North America | 2 | -5.9 | -5.9 | -6.4 | -5.3 |
| Western Europe | 19 | -4.2 | -4.8 | -7.3 | 6.1 |

## CCR Base Cost of Equity Capital:

| India | COE (%) |
|---|---|
| March 2017 | 18.1 |
| December 2016 | 18.0 |

CCR base country-level COE for an India-based investor investing in India.

§ S&P Credit Rating based on long-term foreign currency issuer rating. See http://www.standardandpoors.com/.

* World rank based on 175 countries covered by Euromoney. Ranking based on ascending order in which '1' equals the smallest country risk premium (CRP) and '175' equals the largest country risk premium (CRP).

† MSCI Market Classification based on MSCI Market Classification Framework. See http://www.msci.com/products/indexes/market_classification.html

‡ Regional classification based on Euromoney. Regional rankings based on ascending order in which '1' equals the smallest country risk premium (CRP) for each region.

** Investment grade based on S&P sovereign credit rating from AAA to BBB-. Non-Investment grade based on S&P sovereign credit rating from BB+ to SD. For purposes of this analysis, the U.S. is being treated as if it were rated AAA by S&P.

Note: A CRP of 0.0% is assumed in the following cases: (i) when the investor country and the investee country both have an S&P sovereign credit rating of AAA; or (ii) when the investor country has an S&P credit rating of AAA, and the investee country has a sovereign credit rating below AAA, but has a calculated CRP below 0.0% (which would imply lower risk than a country rated AAA); or (iii) when the investor country has an S&P credit rating below AAA, and the investee country has a sovereign credit rating of AAA, but has a calculated CRP above 0.0% (which would imply greater risk than a country rated below AAA). For purposes of this analysis, the U.S. is treated as having a sovereign credit rating equivalent to AAA.

The country risk premium (CRP) is not the cost of equity capital (COE). The CRP is to be added to base COE. See Chapter 6 for proper application.

### Data Updated Through March 2017

| Investee Country | December 2016 Country Risk Premium (CRP) (%) | March 2017 Country Risk Premium (CRP) (%) | S&P Sovereign Credit Rating § | World Rank Out of 175* | MSCI Market Classification † | Euromoney Region ‡ | Regional Rank ‡ |
|---|---|---|---|---|---|---|---|
| Afghanistan | 9.6 | 9.5 | | 139 | | Asia | 23 out of 29 |
| Albania | 4.4 | 4.6 | B+ | 93 | | Central and Eastern Europe | 18 out of 25 |
| Algeria | 4.5 | 4.5 | | 91 | | Africa | 10 out of 51 |
| Angola | 6.7 | 6.8 | B | 121 | | Africa | 26 out of 51 |
| Argentina | 5.0 | 4.8 | B- | 96 | Frontier | Latin America | 13 out of 20 |
| Armenia | 2.1 | 2.3 | | 77 | | Asia | 15 out of 29 |
| Australia | -6.5 | -6.7 | AAA | 12 | Developed | Australasia | 2 out of 7 |
| Austria | -6.4 | -6.5 | AA+ | 13 | Developed | Western Europe | 9 out of 19 |
| Azerbaijan | 3.3 | 3.6 | BB+ | 85 | | Asia | 17 out of 29 |
| Bahamas | 0.7 | 0.4 | BB+ | 65 | | Caribbean | 3 out of 9 |
| Bahrain | 0.6 | 0.4 | BB- | 64 | Frontier | Middle East | 7 out of 13 |
| Bangladesh | 7.2 | 7.0 | BB- | 126 | Frontier | Asia | 20 out of 29 |
| Barbados | 2.3 | 3.3 | CCC+ | 82 | | Caribbean | 4 out of 9 |
| Belarus | 9.3 | 9.8 | B- | 143 | | Central and Eastern Europe | 23 out of 25 |
| Belgium | -5.1 | -5.3 | AA | 17 | Developed | Western Europe | 10 out of 19 |
| Belize | 5.4 | 5.5 | B- | 106 | | Latin America | 17 out of 20 |
| Benin | 11.0 | 11.1 | | 150 | | Africa | 37 out of 51 |
| Bermuda | -1.6 | -1.7 | A+ | 44 | | Caribbean | 1 out of 9 |
| Bhutan | 10.7 | 10.6 | | 148 | | Asia | 25 out of 29 |
| Bolivia | 4.0 | 4.3 | BB | 88 | | Latin America | 12 out of 20 |
| Bosnia & Herzegovina | 9.8 | 10.0 | B | 144 | | Central and Eastern Europe | 24 out of 25 |
| Botswana | -1.6 | -1.6 | A- | 48 | | Africa | 1 out of 51 |
| Brazil | -0.1 | -0.3 | BB | 59 | Emerging | Latin America | 7 out of 20 |
| Bulgaria | -0.3 | -0.1 | BB+ | 61 | | Central and Eastern Europe | 12 out of 25 |
| Burkina Faso | 8.2 | 8.3 | B- | 133 | | Africa | 33 out of 51 |
| Burundi | 19.7 | 19.9 | | 169 | | Africa | 47 out of 51 |
| Cambodia | 11.5 | 11.3 | | 151 | | Asia | 27 out of 29 |
| Cameroon | 6.9 | 6.9 | B | 124 | | Africa | 28 out of 51 |
| Canada | -6.7 | -6.9 | AAA | 9 | Developed | North America | 1 out of 2 |
| Cape Verde | 4.6 | 4.7 | B | 94 | | Africa | 12 out of 51 |
| Central African Republic | 23.0 | 23.3 | | 172 | | Africa | 49 out of 51 |
| Chad | 21.8 | 22.0 | | 171 | | Africa | 48 out of 51 |
| Chile | -5.6 | -5.5 | AA- | 16 | Emerging | Latin America | 1 out of 20 |
| China | -1.8 | -1.8 | AA- | 42 | Emerging | Asia | 7 out of 29 |
| Colombia | -1.8 | -1.9 | BBB | 41 | Emerging | Latin America | 4 out of 20 |
| Congo Republic | 6.5 | 6.4 | B- | 117 | | Africa | 24 out of 51 |
| Congo, DR | 7.7 | 7.7 | B- | 131 | | Africa | 32 out of 51 |
| Costa Rica | 1.1 | 1.3 | BB- | 71 | | Latin America | 8 out of 20 |
| Côte d'Ivoire | 4.5 | 4.5 | | 92 | | Africa | 11 out of 51 |
| Croatia | 0.2 | 0.1 | BB | 63 | Frontier | Central and Eastern Europe | 13 out of 25 |
| Cuba | 13.8 | 14.0 | | 160 | | Caribbean | 9 out of 9 |
| Cyprus | -2.1 | -2.0 | BB+ | 40 | | Central and Eastern Europe | 7 out of 25 |
| Czech Republic | -4.4 | -4.5 | AA- | 23 | Emerging | Central and Eastern Europe | 1 out of 25 |
| Denmark | -7.3 | -7.5 | AAA | 4 | Developed | Western Europe | 3 out of 19 |
| Djibouti | 30.7 | 28.8 | | 175 | | Africa | 51 out of 51 |
| Dominican Republic | 4.3 | 4.4 | BB- | 90 | | Caribbean | 5 out of 9 |
| Ecuador | 5.9 | 5.7 | B | 109 | | Latin America | 18 out of 20 |
| Egypt | 6.3 | 6.3 | B- | 116 | Emerging | Africa | 23 out of 51 |
| El Salvador | 3.4 | 3.2 | B- | 81 | | Latin America | 10 out of 20 |
| Equatorial Guinea | 16.2 | 16.4 | | 165 | | Africa | 45 out of 51 |

§ S&P Credit Rating based on long-term foreign currency issuer rating. See http://www.standardandpoors.com/.

* World rank based on 175 countries covered by Euromoney. Ranking based on ascending order in which '1' equals the smallest country risk premium (CRP) and '175' equals the largest country risk premium (CRP).

† MSCI Market Classification based on MSCI Market Classification Framework. See http://www.msci.com/products/indexes/market_classification.html.

‡ Regional classification based on Euromoney. Regional rankings based on ascending order in which '1' equals the smallest country risk premium (CRP) for each region.

Note: A CRP of 0.0% is assumed in the following cases: (i) when the investor country and the investee country both have an S&P sovereign credit rating of AAA; or (ii) when the investor country has an S&P credit rating of AAA, and the investee country has a sovereign credit rating below AAA, but has a calculated CRP below 0.0% (which would imply lower risk than a country rated AAA); or (iii) when the investor country has an S&P credit rating below AAA, and the investee country has a sovereign credit rating of AAA, but has a calculated CRP above 0.0% (which would imply greater risk than a country rated below AAA). For purposes of this analysis, the U.S. is treated as having a sovereign credit rating equivalent to AAA.

The country risk premium (CRP) is not the cost of equity capital (COE). The CRP is to be added to base COE. See Chapter 6 for proper application.

### Data Updated Through March 2017

| Investee Country | December 2016 Country Risk Premium (CRP) (%) | March 2017 Country Risk Premium (CRP) (%) | S&P Sovereign Credit Rating § | World Rank Out of 175∗ | MSCI Market Classification † | Euromoney Region ‡ | Regional Rank ‡ |
|---|---|---|---|---|---|---|---|
| Eritrea | 27.1 | 25.6 | | 173 | | Africa | 50 out of 51 |
| Estonia | -3.8 | -3.6 | AA- | 32 | Frontier | Central and Eastern Europe | 4 out of 25 |
| Ethiopia | 5.2 | 5.2 | B | 101 | | Africa | 16 out of 51 |
| Fiji | 10.3 | 10.3 | B+ | 147 | | Australasia | 5 out of 7 |
| Finland | -6.6 | -6.7 | AA+ | 11 | Developed | Western Europe | 8 out of 19 |
| France | -4.3 | -4.6 | AA | 22 | Developed | Western Europe | 12 out of 19 |
| Gabon | 3.0 | 3.4 | | 83 | | Africa | 7 out of 51 |
| Gambia | 8.9 | 8.9 | | 138 | | Africa | 34 out of 51 |
| Georgia | 1.8 | 2.1 | BB- | 74 | | Central and Eastern Europe | 15 out of 25 |
| Germany | -6.6 | -6.8 | AAA | 10 | Developed | Western Europe | 7 out of 19 |
| Ghana | 4.7 | 4.4 | B- | 89 | | Africa | 9 out of 51 |
| Greece | 5.8 | 5.6 | B- | 108 | Emerging | Western Europe | 19 out of 19 |
| Grenada | 5.4 | 5.5 | | 105 | | Caribbean | 7 out of 9 |
| Guatemala | 3.4 | 3.5 | BB | 84 | | Latin America | 11 out of 20 |
| Guinea | 12.4 | 12.5 | | 156 | | Africa | 41 out of 51 |
| Guinea-Bissau | 6.2 | 6.3 | | 115 | | Africa | 22 out of 51 |
| Guyana | 5.1 | 5.1 | | 100 | | Latin America | 15 out of 20 |
| Haiti | 15.2 | 13.3 | | 157 | | Caribbean | 8 out of 9 |
| Honduras | 4.8 | 4.9 | B+ | 98 | | Latin America | 14 out of 20 |
| Hong Kong | -6.0 | -6.2 | AAA | 14 | Developed | Asia | 2 out of 29 |
| Hungary | -0.5 | -0.4 | BBB- | 57 | Emerging | Central and Eastern Europe | 10 out of 25 |
| Iceland | -3.4 | -3.7 | A | 30 | | Western Europe | 15 out of 19 |
| India | -0.7 | -0.5 | BBB- | 55 | Emerging | Asia | 10 out of 29 |
| Indonesia | 0.0 | 0.0 | BB+ | 62 | Emerging | Asia | 11 out of 29 |
| Iran | 6.7 | 7.0 | | 125 | | Middle East | 10 out of 13 |
| Iraq | 8.5 | 8.6 | B- | 136 | | Middle East | 11 out of 13 |
| Ireland | -3.9 | -4.0 | A+ | 27 | Developed | Western Europe | 14 out of 19 |
| Israel | -3.9 | -4.0 | A+ | 28 | Developed | Middle East | 2 out of 13 |
| Italy | -1.1 | -1.3 | BBB- | 50 | Developed | Western Europe | 18 out of 19 |
| Jamaica | 4.9 | 5.5 | B | 104 | | Caribbean | 6 out of 9 |
| Japan | -4.0 | -4.1 | A+ | 25 | Developed | Asia | 5 out of 29 |
| Jordan | 2.1 | 2.2 | BB- | 76 | Frontier | Middle East | 8 out of 13 |
| Kazakhstan | 1.6 | 1.2 | BBB- | 70 | Frontier | Asia | 13 out of 29 |
| Kenya | 4.9 | 5.0 | B+ | 99 | Frontier | Africa | 15 out of 51 |
| Korea (North) | 26.4 | 26.2 | | 174 | | Asia | 29 out of 29 |
| Korea (South) | -4.8 | -4.8 | AA | 19 | Emerging | Asia | 4 out of 29 |
| Kuwait | -3.7 | -3.7 | AA | 31 | Frontier | Middle East | 3 out of 13 |
| Kyrgyz Republic | 9.8 | 9.8 | | 142 | | Central and Eastern Europe | 22 out of 25 |
| Laos | 14.0 | 13.6 | | 158 | | Asia | 28 out of 29 |
| Latvia | -1.8 | -1.7 | A- | 43 | | Central and Eastern Europe | 8 out of 25 |
| Lebanon | 6.6 | 6.0 | B- | 112 | Frontier | Middle East | 9 out of 13 |
| Lesotho | 10.0 | 10.2 | | 146 | | Africa | 36 out of 51 |
| Liberia | 5.5 | 5.6 | | 107 | | Africa | 17 out of 51 |
| Libya | 11.5 | 12.0 | | 153 | | Africa | 39 out of 51 |
| Lithuania | -2.6 | -2.5 | A- | 36 | Frontier | Central and Eastern Europe | 6 out of 25 |
| Luxembourg | -7.0 | -7.2 | AAA | 5 | | Western Europe | 4 out of 19 |
| Macedonia | 4.0 | 4.2 | BB- | 87 | | Central and Eastern Europe | 17 out of 25 |
| Madagascar | 6.3 | 6.9 | | 123 | | Africa | 27 out of 51 |
| Malawi | 6.1 | 6.1 | | 114 | | Africa | 21 out of 51 |
| Malaysia | -2.4 | -2.6 | A- | 35 | Emerging | Asia | 6 out of 29 |

§ S&P Credit Rating based on long-term foreign currency issuer rating. See http://www.standardandpoors.com/.

∗ World rank based on 175 countries covered by Euromoney. Ranking based on ascending order in which '1' equals the smallest country risk premium (CRP) and '175' equals the largest country risk premium (CRP).

† MSCI Market Classification based on MSCI Market Classification Framework. See http://www.msci.com/products/indexes/market_classification.html.

‡ Regional classification based on Euromoney. Regional rankings based on ascending order in which '1' equals the smallest country risk premium (CRP) for each region.

Note: A CRP of 0.0% is assumed in the following cases: (i) when the investor country and the investee country both have an S&P sovereign credit rating of AAA; or (ii) when the investor country has an S&P credit rating of AAA, and the investee country has a sovereign credit rating below AAA, but has a calculated CRP below 0.0% (which would imply lower risk than a country rated AAA); or (iii) when the investor country has an S&P credit rating below AAA, and the investee country has a sovereign credit rating of AAA, but has a calculated CRP above 0.0% (which would imply greater risk than a country rated below AAA). For purposes of this analysis, the U.S. is treated as having a sovereign credit rating equivalent to AAA.

The country risk premium (CRP) is not the cost of equity capital (COE). The CRP is to be added to base COE. See Chapter 6 for proper application.

## Data Updated Through March 2017

| Investee Country | December 2016 Country Risk Premium (CRP) (%) | March 2017 Country Risk Premium (CRP) (%) | S&P Sovereign Credit Rating § | World Rank Out of 175* | MSCI Market Classification † | Euromoney Region ‡ | Regional Rank ‡ |
|---|---|---|---|---|---|---|---|
| Mali | 9.7 | 9.8 | | 141 | | Africa | 35 out of 51 |
| Malta | -4.0 | -4.0 | A- | 26 | | Western Europe | 13 out of 19 |
| Mauritania | 13.6 | 13.7 | | 159 | | Africa | 42 out of 51 |
| Mauritius | 0.9 | 0.9 | | 67 | Frontier | Asia | 12 out of 29 |
| Mexico | -2.5 | -2.4 | BBB+ | 37 | Emerging | Latin America | 2 out of 20 |
| Moldova | 8.2 | 8.6 | | 137 | | Central and Eastern Europe | 21 out of 25 |
| Mongolia | 6.4 | 6.8 | B- | 119 | | Asia | 18 out of 29 |
| Montenegro | 5.6 | 5.5 | B+ | 103 | | Central and Eastern Europe | 19 out of 25 |
| Morocco | 0.9 | 1.1 | BBB- | 69 | Frontier | Africa | 4 out of 51 |
| Mozambique | 7.4 | 7.4 | SD | 128 | | Africa | 29 out of 51 |
| Myanmar | 8.3 | 8.3 | | 134 | | Asia | 22 out of 29 |
| Namibia | 0.6 | 0.7 | | 66 | | Africa | 3 out of 51 |
| Nepal | 10.9 | 11.0 | | 149 | | Asia | 26 out of 29 |
| Netherlands | -7.0 | -7.1 | AAA | 6 | Developed | Western Europe | 5 out of 19 |
| New Zealand | -6.8 | -6.9 | AA | 8 | Developed | Australasia | 1 out of 7 |
| Nicaragua | 7.1 | 7.2 | B+ | 127 | | Latin America | 19 out of 20 |
| Niger | 6.7 | 6.8 | | 120 | | Africa | 25 out of 51 |
| Nigeria | 4.8 | 4.9 | B | 97 | Frontier | Africa | 14 out of 51 |
| Norway | -7.6 | -7.8 | AAA | 3 | Developed | Western Europe | 2 out of 19 |
| Oman | -1.7 | -1.7 | BBB- | 46 | Frontier | Middle East | 5 out of 13 |
| Pakistan | 6.8 | 6.8 | B | 122 | Frontier | Asia | 19 out of 29 |
| Panama | -1.0 | -1.0 | BBB | 52 | | Latin America | 6 out of 20 |
| Papua New Guinea | 6.4 | 6.5 | B+ | 118 | | Australasia | 3 out of 7 |
| Paraguay | 2.4 | 2.6 | BB | 80 | | Latin America | 9 out of 20 |
| Peru | -2.2 | -2.1 | BBB+ | 39 | Emerging | Latin America | 3 out of 20 |
| Philippines | -0.6 | -0.7 | BBB | 53 | Emerging | Asia | 9 out of 29 |
| Poland | -3.6 | -3.7 | BBB+ | 29 | Emerging | Central and Eastern Europe | 3 out of 25 |
| Portugal | -1.2 | -1.5 | BB+ | 49 | Developed | Western Europe | 17 out of 19 |
| Qatar | -4.6 | -4.7 | AA | 21 | Emerging | Middle East | 1 out of 13 |
| Romania | -0.5 | -0.5 | BBB- | 56 | Frontier | Central and Eastern Europe | 9 out of 25 |
| Russia | 1.7 | 1.1 | BB+ | 68 | Emerging | Central and Eastern Europe | 14 out of 25 |
| Rwanda | 7.5 | 7.6 | B | 130 | | Africa | 31 out of 51 |
| São Tomé & Príncipe | 13.7 | 14.3 | | 163 | | Africa | 43 out of 51 |
| Saudi Arabia | -1.3 | -1.7 | A- | 47 | | Middle East | 6 out of 13 |
| Senegal | 4.2 | 4.2 | B+ | 86 | | Africa | 8 out of 51 |
| Serbia | 2.4 | 2.1 | BB- | 75 | Frontier | Central and Eastern Europe | 16 out of 25 |
| Seychelles | 1.8 | 1.8 | | 73 | | Africa | 5 out of 51 |
| Sierra Leone | 7.5 | 7.6 | | 129 | | Africa | 30 out of 51 |
| Singapore | -7.8 | -7.9 | AAA | 1 | Developed | Asia | 1 out of 29 |
| Slovakia | -4.3 | -4.3 | A+ | 24 | | Central and Eastern Europe | 2 out of 25 |
| Slovenia | -2.9 | -2.9 | A | 34 | Frontier | Central and Eastern Europe | 5 out of 25 |
| Solomon Islands | 17.9 | 18.1 | | 168 | | Australasia | 6 out of 7 |
| Somalia | 16.2 | 16.4 | | 166 | | Africa | 46 out of 51 |
| South Africa | -0.4 | -0.2 | BBB- | 60 | Emerging | Africa | 2 out of 51 |
| Spain | -2.1 | -2.1 | BBB+ | 38 | Developed | Western Europe | 16 out of 19 |
| Sri Lanka | 1.8 | 1.5 | B+ | 72 | Frontier | Asia | 14 out of 29 |
| Sudan | 12.4 | 12.4 | | 154 | | Africa | 40 out of 51 |
| Suriname | 5.1 | 5.3 | B+ | 102 | | Latin America | 16 out of 20 |
| Swaziland | 10.7 | 11.8 | | 152 | | Africa | 38 out of 51 |
| Sweden | -6.9 | -7.1 | AAA | 7 | Developed | Western Europe | 6 out of 19 |

§ S&P Credit Rating based on long-term foreign currency issuer rating. See http://www.standardandpoors.com/.

* World rank based on 175 countries covered by Euromoney. Ranking based on ascending order in which '1' equals the smallest country risk premium (CRP) and '175' equals the largest country risk premium (CRP).

† MSCI Market Classification based on MSCI Market Classification Framework. See http://www.msci.com/products/indexes/market_classification.html

‡ Regional classification based on Euromoney. Regional rankings based on ascending order in which '1' equals the smallest country risk premium (CRP) for each region.

Note: A CRP of 0.0% is assumed in the following cases: (i) when the investor country and the investee country both have an S&P sovereign credit rating of AAA; or (ii) when the investor country has an S&P credit rating of AAA, and the investee country has a sovereign credit rating below AAA, but has a calculated CRP below 0.0% (which would imply lower risk than a country rated AAA); or (iii) when the investor country has an S&P credit rating below AAA, and the investee country has a sovereign credit rating of AAA, but has a calculated CRP above 0.0% (which would imply greater risk than a country rated below AAA). For purposes of this analysis, the U.S. is treated as having a sovereign credit rating equivalent to AAA.

The country risk premium (CRP) is not the cost of equity capital (COE). The CRP is to be added to base COE. See Chapter 6 for proper application.

## Data Updated Through March 2017

| Investee Country | December 2016 Country Risk Premium (CRP) (%) | March 2017 Country Risk Premium (CRP) (%) | S&P Sovereign Credit Rating § | World Rank Out of 175* | MSCI Market Classification † | Euromoney Region ‡ | Regional Rank ‡ |
|---|---|---|---|---|---|---|---|
| Switzerland | -7.6 | -7.8 | AAA | 2 | Developed | Western Europe | 1 out of 19 |
| Syria | 17.0 | 17.4 | | 167 | | Middle East | 13 out of 13 |
| Taiwan | -5.0 | -5.1 | AA- | 18 | Emerging | Asia | 3 out of 29 |
| Tajikistan | 12.0 | 12.4 | | 155 | | Central and Eastern Europe | 25 out of 25 |
| Tanzania | 4.5 | 4.7 | | 95 | | Africa | 13 out of 51 |
| Thailand | -1.0 | -1.1 | BBB+ | 51 | Emerging | Asia | 8 out of 29 |
| Togo | 6.0 | 6.1 | | 113 | | Africa | 20 out of 51 |
| Tonga | 20.3 | 20.5 | | 170 | | Australasia | 7 out of 7 |
| Trinidad & Tobago | -0.6 | -0.6 | A- | 54 | | Caribbean | 2 out of 9 |
| Tunisia | 2.2 | 2.5 | | 79 | Frontier | Africa | 6 out of 51 |
| Turkey | -0.3 | -0.4 | BB | 58 | Emerging | Central and Eastern Europe | 11 out of 25 |
| Turkmenistan | 9.2 | 9.6 | | 140 | | Asia | 24 out of 29 |
| Uganda | 5.5 | 5.9 | B | 110 | | Africa | 18 out of 51 |
| Ukraine | 8.3 | 8.4 | B- | 135 | | Central and Eastern Europe | 20 out of 25 |
| United Arab Emirates | -3.3 | -3.3 | AA | 33 | Emerging | Middle East | 4 out of 13 |
| United Kingdom | -4.8 | -4.7 | AA | 20 | Developed | Western Europe | 11 out of 19 |
| United States | -5.8 | -5.8 | AA+ | 15 | Developed | North America | 2 out of 2 |
| Uruguay | -1.6 | -1.7 | BBB | 45 | | Latin America | 5 out of 20 |
| Uzbekistan | 8.4 | 8.0 | | 132 | | Asia | 21 out of 29 |
| Vanuatu | 10.0 | 10.1 | | 145 | | Australasia | 4 out of 7 |
| Venezuela | 13.7 | 14.3 | CCC | 162 | | Latin America | 20 out of 20 |
| Vietnam | 2.7 | 2.4 | BB- | 78 | Frontier | Asia | 16 out of 29 |
| Yemen | 14.0 | 14.2 | | 161 | | Middle East | 12 out of 13 |
| Zambia | 5.9 | 6.0 | B | 111 | | Africa | 19 out of 51 |
| Zimbabwe | 15.6 | 15.7 | | 164 | | Africa | 44 out of 51 |

## March 2017 Country Risk Premium (CRP) Summary Statistics:

| S&P Rating | Country Count | Average CRP (%) | Median CRP (%) | Min CRP (%) | Max CRP (%) |
|---|---|---|---|---|---|
| AAA ** | 12 | -7.1 | -7.1 | -7.9 | -5.8 |
| AA (AA+, AA, AA-) | 15 | -4.8 | -4.7 | -6.9 | -1.8 |
| A (A+, A, A-) | 14 | -2.8 | -2.8 | -4.3 | -0.6 |
| BBB (BBB+, BBB, BBB-) | 17 | -1.1 | -1.1 | -3.7 | 1.2 |
| BB (BB+, BB, BB-) | 22 | 1.7 | 1.7 | -2.0 | 7.0 |
| B+ − SD | 39 | 6.3 | 6.0 | 1.5 | 14.3 |
| Investment Grade ** | 58 | -3.7 | -3.7 | -7.9 | 1.2 |
| Non-Investment Grade ** | 61 | 4.7 | 4.9 | -2.0 | 14.3 |
| **MSCI Market Classification** | | | | | |
| Developed Markets | 23 | -5.6 | -6.5 | -7.9 | -1.3 |
| Emerging Markets | 23 | -1.4 | -1.8 | -5.5 | 6.3 |
| Frontier Markets | 22 | 1.5 | 1.4 | -3.7 | 7.0 |
| **Euromoney Region ‡** | | | | | |
| Africa | 51 | 8.8 | 6.8 | -1.6 | 28.8 |
| Asia | 29 | 3.6 | 2.3 | -7.9 | 26.2 |
| Australasia | 7 | 7.4 | 10.1 | -6.9 | 20.5 |
| Caribbean | 9 | 4.9 | 4.4 | -1.7 | 14.0 |
| Central and Eastern Europe | 25 | 2.1 | 0.1 | -4.5 | 12.4 |
| Latin America | 20 | 2.6 | 3.3 | -5.5 | 14.3 |
| Middle East | 13 | 2.8 | 0.4 | -4.7 | 17.4 |
| North America | 2 | -6.4 | -6.4 | -6.9 | -5.8 |
| Western Europe | 19 | -4.7 | -5.3 | -7.8 | 5.6 |

## CCR Base Cost of Equity Capital:

| Indonesia | COE (%) |
|---|---|
| March 2017 | 22.1 |
| December 2016 | 22.1 |

CCR base country-level COE for an Indonesia-based investor investing in Indonesia.

§ S&P Credit Rating based on long-term foreign currency issuer rating. See http://www.standardandpoors.com/.

* World rank based on 175 countries covered by Euromoney. Ranking based on ascending order in which '1' equals the smallest country risk premium (CRP) and '175' equals the largest country risk premium (CRP).

† MSCI Market Classification based on MSCI Market Classification Framework. See http://www.msci.com/products/indexes/market_classification.html

‡ Regional classification based on Euromoney. Regional rankings based on ascending order in which '1' equals the smallest country risk premium (CRP) for each region.

** Investment grade based on S&P sovereign credit rating from AAA to BBB-. Non-Investment grade based on S&P sovereign credit rating from BB+ to SD. For purposes of this analysis, the U.S. is being treated as if it were rated AAA by S&P.

Note: A CRP of 0.0% is assumed in the following cases: (i) when the investor country and the investee country both have an S&P sovereign credit rating of AAA; or (ii) when the investor country has an S&P credit rating of AAA, and the investee country has a sovereign credit rating below AAA, but has a calculated CRP below 0.0% (which would imply lower risk than a country rated AAA); or (iii) when the investor country has an S&P credit rating below AAA, and the investee country has a sovereign credit rating of AAA, but has a calculated CRP above 0.0% (which would imply greater risk than a country rated below AAA). For purposes of this analysis, the U.S. is treated as having a sovereign credit rating equivalent to AAA.

The country risk premium (CRP) is not the cost of equity capital (COE).  The CRP is to be added to base COE. See Chapter 6 for proper application.

## Data Updated Through March 2017

| Investee Country | December 2016 Country Risk Premium (CRP) (%) | March 2017 Country Risk Premium (CRP) (%) | S&P Sovereign Credit Rating § | World Rank Out of 175* | MSCI Market Classification † | Euromoney Region ‡ | Regional Rank ‡ |
|---|---|---|---|---|---|---|---|
| Afghanistan | 14.1 | 14.0 | | 139 | | Asia | 23 out of 29 |
| Albania | 8.7 | 8.9 | B+ | 93 | | Central and Eastern Europe | 18 out of 25 |
| Algeria | 8.7 | 8.9 | | 91 | | Africa | 10 out of 51 |
| Angola | 11.1 | 11.3 | B | 121 | | Africa | 26 out of 51 |
| Argentina | 9.3 | 9.1 | B- | 96 | Frontier | Latin America | 13 out of 20 |
| Armenia | 6.3 | 6.5 | | 77 | | Asia | 15 out of 29 |
| Australia | -2.8 | -2.8 | AAA | 12 | Developed | Australasia | 2 out of 7 |
| Austria | -2.6 | -2.6 | AA+ | 13 | Developed | Western Europe | 9 out of 19 |
| Azerbaijan | 7.5 | 7.9 | BB+ | 85 | | Asia | 17 out of 29 |
| Bahamas | 4.8 | 4.6 | BB+ | 65 | | Caribbean | 3 out of 9 |
| Bahrain | 4.7 | 4.6 | BB- | 64 | Frontier | Middle East | 7 out of 13 |
| Bangladesh | 11.6 | 11.5 | BB- | 126 | Frontier | Asia | 20 out of 29 |
| Barbados | 6.5 | 7.6 | CCC+ | 82 | | Caribbean | 4 out of 9 |
| Belarus | 13.8 | 14.4 | B- | 143 | | Central and Eastern Europe | 23 out of 25 |
| Belgium | -1.3 | -1.3 | AA | 17 | Developed | Western Europe | 10 out of 19 |
| Belize | 9.7 | 9.9 | B- | 106 | | Latin America | 17 out of 20 |
| Benin | 15.5 | 15.7 | | 150 | | Africa | 37 out of 51 |
| Bermuda | 2.4 | 2.4 | A+ | 44 | | Caribbean | 1 out of 9 |
| Bhutan | 15.2 | 15.2 | | 148 | | Asia | 25 out of 29 |
| Bolivia | 8.2 | 8.6 | BB | 88 | | Latin America | 12 out of 20 |
| Bosnia & Herzegovina | 14.3 | 14.5 | B | 144 | | Central and Eastern Europe | 24 out of 25 |
| Botswana | 2.4 | 2.5 | A- | 48 | | Africa | 1 out of 51 |
| Brazil | 3.9 | 3.9 | BB | 59 | Emerging | Latin America | 7 out of 20 |
| Bulgaria | 3.8 | 4.0 | BB+ | 61 | | Central and Eastern Europe | 12 out of 25 |
| Burkina Faso | 12.7 | 12.8 | B- | 133 | | Africa | 33 out of 51 |
| Burundi | 24.6 | 24.8 | | 169 | | Africa | 47 out of 51 |
| Cambodia | 16.1 | 15.9 | | 151 | | Asia | 27 out of 29 |
| Cameroon | 11.3 | 11.4 | B | 124 | | Africa | 28 out of 51 |
| Canada | -3.0 | -3.0 | AAA | 9 | Developed | North America | 1 out of 2 |
| Cape Verde | 8.9 | 9.0 | B | 94 | | Africa | 12 out of 51 |
| Central African Republic | 28.2 | 28.3 | | 172 | | Africa | 49 out of 51 |
| Chad | 26.8 | 27.0 | | 171 | | Africa | 48 out of 51 |
| Chile | -1.8 | -1.5 | AA- | 16 | Emerging | Latin America | 1 out of 20 |
| China | 2.2 | 2.2 | AA- | 42 | Emerging | Asia | 7 out of 29 |
| Colombia | 2.1 | 2.2 | BBB | 41 | Emerging | Latin America | 4 out of 20 |
| Congo Republic | 10.9 | 10.8 | B- | 117 | | Africa | 24 out of 51 |
| Congo, DR | 12.2 | 12.2 | B- | 131 | | Africa | 32 out of 51 |
| Costa Rica | 5.2 | 5.5 | BB- | 71 | | Latin America | 8 out of 20 |
| Côte d'Ivoire | 8.8 | 8.9 | | 92 | | Africa | 11 out of 51 |
| Croatia | 4.3 | 4.2 | BB | 63 | Frontier | Central and Eastern Europe | 13 out of 25 |
| Cuba | 18.5 | 18.7 | | 160 | | Caribbean | 9 out of 9 |
| Cyprus | 1.9 | 2.1 | BB+ | 40 | | Central and Eastern Europe | 7 out of 25 |
| Czech Republic | -0.5 | -0.5 | AA- | 23 | Emerging | Central and Eastern Europe | 1 out of 25 |
| Denmark | -3.6 | -3.6 | AAA | 4 | Developed | Western Europe | 3 out of 19 |
| Djibouti | 36.2 | 34.0 | | 175 | | Africa | 51 out of 51 |
| Dominican Republic | 8.6 | 8.8 | BB- | 90 | | Caribbean | 5 out of 9 |
| Ecuador | 10.2 | 10.1 | B | 109 | | Latin America | 18 out of 20 |
| Egypt | 10.6 | 10.7 | B- | 116 | Emerging | Africa | 23 out of 51 |
| El Salvador | 7.6 | 7.5 | B- | 81 | | Latin America | 10 out of 20 |
| Equatorial Guinea | 21.0 | 21.1 | | 165 | | Africa | 45 out of 51 |

§ S&P Credit Rating based on long-term foreign currency issuer rating. See http://www.standardandpoors.com/.

* World rank based on 175 countries covered by Euromoney. Ranking based on ascending order in which '1' equals the smallest country risk premium (CRP) and '175' equals the largest country risk premium (CRP).

† MSCI Market Classification based on MSCI Market Classification Framework.  See http://www.msci.com/products/indexes/market_classification.html

‡ Regional classification based on Euromoney. Regional rankings based on ascending order in which '1' equals the smallest country risk premium (CRP) for each region.

Note: A CRP of 0.0% is assumed in the following cases: (i) when the investor country and the investee country both have an S&P sovereign credit rating of AAA; or (ii) when the investor country has an S&P credit rating of AAA, and the investee country has a sovereign credit rating below AAA, but has a calculated CRP below 0.0% (which would imply lower risk than a country rated AAA); or (iii) when the investor country has an S&P credit rating below AAA, and the investee country has a sovereign credit rating of AAA, but has a calculated CRP above 0.0% (which would imply greater risk than a country rated below AAA). For purposes of this analysis, the U.S. is treated as having a sovereign credit rating equivalent to AAA.

The country risk premium (CRP) is not the cost of equity capital (COE). The CRP is to be added to base COE. See Chapter 6 for proper application.

## Data Updated Through March 2017

| Investee Country | December 2016 Country Risk Premium (CRP) (%) | March 2017 Country Risk Premium (CRP) (%) | S&P Sovereign Credit Rating § | World Rank Out of 175∗ | MSCI Market Classification † | Euromoney Region ‡ | Regional Rank ‡ |
|---|---|---|---|---|---|---|---|
| Eritrea | 32.4 | 30.7 | | 173 | | Africa | 50 out of 51 |
| Estonia | 0.1 | 0.4 | AA- | 32 | Frontier | Central and Eastern Europe | 4 out of 25 |
| Ethiopia | 9.4 | 9.6 | B | 101 | | Africa | 16 out of 51 |
| Fiji | 14.9 | 14.9 | B+ | 147 | | Australasia | 5 out of 7 |
| Finland | -2.9 | -2.8 | AA+ | 11 | Developed | Western Europe | 8 out of 19 |
| France | -0.5 | -0.6 | AA | 22 | Developed | Western Europe | 12 out of 19 |
| Gabon | 7.2 | 7.7 | | 83 | | Africa | 7 out of 51 |
| Gambia | 13.3 | 13.4 | | 138 | | Africa | 34 out of 51 |
| Georgia | 6.0 | 6.3 | BB- | 74 | | Central and Eastern Europe | 15 out of 25 |
| Germany | -2.9 | -2.9 | AAA | 10 | Developed | Western Europe | 7 out of 19 |
| Ghana | 9.0 | 8.7 | B- | 89 | | Africa | 9 out of 51 |
| Greece | 10.1 | 10.0 | B- | 108 | Emerging | Western Europe | 19 out of 19 |
| Grenada | 9.7 | 9.9 | | 105 | | Caribbean | 7 out of 9 |
| Guatemala | 7.6 | 7.8 | BB | 84 | | Latin America | 11 out of 20 |
| Guinea | 17.1 | 17.2 | | 156 | | Africa | 41 out of 51 |
| Guinea-Bissau | 10.6 | 10.7 | | 115 | | Africa | 22 out of 51 |
| Guyana | 9.4 | 9.5 | | 100 | | Latin America | 15 out of 20 |
| Haiti | 19.9 | 18.0 | | 157 | | Caribbean | 8 out of 9 |
| Honduras | 9.1 | 9.2 | B+ | 98 | | Latin America | 14 out of 20 |
| Hong Kong | -2.3 | -2.2 | AAA | 14 | Developed | Asia | 2 out of 29 |
| Hungary | 3.5 | 3.7 | BBB- | 57 | Emerging | Central and Eastern Europe | 10 out of 25 |
| Iceland | 0.5 | 0.4 | A | 30 | | Western Europe | 15 out of 19 |
| India | 3.3 | 3.7 | BBB- | 55 | Emerging | Asia | 10 out of 29 |
| Indonesia | 4.1 | 4.2 | BB+ | 62 | Emerging | Asia | 11 out of 29 |
| Iran | 11.1 | 11.4 | | 125 | | Middle East | 10 out of 13 |
| Iraq | 12.9 | 13.1 | B- | 136 | | Middle East | 11 out of 13 |
| Ireland | 0.0 | 0.0 | A+ | 27 | Developed | Western Europe | 14 out of 19 |
| Israel | 0.0 | 0.0 | A+ | 28 | Developed | Middle East | 2 out of 13 |
| Italy | 2.9 | 2.8 | BBB- | 50 | Developed | Western Europe | 18 out of 19 |
| Jamaica | 9.1 | 9.8 | B | 104 | | Caribbean | 6 out of 9 |
| Japan | -0.2 | -0.1 | A+ | 25 | Developed | Asia | 5 out of 29 |
| Jordan | 6.2 | 6.5 | BB- | 76 | Frontier | Middle East | 8 out of 13 |
| Kazakhstan | 5.7 | 5.4 | BBB- | 70 | Frontier | Asia | 13 out of 29 |
| Kenya | 9.2 | 9.3 | B+ | 99 | Frontier | Africa | 15 out of 51 |
| Korea (North) | 31.7 | 31.4 | | 174 | | Asia | 29 out of 29 |
| Korea (South) | -0.9 | -0.8 | AA | 19 | Emerging | Asia | 4 out of 29 |
| Kuwait | 0.2 | 0.4 | AA | 31 | Frontier | Middle East | 3 out of 13 |
| Kyrgyz Republic | 14.4 | 14.3 | | 142 | | Central and Eastern Europe | 22 out of 25 |
| Laos | 18.7 | 18.2 | | 158 | | Asia | 28 out of 29 |
| Latvia | 2.2 | 2.4 | A- | 43 | | Central and Eastern Europe | 8 out of 25 |
| Lebanon | 10.9 | 10.4 | B- | 112 | Frontier | Middle East | 9 out of 13 |
| Lesotho | 14.6 | 14.7 | | 146 | | Africa | 36 out of 51 |
| Liberia | 9.8 | 9.9 | | 107 | | Africa | 17 out of 51 |
| Libya | 16.1 | 16.6 | | 153 | | Africa | 39 out of 51 |
| Lithuania | 1.4 | 1.6 | A- | 36 | Frontier | Central and Eastern Europe | 6 out of 25 |
| Luxembourg | -3.3 | -3.3 | AAA | 5 | | Western Europe | 4 out of 19 |
| Macedonia | 8.2 | 8.5 | BB- | 87 | | Central and Eastern Europe | 17 out of 25 |
| Madagascar | 10.7 | 11.3 | | 123 | | Africa | 27 out of 51 |
| Malawi | 10.4 | 10.5 | | 114 | | Africa | 21 out of 51 |
| Malaysia | 1.6 | 1.5 | A- | 35 | Emerging | Asia | 6 out of 29 |

§ S&P Credit Rating based on long-term foreign currency issuer rating. See http://www.standardandpoors.com/.
∗ World rank based on 175 countries covered by Euromoney. Ranking based on ascending order in which '1' equals the smallest country risk premium (CRP) and '175' equals the largest country risk premium (CRP).
† MSCI Market Classification based on MSCI Market Classification Framework. See http://www.msci.com/products/indexes/market_classification.html.
‡ Regional classification based on Euromoney. Regional rankings based on ascending order in which '1' equals the smallest country risk premium (CRP) for each region.
Note: A CRP of 0.0% is assumed in the following cases: (i) when the investor country and the investee country both have an S&P sovereign credit rating of AAA; or (ii) when the investor country has an S&P credit rating of AAA, and the investee country has a sovereign credit rating below AAA, but has a calculated CRP below 0.0% (which would imply lower risk than a country rated AAA); or (iii) when the investor country has an S&P credit rating below AAA, and the investee country has a sovereign credit rating of AAA, but has a calculated CRP above 0.0% (which would imply greater risk than a country rated below AAA). For purposes of this analysis, the U.S. is treated as having a sovereign credit rating equivalent to AAA.

The country risk premium (CRP) is not the cost of equity capital (COE). The CRP is to be added to base COE. See Chapter 6 for proper application.

Data Updated Through March 2017

| Investee Country | December 2016 Country Risk Premium (CRP) (%) | March 2017 Country Risk Premium (CRP) (%) | S&P Sovereign Credit Rating § | World Rank Out of 175* | MSCI Market Classification † | Euromoney Region ‡ | Regional Rank ‡ |
|---|---|---|---|---|---|---|---|
| Mali | 14.2 | 14.3 | | 141 | | Africa | 35 out of 51 |
| Malta | -0.2 | 0.0 | A- | 26 | | Western Europe | 13 out of 19 |
| Mauritania | 18.3 | 18.4 | | 159 | | Africa | 42 out of 51 |
| Mauritius | 5.0 | 5.1 | | 67 | Frontier | Asia | 12 out of 29 |
| Mexico | 1.4 | 1.6 | BBB+ | 37 | Emerging | Latin America | 2 out of 20 |
| Moldova | 12.6 | 13.1 | | 137 | | Central and Eastern Europe | 21 out of 25 |
| Mongolia | 10.7 | 11.2 | B- | 119 | | Asia | 18 out of 29 |
| Montenegro | 9.9 | 9.8 | B+ | 103 | | Central and Eastern Europe | 19 out of 25 |
| Morocco | 5.0 | 5.3 | BBB- | 69 | Frontier | Africa | 4 out of 51 |
| Mozambique | 11.8 | 11.8 | SD | 128 | | Africa | 29 out of 51 |
| Myanmar | 12.8 | 12.8 | | 134 | | Asia | 22 out of 29 |
| Namibia | 4.7 | 4.9 | | 66 | | Africa | 3 out of 51 |
| Nepal | 15.5 | 15.6 | | 149 | | Asia | 26 out of 29 |
| Netherlands | -3.3 | -3.2 | AAA | 6 | Developed | Western Europe | 5 out of 19 |
| New Zealand | -3.1 | -3.0 | AA | 8 | Developed | Australasia | 1 out of 7 |
| Nicaragua | 11.5 | 11.6 | B+ | 127 | | Latin America | 19 out of 20 |
| Niger | 11.1 | 11.2 | | 120 | | Africa | 25 out of 51 |
| Nigeria | 9.1 | 9.2 | B | 97 | Frontier | Africa | 14 out of 51 |
| Norway | -3.9 | -3.9 | AAA | 3 | Developed | Western Europe | 2 out of 19 |
| Oman | 2.3 | 2.4 | BBB- | 46 | Frontier | Middle East | 5 out of 13 |
| Pakistan | 11.2 | 11.3 | B | 122 | Frontier | Asia | 19 out of 29 |
| Panama | 3.0 | 3.2 | BBB | 52 | | Latin America | 6 out of 20 |
| Papua New Guinea | 10.7 | 10.9 | B+ | 118 | | Australasia | 3 out of 7 |
| Paraguay | 6.6 | 6.9 | BB | 80 | | Latin America | 9 out of 20 |
| Peru | 1.7 | 2.0 | BBB+ | 39 | Emerging | Latin America | 3 out of 20 |
| Philippines | 3.4 | 3.4 | BBB | 53 | Emerging | Asia | 9 out of 29 |
| Poland | 0.3 | 0.3 | BBB+ | 29 | Emerging | Central and Eastern Europe | 3 out of 25 |
| Portugal | 2.8 | 2.6 | BB+ | 49 | Developed | Western Europe | 17 out of 19 |
| Qatar | -0.8 | -0.7 | AA | 21 | Emerging | Middle East | 1 out of 13 |
| Romania | 3.6 | 3.7 | BBB- | 56 | Frontier | Central and Eastern Europe | 9 out of 25 |
| Russia | 5.8 | 5.3 | BB+ | 68 | Emerging | Central and Eastern Europe | 14 out of 25 |
| Rwanda | 11.9 | 12.0 | B | 130 | | Africa | 31 out of 51 |
| São Tomé & Principe | 18.4 | 19.0 | | 163 | | Africa | 43 out of 51 |
| Saudi Arabia | 2.7 | 2.4 | A- | 47 | | Middle East | 6 out of 13 |
| Senegal | 8.4 | 8.5 | B+ | 86 | | Africa | 8 out of 51 |
| Serbia | 6.5 | 6.3 | BB- | 75 | Frontier | Central and Eastern Europe | 16 out of 25 |
| Seychelles | 6.0 | 6.1 | | 73 | | Africa | 5 out of 51 |
| Sierra Leone | 11.9 | 12.0 | | 129 | | Africa | 30 out of 51 |
| Singapore | -4.1 | -4.1 | AAA | 1 | Developed | Asia | 1 out of 29 |
| Slovakia | -0.4 | -0.3 | A+ | 24 | | Central and Eastern Europe | 2 out of 25 |
| Slovenia | 1.0 | 1.1 | A | 34 | Frontier | Central and Eastern Europe | 5 out of 25 |
| Solomon Islands | 22.8 | 22.9 | | 168 | | Australasia | 6 out of 7 |
| Somalia | 21.0 | 21.2 | | 166 | | Africa | 46 out of 51 |
| South Africa | 3.6 | 3.9 | BBB- | 60 | Emerging | Africa | 2 out of 51 |
| Spain | 1.8 | 1.9 | BBB+ | 38 | Developed | Western Europe | 16 out of 19 |
| Sri Lanka | 5.9 | 5.7 | B+ | 72 | Frontier | Asia | 14 out of 29 |
| Sudan | 17.0 | 17.0 | | 154 | | Africa | 40 out of 51 |
| Suriname | 9.4 | 9.6 | B+ | 102 | | Latin America | 16 out of 20 |
| Swaziland | 15.3 | 16.4 | | 152 | | Africa | 38 out of 51 |
| Sweden | -3.2 | -3.2 | AAA | 7 | Developed | Western Europe | 6 out of 19 |

§ S&P Credit Rating based on long-term foreign currency issuer rating. See http://www.standardandpoors.com/.

* World rank based on 175 countries covered by Euromoney. Ranking based on ascending order in which '1' equals the smallest country risk premium (CRP) and '175' equals the largest country risk premium (CRP).

† MSCI Market Classification based on MSCI Market Classification Framework. See http://www.msci.com/products/indexes/market_classification.html.

‡ Regional classification based on Euromoney. Regional rankings based on ascending order in which '1' equals the smallest country risk premium (CRP) for each region.

Note: A CRP of 0.0% is assumed in the following cases: (i) when the investor country and the investee country both have an S&P sovereign credit rating of AAA; or (ii) when the investor country has an S&P credit rating of AAA, and the investee country has a sovereign credit rating below AAA, but has a calculated CRP below 0.0% (which would imply lower risk than a country rated AAA); or (iii) when the investor country has an S&P credit rating below AAA, and the investee country has a sovereign credit rating of AAA, but has a calculated CRP above 0.0% (which would imply greater risk than a country rated below AAA). For purposes of this analysis, the U.S. is treated as having a sovereign credit rating equivalent to AAA.

The country risk premium (CRP) is not the cost of equity capital (COE). The CRP is to be added to base COE. See Chapter 6 for proper application.

## Data Updated Through March 2017

| Investee Country | December 2016 Country Risk Premium (CRP) (%) | March 2017 Country Risk Premium (CRP) (%) | S&P Sovereign Credit Rating § | World Rank Out of 175∗ | MSCI Market Classification † | Euromoney Region ‡ | Regional Rank ‡ |
|---|---|---|---|---|---|---|---|
| Switzerland | -3.9 | -4.0 | AAA | 2 | Developed | Western Europe | 1 out of 19 |
| Syria | 21.8 | 22.2 | | 167 | | Middle East | 13 out of 13 |
| Taiwan | -1.2 | -1.1 | AA- | 18 | Emerging | Asia | 3 out of 29 |
| Tajikistan | 16.6 | 17.0 | | 155 | | Central and Eastern Europe | 25 out of 25 |
| Tanzania | 8.8 | 9.1 | | 95 | | Africa | 13 out of 51 |
| Thailand | 3.1 | 3.0 | BBB+ | 51 | Emerging | Asia | 8 out of 29 |
| Togo | 10.4 | 10.5 | | 113 | | Africa | 20 out of 51 |
| Tonga | 25.3 | 25.4 | | 170 | | Australasia | 7 out of 7 |
| Trinidad & Tobago | 3.4 | 3.5 | A- | 54 | | Caribbean | 2 out of 9 |
| Tunisia | 6.3 | 6.8 | | 79 | Frontier | Africa | 6 out of 51 |
| Turkey | 3.8 | 3.8 | BB | 58 | Emerging | Central and Eastern Europe | 11 out of 25 |
| Turkmenistan | 13.7 | 14.1 | | 140 | | Asia | 24 out of 29 |
| Uganda | 9.8 | 10.3 | B | 110 | | Africa | 18 out of 51 |
| Ukraine | 12.7 | 12.9 | B- | 135 | | Central and Eastern Europe | 20 out of 25 |
| United Arab Emirates | 0.6 | 0.7 | AA | 33 | Emerging | Middle East | 4 out of 13 |
| United Kingdom | -0.9 | -0.7 | AA | 20 | Developed | Western Europe | 11 out of 19 |
| United States | -2.0 | -1.9 | AA+ | 15 | Developed | North America | 2 out of 2 |
| Uruguay | 2.4 | 2.4 | BBB | 45 | | Latin America | 5 out of 20 |
| Uzbekistan | 12.9 | 12.4 | | 132 | | Asia | 21 out of 29 |
| Vanuatu | 14.6 | 14.7 | | 145 | | Australasia | 4 out of 7 |
| Venezuela | 18.4 | 19.0 | CCC | 162 | | Latin America | 20 out of 20 |
| Vietnam | 6.9 | 6.7 | BB- | 78 | Frontier | Asia | 16 out of 29 |
| Yemen | 18.7 | 18.9 | | 161 | | Middle East | 12 out of 13 |
| Zambia | 10.2 | 10.3 | B | 111 | | Africa | 19 out of 51 |
| Zimbabwe | 20.3 | 20.4 | | 164 | | Africa | 44 out of 51 |

## March 2017 Country Risk Premium (CRP) Summary Statistics:

| S&P Rating | Country Count | Average CRP (%) | Median CRP (%) | Min CRP (%) | Max CRP (%) |
|---|---|---|---|---|---|
| AAA ∗∗ | 12 | -3.2 | -3.2 | -4.1 | -1.9 |
| AA (AA+, AA, AA-) | 15 | -0.8 | -0.7 | -3.0 | 2.2 |
| A (A+, A, A-) | 14 | 1.2 | 1.3 | -0.3 | 3.5 |
| BBB (BBB+, BBB, BBB-) | 17 | 3.0 | 3.0 | 0.3 | 5.4 |
| BB (BB+, BB, BB-) | 22 | 5.9 | 5.9 | 2.1 | 11.5 |
| B+ − SD | 39 | 10.7 | 10.3 | 5.7 | 19.0 |
| Investment Grade ∗∗ | 58 | 0.3 | 0.3 | -4.1 | 5.4 |
| Non-Investment Grade ∗∗ | 61 | 9.0 | 9.2 | 2.1 | 19.0 |
| **MSCI Market Classification** | | | | | |
| Developed Markets | 23 | -1.7 | -2.6 | -4.1 | 2.8 |
| Emerging Markets | 23 | 2.7 | 2.2 | -1.5 | 10.7 |
| Frontier Markets | 22 | 5.8 | 5.6 | 0.4 | 11.5 |
| **Euromoney Region ‡** | | | | | |
| Africa | 51 | 13.3 | 11.3 | 2.5 | 34.0 |
| Asia | 29 | 7.9 | 6.5 | -4.1 | 31.4 |
| Australasia | 7 | 11.9 | 14.7 | -3.0 | 25.4 |
| Caribbean | 9 | 9.2 | 8.8 | 2.4 | 18.7 |
| Central and Eastern Europe | 25 | 6.3 | 4.2 | -0.5 | 17.0 |
| Latin America | 20 | 6.9 | 7.6 | -1.5 | 19.0 |
| Middle East | 13 | 7.1 | 4.6 | -0.7 | 22.2 |
| North America | 2 | -2.5 | -2.5 | -3.0 | -1.9 |
| Western Europe | 19 | -0.8 | -1.3 | -4.0 | 10.0 |

## CCR Base Cost of Equity Capital:

| Ireland | COE (%) |
|---|---|
| March 2017 | 10.4 |
| December 2016 | 10.4 |

CCR base country-level COE for an Ireland-based investor investing in Ireland.

§ S&P Credit Rating based on long-term foreign currency issuer rating. See http://www.standardandpoors.com/.

∗ World rank based on 175 countries covered by Euromoney. Ranking based on ascending order in which '1' equals the smallest country risk premium (CRP) and '175' equals the largest country risk premium (CRP).

† MSCI Market Classification based on MSCI Market Classification Framework. See http://www.msci.com/products/indexes/market_classification.html

‡ Regional classification based on Euromoney. Regional rankings based on ascending order in which '1' equals the smallest country risk premium (CRP) for each region.

∗∗ Investment grade based on S&P sovereign credit rating from AAA to BBB-. Non-Investment grade based on S&P sovereign credit rating from BB+ to SD. For purposes of this analysis, the U.S. is being treated as if it were rated AAA by S&P.

Note: A CRP of 0.0% is assumed in the following cases: (i) when the investor country and the investee country both have an S&P sovereign credit rating of AAA; or (ii) when the investor country has an S&P credit rating of AAA, and the investee country has a sovereign credit rating below AAA, but has a calculated CRP below 0.0% (which would imply lower risk than a country rated AAA); or (iii) when the investor country has an S&P credit rating below AAA, and the investee country has a sovereign credit rating of AAA, but has a calculated CRP above 0.0% (which would imply greater risk than a country rated below AAA). For purposes of this analysis, the U.S. is treated as having a sovereign credit rating equivalent to AAA.

The country risk premium (CRP) is not the cost of equity capital (COE). The CRP is to be added to base COE. See Chapter 6 for proper application.

### Data Updated Through March 2017

| Investee Country | December 2016 Country Risk Premium (CRP) (%) | March 2017 Country Risk Premium (CRP) (%) | S&P Sovereign Credit Rating § | World Rank Out of 175∗ | MSCI Market Classification † | Euromoney Region ‡ | Regional Rank ‡ |
|---|---|---|---|---|---|---|---|
| Afghanistan | 11.2 | 11.2 | | 139 | | Asia | 23 out of 29 |
| Albania | 5.8 | 6.1 | B+ | 93 | | Central and Eastern Europe | 18 out of 25 |
| Algeria | 5.8 | 6.1 | | 91 | | Africa | 10 out of 51 |
| Angola | 8.2 | 8.4 | B | 121 | | Africa | 26 out of 51 |
| Argentina | 6.4 | 6.3 | B- | 96 | Frontier | Latin America | 13 out of 20 |
| Armenia | 3.3 | 3.7 | | 77 | | Asia | 15 out of 29 |
| Australia | -5.7 | -5.6 | AAA | 12 | Developed | Australasia | 2 out of 7 |
| Austria | -5.5 | -5.4 | AA+ | 13 | Developed | Western Europe | 9 out of 19 |
| Azerbaijan | 4.6 | 5.1 | BB+ | 85 | | Asia | 17 out of 29 |
| Bahamas | 1.9 | 1.8 | BB+ | 65 | | Caribbean | 3 out of 9 |
| Bahrain | 1.8 | 1.8 | BB- | 64 | Frontier | Middle East | 7 out of 13 |
| Bangladesh | 8.7 | 8.7 | BB- | 126 | Frontier | Asia | 20 out of 29 |
| Barbados | 3.5 | 4.8 | CCC+ | 82 | | Caribbean | 4 out of 9 |
| Belarus | 10.9 | 11.6 | B- | 143 | | Central and Eastern Europe | 23 out of 25 |
| Belgium | -4.2 | -4.1 | AA | 17 | Developed | Western Europe | 10 out of 19 |
| Belize | 6.8 | 7.1 | B- | 106 | | Latin America | 17 out of 20 |
| Benin | 12.6 | 12.9 | | 150 | | Africa | 37 out of 51 |
| Bermuda | -0.5 | -0.4 | A+ | 44 | | Caribbean | 1 out of 9 |
| Bhutan | 12.3 | 12.4 | | 148 | | Asia | 25 out of 29 |
| Bolivia | 5.3 | 5.8 | BB | 88 | | Latin America | 12 out of 20 |
| Bosnia & Herzegovina | 11.4 | 11.7 | B | 144 | | Central and Eastern Europe | 24 out of 25 |
| Botswana | -0.5 | -0.4 | A- | 48 | | Africa | 1 out of 51 |
| Brazil | 1.0 | 1.1 | BB | 59 | Emerging | Latin America | 7 out of 20 |
| Bulgaria | 0.9 | 1.2 | BB+ | 61 | | Central and Eastern Europe | 12 out of 25 |
| Burkina Faso | 9.7 | 10.0 | B- | 133 | | Africa | 33 out of 51 |
| Burundi | 21.7 | 21.9 | | 169 | | Africa | 47 out of 51 |
| Cambodia | 13.2 | 13.1 | | 151 | | Asia | 27 out of 29 |
| Cameroon | 8.4 | 8.6 | B | 124 | | Africa | 28 out of 51 |
| Canada | -5.9 | -5.8 | AAA | 9 | Developed | North America | 1 out of 2 |
| Cape Verde | 6.0 | 6.2 | B | 94 | | Africa | 12 out of 51 |
| Central African Republic | 25.3 | 25.5 | | 172 | | Africa | 49 out of 51 |
| Chad | 23.9 | 24.2 | | 171 | | Africa | 48 out of 51 |
| Chile | -4.7 | -4.3 | AA- | 16 | Emerging | Latin America | 1 out of 20 |
| China | -0.7 | -0.6 | AA- | 42 | Emerging | Asia | 7 out of 29 |
| Colombia | -0.8 | -0.6 | BBB | 41 | Emerging | Latin America | 4 out of 20 |
| Congo Republic | 8.0 | 8.0 | B- | 117 | | Africa | 24 out of 51 |
| Congo, DR | 9.3 | 9.4 | B- | 131 | | Africa | 32 out of 51 |
| Costa Rica | 2.3 | 2.7 | BB- | 71 | | Latin America | 8 out of 20 |
| Côte d'Ivoire | 5.8 | 6.1 | | 92 | | Africa | 11 out of 51 |
| Croatia | 1.4 | 1.4 | BB | 63 | Frontier | Central and Eastern Europe | 13 out of 25 |
| Cuba | 15.6 | 15.9 | | 160 | | Caribbean | 9 out of 9 |
| Cyprus | -1.0 | -0.8 | BB+ | 40 | | Central and Eastern Europe | 7 out of 25 |
| Czech Republic | -3.4 | -3.3 | AA- | 23 | Emerging | Central and Eastern Europe | 1 out of 25 |
| Denmark | -6.5 | -6.4 | AAA | 4 | Developed | Western Europe | 3 out of 19 |
| Djibouti | 33.3 | 31.2 | | 175 | | Africa | 51 out of 51 |
| Dominican Republic | 5.7 | 6.0 | BB- | 90 | | Caribbean | 5 out of 9 |
| Ecuador | 7.3 | 7.3 | B | 109 | | Latin America | 18 out of 20 |
| Egypt | 7.7 | 7.9 | B- | 116 | Emerging | Africa | 23 out of 51 |
| El Salvador | 4.7 | 4.7 | B- | 81 | | Latin America | 10 out of 20 |
| Equatorial Guinea | 18.1 | 18.3 | | 165 | | Africa | 45 out of 51 |

§ S&P Credit Rating based on long-term foreign currency issuer rating. See http://www.standardandpoors.com/.

∗ World rank based on 175 countries covered by Euromoney. Ranking based on ascending order in which '1' equals the smallest country risk premium (CRP) and '175' equals the largest country risk premium (CRP).

† MSCI Market Classification based on MSCI Market Classification Framework. See http://www.msci.com/products/indexes/market_classification.html

‡ Regional classification based on Euromoney. Regional rankings based on ascending order in which '1' equals the smallest country risk premium (CRP) for each region.

Note: A CRP of 0.0% is assumed in the following cases: (i) when the investor country and the investee country both have an S&P sovereign credit rating of AAA; or (ii) when the investor country has an S&P credit rating of AAA, and the investee country has a sovereign credit rating below AAA, but has a calculated CRP below 0.0% (which would imply lower risk than a country rated AAA); or (iii) when the investor country has an S&P credit rating below AAA, and the investee country has a sovereign credit rating of AAA, but has a calculated CRP above 0.0% (which would imply greater risk than a country rated below AAA). For purposes of this analysis, the U.S. is treated as having a sovereign credit rating equivalent to AAA.

The country risk premium (CRP) is not the cost of equity capital (COE). The CRP is to be added to base COE. See Chapter 6 for proper application.

### Data Updated Through March 2017

| Investee Country | December 2016 Country Risk Premium (CRP) (%) | March 2017 Country Risk Premium (CRP) (%) | S&P Sovereign Credit Rating § | World Rank Out of 175* | MSCI Market Classification † | Euromoney Region ‡ | Regional Rank ‡ |
|---|---|---|---|---|---|---|---|
| Eritrea | 29.5 | 27.9 | | 173 | | Africa | 50 out of 51 |
| Estonia | -2.8 | -2.4 | AA- | 32 | Frontier | Central and Eastern Europe | 4 out of 25 |
| Ethiopia | 6.5 | 6.8 | B | 101 | | Africa | 16 out of 51 |
| Fiji | 12.0 | 12.0 | B+ | 147 | | Australasia | 5 out of 7 |
| Finland | -5.8 | -5.6 | AA+ | 11 | Developed | Western Europe | 8 out of 19 |
| France | -3.4 | -3.4 | AA | 22 | Developed | Western Europe | 12 out of 19 |
| Gabon | 4.3 | 4.8 | | 83 | | Africa | 7 out of 51 |
| Gambia | 10.4 | 10.6 | | 138 | | Africa | 34 out of 51 |
| Georgia | 3.1 | 3.5 | BB- | 74 | | Central and Eastern Europe | 15 out of 25 |
| Germany | -5.8 | -5.7 | AAA | 10 | Developed | Western Europe | 7 out of 19 |
| Ghana | 6.1 | 5.9 | B- | 89 | | Africa | 9 out of 51 |
| Greece | 7.2 | 7.2 | B- | 108 | Emerging | Western Europe | 19 out of 19 |
| Grenada | 6.8 | 7.1 | | 105 | | Caribbean | 7 out of 9 |
| Guatemala | 4.7 | 5.0 | BB | 84 | | Latin America | 11 out of 20 |
| Guinea | 14.1 | 14.4 | | 156 | | Africa | 41 out of 51 |
| Guinea-Bissau | 7.7 | 7.9 | | 115 | | Africa | 22 out of 51 |
| Guyana | 6.5 | 6.7 | | 100 | | Latin America | 15 out of 20 |
| Haiti | 17.0 | 15.2 | | 157 | | Caribbean | 8 out of 9 |
| Honduras | 6.2 | 6.4 | B+ | 98 | | Latin America | 14 out of 20 |
| Hong Kong | -5.2 | -5.0 | AAA | 14 | Developed | Asia | 2 out of 29 |
| Hungary | 0.6 | 0.9 | BBB- | 57 | Emerging | Central and Eastern Europe | 10 out of 25 |
| Iceland | -2.4 | -2.5 | A | 30 | | Western Europe | 15 out of 19 |
| India | 0.4 | 0.9 | BBB- | 55 | Emerging | Asia | 10 out of 29 |
| Indonesia | 1.2 | 1.4 | BB+ | 62 | Emerging | Asia | 11 out of 29 |
| Iran | 8.2 | 8.6 | | 125 | | Middle East | 10 out of 13 |
| Iraq | 10.0 | 10.2 | B- | 136 | | Middle East | 11 out of 13 |
| Ireland | -2.9 | -2.8 | A+ | 27 | Developed | Western Europe | 14 out of 19 |
| Israel | -2.9 | -2.8 | A+ | 28 | Developed | Middle East | 2 out of 13 |
| Italy | 0.0 | 0.0 | BBB- | 50 | Developed | Western Europe | 18 out of 19 |
| Jamaica | 6.2 | 7.0 | B | 104 | | Caribbean | 6 out of 9 |
| Japan | -3.1 | -2.9 | A+ | 25 | Developed | Asia | 5 out of 29 |
| Jordan | 3.3 | 3.7 | BB- | 76 | Frontier | Middle East | 8 out of 13 |
| Kazakhstan | 2.8 | 2.6 | BBB- | 70 | Frontier | Asia | 13 out of 29 |
| Kenya | 6.3 | 6.5 | B+ | 99 | Frontier | Africa | 15 out of 51 |
| Korea (North) | 28.8 | 28.6 | | 174 | | Asia | 29 out of 29 |
| Korea (South) | -3.8 | -3.6 | AA | 19 | Emerging | Asia | 4 out of 29 |
| Kuwait | -2.8 | -2.4 | AA | 31 | Frontier | Middle East | 3 out of 13 |
| Kyrgyz Republic | 11.4 | 11.5 | | 142 | | Central and Eastern Europe | 22 out of 25 |
| Laos | 15.8 | 15.4 | | 158 | | Asia | 28 out of 29 |
| Latvia | -0.7 | -0.4 | A- | 43 | | Central and Eastern Europe | 8 out of 25 |
| Lebanon | 8.0 | 7.6 | B- | 112 | Frontier | Middle East | 9 out of 13 |
| Lesotho | 11.7 | 11.9 | | 146 | | Africa | 36 out of 51 |
| Liberia | 6.9 | 7.1 | | 107 | | Africa | 17 out of 51 |
| Libya | 13.2 | 13.8 | | 153 | | Africa | 39 out of 51 |
| Lithuania | -1.5 | -1.2 | A- | 36 | Frontier | Central and Eastern Europe | 6 out of 25 |
| Luxembourg | -6.2 | -6.1 | AAA | 5 | | Western Europe | 4 out of 19 |
| Macedonia | 5.3 | 5.7 | BB- | 87 | | Central and Eastern Europe | 17 out of 25 |
| Madagascar | 7.8 | 8.5 | | 123 | | Africa | 27 out of 51 |
| Malawi | 7.5 | 7.7 | | 114 | | Africa | 21 out of 51 |
| Malaysia | -1.3 | -1.3 | A- | 35 | Emerging | Asia | 6 out of 29 |

§ S&P Credit Rating based on long-term foreign currency issuer rating. See http://www.standardandpoors.com/.
* World rank based on 175 countries covered by Euromoney. Ranking based on ascending order in which '1' equals the smallest country risk premium (CRP) and '175' equals the largest country risk premium (CRP).
† MSCI Market Classification based on MSCI Market Classification Framework. See http://www.msci.com/products/indexes/market_classification.html
‡ Regional classification based on Euromoney. Regional rankings based on ascending order in which '1' equals the smallest country risk premium (CRP) for each region.
Note: A CRP of 0.0% is assumed in the following cases: (i) when the investor country and the investee country both have an S&P sovereign credit rating of AAA; or (ii) when the investor country has an S&P credit rating of AAA, and the investee country has a sovereign credit rating below AAA, but has a calculated CRP below 0.0% (which would imply lower risk than a country rated AAA); or (iii) when the investor country has an S&P credit rating below AAA, and the investee country has a sovereign credit rating of AAA, but has a calculated CRP above 0.0% (which would imply greater risk than a country rated below AAA). For purposes of this analysis, the U.S. is treated as having a sovereign credit rating equivalent to AAA.

The country risk premium (CRP) is not the cost of equity capital (COE). The CRP is to be added to base COE. See Chapter 6 for proper application.

Data Updated Through March 2017

| Investee Country | December 2016 Country Risk Premium (CRP) (%) | March 2017 Country Risk Premium (CRP) (%) | S&P Sovereign Credit Rating § | World Rank Out of 175* | MSCI Market Classification † | Euromoney Region ‡ | Regional Rank ‡ |
|---|---|---|---|---|---|---|---|
| Mali | 11.3 | 11.5 | | 141 | | Africa | 35 out of 51 |
| Malta | -3.1 | -2.8 | A- | 26 | | Western Europe | 13 out of 19 |
| Mauritania | 15.4 | 15.6 | | 159 | | Africa | 42 out of 51 |
| Mauritius | 2.1 | 2.3 | | 67 | Frontier | Asia | 12 out of 29 |
| Mexico | -1.5 | -1.2 | BBB+ | 37 | Emerging | Latin America | 2 out of 20 |
| Moldova | 9.7 | 10.3 | | 137 | | Central and Eastern Europe | 21 out of 25 |
| Mongolia | 7.8 | 8.4 | B- | 119 | | Asia | 18 out of 29 |
| Montenegro | 7.0 | 7.0 | B+ | 103 | | Central and Eastern Europe | 19 out of 25 |
| Morocco | 2.1 | 2.5 | BBB- | 69 | Frontier | Africa | 4 out of 51 |
| Mozambique | 8.9 | 9.0 | SD | 128 | | Africa | 29 out of 51 |
| Myanmar | 9.9 | 10.0 | | 134 | | Asia | 22 out of 29 |
| Namibia | 1.7 | 2.1 | | 66 | | Africa | 3 out of 51 |
| Nepal | 12.6 | 12.8 | | 149 | | Asia | 26 out of 29 |
| Netherlands | -6.2 | -6.0 | AAA | 6 | Developed | Western Europe | 5 out of 19 |
| New Zealand | -6.0 | -5.8 | AA | 8 | Developed | Australasia | 1 out of 7 |
| Nicaragua | 8.6 | 8.8 | B+ | 127 | | Latin America | 19 out of 20 |
| Niger | 8.2 | 8.4 | | 120 | | Africa | 25 out of 51 |
| Nigeria | 6.2 | 6.4 | B | 97 | Frontier | Africa | 14 out of 51 |
| Norway | -6.8 | -6.7 | AAA | 3 | Developed | Western Europe | 2 out of 19 |
| Oman | -0.6 | -0.4 | BBB- | 46 | Frontier | Middle East | 5 out of 13 |
| Pakistan | 8.3 | 8.4 | B | 122 | Frontier | Asia | 19 out of 29 |
| Panama | 0.1 | 0.4 | BBB | 52 | | Latin America | 6 out of 20 |
| Papua New Guinea | 7.8 | 8.1 | B+ | 118 | | Australasia | 3 out of 7 |
| Paraguay | 3.7 | 4.1 | BB | 80 | | Latin America | 9 out of 20 |
| Peru | -1.2 | -0.9 | BBB+ | 39 | Emerging | Latin America | 3 out of 20 |
| Philippines | 0.5 | 0.6 | BBB | 53 | Emerging | Asia | 9 out of 29 |
| Poland | -2.6 | -2.5 | BBB+ | 29 | Emerging | Central and Eastern Europe | 3 out of 25 |
| Portugal | -0.2 | -0.2 | BB+ | 49 | Developed | Western Europe | 17 out of 19 |
| Qatar | -3.7 | -3.5 | AA | 21 | Emerging | Middle East | 1 out of 13 |
| Romania | 0.6 | 0.9 | BBB- | 56 | Frontier | Central and Eastern Europe | 9 out of 25 |
| Russia | 2.9 | 2.5 | BB+ | 68 | Emerging | Central and Eastern Europe | 14 out of 25 |
| Rwanda | 9.0 | 9.2 | B | 130 | | Africa | 31 out of 51 |
| São Tomé & Príncipe | 15.5 | 16.2 | | 163 | | Africa | 43 out of 51 |
| Saudi Arabia | -0.2 | -0.4 | A- | 47 | | Middle East | 6 out of 13 |
| Senegal | 5.5 | 5.7 | B+ | 86 | | Africa | 8 out of 51 |
| Serbia | 3.6 | 3.5 | BB- | 75 | Frontier | Central and Eastern Europe | 16 out of 25 |
| Seychelles | 3.1 | 3.3 | | 73 | | Africa | 5 out of 51 |
| Sierra Leone | 9.0 | 9.2 | | 129 | | Africa | 30 out of 51 |
| Singapore | -7.0 | -6.9 | AAA | 1 | Developed | Asia | 1 out of 29 |
| Slovakia | -3.3 | -3.1 | A+ | 24 | | Central and Eastern Europe | 2 out of 25 |
| Slovenia | -1.9 | -1.7 | A | 34 | Frontier | Central and Eastern Europe | 5 out of 25 |
| Solomon Islands | 19.9 | 20.1 | | 168 | | Australasia | 6 out of 7 |
| Somalia | 18.1 | 18.4 | | 166 | | Africa | 46 out of 51 |
| South Africa | 0.7 | 1.1 | BBB- | 60 | Emerging | Africa | 2 out of 51 |
| Spain | -1.1 | -0.9 | BBB+ | 38 | Developed | Western Europe | 16 out of 19 |
| Sri Lanka | 3.0 | 2.9 | B+ | 72 | Frontier | Asia | 14 out of 29 |
| Sudan | 14.1 | 14.2 | | 154 | | Africa | 40 out of 51 |
| Suriname | 6.5 | 6.8 | B+ | 102 | | Latin America | 16 out of 20 |
| Swaziland | 12.4 | 13.6 | | 152 | | Africa | 38 out of 51 |
| Sweden | -6.1 | -6.0 | AAA | 7 | Developed | Western Europe | 6 out of 19 |

§ S&P Credit Rating based on long-term foreign currency issuer rating. See http://www.standardandpoors.com/.

* World rank based on 175 countries covered by Euromoney. Ranking based on ascending order in which '1' equals the smallest country risk premium (CRP) and '175' equals the largest country risk premium (CRP).

† MSCI Market Classification based on MSCI Market Classification Framework. See http://www.msci.com/products/indexes/market_classification.html

‡ Regional classification based on Euromoney. Regional rankings based on ascending order in which '1' equals the smallest country risk premium (CRP) for each region.

Note: A CRP of 0.0% is assumed in the following cases: (i) when the investor country and the investee country both have an S&P sovereign credit rating of AAA; or (ii) when the investor country has an S&P credit rating of AAA, and the investee country has a sovereign credit rating below AAA, but has a calculated CRP below 0.0% (which would imply lower risk than a country rated AAA); or (iii) when the investor country has an S&P credit rating below AAA, and the investee country has a sovereign credit rating of AAA, but has a calculated CRP above 0.0% (which would imply greater risk than a country rated below AAA). For purposes of this analysis, the U.S. is treated as having a sovereign credit rating equivalent to AAA.

The country risk premium (CRP) is not the cost of equity capital (COE). The CRP is to be added to base COE. See Chapter 6 for proper application.

### Data Updated Through March 2017

| Investee Country | December 2016 Country Risk Premium (CRP) (%) | March 2017 Country Risk Premium (CRP) (%) | S&P Sovereign Credit Rating § | World Rank Out of 175* | MSCI Market Classification † | Euromoney Region ‡ | Regional Rank ‡ |
|---|---|---|---|---|---|---|---|
| Switzerland | -6.8 | -6.8 | AAA | 2 | Developed | Western Europe | 1 out of 19 |
| Syria | 18.9 | 19.4 | | 167 | | Middle East | 13 out of 13 |
| Taiwan | -4.1 | -3.9 | AA- | 18 | Emerging | Asia | 3 out of 29 |
| Tajikistan | 13.7 | 14.2 | | 155 | | Central and Eastern Europe | 25 out of 25 |
| Tanzania | 5.8 | 6.2 | | 95 | | Africa | 13 out of 51 |
| Thailand | 0.2 | 0.2 | BBB+ | 51 | Emerging | Asia | 8 out of 29 |
| Togo | 7.4 | 7.7 | | 113 | | Africa | 20 out of 51 |
| Tonga | 22.4 | 22.6 | | 170 | | Australasia | 7 out of 7 |
| Trinidad & Tobago | 0.5 | 0.7 | A- | 54 | | Caribbean | 2 out of 9 |
| Tunisia | 3.4 | 4.0 | | 79 | Frontier | Africa | 6 out of 51 |
| Turkey | 0.9 | 0.9 | BB | 58 | Emerging | Central and Eastern Europe | 11 out of 25 |
| Turkmenistan | 10.8 | 11.3 | | 140 | | Asia | 24 out of 29 |
| Uganda | 6.9 | 7.5 | B | 110 | | Africa | 18 out of 51 |
| Ukraine | 9.8 | 10.1 | B- | 135 | | Central and Eastern Europe | 20 out of 25 |
| United Arab Emirates | -2.3 | -2.1 | AA | 33 | Emerging | Middle East | 4 out of 13 |
| United Kingdom | -3.8 | -3.5 | AA | 20 | Developed | Western Europe | 11 out of 19 |
| United States | -4.9 | -4.7 | AA+ | 15 | Developed | North America | 2 out of 2 |
| Uruguay | -0.5 | -0.4 | BBB | 45 | | Latin America | 5 out of 20 |
| Uzbekistan | 10.0 | 9.6 | | 132 | | Asia | 21 out of 29 |
| Vanuatu | 11.7 | 11.9 | | 145 | | Australasia | 4 out of 7 |
| Venezuela | 15.5 | 16.2 | CCC | 162 | | Latin America | 20 out of 20 |
| Vietnam | 4.0 | 3.9 | BB- | 78 | Frontier | Asia | 16 out of 29 |
| Yemen | 15.8 | 16.1 | | 161 | | Middle East | 12 out of 13 |
| Zambia | 7.3 | 7.5 | B | 111 | | Africa | 19 out of 51 |
| Zimbabwe | 17.4 | 17.6 | | 164 | | Africa | 44 out of 51 |

### March 2017 Country Risk Premium (CRP) Summary Statistics:

| S&P Rating | Country Count | Average CRP (%) | Median CRP (%) | Min CRP (%) | Max CRP (%) |
|---|---|---|---|---|---|
| AAA ** | 12 | -6.0 | -6.0 | -6.9 | -4.7 |
| AA (AA+, AA, AA-) | 15 | -3.6 | -3.5 | -5.8 | -0.6 |
| A (A+, A, A-) | 14 | -1.6 | -1.5 | -3.1 | 0.7 |
| BBB (BBB+, BBB, BBB-) | 17 | 0.2 | 0.2 | -2.5 | 2.6 |
| BB (BB+, BB, BB-) | 22 | 3.1 | 3.1 | -0.8 | 8.7 |
| B+ − SD | 39 | 7.9 | 7.5 | 2.9 | 16.2 |
| Investment Grade ** | 58 | -2.5 | -2.5 | -6.9 | 2.6 |
| Non-Investment Grade ** | 61 | 6.2 | 6.4 | -0.8 | 16.2 |
| **MSCI Market Classification** | | | | | |
| Developed Markets | 23 | -4.5 | -5.4 | -6.9 | 0.0 |
| Emerging Markets | 23 | -0.1 | -0.6 | -4.3 | 7.9 |
| Frontier Markets | 22 | 3.0 | 2.8 | -2.4 | 8.7 |
| **Euromoney Region ‡** | | | | | |
| Africa | 51 | 10.5 | 8.4 | -0.4 | 31.2 |
| Asia | 29 | 5.1 | 3.7 | -6.9 | 28.6 |
| Australasia | 7 | 9.1 | 11.9 | -5.8 | 22.6 |
| Caribbean | 9 | 6.4 | 6.0 | -0.4 | 15.9 |
| Central and Eastern Europe | 25 | 3.5 | 1.4 | -3.3 | 14.2 |
| Latin America | 20 | 4.1 | 4.8 | -4.3 | 16.2 |
| Middle East | 13 | 4.3 | 1.8 | -3.5 | 19.4 |
| North America | 2 | -5.3 | -5.3 | -5.8 | -4.7 |
| Western Europe | 19 | -3.6 | -4.1 | -6.8 | 7.2 |

### CCR Base Cost of Equity Capital:

| Italy | COE (%) |
|---|---|
| March 2017 | 13.2 |
| December 2016 | 13.3 |

CCR base country-level COE for an Italy-based investor investing in Italy.

§ S&P Credit Rating based on long-term foreign currency issuer rating. See http://www.standardandpoors.com/.

* World rank based on 175 countries covered by Euromoney. Ranking based on ascending order in which '1' equals the smallest country risk premium (CRP) and '175' equals the largest country risk premium (CRP).

† MSCI Market Classification based on MSCI Market Classification Framework. See http://www.msci.com/products/indexes/market_classification.html

‡ Regional classification based on Euromoney. Regional rankings based on ascending order in which '1' equals the smallest country risk premium (CRP) for each region.

** Investment grade based on S&P sovereign credit rating from AAA to BBB-. Non-Investment grade based on S&P sovereign credit rating from BB+ to SD. For purposes of this analysis, the U.S. is being treated as if it were rated AAA by S&P.

Note: A CRP of 0.0% is assumed in the following cases: (i) when the investor country and the investee country both have an S&P sovereign credit rating of AAA; or (ii) when the investor country has an S&P credit rating of AAA, and the investee country has a sovereign credit rating below AAA, but has a calculated CRP below 0.0% (which would imply lower risk than a country rated AAA); or (iii) when the investor country has an S&P credit rating below AAA, and the investee country has a sovereign credit rating of AAA, but has a calculated CRP above 0.0% (which would imply greater risk than a country rated below AAA). For purposes of this analysis, the U.S. is treated as having a sovereign credit rating equivalent to AAA.

The country risk premium (CRP) is not the cost of equity capital (COE). The CRP is to be added to base COE. See Chapter 6 for proper application.

## Data Updated Through March 2017

| Investee Country | December 2016 Country Risk Premium (CRP) (%) | March 2017 Country Risk Premium (CRP) (%) | S&P Sovereign Credit Rating § | World Rank Out of 175∗ | MSCI Market Classification † | Euromoney Region ‡ | Regional Rank ‡ |
|---|---|---|---|---|---|---|---|
| Afghanistan | 14.5 | 14.1 | | 139 | | Asia | 23 out of 29 |
| Albania | 8.9 | 9.0 | B+ | 93 | | Central and Eastern Europe | 18 out of 25 |
| Algeria | 9.0 | 9.0 | | 91 | | Africa | 10 out of 51 |
| Angola | 11.4 | 11.4 | B | 121 | | Africa | 26 out of 51 |
| Argentina | 9.5 | 9.2 | B- | 96 | Frontier | Latin America | 13 out of 20 |
| Armenia | 6.5 | 6.6 | | 77 | | Asia | 15 out of 29 |
| Australia | -2.6 | -2.7 | AAA | 12 | Developed | Australasia | 2 out of 7 |
| Austria | -2.5 | -2.5 | AA+ | 13 | Developed | Western Europe | 9 out of 19 |
| Azerbaijan | 7.7 | 8.0 | BB+ | 85 | | Asia | 17 out of 29 |
| Bahamas | 5.0 | 4.7 | BB+ | 65 | | Caribbean | 3 out of 9 |
| Bahrain | 4.9 | 4.7 | BB- | 64 | Frontier | Middle East | 7 out of 13 |
| Bangladesh | 11.9 | 11.6 | BB- | 126 | Frontier | Asia | 20 out of 29 |
| Barbados | 6.7 | 7.7 | CCC+ | 82 | | Caribbean | 4 out of 9 |
| Belarus | 14.1 | 14.5 | B- | 143 | | Central and Eastern Europe | 23 out of 25 |
| Belgium | -1.2 | -1.3 | AA | 17 | Developed | Western Europe | 10 out of 19 |
| Belize | 10.0 | 10.0 | B- | 106 | | Latin America | 17 out of 20 |
| Benin | 15.9 | 15.8 | | 150 | | Africa | 37 out of 51 |
| Bermuda | 2.6 | 2.5 | A+ | 44 | | Caribbean | 1 out of 9 |
| Bhutan | 15.5 | 15.3 | | 148 | | Asia | 25 out of 29 |
| Bolivia | 8.5 | 8.7 | BB | 88 | | Latin America | 12 out of 20 |
| Bosnia & Herzegovina | 14.6 | 14.7 | B | 144 | | Central and Eastern Europe | 24 out of 25 |
| Botswana | 2.6 | 2.5 | A- | 48 | | Africa | 1 out of 51 |
| Brazil | 4.1 | 4.0 | BB | 59 | Emerging | Latin America | 7 out of 20 |
| Bulgaria | 4.0 | 4.1 | BB+ | 61 | | Central and Eastern Europe | 12 out of 25 |
| Burkina Faso | 12.9 | 12.9 | B- | 133 | | Africa | 33 out of 51 |
| Burundi | 25.1 | 24.9 | | 169 | | Africa | 47 out of 51 |
| Cambodia | 16.5 | 16.0 | | 151 | | Asia | 27 out of 29 |
| Cameroon | 11.6 | 11.5 | B | 124 | | Africa | 28 out of 51 |
| Canada | -2.9 | -2.9 | AAA | 9 | Developed | North America | 1 out of 2 |
| Cape Verde | 9.1 | 9.1 | B | 94 | | Africa | 12 out of 51 |
| Central African Republic | 28.7 | 28.5 | | 172 | | Africa | 49 out of 51 |
| Chad | 27.3 | 27.2 | | 171 | | Africa | 48 out of 51 |
| Chile | -1.6 | -1.4 | AA- | 16 | Emerging | Latin America | 1 out of 20 |
| China | 2.4 | 2.3 | AA- | 42 | Emerging | Asia | 7 out of 29 |
| Colombia | 2.3 | 2.3 | BBB | 41 | Emerging | Latin America | 4 out of 20 |
| Congo Republic | 11.2 | 10.9 | B- | 117 | | Africa | 24 out of 51 |
| Congo, DR | 12.5 | 12.3 | B- | 131 | | Africa | 32 out of 51 |
| Costa Rica | 5.4 | 5.6 | BB- | 71 | | Latin America | 8 out of 20 |
| Côte d'Ivoire | 9.0 | 9.0 | | 92 | | Africa | 11 out of 51 |
| Croatia | 4.5 | 4.3 | BB | 63 | Frontier | Central and Eastern Europe | 13 out of 25 |
| Cuba | 18.8 | 18.8 | | 160 | | Caribbean | 9 out of 9 |
| Cyprus | 2.1 | 2.1 | BB+ | 40 | | Central and Eastern Europe | 7 out of 25 |
| Czech Republic | -0.4 | -0.4 | AA- | 23 | Emerging | Central and Eastern Europe | 1 out of 25 |
| Denmark | -3.5 | -3.5 | AAA | 4 | Developed | Western Europe | 3 out of 19 |
| Djibouti | 36.8 | 34.2 | | 175 | | Africa | 51 out of 51 |
| Dominican Republic | 8.8 | 8.9 | BB- | 90 | | Caribbean | 5 out of 9 |
| Ecuador | 10.5 | 10.2 | B | 109 | | Latin America | 18 out of 20 |
| Egypt | 10.9 | 10.8 | B- | 116 | Emerging | Africa | 23 out of 51 |
| El Salvador | 7.8 | 7.6 | B- | 81 | | Latin America | 10 out of 20 |
| Equatorial Guinea | 21.4 | 21.3 | | 165 | | Africa | 45 out of 51 |

§ S&P Credit Rating based on long-term foreign currency issuer rating. See http://www.standardandpoors.com/.

∗ World rank based on 175 countries covered by Euromoney. Ranking based on ascending order in which '1' equals the smallest country risk premium (CRP) and '175' equals the largest country risk premium (CRP).

† MSCI Market Classification based on MSCI Market Classification Framework. See http://www.msci.com/products/indexes/market_classification.html

‡ Regional classification based on Euromoney. Regional rankings based on ascending order in which '1' equals the smallest country risk premium (CRP) for each region.

Note: A CRP of 0.0% is assumed in the following cases: (i) when the investor country and the investee country both have an S&P sovereign credit rating of AAA; or (ii) when the investor country has an S&P credit rating of AAA, and the investee country has a sovereign credit rating below AAA, but has a calculated CRP below 0.0% (which would imply lower risk than a country rated AAA); or (iii) when the investor country has an S&P credit rating below AAA, and the investee country has a sovereign credit rating of AAA, but has a calculated CRP above 0.0% (which would imply greater risk than a country rated below AAA). For purposes of this analysis, the U.S. is treated as having a sovereign credit rating equivalent to AAA.

The country risk premium (CRP) is not the cost of equity capital (COE). The CRP is to be added to base COE. See Chapter 6 for proper application.

## Data Updated Through March 2017

| Investee Country | December 2016 Country Risk Premium (CRP) (%) | March 2017 Country Risk Premium (CRP) (%) | S&P Sovereign Credit Rating § | World Rank Out of 175* | MSCI Market Classification † | Euromoney Region ‡ | Regional Rank ‡ |
|---|---|---|---|---|---|---|---|
| Eritrea | 32.9 | 30.9 | | 173 | | Africa | 50 out of 51 |
| Estonia | 0.3 | 0.5 | AA- | 32 | Frontier | Central and Eastern Europe | 4 out of 25 |
| Ethiopia | 9.7 | 9.7 | B | 101 | | Africa | 16 out of 51 |
| Fiji | 15.2 | 15.0 | B+ | 147 | | Australasia | 5 out of 7 |
| Finland | -2.7 | -2.7 | AA+ | 11 | Developed | Western Europe | 8 out of 19 |
| France | -0.3 | -0.5 | AA | 22 | Developed | Western Europe | 12 out of 19 |
| Gabon | 7.5 | 7.8 | | 83 | | Africa | 7 out of 51 |
| Gambia | 13.6 | 13.6 | | 138 | | Africa | 34 out of 51 |
| Georgia | 6.2 | 6.4 | BB- | 74 | | Central and Eastern Europe | 15 out of 25 |
| Germany | -2.7 | -2.8 | AAA | 10 | Developed | Western Europe | 7 out of 19 |
| Ghana | 9.2 | 8.8 | B- | 89 | | Africa | 9 out of 51 |
| Greece | 10.4 | 10.1 | B- | 108 | Emerging | Western Europe | 19 out of 19 |
| Grenada | 10.0 | 10.0 | | 105 | | Caribbean | 7 out of 9 |
| Guatemala | 7.9 | 7.9 | BB | 84 | | Latin America | 11 out of 20 |
| Guinea | 17.4 | 17.3 | | 156 | | Africa | 41 out of 51 |
| Guinea-Bissau | 10.8 | 10.8 | | 115 | | Africa | 22 out of 51 |
| Guyana | 9.6 | 9.6 | | 100 | | Latin America | 15 out of 20 |
| Haiti | 20.3 | 18.1 | | 157 | | Caribbean | 8 out of 9 |
| Honduras | 9.3 | 9.3 | B+ | 98 | | Latin America | 14 out of 20 |
| Hong Kong | -2.1 | -2.1 | AAA | 14 | Developed | Asia | 2 out of 29 |
| Hungary | 3.7 | 3.8 | BBB- | 57 | Emerging | Central and Eastern Europe | 10 out of 25 |
| Iceland | 0.6 | 0.4 | A | 30 | | Western Europe | 15 out of 19 |
| India | 3.5 | 3.8 | BBB- | 55 | Emerging | Asia | 10 out of 29 |
| Indonesia | 4.3 | 4.3 | BB+ | 62 | Emerging | Asia | 11 out of 29 |
| Iran | 11.3 | 11.5 | | 125 | | Middle East | 10 out of 13 |
| Iraq | 13.2 | 13.2 | B- | 136 | | Middle East | 11 out of 13 |
| Ireland | 0.2 | 0.1 | A+ | 27 | Developed | Western Europe | 14 out of 19 |
| Israel | 0.1 | 0.1 | A+ | 28 | Developed | Middle East | 2 out of 13 |
| Italy | 3.1 | 2.9 | BBB- | 50 | Developed | Western Europe | 18 out of 19 |
| Jamaica | 9.4 | 9.9 | B | 104 | | Caribbean | 6 out of 9 |
| Japan | 0.0 | 0.0 | A+ | 25 | Developed | Asia | 5 out of 29 |
| Jordan | 6.4 | 6.6 | BB- | 76 | Frontier | Middle East | 8 out of 13 |
| Kazakhstan | 5.9 | 5.5 | BBB- | 70 | Frontier | Asia | 13 out of 29 |
| Kenya | 9.4 | 9.4 | B+ | 99 | Frontier | Africa | 15 out of 51 |
| Korea (North) | 32.2 | 31.6 | | 174 | | Asia | 29 out of 29 |
| Korea (South) | -0.8 | -0.8 | AA | 19 | Emerging | Asia | 4 out of 29 |
| Kuwait | 0.3 | 0.5 | AA | 31 | Frontier | Middle East | 3 out of 13 |
| Kyrgyz Republic | 14.7 | 14.5 | | 142 | | Central and Eastern Europe | 22 out of 25 |
| Laos | 19.0 | 18.4 | | 158 | | Asia | 28 out of 29 |
| Latvia | 2.4 | 2.5 | A- | 43 | | Central and Eastern Europe | 8 out of 25 |
| Lebanon | 11.2 | 10.5 | B- | 112 | Frontier | Middle East | 9 out of 13 |
| Lesotho | 14.9 | 14.8 | | 146 | | Africa | 36 out of 51 |
| Liberia | 10.1 | 10.0 | | 107 | | Africa | 17 out of 51 |
| Libya | 16.5 | 16.7 | | 153 | | Africa | 39 out of 51 |
| Lithuania | 1.6 | 1.6 | A- | 36 | Frontier | Central and Eastern Europe | 6 out of 25 |
| Luxembourg | -3.2 | -3.2 | AAA | 5 | | Western Europe | 4 out of 19 |
| Macedonia | 8.5 | 8.7 | BB- | 87 | | Central and Eastern Europe | 17 out of 25 |
| Madagascar | 11.0 | 11.4 | | 123 | | Africa | 27 out of 51 |
| Malawi | 10.7 | 10.6 | | 114 | | Africa | 21 out of 51 |
| Malaysia | 1.7 | 1.6 | A- | 35 | Emerging | Asia | 6 out of 29 |

§ S&P Credit Rating based on long-term foreign currency issuer rating. See http://www.standardandpoors.com/.

* World rank based on 175 countries covered by Euromoney. Ranking based on ascending order in which '1' equals the smallest country risk premium (CRP) and '175' equals the largest country risk premium (CRP).

† MSCI Market Classification based on MSCI Market Classification Framework. See http://www.msci.com/products/indexes/market_classification.html

‡ Regional classification based on Euromoney. Regional rankings based on ascending order in which '1' equals the smallest country risk premium (CRP) for each region.

Note: A CRP of 0.0% is assumed in the following cases: (i) when the investor country and the investee country both have an S&P sovereign credit rating of AAA; or (ii) when the investor country has an S&P credit rating of AAA, and the investee country has a sovereign credit rating below AAA, but has a calculated CRP below 0.0% (which would imply lower risk than a country rated AAA); or (iii) when the investor country has an S&P credit rating below AAA, and the investee country has a sovereign credit rating of AAA, but has a calculated CRP above 0.0% (which would imply greater risk than a country rated below AAA). For purposes of this analysis, the U.S. is treated as having a sovereign credit rating equivalent to AAA.

The country risk premium (CRP) is not the cost of equity capital (COE). The CRP is to be added to base COE. See Chapter 6 for proper application.

## Data Updated Through March 2017

| Investee Country | December 2016 Country Risk Premium (CRP) (%) | March 2017 Country Risk Premium (CRP) (%) | S&P Sovereign Credit Rating § | World Rank Out of 175* | MSCI Market Classification † | Euromoney Region ‡ | Regional Rank ‡ |
|---|---|---|---|---|---|---|---|
| Mali | 14.5 | 14.4 | | 141 | | Africa | 35 out of 51 |
| Malta | 0.0 | 0.1 | A- | 26 | | Western Europe | 13 out of 19 |
| Mauritania | 18.6 | 18.5 | | 159 | | Africa | 42 out of 51 |
| Mauritius | 5.2 | 5.2 | | 67 | Frontier | Asia | 12 out of 29 |
| Mexico | 1.6 | 1.7 | BBB+ | 37 | Emerging | Latin America | 2 out of 20 |
| Moldova | 12.9 | 13.2 | | 137 | | Central and Eastern Europe | 21 out of 25 |
| Mongolia | 11.0 | 11.3 | B- | 119 | | Asia | 18 out of 29 |
| Montenegro | 10.2 | 9.9 | B+ | 103 | | Central and Eastern Europe | 19 out of 25 |
| Morocco | 5.3 | 5.4 | BBB- | 69 | Frontier | Africa | 4 out of 51 |
| Mozambique | 12.1 | 11.9 | SD | 128 | | Africa | 29 out of 51 |
| Myanmar | 13.1 | 12.9 | | 134 | | Asia | 22 out of 29 |
| Namibia | 4.9 | 5.0 | | 66 | | Africa | 3 out of 51 |
| Nepal | 15.8 | 15.7 | | 149 | | Asia | 26 out of 29 |
| Netherlands | -3.1 | -3.2 | AAA | 6 | Developed | Western Europe | 5 out of 19 |
| New Zealand | -3.0 | -2.9 | AA | 8 | Developed | Australasia | 1 out of 7 |
| Nicaragua | 11.8 | 11.8 | B+ | 127 | | Latin America | 19 out of 20 |
| Niger | 11.4 | 11.3 | | 120 | | Africa | 25 out of 51 |
| Nigeria | 9.4 | 9.3 | B | 97 | Frontier | Africa | 14 out of 51 |
| Norway | -3.8 | -3.9 | AAA | 3 | Developed | Western Europe | 2 out of 19 |
| Oman | 2.5 | 2.5 | BBB- | 46 | Frontier | Middle East | 5 out of 13 |
| Pakistan | 11.5 | 11.4 | B | 122 | Frontier | Asia | 19 out of 29 |
| Panama | 3.2 | 3.3 | BBB | 52 | | Latin America | 6 out of 20 |
| Papua New Guinea | 11.0 | 11.0 | B+ | 118 | | Australasia | 3 out of 7 |
| Paraguay | 6.8 | 7.0 | BB | 80 | | Latin America | 9 out of 20 |
| Peru | 1.9 | 2.0 | BBB+ | 39 | Emerging | Latin America | 3 out of 20 |
| Philippines | 3.6 | 3.5 | BBB | 53 | Emerging | Asia | 9 out of 29 |
| Poland | 0.5 | 0.4 | BBB+ | 29 | Emerging | Central and Eastern Europe | 3 out of 25 |
| Portugal | 2.9 | 2.7 | BB+ | 49 | Developed | Western Europe | 17 out of 19 |
| Qatar | -0.7 | -0.6 | AA | 21 | Emerging | Middle East | 1 out of 13 |
| Romania | 3.7 | 3.8 | BBB- | 56 | Frontier | Central and Eastern Europe | 9 out of 25 |
| Russia | 6.1 | 5.4 | BB+ | 68 | Emerging | Central and Eastern Europe | 14 out of 25 |
| Rwanda | 12.2 | 12.1 | B | 130 | | Africa | 31 out of 51 |
| São Tomé & Príncipe | 18.7 | 19.1 | | 163 | | Africa | 43 out of 51 |
| Saudi Arabia | 2.9 | 2.5 | A- | 47 | | Middle East | 6 out of 13 |
| Senegal | 8.7 | 8.6 | B+ | 86 | | Africa | 8 out of 51 |
| Serbia | 6.7 | 6.4 | BB- | 75 | Frontier | Central and Eastern Europe | 16 out of 25 |
| Seychelles | 6.2 | 6.2 | | 73 | | Africa | 5 out of 51 |
| Sierra Leone | 12.2 | 12.1 | | 129 | | Africa | 30 out of 51 |
| Singapore | -4.0 | -4.0 | AAA | 1 | Developed | Asia | 1 out of 29 |
| Slovakia | -0.3 | -0.2 | A+ | 24 | | Central and Eastern Europe | 2 out of 25 |
| Slovenia | 1.2 | 1.2 | A | 34 | Frontier | Central and Eastern Europe | 5 out of 25 |
| Solomon Islands | 23.2 | 23.1 | | 168 | | Australasia | 6 out of 7 |
| Somalia | 21.4 | 21.3 | | 166 | | Africa | 46 out of 51 |
| South Africa | 3.8 | 4.0 | BBB- | 60 | Emerging | Africa | 2 out of 51 |
| Spain | 2.0 | 2.0 | BBB+ | 38 | Developed | Western Europe | 16 out of 19 |
| Sri Lanka | 6.1 | 5.8 | B+ | 72 | Frontier | Asia | 14 out of 29 |
| Sudan | 17.3 | 17.2 | | 154 | | Africa | 40 out of 51 |
| Suriname | 9.6 | 9.8 | B+ | 102 | | Latin America | 16 out of 20 |
| Swaziland | 15.6 | 16.5 | | 152 | | Africa | 38 out of 51 |
| Sweden | -3.1 | -3.1 | AAA | 7 | Developed | Western Europe | 6 out of 19 |

§ S&P Credit Rating based on long-term foreign currency issuer rating. See http://www.standardandpoors.com/.

* World rank based on 175 countries covered by Euromoney. Ranking based on ascending order in which '1' equals the smallest country risk premium (CRP) and '175' equals the largest country risk premium (CRP).

† MSCI Market Classification based on MSCI Market Classification Framework. See http://www.msci.com/products/indexes/market_classification.html

‡ Regional classification based on Euromoney. Regional rankings based on ascending order in which '1' equals the smallest country risk premium (CRP) for each region.

Note: A CRP of 0.0% is assumed in the following cases: (i) when the investor country and the investee country both have an S&P sovereign credit rating of AAA; or (ii) when the investor country has an S&P credit rating of AAA, and the investee country has a sovereign credit rating below AAA, but has a calculated CRP below 0.0% (which would imply lower risk than a country rated AAA); or (iii) when the investor country has an S&P credit rating below AAA, and the investee country has a sovereign credit rating of AAA, but has a calculated CRP above 0.0% (which would imply greater risk than a country rated below AAA). For purposes of this analysis, the U.S. is treated as having a sovereign credit rating equivalent to AAA.

The country risk premium (CRP) is not the cost of equity capital (COE). The CRP is to be added to base COE. See Chapter 6 for proper application.

## Data Updated Through March 2017

| Investee Country | December 2016 Country Risk Premium (CRP) (%) | March 2017 Country Risk Premium (CRP) (%) | S&P Sovereign Credit Rating § | World Rank Out of 175* | MSCI Market Classification † | Euromoney Region ‡ | Regional Rank ‡ |
|---|---|---|---|---|---|---|---|
| Switzerland | -3.8 | -3.9 | AAA | 2 | Developed | Western Europe | 1 out of 19 |
| Syria | 22.2 | 22.3 | | 167 | | Middle East | 13 out of 13 |
| Taiwan | -1.1 | -1.0 | AA- | 18 | Emerging | Asia | 3 out of 29 |
| Tajikistan | 16.9 | 17.2 | | 155 | | Central and Eastern Europe | 25 out of 25 |
| Tanzania | 9.0 | 9.2 | | 95 | | Africa | 13 out of 51 |
| Thailand | 3.2 | 3.1 | BBB+ | 51 | Emerging | Asia | 8 out of 29 |
| Togo | 10.6 | 10.6 | | 113 | | Africa | 20 out of 51 |
| Tonga | 25.7 | 25.6 | | 170 | | Australasia | 7 out of 7 |
| Trinidad & Tobago | 3.6 | 3.6 | A- | 54 | | Caribbean | 2 out of 9 |
| Tunisia | 6.5 | 6.9 | | 79 | Frontier | Africa | 6 out of 51 |
| Turkey | 4.0 | 3.8 | BB | 58 | Emerging | Central and Eastern Europe | 11 out of 25 |
| Turkmenistan | 14.0 | 14.2 | | 140 | | Asia | 24 out of 29 |
| Uganda | 10.1 | 10.4 | B | 110 | | Africa | 18 out of 51 |
| Ukraine | 13.0 | 13.0 | B- | 135 | | Central and Eastern Europe | 20 out of 25 |
| United Arab Emirates | 0.8 | 0.8 | AA | 33 | Emerging | Middle East | 4 out of 13 |
| United Kingdom | -0.8 | -0.6 | AA | 20 | Developed | Western Europe | 11 out of 19 |
| United States | -1.8 | -1.8 | AA+ | 15 | Developed | North America | 2 out of 2 |
| Uruguay | 2.6 | 2.5 | BBB | 45 | | Latin America | 5 out of 20 |
| Uzbekistan | 13.2 | 12.6 | | 132 | | Asia | 21 out of 29 |
| Vanuatu | 14.9 | 14.8 | | 145 | | Australasia | 4 out of 7 |
| Venezuela | 18.7 | 19.1 | CCC | 162 | | Latin America | 20 out of 20 |
| Vietnam | 7.1 | 6.8 | BB- | 78 | Frontier | Asia | 16 out of 29 |
| Yemen | 19.1 | 19.0 | | 161 | | Middle East | 12 out of 13 |
| Zambia | 10.5 | 10.5 | B | 111 | | Africa | 19 out of 51 |
| Zimbabwe | 20.7 | 20.5 | | 164 | | Africa | 44 out of 51 |

## March 2017 Country Risk Premium (CRP) Summary Statistics:

| S&P Rating | Country Count | Average CRP (%) | Median CRP (%) | Min CRP (%) | Max CRP (%) |
|---|---|---|---|---|---|
| AAA ** | 12 | -3.1 | -3.2 | -4.0 | -1.8 |
| AA (AA+, AA, AA-) | 15 | -0.7 | -0.6 | -2.9 | 2.3 |
| A (A+, A, A-) | 14 | 1.3 | 1.4 | -0.2 | 3.6 |
| BBB (BBB+, BBB, BBB-) | 17 | 3.1 | 3.1 | 0.4 | 5.5 |
| BB (BB+, BB, BB-) | 22 | 6.0 | 6.0 | 2.1 | 11.6 |
| B+ − SD | 39 | 10.9 | 10.5 | 5.8 | 19.1 |
| Investment Grade ** | 58 | 0.4 | 0.4 | -4.0 | 5.5 |
| Non-Investment Grade ** | 61 | 9.1 | 9.3 | 2.1 | 19.1 |
| **MSCI Market Classification** | | | | | |
| Developed Markets | 23 | -1.6 | -2.5 | -4.0 | 2.9 |
| Emerging Markets | 23 | 2.8 | 2.3 | -1.4 | 10.8 |
| Frontier Markets | 22 | 5.9 | 5.7 | 0.5 | 11.6 |
| **Euromoney Region ‡** | | | | | |
| Africa | 51 | 13.4 | 11.4 | 2.5 | 34.2 |
| Asia | 29 | 8.1 | 6.6 | -4.0 | 31.6 |
| Australasia | 7 | 12.0 | 14.8 | -2.9 | 25.6 |
| Caribbean | 9 | 9.4 | 8.9 | 2.5 | 18.8 |
| Central and Eastern Europe | 25 | 6.4 | 4.3 | -0.4 | 17.2 |
| Latin America | 20 | 7.0 | 7.7 | -1.4 | 19.1 |
| Middle East | 13 | 7.2 | 4.7 | -0.6 | 22.3 |
| North America | 2 | -2.4 | -2.4 | -2.9 | -1.8 |
| Western Europe | 19 | -0.7 | -1.3 | -3.9 | 10.1 |

## CCR Base Cost of Equity Capital:

| Japan | COE (%) |
|---|---|
| March 2017 | 10.2 |
| December 2016 | 10.3 |

CCR base country-level COE for a Japan-based investor investing in Japan.

§ S&P Credit Rating based on long-term foreign currency issuer rating. See http://www.standardandpoors.com/.

* World rank based on 175 countries covered by Euromoney. Ranking based on ascending order in which '1' equals the smallest country risk premium (CRP) and '175' equals the largest country risk premium (CRP).

† MSCI Market Classification based on MSCI Market Classification Framework. See http://www.msci.com/products/indexes/market_classification.html.

‡ Regional classification based on Euromoney. Regional rankings based on ascending order in which '1' equals the smallest country risk premium (CRP) for each region.

** Investment grade based on S&P sovereign credit rating from AAA to BBB-. Non-Investment grade based on S&P sovereign credit rating from BB+ to SD. For purposes of this analysis, the U.S. is being treated as if it were rated AAA by S&P.

Note: A CRP of 0.0% is assumed in the following cases: (i) when the investor country and the investee country both have an S&P sovereign credit rating of AAA; or (ii) when the investor country has an S&P credit rating of AAA, and the investee country has a sovereign credit rating below AAA, but has a calculated CRP below 0.0% (which would imply lower risk than a country rated AAA); or (iii) when the investor country has an S&P credit rating below AAA, and the investee country has a sovereign credit rating of AAA, but has a calculated CRP above 0.0% (which would imply greater risk than a country rated below AAA). For purposes of this analysis, the U.S. is treated as having a sovereign credit rating equivalent to AAA.

The country risk premium (CRP) is not the cost of equity capital (COE). The CRP is to be added to base COE. See Chapter 6 for proper application.

## Data Updated Through March 2017

| Investee Country | December 2016 Country Risk Premium (CRP) (%) | March 2017 Country Risk Premium (CRP) (%) | S&P Sovereign Credit Rating § | World Rank Out of 175* | MSCI Market Classification † | Euromoney Region ‡ | Regional Rank ‡ |
|---|---|---|---|---|---|---|---|
| Afghanistan | 13.9 | 13.7 | | 139 | | Asia | 23 out of 29 |
| Albania | 8.9 | 9.0 | B+ | 93 | | Central and Eastern Europe | 18 out of 25 |
| Algeria | 8.9 | 8.9 | | 91 | | Africa | 10 out of 51 |
| Angola | 11.1 | 11.2 | B | 121 | | Africa | 26 out of 51 |
| Argentina | 9.4 | 9.2 | B- | 96 | Frontier | Latin America | 13 out of 20 |
| Armenia | 6.6 | 6.8 | | 77 | | Asia | 15 out of 29 |
| Australia | -1.7 | -1.8 | AAA | 12 | Developed | Australasia | 2 out of 7 |
| Austria | -1.5 | -1.6 | AA+ | 13 | Developed | Western Europe | 9 out of 19 |
| Azerbaijan | 7.8 | 8.0 | BB+ | 85 | | Asia | 17 out of 29 |
| Bahamas | 5.3 | 5.0 | BB+ | 65 | | Caribbean | 3 out of 9 |
| Bahrain | 5.2 | 5.0 | BB- | 64 | Frontier | Middle East | 7 out of 13 |
| Bangladesh | 11.6 | 11.3 | BB- | 126 | Frontier | Asia | 20 out of 29 |
| Barbados | 6.8 | 7.8 | CCC+ | 82 | | Caribbean | 4 out of 9 |
| Belarus | 13.7 | 14.0 | B- | 143 | | Central and Eastern Europe | 23 out of 25 |
| Belgium | -0.3 | -0.5 | AA | 17 | Developed | Western Europe | 10 out of 19 |
| Belize | 9.9 | 9.9 | B- | 106 | | Latin America | 17 out of 20 |
| Benin | 15.2 | 15.2 | | 150 | | Africa | 37 out of 51 |
| Bermuda | 3.1 | 3.0 | A+ | 44 | | Caribbean | 1 out of 9 |
| Bhutan | 14.9 | 14.8 | | 148 | | Asia | 25 out of 29 |
| Bolivia | 8.5 | 8.7 | BB | 88 | | Latin America | 12 out of 20 |
| Bosnia & Herzegovina | 14.1 | 14.2 | B | 144 | | Central and Eastern Europe | 24 out of 25 |
| Botswana | 3.1 | 3.0 | A- | 48 | | Africa | 1 out of 51 |
| Brazil | 4.5 | 4.3 | BB | 59 | Emerging | Latin America | 7 out of 20 |
| Bulgaria | 4.3 | 4.5 | BB+ | 61 | | Central and Eastern Europe | 12 out of 25 |
| Burkina Faso | 12.6 | 12.5 | B- | 133 | | Africa | 33 out of 51 |
| Burundi | 23.6 | 23.6 | | 169 | | Africa | 47 out of 51 |
| Cambodia | 15.8 | 15.4 | | 151 | | Asia | 27 out of 29 |
| Cameroon | 11.3 | 11.3 | B | 124 | | Africa | 28 out of 51 |
| Canada | -1.9 | -2.0 | AAA | 9 | Developed | North America | 1 out of 2 |
| Cape Verde | 9.1 | 9.1 | B | 94 | | Africa | 12 out of 51 |
| Central African Republic | 26.9 | 26.9 | | 172 | | Africa | 49 out of 51 |
| Chad | 25.7 | 25.7 | | 171 | | Africa | 48 out of 51 |
| Chile | -0.8 | -0.6 | AA- | 16 | Emerging | Latin America | 1 out of 20 |
| China | 2.9 | 2.8 | AA- | 42 | Emerging | Asia | 7 out of 29 |
| Colombia | 2.8 | 2.8 | BBB | 41 | Emerging | Latin America | 4 out of 20 |
| Congo Republic | 10.9 | 10.7 | B- | 117 | | Africa | 24 out of 51 |
| Congo, DR | 12.1 | 12.0 | B- | 131 | | Africa | 32 out of 51 |
| Costa Rica | 5.7 | 5.9 | BB- | 71 | | Latin America | 8 out of 20 |
| Côte d'Ivoire | 9.0 | 9.0 | | 92 | | Africa | 11 out of 51 |
| Croatia | 4.8 | 4.7 | BB | 63 | Frontier | Central and Eastern Europe | 13 out of 25 |
| Cuba | 17.9 | 18.0 | | 160 | | Caribbean | 9 out of 9 |
| Cyprus | 2.6 | 2.7 | BB+ | 40 | | Central and Eastern Europe | 7 out of 25 |
| Czech Republic | 0.4 | 0.3 | AA- | 23 | Emerging | Central and Eastern Europe | 1 out of 25 |
| Denmark | -2.5 | -2.5 | AAA | 4 | Developed | Western Europe | 3 out of 19 |
| Djibouti | 34.4 | 32.2 | | 175 | | Africa | 51 out of 51 |
| Dominican Republic | 8.8 | 8.9 | BB- | 90 | | Caribbean | 5 out of 9 |
| Ecuador | 10.3 | 10.1 | B | 109 | | Latin America | 18 out of 20 |
| Egypt | 10.7 | 10.6 | B- | 116 | Emerging | Africa | 23 out of 51 |
| El Salvador | 7.9 | 7.7 | B- | 81 | | Latin America | 10 out of 20 |
| Equatorial Guinea | 20.3 | 20.3 | | 165 | | Africa | 45 out of 51 |

§ S&P Credit Rating based on long-term foreign currency issuer rating. See http://www.standardandpoors.com/.

• World rank based on 175 countries covered by Euromoney. Ranking based on ascending order in which '1' equals the smallest country risk premium (CRP) and '175' equals the largest country risk premium (CRP).

† MSCI Market Classification based on MSCI Market Classification Framework. See http://www.msci.com/products/indexes/market_classification.html.

‡ Regional classification based on Euromoney. Regional rankings based on ascending order in which '1' equals the smallest country risk premium (CRP) for each region.

Note: A CRP of 0.0% is assumed in the following cases: (i) when the investor country and the investee country both have an S&P sovereign credit rating of AAA; or (ii) when the investor country has an S&P credit rating of AAA, and the investee country has a sovereign credit rating below AAA, but has a calculated CRP below 0.0% (which would imply lower risk than a country rated AAA); or (iii) when the investor country has an S&P credit rating below AAA, and the investee country has a sovereign credit rating of AAA, but has a calculated CRP above 0.0% (which would imply greater risk than a country rated below AAA). For purposes of this analysis, the U.S. is treated as having a sovereign credit rating equivalent to AAA.

The country risk premium (CRP) is not the cost of equity capital (COE). The CRP is to be added to base COE. See Chapter 6 for proper application.

## Data Updated Through March 2017

| Investee Country | December 2016 Country Risk Premium (CRP) (%) | March 2017 Country Risk Premium (CRP) (%) | S&P Sovereign Credit Rating § | World Rank Out of 175∗ | MSCI Market Classification † | Euromoney Region ‡ | Regional Rank ‡ |
|---|---|---|---|---|---|---|---|
| Eritrea | 30.8 | 29.1 | | 173 | | Africa | 50 out of 51 |
| Estonia | 1.0 | 1.1 | AA- | 32 | Frontier | Central and Eastern Europe | 4 out of 25 |
| Ethiopia | 9.6 | 9.6 | B | 101 | | Africa | 16 out of 51 |
| Fiji | 14.6 | 14.5 | B+ | 147 | | Australasia | 5 out of 7 |
| Finland | -1.8 | -1.8 | AA+ | 11 | Developed | Western Europe | 8 out of 19 |
| France | 0.4 | 0.2 | AA | 22 | Developed | Western Europe | 12 out of 19 |
| Gabon | 7.5 | 7.8 | | 83 | | Africa | 7 out of 51 |
| Gambia | 13.2 | 13.2 | | 138 | | Africa | 34 out of 51 |
| Georgia | 6.4 | 6.6 | BB- | 74 | | Central and Eastern Europe | 15 out of 25 |
| Germany | -1.8 | -1.9 | AAA | 10 | Developed | Western Europe | 7 out of 19 |
| Ghana | 9.2 | 8.8 | B- | 89 | | Africa | 9 out of 51 |
| Greece | 10.2 | 10.0 | B- | 108 | Emerging | Western Europe | 19 out of 19 |
| Grenada | 9.8 | 9.9 | | 105 | | Caribbean | 7 out of 9 |
| Guatemala | 7.9 | 7.9 | BB | 84 | | Latin America | 11 out of 20 |
| Guinea | 16.6 | 16.6 | | 156 | | Africa | 41 out of 51 |
| Guinea-Bissau | 10.6 | 10.6 | | 115 | | Africa | 22 out of 51 |
| Guyana | 9.5 | 9.5 | | 100 | | Latin America | 15 out of 20 |
| Haiti | 19.3 | 17.4 | | 157 | | Caribbean | 8 out of 9 |
| Honduras | 9.2 | 9.3 | B+ | 98 | | Latin America | 14 out of 20 |
| Hong Kong | -1.2 | -1.3 | AAA | 14 | Developed | Asia | 2 out of 29 |
| Hungary | 4.1 | 4.2 | BBB- | 57 | Emerging | Central and Eastern Europe | 10 out of 25 |
| Iceland | 1.3 | 1.1 | A | 30 | | Western Europe | 15 out of 19 |
| India | 3.9 | 4.1 | BBB- | 55 | Emerging | Asia | 10 out of 29 |
| Indonesia | 4.6 | 4.6 | BB+ | 62 | Emerging | Asia | 11 out of 29 |
| Iran | 11.1 | 11.3 | | 125 | | Middle East | 10 out of 13 |
| Iraq | 12.8 | 12.8 | B- | 136 | | Middle East | 11 out of 13 |
| Ireland | 0.9 | 0.8 | A+ | 27 | Developed | Western Europe | 14 out of 19 |
| Israel | 0.8 | 0.8 | A+ | 28 | Developed | Middle East | 2 out of 13 |
| Italy | 3.5 | 3.4 | BBB- | 50 | Developed | Western Europe | 18 out of 19 |
| Jamaica | 9.3 | 9.8 | B | 104 | | Caribbean | 6 out of 9 |
| Japan | 0.7 | 0.7 | A+ | 25 | Developed | Asia | 5 out of 29 |
| Jordan | 6.6 | 6.7 | BB- | 76 | Frontier | Middle East | 8 out of 13 |
| Kazakhstan | 6.1 | 5.8 | BBB- | 70 | Frontier | Asia | 13 out of 29 |
| Kenya | 9.3 | 9.4 | B+ | 99 | Frontier | Africa | 15 out of 51 |
| Korea (North) | 30.2 | 29.7 | | 174 | | Asia | 29 out of 29 |
| Korea (South) | 0.0 | 0.0 | AA | 19 | Emerging | Asia | 4 out of 29 |
| Kuwait | 1.0 | 1.1 | AA | 31 | Frontier | Middle East | 3 out of 13 |
| Kyrgyz Republic | 14.1 | 14.0 | | 142 | | Central and Eastern Europe | 22 out of 25 |
| Laos | 18.1 | 17.6 | | 158 | | Asia | 28 out of 29 |
| Latvia | 2.9 | 3.0 | A- | 43 | | Central and Eastern Europe | 8 out of 25 |
| Lebanon | 11.0 | 10.4 | B- | 112 | Frontier | Middle East | 9 out of 13 |
| Lesotho | 14.3 | 14.3 | | 146 | | Africa | 36 out of 51 |
| Liberia | 9.9 | 9.9 | | 107 | | Africa | 17 out of 51 |
| Libya | 15.8 | 16.1 | | 153 | | Africa | 39 out of 51 |
| Lithuania | 2.1 | 2.2 | A- | 36 | Frontier | Central and Eastern Europe | 6 out of 25 |
| Luxembourg | -2.2 | -2.3 | AAA | 5 | | Western Europe | 4 out of 19 |
| Macedonia | 8.5 | 8.7 | BB- | 87 | | Central and Eastern Europe | 17 out of 25 |
| Madagascar | 10.7 | 11.2 | | 123 | | Africa | 27 out of 51 |
| Malawi | 10.5 | 10.5 | | 114 | | Africa | 21 out of 51 |
| Malaysia | 2.3 | 2.1 | A- | 35 | Emerging | Asia | 6 out of 29 |

§ S&P Credit Rating based on long-term foreign currency issuer rating. See http://www.standardandpoors.com/.

∗ World rank based on 175 countries covered by Euromoney. Ranking based on ascending order in which '1' equals the smallest country risk premium (CRP) and '175' equals the largest country risk premium (CRP).

† MSCI Market Classification based on MSCI Market Classification Framework. See http://www.msci.com/products/indexes/market_classification.html

‡ Regional classification based on Euromoney. Regional rankings based on ascending order in which '1' equals the smallest country risk premium (CRP) for each region.

Note: A CRP of 0.0% is assumed in the following cases: (i) when the investor country and the investee country both have an S&P sovereign credit rating of AAA; or (ii) when the investor country has an S&P credit rating of AAA, and the investee country has a sovereign credit rating below AAA, but has a calculated CRP below 0.0% (which would imply lower risk than a country rated AAA); or (iii) when the investor country has an S&P credit rating below AAA, and the investee country has a sovereign credit rating of AAA, but has a calculated CRP above 0.0% (which would imply greater risk than a country rated below AAA). For purposes of this analysis, the U.S. is treated as having a sovereign credit rating equivalent to AAA.

The country risk premium (CRP) is not the cost of equity capital (COE). The CRP is to be added to base COE. See Chapter 6 for proper application.

## Data Updated Through March 2017

| Investee Country | December 2016 Country Risk Premium (CRP) (%) | March 2017 Country Risk Premium (CRP) (%) | S&P Sovereign Credit Rating § | World Rank Out of 175∗ | MSCI Market Classification † | Euromoney Region ‡ | Regional Rank ‡ |
|---|---|---|---|---|---|---|---|
| Mali | 14.0 | 14.0 | | 141 | | Africa | 35 out of 51 |
| Malta | 0.7 | 0.7 | A- | 26 | | Western Europe | 13 out of 19 |
| Mauritania | 17.8 | 17.7 | | 159 | | Africa | 42 out of 51 |
| Mauritius | 5.5 | 5.4 | | 67 | Frontier | Asia | 12 out of 29 |
| Mexico | 2.2 | 2.3 | BBB+ | 37 | Emerging | Latin America | 2 out of 20 |
| Moldova | 12.5 | 12.9 | | 137 | | Central and Eastern Europe | 21 out of 25 |
| Mongolia | 10.8 | 11.1 | B- | 119 | | Asia | 18 out of 29 |
| Montenegro | 10.1 | 9.8 | B+ | 103 | | Central and Eastern Europe | 19 out of 25 |
| Morocco | 5.5 | 5.7 | BBB- | 69 | Frontier | Africa | 4 out of 51 |
| Mozambique | 11.8 | 11.7 | SD | 128 | | Africa | 29 out of 51 |
| Myanmar | 12.7 | 12.6 | | 134 | | Asia | 22 out of 29 |
| Namibia | 5.2 | 5.3 | | 66 | | Africa | 3 out of 51 |
| Nepal | 15.2 | 15.2 | | 149 | | Asia | 26 out of 29 |
| Netherlands | -2.1 | -2.2 | AAA | 6 | Developed | Western Europe | 5 out of 19 |
| New Zealand | -2.0 | -2.0 | AA | 8 | Developed | Australasia | 1 out of 7 |
| Nicaragua | 11.5 | 11.5 | B+ | 127 | | Latin America | 19 out of 20 |
| Niger | 11.1 | 11.1 | | 120 | | Africa | 25 out of 51 |
| Nigeria | 9.3 | 9.3 | B | 97 | Frontier | Africa | 14 out of 51 |
| Norway | -2.8 | -2.9 | AAA | 3 | Developed | Western Europe | 2 out of 19 |
| Oman | 3.0 | 3.0 | BBB- | 46 | Frontier | Middle East | 5 out of 13 |
| Pakistan | 11.2 | 11.2 | B | 122 | Frontier | Asia | 19 out of 29 |
| Panama | 3.7 | 3.7 | BBB | 52 | | Latin America | 6 out of 20 |
| Papua New Guinea | 10.8 | 10.8 | B+ | 118 | | Australasia | 3 out of 7 |
| Paraguay | 7.0 | 7.1 | BB | 80 | | Latin America | 9 out of 20 |
| Peru | 2.5 | 2.6 | BBB+ | 39 | Emerging | Latin America | 3 out of 20 |
| Philippines | 4.0 | 3.9 | BBB | 53 | Emerging | Asia | 9 out of 29 |
| Poland | 1.2 | 1.0 | BBB+ | 29 | Emerging | Central and Eastern Europe | 3 out of 25 |
| Portugal | 3.4 | 3.2 | BB+ | 49 | Developed | Western Europe | 17 out of 19 |
| Qatar | 0.1 | 0.2 | AA | 21 | Emerging | Middle East | 1 out of 13 |
| Romania | 4.1 | 4.2 | BBB- | 56 | Frontier | Central and Eastern Europe | 9 out of 25 |
| Russia | 6.3 | 5.6 | BB+ | 68 | Emerging | Central and Eastern Europe | 14 out of 25 |
| Rwanda | 11.9 | 11.9 | B | 130 | | Africa | 31 out of 51 |
| São Tomé & Príncipe | 17.9 | 18.3 | | 163 | | Africa | 43 out of 51 |
| Saudi Arabia | 3.4 | 3.0 | A- | 47 | | Middle East | 6 out of 13 |
| Senegal | 8.6 | 8.6 | B+ | 86 | | Africa | 8 out of 51 |
| Serbia | 6.9 | 6.6 | BB- | 75 | Frontier | Central and Eastern Europe | 16 out of 25 |
| Seychelles | 6.4 | 6.4 | | 73 | | Africa | 5 out of 51 |
| Sierra Leone | 11.9 | 11.9 | | 129 | | Africa | 30 out of 51 |
| Singapore | -2.9 | -3.0 | AAA | 1 | Developed | Asia | 1 out of 29 |
| Slovakia | 0.5 | 0.5 | A+ | 24 | | Central and Eastern Europe | 2 out of 25 |
| Slovenia | 1.8 | 1.8 | A | 34 | Frontier | Central and Eastern Europe | 5 out of 25 |
| Solomon Islands | 21.9 | 21.9 | | 168 | | Australasia | 6 out of 7 |
| Somalia | 20.3 | 20.3 | | 166 | | Africa | 46 out of 51 |
| South Africa | 4.2 | 4.4 | BBB- | 60 | Emerging | Africa | 2 out of 51 |
| Spain | 2.6 | 2.6 | BBB+ | 38 | Developed | Western Europe | 16 out of 19 |
| Sri Lanka | 6.3 | 6.0 | B+ | 72 | Frontier | Asia | 14 out of 29 |
| Sudan | 16.6 | 16.5 | | 154 | | Africa | 40 out of 51 |
| Suriname | 9.5 | 9.7 | B+ | 102 | | Latin America | 16 out of 20 |
| Swaziland | 15.0 | 15.9 | | 152 | | Africa | 38 out of 51 |
| Sweden | -2.1 | -2.2 | AAA | 7 | Developed | Western Europe | 6 out of 19 |

§ S&P Credit Rating based on long-term foreign currency issuer rating. See http://www.standardandpoors.com/.

∗ World rank based on 175 countries covered by Euromoney. Ranking based on ascending order in which '1' equals the smallest country risk premium (CRP) and '175' equals the largest country risk premium (CRP).

† MSCI Market Classification based on MSCI Market Classification Framework. See http://www.msci.com/products/indexes/market_classification.html

‡ Regional classification based on Euromoney. Regional rankings based on ascending order in which '1' equals the smallest country risk premium (CRP) for each region.

Note: A CRP of 0.0% is assumed in the following cases: (i) when the investor country and the investee country both have an S&P sovereign credit rating of AAA, or (ii) when the investor country has an S&P credit rating of AAA, and the investee country has a sovereign credit rating below AAA, but has a calculated CRP below 0.0% (which would imply lower risk than a country rated AAA); or (iii) when the investor country has an S&P credit rating below AAA, and the investee country has a sovereign credit rating of AAA, but has a calculated CRP above 0.0% (which would imply greater risk than a country rated below AAA). For purposes of this analysis, the U.S. is treated as having a sovereign credit rating equivalent to AAA.

The country risk premium (CRP) is not the cost of equity capital (COE). The CRP is to be added to base COE. See Chapter 6 for proper application.

## Data Updated Through March 2017

| Investee Country | December 2016 Country Risk Premium (CRP) (%) | March 2017 Country Risk Premium (CRP) (%) | S&P Sovereign Credit Rating § | World Rank Out of 175* | MSCI Market Classification † | Euromoney Region ‡ | Regional Rank ‡ |
|---|---|---|---|---|---|---|---|
| Switzerland | -2.7 | -2.9 | AAA | 2 | Developed | Western Europe | 1 out of 19 |
| Syria | 21.0 | 21.2 | | 167 | | Middle East | 13 out of 13 |
| Taiwan | -0.2 | -0.3 | AA- | 18 | Emerging | Asia | 3 out of 29 |
| Tajikistan | 16.2 | 16.5 | | 155 | | Central and Eastern Europe | 25 out of 25 |
| Tanzania | 9.0 | 9.1 | | 95 | | Africa | 13 out of 51 |
| Thailand | 3.7 | 3.5 | BBB+ | 51 | Emerging | Asia | 8 out of 29 |
| Togo | 10.4 | 10.4 | | 113 | | Africa | 20 out of 51 |
| Tonga | 24.2 | 24.2 | | 170 | | Australasia | 7 out of 7 |
| Trinidad & Tobago | 4.0 | 4.0 | A- | 54 | | Caribbean | 2 out of 9 |
| Tunisia | 6.7 | 7.0 | | 79 | Frontier | Africa | 6 out of 51 |
| Turkey | 4.4 | 4.2 | BB | 58 | Emerging | Central and Eastern Europe | 11 out of 25 |
| Turkmenistan | 13.5 | 13.8 | | 140 | | Asia | 24 out of 29 |
| Uganda | 10.0 | 10.2 | B | 110 | | Africa | 18 out of 51 |
| Ukraine | 12.6 | 12.7 | B- | 135 | | Central and Eastern Europe | 20 out of 25 |
| United Arab Emirates | 1.4 | 1.5 | AA | 33 | Emerging | Middle East | 4 out of 13 |
| United Kingdom | 0.0 | 0.1 | AA | 20 | Developed | Western Europe | 11 out of 19 |
| United States | -1.0 | -1.0 | AA+ | 15 | Developed | North America | 2 out of 2 |
| Uruguay | 3.1 | 3.0 | BBB | 45 | | Latin America | 5 out of 20 |
| Uzbekistan | 12.8 | 12.3 | | 132 | | Asia | 21 out of 29 |
| Vanuatu | 14.3 | 14.3 | | 145 | | Australasia | 4 out of 7 |
| Venezuela | 17.9 | 18.3 | CCC | 162 | | Latin America | 20 out of 20 |
| Vietnam | 7.2 | 6.9 | BB- | 78 | Frontier | Asia | 16 out of 29 |
| Yemen | 18.1 | 18.2 | | 161 | | Middle East | 12 out of 13 |
| Zambia | 10.3 | 10.3 | B | 111 | | Africa | 19 out of 51 |
| Zimbabwe | 19.7 | 19.6 | | 164 | | Africa | 44 out of 51 |

## March 2017 Country Risk Premium (CRP) Summary Statistics:

| S&P Rating | Country Count | Average CRP (%) | Median CRP (%) | Min CRP (%) | Max CRP (%) |
|---|---|---|---|---|---|
| AAA ** | 12 | -2.2 | -2.2 | -3.0 | -1.0 |
| AA (AA+, AA, AA-) | 15 | 0.0 | 0.1 | -2.0 | 2.8 |
| A (A+, A, A-) | 14 | 1.9 | 2.0 | 0.5 | 4.0 |
| BBB (BBB+, BBB, BBB-) | 17 | 3.5 | 3.5 | 1.0 | 5.8 |
| BB (BB+, BB, BB-) | 22 | 6.2 | 6.2 | 2.7 | 11.3 |
| B+ − SD | 39 | 10.7 | 10.3 | 6.0 | 18.3 |
| Investment Grade ** | 58 | 1.1 | 1.1 | -3.0 | 5.8 |
| Non-Investment Grade ** | 61 | 9.1 | 9.3 | 2.7 | 18.3 |
| **MSCI Market Classification §** | | | | | |
| Developed Markets | 23 | -0.8 | -1.6 | -3.0 | 3.4 |
| Emerging Markets | 23 | 3.2 | 2.8 | -0.6 | 10.6 |
| Frontier Markets | 22 | 6.1 | 5.9 | 1.1 | 11.3 |
| **Euromoney Region ‡** | | | | | |
| Africa | 51 | 13.0 | 11.2 | 3.0 | 32.2 |
| Asia | 29 | 8.1 | 6.8 | -3.0 | 29.7 |
| Australasia | 7 | 11.7 | 14.3 | -2.0 | 24.2 |
| Caribbean | 9 | 9.3 | 8.9 | 3.0 | 18.0 |
| Central and Eastern Europe | 25 | 6.6 | 4.7 | 0.3 | 16.5 |
| Latin America | 20 | 7.1 | 7.8 | -0.6 | 18.3 |
| Middle East | 13 | 7.3 | 5.0 | 0.2 | 21.2 |
| North America | 2 | -1.5 | -1.5 | -2.0 | -1.0 |
| Western Europe | 19 | 0.1 | -0.5 | -2.9 | 10.0 |

## CCR Base Cost of Equity Capital:

| Korea (South) | COE (%) |
|---|---|
| March 2017 | 10.3 |
| December 2016 | 10.6 |

CCR base country-level COE for a Korea (South)-based investor investing in Korea (South).

§ S&P Credit Rating based on long-term foreign currency issuer rating. See http://www.standardandpoors.com/.

* World rank based on 175 countries covered by Euromoney. Ranking based on ascending order in which '1' equals the smallest country risk premium (CRP) and '175' equals the largest country risk premium (CRP).

† MSCI Market Classification based on MSCI Market Classification Framework. See http://www.msci.com/products/indexes/market_classification.html.

‡ Regional classification based on Euromoney. Regional rankings based on ascending order in which '1' equals the smallest country risk premium (CRP) for each region.

** Investment grade based on S&P sovereign credit rating from AAA to BBB-. Non-Investment grade based on S&P sovereign credit rating from BB+ to SD. For purposes of this analysis, the U.S. is being treated as if it were rated AAA by S&P.

Note: A CRP of 0.0% is assumed in the following cases: (i) when the investor country and the investee country both have an S&P sovereign credit rating of AAA; or (ii) when the investor country has an S&P credit rating of AAA, and the investee country has a sovereign credit rating below AAA, but has a calculated CRP below 0.0% (which would imply lower risk than a country rated AAA); or (iii) when the investor country has an S&P credit rating below AAA, and the investee country has a sovereign credit rating of AAA, but has a calculated CRP above 0.0% (which would imply greater risk than a country rated below AAA). For purposes of this analysis, the U.S. is treated as having a sovereign credit rating equivalent to AAA.

The country risk premium (CRP) is not the cost of equity capital (COE). The CRP is to be added to base COE. See Chapter 6 for proper application.

### Data Updated Through March 2017

| Investee Country | December 2016 Country Risk Premium (CRP) (%) | March 2017 Country Risk Premium (CRP) (%) | S&P Sovereign Credit Rating § | World Rank Out of 175• | MSCI Market Classification † | Euromoney Region ‡ | Regional Rank ‡ |
|---|---|---|---|---|---|---|---|
| Afghanistan | 13.4 | 13.0 | | 139 | | Asia | 23 out of 29 |
| Albania | 8.1 | 8.2 | B+ | 93 | | Central and Eastern Europe | 18 out of 25 |
| Algeria | 8.2 | 8.1 | | 91 | | Africa | 10 out of 51 |
| Angola | 10.5 | 10.4 | B | 121 | | Africa | 26 out of 51 |
| Argentina | 8.7 | 8.4 | B- | 96 | Frontier | Latin America | 13 out of 20 |
| Armenia | 5.8 | 5.9 | | 77 | | Asia | 15 out of 29 |
| Australia | -2.8 | -3.0 | AAA | 12 | Developed | Australasia | 2 out of 7 |
| Austria | -2.6 | -2.8 | AA+ | 13 | Developed | Western Europe | 9 out of 19 |
| Azerbaijan | 7.0 | 7.2 | BB+ | 85 | | Asia | 17 out of 29 |
| Bahamas | 4.4 | 4.0 | BB+ | 65 | | Caribbean | 3 out of 9 |
| Bahrain | 4.4 | 4.0 | BB- | 64 | Frontier | Middle East | 7 out of 13 |
| Bangladesh | 10.9 | 10.6 | BB- | 126 | Frontier | Asia | 20 out of 29 |
| Barbados | 6.0 | 6.9 | CCC+ | 82 | | Caribbean | 4 out of 9 |
| Belarus | 13.1 | 13.4 | B- | 143 | | Central and Eastern Europe | 23 out of 25 |
| Belgium | -1.4 | -1.6 | AA | 17 | Developed | Western Europe | 10 out of 19 |
| Belize | 9.2 | 9.1 | B- | 106 | | Latin America | 17 out of 20 |
| Benin | 14.7 | 14.6 | | 150 | | Africa | 37 out of 51 |
| Bermuda | 2.1 | 1.9 | A+ | 44 | | Caribbean | 1 out of 9 |
| Bhutan | 14.4 | 14.2 | | 148 | | Asia | 25 out of 29 |
| Bolivia | 7.7 | 7.9 | BB | 88 | | Latin America | 12 out of 20 |
| Bosnia & Herzegovina | 13.5 | 13.5 | B | 144 | | Central and Eastern Europe | 24 out of 25 |
| Botswana | 2.1 | 2.0 | A- | 48 | | Africa | 1 out of 51 |
| Brazil | 3.6 | 3.4 | BB | 59 | Emerging | Latin America | 7 out of 20 |
| Bulgaria | 3.5 | 3.5 | BB+ | 61 | | Central and Eastern Europe | 12 out of 25 |
| Burkina Faso | 11.9 | 11.9 | B- | 133 | | Africa | 33 out of 51 |
| Burundi | 23.4 | 23.3 | | 169 | | Africa | 47 out of 51 |
| Cambodia | 15.3 | 14.9 | | 151 | | Asia | 27 out of 29 |
| Cameroon | 10.6 | 10.5 | B | 124 | | Africa | 28 out of 51 |
| Canada | -3.0 | -3.2 | AAA | 9 | Developed | North America | 1 out of 2 |
| Cape Verde | 8.4 | 8.3 | B | 94 | | Africa | 12 out of 51 |
| Central African Republic | 26.8 | 26.8 | | 172 | | Africa | 49 out of 51 |
| Chad | 25.5 | 25.5 | | 171 | | Africa | 48 out of 51 |
| Chile | -1.8 | -1.8 | AA- | 16 | Emerging | Latin America | 1 out of 20 |
| China | 1.9 | 1.8 | AA- | 42 | Emerging | Asia | 7 out of 29 |
| Colombia | 1.9 | 1.8 | BBB | 41 | Emerging | Latin America | 4 out of 20 |
| Congo Republic | 10.2 | 10.0 | B- | 117 | | Africa | 24 out of 51 |
| Congo, DR | 11.5 | 11.3 | B- | 131 | | Africa | 32 out of 51 |
| Costa Rica | 4.8 | 4.9 | BB- | 71 | | Latin America | 8 out of 20 |
| Côte d'Ivoire | 8.2 | 8.1 | | 92 | | Africa | 11 out of 51 |
| Croatia | 4.0 | 3.7 | BB | 63 | Frontier | Central and Eastern Europe | 13 out of 25 |
| Cuba | 17.5 | 17.5 | | 160 | | Caribbean | 9 out of 9 |
| Cyprus | 1.7 | 1.6 | BB+ | 40 | | Central and Eastern Europe | 7 out of 25 |
| Czech Republic | -0.6 | -0.8 | AA- | 23 | Emerging | Central and Eastern Europe | 1 out of 25 |
| Denmark | -3.6 | -3.8 | AAA | 4 | Developed | Western Europe | 3 out of 19 |
| Djibouti | 34.5 | 32.2 | | 175 | | Africa | 51 out of 51 |
| Dominican Republic | 8.1 | 8.0 | BB- | 90 | | Caribbean | 5 out of 9 |
| Ecuador | 9.6 | 9.3 | B | 109 | | Latin America | 18 out of 20 |
| Egypt | 10.0 | 9.9 | B- | 116 | Emerging | Africa | 23 out of 51 |
| El Salvador | 7.1 | 6.8 | B- | 81 | | Latin America | 10 out of 20 |
| Equatorial Guinea | 19.9 | 19.9 | | 165 | | Africa | 45 out of 51 |

§ S&P Credit Rating based on long-term foreign currency issuer rating. See http://www.standardandpoors.com/.

• World rank based on 175 countries covered by Euromoney. Ranking based on ascending order in which '1' equals the smallest country risk premium (CRP) and '175' equals the largest country risk premium (CRP).

† MSCI Market Classification based on MSCI Market Classification Framework. See http://www.msci.com/products/indexes/market_classification.html

‡ Regional classification based on Euromoney. Regional rankings based on ascending order in which '1' equals the smallest country risk premium (CRP) for each region.

Note: A CRP of 0.0% is assumed in the following cases: (i) when the investor country and the investee country both have an S&P sovereign credit rating of AAA; or (ii) when the investor country has an S&P credit rating of AAA, and the investee country has a sovereign credit rating below AAA, but has a calculated CRP below 0.0% (which would imply lower risk than a country rated AAA); or (iii) when the investor country has an S&P credit rating below AAA, and the investee country has a sovereign credit rating of AAA, but has a calculated CRP above 0.0% (which would imply greater risk than a country rated below AAA). For purposes of this analysis, the U.S. is treated as having a sovereign credit rating equivalent to AAA.

The country risk premium (CRP) is not the cost of equity capital (COE). The CRP is to be added to base COE. See Chapter 6 for proper application.

## Data Updated Through March 2017

| Investee Country | December 2016 Country Risk Premium (CRP) (%) | March 2017 Country Risk Premium (CRP) (%) | S&P Sovereign Credit Rating § | World Rank Out of 175∗ | MSCI Market Classification † | Euromoney Region ‡ | Regional Rank ‡ |
|---|---|---|---|---|---|---|---|
| Eritrea | 30.8 | 29.0 | | 173 | | Africa | 50 out of 51 |
| Estonia | -0.1 | 0.0 | AA- | 32 | Frontier | Central and Eastern Europe | 4 out of 25 |
| Ethiopia | 8.9 | 8.8 | B | 101 | | Africa | 16 out of 51 |
| Fiji | 14.1 | 13.9 | B+ | 147 | | Australasia | 5 out of 7 |
| Finland | -2.9 | -3.0 | AA+ | 11 | Developed | Western Europe | 8 out of 19 |
| France | -0.6 | -0.9 | AA | 22 | Developed | Western Europe | 12 out of 19 |
| Gabon | 6.8 | 7.0 | | 83 | | Africa | 7 out of 51 |
| Gambia | 12.6 | 12.5 | | 138 | | Africa | 34 out of 51 |
| Georgia | 5.5 | 5.7 | BB- | 74 | | Central and Eastern Europe | 15 out of 25 |
| Germany | -2.9 | -3.1 | AAA | 10 | Developed | Western Europe | 7 out of 19 |
| Ghana | 8.4 | 8.0 | B- | 89 | | Africa | 9 out of 51 |
| Greece | 9.5 | 9.2 | B- | 108 | Emerging | Western Europe | 19 out of 19 |
| Grenada | 9.1 | 9.1 | | 105 | | Caribbean | 7 out of 9 |
| Guatemala | 7.1 | 7.1 | BB | 84 | | Latin America | 11 out of 20 |
| Guinea | 16.1 | 16.1 | | 156 | | Africa | 41 out of 51 |
| Guinea-Bissau | 9.9 | 9.9 | | 115 | | Africa | 22 out of 51 |
| Guyana | 8.8 | 8.7 | | 100 | | Latin America | 15 out of 20 |
| Haiti | 18.9 | 16.9 | | 157 | | Caribbean | 8 out of 9 |
| Honduras | 8.5 | 8.4 | B+ | 98 | | Latin America | 14 out of 20 |
| Hong Kong | -2.3 | -2.5 | AAA | 14 | Developed | Asia | 2 out of 29 |
| Hungary | 3.2 | 3.2 | BBB- | 57 | Emerging | Central and Eastern Europe | 10 out of 25 |
| Iceland | 0.3 | 0.0 | A | 30 | | Western Europe | 15 out of 19 |
| India | 3.0 | 3.1 | BBB- | 55 | Emerging | Asia | 10 out of 29 |
| Indonesia | 3.7 | 3.6 | BB+ | 62 | Emerging | Asia | 11 out of 29 |
| Iran | 10.4 | 10.6 | | 125 | | Middle East | 10 out of 13 |
| Iraq | 12.2 | 12.1 | B- | 136 | | Middle East | 11 out of 13 |
| Ireland | -0.1 | -0.4 | A+ | 27 | Developed | Western Europe | 14 out of 19 |
| Israel | -0.2 | -0.3 | A+ | 28 | Developed | Middle East | 2 out of 13 |
| Italy | 2.6 | 2.3 | BBB- | 50 | Developed | Western Europe | 18 out of 19 |
| Jamaica | 8.6 | 9.1 | B | 104 | | Caribbean | 6 out of 9 |
| Japan | -0.3 | -0.4 | A+ | 25 | Developed | Asia | 5 out of 29 |
| Jordan | 5.8 | 5.8 | BB- | 76 | Frontier | Middle East | 8 out of 13 |
| Kazakhstan | 5.3 | 4.8 | BBB- | 70 | Frontier | Asia | 13 out of 29 |
| Kenya | 8.6 | 8.6 | B+ | 99 | Frontier | Africa | 15 out of 51 |
| Korea (North) | 30.2 | 29.7 | | 174 | | Asia | 29 out of 29 |
| Korea (South) | -1.0 | -1.2 | AA | 19 | Emerging | Asia | 4 out of 29 |
| Kuwait | 0.0 | 0.0 | AA | 31 | Frontier | Middle East | 3 out of 13 |
| Kyrgyz Republic | 13.6 | 13.4 | | 142 | | Central and Eastern Europe | 22 out of 25 |
| Laos | 17.7 | 17.1 | | 158 | | Asia | 28 out of 29 |
| Latvia | 1.9 | 1.9 | A- | 43 | | Central and Eastern Europe | 8 out of 25 |
| Lebanon | 10.3 | 9.6 | B- | 112 | Frontier | Middle East | 9 out of 13 |
| Lesotho | 13.8 | 13.7 | | 146 | | Africa | 36 out of 51 |
| Liberia | 9.2 | 9.1 | | 107 | | Africa | 17 out of 51 |
| Libya | 15.3 | 15.5 | | 153 | | Africa | 39 out of 51 |
| Lithuania | 1.2 | 1.1 | A- | 36 | Frontier | Central and Eastern Europe | 6 out of 25 |
| Luxembourg | -3.3 | -3.5 | AAA | 5 | | Western Europe | 4 out of 19 |
| Macedonia | 7.7 | 7.8 | BB- | 87 | | Central and Eastern Europe | 17 out of 25 |
| Madagascar | 10.1 | 10.5 | | 123 | | Africa | 27 out of 51 |
| Malawi | 9.8 | 9.7 | | 114 | | Africa | 21 out of 51 |
| Malaysia | 1.4 | 1.1 | A- | 35 | Emerging | Asia | 6 out of 29 |

§ S&P Credit Rating based on long-term foreign currency issuer rating. See http://www.standardandpoors.com/.

∗ World rank based on 175 countries covered by Euromoney. Ranking based on ascending order in which '1' equals the smallest country risk premium (CRP) and '175' equals the largest country risk premium (CRP).

† MSCI Market Classification based on MSCI Market Classification Framework. See http://www.msci.com/products/indexes/market_classification.html

‡ Regional classification based on Euromoney. Regional rankings based on ascending order in which '1' equals the smallest country risk premium (CRP) for each region.

Note: A CRP of 0.0% is assumed in the following cases: (i) when the investor country and the investee country both have an S&P sovereign credit rating of AAA; or (ii) when the investor country has an S&P credit rating of AAA, and the investee country has a sovereign credit rating below AAA, but has a calculated CRP below 0.0% (which would imply lower risk than a country rated AAA); or (iii) when the investor country has an S&P credit rating below AAA, and the investee country has a sovereign credit rating of AAA, but has a calculated CRP above 0.0% (which would imply greater risk than a country rated below AAA). For purposes of this analysis, the U.S. is treated as having a sovereign credit rating equivalent to AAA.

The country risk premium (CRP) is not the cost of equity capital (COE). The CRP is to be added to base COE. See Chapter 6 for proper application.

### Data Updated Through March 2017

| Investee Country | December 2016 Country Risk Premium (CRP) (%) | March 2017 Country Risk Premium (CRP) (%) | S&P Sovereign Credit Rating § | World Rank Out of 175* | MSCI Market Classification † | Euromoney Region ‡ | Regional Rank ‡ |
|---|---|---|---|---|---|---|---|
| Mali | 13.4 | 13.3 | | 141 | | Africa | 35 out of 51 |
| Malta | -0.3 | -0.4 | A- | 26 | | Western Europe | 13 out of 19 |
| Mauritania | 17.3 | 17.3 | | 159 | | Africa | 42 out of 51 |
| Mauritius | 4.6 | 4.5 | | 67 | Frontier | Asia | 12 out of 29 |
| Mexico | 1.2 | 1.2 | BBB+ | 37 | Emerging | Latin America | 2 out of 20 |
| Moldova | 11.9 | 12.2 | | 137 | | Central and Eastern Europe | 21 out of 25 |
| Mongolia | 10.1 | 10.4 | B- | 119 | | Asia | 18 out of 29 |
| Montenegro | 9.4 | 9.0 | B+ | 103 | | Central and Eastern Europe | 19 out of 25 |
| Morocco | 4.7 | 4.7 | BBB- | 69 | Frontier | Africa | 4 out of 51 |
| Mozambique | 11.2 | 10.9 | SD | 128 | | Africa | 29 out of 51 |
| Myanmar | 12.1 | 11.9 | | 134 | | Asia | 22 out of 29 |
| Namibia | 4.3 | 4.3 | | 66 | | Africa | 3 out of 51 |
| Nepal | 14.7 | 14.6 | | 149 | | Asia | 26 out of 29 |
| Netherlands | -3.3 | -3.5 | AAA | 6 | Developed | Western Europe | 5 out of 19 |
| New Zealand | -3.1 | -3.2 | AA | 8 | Developed | Australasia | 1 out of 7 |
| Nicaragua | 10.9 | 10.8 | B+ | 127 | | Latin America | 19 out of 20 |
| Niger | 10.5 | 10.4 | | 120 | | Africa | 25 out of 51 |
| Nigeria | 8.6 | 8.4 | B | 97 | Frontier | Africa | 14 out of 51 |
| Norway | -3.9 | -4.1 | AAA | 3 | Developed | Western Europe | 2 out of 19 |
| Oman | 2.1 | 2.0 | BBB- | 46 | Frontier | Middle East | 5 out of 13 |
| Pakistan | 10.6 | 10.4 | B | 122 | Frontier | Asia | 19 out of 29 |
| Panama | 2.8 | 2.7 | BBB | 52 | | Latin America | 6 out of 20 |
| Papua New Guinea | 10.1 | 10.1 | B+ | 118 | | Australasia | 3 out of 7 |
| Paraguay | 6.2 | 6.2 | BB | 80 | | Latin America | 9 out of 20 |
| Peru | 1.5 | 1.5 | BBB+ | 39 | Emerging | Latin America | 3 out of 20 |
| Philippines | 3.1 | 2.9 | BBB | 53 | Emerging | Asia | 9 out of 29 |
| Poland | 0.2 | -0.1 | BBB+ | 29 | Emerging | Central and Eastern Europe | 3 out of 25 |
| Portugal | 2.5 | 2.2 | BB+ | 49 | Developed | Western Europe | 17 out of 19 |
| Qatar | -0.9 | -1.0 | AA | 21 | Emerging | Middle East | 1 out of 13 |
| Romania | 3.2 | 3.2 | BBB- | 56 | Frontier | Central and Eastern Europe | 9 out of 25 |
| Russia | 5.4 | 4.7 | BB+ | 68 | Emerging | Central and Eastern Europe | 14 out of 25 |
| Rwanda | 11.2 | 11.1 | B | 130 | | Africa | 31 out of 51 |
| São Tomé & Príncipe | 17.4 | 17.8 | | 163 | | Africa | 43 out of 51 |
| Saudi Arabia | 2.4 | 2.0 | A- | 47 | | Middle East | 6 out of 13 |
| Senegal | 7.9 | 7.8 | B+ | 86 | | Africa | 8 out of 51 |
| Serbia | 6.1 | 5.7 | BB- | 75 | Frontier | Central and Eastern Europe | 16 out of 25 |
| Seychelles | 5.6 | 5.5 | | 73 | | Africa | 5 out of 51 |
| Sierra Leone | 11.2 | 11.1 | | 129 | | Africa | 30 out of 51 |
| Singapore | -4.1 | -4.2 | AAA | 1 | Developed | Asia | 1 out of 29 |
| Slovakia | -0.5 | -0.6 | A+ | 24 | | Central and Eastern Europe | 2 out of 25 |
| Slovenia | 0.8 | 0.7 | A | 34 | Frontier | Central and Eastern Europe | 5 out of 25 |
| Solomon Islands | 21.6 | 21.6 | | 168 | | Australasia | 6 out of 7 |
| Somalia | 20.0 | 19.9 | | 166 | | Africa | 46 out of 51 |
| South Africa | 3.3 | 3.4 | BBB- | 60 | Emerging | Africa | 2 out of 51 |
| Spain | 1.6 | 1.5 | BBB+ | 38 | Developed | Western Europe | 16 out of 19 |
| Sri Lanka | 5.5 | 5.1 | B+ | 72 | Frontier | Asia | 14 out of 29 |
| Sudan | 16.1 | 16.0 | | 154 | | Africa | 40 out of 51 |
| Suriname | 8.8 | 8.9 | B+ | 102 | | Latin America | 16 out of 20 |
| Swaziland | 14.5 | 15.3 | | 152 | | Africa | 38 out of 51 |
| Sweden | -3.2 | -3.4 | AAA | 7 | Developed | Western Europe | 6 out of 19 |

§ S&P Credit Rating based on long-term foreign currency issuer rating. See http://www.standardandpoors.com/.

* World rank based on 175 countries covered by Euromoney. Ranking based on ascending order in which '1' equals the smallest country risk premium (CRP) and '175' equals the largest country risk premium (CRP).

† MSCI Market Classification based on MSCI Market Classification Framework. See http://www.msci.com/products/indexes/market_classification.html.

‡ Regional classification based on Euromoney. Regional rankings based on ascending order in which '1' equals the smallest country risk premium (CRP) for each region.

Note: A CRP of 0.0% is assumed in the following cases: (i) when the investor country and the investee country both have an S&P sovereign credit rating of AAA; or (ii) when the investor country has an S&P credit rating of AAA, and the investee country has a sovereign credit rating below AAA, but has a calculated CRP below 0.0% (which would imply lower risk than a country rated AAA); or (iii) when the investor country has an S&P credit rating below AAA, and the investee country has a sovereign credit rating of AAA, but has a calculated CRP above 0.0% (which would imply greater risk than a country rated below AAA). For purposes of this analysis, the U.S. is treated as having a sovereign credit rating equivalent to AAA.

The country risk premium (CRP) is not the cost of equity capital (COE). The CRP is to be added to base COE. See Chapter 6 for proper application.

## Data Updated Through March 2017

| Investee Country | December 2016 Country Risk Premium (CRP) (%) | March 2017 Country Risk Premium (CRP) (%) | S&P Sovereign Credit Rating § | World Rank Out of 175∗ | MSCI Market Classification † | Euromoney Region ‡ | Regional Rank ‡ |
|---|---|---|---|---|---|---|---|
| Switzerland | -3.9 | -4.1 | AAA | 2 | Developed | Western Europe | 1 out of 19 |
| Syria | 20.7 | 20.9 | | 167 | | Middle East | 13 out of 13 |
| Taiwan | -1.3 | -1.4 | AA- | 18 | Emerging | Asia | 3 out of 29 |
| Tajikistan | 15.7 | 16.0 | | 155 | | Central and Eastern Europe | 25 out of 25 |
| Tanzania | 8.2 | 8.3 | | 95 | | Africa | 13 out of 51 |
| Thailand | 2.8 | 2.5 | BBB+ | 51 | Emerging | Asia | 8 out of 29 |
| Togo | 9.7 | 9.7 | | 113 | | Africa | 20 out of 51 |
| Tonga | 24.0 | 24.0 | | 170 | | Australasia | 7 out of 7 |
| Trinidad & Tobago | 3.1 | 3.0 | A- | 54 | | Caribbean | 2 out of 9 |
| Tunisia | 5.9 | 6.1 | | 79 | Frontier | Africa | 6 out of 51 |
| Turkey | 3.5 | 3.2 | BB | 58 | Emerging | Central and Eastern Europe | 11 out of 25 |
| Turkmenistan | 13.0 | 13.1 | | 140 | | Asia | 24 out of 29 |
| Uganda | 9.3 | 9.5 | B | 110 | | Africa | 18 out of 51 |
| Ukraine | 12.0 | 12.0 | B- | 135 | | Central and Eastern Europe | 20 out of 25 |
| United Arab Emirates | 0.4 | 0.4 | AA | 33 | Emerging | Middle East | 4 out of 13 |
| United Kingdom | -1.0 | -1.1 | AA | 20 | Developed | Western Europe | 11 out of 19 |
| United States | -2.0 | -2.2 | AA+ | 15 | Developed | North America | 2 out of 2 |
| Uruguay | 2.2 | 1.9 | BBB | 45 | | Latin America | 5 out of 20 |
| Uzbekistan | 12.2 | 11.6 | | 132 | | Asia | 21 out of 29 |
| Vanuatu | 13.8 | 13.7 | | 145 | | Australasia | 4 out of 7 |
| Venezuela | 17.4 | 17.8 | CCC | 162 | | Latin America | 20 out of 20 |
| Vietnam | 6.4 | 6.0 | BB- | 78 | Frontier | Asia | 16 out of 29 |
| Yemen | 17.7 | 17.7 | | 161 | | Middle East | 12 out of 13 |
| Zambia | 9.6 | 9.5 | B | 111 | | Africa | 19 out of 51 |
| Zimbabwe | 19.3 | 19.2 | | 164 | | Africa | 44 out of 51 |

## March 2017 Country Risk Premium (CRP) Summary Statistics:

| S&P Rating | Country Count | Average CRP (%) | Median CRP (%) | Min CRP (%) | Max CRP (%) |
|---|---|---|---|---|---|
| AAA ∗∗ | 12 | -3.4 | -3.4 | -4.2 | -2.2 |
| AA (AA+, AA, AA-) | 15 | -1.1 | -1.1 | -3.2 | 1.8 |
| A (A+, A, A-) | 14 | 0.8 | 0.9 | -0.6 | 3.0 |
| BBB (BBB+, BBB, BBB-) | 17 | 2.5 | 2.5 | -0.1 | 4.8 |
| BB (BB+, BB, BB-) | 22 | 5.3 | 5.3 | 1.6 | 10.6 |
| B+ − SD | 39 | 9.9 | 9.5 | 5.1 | 17.8 |
| Investment Grade ∗∗ | 58 | -0.1 | -0.1 | -4.2 | 4.8 |
| Non-Investment Grade ∗∗ | 61 | 8.3 | 8.4 | 1.6 | 17.8 |
| **MSCI Market Classification** | | | | | |
| Developed Markets | 23 | -2.0 | -2.8 | -4.2 | 2.3 |
| Emerging Markets | 23 | 2.2 | 1.8 | -1.8 | 9.9 |
| Frontier Markets | 22 | 5.2 | 5.0 | 0.0 | 10.6 |
| **Euromoney Region ‡** | | | | | |
| Africa | 51 | 12.4 | 10.4 | 2.0 | 32.2 |
| Asia | 29 | 7.2 | 5.9 | -4.2 | 29.7 |
| Australasia | 7 | 11.0 | 13.7 | -3.2 | 24.0 |
| Caribbean | 9 | 8.5 | 8.0 | 1.9 | 17.5 |
| Central and Eastern Europe | 25 | 5.7 | 3.7 | -0.8 | 16.0 |
| Latin America | 20 | 6.2 | 6.9 | -1.8 | 17.8 |
| Middle East | 13 | 6.4 | 4.0 | -1.0 | 20.9 |
| North America | 2 | -2.7 | -2.7 | -3.2 | -2.2 |
| Western Europe | 19 | -1.1 | -1.6 | -4.1 | 9.2 |

## CCR Base Cost of Equity Capital:

| Kuwait | COE (%) |
|---|---|
| March 2017 | 10.8 |
| December 2016 | 10.6 |

CCR base country-level COE for a Kuwait-based investor investing in Kuwait.

§ S&P Credit Rating based on long-term foreign currency issuer rating. See http://www.standardandpoors.com/.

∗ World rank based on 175 countries covered by Euromoney. Ranking based on ascending order in which '1' equals the smallest country risk premium (CRP) and '175' equals the largest country risk premium (CRP).

† MSCI Market Classification based on MSCI Market Classification Framework. See http://www.msci.com/products/indexes/market_classification.html.

‡ Regional classification based on Euromoney. Regional rankings based on ascending order in which '1' equals the smallest country risk premium (CRP) for each region.

∗∗ Investment grade based on S&P sovereign credit rating from AAA to BBB-. Non-Investment grade based on S&P sovereign credit rating from BB+ to SD. For purposes of this analysis, the U.S. is being treated as if it were rated AAA by S&P.

Note: A CRP of 0.0% is assumed in the following cases: (i) when the investor country and the investee country both have an S&P sovereign credit rating of AAA; or (ii) when the investor country has an S&P sovereign credit rating of AAA, and the investee country has a sovereign credit rating below AAA, but has a calculated CRP below 0.0% (which would imply lower risk than a country rated AAA); or (iii) when the investor country has an S&P credit rating below AAA, and the investee country has a sovereign credit rating of AAA, but has a calculated CRP above 0.0% (which would imply greater risk than a country rated below AAA). For purposes of this analysis, the U.S. is treated as having a sovereign credit rating equivalent to AAA.

The country risk premium (CRP) is not the cost of equity capital (COE). The CRP is to be added to base COE. See Chapter 6 for proper application.

## Data Updated Through March 2017

| Investee Country | December 2016 Country Risk Premium (CRP) (%) | March 2017 Country Risk Premium (CRP) (%) | S&P Sovereign Credit Rating § | World Rank Out of 175* | MSCI Market Classification † | Euromoney Region ‡ | Regional Rank ‡ |
|---|---|---|---|---|---|---|---|
| Afghanistan | 12.0 | 11.6 | | 139 | | Asia | 23 out of 29 |
| Albania | 6.5 | 6.6 | B+ | 93 | | Central and Eastern Europe | 18 out of 25 |
| Algeria | 6.5 | 6.5 | | 91 | | Africa | 10 out of 51 |
| Angola | 8.9 | 8.9 | B | 121 | | Africa | 26 out of 51 |
| Argentina | 7.1 | 6.7 | B- | 96 | Frontier | Latin America | 13 out of 20 |
| Armenia | 4.1 | 4.1 | | 77 | | Asia | 15 out of 29 |
| Australia | -5.0 | -5.1 | AAA | 12 | Developed | Australasia | 2 out of 7 |
| Austria | -4.8 | -4.9 | AA+ | 13 | Developed | Western Europe | 9 out of 19 |
| Azerbaijan | 5.3 | 5.5 | BB+ | 85 | | Asia | 17 out of 29 |
| Bahamas | 2.6 | 2.2 | BB+ | 65 | | Caribbean | 3 out of 9 |
| Bahrain | 2.5 | 2.2 | BB- | 64 | Frontier | Middle East | 7 out of 13 |
| Bangladesh | 9.4 | 9.1 | BB- | 126 | Frontier | Asia | 20 out of 29 |
| Barbados | 4.3 | 5.2 | CCC+ | 82 | | Caribbean | 4 out of 9 |
| Belarus | 11.7 | 12.0 | B- | 143 | | Central and Eastern Europe | 23 out of 25 |
| Belgium | -3.5 | -3.7 | AA | 17 | Developed | Western Europe | 10 out of 19 |
| Belize | 7.5 | 7.5 | B- | 106 | | Latin America | 17 out of 20 |
| Benin | 13.4 | 13.3 | | 150 | | Africa | 37 out of 51 |
| Bermuda | 0.2 | 0.0 | A+ | 44 | | Caribbean | 1 out of 9 |
| Bhutan | 13.0 | 12.8 | | 148 | | Asia | 25 out of 29 |
| Bolivia | 6.0 | 6.2 | BB | 88 | | Latin America | 12 out of 20 |
| Bosnia & Herzegovina | 12.1 | 12.2 | B | 144 | | Central and Eastern Europe | 24 out of 25 |
| Botswana | 0.2 | 0.1 | A- | 48 | | Africa | 1 out of 51 |
| Brazil | 1.7 | 1.5 | BB | 59 | Emerging | Latin America | 7 out of 20 |
| Bulgaria | 1.6 | 1.6 | BB+ | 61 | | Central and Eastern Europe | 12 out of 25 |
| Burkina Faso | 10.5 | 10.4 | B- | 133 | | Africa | 33 out of 51 |
| Burundi | 22.4 | 22.4 | | 169 | | Africa | 47 out of 51 |
| Cambodia | 13.9 | 13.5 | | 151 | | Asia | 27 out of 29 |
| Cameroon | 9.1 | 9.0 | B | 124 | | Africa | 28 out of 51 |
| Canada | -5.2 | -5.4 | AAA | 9 | Developed | North America | 1 out of 2 |
| Cape Verde | 6.7 | 6.6 | B | 94 | | Africa | 12 out of 51 |
| Central African Republic | 26.0 | 26.0 | | 172 | | Africa | 49 out of 51 |
| Chad | 24.7 | 24.6 | | 171 | | Africa | 48 out of 51 |
| Chile | -4.0 | -3.9 | AA- | 16 | Emerging | Latin America | 1 out of 20 |
| China | 0.0 | -0.1 | AA- | 42 | Emerging | Asia | 7 out of 29 |
| Colombia | 0.0 | -0.2 | BBB | 41 | Emerging | Latin America | 4 out of 20 |
| Congo Republic | 8.7 | 8.4 | B- | 117 | | Africa | 24 out of 51 |
| Congo, DR | 10.0 | 9.8 | B- | 131 | | Africa | 32 out of 51 |
| Costa Rica | 3.0 | 3.1 | BB- | 71 | | Latin America | 8 out of 20 |
| Côte d'Ivoire | 6.6 | 6.5 | | 92 | | Africa | 11 out of 51 |
| Croatia | 2.1 | 1.9 | BB | 63 | Frontier | Central and Eastern Europe | 13 out of 25 |
| Cuba | 16.3 | 16.3 | | 160 | | Caribbean | 9 out of 9 |
| Cyprus | -0.3 | -0.3 | BB+ | 40 | | Central and Eastern Europe | 7 out of 25 |
| Czech Republic | -2.7 | -2.8 | AA- | 23 | Emerging | Central and Eastern Europe | 1 out of 25 |
| Denmark | -5.8 | -6.0 | AAA | 4 | Developed | Western Europe | 3 out of 19 |
| Djibouti | 34.0 | 31.7 | | 175 | | Africa | 51 out of 51 |
| Dominican Republic | 6.4 | 6.4 | BB- | 90 | | Caribbean | 5 out of 9 |
| Ecuador | 8.0 | 7.7 | B | 109 | | Latin America | 18 out of 20 |
| Egypt | 8.5 | 8.3 | B- | 116 | Emerging | Africa | 23 out of 51 |
| El Salvador | 5.4 | 5.1 | B- | 81 | | Latin America | 10 out of 20 |
| Equatorial Guinea | 18.8 | 18.8 | | 165 | | Africa | 45 out of 51 |

§ S&P Credit Rating based on long-term foreign currency issuer rating. See http://www.standardandpoors.com/.

* World rank based on 175 countries covered by Euromoney. Ranking based on ascending order in which '1' equals the smallest country risk premium (CRP) and '175' equals the largest country risk premium (CRP).

† MSCI Market Classification based on MSCI Market Classification Framework. See http://www.msci.com/products/indexes/market_classification.html

‡ Regional classification based on Euromoney. Regional rankings based on ascending order in which '1' equals the smallest country risk premium (CRP) for each region.

Note: A CRP of 0.0% is assumed in the following cases: (i) when the investor country and the investee country both have an S&P sovereign credit rating of AAA; or (ii) when the investor country has an S&P credit rating of AAA, and the investee country has a sovereign credit rating below AAA, but has a calculated CRP below 0.0% (which would imply lower risk than a country rated AAA); or (iii) when the investor country has an S&P credit rating below AAA, and the investee country has a sovereign credit rating of AAA, but has a calculated CRP above 0.0% (which would imply greater risk than a country rated below AAA). For purposes of this analysis, the U.S. is treated as having a sovereign credit rating equivalent to AAA.

2017 Valuation Handbook – International Guide to Cost of Capital          Data Exhibit 4          Investor Perspective: Latvia (EUR); Page 1 of 4

The country risk premium (CRP) is not the cost of equity capital (COE). The CRP is to be added to base COE. See Chapter 6 for proper application.

## Data Updated Through March 2017

| Investee Country | December 2016 Country Risk Premium (CRP) (%) | March 2017 Country Risk Premium (CRP) (%) | S&P Sovereign Credit Rating § | World Rank Out of 175• | MSCI Market Classification † | Euromoney Region ‡ | Regional Rank ‡ |
|---|---|---|---|---|---|---|---|
| Eritrea | 30.2 | 28.3 | | 173 | | Africa | 50 out of 51 |
| Estonia | -2.1 | -2.0 | AA- | 32 | Frontier | Central and Eastern Europe | 4 out of 25 |
| Ethiopia | 7.3 | 7.2 | B | 101 | | Africa | 16 out of 51 |
| Fiji | 12.7 | 12.5 | B+ | 147 | | Australasia | 5 out of 7 |
| Finland | -5.0 | -5.2 | AA+ | 11 | Developed | Western Europe | 8 out of 19 |
| France | -2.7 | -3.0 | AA | 22 | Developed | Western Europe | 12 out of 19 |
| Gabon | 5.0 | 5.3 | | 83 | | Africa | 7 out of 51 |
| Gambia | 11.1 | 11.1 | | 138 | | Africa | 34 out of 51 |
| Georgia | 3.8 | 3.9 | BB- | 74 | | Central and Eastern Europe | 15 out of 25 |
| Germany | -5.0 | -5.2 | AAA | 10 | Developed | Western Europe | 7 out of 19 |
| Ghana | 6.8 | 6.3 | B- | 89 | | Africa | 9 out of 51 |
| Greece | 7.9 | 7.6 | B- | 108 | Emerging | Western Europe | 19 out of 19 |
| Grenada | 7.5 | 7.5 | | 105 | | Caribbean | 7 out of 9 |
| Guatemala | 5.4 | 5.4 | BB | 84 | | Latin America | 11 out of 20 |
| Guinea | 14.9 | 14.8 | | 156 | | Africa | 41 out of 51 |
| Guinea-Bissau | 8.4 | 8.3 | | 115 | | Africa | 22 out of 51 |
| Guyana | 7.2 | 7.1 | | 100 | | Latin America | 15 out of 20 |
| Haiti | 17.8 | 15.6 | | 157 | | Caribbean | 8 out of 9 |
| Honduras | 6.9 | 6.8 | B+ | 98 | | Latin America | 14 out of 20 |
| Hong Kong | -4.5 | -4.6 | AAA | 14 | Developed | Asia | 2 out of 29 |
| Hungary | 1.3 | 1.4 | BBB- | 57 | Emerging | Central and Eastern Europe | 10 out of 25 |
| Iceland | -1.7 | -2.0 | A | 30 | | Western Europe | 15 out of 19 |
| India | 1.1 | 1.3 | BBB- | 55 | Emerging | Asia | 10 out of 29 |
| Indonesia | 1.9 | 1.8 | BB+ | 62 | Emerging | Asia | 11 out of 29 |
| Iran | 8.9 | 9.0 | | 125 | | Middle East | 10 out of 13 |
| Iraq | 10.7 | 10.7 | B- | 136 | | Middle East | 11 out of 13 |
| Ireland | -2.2 | -2.4 | A+ | 27 | Developed | Western Europe | 14 out of 19 |
| Israel | -2.2 | -2.4 | A+ | 28 | Developed | Middle East | 2 out of 13 |
| Italy | 0.7 | 0.4 | BBB- | 50 | Developed | Western Europe | 18 out of 19 |
| Jamaica | 6.9 | 7.5 | B | 104 | | Caribbean | 6 out of 9 |
| Japan | -2.3 | -2.5 | A+ | 25 | Developed | Asia | 5 out of 29 |
| Jordan | 4.0 | 4.1 | BB- | 76 | Frontier | Middle East | 8 out of 13 |
| Kazakhstan | 3.5 | 3.0 | BBB- | 70 | Frontier | Asia | 13 out of 29 |
| Kenya | 7.0 | 7.0 | B+ | 99 | Frontier | Africa | 15 out of 51 |
| Korea (North) | 29.5 | 29.0 | | 174 | | Asia | 29 out of 29 |
| Korea (South) | -3.1 | -3.2 | AA | 19 | Emerging | Asia | 4 out of 29 |
| Kuwait | -2.0 | -2.0 | AA | 31 | Frontier | Middle East | 3 out of 13 |
| Kyrgyz Republic | 12.2 | 12.0 | | 142 | | Central and Eastern Europe | 22 out of 25 |
| Laos | 16.5 | 15.9 | | 158 | | Asia | 28 out of 29 |
| Latvia | 0.0 | 0.0 | A- | 43 | | Central and Eastern Europe | 8 out of 25 |
| Lebanon | 8.8 | 8.0 | B- | 112 | Frontier | Middle East | 9 out of 13 |
| Lesotho | 12.4 | 12.3 | | 146 | | Africa | 36 out of 51 |
| Liberia | 7.6 | 7.6 | | 107 | | Africa | 17 out of 51 |
| Libya | 13.9 | 14.2 | | 153 | | Africa | 39 out of 51 |
| Lithuania | -0.8 | -0.8 | A- | 36 | Frontier | Central and Eastern Europe | 6 out of 25 |
| Luxembourg | -5.5 | -5.7 | AAA | 5 | | Western Europe | 4 out of 19 |
| Macedonia | 6.1 | 6.2 | BB- | 87 | | Central and Eastern Europe | 17 out of 25 |
| Madagascar | 8.5 | 8.9 | | 123 | | Africa | 27 out of 51 |
| Malawi | 8.2 | 8.1 | | 114 | | Africa | 21 out of 51 |
| Malaysia | -0.6 | -0.9 | A- | 35 | Emerging | Asia | 6 out of 29 |

§ S&P Credit Rating based on long-term foreign currency issuer rating. See http://www.standardandpoors.com/.

• World rank based on 175 countries covered by Euromoney. Ranking based on ascending order in which '1' equals the smallest country risk premium (CRP) and '175' equals the largest country risk premium (CRP).

† MSCI Market Classification based on MSCI Market Classification Framework. See http://www.msci.com/products/indexes/market_classification.html

‡ Regional classification based on Euromoney. Regional rankings based on ascending order in which '1' equals the smallest country risk premium (CRP) for each region.

Note: A CRP of 0.0% is assumed in the following cases: (i) when the investor country and the investee country both have an S&P sovereign credit rating of AAA; or (ii) when the investor country has an S&P credit rating of AAA, and the investee country has a sovereign credit rating below AAA, but has a calculated CRP below 0.0% (which would imply lower risk than a country rated AAA); or (iii) when the investor country has an S&P credit rating below AAA, and the investee country has a sovereign credit rating of AAA, but has a calculated CRP above 0.0% (which would imply greater risk than a country rated below AAA). For purposes of this analysis, the U.S. is treated as having a sovereign credit rating equivalent to AAA.

The country risk premium (CRP) is not the cost of equity capital (COE).  The CRP is to be added to base COE. See Chapter 6 for proper application.

### Data Updated Through March 2017

| Investee Country | December 2016 Country Risk Premium (CRP) (%) | March 2017 Country Risk Premium (CRP) (%) | S&P Sovereign Credit Rating § | World Rank Out of 175∗ | MSCI Market Classification † | Euromoney Region ‡ | Regional Rank ‡ |
|---|---|---|---|---|---|---|---|
| Mali | 12.0 | 11.9 | | 141 | | Africa | 35 out of 51 |
| Malta | -2.3 | -2.4 | A- | 26 | | Western Europe | 13 out of 19 |
| Mauritania | 16.1 | 16.0 | | 159 | | Africa | 42 out of 51 |
| Mauritius | 2.8 | 2.7 | | 67 | Frontier | Asia | 12 out of 29 |
| Mexico | -0.7 | -0.7 | BBB+ | 37 | Emerging | Latin America | 2 out of 20 |
| Moldova | 10.4 | 10.7 | | 137 | | Central and Eastern Europe | 21 out of 25 |
| Mongolia | 8.6 | 8.8 | B- | 119 | | Asia | 18 out of 29 |
| Montenegro | 7.8 | 7.5 | B+ | 103 | | Central and Eastern Europe | 19 out of 25 |
| Morocco | 2.9 | 3.0 | BBB- | 69 | Frontier | Africa | 4 out of 51 |
| Mozambique | 9.7 | 9.4 | SD | 128 | | Africa | 29 out of 51 |
| Myanmar | 10.6 | 10.4 | | 134 | | Asia | 22 out of 29 |
| Namibia | 2.5 | 2.5 | | 66 | | Africa | 3 out of 51 |
| Nepal | 13.3 | 13.2 | | 149 | | Asia | 26 out of 29 |
| Netherlands | -5.4 | -5.6 | AAA | 6 | Developed | Western Europe | 5 out of 19 |
| New Zealand | -5.3 | -5.4 | AA | 8 | Developed | Australasia | 1 out of 7 |
| Nicaragua | 9.3 | 9.3 | B+ | 127 | | Latin America | 19 out of 20 |
| Niger | 8.9 | 8.8 | | 120 | | Africa | 25 out of 51 |
| Nigeria | 6.9 | 6.8 | B | 97 | Frontier | Africa | 14 out of 51 |
| Norway | -6.1 | -6.3 | AAA | 3 | Developed | Western Europe | 2 out of 19 |
| Oman | 0.1 | 0.1 | BBB- | 46 | Frontier | Middle East | 5 out of 13 |
| Pakistan | 9.0 | 8.9 | B | 122 | Frontier | Asia | 19 out of 29 |
| Panama | 0.9 | 0.8 | BBB | 52 | | Latin America | 6 out of 20 |
| Papua New Guinea | 8.5 | 8.5 | B+ | 118 | | Australasia | 3 out of 7 |
| Paraguay | 4.4 | 4.5 | BB | 80 | | Latin America | 9 out of 20 |
| Peru | -0.5 | -0.4 | BBB+ | 39 | Emerging | Latin America | 3 out of 20 |
| Philippines | 1.2 | 1.1 | BBB | 53 | Emerging | Asia | 9 out of 29 |
| Poland | -1.9 | -2.1 | BBB+ | 29 | Emerging | Central and Eastern Europe | 3 out of 25 |
| Portugal | 0.6 | 0.3 | BB+ | 49 | Developed | Western Europe | 17 out of 19 |
| Qatar | -3.0 | -3.0 | AA | 21 | Emerging | Middle East | 1 out of 13 |
| Romania | 1.4 | 1.3 | BBB- | 56 | Frontier | Central and Eastern Europe | 9 out of 25 |
| Russia | 3.6 | 2.9 | BB+ | 68 | Emerging | Central and Eastern Europe | 14 out of 25 |
| Rwanda | 9.7 | 9.6 | B | 130 | | Africa | 31 out of 51 |
| São Tomé & Príncipe | 16.2 | 16.6 | | 163 | | Africa | 43 out of 51 |
| Saudi Arabia | 0.5 | 0.1 | A- | 47 | | Middle East | 6 out of 13 |
| Senegal | 6.2 | 6.1 | B+ | 86 | | Africa | 8 out of 51 |
| Serbia | 4.3 | 3.9 | BB- | 75 | Frontier | Central and Eastern Europe | 16 out of 25 |
| Seychelles | 3.8 | 3.7 | | 73 | | Africa | 5 out of 51 |
| Sierra Leone | 9.7 | 9.6 | | 129 | | Africa | 30 out of 51 |
| Singapore | -6.3 | -6.4 | AAA | 1 | Developed | Asia | 1 out of 29 |
| Slovakia | -2.6 | -2.6 | A+ | 24 | | Central and Eastern Europe | 2 out of 25 |
| Slovenia | -1.2 | -1.3 | A | 34 | Frontier | Central and Eastern Europe | 5 out of 25 |
| Solomon Islands | 20.6 | 20.6 | | 168 | | Australasia | 6 out of 7 |
| Somalia | 18.9 | 18.8 | | 166 | | Africa | 46 out of 51 |
| South Africa | 1.4 | 1.6 | BBB- | 60 | Emerging | Africa | 2 out of 51 |
| Spain | -0.3 | -0.4 | BBB+ | 38 | Developed | Western Europe | 16 out of 19 |
| Sri Lanka | 3.7 | 3.3 | B+ | 72 | Frontier | Asia | 14 out of 29 |
| Sudan | 14.8 | 14.7 | | 154 | | Africa | 40 out of 51 |
| Suriname | 7.2 | 7.3 | B+ | 102 | | Latin America | 16 out of 20 |
| Swaziland | 13.1 | 14.0 | | 152 | | Africa | 38 out of 51 |
| Sweden | -5.4 | -5.6 | AAA | 7 | Developed | Western Europe | 6 out of 19 |

§ S&P Credit Rating based on long-term foreign currency issuer rating. See http://www.standardandpoors.com/.

∗ World rank based on 175 countries covered by Euromoney. Ranking based on ascending order in which '1' equals the smallest country risk premium (CRP) and '175' equals the largest country risk premium (CRP).

† MSCI Market Classification based on MSCI Market Classification Framework.  See http://www.msci.com/products/indexes/market_classification.html

‡ Regional classification based on Euromoney. Regional rankings based on ascending order in which '1' equals the smallest country risk premium (CRP) for each region.

Note: A CRP of 0.0% is assumed in the following cases: (i) when the investor country and the investee country both have an S&P sovereign credit rating of AAA; or (ii) when the investor country has an S&P credit rating of AAA, and the investee country has a sovereign credit rating below AAA, but has a calculated CRP below 0.0% (which would imply lower risk than a country rated AAA); or (iii) when the investor country has an S&P credit rating below AAA, and the investee country has a sovereign credit rating of AAA, but has a calculated CRP above 0.0% (which would imply greater risk than a country rated below AAA). For purposes of this analysis, the U.S. is treated as having a sovereign credit rating equivalent to AAA.

The country risk premium (CRP) is not the cost of equity capital (COE). The CRP is to be added to base COE. See Chapter 6 for proper application.

## Data Updated Through March 2017

| Investee Country | December 2016 Country Risk Premium (CRP) (%) | March 2017 Country Risk Premium (CRP) (%) | S&P Sovereign Credit Rating § | World Rank Out of 175* | MSCI Market Classification † | Euromoney Region ‡ | Regional Rank ‡ |
|---|---|---|---|---|---|---|---|
| Switzerland | -6.1 | -6.3 | AAA | 2 | Developed | Western Europe | 1 out of 19 |
| Syria | 19.6 | 19.8 | | 167 | | Middle East | 13 out of 13 |
| Taiwan | -3.4 | -3.5 | AA- | 18 | Emerging | Asia | 3 out of 29 |
| Tajikistan | 14.4 | 14.7 | | 155 | | Central and Eastern Europe | 25 out of 25 |
| Tanzania | 6.6 | 6.7 | | 95 | | Africa | 13 out of 51 |
| Thailand | 0.9 | 0.6 | BBB+ | 51 | Emerging | Asia | 8 out of 29 |
| Togo | 8.2 | 8.1 | | 113 | | Africa | 20 out of 51 |
| Tonga | 23.1 | 23.1 | | 170 | | Australasia | 7 out of 7 |
| Trinidad & Tobago | 1.2 | 1.1 | A- | 54 | | Caribbean | 2 out of 9 |
| Tunisia | 4.1 | 4.4 | | 79 | Frontier | Africa | 6 out of 51 |
| Turkey | 1.6 | 1.4 | BB | 58 | Emerging | Central and Eastern Europe | 11 out of 25 |
| Turkmenistan | 11.5 | 11.7 | | 140 | | Asia | 24 out of 29 |
| Uganda | 7.7 | 7.9 | B | 110 | | Africa | 18 out of 51 |
| Ukraine | 10.5 | 10.5 | B- | 135 | | Central and Eastern Europe | 20 out of 25 |
| United Arab Emirates | -1.6 | -1.6 | AA | 33 | Emerging | Middle East | 4 out of 13 |
| United Kingdom | -3.1 | -3.1 | AA | 20 | Developed | Western Europe | 11 out of 19 |
| United States | -4.2 | -4.3 | AA+ | 15 | Developed | North America | 2 out of 2 |
| Uruguay | 0.2 | 0.0 | BBB | 45 | | Latin America | 5 out of 20 |
| Uzbekistan | 10.7 | 10.1 | | 132 | | Asia | 21 out of 29 |
| Vanuatu | 12.4 | 12.3 | | 145 | | Australasia | 4 out of 7 |
| Venezuela | 16.2 | 16.6 | CCC | 162 | | Latin America | 20 out of 20 |
| Vietnam | 4.7 | 4.3 | BB- | 78 | Frontier | Asia | 16 out of 29 |
| Yemen | 16.5 | 16.5 | | 161 | | Middle East | 12 out of 13 |
| Zambia | 8.0 | 8.0 | B | 111 | | Africa | 19 out of 51 |
| Zimbabwe | 18.1 | 18.0 | | 164 | | Africa | 44 out of 51 |

## March 2017 Country Risk Premium (CRP) Summary Statistics:

| S&P Rating | Country Count | Average CRP (%) | Median CRP (%) | Min CRP (%) | Max CRP (%) |
|---|---|---|---|---|---|
| AAA ** | 12 | -5.5 | -5.6 | -6.4 | -4.3 |
| AA (AA+, AA, AA-) | 15 | -3.2 | -3.1 | -5.4 | -0.1 |
| A (A+, A, A-) | 14 | -1.1 | -1.1 | -2.6 | 1.1 |
| BBB (BBB+, BBB, BBB-) | 17 | 0.6 | 0.6 | -2.1 | 3.0 |
| BB (BB+, BB, BB-) | 22 | 3.6 | 3.5 | -0.3 | 9.1 |
| B+ − SD | 39 | 8.4 | 8.0 | 3.3 | 16.6 |
| Investment Grade ** | 58 | -2.1 | -2.1 | -6.4 | 3.0 |
| Non-Investment Grade ** | 61 | 6.6 | 6.8 | -0.3 | 16.6 |

| MSCI Market Classification | | | | | |
|---|---|---|---|---|---|
| Developed Markets | 23 | -4.0 | -4.9 | -6.4 | 0.4 |
| Emerging Markets | 23 | 0.3 | -0.1 | -3.9 | 8.3 |
| Frontier Markets | 22 | 3.4 | 3.2 | -2.0 | 9.1 |

| Euromoney Region ‡ | | | | | |
|---|---|---|---|---|---|
| Africa | 51 | 10.9 | 8.9 | 0.1 | 31.7 |
| Asia | 29 | 5.6 | 4.1 | -6.4 | 29.0 |
| Australasia | 7 | 9.5 | 12.3 | -5.4 | 23.1 |
| Caribbean | 9 | 6.9 | 6.4 | 0.0 | 16.3 |
| Central and Eastern Europe | 25 | 3.9 | 1.9 | -2.8 | 14.7 |
| Latin America | 20 | 4.5 | 5.3 | -3.9 | 16.6 |
| Middle East | 13 | 4.7 | 2.2 | -3.0 | 19.8 |
| North America | 2 | -4.8 | -4.8 | -5.4 | -4.3 |
| Western Europe | 19 | -3.1 | -3.7 | -6.3 | 7.6 |

## CCR Base Cost of Equity Capital:

| Latvia | COE (%) |
|---|---|
| March 2017 | 12.8 |
| December 2016 | 12.6 |

CCR base country-level COE for a Latvia-based investor investing in Latvia.

§ S&P Credit Rating based on long-term foreign currency issuer rating. See http://www.standardandpoors.com/.

• World rank based on 175 countries covered by Euromoney. Ranking based on ascending order in which '1' equals the smallest country risk premium (CRP) and '175' equals the largest country risk premium (CRP).

† MSCI Market Classification based on MSCI Market Classification Framework. See http://www.msci.com/products/indexes/market_classification.html.

‡ Regional classification based on Euromoney. Regional rankings based on ascending order in which '1' equals the smallest country risk premium (CRP) for each region.

** Investment grade based on S&P sovereign credit rating from AAA to BBB-. Non-Investment grade based on S&P sovereign credit rating from BB+ to SD. For purposes of this analysis, the U.S. is being treated as if it were rated AAA by S&P.

Note: A CRP of 0.0% is assumed in the following cases: (i) when the investor country and the investee country both have an S&P sovereign credit rating of AAA; or (ii) when the investor country has an S&P credit rating of AAA, and the investee country has a sovereign credit rating below AAA, but has a calculated CRP below 0.0% (which would imply lower risk than a country rated AAA); or (iii) when the investor country has an S&P credit rating below AAA, and the investee country has a sovereign credit rating of AAA, but has a calculated CRP above 0.0% (which would imply greater risk than a country rated below AAA). For purposes of this analysis, the U.S. is treated as having a sovereign credit rating equivalent to AAA.

The country risk premium (CRP) is not the cost of equity capital (COE). The CRP is to be added to base COE. See Chapter 6 for proper application.

## Data Updated Through March 2017

| Investee Country | December 2016 Country Risk Premium (CRP) (%) | March 2017 Country Risk Premium (CRP) (%) | S&P Sovereign Credit Rating § | World Rank Out of 175* | MSCI Market Classification † | Euromoney Region ‡ | Regional Rank ‡ |
|---|---|---|---|---|---|---|---|
| Afghanistan | 12.8 | 12.4 | | 139 | | Asia | 23 out of 29 |
| Albania | 7.3 | 7.4 | B+ | 93 | | Central and Eastern Europe | 18 out of 25 |
| Algeria | 7.3 | 7.3 | | 91 | | Africa | 10 out of 51 |
| Angola | 9.7 | 9.7 | B | 121 | | Africa | 26 out of 51 |
| Argentina | 7.9 | 7.5 | B- | 96 | Frontier | Latin America | 13 out of 20 |
| Armenia | 4.9 | 5.0 | | 77 | | Asia | 15 out of 29 |
| Australia | -4.2 | -4.3 | AAA | 12 | Developed | Australasia | 2 out of 7 |
| Austria | -4.0 | -4.1 | AA+ | 13 | Developed | Western Europe | 9 out of 19 |
| Azerbaijan | 6.1 | 6.3 | BB+ | 85 | | Asia | 17 out of 29 |
| Bahamas | 3.4 | 3.0 | BB+ | 65 | | Caribbean | 3 out of 9 |
| Bahrain | 3.3 | 3.0 | BB- | 64 | Frontier | Middle East | 7 out of 13 |
| Bangladesh | 10.2 | 9.9 | BB- | 126 | Frontier | Asia | 20 out of 29 |
| Barbados | 5.1 | 6.1 | CCC+ | 82 | | Caribbean | 4 out of 9 |
| Belarus | 12.5 | 12.8 | B- | 143 | | Central and Eastern Europe | 23 out of 25 |
| Belgium | -2.7 | -2.9 | AA | 17 | Developed | Western Europe | 10 out of 19 |
| Belize | 8.3 | 8.4 | B- | 106 | | Latin America | 17 out of 20 |
| Benin | 14.2 | 14.1 | | 150 | | Africa | 37 out of 51 |
| Bermuda | 1.0 | 0.8 | A+ | 44 | | Caribbean | 1 out of 9 |
| Bhutan | 13.8 | 13.6 | | 148 | | Asia | 25 out of 29 |
| Bolivia | 6.9 | 7.0 | BB | 88 | | Latin America | 12 out of 20 |
| Bosnia & Herzegovina | 12.9 | 13.0 | B | 144 | | Central and Eastern Europe | 24 out of 25 |
| Botswana | 1.0 | 0.9 | A- | 48 | | Africa | 1 out of 51 |
| Brazil | 2.5 | 2.3 | BB | 59 | Emerging | Latin America | 7 out of 20 |
| Bulgaria | 2.4 | 2.5 | BB+ | 61 | | Central and Eastern Europe | 12 out of 25 |
| Burkina Faso | 11.3 | 11.2 | B- | 133 | | Africa | 33 out of 51 |
| Burundi | 23.2 | 23.2 | | 169 | | Africa | 47 out of 51 |
| Cambodia | 14.7 | 14.3 | | 151 | | Asia | 27 out of 29 |
| Cameroon | 9.9 | 9.8 | B | 124 | | Africa | 28 out of 51 |
| Canada | -4.4 | -4.5 | AAA | 9 | Developed | North America | 1 out of 2 |
| Cape Verde | 7.5 | 7.4 | B | 94 | | Africa | 12 out of 51 |
| Central African Republic | 26.8 | 26.8 | | 172 | | Africa | 49 out of 51 |
| Chad | 25.5 | 25.4 | | 171 | | Africa | 48 out of 51 |
| Chile | -3.2 | -3.1 | AA- | 16 | Emerging | Latin America | 1 out of 20 |
| China | 0.8 | 0.7 | AA- | 42 | Emerging | Asia | 7 out of 29 |
| Colombia | 0.8 | 0.6 | BBB | 41 | Emerging | Latin America | 4 out of 20 |
| Congo Republic | 9.5 | 9.2 | B- | 117 | | Africa | 24 out of 51 |
| Congo, DR | 10.8 | 10.6 | B- | 131 | | Africa | 32 out of 51 |
| Costa Rica | 3.8 | 4.0 | BB- | 71 | | Latin America | 8 out of 20 |
| Côte d'Ivoire | 7.4 | 7.3 | | 92 | | Africa | 11 out of 51 |
| Croatia | 2.9 | 2.7 | BB | 63 | Frontier | Central and Eastern Europe | 13 out of 25 |
| Cuba | 17.1 | 17.1 | | 160 | | Caribbean | 9 out of 9 |
| Cyprus | 0.5 | 0.5 | BB+ | 40 | | Central and Eastern Europe | 7 out of 25 |
| Czech Republic | -1.9 | -2.0 | AA- | 23 | Emerging | Central and Eastern Europe | 1 out of 25 |
| Denmark | -5.0 | -5.1 | AAA | 4 | Developed | Western Europe | 3 out of 19 |
| Djibouti | 34.8 | 32.5 | | 175 | | Africa | 51 out of 51 |
| Dominican Republic | 7.2 | 7.2 | BB- | 90 | | Caribbean | 5 out of 9 |
| Ecuador | 8.8 | 8.6 | B | 109 | | Latin America | 18 out of 20 |
| Egypt | 9.3 | 9.1 | B- | 116 | Emerging | Africa | 23 out of 51 |
| El Salvador | 6.2 | 5.9 | B- | 81 | | Latin America | 10 out of 20 |
| Equatorial Guinea | 19.6 | 19.6 | | 165 | | Africa | 45 out of 51 |

§ S&P Credit Rating based on long-term foreign currency issuer rating. See http://www.standardandpoors.com/.

• World rank based on 175 countries covered by Euromoney. Ranking based on ascending order in which '1' equals the smallest country risk premium (CRP) and '175' equals the largest country risk premium (CRP).

† MSCI Market Classification based on MSCI Market Classification Framework. See http://www.msci.com/products/indexes/market_classification.html

‡ Regional classification based on Euromoney. Regional rankings based on ascending order in which '1' equals the smallest country risk premium (CRP) for each region.

Note: A CRP of 0.0% is assumed in the following cases: (i) when the investor country and the investee country both have an S&P sovereign credit rating of AAA; or (ii) when the investor country has an S&P credit rating of AAA, and the investee country has a sovereign credit rating below AAA, but has a calculated CRP below 0.0% (which would imply lower risk than a country rated AAA); or (iii) when the investor country has an S&P credit rating below AAA, and the investee country has a sovereign credit rating of AAA, but has a calculated CRP above 0.0% (which would imply greater risk than a country rated below AAA). For purposes of this analysis, the U.S. is treated as having a sovereign credit rating equivalent to AAA.

The country risk premium (CRP) is not the cost of equity capital (COE). The CRP is to be added to base COE. See Chapter 6 for proper application.

## Data Updated Through March 2017

| Investee Country | December 2016 Country Risk Premium (CRP) (%) | March 2017 Country Risk Premium (CRP) (%) | S&P Sovereign Credit Rating § | World Rank Out of 175• | MSCI Market Classification † | Euromoney Region ‡ | Regional Rank ‡ |
|---|---|---|---|---|---|---|---|
| Eritrea | 31.0 | 29.1 | | 173 | | Africa | 50 out of 51 |
| Estonia | -1.3 | -1.2 | AA- | 32 | Frontier | Central and Eastern Europe | 4 out of 25 |
| Ethiopia | 8.1 | 8.0 | B | 101 | | Africa | 16 out of 51 |
| Fiji | 13.5 | 13.3 | B+ | 147 | | Australasia | 5 out of 7 |
| Finland | -4.2 | -4.4 | AA+ | 11 | Developed | Western Europe | 8 out of 19 |
| France | -1.9 | -2.1 | AA | 22 | Developed | Western Europe | 12 out of 19 |
| Gabon | 5.8 | 6.1 | | 83 | | Africa | 7 out of 51 |
| Gambia | 11.9 | 11.9 | | 138 | | Africa | 34 out of 51 |
| Georgia | 4.6 | 4.7 | BB- | 74 | | Central and Eastern Europe | 15 out of 25 |
| Germany | -4.2 | -4.4 | AAA | 10 | Developed | Western Europe | 7 out of 19 |
| Ghana | 7.6 | 7.1 | B- | 89 | | Africa | 9 out of 51 |
| Greece | 8.7 | 8.4 | B- | 108 | Emerging | Western Europe | 19 out of 19 |
| Grenada | 8.3 | 8.3 | | 105 | | Caribbean | 7 out of 9 |
| Guatemala | 6.2 | 6.2 | BB | 84 | | Latin America | 11 out of 20 |
| Guinea | 15.7 | 15.6 | | 156 | | Africa | 41 out of 51 |
| Guinea-Bissau | 9.2 | 9.1 | | 115 | | Africa | 22 out of 51 |
| Guyana | 8.0 | 7.9 | | 100 | | Latin America | 15 out of 20 |
| Haiti | 18.6 | 16.4 | | 157 | | Caribbean | 8 out of 9 |
| Honduras | 7.7 | 7.6 | B+ | 98 | | Latin America | 14 out of 20 |
| Hong Kong | -3.7 | -3.8 | AAA | 14 | Developed | Asia | 2 out of 29 |
| Hungary | 2.1 | 2.2 | BBB- | 57 | Emerging | Central and Eastern Europe | 10 out of 25 |
| Iceland | -0.9 | -1.2 | A | 30 | | Western Europe | 15 out of 19 |
| India | 1.9 | 2.1 | BBB- | 55 | Emerging | Asia | 10 out of 29 |
| Indonesia | 2.7 | 2.6 | BB+ | 62 | Emerging | Asia | 11 out of 29 |
| Iran | 9.7 | 9.9 | | 125 | | Middle East | 10 out of 13 |
| Iraq | 11.5 | 11.5 | B- | 136 | | Middle East | 11 out of 13 |
| Ireland | -1.4 | -1.6 | A+ | 27 | Developed | Western Europe | 14 out of 19 |
| Israel | -1.4 | -1.5 | A+ | 28 | Developed | Middle East | 2 out of 13 |
| Italy | 1.5 | 1.2 | BBB- | 50 | Developed | Western Europe | 18 out of 19 |
| Jamaica | 7.8 | 8.3 | B | 104 | | Caribbean | 6 out of 9 |
| Japan | -1.5 | -1.6 | A+ | 25 | Developed | Asia | 5 out of 29 |
| Jordan | 4.8 | 4.9 | BB- | 76 | Frontier | Middle East | 8 out of 13 |
| Kazakhstan | 4.3 | 3.9 | BBB- | 70 | Frontier | Asia | 13 out of 29 |
| Kenya | 7.8 | 7.8 | B+ | 99 | Frontier | Africa | 15 out of 51 |
| Korea (North) | 30.3 | 29.8 | | 174 | | Asia | 29 out of 29 |
| Korea (South) | -2.3 | -2.4 | AA | 19 | Emerging | Asia | 4 out of 29 |
| Kuwait | -1.2 | -1.2 | AA | 31 | Frontier | Middle East | 3 out of 13 |
| Kyrgyz Republic | 13.0 | 12.8 | | 142 | | Central and Eastern Europe | 22 out of 25 |
| Laos | 17.3 | 16.7 | | 158 | | Asia | 28 out of 29 |
| Latvia | 0.8 | 0.8 | A- | 43 | | Central and Eastern Europe | 8 out of 25 |
| Lebanon | 9.6 | 8.8 | B- | 112 | Frontier | Middle East | 9 out of 13 |
| Lesotho | 13.2 | 13.1 | | 146 | | Africa | 36 out of 51 |
| Liberia | 8.4 | 8.4 | | 107 | | Africa | 17 out of 51 |
| Libya | 14.7 | 15.0 | | 153 | | Africa | 39 out of 51 |
| Lithuania | 0.0 | 0.0 | A- | 36 | Frontier | Central and Eastern Europe | 6 out of 25 |
| Luxembourg | -4.7 | -4.8 | AAA | 5 | | Western Europe | 4 out of 19 |
| Macedonia | 6.9 | 7.0 | BB- | 87 | | Central and Eastern Europe | 17 out of 25 |
| Madagascar | 9.3 | 9.7 | | 123 | | Africa | 27 out of 51 |
| Malawi | 9.0 | 9.0 | | 114 | | Africa | 21 out of 51 |
| Malaysia | 0.2 | -0.1 | A- | 35 | Emerging | Asia | 6 out of 29 |

§ S&P Credit Rating based on long-term foreign currency issuer rating. See http://www.standardandpoors.com/.

• World rank based on 175 countries covered by Euromoney. Ranking based on ascending order in which '1' equals the smallest country risk premium (CRP) and '175' equals the largest country risk premium (CRP).

† MSCI Market Classification based on MSCI Market Classification Framework. See http://www.msci.com/products/indexes/market_classification.html

‡ Regional classification based on Euromoney. Regional rankings based on ascending order in which '1' equals the smallest country risk premium (CRP) for each region.

Note: A CRP of 0.0% is assumed in the following cases: (i) when the investor country and the investee country both have an S&P sovereign credit rating of AAA; or (ii) when the investor country has an S&P credit rating of AAA, and the investee country has a sovereign credit rating below AAA, but has a calculated CRP below 0.0% (which would imply lower risk than a country rated AAA); or (iii) when the investor country has an S&P credit rating below AAA, and the investee country has a sovereign credit rating of AAA, but has a calculated CRP above 0.0% (which would imply greater risk than a country rated below AAA). For purposes of this analysis, the U.S. is treated as having a sovereign credit rating equivalent to AAA.

2017 Valuation Handbook – International Guide to Cost of Capital     Data Exhibit 4     Investor Perspective: Lithuania (EUR); Page 2 of 4

The country risk premium (CRP) is not the cost of equity capital (COE). The CRP is to be added to base COE. See Chapter 6 for proper application.

### Data Updated Through March 2017

| Investee Country | December 2016 Country Risk Premium (CRP) (%) | March 2017 Country Risk Premium (CRP) (%) | S&P Sovereign Credit Rating § | World Rank Out of 175* | MSCI Market Classification † | Euromoney Region ‡ | Regional Rank ‡ |
|---|---|---|---|---|---|---|---|
| Mali | 12.8 | 12.7 | | 141 | | Africa | 35 out of 51 |
| Malta | -1.5 | -1.6 | A- | 26 | | Western Europe | 13 out of 19 |
| Mauritania | 16.9 | 16.8 | | 159 | | Africa | 42 out of 51 |
| Mauritius | 3.6 | 3.5 | | 67 | Frontier | Asia | 12 out of 29 |
| Mexico | 0.1 | 0.1 | BBB+ | 37 | Emerging | Latin America | 2 out of 20 |
| Moldova | 11.2 | 11.6 | | 137 | | Central and Eastern Europe | 21 out of 25 |
| Mongolia | 9.4 | 9.6 | B- | 119 | | Asia | 18 out of 29 |
| Montenegro | 8.6 | 8.3 | B+ | 103 | | Central and Eastern Europe | 19 out of 25 |
| Morocco | 3.7 | 3.8 | BBB- | 69 | Frontier | Africa | 4 out of 51 |
| Mozambique | 10.5 | 10.2 | SD | 128 | | Africa | 29 out of 51 |
| Myanmar | 11.4 | 11.2 | | 134 | | Asia | 22 out of 29 |
| Namibia | 3.3 | 3.3 | | 66 | | Africa | 3 out of 51 |
| Nepal | 14.1 | 14.1 | | 149 | | Asia | 26 out of 29 |
| Netherlands | -4.6 | -4.8 | AAA | 6 | Developed | Western Europe | 5 out of 19 |
| New Zealand | -4.5 | -4.6 | AA | 8 | Developed | Australasia | 1 out of 7 |
| Nicaragua | 10.1 | 10.1 | B+ | 127 | | Latin America | 19 out of 20 |
| Niger | 9.7 | 9.7 | | 120 | | Africa | 25 out of 51 |
| Nigeria | 7.7 | 7.6 | B | 97 | Frontier | Africa | 14 out of 51 |
| Norway | -5.3 | -5.5 | AAA | 3 | Developed | Western Europe | 2 out of 19 |
| Oman | 0.9 | 0.9 | BBB- | 46 | Frontier | Middle East | 5 out of 13 |
| Pakistan | 9.8 | 9.7 | B | 122 | Frontier | Asia | 19 out of 29 |
| Panama | 1.7 | 1.6 | BBB | 52 | | Latin America | 6 out of 20 |
| Papua New Guinea | 9.3 | 9.4 | B+ | 118 | | Australasia | 3 out of 7 |
| Paraguay | 5.2 | 5.3 | BB | 80 | | Latin America | 9 out of 20 |
| Peru | 0.3 | 0.4 | BBB+ | 39 | Emerging | Latin America | 3 out of 20 |
| Philippines | 2.0 | 1.9 | BBB | 53 | Emerging | Asia | 9 out of 29 |
| Poland | -1.1 | -1.3 | BBB+ | 29 | Emerging | Central and Eastern Europe | 3 out of 25 |
| Portugal | 1.4 | 1.1 | BB+ | 49 | Developed | Western Europe | 17 out of 19 |
| Qatar | -2.2 | -2.2 | AA | 21 | Emerging | Middle East | 1 out of 13 |
| Romania | 2.2 | 2.1 | BBB- | 56 | Frontier | Central and Eastern Europe | 9 out of 25 |
| Russia | 4.5 | 3.7 | BB+ | 68 | Emerging | Central and Eastern Europe | 14 out of 25 |
| Rwanda | 10.5 | 10.5 | B | 130 | | Africa | 31 out of 51 |
| São Tomé & Príncipe | 17.0 | 17.4 | | 163 | | Africa | 43 out of 51 |
| Saudi Arabia | 1.3 | 0.9 | A- | 47 | | Middle East | 6 out of 13 |
| Senegal | 7.0 | 7.0 | B+ | 86 | | Africa | 8 out of 51 |
| Serbia | 5.1 | 4.8 | BB- | 75 | Frontier | Central and Eastern Europe | 16 out of 25 |
| Seychelles | 4.6 | 4.5 | | 73 | | Africa | 5 out of 51 |
| Sierra Leone | 10.5 | 10.5 | | 129 | | Africa | 30 out of 51 |
| Singapore | -5.5 | -5.6 | AAA | 1 | Developed | Asia | 1 out of 29 |
| Slovakia | -1.8 | -1.8 | A+ | 24 | | Central and Eastern Europe | 2 out of 25 |
| Slovenia | -0.4 | -0.4 | A | 34 | Frontier | Central and Eastern Europe | 5 out of 25 |
| Solomon Islands | 21.4 | 21.4 | | 168 | | Australasia | 6 out of 7 |
| Somalia | 19.7 | 19.6 | | 166 | | Africa | 46 out of 51 |
| South Africa | 2.2 | 2.4 | BBB- | 60 | Emerging | Africa | 2 out of 51 |
| Spain | 0.5 | 0.4 | BBB+ | 38 | Developed | Western Europe | 16 out of 19 |
| Sri Lanka | 4.5 | 4.1 | B+ | 72 | Frontier | Asia | 14 out of 29 |
| Sudan | 15.6 | 15.5 | | 154 | | Africa | 40 out of 51 |
| Suriname | 8.0 | 8.1 | B+ | 102 | | Latin America | 16 out of 20 |
| Swaziland | 13.9 | 14.8 | | 152 | | Africa | 38 out of 51 |
| Sweden | -4.6 | -4.8 | AAA | 7 | Developed | Western Europe | 6 out of 19 |

§ S&P Credit Rating based on long-term foreign currency issuer rating. See http://www.standardandpoors.com/.

* World rank based on 175 countries covered by Euromoney. Ranking based on ascending order in which '1' equals the smallest country risk premium (CRP) and '175' equals the largest country risk premium (CRP).

† MSCI Market Classification based on MSCI Market Classification Framework. See http://www.msci.com/products/indexes/market_classification.html.

‡ Regional classification based on Euromoney. Regional rankings based on ascending order in which '1' equals the smallest country risk premium (CRP) for each region.

Note: A CRP of 0.0% is assumed in the following cases: (i) when the investor country and the investee country both have an S&P sovereign credit rating of AAA; or (ii) when the investor country has an S&P credit rating of AAA, and the investee country has a sovereign credit rating below AAA, but has a calculated CRP below 0.0% (which would imply lower risk than a country rated AAA); or (iii) when the investor country has an S&P credit rating below AAA, and the investee country has a sovereign credit rating of AAA, but has a calculated CRP above 0.0% (which would imply greater risk than a country rated below AAA). For purposes of this analysis, the U.S. is treated as having a sovereign credit rating equivalent to AAA.

The country risk premium (CRP) is not the cost of equity capital (COE). The CRP is to be added to base COE. See Chapter 6 for proper application.

## Data Updated Through March 2017

| Investee Country | December 2016 Country Risk Premium (CRP) (%) | March 2017 Country Risk Premium (CRP) (%) | S&P Sovereign Credit Rating § | World Rank Out of 175∗ | MSCI Market Classification † | Euromoney Region ‡ | Regional Rank ‡ |
|---|---|---|---|---|---|---|---|
| Switzerland | -5.3 | -5.5 | AAA | 2 | Developed | Western Europe | 1 out of 19 |
| Syria | 20.4 | 20.6 | | 167 | | Middle East | 13 out of 13 |
| Taiwan | -2.6 | -2.7 | AA- | 18 | Emerging | Asia | 3 out of 29 |
| Tajikistan | 15.2 | 15.5 | | 155 | | Central and Eastern Europe | 25 out of 25 |
| Tanzania | 7.4 | 7.5 | | 95 | | Africa | 13 out of 51 |
| Thailand | 1.7 | 1.4 | BBB+ | 51 | Emerging | Asia | 8 out of 29 |
| Togo | 9.0 | 8.9 | | 113 | | Africa | 20 out of 51 |
| Tonga | 23.9 | 23.9 | | 170 | | Australasia | 7 out of 7 |
| Trinidad & Tobago | 2.0 | 1.9 | A- | 54 | | Caribbean | 2 out of 9 |
| Tunisia | 4.9 | 5.2 | | 79 | Frontier | Africa | 6 out of 51 |
| Turkey | 2.4 | 2.2 | BB | 58 | Emerging | Central and Eastern Europe | 11 out of 25 |
| Turkmenistan | 12.3 | 12.5 | | 140 | | Asia | 24 out of 29 |
| Uganda | 8.5 | 8.7 | B | 110 | | Africa | 18 out of 51 |
| Ukraine | 11.3 | 11.4 | B- | 135 | | Central and Eastern Europe | 20 out of 25 |
| United Arab Emirates | -0.8 | -0.8 | AA | 33 | Emerging | Middle East | 4 out of 13 |
| United Kingdom | -2.3 | -2.3 | AA | 20 | Developed | Western Europe | 11 out of 19 |
| United States | -3.4 | -3.5 | AA+ | 15 | Developed | North America | 2 out of 2 |
| Uruguay | 1.0 | 0.8 | BBB | 45 | | Latin America | 5 out of 20 |
| Uzbekistan | 11.5 | 10.9 | | 132 | | Asia | 21 out of 29 |
| Vanuatu | 13.2 | 13.1 | | 145 | | Australasia | 4 out of 7 |
| Venezuela | 17.0 | 17.4 | CCC | 162 | | Latin America | 20 out of 20 |
| Vietnam | 5.5 | 5.1 | BB- | 78 | Frontier | Asia | 16 out of 29 |
| Yemen | 17.3 | 17.3 | | 161 | | Middle East | 12 out of 13 |
| Zambia | 8.8 | 8.8 | B | 111 | | Africa | 19 out of 51 |
| Zimbabwe | 19.0 | 18.8 | | 164 | | Africa | 44 out of 51 |

## March 2017 Country Risk Premium (CRP) Summary Statistics:

| S&P Rating | Country Count | Average CRP (%) | Median CRP (%) | Min CRP (%) | Max CRP (%) |
|---|---|---|---|---|---|
| AAA ∗∗ | 12 | -4.7 | -4.8 | -5.6 | -3.5 |
| AA (AA+, AA, AA-) | 15 | -2.3 | -2.3 | -4.6 | 0.7 |
| A (A+, A, A-) | 14 | -0.3 | -0.3 | -1.8 | 1.9 |
| BBB (BBB+, BBB, BBB-) | 17 | 1.4 | 1.4 | -1.3 | 3.9 |
| BB (BB+, BB, BB-) | 22 | 4.4 | 4.3 | 0.5 | 9.9 |
| B+ − SD | 39 | 9.2 | 8.8 | 4.1 | 17.4 |
| Investment Grade ∗∗ | 58 | -1.2 | -1.2 | -5.6 | 3.9 |
| Non-Investment Grade ∗∗ | 61 | 7.5 | 7.6 | 0.5 | 17.4 |
| **MSCI Market Classification** | | | | | |
| Developed Markets | 23 | -3.2 | -4.1 | -5.6 | 1.2 |
| Emerging Markets | 23 | 1.1 | 0.7 | -3.1 | 9.1 |
| Frontier Markets | 22 | 4.2 | 4.0 | -1.2 | 9.9 |
| **Euromoney Region ‡** | | | | | |
| Africa | 51 | 11.7 | 9.7 | 0.9 | 32.5 |
| Asia | 29 | 6.4 | 5.0 | -5.6 | 29.8 |
| Australasia | 7 | 10.3 | 13.1 | -4.6 | 23.9 |
| Caribbean | 9 | 7.7 | 7.2 | 0.8 | 17.1 |
| Central and Eastern Europe | 25 | 4.8 | 2.7 | -2.0 | 15.5 |
| Latin America | 20 | 5.3 | 6.1 | -3.1 | 17.4 |
| Middle East | 13 | 5.5 | 3.0 | -2.2 | 20.6 |
| North America | 2 | -4.0 | -4.0 | -4.5 | -3.5 |
| Western Europe | 19 | -2.3 | -2.9 | -5.5 | 8.4 |

## CCR Base Cost of Equity Capital:

| Lithuania | COE (%) |
|---|---|
| March 2017 | 12.0 |
| December 2016 | 11.8 |

CCR base country-level COE for a Lithuania-based investor investing in Lithuania.

§ S&P Credit Rating based on long-term foreign currency issuer rating. See http://www.standardandpoors.com/.

∗ World rank based on 175 countries covered by Euromoney. Ranking based on ascending order in which '1' equals the smallest country risk premium (CRP) and '175' equals the largest country risk premium (CRP).

† MSCI Market Classification based on MSCI Market Classification Framework. See http://www.msci.com/products/indexes/market_classification.html

‡ Regional classification based on Euromoney. Regional rankings based on ascending order in which '1' equals the smallest country risk premium (CRP) for each region.

∗∗ Investment grade based on S&P sovereign credit rating from AAA to BBB-. Non-Investment grade based on S&P sovereign credit rating from BB+ to SD. For purposes of this analysis, the U.S. is being treated as if it were rated AAA by S&P.

Note: A CRP of 0.0% is assumed in the following cases: (i) when the investor country and the investee country both have an S&P sovereign credit rating of AAA; or (ii) when the investor country has an S&P credit rating of AAA, and the investee country has a sovereign credit rating below AAA, but has a calculated CRP below 0.0% (which would imply lower risk than a country rated AAA); or (iii) when the investor country has an S&P credit rating below AAA, and the investee country has a sovereign credit rating of AAA, but has a calculated CRP above 0.0% (which would imply greater risk than a country rated below AAA). For purposes of this analysis, the U.S. is treated as having a sovereign credit rating equivalent to AAA.

The country risk premium (CRP) is not the cost of equity capital (COE). The CRP is to be added to base COE. See Chapter 6 for proper application.

Data Updated Through March 2017

| Investee Country | December 2016 Country Risk Premium (CRP) (%) | March 2017 Country Risk Premium (CRP) (%) | S&P Sovereign Credit Rating § | World Rank Out of 175* | MSCI Market Classification † | Euromoney Region ‡ | Regional Rank ‡ |
|---|---|---|---|---|---|---|---|
| Afghanistan | 17.4 | 17.3 | | 139 | | Asia | 23 out of 29 |
| Albania | 12.0 | 12.2 | B+ | 93 | | Central and Eastern Europe | 18 out of 25 |
| Algeria | 12.0 | 12.1 | | 91 | | Africa | 10 out of 51 |
| Angola | 14.4 | 14.5 | B | 121 | | Africa | 26 out of 51 |
| Argentina | 12.6 | 12.4 | B- | 96 | Frontier | Latin America | 13 out of 20 |
| Armenia | 9.5 | 9.8 | | 77 | | Asia | 15 out of 29 |
| Australia | 0.0 | 0.0 | AAA | 12 | Developed | Australasia | 2 out of 7 |
| Austria | 0.7 | 0.7 | AA+ | 13 | Developed | Western Europe | 9 out of 19 |
| Azerbaijan | 10.8 | 11.2 | BB+ | 85 | | Asia | 17 out of 29 |
| Bahamas | 8.1 | 7.9 | BB+ | 65 | | Caribbean | 3 out of 9 |
| Bahrain | 8.0 | 7.9 | BB- | 64 | Frontier | Middle East | 7 out of 13 |
| Bangladesh | 14.9 | 14.7 | BB- | 126 | Frontier | Asia | 20 out of 29 |
| Barbados | 9.7 | 10.9 | CCC+ | 82 | | Caribbean | 4 out of 9 |
| Belarus | 17.1 | 17.6 | B- | 143 | | Central and Eastern Europe | 23 out of 25 |
| Belgium | 2.0 | 1.9 | AA | 17 | Developed | Western Europe | 10 out of 19 |
| Belize | 13.0 | 13.2 | B- | 106 | | Latin America | 17 out of 20 |
| Benin | 18.8 | 19.0 | | 150 | | Africa | 37 out of 51 |
| Bermuda | 5.7 | 5.7 | A+ | 44 | | Caribbean | 1 out of 9 |
| Bhutan | 18.5 | 18.5 | | 148 | | Asia | 25 out of 29 |
| Bolivia | 11.5 | 11.9 | BB | 88 | | Latin America | 12 out of 20 |
| Bosnia & Herzegovina | 17.6 | 17.8 | B | 144 | | Central and Eastern Europe | 24 out of 25 |
| Botswana | 5.7 | 5.7 | A- | 48 | | Africa | 1 out of 51 |
| Brazil | 7.2 | 7.2 | BB | 59 | Emerging | Latin America | 7 out of 20 |
| Bulgaria | 7.1 | 7.3 | BB+ | 61 | | Central and Eastern Europe | 12 out of 25 |
| Burkina Faso | 16.0 | 16.1 | B- | 133 | | Africa | 33 out of 51 |
| Burundi | 27.9 | 28.0 | | 169 | | Africa | 47 out of 51 |
| Cambodia | 19.4 | 19.2 | | 151 | | Asia | 27 out of 29 |
| Cameroon | 14.6 | 14.6 | B | 124 | | Africa | 28 out of 51 |
| Canada | 0.0 | 0.0 | AAA | 9 | Developed | North America | 1 out of 2 |
| Cape Verde | 12.2 | 12.3 | B | 94 | | Africa | 12 out of 51 |
| Central African Republic | 31.5 | 31.6 | | 172 | | Africa | 49 out of 51 |
| Chad | 30.1 | 30.3 | | 171 | | Africa | 48 out of 51 |
| Chile | 1.5 | 1.8 | AA- | 16 | Emerging | Latin America | 1 out of 20 |
| China | 5.5 | 5.5 | AA- | 42 | Emerging | Asia | 7 out of 29 |
| Colombia | 5.4 | 5.5 | BBB | 41 | Emerging | Latin America | 4 out of 20 |
| Congo Republic | 14.2 | 14.1 | B- | 117 | | Africa | 24 out of 51 |
| Congo, DR | 15.5 | 15.5 | B- | 131 | | Africa | 32 out of 51 |
| Costa Rica | 8.5 | 8.8 | BB- | 71 | | Latin America | 8 out of 20 |
| Côte d'Ivoire | 12.1 | 12.2 | | 92 | | Africa | 11 out of 51 |
| Croatia | 7.6 | 7.5 | BB | 63 | Frontier | Central and Eastern Europe | 13 out of 25 |
| Cuba | 21.8 | 22.0 | | 160 | | Caribbean | 9 out of 9 |
| Cyprus | 5.2 | 5.3 | BB+ | 40 | | Central and Eastern Europe | 7 out of 25 |
| Czech Republic | 2.8 | 2.8 | AA- | 23 | Emerging | Central and Eastern Europe | 1 out of 25 |
| Denmark | 0.0 | 0.0 | AAA | 4 | Developed | Western Europe | 3 out of 19 |
| Djibouti | 39.5 | 37.3 | | 175 | | Africa | 51 out of 51 |
| Dominican Republic | 11.9 | 12.1 | BB- | 90 | | Caribbean | 5 out of 9 |
| Ecuador | 13.5 | 13.4 | B | 109 | | Latin America | 18 out of 20 |
| Egypt | 13.9 | 14.0 | B- | 116 | Emerging | Africa | 23 out of 51 |
| El Salvador | 10.9 | 10.8 | B- | 81 | | Latin America | 10 out of 20 |
| Equatorial Guinea | 24.3 | 24.4 | | 165 | | Africa | 45 out of 51 |

§ S&P Credit Rating based on long-term foreign currency issuer rating. See http://www.standardandpoors.com/.

* World rank based on 175 countries covered by Euromoney. Ranking based on ascending order in which '1' equals the smallest country risk premium (CRP) and '175' equals the largest country risk premium (CRP).

† MSCI Market Classification based on MSCI Market Classification Framework. See http://www.msci.com/products/indexes/market_classification.html

‡ Regional classification based on Euromoney. Regional rankings based on ascending order in which '1' equals the smallest country risk premium (CRP) for each region.

Note: A CRP of 0.0% is assumed in the following cases: (i) when the investor country and the investee country both have an S&P sovereign credit rating of AAA; or (ii) when the investor country has an S&P credit rating of AAA, and the investee country has a sovereign credit rating below AAA, but has a calculated CRP below 0.0% (which would imply lower risk than a country rated AAA); or (iii) when the investor country has an S&P credit rating below AAA, and the investee country has a sovereign credit rating of AAA, but has a calculated CRP above 0.0% (which would imply greater risk than a country rated below AAA). For purposes of this analysis, the U.S. is treated as having a sovereign credit rating equivalent to AAA.

Investor Perspective: Luxembourg
Currency: Euro (EUR)

Erb-Harvey-Viskanta
Country Credit Rating (CCR) Model

The country risk premium (CRP) is not the cost of equity capital (COE). The CRP is to be added to base COE. See Chapter 6 for proper application.

## Data Updated Through March 2017

| Investee Country | December 2016 Country Risk Premium (CRP) (%) | March 2017 Country Risk Premium (CRP) (%) | S&P Sovereign Credit Rating § | World Rank Out of 175* | MSCI Market Classification † | Euromoney Region ‡ | Regional Rank ‡ |
|---|---|---|---|---|---|---|---|
| Eritrea | 35.7 | 34.0 | | 173 | | Africa | 50 out of 51 |
| Estonia | 3.4 | 3.7 | AA- | 32 | Frontier | Central and Eastern Europe | 4 out of 25 |
| Ethiopia | 12.7 | 12.9 | B | 101 | | Africa | 16 out of 51 |
| Fiji | 18.2 | 18.1 | B+ | 147 | | Australasia | 5 out of 7 |
| Finland | 0.4 | 0.5 | AA+ | 11 | Developed | Western Europe | 8 out of 19 |
| France | 2.8 | 2.7 | AA | 22 | Developed | Western Europe | 12 out of 19 |
| Gabon | 10.5 | 10.9 | | 83 | | Africa | 7 out of 51 |
| Gambia | 16.6 | 16.7 | | 138 | | Africa | 34 out of 51 |
| Georgia | 9.3 | 9.6 | BB- | 74 | | Central and Eastern Europe | 15 out of 25 |
| Germany | 0.0 | 0.0 | AAA | 10 | Developed | Western Europe | 7 out of 19 |
| Ghana | 12.3 | 12.0 | B- | 89 | | Africa | 9 out of 51 |
| Greece | 13.4 | 13.3 | B- | 108 | Emerging | Western Europe | 19 out of 19 |
| Grenada | 13.0 | 13.2 | | 105 | | Caribbean | 7 out of 9 |
| Guatemala | 10.9 | 11.1 | BB | 84 | | Latin America | 11 out of 20 |
| Guinea | 20.3 | 20.5 | | 156 | | Africa | 41 out of 51 |
| Guinea-Bissau | 13.9 | 14.0 | | 115 | | Africa | 22 out of 51 |
| Guyana | 12.7 | 12.8 | | 100 | | Latin America | 15 out of 20 |
| Haiti | 23.2 | 21.3 | | 157 | | Caribbean | 8 out of 9 |
| Honduras | 12.4 | 12.5 | B+ | 98 | | Latin America | 14 out of 20 |
| Hong Kong | 0.0 | 0.0 | AAA | 14 | Developed | Asia | 2 out of 29 |
| Hungary | 6.8 | 7.0 | BBB- | 57 | Emerging | Central and Eastern Europe | 10 out of 25 |
| Iceland | 3.8 | 3.6 | A | 30 | | Western Europe | 15 out of 19 |
| India | 6.6 | 6.9 | BBB- | 55 | Emerging | Asia | 10 out of 29 |
| Indonesia | 7.4 | 7.4 | BB+ | 62 | Emerging | Asia | 11 out of 29 |
| Iran | 14.4 | 14.7 | | 125 | | Middle East | 10 out of 13 |
| Iraq | 16.2 | 16.3 | B- | 136 | | Middle East | 11 out of 13 |
| Ireland | 3.3 | 3.3 | A+ | 27 | Developed | Western Europe | 14 out of 19 |
| Israel | 3.3 | 3.3 | A+ | 28 | Developed | Middle East | 2 out of 13 |
| Italy | 6.2 | 6.1 | BBB- | 50 | Developed | Western Europe | 18 out of 19 |
| Jamaica | 12.4 | 13.1 | B | 104 | | Caribbean | 6 out of 9 |
| Japan | 3.1 | 3.2 | A+ | 25 | Developed | Asia | 5 out of 29 |
| Jordan | 9.5 | 9.8 | BB- | 76 | Frontier | Middle East | 8 out of 13 |
| Kazakhstan | 9.0 | 8.7 | BBB- | 70 | Frontier | Asia | 13 out of 29 |
| Kenya | 12.5 | 12.6 | B+ | 99 | Frontier | Africa | 15 out of 51 |
| Korea (North) | 35.0 | 34.7 | | 174 | | Asia | 29 out of 29 |
| Korea (South) | 2.4 | 2.5 | AA | 19 | Emerging | Asia | 4 out of 29 |
| Kuwait | 3.5 | 3.7 | AA | 31 | Frontier | Middle East | 3 out of 13 |
| Kyrgyz Republic | 17.7 | 17.6 | | 142 | | Central and Eastern Europe | 22 out of 25 |
| Laos | 22.0 | 21.5 | | 158 | | Asia | 28 out of 29 |
| Latvia | 5.5 | 5.7 | A- | 43 | | Central and Eastern Europe | 8 out of 25 |
| Lebanon | 14.2 | 13.7 | B- | 112 | Frontier | Middle East | 9 out of 13 |
| Lesotho | 17.9 | 18.0 | | 146 | | Africa | 36 out of 51 |
| Liberia | 13.1 | 13.2 | | 107 | | Africa | 17 out of 51 |
| Libya | 19.4 | 19.9 | | 153 | | Africa | 39 out of 51 |
| Lithuania | 4.7 | 4.8 | A- | 36 | Frontier | Central and Eastern Europe | 6 out of 25 |
| Luxembourg | 0.0 | 0.0 | AAA | 5 | | Western Europe | 4 out of 19 |
| Macedonia | 11.5 | 11.8 | BB- | 87 | | Central and Eastern Europe | 17 out of 25 |
| Madagascar | 14.0 | 14.6 | | 123 | | Africa | 27 out of 51 |
| Malawi | 13.7 | 13.8 | | 114 | | Africa | 21 out of 51 |
| Malaysia | 4.9 | 4.8 | A- | 35 | Emerging | Asia | 6 out of 29 |

§ S&P Credit Rating based on long-term foreign currency issuer rating. See http://www.standardandpoors.com/.
∗ World rank based on 175 countries covered by Euromoney. Ranking based on ascending order in which '1' equals the smallest country risk premium (CRP) and '175' equals the largest country risk premium (CRP).
† MSCI Market Classification based on MSCI Market Classification Framework. See http://www.msci.com/products/indexes/market_classification.html.
‡ Regional classification based on Euromoney. Regional rankings based on ascending order in which '1' equals the smallest country risk premium (CRP) for each region.
Note: A CRP of 0.0% is assumed in the following cases: (i) when the investor country and the investee country both have an S&P sovereign credit rating of AAA; or (ii) when the investor country has an S&P credit rating of AAA, and the investee country has a sovereign credit rating below AAA, but has a calculated CRP below 0.0% (which would imply lower risk than a country rated AAA); or (iii) when the investor country has an S&P credit rating below AAA, and the investee country has a sovereign credit rating of AAA, but has a calculated CRP above 0.0% (which would imply greater risk than a country rated below AAA). For purposes of this analysis, the U.S. is treated as having a sovereign credit rating equivalent to AAA.


2017 Valuation Handbook – International Guide to Cost of Capital    Data Exhibit 4    Investor Perspective: Luxembourg (EUR); Page 2 of 4

The country risk premium (CRP) is not the cost of equity capital (COE). The CRP is to be added to base COE. See Chapter 6 for proper application.

## Data Updated Through March 2017

| Investee Country | December 2016 Country Risk Premium (CRP) (%) | March 2017 Country Risk Premium (CRP) (%) | S&P Sovereign Credit Rating § | World Rank Out of 175• | MSCI Market Classification † | Euromoney Region ‡ | Regional Rank ‡ |
|---|---|---|---|---|---|---|---|
| Mali | 17.5 | 17.6 | | 141 | | Africa | 35 out of 51 |
| Malta | 3.1 | 3.3 | A- | 26 | | Western Europe | 13 out of 19 |
| Mauritania | 21.6 | 21.7 | | 159 | | Africa | 42 out of 51 |
| Mauritius | 8.3 | 8.3 | | 67 | Frontier | Asia | 12 out of 29 |
| Mexico | 4.7 | 4.9 | BBB+ | 37 | Emerging | Latin America | 2 out of 20 |
| Moldova | 15.9 | 16.4 | | 137 | | Central and Eastern Europe | 21 out of 25 |
| Mongolia | 14.0 | 14.5 | B- | 119 | | Asia | 18 out of 29 |
| Montenegro | 13.2 | 13.1 | B+ | 103 | | Central and Eastern Europe | 19 out of 25 |
| Morocco | 8.3 | 8.6 | BBB- | 69 | Frontier | Africa | 4 out of 51 |
| Mozambique | 15.1 | 15.1 | SD | 128 | | Africa | 29 out of 51 |
| Myanmar | 16.1 | 16.1 | | 134 | | Asia | 22 out of 29 |
| Namibia | 8.0 | 8.2 | | 66 | | Africa | 3 out of 51 |
| Nepal | 18.8 | 18.9 | | 149 | | Asia | 26 out of 29 |
| Netherlands | 0.0 | 0.0 | AAA | 6 | Developed | Western Europe | 5 out of 19 |
| New Zealand | 0.2 | 0.3 | AA | 8 | Developed | Australasia | 1 out of 7 |
| Nicaragua | 14.8 | 14.9 | B+ | 127 | | Latin America | 19 out of 20 |
| Niger | 14.4 | 14.5 | | 120 | | Africa | 25 out of 51 |
| Nigeria | 12.4 | 12.5 | B | 97 | Frontier | Africa | 14 out of 51 |
| Norway | 0.0 | 0.0 | AAA | 3 | Developed | Western Europe | 2 out of 19 |
| Oman | 5.6 | 5.7 | BBB- | 46 | Frontier | Middle East | 5 out of 13 |
| Pakistan | 14.5 | 14.5 | B | 122 | Frontier | Asia | 19 out of 29 |
| Panama | 6.3 | 6.5 | BBB | 52 | | Latin America | 6 out of 20 |
| Papua New Guinea | 14.0 | 14.2 | B+ | 118 | | Australasia | 3 out of 7 |
| Paraguay | 9.9 | 10.2 | BB | 80 | | Latin America | 9 out of 20 |
| Peru | 5.0 | 5.2 | BBB+ | 39 | Emerging | Latin America | 3 out of 20 |
| Philippines | 6.7 | 6.7 | BBB | 53 | Emerging | Asia | 9 out of 29 |
| Poland | 3.6 | 3.6 | BBB+ | 29 | Emerging | Central and Eastern Europe | 3 out of 25 |
| Portugal | 6.1 | 5.9 | BB+ | 49 | Developed | Western Europe | 17 out of 19 |
| Qatar | 2.5 | 2.6 | AA | 21 | Emerging | Middle East | 1 out of 13 |
| Romania | 6.9 | 7.0 | BBB- | 56 | Frontier | Central and Eastern Europe | 9 out of 25 |
| Russia | 9.1 | 8.6 | BB+ | 68 | Emerging | Central and Eastern Europe | 14 out of 25 |
| Rwanda | 15.2 | 15.3 | B | 130 | | Africa | 31 out of 51 |
| São Tomé & Príncipe | 21.7 | 22.3 | | 163 | | Africa | 43 out of 51 |
| Saudi Arabia | 6.0 | 5.7 | A- | 47 | | Middle East | 6 out of 13 |
| Senegal | 11.7 | 11.8 | B+ | 86 | | Africa | 8 out of 51 |
| Serbia | 9.8 | 9.6 | BB- | 75 | Frontier | Central and Eastern Europe | 16 out of 25 |
| Seychelles | 9.3 | 9.4 | | 73 | | Africa | 5 out of 51 |
| Sierra Leone | 15.2 | 15.3 | | 129 | | Africa | 30 out of 51 |
| Singapore | 0.0 | 0.0 | AAA | 1 | Developed | Asia | 1 out of 29 |
| Slovakia | 2.9 | 3.0 | A+ | 24 | | Central and Eastern Europe | 2 out of 25 |
| Slovenia | 4.3 | 4.4 | A | 34 | Frontier | Central and Eastern Europe | 5 out of 25 |
| Solomon Islands | 26.1 | 26.2 | | 168 | | Australasia | 6 out of 7 |
| Somalia | 24.3 | 24.5 | | 166 | | Africa | 46 out of 51 |
| South Africa | 6.9 | 7.2 | BBB- | 60 | Emerging | Africa | 2 out of 51 |
| Spain | 5.1 | 5.2 | BBB+ | 38 | Developed | Western Europe | 16 out of 19 |
| Sri Lanka | 9.2 | 9.0 | B+ | 72 | Frontier | Asia | 14 out of 29 |
| Sudan | 20.3 | 20.3 | | 154 | | Africa | 40 out of 51 |
| Suriname | 12.7 | 12.9 | B+ | 102 | | Latin America | 16 out of 20 |
| Swaziland | 18.6 | 19.7 | | 152 | | Africa | 38 out of 51 |
| Sweden | 0.0 | 0.0 | AAA | 7 | Developed | Western Europe | 6 out of 19 |

§ S&P Credit Rating based on long-term foreign currency issuer rating. See http://www.standardandpoors.com/.

• World rank based on 175 countries covered by Euromoney. Ranking based on ascending order in which '1' equals the smallest country risk premium (CRP) and '175' equals the largest country risk premium (CRP).

† MSCI Market Classification based on MSCI Market Classification Framework. See http://www.msci.com/products/indexes/market_classification.html.

‡ Regional classification based on Euromoney. Regional rankings based on ascending order in which '1' equals the smallest country risk premium (CRP) for each region.

Note: A CRP of 0.0% is assumed in the following cases: (i) when the investor country and the investee country both have an S&P sovereign credit rating of AAA; or (ii) when the investor country has an S&P credit rating of AAA, and the investee country has a sovereign credit rating below AAA, but has a calculated CRP below 0.0% (which would imply lower risk than a country rated AAA); or (iii) when the investor country has an S&P credit rating below AAA, and the investee country has a sovereign credit rating of AAA, but has a calculated CRP above 0.0% (which would imply greater risk than a country rated below AAA). For purposes of this analysis, the U.S. is treated as having a sovereign credit rating equivalent to AAA.

The country risk premium (CRP) is not the cost of equity capital (COE). The CRP is to be added to base COE. See Chapter 6 for proper application.

## Data Updated Through March 2017

| Investee Country | December 2016 Country Risk Premium (CRP) (%) | March 2017 Country Risk Premium (CRP) (%) | S&P Sovereign Credit Rating § | World Rank Out of 175* | MSCI Market Classification † | Euromoney Region ‡ | Regional Rank ‡ |
|---|---|---|---|---|---|---|---|
| Switzerland | 0.0 | 0.0 | AAA | 2 | Developed | Western Europe | 1 out of 19 |
| Syria | 25.1 | 25.5 | | 167 | | Middle East | 13 out of 13 |
| Taiwan | 2.1 | 2.2 | AA- | 18 | Emerging | Asia | 3 out of 29 |
| Tajikistan | 19.9 | 20.3 | | 155 | | Central and Eastern Europe | 25 out of 25 |
| Tanzania | 12.1 | 12.3 | | 95 | | Africa | 13 out of 51 |
| Thailand | 6.4 | 6.3 | BBB+ | 51 | Emerging | Asia | 8 out of 29 |
| Togo | 13.7 | 13.7 | | 113 | | Africa | 20 out of 51 |
| Tonga | 28.6 | 28.7 | | 170 | | Australasia | 7 out of 7 |
| Trinidad & Tobago | 6.7 | 6.8 | A- | 54 | | Caribbean | 2 out of 9 |
| Tunisia | 9.6 | 10.0 | | 79 | Frontier | Africa | 6 out of 51 |
| Turkey | 7.1 | 7.0 | BB | 58 | Emerging | Central and Eastern Europe | 11 out of 25 |
| Turkmenistan | 17.0 | 17.4 | | 140 | | Asia | 24 out of 29 |
| Uganda | 13.1 | 13.6 | B | 110 | | Africa | 18 out of 51 |
| Ukraine | 16.0 | 16.2 | B- | 135 | | Central and Eastern Europe | 20 out of 25 |
| United Arab Emirates | 3.9 | 4.0 | AA | 33 | Emerging | Middle East | 4 out of 13 |
| United Kingdom | 2.4 | 2.6 | AA | 20 | Developed | Western Europe | 11 out of 19 |
| United States | 0.0 | 0.0 | AA+ | 15 | Developed | North America | 2 out of 2 |
| Uruguay | 5.7 | 5.7 | BBB | 45 | | Latin America | 5 out of 20 |
| Uzbekistan | 16.2 | 15.7 | | 132 | | Asia | 21 out of 29 |
| Vanuatu | 17.9 | 18.0 | | 145 | | Australasia | 4 out of 7 |
| Venezuela | 21.7 | 22.3 | CCC | 162 | | Latin America | 20 out of 20 |
| Vietnam | 10.2 | 10.0 | BB- | 78 | Frontier | Asia | 16 out of 29 |
| Yemen | 22.0 | 22.2 | | 161 | | Middle East | 12 out of 13 |
| Zambia | 13.5 | 13.6 | B | 111 | | Africa | 19 out of 51 |
| Zimbabwe | 23.6 | 23.7 | | 164 | | Africa | 44 out of 51 |

## March 2017 Country Risk Premium (CRP) Summary Statistics:

| S&P Rating | Country Count | Average CRP (%) | Median CRP (%) | Min CRP (%) | Max CRP (%) |
|---|---|---|---|---|---|
| AAA ** | 12 | 0.0 | 0.0 | 0.0 | 0.0 |
| AA (AA+, AA, AA-) | 15 | 2.5 | 2.6 | 0.3 | 5.5 |
| A (A+, A, A-) | 14 | 4.5 | 4.6 | 3.0 | 6.8 |
| BBB (BBB+, BBB, BBB-) | 17 | 6.3 | 6.3 | 3.6 | 8.7 |
| BB (BB+, BB, BB-) | 22 | 9.2 | 9.2 | 5.3 | 14.7 |
| B+ − SD | 39 | 14.0 | 13.6 | 9.0 | 22.3 |
| Investment Grade ** | 58 | 3.6 | 3.6 | 0.0 | 8.7 |
| Non-Investment Grade ** | 61 | 12.3 | 12.5 | 5.3 | 22.3 |
| **MSCI Market Classification** | | | | | |
| Developed Markets | 23 | 1.6 | 0.3 | 0.0 | 6.1 |
| Emerging Markets | 23 | 6.0 | 5.5 | 1.8 | 14.0 |
| Frontier Markets | 22 | 9.1 | 8.8 | 3.7 | 14.7 |
| **Euromoney Region ‡** | | | | | |
| Africa | 51 | 16.6 | 14.5 | 5.7 | 37.3 |
| Asia | 29 | 11.2 | 9.8 | 0.0 | 34.7 |
| Australasia | 7 | 15.1 | 18.0 | 0.0 | 28.7 |
| Caribbean | 9 | 12.5 | 12.1 | 5.7 | 22.0 |
| Central and Eastern Europe | 25 | 9.6 | 7.5 | 2.8 | 20.3 |
| Latin America | 20 | 10.2 | 10.9 | 1.8 | 22.3 |
| Middle East | 13 | 10.4 | 7.9 | 2.6 | 25.5 |
| North America | 2 | 0.0 | 0.0 | 0.0 | 0.0 |
| Western Europe | 19 | 2.6 | 1.9 | 0.0 | 13.3 |

## CCR Base Cost of Equity Capital:

| Luxembourg | COE (%) |
|---|---|
| March 2017 | 7.1 |
| December 2016 | 7.1 |

CCR base country-level COE for a Luxembourg-based investor investing in Luxembourg.

§ S&P Credit Rating based on long-term foreign currency issuer rating. See http://www.standardandpoors.com/.

* World rank based on 175 countries covered by Euromoney. Ranking based on ascending order in which '1' equals the smallest country risk premium (CRP) and '175' equals the largest country risk premium (CRP).

† MSCI Market Classification based on MSCI Market Classification Framework. See http://www.msci.com/products/indexes/market_classification.html

‡ Regional classification based on Euromoney. Regional rankings based on ascending order in which '1' equals the smallest country risk premium (CRP) for each region.

** Investment grade based on S&P sovereign credit rating from AAA to BBB-. Non-Investment grade based on S&P sovereign credit rating from BB+ to SD. For purposes of this analysis, the U.S. is being treated as if it were rated AAA by S&P.

Note: A CRP of 0.0% is assumed in the following cases: (i) when the investor country and the investee country both have an S&P sovereign credit rating of AAA; or (ii) when the investor country has an S&P credit rating of AAA, and the investee country has a sovereign credit rating below AAA, but has a calculated CRP below 0.0% (which would imply lower risk than a country rated AAA); or (iii) when the investor country has an S&P credit rating below AAA, and the investee country has a sovereign credit rating of AAA, but has a calculated CRP above 0.0% (which would imply greater risk than a country rated below AAA). For purposes of this analysis, the U.S. is treated as having a sovereign credit rating equivalent to AAA.

The country risk premium (CRP) is not the cost of equity capital (COE). The CRP is to be added to base COE. See Chapter 6 for proper application.

## Data Updated Through March 2017

| Investee Country | December 2016 Country Risk Premium (CRP) (%) | March 2017 Country Risk Premium (CRP) (%) | S&P Sovereign Credit Rating § | World Rank Out of 175* | MSCI Market Classification † | Euromoney Region ‡ | Regional Rank ‡ |
|---|---|---|---|---|---|---|---|
| Afghanistan | 12.4 | 12.4 | | 139 | | Asia | 23 out of 29 |
| Albania | 7.0 | 7.4 | B+ | 93 | | Central and Eastern Europe | 18 out of 25 |
| Algeria | 7.1 | 7.3 | | 91 | | Africa | 10 out of 51 |
| Angola | 9.4 | 9.7 | B | 121 | | Africa | 26 out of 51 |
| Argentina | 7.6 | 7.5 | B- | 96 | Frontier | Latin America | 13 out of 20 |
| Armenia | 4.6 | 5.0 | | 77 | | Asia | 15 out of 29 |
| Australia | -4.3 | -4.2 | AAA | 12 | Developed | Australasia | 2 out of 7 |
| Austria | -4.1 | -4.0 | AA+ | 13 | Developed | Western Europe | 9 out of 19 |
| Azerbaijan | 5.8 | 6.3 | BB+ | 85 | | Asia | 17 out of 29 |
| Bahamas | 3.2 | 3.1 | BB+ | 65 | | Caribbean | 3 out of 9 |
| Bahrain | 3.1 | 3.1 | BB- | 64 | Frontier | Middle East | 7 out of 13 |
| Bangladesh | 9.9 | 9.9 | BB- | 126 | Frontier | Asia | 20 out of 29 |
| Barbados | 4.8 | 6.1 | CCC+ | 82 | | Caribbean | 4 out of 9 |
| Belarus | 12.1 | 12.7 | B- | 143 | | Central and Eastern Europe | 23 out of 25 |
| Belgium | -2.8 | -2.8 | AA | 17 | Developed | Western Europe | 10 out of 19 |
| Belize | 8.1 | 8.3 | B- | 106 | | Latin America | 17 out of 20 |
| Benin | 13.8 | 14.0 | | 150 | | Africa | 37 out of 51 |
| Bermuda | 0.8 | 0.9 | A+ | 44 | | Caribbean | 1 out of 9 |
| Bhutan | 13.5 | 13.5 | | 148 | | Asia | 25 out of 29 |
| Bolivia | 6.6 | 7.0 | BB | 88 | | Latin America | 12 out of 20 |
| Bosnia & Herzegovina | 12.6 | 12.9 | B | 144 | | Central and Eastern Europe | 24 out of 25 |
| Botswana | 0.8 | 0.9 | A- | 48 | | Africa | 1 out of 51 |
| Brazil | 2.3 | 2.4 | BB | 59 | Emerging | Latin America | 7 out of 20 |
| Bulgaria | 2.2 | 2.5 | BB+ | 61 | | Central and Eastern Europe | 12 out of 25 |
| Burkina Faso | 10.9 | 11.2 | B- | 133 | | Africa | 33 out of 51 |
| Burundi | 22.8 | 23.0 | | 169 | | Africa | 47 out of 51 |
| Cambodia | 14.4 | 14.2 | | 151 | | Asia | 27 out of 29 |
| Cameroon | 9.6 | 9.8 | B | 124 | | Africa | 28 out of 51 |
| Canada | -4.5 | -4.4 | AAA | 9 | Developed | North America | 1 out of 2 |
| Cape Verde | 7.2 | 7.4 | B | 94 | | Africa | 12 out of 51 |
| Central African Republic | 26.2 | 26.6 | | 172 | | Africa | 49 out of 51 |
| Chad | 24.9 | 25.2 | | 171 | | Africa | 48 out of 51 |
| Chile | -3.3 | -3.0 | AA- | 16 | Emerging | Latin America | 1 out of 20 |
| China | 0.6 | 0.7 | AA- | 42 | Emerging | Asia | 7 out of 29 |
| Colombia | 0.6 | 0.7 | BBB | 41 | Emerging | Latin America | 4 out of 20 |
| Congo Republic | 9.2 | 9.2 | B- | 117 | | Africa | 24 out of 51 |
| Congo, DR | 10.4 | 10.6 | B- | 131 | | Africa | 32 out of 51 |
| Costa Rica | 3.6 | 4.0 | BB- | 71 | | Latin America | 8 out of 20 |
| Côte d'Ivoire | 7.1 | 7.3 | | 92 | | Africa | 11 out of 51 |
| Croatia | 2.7 | 2.7 | BB | 63 | Frontier | Central and Eastern Europe | 13 out of 25 |
| Cuba | 16.7 | 17.0 | | 160 | | Caribbean | 9 out of 9 |
| Cyprus | 0.3 | 0.6 | BB+ | 40 | | Central and Eastern Europe | 7 out of 25 |
| Czech Republic | -2.1 | -1.9 | AA- | 23 | Emerging | Central and Eastern Europe | 1 out of 25 |
| Denmark | -5.1 | -5.0 | AAA | 4 | Developed | Western Europe | 3 out of 19 |
| Djibouti | 34.2 | 32.2 | | 175 | | Africa | 51 out of 51 |
| Dominican Republic | 6.9 | 7.2 | BB- | 90 | | Caribbean | 5 out of 9 |
| Ecuador | 8.5 | 8.5 | B | 109 | | Latin America | 18 out of 20 |
| Egypt | 8.9 | 9.1 | B- | 116 | Emerging | Africa | 23 out of 51 |
| El Salvador | 6.0 | 5.9 | B- | 81 | | Latin America | 10 out of 20 |
| Equatorial Guinea | 19.2 | 19.4 | | 165 | | Africa | 45 out of 51 |

§ S&P Credit Rating based on long-term foreign currency issuer rating. See http://www.standardandpoors.com/.

* World rank based on 175 countries covered by Euromoney. Ranking based on ascending order in which '1' equals the smallest country risk premium (CRP) and '175' equals the largest country risk premium (CRP).

† MSCI Market Classification based on MSCI Market Classification Framework. See http://www.msci.com/products/indexes/market_classification.html.

‡ Regional classification based on Euromoney. Regional rankings based on ascending order in which '1' equals the smallest country risk premium (CRP) for each region.

Note: A CRP of 0.0% is assumed in the following cases: (i) when the investor country and the investee country both have an S&P sovereign credit rating of AAA; or (ii) when the investor country has an S&P credit rating of AAA, and the investee country has a sovereign credit rating below AAA, but has a calculated CRP below 0.0% (which would imply lower risk than a country rated AAA); or (iii) when the investor country has an S&P credit rating below AAA, and the investee country has a sovereign credit rating of AAA, but has a calculated CRP above 0.0% (which would imply greater risk than a country rated below AAA). For purposes of this analysis, the U.S. is treated as having a sovereign credit rating equivalent to AAA.

The country risk premium (CRP) is not the cost of equity capital (COE). The CRP is to be added to base COE. See Chapter 6 for proper application.

## Data Updated Through March 2017

| Investee Country | December 2016 Country Risk Premium (CRP) (%) | March 2017 Country Risk Premium (CRP) (%) | S&P Sovereign Credit Rating § | World Rank Out of 175∗ | MSCI Market Classification † | Euromoney Region ‡ | Regional Rank ‡ |
|---|---|---|---|---|---|---|---|
| Eritrea | 30.4 | 28.9 | | 173 | | Africa | 50 out of 51 |
| Estonia | -1.5 | -1.1 | AA- | 32 | Frontier | Central and Eastern Europe | 4 out of 25 |
| Ethiopia | 7.8 | 8.0 | B | 101 | | Africa | 16 out of 51 |
| Fiji | 13.1 | 13.2 | B+ | 147 | | Australasia | 5 out of 7 |
| Finland | -4.4 | -4.3 | AA+ | 11 | Developed | Western Europe | 8 out of 19 |
| France | -2.0 | -2.1 | AA | 22 | Developed | Western Europe | 12 out of 19 |
| Gabon | 5.6 | 6.1 | | 83 | | Africa | 7 out of 51 |
| Gambia | 11.6 | 11.8 | | 138 | | Africa | 34 out of 51 |
| Georgia | 4.3 | 4.7 | BB- | 74 | | Central and Eastern Europe | 15 out of 25 |
| Germany | -4.4 | -4.3 | AAA | 10 | Developed | Western Europe | 7 out of 19 |
| Ghana | 7.3 | 7.1 | B- | 89 | | Africa | 9 out of 51 |
| Greece | 8.4 | 8.4 | B- | 108 | Emerging | Western Europe | 19 out of 19 |
| Grenada | 8.0 | 8.3 | | 105 | | Caribbean | 7 out of 9 |
| Guatemala | 6.0 | 6.2 | BB | 84 | | Latin America | 11 out of 20 |
| Guinea | 15.3 | 15.5 | | 156 | | Africa | 41 out of 51 |
| Guinea-Bissau | 8.9 | 9.1 | | 115 | | Africa | 22 out of 51 |
| Guyana | 7.7 | 7.9 | | 100 | | Latin America | 15 out of 20 |
| Haiti | 18.1 | 16.3 | | 157 | | Caribbean | 8 out of 9 |
| Honduras | 7.4 | 7.6 | B+ | 98 | | Latin America | 14 out of 20 |
| Hong Kong | -3.8 | -3.7 | AAA | 14 | Developed | Asia | 2 out of 29 |
| Hungary | 1.9 | 2.2 | BBB- | 57 | Emerging | Central and Eastern Europe | 10 out of 25 |
| Iceland | -1.1 | -1.1 | A | 30 | | Western Europe | 15 out of 19 |
| India | 1.7 | 2.1 | BBB- | 55 | Emerging | Asia | 10 out of 29 |
| Indonesia | 2.5 | 2.6 | BB+ | 62 | Emerging | Asia | 11 out of 29 |
| Iran | 9.4 | 9.8 | | 125 | | Middle East | 10 out of 13 |
| Iraq | 11.2 | 11.4 | B- | 136 | | Middle East | 11 out of 13 |
| Ireland | -1.5 | -1.5 | A+ | 27 | Developed | Western Europe | 14 out of 19 |
| Israel | -1.6 | -1.5 | A+ | 28 | Developed | Middle East | 2 out of 13 |
| Italy | 1.3 | 1.3 | BBB- | 50 | Developed | Western Europe | 18 out of 19 |
| Jamaica | 7.5 | 8.3 | B | 104 | | Caribbean | 6 out of 9 |
| Japan | -1.7 | -1.6 | A+ | 25 | Developed | Asia | 5 out of 29 |
| Jordan | 4.6 | 4.9 | BB- | 76 | Frontier | Middle East | 8 out of 13 |
| Kazakhstan | 4.1 | 3.9 | BBB- | 70 | Frontier | Asia | 13 out of 29 |
| Kenya | 7.5 | 7.8 | B+ | 99 | Frontier | Africa | 15 out of 51 |
| Korea (North) | 29.7 | 29.6 | | 174 | | Asia | 29 out of 29 |
| Korea (South) | -2.5 | -2.3 | AA | 19 | Emerging | Asia | 4 out of 29 |
| Kuwait | -1.4 | -1.1 | AA | 31 | Frontier | Middle East | 3 out of 13 |
| Kyrgyz Republic | 12.6 | 12.7 | | 142 | | Central and Eastern Europe | 22 out of 25 |
| Laos | 16.9 | 16.6 | | 158 | | Asia | 28 out of 29 |
| Latvia | 0.6 | 0.9 | A- | 43 | | Central and Eastern Europe | 8 out of 25 |
| Lebanon | 9.3 | 8.8 | B- | 112 | Frontier | Middle East | 9 out of 13 |
| Lesotho | 12.8 | 13.1 | | 146 | | Africa | 36 out of 51 |
| Liberia | 8.1 | 8.3 | | 107 | | Africa | 17 out of 51 |
| Libya | 14.4 | 14.9 | | 153 | | Africa | 39 out of 51 |
| Lithuania | -0.2 | 0.1 | A- | 36 | Frontier | Central and Eastern Europe | 6 out of 25 |
| Luxembourg | -4.8 | -4.7 | AAA | 5 | | Western Europe | 4 out of 19 |
| Macedonia | 6.6 | 7.0 | BB- | 87 | | Central and Eastern Europe | 17 out of 25 |
| Madagascar | 9.0 | 9.7 | | 123 | | Africa | 27 out of 51 |
| Malawi | 8.7 | 8.9 | | 114 | | Africa | 21 out of 51 |
| Malaysia | 0.0 | 0.0 | A- | 35 | Emerging | Asia | 6 out of 29 |

§ S&P Credit Rating based on long-term foreign currency issuer rating. See http://www.standardandpoors.com/.

∗ World rank based on 175 countries covered by Euromoney. Ranking based on ascending order in which '1' equals the smallest country risk premium (CRP) and '175' equals the largest country risk premium (CRP).

† MSCI Market Classification based on MSCI Market Classification Framework. See http://www.msci.com/products/indexes/market_classification.html

‡ Regional classification based on Euromoney. Regional rankings based on ascending order in which '1' equals the smallest country risk premium (CRP) for each region.

Note: A CRP of 0.0% is assumed in the following cases: (i) when the investor country and the investee country both have an S&P sovereign credit rating of AAA; or (ii) when the investor country has an S&P credit rating of AAA, and the investee country has a sovereign credit rating below AAA, but has a calculated CRP below 0.0% (which would imply lower risk than a country rated AAA); or (iii) when the investor country has an S&P credit rating below AAA, and the investee country has a sovereign credit rating of AAA, but has a calculated CRP above 0.0% (which would imply greater risk than a country rated below AAA). For purposes of this analysis, the U.S. is treated as having a sovereign credit rating equivalent to AAA.

The country risk premium (CRP) is not the cost of equity capital (COE). The CRP is to be added to base COE. See Chapter 6 for proper application.

## Data Updated Through March 2017

| Investee Country | December 2016 Country Risk Premium (CRP) (%) | March 2017 Country Risk Premium (CRP) (%) | S&P Sovereign Credit Rating § | World Rank Out of 175* | MSCI Market Classification † | Euromoney Region ‡ | Regional Rank ‡ |
|---|---|---|---|---|---|---|---|
| Mali | 12.4 | 12.7 | | 141 | | Africa | 35 out of 51 |
| Malta | -1.7 | -1.5 | A- | 26 | | Western Europe | 13 out of 19 |
| Mauritania | 16.5 | 16.7 | | 159 | | Africa | 42 out of 51 |
| Mauritius | 3.4 | 3.5 | | 67 | Frontier | Asia | 12 out of 29 |
| Mexico | -0.1 | 0.1 | BBB+ | 37 | Emerging | Latin America | 2 out of 20 |
| Moldova | 10.9 | 11.5 | | 137 | | Central and Eastern Europe | 21 out of 25 |
| Mongolia | 9.1 | 9.6 | B- | 119 | | Asia | 18 out of 29 |
| Montenegro | 8.3 | 8.2 | B+ | 103 | | Central and Eastern Europe | 19 out of 25 |
| Morocco | 3.4 | 3.8 | BBB- | 69 | Frontier | Africa | 4 out of 51 |
| Mozambique | 10.1 | 10.2 | SD | 128 | | Africa | 29 out of 51 |
| Myanmar | 11.1 | 11.2 | | 134 | | Asia | 22 out of 29 |
| Namibia | 3.0 | 3.4 | | 66 | | Africa | 3 out of 51 |
| Nepal | 13.7 | 14.0 | | 149 | | Asia | 26 out of 29 |
| Netherlands | -4.8 | -4.7 | AAA | 6 | Developed | Western Europe | 5 out of 19 |
| New Zealand | -4.6 | -4.5 | AA | 8 | Developed | Australasia | 1 out of 7 |
| Nicaragua | 9.8 | 10.0 | B+ | 127 | | Latin America | 19 out of 20 |
| Niger | 9.4 | 9.6 | | 120 | | Africa | 25 out of 51 |
| Nigeria | 7.4 | 7.6 | B | 97 | Frontier | Africa | 14 out of 51 |
| Norway | -5.4 | -5.4 | AAA | 3 | Developed | Western Europe | 2 out of 19 |
| Oman | 0.7 | 0.9 | BBB- | 46 | Frontier | Middle East | 5 out of 13 |
| Pakistan | 9.5 | 9.7 | B | 122 | Frontier | Asia | 19 out of 29 |
| Panama | 1.4 | 1.7 | BBB | 52 | | Latin America | 6 out of 20 |
| Papua New Guinea | 9.0 | 9.3 | B+ | 118 | | Australasia | 3 out of 7 |
| Paraguay | 5.0 | 5.3 | BB | 80 | | Latin America | 9 out of 20 |
| Peru | 0.2 | 0.5 | BBB+ | 39 | Emerging | Latin America | 3 out of 20 |
| Philippines | 1.8 | 1.9 | BBB | 53 | Emerging | Asia | 9 out of 29 |
| Poland | -1.2 | -1.2 | BBB+ | 29 | Emerging | Central and Eastern Europe | 3 out of 25 |
| Portugal | 1.2 | 1.1 | BB+ | 49 | Developed | Western Europe | 17 out of 19 |
| Qatar | -2.3 | -2.1 | AA | 21 | Emerging | Middle East | 1 out of 13 |
| Romania | 2.0 | 2.2 | BBB- | 56 | Frontier | Central and Eastern Europe | 9 out of 25 |
| Russia | 4.2 | 3.8 | BB+ | 68 | Emerging | Central and Eastern Europe | 14 out of 25 |
| Rwanda | 10.2 | 10.4 | B | 130 | | Africa | 31 out of 51 |
| São Tomé & Príncipe | 16.6 | 17.3 | | 163 | | Africa | 43 out of 51 |
| Saudi Arabia | 1.1 | 0.9 | A- | 47 | | Middle East | 6 out of 13 |
| Senegal | 6.8 | 6.9 | B+ | 86 | | Africa | 8 out of 51 |
| Serbia | 4.9 | 4.8 | BB- | 75 | Frontier | Central and Eastern Europe | 16 out of 25 |
| Seychelles | 4.4 | 4.5 | | 73 | | Africa | 5 out of 51 |
| Sierra Leone | 10.2 | 10.4 | | 129 | | Africa | 30 out of 51 |
| Singapore | -5.6 | -5.5 | AAA | 1 | Developed | Asia | 1 out of 29 |
| Slovakia | -2.0 | -1.8 | A+ | 24 | | Central and Eastern Europe | 2 out of 25 |
| Slovenia | -0.5 | -0.4 | A | 34 | Frontier | Central and Eastern Europe | 5 out of 25 |
| Solomon Islands | 20.9 | 21.2 | | 168 | | Australasia | 6 out of 7 |
| Somalia | 19.2 | 19.5 | | 166 | | Africa | 46 out of 51 |
| South Africa | 2.0 | 2.4 | BBB- | 60 | Emerging | Africa | 2 out of 51 |
| Spain | 0.3 | 0.4 | BBB+ | 38 | Developed | Western Europe | 16 out of 19 |
| Sri Lanka | 4.3 | 4.2 | B+ | 72 | Frontier | Asia | 14 out of 29 |
| Sudan | 15.2 | 15.4 | | 154 | | Africa | 40 out of 51 |
| Suriname | 7.7 | 8.1 | B+ | 102 | | Latin America | 16 out of 20 |
| Swaziland | 13.5 | 14.7 | | 152 | | Africa | 38 out of 51 |
| Sweden | -4.7 | -4.7 | AAA | 7 | Developed | Western Europe | 6 out of 19 |

§ S&P Credit Rating based on long-term foreign currency issuer rating. See http://www.standardandpoors.com/.

* World rank based on 175 countries covered by Euromoney. Ranking based on ascending order in which '1' equals the smallest country risk premium (CRP) and '175' equals the largest country risk premium (CRP).

† MSCI Market Classification based on MSCI Market Classification Framework. See http://www.msci.com/products/indexes/market_classification.html

‡ Regional classification based on Euromoney. Regional rankings based on ascending order in which '1' equals the smallest country risk premium (CRP) for each region.

Note: A CRP of 0.0% is assumed in the following cases: (i) when the investor country and the investee country both have an S&P sovereign credit rating of AAA; or (ii) when the investor country has an S&P credit rating of AAA, and the investee country has a sovereign credit rating below AAA, but has a calculated CRP below 0.0% (which would imply lower risk than a country rated AAA); or (iii) when the investor country has an S&P credit rating below AAA, and the investee country has a sovereign credit rating of AAA, but has a calculated CRP above 0.0% (which would imply greater risk than a country rated below AAA). For purposes of this analysis, the U.S. is treated as having a sovereign credit rating equivalent to AAA.

The country risk premium (CRP) is not the cost of equity capital (COE). The CRP is to be added to base COE. See Chapter 6 for proper application.

## Data Updated Through March 2017

| Investee Country | December 2016 Country Risk Premium (CRP) (%) | March 2017 Country Risk Premium (CRP) (%) | S&P Sovereign Credit Rating § | World Rank Out of 175** | MSCI Market Classification † | Euromoney Region ‡ | Regional Rank ‡ |
|---|---|---|---|---|---|---|---|
| Switzerland | -5.4 | -5.4 | AAA | 2 | Developed | Western Europe | 1 out of 19 |
| Syria | 20.0 | 20.5 | | 167 | | Middle East | 13 out of 13 |
| Taiwan | -2.7 | -2.6 | AA- | 18 | Emerging | Asia | 3 out of 29 |
| Tajikistan | 14.8 | 15.4 | | 155 | | Central and Eastern Europe | 25 out of 25 |
| Tanzania | 7.1 | 7.5 | | 95 | | Africa | 13 out of 51 |
| Thailand | 1.5 | 1.5 | BBB+ | 51 | Emerging | Asia | 8 out of 29 |
| Togo | 8.7 | 8.9 | | 113 | | Africa | 20 out of 51 |
| Tonga | 23.4 | 23.7 | | 170 | | Australasia | 7 out of 7 |
| Trinidad & Tobago | 1.8 | 2.0 | A- | 54 | | Caribbean | 2 out of 9 |
| Tunisia | 4.7 | 5.2 | | 79 | Frontier | Africa | 6 out of 51 |
| Turkey | 2.2 | 2.2 | BB | 58 | Emerging | Central and Eastern Europe | 11 out of 25 |
| Turkmenistan | 12.0 | 12.5 | | 140 | | Asia | 24 out of 29 |
| Uganda | 8.2 | 8.7 | B | 110 | | Africa | 18 out of 51 |
| Ukraine | 11.0 | 11.3 | B- | 135 | | Central and Eastern Europe | 20 out of 25 |
| United Arab Emirates | -1.0 | -0.7 | AA | 33 | Emerging | Middle East | 4 out of 13 |
| United Kingdom | -2.5 | -2.2 | AA | 20 | Developed | Western Europe | 11 out of 19 |
| United States | -3.5 | -3.4 | AA+ | 15 | Developed | North America | 2 out of 2 |
| Uruguay | 0.8 | 0.9 | BBB | 45 | | Latin America | 5 out of 20 |
| Uzbekistan | 11.2 | 10.8 | | 132 | | Asia | 21 out of 29 |
| Vanuatu | 12.8 | 13.0 | | 145 | | Australasia | 4 out of 7 |
| Venezuela | 16.6 | 17.3 | CCC | 162 | | Latin America | 20 out of 20 |
| Vietnam | 5.2 | 5.1 | BB- | 78 | Frontier | Asia | 16 out of 29 |
| Yemen | 16.9 | 17.2 | | 161 | | Middle East | 12 out of 13 |
| Zambia | 8.5 | 8.8 | B | 111 | | Africa | 19 out of 51 |
| Zimbabwe | 18.5 | 18.7 | | 164 | | Africa | 44 out of 51 |

## March 2017 Country Risk Premium (CRP) Summary Statistics:

| S&P Rating | Country Count | Average CRP (%) | Median CRP (%) | Min CRP (%) | Max CRP (%) |
|---|---|---|---|---|---|
| AAA ** | 12 | -4.6 | -4.7 | -5.5 | -3.4 |
| AA (AA+, AA, AA-) | 15 | -2.3 | -2.2 | -4.5 | 0.7 |
| A (A+, A, A-) | 14 | -0.3 | -0.2 | -1.8 | 2.0 |
| BBB (BBB+, BBB, BBB-) | 17 | 1.5 | 1.5 | -1.2 | 3.9 |
| BB (BB+, BB, BB-) | 22 | 4.4 | 4.4 | 0.6 | 9.9 |
| B+ − SD | 39 | 9.2 | 8.8 | 4.2 | 17.3 |
| Investment Grade ** | 58 | -1.2 | -1.2 | -5.5 | 3.9 |
| Non-Investment Grade ** | 61 | 7.4 | 7.6 | 0.6 | 17.3 |
| **MSCI Market Classification** | | | | | |
| Developed Markets | 23 | -3.1 | -4.0 | -5.5 | 1.3 |
| Emerging Markets | 23 | 1.2 | 0.7 | -3.0 | 9.1 |
| Frontier Markets | 22 | 4.2 | 4.0 | -1.1 | 9.9 |
| **Euromoney Region ‡** | | | | | |
| Africa | 51 | 11.7 | 9.7 | 0.9 | 32.2 |
| Asia | 29 | 6.4 | 5.0 | -5.5 | 29.6 |
| Australasia | 7 | 10.3 | 13.0 | -4.5 | 23.7 |
| Caribbean | 9 | 7.7 | 7.2 | 0.9 | 17.0 |
| Central and Eastern Europe | 25 | 4.8 | 2.7 | -1.9 | 15.4 |
| Latin America | 20 | 5.3 | 6.1 | -3.0 | 17.3 |
| Middle East | 13 | 5.6 | 3.1 | -2.1 | 20.5 |
| North America | 2 | -3.9 | -3.9 | -4.4 | -3.4 |
| Western Europe | 19 | -2.2 | -2.8 | -5.4 | 8.4 |

## CCR Base Cost of Equity Capital:

| Malaysia | COE (%) |
|---|---|
| March 2017 | 13.8 |
| December 2016 | 13.9 |

CCR base country-level COE for a Malaysia-based investor investing in Malaysia.

§ S&P Credit Rating based on long-term foreign currency issuer rating. See http://www.standardandpoors.com/.

* World rank based on 175 countries covered by Euromoney. Ranking based on ascending order in which '1' equals the smallest country risk premium (CRP) and '175' equals the largest country risk premium (CRP).

† MSCI Market Classification based on MSCI Market Classification Framework. See http://www.msci.com/products/indexes/market_classification.html

‡ Regional classification based on Euromoney. Regional rankings based on ascending order in which '1' equals the smallest country risk premium (CRP) for each region.

** Investment grade based on S&P sovereign credit rating from AAA to BBB-. Non-Investment grade based on S&P sovereign credit rating from BB+ to SD. For purposes of this analysis, the U.S. is being treated as if it were rated AAA by S&P.

Note: A CRP of 0.0% is assumed in the following cases: (i) when the investor country and the investee country both have an S&P sovereign credit rating of AAA; or (ii) when the investor country has an S&P credit rating of AAA, and the investee country has a sovereign credit rating below AAA, but has a calculated CRP below 0.0% (which would imply lower risk than a country rated AAA); or (iii) when the investor country has an S&P credit rating below AAA, and the investee country has a sovereign credit rating of AAA, but has a calculated CRP above 0.0% (which would imply greater risk than a country rated below AAA). For purposes of this analysis, the U.S. is treated as having a sovereign credit rating equivalent to AAA.

The country risk premium (CRP) is not the cost of equity capital (COE). The CRP is to be added to base COE. See Chapter 6 for proper application.

## Data Updated Through March 2017

| Investee Country | December 2016 Country Risk Premium (CRP) (%) | March 2017 Country Risk Premium (CRP) (%) | S&P Sovereign Credit Rating § | World Rank Out of 175• | MSCI Market Classification † | Euromoney Region ‡ | Regional Rank ‡ |
|---|---|---|---|---|---|---|---|
| Afghanistan | 14.3 | 14.0 | | 139 | | Asia | 23 out of 29 |
| Albania | 8.8 | 9.0 | B+ | 93 | | Central and Eastern Europe | 18 out of 25 |
| Algeria | 8.9 | 8.9 | | 91 | | Africa | 10 out of 51 |
| Angola | 11.2 | 11.3 | B | 121 | | Africa | 26 out of 51 |
| Argentina | 9.4 | 9.1 | B- | 96 | Frontier | Latin America | 13 out of 20 |
| Armenia | 6.4 | 6.5 | | 77 | | Asia | 15 out of 29 |
| Australia | -2.6 | -2.7 | AAA | 12 | Developed | Australasia | 2 out of 7 |
| Austria | -2.4 | -2.5 | AA+ | 13 | Developed | Western Europe | 9 out of 19 |
| Azerbaijan | 7.6 | 7.9 | BB+ | 85 | | Asia | 17 out of 29 |
| Bahamas | 5.0 | 4.6 | BB+ | 65 | | Caribbean | 3 out of 9 |
| Bahrain | 4.9 | 4.6 | BB- | 64 | Frontier | Middle East | 7 out of 13 |
| Bangladesh | 11.7 | 11.5 | BB- | 126 | Frontier | Asia | 20 out of 29 |
| Barbados | 6.6 | 7.6 | CCC+ | 82 | | Caribbean | 4 out of 9 |
| Belarus | 14.0 | 14.4 | B- | 143 | | Central and Eastern Europe | 23 out of 25 |
| Belgium | -1.2 | -1.3 | AA | 17 | Developed | Western Europe | 10 out of 19 |
| Belize | 9.9 | 9.9 | B- | 106 | | Latin America | 17 out of 20 |
| Benin | 15.7 | 15.7 | | 150 | | Africa | 37 out of 51 |
| Bermuda | 2.5 | 2.4 | A+ | 44 | | Caribbean | 1 out of 9 |
| Bhutan | 15.4 | 15.2 | | 148 | | Asia | 25 out of 29 |
| Bolivia | 8.4 | 8.6 | BB | 88 | | Latin America | 12 out of 20 |
| Bosnia & Herzegovina | 14.5 | 14.6 | B | 144 | | Central and Eastern Europe | 24 out of 25 |
| Botswana | 2.5 | 2.5 | A- | 48 | | Africa | 1 out of 51 |
| Brazil | 4.1 | 3.9 | BB | 59 | Emerging | Latin America | 7 out of 20 |
| Bulgaria | 3.9 | 4.0 | BB+ | 61 | | Central and Eastern Europe | 12 out of 25 |
| Burkina Faso | 12.8 | 12.8 | B- | 133 | | Africa | 33 out of 51 |
| Burundi | 24.8 | 24.8 | | 169 | | Africa | 47 out of 51 |
| Cambodia | 16.3 | 15.9 | | 151 | | Asia | 27 out of 29 |
| Cameroon | 11.4 | 11.4 | B | 124 | | Africa | 28 out of 51 |
| Canada | -2.8 | -3.0 | AAA | 9 | Developed | North America | 1 out of 2 |
| Cape Verde | 9.0 | 9.0 | B | 94 | | Africa | 12 out of 51 |
| Central African Republic | 28.3 | 28.4 | | 172 | | Africa | 49 out of 51 |
| Chad | 27.0 | 27.0 | | 171 | | Africa | 48 out of 51 |
| Chile | -1.6 | -1.5 | AA- | 16 | Emerging | Latin America | 1 out of 20 |
| China | 2.3 | 2.3 | AA- | 42 | Emerging | Asia | 7 out of 29 |
| Colombia | 2.3 | 2.2 | BBB | 41 | Emerging | Latin America | 4 out of 20 |
| Congo Republic | 11.0 | 10.8 | B- | 117 | | Africa | 24 out of 51 |
| Congo, DR | 12.3 | 12.2 | B- | 131 | | Africa | 32 out of 51 |
| Costa Rica | 5.4 | 5.5 | BB- | 71 | | Latin America | 8 out of 20 |
| Côte d'Ivoire | 8.9 | 8.9 | | 92 | | Africa | 11 out of 51 |
| Croatia | 4.5 | 4.3 | BB | 63 | Frontier | Central and Eastern Europe | 13 out of 25 |
| Cuba | 18.6 | 18.7 | | 160 | | Caribbean | 9 out of 9 |
| Cyprus | 2.0 | 2.1 | BB+ | 40 | | Central and Eastern Europe | 7 out of 25 |
| Czech Republic | -0.4 | -0.4 | AA- | 23 | Emerging | Central and Eastern Europe | 1 out of 25 |
| Denmark | -3.5 | -3.6 | AAA | 4 | Developed | Western Europe | 3 out of 19 |
| Djibouti | 36.4 | 34.1 | | 175 | | Africa | 51 out of 51 |
| Dominican Republic | 8.7 | 8.8 | BB- | 90 | | Caribbean | 5 out of 9 |
| Ecuador | 10.3 | 10.1 | B | 109 | | Latin America | 18 out of 20 |
| Egypt | 10.8 | 10.7 | B- | 116 | Emerging | Africa | 23 out of 51 |
| El Salvador | 7.8 | 7.5 | B- | 81 | | Latin America | 10 out of 20 |
| Equatorial Guinea | 21.1 | 21.2 | | 165 | | Africa | 45 out of 51 |

§ S&P Credit Rating based on long-term foreign currency issuer rating. See http://www.standardandpoors.com/.

• World rank based on 175 countries covered by Euromoney. Ranking based on ascending order in which '1' equals the smallest country risk premium (CRP) and '175' equals the largest country risk premium (CRP).

† MSCI Market Classification based on MSCI Market Classification Framework. See http://www.msci.com/products/indexes/market_classification.html

‡ Regional classification based on Euromoney. Regional rankings based on ascending order in which '1' equals the smallest country risk premium (CRP) for each region.

Note: A CRP of 0.0% is assumed in the following cases: (i) when the investor country and the investee country both have an S&P sovereign credit rating of AAA; or (ii) when the investor country has an S&P credit rating of AAA, and the investee country has a sovereign credit rating below AAA, but has a calculated CRP below 0.0% (which would imply lower risk than a country rated AAA); or (iii) when the investor country has an S&P credit rating below AAA, and the investee country has a sovereign credit rating of AAA, but has a calculated CRP above 0.0% (which would imply greater risk than a country rated below AAA). For purposes of this analysis, the U.S. is treated as having a sovereign credit rating equivalent to AAA.

The country risk premium (CRP) is not the cost of equity capital (COE). The CRP is to be added to base COE. See Chapter 6 for proper application.

## Data Updated Through March 2017

| Investee Country | December 2016 Country Risk Premium (CRP) (%) | March 2017 Country Risk Premium (CRP) (%) | S&P Sovereign Credit Rating § | World Rank Out of 175* | MSCI Market Classification † | Euromoney Region ‡ | Regional Rank ‡ |
|---|---|---|---|---|---|---|---|
| Eritrea | 32.5 | 30.7 | | 173 | | Africa | 50 out of 51 |
| Estonia | 0.3 | 0.4 | AA- | 32 | Frontier | Central and Eastern Europe | 4 out of 25 |
| Ethiopia | 9.6 | 9.6 | B | 101 | | Africa | 16 out of 51 |
| Fiji | 15.0 | 14.9 | B+ | 147 | | Australasia | 5 out of 7 |
| Finland | -2.7 | -2.8 | AA+ | 11 | Developed | Western Europe | 8 out of 19 |
| France | -0.3 | -0.6 | AA | 22 | Developed | Western Europe | 12 out of 19 |
| Gabon | 7.4 | 7.7 | | 83 | | Africa | 7 out of 51 |
| Gambia | 13.5 | 13.5 | | 138 | | Africa | 34 out of 51 |
| Georgia | 6.1 | 6.3 | BB- | 74 | | Central and Eastern Europe | 15 out of 25 |
| Germany | -2.7 | -2.8 | AAA | 10 | Developed | Western Europe | 7 out of 19 |
| Ghana | 9.1 | 8.7 | B- | 89 | | Africa | 9 out of 51 |
| Greece | 10.3 | 10.0 | B- | 108 | Emerging | Western Europe | 19 out of 19 |
| Grenada | 9.9 | 9.9 | | 105 | | Caribbean | 7 out of 9 |
| Guatemala | 7.8 | 7.8 | BB | 84 | | Latin America | 11 out of 20 |
| Guinea | 17.2 | 17.2 | | 156 | | Africa | 41 out of 51 |
| Guinea-Bissau | 10.7 | 10.7 | | 115 | | Africa | 22 out of 51 |
| Guyana | 9.5 | 9.5 | | 100 | | Latin America | 15 out of 20 |
| Haiti | 20.1 | 18.0 | | 157 | | Caribbean | 8 out of 9 |
| Honduras | 9.2 | 9.2 | B+ | 98 | | Latin America | 14 out of 20 |
| Hong Kong | -2.1 | -2.2 | AAA | 14 | Developed | Asia | 2 out of 29 |
| Hungary | 3.7 | 3.8 | BBB- | 57 | Emerging | Central and Eastern Europe | 10 out of 25 |
| Iceland | 0.6 | 0.4 | A | 30 | | Western Europe | 15 out of 19 |
| India | 3.4 | 3.7 | BBB- | 55 | Emerging | Asia | 10 out of 29 |
| Indonesia | 4.2 | 4.2 | BB+ | 62 | Emerging | Asia | 11 out of 29 |
| Iran | 11.2 | 11.4 | | 125 | | Middle East | 10 out of 13 |
| Iraq | 13.1 | 13.1 | B- | 136 | | Middle East | 11 out of 13 |
| Ireland | 0.2 | 0.0 | A+ | 27 | Developed | Western Europe | 14 out of 19 |
| Israel | 0.1 | 0.0 | A+ | 28 | Developed | Middle East | 2 out of 13 |
| Italy | 3.1 | 2.8 | BBB- | 50 | Developed | Western Europe | 18 out of 19 |
| Jamaica | 9.3 | 9.9 | B | 104 | | Caribbean | 6 out of 9 |
| Japan | 0.0 | -0.1 | A+ | 25 | Developed | Asia | 5 out of 29 |
| Jordan | 6.4 | 6.5 | BB- | 76 | Frontier | Middle East | 8 out of 13 |
| Kazakhstan | 5.8 | 5.4 | BBB- | 70 | Frontier | Asia | 13 out of 29 |
| Kenya | 9.3 | 9.4 | B+ | 99 | Frontier | Africa | 15 out of 51 |
| Korea (North) | 31.9 | 31.4 | | 174 | | Asia | 29 out of 29 |
| Korea (South) | -0.8 | -0.8 | AA | 19 | Emerging | Asia | 4 out of 29 |
| Kuwait | 0.3 | 0.4 | AA | 31 | Frontier | Middle East | 3 out of 13 |
| Kyrgyz Republic | 14.5 | 14.3 | | 142 | | Central and Eastern Europe | 22 out of 25 |
| Laos | 18.8 | 18.2 | | 158 | | Asia | 28 out of 29 |
| Latvia | 2.3 | 2.4 | A- | 43 | | Central and Eastern Europe | 8 out of 25 |
| Lebanon | 11.1 | 10.4 | B- | 112 | Frontier | Middle East | 9 out of 13 |
| Lesotho | 14.7 | 14.7 | | 146 | | Africa | 36 out of 51 |
| Liberia | 10.0 | 9.9 | | 107 | | Africa | 17 out of 51 |
| Libya | 16.3 | 16.6 | | 153 | | Africa | 39 out of 51 |
| Lithuania | 1.5 | 1.6 | A- | 36 | Frontier | Central and Eastern Europe | 6 out of 25 |
| Luxembourg | -3.1 | -3.3 | AAA | 5 | | Western Europe | 4 out of 19 |
| Macedonia | 8.4 | 8.6 | BB- | 87 | | Central and Eastern Europe | 17 out of 25 |
| Madagascar | 10.8 | 11.3 | | 123 | | Africa | 27 out of 51 |
| Malawi | 10.6 | 10.5 | | 114 | | Africa | 21 out of 51 |
| Malaysia | 1.7 | 1.5 | A- | 35 | Emerging | Asia | 6 out of 29 |

§ S&P Credit Rating based on long-term foreign currency issuer rating. See http://www.standardandpoors.com/.

* World rank based on 175 countries covered by Euromoney. Ranking based on ascending order in which '1' equals the smallest country risk premium (CRP) and '175' equals the largest country risk premium (CRP).

† MSCI Market Classification based on MSCI Market Classification Framework. See http://www.msci.com/products/indexes/market_classification.html.

‡ Regional classification based on Euromoney. Regional rankings based on ascending order in which '1' equals the smallest country risk premium (CRP) for each region.

Note: A CRP of 0.0% is assumed in the following cases: (i) when the investor country and the investee country both have an S&P sovereign credit rating of AAA; or (ii) when the investor country has an S&P credit rating of AAA, and the investee country has a sovereign credit rating below AAA, but has a calculated CRP below 0.0% (which would imply lower risk than a country rated AAA); or (iii) when the investor country has an S&P credit rating below AAA, and the investee country has a sovereign credit rating of AAA, but has a calculated CRP above 0.0% (which would imply greater risk than a country rated below AAA). For purposes of this analysis, the U.S. is treated as having a sovereign credit rating equivalent to AAA.

The country risk premium (CRP) is not the cost of equity capital (COE).  The CRP is to be added to base COE. See Chapter 6 for proper application.

## Data Updated Through March 2017

| Investee Country | December 2016 Country Risk Premium (CRP) (%) | March 2017 Country Risk Premium (CRP) (%) | S&P Sovereign Credit Rating § | World Rank Out of 175* | MSCI Market Classification † | Euromoney Region ‡ | Regional Rank ‡ |
|---|---|---|---|---|---|---|---|
| Mali | 14.3 | 14.3 | | 141 | | Africa | 35 out of 51 |
| Malta | 0.0 | 0.0 | A- | 26 | | Western Europe | 13 out of 19 |
| Mauritania | 18.4 | 18.4 | | 159 | | Africa | 42 out of 51 |
| Mauritius | 5.1 | 5.1 | | 67 | Frontier | Asia | 12 out of 29 |
| Mexico | 1.6 | 1.7 | BBB+ | 37 | Emerging | Latin America | 2 out of 20 |
| Moldova | 12.7 | 13.1 | | 137 | | Central and Eastern Europe | 21 out of 25 |
| Mongolia | 10.9 | 11.2 | B- | 119 | | Asia | 18 out of 29 |
| Montenegro | 10.1 | 9.8 | B+ | 103 | | Central and Eastern Europe | 19 out of 25 |
| Morocco | 5.2 | 5.4 | BBB- | 69 | Frontier | Africa | 4 out of 51 |
| Mozambique | 12.0 | 11.8 | SD | 128 | | Africa | 29 out of 51 |
| Myanmar | 12.9 | 12.8 | | 134 | | Asia | 22 out of 29 |
| Namibia | 4.8 | 4.9 | | 66 | | Africa | 3 out of 51 |
| Nepal | 15.6 | 15.6 | | 149 | | Asia | 26 out of 29 |
| Netherlands | -3.1 | -3.2 | AAA | 6 | Developed | Western Europe | 5 out of 19 |
| New Zealand | -3.0 | -3.0 | AA | 8 | Developed | Australasia | 1 out of 7 |
| Nicaragua | 11.7 | 11.7 | B+ | 127 | | Latin America | 19 out of 20 |
| Niger | 11.3 | 11.2 | | 120 | | Africa | 25 out of 51 |
| Nigeria | 9.3 | 9.2 | B | 97 | Frontier | Africa | 14 out of 51 |
| Norway | -3.8 | -3.9 | AAA | 3 | Developed | Western Europe | 2 out of 19 |
| Oman | 2.5 | 2.5 | BBB- | 46 | Frontier | Middle East | 5 out of 13 |
| Pakistan | 11.4 | 11.3 | B | 122 | Frontier | Asia | 19 out of 29 |
| Panama | 3.2 | 3.2 | BBB | 52 | | Latin America | 6 out of 20 |
| Papua New Guinea | 10.9 | 10.9 | B+ | 118 | | Australasia | 3 out of 7 |
| Paraguay | 6.8 | 6.9 | BB | 80 | | Latin America | 9 out of 20 |
| Peru | 1.9 | 2.0 | BBB+ | 39 | Emerging | Latin America | 3 out of 20 |
| Philippines | 3.6 | 3.5 | BBB | 53 | Emerging | Asia | 9 out of 29 |
| Poland | 0.5 | 0.3 | BBB+ | 29 | Emerging | Central and Eastern Europe | 3 out of 25 |
| Portugal | 2.9 | 2.7 | BB+ | 49 | Developed | Western Europe | 17 out of 19 |
| Qatar | -0.7 | -0.6 | AA | 21 | Emerging | Middle East | 1 out of 13 |
| Romania | 3.7 | 3.7 | BBB- | 56 | Frontier | Central and Eastern Europe | 9 out of 25 |
| Russia | 6.0 | 5.3 | BB+ | 68 | Emerging | Central and Eastern Europe | 14 out of 25 |
| Rwanda | 12.1 | 12.0 | B | 130 | | Africa | 31 out of 51 |
| São Tomé & Príncipe | 18.5 | 19.0 | | 163 | | Africa | 43 out of 51 |
| Saudi Arabia | 2.8 | 2.5 | A- | 47 | | Middle East | 6 out of 13 |
| Senegal | 8.6 | 8.5 | B+ | 86 | | Africa | 8 out of 51 |
| Serbia | 6.7 | 6.3 | BB- | 75 | Frontier | Central and Eastern Europe | 16 out of 25 |
| Seychelles | 6.1 | 6.1 | | 73 | | Africa | 5 out of 51 |
| Sierra Leone | 12.1 | 12.0 | | 129 | | Africa | 30 out of 51 |
| Singapore | -4.0 | -4.0 | AAA | 1 | Developed | Asia | 1 out of 29 |
| Slovakia | -0.3 | -0.3 | A+ | 24 | | Central and Eastern Europe | 2 out of 25 |
| Slovenia | 1.2 | 1.1 | A | 34 | Frontier | Central and Eastern Europe | 5 out of 25 |
| Solomon Islands | 23.0 | 23.0 | | 168 | | Australasia | 6 out of 7 |
| Somalia | 21.2 | 21.2 | | 166 | | Africa | 46 out of 51 |
| South Africa | 3.8 | 4.0 | BBB- | 60 | Emerging | Africa | 2 out of 51 |
| Spain | 2.0 | 2.0 | BBB+ | 38 | Developed | Western Europe | 16 out of 19 |
| Sri Lanka | 6.1 | 5.7 | B+ | 72 | Frontier | Asia | 14 out of 29 |
| Sudan | 17.1 | 17.1 | | 154 | | Africa | 40 out of 51 |
| Suriname | 9.5 | 9.7 | B+ | 102 | | Latin America | 16 out of 20 |
| Swaziland | 15.4 | 16.4 | | 152 | | Africa | 38 out of 51 |
| Sweden | -3.0 | -3.2 | AAA | 7 | Developed | Western Europe | 6 out of 19 |

§ S&P Credit Rating based on long-term foreign currency issuer rating. See http://www.standardandpoors.com/.

* World rank based on 175 countries covered by Euromoney. Ranking based on ascending order in which '1' equals the smallest country risk premium (CRP) and '175' equals the largest country risk premium (CRP).

† MSCI Market Classification based on MSCI Market Classification Framework.  See http://www.msci.com/products/indexes/market_classification.html

‡ Regional classification based on Euromoney. Regional rankings based on ascending order in which '1' equals the smallest country risk premium (CRP) for each region.

Note: A CRP of 0.0% is assumed in the following cases: (i) when the investor country and the investee country both have an S&P sovereign credit rating of AAA; or (ii) when the investor country has an S&P credit rating of AAA, and the investee country has a sovereign credit rating below AAA, but has a calculated CRP below 0.0% (which would imply lower risk than a country rated AAA), or (iii) when the investor country has an S&P credit rating below AAA, and the investee country has a sovereign credit rating of AAA, but has a calculated CRP above 0.0% (which would imply greater risk than a country rated below AAA). For purposes of this analysis, the U.S. is treated as having a sovereign credit rating equivalent to AAA.

The country risk premium (CRP) is not the cost of equity capital (COE). The CRP is to be added to base COE. See Chapter 6 for proper application.

## Data Updated Through March 2017

| Investee Country | December 2016 Country Risk Premium (CRP) (%) | March 2017 Country Risk Premium (CRP) (%) | S&P Sovereign Credit Rating § | World Rank Out of 175* | MSCI Market Classification † | Euromoney Region ‡ | Regional Rank ‡ |
|---|---|---|---|---|---|---|---|
| Switzerland | -3.7 | -3.9 | AAA | 2 | Developed | Western Europe | 1 out of 19 |
| Syria | 22.0 | 22.2 | | 167 | | Middle East | 13 out of 13 |
| Taiwan | -1.0 | -1.1 | AA- | 18 | Emerging | Asia | 3 out of 29 |
| Tajikistan | 16.7 | 17.1 | | 155 | | Central and Eastern Europe | 25 out of 25 |
| Tanzania | 8.9 | 9.1 | | 95 | | Africa | 13 out of 51 |
| Thailand | 3.2 | 3.0 | BBB+ | 51 | Emerging | Asia | 8 out of 29 |
| Togo | 10.5 | 10.5 | | 113 | | Africa | 20 out of 51 |
| Tonga | 25.4 | 25.5 | | 170 | | Australasia | 7 out of 7 |
| Trinidad & Tobago | 3.6 | 3.5 | A- | 54 | | Caribbean | 2 out of 9 |
| Tunisia | 6.5 | 6.8 | | 79 | Frontier | Africa | 6 out of 51 |
| Turkey | 3.9 | 3.8 | BB | 58 | Emerging | Central and Eastern Europe | 11 out of 25 |
| Turkmenistan | 13.9 | 14.1 | | 140 | | Asia | 24 out of 29 |
| Uganda | 10.0 | 10.3 | B | 110 | | Africa | 18 out of 51 |
| Ukraine | 12.9 | 12.9 | B- | 135 | | Central and Eastern Europe | 20 out of 25 |
| United Arab Emirates | 0.7 | 0.8 | AA | 33 | Emerging | Middle East | 4 out of 13 |
| United Kingdom | -0.8 | -0.7 | AA | 20 | Developed | Western Europe | 11 out of 19 |
| United States | -1.8 | -1.9 | AA+ | 15 | Developed | North America | 2 out of 2 |
| Uruguay | 2.6 | 2.4 | BBB | 45 | | Latin America | 5 out of 20 |
| Uzbekistan | 13.0 | 12.5 | | 132 | | Asia | 21 out of 29 |
| Vanuatu | 14.7 | 14.7 | | 145 | | Australasia | 4 out of 7 |
| Venezuela | 18.5 | 19.0 | CCC | 162 | | Latin America | 20 out of 20 |
| Vietnam | 7.0 | 6.7 | BB- | 78 | Frontier | Asia | 16 out of 29 |
| Yemen | 18.8 | 18.9 | | 161 | | Middle East | 12 out of 13 |
| Zambia | 10.4 | 10.4 | B | 111 | | Africa | 19 out of 51 |
| Zimbabwe | 20.5 | 20.4 | | 164 | | Africa | 44 out of 51 |

## March 2017 Country Risk Premium (CRP) Summary Statistics:

| S&P Rating | Country Count | Average CRP (%) | Median CRP (%) | Min CRP (%) | Max CRP (%) |
|---|---|---|---|---|---|
| AAA ** | 12 | -3.1 | -3.2 | -4.0 | -1.9 |
| AA (AA+, AA, AA-) | 15 | -0.8 | -0.7 | -3.0 | 2.3 |
| A (A+, A, A-) | 14 | 1.3 | 1.3 | -0.3 | 3.5 |
| BBB (BBB+, BBB, BBB-) | 17 | 3.0 | 3.0 | 0.3 | 5.4 |
| BB (BB+, BB, BB-) | 22 | 6.0 | 5.9 | 2.1 | 11.5 |
| B+ − SD | 39 | 10.8 | 10.4 | 5.7 | 19.0 |
| Investment Grade ** | 58 | 0.3 | 0.3 | -4.0 | 5.4 |
| Non-Investment Grade ** | 61 | 9.0 | 9.2 | 2.1 | 19.0 |
| **MSCI Market Classification** | | | | | |
| Developed Markets | 23 | -1.6 | -2.5 | -4.0 | 2.8 |
| Emerging Markets | 23 | 2.7 | 2.3 | -1.5 | 10.7 |
| Frontier Markets | 22 | 5.8 | 5.6 | 0.4 | 11.5 |
| **Euromoney Region ‡** | | | | | |
| Africa | 51 | 13.3 | 11.3 | 2.5 | 34.1 |
| Asia | 29 | 8.0 | 6.5 | -4.0 | 31.4 |
| Australasia | 7 | 11.9 | 14.7 | -3.0 | 25.5 |
| Caribbean | 9 | 9.3 | 8.8 | 2.4 | 18.7 |
| Central and Eastern Europe | 25 | 6.3 | 4.3 | -0.4 | 17.1 |
| Latin America | 20 | 6.9 | 7.7 | -1.5 | 19.0 |
| Middle East | 13 | 7.1 | 4.6 | -0.6 | 22.2 |
| North America | 2 | -2.4 | -2.4 | -3.0 | -1.9 |
| Western Europe | 19 | -0.7 | -1.3 | -3.9 | 10.0 |

## CCR Base Cost of Equity Capital:

| Malta | COE (%) |
|---|---|
| March 2017 | 10.4 |
| December 2016 | 10.3 |

CCR base country-level COE for a Malta-based investor investing in Malta.

§ S&P Credit Rating based on long-term foreign currency issuer rating. See http://www.standardandpoors.com/.

* World rank based on 175 countries covered by Euromoney. Ranking based on ascending order in which '1' equals the smallest country risk premium (CRP) and '175' equals the largest country risk premium (CRP).

† MSCI Market Classification based on MSCI Market Classification Framework. See http://www.msci.com/products/indexes/market_classification.html.

‡ Regional classification based on Euromoney. Regional rankings based on ascending order in which '1' equals the smallest country risk premium (CRP) for each region.

** Investment grade based on S&P sovereign credit rating from AAA to BBB-. Non-Investment grade based on S&P sovereign credit rating from BB+ to SD. For purposes of this analysis, the U.S. is being treated as if it were rated AAA by S&P.

Note: A CRP of 0.0% is assumed in the following cases: (i) when the investor country and the investee country both have an S&P sovereign credit rating of AAA; or (ii) when the investor country has an S&P credit rating of AAA, and the investee country has a sovereign credit rating below AAA, but has a calculated CRP below 0.0% (which would imply lower risk than a country rated AAA); or (iii) when the investor country has an S&P credit rating below AAA, and the investee country has a sovereign credit rating of AAA, but has a calculated CRP above 0.0% (which would imply greater risk than a country rated below AAA). For purposes of this analysis, the U.S. is treated as having a sovereign credit rating equivalent to AAA.

The country risk premium (CRP) is not the cost of equity capital (COE).  The CRP is to be added to base COE. See Chapter 6 for proper application.

### Data Updated Through March 2017

| Investee Country | December 2016 Country Risk Premium (CRP) (%) | March 2017 Country Risk Premium (CRP) (%) | S&P Sovereign Credit Rating § | World Rank Out of 175* | MSCI Market Classification † | Euromoney Region ‡ | Regional Rank ‡ |
|---|---|---|---|---|---|---|---|
| Afghanistan | 8.9 | 8.5 | | 139 | | Asia | 23 out of 29 |
| Albania | 3.5 | 3.5 | B+ | 93 | | Central and Eastern Europe | 18 out of 25 |
| Algeria | 3.6 | 3.5 | | 91 | | Africa | 10 out of 51 |
| Angola | 5.9 | 5.8 | B | 121 | | Africa | 26 out of 51 |
| Argentina | 4.1 | 3.7 | B- | 96 | Frontier | Latin America | 13 out of 20 |
| Armenia | 1.2 | 1.2 | | 77 | | Asia | 15 out of 29 |
| Australia | -7.6 | -8.0 | AAA | 12 | Developed | Australasia | 2 out of 7 |
| Austria | -7.4 | -7.7 | AA+ | 13 | Developed | Western Europe | 9 out of 19 |
| Azerbaijan | 2.4 | 2.5 | BB+ | 85 | | Asia | 17 out of 29 |
| Bahamas | -0.2 | -0.7 | BB+ | 65 | | Caribbean | 3 out of 9 |
| Bahrain | -0.3 | -0.7 | BB- | 64 | Frontier | Middle East | 7 out of 13 |
| Bangladesh | 6.4 | 6.0 | BB- | 126 | Frontier | Asia | 20 out of 29 |
| Barbados | 1.4 | 2.2 | CCC+ | 82 | | Caribbean | 4 out of 9 |
| Belarus | 8.6 | 8.9 | B- | 143 | | Central and Eastern Europe | 23 out of 25 |
| Belgium | -6.2 | -6.5 | AA | 17 | Developed | Western Europe | 10 out of 19 |
| Belize | 4.6 | 4.5 | B- | 106 | | Latin America | 17 out of 20 |
| Benin | 10.2 | 10.1 | | 150 | | Africa | 37 out of 51 |
| Bermuda | -2.6 | -2.9 | A+ | 44 | | Caribbean | 1 out of 9 |
| Bhutan | 9.9 | 9.7 | | 148 | | Asia | 25 out of 29 |
| Bolivia | 3.1 | 3.2 | BB | 88 | | Latin America | 12 out of 20 |
| Bosnia & Herzegovina | 9.0 | 9.0 | B | 144 | | Central and Eastern Europe | 24 out of 25 |
| Botswana | -2.6 | -2.8 | A- | 48 | | Africa | 1 out of 51 |
| Brazil | -1.1 | -1.4 | BB | 59 | Emerging | Latin America | 7 out of 20 |
| Bulgaria | -1.2 | -1.3 | BB+ | 61 | | Central and Eastern Europe | 12 out of 25 |
| Burkina Faso | 7.4 | 7.3 | B- | 133 | | Africa | 33 out of 51 |
| Burundi | 19.1 | 19.1 | | 169 | | Africa | 47 out of 51 |
| Cambodia | 10.8 | 10.4 | | 151 | | Asia | 27 out of 29 |
| Cameroon | 6.1 | 5.9 | B | 124 | | Africa | 28 out of 51 |
| Canada | -7.8 | -8.2 | AAA | 9 | Developed | North America | 1 out of 2 |
| Cape Verde | 3.7 | 3.6 | B | 94 | | Africa | 12 out of 51 |
| Central African Republic | 22.5 | 22.6 | | 172 | | Africa | 49 out of 51 |
| Chad | 21.2 | 21.3 | | 171 | | Africa | 48 out of 51 |
| Chile | -6.6 | -6.7 | AA- | 16 | Emerging | Latin America | 1 out of 20 |
| China | -2.8 | -3.0 | AA- | 42 | Emerging | Asia | 7 out of 29 |
| Colombia | -2.8 | -3.1 | BBB | 41 | Emerging | Latin America | 4 out of 20 |
| Congo Republic | 5.7 | 5.4 | B- | 117 | | Africa | 24 out of 51 |
| Congo, DR | 6.9 | 6.7 | B- | 131 | | Africa | 32 out of 51 |
| Costa Rica | 0.2 | 0.2 | BB- | 71 | | Latin America | 8 out of 20 |
| Côte d'Ivoire | 3.6 | 3.5 | | 92 | | Africa | 11 out of 51 |
| Croatia | -0.7 | -1.1 | BB | 63 | Frontier | Central and Eastern Europe | 13 out of 25 |
| Cuba | 13.1 | 13.1 | | 160 | | Caribbean | 9 out of 9 |
| Cyprus | -3.1 | -3.2 | BB+ | 40 | | Central and Eastern Europe | 7 out of 25 |
| Czech Republic | -5.4 | -5.7 | AA- | 23 | Emerging | Central and Eastern Europe | 1 out of 25 |
| Denmark | -8.4 | -8.7 | AAA | 4 | Developed | Western Europe | 3 out of 19 |
| Djibouti | 30.3 | 28.2 | | 175 | | Africa | 51 out of 51 |
| Dominican Republic | 3.4 | 3.4 | BB- | 90 | | Caribbean | 5 out of 9 |
| Ecuador | 5.0 | 4.7 | B | 109 | | Latin America | 18 out of 20 |
| Egypt | 5.4 | 5.2 | B- | 116 | Emerging | Africa | 23 out of 51 |
| El Salvador | 2.5 | 2.1 | B- | 81 | | Latin America | 10 out of 20 |
| Equatorial Guinea | 15.5 | 15.5 | | 165 | | Africa | 45 out of 51 |

§ S&P Credit Rating based on long-term foreign currency issuer rating. See http://www.standardandpoors.com/.
• World rank based on 175 countries covered by Euromoney. Ranking based on ascending order in which '1' equals the smallest country risk premium (CRP) and '175' equals the largest country risk premium (CRP).
† MSCI Market Classification based on MSCI Market Classification Framework.  See http://www.msci.com/products/indexes/market_classification.html
‡ Regional classification based on Euromoney. Regional rankings based on ascending order in which '1' equals the smallest country risk premium (CRP) for each region.
Note: A CRP of 0.0% is assumed in the following cases: (i) when the investor country and the investee country both have an S&P sovereign credit rating of AAA; or (ii) when the investor country has an S&P credit rating of AAA, and the investee country has a sovereign credit rating below AAA, but has a calculated CRP below 0.0% (which would imply lower risk than a country rated AAA); or (iii) when the investor country has an S&P credit rating below AAA, and the investee country has a sovereign credit rating of AAA, but has a calculated CRP above 0.0% (which would imply greater risk than a country rated below AAA). For purposes of this analysis, the U.S. is treated as having a sovereign credit rating equivalent to AAA.

The country risk premium (CRP) is not the cost of equity capital (COE). The CRP is to be added to base COE. See Chapter 6 for proper application.

## Data Updated Through March 2017

| Investee Country | December 2016 Country Risk Premium (CRP) (%) | March 2017 Country Risk Premium (CRP) (%) | S&P Sovereign Credit Rating § | World Rank Out of 175* | MSCI Market Classification † | Euromoney Region ‡ | Regional Rank ‡ |
|---|---|---|---|---|---|---|---|
| Eritrea | 26.6 | 24.9 | | 173 | | Africa | 50 out of 51 |
| Estonia | -4.8 | -4.8 | AA- | 32 | Frontier | Central and Eastern Europe | 4 out of 25 |
| Ethiopia | 4.3 | 4.2 | B | 101 | | Africa | 16 out of 51 |
| Fiji | 9.6 | 9.3 | B+ | 147 | | Australasia | 5 out of 7 |
| Finland | -7.7 | -8.0 | AA+ | 11 | Developed | Western Europe | 8 out of 19 |
| France | -5.4 | -5.8 | AA | 22 | Developed | Western Europe | 12 out of 19 |
| Gabon | 2.1 | 2.3 | | 83 | | Africa | 7 out of 51 |
| Gambia | 8.1 | 8.0 | | 138 | | Africa | 34 out of 51 |
| Georgia | 0.9 | 0.9 | BB- | 74 | | Central and Eastern Europe | 15 out of 25 |
| Germany | -7.7 | -8.0 | AAA | 10 | Developed | Western Europe | 7 out of 19 |
| Ghana | 3.8 | 3.3 | B- | 89 | | Africa | 9 out of 51 |
| Greece | 4.9 | 4.6 | B- | 108 | Emerging | Western Europe | 19 out of 19 |
| Grenada | 4.5 | 4.5 | | 105 | | Caribbean | 7 out of 9 |
| Guatemala | 2.5 | 2.4 | BB | 84 | | Latin America | 11 out of 20 |
| Guinea | 11.7 | 11.6 | | 156 | | Africa | 41 out of 51 |
| Guinea-Bissau | 5.4 | 5.2 | | 115 | | Africa | 22 out of 51 |
| Guyana | 4.2 | 4.1 | | 100 | | Latin America | 15 out of 20 |
| Haiti | 14.5 | 12.4 | | 157 | | Caribbean | 8 out of 9 |
| Honduras | 3.9 | 3.8 | B+ | 98 | | Latin America | 14 out of 20 |
| Hong Kong | -7.1 | -7.4 | AAA | 14 | Developed | Asia | 2 out of 29 |
| Hungary | -1.5 | -1.6 | BBB- | 57 | Emerging | Central and Eastern Europe | 10 out of 25 |
| Iceland | -4.4 | -4.9 | A | 30 | | Western Europe | 15 out of 19 |
| India | -1.7 | -1.6 | BBB- | 55 | Emerging | Asia | 10 out of 29 |
| Indonesia | -1.0 | -1.1 | BB+ | 62 | Emerging | Asia | 11 out of 29 |
| Iran | 5.9 | 6.0 | | 125 | | Middle East | 10 out of 13 |
| Iraq | 7.7 | 7.6 | B- | 136 | | Middle East | 11 out of 13 |
| Ireland | -4.9 | -5.2 | A+ | 27 | Developed | Western Europe | 14 out of 19 |
| Israel | -4.9 | -5.2 | A+ | 28 | Developed | Middle East | 2 out of 13 |
| Italy | -2.1 | -2.5 | BBB- | 50 | Developed | Western Europe | 18 out of 19 |
| Jamaica | 4.0 | 4.4 | B | 104 | | Caribbean | 6 out of 9 |
| Japan | -5.1 | -5.3 | A+ | 25 | Developed | Asia | 5 out of 29 |
| Jordan | 1.1 | 1.1 | BB- | 76 | Frontier | Middle East | 8 out of 13 |
| Kazakhstan | 0.6 | 0.1 | BBB- | 70 | Frontier | Asia | 13 out of 29 |
| Kenya | 4.0 | 3.9 | B+ | 99 | Frontier | Africa | 15 out of 51 |
| Korea (North) | 26.0 | 25.6 | | 174 | | Asia | 29 out of 29 |
| Korea (South) | -5.8 | -6.0 | AA | 19 | Emerging | Asia | 4 out of 29 |
| Kuwait | -4.8 | -4.9 | AA | 31 | Frontier | Middle East | 3 out of 13 |
| Kyrgyz Republic | 9.1 | 8.8 | | 142 | | Central and Eastern Europe | 22 out of 25 |
| Laos | 13.3 | 12.7 | | 158 | | Asia | 28 out of 29 |
| Latvia | -2.8 | -2.9 | A- | 43 | | Central and Eastern Europe | 8 out of 25 |
| Lebanon | 5.7 | 5.0 | B- | 112 | Frontier | Middle East | 9 out of 13 |
| Lesotho | 9.3 | 9.2 | | 146 | | Africa | 36 out of 51 |
| Liberia | 4.6 | 4.5 | | 107 | | Africa | 17 out of 51 |
| Libya | 10.8 | 11.1 | | 153 | | Africa | 39 out of 51 |
| Lithuania | -3.6 | -3.7 | A- | 36 | Frontier | Central and Eastern Europe | 6 out of 25 |
| Luxembourg | -8.1 | -8.5 | AAA | 5 | | Western Europe | 4 out of 19 |
| Macedonia | 3.1 | 3.2 | BB- | 87 | | Central and Eastern Europe | 17 out of 25 |
| Madagascar | 5.5 | 5.9 | | 123 | | Africa | 27 out of 51 |
| Malawi | 5.2 | 5.1 | | 114 | | Africa | 21 out of 51 |
| Malaysia | -3.4 | -3.8 | A- | 35 | Emerging | Asia | 6 out of 29 |

§ S&P Credit Rating based on long-term foreign currency issuer rating. See http://www.standardandpoors.com/.
* World rank based on 175 countries covered by Euromoney. Ranking based on ascending order in which '1' equals the smallest country risk premium (CRP) and '175' equals the largest country risk premium (CRP).
† MSCI Market Classification based on MSCI Market Classification Framework. See http://www.msci.com/products/indexes/market_classification.html
‡ Regional classification based on Euromoney. Regional rankings based on ascending order in which '1' equals the smallest country risk premium (CRP) for each region.
Note: A CRP of 0.0% is assumed in the following cases: (i) when the investor country and the investee country both have an S&P sovereign credit rating of AAA; or (ii) when the investor country has an S&P credit rating of AAA, and the investee country has a sovereign credit rating below AAA, but has a calculated CRP below 0.0% (which would imply lower risk than a country rated AAA); or (iii) when the investor country has an S&P credit rating below AAA, and the investee country has a sovereign credit rating of AAA, but has a calculated CRP above 0.0% (which would imply greater risk than a country rated below AAA). For purposes of this analysis, the U.S. is treated as having a sovereign credit rating equivalent to AAA.

The country risk premium (CRP) is not the cost of equity capital (COE). The CRP is to be added to base COE. See Chapter 6 for proper application.

### Data Updated Through March 2017

| Investee Country | December 2016 Country Risk Premium (CRP) (%) | March 2017 Country Risk Premium (CRP) (%) | S&P Sovereign Credit Rating § | World Rank Out of 175* | MSCI Market Classification † | Euromoney Region ‡ | Regional Rank ‡ |
|---|---|---|---|---|---|---|---|
| Mali | 8.9 | 8.8 | | 141 | | Africa | 35 out of 51 |
| Malta | -5.1 | -5.3 | A- | 26 | | Western Europe | 13 out of 19 |
| Mauritania | 12.9 | 12.8 | | 159 | | Africa | 42 out of 51 |
| Mauritius | -0.1 | -0.3 | | 67 | Frontier | Asia | 12 out of 29 |
| Mexico | -3.5 | -3.6 | BBB+ | 37 | Emerging | Latin America | 2 out of 20 |
| Moldova | 7.3 | 7.6 | | 137 | | Central and Eastern Europe | 21 out of 25 |
| Mongolia | 5.6 | 5.8 | B- | 119 | | Asia | 18 out of 29 |
| Montenegro | 4.8 | 4.4 | B+ | 103 | | Central and Eastern Europe | 19 out of 25 |
| Morocco | 0.0 | 0.0 | BBB- | 69 | Frontier | Africa | 4 out of 51 |
| Mozambique | 6.6 | 6.3 | SD | 128 | | Africa | 29 out of 51 |
| Myanmar | 7.5 | 7.3 | | 134 | | Asia | 22 out of 29 |
| Namibia | -0.4 | -0.4 | | 66 | | Africa | 3 out of 51 |
| Nepal | 10.2 | 10.1 | | 149 | | Asia | 26 out of 29 |
| Netherlands | -8.1 | -8.4 | AAA | 6 | Developed | Western Europe | 5 out of 19 |
| New Zealand | -7.9 | -8.2 | AA | 8 | Developed | Australasia | 1 out of 7 |
| Nicaragua | 6.3 | 6.2 | B+ | 127 | | Latin America | 19 out of 20 |
| Niger | 5.9 | 5.8 | | 120 | | Africa | 25 out of 51 |
| Nigeria | 4.0 | 3.8 | B | 97 | Frontier | Africa | 14 out of 51 |
| Norway | -8.7 | -9.1 | AAA | 3 | Developed | Western Europe | 2 out of 19 |
| Oman | -2.6 | -2.8 | BBB- | 46 | Frontier | Middle East | 5 out of 13 |
| Pakistan | 6.0 | 5.8 | B | 122 | Frontier | Asia | 19 out of 29 |
| Panama | -2.0 | -2.1 | BBB | 52 | | Latin America | 6 out of 20 |
| Papua New Guinea | 5.5 | 5.5 | B+ | 118 | | Australasia | 3 out of 7 |
| Paraguay | 1.5 | 1.5 | BB | 80 | | Latin America | 9 out of 20 |
| Peru | -3.2 | -3.3 | BBB+ | 39 | Emerging | Latin America | 3 out of 20 |
| Philippines | -1.6 | -1.9 | BBB | 53 | Emerging | Asia | 9 out of 29 |
| Poland | -4.6 | -5.0 | BBB+ | 29 | Emerging | Central and Eastern Europe | 3 out of 25 |
| Portugal | -2.2 | -2.6 | BB+ | 49 | Developed | Western Europe | 17 out of 19 |
| Qatar | -5.7 | -5.9 | AA | 21 | Emerging | Middle East | 1 out of 13 |
| Romania | -1.5 | -1.6 | BBB- | 56 | Frontier | Central and Eastern Europe | 9 out of 25 |
| Russia | 0.8 | 0.0 | BB+ | 68 | Emerging | Central and Eastern Europe | 14 out of 25 |
| Rwanda | 6.7 | 6.6 | B | 130 | | Africa | 31 out of 51 |
| São Tomé & Príncipe | 13.0 | 13.4 | | 163 | | Africa | 43 out of 51 |
| Saudi Arabia | -2.3 | -2.8 | A- | 47 | | Middle East | 6 out of 13 |
| Senegal | 3.3 | 3.1 | B+ | 86 | | Africa | 8 out of 51 |
| Serbia | 1.4 | 1.0 | BB- | 75 | Frontier | Central and Eastern Europe | 16 out of 25 |
| Seychelles | 0.9 | 0.7 | | 73 | | Africa | 5 out of 51 |
| Sierra Leone | 6.7 | 6.6 | | 129 | | Africa | 30 out of 51 |
| Singapore | -8.9 | -9.2 | AAA | 1 | Developed | Asia | 1 out of 29 |
| Slovakia | -5.3 | -5.5 | A+ | 24 | | Central and Eastern Europe | 2 out of 25 |
| Slovenia | -3.9 | -4.1 | A | 34 | Frontier | Central and Eastern Europe | 5 out of 25 |
| Solomon Islands | 17.3 | 17.3 | | 168 | | Australasia | 6 out of 7 |
| Somalia | 15.6 | 15.6 | | 166 | | Africa | 46 out of 51 |
| South Africa | -1.4 | -1.4 | BBB- | 60 | Emerging | Africa | 2 out of 51 |
| Spain | -3.1 | -3.3 | BBB+ | 38 | Developed | Western Europe | 16 out of 19 |
| Sri Lanka | 0.8 | 0.4 | B+ | 72 | Frontier | Asia | 14 out of 29 |
| Sudan | 11.6 | 11.5 | | 154 | | Africa | 40 out of 51 |
| Suriname | 4.2 | 4.2 | B+ | 102 | | Latin America | 16 out of 20 |
| Swaziland | 10.0 | 10.8 | | 152 | | Africa | 38 out of 51 |
| Sweden | -8.0 | -8.4 | AAA | 7 | Developed | Western Europe | 6 out of 19 |

§ S&P Credit Rating based on long-term foreign currency issuer rating. See http://www.standardandpoors.com/.

* World rank based on 175 countries covered by Euromoney. Ranking based on ascending order in which '1' equals the smallest country risk premium (CRP) and '175' equals the largest country risk premium (CRP).

† MSCI Market Classification based on MSCI Market Classification Framework. See http://www.msci.com/products/indexes/market_classification.html.

‡ Regional classification based on Euromoney. Regional rankings based on ascending order in which '1' equals the smallest country risk premium (CRP) for each region.

Note: A CRP of 0.0% is assumed in the following cases: (i) when the investor country and the investee country both have an S&P sovereign credit rating of AAA; or (ii) when the investor country has an S&P credit rating of AAA, and the investee country has a sovereign credit rating below AAA, but has a calculated CRP below 0.0% (which would imply lower risk than a country rated AAA); or (iii) when the investor country has an S&P credit rating below AAA, and the investee country has a sovereign credit rating of AAA, but has a calculated CRP above 0.0% (which would imply greater risk than a country rated below AAA). For purposes of this analysis, the U.S. is treated as having a sovereign credit rating equivalent to AAA.

The country risk premium (CRP) is not the cost of equity capital (COE). The CRP is to be added to base COE. See Chapter 6 for proper application.

## Data Updated Through March 2017

| Investee Country | December 2016 Country Risk Premium (CRP) (%) | March 2017 Country Risk Premium (CRP) (%) | S&P Sovereign Credit Rating § | World Rank Out of 175* | MSCI Market Classification † | Euromoney Region ‡ | Regional Rank ‡ |
|---|---|---|---|---|---|---|---|
| Switzerland | -8.7 | -9.1 | AAA | 2 | Developed | Western Europe | 1 out of 19 |
| Syria | 16.3 | 16.5 | | 167 | | Middle East | 13 out of 13 |
| Taiwan | -6.1 | -6.3 | AA- | 18 | Emerging | Asia | 3 out of 29 |
| Tajikistan | 11.2 | 11.5 | | 155 | | Central and Eastern Europe | 25 out of 25 |
| Tanzania | 3.6 | 3.7 | | 95 | | Africa | 13 out of 51 |
| Thailand | -1.9 | -2.3 | BBB+ | 51 | Emerging | Asia | 8 out of 29 |
| Togo | 5.2 | 5.0 | | 113 | | Africa | 20 out of 51 |
| Tonga | 19.7 | 19.7 | | 170 | | Australasia | 7 out of 7 |
| Trinidad & Tobago | -1.6 | -1.8 | A- | 54 | | Caribbean | 2 out of 9 |
| Tunisia | 1.2 | 1.4 | | 79 | Frontier | Africa | 6 out of 51 |
| Turkey | -1.2 | -1.5 | BB | 58 | Emerging | Central and Eastern Europe | 11 out of 25 |
| Turkmenistan | 8.4 | 8.6 | | 140 | | Asia | 24 out of 29 |
| Uganda | 4.7 | 4.8 | B | 110 | | Africa | 18 out of 51 |
| Ukraine | 7.5 | 7.4 | B- | 135 | | Central and Eastern Europe | 20 out of 25 |
| United Arab Emirates | -4.3 | -4.5 | AA | 33 | Emerging | Middle East | 4 out of 13 |
| United Kingdom | -5.8 | -5.9 | AA | 20 | Developed | Western Europe | 11 out of 19 |
| United States | -6.8 | -7.1 | AA+ | 15 | Developed | North America | 2 out of 2 |
| Uruguay | -2.5 | -2.9 | BBB | 45 | | Latin America | 5 out of 20 |
| Uzbekistan | 7.6 | 7.0 | | 132 | | Asia | 21 out of 29 |
| Vanuatu | 9.3 | 9.2 | | 145 | | Australasia | 4 out of 7 |
| Venezuela | 13.0 | 13.4 | CCC | 162 | | Latin America | 20 out of 20 |
| Vietnam | 1.8 | 1.3 | BB- | 78 | Frontier | Asia | 16 out of 29 |
| Yemen | 13.3 | 13.3 | | 161 | | Middle East | 12 out of 13 |
| Zambia | 5.0 | 4.9 | B | 111 | | Africa | 19 out of 51 |
| Zimbabwe | 14.9 | 14.8 | | 164 | | Africa | 44 out of 51 |

## March 2017 Country Risk Premium (CRP) Summary Statistics:

| S&P Rating | Country Count | Average CRP (%) | Median CRP (%) | Min CRP (%) | Max CRP (%) |
|---|---|---|---|---|---|
| AAA ** | 12 | -8.3 | -8.4 | -9.2 | -7.1 |
| AA (AA+, AA, AA-) | 15 | -6.0 | -5.9 | -8.2 | -3.0 |
| A (A+, A, A-) | 14 | -4.0 | -4.0 | -5.5 | -1.8 |
| BBB (BBB+, BBB, BBB-) | 17 | -2.3 | -2.3 | -5.0 | 0.1 |
| BB (BB+, BB, BB-) | 22 | 0.6 | 0.6 | -3.2 | 6.0 |
| B+ − SD | 39 | 5.3 | 4.9 | 0.4 | 13.4 |
| Investment Grade ** | 58 | -4.9 | -4.9 | -9.2 | 0.1 |
| Non-Investment Grade ** | 61 | 3.6 | 3.8 | -3.2 | 13.4 |
| **MSCI Market Classification** | | | | | |
| Developed Markets | 23 | -6.9 | -7.7 | -9.2 | -2.5 |
| Emerging Markets | 23 | -2.6 | -3.0 | -6.7 | 5.2 |
| Frontier Markets | 22 | 0.4 | 0.2 | -4.9 | 6.0 |
| **Euromoney Region ‡** | | | | | |
| Africa | 51 | 7.8 | 5.8 | -2.8 | 28.2 |
| Asia | 29 | 2.6 | 1.2 | -9.2 | 25.6 |
| Australasia | 7 | 6.4 | 9.2 | -8.2 | 19.7 |
| Caribbean | 9 | 3.8 | 3.4 | -2.9 | 13.1 |
| Central and Eastern Europe | 25 | 1.0 | -1.1 | -5.7 | 11.5 |
| Latin America | 20 | 1.5 | 2.3 | -6.7 | 13.4 |
| Middle East | 13 | 1.7 | -0.7 | -5.9 | 16.5 |
| North America | 2 | -7.6 | -7.6 | -8.2 | -7.1 |
| Western Europe | 19 | -6.0 | -6.5 | -9.1 | 4.6 |

## CCR Base Cost of Equity Capital:

| Morocco | COE (%) |
|---|---|
| March 2017 | 16.0 |
| December 2016 | 15.7 |

CCR base country-level COE for a Morocco-based investor investing in Morocco.

§ S&P Credit Rating based on long-term foreign currency issuer rating. See http://www.standardandpoors.com/.

* World rank based on 175 countries covered by Euromoney. Ranking based on ascending order in which '1' equals the smallest country risk premium (CRP) and '175' equals the largest country risk premium (CRP).

† MSCI Market Classification based on MSCI Market Classification Framework. See http://www.msci.com/products/indexes/market_classification.html.

‡ Regional classification based on Euromoney. Regional rankings based on ascending order in which '1' equals the smallest country risk premium (CRP) for each region.

** Investment grade based on S&P sovereign credit rating from AAA to BBB-. Non-Investment grade based on S&P sovereign credit rating from BB+ to SD. For purposes of this analysis, the U.S. is being treated as if it were rated AAA by S&P.

Note: A CRP of 0.0% is assumed in the following cases: (i) when the investor country and the investee country both have an S&P sovereign credit rating of AAA; or (ii) when the investor country has an S&P credit rating of AAA, and the investee country has a sovereign credit rating below AAA, but has a calculated CRP below 0.0% (which would imply lower risk than a country rated AAA); or (iii) when the investor country has an S&P credit rating below AAA, and the investee country has a sovereign credit rating of AAA, but has a calculated CRP above 0.0% (which would imply greater risk than a country rated below AAA). For purposes of this analysis, the U.S. is treated as having a sovereign credit rating equivalent to AAA.

The country risk premium (CRP) is not the cost of equity capital (COE). The CRP is to be added to base COE. See Chapter 6 for proper application.

## Data Updated Through March 2017

| Investee Country | December 2016 Country Risk Premium (CRP) (%) | March 2017 Country Risk Premium (CRP) (%) | S&P Sovereign Credit Rating § | World Rank Out of 175* | MSCI Market Classification † | Euromoney Region ‡ | Regional Rank ‡ |
|---|---|---|---|---|---|---|---|
| Afghanistan | 17.4 | 17.2 | | 139 | | Asia | 23 out of 29 |
| Albania | 11.9 | 12.2 | B+ | 93 | | Central and Eastern Europe | 18 out of 25 |
| Algeria | 12.0 | 12.1 | | 91 | | Africa | 10 out of 51 |
| Angola | 14.3 | 14.5 | B | 121 | | Africa | 26 out of 51 |
| Argentina | 12.5 | 12.3 | B- | 96 | Frontier | Latin America | 13 out of 20 |
| Armenia | 9.5 | 9.8 | | 77 | | Asia | 15 out of 29 |
| Australia | 0.0 | 0.0 | AAA | 12 | Developed | Australasia | 2 out of 7 |
| Austria | 0.7 | 0.7 | AA+ | 13 | Developed | Western Europe | 9 out of 19 |
| Azerbaijan | 10.7 | 11.1 | BB+ | 85 | | Asia | 17 out of 29 |
| Bahamas | 8.1 | 7.8 | BB+ | 65 | | Caribbean | 3 out of 9 |
| Bahrain | 8.0 | 7.8 | BB- | 64 | Frontier | Middle East | 7 out of 13 |
| Bangladesh | 14.8 | 14.7 | BB- | 126 | Frontier | Asia | 20 out of 29 |
| Barbados | 9.7 | 10.9 | CCC+ | 82 | | Caribbean | 4 out of 9 |
| Belarus | 17.1 | 17.6 | B- | 143 | | Central and Eastern Europe | 23 out of 25 |
| Belgium | 1.9 | 1.9 | AA | 17 | Developed | Western Europe | 10 out of 19 |
| Belize | 13.0 | 13.2 | B- | 106 | | Latin America | 17 out of 20 |
| Benin | 18.8 | 18.9 | | 150 | | Africa | 37 out of 51 |
| Bermuda | 5.6 | 5.6 | A+ | 44 | | Caribbean | 1 out of 9 |
| Bhutan | 18.5 | 18.4 | | 148 | | Asia | 25 out of 29 |
| Bolivia | 11.5 | 11.8 | BB | 88 | | Latin America | 12 out of 20 |
| Bosnia & Herzegovina | 17.6 | 17.8 | B | 144 | | Central and Eastern Europe | 24 out of 25 |
| Botswana | 5.6 | 5.7 | A- | 48 | | Africa | 1 out of 51 |
| Brazil | 7.2 | 7.1 | BB | 59 | Emerging | Latin America | 7 out of 20 |
| Bulgaria | 7.0 | 7.3 | BB+ | 61 | | Central and Eastern Europe | 12 out of 25 |
| Burkina Faso | 15.9 | 16.0 | B- | 133 | | Africa | 33 out of 51 |
| Burundi | 27.9 | 28.0 | | 169 | | Africa | 47 out of 51 |
| Cambodia | 19.4 | 19.1 | | 151 | | Asia | 27 out of 29 |
| Cameroon | 14.5 | 14.6 | B | 124 | | Africa | 28 out of 51 |
| Canada | 0.0 | 0.0 | AAA | 9 | Developed | North America | 1 out of 2 |
| Cape Verde | 12.1 | 12.2 | B | 94 | | Africa | 12 out of 51 |
| Central African Republic | 31.4 | 31.6 | | 172 | | Africa | 49 out of 51 |
| Chad | 30.1 | 30.2 | | 171 | | Africa | 48 out of 51 |
| Chile | 1.5 | 1.7 | AA- | 16 | Emerging | Latin America | 1 out of 20 |
| China | 5.4 | 5.5 | AA- | 42 | Emerging | Asia | 7 out of 29 |
| Colombia | 5.4 | 5.4 | BBB | 41 | Emerging | Latin America | 4 out of 20 |
| Congo Republic | 14.1 | 14.0 | B- | 117 | | Africa | 24 out of 51 |
| Congo, DR | 15.4 | 15.4 | B- | 131 | | Africa | 32 out of 51 |
| Costa Rica | 8.5 | 8.8 | BB- | 71 | | Latin America | 8 out of 20 |
| Côte d'Ivoire | 12.0 | 12.1 | | 92 | | Africa | 11 out of 51 |
| Croatia | 7.6 | 7.5 | BB | 63 | Frontier | Central and Eastern Europe | 13 out of 25 |
| Cuba | 21.7 | 21.9 | | 160 | | Caribbean | 9 out of 9 |
| Cyprus | 5.1 | 5.3 | BB+ | 40 | | Central and Eastern Europe | 7 out of 25 |
| Czech Republic | 2.7 | 2.8 | AA- | 23 | Emerging | Central and Eastern Europe | 1 out of 25 |
| Denmark | 0.0 | 0.0 | AAA | 4 | Developed | Western Europe | 3 out of 19 |
| Djibouti | 39.5 | 37.3 | | 175 | | Africa | 51 out of 51 |
| Dominican Republic | 11.8 | 12.0 | BB- | 90 | | Caribbean | 5 out of 9 |
| Ecuador | 13.4 | 13.3 | B | 109 | | Latin America | 18 out of 20 |
| Egypt | 13.9 | 13.9 | B- | 116 | Emerging | Africa | 23 out of 51 |
| El Salvador | 10.9 | 10.7 | B- | 81 | | Latin America | 10 out of 20 |
| Equatorial Guinea | 24.2 | 24.4 | | 165 | | Africa | 45 out of 51 |

§ S&P Credit Rating based on long-term foreign currency issuer rating. See http://www.standardandpoors.com/.

• World rank based on 175 countries covered by Euromoney. Ranking based on ascending order in which '1' equals the smallest country risk premium (CRP) and '175' equals the largest country risk premium (CRP).

† MSCI Market Classification based on MSCI Market Classification Framework. See http://www.msci.com/products/indexes/market_classification.html.

‡ Regional classification based on Euromoney. Regional rankings based on ascending order in which '1' equals the smallest country risk premium (CRP) for each region.

Note: A CRP of 0.0% is assumed in the following cases: (i) when the investor country and the investee country both have an S&P sovereign credit rating of AAA; or (ii) when the investor country has an S&P credit rating of AAA, and the investee country has a sovereign credit rating below AAA, but has a calculated CRP below 0.0% (which would imply lower risk than a country rated AAA); or (iii) when the investor country has an S&P credit rating below AAA, and the investee country has a sovereign credit rating of AAA, but has a calculated CRP above 0.0% (which would imply greater risk than a country rated below AAA). For purposes of this analysis, the U.S. is treated as having a sovereign credit rating equivalent to AAA.

The country risk premium (CRP) is not the cost of equity capital (COE).  The CRP is to be added to base COE. See Chapter 6 for proper application.

## Data Updated Through March 2017

| Investee Country | December 2016 Country Risk Premium (CRP) (%) | March 2017 Country Risk Premium (CRP) (%) | S&P Sovereign Credit Rating § | World Rank Out of 175* | MSCI Market Classification † | Euromoney Region ‡ | Regional Rank ‡ |
|---|---|---|---|---|---|---|---|
| Eritrea | 35.6 | 33.9 | | 173 | | Africa | 50 out of 51 |
| Estonia | 3.4 | 3.6 | AA- | 32 | Frontier | Central and Eastern Europe | 4 out of 25 |
| Ethiopia | 12.7 | 12.8 | B | 101 | | Africa | 16 out of 51 |
| Fiji | 18.1 | 18.1 | B+ | 147 | | Australasia | 5 out of 7 |
| Finland | 0.4 | 0.4 | AA+ | 11 | Developed | Western Europe | 8 out of 19 |
| France | 2.8 | 2.6 | AA | 22 | Developed | Western Europe | 12 out of 19 |
| Gabon | 10.5 | 10.9 | | 83 | | Africa | 7 out of 51 |
| Gambia | 16.6 | 16.7 | | 138 | | Africa | 34 out of 51 |
| Georgia | 9.2 | 9.5 | BB- | 74 | | Central and Eastern Europe | 15 out of 25 |
| Germany | 0.0 | 0.0 | AAA | 10 | Developed | Western Europe | 7 out of 19 |
| Ghana | 12.2 | 11.9 | B- | 89 | | Africa | 9 out of 51 |
| Greece | 13.4 | 13.2 | B- | 108 | Emerging | Western Europe | 19 out of 19 |
| Grenada | 13.0 | 13.1 | | 105 | | Caribbean | 7 out of 9 |
| Guatemala | 10.9 | 11.0 | BB | 84 | | Latin America | 11 out of 20 |
| Guinea | 20.3 | 20.4 | | 156 | | Africa | 41 out of 51 |
| Guinea-Bissau | 13.8 | 13.9 | | 115 | | Africa | 22 out of 51 |
| Guyana | 12.6 | 12.7 | | 100 | | Latin America | 15 out of 20 |
| Haiti | 23.2 | 21.2 | | 157 | | Caribbean | 8 out of 9 |
| Honduras | 12.3 | 12.4 | B+ | 98 | | Latin America | 14 out of 20 |
| Hong Kong | 0.0 | 0.0 | AAA | 14 | Developed | Asia | 2 out of 29 |
| Hungary | 6.8 | 7.0 | BBB- | 57 | Emerging | Central and Eastern Europe | 10 out of 25 |
| Iceland | 3.7 | 3.6 | A | 30 | | Western Europe | 15 out of 19 |
| India | 6.5 | 6.9 | BBB- | 55 | Emerging | Asia | 10 out of 29 |
| Indonesia | 7.3 | 7.4 | BB+ | 62 | Emerging | Asia | 11 out of 29 |
| Iran | 14.3 | 14.6 | | 125 | | Middle East | 10 out of 13 |
| Iraq | 16.2 | 16.3 | B- | 136 | | Middle East | 11 out of 13 |
| Ireland | 3.3 | 3.2 | A+ | 27 | Developed | Western Europe | 14 out of 19 |
| Israel | 3.2 | 3.3 | A+ | 28 | Developed | Middle East | 2 out of 13 |
| Italy | 6.2 | 6.0 | BBB- | 50 | Developed | Western Europe | 18 out of 19 |
| Jamaica | 12.4 | 13.1 | B | 104 | | Caribbean | 6 out of 9 |
| Japan | 3.1 | 3.2 | A+ | 25 | Developed | Asia | 5 out of 29 |
| Jordan | 9.5 | 9.7 | BB- | 76 | Frontier | Middle East | 8 out of 13 |
| Kazakhstan | 8.9 | 8.7 | BBB- | 70 | Frontier | Asia | 13 out of 29 |
| Kenya | 12.4 | 12.6 | B+ | 99 | Frontier | Africa | 15 out of 51 |
| Korea (North) | 35.0 | 34.6 | | 174 | | Asia | 29 out of 29 |
| Korea (South) | 2.3 | 2.4 | AA | 19 | Emerging | Asia | 4 out of 29 |
| Kuwait | 3.4 | 3.6 | AA | 31 | Frontier | Middle East | 3 out of 13 |
| Kyrgyz Republic | 17.6 | 17.6 | | 142 | | Central and Eastern Europe | 22 out of 25 |
| Laos | 21.9 | 21.5 | | 158 | | Asia | 28 out of 29 |
| Latvia | 5.4 | 5.6 | A- | 43 | | Central and Eastern Europe | 8 out of 25 |
| Lebanon | 14.2 | 13.6 | B- | 112 | Frontier | Middle East | 9 out of 13 |
| Lesotho | 17.8 | 17.9 | | 146 | | Africa | 36 out of 51 |
| Liberia | 13.1 | 13.2 | | 107 | | Africa | 17 out of 51 |
| Libya | 19.4 | 19.8 | | 153 | | Africa | 39 out of 51 |
| Lithuania | 4.6 | 4.8 | A- | 36 | Frontier | Central and Eastern Europe | 6 out of 25 |
| Luxembourg | 0.0 | 0.0 | AAA | 5 | | Western Europe | 4 out of 19 |
| Macedonia | 11.5 | 11.8 | BB- | 87 | | Central and Eastern Europe | 17 out of 25 |
| Madagascar | 13.9 | 14.5 | | 123 | | Africa | 27 out of 51 |
| Malawi | 13.7 | 13.8 | | 114 | | Africa | 21 out of 51 |
| Malaysia | 4.8 | 4.7 | A- | 35 | Emerging | Asia | 6 out of 29 |

§ S&P Credit Rating based on long-term foreign currency issuer rating. See http://www.standardandpoors.com/.
* World rank based on 175 countries covered by Euromoney. Ranking based on ascending order in which '1' equals the smallest country risk premium (CRP) and '175' equals the largest country risk premium (CRP).
† MSCI Market Classification based on MSCI Market Classification Framework.  See http://www.msci.com/products/indexes/market_classification.html.
‡ Regional classification based on Euromoney. Regional rankings based on ascending order in which '1' equals the smallest country risk premium (CRP) for each region.
Note: A CRP of 0.0% is assumed in the following cases: (i) when the investor country and the investee country both have an S&P sovereign credit rating of AAA; or (ii) when the investor country has an S&P sovereign credit rating of AAA, and the investee country has a sovereign credit rating below AAA, but has a calculated CRP below 0.0% (which would imply lower risk than a country rated AAA); or (iii) when the investor country has an S&P credit rating below AAA, and the investee country has a sovereign credit rating of AAA, but has a calculated CRP above 0.0% (which would imply greater risk than a country rated below AAA). For purposes of this analysis, the U.S. is treated as having a sovereign credit rating equivalent to AAA.

The country risk premium (CRP) is not the cost of equity capital (COE). The CRP is to be added to base COE. See Chapter 6 for proper application.

### Data Updated Through March 2017

| Investee Country | December 2016 Country Risk Premium (CRP) (%) | March 2017 Country Risk Premium (CRP) (%) | S&P Sovereign Credit Rating § | World Rank Out of 175• | MSCI Market Classification † | Euromoney Region ‡ | Regional Rank ‡ |
|---|---|---|---|---|---|---|---|
| Mali | 17.4 | 17.5 | | 141 | | Africa | 35 out of 51 |
| Malta | 3.1 | 3.2 | A- | 26 | | Western Europe | 13 out of 19 |
| Mauritania | 21.5 | 21.6 | | 159 | | Africa | 42 out of 51 |
| Mauritius | 8.2 | 8.3 | | 67 | Frontier | Asia | 12 out of 29 |
| Mexico | 4.7 | 4.9 | BBB+ | 37 | Emerging | Latin America | 2 out of 20 |
| Moldova | 15.8 | 16.4 | | 137 | | Central and Eastern Europe | 21 out of 25 |
| Mongolia | 14.0 | 14.4 | B- | 119 | | Asia | 18 out of 29 |
| Montenegro | 13.2 | 13.1 | B+ | 103 | | Central and Eastern Europe | 19 out of 25 |
| Morocco | 8.3 | 8.6 | BBB- | 69 | Frontier | Africa | 4 out of 51 |
| Mozambique | 15.1 | 15.0 | SD | 128 | | Africa | 29 out of 51 |
| Myanmar | 16.0 | 16.0 | | 134 | | Asia | 22 out of 29 |
| Namibia | 7.9 | 8.1 | | 66 | | Africa | 3 out of 51 |
| Nepal | 18.8 | 18.9 | | 149 | | Asia | 26 out of 29 |
| Netherlands | 0.0 | 0.0 | AAA | 6 | Developed | Western Europe | 5 out of 19 |
| New Zealand | 0.1 | 0.2 | AA | 8 | Developed | Australasia | 1 out of 7 |
| Nicaragua | 14.8 | 14.9 | B+ | 127 | | Latin America | 19 out of 20 |
| Niger | 14.4 | 14.5 | | 120 | | Africa | 25 out of 51 |
| Nigeria | 12.4 | 12.4 | B | 97 | Frontier | Africa | 14 out of 51 |
| Norway | 0.0 | 0.0 | AAA | 3 | Developed | Western Europe | 2 out of 19 |
| Oman | 5.6 | 5.7 | BBB- | 46 | Frontier | Middle East | 5 out of 13 |
| Pakistan | 14.5 | 14.5 | B | 122 | Frontier | Asia | 19 out of 29 |
| Panama | 6.3 | 6.4 | BBB | 52 | | Latin America | 6 out of 20 |
| Papua New Guinea | 14.0 | 14.1 | B+ | 118 | | Australasia | 3 out of 7 |
| Paraguay | 9.9 | 10.1 | BB | 80 | | Latin America | 9 out of 20 |
| Peru | 5.0 | 5.2 | BBB+ | 39 | Emerging | Latin America | 3 out of 20 |
| Philippines | 6.7 | 6.7 | BBB | 53 | Emerging | Asia | 9 out of 29 |
| Poland | 3.6 | 3.5 | BBB+ | 29 | Emerging | Central and Eastern Europe | 3 out of 25 |
| Portugal | 6.0 | 5.9 | BB+ | 49 | Developed | Western Europe | 17 out of 19 |
| Qatar | 2.4 | 2.6 | AA | 21 | Emerging | Middle East | 1 out of 13 |
| Romania | 6.8 | 6.9 | BBB- | 56 | Frontier | Central and Eastern Europe | 9 out of 25 |
| Russia | 9.1 | 8.5 | BB+ | 68 | Emerging | Central and Eastern Europe | 14 out of 25 |
| Rwanda | 15.2 | 15.3 | B | 130 | | Africa | 31 out of 51 |
| São Tomé & Príncipe | 21.6 | 22.2 | | 163 | | Africa | 43 out of 51 |
| Saudi Arabia | 5.9 | 5.7 | A- | 47 | | Middle East | 6 out of 13 |
| Senegal | 11.7 | 11.7 | B+ | 86 | | Africa | 8 out of 51 |
| Serbia | 9.8 | 9.6 | BB- | 75 | Frontier | Central and Eastern Europe | 16 out of 25 |
| Seychelles | 9.2 | 9.3 | | 73 | | Africa | 5 out of 51 |
| Sierra Leone | 15.2 | 15.3 | | 129 | | Africa | 30 out of 51 |
| Singapore | 0.0 | 0.0 | AAA | 1 | Developed | Asia | 1 out of 29 |
| Slovakia | 2.8 | 3.0 | A+ | 24 | | Central and Eastern Europe | 2 out of 25 |
| Slovenia | 4.3 | 4.3 | A | 34 | Frontier | Central and Eastern Europe | 5 out of 25 |
| Solomon Islands | 26.1 | 26.2 | | 168 | | Australasia | 6 out of 7 |
| Somalia | 24.3 | 24.4 | | 166 | | Africa | 46 out of 51 |
| South Africa | 6.9 | 7.2 | BBB- | 60 | Emerging | Africa | 2 out of 51 |
| Spain | 5.1 | 5.2 | BBB+ | 38 | Developed | Western Europe | 16 out of 19 |
| Sri Lanka | 9.2 | 8.9 | B+ | 72 | Frontier | Asia | 14 out of 29 |
| Sudan | 20.2 | 20.3 | | 154 | | Africa | 40 out of 51 |
| Suriname | 12.6 | 12.9 | B+ | 102 | | Latin America | 16 out of 20 |
| Swaziland | 18.5 | 19.6 | | 152 | | Africa | 38 out of 51 |
| Sweden | 0.0 | 0.0 | AAA | 7 | Developed | Western Europe | 6 out of 19 |

The country risk premium (CRP) is not the cost of equity capital (COE). The CRP is to be added to base COE. See Chapter 6 for proper application.

## Data Updated Through March 2017

| Investee Country | December 2016 Country Risk Premium (CRP) (%) | March 2017 Country Risk Premium (CRP) (%) | S&P Sovereign Credit Rating § | World Rank Out of 175* | MSCI Market Classification † | Euromoney Region ‡ | Regional Rank ‡ |
|---|---|---|---|---|---|---|---|
| Switzerland | 0.0 | 0.0 | AAA | 2 | Developed | Western Europe | 1 out of 19 |
| Syria | 25.1 | 25.4 | | 167 | | Middle East | 13 out of 13 |
| Taiwan | 2.1 | 2.1 | AA- | 18 | Emerging | Asia | 3 out of 29 |
| Tajikistan | 19.8 | 20.3 | | 155 | | Central and Eastern Europe | 25 out of 25 |
| Tanzania | 12.0 | 12.3 | | 95 | | Africa | 13 out of 51 |
| Thailand | 6.3 | 6.2 | BBB+ | 51 | Emerging | Asia | 8 out of 29 |
| Togo | 13.6 | 13.7 | | 113 | | Africa | 20 out of 51 |
| Tonga | 28.5 | 28.7 | | 170 | | Australasia | 7 out of 7 |
| Trinidad & Tobago | 6.7 | 6.7 | A- | 54 | | Caribbean | 2 out of 9 |
| Tunisia | 9.6 | 10.0 | | 79 | Frontier | Africa | 6 out of 51 |
| Turkey | 7.0 | 7.0 | BB | 58 | Emerging | Central and Eastern Europe | 11 out of 25 |
| Turkmenistan | 17.0 | 17.3 | | 140 | | Asia | 24 out of 29 |
| Uganda | 13.1 | 13.5 | B | 110 | | Africa | 18 out of 51 |
| Ukraine | 16.0 | 16.2 | B- | 135 | | Central and Eastern Europe | 20 out of 25 |
| United Arab Emirates | 3.9 | 4.0 | AA | 33 | Emerging | Middle East | 4 out of 13 |
| United Kingdom | 2.3 | 2.5 | AA | 20 | Developed | Western Europe | 11 out of 19 |
| United States | 0.0 | 0.0 | AA+ | 15 | Developed | North America | 2 out of 2 |
| Uruguay | 5.7 | 5.6 | BBB | 45 | | Latin America | 5 out of 20 |
| Uzbekistan | 16.1 | 15.7 | | 132 | | Asia | 21 out of 29 |
| Vanuatu | 17.8 | 17.9 | | 145 | | Australasia | 4 out of 7 |
| Venezuela | 21.6 | 22.2 | CCC | 162 | | Latin America | 20 out of 20 |
| Vietnam | 10.1 | 9.9 | BB- | 78 | Frontier | Asia | 16 out of 29 |
| Yemen | 21.9 | 22.1 | | 161 | | Middle East | 12 out of 13 |
| Zambia | 13.5 | 13.6 | B | 111 | | Africa | 19 out of 51 |
| Zimbabwe | 23.6 | 23.6 | | 164 | | Africa | 44 out of 51 |

## March 2017 Country Risk Premium (CRP) Summary Statistics:

| S&P Rating | Country Count | Average CRP (%) | Median CRP (%) | Min CRP (%) | Max CRP (%) |
|---|---|---|---|---|---|
| AAA ** | 12 | 0.0 | 0.0 | 0.0 | 0.0 |
| AA (AA+, AA, AA-) | 15 | 2.5 | 2.5 | 0.2 | 5.5 |
| A (A+, A, A-) | 14 | 4.5 | 4.5 | 3.0 | 6.7 |
| BBB (BBB+, BBB, BBB-) | 17 | 6.2 | 6.2 | 3.5 | 8.7 |
| BB (BB+, BB, BB-) | 22 | 9.2 | 9.1 | 5.3 | 14.7 |
| B+ − SD | 39 | 14.0 | 13.6 | 8.9 | 22.2 |
| Investment Grade ** | 58 | 3.5 | 3.6 | 0.0 | 8.7 |
| Non-Investment Grade ** | 61 | 12.2 | 12.4 | 5.3 | 22.2 |
| **MSCI Market Classification** | | | | | |
| Developed Markets | 23 | 1.5 | 0.2 | 0.0 | 6.0 |
| Emerging Markets | 23 | 5.9 | 5.5 | 1.7 | 13.9 |
| Frontier Markets | 22 | 9.0 | 8.8 | 3.6 | 14.7 |
| **Euromoney Region ‡** | | | | | |
| Africa | 51 | 16.5 | 14.5 | 5.7 | 37.3 |
| Asia | 29 | 11.2 | 9.8 | 0.0 | 34.6 |
| Australasia | 7 | 15.0 | 17.9 | 0.0 | 28.7 |
| Caribbean | 9 | 12.5 | 12.0 | 5.6 | 21.9 |
| Central and Eastern Europe | 25 | 9.6 | 7.5 | 2.8 | 20.3 |
| Latin America | 20 | 10.1 | 10.9 | 1.7 | 22.2 |
| Middle East | 13 | 10.3 | 7.8 | 2.6 | 25.4 |
| North America | 2 | 0.0 | 0.0 | 0.0 | 0.0 |
| Western Europe | 19 | 2.6 | 1.9 | 0.0 | 13.2 |

## CCR Base Cost of Equity Capital:

| Netherlands | COE (%) |
|---|---|
| March 2017 | 7.2 |
| December 2016 | 7.2 |

CCR base country-level COE for a Netherlands-based investor investing in the Netherlands.

§ S&P Credit Rating based on long-term foreign currency issuer rating. See http://www.standardandpoors.com/.

* World rank based on 175 countries covered by Euromoney. Ranking based on ascending order in which '1' equals the smallest country risk premium (CRP) and '175' equals the largest country risk premium (CRP).

† MSCI Market Classification based on MSCI Market Classification Framework. See http://www.msci.com/products/indexes/market_classification.html.

‡ Regional classification based on Euromoney. Regional rankings based on ascending order in which '1' equals the smallest country risk premium (CRP) for each region.

** Investment grade based on S&P sovereign credit rating from AAA to BBB-. Non-Investment grade based on S&P sovereign credit rating from BB+ to SD. For purposes of this analysis, the U.S. is being treated as if it were rated AAA by S&P.

Note: A CRP of 0.0% is assumed in the following cases: (i) when the investor country and the investee country both have an S&P sovereign credit rating of AAA; or (ii) when the investor country has an S&P credit rating of AAA, and the investee country has a sovereign credit rating below AAA, but has a calculated CRP below 0.0% (which would imply lower risk than a country rated AAA); or (iii) when the investor country has an S&P credit rating below AAA, and the investee country has a sovereign credit rating of AAA, but has a calculated CRP above 0.0% (which would imply greater risk than a country rated below AAA). For purposes of this analysis, the U.S. is treated as having a sovereign credit rating equivalent to AAA.

The country risk premium (CRP) is not the cost of equity capital (COE). The CRP is to be added to base COE. See Chapter 6 for proper application.

## Data Updated Through March 2017

| Investee Country | December 2016 Country Risk Premium (CRP) (%) | March 2017 Country Risk Premium (CRP) (%) | S&P Sovereign Credit Rating § | World Rank Out of 175* | MSCI Market Classification † | Euromoney Region ‡ | Regional Rank ‡ |
|---|---|---|---|---|---|---|---|
| Afghanistan | 15.7 | 15.5 | | 139 | | Asia | 23 out of 29 |
| Albania | 10.7 | 10.9 | B+ | 93 | | Central and Eastern Europe | 18 out of 25 |
| Algeria | 10.8 | 10.8 | | 91 | | Africa | 10 out of 51 |
| Angola | 12.9 | 13.0 | B | 121 | | Africa | 26 out of 51 |
| Argentina | 11.3 | 11.1 | B- | 96 | Frontier | Latin America | 13 out of 20 |
| Armenia | 8.5 | 8.7 | | 77 | | Asia | 15 out of 29 |
| Australia | 0.0 | 0.0 | AAA | 12 | Developed | Australasia | 2 out of 7 |
| Austria | 0.5 | 0.4 | AA+ | 13 | Developed | Western Europe | 9 out of 19 |
| Azerbaijan | 9.6 | 10.0 | BB+ | 85 | | Asia | 17 out of 29 |
| Bahamas | 7.2 | 6.9 | BB+ | 65 | | Caribbean | 3 out of 9 |
| Bahrain | 7.1 | 6.9 | BB- | 64 | Frontier | Middle East | 7 out of 13 |
| Bangladesh | 13.4 | 13.2 | BB- | 126 | Frontier | Asia | 20 out of 29 |
| Barbados | 8.7 | 9.7 | CCC+ | 82 | | Caribbean | 4 out of 9 |
| Belarus | 15.4 | 15.9 | B- | 143 | | Central and Eastern Europe | 23 out of 25 |
| Belgium | 1.6 | 1.5 | AA | 17 | Developed | Western Europe | 10 out of 19 |
| Belize | 11.7 | 11.8 | B- | 106 | | Latin America | 17 out of 20 |
| Benin | 17.0 | 17.1 | | 150 | | Africa | 37 out of 51 |
| Bermuda | 5.0 | 4.9 | A+ | 44 | | Caribbean | 1 out of 9 |
| Bhutan | 16.7 | 16.6 | | 148 | | Asia | 25 out of 29 |
| Bolivia | 10.3 | 10.6 | BB | 88 | | Latin America | 12 out of 20 |
| Bosnia & Herzegovina | 15.8 | 16.0 | B | 144 | | Central and Eastern Europe | 24 out of 25 |
| Botswana | 5.0 | 5.0 | A- | 48 | | Africa | 1 out of 51 |
| Brazil | 6.4 | 6.3 | BB | 59 | Emerging | Latin America | 7 out of 20 |
| Bulgaria | 6.3 | 6.4 | BB+ | 61 | | Central and Eastern Europe | 12 out of 25 |
| Burkina Faso | 14.3 | 14.4 | B- | 133 | | Africa | 33 out of 51 |
| Burundi | 25.2 | 25.3 | | 169 | | Africa | 47 out of 51 |
| Cambodia | 17.5 | 17.3 | | 151 | | Asia | 27 out of 29 |
| Cameroon | 13.1 | 13.1 | B | 124 | | Africa | 28 out of 51 |
| Canada | 0.0 | 0.0 | AAA | 9 | Developed | North America | 1 out of 2 |
| Cape Verde | 10.9 | 11.0 | B | 94 | | Africa | 12 out of 51 |
| Central African Republic | 28.5 | 28.6 | | 172 | | Africa | 49 out of 51 |
| Chad | 27.2 | 27.4 | | 171 | | Africa | 48 out of 51 |
| Chile | 1.2 | 1.4 | AA- | 16 | Emerging | Latin America | 1 out of 20 |
| China | 4.8 | 4.8 | AA- | 42 | Emerging | Asia | 7 out of 29 |
| Colombia | 4.8 | 4.8 | BBB | 41 | Emerging | Latin America | 4 out of 20 |
| Congo Republic | 12.7 | 12.6 | B- | 117 | | Africa | 24 out of 51 |
| Congo, DR | 13.9 | 13.9 | B- | 131 | | Africa | 32 out of 51 |
| Costa Rica | 7.6 | 7.8 | BB- | 71 | | Latin America | 8 out of 20 |
| Côte d'Ivoire | 10.8 | 10.9 | | 92 | | Africa | 11 out of 51 |
| Croatia | 6.7 | 6.6 | BB | 63 | Frontier | Central and Eastern Europe | 13 out of 25 |
| Cuba | 19.6 | 19.8 | | 160 | | Caribbean | 9 out of 9 |
| Cyprus | 4.5 | 4.6 | BB+ | 40 | | Central and Eastern Europe | 7 out of 25 |
| Czech Republic | 2.3 | 2.3 | AA- | 23 | Emerging | Central and Eastern Europe | 1 out of 25 |
| Denmark | -0.5 | -0.5 | AAA | 4 | Developed | Western Europe | 3 out of 19 |
| Djibouti | 35.8 | 33.8 | | 175 | | Africa | 51 out of 51 |
| Dominican Republic | 10.6 | 10.8 | BB- | 90 | | Caribbean | 5 out of 9 |
| Ecuador | 12.1 | 12.0 | B | 109 | | Latin America | 18 out of 20 |
| Egypt | 12.5 | 12.5 | B- | 116 | Emerging | Africa | 23 out of 51 |
| El Salvador | 9.7 | 9.6 | B- | 81 | | Latin America | 10 out of 20 |
| Equatorial Guinea | 21.9 | 22.0 | | 165 | | Africa | 45 out of 51 |

§ S&P Credit Rating based on long-term foreign currency issuer rating. See http://www.standardandpoors.com/.

* World rank based on 175 countries covered by Euromoney. Ranking based on ascending order in which '1' equals the smallest country risk premium (CRP) and '175' equals the largest country risk premium (CRP).

† MSCI Market Classification based on MSCI Market Classification Framework. See http://www.msci.com/products/indexes/market_classification.html

‡ Regional classification based on Euromoney. Regional rankings based on ascending order in which '1' equals the smallest country risk premium (CRP) for each region.

Note: A CRP of 0.0% is assumed in the following cases: (i) when the investor country and the investee country both have an S&P sovereign credit rating of AAA; or (ii) when the investor country has an S&P credit rating of AAA, and the investee country has a sovereign credit rating below AAA, but has a calculated CRP below 0.0% (which would imply lower risk than a country rated AAA); or (iii) when the investor country has an S&P credit rating below AAA, and the investee country has a sovereign credit rating of AAA, but has a calculated CRP above 0.0% (which would imply greater risk than a country rated below AAA). For purposes of this analysis, the U.S. is treated as having a sovereign credit rating equivalent to AAA.

The country risk premium (CRP) is not the cost of equity capital (COE). The CRP is to be added to base COE. See Chapter 6 for proper application.

## Data Updated Through March 2017

| Investee Country | December 2016 Country Risk Premium (CRP) (%) | March 2017 Country Risk Premium (CRP) (%) | S&P Sovereign Credit Rating § | World Rank Out of 175∗ | MSCI Market Classification † | Euromoney Region ‡ | Regional Rank ‡ |
|---|---|---|---|---|---|---|---|
| Eritrea | 32.3 | 30.8 | | 173 | | Africa | 50 out of 51 |
| Estonia | 2.9 | 3.1 | AA- | 32 | Frontier | Central and Eastern Europe | 4 out of 25 |
| Ethiopia | 11.4 | 11.5 | B | 101 | | Africa | 16 out of 51 |
| Fiji | 16.4 | 16.3 | B+ | 147 | | Australasia | 5 out of 7 |
| Finland | 0.2 | 0.2 | AA+ | 11 | Developed | Western Europe | 8 out of 19 |
| France | 2.4 | 2.2 | AA | 22 | Developed | Western Europe | 12 out of 19 |
| Gabon | 9.4 | 9.7 | | 83 | | Africa | 7 out of 51 |
| Gambia | 14.9 | 15.0 | | 138 | | Africa | 34 out of 51 |
| Georgia | 8.2 | 8.5 | BB- | 74 | | Central and Eastern Europe | 15 out of 25 |
| Germany | 0.0 | 0.0 | AAA | 10 | Developed | Western Europe | 7 out of 19 |
| Ghana | 11.0 | 10.7 | B- | 89 | | Africa | 9 out of 51 |
| Greece | 12.0 | 11.9 | B- | 108 | Emerging | Western Europe | 19 out of 19 |
| Grenada | 11.7 | 11.8 | | 105 | | Caribbean | 7 out of 9 |
| Guatemala | 9.8 | 9.8 | BB | 84 | | Latin America | 11 out of 20 |
| Guinea | 18.3 | 18.4 | | 156 | | Africa | 41 out of 51 |
| Guinea-Bissau | 12.4 | 12.5 | | 115 | | Africa | 22 out of 51 |
| Guyana | 11.4 | 11.4 | | 100 | | Latin America | 15 out of 20 |
| Haiti | 21.0 | 19.2 | | 157 | | Caribbean | 8 out of 9 |
| Honduras | 11.1 | 11.2 | B+ | 98 | | Latin America | 14 out of 20 |
| Hong Kong | 0.0 | 0.0 | AAA | 14 | Developed | Asia | 2 out of 29 |
| Hungary | 6.0 | 6.2 | BBB- | 57 | Emerging | Central and Eastern Europe | 10 out of 25 |
| Iceland | 3.3 | 3.1 | A | 30 | | Western Europe | 15 out of 19 |
| India | 5.8 | 6.1 | BBB- | 55 | Emerging | Asia | 10 out of 29 |
| Indonesia | 6.5 | 6.6 | BB+ | 62 | Emerging | Asia | 11 out of 29 |
| Iran | 12.9 | 13.2 | | 125 | | Middle East | 10 out of 13 |
| Iraq | 14.6 | 14.7 | B- | 136 | | Middle East | 11 out of 13 |
| Ireland | 2.8 | 2.8 | A+ | 27 | Developed | Western Europe | 14 out of 19 |
| Israel | 2.8 | 2.8 | A+ | 28 | Developed | Middle East | 2 out of 13 |
| Italy | 5.5 | 5.3 | BBB- | 50 | Developed | Western Europe | 18 out of 19 |
| Jamaica | 11.1 | 11.7 | B | 104 | | Caribbean | 6 out of 9 |
| Japan | 2.7 | 2.7 | A+ | 25 | Developed | Asia | 5 out of 29 |
| Jordan | 8.5 | 8.7 | BB- | 76 | Frontier | Middle East | 8 out of 13 |
| Kazakhstan | 8.0 | 7.7 | BBB- | 70 | Frontier | Asia | 13 out of 29 |
| Kenya | 11.2 | 11.3 | B+ | 99 | Frontier | Africa | 15 out of 51 |
| Korea (North) | 31.7 | 31.4 | | 174 | | Asia | 29 out of 29 |
| Korea (South) | 2.0 | 2.0 | AA | 19 | Emerging | Asia | 4 out of 29 |
| Kuwait | 3.0 | 3.1 | AA | 31 | Frontier | Middle East | 3 out of 13 |
| Kyrgyz Republic | 15.9 | 15.8 | | 142 | | Central and Eastern Europe | 22 out of 25 |
| Laos | 19.8 | 19.4 | | 158 | | Asia | 28 out of 29 |
| Latvia | 4.8 | 4.9 | A- | 43 | | Central and Eastern Europe | 8 out of 25 |
| Lebanon | 12.8 | 12.2 | B- | 112 | Frontier | Middle East | 9 out of 13 |
| Lesotho | 16.1 | 16.2 | | 146 | | Africa | 36 out of 51 |
| Liberia | 11.8 | 11.8 | | 107 | | Africa | 17 out of 51 |
| Libya | 17.5 | 17.9 | | 153 | | Africa | 39 out of 51 |
| Lithuania | 4.1 | 4.2 | A- | 36 | Frontier | Central and Eastern Europe | 6 out of 25 |
| Luxembourg | -0.2 | -0.2 | AAA | 5 | | Western Europe | 4 out of 19 |
| Macedonia | 10.3 | 10.6 | BB- | 87 | | Central and Eastern Europe | 17 out of 25 |
| Madagascar | 12.5 | 13.1 | | 123 | | Africa | 27 out of 51 |
| Malawi | 12.3 | 12.3 | | 114 | | Africa | 21 out of 51 |
| Malaysia | 4.3 | 4.1 | A- | 35 | Emerging | Asia | 6 out of 29 |

§ S&P Credit Rating based on long-term foreign currency issuer rating. See http://www.standardandpoors.com/.

∗ World rank based on 175 countries covered by Euromoney. Ranking based on ascending order in which '1' equals the smallest country risk premium (CRP) and '175' equals the largest country risk premium (CRP).

† MSCI Market Classification based on MSCI Market Classification Framework. See http://www.msci.com/products/indexes/market_classification.html

‡ Regional classification based on Euromoney. Regional rankings based on ascending order in which '1' equals the smallest country risk premium (CRP) for each region.

Note: A CRP of 0.0% is assumed in the following cases: (i) when the investor country and the investee country both have an S&P sovereign credit rating of AAA; or (ii) when the investor country has an S&P credit rating of AAA, and the investee country has a sovereign credit rating below AAA, but has a calculated CRP below 0.0% (which would imply lower risk than a country rated AAA); or (iii) when the investor country has an S&P credit rating below AAA, and the investee country has a sovereign credit rating of AAA, but has a calculated CRP above 0.0% (which would imply greater risk than a country rated below AAA). For purposes of this analysis, the U.S. is treated as having a sovereign credit rating equivalent to AAA.

2017 Valuation Handbook – International Guide to Cost of Capital      Data Exhibit 4      Investor Perspective: New Zealand (NZD); Page 2 of 4

The country risk premium (CRP) is not the cost of equity capital (COE). The CRP is to be added to base COE. See Chapter 6 for proper application.

## Data Updated Through March 2017

| Investee Country | December 2016 Country Risk Premium (CRP) (%) | March 2017 Country Risk Premium (CRP) (%) | S&P Sovereign Credit Rating § | World Rank Out of 175∗ | MSCI Market Classification † | Euromoney Region ‡ | Regional Rank ‡ |
|---|---|---|---|---|---|---|---|
| Mali | 15.7 | 15.8 | | 141 | | Africa | 35 out of 51 |
| Malta | 2.7 | 2.7 | A- | 26 | | Western Europe | 13 out of 19 |
| Mauritania | 19.4 | 19.5 | | 159 | | Africa | 42 out of 51 |
| Mauritius | 7.4 | 7.4 | | 67 | Frontier | Asia | 12 out of 29 |
| Mexico | 4.1 | 4.2 | BBB+ | 37 | Emerging | Latin America | 2 out of 20 |
| Moldova | 14.3 | 14.7 | | 137 | | Central and Eastern Europe | 21 out of 25 |
| Mongolia | 12.6 | 13.0 | B- | 119 | | Asia | 18 out of 29 |
| Montenegro | 11.9 | 11.7 | B+ | 103 | | Central and Eastern Europe | 19 out of 25 |
| Morocco | 7.4 | 7.6 | BBB- | 69 | Frontier | Africa | 4 out of 51 |
| Mozambique | 13.6 | 13.5 | SD | 128 | | Africa | 29 out of 51 |
| Myanmar | 14.5 | 14.4 | | 134 | | Asia | 22 out of 29 |
| Namibia | 7.1 | 7.2 | | 66 | | Africa | 3 out of 51 |
| Nepal | 16.9 | 17.0 | | 149 | | Asia | 26 out of 29 |
| Netherlands | -0.1 | -0.2 | AAA | 6 | Developed | Western Europe | 5 out of 19 |
| New Zealand | 0.0 | 0.0 | AA | 8 | Developed | Australasia | 1 out of 7 |
| Nicaragua | 13.3 | 13.4 | B+ | 127 | | Latin America | 19 out of 20 |
| Niger | 12.9 | 13.0 | | 120 | | Africa | 25 out of 51 |
| Nigeria | 11.1 | 11.1 | B | 97 | Frontier | Africa | 14 out of 51 |
| Norway | -0.7 | -0.8 | AAA | 3 | Developed | Western Europe | 2 out of 19 |
| Oman | 4.9 | 5.0 | BBB- | 46 | Frontier | Middle East | 5 out of 13 |
| Pakistan | 13.0 | 13.0 | B | 122 | Frontier | Asia | 19 out of 29 |
| Panama | 5.6 | 5.6 | BBB | 52 | | Latin America | 6 out of 20 |
| Papua New Guinea | 12.6 | 12.7 | B+ | 118 | | Australasia | 3 out of 7 |
| Paraguay | 8.8 | 9.0 | BB | 80 | | Latin America | 9 out of 20 |
| Peru | 4.4 | 4.5 | BBB+ | 39 | Emerging | Latin America | 3 out of 20 |
| Philippines | 5.9 | 5.9 | BBB | 53 | Emerging | Asia | 9 out of 29 |
| Poland | 3.1 | 3.0 | BBB+ | 29 | Emerging | Central and Eastern Europe | 3 out of 25 |
| Portugal | 5.3 | 5.2 | BB+ | 49 | Developed | Western Europe | 17 out of 19 |
| Qatar | 2.1 | 2.1 | AA | 21 | Emerging | Middle East | 1 out of 13 |
| Romania | 6.1 | 6.1 | BBB- | 56 | Frontier | Central and Eastern Europe | 9 out of 25 |
| Russia | 8.1 | 7.6 | BB+ | 68 | Emerging | Central and Eastern Europe | 14 out of 25 |
| Rwanda | 13.7 | 13.7 | B | 130 | | Africa | 31 out of 51 |
| São Tomé & Príncipe | 19.6 | 20.1 | | 163 | | Africa | 43 out of 51 |
| Saudi Arabia | 5.3 | 5.0 | A- | 47 | | Middle East | 6 out of 13 |
| Senegal | 10.5 | 10.5 | B+ | 86 | | Africa | 8 out of 51 |
| Serbia | 8.8 | 8.5 | BB- | 75 | Frontier | Central and Eastern Europe | 16 out of 25 |
| Seychelles | 8.3 | 8.3 | | 73 | | Africa | 5 out of 51 |
| Sierra Leone | 13.7 | 13.7 | | 129 | | Africa | 30 out of 51 |
| Singapore | -0.9 | -1.0 | AAA | 1 | Developed | Asia | 1 out of 29 |
| Slovakia | 2.5 | 2.5 | A+ | 24 | | Central and Eastern Europe | 2 out of 25 |
| Slovenia | 3.8 | 3.8 | A | 34 | Frontier | Central and Eastern Europe | 5 out of 25 |
| Solomon Islands | 23.6 | 23.7 | | 168 | | Australasia | 6 out of 7 |
| Somalia | 22.0 | 22.1 | | 166 | | Africa | 46 out of 51 |
| South Africa | 6.1 | 6.3 | BBB- | 60 | Emerging | Africa | 2 out of 51 |
| Spain | 4.5 | 4.5 | BBB+ | 38 | Developed | Western Europe | 16 out of 19 |
| Sri Lanka | 8.2 | 8.0 | B+ | 72 | Frontier | Asia | 14 out of 29 |
| Sudan | 18.3 | 18.3 | | 154 | | Africa | 40 out of 51 |
| Suriname | 11.3 | 11.5 | B+ | 102 | | Latin America | 16 out of 20 |
| Swaziland | 16.7 | 17.7 | | 152 | | Africa | 38 out of 51 |
| Sweden | -0.1 | -0.2 | AAA | 7 | Developed | Western Europe | 6 out of 19 |

§ S&P Credit Rating based on long-term foreign currency issuer rating. See http://www.standardandpoors.com/.

∗ World rank based on 175 countries covered by Euromoney. Ranking based on ascending order in which '1' equals the smallest country risk premium (CRP) and '175' equals the largest country risk premium (CRP).

† MSCI Market Classification based on MSCI Market Classification Framework. See http://www.msci.com/products/indexes/market_classification.html.

‡ Regional classification based on Euromoney. Regional rankings based on ascending order in which '1' equals the smallest country risk premium (CRP) for each region.

Note: A CRP of 0.0% is assumed in the following cases: (i) when the investor country and the investee country both have an S&P sovereign credit rating of AAA; or (ii) when the investor country has an S&P credit rating of AAA, and the investee country has a sovereign credit rating below AAA, but has a calculated CRP below 0.0% (which would imply lower risk than a country rated AAA); or (iii) when the investor country has an S&P credit rating below AAA, and the investee country has a sovereign credit rating of AAA, but has a calculated CRP above 0.0% (which would imply greater risk than a country rated below AAA). For purposes of this analysis, the U.S. is treated as having a sovereign credit rating equivalent to AAA.

The country risk premium (CRP) is not the cost of equity capital (COE). The CRP is to be added to base COE. See Chapter 6 for proper application.

## Data Updated Through March 2017

| Investee Country | December 2016 Country Risk Premium (CRP) (%) | March 2017 Country Risk Premium (CRP) (%) | S&P Sovereign Credit Rating § | World Rank Out of 175∗ | MSCI Market Classification † | Euromoney Region ‡ | Regional Rank ‡ |
|---|---|---|---|---|---|---|---|
| Switzerland | -0.7 | -0.9 | AAA | 2 | Developed | Western Europe | 1 out of 19 |
| Syria | 22.7 | 23.0 | | 167 | | Middle East | 13 out of 13 |
| Taiwan | 1.7 | 1.7 | AA- | 18 | Emerging | Asia | 3 out of 29 |
| Tajikistan | 17.9 | 18.3 | | 155 | | Central and Eastern Europe | 25 out of 25 |
| Tanzania | 10.8 | 11.0 | | 95 | | Africa | 13 out of 51 |
| Thailand | 5.6 | 5.5 | BBB+ | 51 | Emerging | Asia | 8 out of 29 |
| Togo | 12.2 | 12.3 | | 113 | | Africa | 20 out of 51 |
| Tonga | 25.8 | 26.0 | | 170 | | Australasia | 7 out of 7 |
| Trinidad & Tobago | 5.9 | 5.9 | A- | 54 | | Caribbean | 2 out of 9 |
| Tunisia | 8.6 | 8.9 | | 79 | Frontier | Africa | 6 out of 51 |
| Turkey | 6.3 | 6.2 | BB | 58 | Emerging | Central and Eastern Europe | 11 out of 25 |
| Turkmenistan | 15.3 | 15.6 | | 140 | | Asia | 24 out of 29 |
| Uganda | 11.8 | 12.1 | B | 110 | | Africa | 18 out of 51 |
| Ukraine | 14.4 | 14.5 | B- | 135 | | Central and Eastern Europe | 20 out of 25 |
| United Arab Emirates | 3.4 | 3.4 | AA | 33 | Emerging | Middle East | 4 out of 13 |
| United Kingdom | 2.0 | 2.1 | AA | 20 | Developed | Western Europe | 11 out of 19 |
| United States | 0.0 | 0.0 | AA+ | 15 | Developed | North America | 2 out of 2 |
| Uruguay | 5.0 | 4.9 | BBB | 45 | | Latin America | 5 out of 20 |
| Uzbekistan | 14.6 | 14.1 | | 132 | | Asia | 21 out of 29 |
| Vanuatu | 16.1 | 16.2 | | 145 | | Australasia | 4 out of 7 |
| Venezuela | 19.5 | 20.1 | CCC | 162 | | Latin America | 20 out of 20 |
| Vietnam | 9.1 | 8.9 | BB- | 78 | Frontier | Asia | 16 out of 29 |
| Yemen | 19.8 | 20.0 | | 161 | | Middle East | 12 out of 13 |
| Zambia | 12.1 | 12.2 | B | 111 | | Africa | 19 out of 51 |
| Zimbabwe | 21.3 | 21.4 | | 164 | | Africa | 44 out of 51 |

## March 2017 Country Risk Premium (CRP) Summary Statistics:

| S&P Rating | Country Count | Average CRP (%) | Median CRP (%) | Min CRP (%) | Max CRP (%) |
|---|---|---|---|---|---|
| AAA ∗∗ | 12 | -0.3 | -0.2 | -1.0 | 0.0 |
| AA (AA+, AA, AA-) | 15 | 2.0 | 2.1 | 0.0 | 4.8 |
| A (A+, A, A-) | 14 | 3.9 | 3.9 | 2.5 | 5.9 |
| BBB (BBB+, BBB, BBB-) | 17 | 5.5 | 5.5 | 3.0 | 7.7 |
| BB (BB+, BB, BB-) | 22 | 8.2 | 8.1 | 4.6 | 13.2 |
| B+ − SD | 39 | 12.6 | 12.2 | 8.0 | 20.1 |
| Investment Grade ∗∗ | 58 | 3.0 | 3.0 | -1.0 | 7.7 |
| Non-Investment Grade ∗∗ | 61 | 11.0 | 11.2 | 4.6 | 20.1 |
| **MSCI Market Classification** | | | | | |
| Developed Markets | 23 | 1.1 | 0.0 | -1.0 | 5.3 |
| Emerging Markets | 23 | 5.2 | 4.8 | 1.4 | 12.5 |
| Frontier Markets | 22 | 8.0 | 7.8 | 3.1 | 13.2 |
| **Euromoney Region ‡** | | | | | |
| Africa | 51 | 14.9 | 13.0 | 5.0 | 33.8 |
| Asia | 29 | 10.0 | 8.7 | -1.0 | 31.4 |
| Australasia | 7 | 13.5 | 16.2 | 0.0 | 26.0 |
| Caribbean | 9 | 11.2 | 10.8 | 4.9 | 19.8 |
| Central and Eastern Europe | 25 | 8.5 | 6.6 | 2.3 | 18.3 |
| Latin America | 20 | 9.1 | 9.7 | 1.4 | 20.1 |
| Middle East | 13 | 9.2 | 6.9 | 2.1 | 23.0 |
| North America | 2 | 0.0 | 0.0 | 0.0 | 0.0 |
| Western Europe | 19 | 2.1 | 1.5 | -0.9 | 11.9 |

### CCR Base Cost of Equity Capital:

| New Zealand | COE (%) |
|---|---|
| March 2017 | 6.3 |
| December 2016 | 6.2 |

CCR base country-level COE for a New Zealand-based investor investing in New Zealand.

§ S&P Credit Rating based on long-term foreign currency issuer rating. See http://www.standardandpoors.com/.
∗ World rank based on 175 countries covered by Euromoney. Ranking based on ascending order in which '1' equals the smallest country risk premium (CRP) and '175' equals the largest country risk premium (CRP).
† MSCI Market Classification based on MSCI Market Classification Framework. See http://www.msci.com/products/indexes/market_classification.html.
‡ Regional classification based on Euromoney. Regional rankings based on ascending order in which '1' equals the smallest country risk premium (CRP) for each region.
∗∗ Investment grade based on S&P sovereign credit rating from AAA to BBB-. Non-Investment grade based on S&P sovereign credit rating from BB+ to SD. For purposes of this analysis, the U.S. is being treated as if it were rated AAA by S&P.
Note: A CRP of 0.0% is assumed in the following cases: (i) when the investor country and the investee country both have an S&P sovereign credit rating of AAA; or (ii) when the investor country has an S&P credit rating of AAA, and the investee country has a sovereign credit rating below AAA, but has a calculated CRP below 0.0% (which would imply lower risk than a country rated AAA); or (iii) when the investor country has an S&P credit rating below AAA, and the investee country has a sovereign credit rating of AAA, but has a calculated CRP above 0.0% (which would imply greater risk than a country rated below AAA). For purposes of this analysis, the U.S. is treated as having a sovereign credit rating equivalent to AAA.

The country risk premium (CRP) is not the cost of equity capital (COE). The CRP is to be added to base COE. See Chapter 6 for proper application.

### Data Updated Through March 2017

| Investee Country | December 2016 Country Risk Premium (CRP) (%) | March 2017 Country Risk Premium (CRP) (%) | S&P Sovereign Credit Rating § | World Rank Out of 175* | MSCI Market Classification † | Euromoney Region ‡ | Regional Rank ‡ |
|---|---|---|---|---|---|---|---|
| Afghanistan | 17.9 | 17.7 | | 139 | | Asia | 23 out of 29 |
| Albania | 12.5 | 12.7 | B+ | 93 | | Central and Eastern Europe | 18 out of 25 |
| Algeria | 12.5 | 12.7 | | 91 | | Africa | 10 out of 51 |
| Angola | 14.9 | 15.0 | B | 121 | | Africa | 26 out of 51 |
| Argentina | 13.0 | 12.9 | B- | 96 | Frontier | Latin America | 13 out of 20 |
| Armenia | 10.1 | 10.3 | | 77 | | Asia | 15 out of 29 |
| Australia | 0.0 | 0.0 | AAA | 12 | Developed | Australasia | 2 out of 7 |
| Austria | 1.3 | 1.4 | AA+ | 13 | Developed | Western Europe | 9 out of 19 |
| Azerbaijan | 11.3 | 11.7 | BB+ | 85 | | Asia | 17 out of 29 |
| Bahamas | 8.6 | 8.4 | BB+ | 65 | | Caribbean | 3 out of 9 |
| Bahrain | 8.5 | 8.4 | BB- | 64 | Frontier | Middle East | 7 out of 13 |
| Bangladesh | 15.4 | 15.2 | BB- | 126 | Frontier | Asia | 20 out of 29 |
| Barbados | 10.3 | 11.4 | CCC+ | 82 | | Caribbean | 4 out of 9 |
| Belarus | 17.6 | 18.1 | B- | 143 | | Central and Eastern Europe | 23 out of 25 |
| Belgium | 2.6 | 2.6 | AA | 17 | Developed | Western Europe | 10 out of 19 |
| Belize | 13.5 | 13.7 | B- | 106 | | Latin America | 17 out of 20 |
| Benin | 19.3 | 19.4 | | 150 | | Africa | 37 out of 51 |
| Bermuda | 6.2 | 6.2 | A+ | 44 | | Caribbean | 1 out of 9 |
| Bhutan | 18.9 | 18.9 | | 148 | | Asia | 25 out of 29 |
| Bolivia | 12.0 | 12.4 | BB | 88 | | Latin America | 12 out of 20 |
| Bosnia & Herzegovina | 18.0 | 18.3 | B | 144 | | Central and Eastern Europe | 24 out of 25 |
| Botswana | 6.2 | 6.3 | A- | 48 | | Africa | 1 out of 51 |
| Brazil | 7.8 | 7.7 | BB | 59 | Emerging | Latin America | 7 out of 20 |
| Bulgaria | 7.6 | 7.9 | BB+ | 61 | | Central and Eastern Europe | 12 out of 25 |
| Burkina Faso | 16.4 | 16.5 | B- | 133 | | Africa | 33 out of 51 |
| Burundi | 28.3 | 28.4 | | 169 | | Africa | 47 out of 51 |
| Cambodia | 19.8 | 19.6 | | 151 | | Asia | 27 out of 29 |
| Cameroon | 15.1 | 15.1 | B | 124 | | Africa | 28 out of 51 |
| Canada | 0.0 | 0.0 | AAA | 9 | Developed | North America | 1 out of 2 |
| Cape Verde | 12.7 | 12.8 | B | 94 | | Africa | 12 out of 51 |
| Central African Republic | 31.8 | 31.9 | | 172 | | Africa | 49 out of 51 |
| Chad | 30.4 | 30.6 | | 171 | | Africa | 48 out of 51 |
| Chile | 2.1 | 2.4 | AA- | 16 | Emerging | Latin America | 1 out of 20 |
| China | 6.0 | 6.1 | AA- | 42 | Emerging | Asia | 7 out of 29 |
| Colombia | 6.0 | 6.1 | BBB | 41 | Emerging | Latin America | 4 out of 20 |
| Congo Republic | 14.6 | 14.6 | B- | 117 | | Africa | 24 out of 51 |
| Congo, DR | 15.9 | 15.9 | B- | 131 | | Africa | 32 out of 51 |
| Costa Rica | 9.0 | 9.3 | BB- | 71 | | Latin America | 8 out of 20 |
| Côte d'Ivoire | 12.5 | 12.7 | | 92 | | Africa | 11 out of 51 |
| Croatia | 8.1 | 8.1 | BB | 63 | Frontier | Central and Eastern Europe | 13 out of 25 |
| Cuba | 22.1 | 22.4 | | 160 | | Caribbean | 9 out of 9 |
| Cyprus | 5.7 | 5.9 | BB+ | 40 | | Central and Eastern Europe | 7 out of 25 |
| Czech Republic | 3.4 | 3.4 | AA- | 23 | Emerging | Central and Eastern Europe | 1 out of 25 |
| Denmark | 0.0 | 0.0 | AAA | 4 | Developed | Western Europe | 3 out of 19 |
| Djibouti | 39.7 | 37.6 | | 175 | | Africa | 51 out of 51 |
| Dominican Republic | 12.4 | 12.6 | BB- | 90 | | Caribbean | 5 out of 9 |
| Ecuador | 14.0 | 13.9 | B | 109 | | Latin America | 18 out of 20 |
| Egypt | 14.4 | 14.5 | B- | 116 | Emerging | Africa | 23 out of 51 |
| El Salvador | 11.4 | 11.3 | B- | 81 | | Latin America | 10 out of 20 |
| Equatorial Guinea | 24.7 | 24.8 | | 165 | | Africa | 45 out of 51 |

The country risk premium (CRP) is not the cost of equity capital (COE). The CRP is to be added to base COE. See Chapter 6 for proper application.

## Data Updated Through March 2017

| Investee Country | December 2016 Country Risk Premium (CRP) (%) | March 2017 Country Risk Premium (CRP) (%) | S&P Sovereign Credit Rating § | World Rank Out of 175∗ | MSCI Market Classification † | Euromoney Region ‡ | Regional Rank ‡ |
|---|---|---|---|---|---|---|---|
| Eritrea | 35.9 | 34.3 | | 173 | | Africa | 50 out of 51 |
| Estonia | 4.0 | 4.3 | AA- | 32 | Frontier | Central and Eastern Europe | 4 out of 25 |
| Ethiopia | 13.2 | 13.4 | B | 101 | | Africa | 16 out of 51 |
| Fiji | 18.6 | 18.6 | B+ | 147 | | Australasia | 5 out of 7 |
| Finland | 1.1 | 1.1 | AA+ | 11 | Developed | Western Europe | 8 out of 19 |
| France | 3.4 | 3.3 | AA | 22 | Developed | Western Europe | 12 out of 19 |
| Gabon | 11.0 | 11.5 | | 83 | | Africa | 7 out of 51 |
| Gambia | 17.1 | 17.2 | | 138 | | Africa | 34 out of 51 |
| Georgia | 9.8 | 10.1 | BB- | 74 | | Central and Eastern Europe | 15 out of 25 |
| Germany | 0.0 | 0.0 | AAA | 10 | Developed | Western Europe | 7 out of 19 |
| Ghana | 12.8 | 12.5 | B- | 89 | | Africa | 9 out of 51 |
| Greece | 13.9 | 13.8 | B- | 108 | Emerging | Western Europe | 19 out of 19 |
| Grenada | 13.5 | 13.7 | | 105 | | Caribbean | 7 out of 9 |
| Guatemala | 11.4 | 11.6 | BB | 84 | | Latin America | 11 out of 20 |
| Guinea | 20.8 | 20.9 | | 156 | | Africa | 41 out of 51 |
| Guinea-Bissau | 14.3 | 14.4 | | 115 | | Africa | 22 out of 51 |
| Guyana | 13.2 | 13.3 | | 100 | | Latin America | 15 out of 20 |
| Haiti | 23.6 | 21.7 | | 157 | | Caribbean | 8 out of 9 |
| Honduras | 12.9 | 13.0 | B+ | 98 | | Latin America | 14 out of 20 |
| Hong Kong | 0.0 | 0.0 | AAA | 14 | Developed | Asia | 2 out of 29 |
| Hungary | 7.4 | 7.6 | BBB- | 57 | Emerging | Central and Eastern Europe | 10 out of 25 |
| Iceland | 4.4 | 4.2 | A | 30 | | Western Europe | 15 out of 19 |
| India | 7.1 | 7.5 | BBB- | 55 | Emerging | Asia | 10 out of 29 |
| Indonesia | 7.9 | 8.0 | BB+ | 62 | Emerging | Asia | 11 out of 29 |
| Iran | 14.8 | 15.2 | | 125 | | Middle East | 10 out of 13 |
| Iraq | 16.7 | 16.8 | B- | 136 | | Middle East | 11 out of 13 |
| Ireland | 3.9 | 3.9 | A+ | 27 | Developed | Western Europe | 14 out of 19 |
| Israel | 3.8 | 3.9 | A+ | 28 | Developed | Middle East | 2 out of 13 |
| Italy | 6.8 | 6.7 | BBB- | 50 | Developed | Western Europe | 18 out of 19 |
| Jamaica | 12.9 | 13.6 | B | 104 | | Caribbean | 6 out of 9 |
| Japan | 3.7 | 3.8 | A+ | 25 | Developed | Asia | 5 out of 29 |
| Jordan | 10.0 | 10.3 | BB- | 76 | Frontier | Middle East | 8 out of 13 |
| Kazakhstan | 9.5 | 9.3 | BBB- | 70 | Frontier | Asia | 13 out of 29 |
| Kenya | 13.0 | 13.1 | B+ | 99 | Frontier | Africa | 15 out of 51 |
| Korea (North) | 35.3 | 34.9 | | 174 | | Asia | 29 out of 29 |
| Korea (South) | 3.0 | 3.1 | AA | 19 | Emerging | Asia | 4 out of 29 |
| Kuwait | 4.0 | 4.3 | AA | 31 | Frontier | Middle East | 3 out of 13 |
| Kyrgyz Republic | 18.1 | 18.1 | | 142 | | Central and Eastern Europe | 22 out of 25 |
| Laos | 22.4 | 21.9 | | 158 | | Asia | 28 out of 29 |
| Latvia | 6.0 | 6.2 | A- | 43 | | Central and Eastern Europe | 8 out of 25 |
| Lebanon | 14.7 | 14.2 | B- | 112 | Frontier | Middle East | 9 out of 13 |
| Lesotho | 18.3 | 18.4 | | 146 | | Africa | 36 out of 51 |
| Liberia | 13.6 | 13.7 | | 107 | | Africa | 17 out of 51 |
| Libya | 19.8 | 20.3 | | 153 | | Africa | 39 out of 51 |
| Lithuania | 5.2 | 5.4 | A- | 36 | Frontier | Central and Eastern Europe | 6 out of 25 |
| Luxembourg | 0.0 | 0.0 | AAA | 5 | | Western Europe | 4 out of 19 |
| Macedonia | 12.0 | 12.3 | BB- | 87 | | Central and Eastern Europe | 17 out of 25 |
| Madagascar | 14.5 | 15.1 | | 123 | | Africa | 27 out of 51 |
| Malawi | 14.2 | 14.3 | | 114 | | Africa | 21 out of 51 |
| Malaysia | 5.4 | 5.4 | A- | 35 | Emerging | Asia | 6 out of 29 |

§ S&P Credit Rating based on long-term foreign currency issuer rating. See http://www.standardandpoors.com/.
∗ World rank based on 175 countries covered by Euromoney. Ranking based on ascending order in which '1' equals the smallest country risk premium (CRP) and '175' equals the largest country risk premium (CRP).
† MSCI Market Classification based on MSCI Market Classification Framework. See http://www.msci.com/products/indexes/market_classification.html
‡ Regional classification based on Euromoney. Regional rankings based on ascending order in which '1' equals the smallest country risk premium (CRP) for each region.
Note: A CRP of 0.0% is assumed in the following cases: (i) when the investor country and the investee country both have an S&P sovereign credit rating of AAA; or (ii) when the investor country has an S&P credit rating of AAA, and the investee country has a sovereign credit rating below AAA, but has a calculated CRP below 0.0% (which would imply lower risk than a country rated AAA); or (iii) when the investor country has an S&P credit rating below AAA, and the investee country has a sovereign credit rating of AAA, but has a calculated CRP above 0.0% (which would imply greater risk than a country rated below AAA). For purposes of this analysis, the U.S. is treated as having a sovereign credit rating equivalent to AAA.

2017 Valuation Handbook – International Guide to Cost of Capital          Data Exhibit 4          Investor Perspective: Norway (NOK); Page 2 of 4

The country risk premium (CRP) is not the cost of equity capital (COE). The CRP is to be added to base COE. See Chapter 6 for proper application.

### Data Updated Through March 2017

| Investee Country | December 2016 Country Risk Premium (CRP) (%) | March 2017 Country Risk Premium (CRP) (%) | S&P Sovereign Credit Rating § | World Rank Out of 175∗ | MSCI Market Classification † | Euromoney Region ‡ | Regional Rank ‡ |
|---|---|---|---|---|---|---|---|
| Mali | 17.9 | 18.0 | | 141 | | Africa | 35 out of 51 |
| Malta | 3.7 | 3.9 | A- | 26 | | Western Europe | 13 out of 19 |
| Mauritania | 22.0 | 22.1 | | 159 | | Africa | 42 out of 51 |
| Mauritius | 8.8 | 8.9 | | 67 | Frontier | Asia | 12 out of 29 |
| Mexico | 5.3 | 5.5 | BBB+ | 37 | Emerging | Latin America | 2 out of 20 |
| Moldova | 16.3 | 16.9 | | 137 | | Central and Eastern Europe | 21 out of 25 |
| Mongolia | 14.5 | 15.0 | B- | 119 | | Asia | 18 out of 29 |
| Montenegro | 13.7 | 13.6 | B+ | 103 | | Central and Eastern Europe | 19 out of 25 |
| Morocco | 8.9 | 9.2 | BBB- | 69 | Frontier | Africa | 4 out of 51 |
| Mozambique | 15.6 | 15.6 | SD | 128 | | Africa | 29 out of 51 |
| Myanmar | 16.5 | 16.5 | | 134 | | Asia | 22 out of 29 |
| Namibia | 8.5 | 8.7 | | 66 | | Africa | 3 out of 51 |
| Nepal | 19.2 | 19.3 | | 149 | | Asia | 26 out of 29 |
| Netherlands | 0.0 | 0.0 | AAA | 6 | Developed | Western Europe | 5 out of 19 |
| New Zealand | 0.8 | 0.9 | AA | 8 | Developed | Australasia | 1 out of 7 |
| Nicaragua | 15.3 | 15.4 | B+ | 127 | | Latin America | 19 out of 20 |
| Niger | 14.9 | 15.0 | | 120 | | Africa | 25 out of 51 |
| Nigeria | 12.9 | 13.0 | B | 97 | Frontier | Africa | 14 out of 51 |
| Norway | 0.0 | 0.0 | AAA | 3 | Developed | Western Europe | 2 out of 19 |
| Oman | 6.2 | 6.3 | BBB- | 46 | Frontier | Middle East | 5 out of 13 |
| Pakistan | 15.0 | 15.0 | B | 122 | Frontier | Asia | 19 out of 29 |
| Panama | 6.9 | 7.0 | BBB | 52 | | Latin America | 6 out of 20 |
| Papua New Guinea | 14.5 | 14.7 | B+ | 118 | | Australasia | 3 out of 7 |
| Paraguay | 10.4 | 10.7 | BB | 80 | | Latin America | 9 out of 20 |
| Peru | 5.6 | 5.8 | BBB+ | 39 | Emerging | Latin America | 3 out of 20 |
| Philippines | 7.3 | 7.3 | BBB | 53 | Emerging | Asia | 9 out of 29 |
| Poland | 4.2 | 4.2 | BBB+ | 29 | Emerging | Central and Eastern Europe | 3 out of 25 |
| Portugal | 6.6 | 6.5 | BB+ | 49 | Developed | Western Europe | 17 out of 19 |
| Qatar | 3.1 | 3.2 | AA | 21 | Emerging | Middle East | 1 out of 13 |
| Romania | 7.4 | 7.5 | BBB- | 56 | Frontier | Central and Eastern Europe | 9 out of 25 |
| Russia | 9.7 | 9.1 | BB+ | 68 | Emerging | Central and Eastern Europe | 14 out of 25 |
| Rwanda | 15.7 | 15.8 | B | 130 | | Africa | 31 out of 51 |
| São Tomé & Príncipe | 22.1 | 22.7 | | 163 | | Africa | 43 out of 51 |
| Saudi Arabia | 6.5 | 6.3 | A- | 47 | | Middle East | 6 out of 13 |
| Senegal | 12.2 | 12.3 | B+ | 86 | | Africa | 8 out of 51 |
| Serbia | 10.3 | 10.1 | BB- | 75 | Frontier | Central and Eastern Europe | 16 out of 25 |
| Seychelles | 9.8 | 9.9 | | 73 | | Africa | 5 out of 51 |
| Sierra Leone | 15.7 | 15.8 | | 129 | | Africa | 30 out of 51 |
| Singapore | 0.0 | 0.0 | AAA | 1 | Developed | Asia | 1 out of 29 |
| Slovakia | 3.5 | 3.6 | A+ | 24 | | Central and Eastern Europe | 2 out of 25 |
| Slovenia | 4.9 | 5.0 | A | 34 | Frontier | Central and Eastern Europe | 5 out of 25 |
| Solomon Islands | 26.5 | 26.6 | | 168 | | Australasia | 6 out of 7 |
| Somalia | 24.7 | 24.9 | | 166 | | Africa | 46 out of 51 |
| South Africa | 7.5 | 7.8 | BBB- | 60 | Emerging | Africa | 2 out of 51 |
| Spain | 5.7 | 5.8 | BBB+ | 38 | Developed | Western Europe | 16 out of 19 |
| Sri Lanka | 9.7 | 9.5 | B+ | 72 | Frontier | Asia | 14 out of 29 |
| Sudan | 20.7 | 20.8 | | 154 | | Africa | 40 out of 51 |
| Suriname | 13.1 | 13.4 | B+ | 102 | | Latin America | 16 out of 20 |
| Swaziland | 19.0 | 20.1 | | 152 | | Africa | 38 out of 51 |
| Sweden | 0.0 | 0.0 | AAA | 7 | Developed | Western Europe | 6 out of 19 |

§ S&P Credit Rating based on long-term foreign currency issuer rating. See http://www.standardandpoors.com/.

∗ World rank based on 175 countries covered by Euromoney. Ranking based on ascending order in which '1' equals the smallest country risk premium (CRP) and '175' equals the largest country risk premium (CRP).

† MSCI Market Classification based on MSCI Market Classification Framework. See http://www.msci.com/products/indexes/market_classification.html.

‡ Regional classification based on Euromoney. Regional rankings based on ascending order in which '1' equals the smallest country risk premium (CRP) for each region.

Note: A CRP of 0.0% is assumed in the following cases: (i) when the investor country and the investee country both have an S&P sovereign credit rating of AAA; or (ii) when the investor country has an S&P credit rating of AAA, and the investee country has a sovereign credit rating below AAA, but has a calculated CRP below 0.0% (which would imply lower risk than a country rated AAA); or (iii) when the investor country has an S&P credit rating below AAA, and the investee country has a sovereign credit rating of AAA, but has a calculated CRP above 0.0% (which would imply greater risk than a country rated below AAA). For purposes of this analysis, the U.S. is treated as having a sovereign credit rating equivalent to AAA.

The country risk premium (CRP) is not the cost of equity capital (COE). The CRP is to be added to base COE. See Chapter 6 for proper application.

## Data Updated Through March 2017

| Investee Country | December 2016 Country Risk Premium (CRP) (%) | March 2017 Country Risk Premium (CRP) (%) | S&P Sovereign Credit Rating § | World Rank Out of 175* | MSCI Market Classification † | Euromoney Region ‡ | Regional Rank ‡ |
|---|---|---|---|---|---|---|---|
| Switzerland | 0.0 | 0.0 | AAA | 2 | Developed | Western Europe | 1 out of 19 |
| Syria | 25.5 | 25.8 | | 167 | | Middle East | 13 out of 13 |
| Taiwan | 2.7 | 2.8 | AA- | 18 | Emerging | Asia | 3 out of 29 |
| Tajikistan | 20.3 | 20.8 | | 155 | | Central and Eastern Europe | 25 out of 25 |
| Tanzania | 12.5 | 12.9 | | 95 | | Africa | 13 out of 51 |
| Thailand | 6.9 | 6.8 | BBB+ | 51 | Emerging | Asia | 8 out of 29 |
| Togo | 14.1 | 14.2 | | 113 | | Africa | 20 out of 51 |
| Tonga | 28.9 | 29.1 | | 170 | | Australasia | 7 out of 7 |
| Trinidad & Tobago | 7.3 | 7.3 | A- | 54 | | Caribbean | 2 out of 9 |
| Tunisia | 10.1 | 10.6 | | 79 | Frontier | Africa | 6 out of 51 |
| Turkey | 7.6 | 7.6 | BB | 58 | Emerging | Central and Eastern Europe | 11 out of 25 |
| Turkmenistan | 17.4 | 17.8 | | 140 | | Asia | 24 out of 29 |
| Uganda | 13.6 | 14.1 | B | 110 | | Africa | 18 out of 51 |
| Ukraine | 16.5 | 16.7 | B- | 135 | | Central and Eastern Europe | 20 out of 25 |
| United Arab Emirates | 4.5 | 4.6 | AA | 33 | Emerging | Middle East | 4 out of 13 |
| United Kingdom | 3.0 | 3.2 | AA | 20 | Developed | Western Europe | 11 out of 19 |
| United States | 0.0 | 0.0 | AA+ | 15 | Developed | North America | 2 out of 2 |
| Uruguay | 6.3 | 6.2 | BBB | 45 | | Latin America | 5 out of 20 |
| Uzbekistan | 16.6 | 16.2 | | 132 | | Asia | 21 out of 29 |
| Vanuatu | 18.3 | 18.4 | | 145 | | Australasia | 4 out of 7 |
| Venezuela | 22.1 | 22.7 | CCC | 162 | | Latin America | 20 out of 20 |
| Vietnam | 10.7 | 10.5 | BB- | 78 | Frontier | Asia | 16 out of 29 |
| Yemen | 22.4 | 22.6 | | 161 | | Middle East | 12 out of 13 |
| Zambia | 14.0 | 14.1 | B | 111 | | Africa | 19 out of 51 |
| Zimbabwe | 24.0 | 24.1 | | 164 | | Africa | 44 out of 51 |

## March 2017 Country Risk Premium (CRP) Summary Statistics:

| S&P Rating | Country Count | Average CRP (%) | Median CRP (%) | Min CRP (%) | Max CRP (%) |
|---|---|---|---|---|---|
| AAA ** | 12 | 0.0 | 0.0 | 0.0 | 0.0 |
| AA (AA+, AA, AA-) | 15 | 3.1 | 3.2 | 0.9 | 6.1 |
| A (A+, A, A-) | 14 | 5.1 | 5.2 | 3.6 | 7.3 |
| BBB (BBB+, BBB, BBB-) | 17 | 6.9 | 6.8 | 4.2 | 9.3 |
| BB (BB+, BB, BB-) | 22 | 9.8 | 9.7 | 5.9 | 15.2 |
| B+ − SD | 39 | 14.5 | 14.1 | 9.5 | 22.7 |
| Investment Grade ** | 58 | 4.1 | 4.2 | 0.0 | 9.3 |
| Non-Investment Grade ** | 61 | 12.8 | 13.0 | 5.9 | 22.7 |
| **MSCI Market Classification** | | | | | |
| Developed Markets | 23 | 1.9 | 0.9 | 0.0 | 6.7 |
| Emerging Markets | 23 | 6.5 | 6.1 | 2.4 | 14.5 |
| Frontier Markets | 22 | 9.6 | 9.4 | 4.3 | 15.2 |
| **Euromoney Region ‡** | | | | | |
| Africa | 51 | 17.0 | 15.0 | 6.3 | 37.6 |
| Asia | 29 | 11.7 | 10.3 | 0.0 | 34.9 |
| Australasia | 7 | 15.5 | 18.4 | 0.0 | 29.1 |
| Caribbean | 9 | 13.0 | 12.6 | 6.2 | 22.4 |
| Central and Eastern Europe | 25 | 10.1 | 8.1 | 3.4 | 20.8 |
| Latin America | 20 | 10.7 | 11.4 | 2.4 | 22.7 |
| Middle East | 13 | 10.9 | 8.4 | 3.2 | 25.8 |
| North America | 2 | 0.0 | 0.0 | 0.0 | 0.0 |
| Western Europe | 19 | 3.0 | 2.6 | 0.0 | 13.8 |

## CCR Base Cost of Equity Capital:

| Norway | COE (%) |
|---|---|
| March 2017 | 7.1 |
| December 2016 | 7.0 |

CCR base country-level COE for a Norway-based investor investing in Norway.

§ S&P Credit Rating based on long-term foreign currency issuer rating. See http://www.standardandpoors.com/.

* World rank based on 175 countries covered by Euromoney. Ranking based on ascending order in which '1' equals the smallest country risk premium (CRP) and '175' equals the largest country risk premium (CRP).

† MSCI Market Classification based on MSCI Market Classification Framework. See http://www.msci.com/products/indexes/market_classification.html.

‡ Regional classification based on Euromoney. Regional rankings based on ascending order in which '1' equals the smallest country risk premium (CRP) for each region.

** Investment grade based on S&P sovereign credit rating from AAA to BBB-. Non-Investment grade based on S&P sovereign credit rating from BB+ to SD. For purposes of this analysis, the U.S. is being treated as if it were rated AAA by S&P.

Note: A CRP of 0.0% is assumed in the following cases: (i) when the investor country and the investee country both have an S&P sovereign credit rating of AAA; or (ii) when the investor country has an S&P credit rating of AAA, and the investee country has a sovereign credit rating below AAA, but has a calculated CRP below 0.0% (which would imply lower risk than a country rated AAA); or (iii) when the investor country has an S&P credit rating below AAA, and the investee country has a sovereign credit rating of AAA, but has a calculated CRP above 0.0% (which would imply greater risk than a country rated below AAA). For purposes of this analysis, the U.S. is treated as having a sovereign credit rating equivalent to AAA.

The country risk premium (CRP) is not the cost of equity capital (COE). The CRP is to be added to base COE. See Chapter 6 for proper application.

## Data Updated Through March 2017

| Investee Country | December 2016 Country Risk Premium (CRP) (%) | March 2017 Country Risk Premium (CRP) (%) | S&P Sovereign Credit Rating § | World Rank Out of 175* | MSCI Market Classification † | Euromoney Region ‡ | Regional Rank ‡ |
|---|---|---|---|---|---|---|---|
| Afghanistan | 10.8 | 10.8 | | 139 | | Asia | 23 out of 29 |
| Albania | 5.3 | 5.6 | B+ | 93 | | Central and Eastern Europe | 18 out of 25 |
| Algeria | 5.4 | 5.6 | | 91 | | Africa | 10 out of 51 |
| Angola | 7.8 | 8.0 | B | 121 | | Africa | 26 out of 51 |
| Argentina | 5.9 | 5.8 | B- | 96 | Frontier | Latin America | 13 out of 20 |
| Armenia | 2.9 | 3.2 | | 77 | | Asia | 15 out of 29 |
| Australia | -6.3 | -6.4 | AAA | 12 | Developed | Australasia | 2 out of 7 |
| Austria | -6.1 | -6.1 | AA+ | 13 | Developed | Western Europe | 9 out of 19 |
| Azerbaijan | 4.1 | 4.6 | BB+ | 85 | | Asia | 17 out of 29 |
| Bahamas | 1.4 | 1.2 | BB+ | 65 | | Caribbean | 3 out of 9 |
| Bahrain | 1.3 | 1.2 | BB- | 64 | Frontier | Middle East | 7 out of 13 |
| Bangladesh | 8.3 | 8.2 | BB- | 126 | Frontier | Asia | 20 out of 29 |
| Barbados | 3.1 | 4.3 | CCC+ | 82 | | Caribbean | 4 out of 9 |
| Belarus | 10.5 | 11.2 | B- | 143 | | Central and Eastern Europe | 23 out of 25 |
| Belgium | -4.8 | -4.9 | AA | 17 | Developed | Western Europe | 10 out of 19 |
| Belize | 6.4 | 6.6 | B- | 106 | | Latin America | 17 out of 20 |
| Benin | 12.3 | 12.6 | | 150 | | Africa | 37 out of 51 |
| Bermuda | -1.0 | -1.1 | A+ | 44 | | Caribbean | 1 out of 9 |
| Bhutan | 11.9 | 12.1 | | 148 | | Asia | 25 out of 29 |
| Bolivia | 4.9 | 5.3 | BB | 88 | | Latin America | 12 out of 20 |
| Bosnia & Herzegovina | 11.0 | 11.4 | B | 144 | | Central and Eastern Europe | 24 out of 25 |
| Botswana | -1.0 | -1.0 | A- | 48 | | Africa | 1 out of 51 |
| Brazil | 0.5 | 0.5 | BB | 59 | Emerging | Latin America | 7 out of 20 |
| Bulgaria | 0.4 | 0.6 | BB+ | 61 | | Central and Eastern Europe | 12 out of 25 |
| Burkina Faso | 9.3 | 9.6 | B- | 133 | | Africa | 33 out of 51 |
| Burundi | 21.4 | 21.9 | | 169 | | Africa | 47 out of 51 |
| Cambodia | 12.8 | 12.8 | | 151 | | Asia | 27 out of 29 |
| Cameroon | 8.0 | 8.1 | B | 124 | | Africa | 28 out of 51 |
| Canada | -6.5 | -6.6 | AAA | 9 | Developed | North America | 1 out of 2 |
| Cape Verde | 5.5 | 5.7 | B | 94 | | Africa | 12 out of 51 |
| Central African Republic | 25.0 | 25.6 | | 172 | | Africa | 49 out of 51 |
| Chad | 23.7 | 24.2 | | 171 | | Africa | 48 out of 51 |
| Chile | -5.3 | -5.1 | AA- | 16 | Emerging | Latin America | 1 out of 20 |
| China | -1.3 | -1.2 | AA- | 42 | Emerging | Asia | 7 out of 29 |
| Colombia | -1.3 | -1.3 | BBB | 41 | Emerging | Latin America | 4 out of 20 |
| Congo Republic | 7.5 | 7.6 | B- | 117 | | Africa | 24 out of 51 |
| Congo, DR | 8.8 | 9.0 | B- | 131 | | Africa | 32 out of 51 |
| Costa Rica | 1.8 | 2.1 | BB- | 71 | | Latin America | 8 out of 20 |
| Côte d'Ivoire | 5.4 | 5.6 | | 92 | | Africa | 11 out of 51 |
| Croatia | 0.9 | 0.8 | BB | 63 | Frontier | Central and Eastern Europe | 13 out of 25 |
| Cuba | 15.2 | 15.6 | | 160 | | Caribbean | 9 out of 9 |
| Cyprus | -1.6 | -1.4 | BB+ | 40 | | Central and Eastern Europe | 7 out of 25 |
| Czech Republic | -4.0 | -4.0 | AA- | 23 | Emerging | Central and Eastern Europe | 1 out of 25 |
| Denmark | -7.1 | -7.2 | AAA | 4 | Developed | Western Europe | 3 out of 19 |
| Djibouti | 33.2 | 31.4 | | 175 | | Africa | 51 out of 51 |
| Dominican Republic | 5.2 | 5.5 | BB- | 90 | | Caribbean | 5 out of 9 |
| Ecuador | 6.8 | 6.8 | B | 109 | | Latin America | 18 out of 20 |
| Egypt | 7.3 | 7.4 | B- | 116 | Emerging | Africa | 23 out of 51 |
| El Salvador | 4.2 | 4.2 | B- | 81 | | Latin America | 10 out of 20 |
| Equatorial Guinea | 17.8 | 18.2 | | 165 | | Africa | 45 out of 51 |

§ S&P Credit Rating based on long-term foreign currency issuer rating. See http://www.standardandpoors.com/.

* World rank based on 175 countries covered by Euromoney. Ranking based on ascending order in which '1' equals the smallest country risk premium (CRP) and '175' equals the largest country risk premium (CRP).

† MSCI Market Classification based on MSCI Market Classification Framework. See http://www.msci.com/products/indexes/market_classification.html

‡ Regional classification based on Euromoney. Regional rankings based on ascending order in which '1' equals the smallest country risk premium (CRP) for each region.

Note: A CRP of 0.0% is assumed in the following cases: (i) when the investor country and the investee country both have an S&P sovereign credit rating of AAA; or (ii) when the investor country has an S&P credit rating of AAA, and the investee country has a sovereign credit rating below AAA, but has a calculated CRP below 0.0% (which would imply lower risk than a country rated AAA); or (iii) when the investor country has an S&P credit rating below AAA, and the investee country has a sovereign credit rating of AAA, but has a calculated CRP above 0.0% (which would imply greater risk than a country rated below AAA). For purposes of this analysis, the U.S. is treated as having a sovereign credit rating equivalent to AAA.

The country risk premium (CRP) is not the cost of equity capital (COE).  The CRP is to be added to base COE. See Chapter 6 for proper application.

### Data Updated Through March 2017

| Investee Country | December 2016 Country Risk Premium (CRP) (%) | March 2017 Country Risk Premium (CRP) (%) | S&P Sovereign Credit Rating § | World Rank Out of 175∗ | MSCI Market Classification † | Euromoney Region ‡ | Regional Rank ‡ |
|---|---|---|---|---|---|---|---|
| Eritrea | 29.3 | 28.0 | | 173 | | Africa | 50 out of 51 |
| Estonia | -3.4 | -3.1 | AA- | 32 | Frontier | Central and Eastern Europe | 4 out of 25 |
| Ethiopia | 6.1 | 6.3 | B | 101 | | Africa | 16 out of 51 |
| Fiji | 11.6 | 11.7 | B+ | 147 | | Australasia | 5 out of 7 |
| Finland | -6.3 | -6.4 | AA+ | 11 | Developed | Western Europe | 8 out of 19 |
| France | -3.9 | -4.1 | AA | 22 | Developed | Western Europe | 12 out of 19 |
| Gabon | 3.8 | 4.3 | | 83 | | Africa | 7 out of 51 |
| Gambia | 10.0 | 10.3 | | 138 | | Africa | 34 out of 51 |
| Georgia | 2.6 | 2.9 | BB- | 74 | | Central and Eastern Europe | 15 out of 25 |
| Germany | -6.3 | -6.5 | AAA | 10 | Developed | Western Europe | 7 out of 19 |
| Ghana | 5.6 | 5.4 | B- | 89 | | Africa | 9 out of 51 |
| Greece | 6.8 | 6.7 | B- | 108 | Emerging | Western Europe | 19 out of 19 |
| Grenada | 6.4 | 6.6 | | 105 | | Caribbean | 7 out of 9 |
| Guatemala | 4.3 | 4.4 | BB | 84 | | Latin America | 11 out of 20 |
| Guinea | 13.8 | 14.1 | | 156 | | Africa | 41 out of 51 |
| Guinea-Bissau | 7.2 | 7.4 | | 115 | | Africa | 22 out of 51 |
| Guyana | 6.0 | 6.2 | | 100 | | Latin America | 15 out of 20 |
| Haiti | 16.7 | 14.9 | | 157 | | Caribbean | 8 out of 9 |
| Honduras | 5.7 | 5.9 | B+ | 98 | | Latin America | 14 out of 20 |
| Hong Kong | -5.8 | -5.8 | AAA | 14 | Developed | Asia | 2 out of 29 |
| Hungary | 0.1 | 0.3 | BBB- | 57 | Emerging | Central and Eastern Europe | 10 out of 25 |
| Iceland | -3.0 | -3.2 | A | 30 | | Western Europe | 15 out of 19 |
| India | -0.1 | 0.2 | BBB- | 55 | Emerging | Asia | 10 out of 29 |
| Indonesia | 0.6 | 0.7 | BB+ | 62 | Emerging | Asia | 11 out of 29 |
| Iran | 7.7 | 8.2 | | 125 | | Middle East | 10 out of 13 |
| Iraq | 9.6 | 9.9 | B- | 136 | | Middle East | 11 out of 13 |
| Ireland | -3.5 | -3.5 | A+ | 27 | Developed | Western Europe | 14 out of 19 |
| Israel | -3.5 | -3.5 | A+ | 28 | Developed | Middle East | 2 out of 13 |
| Italy | -0.5 | -0.6 | BBB- | 50 | Developed | Western Europe | 18 out of 19 |
| Jamaica | 5.8 | 6.6 | B | 104 | | Caribbean | 6 out of 9 |
| Japan | -3.6 | -3.6 | A+ | 25 | Developed | Asia | 5 out of 29 |
| Jordan | 2.8 | 3.1 | BB- | 76 | Frontier | Middle East | 8 out of 13 |
| Kazakhstan | 2.3 | 2.0 | BBB- | 70 | Frontier | Asia | 13 out of 29 |
| Kenya | 5.8 | 6.0 | B+ | 99 | Frontier | Africa | 15 out of 51 |
| Korea (North) | 28.6 | 28.7 | | 174 | | Asia | 29 out of 29 |
| Korea (South) | -4.4 | -4.4 | AA | 19 | Emerging | Asia | 4 out of 29 |
| Kuwait | -3.3 | -3.1 | AA | 31 | Frontier | Middle East | 3 out of 13 |
| Kyrgyz Republic | 11.1 | 11.2 | | 142 | | Central and Eastern Europe | 22 out of 25 |
| Laos | 15.4 | 15.2 | | 158 | | Asia | 28 out of 29 |
| Latvia | -1.2 | -1.1 | A- | 43 | | Central and Eastern Europe | 8 out of 25 |
| Lebanon | 7.6 | 7.1 | B- | 112 | Frontier | Middle East | 9 out of 13 |
| Lesotho | 11.3 | 11.6 | | 146 | | Africa | 36 out of 51 |
| Liberia | 6.5 | 6.7 | | 107 | | Africa | 17 out of 51 |
| Libya | 12.8 | 13.5 | | 153 | | Africa | 39 out of 51 |
| Lithuania | -2.1 | -1.9 | A- | 36 | Frontier | Central and Eastern Europe | 6 out of 25 |
| Luxembourg | -6.8 | -6.9 | AAA | 5 | | Western Europe | 4 out of 19 |
| Macedonia | 4.9 | 5.2 | BB- | 87 | | Central and Eastern Europe | 17 out of 25 |
| Madagascar | 7.3 | 8.1 | | 123 | | Africa | 27 out of 51 |
| Malawi | 7.1 | 7.3 | | 114 | | Africa | 21 out of 51 |
| Malaysia | -1.9 | -2.0 | A- | 35 | Emerging | Asia | 6 out of 29 |

§ S&P Credit Rating based on long-term foreign currency issuer rating. See http://www.standardandpoors.com/.

∗ World rank based on 175 countries covered by Euromoney. Ranking based on ascending order in which '1' equals the smallest country risk premium (CRP) and '175' equals the largest country risk premium (CRP).

† MSCI Market Classification based on MSCI Market Classification Framework.  See http://www.msci.com/products/indexes/market_classification.html

‡ Regional classification based on Euromoney. Regional rankings based on ascending order in which '1' equals the smallest country risk premium (CRP) for each region.

Note: A CRP of 0.0% is assumed in the following cases: (i) when the investor country and the investee country both have an S&P sovereign credit rating of AAA; or (ii) when the investor country has an S&P sovereign credit rating of AAA, and the investee country has a sovereign credit rating below AAA, but has a calculated CRP below 0.0% (which would imply lower risk than a country rated AAA); or (iii) when the investor country has an S&P sovereign credit rating below AAA, and the investee country has a sovereign credit rating of AAA, but has a calculated CRP above 0.0% (which would imply greater risk than a country rated below AAA). For purposes of this analysis, the U.S. is treated as having a sovereign credit rating equivalent to AAA.

The country risk premium (CRP) is not the cost of equity capital (COE). The CRP is to be added to base COE. See Chapter 6 for proper application.

### Data Updated Through March 2017

| Investee Country | December 2016 Country Risk Premium (CRP) (%) | March 2017 Country Risk Premium (CRP) (%) | S&P Sovereign Credit Rating § | World Rank Out of 175* | MSCI Market Classification † | Euromoney Region ‡ | Regional Rank ‡ |
|---|---|---|---|---|---|---|---|
| Mali | 10.9 | 11.2 | | 141 | | Africa | 35 out of 51 |
| Malta | -3.6 | -3.6 | A- | 26 | | Western Europe | 13 out of 19 |
| Mauritania | 15.0 | 15.4 | | 159 | | Africa | 42 out of 51 |
| Mauritius | 1.6 | 1.7 | | 67 | Frontier | Asia | 12 out of 29 |
| Mexico | -2.0 | -1.9 | BBB+ | 37 | Emerging | Latin America | 2 out of 20 |
| Moldova | 9.3 | 9.9 | | 137 | | Central and Eastern Europe | 21 out of 25 |
| Mongolia | 7.4 | 8.0 | B- | 119 | | Asia | 18 out of 29 |
| Montenegro | 6.6 | 6.6 | B+ | 103 | | Central and Eastern Europe | 19 out of 25 |
| Morocco | 1.6 | 1.9 | BBB- | 69 | Frontier | Africa | 4 out of 51 |
| Mozambique | 8.5 | 8.6 | SD | 128 | | Africa | 29 out of 51 |
| Myanmar | 9.5 | 9.6 | | 134 | | Asia | 22 out of 29 |
| Namibia | 1.2 | 1.5 | | 66 | | Africa | 3 out of 51 |
| Nepal | 12.2 | 12.5 | | 149 | | Asia | 26 out of 29 |
| Netherlands | -6.7 | -6.9 | AAA | 6 | Developed | Western Europe | 5 out of 19 |
| New Zealand | -6.6 | -6.6 | AA | 8 | Developed | Australasia | 1 out of 7 |
| Nicaragua | 8.2 | 8.4 | B+ | 127 | | Latin America | 19 out of 20 |
| Niger | 7.8 | 8.0 | | 120 | | Africa | 25 out of 51 |
| Nigeria | 5.7 | 5.9 | B | 97 | Frontier | Africa | 14 out of 51 |
| Norway | -7.4 | -7.6 | AAA | 3 | Developed | Western Europe | 2 out of 19 |
| Oman | -1.1 | -1.0 | BBB- | 46 | Frontier | Middle East | 5 out of 13 |
| Pakistan | 7.9 | 8.0 | B | 122 | Frontier | Asia | 19 out of 29 |
| Panama | -0.4 | -0.3 | BBB | 52 | | Latin America | 6 out of 20 |
| Papua New Guinea | 7.4 | 7.7 | B+ | 118 | | Australasia | 3 out of 7 |
| Paraguay | 3.2 | 3.6 | BB | 80 | | Latin America | 9 out of 20 |
| Peru | -1.7 | -1.5 | BBB+ | 39 | Emerging | Latin America | 3 out of 20 |
| Philippines | 0.0 | 0.0 | BBB | 53 | Emerging | Asia | 9 out of 29 |
| Poland | -3.1 | -3.2 | BBB+ | 29 | Emerging | Central and Eastern Europe | 3 out of 25 |
| Portugal | -0.7 | -0.8 | BB+ | 49 | Developed | Western Europe | 17 out of 19 |
| Qatar | -4.3 | -4.2 | AA | 21 | Emerging | Middle East | 1 out of 13 |
| Romania | 0.1 | 0.3 | BBB- | 56 | Frontier | Central and Eastern Europe | 9 out of 25 |
| Russia | 2.4 | 1.9 | BB+ | 68 | Emerging | Central and Eastern Europe | 14 out of 25 |
| Rwanda | 8.6 | 8.8 | B | 130 | | Africa | 31 out of 51 |
| São Tomé & Príncipe | 15.1 | 16.0 | | 163 | | Africa | 43 out of 51 |
| Saudi Arabia | -0.7 | -1.0 | A- | 47 | | Middle East | 6 out of 13 |
| Senegal | 5.1 | 5.2 | B+ | 86 | | Africa | 8 out of 51 |
| Serbia | 3.1 | 3.0 | BB- | 75 | Frontier | Central and Eastern Europe | 16 out of 25 |
| Seychelles | 2.6 | 2.7 | | 73 | | Africa | 5 out of 51 |
| Sierra Leone | 8.6 | 8.8 | | 129 | | Africa | 30 out of 51 |
| Singapore | -7.6 | -7.7 | AAA | 1 | Developed | Asia | 1 out of 29 |
| Slovakia | -3.9 | -3.8 | A+ | 24 | | Central and Eastern Europe | 2 out of 25 |
| Slovenia | -2.4 | -2.4 | A | 34 | Frontier | Central and Eastern Europe | 5 out of 25 |
| Solomon Islands | 19.6 | 20.0 | | 168 | | Australasia | 6 out of 7 |
| Somalia | 17.8 | 18.2 | | 166 | | Africa | 46 out of 51 |
| South Africa | 0.2 | 0.5 | BBB- | 60 | Emerging | Africa | 2 out of 51 |
| Spain | -1.6 | -1.5 | BBB+ | 38 | Developed | Western Europe | 16 out of 19 |
| Sri Lanka | 2.5 | 2.3 | B+ | 72 | Frontier | Asia | 14 out of 29 |
| Sudan | 13.7 | 14.0 | | 154 | | Africa | 40 out of 51 |
| Suriname | 6.0 | 6.4 | B+ | 102 | | Latin America | 16 out of 20 |
| Swaziland | 12.0 | 13.3 | | 152 | | Africa | 38 out of 51 |
| Sweden | -6.7 | -6.8 | AAA | 7 | Developed | Western Europe | 6 out of 19 |

§ S&P Credit Rating based on long-term foreign currency issuer rating. See http://www.standardandpoors.com/.

* World rank based on 175 countries covered by Euromoney. Ranking based on ascending order in which '1' equals the smallest country risk premium (CRP) and '175' equals the largest country risk premium (CRP).

† MSCI Market Classification based on MSCI Market Classification Framework. See http://www.msci.com/products/indexes/market_classification.html

‡ Regional classification based on Euromoney. Regional rankings based on ascending order in which '1' equals the smallest country risk premium (CRP) for each region.

Note: A CRP of 0.0% is assumed in the following cases: (i) when the investor country and the investee country both have an S&P sovereign credit rating of AAA; or (ii) when the investor country has an S&P credit rating of AAA, and the investee country has a sovereign credit rating below AAA, but has a calculated CRP below 0.0% (which would imply lower risk than a country rated AAA); or (iii) when the investor country has an S&P credit rating below AAA, and the investee country has a sovereign credit rating of AAA, but has a calculated CRP above 0.0% (which would imply greater risk than a country rated AAA). For purposes of this analysis, the U.S. is treated as having a sovereign credit rating equivalent to AAA.

The country risk premium (CRP) is not the cost of equity capital (COE). The CRP is to be added to base COE. See Chapter 6 for proper application.

## Data Updated Through March 2017

| Investee Country | December 2016 Country Risk Premium (CRP) (%) | March 2017 Country Risk Premium (CRP) (%) | S&P Sovereign Credit Rating § | World Rank Out of 175∗ | MSCI Market Classification † | Euromoney Region ‡ | Regional Rank ‡ |
|---|---|---|---|---|---|---|---|
| Switzerland | -7.4 | -7.6 | AAA | 2 | Developed | Western Europe | 1 out of 19 |
| Syria | 18.6 | 19.2 | | 167 | | Middle East | 13 out of 13 |
| Taiwan | -4.7 | -4.7 | AA- | 18 | Emerging | Asia | 3 out of 29 |
| Tajikistan | 13.3 | 14.0 | | 155 | | Central and Eastern Europe | 25 out of 25 |
| Tanzania | 5.4 | 5.8 | | 95 | | Africa | 13 out of 51 |
| Thailand | -0.4 | -0.5 | BBB+ | 51 | Emerging | Asia | 8 out of 29 |
| Togo | 7.0 | 7.2 | | 113 | | Africa | 20 out of 51 |
| Tonga | 22.1 | 22.6 | | 170 | | Australasia | 7 out of 7 |
| Trinidad & Tobago | 0.0 | 0.1 | A- | 54 | | Caribbean | 2 out of 9 |
| Tunisia | 2.9 | 3.4 | | 79 | Frontier | Africa | 6 out of 51 |
| Turkey | 0.4 | 0.3 | BB | 58 | Emerging | Central and Eastern Europe | 11 out of 25 |
| Turkmenistan | 10.4 | 11.0 | | 140 | | Asia | 24 out of 29 |
| Uganda | 6.5 | 7.0 | B | 110 | | Africa | 18 out of 51 |
| Ukraine | 9.4 | 9.7 | B- | 135 | | Central and Eastern Europe | 20 out of 25 |
| United Arab Emirates | -2.9 | -2.8 | AA | 33 | Emerging | Middle East | 4 out of 13 |
| United Kingdom | -4.4 | -4.3 | AA | 20 | Developed | Western Europe | 11 out of 19 |
| United States | -5.5 | -5.5 | AA+ | 15 | Developed | North America | 2 out of 2 |
| Uruguay | -1.0 | -1.1 | BBB | 45 | | Latin America | 5 out of 20 |
| Uzbekistan | 9.6 | 9.2 | | 132 | | Asia | 21 out of 29 |
| Vanuatu | 11.3 | 11.5 | | 145 | | Australasia | 4 out of 7 |
| Venezuela | 15.1 | 15.9 | CCC | 162 | | Latin America | 20 out of 20 |
| Vietnam | 3.5 | 3.3 | BB- | 78 | Frontier | Asia | 16 out of 29 |
| Yemen | 15.4 | 15.9 | | 161 | | Middle East | 12 out of 13 |
| Zambia | 6.9 | 7.1 | B | 111 | | Africa | 19 out of 51 |
| Zimbabwe | 17.1 | 17.4 | | 164 | | Africa | 44 out of 51 |

## March 2017 Country Risk Premium (CRP) Summary Statistics:

| S&P Rating | Country Count | Average CRP (%) | Median CRP (%) | Min CRP (%) | Max CRP (%) |
|---|---|---|---|---|---|
| AAA ∗∗ | 12 | -6.8 | -6.8 | -7.7 | -5.5 |
| AA (AA+, AA, AA-) | 15 | -4.3 | -4.3 | -6.6 | -1.2 |
| A (A+, A, A-) | 14 | -2.3 | -2.2 | -3.8 | 0.1 |
| BBB (BBB+, BBB, BBB-) | 17 | -0.4 | -0.5 | -3.2 | 2.0 |
| BB (BB+, BB, BB-) | 22 | 2.6 | 2.5 | -1.4 | 8.2 |
| B+ − SD | 39 | 7.5 | 7.1 | 2.3 | 15.9 |
| Investment Grade ∗∗ | 58 | -3.2 | -3.2 | -7.7 | 2.0 |
| Non-Investment Grade ∗∗ | 61 | 5.7 | 5.9 | -1.4 | 15.9 |
| **MSCI Market Classification** | | | | | |
| Developed Markets | 23 | -5.2 | -6.1 | -7.7 | -0.6 |
| Emerging Markets | 23 | -0.8 | -1.2 | -5.1 | 7.4 |
| Frontier Markets | 22 | 2.4 | 2.2 | -3.1 | 8.2 |
| **Euromoney Region ‡** | | | | | |
| Africa | 51 | 10.1 | 8.0 | -1.0 | 31.4 |
| Asia | 29 | 4.6 | 3.2 | -7.7 | 28.7 |
| Australasia | 7 | 8.6 | 11.5 | -6.6 | 22.6 |
| Caribbean | 9 | 6.0 | 5.5 | -1.1 | 15.6 |
| Central and Eastern Europe | 25 | 3.0 | 0.8 | -4.0 | 14.0 |
| Latin America | 20 | 3.6 | 4.3 | -5.1 | 15.9 |
| Middle East | 13 | 3.8 | 1.2 | -4.2 | 19.2 |
| North America | 2 | -6.0 | -6.0 | -6.6 | -5.5 |
| Western Europe | 19 | -4.3 | -4.9 | -7.6 | 6.7 |

### CCR Base Cost of Equity Capital:

| Philippines | COE (%) |
|---|---|
| March 2017 | 16.0 |
| December 2016 | 16.0 |

CCR base country-level COE for a Philippines-based investor investing in the Philippines.

§ S&P Credit Rating based on long-term foreign currency issuer rating. See http://www.standardandpoors.com/.

∗ World rank based on 175 countries covered by Euromoney. Ranking based on ascending order in which '1' equals the smallest country risk premium (CRP) and '175' equals the largest country risk premium (CRP).

† MSCI Market Classification based on MSCI Market Classification Framework. See http://www.msci.com/products/indexes/market_classification.html

‡ Regional classification based on Euromoney. Regional rankings based on ascending order in which '1' equals the smallest country risk premium (CRP) for each region.

∗∗ Investment grade based on S&P sovereign credit rating from AAA to BBB-. Non-Investment grade based on S&P sovereign credit rating from BB+ to SD. For purposes of this analysis, the U.S. is being treated as if it were rated AAA by S&P.

Note: A CRP of 0.0% is assumed in the following cases: (i) when the investor country and the investee country both have an S&P sovereign credit rating of AAA; or (ii) when the investor country has an S&P credit rating of AAA, and the investee country has a sovereign credit rating below AAA, but has a calculated CRP below 0.0% (which would imply lower risk than a country rated AAA); or (iii) when the investor country has an S&P credit rating below AAA, and the investee country has a sovereign credit rating of AAA, but has a calculated CRP above 0.0% (which would imply greater risk than a country rated below AAA). For purposes of this analysis, the U.S. is treated as having a sovereign credit rating equivalent to AAA.

The country risk premium (CRP) is not the cost of equity capital (COE).  The CRP is to be added to base COE. See Chapter 6 for proper application.

## Data Updated Through March 2017

| Investee Country | December 2016 Country Risk Premium (CRP) (%) | March 2017 Country Risk Premium (CRP) (%) | S&P Sovereign Credit Rating § | World Rank Out of 175∗ | MSCI Market Classification † | Euromoney Region ‡ | Regional Rank ‡ |
|---|---|---|---|---|---|---|---|
| Afghanistan | 12.3 | 12.0 | | 139 | | Asia | 23 out of 29 |
| Albania | 7.4 | 7.6 | B+ | 93 | | Central and Eastern Europe | 18 out of 25 |
| Algeria | 7.5 | 7.5 | | 91 | | Africa | 10 out of 51 |
| Angola | 9.6 | 9.6 | B | 121 | | Africa | 26 out of 51 |
| Argentina | 8.0 | 7.7 | B- | 96 | Frontier | Latin America | 13 out of 20 |
| Armenia | 5.3 | 5.5 | | 77 | | Asia | 15 out of 29 |
| Australia | -2.8 | -2.7 | AAA | 12 | Developed | Australasia | 2 out of 7 |
| Austria | -2.6 | -2.5 | AA+ | 13 | Developed | Western Europe | 9 out of 19 |
| Azerbaijan | 6.4 | 6.7 | BB+ | 85 | | Asia | 17 out of 29 |
| Bahamas | 4.0 | 3.8 | BB+ | 65 | | Caribbean | 3 out of 9 |
| Bahrain | 3.9 | 3.8 | BB- | 64 | Frontier | Middle East | 7 out of 13 |
| Bangladesh | 10.0 | 9.8 | BB- | 126 | Frontier | Asia | 20 out of 29 |
| Barbados | 5.5 | 6.4 | CCC+ | 82 | | Caribbean | 4 out of 9 |
| Belarus | 12.0 | 12.3 | B- | 143 | | Central and Eastern Europe | 23 out of 25 |
| Belgium | -1.5 | -1.4 | AA | 17 | Developed | Western Europe | 10 out of 19 |
| Belize | 8.4 | 8.4 | B- | 106 | | Latin America | 17 out of 20 |
| Benin | 13.6 | 13.5 | | 150 | | Africa | 37 out of 51 |
| Bermuda | 1.8 | 1.8 | A+ | 44 | | Caribbean | 1 out of 9 |
| Bhutan | 13.3 | 13.0 | | 148 | | Asia | 25 out of 29 |
| Bolivia | 7.0 | 7.3 | BB | 88 | | Latin America | 12 out of 20 |
| Bosnia & Herzegovina | 12.5 | 12.5 | B | 144 | | Central and Eastern Europe | 24 out of 25 |
| Botswana | 1.8 | 1.9 | A- | 48 | | Africa | 1 out of 51 |
| Brazil | 3.2 | 3.2 | BB | 59 | Emerging | Latin America | 7 out of 20 |
| Bulgaria | 3.1 | 3.3 | BB+ | 61 | | Central and Eastern Europe | 12 out of 25 |
| Burkina Faso | 11.0 | 10.9 | B- | 133 | | Africa | 33 out of 51 |
| Burundi | 21.7 | 21.4 | | 169 | | Africa | 47 out of 51 |
| Cambodia | 14.1 | 13.6 | | 151 | | Asia | 27 out of 29 |
| Cameroon | 9.8 | 9.7 | B | 124 | | Africa | 28 out of 51 |
| Canada | -2.9 | -2.9 | AAA | 9 | Developed | North America | 1 out of 2 |
| Cape Verde | 7.6 | 7.6 | B | 94 | | Africa | 12 out of 51 |
| Central African Republic | 24.8 | 24.5 | | 172 | | Africa | 49 out of 51 |
| Chad | 23.6 | 23.3 | | 171 | | Africa | 48 out of 51 |
| Chile | -1.9 | -1.6 | AA- | 16 | Emerging | Latin America | 1 out of 20 |
| China | 1.6 | 1.7 | AA- | 42 | Emerging | Asia | 7 out of 29 |
| Colombia | 1.6 | 1.7 | BBB | 41 | Emerging | Latin America | 4 out of 20 |
| Congo Republic | 9.4 | 9.2 | B- | 117 | | Africa | 24 out of 51 |
| Congo, DR | 10.5 | 10.4 | B- | 131 | | Africa | 32 out of 51 |
| Costa Rica | 4.4 | 4.6 | BB- | 71 | | Latin America | 8 out of 20 |
| Côte d'Ivoire | 7.5 | 7.5 | | 92 | | Africa | 11 out of 51 |
| Croatia | 3.5 | 3.5 | BB | 63 | Frontier | Central and Eastern Europe | 13 out of 25 |
| Cuba | 16.2 | 16.1 | | 160 | | Caribbean | 9 out of 9 |
| Cyprus | 1.4 | 1.6 | BB+ | 40 | | Central and Eastern Europe | 7 out of 25 |
| Czech Republic | -0.8 | -0.6 | AA- | 23 | Emerging | Central and Eastern Europe | 1 out of 25 |
| Denmark | -3.5 | -3.4 | AAA | 4 | Developed | Western Europe | 3 out of 19 |
| Djibouti | 32.0 | 29.5 | | 175 | | Africa | 51 out of 51 |
| Dominican Republic | 7.4 | 7.4 | BB- | 90 | | Caribbean | 5 out of 9 |
| Ecuador | 8.8 | 8.6 | B | 109 | | Latin America | 18 out of 20 |
| Egypt | 9.2 | 9.1 | B- | 116 | Emerging | Africa | 23 out of 51 |
| El Salvador | 6.5 | 6.3 | B- | 81 | | Latin America | 10 out of 20 |
| Equatorial Guinea | 18.4 | 18.2 | | 165 | | Africa | 45 out of 51 |

§ S&P Credit Rating based on long-term foreign currency issuer rating. See http://www.standardandpoors.com/.

∗ World rank based on 175 countries covered by Euromoney. Ranking based on ascending order in which '1' equals the smallest country risk premium (CRP) and '175' equals the largest country risk premium (CRP).

† MSCI Market Classification based on MSCI Market Classification Framework.  See http://www.msci.com/products/indexes/market_classification.html

‡ Regional classification based on Euromoney. Regional rankings based on ascending order in which '1' equals the smallest country risk premium (CRP) for each region.

Note: A CRP of 0.0% is assumed in the following cases: (i) when the investor country and the investee country both have an S&P sovereign credit rating of AAA; or (ii) when the investor country has an S&P credit rating of AAA, and the investee country has a sovereign credit rating below AAA, but has a calculated CRP below 0.0% (which would imply lower risk than a country rated AAA); or (iii) when the investor country has an S&P credit rating below AAA, and the investee country has a sovereign credit rating of AAA, but has a calculated CRP above 0.0% (which would imply greater risk than a country rated below AAA). For purposes of this analysis, the U.S. is treated as having a sovereign credit rating equivalent to AAA.

The country risk premium (CRP) is not the cost of equity capital (COE).  The CRP is to be added to base COE. See Chapter 6 for proper application.

## Data Updated Through March 2017

| Investee Country | December 2016 Country Risk Premium (CRP) (%) | March 2017 Country Risk Premium (CRP) (%) | S&P Sovereign Credit Rating § | World Rank Out of 175∗ | MSCI Market Classification † | Euromoney Region ‡ | Regional Rank ‡ |
|---|---|---|---|---|---|---|---|
| Eritrea | 28.6 | 26.6 | | 173 | | Africa | 50 out of 51 |
| Estonia | -0.2 | 0.1 | AA- | 32 | Frontier | Central and Eastern Europe | 4 out of 25 |
| Ethiopia | 8.1 | 8.1 | B | 101 | | Africa | 16 out of 51 |
| Fiji | 13.0 | 12.7 | B+ | 147 | | Australasia | 5 out of 7 |
| Finland | -2.8 | -2.7 | AA+ | 11 | Developed | Western Europe | 8 out of 19 |
| France | -0.7 | -0.8 | AA | 22 | Developed | Western Europe | 12 out of 19 |
| Gabon | 6.1 | 6.5 | | 83 | | Africa | 7 out of 51 |
| Gambia | 11.6 | 11.5 | | 138 | | Africa | 34 out of 51 |
| Georgia | 5.0 | 5.3 | BB- | 74 | | Central and Eastern Europe | 15 out of 25 |
| Germany | -2.8 | -2.7 | AAA | 10 | Developed | Western Europe | 7 out of 19 |
| Ghana | 7.7 | 7.3 | B- | 89 | | Africa | 9 out of 51 |
| Greece | 8.7 | 8.5 | B- | 108 | Emerging | Western Europe | 19 out of 19 |
| Grenada | 8.4 | 8.4 | | 105 | | Caribbean | 7 out of 9 |
| Guatemala | 6.5 | 6.5 | BB | 84 | | Latin America | 11 out of 20 |
| Guinea | 14.9 | 14.8 | | 156 | | Africa | 41 out of 51 |
| Guinea-Bissau | 9.1 | 9.1 | | 115 | | Africa | 22 out of 51 |
| Guyana | 8.1 | 8.1 | | 100 | | Latin America | 15 out of 20 |
| Haiti | 17.5 | 15.5 | | 157 | | Caribbean | 8 out of 9 |
| Honduras | 7.8 | 7.8 | B+ | 98 | | Latin America | 14 out of 20 |
| Hong Kong | -2.3 | -2.2 | AAA | 14 | Developed | Asia | 2 out of 29 |
| Hungary | 2.8 | 3.0 | BBB- | 57 | Emerging | Central and Eastern Europe | 10 out of 25 |
| Iceland | 0.1 | 0.1 | A | 30 | | Western Europe | 15 out of 19 |
| India | 2.6 | 3.0 | BBB- | 55 | Emerging | Asia | 10 out of 29 |
| Indonesia | 3.3 | 3.4 | BB+ | 62 | Emerging | Asia | 11 out of 29 |
| Iran | 9.6 | 9.7 | | 125 | | Middle East | 10 out of 13 |
| Iraq | 11.2 | 11.2 | B- | 136 | | Middle East | 11 out of 13 |
| Ireland | -0.3 | -0.2 | A+ | 27 | Developed | Western Europe | 14 out of 19 |
| Israel | -0.3 | -0.2 | A+ | 28 | Developed | Middle East | 2 out of 13 |
| Italy | 2.3 | 2.2 | BBB- | 50 | Developed | Western Europe | 18 out of 19 |
| Jamaica | 7.8 | 8.4 | B | 104 | | Caribbean | 6 out of 9 |
| Japan | -0.4 | -0.3 | A+ | 25 | Developed | Asia | 5 out of 29 |
| Jordan | 5.2 | 5.4 | BB- | 76 | Frontier | Middle East | 8 out of 13 |
| Kazakhstan | 4.8 | 4.5 | BBB- | 70 | Frontier | Asia | 13 out of 29 |
| Kenya | 7.9 | 7.9 | B+ | 99 | Frontier | Africa | 15 out of 51 |
| Korea (North) | 28.0 | 27.2 | | 174 | | Asia | 29 out of 29 |
| Korea (South) | -1.1 | -1.0 | AA | 19 | Emerging | Asia | 4 out of 29 |
| Kuwait | -0.2 | 0.1 | AA | 31 | Frontier | Middle East | 3 out of 13 |
| Kyrgyz Republic | 12.5 | 12.3 | | 142 | | Central and Eastern Europe | 22 out of 25 |
| Laos | 16.3 | 15.7 | | 158 | | Asia | 28 out of 29 |
| Latvia | 1.7 | 1.8 | A- | 43 | | Central and Eastern Europe | 8 out of 25 |
| Lebanon | 9.5 | 8.8 | B- | 112 | Frontier | Middle East | 9 out of 13 |
| Lesotho | 12.7 | 12.6 | | 146 | | Africa | 36 out of 51 |
| Liberia | 8.5 | 8.4 | | 107 | | Africa | 17 out of 51 |
| Libya | 14.1 | 14.3 | | 153 | | Africa | 39 out of 51 |
| Lithuania | 0.9 | 1.1 | A- | 36 | Frontier | Central and Eastern Europe | 6 out of 25 |
| Luxembourg | -3.2 | -3.1 | AAA | 5 | | Western Europe | 4 out of 19 |
| Macedonia | 7.0 | 7.2 | BB- | 87 | | Central and Eastern Europe | 17 out of 25 |
| Madagascar | 9.2 | 9.6 | | 123 | | Africa | 27 out of 51 |
| Malawi | 9.0 | 8.9 | | 114 | | Africa | 21 out of 51 |
| Malaysia | 1.1 | 1.1 | A- | 35 | Emerging | Asia | 6 out of 29 |

§ S&P Credit Rating based on long-term foreign currency issuer rating. See http://www.standardandpoors.com/.

∗ World rank based on 175 countries covered by Euromoney. Ranking based on ascending order in which '1' equals the smallest country risk premium (CRP) and '175' equals the largest country risk premium (CRP).

† MSCI Market Classification based on MSCI Market Classification Framework.  See http://www.msci.com/products/indexes/market_classification.html

‡ Regional classification based on Euromoney. Regional rankings based on ascending order in which '1' equals the smallest country risk premium (CRP) for each region.

Note: A CRP of 0.0% is assumed in the following cases: (i) when the investor country and the investee country both have an S&P sovereign credit rating of AAA; or (ii) when the investor country has an S&P credit rating of AAA, and the investee country has a sovereign credit rating below AAA, but has a calculated CRP below 0.0% (which would imply lower risk than a country rated AAA); or (iii) when the investor country has an S&P credit rating below AAA, and the investee country has a sovereign credit rating of AAA, but has a calculated CRP above 0.0% (which would imply greater risk than a country rated below AAA). For purposes of this analysis, the U.S. is treated as having a sovereign credit rating equivalent to AAA.

The country risk premium (CRP) is not the cost of equity capital (COE). The CRP is to be added to base COE. See Chapter 6 for proper application.

## Data Updated Through March 2017

| Investee Country | December 2016 Country Risk Premium (CRP) (%) | March 2017 Country Risk Premium (CRP) (%) | S&P Sovereign Credit Rating § | World Rank Out of 175* | MSCI Market Classification † | Euromoney Region ‡ | Regional Rank ‡ |
|---|---|---|---|---|---|---|---|
| Mali | 12.3 | 12.3 | | 141 | | Africa | 35 out of 51 |
| Malta | -0.4 | -0.3 | A- | 26 | | Western Europe | 13 out of 19 |
| Mauritania | 16.0 | 15.8 | | 159 | | Africa | 42 out of 51 |
| Mauritius | 4.2 | 4.2 | | 67 | Frontier | Asia | 12 out of 29 |
| Mexico | 1.0 | 1.2 | BBB+ | 37 | Emerging | Latin America | 2 out of 20 |
| Moldova | 10.9 | 11.2 | | 137 | | Central and Eastern Europe | 21 out of 25 |
| Mongolia | 9.3 | 9.5 | B- | 119 | | Asia | 18 out of 29 |
| Montenegro | 8.6 | 8.3 | B+ | 103 | | Central and Eastern Europe | 19 out of 25 |
| Morocco | 4.2 | 4.4 | BBB- | 69 | Frontier | Africa | 4 out of 51 |
| Mozambique | 10.3 | 10.1 | SD | 128 | | Africa | 29 out of 51 |
| Myanmar | 11.1 | 10.9 | | 134 | | Asia | 22 out of 29 |
| Namibia | 3.9 | 4.0 | | 66 | | Africa | 3 out of 51 |
| Nepal | 13.5 | 13.4 | | 149 | | Asia | 26 out of 29 |
| Netherlands | -3.2 | -3.1 | AAA | 6 | Developed | Western Europe | 5 out of 19 |
| New Zealand | -3.1 | -2.9 | AA | 8 | Developed | Australasia | 1 out of 7 |
| Nicaragua | 10.0 | 9.9 | B+ | 127 | | Latin America | 19 out of 20 |
| Niger | 9.6 | 9.6 | | 120 | | Africa | 25 out of 51 |
| Nigeria | 7.8 | 7.8 | B | 97 | Frontier | Africa | 14 out of 51 |
| Norway | -3.8 | -3.7 | AAA | 3 | Developed | Western Europe | 2 out of 19 |
| Oman | 1.8 | 1.9 | BBB- | 46 | Frontier | Middle East | 5 out of 13 |
| Pakistan | 9.7 | 9.6 | B | 122 | Frontier | Asia | 19 out of 29 |
| Panama | 2.4 | 2.5 | BBB | 52 | | Latin America | 6 out of 20 |
| Papua New Guinea | 9.3 | 9.3 | B+ | 118 | | Australasia | 3 out of 7 |
| Paraguay | 5.6 | 5.8 | BB | 80 | | Latin America | 9 out of 20 |
| Peru | 1.2 | 1.5 | BBB+ | 39 | Emerging | Latin America | 3 out of 20 |
| Philippines | 2.8 | 2.8 | BBB | 53 | Emerging | Asia | 9 out of 29 |
| Poland | 0.0 | 0.0 | BBB+ | 29 | Emerging | Central and Eastern Europe | 3 out of 25 |
| Portugal | 2.2 | 2.1 | BB+ | 49 | Developed | Western Europe | 17 out of 19 |
| Qatar | -1.0 | -0.8 | AA | 21 | Emerging | Middle East | 1 out of 13 |
| Romania | 2.9 | 3.0 | BBB- | 56 | Frontier | Central and Eastern Europe | 9 out of 25 |
| Russia | 4.9 | 4.4 | BB+ | 68 | Emerging | Central and Eastern Europe | 14 out of 25 |
| Rwanda | 10.3 | 10.3 | B | 130 | | Africa | 31 out of 51 |
| São Tomé & Príncipe | 16.1 | 16.4 | | 163 | | Africa | 43 out of 51 |
| Saudi Arabia | 2.1 | 1.9 | A- | 47 | | Middle East | 6 out of 13 |
| Senegal | 7.2 | 7.2 | B+ | 86 | | Africa | 8 out of 51 |
| Serbia | 5.5 | 5.3 | BB- | 75 | Frontier | Central and Eastern Europe | 16 out of 25 |
| Seychelles | 5.0 | 5.1 | | 73 | | Africa | 5 out of 51 |
| Sierra Leone | 10.3 | 10.3 | | 129 | | Africa | 30 out of 51 |
| Singapore | -4.0 | -3.8 | AAA | 1 | Developed | Asia | 1 out of 29 |
| Slovakia | -0.7 | -0.5 | A+ | 24 | | Central and Eastern Europe | 2 out of 25 |
| Slovenia | 0.6 | 0.7 | A | 34 | Frontier | Central and Eastern Europe | 5 out of 25 |
| Solomon Islands | 20.0 | 19.8 | | 168 | | Australasia | 6 out of 7 |
| Somalia | 18.5 | 18.3 | | 166 | | Africa | 46 out of 51 |
| South Africa | 2.9 | 3.2 | BBB- | 60 | Emerging | Africa | 2 out of 51 |
| Spain | 1.3 | 1.5 | BBB+ | 38 | Developed | Western Europe | 16 out of 19 |
| Sri Lanka | 5.0 | 4.7 | B+ | 72 | Frontier | Asia | 14 out of 29 |
| Sudan | 14.9 | 14.7 | | 154 | | Africa | 40 out of 51 |
| Suriname | 8.0 | 8.2 | B+ | 102 | | Latin America | 16 out of 20 |
| Swaziland | 13.3 | 14.1 | | 152 | | Africa | 38 out of 51 |
| Sweden | -3.1 | -3.0 | AAA | 7 | Developed | Western Europe | 6 out of 19 |

§ S&P Credit Rating based on long-term foreign currency issuer rating. See http://www.standardandpoors.com/.

* World rank based on 175 countries covered by Euromoney. Ranking based on ascending order in which '1' equals the smallest country risk premium (CRP) and '175' equals the largest country risk premium (CRP).

† MSCI Market Classification based on MSCI Market Classification Framework. See http://www.msci.com/products/indexes/market_classification.html.

‡ Regional classification based on Euromoney. Regional rankings based on ascending order in which '1' equals the smallest country risk premium (CRP) for each region.

Note: A CRP of 0.0% is assumed in the following cases: (i) when the investor country and the investee country both have an S&P sovereign credit rating of AAA; or (ii) when the investor country has an S&P credit rating of AAA, and the investee country has a sovereign credit rating below AAA, but has a calculated CRP below 0.0% (which would imply lower risk than a country rated AAA); or (iii) when the investor country has an S&P credit rating below AAA, and the investee country has a sovereign credit rating of AAA, but has a calculated CRP above 0.0% (which would imply greater risk than a country rated below AAA). For purposes of this analysis, the U.S. is treated as having a sovereign credit rating equivalent to AAA.

The country risk premium (CRP) is not the cost of equity capital (COE). The CRP is to be added to base COE. See Chapter 6 for proper application.

## Data Updated Through March 2017

| Investee Country | December 2016 Country Risk Premium (CRP) (%) | March 2017 Country Risk Premium (CRP) (%) | S&P Sovereign Credit Rating § | World Rank Out of 175* | MSCI Market Classification † | Euromoney Region ‡ | Regional Rank ‡ |
|---|---|---|---|---|---|---|---|
| Switzerland | -3.8 | -3.7 | AAA | 2 | Developed | Western Europe | 1 out of 19 |
| Syria | 19.1 | 19.1 | | 167 | | Middle East | 13 out of 13 |
| Taiwan | -1.4 | -1.2 | AA- | 18 | Emerging | Asia | 3 out of 29 |
| Tajikistan | 14.5 | 14.7 | | 155 | | Central and Eastern Europe | 25 out of 25 |
| Tanzania | 7.5 | 7.7 | | 95 | | Africa | 13 out of 51 |
| Thailand | 2.4 | 2.4 | BBB+ | 51 | Emerging | Asia | 8 out of 29 |
| Togo | 8.9 | 8.9 | | 113 | | Africa | 20 out of 51 |
| Tonga | 22.2 | 22.0 | | 170 | | Australasia | 7 out of 7 |
| Trinidad & Tobago | 2.8 | 2.8 | A- | 54 | | Caribbean | 2 out of 9 |
| Tunisia | 5.3 | 5.7 | | 79 | Frontier | Africa | 6 out of 51 |
| Turkey | 3.1 | 3.0 | BB | 58 | Emerging | Central and Eastern Europe | 11 out of 25 |
| Turkmenistan | 11.9 | 12.1 | | 140 | | Asia | 24 out of 29 |
| Uganda | 8.5 | 8.7 | B | 110 | | Africa | 18 out of 51 |
| Ukraine | 11.0 | 11.0 | B- | 135 | | Central and Eastern Europe | 20 out of 25 |
| United Arab Emirates | 0.2 | 0.4 | AA | 33 | Emerging | Middle East | 4 out of 13 |
| United Kingdom | -1.1 | -0.9 | AA | 20 | Developed | Western Europe | 11 out of 19 |
| United States | -2.1 | -1.9 | AA+ | 15 | Developed | North America | 2 out of 2 |
| Uruguay | 1.9 | 1.8 | BBB | 45 | | Latin America | 5 out of 20 |
| Uzbekistan | 11.2 | 10.6 | | 132 | | Asia | 21 out of 29 |
| Vanuatu | 12.7 | 12.6 | | 145 | | Australasia | 4 out of 7 |
| Venezuela | 16.1 | 16.3 | CCC | 162 | | Latin America | 20 out of 20 |
| Vietnam | 5.8 | 5.6 | BB- | 78 | Frontier | Asia | 16 out of 29 |
| Yemen | 16.4 | 16.3 | | 161 | | Middle East | 12 out of 13 |
| Zambia | 8.8 | 8.8 | B | 111 | | Africa | 19 out of 51 |
| Zimbabwe | 17.8 | 17.6 | | 164 | | Africa | 44 out of 51 |

## March 2017 Country Risk Premium (CRP) Summary Statistics:

| S&P Rating | Country Count | Average CRP (%) | Median CRP (%) | Min CRP (%) | Max CRP (%) |
|---|---|---|---|---|---|
| AAA ** | 12 | -3.0 | -3.1 | -3.8 | -1.9 |
| AA (AA+, AA, AA-) | 15 | -0.9 | -0.9 | -2.9 | 1.7 |
| A (A+, A, A-) | 14 | 0.8 | 0.9 | -0.5 | 2.8 |
| BBB (BBB+, BBB, BBB-) | 17 | 2.4 | 2.4 | 0.0 | 4.5 |
| BB (BB+, BB, BB-) | 22 | 4.9 | 4.9 | 1.6 | 9.8 |
| B+ − SD | 39 | 9.2 | 8.8 | 4.7 | 16.3 |
| Investment Grade ** | 58 | 0.0 | 0.0 | -3.8 | 4.5 |
| Non-Investment Grade ** | 61 | 7.6 | 7.8 | 1.6 | 16.3 |
| **MSCI Market Classification** | | | | | |
| Developed Markets | 23 | -1.7 | -2.5 | -3.8 | 2.2 |
| Emerging Markets | 23 | 2.1 | 1.7 | -1.6 | 9.1 |
| Frontier Markets | 22 | 4.8 | 4.6 | 0.1 | 9.8 |
| **Euromoney Region ‡** | | | | | |
| Africa | 51 | 11.4 | 9.6 | 1.9 | 29.5 |
| Asia | 29 | 6.7 | 5.5 | -3.8 | 27.2 |
| Australasia | 7 | 10.1 | 12.6 | -2.9 | 22.0 |
| Caribbean | 9 | 7.8 | 7.4 | 1.8 | 16.1 |
| Central and Eastern Europe | 25 | 5.3 | 3.5 | -0.6 | 14.7 |
| Latin America | 20 | 5.8 | 6.4 | -1.6 | 16.3 |
| Middle East | 13 | 6.0 | 3.8 | -0.8 | 19.1 |
| North America | 2 | -2.4 | -2.4 | -2.9 | -1.9 |
| Western Europe | 19 | -0.9 | -1.4 | -3.7 | 8.5 |

## CCR Base Cost of Equity Capital:

| Poland | COE (%) |
|---|---|
| March 2017 | 13.1 |
| December 2016 | 13.3 |

CCR base country-level COE for a Poland-based investor investing in Poland.

§ S&P Credit Rating based on long-term foreign currency issuer rating. See http://www.standardandpoors.com/.

* World rank based on 175 countries covered by Euromoney. Ranking based on ascending order in which '1' equals the smallest country risk premium (CRP) and '175' equals the largest country risk premium (CRP).

† MSCI Market Classification based on MSCI Market Classification Framework. See http://www.msci.com/products/indexes/market_classification.html

‡ Regional classification based on Euromoney. Regional rankings based on ascending order in which '1' equals the smallest country risk premium (CRP) for each region.

** Investment grade based on S&P sovereign credit rating from AAA to BBB-. Non-Investment grade based on S&P sovereign credit rating from BB+ to SD. For purposes of this analysis, the U.S. is being treated as if it were rated AAA by S&P.

Note: A CRP of 0.0% is assumed in the following cases: (i) when the investor country and the investee country both have an S&P sovereign credit rating of AAA; or (ii) when the investor country has an S&P credit rating of AAA, and the investee country has a sovereign credit rating below AAA, but has a calculated CRP below 0.0% (which would imply lower risk than a country rated AAA); or (iii) when the investor country has an S&P credit rating below AAA, and the investee country has a sovereign credit rating of AAA, but has a calculated CRP above 0.0% (which would imply greater risk than a country rated below AAA). For purposes of this analysis, the U.S. is treated as having a sovereign credit rating equivalent to AAA.

The country risk premium (CRP) is not the cost of equity capital (COE).  The CRP is to be added to base COE. See Chapter 6 for proper application.

### Data Updated Through March 2017

| Investee Country | December 2016 Country Risk Premium (CRP) (%) | March 2017 Country Risk Premium (CRP) (%) | S&P Sovereign Credit Rating § | World Rank Out of 175* | MSCI Market Classification † | Euromoney Region ‡ | Regional Rank ‡ |
|---|---|---|---|---|---|---|---|
| Afghanistan | 11.4 | 11.3 | | 139 | | Asia | 23 out of 29 |
| Albania | 5.9 | 6.3 | B+ | 93 | | Central and Eastern Europe | 18 out of 25 |
| Algeria | 6.0 | 6.2 | | 91 | | Africa | 10 out of 51 |
| Angola | 8.3 | 8.6 | B | 121 | | Africa | 26 out of 51 |
| Argentina | 6.5 | 6.5 | B- | 96 | Frontier | Latin America | 13 out of 20 |
| Armenia | 3.5 | 3.9 | | 77 | | Asia | 15 out of 29 |
| Australia | -5.5 | -5.4 | AAA | 12 | Developed | Australasia | 2 out of 7 |
| Austria | -5.4 | -5.2 | AA+ | 13 | Developed | Western Europe | 9 out of 19 |
| Azerbaijan | 4.7 | 5.3 | BB+ | 85 | | Asia | 17 out of 29 |
| Bahamas | 2.1 | 2.0 | BB+ | 65 | | Caribbean | 3 out of 9 |
| Bahrain | 2.0 | 2.0 | BB- | 64 | Frontier | Middle East | 7 out of 13 |
| Bangladesh | 8.8 | 8.8 | BB- | 126 | Frontier | Asia | 20 out of 29 |
| Barbados | 3.7 | 5.0 | CCC+ | 82 | | Caribbean | 4 out of 9 |
| Belarus | 11.1 | 11.7 | B- | 143 | | Central and Eastern Europe | 23 out of 25 |
| Belgium | -4.1 | -4.0 | AA | 17 | Developed | Western Europe | 10 out of 19 |
| Belize | 7.0 | 7.3 | B- | 106 | | Latin America | 17 out of 20 |
| Benin | 12.8 | 13.0 | | 150 | | Africa | 37 out of 51 |
| Bermuda | -0.4 | -0.3 | A+ | 44 | | Caribbean | 1 out of 9 |
| Bhutan | 12.5 | 12.5 | | 148 | | Asia | 25 out of 29 |
| Bolivia | 5.5 | 6.0 | BB | 88 | | Latin America | 12 out of 20 |
| Bosnia & Herzegovina | 11.6 | 11.9 | B | 144 | | Central and Eastern Europe | 24 out of 25 |
| Botswana | -0.4 | -0.2 | A- | 48 | | Africa | 1 out of 51 |
| Brazil | 1.2 | 1.2 | BB | 59 | Emerging | Latin America | 7 out of 20 |
| Bulgaria | 1.0 | 1.4 | BB+ | 61 | | Central and Eastern Europe | 12 out of 25 |
| Burkina Faso | 9.9 | 10.1 | B- | 133 | | Africa | 33 out of 51 |
| Burundi | 21.9 | 22.1 | | 169 | | Africa | 47 out of 51 |
| Cambodia | 13.4 | 13.3 | | 151 | | Asia | 27 out of 29 |
| Cameroon | 8.5 | 8.7 | B | 124 | | Africa | 28 out of 51 |
| Canada | -5.7 | -5.6 | AAA | 9 | Developed | North America | 1 out of 2 |
| Cape Verde | 6.1 | 6.4 | B | 94 | | Africa | 12 out of 51 |
| Central African Republic | 25.4 | 25.7 | | 172 | | Africa | 49 out of 51 |
| Chad | 24.1 | 24.4 | | 171 | | Africa | 48 out of 51 |
| Chile | -4.5 | -4.1 | AA- | 16 | Emerging | Latin America | 1 out of 20 |
| China | -0.6 | -0.4 | AA- | 42 | Emerging | Asia | 7 out of 29 |
| Colombia | -0.6 | -0.4 | BBB | 41 | Emerging | Latin America | 4 out of 20 |
| Congo Republic | 8.1 | 8.2 | B- | 117 | | Africa | 24 out of 51 |
| Congo, DR | 9.4 | 9.5 | B- | 131 | | Africa | 32 out of 51 |
| Costa Rica | 2.5 | 2.9 | BB- | 71 | | Latin America | 8 out of 20 |
| Côte d'Ivoire | 6.0 | 6.2 | | 92 | | Africa | 11 out of 51 |
| Croatia | 1.5 | 1.6 | BB | 63 | Frontier | Central and Eastern Europe | 13 out of 25 |
| Cuba | 15.7 | 16.0 | | 160 | | Caribbean | 9 out of 9 |
| Cyprus | -0.9 | -0.6 | BB+ | 40 | | Central and Eastern Europe | 7 out of 25 |
| Czech Republic | -3.3 | -3.1 | AA- | 23 | Emerging | Central and Eastern Europe | 1 out of 25 |
| Denmark | -6.4 | -6.2 | AAA | 4 | Developed | Western Europe | 3 out of 19 |
| Djibouti | 33.5 | 31.4 | | 175 | | Africa | 51 out of 51 |
| Dominican Republic | 5.8 | 6.1 | BB- | 90 | | Caribbean | 5 out of 9 |
| Ecuador | 7.4 | 7.5 | B | 109 | | Latin America | 18 out of 20 |
| Egypt | 7.9 | 8.0 | B- | 116 | Emerging | Africa | 23 out of 51 |
| El Salvador | 4.9 | 4.9 | B- | 81 | | Latin America | 10 out of 20 |
| Equatorial Guinea | 18.2 | 18.5 | | 165 | | Africa | 45 out of 51 |

§ S&P Credit Rating based on long-term foreign currency issuer rating. See http://www.standardandpoors.com/.

* World rank based on 175 countries covered by Euromoney. Ranking based on ascending order in which '1' equals the smallest country risk premium (CRP) and '175' equals the largest country risk premium (CRP).

† MSCI Market Classification based on MSCI Market Classification Framework.  See http://www.msci.com/products/indexes/market_classification.html.

‡ Regional classification based on Euromoney. Regional rankings based on ascending order in which '1' equals the smallest country risk premium (CRP) for each region.

Note: A CRP of 0.0% is assumed in the following cases: (i) when the investor country and the investee country both have an S&P sovereign credit rating of AAA; or (ii) when the investor country has an S&P credit rating of AAA, and the investee country has a sovereign credit rating below AAA, but has a calculated CRP below 0.0% (which would imply lower risk than a country rated AAA); or (iii) when the investor country has an S&P credit rating below AAA, and the investee country has a sovereign credit rating of AAA, but has a calculated CRP above 0.0% (which would imply greater risk than a country rated below AAA). For purposes of this analysis, the U.S. is treated as having a sovereign credit rating equivalent to AAA.

The country risk premium (CRP) is not the cost of equity capital (COE). The CRP is to be added to base COE. See Chapter 6 for proper application.

## Data Updated Through March 2017

| Investee Country | December 2016 Country Risk Premium (CRP) (%) | March 2017 Country Risk Premium (CRP) (%) | S&P Sovereign Credit Rating § | World Rank Out of 175* | MSCI Market Classification † | Euromoney Region ‡ | Regional Rank ‡ |
|---|---|---|---|---|---|---|---|
| Eritrea | 29.6 | 28.0 | | 173 | | Africa | 50 out of 51 |
| Estonia | -2.7 | -2.2 | AA- | 32 | Frontier | Central and Eastern Europe | 4 out of 25 |
| Ethiopia | 6.7 | 7.0 | B | 101 | | Africa | 16 out of 51 |
| Fiji | 12.1 | 12.2 | B+ | 147 | | Australasia | 5 out of 7 |
| Finland | -5.6 | -5.4 | AA+ | 11 | Developed | Western Europe | 8 out of 19 |
| France | -3.2 | -3.2 | AA | 22 | Developed | Western Europe | 12 out of 19 |
| Gabon | 4.5 | 5.0 | | 83 | | Africa | 7 out of 51 |
| Gambia | 10.6 | 10.8 | | 138 | | Africa | 34 out of 51 |
| Georgia | 3.2 | 3.7 | BB- | 74 | | Central and Eastern Europe | 15 out of 25 |
| Germany | -5.6 | -5.5 | AAA | 10 | Developed | Western Europe | 7 out of 19 |
| Ghana | 6.2 | 6.0 | B- | 89 | | Africa | 9 out of 51 |
| Greece | 7.4 | 7.3 | B- | 108 | Emerging | Western Europe | 19 out of 19 |
| Grenada | 7.0 | 7.2 | | 105 | | Caribbean | 7 out of 9 |
| Guatemala | 4.9 | 5.1 | BB | 84 | | Latin America | 11 out of 20 |
| Guinea | 14.3 | 14.5 | | 156 | | Africa | 41 out of 51 |
| Guinea-Bissau | 7.8 | 8.0 | | 115 | | Africa | 22 out of 51 |
| Guyana | 6.6 | 6.9 | | 100 | | Latin America | 15 out of 20 |
| Haiti | 17.2 | 15.4 | | 157 | | Caribbean | 8 out of 9 |
| Honduras | 6.3 | 6.6 | B+ | 98 | | Latin America | 14 out of 20 |
| Hong Kong | -5.0 | -4.9 | AAA | 14 | Developed | Asia | 2 out of 29 |
| Hungary | 0.8 | 1.1 | BBB- | 57 | Emerging | Central and Eastern Europe | 10 out of 25 |
| Iceland | -2.3 | -2.3 | A | 30 | | Western Europe | 15 out of 19 |
| India | 0.5 | 1.0 | BBB- | 55 | Emerging | Asia | 10 out of 29 |
| Indonesia | 1.3 | 1.5 | BB+ | 62 | Emerging | Asia | 11 out of 29 |
| Iran | 8.3 | 8.8 | | 125 | | Middle East | 10 out of 13 |
| Iraq | 10.2 | 10.4 | B- | 136 | | Middle East | 11 out of 13 |
| Ireland | -2.8 | -2.6 | A+ | 27 | Developed | Western Europe | 14 out of 19 |
| Israel | -2.8 | -2.6 | A+ | 28 | Developed | Middle East | 2 out of 13 |
| Italy | 0.2 | 0.2 | BBB- | 50 | Developed | Western Europe | 18 out of 19 |
| Jamaica | 6.4 | 7.2 | B | 104 | | Caribbean | 6 out of 9 |
| Japan | -2.9 | -2.7 | A+ | 25 | Developed | Asia | 5 out of 29 |
| Jordan | 3.4 | 3.8 | BB- | 76 | Frontier | Middle East | 8 out of 13 |
| Kazakhstan | 2.9 | 2.8 | BBB- | 70 | Frontier | Asia | 13 out of 29 |
| Kenya | 6.4 | 6.7 | B+ | 99 | Frontier | Africa | 15 out of 51 |
| Korea (North) | 29.0 | 28.7 | | 174 | | Asia | 29 out of 29 |
| Korea (South) | -3.7 | -3.5 | AA | 19 | Emerging | Asia | 4 out of 29 |
| Kuwait | -2.6 | -2.3 | AA | 31 | Frontier | Middle East | 3 out of 13 |
| Kyrgyz Republic | 11.6 | 11.7 | | 142 | | Central and Eastern Europe | 22 out of 25 |
| Laos | 15.9 | 15.6 | | 158 | | Asia | 28 out of 29 |
| Latvia | -0.6 | -0.3 | A- | 43 | | Central and Eastern Europe | 8 out of 25 |
| Lebanon | 8.2 | 7.8 | B- | 112 | Frontier | Middle East | 9 out of 13 |
| Lesotho | 11.8 | 12.1 | | 146 | | Africa | 36 out of 51 |
| Liberia | 7.1 | 7.3 | | 107 | | Africa | 17 out of 51 |
| Libya | 13.4 | 14.0 | | 153 | | Africa | 39 out of 51 |
| Lithuania | -1.4 | -1.1 | A- | 36 | Frontier | Central and Eastern Europe | 6 out of 25 |
| Luxembourg | -6.1 | -5.9 | AAA | 5 | | Western Europe | 4 out of 19 |
| Macedonia | 5.5 | 5.9 | BB- | 87 | | Central and Eastern Europe | 17 out of 25 |
| Madagascar | 7.9 | 8.7 | | 123 | | Africa | 27 out of 51 |
| Malawi | 7.7 | 7.9 | | 114 | | Africa | 21 out of 51 |
| Malaysia | -1.2 | -1.1 | A- | 35 | Emerging | Asia | 6 out of 29 |

§ S&P Credit Rating based on long-term foreign currency issuer rating. See http://www.standardandpoors.com/.

* World rank based on 175 countries covered by Euromoney. Ranking based on ascending order in which '1' equals the smallest country risk premium (CRP) and '175' equals the largest country risk premium (CRP).

† MSCI Market Classification based on MSCI Market Classification Framework. See http://www.msci.com/products/indexes/market_classification.html

‡ Regional classification based on Euromoney. Regional rankings based on ascending order in which '1' equals the smallest country risk premium (CRP) for each region.

Note: A CRP of 0.0% is assumed in the following cases: (i) when the investor country and the investee country both have an S&P sovereign credit rating of AAA; or (ii) when the investor country has an S&P credit rating of AAA, and the investee country has a sovereign credit rating below AAA, but has a calculated CRP below 0.0% (which would imply lower risk than a country rated AAA); or (iii) when the investor country has an S&P credit rating below AAA, and the investee country has a sovereign credit rating of AAA, but has a calculated CRP above 0.0% (which would imply greater risk than a country rated below AAA). For purposes of this analysis, the U.S. is treated as having a sovereign credit rating equivalent to AAA.

The country risk premium (CRP) is not the cost of equity capital (COE). The CRP is to be added to base COE. See Chapter 6 for proper application.

## Data Updated Through March 2017

| Investee Country | December 2016 Country Risk Premium (CRP) (%) | March 2017 Country Risk Premium (CRP) (%) | S&P Sovereign Credit Rating § | World Rank Out of 175* | MSCI Market Classification † | Euromoney Region ‡ | Regional Rank ‡ |
|---|---|---|---|---|---|---|---|
| Mali | 11.4 | 11.7 | | 141 | | Africa | 35 out of 51 |
| Malta | -2.9 | -2.7 | A- | 26 | | Western Europe | 13 out of 19 |
| Mauritania | 15.5 | 15.8 | | 159 | | Africa | 42 out of 51 |
| Mauritius | 2.2 | 2.4 | | 67 | Frontier | Asia | 12 out of 29 |
| Mexico | -1.3 | -1.0 | BBB+ | 37 | Emerging | Latin America | 2 out of 20 |
| Moldova | 9.8 | 10.5 | | 137 | | Central and Eastern Europe | 21 out of 25 |
| Mongolia | 8.0 | 8.6 | B- | 119 | | Asia | 18 out of 29 |
| Montenegro | 7.2 | 7.2 | B+ | 103 | | Central and Eastern Europe | 19 out of 25 |
| Morocco | 2.3 | 2.7 | BBB- | 69 | Frontier | Africa | 4 out of 51 |
| Mozambique | 9.1 | 9.2 | SD | 128 | | Africa | 29 out of 51 |
| Myanmar | 10.0 | 10.2 | | 134 | | Asia | 22 out of 29 |
| Namibia | 1.9 | 2.3 | | 66 | | Africa | 3 out of 51 |
| Nepal | 12.7 | 13.0 | | 149 | | Asia | 26 out of 29 |
| Netherlands | -6.0 | -5.9 | AAA | 6 | Developed | Western Europe | 5 out of 19 |
| New Zealand | -5.9 | -5.7 | AA | 8 | Developed | Australasia | 1 out of 7 |
| Nicaragua | 8.8 | 9.0 | B+ | 127 | | Latin America | 19 out of 20 |
| Niger | 8.4 | 8.6 | | 120 | | Africa | 25 out of 51 |
| Nigeria | 6.4 | 6.6 | B | 97 | Frontier | Africa | 14 out of 51 |
| Norway | -6.7 | -6.6 | AAA | 3 | Developed | Western Europe | 2 out of 19 |
| Oman | -0.4 | -0.2 | BBB- | 46 | Frontier | Middle East | 5 out of 13 |
| Pakistan | 8.5 | 8.6 | B | 122 | Frontier | Asia | 19 out of 29 |
| Panama | 0.3 | 0.5 | BBB | 52 | | Latin America | 6 out of 20 |
| Papua New Guinea | 8.0 | 8.3 | B+ | 118 | | Australasia | 3 out of 7 |
| Paraguay | 3.9 | 4.3 | BB | 80 | | Latin America | 9 out of 20 |
| Peru | -1.0 | -0.7 | BBB+ | 39 | Emerging | Latin America | 3 out of 20 |
| Philippines | 0.7 | 0.8 | BBB | 53 | Emerging | Asia | 9 out of 29 |
| Poland | -2.4 | -2.4 | BBB+ | 29 | Emerging | Central and Eastern Europe | 3 out of 25 |
| Portugal | 0.0 | 0.0 | BB+ | 49 | Developed | Western Europe | 17 out of 19 |
| Qatar | -3.6 | -3.3 | AA | 21 | Emerging | Middle East | 1 out of 13 |
| Romania | 0.8 | 1.1 | BBB- | 56 | Frontier | Central and Eastern Europe | 9 out of 25 |
| Russia | 3.1 | 2.7 | BB+ | 68 | Emerging | Central and Eastern Europe | 14 out of 25 |
| Rwanda | 9.2 | 9.4 | B | 130 | | Africa | 31 out of 51 |
| São Tomé & Príncipe | 15.6 | 16.4 | | 163 | | Africa | 43 out of 51 |
| Saudi Arabia | -0.1 | -0.2 | A- | 47 | | Middle East | 6 out of 13 |
| Senegal | 5.7 | 5.9 | B+ | 86 | | Africa | 8 out of 51 |
| Serbia | 3.8 | 3.7 | BB- | 75 | Frontier | Central and Eastern Europe | 16 out of 25 |
| Seychelles | 3.2 | 3.4 | | 73 | | Africa | 5 out of 51 |
| Sierra Leone | 9.2 | 9.4 | | 129 | | Africa | 30 out of 51 |
| Singapore | -6.9 | -6.7 | AAA | 1 | Developed | Asia | 1 out of 29 |
| Slovakia | -3.2 | -2.9 | A+ | 24 | | Central and Eastern Europe | 2 out of 25 |
| Slovenia | -1.7 | -1.5 | A | 34 | Frontier | Central and Eastern Europe | 5 out of 25 |
| Solomon Islands | 20.1 | 20.3 | | 168 | | Australasia | 6 out of 7 |
| Somalia | 18.3 | 18.6 | | 166 | | Africa | 46 out of 51 |
| South Africa | 0.9 | 1.3 | BBB- | 60 | Emerging | Africa | 2 out of 51 |
| Spain | -0.9 | -0.7 | BBB+ | 38 | Developed | Western Europe | 16 out of 19 |
| Sri Lanka | 3.2 | 3.1 | B+ | 72 | Frontier | Asia | 14 out of 29 |
| Sudan | 14.2 | 14.4 | | 154 | | Africa | 40 out of 51 |
| Suriname | 6.6 | 7.0 | B+ | 102 | | Latin America | 16 out of 20 |
| Swaziland | 12.5 | 13.7 | | 152 | | Africa | 38 out of 51 |
| Sweden | -6.0 | -5.8 | AAA | 7 | Developed | Western Europe | 6 out of 19 |

§ S&P Credit Rating based on long-term foreign currency issuer rating. See http://www.standardandpoors.com/.

* World rank based on 175 countries covered by Euromoney. Ranking based on ascending order in which '1' equals the smallest country risk premium (CRP) and '175' equals the largest country risk premium (CRP).

† MSCI Market Classification based on MSCI Market Classification Framework. See http://www.msci.com/products/indexes/market_classification.html

‡ Regional classification based on Euromoney. Regional rankings based on ascending order in which '1' equals the smallest country risk premium (CRP) for each region.

Note: A CRP of 0.0% is assumed in the following cases: (i) when the investor country and the investee country both have an S&P sovereign credit rating of AAA; or (ii) when the investor country has an S&P credit rating of AAA, and the investee country has a sovereign credit rating below AAA, but has a calculated CRP below 0.0% (which would imply lower risk than a country rated AAA); or (iii) when the investor country has an S&P credit rating below AAA, and the investee country has a sovereign credit rating of AAA, but has a calculated CRP above 0.0% (which would imply greater risk than a country rated below AAA). For purposes of this analysis, the U.S. is treated as having a sovereign credit rating equivalent to AAA.

The country risk premium (CRP) is not the cost of equity capital (COE). The CRP is to be added to base COE. See Chapter 6 for proper application.

## Data Updated Through March 2017

| Investee Country | December 2016 Country Risk Premium (CRP) (%) | March 2017 Country Risk Premium (CRP) (%) | S&P Sovereign Credit Rating § | World Rank Out of 175* | MSCI Market Classification † | Euromoney Region ‡ | Regional Rank ‡ |
|---|---|---|---|---|---|---|---|
| Switzerland | -6.6 | -6.6 | AAA | 2 | Developed | Western Europe | 1 out of 19 |
| Syria | 19.1 | 19.6 | | 167 | | Middle East | 13 out of 13 |
| Taiwan | -4.0 | -3.8 | AA- | 18 | Emerging | Asia | 3 out of 29 |
| Tajikistan | 13.8 | 14.4 | | 155 | | Central and Eastern Europe | 25 out of 25 |
| Tanzania | 6.0 | 6.4 | | 95 | | Africa | 13 out of 51 |
| Thailand | 0.3 | 0.3 | BBB+ | 51 | Emerging | Asia | 8 out of 29 |
| Togo | 7.6 | 7.8 | | 113 | | Africa | 20 out of 51 |
| Tonga | 22.5 | 22.8 | | 170 | | Australasia | 7 out of 7 |
| Trinidad & Tobago | 0.7 | 0.9 | A- | 54 | | Caribbean | 2 out of 9 |
| Tunisia | 3.6 | 4.1 | | 79 | Frontier | Africa | 6 out of 51 |
| Turkey | 1.0 | 1.1 | BB | 58 | Emerging | Central and Eastern Europe | 11 out of 25 |
| Turkmenistan | 11.0 | 11.5 | | 140 | | Asia | 24 out of 29 |
| Uganda | 7.1 | 7.6 | B | 110 | | Africa | 18 out of 51 |
| Ukraine | 10.0 | 10.3 | B- | 135 | | Central and Eastern Europe | 20 out of 25 |
| United Arab Emirates | -2.2 | -1.9 | AA | 33 | Emerging | Middle East | 4 out of 13 |
| United Kingdom | -3.7 | -3.4 | AA | 20 | Developed | Western Europe | 11 out of 19 |
| United States | -4.7 | -4.5 | AA+ | 15 | Developed | North America | 2 out of 2 |
| Uruguay | -0.3 | -0.3 | BBB | 45 | | Latin America | 5 out of 20 |
| Uzbekistan | 10.1 | 9.8 | | 132 | | Asia | 21 out of 29 |
| Vanuatu | 11.8 | 12.0 | | 145 | | Australasia | 4 out of 7 |
| Venezuela | 15.6 | 16.3 | CCC | 162 | | Latin America | 20 out of 20 |
| Vietnam | 4.1 | 4.0 | BB- | 78 | Frontier | Asia | 16 out of 29 |
| Yemen | 15.9 | 16.3 | | 161 | | Middle East | 12 out of 13 |
| Zambia | 7.5 | 7.7 | B | 111 | | Africa | 19 out of 51 |
| Zimbabwe | 17.6 | 17.8 | | 164 | | Africa | 44 out of 51 |

## March 2017 Country Risk Premium (CRP) Summary Statistics:

| S&P Rating | Country Count | Average CRP (%) | Median CRP (%) | Min CRP (%) | Max CRP (%) |
|---|---|---|---|---|---|
| AAA ** | 12 | -5.8 | -5.9 | -6.7 | -4.5 |
| AA (AA+, AA, AA-) | 15 | -3.4 | -3.4 | -5.7 | -0.4 |
| A (A+, A, A-) | 14 | -1.4 | -1.3 | -2.9 | 0.9 |
| BBB (BBB+, BBB, BBB-) | 17 | 0.4 | 0.3 | -2.4 | 2.8 |
| BB (BB+, BB, BB-) | 22 | 3.3 | 3.3 | -0.6 | 8.8 |
| B+ − SD | 39 | 8.1 | 7.7 | 3.1 | 16.3 |
| Investment Grade ** | 58 | -2.3 | -2.3 | -6.7 | 2.8 |
| Non-Investment Grade ** | 61 | 6.4 | 6.6 | -0.6 | 16.3 |
| **MSCI Market Classification** | | | | | |
| Developed Markets | 23 | -4.3 | -5.2 | -6.7 | 0.2 |
| Emerging Markets | 23 | 0.0 | -0.4 | -4.1 | 8.0 |
| Frontier Markets | 22 | 3.1 | 2.9 | -2.3 | 8.8 |
| **Euromoney Region ‡** | | | | | |
| Africa | 51 | 10.7 | 8.6 | -0.2 | 31.4 |
| Asia | 29 | 5.3 | 3.9 | -6.7 | 28.7 |
| Australasia | 7 | 9.2 | 12.0 | -5.7 | 22.8 |
| Caribbean | 9 | 6.6 | 6.1 | -0.3 | 16.0 |
| Central and Eastern Europe | 25 | 3.7 | 1.6 | -3.1 | 14.4 |
| Latin America | 20 | 4.3 | 5.0 | -4.1 | 16.3 |
| Middle East | 13 | 4.5 | 2.0 | -3.3 | 19.6 |
| North America | 2 | -5.1 | -5.1 | -5.6 | -4.5 |
| Western Europe | 19 | -3.4 | -4.0 | -6.6 | 7.3 |

## CCR Base Cost of Equity Capital:

| Portugal | COE (%) |
|---|---|
| March 2017 | 13.0 |
| December 2016 | 13.2 |

CCR base country-level COE for a Portugal-based investor investing in Portugal.

§ S&P Credit Rating based on long-term foreign currency issuer rating. See http://www.standardandpoors.com/.

* World rank based on 175 countries covered by Euromoney. Ranking based on ascending order in which '1' equals the smallest country risk premium (CRP) and '175' equals the largest country risk premium (CRP).

† MSCI Market Classification based on MSCI Market Classification Framework. See http://www.msci.com/products/indexes/market_classification.html.

‡ Regional classification based on Euromoney. Regional rankings based on ascending order in which '1' equals the smallest country risk premium (CRP) for each region.

** Investment grade based on S&P sovereign credit rating from AAA to BBB-. Non-Investment grade based on S&P sovereign credit rating from BB+ to SD. For purposes of this analysis, the U.S. is being treated as if it were rated AAA by S&P.

Note: A CRP of 0.0% is assumed in the following cases: (i) when the investor country and the investee country both have an S&P sovereign credit rating of AAA; or (ii) when the investor country has an S&P credit rating of AAA, and the investee country has a sovereign credit rating below AAA, but has a calculated CRP below 0.0% (which would imply lower risk than a country rated AAA); or (iii) when the investor country has an S&P credit rating below AAA, and the investee country has a sovereign credit rating of AAA, but has a calculated CRP above 0.0% (which would imply greater risk than a country rated below AAA). For purposes of this analysis, the U.S. is treated as having a sovereign credit rating equivalent to AAA.

The country risk premium (CRP) is not the cost of equity capital (COE). The CRP is to be added to base COE. See Chapter 6 for proper application.

## Data Updated Through March 2017

| Investee Country | December 2016 Country Risk Premium (CRP) (%) | March 2017 Country Risk Premium (CRP) (%) | S&P Sovereign Credit Rating § | World Rank Out of 175∗ | MSCI Market Classification † | Euromoney Region ‡ | Regional Rank ‡ |
|---|---|---|---|---|---|---|---|
| Afghanistan | 14.0 | 13.9 | | 139 | | Asia | 23 out of 29 |
| Albania | 8.9 | 9.1 | B+ | 93 | | Central and Eastern Europe | 18 out of 25 |
| Algeria | 8.9 | 9.1 | | 91 | | Africa | 10 out of 51 |
| Angola | 11.1 | 11.3 | B | 121 | | Africa | 26 out of 51 |
| Argentina | 9.4 | 9.3 | B- | 96 | Frontier | Latin America | 13 out of 20 |
| Armenia | 6.6 | 6.8 | | 77 | | Asia | 15 out of 29 |
| Australia | -1.8 | -2.0 | AAA | 12 | Developed | Australasia | 2 out of 7 |
| Austria | -1.7 | -1.8 | AA+ | 13 | Developed | Western Europe | 9 out of 19 |
| Azerbaijan | 7.7 | 8.1 | BB+ | 85 | | Asia | 17 out of 29 |
| Bahamas | 5.2 | 5.0 | BB+ | 65 | | Caribbean | 3 out of 9 |
| Bahrain | 5.2 | 5.0 | BB- | 64 | Frontier | Middle East | 7 out of 13 |
| Bangladesh | 11.6 | 11.5 | BB- | 126 | Frontier | Asia | 20 out of 29 |
| Barbados | 6.8 | 7.9 | CCC+ | 82 | | Caribbean | 4 out of 9 |
| Belarus | 13.7 | 14.3 | B- | 143 | | Central and Eastern Europe | 23 out of 25 |
| Belgium | -0.5 | -0.6 | AA | 17 | Developed | Western Europe | 10 out of 19 |
| Belize | 9.8 | 10.1 | B- | 106 | | Latin America | 17 out of 20 |
| Benin | 15.3 | 15.5 | | 150 | | Africa | 37 out of 51 |
| Bermuda | 3.0 | 2.9 | A+ | 44 | | Caribbean | 1 out of 9 |
| Bhutan | 15.0 | 15.1 | | 148 | | Asia | 25 out of 29 |
| Bolivia | 8.4 | 8.8 | BB | 88 | | Latin America | 12 out of 20 |
| Bosnia & Herzegovina | 14.1 | 14.4 | B | 144 | | Central and Eastern Europe | 24 out of 25 |
| Botswana | 3.0 | 3.0 | A- | 48 | | Africa | 1 out of 51 |
| Brazil | 4.4 | 4.3 | BB | 59 | Emerging | Latin America | 7 out of 20 |
| Bulgaria | 4.3 | 4.4 | BB+ | 61 | | Central and Eastern Europe | 12 out of 25 |
| Burkina Faso | 12.6 | 12.8 | B- | 133 | | Africa | 33 out of 51 |
| Burundi | 23.8 | 24.2 | | 169 | | Africa | 47 out of 51 |
| Cambodia | 15.8 | 15.7 | | 151 | | Asia | 27 out of 29 |
| Cameroon | 11.3 | 11.4 | B | 124 | | Africa | 28 out of 51 |
| Canada | -2.0 | -2.2 | AAA | 9 | Developed | North America | 1 out of 2 |
| Cape Verde | 9.1 | 9.2 | B | 94 | | Africa | 12 out of 51 |
| Central African Republic | 27.1 | 27.6 | | 172 | | Africa | 49 out of 51 |
| Chad | 25.8 | 26.3 | | 171 | | Africa | 48 out of 51 |
| Chile | -0.9 | -0.8 | AA- | 16 | Emerging | Latin America | 1 out of 20 |
| China | 2.8 | 2.8 | AA- | 42 | Emerging | Asia | 7 out of 29 |
| Colombia | 2.8 | 2.7 | BBB | 41 | Emerging | Latin America | 4 out of 20 |
| Congo Republic | 10.9 | 10.9 | B- | 117 | | Africa | 24 out of 51 |
| Congo, DR | 12.1 | 12.2 | B- | 131 | | Africa | 32 out of 51 |
| Costa Rica | 5.6 | 5.9 | BB- | 71 | | Latin America | 8 out of 20 |
| Côte d'Ivoire | 8.9 | 9.1 | | 92 | | Africa | 11 out of 51 |
| Croatia | 4.8 | 4.7 | BB | 63 | Frontier | Central and Eastern Europe | 13 out of 25 |
| Cuba | 18.0 | 18.4 | | 160 | | Caribbean | 9 out of 9 |
| Cyprus | 2.5 | 2.6 | BB+ | 40 | | Central and Eastern Europe | 7 out of 25 |
| Czech Republic | 0.3 | 0.2 | AA- | 23 | Emerging | Central and Eastern Europe | 1 out of 25 |
| Denmark | -2.6 | -2.8 | AAA | 4 | Developed | Western Europe | 3 out of 19 |
| Djibouti | 34.6 | 33.0 | | 175 | | Africa | 51 out of 51 |
| Dominican Republic | 8.8 | 9.0 | BB- | 90 | | Caribbean | 5 out of 9 |
| Ecuador | 10.3 | 10.2 | B | 109 | | Latin America | 18 out of 20 |
| Egypt | 10.7 | 10.8 | B- | 116 | Emerging | Africa | 23 out of 51 |
| El Salvador | 7.9 | 7.8 | B- | 81 | | Latin America | 10 out of 20 |
| Equatorial Guinea | 20.4 | 20.7 | | 165 | | Africa | 45 out of 51 |

§ S&P Credit Rating based on long-term foreign currency issuer rating. See http://www.standardandpoors.com/.

∗ World rank based on 175 countries covered by Euromoney. Ranking based on ascending order in which '1' equals the smallest country risk premium (CRP) and '175' equals the largest country risk premium (CRP).

† MSCI Market Classification based on MSCI Market Classification Framework. See http://www.msci.com/products/indexes/market_classification.html.

‡ Regional classification based on Euromoney. Regional rankings based on ascending order in which '1' equals the smallest country risk premium (CRP) for each region.

Note: A CRP of 0.0% is assumed in the following cases: (i) when the investor country and the investee country both have an S&P sovereign credit rating of AAA; or (ii) when the investor country has an S&P credit rating of AAA, and the investee country has a sovereign credit rating below AAA, but has a calculated CRP below 0.0% (which would imply lower risk than a country rated AAA); or (iii) when the investor country has an S&P credit rating below AAA, and the investee country has a sovereign credit rating of AAA, but has a calculated CRP above 0.0% (which would imply greater risk than a country rated below AAA). For purposes of this analysis, the U.S. is treated as having a sovereign credit rating equivalent to AAA.

The country risk premium (CRP) is not the cost of equity capital (COE). The CRP is to be added to base COE. See Chapter 6 for proper application.

### Data Updated Through March 2017

| Investee Country | December 2016 Country Risk Premium (CRP) (%) | March 2017 Country Risk Premium (CRP) (%) | S&P Sovereign Credit Rating § | World Rank Out of 175* | MSCI Market Classification † | Euromoney Region ‡ | Regional Rank ‡ |
|---|---|---|---|---|---|---|---|
| Eritrea | 31.0 | 29.8 | | 173 | | Africa | 50 out of 51 |
| Estonia | 0.8 | 1.0 | AA- | 32 | Frontier | Central and Eastern Europe | 4 out of 25 |
| Ethiopia | 9.6 | 9.8 | B | 101 | | Africa | 16 out of 51 |
| Fiji | 14.7 | 14.8 | B+ | 147 | | Australasia | 5 out of 7 |
| Finland | -1.9 | -2.0 | AA+ | 11 | Developed | Western Europe | 8 out of 19 |
| France | 0.3 | 0.1 | AA | 22 | Developed | Western Europe | 12 out of 19 |
| Gabon | 7.5 | 7.9 | | 83 | | Africa | 7 out of 51 |
| Gambia | 13.2 | 13.4 | | 138 | | Africa | 34 out of 51 |
| Georgia | 6.3 | 6.6 | BB- | 74 | | Central and Eastern Europe | 15 out of 25 |
| Germany | -1.9 | -2.1 | AAA | 10 | Developed | Western Europe | 7 out of 19 |
| Ghana | 9.1 | 8.9 | B- | 89 | | Africa | 9 out of 51 |
| Greece | 10.2 | 10.1 | B- | 108 | Emerging | Western Europe | 19 out of 19 |
| Grenada | 9.8 | 10.0 | | 105 | | Caribbean | 7 out of 9 |
| Guatemala | 7.9 | 8.0 | BB | 84 | | Latin America | 11 out of 20 |
| Guinea | 16.7 | 17.0 | | 156 | | Africa | 41 out of 51 |
| Guinea-Bissau | 10.6 | 10.8 | | 115 | | Africa | 22 out of 51 |
| Guyana | 9.5 | 9.7 | | 100 | | Latin America | 15 out of 20 |
| Haiti | 19.4 | 17.7 | | 157 | | Caribbean | 8 out of 9 |
| Honduras | 9.2 | 9.4 | B+ | 98 | | Latin America | 14 out of 20 |
| Hong Kong | -1.4 | -1.5 | AAA | 14 | Developed | Asia | 2 out of 29 |
| Hungary | 4.0 | 4.2 | BBB- | 57 | Emerging | Central and Eastern Europe | 10 out of 25 |
| Iceland | 1.2 | 1.0 | A | 30 | | Western Europe | 15 out of 19 |
| India | 3.8 | 4.1 | BBB- | 55 | Emerging | Asia | 10 out of 29 |
| Indonesia | 4.5 | 4.6 | BB+ | 62 | Emerging | Asia | 11 out of 29 |
| Iran | 11.1 | 11.5 | | 125 | | Middle East | 10 out of 13 |
| Iraq | 12.8 | 13.0 | B- | 136 | | Middle East | 11 out of 13 |
| Ireland | 0.8 | 0.6 | A+ | 27 | Developed | Western Europe | 14 out of 19 |
| Israel | 0.7 | 0.7 | A+ | 28 | Developed | Middle East | 2 out of 13 |
| Italy | 3.5 | 3.3 | BBB- | 50 | Developed | Western Europe | 18 out of 19 |
| Jamaica | 9.3 | 10.0 | B | 104 | | Caribbean | 6 out of 9 |
| Japan | 0.6 | 0.6 | A+ | 25 | Developed | Asia | 5 out of 29 |
| Jordan | 6.5 | 6.8 | BB- | 76 | Frontier | Middle East | 8 out of 13 |
| Kazakhstan | 6.1 | 5.8 | BBB- | 70 | Frontier | Asia | 13 out of 29 |
| Kenya | 9.3 | 9.5 | B+ | 99 | Frontier | Africa | 15 out of 51 |
| Korea (North) | 30.4 | 30.5 | | 174 | | Asia | 29 out of 29 |
| Korea (South) | -0.1 | -0.2 | AA | 19 | Emerging | Asia | 4 out of 29 |
| Kuwait | 0.9 | 1.0 | AA | 31 | Frontier | Middle East | 3 out of 13 |
| Kyrgyz Republic | 14.2 | 14.3 | | 142 | | Central and Eastern Europe | 22 out of 25 |
| Laos | 18.2 | 18.0 | | 158 | | Asia | 28 out of 29 |
| Latvia | 2.8 | 2.9 | A- | 43 | | Central and Eastern Europe | 8 out of 25 |
| Lebanon | 11.0 | 10.5 | B- | 112 | Frontier | Middle East | 9 out of 13 |
| Lesotho | 14.4 | 14.6 | | 146 | | Africa | 36 out of 51 |
| Liberia | 9.9 | 10.1 | | 107 | | Africa | 17 out of 51 |
| Libya | 15.8 | 16.4 | | 153 | | Africa | 39 out of 51 |
| Lithuania | 2.0 | 2.1 | A- | 36 | Frontier | Central and Eastern Europe | 6 out of 25 |
| Luxembourg | -2.3 | -2.5 | AAA | 5 | | Western Europe | 4 out of 19 |
| Macedonia | 8.5 | 8.8 | BB- | 87 | | Central and Eastern Europe | 17 out of 25 |
| Madagascar | 10.7 | 11.4 | | 123 | | Africa | 27 out of 51 |
| Malawi | 10.5 | 10.6 | | 114 | | Africa | 21 out of 51 |
| Malaysia | 2.2 | 2.1 | A- | 35 | Emerging | Asia | 6 out of 29 |

§ S&P Credit Rating based on long-term foreign currency issuer rating. See http://www.standardandpoors.com/.

• World rank based on 175 countries covered by Euromoney. Ranking based on ascending order in which '1' equals the smallest country risk premium (CRP) and '175' equals the largest country risk premium (CRP).

† MSCI Market Classification based on MSCI Market Classification Framework. See http://www.msci.com/products/indexes/market_classification.html.

‡ Regional classification based on Euromoney. Regional rankings based on ascending order in which '1' equals the smallest country risk premium (CRP) for each region.

Note: A CRP of 0.0% is assumed in the following cases: (i) when the investor country and the investee country both have an S&P sovereign credit rating of AAA; or (ii) when the investor country has an S&P credit rating of AAA, and the investee country has a sovereign credit rating below AAA, but has a calculated CRP below 0.0% (which would imply lower risk than a country rated AAA); or (iii) when the investor country has an S&P credit rating below AAA, and the investee country has a sovereign credit rating of AAA, but has a calculated CRP above 0.0% (which would imply greater risk than a country rated below AAA). For purposes of this analysis, the U.S. is treated as having a sovereign credit rating equivalent to AAA.

The country risk premium (CRP) is not the cost of equity capital (COE). The CRP is to be added to base COE. See Chapter 6 for proper application.

## Data Updated Through March 2017

| Investee Country | December 2016 Country Risk Premium (CRP) (%) | March 2017 Country Risk Premium (CRP) (%) | S&P Sovereign Credit Rating § | World Rank Out of 175* | MSCI Market Classification † | Euromoney Region ‡ | Regional Rank ‡ |
|---|---|---|---|---|---|---|---|
| Mali | 14.0 | 14.2 | | 141 | | Africa | 35 out of 51 |
| Malta | 0.6 | 0.6 | A- | 26 | | Western Europe | 13 out of 19 |
| Mauritania | 17.8 | 18.1 | | 159 | | Africa | 42 out of 51 |
| Mauritius | 5.4 | 5.4 | | 67 | Frontier | Asia | 12 out of 29 |
| Mexico | 2.1 | 2.2 | BBB+ | 37 | Emerging | Latin America | 2 out of 20 |
| Moldova | 12.5 | 13.1 | | 137 | | Central and Eastern Europe | 21 out of 25 |
| Mongolia | 10.8 | 11.3 | B- | 119 | | Asia | 18 out of 29 |
| Montenegro | 10.1 | 10.0 | B+ | 103 | | Central and Eastern Europe | 19 out of 25 |
| Morocco | 5.5 | 5.7 | BBB- | 69 | Frontier | Africa | 4 out of 51 |
| Mozambique | 11.8 | 11.8 | SD | 128 | | Africa | 29 out of 51 |
| Myanmar | 12.7 | 12.8 | | 134 | | Asia | 22 out of 29 |
| Namibia | 5.1 | 5.3 | | 66 | | Africa | 3 out of 51 |
| Nepal | 15.2 | 15.5 | | 149 | | Asia | 26 out of 29 |
| Netherlands | -2.3 | -2.4 | AAA | 6 | Developed | Western Europe | 5 out of 19 |
| New Zealand | -2.1 | -2.2 | AA | 8 | Developed | Australasia | 1 out of 7 |
| Nicaragua | 11.5 | 11.7 | B+ | 127 | | Latin America | 19 out of 20 |
| Niger | 11.1 | 11.3 | | 120 | | Africa | 25 out of 51 |
| Nigeria | 9.3 | 9.4 | B | 97 | Frontier | Africa | 14 out of 51 |
| Norway | -2.9 | -3.1 | AAA | 3 | Developed | Western Europe | 2 out of 19 |
| Oman | 2.9 | 3.0 | BBB- | 46 | Frontier | Middle East | 5 out of 13 |
| Pakistan | 11.2 | 11.3 | B | 122 | Frontier | Asia | 19 out of 29 |
| Panama | 3.6 | 3.6 | BBB | 52 | | Latin America | 6 out of 20 |
| Papua New Guinea | 10.8 | 11.0 | B+ | 118 | | Australasia | 3 out of 7 |
| Paraguay | 6.9 | 7.2 | BB | 80 | | Latin America | 9 out of 20 |
| Peru | 2.4 | 2.5 | BBB+ | 39 | Emerging | Latin America | 3 out of 20 |
| Philippines | 3.9 | 3.9 | BBB | 53 | Emerging | Asia | 9 out of 29 |
| Poland | 1.1 | 0.9 | BBB+ | 29 | Emerging | Central and Eastern Europe | 3 out of 25 |
| Portugal | 3.3 | 3.1 | BB+ | 49 | Developed | Western Europe | 17 out of 19 |
| Qatar | 0.0 | 0.0 | AA | 21 | Emerging | Middle East | 1 out of 13 |
| Romania | 4.1 | 4.1 | BBB- | 56 | Frontier | Central and Eastern Europe | 9 out of 25 |
| Russia | 6.2 | 5.7 | BB+ | 68 | Emerging | Central and Eastern Europe | 14 out of 25 |
| Rwanda | 11.9 | 12.1 | B | 130 | | Africa | 31 out of 51 |
| São Tomé & Príncipe | 17.9 | 18.7 | | 163 | | Africa | 43 out of 51 |
| Saudi Arabia | 3.3 | 3.0 | A- | 47 | | Middle East | 6 out of 13 |
| Senegal | 8.6 | 8.7 | B+ | 86 | | Africa | 8 out of 51 |
| Serbia | 6.8 | 6.6 | BB- | 75 | Frontier | Central and Eastern Europe | 16 out of 25 |
| Seychelles | 6.3 | 6.4 | | 73 | | Africa | 5 out of 51 |
| Sierra Leone | 11.9 | 12.1 | | 129 | | Africa | 30 out of 51 |
| Singapore | -3.1 | -3.2 | AAA | 1 | Developed | Asia | 1 out of 29 |
| Slovakia | 0.4 | 0.4 | A+ | 24 | | Central and Eastern Europe | 2 out of 25 |
| Slovenia | 1.7 | 1.7 | A | 34 | Frontier | Central and Eastern Europe | 5 out of 25 |
| Solomon Islands | 22.1 | 22.5 | | 168 | | Australasia | 6 out of 7 |
| Somalia | 20.4 | 20.8 | | 166 | | Africa | 46 out of 51 |
| South Africa | 4.1 | 4.4 | BBB- | 60 | Emerging | Africa | 2 out of 51 |
| Spain | 2.5 | 2.5 | BBB+ | 38 | Developed | Western Europe | 16 out of 19 |
| Sri Lanka | 6.3 | 6.1 | B+ | 72 | Frontier | Asia | 14 out of 29 |
| Sudan | 16.6 | 16.8 | | 154 | | Africa | 40 out of 51 |
| Suriname | 9.5 | 9.8 | B+ | 102 | | Latin America | 16 out of 20 |
| Swaziland | 15.0 | 16.2 | | 152 | | Africa | 38 out of 51 |
| Sweden | -2.2 | -2.4 | AAA | 7 | Developed | Western Europe | 6 out of 19 |

§ S&P Credit Rating based on long-term foreign currency issuer rating. See http://www.standardandpoors.com/.

* World rank based on 175 countries covered by Euromoney. Ranking based on ascending order in which '1' equals the smallest country risk premium (CRP) and '175' equals the largest country risk premium (CRP).

† MSCI Market Classification based on MSCI Market Classification Framework. See http://www.msci.com/products/indexes/market_classification.html

‡ Regional classification based on Euromoney. Regional rankings based on ascending order in which '1' equals the smallest country risk premium (CRP) for each region.

Note: A CRP of 0.0% is assumed in the following cases: (i) when the investor country and the investee country both have an S&P sovereign credit rating of AAA; or (ii) when the investor country has an S&P credit rating of AAA, and the investee country has a sovereign credit rating below AAA, but has a calculated CRP below 0.0% (which would imply lower risk than a country rated AAA); or (iii) when the investor country has an S&P credit rating below AAA, and the investee country has a sovereign credit rating of AAA, but has a calculated CRP above 0.0% (which would imply greater risk than a country rated below AAA). For purposes of this analysis, the U.S. is treated as having a sovereign credit rating equivalent to AAA.

The country risk premium (CRP) is not the cost of equity capital (COE). The CRP is to be added to base COE. See Chapter 6 for proper application.

## Data Updated Through March 2017

| Investee Country | December 2016 Country Risk Premium (CRP) (%) | March 2017 Country Risk Premium (CRP) (%) | S&P Sovereign Credit Rating § | World Rank Out of 175∗ | MSCI Market Classification † | Euromoney Region ‡ | Regional Rank ‡ |
|---|---|---|---|---|---|---|---|
| Switzerland | -2.9 | -3.1 | AAA | 2 | Developed | Western Europe | 1 out of 19 |
| Syria | 21.1 | 21.7 | | 167 | | Middle East | 13 out of 13 |
| Taiwan | -0.4 | -0.4 | AA- | 18 | Emerging | Asia | 3 out of 29 |
| Tajikistan | 16.2 | 16.8 | | 155 | | Central and Eastern Europe | 25 out of 25 |
| Tanzania | 8.9 | 9.2 | | 95 | | Africa | 13 out of 51 |
| Thailand | 3.6 | 3.5 | BBB+ | 51 | Emerging | Asia | 8 out of 29 |
| Togo | 10.4 | 10.6 | | 113 | | Africa | 20 out of 51 |
| Tonga | 24.4 | 24.8 | | 170 | | Australasia | 7 out of 7 |
| Trinidad & Tobago | 4.0 | 4.0 | A- | 54 | | Caribbean | 2 out of 9 |
| Tunisia | 6.6 | 7.1 | | 79 | Frontier | Africa | 6 out of 51 |
| Turkey | 4.3 | 4.2 | BB | 58 | Emerging | Central and Eastern Europe | 11 out of 25 |
| Turkmenistan | 13.6 | 14.0 | | 140 | | Asia | 24 out of 29 |
| Uganda | 10.0 | 10.4 | B | 110 | | Africa | 18 out of 51 |
| Ukraine | 12.6 | 12.9 | B- | 135 | | Central and Eastern Europe | 20 out of 25 |
| United Arab Emirates | 1.3 | 1.3 | AA | 33 | Emerging | Middle East | 4 out of 13 |
| United Kingdom | -0.1 | -0.1 | AA | 20 | Developed | Western Europe | 11 out of 19 |
| United States | -1.1 | -1.2 | AA+ | 15 | Developed | North America | 2 out of 2 |
| Uruguay | 3.0 | 2.9 | BBB | 45 | | Latin America | 5 out of 20 |
| Uzbekistan | 12.8 | 12.5 | | 132 | | Asia | 21 out of 29 |
| Vanuatu | 14.4 | 14.6 | | 145 | | Australasia | 4 out of 7 |
| Venezuela | 17.9 | 18.7 | CCC | 162 | | Latin America | 20 out of 20 |
| Vietnam | 7.2 | 7.0 | BB- | 78 | Frontier | Asia | 16 out of 29 |
| Yemen | 18.2 | 18.6 | | 161 | | Middle East | 12 out of 13 |
| Zambia | 10.3 | 10.5 | B | 111 | | Africa | 19 out of 51 |
| Zimbabwe | 19.8 | 20.0 | | 164 | | Africa | 44 out of 51 |

## March 2017 Country Risk Premium (CRP) Summary Statistics:

| S&P Rating | Country Count | Average CRP (%) | Median CRP (%) | Min CRP (%) | Max CRP (%) |
|---|---|---|---|---|---|
| AAA ∗∗ | 12 | -2.4 | -2.4 | -3.2 | -1.2 |
| AA (AA+, AA, AA-) | 15 | -0.1 | -0.1 | -2.2 | 2.8 |
| A (A+, A, A-) | 14 | 1.8 | 1.9 | 0.4 | 4.0 |
| BBB (BBB+, BBB, BBB-) | 17 | 3.5 | 3.5 | 0.9 | 5.8 |
| BB (BB+, BB, BB-) | 22 | 6.3 | 6.2 | 2.6 | 11.5 |
| B+ − SD | 39 | 10.9 | 10.5 | 6.1 | 18.7 |
| Investment Grade ∗∗ | 58 | 0.9 | 0.9 | -3.2 | 5.8 |
| Non-Investment Grade ∗∗ | 61 | 9.2 | 9.4 | 2.6 | 18.7 |
| **MSCI Market Classification** | | | | | |
| Developed Markets | 23 | -1.0 | -1.8 | -3.2 | 3.3 |
| Emerging Markets | 23 | 3.2 | 2.8 | -0.8 | 10.8 |
| Frontier Markets | 22 | 6.1 | 5.9 | 1.0 | 11.5 |
| **Euromoney Region ‡** | | | | | |
| Africa | 51 | 13.3 | 11.3 | 3.0 | 33.0 |
| Asia | 29 | 8.2 | 6.8 | -3.2 | 30.5 |
| Australasia | 7 | 11.9 | 14.6 | -2.2 | 24.8 |
| Caribbean | 9 | 9.4 | 9.0 | 2.9 | 18.4 |
| Central and Eastern Europe | 25 | 6.6 | 4.7 | 0.2 | 16.8 |
| Latin America | 20 | 7.2 | 7.9 | -0.8 | 18.7 |
| Middle East | 13 | 7.4 | 5.0 | 0.0 | 21.7 |
| North America | 2 | -1.7 | -1.7 | -2.2 | -1.2 |
| Western Europe | 19 | -0.1 | -0.6 | -3.1 | 10.1 |

## CCR Base Cost of Equity Capital:

| Qatar | COE (%) |
|---|---|
| March 2017 | 9.6 |
| December 2016 | 9.6 |

CCR base country-level COE for a Qatar-based investor investing in Qatar.

§ S&P Credit Rating based on long-term foreign currency issuer rating. See http://www.standardandpoors.com/.

∗ World rank based on 175 countries covered by Euromoney. Ranking based on ascending order in which '1' equals the smallest country risk premium (CRP) and '175' equals the largest country risk premium (CRP).

† MSCI Market Classification based on MSCI Market Classification Framework. See http://www.msci.com/products/indexes/market_classification.html.

‡ Regional classification based on Euromoney. Regional rankings based on ascending order in which '1' equals the smallest country risk premium (CRP) for each region.

∗∗ Investment grade based on S&P sovereign credit rating from AAA to BBB-. Non-Investment grade based on S&P sovereign credit rating from BB+ to SD. For purposes of this analysis, the U.S. is being treated as if it were rated AAA by S&P.

Note: A CRP of 0.0% is assumed in the following cases: (i) when the investor country and the investee country both have an S&P sovereign credit rating of AAA; or (ii) when the investor country has an S&P credit rating of AAA, and the investee country has a sovereign credit rating below AAA, but has a calculated CRP below 0.0% (which would imply lower risk than a country rated AAA); or (iii) when the investor country has an S&P credit rating below AAA, and the investee country has a sovereign credit rating of AAA, but has a calculated CRP above 0.0% (which would imply greater risk than a country rated below AAA). For purposes of this analysis, the U.S. is treated as having a sovereign credit rating equivalent to AAA.

The country risk premium (CRP) is not the cost of equity capital (COE). The CRP is to be added to base COE. See Chapter 6 for proper application.

## Data Updated Through March 2017

| Investee Country | December 2016 Country Risk Premium (CRP) (%) | March 2017 Country Risk Premium (CRP) (%) | S&P Sovereign Credit Rating § | World Rank Out of 175* | MSCI Market Classification † | Euromoney Region ‡ | Regional Rank ‡ |
|---|---|---|---|---|---|---|---|
| Afghanistan | 7.2 | 7.3 | | 139 | | Asia | 23 out of 29 |
| Albania | 2.5 | 3.0 | B+ | 93 | | Central and Eastern Europe | 18 out of 25 |
| Algeria | 2.5 | 3.0 | | 91 | | Africa | 10 out of 51 |
| Angola | 4.6 | 5.0 | B | 121 | | Africa | 26 out of 51 |
| Argentina | 3.0 | 3.2 | B- | 96 | Frontier | Latin America | 13 out of 20 |
| Armenia | 0.4 | 1.0 | | 77 | | Asia | 15 out of 29 |
| Australia | -7.5 | -6.7 | AAA | 12 | Developed | Australasia | 2 out of 7 |
| Austria | -7.3 | -6.5 | AA+ | 13 | Developed | Western Europe | 9 out of 19 |
| Azerbaijan | 1.4 | 2.2 | BB+ | 85 | | Asia | 17 out of 29 |
| Bahamas | -0.9 | -0.6 | BB+ | 65 | | Caribbean | 3 out of 9 |
| Bahrain | -1.0 | -0.6 | BB- | 64 | Frontier | Middle East | 7 out of 13 |
| Bangladesh | 5.0 | 5.2 | BB- | 126 | Frontier | Asia | 20 out of 29 |
| Barbados | 0.5 | 1.9 | CCC+ | 82 | | Caribbean | 4 out of 9 |
| Belarus | 6.9 | 7.6 | B- | 143 | | Central and Eastern Europe | 23 out of 25 |
| Belgium | -6.2 | -5.5 | AA | 17 | Developed | Western Europe | 10 out of 19 |
| Belize | 3.4 | 3.9 | B- | 106 | | Latin America | 17 out of 20 |
| Benin | 8.4 | 8.7 | | 150 | | Africa | 37 out of 51 |
| Bermuda | -3.0 | -2.4 | A+ | 44 | | Caribbean | 1 out of 9 |
| Bhutan | 8.1 | 8.2 | | 148 | | Asia | 25 out of 29 |
| Bolivia | 2.1 | 2.8 | BB | 88 | | Latin America | 12 out of 20 |
| Bosnia & Herzegovina | 7.3 | 7.7 | B | 144 | | Central and Eastern Europe | 24 out of 25 |
| Botswana | -3.0 | -2.4 | A- | 48 | | Africa | 1 out of 51 |
| Brazil | -1.6 | -1.2 | BB | 59 | Emerging | Latin America | 7 out of 20 |
| Bulgaria | -1.8 | -1.1 | BB+ | 61 | | Central and Eastern Europe | 12 out of 25 |
| Burkina Faso | 5.9 | 6.2 | B- | 133 | | Africa | 33 out of 51 |
| Burundi | 16.3 | 16.2 | | 169 | | Africa | 47 out of 51 |
| Cambodia | 8.9 | 8.8 | | 151 | | Asia | 27 out of 29 |
| Cameroon | 4.7 | 5.1 | B | 124 | | Africa | 28 out of 51 |
| Canada | -7.6 | -6.9 | AAA | 9 | Developed | North America | 1 out of 2 |
| Cape Verde | 2.7 | 3.1 | B | 94 | | Africa | 12 out of 51 |
| Central African Republic | 19.4 | 19.2 | | 172 | | Africa | 49 out of 51 |
| Chad | 18.2 | 18.1 | | 171 | | Africa | 48 out of 51 |
| Chile | -6.6 | -5.7 | AA- | 16 | Emerging | Latin America | 1 out of 20 |
| China | -3.2 | -2.5 | AA- | 42 | Emerging | Asia | 7 out of 29 |
| Colombia | -3.2 | -2.6 | BBB | 41 | Emerging | Latin America | 4 out of 20 |
| Congo Republic | 4.4 | 4.6 | B- | 117 | | Africa | 24 out of 51 |
| Congo, DR | 5.5 | 5.7 | B- | 131 | | Africa | 32 out of 51 |
| Costa Rica | -0.5 | 0.2 | BB- | 71 | | Latin America | 8 out of 20 |
| Côte d'Ivoire | 2.5 | 3.0 | | 92 | | Africa | 11 out of 51 |
| Croatia | -1.3 | -0.9 | BB | 63 | Frontier | Central and Eastern Europe | 13 out of 25 |
| Cuba | 10.9 | 11.2 | | 160 | | Caribbean | 9 out of 9 |
| Cyprus | -3.4 | -2.7 | BB+ | 40 | | Central and Eastern Europe | 7 out of 25 |
| Czech Republic | -5.5 | -4.8 | AA- | 23 | Emerging | Central and Eastern Europe | 1 out of 25 |
| Denmark | -8.2 | -7.4 | AAA | 4 | Developed | Western Europe | 3 out of 19 |
| Djibouti | 26.3 | 24.0 | | 175 | | Africa | 51 out of 51 |
| Dominican Republic | 2.4 | 2.9 | BB- | 90 | | Caribbean | 5 out of 9 |
| Ecuador | 3.8 | 4.0 | B | 109 | | Latin America | 18 out of 20 |
| Egypt | 4.2 | 4.5 | B- | 116 | Emerging | Africa | 23 out of 51 |
| El Salvador | 1.5 | 1.8 | B- | 81 | | Latin America | 10 out of 20 |
| Equatorial Guinea | 13.1 | 13.2 | | 165 | | Africa | 45 out of 51 |

§ S&P Credit Rating based on long-term foreign currency issuer rating. See http://www.standardandpoors.com/.

* World rank based on 175 countries covered by Euromoney. Ranking based on ascending order in which '1' equals the smallest country risk premium (CRP) and '175' equals the largest country risk premium (CRP).

† MSCI Market Classification based on MSCI Market Classification Framework. See http://www.msci.com/products/indexes/market_classification.html

‡ Regional classification based on Euromoney. Regional rankings based on ascending order in which '1' equals the smallest country risk premium (CRP) for each region.

Note: A CRP of 0.0% is assumed in the following cases: (i) when the investor country and the investee country both have an S&P sovereign credit rating of AAA; or (ii) when the investor country has an S&P credit rating of AAA, and the investee country has a sovereign credit rating below AAA, but has a calculated CRP below 0.0% (which would imply lower risk than a country rated AAA); or (iii) when the investor country has an S&P credit rating below AAA, and the investee country has a sovereign credit rating of AAA, but has a calculated CRP above 0.0% (which would imply greater risk than a country rated below AAA). For purposes of this analysis, the U.S. is treated as having a sovereign credit rating equivalent to AAA.

The country risk premium (CRP) is not the cost of equity capital (COE). The CRP is to be added to base COE. See Chapter 6 for proper application.

### Data Updated Through March 2017

| Investee Country | December 2016 Country Risk Premium (CRP) (%) | March 2017 Country Risk Premium (CRP) (%) | S&P Sovereign Credit Rating § | World Rank Out of 175* | MSCI Market Classification † | Euromoney Region ‡ | Regional Rank ‡ |
|---|---|---|---|---|---|---|---|
| Eritrea | 23.0 | 21.2 | | 173 | | Africa | 50 out of 51 |
| Estonia | -5.0 | -4.1 | AA- | 32 | Frontier | Central and Eastern Europe | 4 out of 25 |
| Ethiopia | 3.1 | 3.6 | B | 101 | | Africa | 16 out of 51 |
| Fiji | 7.8 | 8.0 | B+ | 147 | | Australasia | 5 out of 7 |
| Finland | -7.5 | -6.8 | AA+ | 11 | Developed | Western Europe | 8 out of 19 |
| France | -5.5 | -4.9 | AA | 22 | Developed | Western Europe | 12 out of 19 |
| Gabon | 1.2 | 2.0 | | 83 | | Africa | 7 out of 51 |
| Gambia | 6.5 | 6.8 | | 138 | | Africa | 34 out of 51 |
| Georgia | 0.1 | 0.8 | BB- | 74 | | Central and Eastern Europe | 15 out of 25 |
| Germany | -7.5 | -6.8 | AAA | 10 | Developed | Western Europe | 7 out of 19 |
| Ghana | 2.7 | 2.8 | B- | 89 | | Africa | 9 out of 51 |
| Greece | 3.7 | 3.9 | B- | 108 | Emerging | Western Europe | 19 out of 19 |
| Grenada | 3.4 | 3.8 | | 105 | | Caribbean | 7 out of 9 |
| Guatemala | 1.6 | 2.1 | BB | 84 | | Latin America | 11 out of 20 |
| Guinea | 9.7 | 9.9 | | 156 | | Africa | 41 out of 51 |
| Guinea-Bissau | 4.1 | 4.5 | | 115 | | Africa | 22 out of 51 |
| Guyana | 3.1 | 3.5 | | 100 | | Latin America | 15 out of 20 |
| Haiti | 12.2 | 10.6 | | 157 | | Caribbean | 8 out of 9 |
| Honduras | 2.8 | 3.3 | B+ | 98 | | Latin America | 14 out of 20 |
| Hong Kong | -7.0 | -6.3 | AAA | 14 | Developed | Asia | 2 out of 29 |
| Hungary | -2.0 | -1.3 | BBB- | 57 | Emerging | Central and Eastern Europe | 10 out of 25 |
| Iceland | -4.6 | -4.1 | A | 30 | | Western Europe | 15 out of 19 |
| India | -2.2 | -1.4 | BBB- | 55 | Emerging | Asia | 10 out of 29 |
| Indonesia | -1.5 | -0.9 | BB+ | 62 | Emerging | Asia | 11 out of 29 |
| Iran | 4.5 | 5.1 | | 125 | | Middle East | 10 out of 13 |
| Iraq | 6.1 | 6.5 | B- | 136 | | Middle East | 11 out of 13 |
| Ireland | -5.1 | -4.4 | A+ | 27 | Developed | Western Europe | 14 out of 19 |
| Israel | -5.1 | -4.4 | A+ | 28 | Developed | Middle East | 2 out of 13 |
| Italy | -2.5 | -2.1 | BBB- | 50 | Developed | Western Europe | 18 out of 19 |
| Jamaica | 2.9 | 3.8 | B | 104 | | Caribbean | 6 out of 9 |
| Japan | -5.2 | -4.5 | A+ | 25 | Developed | Asia | 5 out of 29 |
| Jordan | 0.3 | 1.0 | BB- | 76 | Frontier | Middle East | 8 out of 13 |
| Kazakhstan | -0.1 | 0.1 | BBB- | 70 | Frontier | Asia | 13 out of 29 |
| Kenya | 2.9 | 3.4 | B+ | 99 | Frontier | Africa | 15 out of 51 |
| Korea (North) | 22.4 | 21.8 | | 174 | | Asia | 29 out of 29 |
| Korea (South) | -5.9 | -5.1 | AA | 19 | Emerging | Asia | 4 out of 29 |
| Kuwait | -4.9 | -4.1 | AA | 31 | Frontier | Middle East | 3 out of 13 |
| Kyrgyz Republic | 7.4 | 7.5 | | 142 | | Central and Eastern Europe | 22 out of 25 |
| Laos | 11.1 | 10.8 | | 158 | | Asia | 28 out of 29 |
| Latvia | -3.2 | -2.4 | A- | 43 | | Central and Eastern Europe | 8 out of 25 |
| Lebanon | 4.4 | 4.3 | B- | 112 | Frontier | Middle East | 9 out of 13 |
| Lesotho | 7.6 | 7.9 | | 146 | | Africa | 36 out of 51 |
| Liberia | 3.5 | 3.9 | | 107 | | Africa | 17 out of 51 |
| Libya | 8.9 | 9.4 | | 153 | | Africa | 39 out of 51 |
| Lithuania | -3.9 | -3.1 | A- | 36 | Frontier | Central and Eastern Europe | 6 out of 25 |
| Luxembourg | -7.9 | -7.2 | AAA | 5 | | Western Europe | 4 out of 19 |
| Macedonia | 2.1 | 2.7 | BB- | 87 | | Central and Eastern Europe | 17 out of 25 |
| Madagascar | 4.2 | 5.0 | | 123 | | Africa | 27 out of 51 |
| Malawi | 4.0 | 4.4 | | 114 | | Africa | 21 out of 51 |
| Malaysia | -3.7 | -3.2 | A- | 35 | Emerging | Asia | 6 out of 29 |

§ S&P Credit Rating based on long-term foreign currency issuer rating. See http://www.standardandpoors.com/.

* World rank based on 175 countries covered by Euromoney. Ranking based on ascending order in which '1' equals the smallest country risk premium (CRP) and '175' equals the largest country risk premium (CRP).

† MSCI Market Classification based on MSCI Market Classification Framework. See http://www.msci.com/products/indexes/market_classification.html

‡ Regional classification based on Euromoney. Regional rankings based on ascending order in which '1' equals the smallest country risk premium (CRP) for each region.

Note: A CRP of 0.0% is assumed in the following cases: (i) when the investor country and the investee country both have an S&P sovereign credit rating of AAA; or (ii) when the investor country has an S&P credit rating of AAA, and the investee country has a sovereign credit rating below AAA, but has a calculated CRP below 0.0% (which would imply lower risk than a country rated AAA); or (iii) when the investor country has an S&P credit rating below AAA, and the investee country has a sovereign credit rating of AAA, but has a calculated CRP above 0.0% (which would imply greater risk than a country rated below AAA). For purposes of this analysis, the U.S. is treated as having a sovereign credit rating equivalent to AAA.

The country risk premium (CRP) is not the cost of equity capital (COE). The CRP is to be added to base COE. See Chapter 6 for proper application.

### Data Updated Through March 2017

| Investee Country | December 2016 Country Risk Premium (CRP) (%) | March 2017 Country Risk Premium (CRP) (%) | S&P Sovereign Credit Rating § | World Rank Out of 175* | MSCI Market Classification † | Euromoney Region ‡ | Regional Rank ‡ |
|---|---|---|---|---|---|---|---|
| Mali | 7.2 | 7.5 | | 141 | | Africa | 35 out of 51 |
| Malta | -5.2 | -4.4 | A- | 26 | | Western Europe | 13 out of 19 |
| Mauritania | 10.8 | 10.9 | | 159 | | Africa | 42 out of 51 |
| Mauritius | -0.7 | -0.2 | | 67 | Frontier | Asia | 12 out of 29 |
| Mexico | -3.8 | -3.1 | BBB+ | 37 | Emerging | Latin America | 2 out of 20 |
| Moldova | 5.9 | 6.5 | | 137 | | Central and Eastern Europe | 21 out of 25 |
| Mongolia | 4.3 | 4.9 | B- | 119 | | Asia | 18 out of 29 |
| Montenegro | 3.6 | 3.8 | B+ | 103 | | Central and Eastern Europe | 19 out of 25 |
| Morocco | -0.7 | 0.0 | BBB- | 69 | Frontier | Africa | 4 out of 51 |
| Mozambique | 5.2 | 5.4 | SD | 128 | | Africa | 29 out of 51 |
| Myanmar | 6.0 | 6.3 | | 134 | | Asia | 22 out of 29 |
| Namibia | -1.0 | -0.3 | | 66 | | Africa | 3 out of 51 |
| Nepal | 8.4 | 8.6 | | 149 | | Asia | 26 out of 29 |
| Netherlands | -7.9 | -7.1 | AAA | 6 | Developed | Western Europe | 5 out of 19 |
| New Zealand | -7.7 | -6.9 | AA | 8 | Developed | Australasia | 1 out of 7 |
| Nicaragua | 4.9 | 5.3 | B+ | 127 | | Latin America | 19 out of 20 |
| Niger | 4.6 | 4.9 | | 120 | | Africa | 25 out of 51 |
| Nigeria | 2.8 | 3.3 | B | 97 | Frontier | Africa | 14 out of 51 |
| Norway | -8.4 | -7.7 | AAA | 3 | Developed | Western Europe | 2 out of 19 |
| Oman | -3.0 | -2.4 | BBB- | 46 | Frontier | Middle East | 5 out of 13 |
| Pakistan | 4.7 | 5.0 | B | 122 | Frontier | Asia | 19 out of 29 |
| Panama | -2.4 | -1.8 | BBB | 52 | | Latin America | 6 out of 20 |
| Papua New Guinea | 4.2 | 4.7 | B+ | 118 | | Australasia | 3 out of 7 |
| Paraguay | 0.7 | 1.3 | BB | 80 | | Latin America | 9 out of 20 |
| Peru | -3.6 | -2.8 | BBB+ | 39 | Emerging | Latin America | 3 out of 20 |
| Philippines | -2.1 | -1.5 | BBB | 53 | Emerging | Asia | 9 out of 29 |
| Poland | -4.8 | -4.2 | BBB+ | 29 | Emerging | Central and Eastern Europe | 3 out of 25 |
| Portugal | -2.7 | -2.2 | BB+ | 49 | Developed | Western Europe | 17 out of 19 |
| Qatar | -5.8 | -5.0 | AA | 21 | Emerging | Middle East | 1 out of 13 |
| Romania | -2.0 | -1.3 | BBB- | 56 | Frontier | Central and Eastern Europe | 9 out of 25 |
| Russia | 0.0 | 0.0 | BB+ | 68 | Emerging | Central and Eastern Europe | 14 out of 25 |
| Rwanda | 5.3 | 5.6 | B | 130 | | Africa | 31 out of 51 |
| São Tomé & Príncipe | 10.9 | 11.4 | | 163 | | Africa | 43 out of 51 |
| Saudi Arabia | -2.7 | -2.4 | A- | 47 | | Middle East | 6 out of 13 |
| Senegal | 2.2 | 2.7 | B+ | 86 | | Africa | 8 out of 51 |
| Serbia | 0.6 | 0.9 | BB- | 75 | Frontier | Central and Eastern Europe | 16 out of 25 |
| Seychelles | 0.1 | 0.7 | | 73 | | Africa | 5 out of 51 |
| Sierra Leone | 5.3 | 5.6 | | 129 | | Africa | 30 out of 51 |
| Singapore | -8.6 | -7.8 | AAA | 1 | Developed | Asia | 1 out of 29 |
| Slovakia | -5.4 | -4.6 | A+ | 24 | | Central and Eastern Europe | 2 out of 25 |
| Slovenia | -4.2 | -3.5 | A | 34 | Frontier | Central and Eastern Europe | 5 out of 25 |
| Solomon Islands | 14.7 | 14.7 | | 168 | | Australasia | 6 out of 7 |
| Somalia | 13.2 | 13.3 | | 166 | | Africa | 46 out of 51 |
| South Africa | -1.9 | -1.1 | BBB- | 60 | Emerging | Africa | 2 out of 51 |
| Spain | -3.5 | -2.8 | BBB+ | 38 | Developed | Western Europe | 16 out of 19 |
| Sri Lanka | 0.1 | 0.3 | B+ | 72 | Frontier | Asia | 14 out of 29 |
| Sudan | 9.7 | 9.8 | | 154 | | Africa | 40 out of 51 |
| Suriname | 3.1 | 3.6 | B+ | 102 | | Latin America | 16 out of 20 |
| Swaziland | 8.2 | 9.2 | | 152 | | Africa | 38 out of 51 |
| Sweden | -7.8 | -7.1 | AAA | 7 | Developed | Western Europe | 6 out of 19 |

§ S&P Credit Rating based on long-term foreign currency issuer rating. See http://www.standardandpoors.com/.

* World rank based on 175 countries covered by Euromoney. Ranking based on ascending order in which '1' equals the smallest country risk premium (CRP) and '175' equals the largest country risk premium (CRP).

† MSCI Market Classification based on MSCI Market Classification Framework. See http://www.msci.com/products/indexes/market_classification.html

‡ Regional classification based on Euromoney. Regional rankings based on ascending order in which '1' equals the smallest country risk premium (CRP) for each region.

Note: A CRP of 0.0% is assumed in the following cases: (i) when the investor country and the investee country both have an S&P sovereign credit rating of AAA; or (ii) when the investor country has an S&P credit rating of AAA, and the investee country has a sovereign credit rating below AAA, but has a calculated CRP below 0.0% (which would imply lower risk than a country rated AAA); or (iii) when the investor country has an S&P credit rating below AAA, and the investee country has a sovereign credit rating of AAA, but has a calculated CRP above 0.0% (which would imply greater risk than a country rated below AAA). For purposes of this analysis, the U.S. is treated as having a sovereign credit rating equivalent to AAA.

The country risk premium (CRP) is not the cost of equity capital (COE). The CRP is to be added to base COE. See Chapter 6 for proper application.

## Data Updated Through March 2017

| Investee Country | December 2016 Country Risk Premium (CRP) (%) | March 2017 Country Risk Premium (CRP) (%) | S&P Sovereign Credit Rating § | World Rank Out of 175* | MSCI Market Classification † | Euromoney Region ‡ | Regional Rank ‡ |
|---|---|---|---|---|---|---|---|
| Switzerland | -8.4 | -7.7 | AAA | 2 | Developed | Western Europe | 1 out of 19 |
| Syria | 13.8 | 14.1 | | 167 | | Middle East | 13 out of 13 |
| Taiwan | -6.1 | -5.3 | AA- | 18 | Emerging | Asia | 3 out of 29 |
| Tajikistan | 9.3 | 9.8 | | 155 | | Central and Eastern Europe | 25 out of 25 |
| Tanzania | 2.5 | 3.1 | | 95 | | Africa | 13 out of 51 |
| Thailand | -2.4 | -1.9 | BBB+ | 51 | Emerging | Asia | 8 out of 29 |
| Togo | 3.9 | 4.3 | | 113 | | Africa | 20 out of 51 |
| Tonga | 16.8 | 16.8 | | 170 | | Australasia | 7 out of 7 |
| Trinidad & Tobago | -2.1 | -1.5 | A- | 54 | | Caribbean | 2 out of 9 |
| Tunisia | 0.4 | 1.2 | | 79 | Frontier | Africa | 6 out of 51 |
| Turkey | -1.8 | -1.3 | BB | 58 | Emerging | Central and Eastern Europe | 11 out of 25 |
| Turkmenistan | 6.8 | 7.4 | | 140 | | Asia | 24 out of 29 |
| Uganda | 3.5 | 4.2 | B | 110 | | Africa | 18 out of 51 |
| Ukraine | 6.0 | 6.4 | B- | 135 | | Central and Eastern Europe | 20 out of 25 |
| United Arab Emirates | -4.5 | -3.8 | AA | 33 | Emerging | Middle East | 4 out of 13 |
| United Kingdom | -5.9 | -5.0 | AA | 20 | Developed | Western Europe | 11 out of 19 |
| United States | -6.8 | -6.0 | AA+ | 15 | Developed | North America | 2 out of 2 |
| Uruguay | -3.0 | -2.4 | BBB | 45 | | Latin America | 5 out of 20 |
| Uzbekistan | 6.1 | 6.0 | | 132 | | Asia | 21 out of 29 |
| Vanuatu | 7.6 | 7.8 | | 145 | | Australasia | 4 out of 7 |
| Venezuela | 10.9 | 11.4 | CCC | 162 | | Latin America | 20 out of 20 |
| Vietnam | 0.9 | 1.2 | BB- | 78 | Frontier | Asia | 16 out of 29 |
| Yemen | 11.1 | 11.4 | | 161 | | Middle East | 12 out of 13 |
| Zambia | 3.8 | 4.2 | B | 111 | | Africa | 19 out of 51 |
| Zimbabwe | 12.6 | 12.6 | | 164 | | Africa | 44 out of 51 |

### March 2017 Country Risk Premium (CRP) Summary Statistics:

| S&P Rating | Country Count | Average CRP (%) | Median CRP (%) | Min CRP (%) | Max CRP (%) |
|---|---|---|---|---|---|
| AAA ** | 12 | -7.1 | -7.1 | -7.8 | -6.0 |
| AA (AA+, AA, AA-) | 15 | -5.1 | -5.0 | -6.9 | -2.5 |
| A (A+, A, A-) | 14 | -3.4 | -3.3 | -4.6 | -1.5 |
| BBB (BBB+, BBB, BBB-) | 17 | -1.9 | -1.9 | -4.2 | 0.1 |
| BB (BB+, BB, BB-) | 22 | 0.5 | 0.5 | -2.7 | 5.2 |
| B+ − SD | 39 | 4.6 | 4.2 | 0.3 | 11.4 |
| Investment Grade ** | 58 | -4.1 | -4.2 | -7.8 | 0.1 |
| Non-Investment Grade ** | 61 | 3.1 | 3.3 | -2.7 | 11.4 |
| **MSCI Market Classification** | | | | | |
| Developed Markets | 23 | -5.8 | -6.5 | -7.8 | -2.1 |
| Emerging Markets | 23 | -2.2 | -2.5 | -5.7 | 4.5 |
| Frontier Markets | 22 | 0.4 | 0.2 | -4.1 | 5.2 |
| **Euromoney Region ‡** | | | | | |
| Africa | 51 | 6.7 | 5.0 | -2.4 | 24.0 |
| Asia | 29 | 2.2 | 1.0 | -7.8 | 21.8 |
| Australasia | 7 | 5.5 | 7.8 | -6.9 | 16.8 |
| Caribbean | 9 | 3.3 | 2.9 | -2.4 | 11.2 |
| Central and Eastern Europe | 25 | 0.9 | -0.9 | -4.8 | 9.8 |
| Latin America | 20 | 1.3 | 2.0 | -5.7 | 11.4 |
| Middle East | 13 | 1.5 | -0.6 | -5.0 | 14.1 |
| North America | 2 | -6.5 | -6.5 | -6.9 | -6.0 |
| Western Europe | 19 | -5.0 | -5.5 | -7.7 | 3.9 |

### CCR Base Cost of Equity Capital:

| Russia | COE (%) |
|---|---|
| March 2017 | 24.1 |
| December 2016 | 25.1 |

CCR base country-level COE for a Russia-based investor investing in Russia.

§ S&P Credit Rating based on long-term foreign currency issuer rating. See http://www.standardandpoors.com/.

* World rank based on 175 countries covered by Euromoney. Ranking based on ascending order in which '1' equals the smallest country risk premium (CRP) and '175' equals the largest country risk premium (CRP).

† MSCI Market Classification based on MSCI Market Classification Framework. See http://www.msci.com/products/indexes/market_classification.html

‡ Regional classification based on Euromoney. Regional rankings based on ascending order in which '1' equals the smallest country risk premium (CRP) for each region.

** Investment grade based on S&P sovereign credit rating from AAA to BBB-. Non-Investment grade based on S&P sovereign credit rating from BB+ to SD. For purposes of this analysis, the U.S. is being treated as if it were rated AAA by S&P.

Note: A CRP of 0.0% is assumed in the following cases: (i) when the investor country and the investee country both have an S&P sovereign credit rating of AAA; or (ii) when the investor country has an S&P credit rating of AAA, and the investee country has a sovereign credit rating below AAA, but has a calculated CRP below 0.0% (which would imply lower risk than a country rated AAA); or (iii) when the investor country has an S&P credit rating below AAA, and the investee country has a sovereign credit rating of AAA, but has a calculated CRP above 0.0% (which would imply greater risk than a country rated below AAA). For purposes of this analysis, the U.S. is treated as having a sovereign credit rating equivalent to AAA.

The country risk premium (CRP) is not the cost of equity capital (COE). The CRP is to be added to base COE. See Chapter 6 for proper application.

## Data Updated Through March 2017

| Investee Country | December 2016 Country Risk Premium (CRP) (%) | March 2017 Country Risk Premium (CRP) (%) | S&P Sovereign Credit Rating § | World Rank Out of 175* | MSCI Market Classification † | Euromoney Region ‡ | Regional Rank ‡ |
|---|---|---|---|---|---|---|---|
| Afghanistan | 10.7 | 10.9 | | 139 | | Asia | 23 out of 29 |
| Albania | 5.6 | 6.1 | B+ | 93 | | Central and Eastern Europe | 18 out of 25 |
| Algeria | 5.6 | 6.1 | | 91 | | Africa | 10 out of 51 |
| Angola | 7.8 | 8.3 | B | 121 | | Africa | 26 out of 51 |
| Argentina | 6.1 | 6.3 | B- | 96 | Frontier | Latin America | 13 out of 20 |
| Armenia | 3.3 | 3.8 | | 77 | | Asia | 15 out of 29 |
| Australia | -5.1 | -4.9 | AAA | 12 | Developed | Australasia | 2 out of 7 |
| Austria | -4.9 | -4.7 | AA+ | 13 | Developed | Western Europe | 9 out of 19 |
| Azerbaijan | 4.4 | 5.1 | BB+ | 85 | | Asia | 17 out of 29 |
| Bahamas | 2.0 | 2.0 | BB+ | 65 | | Caribbean | 3 out of 9 |
| Bahrain | 1.9 | 2.0 | BB- | 64 | Frontier | Middle East | 7 out of 13 |
| Bangladesh | 8.3 | 8.5 | BB- | 126 | Frontier | Asia | 20 out of 29 |
| Barbados | 3.5 | 4.9 | CCC+ | 82 | | Caribbean | 4 out of 9 |
| Belarus | 10.4 | 11.2 | B- | 143 | | Central and Eastern Europe | 23 out of 25 |
| Belgium | -3.7 | -3.6 | AA | 17 | Developed | Western Europe | 10 out of 19 |
| Belize | 6.5 | 7.0 | B- | 106 | | Latin America | 17 out of 20 |
| Benin | 12.0 | 12.5 | | 150 | | Africa | 37 out of 51 |
| Bermuda | -0.3 | -0.1 | A+ | 44 | | Caribbean | 1 out of 9 |
| Bhutan | 11.7 | 12.0 | | 148 | | Asia | 25 out of 29 |
| Bolivia | 5.2 | 5.8 | BB | 88 | | Latin America | 12 out of 20 |
| Bosnia & Herzegovina | 10.8 | 11.4 | B | 144 | | Central and Eastern Europe | 24 out of 25 |
| Botswana | -0.3 | 0.0 | A- | 48 | | Africa | 1 out of 51 |
| Brazil | 1.2 | 1.4 | BB | 59 | Emerging | Latin America | 7 out of 20 |
| Bulgaria | 1.0 | 1.5 | BB+ | 61 | | Central and Eastern Europe | 12 out of 25 |
| Burkina Faso | 9.3 | 9.7 | B- | 133 | | Africa | 33 out of 51 |
| Burundi | 20.4 | 21.0 | | 169 | | Africa | 47 out of 51 |
| Cambodia | 12.5 | 12.7 | | 151 | | Asia | 27 out of 29 |
| Cameroon | 8.0 | 8.4 | B | 124 | | Africa | 28 out of 51 |
| Canada | -5.3 | -5.1 | AAA | 9 | Developed | North America | 1 out of 2 |
| Cape Verde | 5.8 | 6.2 | B | 94 | | Africa | 12 out of 51 |
| Central African Republic | 23.7 | 24.4 | | 172 | | Africa | 49 out of 51 |
| Chad | 22.5 | 23.2 | | 171 | | Africa | 48 out of 51 |
| Chile | -4.2 | -3.7 | AA- | 16 | Emerging | Latin America | 1 out of 20 |
| China | -0.5 | -0.2 | AA- | 42 | Emerging | Asia | 7 out of 29 |
| Colombia | -0.5 | -0.2 | BBB | 41 | Emerging | Latin America | 4 out of 20 |
| Congo Republic | 7.6 | 7.9 | B- | 117 | | Africa | 24 out of 51 |
| Congo, DR | 8.8 | 9.2 | B- | 131 | | Africa | 32 out of 51 |
| Costa Rica | 2.3 | 2.9 | BB- | 71 | | Latin America | 8 out of 20 |
| Côte d'Ivoire | 5.6 | 6.1 | | 92 | | Africa | 11 out of 51 |
| Croatia | 1.5 | 1.7 | BB | 63 | Frontier | Central and Eastern Europe | 13 out of 25 |
| Cuba | 14.7 | 15.3 | | 160 | | Caribbean | 9 out of 9 |
| Cyprus | -0.8 | -0.4 | BB+ | 40 | | Central and Eastern Europe | 7 out of 25 |
| Czech Republic | -3.0 | -2.7 | AA- | 23 | Emerging | Central and Eastern Europe | 1 out of 25 |
| Denmark | -5.9 | -5.7 | AAA | 4 | Developed | Western Europe | 3 out of 19 |
| Djibouti | 31.2 | 29.8 | | 175 | | Africa | 51 out of 51 |
| Dominican Republic | 5.5 | 6.0 | BB- | 90 | | Caribbean | 5 out of 9 |
| Ecuador | 7.0 | 7.2 | B | 109 | | Latin America | 18 out of 20 |
| Egypt | 7.4 | 7.8 | B- | 116 | Emerging | Africa | 23 out of 51 |
| El Salvador | 4.6 | 4.8 | B- | 81 | | Latin America | 10 out of 20 |
| Equatorial Guinea | 17.0 | 17.6 | | 165 | | Africa | 45 out of 51 |

§ S&P Credit Rating based on long-term foreign currency issuer rating. See http://www.standardandpoors.com/.
• World rank based on 175 countries covered by Euromoney. Ranking based on ascending order in which '1' equals the smallest country risk premium (CRP) and '175' equals the largest country risk premium (CRP).
† MSCI Market Classification based on MSCI Market Classification Framework. See http://www.msci.com/products/indexes/market_classification.html
‡ Regional classification based on Euromoney. Regional rankings based on ascending order in which '1' equals the smallest country risk premium (CRP) for each region.
Note: A CRP of 0.0% is assumed in the following cases: (i) when the investor country and the investee country both have an S&P sovereign credit rating of AAA; or (ii) when the investor country has an S&P credit rating of AAA, and the investee country has a sovereign credit rating below AAA, but has a calculated CRP below 0.0% (which would imply lower risk than a country rated AAA); or (iii) when the investor country has an S&P credit rating below AAA, and the investee country has a sovereign credit rating of AAA, but has a calculated CRP above 0.0% (which would imply greater risk than a country rated below AAA). For purposes of this analysis, the U.S. is treated as having a sovereign credit rating equivalent to AAA.

2017 Valuation Handbook – International Guide to Cost of Capital          Data Exhibit 4          Investor Perspective: Saudi Arabia (SAR); Page 1 of 4

The country risk premium (CRP) is not the cost of equity capital (COE). The CRP is to be added to base COE. See Chapter 6 for proper application.

### Data Updated Through March 2017

| Investee Country | December 2016 Country Risk Premium (CRP) (%) | March 2017 Country Risk Premium (CRP) (%) | S&P Sovereign Credit Rating § | World Rank Out of 175* | MSCI Market Classification † | Euromoney Region ‡ | Regional Rank ‡ |
|---|---|---|---|---|---|---|---|
| Eritrea | 27.6 | 26.6 | | 173 | | Africa | 50 out of 51 |
| Estonia | -2.4 | -1.9 | AA- | 32 | Frontier | Central and Eastern Europe | 4 out of 25 |
| Ethiopia | 6.3 | 6.7 | B | 101 | | Africa | 16 out of 51 |
| Fiji | 11.3 | 11.7 | B+ | 147 | | Australasia | 5 out of 7 |
| Finland | -5.2 | -5.0 | AA+ | 11 | Developed | Western Europe | 8 out of 19 |
| France | -3.0 | -2.9 | AA | 22 | Developed | Western Europe | 12 out of 19 |
| Gabon | 4.2 | 4.9 | | 83 | | Africa | 7 out of 51 |
| Gambia | 9.9 | 10.4 | | 138 | | Africa | 34 out of 51 |
| Georgia | 3.0 | 3.6 | BB- | 74 | | Central and Eastern Europe | 15 out of 25 |
| Germany | -5.2 | -5.0 | AAA | 10 | Developed | Western Europe | 7 out of 19 |
| Ghana | 5.8 | 5.9 | B- | 89 | | Africa | 9 out of 51 |
| Greece | 6.9 | 7.1 | B- | 108 | Emerging | Western Europe | 19 out of 19 |
| Grenada | 6.5 | 7.0 | | 105 | | Caribbean | 7 out of 9 |
| Guatemala | 4.6 | 5.0 | BB | 84 | | Latin America | 11 out of 20 |
| Guinea | 13.4 | 13.9 | | 156 | | Africa | 41 out of 51 |
| Guinea-Bissau | 7.3 | 7.8 | | 115 | | Africa | 22 out of 51 |
| Guyana | 6.2 | 6.6 | | 100 | | Latin America | 15 out of 20 |
| Haiti | 16.0 | 14.7 | | 157 | | Caribbean | 8 out of 9 |
| Honduras | 5.9 | 6.4 | B+ | 98 | | Latin America | 14 out of 20 |
| Hong Kong | -4.6 | -4.4 | AAA | 14 | Developed | Asia | 2 out of 29 |
| Hungary | 0.8 | 1.2 | BBB- | 57 | Emerging | Central and Eastern Europe | 10 out of 25 |
| Iceland | -2.1 | -2.0 | A | 30 | | Western Europe | 15 out of 19 |
| India | 0.5 | 1.1 | BBB- | 55 | Emerging | Asia | 10 out of 29 |
| Indonesia | 1.3 | 1.6 | BB+ | 62 | Emerging | Asia | 11 out of 29 |
| Iran | 7.8 | 8.5 | | 125 | | Middle East | 10 out of 13 |
| Iraq | 9.5 | 10.0 | B- | 136 | | Middle East | 11 out of 13 |
| Ireland | -2.5 | -2.3 | A+ | 27 | Developed | Western Europe | 14 out of 19 |
| Israel | -2.5 | -2.3 | A+ | 28 | Developed | Middle East | 2 out of 13 |
| Italy | 0.2 | 0.3 | BBB- | 50 | Developed | Western Europe | 18 out of 19 |
| Jamaica | 6.0 | 7.0 | B | 104 | | Caribbean | 6 out of 9 |
| Japan | -2.6 | -2.4 | A+ | 25 | Developed | Asia | 5 out of 29 |
| Jordan | 3.3 | 3.8 | BB- | 76 | Frontier | Middle East | 8 out of 13 |
| Kazakhstan | 2.8 | 2.8 | BBB- | 70 | Frontier | Asia | 13 out of 29 |
| Kenya | 6.0 | 6.5 | B+ | 99 | Frontier | Africa | 15 out of 51 |
| Korea (North) | 27.0 | 27.3 | | 174 | | Asia | 29 out of 29 |
| Korea (South) | -3.4 | -3.1 | AA | 19 | Emerging | Asia | 4 out of 29 |
| Kuwait | -2.4 | -2.0 | AA | 31 | Frontier | Middle East | 3 out of 13 |
| Kyrgyz Republic | 10.9 | 11.2 | | 142 | | Central and Eastern Europe | 22 out of 25 |
| Laos | 14.9 | 14.9 | | 158 | | Asia | 28 out of 29 |
| Latvia | -0.5 | -0.1 | A- | 43 | | Central and Eastern Europe | 8 out of 25 |
| Lebanon | 7.7 | 7.5 | B- | 112 | Frontier | Middle East | 9 out of 13 |
| Lesotho | 11.0 | 11.6 | | 146 | | Africa | 36 out of 51 |
| Liberia | 6.6 | 7.1 | | 107 | | Africa | 17 out of 51 |
| Libya | 12.5 | 13.4 | | 153 | | Africa | 39 out of 51 |
| Lithuania | -1.2 | -0.8 | A- | 36 | Frontier | Central and Eastern Europe | 6 out of 25 |
| Luxembourg | -5.6 | -5.4 | AAA | 5 | | Western Europe | 4 out of 19 |
| Macedonia | 5.2 | 5.8 | BB- | 87 | | Central and Eastern Europe | 17 out of 25 |
| Madagascar | 7.4 | 8.4 | | 123 | | Africa | 27 out of 51 |
| Malawi | 7.2 | 7.6 | | 114 | | Africa | 21 out of 51 |
| Malaysia | -1.0 | -0.9 | A- | 35 | Emerging | Asia | 6 out of 29 |

§ S&P Credit Rating based on long-term foreign currency issuer rating. See http://www.standardandpoors.com/.
• World rank based on 175 countries covered by Euromoney. Ranking based on ascending order in which '1' equals the smallest country risk premium (CRP) and '175' equals the largest country risk premium (CRP).
† MSCI Market Classification based on MSCI Market Classification Framework. See http://www.msci.com/products/indexes/market_classification.html.
‡ Regional classification based on Euromoney. Regional rankings based on ascending order in which '1' equals the smallest country risk premium (CRP) for each region.
Note: A CRP of 0.0% is assumed in the following cases: (i) when the investor country and the investee country both have an S&P sovereign credit rating of AAA; or (ii) when the investor country has an S&P credit rating of AAA, and the investee country has a sovereign credit rating below AAA, but has a calculated CRP below 0.0% (which would imply lower risk than a country rated AAA); or (iii) when the investor country has an S&P credit rating below AAA, and the investee country has a sovereign credit rating of AAA, but has a calculated CRP above 0.0% (which would imply greater risk than a country rated below AAA). For purposes of this analysis, the U.S. is treated as having a sovereign credit rating equivalent to AAA.

The country risk premium (CRP) is not the cost of equity capital (COE). The CRP is to be added to base COE. See Chapter 6 for proper application.

### Data Updated Through March 2017

| Investee Country | December 2016 Country Risk Premium (CRP) (%) | March 2017 Country Risk Premium (CRP) (%) | S&P Sovereign Credit Rating § | World Rank Out of 175∗ | MSCI Market Classification † | Euromoney Region ‡ | Regional Rank ‡ |
|---|---|---|---|---|---|---|---|
| Mali | 10.7 | 11.2 | | 141 | | Africa | 35 out of 51 |
| Malta | -2.6 | -2.3 | A- | 26 | | Western Europe | 13 out of 19 |
| Mauritania | 14.5 | 15.1 | | 159 | | Africa | 42 out of 51 |
| Mauritius | 2.1 | 2.5 | | 67 | Frontier | Asia | 12 out of 29 |
| Mexico | -1.2 | -0.8 | BBB+ | 37 | Emerging | Latin America | 2 out of 20 |
| Moldova | 9.2 | 10.1 | | 137 | | Central and Eastern Europe | 21 out of 25 |
| Mongolia | 7.5 | 8.3 | B- | 119 | | Asia | 18 out of 29 |
| Montenegro | 6.8 | 7.0 | B+ | 103 | | Central and Eastern Europe | 19 out of 25 |
| Morocco | 2.2 | 2.7 | BBB- | 69 | Frontier | Africa | 4 out of 51 |
| Mozambique | 8.5 | 8.8 | SD | 128 | | Africa | 29 out of 51 |
| Myanmar | 9.4 | 9.8 | | 134 | | Asia | 22 out of 29 |
| Namibia | 1.8 | 2.3 | | 66 | | Africa | 3 out of 51 |
| Nepal | 11.9 | 12.4 | | 149 | | Asia | 26 out of 29 |
| Netherlands | -5.5 | -5.4 | AAA | 6 | Developed | Western Europe | 5 out of 19 |
| New Zealand | -5.4 | -5.2 | AA | 8 | Developed | Australasia | 1 out of 7 |
| Nicaragua | 8.2 | 8.7 | B+ | 127 | | Latin America | 19 out of 20 |
| Niger | 7.8 | 8.3 | | 120 | | Africa | 25 out of 51 |
| Nigeria | 6.0 | 6.4 | B | 97 | Frontier | Africa | 14 out of 51 |
| Norway | -6.2 | -6.0 | AAA | 3 | Developed | Western Europe | 2 out of 19 |
| Oman | -0.3 | 0.0 | BBB- | 46 | Frontier | Middle East | 5 out of 13 |
| Pakistan | 7.9 | 8.3 | B | 122 | Frontier | Asia | 19 out of 29 |
| Panama | 0.3 | 0.7 | BBB | 52 | | Latin America | 6 out of 20 |
| Papua New Guinea | 7.5 | 8.0 | B+ | 118 | | Australasia | 3 out of 7 |
| Paraguay | 3.6 | 4.2 | BB | 80 | | Latin America | 9 out of 20 |
| Peru | -0.9 | -0.5 | BBB+ | 39 | Emerging | Latin America | 3 out of 20 |
| Philippines | 0.7 | 0.9 | BBB | 53 | Emerging | Asia | 9 out of 29 |
| Poland | -2.2 | -2.1 | BBB+ | 29 | Emerging | Central and Eastern Europe | 3 out of 25 |
| Portugal | 0.1 | 0.2 | BB+ | 49 | Developed | Western Europe | 17 out of 19 |
| Qatar | -3.3 | -2.9 | AA | 21 | Emerging | Middle East | 1 out of 13 |
| Romania | 0.8 | 1.2 | BBB- | 56 | Frontier | Central and Eastern Europe | 9 out of 25 |
| Russia | 2.9 | 2.7 | BB+ | 68 | Emerging | Central and Eastern Europe | 14 out of 25 |
| Rwanda | 8.6 | 9.0 | B | 130 | | Africa | 31 out of 51 |
| São Tomé & Príncipe | 14.6 | 15.6 | | 163 | | Africa | 43 out of 51 |
| Saudi Arabia | 0.0 | 0.0 | A- | 47 | | Middle East | 6 out of 13 |
| Senegal | 5.3 | 5.7 | B+ | 86 | | Africa | 8 out of 51 |
| Serbia | 3.6 | 3.6 | BB- | 75 | Frontier | Central and Eastern Europe | 16 out of 25 |
| Seychelles | 3.1 | 3.4 | | 73 | | Africa | 5 out of 51 |
| Sierra Leone | 8.6 | 9.0 | | 129 | | Africa | 30 out of 51 |
| Singapore | -6.3 | -6.1 | AAA | 1 | Developed | Asia | 1 out of 29 |
| Slovakia | -2.9 | -2.6 | A+ | 24 | | Central and Eastern Europe | 2 out of 25 |
| Slovenia | -1.6 | -1.3 | A | 34 | Frontier | Central and Eastern Europe | 5 out of 25 |
| Solomon Islands | 18.7 | 19.3 | | 168 | | Australasia | 6 out of 7 |
| Somalia | 17.1 | 17.7 | | 166 | | Africa | 46 out of 51 |
| South Africa | 0.9 | 1.4 | BBB- | 60 | Emerging | Africa | 2 out of 51 |
| Spain | -0.8 | -0.5 | BBB+ | 38 | Developed | Western Europe | 16 out of 19 |
| Sri Lanka | 3.0 | 3.1 | B+ | 72 | Frontier | Asia | 14 out of 29 |
| Sudan | 13.3 | 13.8 | | 154 | | Africa | 40 out of 51 |
| Suriname | 6.2 | 6.8 | B+ | 102 | | Latin America | 16 out of 20 |
| Swaziland | 11.7 | 13.1 | | 152 | | Africa | 38 out of 51 |
| Sweden | -5.5 | -5.3 | AAA | 7 | Developed | Western Europe | 6 out of 19 |

§ S&P Credit Rating based on long-term foreign currency issuer rating. See http://www.standardandpoors.com/.

∗ World rank based on 175 countries covered by Euromoney. Ranking based on ascending order in which '1' equals the smallest country risk premium (CRP) and '175' equals the largest country risk premium (CRP).

† MSCI Market Classification based on MSCI Market Classification Framework. See http://www.msci.com/products/indexes/market_classification.html

‡ Regional classification based on Euromoney. Regional rankings based on ascending order in which '1' equals the smallest country risk premium (CRP) for each region.

Note: A CRP of 0.0% is assumed in the following cases: (i) when the investor country and the investee country both have an S&P sovereign credit rating of AAA; or (ii) when the investor country has an S&P credit rating of AAA, and the investee country has a sovereign credit rating below AAA, but has a calculated CRP below 0.0% (which would imply lower risk than a country rated AAA); or (iii) when the investor country has an S&P credit rating below AAA, and the investee country has a sovereign credit rating of AAA, but has a calculated CRP above 0.0% (which would imply greater risk than a country rated below AAA). For purposes of this analysis, the U.S. is treated as having a sovereign credit rating equivalent to AAA.

The country risk premium (CRP) is not the cost of equity capital (COE). The CRP is to be added to base COE. See Chapter 6 for proper application.

## Data Updated Through March 2017

| Investee Country | December 2016 Country Risk Premium (CRP) (%) | March 2017 Country Risk Premium (CRP) (%) | S&P Sovereign Credit Rating § | World Rank Out of 175∗ | MSCI Market Classification † | Euromoney Region ‡ | Regional Rank ‡ |
|---|---|---|---|---|---|---|---|
| Switzerland | -6.1 | -6.0 | AAA | 2 | Developed | Western Europe | 1 out of 19 |
| Syria | 17.8 | 18.6 | | 167 | | Middle East | 13 out of 13 |
| Taiwan | -3.6 | -3.4 | AA- | 18 | Emerging | Asia | 3 out of 29 |
| Tajikistan | 12.9 | 13.8 | | 155 | | Central and Eastern Europe | 25 out of 25 |
| Tanzania | 5.6 | 6.2 | | 95 | | Africa | 13 out of 51 |
| Thailand | 0.3 | 0.5 | BBB+ | 51 | Emerging | Asia | 8 out of 29 |
| Togo | 7.1 | 7.6 | | 113 | | Africa | 20 out of 51 |
| Tonga | 21.0 | 21.7 | | 170 | | Australasia | 7 out of 7 |
| Trinidad & Tobago | 0.7 | 1.0 | A- | 54 | | Caribbean | 2 out of 9 |
| Tunisia | 3.4 | 4.1 | | 79 | Frontier | Africa | 6 out of 51 |
| Turkey | 1.0 | 1.2 | BB | 58 | Emerging | Central and Eastern Europe | 11 out of 25 |
| Turkmenistan | 10.3 | 11.0 | | 140 | | Asia | 24 out of 29 |
| Uganda | 6.7 | 7.4 | B | 110 | | Africa | 18 out of 51 |
| Ukraine | 9.3 | 9.9 | B- | 135 | | Central and Eastern Europe | 20 out of 25 |
| United Arab Emirates | -2.0 | -1.6 | AA | 33 | Emerging | Middle East | 4 out of 13 |
| United Kingdom | -3.4 | -3.0 | AA | 20 | Developed | Western Europe | 11 out of 19 |
| United States | -4.4 | -4.1 | AA+ | 15 | Developed | North America | 2 out of 2 |
| Uruguay | -0.2 | -0.1 | BBB | 45 | | Latin America | 5 out of 20 |
| Uzbekistan | 9.5 | 9.4 | | 132 | | Asia | 21 out of 29 |
| Vanuatu | 11.0 | 11.5 | | 145 | | Australasia | 4 out of 7 |
| Venezuela | 14.6 | 15.6 | CCC | 162 | | Latin America | 20 out of 20 |
| Vietnam | 3.9 | 4.0 | BB- | 78 | Frontier | Asia | 16 out of 29 |
| Yemen | 14.9 | 15.5 | | 161 | | Middle East | 12 out of 13 |
| Zambia | 7.0 | 7.4 | B | 111 | | Africa | 19 out of 51 |
| Zimbabwe | 16.4 | 16.9 | | 164 | | Africa | 44 out of 51 |

## March 2017 Country Risk Premium (CRP) Summary Statistics:

| S&P Rating | Country Count | Average CRP (%) | Median CRP (%) | Min CRP (%) | Max CRP (%) |
|---|---|---|---|---|---|
| AAA ∗∗ | 12 | -5.3 | -5.4 | -6.1 | -4.1 |
| AA (AA+, AA, AA-) | 15 | -3.1 | -3.0 | -5.2 | -0.2 |
| A (A+, A, A-) | 14 | -1.1 | -1.1 | -2.6 | 1.0 |
| BBB (BBB+, BBB, BBB-) | 17 | 0.5 | 0.5 | -2.1 | 2.8 |
| BB (BB+, BB, BB-) | 22 | 3.3 | 3.3 | -0.4 | 8.5 |
| B+ − SD | 39 | 7.8 | 7.4 | 3.1 | 15.6 |
| Investment Grade ∗∗ | 58 | -2.0 | -2.0 | -6.1 | 2.8 |
| Non-Investment Grade ∗∗ | 61 | 6.2 | 6.4 | -0.4 | 15.6 |
| **MSCI Market Classification** | | | | | |
| Developed Markets | 23 | -3.9 | -4.7 | -6.1 | 0.3 |
| Emerging Markets | 23 | 0.2 | -0.2 | -3.7 | 7.8 |
| Frontier Markets | 22 | 3.1 | 2.9 | -2.0 | 8.5 |
| **Euromoney Region ‡** | | | | | |
| Africa | 51 | 10.2 | 8.3 | 0.0 | 29.8 |
| Asia | 29 | 5.2 | 3.8 | -6.1 | 27.3 |
| Australasia | 7 | 8.9 | 11.5 | -5.2 | 21.7 |
| Caribbean | 9 | 6.4 | 6.0 | -0.1 | 15.3 |
| Central and Eastern Europe | 25 | 3.7 | 1.7 | -2.7 | 13.8 |
| Latin America | 20 | 4.2 | 4.9 | -3.7 | 15.6 |
| Middle East | 13 | 4.4 | 2.0 | -2.9 | 18.6 |
| North America | 2 | -4.6 | -4.6 | -5.1 | -4.1 |
| Western Europe | 19 | -3.0 | -3.6 | -6.0 | 7.1 |

## CCR Base Cost of Equity Capital:

| Saudi Arabia | COE (%) |
|---|---|
| March 2017 | 12.5 |
| December 2016 | 12.8 |

CCR base country-level COE for a Saudi Arabia-based investor investing in Saudi Arabia.

§ S&P Credit Rating based on long-term foreign currency issuer rating. See http://www.standardandpoors.com/.

∗ World rank based on 175 countries covered by Euromoney. Ranking based on ascending order in which '1' equals the smallest country risk premium (CRP) and '175' equals the largest country risk premium (CRP).

† MSCI Market Classification based on MSCI Market Classification Framework. See http://www.msci.com/products/indexes/market_classification.html.

‡ Regional classification based on Euromoney. Regional rankings based on ascending order in which '1' equals the smallest country risk premium (CRP) for each region.

∗∗ Investment grade based on S&P sovereign credit rating from AAA to BBB-. Non-Investment grade based on S&P sovereign credit rating from BB+ to SD. For purposes of this analysis, the U.S. is being treated as if it were rated AAA by S&P.

Note: A CRP of 0.0% is assumed in the following cases: (i) when the investor country and the investee country both have an S&P sovereign credit rating of AAA; or (ii) when the investor country has an S&P credit rating of AAA, and the investee country has a sovereign credit rating below AAA, but has a calculated CRP below 0.0% (which would imply lower risk than a country rated AAA); or (iii) when the investor country has an S&P sovereign credit rating below AAA, and the investee country has a sovereign credit rating of AAA, but has a calculated CRP above 0.0% (which would imply greater risk than a country rated below AAA). For purposes of this analysis, the U.S. is treated as having a sovereign credit rating equivalent to AAA.

The country risk premium (CRP) is not the cost of equity capital (COE). The CRP is to be added to base COE. See Chapter 6 for proper application.

## Data Updated Through March 2017

| Investee Country | December 2016 Country Risk Premium (CRP) (%) | March 2017 Country Risk Premium (CRP) (%) | S&P Sovereign Credit Rating § | World Rank Out of 175• | MSCI Market Classification † | Euromoney Region ‡ | Regional Rank ‡ |
|---|---|---|---|---|---|---|---|
| Afghanistan | 17.8 | 17.6 | | 139 | | Asia | 23 out of 29 |
| Albania | 12.4 | 12.7 | B+ | 93 | | Central and Eastern Europe | 18 out of 25 |
| Algeria | 12.5 | 12.6 | | 91 | | Africa | 10 out of 51 |
| Angola | 14.8 | 15.0 | B | 121 | | Africa | 26 out of 51 |
| Argentina | 13.0 | 12.9 | B- | 96 | Frontier | Latin America | 13 out of 20 |
| Armenia | 10.1 | 10.3 | | 77 | | Asia | 15 out of 29 |
| Australia | 0.0 | 0.0 | AAA | 12 | Developed | Australasia | 2 out of 7 |
| Austria | 1.5 | 1.5 | AA+ | 13 | Developed | Western Europe | 9 out of 19 |
| Azerbaijan | 11.3 | 11.7 | BB+ | 85 | | Asia | 17 out of 29 |
| Bahamas | 8.7 | 8.5 | BB+ | 65 | | Caribbean | 3 out of 9 |
| Bahrain | 8.6 | 8.5 | BB- | 64 | Frontier | Middle East | 7 out of 13 |
| Bangladesh | 15.3 | 15.2 | BB- | 126 | Frontier | Asia | 20 out of 29 |
| Barbados | 10.3 | 11.4 | CCC+ | 82 | | Caribbean | 4 out of 9 |
| Belarus | 17.5 | 18.0 | B- | 143 | | Central and Eastern Europe | 23 out of 25 |
| Belgium | 2.7 | 2.7 | AA | 17 | Developed | Western Europe | 10 out of 19 |
| Belize | 13.5 | 13.7 | B- | 106 | | Latin America | 17 out of 20 |
| Benin | 19.1 | 19.3 | | 150 | | Africa | 37 out of 51 |
| Bermuda | 6.3 | 6.3 | A+ | 44 | | Caribbean | 1 out of 9 |
| Bhutan | 18.8 | 18.8 | | 148 | | Asia | 25 out of 29 |
| Bolivia | 12.0 | 12.4 | BB | 88 | | Latin America | 12 out of 20 |
| Bosnia & Herzegovina | 17.9 | 18.2 | B | 144 | | Central and Eastern Europe | 24 out of 25 |
| Botswana | 6.3 | 6.4 | A- | 48 | | Africa | 1 out of 51 |
| Brazil | 7.8 | 7.8 | BB | 59 | Emerging | Latin America | 7 out of 20 |
| Bulgaria | 7.7 | 7.9 | BB+ | 61 | | Central and Eastern Europe | 12 out of 25 |
| Burkina Faso | 16.3 | 16.4 | B- | 133 | | Africa | 33 out of 51 |
| Burundi | 27.9 | 28.1 | | 169 | | Africa | 47 out of 51 |
| Cambodia | 19.7 | 19.5 | | 151 | | Asia | 27 out of 29 |
| Cameroon | 15.0 | 15.1 | B | 124 | | Africa | 28 out of 51 |
| Canada | 0.0 | 0.0 | AAA | 9 | Developed | North America | 1 out of 2 |
| Cape Verde | 12.6 | 12.8 | B | 94 | | Africa | 12 out of 51 |
| Central African Republic | 31.4 | 31.6 | | 172 | | Africa | 49 out of 51 |
| Chad | 30.1 | 30.3 | | 171 | | Africa | 48 out of 51 |
| Chile | 2.3 | 2.5 | AA- | 16 | Emerging | Latin America | 1 out of 20 |
| China | 6.1 | 6.2 | AA- | 42 | Emerging | Asia | 7 out of 29 |
| Colombia | 6.1 | 6.1 | BBB | 41 | Emerging | Latin America | 4 out of 20 |
| Congo Republic | 14.6 | 14.5 | B- | 117 | | Africa | 24 out of 51 |
| Congo, DR | 15.8 | 15.9 | B- | 131 | | Africa | 32 out of 51 |
| Costa Rica | 9.1 | 9.4 | BB- | 71 | | Latin America | 8 out of 20 |
| Côte d'Ivoire | 12.5 | 12.6 | | 92 | | Africa | 11 out of 51 |
| Croatia | 8.2 | 8.1 | BB | 63 | Frontier | Central and Eastern Europe | 13 out of 25 |
| Cuba | 21.9 | 22.2 | | 160 | | Caribbean | 9 out of 9 |
| Cyprus | 5.8 | 6.0 | BB+ | 40 | | Central and Eastern Europe | 7 out of 25 |
| Czech Republic | 3.5 | 3.5 | AA- | 23 | Emerging | Central and Eastern Europe | 1 out of 25 |
| Denmark | 0.0 | 0.0 | AAA | 4 | Developed | Western Europe | 3 out of 19 |
| Djibouti | 39.2 | 37.2 | | 175 | | Africa | 51 out of 51 |
| Dominican Republic | 12.3 | 12.5 | BB- | 90 | | Caribbean | 5 out of 9 |
| Ecuador | 13.9 | 13.8 | B | 109 | | Latin America | 18 out of 20 |
| Egypt | 14.3 | 14.4 | B- | 116 | Emerging | Africa | 23 out of 51 |
| El Salvador | 11.4 | 11.3 | B- | 81 | | Latin America | 10 out of 20 |
| Equatorial Guinea | 24.4 | 24.6 | | 165 | | Africa | 45 out of 51 |

§ S&P Credit Rating based on long-term foreign currency issuer rating. See http://www.standardandpoors.com/.

• World rank based on 175 countries covered by Euromoney. Ranking based on ascending order in which '1' equals the smallest country risk premium (CRP) and '175' equals the largest country risk premium (CRP).

† MSCI Market Classification based on MSCI Market Classification Framework. See http://www.msci.com/products/indexes/market_classification.html.

‡ Regional classification based on Euromoney. Regional rankings based on ascending order in which '1' equals the smallest country risk premium (CRP) for each region.

Note: A CRP of 0.0% is assumed in the following cases: (i) when the investor country and the investee country both have an S&P sovereign credit rating of AAA; or (ii) when the investor country has an S&P credit rating of AAA, and the investee country has a sovereign credit rating below AAA, but has a calculated CRP below 0.0% (which would imply lower risk than a country rated AAA); or (iii) when the investor country has an S&P credit rating below AAA, and the investee country has a sovereign credit rating of AAA, but has a calculated CRP above 0.0% (which would imply greater risk than a country rated below AAA). For purposes of this analysis, the U.S. is treated as having a sovereign credit rating equivalent to AAA.

The country risk premium (CRP) is not the cost of equity capital (COE). The CRP is to be added to base COE. See Chapter 6 for proper application.

### Data Updated Through March 2017

| Investee Country | December 2016 Country Risk Premium (CRP) (%) | March 2017 Country Risk Premium (CRP) (%) | S&P Sovereign Credit Rating § | World Rank Out of 175* | MSCI Market Classification † | Euromoney Region ‡ | Regional Rank ‡ |
|---|---|---|---|---|---|---|---|
| Eritrea | 35.5 | 33.9 | | 173 | | Africa | 50 out of 51 |
| Estonia | 4.1 | 4.4 | AA- | 32 | Frontier | Central and Eastern Europe | 4 out of 25 |
| Ethiopia | 13.2 | 13.3 | B | 101 | | Africa | 16 out of 51 |
| Fiji | 18.5 | 18.5 | B+ | 147 | | Australasia | 5 out of 7 |
| Finland | 1.2 | 1.2 | AA+ | 11 | Developed | Western Europe | 8 out of 19 |
| France | 3.5 | 3.4 | AA | 22 | Developed | Western Europe | 12 out of 19 |
| Gabon | 11.0 | 11.4 | | 83 | | Africa | 7 out of 51 |
| Gambia | 16.9 | 17.1 | | 138 | | Africa | 34 out of 51 |
| Georgia | 9.8 | 10.1 | BB- | 74 | | Central and Eastern Europe | 15 out of 25 |
| Germany | 0.0 | 0.0 | AAA | 10 | Developed | Western Europe | 7 out of 19 |
| Ghana | 12.7 | 12.4 | B- | 89 | | Africa | 9 out of 51 |
| Greece | 13.8 | 13.7 | B- | 108 | Emerging | Western Europe | 19 out of 19 |
| Grenada | 13.4 | 13.6 | | 105 | | Caribbean | 7 out of 9 |
| Guatemala | 11.4 | 11.5 | BB | 84 | | Latin America | 11 out of 20 |
| Guinea | 20.6 | 20.7 | | 156 | | Africa | 41 out of 51 |
| Guinea-Bissau | 14.3 | 14.4 | | 115 | | Africa | 22 out of 51 |
| Guyana | 13.1 | 13.2 | | 100 | | Latin America | 15 out of 20 |
| Haiti | 23.4 | 21.5 | | 157 | | Caribbean | 8 out of 9 |
| Honduras | 12.8 | 13.0 | B+ | 98 | | Latin America | 14 out of 20 |
| Hong Kong | 0.0 | 0.0 | AAA | 14 | Developed | Asia | 2 out of 29 |
| Hungary | 7.4 | 7.6 | BBB- | 57 | Emerging | Central and Eastern Europe | 10 out of 25 |
| Iceland | 4.5 | 4.3 | A | 30 | | Western Europe | 15 out of 19 |
| India | 7.2 | 7.5 | BBB- | 55 | Emerging | Asia | 10 out of 29 |
| Indonesia | 7.9 | 8.0 | BB+ | 62 | Emerging | Asia | 11 out of 29 |
| Iran | 14.8 | 15.1 | | 125 | | Middle East | 10 out of 13 |
| Iraq | 16.6 | 16.7 | B- | 136 | | Middle East | 11 out of 13 |
| Ireland | 4.0 | 4.0 | A+ | 27 | Developed | Western Europe | 14 out of 19 |
| Israel | 4.0 | 4.0 | A+ | 28 | Developed | Middle East | 2 out of 13 |
| Italy | 6.8 | 6.7 | BBB- | 50 | Developed | Western Europe | 18 out of 19 |
| Jamaica | 12.9 | 13.6 | B | 104 | | Caribbean | 6 out of 9 |
| Japan | 3.9 | 3.9 | A+ | 25 | Developed | Asia | 5 out of 29 |
| Jordan | 10.0 | 10.3 | BB- | 76 | Frontier | Middle East | 8 out of 13 |
| Kazakhstan | 9.5 | 9.3 | BBB- | 70 | Frontier | Asia | 13 out of 29 |
| Kenya | 12.9 | 13.1 | B+ | 99 | Frontier | Africa | 15 out of 51 |
| Korea (North) | 34.8 | 34.6 | | 174 | | Asia | 29 out of 29 |
| Korea (South) | 3.1 | 3.2 | AA | 19 | Emerging | Asia | 4 out of 29 |
| Kuwait | 4.2 | 4.3 | AA | 31 | Frontier | Middle East | 3 out of 13 |
| Kyrgyz Republic | 18.0 | 18.0 | | 142 | | Central and Eastern Europe | 22 out of 25 |
| Laos | 22.1 | 21.8 | | 158 | | Asia | 28 out of 29 |
| Latvia | 6.1 | 6.3 | A- | 43 | | Central and Eastern Europe | 8 out of 25 |
| Lebanon | 14.6 | 14.1 | B- | 112 | Frontier | Middle East | 9 out of 13 |
| Lesotho | 18.2 | 18.3 | | 146 | | Africa | 36 out of 51 |
| Liberia | 13.5 | 13.7 | | 107 | | Africa | 17 out of 51 |
| Libya | 19.7 | 20.2 | | 153 | | Africa | 39 out of 51 |
| Lithuania | 5.3 | 5.5 | A- | 36 | Frontier | Central and Eastern Europe | 6 out of 25 |
| Luxembourg | 0.0 | 0.0 | AAA | 5 | | Western Europe | 4 out of 19 |
| Macedonia | 12.0 | 12.3 | BB- | 87 | | Central and Eastern Europe | 17 out of 25 |
| Madagascar | 14.4 | 15.0 | | 123 | | Africa | 27 out of 51 |
| Malawi | 14.1 | 14.2 | | 114 | | Africa | 21 out of 51 |
| Malaysia | 5.5 | 5.4 | A- | 35 | Emerging | Asia | 6 out of 29 |

§ S&P Credit Rating based on long-term foreign currency issuer rating. See http://www.standardandpoors.com/.

* World rank based on 175 countries covered by Euromoney. Ranking based on ascending order in which '1' equals the smallest country risk premium (CRP) and '175' equals the largest country risk premium (CRP).

† MSCI Market Classification based on MSCI Market Classification Framework. See http://www.msci.com/products/indexes/market_classification.html

‡ Regional classification based on Euromoney. Regional rankings based on ascending order in which '1' equals the smallest country risk premium (CRP) for each region.

Note: A CRP of 0.0% is assumed in the following cases: (i) when the investor country and the investee country both have an S&P sovereign credit rating of AAA; or (ii) when the investor country has an S&P sovereign credit rating of AAA, and the investee country has a sovereign credit rating below AAA, but has a calculated CRP below 0.0% (which would imply lower risk than a country rated AAA); or (iii) when the investor country has an S&P sovereign credit rating below AAA, and the investee country has a sovereign credit rating of AAA, but has a calculated CRP above 0.0% (which would imply greater risk than a country rated below AAA). For purposes of this analysis, the U.S. is treated as having a sovereign credit rating equivalent to AAA.

The country risk premium (CRP) is not the cost of equity capital (COE).  The CRP is to be added to base COE. See Chapter 6 for proper application.

### Data Updated Through March 2017

| Investee Country | December 2016 Country Risk Premium (CRP) (%) | March 2017 Country Risk Premium (CRP) (%) | S&P Sovereign Credit Rating § | World Rank Out of 175∗ | MSCI Market Classification † | Euromoney Region ‡ | Regional Rank ‡ |
|---|---|---|---|---|---|---|---|
| Mali | 17.8 | 17.9 | | 141 | | Africa | 35 out of 51 |
| Malta | 3.9 | 3.9 | A- | 26 | | Western Europe | 13 out of 19 |
| Mauritania | 21.8 | 21.9 | | 159 | | Africa | 42 out of 51 |
| Mauritius | 8.9 | 8.9 | | 67 | Frontier | Asia | 12 out of 29 |
| Mexico | 5.4 | 5.6 | BBB+ | 37 | Emerging | Latin America | 2 out of 20 |
| Moldova | 16.2 | 16.8 | | 137 | | Central and Eastern Europe | 21 out of 25 |
| Mongolia | 14.4 | 14.9 | B- | 119 | | Asia | 18 out of 29 |
| Montenegro | 13.7 | 13.6 | B+ | 103 | | Central and Eastern Europe | 19 out of 25 |
| Morocco | 8.9 | 9.2 | BBB- | 69 | Frontier | Africa | 4 out of 51 |
| Mozambique | 15.5 | 15.5 | SD | 128 | | Africa | 29 out of 51 |
| Myanmar | 16.4 | 16.5 | | 134 | | Asia | 22 out of 29 |
| Namibia | 8.5 | 8.8 | | 66 | | Africa | 3 out of 51 |
| Nepal | 19.1 | 19.2 | | 149 | | Asia | 26 out of 29 |
| Netherlands | 0.0 | 0.0 | AAA | 6 | Developed | Western Europe | 5 out of 19 |
| New Zealand | 1.0 | 1.0 | AA | 8 | Developed | Australasia | 1 out of 7 |
| Nicaragua | 15.2 | 15.3 | B+ | 127 | | Latin America | 19 out of 20 |
| Niger | 14.8 | 14.9 | | 120 | | Africa | 25 out of 51 |
| Nigeria | 12.9 | 12.9 | B | 97 | Frontier | Africa | 14 out of 51 |
| Norway | 0.0 | 0.0 | AAA | 3 | Developed | Western Europe | 2 out of 19 |
| Oman | 6.3 | 6.4 | BBB- | 46 | Frontier | Middle East | 5 out of 13 |
| Pakistan | 14.9 | 15.0 | B | 122 | Frontier | Asia | 19 out of 29 |
| Panama | 7.0 | 7.1 | BBB | 52 | | Latin America | 6 out of 20 |
| Papua New Guinea | 14.4 | 14.6 | B+ | 118 | | Australasia | 3 out of 7 |
| Paraguay | 10.4 | 10.7 | BB | 80 | | Latin America | 9 out of 20 |
| Peru | 5.7 | 5.9 | BBB+ | 39 | Emerging | Latin America | 3 out of 20 |
| Philippines | 7.3 | 7.3 | BBB | 53 | Emerging | Asia | 9 out of 29 |
| Poland | 4.3 | 4.2 | BBB+ | 29 | Emerging | Central and Eastern Europe | 3 out of 25 |
| Portugal | 6.7 | 6.5 | BB+ | 49 | Developed | Western Europe | 17 out of 19 |
| Qatar | 3.2 | 3.3 | AA | 21 | Emerging | Middle East | 1 out of 13 |
| Romania | 7.5 | 7.6 | BBB- | 56 | Frontier | Central and Eastern Europe | 9 out of 25 |
| Russia | 9.7 | 9.1 | BB+ | 68 | Emerging | Central and Eastern Europe | 14 out of 25 |
| Rwanda | 15.6 | 15.7 | B | 130 | | Africa | 31 out of 51 |
| São Tomé & Príncipe | 21.9 | 22.5 | | 163 | | Africa | 43 out of 51 |
| Saudi Arabia | 6.6 | 6.4 | A- | 47 | | Middle East | 6 out of 13 |
| Senegal | 12.2 | 12.3 | B+ | 86 | | Africa | 8 out of 51 |
| Serbia | 10.3 | 10.1 | BB- | 75 | Frontier | Central and Eastern Europe | 16 out of 25 |
| Seychelles | 9.8 | 9.9 | | 73 | | Africa | 5 out of 51 |
| Sierra Leone | 15.6 | 15.7 | | 129 | | Africa | 30 out of 51 |
| Singapore | 0.0 | 0.0 | AAA | 1 | Developed | Asia | 1 out of 29 |
| Slovakia | 3.6 | 3.7 | A+ | 24 | | Central and Eastern Europe | 2 out of 25 |
| Slovenia | 5.0 | 5.1 | A | 34 | Frontier | Central and Eastern Europe | 5 out of 25 |
| Solomon Islands | 26.2 | 26.4 | | 168 | | Australasia | 6 out of 7 |
| Somalia | 24.5 | 24.7 | | 166 | | Africa | 46 out of 51 |
| South Africa | 7.5 | 7.8 | BBB- | 60 | Emerging | Africa | 2 out of 51 |
| Spain | 5.8 | 5.9 | BBB+ | 38 | Developed | Western Europe | 16 out of 19 |
| Sri Lanka | 9.7 | 9.5 | B+ | 72 | Frontier | Asia | 14 out of 29 |
| Sudan | 20.5 | 20.6 | | 154 | | Africa | 40 out of 51 |
| Suriname | 13.1 | 13.4 | B+ | 102 | | Latin America | 16 out of 20 |
| Swaziland | 18.9 | 20.0 | | 152 | | Africa | 38 out of 51 |
| Sweden | 0.0 | 0.0 | AAA | 7 | Developed | Western Europe | 6 out of 19 |

§ S&P Credit Rating based on long-term foreign currency issuer rating. See http://www.standardandpoors.com/.

∗ World rank based on 175 countries covered by Euromoney. Ranking based on ascending order in which '1' equals the smallest country risk premium (CRP) and '175' equals the largest country risk premium (CRP).

† MSCI Market Classification based on MSCI Market Classification Framework.  See http://www.msci.com/products/indexes/market_classification.html

‡ Regional classification based on Euromoney. Regional rankings based on ascending order in which '1' equals the smallest country risk premium (CRP) for each region.

Note: A CRP of 0.0% is assumed in the following cases: (i) when the investor country and the investee country both have an S&P sovereign credit rating of AAA; or (ii) when the investor country has an S&P credit rating of AAA, and the investee country has a sovereign credit rating below AAA, but has a calculated CRP below 0.0% (which would imply lower risk than a country rated AAA); or (iii) when the investor country has an S&P credit rating below AAA, and the investee country has a sovereign credit rating of AAA, but has a calculated CRP above 0.0% (which would imply greater risk than a country rated below AAA). For purposes of this analysis, the U.S. is treated as having a sovereign credit rating equivalent to AAA.

The country risk premium (CRP) is not the cost of equity capital (COE). The CRP is to be added to base COE. See Chapter 6 for proper application.

## Data Updated Through March 2017

| Investee Country | December 2016 Country Risk Premium (CRP) (%) | March 2017 Country Risk Premium (CRP) (%) | S&P Sovereign Credit Rating § | World Rank Out of 175∗ | MSCI Market Classification † | Euromoney Region ‡ | Regional Rank ‡ |
|---|---|---|---|---|---|---|---|
| Switzerland | 0.0 | 0.0 | AAA | 2 | Developed | Western Europe | 1 out of 19 |
| Syria | 25.2 | 25.6 | | 167 | | Middle East | 13 out of 13 |
| Taiwan | 2.8 | 2.9 | AA- | 18 | Emerging | Asia | 3 out of 29 |
| Tajikistan | 20.1 | 20.6 | | 155 | | Central and Eastern Europe | 25 out of 25 |
| Tanzania | 12.5 | 12.8 | | 95 | | Africa | 13 out of 51 |
| Thailand | 7.0 | 6.9 | BBB+ | 51 | Emerging | Asia | 8 out of 29 |
| Togo | 14.1 | 14.2 | | 113 | | Africa | 20 out of 51 |
| Tonga | 28.6 | 28.8 | | 170 | | Australasia | 7 out of 7 |
| Trinidad & Tobago | 7.3 | 7.4 | A- | 54 | | Caribbean | 2 out of 9 |
| Tunisia | 10.1 | 10.6 | | 79 | Frontier | Africa | 6 out of 51 |
| Turkey | 7.7 | 7.6 | BB | 58 | Emerging | Central and Eastern Europe | 11 out of 25 |
| Turkmenistan | 17.3 | 17.7 | | 140 | | Asia | 24 out of 29 |
| Uganda | 13.6 | 14.0 | B | 110 | | Africa | 18 out of 51 |
| Ukraine | 16.4 | 16.6 | B- | 135 | | Central and Eastern Europe | 20 out of 25 |
| United Arab Emirates | 4.6 | 4.7 | AA | 33 | Emerging | Middle East | 4 out of 13 |
| United Kingdom | 3.1 | 3.3 | AA | 20 | Developed | Western Europe | 11 out of 19 |
| United States | 0.0 | 0.0 | AA+ | 15 | Developed | North America | 2 out of 2 |
| Uruguay | 6.4 | 6.3 | BBB | 45 | | Latin America | 5 out of 20 |
| Uzbekistan | 16.5 | 16.1 | | 132 | | Asia | 21 out of 29 |
| Vanuatu | 18.2 | 18.3 | | 145 | | Australasia | 4 out of 7 |
| Venezuela | 21.9 | 22.5 | CCC | 162 | | Latin America | 20 out of 20 |
| Vietnam | 10.7 | 10.5 | BB- | 78 | Frontier | Asia | 16 out of 29 |
| Yemen | 22.2 | 22.4 | | 161 | | Middle East | 12 out of 13 |
| Zambia | 13.9 | 14.1 | B | 111 | | Africa | 19 out of 51 |
| Zimbabwe | 23.8 | 23.9 | | 164 | | Africa | 44 out of 51 |

## March 2017 Country Risk Premium (CRP) Summary Statistics:

| S&P Rating | Country Count | Average CRP (%) | Median CRP (%) | Min CRP (%) | Max CRP (%) |
|---|---|---|---|---|---|
| AAA ∗∗ | 12 | 0.0 | 0.0 | 0.0 | 0.0 |
| AA (AA+, AA, AA-) | 15 | 3.2 | 3.3 | 1.0 | 6.2 |
| A (A+, A, A-) | 14 | 5.2 | 5.2 | 3.7 | 7.4 |
| BBB (BBB+, BBB, BBB-) | 17 | 6.9 | 6.9 | 4.2 | 9.3 |
| BB (BB+, BB, BB-) | 22 | 9.8 | 9.7 | 6.0 | 15.2 |
| B+ − SD | 39 | 14.5 | 14.1 | 9.5 | 22.5 |
| Investment Grade ∗∗ | 58 | 4.1 | 4.3 | 0.0 | 9.3 |
| Non-Investment Grade ∗∗ | 61 | 12.8 | 13.0 | 6.0 | 22.5 |
| **MSCI Market Classification** | | | | | |
| Developed Markets | 23 | 1.9 | 1.0 | 0.0 | 6.7 |
| Emerging Markets | 23 | 6.6 | 6.2 | 2.5 | 14.4 |
| Frontier Markets | 22 | 9.6 | 9.4 | 4.3 | 15.2 |
| **Euromoney Region ‡** | | | | | |
| Africa | 51 | 17.0 | 15.0 | 6.4 | 37.2 |
| Asia | 29 | 11.7 | 10.3 | 0.0 | 34.6 |
| Australasia | 7 | 15.4 | 18.3 | 0.0 | 28.8 |
| Caribbean | 9 | 13.0 | 12.5 | 6.3 | 22.2 |
| Central and Eastern Europe | 25 | 10.1 | 8.1 | 3.5 | 20.6 |
| Latin America | 20 | 10.7 | 11.4 | 2.5 | 22.5 |
| Middle East | 13 | 10.9 | 8.5 | 3.3 | 25.6 |
| North America | 2 | 0.0 | 0.0 | 0.0 | 0.0 |
| Western Europe | 19 | 3.0 | 2.7 | 0.0 | 13.7 |

## CCR Base Cost of Equity Capital:

| Singapore | COE (%) |
|---|---|
| March 2017 | 4.7 |
| December 2016 | 4.8 |

CCR base country-level COE for a Singapore-based investor investing in Singapore.

§ S&P Credit Rating based on long-term foreign currency issuer rating. See http://www.standardandpoors.com/.

∗ World rank based on 175 countries covered by Euromoney. Ranking based on ascending order in which '1' equals the smallest country risk premium (CRP) and '175' equals the largest country risk premium (CRP).

† MSCI Market Classification based on MSCI Market Classification Framework. See http://www.msci.com/products/indexes/market_classification.html.

‡ Regional classification based on Euromoney. Regional rankings based on ascending order in which '1' equals the smallest country risk premium (CRP) for each region.

∗∗ Investment grade based on S&P sovereign credit rating from AAA to BBB-. Non-Investment grade based on S&P sovereign credit rating from BB+ to SD. For purposes of this analysis, the U.S. is being treated as if it were rated AAA by S&P.

Note: A CRP of 0.0% is assumed in the following cases: (i) when the investor country and the investee country both have an S&P sovereign credit rating of AAA; or (ii) when the investor country has an S&P credit rating of AAA, and the investee country has a sovereign credit rating below AAA, but has a calculated CRP below 0.0% (which would imply lower risk than a country rated AAA); or (iii) when the investor country has an S&P credit rating below AAA, and the investee country has a sovereign credit rating of AAA, but has a calculated CRP above 0.0% (which would imply greater risk than a country rated below AAA). For purposes of this analysis, the U.S. is treated as having a sovereign credit rating equivalent to AAA.

The country risk premium (CRP) is not the cost of equity capital (COE). The CRP is to be added to base COE. See Chapter 6 for proper application.

### Data Updated Through March 2017

| Investee Country | December 2016 Country Risk Premium (CRP) (%) | March 2017 Country Risk Premium (CRP) (%) | S&P Sovereign Credit Rating § | World Rank Out of 175* | MSCI Market Classification † | Euromoney Region ‡ | Regional Rank ‡ |
|---|---|---|---|---|---|---|---|
| Afghanistan | 14.6 | 14.3 | | 139 | | Asia | 23 out of 29 |
| Albania | 9.1 | 9.2 | B+ | 93 | | Central and Eastern Europe | 18 out of 25 |
| Algeria | 9.1 | 9.1 | | 91 | | Africa | 10 out of 51 |
| Angola | 11.5 | 11.5 | B | 121 | | Africa | 26 out of 51 |
| Argentina | 9.7 | 9.4 | B- | 96 | Frontier | Latin America | 13 out of 20 |
| Armenia | 6.7 | 6.8 | | 77 | | Asia | 15 out of 29 |
| Australia | -2.4 | -2.5 | AAA | 12 | Developed | Australasia | 2 out of 7 |
| Austria | -2.2 | -2.3 | AA+ | 13 | Developed | Western Europe | 9 out of 19 |
| Azerbaijan | 7.9 | 8.2 | BB+ | 85 | | Asia | 17 out of 29 |
| Bahamas | 5.2 | 4.9 | BB+ | 65 | | Caribbean | 3 out of 9 |
| Bahrain | 5.1 | 4.9 | BB- | 64 | Frontier | Middle East | 7 out of 13 |
| Bangladesh | 12.0 | 11.7 | BB- | 126 | Frontier | Asia | 20 out of 29 |
| Barbados | 6.9 | 7.9 | CCC+ | 82 | | Caribbean | 4 out of 9 |
| Belarus | 14.2 | 14.6 | B- | 143 | | Central and Eastern Europe | 23 out of 25 |
| Belgium | -0.9 | -1.1 | AA | 17 | Developed | Western Europe | 10 out of 19 |
| Belize | 10.1 | 10.2 | B- | 106 | | Latin America | 17 out of 20 |
| Benin | 16.0 | 15.9 | | 150 | | Africa | 37 out of 51 |
| Bermuda | 2.8 | 2.6 | A+ | 44 | | Caribbean | 1 out of 9 |
| Bhutan | 15.6 | 15.4 | | 148 | | Asia | 25 out of 29 |
| Bolivia | 8.6 | 8.9 | BB | 88 | | Latin America | 12 out of 20 |
| Bosnia & Herzegovina | 14.7 | 14.8 | B | 144 | | Central and Eastern Europe | 24 out of 25 |
| Botswana | 2.8 | 2.7 | A- | 48 | | Africa | 1 out of 51 |
| Brazil | 4.3 | 4.2 | BB | 59 | Emerging | Latin America | 7 out of 20 |
| Bulgaria | 4.2 | 4.3 | BB+ | 61 | | Central and Eastern Europe | 12 out of 25 |
| Burkina Faso | 13.1 | 13.0 | B- | 133 | | Africa | 33 out of 51 |
| Burundi | 25.0 | 25.0 | | 169 | | Africa | 47 out of 51 |
| Cambodia | 16.5 | 16.2 | | 151 | | Asia | 27 out of 29 |
| Cameroon | 11.7 | 11.6 | B | 124 | | Africa | 28 out of 51 |
| Canada | -2.6 | -2.7 | AAA | 9 | Developed | North America | 1 out of 2 |
| Cape Verde | 9.3 | 9.3 | B | 94 | | Africa | 12 out of 51 |
| Central African Republic | 28.6 | 28.6 | | 172 | | Africa | 49 out of 51 |
| Chad | 27.3 | 27.3 | | 171 | | Africa | 48 out of 51 |
| Chile | -1.4 | -1.2 | AA- | 16 | Emerging | Latin America | 1 out of 20 |
| China | 2.6 | 2.5 | AA- | 42 | Emerging | Asia | 7 out of 29 |
| Colombia | 2.5 | 2.5 | BBB | 41 | Emerging | Latin America | 4 out of 20 |
| Congo Republic | 11.3 | 11.1 | B- | 117 | | Africa | 24 out of 51 |
| Congo, DR | 12.6 | 12.5 | B- | 131 | | Africa | 32 out of 51 |
| Costa Rica | 5.6 | 5.8 | BB- | 71 | | Latin America | 8 out of 20 |
| Côte d'Ivoire | 9.2 | 9.1 | | 92 | | Africa | 11 out of 51 |
| Croatia | 4.7 | 4.5 | BB | 63 | Frontier | Central and Eastern Europe | 13 out of 25 |
| Cuba | 18.9 | 18.9 | | 160 | | Caribbean | 9 out of 9 |
| Cyprus | 2.3 | 2.3 | BB+ | 40 | | Central and Eastern Europe | 7 out of 25 |
| Czech Republic | -0.1 | -0.2 | AA- | 23 | Emerging | Central and Eastern Europe | 1 out of 25 |
| Denmark | -3.2 | -3.3 | AAA | 4 | Developed | Western Europe | 3 out of 19 |
| Djibouti | 36.6 | 34.3 | | 175 | | Africa | 51 out of 51 |
| Dominican Republic | 9.0 | 9.0 | BB- | 90 | | Caribbean | 5 out of 9 |
| Ecuador | 10.6 | 10.4 | B | 109 | | Latin America | 18 out of 20 |
| Egypt | 11.0 | 11.0 | B- | 116 | Emerging | Africa | 23 out of 51 |
| El Salvador | 8.0 | 7.8 | B- | 81 | | Latin America | 10 out of 20 |
| Equatorial Guinea | 21.4 | 21.4 | | 165 | | Africa | 45 out of 51 |

§ S&P Credit Rating based on long-term foreign currency issuer rating. See http://www.standardandpoors.com/.

* World rank based on 175 countries covered by Euromoney. Ranking based on ascending order in which '1' equals the smallest country risk premium (CRP) and '175' equals the largest country risk premium (CRP).

† MSCI Market Classification based on MSCI Market Classification Framework. See http://www.msci.com/products/indexes/market_classification.html.

‡ Regional classification based on Euromoney. Regional rankings based on ascending order in which '1' equals the smallest country risk premium (CRP) for each region.

Note: A CRP of 0.0% is assumed in the following cases: (i) when the investor country and the investee country both have an S&P sovereign credit rating of AAA; or (ii) when the investor country has an S&P credit rating of AAA, and the investee country has a sovereign credit rating below AAA, but has a calculated CRP below 0.0% (which would imply lower risk than a country rated AAA); or (iii) when the investor country has an S&P credit rating below AAA, and the investee country has a sovereign credit rating of AAA, but has a calculated CRP above 0.0% (which would imply greater risk than a country rated below AAA). For purposes of this analysis, the U.S. is treated as having a sovereign credit rating equivalent to AAA.

The country risk premium (CRP) is not the cost of equity capital (COE). The CRP is to be added to base COE. See Chapter 6 for proper application.

## Data Updated Through March 2017

| Investee Country | December 2016 Country Risk Premium (CRP) (%) | March 2017 Country Risk Premium (CRP) (%) | S&P Sovereign Credit Rating § | World Rank Out of 175∗ | MSCI Market Classification † | Euromoney Region ‡ | Regional Rank ‡ |
|---|---|---|---|---|---|---|---|
| Eritrea | 32.8 | 31.0 | | 173 | | Africa | 50 out of 51 |
| Estonia | 0.5 | 0.7 | AA- | 32 | Frontier | Central and Eastern Europe | 4 out of 25 |
| Ethiopia | 9.9 | 9.9 | B | 101 | | Africa | 16 out of 51 |
| Fiji | 15.3 | 15.1 | B+ | 147 | | Australasia | 5 out of 7 |
| Finland | -2.4 | -2.5 | AA+ | 11 | Developed | Western Europe | 8 out of 19 |
| France | -0.1 | -0.3 | AA | 22 | Developed | Western Europe | 12 out of 19 |
| Gabon | 7.6 | 7.9 | | 83 | | Africa | 7 out of 51 |
| Gambia | 13.7 | 13.7 | | 138 | | Africa | 34 out of 51 |
| Georgia | 6.4 | 6.6 | BB- | 74 | | Central and Eastern Europe | 15 out of 25 |
| Germany | -2.4 | -2.6 | AAA | 10 | Developed | Western Europe | 7 out of 19 |
| Ghana | 9.4 | 9.0 | B- | 89 | | Africa | 9 out of 51 |
| Greece | 10.5 | 10.2 | B- | 108 | Emerging | Western Europe | 19 out of 19 |
| Grenada | 10.1 | 10.2 | | 105 | | Caribbean | 7 out of 9 |
| Guatemala | 8.0 | 8.0 | BB | 84 | | Latin America | 11 out of 20 |
| Guinea | 17.5 | 17.5 | | 156 | | Africa | 41 out of 51 |
| Guinea-Bissau | 11.0 | 10.9 | | 115 | | Africa | 22 out of 51 |
| Guyana | 9.8 | 9.8 | | 100 | | Latin America | 15 out of 20 |
| Haiti | 20.3 | 18.3 | | 157 | | Caribbean | 8 out of 9 |
| Honduras | 9.5 | 9.5 | B+ | 98 | | Latin America | 14 out of 20 |
| Hong Kong | -1.9 | -1.9 | AAA | 14 | Developed | Asia | 2 out of 29 |
| Hungary | 3.9 | 4.0 | BBB- | 57 | Emerging | Central and Eastern Europe | 10 out of 25 |
| Iceland | 0.9 | 0.6 | A | 30 | | Western Europe | 15 out of 19 |
| India | 3.7 | 3.9 | BBB- | 55 | Emerging | Asia | 10 out of 29 |
| Indonesia | 4.5 | 4.4 | BB+ | 62 | Emerging | Asia | 11 out of 29 |
| Iran | 11.5 | 11.7 | | 125 | | Middle East | 10 out of 13 |
| Iraq | 13.3 | 13.3 | B- | 136 | | Middle East | 11 out of 13 |
| Ireland | 0.4 | 0.3 | A+ | 27 | Developed | Western Europe | 14 out of 19 |
| Israel | 0.4 | 0.3 | A+ | 28 | Developed | Middle East | 2 out of 13 |
| Italy | 3.3 | 3.1 | BBB- | 50 | Developed | Western Europe | 18 out of 19 |
| Jamaica | 9.5 | 10.1 | B | 104 | | Caribbean | 6 out of 9 |
| Japan | 0.3 | 0.2 | A+ | 25 | Developed | Asia | 5 out of 29 |
| Jordan | 6.6 | 6.8 | BB- | 76 | Frontier | Middle East | 8 out of 13 |
| Kazakhstan | 6.1 | 5.7 | BBB- | 70 | Frontier | Asia | 13 out of 29 |
| Kenya | 9.6 | 9.6 | B+ | 99 | Frontier | Africa | 15 out of 51 |
| Korea (North) | 32.1 | 31.7 | | 174 | | Asia | 29 out of 29 |
| Korea (South) | -0.5 | -0.6 | AA | 19 | Emerging | Asia | 4 out of 29 |
| Kuwait | 0.6 | 0.6 | AA | 31 | Frontier | Middle East | 3 out of 13 |
| Kyrgyz Republic | 14.8 | 14.6 | | 142 | | Central and Eastern Europe | 22 out of 25 |
| Laos | 19.1 | 18.5 | | 158 | | Asia | 28 out of 29 |
| Latvia | 2.6 | 2.6 | A- | 43 | | Central and Eastern Europe | 8 out of 25 |
| Lebanon | 11.4 | 10.7 | B- | 112 | Frontier | Middle East | 9 out of 13 |
| Lesotho | 15.0 | 15.0 | | 146 | | Africa | 36 out of 51 |
| Liberia | 10.2 | 10.2 | | 107 | | Africa | 17 out of 51 |
| Libya | 16.5 | 16.9 | | 153 | | Africa | 39 out of 51 |
| Lithuania | 1.8 | 1.8 | A- | 36 | Frontier | Central and Eastern Europe | 6 out of 25 |
| Luxembourg | -2.9 | -3.0 | AAA | 5 | | Western Europe | 4 out of 19 |
| Macedonia | 8.6 | 8.8 | BB- | 87 | | Central and Eastern Europe | 17 out of 25 |
| Madagascar | 11.1 | 11.6 | | 123 | | Africa | 27 out of 51 |
| Malawi | 10.8 | 10.8 | | 114 | | Africa | 21 out of 51 |
| Malaysia | 2.0 | 1.8 | A- | 35 | Emerging | Asia | 6 out of 29 |

§ S&P Credit Rating based on long-term foreign currency issuer rating. See http://www.standardandpoors.com/.

∗ World rank based on 175 countries covered by Euromoney. Ranking based on ascending order in which '1' equals the smallest country risk premium (CRP) and '175' equals the largest country risk premium (CRP).

† MSCI Market Classification based on MSCI Market Classification Framework. See http://www.msci.com/products/indexes/market_classification.html

‡ Regional classification based on Euromoney. Regional rankings based on ascending order in which '1' equals the smallest country risk premium (CRP) for each region.

Note: A CRP of 0.0% is assumed in the following cases: (i) when the investor country and the investee country both have an S&P sovereign credit rating of AAA; or (ii) when the investor country has an S&P credit rating of AAA, and the investee country has a sovereign credit rating below AAA, but has a calculated CRP below 0.0% (which would imply lower risk than a country rated AAA); or (iii) when the investor country has an S&P credit rating below AAA, and the investee country has a sovereign credit rating of AAA, but has a calculated CRP above 0.0% (which would imply greater risk than a country rated below AAA). For purposes of this analysis, the U.S. is treated as having a sovereign credit rating equivalent to AAA.

The country risk premium (CRP) is not the cost of equity capital (COE). The CRP is to be added to base COE. See Chapter 6 for proper application.

### Data Updated Through March 2017

| Investee Country | December 2016 Country Risk Premium (CRP) (%) | March 2017 Country Risk Premium (CRP) (%) | S&P Sovereign Credit Rating § | World Rank Out of 175* | MSCI Market Classification † | Euromoney Region ‡ | Regional Rank ‡ |
|---|---|---|---|---|---|---|---|
| Mali | 14.6 | 14.6 | | 141 | | Africa | 35 out of 51 |
| Malta | 0.3 | 0.3 | A- | 26 | | Western Europe | 13 out of 19 |
| Mauritania | 18.7 | 18.7 | | 159 | | Africa | 42 out of 51 |
| Mauritius | 5.4 | 5.3 | | 67 | Frontier | Asia | 12 out of 29 |
| Mexico | 1.9 | 1.9 | BBB+ | 37 | Emerging | Latin America | 2 out of 20 |
| Moldova | 13.0 | 13.4 | | 137 | | Central and Eastern Europe | 21 out of 25 |
| Mongolia | 11.2 | 11.5 | B- | 119 | | Asia | 18 out of 29 |
| Montenegro | 10.4 | 10.1 | B+ | 103 | | Central and Eastern Europe | 19 out of 25 |
| Morocco | 5.5 | 5.6 | BBB- | 69 | Frontier | Africa | 4 out of 51 |
| Mozambique | 12.2 | 12.1 | SD | 128 | | Africa | 29 out of 51 |
| Myanmar | 13.2 | 13.1 | | 134 | | Asia | 22 out of 29 |
| Namibia | 5.1 | 5.2 | | 66 | | Africa | 3 out of 51 |
| Nepal | 15.9 | 15.9 | | 149 | | Asia | 26 out of 29 |
| Netherlands | -2.8 | -3.0 | AAA | 6 | Developed | Western Europe | 5 out of 19 |
| New Zealand | -2.7 | -2.7 | AA | 8 | Developed | Australasia | 1 out of 7 |
| Nicaragua | 11.9 | 11.9 | B+ | 127 | | Latin America | 19 out of 20 |
| Niger | 11.5 | 11.5 | | 120 | | Africa | 25 out of 51 |
| Nigeria | 9.5 | 9.5 | B | 97 | Frontier | Africa | 14 out of 51 |
| Norway | -3.5 | -3.7 | AAA | 3 | Developed | Western Europe | 2 out of 19 |
| Oman | 2.7 | 2.7 | BBB- | 46 | Frontier | Middle East | 5 out of 13 |
| Pakistan | 11.6 | 11.5 | B | 122 | Frontier | Asia | 19 out of 29 |
| Panama | 3.4 | 3.4 | BBB | 52 | | Latin America | 6 out of 20 |
| Papua New Guinea | 11.1 | 11.2 | B+ | 118 | | Australasia | 3 out of 7 |
| Paraguay | 7.0 | 7.2 | BB | 80 | | Latin America | 9 out of 20 |
| Peru | 2.1 | 2.2 | BBB+ | 39 | Emerging | Latin America | 3 out of 20 |
| Philippines | 3.8 | 3.7 | BBB | 53 | Emerging | Asia | 9 out of 29 |
| Poland | 0.7 | 0.5 | BBB+ | 29 | Emerging | Central and Eastern Europe | 3 out of 25 |
| Portugal | 3.2 | 2.9 | BB+ | 49 | Developed | Western Europe | 17 out of 19 |
| Qatar | -0.4 | -0.4 | AA | 21 | Emerging | Middle East | 1 out of 13 |
| Romania | 4.0 | 4.0 | BBB- | 56 | Frontier | Central and Eastern Europe | 9 out of 25 |
| Russia | 6.2 | 5.6 | BB+ | 68 | Emerging | Central and Eastern Europe | 14 out of 25 |
| Rwanda | 12.3 | 12.3 | B | 130 | | Africa | 31 out of 51 |
| São Tomé & Príncipe | 18.8 | 19.3 | | 163 | | Africa | 43 out of 51 |
| Saudi Arabia | 3.1 | 2.7 | A- | 47 | | Middle East | 6 out of 13 |
| Senegal | 8.8 | 8.8 | B+ | 86 | | Africa | 8 out of 51 |
| Serbia | 6.9 | 6.6 | BB- | 75 | Frontier | Central and Eastern Europe | 16 out of 25 |
| Seychelles | 6.4 | 6.4 | | 73 | | Africa | 5 out of 51 |
| Sierra Leone | 12.3 | 12.3 | | 129 | | Africa | 30 out of 51 |
| Singapore | -3.7 | -3.8 | AAA | 1 | Developed | Asia | 1 out of 29 |
| Slovakia | 0.0 | 0.0 | A+ | 24 | | Central and Eastern Europe | 2 out of 25 |
| Slovenia | 1.4 | 1.4 | A | 34 | Frontier | Central and Eastern Europe | 5 out of 25 |
| Solomon Islands | 23.2 | 23.2 | | 168 | | Australasia | 6 out of 7 |
| Somalia | 21.5 | 21.5 | | 166 | | Africa | 46 out of 51 |
| South Africa | 4.0 | 4.2 | BBB- | 60 | Emerging | Africa | 2 out of 51 |
| Spain | 2.3 | 2.2 | BBB+ | 38 | Developed | Western Europe | 16 out of 19 |
| Sri Lanka | 6.3 | 6.0 | B+ | 72 | Frontier | Asia | 14 out of 29 |
| Sudan | 17.4 | 17.3 | | 154 | | Africa | 40 out of 51 |
| Suriname | 9.8 | 9.9 | B+ | 102 | | Latin America | 16 out of 20 |
| Swaziland | 15.7 | 16.6 | | 152 | | Africa | 38 out of 51 |
| Sweden | -2.8 | -2.9 | AAA | 7 | Developed | Western Europe | 6 out of 19 |

§ S&P Credit Rating based on long-term foreign currency issuer rating. See http://www.standardandpoors.com/.

* World rank based on 175 countries covered by Euromoney. Ranking based on ascending order in which '1' equals the smallest country risk premium (CRP) and '175' equals the largest country risk premium (CRP).

† MSCI Market Classification based on MSCI Market Classification Framework. See http://www.msci.com/products/indexes/market_classification.html.

‡ Regional classification based on Euromoney. Regional rankings based on ascending order in which '1' equals the smallest country risk premium (CRP) for each region.

Note: A CRP of 0.0% is assumed in the following cases: (i) when the investor country and the investee country both have an S&P sovereign credit rating of AAA; or (ii) when the investor country has an S&P credit rating of AAA, and the investee country has a sovereign credit rating below AAA, but has a calculated CRP below 0.0% (which would imply lower risk than a country rated AAA); or (iii) when the investor country has an S&P credit rating below AAA, and the investee country has a sovereign credit rating of AAA, but has a calculated CRP above 0.0% (which would imply greater risk than a country rated below AAA). For purposes of this analysis, the U.S. is treated as having a sovereign credit rating equivalent to AAA.

The country risk premium (CRP) is not the cost of equity capital (COE). The CRP is to be added to base COE. See Chapter 6 for proper application.

## Data Updated Through March 2017

| Investee Country | December 2016 Country Risk Premium (CRP) (%) | March 2017 Country Risk Premium (CRP) (%) | S&P Sovereign Credit Rating § | World Rank Out of 175* | MSCI Market Classification † | Euromoney Region ‡ | Regional Rank ‡ |
|---|---|---|---|---|---|---|---|
| Switzerland | -3.5 | -3.7 | AAA | 2 | Developed | Western Europe | 1 out of 19 |
| Syria | 22.2 | 22.5 | | 167 | | Middle East | 13 out of 13 |
| Taiwan | -0.8 | -0.8 | AA- | 18 | Emerging | Asia | 3 out of 29 |
| Tajikistan | 17.0 | 17.3 | | 155 | | Central and Eastern Europe | 25 out of 25 |
| Tanzania | 9.2 | 9.3 | | 95 | | Africa | 13 out of 51 |
| Thailand | 3.5 | 3.3 | BBB+ | 51 | Emerging | Asia | 8 out of 29 |
| Togo | 10.8 | 10.7 | | 113 | | Africa | 20 out of 51 |
| Tonga | 25.7 | 25.7 | | 170 | | Australasia | 7 out of 7 |
| Trinidad & Tobago | 3.8 | 3.8 | A- | 54 | | Caribbean | 2 out of 9 |
| Tunisia | 6.7 | 7.0 | | 79 | Frontier | Africa | 6 out of 51 |
| Turkey | 4.2 | 4.0 | BB | 58 | Emerging | Central and Eastern Europe | 11 out of 25 |
| Turkmenistan | 14.1 | 14.4 | | 140 | | Asia | 24 out of 29 |
| Uganda | 10.3 | 10.5 | B | 110 | | Africa | 18 out of 51 |
| Ukraine | 13.1 | 13.2 | B- | 135 | | Central and Eastern Europe | 20 out of 25 |
| United Arab Emirates | 1.0 | 1.0 | AA | 33 | Emerging | Middle East | 4 out of 13 |
| United Kingdom | -0.5 | -0.5 | AA | 20 | Developed | Western Europe | 11 out of 19 |
| United States | -1.6 | -1.6 | AA+ | 15 | Developed | North America | 2 out of 2 |
| Uruguay | 2.8 | 2.7 | BBB | 45 | | Latin America | 5 out of 20 |
| Uzbekistan | 13.3 | 12.7 | | 132 | | Asia | 21 out of 29 |
| Vanuatu | 15.0 | 15.0 | | 145 | | Australasia | 4 out of 7 |
| Venezuela | 18.8 | 19.2 | CCC | 162 | | Latin America | 20 out of 20 |
| Vietnam | 7.3 | 7.0 | BB- | 78 | Frontier | Asia | 16 out of 29 |
| Yemen | 19.1 | 19.2 | | 161 | | Middle East | 12 out of 13 |
| Zambia | 10.6 | 10.6 | B | 111 | | Africa | 19 out of 51 |
| Zimbabwe | 20.7 | 20.7 | | 164 | | Africa | 44 out of 51 |

## March 2017 Country Risk Premium (CRP) Summary Statistics:

| S&P Rating | Country Count | Average CRP (%) | Median CRP (%) | Min CRP (%) | Max CRP (%) |
|---|---|---|---|---|---|
| AAA ** | 12 | -2.9 | -2.9 | -3.8 | -1.6 |
| AA (AA+, AA, AA-) | 15 | -0.5 | -0.5 | -2.7 | 2.5 |
| A (A+, A, A-) | 14 | 1.5 | 1.6 | 0.0 | 3.8 |
| BBB (BBB+, BBB, BBB-) | 17 | 3.3 | 3.3 | 0.5 | 5.7 |
| BB (BB+, BB, BB-) | 22 | 6.2 | 6.2 | 2.3 | 11.7 |
| B+ – SD | 39 | 11.0 | 10.6 | 6.0 | 19.2 |
| Investment Grade ** | 58 | 0.6 | 0.6 | -3.8 | 5.7 |
| Non-Investment Grade ** | 61 | 9.3 | 9.5 | 2.3 | 19.2 |
| **MSCI Market Classification** | | | | | |
| Developed Markets | 23 | -1.4 | -2.3 | -3.8 | 3.1 |
| Emerging Markets | 23 | 2.9 | 2.5 | -1.2 | 11.0 |
| Frontier Markets | 22 | 6.0 | 5.8 | 0.6 | 11.7 |
| **Euromoney Region ‡** | | | | | |
| Africa | 51 | 13.6 | 11.5 | 2.7 | 34.3 |
| Asia | 29 | 8.2 | 6.8 | -3.8 | 31.7 |
| Australasia | 7 | 12.1 | 15.0 | -2.7 | 25.7 |
| Caribbean | 9 | 9.5 | 9.0 | 2.6 | 18.9 |
| Central and Eastern Europe | 25 | 6.6 | 4.5 | -0.2 | 17.3 |
| Latin America | 20 | 7.2 | 7.9 | -1.2 | 19.2 |
| Middle East | 13 | 7.4 | 4.9 | -0.4 | 22.5 |
| North America | 2 | -2.2 | -2.2 | -2.7 | -1.6 |
| Western Europe | 19 | -0.5 | -1.1 | -3.7 | 10.2 |

## CCR Base Cost of Equity Capital:

| Slovakia | COE (%) |
|---|---|
| March 2017 | 10.1 |
| December 2016 | 10.0 |

CCR base country-level COE for a Slovakia-based investor investing in Slovakia.

§ S&P Credit Rating based on long-term foreign currency issuer rating. See http://www.standardandpoors.com/.

* World rank based on 175 countries covered by Euromoney. Ranking based on ascending order in which '1' equals the smallest country risk premium (CRP) and '175' equals the largest country risk premium (CRP).

† MSCI Market Classification based on MSCI Market Classification Framework. See http://www.msci.com/products/indexes/market_classification.html

‡ Regional classification based on Euromoney. Regional rankings based on ascending order in which '1' equals the smallest country risk premium (CRP) for each region.

** Investment grade based on S&P sovereign credit rating from AAA to BBB-. Non-Investment grade based on S&P sovereign credit rating from BB+ to SD. For purposes of this analysis, the U.S. is being treated as if it were rated AAA by S&P.

Note: A CRP of 0.0% is assumed in the following cases: (i) when the investor country and the investee country both have an S&P sovereign credit rating of AAA; or (ii) when the investor country has an S&P credit rating of AAA, and the investee country has a sovereign credit rating below AAA, but has a calculated CRP below 0.0% (which would imply lower risk than a country rated AAA); or (iii) when the investor country has an S&P credit rating below AAA, and the investee country has a sovereign credit rating of AAA, but has a calculated CRP above 0.0% (which would imply greater risk than a country rated below AAA). For purposes of this analysis, the U.S. is treated as having a sovereign credit rating equivalent to AAA.

Investor Perspective: Slovenia
Currency: Euro (EUR)

Erb-Harvey-Viskanta
Country Credit Rating (CCR) Model

The country risk premium (CRP) is not the cost of equity capital (COE). The CRP is to be added to base COE. See Chapter 6 for proper application.

## Data Updated Through March 2017

| Investee Country | December 2016 Country Risk Premium (CRP) (%) | March 2017 Country Risk Premium (CRP) (%) | S&P Sovereign Credit Rating § | World Rank Out of 175• | MSCI Market Classification † | Euromoney Region ‡ | Regional Rank ‡ |
|---|---|---|---|---|---|---|---|
| Afghanistan | 13.1 | 12.9 | | 139 | | Asia | 23 out of 29 |
| Albania | 7.7 | 7.8 | B+ | 93 | | Central and Eastern Europe | 18 out of 25 |
| Algeria | 7.7 | 7.8 | | 91 | | Africa | 10 out of 51 |
| Angola | 10.1 | 10.1 | B | 121 | | Africa | 26 out of 51 |
| Argentina | 8.2 | 8.0 | B- | 96 | Frontier | Latin America | 13 out of 20 |
| Armenia | 5.2 | 5.4 | | 77 | | Asia | 15 out of 29 |
| Australia | -3.8 | -3.9 | AAA | 12 | Developed | Australasia | 2 out of 7 |
| Austria | -3.6 | -3.7 | AA+ | 13 | Developed | Western Europe | 9 out of 19 |
| Azerbaijan | 6.4 | 6.8 | BB+ | 85 | | Asia | 17 out of 29 |
| Bahamas | 3.8 | 3.5 | BB+ | 65 | | Caribbean | 3 out of 9 |
| Bahrain | 3.7 | 3.5 | BB- | 64 | Frontier | Middle East | 7 out of 13 |
| Bangladesh | 10.6 | 10.4 | BB- | 126 | Frontier | Asia | 20 out of 29 |
| Barbados | 5.4 | 6.5 | CCC+ | 82 | | Caribbean | 4 out of 9 |
| Belarus | 12.8 | 13.2 | B- | 143 | | Central and Eastern Europe | 23 out of 25 |
| Belgium | -2.3 | -2.4 | AA | 17 | Developed | Western Europe | 10 out of 19 |
| Belize | 8.7 | 8.8 | B- | 106 | | Latin America | 17 out of 20 |
| Benin | 14.5 | 14.6 | | 150 | | Africa | 37 out of 51 |
| Bermuda | 1.4 | 1.3 | A+ | 44 | | Caribbean | 1 out of 9 |
| Bhutan | 14.2 | 14.1 | | 148 | | Asia | 25 out of 29 |
| Bolivia | 7.2 | 7.5 | BB | 88 | | Latin America | 12 out of 20 |
| Bosnia & Herzegovina | 13.3 | 13.4 | B | 144 | | Central and Eastern Europe | 24 out of 25 |
| Botswana | 1.4 | 1.3 | A- | 48 | | Africa | 1 out of 51 |
| Brazil | 2.9 | 2.8 | BB | 59 | Emerging | Latin America | 7 out of 20 |
| Bulgaria | 2.7 | 2.9 | BB+ | 61 | | Central and Eastern Europe | 12 out of 25 |
| Burkina Faso | 11.6 | 11.7 | B- | 133 | | Africa | 33 out of 51 |
| Burundi | 23.6 | 23.6 | | 169 | | Africa | 47 out of 51 |
| Cambodia | 15.1 | 14.8 | | 151 | | Asia | 27 out of 29 |
| Cameroon | 10.3 | 10.3 | B | 124 | | Africa | 28 out of 51 |
| Canada | -4.0 | -4.1 | AAA | 9 | Developed | North America | 1 out of 2 |
| Cape Verde | 7.9 | 7.9 | B | 94 | | Africa | 12 out of 51 |
| Central African Republic | 27.2 | 27.2 | | 172 | | Africa | 49 out of 51 |
| Chad | 25.8 | 25.9 | | 171 | | Africa | 48 out of 51 |
| Chile | -2.8 | -2.6 | AA- | 16 | Emerging | Latin America | 1 out of 20 |
| China | 1.2 | 1.1 | AA- | 42 | Emerging | Asia | 7 out of 29 |
| Colombia | 1.1 | 1.1 | BBB | 41 | Emerging | Latin America | 4 out of 20 |
| Congo Republic | 9.9 | 9.7 | B- | 117 | | Africa | 24 out of 51 |
| Congo, DR | 11.1 | 11.1 | B- | 131 | | Africa | 32 out of 51 |
| Costa Rica | 4.2 | 4.4 | BB- | 71 | | Latin America | 8 out of 20 |
| Côte d'Ivoire | 7.7 | 7.8 | | 92 | | Africa | 11 out of 51 |
| Croatia | 3.3 | 3.1 | BB | 63 | Frontier | Central and Eastern Europe | 13 out of 25 |
| Cuba | 17.4 | 17.6 | | 160 | | Caribbean | 9 out of 9 |
| Cyprus | 0.9 | 0.9 | BB+ | 40 | | Central and Eastern Europe | 7 out of 25 |
| Czech Republic | -1.5 | -1.6 | AA- | 23 | Emerging | Central and Eastern Europe | 1 out of 25 |
| Denmark | -4.6 | -4.7 | AAA | 4 | Developed | Western Europe | 3 out of 19 |
| Djibouti | 35.2 | 32.9 | | 175 | | Africa | 51 out of 51 |
| Dominican Republic | 7.6 | 7.7 | BB- | 90 | | Caribbean | 5 out of 9 |
| Ecuador | 9.2 | 9.0 | B | 109 | | Latin America | 18 out of 20 |
| Egypt | 9.6 | 9.6 | B- | 116 | Emerging | Africa | 23 out of 51 |
| El Salvador | 6.6 | 6.4 | B- | 81 | | Latin America | 10 out of 20 |
| Equatorial Guinea | 20.0 | 20.0 | | 165 | | Africa | 45 out of 51 |

§ S&P Credit Rating based on long-term foreign currency issuer rating. See http://www.standardandpoors.com/.
• World rank based on 175 countries covered by Euromoney. Ranking based on ascending order in which '1' equals the smallest country risk premium (CRP) and '175' equals the largest country risk premium (CRP).
† MSCI Market Classification based on MSCI Market Classification Framework. See http://www.msci.com/products/indexes/market_classification.html.
‡ Regional classification based on Euromoney. Regional rankings based on ascending order in which '1' equals the smallest country risk premium (CRP) for each region.
Note: A CRP of 0.0% is assumed in the following cases: (i) when the investor country and the investee country both have an S&P sovereign credit rating of AAA; or (ii) when the investor country has an S&P credit rating of AAA, and the investee country has a sovereign credit rating below AAA, but has a calculated CRP below 0.0% (which would imply lower risk than a country rated AAA); or (iii) when the investor country has an S&P credit rating below AAA, and the investee country has a sovereign credit rating of AAA, but has a calculated CRP above 0.0% (which would imply greater risk than a country rated below AAA). For purposes of this analysis, the U.S. is treated as having a sovereign credit rating equivalent to AAA.

2017 Valuation Handbook – International Guide to Cost of Capital          Data Exhibit 4          Investor Perspective: Slovenia (EUR); Page 1 of 4

The country risk premium (CRP) is not the cost of equity capital (COE). The CRP is to be added to base COE. See Chapter 6 for proper application.

### Data Updated Through March 2017

| Investee Country | December 2016 Country Risk Premium (CRP) (%) | March 2017 Country Risk Premium (CRP) (%) | S&P Sovereign Credit Rating § | World Rank Out of 175∗ | MSCI Market Classification † | Euromoney Region ‡ | Regional Rank ‡ |
|---|---|---|---|---|---|---|---|
| Eritrea | 31.4 | 29.6 | | 173 | | Africa | 50 out of 51 |
| Estonia | -0.9 | -0.7 | AA- | 32 | Frontier | Central and Eastern Europe | 4 out of 25 |
| Ethiopia | 8.4 | 8.5 | B | 101 | | Africa | 16 out of 51 |
| Fiji | 13.9 | 13.7 | B+ | 147 | | Australasia | 5 out of 7 |
| Finland | -3.9 | -3.9 | AA+ | 11 | Developed | Western Europe | 8 out of 19 |
| France | -1.5 | -1.7 | AA | 22 | Developed | Western Europe | 12 out of 19 |
| Gabon | 6.2 | 6.5 | | 83 | | Africa | 7 out of 51 |
| Gambia | 12.3 | 12.3 | | 138 | | Africa | 34 out of 51 |
| Georgia | 4.9 | 5.2 | BB- | 74 | | Central and Eastern Europe | 15 out of 25 |
| Germany | -3.9 | -4.0 | AAA | 10 | Developed | Western Europe | 7 out of 19 |
| Ghana | 7.9 | 7.6 | B- | 89 | | Africa | 9 out of 51 |
| Greece | 9.1 | 8.9 | B- | 108 | Emerging | Western Europe | 19 out of 19 |
| Grenada | 8.7 | 8.8 | | 105 | | Caribbean | 7 out of 9 |
| Guatemala | 6.6 | 6.7 | BB | 84 | | Latin America | 11 out of 20 |
| Guinea | 16.0 | 16.1 | | 156 | | Africa | 41 out of 51 |
| Guinea-Bissau | 9.5 | 9.6 | | 115 | | Africa | 22 out of 51 |
| Guyana | 8.4 | 8.4 | | 100 | | Latin America | 15 out of 20 |
| Haiti | 18.9 | 16.9 | | 157 | | Caribbean | 8 out of 9 |
| Honduras | 8.0 | 8.1 | B+ | 98 | | Latin America | 14 out of 20 |
| Hong Kong | -3.3 | -3.3 | AAA | 14 | Developed | Asia | 2 out of 29 |
| Hungary | 2.5 | 2.6 | BBB- | 57 | Emerging | Central and Eastern Europe | 10 out of 25 |
| Iceland | -0.5 | -0.8 | A | 30 | | Western Europe | 15 out of 19 |
| India | 2.3 | 2.5 | BBB- | 55 | Emerging | Asia | 10 out of 29 |
| Indonesia | 3.0 | 3.1 | BB+ | 62 | Emerging | Asia | 11 out of 29 |
| Iran | 10.0 | 10.3 | | 125 | | Middle East | 10 out of 13 |
| Iraq | 11.9 | 11.9 | B- | 136 | | Middle East | 11 out of 13 |
| Ireland | -1.0 | -1.1 | A+ | 27 | Developed | Western Europe | 14 out of 19 |
| Israel | -1.1 | -1.1 | A+ | 28 | Developed | Middle East | 2 out of 13 |
| Italy | 1.9 | 1.7 | BBB- | 50 | Developed | Western Europe | 18 out of 19 |
| Jamaica | 8.1 | 8.7 | B | 104 | | Caribbean | 6 out of 9 |
| Japan | -1.2 | -1.2 | A+ | 25 | Developed | Asia | 5 out of 29 |
| Jordan | 5.2 | 5.4 | BB- | 76 | Frontier | Middle East | 8 out of 13 |
| Kazakhstan | 4.7 | 4.3 | BBB- | 70 | Frontier | Asia | 13 out of 29 |
| Kenya | 8.1 | 8.2 | B+ | 99 | Frontier | Africa | 15 out of 51 |
| Korea (North) | 30.7 | 30.3 | | 174 | | Asia | 29 out of 29 |
| Korea (South) | -2.0 | -1.9 | AA | 19 | Emerging | Asia | 4 out of 29 |
| Kuwait | -0.9 | -0.7 | AA | 31 | Frontier | Middle East | 3 out of 13 |
| Kyrgyz Republic | 13.3 | 13.2 | | 142 | | Central and Eastern Europe | 22 out of 25 |
| Laos | 17.6 | 17.1 | | 158 | | Asia | 28 out of 29 |
| Latvia | 1.2 | 1.3 | A- | 43 | | Central and Eastern Europe | 8 out of 25 |
| Lebanon | 9.9 | 9.3 | B- | 112 | Frontier | Middle East | 9 out of 13 |
| Lesotho | 13.5 | 13.6 | | 146 | | Africa | 36 out of 51 |
| Liberia | 8.8 | 8.8 | | 107 | | Africa | 17 out of 51 |
| Libya | 15.1 | 15.5 | | 153 | | Africa | 39 out of 51 |
| Lithuania | 0.4 | 0.4 | A- | 36 | Frontier | Central and Eastern Europe | 6 out of 25 |
| Luxembourg | -4.3 | -4.4 | AAA | 5 | | Western Europe | 4 out of 19 |
| Macedonia | 7.2 | 7.4 | BB- | 87 | | Central and Eastern Europe | 17 out of 25 |
| Madagascar | 9.7 | 10.2 | | 123 | | Africa | 27 out of 51 |
| Malawi | 9.4 | 9.4 | | 114 | | Africa | 21 out of 51 |
| Malaysia | 0.5 | 0.4 | A- | 35 | Emerging | Asia | 6 out of 29 |

§ S&P Credit Rating based on long-term foreign currency issuer rating. See http://www.standardandpoors.com/.

∗ World rank based on 175 countries covered by Euromoney. Ranking based on ascending order in which '1' equals the smallest country risk premium (CRP) and '175' equals the largest country risk premium (CRP).

† MSCI Market Classification based on MSCI Market Classification Framework. See http://www.msci.com/products/indexes/market_classification.html.

‡ Regional classification based on Euromoney. Regional rankings based on ascending order in which '1' equals the smallest country risk premium (CRP) for each region.

Note: A CRP of 0.0% is assumed in the following cases: (i) when the investor country and the investee country both have an S&P sovereign credit rating of AAA; or (ii) when the investor country has an S&P credit rating of AAA, and the investee country has a sovereign credit rating below AAA, but has a calculated CRP below 0.0% (which would imply lower risk than a country rated AAA); or (iii) when the investor country has an S&P credit rating below AAA, and the investee country has a sovereign credit rating of AAA, but has a calculated CRP above 0.0% (which would imply greater risk than a country rated below AAA). For purposes of this analysis, the U.S. is treated as having a sovereign credit rating equivalent to AAA.

The country risk premium (CRP) is not the cost of equity capital (COE). The CRP is to be added to base COE. See Chapter 6 for proper application.

### Data Updated Through March 2017

| Investee Country | December 2016 Country Risk Premium (CRP) (%) | March 2017 Country Risk Premium (CRP) (%) | S&P Sovereign Credit Rating § | World Rank Out of 175* | MSCI Market Classification † | Euromoney Region ‡ | Regional Rank ‡ |
|---|---|---|---|---|---|---|---|
| Mali | 13.2 | 13.2 | | 141 | | Africa | 35 out of 51 |
| Malta | -1.2 | -1.1 | A- | 26 | | Western Europe | 13 out of 19 |
| Mauritania | 17.2 | 17.3 | | 159 | | Africa | 42 out of 51 |
| Mauritius | 4.0 | 4.0 | | 67 | Frontier | Asia | 12 out of 29 |
| Mexico | 0.4 | 0.5 | BBB+ | 37 | Emerging | Latin America | 2 out of 20 |
| Moldova | 11.6 | 12.0 | | 137 | | Central and Eastern Europe | 21 out of 25 |
| Mongolia | 9.7 | 10.1 | B- | 119 | | Asia | 18 out of 29 |
| Montenegro | 8.9 | 8.7 | B+ | 103 | | Central and Eastern Europe | 19 out of 25 |
| Morocco | 4.0 | 4.2 | BBB- | 69 | Frontier | Africa | 4 out of 51 |
| Mozambique | 10.8 | 10.7 | SD | 128 | | Africa | 29 out of 51 |
| Myanmar | 11.8 | 11.7 | | 134 | | Asia | 22 out of 29 |
| Namibia | 3.6 | 3.8 | | 66 | | Africa | 3 out of 51 |
| Nepal | 14.5 | 14.5 | | 149 | | Asia | 26 out of 29 |
| Netherlands | -4.3 | -4.3 | AAA | 6 | Developed | Western Europe | 5 out of 19 |
| New Zealand | -4.1 | -4.1 | AA | 8 | Developed | Australasia | 1 out of 7 |
| Nicaragua | 10.5 | 10.5 | B+ | 127 | | Latin America | 19 out of 20 |
| Niger | 10.1 | 10.1 | | 120 | | Africa | 25 out of 51 |
| Nigeria | 8.1 | 8.1 | B | 97 | Frontier | Africa | 14 out of 51 |
| Norway | -4.9 | -5.0 | AAA | 3 | Developed | Western Europe | 2 out of 19 |
| Oman | 1.3 | 1.3 | BBB- | 46 | Frontier | Middle East | 5 out of 13 |
| Pakistan | 10.2 | 10.1 | B | 122 | Frontier | Asia | 19 out of 29 |
| Panama | 2.0 | 2.1 | BBB | 52 | | Latin America | 6 out of 20 |
| Papua New Guinea | 9.7 | 9.8 | B+ | 118 | | Australasia | 3 out of 7 |
| Paraguay | 5.6 | 5.8 | BB | 80 | | Latin America | 9 out of 20 |
| Peru | 0.7 | 0.8 | BBB+ | 39 | Emerging | Latin America | 3 out of 20 |
| Philippines | 2.4 | 2.3 | BBB | 53 | Emerging | Asia | 9 out of 29 |
| Poland | -0.7 | -0.8 | BBB+ | 29 | Emerging | Central and Eastern Europe | 3 out of 25 |
| Portugal | 1.7 | 1.5 | BB+ | 49 | Developed | Western Europe | 17 out of 19 |
| Qatar | -1.8 | -1.8 | AA | 21 | Emerging | Middle East | 1 out of 13 |
| Romania | 2.5 | 2.6 | BBB- | 56 | Frontier | Central and Eastern Europe | 9 out of 25 |
| Russia | 4.8 | 4.2 | BB+ | 68 | Emerging | Central and Eastern Europe | 14 out of 25 |
| Rwanda | 10.9 | 10.9 | B | 130 | | Africa | 31 out of 51 |
| São Tomé & Príncipe | 17.4 | 17.9 | | 163 | | Africa | 43 out of 51 |
| Saudi Arabia | 1.7 | 1.3 | A- | 47 | | Middle East | 6 out of 13 |
| Senegal | 7.4 | 7.4 | B+ | 86 | | Africa | 8 out of 51 |
| Serbia | 5.5 | 5.2 | BB- | 75 | Frontier | Central and Eastern Europe | 16 out of 25 |
| Seychelles | 5.0 | 5.0 | | 73 | | Africa | 5 out of 51 |
| Sierra Leone | 10.9 | 10.9 | | 129 | | Africa | 30 out of 51 |
| Singapore | -5.1 | -5.2 | AAA | 1 | Developed | Asia | 1 out of 29 |
| Slovakia | -1.4 | -1.4 | A+ | 24 | | Central and Eastern Europe | 2 out of 25 |
| Slovenia | 0.0 | 0.0 | A | 34 | Frontier | Central and Eastern Europe | 5 out of 25 |
| Solomon Islands | 21.8 | 21.8 | | 168 | | Australasia | 6 out of 7 |
| Somalia | 20.0 | 20.1 | | 166 | | Africa | 46 out of 51 |
| South Africa | 2.6 | 2.8 | BBB- | 60 | Emerging | Africa | 2 out of 51 |
| Spain | 0.8 | 0.8 | BBB+ | 38 | Developed | Western Europe | 16 out of 19 |
| Sri Lanka | 4.9 | 4.6 | B+ | 72 | Frontier | Asia | 14 out of 29 |
| Sudan | 16.0 | 15.9 | | 154 | | Africa | 40 out of 51 |
| Suriname | 8.3 | 8.5 | B+ | 102 | | Latin America | 16 out of 20 |
| Swaziland | 14.3 | 15.3 | | 152 | | Africa | 38 out of 51 |
| Sweden | -4.2 | -4.3 | AAA | 7 | Developed | Western Europe | 6 out of 19 |

§ S&P Credit Rating based on long-term foreign currency issuer rating. See http://www.standardandpoors.com/.
* World rank based on 175 countries covered by Euromoney. Ranking based on ascending order in which '1' equals the smallest country risk premium (CRP) and '175' equals the largest country risk premium (CRP).
† MSCI Market Classification based on MSCI Market Classification Framework. See http://www.msci.com/products/indexes/market_classification.html.
‡ Regional classification based on Euromoney. Regional rankings based on ascending order in which '1' equals the smallest country risk premium (CRP) for each region.
Note: A CRP of 0.0% is assumed in the following cases: (i) when the investor country and the investee country both have an S&P sovereign credit rating of AAA; or (ii) when the investor country has an S&P credit rating of AAA, and the investee country has a sovereign credit rating below AAA, but has a calculated CRP below 0.0% (which would imply lower risk than a country rated AAA); or (iii) when the investor country has an S&P credit rating below AAA, and the investee country has a sovereign credit rating of AAA, but has a calculated CRP above 0.0% (which would imply greater risk than a country rated AAA). For purposes of this analysis, the U.S. is treated as having a sovereign credit rating equivalent to AAA.

The country risk premium (CRP) is not the cost of equity capital (COE). The CRP is to be added to base COE. See Chapter 6 for proper application.

## Data Updated Through March 2017

| Investee Country | December 2016 Country Risk Premium (CRP) (%) | March 2017 Country Risk Premium (CRP) (%) | S&P Sovereign Credit Rating § | World Rank Out of 175* | MSCI Market Classification † | Euromoney Region ‡ | Regional Rank ‡ |
|---|---|---|---|---|---|---|---|
| Switzerland | -4.9 | -5.1 | AAA | 2 | Developed | Western Europe | 1 out of 19 |
| Syria | 20.8 | 21.1 | | 167 | | Middle East | 13 out of 13 |
| Taiwan | -2.2 | -2.2 | AA- | 18 | Emerging | Asia | 3 out of 29 |
| Tajikistan | 15.6 | 15.9 | | 155 | | Central and Eastern Europe | 25 out of 25 |
| Tanzania | 7.7 | 7.9 | | 95 | | Africa | 13 out of 51 |
| Thailand | 2.0 | 1.9 | BBB+ | 51 | Emerging | Asia | 8 out of 29 |
| Togo | 9.3 | 9.3 | | 113 | | Africa | 20 out of 51 |
| Tonga | 24.3 | 24.3 | | 170 | | Australasia | 7 out of 7 |
| Trinidad & Tobago | 2.4 | 2.4 | A- | 54 | | Caribbean | 2 out of 9 |
| Tunisia | 5.3 | 5.6 | | 79 | Frontier | Africa | 6 out of 51 |
| Turkey | 2.8 | 2.6 | BB | 58 | Emerging | Central and Eastern Europe | 11 out of 25 |
| Turkmenistan | 12.7 | 13.0 | | 140 | | Asia | 24 out of 29 |
| Uganda | 8.8 | 9.2 | B | 110 | | Africa | 18 out of 51 |
| Ukraine | 11.7 | 11.8 | B- | 135 | | Central and Eastern Europe | 20 out of 25 |
| United Arab Emirates | -0.4 | -0.4 | AA | 33 | Emerging | Middle East | 4 out of 13 |
| United Kingdom | -2.0 | -1.8 | AA | 20 | Developed | Western Europe | 11 out of 19 |
| United States | -3.0 | -3.0 | AA+ | 15 | Developed | North America | 2 out of 2 |
| Uruguay | 1.4 | 1.3 | BBB | 45 | | Latin America | 5 out of 20 |
| Uzbekistan | 11.9 | 11.3 | | 132 | | Asia | 21 out of 29 |
| Vanuatu | 13.5 | 13.6 | | 145 | | Australasia | 4 out of 7 |
| Venezuela | 17.4 | 17.9 | CCC | 162 | | Latin America | 20 out of 20 |
| Vietnam | 5.8 | 5.6 | BB- | 78 | Frontier | Asia | 16 out of 29 |
| Yemen | 17.7 | 17.8 | | 161 | | Middle East | 12 out of 13 |
| Zambia | 9.2 | 9.2 | B | 111 | | Africa | 19 out of 51 |
| Zimbabwe | 19.3 | 19.3 | | 164 | | Africa | 44 out of 51 |

## March 2017 Country Risk Premium (CRP) Summary Statistics:

| S&P Rating | Country Count | Average CRP (%) | Median CRP (%) | Min CRP (%) | Max CRP (%) |
|---|---|---|---|---|---|
| AAA ** | 12 | -4.3 | -4.3 | -5.2 | -3.0 |
| AA (AA+, AA, AA-) | 15 | -1.9 | -1.8 | -4.1 | 1.1 |
| A (A+, A, A-) | 14 | 0.1 | 0.2 | -1.4 | 2.4 |
| BBB (BBB+, BBB, BBB-) | 17 | 1.9 | 1.9 | -0.8 | 4.3 |
| BB (BB+, BB, BB-) | 22 | 4.8 | 4.8 | 0.9 | 10.4 |
| B+ − SD | 39 | 9.6 | 9.2 | 4.6 | 17.9 |
| Investment Grade ** | 58 | -0.8 | -0.8 | -5.2 | 4.3 |
| Non-Investment Grade ** | 61 | 7.9 | 8.1 | 0.9 | 17.9 |
| **MSCI Market Classification** | | | | | |
| Developed Markets | 23 | -2.8 | -3.7 | -5.2 | 1.7 |
| Emerging Markets | 23 | 1.6 | 1.1 | -2.6 | 9.6 |
| Frontier Markets | 22 | 4.7 | 4.5 | -0.7 | 10.4 |
| **Euromoney Region ‡** | | | | | |
| Africa | 51 | 12.2 | 10.1 | 1.3 | 32.9 |
| Asia | 29 | 6.8 | 5.4 | -5.2 | 30.3 |
| Australasia | 7 | 10.8 | 13.6 | -4.1 | 24.3 |
| Caribbean | 9 | 8.1 | 7.7 | 1.3 | 17.6 |
| Central and Eastern Europe | 25 | 5.2 | 3.1 | -1.6 | 15.9 |
| Latin America | 20 | 5.8 | 6.5 | -2.6 | 17.9 |
| Middle East | 13 | 6.0 | 3.5 | -1.8 | 21.1 |
| North America | 2 | -3.6 | -3.6 | -4.1 | -3.0 |
| Western Europe | 19 | -1.9 | -2.4 | -5.1 | 8.9 |

## CCR Base Cost of Equity Capital:

| Slovenia | COE (%) |
|---|---|
| March 2017 | 11.5 |
| December 2016 | 11.5 |

CCR base country-level COE for a Slovenia-based investor investing in Slovenia.

§ S&P Credit Rating based on long-term foreign currency issuer rating. See http://www.standardandpoors.com/.

* World rank based on 175 countries covered by Euromoney. Ranking based on ascending order in which '1' equals the smallest country risk premium (CRP) and '175' equals the largest country risk premium (CRP).

† MSCI Market Classification based on MSCI Market Classification Framework. See http://www.msci.com/products/indexes/market_classification.html

‡ Regional classification based on Euromoney. Regional rankings based on ascending order in which '1' equals the smallest country risk premium (CRP) for each region.

** Investment grade based on S&P sovereign credit rating from AAA to BBB-. Non-Investment grade based on S&P sovereign credit rating from BB+ to SD. For purposes of this analysis, the U.S. is being treated as if it were rated AAA by S&P.

Note: A CRP of 0.0% is assumed in the following cases: (i) when the investor country and the investee country both have an S&P sovereign credit rating of AAA; or (ii) when the investor country has an S&P credit rating of AAA, and the investee country has a sovereign credit rating below AAA, but has a calculated CRP below 0.0% (which would imply lower risk than a country rated AAA); or (iii) when the investor country has an S&P credit rating below AAA, and the investee country has a sovereign credit rating of AAA, but has a calculated CRP above 0.0% (which would imply greater risk than a country rated below AAA). For purposes of this analysis, the U.S. is treated as having a sovereign credit rating equivalent to AAA.

The country risk premium (CRP) is not the cost of equity capital (COE). The CRP is to be added to base COE. See Chapter 6 for proper application.

## Data Updated Through March 2017

| Investee Country | December 2016 Country Risk Premium (CRP) (%) | March 2017 Country Risk Premium (CRP) (%) | S&P Sovereign Credit Rating § | World Rank Out of 175* | MSCI Market Classification † | Euromoney Region ‡ | Regional Rank ‡ |
|---|---|---|---|---|---|---|---|
| Afghanistan | 10.1 | 9.6 | | 139 | | Asia | 23 out of 29 |
| Albania | 4.9 | 4.8 | B+ | 93 | | Central and Eastern Europe | 18 out of 25 |
| Algeria | 4.9 | 4.7 | | 91 | | Africa | 10 out of 51 |
| Angola | 7.2 | 7.0 | B | 121 | | Africa | 26 out of 51 |
| Argentina | 5.4 | 4.9 | B- | 96 | Frontier | Latin America | 13 out of 20 |
| Armenia | 2.5 | 2.5 | | 77 | | Asia | 15 out of 29 |
| Australia | -6.1 | -6.4 | AAA | 12 | Developed | Australasia | 2 out of 7 |
| Austria | -6.0 | -6.2 | AA+ | 13 | Developed | Western Europe | 9 out of 19 |
| Azerbaijan | 3.7 | 3.8 | BB+ | 85 | | Asia | 17 out of 29 |
| Bahamas | 1.1 | 0.6 | BB+ | 65 | | Caribbean | 3 out of 9 |
| Bahrain | 1.1 | 0.6 | BB- | 64 | Frontier | Middle East | 7 out of 13 |
| Bangladesh | 7.7 | 7.2 | BB- | 126 | Frontier | Asia | 20 out of 29 |
| Barbados | 2.7 | 3.5 | CCC+ | 82 | | Caribbean | 4 out of 9 |
| Belarus | 9.8 | 9.9 | B- | 143 | | Central and Eastern Europe | 23 out of 25 |
| Belgium | -4.7 | -5.0 | AA | 17 | Developed | Western Europe | 10 out of 19 |
| Belize | 5.9 | 5.7 | B- | 106 | | Latin America | 17 out of 20 |
| Benin | 11.5 | 11.2 | | 150 | | Africa | 37 out of 51 |
| Bermuda | -1.2 | -1.5 | A+ | 44 | | Caribbean | 1 out of 9 |
| Bhutan | 11.1 | 10.7 | | 148 | | Asia | 25 out of 29 |
| Bolivia | 4.4 | 4.5 | BB | 88 | | Latin America | 12 out of 20 |
| Bosnia & Herzegovina | 10.3 | 10.1 | B | 144 | | Central and Eastern Europe | 24 out of 25 |
| Botswana | -1.2 | -1.4 | A- | 48 | | Africa | 1 out of 51 |
| Brazil | 0.3 | 0.0 | BB | 59 | Emerging | Latin America | 7 out of 20 |
| Bulgaria | 0.1 | 0.1 | BB+ | 61 | | Central and Eastern Europe | 12 out of 25 |
| Burkina Faso | 8.7 | 8.4 | B- | 133 | | Africa | 33 out of 51 |
| Burundi | 20.2 | 19.9 | | 169 | | Africa | 47 out of 51 |
| Cambodia | 12.0 | 11.4 | | 151 | | Asia | 27 out of 29 |
| Cameroon | 7.4 | 7.1 | B | 124 | | Africa | 28 out of 51 |
| Canada | -6.3 | -6.6 | AAA | 9 | Developed | North America | 1 out of 2 |
| Cape Verde | 5.1 | 4.8 | B | 94 | | Africa | 12 out of 51 |
| Central African Republic | 23.6 | 23.3 | | 172 | | Africa | 49 out of 51 |
| Chad | 22.3 | 22.0 | | 171 | | Africa | 48 out of 51 |
| Chile | -5.2 | -5.2 | AA- | 16 | Emerging | Latin America | 1 out of 20 |
| China | -1.4 | -1.6 | AA- | 42 | Emerging | Asia | 7 out of 29 |
| Colombia | -1.4 | -1.6 | BBB | 41 | Emerging | Latin America | 4 out of 20 |
| Congo Republic | 7.0 | 6.6 | B- | 117 | | Africa | 24 out of 51 |
| Congo, DR | 8.2 | 7.9 | B- | 131 | | Africa | 32 out of 51 |
| Costa Rica | 1.5 | 1.5 | BB- | 71 | | Latin America | 8 out of 20 |
| Côte d'Ivoire | 4.9 | 4.7 | | 92 | | Africa | 11 out of 51 |
| Croatia | 0.7 | 0.3 | BB | 63 | Frontier | Central and Eastern Europe | 13 out of 25 |
| Cuba | 14.3 | 14.1 | | 160 | | Caribbean | 9 out of 9 |
| Cyprus | -1.7 | -1.8 | BB+ | 40 | | Central and Eastern Europe | 7 out of 25 |
| Czech Republic | -4.0 | -4.2 | AA- | 23 | Emerging | Central and Eastern Europe | 1 out of 25 |
| Denmark | -6.9 | -7.2 | AAA | 4 | Developed | Western Europe | 3 out of 19 |
| Djibouti | 31.4 | 28.7 | | 175 | | Africa | 51 out of 51 |
| Dominican Republic | 4.8 | 4.6 | BB- | 90 | | Caribbean | 5 out of 9 |
| Ecuador | 6.3 | 5.9 | B | 109 | | Latin America | 18 out of 20 |
| Egypt | 6.7 | 6.4 | B- | 116 | Emerging | Africa | 23 out of 51 |
| El Salvador | 3.8 | 3.4 | B- | 81 | | Latin America | 10 out of 20 |
| Equatorial Guinea | 16.7 | 16.4 | | 165 | | Africa | 45 out of 51 |

§ S&P Credit Rating based on long-term foreign currency issuer rating. See http://www.standardandpoors.com/.

* World rank based on 175 countries covered by Euromoney. Ranking based on ascending order in which '1' equals the smallest country risk premium (CRP) and '175' equals the largest country risk premium (CRP).

† MSCI Market Classification based on MSCI Market Classification Framework. See http://www.msci.com/products/indexes/market_classification.html

‡ Regional classification based on Euromoney. Regional rankings based on ascending order in which '1' equals the smallest country risk premium (CRP) for each region.

Note: A CRP of 0.0% is assumed in the following cases: (i) when the investor country and the investee country both have an S&P sovereign credit rating of AAA; or (ii) when the investor country has an S&P credit rating of AAA, and the investee country has a sovereign credit rating below AAA, but has a calculated CRP below 0.0% (which would imply lower risk than a country rated AAA); or (iii) when the investor country has an S&P credit rating below AAA, and the investee country has a sovereign credit rating of AAA, but has a calculated CRP above 0.0% (which would imply greater risk than a country rated below AAA). For purposes of this analysis, the U.S. is treated as having a sovereign credit rating equivalent to AAA.

The country risk premium (CRP) is not the cost of equity capital (COE). The CRP is to be added to base COE. See Chapter 6 for proper application.

## Data Updated Through March 2017

| Investee Country | December 2016 Country Risk Premium (CRP) (%) | March 2017 Country Risk Premium (CRP) (%) | S&P Sovereign Credit Rating § | World Rank Out of 175∗ | MSCI Market Classification † | Euromoney Region ‡ | Regional Rank ‡ |
|---|---|---|---|---|---|---|---|
| Eritrea | 27.6 | 25.5 | | 173 | | Africa | 50 out of 51 |
| Estonia | -3.4 | -3.4 | AA- | 32 | Frontier | Central and Eastern Europe | 4 out of 25 |
| Ethiopia | 5.6 | 5.4 | B | 101 | | Africa | 16 out of 51 |
| Fiji | 10.8 | 10.4 | B+ | 147 | | Australasia | 5 out of 7 |
| Finland | -6.2 | -6.4 | AA+ | 11 | Developed | Western Europe | 8 out of 19 |
| France | -3.9 | -4.3 | AA | 22 | Developed | Western Europe | 12 out of 19 |
| Gabon | 3.5 | 3.6 | | 83 | | Africa | 7 out of 51 |
| Gambia | 9.3 | 9.1 | | 138 | | Africa | 34 out of 51 |
| Georgia | 2.2 | 2.3 | BB- | 74 | | Central and Eastern Europe | 15 out of 25 |
| Germany | -6.2 | -6.5 | AAA | 10 | Developed | Western Europe | 7 out of 19 |
| Ghana | 5.1 | 4.5 | B- | 89 | | Africa | 9 out of 51 |
| Greece | 6.3 | 5.8 | B- | 108 | Emerging | Western Europe | 19 out of 19 |
| Grenada | 5.9 | 5.7 | | 105 | | Caribbean | 7 out of 9 |
| Guatemala | 3.9 | 3.7 | BB | 84 | | Latin America | 11 out of 20 |
| Guinea | 12.9 | 12.6 | | 156 | | Africa | 41 out of 51 |
| Guinea-Bissau | 6.7 | 6.4 | | 115 | | Africa | 22 out of 51 |
| Guyana | 5.5 | 5.3 | | 100 | | Latin America | 15 out of 20 |
| Haiti | 15.7 | 13.4 | | 157 | | Caribbean | 8 out of 9 |
| Honduras | 5.2 | 5.0 | B+ | 98 | | Latin America | 14 out of 20 |
| Hong Kong | -5.7 | -5.9 | AAA | 14 | Developed | Asia | 2 out of 29 |
| Hungary | -0.1 | -0.2 | BBB- | 57 | Emerging | Central and Eastern Europe | 10 out of 25 |
| Iceland | -3.0 | -3.4 | A | 30 | | Western Europe | 15 out of 19 |
| India | -0.3 | -0.3 | BBB- | 55 | Emerging | Asia | 10 out of 29 |
| Indonesia | 0.4 | 0.2 | BB+ | 62 | Emerging | Asia | 11 out of 29 |
| Iran | 7.2 | 7.1 | | 125 | | Middle East | 10 out of 13 |
| Iraq | 8.9 | 8.7 | B- | 136 | | Middle East | 11 out of 13 |
| Ireland | -3.5 | -3.7 | A+ | 27 | Developed | Western Europe | 14 out of 19 |
| Israel | -3.5 | -3.7 | A+ | 28 | Developed | Middle East | 2 out of 13 |
| Italy | -0.7 | -1.1 | BBB- | 50 | Developed | Western Europe | 18 out of 19 |
| Jamaica | 5.3 | 5.6 | B | 104 | | Caribbean | 6 out of 9 |
| Japan | -3.6 | -3.8 | A+ | 25 | Developed | Asia | 5 out of 29 |
| Jordan | 2.5 | 2.4 | BB- | 76 | Frontier | Middle East | 8 out of 13 |
| Kazakhstan | 2.0 | 1.4 | BBB- | 70 | Frontier | Asia | 13 out of 29 |
| Kenya | 5.3 | 5.2 | B+ | 99 | Frontier | Africa | 15 out of 51 |
| Korea (North) | 27.0 | 26.2 | | 174 | | Asia | 29 out of 29 |
| Korea (South) | -4.4 | -4.5 | AA | 19 | Emerging | Asia | 4 out of 29 |
| Kuwait | -3.3 | -3.4 | AA | 31 | Frontier | Middle East | 3 out of 13 |
| Kyrgyz Republic | 10.3 | 9.9 | | 142 | | Central and Eastern Europe | 22 out of 25 |
| Laos | 14.5 | 13.6 | | 158 | | Asia | 28 out of 29 |
| Latvia | -1.4 | -1.5 | A- | 43 | | Central and Eastern Europe | 8 out of 25 |
| Lebanon | 7.0 | 6.2 | B- | 112 | Frontier | Middle East | 9 out of 13 |
| Lesotho | 10.5 | 10.3 | | 146 | | Africa | 36 out of 51 |
| Liberia | 6.0 | 5.7 | | 107 | | Africa | 17 out of 51 |
| Libya | 12.0 | 12.1 | | 153 | | Africa | 39 out of 51 |
| Lithuania | -2.1 | -2.3 | A- | 36 | Frontier | Central and Eastern Europe | 6 out of 25 |
| Luxembourg | -6.6 | -6.9 | AAA | 5 | | Western Europe | 4 out of 19 |
| Macedonia | 4.4 | 4.4 | BB- | 87 | | Central and Eastern Europe | 17 out of 25 |
| Madagascar | 6.8 | 7.0 | | 123 | | Africa | 27 out of 51 |
| Malawi | 6.5 | 6.3 | | 114 | | Africa | 21 out of 51 |
| Malaysia | -2.0 | -2.3 | A- | 35 | Emerging | Asia | 6 out of 29 |

§ S&P Credit Rating based on long-term foreign currency issuer rating. See http://www.standardandpoors.com/.

∗ World rank based on 175 countries covered by Euromoney. Ranking based on ascending order in which '1' equals the smallest country risk premium (CRP) and '175' equals the largest country risk premium (CRP).

† MSCI Market Classification based on MSCI Market Classification Framework. See http://www.msci.com/products/indexes/market_classification.html

‡ Regional classification based on Euromoney. Regional rankings based on ascending order in which '1' equals the smallest country risk premium (CRP) for each region.

Note: A CRP of 0.0% is assumed in the following cases: (i) when the investor country and the investee country both have an S&P sovereign credit rating of AAA; or (ii) when the investor country has an S&P credit rating of AAA, and the investee country has a sovereign credit rating below AAA, but has a calculated CRP below 0.0% (which would imply lower risk than a country rated AAA); or (iii) when the investor country has an S&P credit rating below AAA, and the investee country has a sovereign credit rating of AAA, but has a calculated CRP above 0.0% (which would imply greater risk than a country rated below AAA). For purposes of this analysis, the U.S. is treated as having a sovereign credit rating equivalent to AAA.

The country risk premium (CRP) is not the cost of equity capital (COE). The CRP is to be added to base COE. See Chapter 6 for proper application.

## Data Updated Through March 2017

| Investee Country | December 2016 Country Risk Premium (CRP) (%) | March 2017 Country Risk Premium (CRP) (%) | S&P Sovereign Credit Rating § | World Rank Out of 175* | MSCI Market Classification † | Euromoney Region ‡ | Regional Rank ‡ |
|---|---|---|---|---|---|---|---|
| Mali | 10.2 | 9.9 | | 141 | | Africa | 35 out of 51 |
| Malta | -3.6 | -3.8 | A- | 26 | | Western Europe | 13 out of 19 |
| Mauritania | 14.1 | 13.8 | | 159 | | Africa | 42 out of 51 |
| Mauritius | 1.3 | 1.1 | | 67 | Frontier | Asia | 12 out of 29 |
| Mexico | -2.1 | -2.2 | BBB+ | 37 | Emerging | Latin America | 2 out of 20 |
| Moldova | 8.6 | 8.8 | | 137 | | Central and Eastern Europe | 21 out of 25 |
| Mongolia | 6.9 | 6.9 | B- | 119 | | Asia | 18 out of 29 |
| Montenegro | 6.1 | 5.6 | B+ | 103 | | Central and Eastern Europe | 19 out of 25 |
| Morocco | 1.4 | 1.3 | BBB- | 69 | Frontier | Africa | 4 out of 51 |
| Mozambique | 7.9 | 7.5 | SD | 128 | | Africa | 29 out of 51 |
| Myanmar | 8.8 | 8.5 | | 134 | | Asia | 22 out of 29 |
| Namibia | 1.0 | 0.9 | | 66 | | Africa | 3 out of 51 |
| Nepal | 11.4 | 11.2 | | 149 | | Asia | 26 out of 29 |
| Netherlands | -6.6 | -6.8 | AAA | 6 | Developed | Western Europe | 5 out of 19 |
| New Zealand | -6.5 | -6.6 | AA | 8 | Developed | Australasia | 1 out of 7 |
| Nicaragua | 7.6 | 7.4 | B+ | 127 | | Latin America | 19 out of 20 |
| Niger | 7.2 | 7.0 | | 120 | | Africa | 25 out of 51 |
| Nigeria | 5.3 | 5.0 | B | 97 | Frontier | Africa | 14 out of 51 |
| Norway | -7.2 | -7.5 | AAA | 3 | Developed | Western Europe | 2 out of 19 |
| Oman | -1.2 | -1.4 | BBB- | 46 | Frontier | Middle East | 5 out of 13 |
| Pakistan | 7.3 | 7.0 | B | 122 | Frontier | Asia | 19 out of 29 |
| Panama | -0.6 | -0.7 | BBB | 52 | | Latin America | 6 out of 20 |
| Papua New Guinea | 6.8 | 6.7 | B+ | 118 | | Australasia | 3 out of 7 |
| Paraguay | 2.9 | 2.8 | BB | 80 | | Latin America | 9 out of 20 |
| Peru | -1.8 | -1.9 | BBB+ | 39 | Emerging | Latin America | 3 out of 20 |
| Philippines | -0.2 | -0.5 | BBB | 53 | Emerging | Asia | 9 out of 29 |
| Poland | -3.2 | -3.5 | BBB+ | 29 | Emerging | Central and Eastern Europe | 3 out of 25 |
| Portugal | -0.8 | -1.2 | BB+ | 49 | Developed | Western Europe | 17 out of 19 |
| Qatar | -4.3 | -4.4 | AA | 21 | Emerging | Middle East | 1 out of 13 |
| Romania | -0.1 | -0.2 | BBB- | 56 | Frontier | Central and Eastern Europe | 9 out of 25 |
| Russia | 2.1 | 1.3 | BB+ | 68 | Emerging | Central and Eastern Europe | 14 out of 25 |
| Rwanda | 8.0 | 7.7 | B | 130 | | Africa | 31 out of 51 |
| São Tomé & Príncipe | 14.2 | 14.4 | | 163 | | Africa | 43 out of 51 |
| Saudi Arabia | -0.9 | -1.4 | A- | 47 | | Middle East | 6 out of 13 |
| Senegal | 4.6 | 4.4 | B+ | 86 | | Africa | 8 out of 51 |
| Serbia | 2.8 | 2.3 | BB- | 75 | Frontier | Central and Eastern Europe | 16 out of 25 |
| Seychelles | 2.3 | 2.1 | | 73 | | Africa | 5 out of 51 |
| Sierra Leone | 8.0 | 7.7 | | 129 | | Africa | 30 out of 51 |
| Singapore | -7.4 | -7.6 | AAA | 1 | Developed | Asia | 1 out of 29 |
| Slovakia | -3.9 | -4.0 | A+ | 24 | | Central and Eastern Europe | 2 out of 25 |
| Slovenia | -2.5 | -2.7 | A | 34 | Frontier | Central and Eastern Europe | 5 out of 25 |
| Solomon Islands | 18.4 | 18.1 | | 168 | | Australasia | 6 out of 7 |
| Somalia | 16.8 | 16.5 | | 166 | | Africa | 46 out of 51 |
| South Africa | 0.0 | 0.0 | BBB- | 60 | Emerging | Africa | 2 out of 51 |
| Spain | -1.7 | -1.9 | BBB+ | 38 | Developed | Western Europe | 16 out of 19 |
| Sri Lanka | 2.2 | 1.7 | B+ | 72 | Frontier | Asia | 14 out of 29 |
| Sudan | 12.9 | 12.5 | | 154 | | Africa | 40 out of 51 |
| Suriname | 5.5 | 5.4 | B+ | 102 | | Latin America | 16 out of 20 |
| Swaziland | 11.2 | 11.9 | | 152 | | Africa | 38 out of 51 |
| Sweden | -6.6 | -6.8 | AAA | 7 | Developed | Western Europe | 6 out of 19 |

§ S&P Credit Rating based on long-term foreign currency issuer rating. See http://www.standardandpoors.com/.

* World rank based on 175 countries covered by Euromoney. Ranking based on ascending order in which '1' equals the smallest country risk premium (CRP) and '175' equals the largest country risk premium (CRP).

† MSCI Market Classification based on MSCI Market Classification Framework. See http://www.msci.com/products/indexes/market_classification.html

‡ Regional classification based on Euromoney. Regional rankings based on ascending order in which '1' equals the smallest country risk premium (CRP) for each region.

Note: A CRP of 0.0% is assumed in the following cases: (i) when the investor country and the investee country both have an S&P sovereign credit rating of AAA; or (ii) when the investor country has an S&P credit rating of AAA, and the investee country has a sovereign credit rating below AAA, but has a calculated CRP below 0.0% (which would imply lower risk than a country rated AAA); or (iii) when the investor country has an S&P credit rating below AAA, and the investee country has a sovereign credit rating of AAA, but has a calculated CRP above 0.0% (which would imply greater risk than a country rated below AAA). For purposes of this analysis, the U.S. is treated as having a sovereign credit rating equivalent to AAA.

The country risk premium (CRP) is not the cost of equity capital (COE). The CRP is to be added to base COE. See Chapter 6 for proper application.

## Data Updated Through March 2017

| Investee Country | December 2016 Country Risk Premium (CRP) (%) | March 2017 Country Risk Premium (CRP) (%) | S&P Sovereign Credit Rating § | World Rank Out of 175• | MSCI Market Classification † | Euromoney Region ‡ | Regional Rank ‡ |
|---|---|---|---|---|---|---|---|
| Switzerland | -7.2 | -7.5 | AAA | 2 | Developed | Western Europe | 1 out of 19 |
| Syria | 17.5 | 17.4 | | 167 | | Middle East | 13 out of 13 |
| Taiwan | -4.6 | -4.8 | AA- | 18 | Emerging | Asia | 3 out of 29 |
| Tajikistan | 12.5 | 12.5 | | 155 | | Central and Eastern Europe | 25 out of 25 |
| Tanzania | 4.9 | 4.9 | | 95 | | Africa | 13 out of 51 |
| Thailand | -0.5 | -0.9 | BBB+ | 51 | Emerging | Asia | 8 out of 29 |
| Togo | 6.5 | 6.2 | | 113 | | Africa | 20 out of 51 |
| Tonga | 20.8 | 20.5 | | 170 | | Australasia | 7 out of 7 |
| Trinidad & Tobago | -0.2 | -0.4 | A- | 54 | | Caribbean | 2 out of 9 |
| Tunisia | 2.6 | 2.7 | | 79 | Frontier | Africa | 6 out of 51 |
| Turkey | 0.1 | -0.2 | BB | 58 | Emerging | Central and Eastern Europe | 11 out of 25 |
| Turkmenistan | 9.7 | 9.7 | | 140 | | Asia | 24 out of 29 |
| Uganda | 6.0 | 6.0 | B | 110 | | Africa | 18 out of 51 |
| Ukraine | 8.8 | 8.6 | B- | 135 | | Central and Eastern Europe | 20 out of 25 |
| United Arab Emirates | -2.9 | -3.0 | AA | 33 | Emerging | Middle East | 4 out of 13 |
| United Kingdom | -4.4 | -4.4 | AA | 20 | Developed | Western Europe | 11 out of 19 |
| United States | -5.4 | -5.6 | AA+ | 15 | Developed | North America | 2 out of 2 |
| Uruguay | -1.1 | -1.5 | BBB | 45 | | Latin America | 5 out of 20 |
| Uzbekistan | 8.9 | 8.1 | | 132 | | Asia | 21 out of 29 |
| Vanuatu | 10.5 | 10.3 | | 145 | | Australasia | 4 out of 7 |
| Venezuela | 14.2 | 14.3 | CCC | 162 | | Latin America | 20 out of 20 |
| Vietnam | 3.1 | 2.6 | BB- | 78 | Frontier | Asia | 16 out of 29 |
| Yemen | 14.5 | 14.3 | | 161 | | Middle East | 12 out of 13 |
| Zambia | 6.3 | 6.1 | B | 111 | | Africa | 19 out of 51 |
| Zimbabwe | 16.1 | 15.7 | | 164 | | Africa | 44 out of 51 |

## March 2017 Country Risk Premium (CRP) Summary Statistics:

| S&P Rating | Country Count | Average CRP (%) | Median CRP (%) | Min CRP (%) | Max CRP (%) |
|---|---|---|---|---|---|
| AAA ** | 12 | -6.8 | -6.8 | -7.6 | -5.6 |
| AA (AA+, AA, AA-) | 15 | -4.5 | -4.4 | -6.6 | -1.6 |
| A (A+, A, A-) | 14 | -2.6 | -2.5 | -4.0 | -0.4 |
| BBB (BBB+, BBB, BBB-) | 17 | -0.9 | -0.9 | -3.5 | 1.4 |
| BB (BB+, BB, BB-) | 22 | 1.9 | 1.9 | -1.8 | 7.2 |
| B+ − SD | 39 | 6.5 | 6.1 | 1.7 | 14.3 |
| Investment Grade ** | 58 | -3.4 | -3.4 | -7.6 | 1.4 |
| Non-Investment Grade ** | 61 | 4.8 | 5.0 | -1.8 | 14.3 |
| **MSCI Market Classification** | | | | | |
| Developed Markets | 23 | -5.3 | -6.2 | -7.6 | -1.1 |
| Emerging Markets | 23 | -1.2 | -1.6 | -5.2 | 6.4 |
| Frontier Markets | 22 | 1.8 | 1.6 | -3.4 | 7.2 |
| **Euromoney Region ‡** | | | | | |
| Africa | 51 | 8.9 | 7.0 | -1.4 | 28.7 |
| Asia | 29 | 3.8 | 2.5 | -7.6 | 26.2 |
| Australasia | 7 | 7.6 | 10.3 | -6.6 | 20.5 |
| Caribbean | 9 | 5.1 | 4.6 | -1.5 | 14.1 |
| Central and Eastern Europe | 25 | 2.3 | 0.3 | -4.2 | 12.5 |
| Latin America | 20 | 2.8 | 3.5 | -5.2 | 14.3 |
| Middle East | 13 | 3.0 | 0.6 | -4.4 | 17.4 |
| North America | 2 | -6.1 | -6.1 | -6.6 | -5.6 |
| Western Europe | 19 | -4.5 | -5.0 | -7.5 | 5.8 |

## CCR Base Cost of Equity Capital:

| South Africa | COE (%) |
|---|---|
| March 2017 | 19.9 |
| December 2016 | 19.7 |

CCR base country-level COE for a South Africa-based investor investing in South Africa.

§ S&P Credit Rating based on long-term foreign currency issuer rating. See http://www.standardandpoors.com/.

• World rank based on 175 countries covered by Euromoney. Ranking based on ascending order in which '1' equals the smallest country risk premium (CRP) and '175' equals the largest country risk premium (CRP).

† MSCI Market Classification based on MSCI Market Classification Framework. See http://www.msci.com/products/indexes/market_classification.html

‡ Regional classification based on Euromoney. Regional rankings based on ascending order in which '1' equals the smallest country risk premium (CRP) for each region.

** Investment grade based on S&P sovereign credit rating from AAA to BBB-. Non-Investment grade based on S&P sovereign credit rating from BB+ to SD. For purposes of this analysis, the U.S. is being treated as if it were rated AAA by S&P.

Note: A CRP of 0.0% is assumed in the following cases: (i) when the investor country and the investee country both have an S&P sovereign credit rating of AAA; or (ii) when the investor country has an S&P credit rating of AAA, and the investee country has a sovereign credit rating below AAA, but has a calculated CRP below 0.0% (which would imply lower risk than a country rated AAA); or (iii) when the investor country has an S&P credit rating below AAA, and the investee country has a sovereign credit rating of AAA, but has a calculated CRP above 0.0% (which would imply greater risk than a country rated below AAA). For purposes of this analysis, the U.S. is treated as having a sovereign credit rating equivalent to AAA.

The country risk premium (CRP) is not the cost of equity capital (COE).  The CRP is to be added to base COE. See Chapter 6 for proper application.

## Data Updated Through March 2017

| Investee Country | December 2016 Country Risk Premium (CRP) (%) | March 2017 Country Risk Premium (CRP) (%) | S&P Sovereign Credit Rating § | World Rank Out of 175* | MSCI Market Classification † | Euromoney Region ‡ | Regional Rank ‡ |
|---|---|---|---|---|---|---|---|
| Afghanistan | 12.3 | 12.0 | | 139 | | Asia | 23 out of 29 |
| Albania | 6.8 | 7.0 | B+ | 93 | | Central and Eastern Europe | 18 out of 25 |
| Algeria | 6.9 | 6.9 | | 91 | | Africa | 10 out of 51 |
| Angola | 9.2 | 9.3 | B | 121 | | Africa | 26 out of 51 |
| Argentina | 7.4 | 7.2 | B- | 96 | Frontier | Latin America | 13 out of 20 |
| Armenia | 4.4 | 4.6 | | 77 | | Asia | 15 out of 29 |
| Australia | -4.6 | -4.7 | AAA | 12 | Developed | Australasia | 2 out of 7 |
| Austria | -4.4 | -4.5 | AA+ | 13 | Developed | Western Europe | 9 out of 19 |
| Azerbaijan | 5.6 | 5.9 | BB+ | 85 | | Asia | 17 out of 29 |
| Bahamas | 3.0 | 2.7 | BB+ | 65 | | Caribbean | 3 out of 9 |
| Bahrain | 2.9 | 2.7 | BB- | 64 | Frontier | Middle East | 7 out of 13 |
| Bangladesh | 9.8 | 9.5 | BB- | 126 | Frontier | Asia | 20 out of 29 |
| Barbados | 4.6 | 5.7 | CCC+ | 82 | | Caribbean | 4 out of 9 |
| Belarus | 12.0 | 12.4 | B- | 143 | | Central and Eastern Europe | 23 out of 25 |
| Belgium | -3.2 | -3.3 | AA | 17 | Developed | Western Europe | 10 out of 19 |
| Belize | 7.9 | 8.0 | B- | 106 | | Latin America | 17 out of 20 |
| Benin | 13.7 | 13.7 | | 150 | | Africa | 37 out of 51 |
| Bermuda | 0.5 | 0.4 | A+ | 44 | | Caribbean | 1 out of 9 |
| Bhutan | 13.4 | 13.2 | | 148 | | Asia | 25 out of 29 |
| Bolivia | 6.4 | 6.7 | BB | 88 | | Latin America | 12 out of 20 |
| Bosnia & Herzegovina | 12.5 | 12.6 | B | 144 | | Central and Eastern Europe | 24 out of 25 |
| Botswana | 0.6 | 0.5 | A- | 48 | | Africa | 1 out of 51 |
| Brazil | 2.1 | 1.9 | BB | 59 | Emerging | Latin America | 7 out of 20 |
| Bulgaria | 1.9 | 2.1 | BB+ | 61 | | Central and Eastern Europe | 12 out of 25 |
| Burkina Faso | 10.8 | 10.8 | B- | 133 | | Africa | 33 out of 51 |
| Burundi | 22.8 | 22.8 | | 169 | | Africa | 47 out of 51 |
| Cambodia | 14.3 | 14.0 | | 151 | | Asia | 27 out of 29 |
| Cameroon | 9.4 | 9.4 | B | 124 | | Africa | 28 out of 51 |
| Canada | -4.8 | -4.9 | AAA | 9 | Developed | North America | 1 out of 2 |
| Cape Verde | 7.1 | 7.1 | B | 94 | | Africa | 12 out of 51 |
| Central African Republic | 26.3 | 26.4 | | 172 | | Africa | 49 out of 51 |
| Chad | 25.0 | 25.1 | | 171 | | Africa | 48 out of 51 |
| Chile | -3.6 | -3.4 | AA- | 16 | Emerging | Latin America | 1 out of 20 |
| China | 0.3 | 0.3 | AA- | 42 | Emerging | Asia | 7 out of 29 |
| Colombia | 0.3 | 0.3 | BBB | 41 | Emerging | Latin America | 4 out of 20 |
| Congo Republic | 9.0 | 8.9 | B- | 117 | | Africa | 24 out of 51 |
| Congo, DR | 10.3 | 10.2 | B- | 131 | | Africa | 32 out of 51 |
| Costa Rica | 3.4 | 3.6 | BB- | 71 | | Latin America | 8 out of 20 |
| Côte d'Ivoire | 6.9 | 6.9 | | 92 | | Africa | 11 out of 51 |
| Croatia | 2.5 | 2.3 | BB | 63 | Frontier | Central and Eastern Europe | 13 out of 25 |
| Cuba | 16.6 | 16.7 | | 160 | | Caribbean | 9 out of 9 |
| Cyprus | 0.0 | 0.1 | BB+ | 40 | | Central and Eastern Europe | 7 out of 25 |
| Czech Republic | -2.4 | -2.4 | AA- | 23 | Emerging | Central and Eastern Europe | 1 out of 25 |
| Denmark | -5.4 | -5.5 | AAA | 4 | Developed | Western Europe | 3 out of 19 |
| Djibouti | 34.4 | 32.1 | | 175 | | Africa | 51 out of 51 |
| Dominican Republic | 6.7 | 6.8 | BB- | 90 | | Caribbean | 5 out of 9 |
| Ecuador | 8.3 | 8.2 | B | 109 | | Latin America | 18 out of 20 |
| Egypt | 8.8 | 8.7 | B- | 116 | Emerging | Africa | 23 out of 51 |
| El Salvador | 5.8 | 5.6 | B- | 81 | | Latin America | 10 out of 20 |
| Equatorial Guinea | 19.2 | 19.2 | | 165 | | Africa | 45 out of 51 |

§ S&P Credit Rating based on long-term foreign currency issuer rating. See http://www.standardandpoors.com/.

• World rank based on 175 countries covered by Euromoney. Ranking based on ascending order in which '1' equals the smallest country risk premium (CRP) and '175' equals the largest country risk premium (CRP).

† MSCI Market Classification based on MSCI Market Classification Framework.  See http://www.msci.com/products/indexes/market_classification.html.

‡ Regional classification based on Euromoney. Regional rankings based on ascending order in which '1' equals the smallest country risk premium (CRP) for each region.

Note: A CRP of 0.0% is assumed in the following cases: (i) when the investor country and the investee country both have an S&P sovereign credit rating of AAA; or (ii) when the investor country has an S&P credit rating of AAA, and the investee country has a sovereign credit rating below AAA, but has a calculated CRP below 0.0% (which would imply lower risk than a country rated AAA); or (iii) when the investor country has an S&P credit rating below AAA, and the investee country has a sovereign credit rating of AAA, but has a calculated CRP above 0.0% (which would imply greater risk than a country rated below AAA). For purposes of this analysis, the U.S. is treated as having a sovereign credit rating equivalent to AAA.

The country risk premium (CRP) is not the cost of equity capital (COE). The CRP is to be added to base COE. See Chapter 6 for proper application.

### Data Updated Through March 2017

| Investee Country | December 2016 Country Risk Premium (CRP) (%) | March 2017 Country Risk Premium (CRP) (%) | S&P Sovereign Credit Rating § | World Rank Out of 175* | MSCI Market Classification † | Euromoney Region ‡ | Regional Rank ‡ |
|---|---|---|---|---|---|---|---|
| Eritrea | 30.5 | 28.7 | | 173 | | Africa | 50 out of 51 |
| Estonia | -1.7 | -1.5 | AA- | 32 | Frontier | Central and Eastern Europe | 4 out of 25 |
| Ethiopia | 7.6 | 7.7 | B | 101 | | Africa | 16 out of 51 |
| Fiji | 13.0 | 12.9 | B+ | 147 | | Australasia | 5 out of 7 |
| Finland | -4.7 | -4.7 | AA+ | 11 | Developed | Western Europe | 8 out of 19 |
| France | -2.3 | -2.5 | AA | 22 | Developed | Western Europe | 12 out of 19 |
| Gabon | 5.4 | 5.7 | | 83 | | Africa | 7 out of 51 |
| Gambia | 11.5 | 11.5 | | 138 | | Africa | 34 out of 51 |
| Georgia | 4.1 | 4.4 | BB- | 74 | | Central and Eastern Europe | 15 out of 25 |
| Germany | -4.7 | -4.8 | AAA | 10 | Developed | Western Europe | 7 out of 19 |
| Ghana | 7.1 | 6.7 | B- | 89 | | Africa | 9 out of 51 |
| Greece | 8.3 | 8.0 | B | 108 | Emerging | Western Europe | 19 out of 19 |
| Grenada | 7.9 | 7.9 | | 105 | | Caribbean | 7 out of 9 |
| Guatemala | 5.8 | 5.8 | BB | 84 | | Latin America | 11 out of 20 |
| Guinea | 15.2 | 15.2 | | 156 | | Africa | 41 out of 51 |
| Guinea-Bissau | 8.7 | 8.7 | | 115 | | Africa | 22 out of 51 |
| Guyana | 7.5 | 7.6 | | 100 | | Latin America | 15 out of 20 |
| Haiti | 18.1 | 16.1 | | 157 | | Caribbean | 8 out of 9 |
| Honduras | 7.2 | 7.3 | B+ | 98 | | Latin America | 14 out of 20 |
| Hong Kong | -4.1 | -4.2 | AAA | 14 | Developed | Asia | 2 out of 29 |
| Hungary | 1.7 | 1.8 | BBB- | 57 | Emerging | Central and Eastern Europe | 10 out of 25 |
| Iceland | -1.4 | -1.6 | A | 30 | | Western Europe | 15 out of 19 |
| India | 1.4 | 1.7 | BBB- | 55 | Emerging | Asia | 10 out of 29 |
| Indonesia | 2.2 | 2.2 | BB+ | 62 | Emerging | Asia | 11 out of 29 |
| Iran | 9.2 | 9.5 | | 125 | | Middle East | 10 out of 13 |
| Iraq | 11.1 | 11.1 | B- | 136 | | Middle East | 11 out of 13 |
| Ireland | -1.8 | -1.9 | A+ | 27 | Developed | Western Europe | 14 out of 19 |
| Israel | -1.9 | -1.9 | A+ | 28 | Developed | Middle East | 2 out of 13 |
| Italy | 1.1 | 0.9 | BBB- | 50 | Developed | Western Europe | 18 out of 19 |
| Jamaica | 7.3 | 7.9 | B | 104 | | Caribbean | 6 out of 9 |
| Japan | -2.0 | -2.0 | A+ | 25 | Developed | Asia | 5 out of 29 |
| Jordan | 4.4 | 4.5 | BB- | 76 | Frontier | Middle East | 8 out of 13 |
| Kazakhstan | 3.8 | 3.5 | BBB- | 70 | Frontier | Asia | 13 out of 29 |
| Kenya | 7.3 | 7.4 | B+ | 99 | Frontier | Africa | 15 out of 51 |
| Korea (North) | 29.9 | 29.4 | | 174 | | Asia | 29 out of 29 |
| Korea (South) | -2.8 | -2.8 | AA | 19 | Emerging | Asia | 4 out of 29 |
| Kuwait | -1.7 | -1.6 | AA | 31 | Frontier | Middle East | 3 out of 13 |
| Kyrgyz Republic | 12.5 | 12.4 | | 142 | | Central and Eastern Europe | 22 out of 25 |
| Laos | 16.8 | 16.3 | | 158 | | Asia | 28 out of 29 |
| Latvia | 0.3 | 0.4 | A- | 43 | | Central and Eastern Europe | 8 out of 25 |
| Lebanon | 9.1 | 8.5 | B- | 112 | Frontier | Middle East | 9 out of 13 |
| Lesotho | 12.7 | 12.8 | | 146 | | Africa | 36 out of 51 |
| Liberia | 8.0 | 8.0 | | 107 | | Africa | 17 out of 51 |
| Libya | 14.3 | 14.7 | | 153 | | Africa | 39 out of 51 |
| Lithuania | -0.5 | -0.4 | A- | 36 | Frontier | Central and Eastern Europe | 6 out of 25 |
| Luxembourg | -5.1 | -5.2 | AAA | 5 | | Western Europe | 4 out of 19 |
| Macedonia | 6.4 | 6.6 | BB- | 87 | | Central and Eastern Europe | 17 out of 25 |
| Madagascar | 8.8 | 9.4 | | 123 | | Africa | 27 out of 51 |
| Malawi | 8.6 | 8.6 | | 114 | | Africa | 21 out of 51 |
| Malaysia | -0.3 | -0.4 | A- | 35 | Emerging | Asia | 6 out of 29 |

§ S&P Credit Rating based on long-term foreign currency issuer rating. See http://www.standardandpoors.com/.

* World rank based on 175 countries covered by Euromoney. Ranking based on ascending order in which '1' equals the smallest country risk premium (CRP) and '175' equals the largest country risk premium (CRP).

† MSCI Market Classification based on MSCI Market Classification Framework. See http://www.msci.com/products/indexes/market_classification.html.

‡ Regional classification based on Euromoney. Regional rankings based on ascending order in which '1' equals the smallest country risk premium (CRP) for each region.

Note: A CRP of 0.0% is assumed in the following cases: (i) when the investor country and the investee country both have an S&P sovereign credit rating of AAA; or (ii) when the investor country has an S&P credit rating of AAA, and the investee country has a sovereign credit rating below AAA, but has a calculated CRP below 0.0% (which would imply lower risk than a country rated AAA); or (iii) when the investor country has an S&P credit rating below AAA, and the investee country has a sovereign credit rating of AAA, but has a calculated CRP above 0.0% (which would imply greater risk than a country rated below AAA). For purposes of this analysis, the U.S. is treated as having a sovereign credit rating equivalent to AAA.

The country risk premium (CRP) is not the cost of equity capital (COE).  The CRP is to be added to base COE. See Chapter 6 for proper application.

## Data Updated Through March 2017

| Investee Country | December 2016 Country Risk Premium (CRP) (%) | March 2017 Country Risk Premium (CRP) (%) | S&P Sovereign Credit Rating § | World Rank Out of 175* | MSCI Market Classification † | Euromoney Region ‡ | Regional Rank ‡ |
|---|---|---|---|---|---|---|---|
| Mali | 12.3 | 12.4 | | 141 | | Africa | 35 out of 51 |
| Malta | -2.0 | -2.0 | A- | 26 | | Western Europe | 13 out of 19 |
| Mauritania | 16.4 | 16.5 | | 159 | | Africa | 42 out of 51 |
| Mauritius | 3.1 | 3.1 | | 67 | Frontier | Asia | 12 out of 29 |
| Mexico | -0.4 | -0.3 | BBB+ | 37 | Emerging | Latin America | 2 out of 20 |
| Moldova | 10.7 | 11.2 | | 137 | | Central and Eastern Europe | 21 out of 25 |
| Mongolia | 8.9 | 9.3 | B- | 119 | | Asia | 18 out of 29 |
| Montenegro | 8.1 | 7.9 | B+ | 103 | | Central and Eastern Europe | 19 out of 25 |
| Morocco | 3.2 | 3.4 | BBB- | 69 | Frontier | Africa | 4 out of 51 |
| Mozambique | 10.0 | 9.9 | SD | 128 | | Africa | 29 out of 51 |
| Myanmar | 10.9 | 10.9 | | 134 | | Asia | 22 out of 29 |
| Namibia | 2.8 | 3.0 | | 66 | | Africa | 3 out of 51 |
| Nepal | 13.7 | 13.7 | | 149 | | Asia | 26 out of 29 |
| Netherlands | -5.1 | -5.2 | AAA | 6 | Developed | Western Europe | 5 out of 19 |
| New Zealand | -4.9 | -5.0 | AA | 8 | Developed | Australasia | 1 out of 7 |
| Nicaragua | 9.7 | 9.7 | B+ | 127 | | Latin America | 19 out of 20 |
| Niger | 9.3 | 9.3 | | 120 | | Africa | 25 out of 51 |
| Nigeria | 7.3 | 7.3 | B | 97 | Frontier | Africa | 14 out of 51 |
| Norway | -5.8 | -5.9 | AAA | 3 | Developed | Western Europe | 2 out of 19 |
| Oman | 0.5 | 0.5 | BBB- | 46 | Frontier | Middle East | 5 out of 13 |
| Pakistan | 9.4 | 9.3 | B | 122 | Frontier | Asia | 19 out of 29 |
| Panama | 1.2 | 1.2 | BBB | 52 | | Latin America | 6 out of 20 |
| Papua New Guinea | 8.9 | 9.0 | B+ | 118 | | Australasia | 3 out of 7 |
| Paraguay | 4.8 | 5.0 | BB | 80 | | Latin America | 9 out of 20 |
| Peru | -0.1 | 0.0 | BBB+ | 39 | Emerging | Latin America | 3 out of 20 |
| Philippines | 1.6 | 1.5 | BBB | 53 | Emerging | Asia | 9 out of 29 |
| Poland | -1.5 | -1.7 | BBB+ | 29 | Emerging | Central and Eastern Europe | 3 out of 25 |
| Portugal | 0.9 | 0.7 | BB+ | 49 | Developed | Western Europe | 17 out of 19 |
| Qatar | -2.6 | -2.6 | AA | 21 | Emerging | Middle East | 1 out of 13 |
| Romania | 1.7 | 1.8 | BBB- | 56 | Frontier | Central and Eastern Europe | 9 out of 25 |
| Russia | 4.0 | 3.4 | BB+ | 68 | Emerging | Central and Eastern Europe | 14 out of 25 |
| Rwanda | 10.1 | 10.1 | B | 130 | | Africa | 31 out of 51 |
| São Tomé & Príncipe | 16.5 | 17.1 | | 163 | | Africa | 43 out of 51 |
| Saudi Arabia | 0.9 | 0.5 | A- | 47 | | Middle East | 6 out of 13 |
| Senegal | 6.6 | 6.6 | B+ | 86 | | Africa | 8 out of 51 |
| Serbia | 4.7 | 4.4 | BB- | 75 | Frontier | Central and Eastern Europe | 16 out of 25 |
| Seychelles | 4.1 | 4.1 | | 73 | | Africa | 5 out of 51 |
| Sierra Leone | 10.1 | 10.1 | | 129 | | Africa | 30 out of 51 |
| Singapore | -6.0 | -6.0 | AAA | 1 | Developed | Asia | 1 out of 29 |
| Slovakia | -2.3 | -2.2 | A+ | 24 | | Central and Eastern Europe | 2 out of 25 |
| Slovenia | -0.8 | -0.8 | A | 34 | Frontier | Central and Eastern Europe | 5 out of 25 |
| Solomon Islands | 21.0 | 21.0 | | 168 | | Australasia | 6 out of 7 |
| Somalia | 19.2 | 19.2 | | 166 | | Africa | 46 out of 51 |
| South Africa | 1.8 | 2.0 | BBB- | 60 | Emerging | Africa | 2 out of 51 |
| Spain | 0.0 | 0.0 | BBB+ | 38 | Developed | Western Europe | 16 out of 19 |
| Sri Lanka | 4.1 | 3.8 | B+ | 72 | Frontier | Asia | 14 out of 29 |
| Sudan | 15.2 | 15.1 | | 154 | | Africa | 40 out of 51 |
| Suriname | 7.5 | 7.7 | B+ | 102 | | Latin America | 16 out of 20 |
| Swaziland | 13.4 | 14.4 | | 152 | | Africa | 38 out of 51 |
| Sweden | -5.0 | -5.1 | AAA | 7 | Developed | Western Europe | 6 out of 19 |

§ S&P Credit Rating based on long-term foreign currency issuer rating. See http://www.standardandpoors.com/.

* World rank based on 175 countries covered by Euromoney. Ranking based on ascending order in which '1' equals the smallest country risk premium (CRP) and '175' equals the largest country risk premium (CRP).

† MSCI Market Classification based on MSCI Market Classification Framework.  See http://www.msci.com/products/indexes/market_classification.html.

‡ Regional classification based on Euromoney. Regional rankings based on ascending order in which '1' equals the smallest country risk premium (CRP) for each region.

Note: A CRP of 0.0% is assumed in the following cases: (i) when the investor country and the investee country both have an S&P sovereign credit rating of AAA; or (ii) when the investor country has an S&P credit rating of AAA, and the investee country has a sovereign credit rating below AAA, but has a calculated CRP below 0.0% (which would imply lower risk than a country rated AAA); or (iii) when the investor country has an S&P credit rating below AAA, and the investee country has a sovereign credit rating of AAA, but has a calculated CRP above 0.0% (which would imply greater risk than a country rated below AAA). For purposes of this analysis, the U.S. is treated as having a sovereign credit rating equivalent to AAA.

The country risk premium (CRP) is not the cost of equity capital (COE). The CRP is to be added to base COE. See Chapter 6 for proper application.

## Data Updated Through March 2017

| Investee Country | December 2016 Country Risk Premium (CRP) (%) | March 2017 Country Risk Premium (CRP) (%) | S&P Sovereign Credit Rating § | World Rank Out of 175* | MSCI Market Classification † | Euromoney Region ‡ | Regional Rank ‡ |
|---|---|---|---|---|---|---|---|
| Switzerland | -5.7 | -5.9 | AAA | 2 | Developed | Western Europe | 1 out of 19 |
| Syria | 20.0 | 20.3 | | 167 | | Middle East | 13 out of 13 |
| Taiwan | -3.0 | -3.1 | AA- | 18 | Emerging | Asia | 3 out of 29 |
| Tajikistan | 14.7 | 15.1 | | 155 | | Central and Eastern Europe | 25 out of 25 |
| Tanzania | 6.9 | 7.1 | | 95 | | Africa | 13 out of 51 |
| Thailand | 1.2 | 1.0 | BBB+ | 51 | Emerging | Asia | 8 out of 29 |
| Togo | 8.5 | 8.5 | | 113 | | Africa | 20 out of 51 |
| Tonga | 23.4 | 23.5 | | 170 | | Australasia | 7 out of 7 |
| Trinidad & Tobago | 1.6 | 1.6 | A- | 54 | | Caribbean | 2 out of 9 |
| Tunisia | 4.5 | 4.8 | | 79 | Frontier | Africa | 6 out of 51 |
| Turkey | 1.9 | 1.8 | BB | 58 | Emerging | Central and Eastern Europe | 11 out of 25 |
| Turkmenistan | 11.9 | 12.2 | | 140 | | Asia | 24 out of 29 |
| Uganda | 8.0 | 8.3 | B | 110 | | Africa | 18 out of 51 |
| Ukraine | 10.9 | 11.0 | B- | 135 | | Central and Eastern Europe | 20 out of 25 |
| United Arab Emirates | -1.2 | -1.2 | AA | 33 | Emerging | Middle East | 4 out of 13 |
| United Kingdom | -2.8 | -2.7 | AA | 20 | Developed | Western Europe | 11 out of 19 |
| United States | -3.8 | -3.8 | AA+ | 15 | Developed | North America | 2 out of 2 |
| Uruguay | 0.6 | 0.4 | BBB | 45 | | Latin America | 5 out of 20 |
| Uzbekistan | 11.1 | 10.5 | | 132 | | Asia | 21 out of 29 |
| Vanuatu | 12.7 | 12.7 | | 145 | | Australasia | 4 out of 7 |
| Venezuela | 16.5 | 17.0 | CCC | 162 | | Latin America | 20 out of 20 |
| Vietnam | 5.0 | 4.7 | BB- | 78 | Frontier | Asia | 16 out of 29 |
| Yemen | 16.8 | 17.0 | | 161 | | Middle East | 12 out of 13 |
| Zambia | 8.4 | 8.4 | B | 111 | | Africa | 19 out of 51 |
| Zimbabwe | 18.5 | 18.5 | | 164 | | Africa | 44 out of 51 |

### March 2017 Country Risk Premium (CRP) Summary Statistics:

| S&P Rating | Country Count | Average CRP (%) | Median CRP (%) | Min CRP (%) | Max CRP (%) |
|---|---|---|---|---|---|
| AAA ** | 12 | -5.1 | -5.2 | -6.0 | -3.8 |
| AA (AA+, AA, AA-) | 15 | -2.7 | -2.7 | -5.0 | 0.3 |
| A (A+, A, A-) | 14 | -0.7 | -0.6 | -2.2 | 1.6 |
| BBB (BBB+, BBB, BBB-) | 17 | 1.1 | 1.0 | -1.7 | 3.5 |
| BB (BB+, BB, BB-) | 22 | 4.0 | 4.0 | 0.1 | 9.5 |
| B+ − SD | 39 | 8.8 | 8.4 | 3.8 | 17.0 |
| Investment Grade ** | 58 | -1.6 | -1.6 | -6.0 | 3.5 |
| Non-Investment Grade ** | 61 | 7.1 | 7.3 | 0.1 | 17.0 |
| **MSCI Market Classification** | | | | | |
| Developed Markets | 23 | -3.6 | -4.5 | -6.0 | 0.9 |
| Emerging Markets | 23 | 0.7 | 0.3 | -3.4 | 8.7 |
| Frontier Markets | 22 | 3.8 | 3.6 | -1.6 | 9.5 |
| **Euromoney Region ‡** | | | | | |
| Africa | 51 | 11.4 | 9.3 | 0.5 | 32.1 |
| Asia | 29 | 6.0 | 4.6 | -6.0 | 29.4 |
| Australasia | 7 | 9.9 | 12.7 | -5.0 | 23.5 |
| Caribbean | 9 | 7.3 | 6.8 | 0.4 | 16.7 |
| Central and Eastern Europe | 25 | 4.4 | 2.3 | -2.4 | 15.1 |
| Latin America | 20 | 5.0 | 5.7 | -3.4 | 17.0 |
| Middle East | 13 | 5.2 | 2.7 | -2.6 | 20.3 |
| North America | 2 | -4.4 | -4.4 | -4.9 | -3.8 |
| Western Europe | 19 | -2.7 | -3.3 | -5.9 | 8.0 |

### CCR Base Cost of Equity Capital:

| Spain | COE (%) |
|---|---|
| March 2017 | 12.3 |
| December 2016 | 12.3 |

CCR base country-level COE for a Spain-based investor investing in Spain.

§ S&P Credit Rating based on long-term foreign currency issuer rating. See http://www.standardandpoors.com/.

* World rank based on 175 countries covered by Euromoney. Ranking based on ascending order in which '1' equals the smallest country risk premium (CRP) and '175' equals the largest country risk premium (CRP).

† MSCI Market Classification based on MSCI Market Classification Framework. See http://www.msci.com/products/indexes/market_classification.html

‡ Regional classification based on Euromoney. Regional rankings based on ascending order in which '1' equals the smallest country risk premium (CRP) for each region.

** Investment grade based on S&P sovereign credit rating from AAA to BBB-. Non-Investment grade based on S&P sovereign credit rating from BB+ to SD. For purposes of this analysis, the U.S. is being treated as if it were rated AAA by S&P.

Note: A CRP of 0.0% is assumed in the following cases: (i) when the investor country and the investee country both have an S&P sovereign credit rating of AAA; or (ii) when the investor country has an S&P credit rating of AAA, and the investee country has a sovereign credit rating below AAA, but has a calculated CRP below 0.0% (which would imply lower risk than a country rated AAA); or (iii) when the investor country has an S&P credit rating below AAA, and the investee country has a sovereign credit rating of AAA, but has a calculated CRP above 0.0% (which would imply greater risk than a country rated below AAA). For purposes of this analysis, the U.S. is treated as having a sovereign credit rating equivalent to AAA.

The country risk premium (CRP) is not the cost of equity capital (COE). The CRP is to be added to base COE. See Chapter 6 for proper application.

## Data Updated Through March 2017

| Investee Country | December 2016 Country Risk Premium (CRP) (%) | March 2017 Country Risk Premium (CRP) (%) | S&P Sovereign Credit Rating § | World Rank Out of 175∗ | MSCI Market Classification † | Euromoney Region ‡ | Regional Rank ‡ |
|---|---|---|---|---|---|---|---|
| Afghanistan | 16.8 | 16.6 | | 139 | | Asia | 23 out of 29 |
| Albania | 11.5 | 11.7 | B+ | 93 | | Central and Eastern Europe | 18 out of 25 |
| Algeria | 11.5 | 11.6 | | 91 | | Africa | 10 out of 51 |
| Angola | 13.8 | 14.0 | B | 121 | | Africa | 26 out of 51 |
| Argentina | 12.0 | 11.9 | B- | 96 | Frontier | Latin America | 13 out of 20 |
| Armenia | 9.1 | 9.4 | | 77 | | Asia | 15 out of 29 |
| Australia | 0.0 | 0.0 | AAA | 12 | Developed | Australasia | 2 out of 7 |
| Austria | 0.6 | 0.6 | AA+ | 13 | Developed | Western Europe | 9 out of 19 |
| Azerbaijan | 10.3 | 10.7 | BB+ | 85 | | Asia | 17 out of 29 |
| Bahamas | 7.7 | 7.5 | BB+ | 65 | | Caribbean | 3 out of 9 |
| Bahrain | 7.6 | 7.5 | BB- | 64 | Frontier | Middle East | 7 out of 13 |
| Bangladesh | 14.3 | 14.2 | BB- | 126 | Frontier | Asia | 20 out of 29 |
| Barbados | 9.3 | 10.4 | CCC+ | 82 | | Caribbean | 4 out of 9 |
| Belarus | 16.5 | 17.0 | B- | 143 | | Central and Eastern Europe | 23 out of 25 |
| Belgium | 1.8 | 1.8 | AA | 17 | Developed | Western Europe | 10 out of 19 |
| Belize | 12.5 | 12.7 | B- | 106 | | Latin America | 17 out of 20 |
| Benin | 18.1 | 18.2 | | 150 | | Africa | 37 out of 51 |
| Bermuda | 5.4 | 5.4 | A+ | 44 | | Caribbean | 1 out of 9 |
| Bhutan | 17.8 | 17.7 | | 148 | | Asia | 25 out of 29 |
| Bolivia | 11.0 | 11.4 | BB | 88 | | Latin America | 12 out of 20 |
| Bosnia & Herzegovina | 16.9 | 17.1 | B | 144 | | Central and Eastern Europe | 24 out of 25 |
| Botswana | 5.4 | 5.5 | A- | 48 | | Africa | 1 out of 51 |
| Brazil | 6.9 | 6.8 | BB | 59 | Emerging | Latin America | 7 out of 20 |
| Bulgaria | 6.7 | 7.0 | BB+ | 61 | | Central and Eastern Europe | 12 out of 25 |
| Burkina Faso | 15.3 | 15.4 | B- | 133 | | Africa | 33 out of 51 |
| Burundi | 26.9 | 27.0 | | 169 | | Africa | 47 out of 51 |
| Cambodia | 18.7 | 18.4 | | 151 | | Asia | 27 out of 29 |
| Cameroon | 14.0 | 14.1 | B | 124 | | Africa | 28 out of 51 |
| Canada | 0.0 | 0.0 | AAA | 9 | Developed | North America | 1 out of 2 |
| Cape Verde | 11.7 | 11.8 | B | 94 | | Africa | 12 out of 51 |
| Central African Republic | 30.3 | 30.4 | | 172 | | Africa | 49 out of 51 |
| Chad | 29.0 | 29.2 | | 171 | | Africa | 48 out of 51 |
| Chile | 1.4 | 1.6 | AA- | 16 | Emerging | Latin America | 1 out of 20 |
| China | 5.2 | 5.3 | AA- | 42 | Emerging | Asia | 7 out of 29 |
| Colombia | 5.2 | 5.2 | BBB | 41 | Emerging | Latin America | 4 out of 20 |
| Congo Republic | 13.6 | 13.5 | B- | 117 | | Africa | 24 out of 51 |
| Congo, DR | 14.8 | 14.8 | B- | 131 | | Africa | 32 out of 51 |
| Costa Rica | 8.1 | 8.4 | BB- | 71 | | Latin America | 8 out of 20 |
| Côte d'Ivoire | 11.6 | 11.7 | | 92 | | Africa | 11 out of 51 |
| Croatia | 7.2 | 7.2 | BB | 63 | Frontier | Central and Eastern Europe | 13 out of 25 |
| Cuba | 20.9 | 21.1 | | 160 | | Caribbean | 9 out of 9 |
| Cyprus | 4.9 | 5.1 | BB+ | 40 | | Central and Eastern Europe | 7 out of 25 |
| Czech Republic | 2.6 | 2.7 | AA- | 23 | Emerging | Central and Eastern Europe | 1 out of 25 |
| Denmark | 0.0 | 0.0 | AAA | 4 | Developed | Western Europe | 3 out of 19 |
| Djibouti | 38.1 | 35.9 | | 175 | | Africa | 51 out of 51 |
| Dominican Republic | 11.4 | 11.6 | BB- | 90 | | Caribbean | 5 out of 9 |
| Ecuador | 12.9 | 12.9 | B | 109 | | Latin America | 18 out of 20 |
| Egypt | 13.4 | 13.4 | B- | 116 | Emerging | Africa | 23 out of 51 |
| El Salvador | 10.4 | 10.3 | B- | 81 | | Latin America | 10 out of 20 |
| Equatorial Guinea | 23.4 | 23.5 | | 165 | | Africa | 45 out of 51 |

§ S&P Credit Rating based on long-term foreign currency issuer rating. Seehttp://www.standardandpoors.com/.

∗ World rank based on 175 countries covered by Euromoney. Ranking based on ascending order in which '1' equals the smallest country risk premium (CRP) and '175' equals the largest country risk premium (CRP).

† MSCI Market Classification based on MSCI Market Classification Framework. See http://www.msci.com/products/indexes/market_classification.html.

‡ Regional classification based on Euromoney. Regional rankings based on ascending order in which '1' equals the smallest country risk premium (CRP) for each region.

Note: A CRP of 0.0% is assumed in the following cases: (i) when the investor country and the investee country both have an S&P sovereign credit rating of AAA; or (ii) when the investor country has an S&P credit rating of AAA, and the investee country has a sovereign credit rating below AAA, but has a calculated CRP below 0.0% (which would imply lower risk than a country rated AAA); or (iii) when the investor country has an S&P credit rating below AAA, and the investee country has a sovereign credit rating of AAA, but has a calculated CRP above 0.0% (which would imply greater risk than a country rated below AAA). For purposes of this analysis, the U.S. is treated as having a sovereign credit rating equivalent to AAA.

The country risk premium (CRP) is not the cost of equity capital (COE). The CRP is to be added to base COE. See Chapter 6 for proper application.

## Data Updated Through March 2017

| Investee Country | December 2016 Country Risk Premium (CRP) (%) | March 2017 Country Risk Premium (CRP) (%) | S&P Sovereign Credit Rating § | World Rank Out of 175• | MSCI Market Classification † | Euromoney Region ‡ | Regional Rank ‡ |
|---|---|---|---|---|---|---|---|
| Eritrea | 34.4 | 32.7 | | 173 | | Africa | 50 out of 51 |
| Estonia | 3.2 | 3.5 | AA- | 32 | Frontier | Central and Eastern Europe | 4 out of 25 |
| Ethiopia | 12.2 | 12.4 | B | 101 | | Africa | 16 out of 51 |
| Fiji | 17.5 | 17.4 | B+ | 147 | | Australasia | 5 out of 7 |
| Finland | 0.3 | 0.4 | AA+ | 11 | Developed | Western Europe | 8 out of 19 |
| France | 2.6 | 2.5 | AA | 22 | Developed | Western Europe | 12 out of 19 |
| Gabon | 10.1 | 10.5 | | 83 | | Africa | 7 out of 51 |
| Gambia | 16.0 | 16.1 | | 138 | | Africa | 34 out of 51 |
| Georgia | 8.8 | 9.2 | BB- | 74 | | Central and Eastern Europe | 15 out of 25 |
| Germany | 0.0 | 0.0 | AAA | 10 | Developed | Western Europe | 7 out of 19 |
| Ghana | 11.8 | 11.5 | B- | 89 | | Africa | 9 out of 51 |
| Greece | 12.9 | 12.7 | B- | 108 | Emerging | Western Europe | 19 out of 19 |
| Grenada | 12.5 | 12.6 | | 105 | | Caribbean | 7 out of 9 |
| Guatemala | 10.5 | 10.6 | BB | 84 | | Latin America | 11 out of 20 |
| Guinea | 19.6 | 19.7 | | 156 | | Africa | 41 out of 51 |
| Guinea-Bissau | 13.3 | 13.4 | | 115 | | Africa | 22 out of 51 |
| Guyana | 12.2 | 12.3 | | 100 | | Latin America | 15 out of 20 |
| Haiti | 22.4 | 20.5 | | 157 | | Caribbean | 8 out of 9 |
| Honduras | 11.9 | 12.0 | B+ | 98 | | Latin America | 14 out of 20 |
| Hong Kong | 0.0 | 0.0 | AAA | 14 | Developed | Asia | 2 out of 29 |
| Hungary | 6.5 | 6.7 | BBB- | 57 | Emerging | Central and Eastern Europe | 10 out of 25 |
| Iceland | 3.6 | 3.4 | A | 30 | | Western Europe | 15 out of 19 |
| India | 6.3 | 6.6 | BBB- | 55 | Emerging | Asia | 10 out of 29 |
| Indonesia | 7.0 | 7.1 | BB+ | 62 | Emerging | Asia | 11 out of 29 |
| Iran | 13.8 | 14.1 | | 125 | | Middle East | 10 out of 13 |
| Iraq | 15.6 | 15.7 | B- | 136 | | Middle East | 11 out of 13 |
| Ireland | 3.1 | 3.1 | A+ | 27 | Developed | Western Europe | 14 out of 19 |
| Israel | 3.1 | 3.1 | A+ | 28 | Developed | Middle East | 2 out of 13 |
| Italy | 5.9 | 5.8 | BBB- | 50 | Developed | Western Europe | 18 out of 19 |
| Jamaica | 11.9 | 12.6 | B | 104 | | Caribbean | 6 out of 9 |
| Japan | 2.9 | 3.0 | A+ | 25 | Developed | Asia | 5 out of 29 |
| Jordan | 9.1 | 9.4 | BB- | 76 | Frontier | Middle East | 8 out of 13 |
| Kazakhstan | 8.6 | 8.3 | BBB- | 70 | Frontier | Asia | 13 out of 29 |
| Kenya | 12.0 | 12.1 | B+ | 99 | Frontier | Africa | 15 out of 51 |
| Korea (North) | 33.7 | 33.4 | | 174 | | Asia | 29 out of 29 |
| Korea (South) | 2.2 | 2.3 | AA | 19 | Emerging | Asia | 4 out of 29 |
| Kuwait | 3.2 | 3.5 | AA | 31 | Frontier | Middle East | 3 out of 13 |
| Kyrgyz Republic | 17.0 | 16.9 | | 142 | | Central and Eastern Europe | 22 out of 25 |
| Laos | 21.1 | 20.7 | | 158 | | Asia | 28 out of 29 |
| Latvia | 5.2 | 5.4 | A- | 43 | | Central and Eastern Europe | 8 out of 25 |
| Lebanon | 13.7 | 13.1 | B- | 112 | Frontier | Middle East | 9 out of 13 |
| Lesotho | 17.2 | 17.3 | | 146 | | Africa | 36 out of 51 |
| Liberia | 12.6 | 12.7 | | 107 | | Africa | 17 out of 51 |
| Libya | 18.7 | 19.1 | | 153 | | Africa | 39 out of 51 |
| Lithuania | 4.4 | 4.6 | A- | 36 | Frontier | Central and Eastern Europe | 6 out of 25 |
| Luxembourg | 0.0 | 0.0 | AAA | 5 | | Western Europe | 4 out of 19 |
| Macedonia | 11.1 | 11.3 | BB- | 87 | | Central and Eastern Europe | 17 out of 25 |
| Madagascar | 13.4 | 14.0 | | 123 | | Africa | 27 out of 51 |
| Malawi | 13.1 | 13.2 | | 114 | | Africa | 21 out of 51 |
| Malaysia | 4.6 | 4.5 | A- | 35 | Emerging | Asia | 6 out of 29 |

§ S&P Credit Rating based on long-term foreign currency issuer rating. See http://www.standardandpoors.com/.

• World rank based on 175 countries covered by Euromoney. Ranking based on ascending order in which '1' equals the smallest country risk premium (CRP) and '175' equals the largest country risk premium (CRP).

† MSCI Market Classification based on MSCI Market Classification Framework. See http://www.msci.com/products/indexes/market_classification.html

‡ Regional classification based on Euromoney. Regional rankings based on ascending order in which '1' equals the smallest country risk premium (CRP) for each region.

Note: A CRP of 0.0% is assumed in the following cases: (i) when the investor country and the investee country both have an S&P sovereign credit rating of AAA; or (ii) when the investor country has an S&P credit rating of AAA, and the investee country has a sovereign credit rating below AAA, but has a calculated CRP below 0.0% (which would imply lower risk than a country rated AAA); or (iii) when the investor country has an S&P credit rating below AAA, and the investee country has a sovereign credit rating of AAA, but has a calculated CRP above 0.0% (which would imply greater risk than a country rated below AAA). For purposes of this analysis, the U.S. is treated as having a sovereign credit rating equivalent to AAA.

The country risk premium (CRP) is not the cost of equity capital (COE). The CRP is to be added to base COE. See Chapter 6 for proper application.

## Data Updated Through March 2017

| Investee Country | December 2016 Country Risk Premium (CRP) (%) | March 2017 Country Risk Premium (CRP) (%) | S&P Sovereign Credit Rating § | World Rank Out of 175* | MSCI Market Classification † | Euromoney Region ‡ | Regional Rank ‡ |
|---|---|---|---|---|---|---|---|
| Mali | 16.8 | 16.9 | | 141 | | Africa | 35 out of 51 |
| Malta | 2.9 | 3.1 | A- | 26 | | Western Europe | 13 out of 19 |
| Mauritania | 20.7 | 20.9 | | 159 | | Africa | 42 out of 51 |
| Mauritius | 7.9 | 8.0 | | 67 | Frontier | Asia | 12 out of 29 |
| Mexico | 4.5 | 4.7 | BBB+ | 37 | Emerging | Latin America | 2 out of 20 |
| Moldova | 15.3 | 15.8 | | 137 | | Central and Eastern Europe | 21 out of 25 |
| Mongolia | 13.5 | 13.9 | B- | 119 | | Asia | 18 out of 29 |
| Montenegro | 12.7 | 12.6 | B+ | 103 | | Central and Eastern Europe | 19 out of 25 |
| Morocco | 8.0 | 8.2 | BBB- | 69 | Frontier | Africa | 4 out of 51 |
| Mozambique | 14.5 | 14.5 | SD | 128 | | Africa | 29 out of 51 |
| Myanmar | 15.4 | 15.4 | | 134 | | Asia | 22 out of 29 |
| Namibia | 7.6 | 7.8 | | 66 | | Africa | 3 out of 51 |
| Nepal | 18.1 | 18.2 | | 149 | | Asia | 26 out of 29 |
| Netherlands | 0.0 | 0.0 | AAA | 6 | Developed | Western Europe | 5 out of 19 |
| New Zealand | 0.1 | 0.2 | AA | 8 | Developed | Australasia | 1 out of 7 |
| Nicaragua | 14.2 | 14.3 | B+ | 127 | | Latin America | 19 out of 20 |
| Niger | 13.8 | 13.9 | | 120 | | Africa | 25 out of 51 |
| Nigeria | 11.9 | 12.0 | B | 97 | Frontier | Africa | 14 out of 51 |
| Norway | 0.0 | 0.0 | AAA | 3 | Developed | Western Europe | 2 out of 19 |
| Oman | 5.3 | 5.5 | BBB- | 46 | Frontier | Middle East | 5 out of 13 |
| Pakistan | 13.9 | 14.0 | B | 122 | Frontier | Asia | 19 out of 29 |
| Panama | 6.0 | 6.2 | BBB | 52 | | Latin America | 6 out of 20 |
| Papua New Guinea | 13.4 | 13.6 | B+ | 118 | | Australasia | 3 out of 7 |
| Paraguay | 9.5 | 9.8 | BB | 80 | | Latin America | 9 out of 20 |
| Peru | 4.8 | 5.0 | BBB+ | 39 | Emerging | Latin America | 3 out of 20 |
| Philippines | 6.4 | 6.4 | BBB | 53 | Emerging | Asia | 9 out of 29 |
| Poland | 3.4 | 3.4 | BBB+ | 29 | Emerging | Central and Eastern Europe | 3 out of 25 |
| Portugal | 5.8 | 5.6 | BB+ | 49 | Developed | Western Europe | 17 out of 19 |
| Qatar | 2.3 | 2.5 | AA | 21 | Emerging | Middle East | 1 out of 13 |
| Romania | 6.5 | 6.7 | BBB- | 56 | Frontier | Central and Eastern Europe | 9 out of 25 |
| Russia | 8.7 | 8.2 | BB+ | 68 | Emerging | Central and Eastern Europe | 14 out of 25 |
| Rwanda | 14.6 | 14.7 | B | 130 | | Africa | 31 out of 51 |
| São Tomé & Príncipe | 20.9 | 21.4 | | 163 | | Africa | 43 out of 51 |
| Saudi Arabia | 5.7 | 5.5 | A- | 47 | | Middle East | 6 out of 13 |
| Senegal | 11.2 | 11.3 | B+ | 86 | | Africa | 8 out of 51 |
| Serbia | 9.4 | 9.2 | BB- | 75 | Frontier | Central and Eastern Europe | 16 out of 25 |
| Seychelles | 8.9 | 9.0 | | 73 | | Africa | 5 out of 51 |
| Sierra Leone | 14.6 | 14.7 | | 129 | | Africa | 30 out of 51 |
| Singapore | 0.0 | 0.0 | AAA | 1 | Developed | Asia | 1 out of 29 |
| Slovakia | 2.7 | 2.8 | A+ | 24 | | Central and Eastern Europe | 2 out of 25 |
| Slovenia | 4.1 | 4.2 | A | 34 | Frontier | Central and Eastern Europe | 5 out of 25 |
| Solomon Islands | 25.1 | 25.2 | | 168 | | Australasia | 6 out of 7 |
| Somalia | 23.4 | 23.5 | | 166 | | Africa | 46 out of 51 |
| South Africa | 6.6 | 6.9 | BBB- | 60 | Emerging | Africa | 2 out of 51 |
| Spain | 4.9 | 5.0 | BBB+ | 38 | Developed | Western Europe | 16 out of 19 |
| Sri Lanka | 8.8 | 8.6 | B+ | 72 | Frontier | Asia | 14 out of 29 |
| Sudan | 19.5 | 19.6 | | 154 | | Africa | 40 out of 51 |
| Suriname | 12.1 | 12.4 | B+ | 102 | | Latin America | 16 out of 20 |
| Swaziland | 17.9 | 18.9 | | 152 | | Africa | 38 out of 51 |
| Sweden | 0.0 | 0.0 | AAA | 7 | Developed | Western Europe | 6 out of 19 |

§ S&P Credit Rating based on long-term foreign currency issuer rating. See http://www.standardandpoors.com/.

* World rank based on 175 countries covered by Euromoney. Ranking based on ascending order in which '1' equals the smallest country risk premium (CRP) and '175' equals the largest country risk premium (CRP).

† MSCI Market Classification based on MSCI Market Classification Framework. See http://www.msci.com/products/indexes/market_classification.html

‡ Regional classification based on Euromoney. Regional rankings based on ascending order in which '1' equals the smallest country risk premium (CRP) for each region.

Note: A CRP of 0.0% is assumed in the following cases: (i) when the investor country and the investee country both have an S&P sovereign credit rating of AAA; or (ii) when the investor country has an S&P credit rating of AAA, and the investee country has a sovereign credit rating below AAA, but has a calculated CRP below 0.0% (which would imply lower risk than a country rated AAA); or (iii) when the investor country has an S&P credit rating below AAA, and the investee country has a sovereign credit rating of AAA, but has a calculated CRP above 0.0% (which would imply greater risk than a country rated below AAA). For purposes of this analysis, the U.S. is treated as having a sovereign credit rating equivalent to AAA.

The country risk premium (CRP) is not the cost of equity capital (COE).  The CRP is to be added to base COE. See Chapter 6 for proper application.

## Data Updated Through March 2017

| Investee Country | December 2016 Country Risk Premium (CRP) (%) | March 2017 Country Risk Premium (CRP) (%) | S&P Sovereign Credit Rating § | World Rank Out of 175∗ | MSCI Market Classification † | Euromoney Region ‡ | Regional Rank ‡ |
|---|---|---|---|---|---|---|---|
| Switzerland | 0.0 | 0.0 | AAA | 2 | Developed | Western Europe | 1 out of 19 |
| Syria | 24.2 | 24.5 | | 167 | | Middle East | 13 out of 13 |
| Taiwan | 1.9 | 2.0 | AA- | 18 | Emerging | Asia | 3 out of 29 |
| Tajikistan | 19.1 | 19.6 | | 155 | | Central and Eastern Europe | 25 out of 25 |
| Tanzania | 11.6 | 11.8 | | 95 | | Africa | 13 out of 51 |
| Thailand | 6.0 | 6.0 | BBB+ | 51 | Emerging | Asia | 8 out of 29 |
| Togo | 13.1 | 13.2 | | 113 | | Africa | 20 out of 51 |
| Tonga | 27.5 | 27.6 | | 170 | | Australasia | 7 out of 7 |
| Trinidad & Tobago | 6.4 | 6.5 | A- | 54 | | Caribbean | 2 out of 9 |
| Tunisia | 9.2 | 9.6 | | 79 | Frontier | Africa | 6 out of 51 |
| Turkey | 6.7 | 6.7 | BB | 58 | Emerging | Central and Eastern Europe | 11 out of 25 |
| Turkmenistan | 16.3 | 16.7 | | 140 | | Asia | 24 out of 29 |
| Uganda | 12.6 | 13.0 | B | 110 | | Africa | 18 out of 51 |
| Ukraine | 15.4 | 15.6 | B- | 135 | | Central and Eastern Europe | 20 out of 25 |
| United Arab Emirates | 3.7 | 3.8 | AA | 33 | Emerging | Middle East | 4 out of 13 |
| United Kingdom | 2.2 | 2.4 | AA | 20 | Developed | Western Europe | 11 out of 19 |
| United States | 0.0 | 0.0 | AA+ | 15 | Developed | North America | 2 out of 2 |
| Uruguay | 5.4 | 5.4 | BBB | 45 | | Latin America | 5 out of 20 |
| Uzbekistan | 15.6 | 15.1 | | 132 | | Asia | 21 out of 29 |
| Vanuatu | 17.2 | 17.3 | | 145 | | Australasia | 4 out of 7 |
| Venezuela | 20.8 | 21.4 | CCC | 162 | | Latin America | 20 out of 20 |
| Vietnam | 9.7 | 9.5 | BB- | 78 | Frontier | Asia | 16 out of 29 |
| Yemen | 21.1 | 21.3 | | 161 | | Middle East | 12 out of 13 |
| Zambia | 13.0 | 13.1 | B | 111 | | Africa | 19 out of 51 |
| Zimbabwe | 22.7 | 22.8 | | 164 | | Africa | 44 out of 51 |

## March 2017 Country Risk Premium (CRP) Summary Statistics:

| S&P Rating | Country Count | Average CRP (%) | Median CRP (%) | Min CRP (%) | Max CRP (%) |
|---|---|---|---|---|---|
| AAA ∗∗ | 12 | 0.0 | 0.0 | 0.0 | 0.0 |
| AA (AA+, AA, AA-) | 15 | 2.3 | 2.4 | 0.2 | 5.3 |
| A (A+, A, A-) | 14 | 4.3 | 4.4 | 2.8 | 6.5 |
| BBB (BBB+, BBB, BBB-) | 17 | 6.0 | 6.0 | 3.4 | 8.3 |
| BB (BB+, BB, BB-) | 22 | 8.8 | 8.8 | 5.1 | 14.2 |
| B+ − SD | 39 | 13.5 | 13.1 | 8.6 | 21.4 |
| Investment Grade ∗∗ | 58 | 3.4 | 3.4 | 0.0 | 8.3 |
| Non-Investment Grade ∗∗ | 61 | 11.8 | 12.0 | 5.1 | 21.4 |
| **MSCI Market Classification** | | | | | |
| Developed Markets | 23 | 1.5 | 0.2 | 0.0 | 5.8 |
| Emerging Markets | 23 | 5.7 | 5.3 | 1.6 | 13.4 |
| Frontier Markets | 22 | 8.7 | 8.5 | 3.5 | 14.2 |
| **Euromoney Region ‡** | | | | | |
| Africa | 51 | 15.9 | 14.0 | 5.5 | 35.9 |
| Asia | 29 | 10.8 | 9.4 | 0.0 | 33.4 |
| Australasia | 7 | 14.5 | 17.3 | 0.0 | 27.6 |
| Caribbean | 9 | 12.0 | 11.6 | 5.4 | 21.1 |
| Central and Eastern Europe | 25 | 9.2 | 7.2 | 2.7 | 19.6 |
| Latin America | 20 | 9.8 | 10.5 | 1.6 | 21.4 |
| Middle East | 13 | 10.0 | 7.5 | 2.5 | 24.5 |
| North America | 2 | 0.0 | 0.0 | 0.0 | 0.0 |
| Western Europe | 19 | 2.4 | 1.8 | 0.0 | 12.7 |

### CCR Base Cost of Equity Capital:

| Sweden | COE (%) |
|---|---|
| March 2017 | 7.9 |
| December 2016 | 8.0 |

CCR base country-level COE for a Sweden-based investor investing in Sweden.

§ S&P Credit Rating based on long-term foreign currency issuer rating. Seehttp://www.standardandpoors.com/.
∗ World rank based on 175 countries covered by Euromoney. Ranking based on ascending order in which '1' equals the smallest country risk premium (CRP) and '175' equals the largest country risk premium (CRP).
† MSCI Market Classification based on MSCI Market Classification Framework.  See http://www.msci.com/products/indexes/market_classification.html.
‡ Regional classification based on Euromoney. Regional rankings based on ascending order in which '1' equals the smallest country risk premium (CRP) for each region.
∗∗ Investment grade based on S&P sovereign credit rating from AAA to BBB-. Non-Investment grade based on S&P sovereign credit rating from BB+ to SD. For purposes of this analysis, the U.S. is being treated as if it were rated AAA by S&P.
Note: A CRP of 0.0% is assumed in the following cases: (i) when the investor country and the investee country both have an S&P sovereign credit rating of AAA; or (ii) when the investor country has an S&P credit rating of AAA, and the investee country has a sovereign credit rating below AAA, but has a calculated CRP below 0.0% (which would imply lower risk than a country rated AAA); or (iii) when the investor country has an S&P credit rating below AAA, and the investee country has a sovereign credit rating of AAA, but has a calculated CRP above 0.0% (which would imply greater risk than a country rated below AAA). For purposes of this analysis, the U.S. is treated as having a sovereign credit rating equivalent to AAA.

The country risk premium (CRP) is not the cost of equity capital (COE). The CRP is to be added to base COE. See Chapter 6 for proper application.

## Data Updated Through March 2017

| Investee Country | December 2016 Country Risk Premium (CRP) (%) | March 2017 Country Risk Premium (CRP) (%) | S&P Sovereign Credit Rating § | World Rank Out of 175∗ | MSCI Market Classification † | Euromoney Region ‡ | Regional Rank ‡ |
|---|---|---|---|---|---|---|---|
| Afghanistan | 18.4 | 18.3 | | 139 | | Asia | 23 out of 29 |
| Albania | 12.8 | 13.2 | B+ | 93 | | Central and Eastern Europe | 18 out of 25 |
| Algeria | 12.9 | 13.1 | | 91 | | Africa | 10 out of 51 |
| Angola | 15.3 | 15.6 | B | 121 | | Africa | 26 out of 51 |
| Argentina | 13.4 | 13.3 | B- | 96 | Frontier | Latin America | 13 out of 20 |
| Armenia | 10.4 | 10.7 | | 77 | | Asia | 15 out of 29 |
| Australia | 0.0 | 0.0 | AAA | 12 | Developed | Australasia | 2 out of 7 |
| Austria | 1.3 | 1.4 | AA+ | 13 | Developed | Western Europe | 9 out of 19 |
| Azerbaijan | 11.6 | 12.1 | BB+ | 85 | | Asia | 17 out of 29 |
| Bahamas | 8.9 | 8.7 | BB+ | 65 | | Caribbean | 3 out of 9 |
| Bahrain | 8.8 | 8.7 | BB- | 64 | Frontier | Middle East | 7 out of 13 |
| Bangladesh | 15.8 | 15.8 | BB- | 126 | Frontier | Asia | 20 out of 29 |
| Barbados | 10.6 | 11.8 | CCC+ | 82 | | Caribbean | 4 out of 9 |
| Belarus | 18.1 | 18.7 | B- | 143 | | Central and Eastern Europe | 23 out of 25 |
| Belgium | 2.6 | 2.7 | AA | 17 | Developed | Western Europe | 10 out of 19 |
| Belize | 13.9 | 14.2 | B- | 106 | | Latin America | 17 out of 20 |
| Benin | 19.9 | 20.1 | | 150 | | Africa | 37 out of 51 |
| Bermuda | 6.4 | 6.5 | A+ | 44 | | Caribbean | 1 out of 9 |
| Bhutan | 19.5 | 19.6 | | 148 | | Asia | 25 out of 29 |
| Bolivia | 12.4 | 12.8 | BB | 88 | | Latin America | 12 out of 20 |
| Bosnia & Herzegovina | 18.6 | 18.9 | B | 144 | | Central and Eastern Europe | 24 out of 25 |
| Botswana | 6.4 | 6.6 | A- | 48 | | Africa | 1 out of 51 |
| Brazil | 8.0 | 8.0 | BB | 59 | Emerging | Latin America | 7 out of 20 |
| Bulgaria | 7.8 | 8.1 | BB+ | 61 | | Central and Eastern Europe | 12 out of 25 |
| Burkina Faso | 16.9 | 17.1 | B- | 133 | | Africa | 33 out of 51 |
| Burundi | 29.2 | 29.4 | | 169 | | Africa | 47 out of 51 |
| Cambodia | 20.5 | 20.3 | | 151 | | Asia | 27 out of 29 |
| Cameroon | 15.5 | 15.7 | B | 124 | | Africa | 28 out of 51 |
| Canada | 0.0 | 0.0 | AAA | 9 | Developed | North America | 1 out of 2 |
| Cape Verde | 13.1 | 13.2 | B | 94 | | Africa | 12 out of 51 |
| Central African Republic | 32.8 | 33.0 | | 172 | | Africa | 49 out of 51 |
| Chad | 31.4 | 31.6 | | 171 | | Africa | 48 out of 51 |
| Chile | 2.2 | 2.5 | AA- | 16 | Emerging | Latin America | 1 out of 20 |
| China | 6.2 | 6.3 | AA- | 42 | Emerging | Asia | 7 out of 29 |
| Colombia | 6.2 | 6.3 | BBB | 41 | Emerging | Latin America | 4 out of 20 |
| Congo Republic | 15.1 | 15.1 | B- | 117 | | Africa | 24 out of 51 |
| Congo, DR | 16.4 | 16.5 | B- | 131 | | Africa | 32 out of 51 |
| Costa Rica | 9.3 | 9.7 | BB- | 71 | | Latin America | 8 out of 20 |
| Côte d'Ivoire | 12.9 | 13.1 | | 92 | | Africa | 11 out of 51 |
| Croatia | 8.4 | 8.4 | BB | 63 | Frontier | Central and Eastern Europe | 13 out of 25 |
| Cuba | 22.8 | 23.1 | | 160 | | Caribbean | 9 out of 9 |
| Cyprus | 5.9 | 6.1 | BB+ | 40 | | Central and Eastern Europe | 7 out of 25 |
| Czech Republic | 3.4 | 3.6 | AA- | 23 | Emerging | Central and Eastern Europe | 1 out of 25 |
| Denmark | 0.0 | 0.0 | AAA | 4 | Developed | Western Europe | 3 out of 19 |
| Djibouti | 41.0 | 38.8 | | 175 | | Africa | 51 out of 51 |
| Dominican Republic | 12.7 | 13.0 | BB- | 90 | | Caribbean | 5 out of 9 |
| Ecuador | 14.4 | 14.4 | B | 109 | | Latin America | 18 out of 20 |
| Egypt | 14.8 | 15.0 | B- | 116 | Emerging | Africa | 23 out of 51 |
| El Salvador | 11.7 | 11.7 | B- | 81 | | Latin America | 10 out of 20 |
| Equatorial Guinea | 25.4 | 25.7 | | 165 | | Africa | 45 out of 51 |

§ S&P Credit Rating based on long-term foreign currency issuer rating. See http://www.standardandpoors.com/.

∗ World rank based on 175 countries covered by Euromoney. Ranking based on ascending order in which '1' equals the smallest country risk premium (CRP) and '175' equals the largest country risk premium (CRP).

† MSCI Market Classification based on MSCI Market Classification Framework. See http://www.msci.com/products/indexes/market_classification.html

‡ Regional classification based on Euromoney. Regional rankings based on ascending order in which '1' equals the smallest country risk premium (CRP) for each region.

Note: A CRP of 0.0% is assumed in the following cases: (i) when the investor country and the investee country both have an S&P sovereign credit rating of AAA; or (ii) when the investor country has an S&P credit rating of AAA, and the investee country has a sovereign credit rating below AAA, but has a calculated CRP below 0.0% (which would imply lower risk than a country rated AAA); or (iii) when the investor country has an S&P credit rating below AAA, and the investee country has a sovereign credit rating of AAA, but has a calculated CRP above 0.0% (which would imply greater risk than a country rated below AAA). For purposes of this analysis, the U.S. is treated as having a sovereign credit rating equivalent to AAA.

The country risk premium (CRP) is not the cost of equity capital (COE). The CRP is to be added to base COE. See Chapter 6 for proper application.

## Data Updated Through March 2017

| Investee Country | December 2016 Country Risk Premium (CRP) (%) | March 2017 Country Risk Premium (CRP) (%) | S&P Sovereign Credit Rating § | World Rank Out of 175∗ | MSCI Market Classification † | Euromoney Region ‡ | Regional Rank ‡ |
|---|---|---|---|---|---|---|---|
| Eritrea | 37.1 | 35.4 | | 173 | | Africa | 50 out of 51 |
| Estonia | 4.1 | 4.5 | AA- | 32 | Frontier | Central and Eastern Europe | 4 out of 25 |
| Ethiopia | 13.6 | 13.9 | B | 101 | | Africa | 16 out of 51 |
| Fiji | 19.2 | 19.2 | B+ | 147 | | Australasia | 5 out of 7 |
| Finland | 1.1 | 1.2 | AA+ | 11 | Developed | Western Europe | 8 out of 19 |
| France | 3.5 | 3.4 | AA | 22 | Developed | Western Europe | 12 out of 19 |
| Gabon | 11.4 | 11.9 | | 83 | | Africa | 7 out of 51 |
| Gambia | 17.6 | 17.8 | | 138 | | Africa | 34 out of 51 |
| Georgia | 10.1 | 10.5 | BB- | 74 | | Central and Eastern Europe | 15 out of 25 |
| Germany | 0.0 | 0.0 | AAA | 10 | Developed | Western Europe | 7 out of 19 |
| Ghana | 13.1 | 12.9 | B- | 89 | | Africa | 9 out of 51 |
| Greece | 14.3 | 14.2 | B- | 108 | Emerging | Western Europe | 19 out of 19 |
| Grenada | 13.9 | 14.1 | | 105 | | Caribbean | 7 out of 9 |
| Guatemala | 11.8 | 12.0 | BB | 84 | | Latin America | 11 out of 20 |
| Guinea | 21.4 | 21.6 | | 156 | | Africa | 41 out of 51 |
| Guinea-Bissau | 14.8 | 15.0 | | 115 | | Africa | 22 out of 51 |
| Guyana | 13.6 | 13.7 | | 100 | | Latin America | 15 out of 20 |
| Haiti | 24.4 | 22.5 | | 157 | | Caribbean | 8 out of 9 |
| Honduras | 13.2 | 13.5 | B+ | 98 | | Latin America | 14 out of 20 |
| Hong Kong | 0.0 | 0.0 | AAA | 14 | Developed | Asia | 2 out of 29 |
| Hungary | 7.6 | 7.9 | BBB- | 57 | Emerging | Central and Eastern Europe | 10 out of 25 |
| Iceland | 4.5 | 4.4 | A | 30 | | Western Europe | 15 out of 19 |
| India | 7.3 | 7.8 | BBB- | 55 | Emerging | Asia | 10 out of 29 |
| Indonesia | 8.1 | 8.3 | BB+ | 62 | Emerging | Asia | 11 out of 29 |
| Iran | 15.3 | 15.7 | | 125 | | Middle East | 10 out of 13 |
| Iraq | 17.2 | 17.4 | B- | 136 | | Middle East | 11 out of 13 |
| Ireland | 4.0 | 4.0 | A+ | 27 | Developed | Western Europe | 14 out of 19 |
| Israel | 3.9 | 4.1 | A+ | 28 | Developed | Middle East | 2 out of 13 |
| Italy | 6.9 | 6.9 | BBB- | 50 | Developed | Western Europe | 18 out of 19 |
| Jamaica | 13.3 | 14.1 | B | 104 | | Caribbean | 6 out of 9 |
| Japan | 3.8 | 4.0 | A+ | 25 | Developed | Asia | 5 out of 29 |
| Jordan | 10.3 | 10.7 | BB- | 76 | Frontier | Middle East | 8 out of 13 |
| Kazakhstan | 9.8 | 9.6 | BBB- | 70 | Frontier | Asia | 13 out of 29 |
| Kenya | 13.4 | 13.6 | B+ | 99 | Frontier | Africa | 15 out of 51 |
| Korea (North) | 36.4 | 36.1 | | 174 | | Asia | 29 out of 29 |
| Korea (South) | 3.0 | 3.2 | AA | 19 | Emerging | Asia | 4 out of 29 |
| Kuwait | 4.1 | 4.4 | AA | 31 | Frontier | Middle East | 3 out of 13 |
| Kyrgyz Republic | 18.6 | 18.7 | | 142 | | Central and Eastern Europe | 22 out of 25 |
| Laos | 23.1 | 22.7 | | 158 | | Asia | 28 out of 29 |
| Latvia | 6.2 | 6.5 | A- | 43 | | Central and Eastern Europe | 8 out of 25 |
| Lebanon | 15.2 | 14.7 | B- | 112 | Frontier | Middle East | 9 out of 13 |
| Lesotho | 18.9 | 19.1 | | 146 | | Africa | 36 out of 51 |
| Liberia | 14.0 | 14.2 | | 107 | | Africa | 17 out of 51 |
| Libya | 20.5 | 21.0 | | 153 | | Africa | 39 out of 51 |
| Lithuania | 5.4 | 5.6 | A- | 36 | Frontier | Central and Eastern Europe | 6 out of 25 |
| Luxembourg | 0.0 | 0.0 | AAA | 5 | | Western Europe | 4 out of 19 |
| Macedonia | 12.4 | 12.8 | BB- | 87 | | Central and Eastern Europe | 17 out of 25 |
| Madagascar | 14.9 | 15.6 | | 123 | | Africa | 27 out of 51 |
| Malawi | 14.6 | 14.8 | | 114 | | Africa | 21 out of 51 |
| Malaysia | 5.6 | 5.6 | A- | 35 | Emerging | Asia | 6 out of 29 |

§ S&P Credit Rating based on long-term foreign currency issuer rating. See http://www.standardandpoors.com/.

∗ World rank based on 175 countries covered by Euromoney. Ranking based on ascending order in which '1' equals the smallest country risk premium (CRP) and '175' equals the largest country risk premium (CRP).

† MSCI Market Classification based on MSCI Market Classification Framework. See http://www.msci.com/products/indexes/market_classification.html

‡ Regional classification based on Euromoney. Regional rankings based on ascending order in which '1' equals the smallest country risk premium (CRP) for each region.

Note: A CRP of 0.0% is assumed in the following cases: (i) when the investor country and the investee country both have an S&P sovereign credit rating of AAA; or (ii) when the investor country has an S&P credit rating of AAA, and the investee country has a sovereign credit rating below AAA, but has a calculated CRP below 0.0% (which would imply lower risk than a country rated AAA); or (iii) when the investor country has an S&P credit rating below AAA, and the investee country has a sovereign credit rating of AAA, but has a calculated CRP above 0.0% (which would imply greater risk than a country rated below AAA). For purposes of this analysis, the U.S. is treated as having a sovereign credit rating equivalent to AAA.

The country risk premium (CRP) is not the cost of equity capital (COE). The CRP is to be added to base COE. See Chapter 6 for proper application.

Data Updated Through March 2017

| Investee Country | December 2016 Country Risk Premium (CRP) (%) | March 2017 Country Risk Premium (CRP) (%) | S&P Sovereign Credit Rating § | World Rank Out of 175* | MSCI Market Classification † | Euromoney Region ‡ | Regional Rank ‡ |
|---|---|---|---|---|---|---|---|
| Mali | 18.5 | 18.7 | | 141 | | Africa | 35 out of 51 |
| Malta | 3.8 | 4.0 | A- | 26 | | Western Europe | 13 out of 19 |
| Mauritania | 22.7 | 22.9 | | 159 | | Africa | 42 out of 51 |
| Mauritius | 9.1 | 9.2 | | 67 | Frontier | Asia | 12 out of 29 |
| Mexico | 5.5 | 5.7 | BBB+ | 37 | Emerging | Latin America | 2 out of 20 |
| Moldova | 16.8 | 17.5 | | 137 | | Central and Eastern Europe | 21 out of 25 |
| Mongolia | 15.0 | 15.5 | B- | 119 | | Asia | 18 out of 29 |
| Montenegro | 14.1 | 14.1 | B+ | 103 | | Central and Eastern Europe | 19 out of 25 |
| Morocco | 9.1 | 9.5 | BBB- | 69 | Frontier | Africa | 4 out of 51 |
| Mozambique | 16.1 | 16.1 | SD | 128 | | Africa | 29 out of 51 |
| Myanmar | 17.0 | 17.1 | | 134 | | Asia | 22 out of 29 |
| Namibia | 8.7 | 9.1 | | 66 | | Africa | 3 out of 51 |
| Nepal | 19.8 | 20.0 | | 149 | | Asia | 26 out of 29 |
| Netherlands | 0.0 | 0.0 | AAA | 6 | Developed | Western Europe | 5 out of 19 |
| New Zealand | 0.8 | 1.0 | AA | 8 | Developed | Australasia | 1 out of 7 |
| Nicaragua | 15.8 | 15.9 | B+ | 127 | | Latin America | 19 out of 20 |
| Niger | 15.3 | 15.5 | | 120 | | Africa | 25 out of 51 |
| Nigeria | 13.3 | 13.4 | B | 97 | Frontier | Africa | 14 out of 51 |
| Norway | 0.0 | 0.0 | AAA | 3 | Developed | Western Europe | 2 out of 19 |
| Oman | 6.4 | 6.5 | BBB- | 46 | Frontier | Middle East | 5 out of 13 |
| Pakistan | 15.4 | 15.6 | B | 122 | Frontier | Asia | 19 out of 29 |
| Panama | 7.1 | 7.3 | BBB | 52 | | Latin America | 6 out of 20 |
| Papua New Guinea | 14.9 | 15.2 | B+ | 118 | | Australasia | 3 out of 7 |
| Paraguay | 10.7 | 11.1 | BB | 80 | | Latin America | 9 out of 20 |
| Peru | 5.7 | 6.0 | BBB+ | 39 | Emerging | Latin America | 3 out of 20 |
| Philippines | 7.5 | 7.6 | BBB | 53 | Emerging | Asia | 9 out of 29 |
| Poland | 4.3 | 4.3 | BBB+ | 29 | Emerging | Central and Eastern Europe | 3 out of 25 |
| Portugal | 6.8 | 6.7 | BB+ | 49 | Developed | Western Europe | 17 out of 19 |
| Qatar | 3.1 | 3.4 | AA | 21 | Emerging | Middle East | 1 out of 13 |
| Romania | 7.6 | 7.8 | BBB- | 56 | Frontier | Central and Eastern Europe | 9 out of 25 |
| Russia | 9.9 | 9.5 | BB+ | 68 | Emerging | Central and Eastern Europe | 14 out of 25 |
| Rwanda | 16.2 | 16.3 | B | 130 | | Africa | 31 out of 51 |
| São Tomé & Príncipe | 22.8 | 23.5 | | 163 | | Africa | 43 out of 51 |
| Saudi Arabia | 6.7 | 6.5 | A- | 47 | | Middle East | 6 out of 13 |
| Senegal | 12.6 | 12.7 | B+ | 86 | | Africa | 8 out of 51 |
| Serbia | 10.6 | 10.5 | BB- | 75 | Frontier | Central and Eastern Europe | 16 out of 25 |
| Seychelles | 10.1 | 10.3 | | 73 | | Africa | 5 out of 51 |
| Sierra Leone | 16.1 | 16.3 | | 129 | | Africa | 30 out of 51 |
| Singapore | 0.0 | 0.0 | AAA | 1 | Developed | Asia | 1 out of 29 |
| Slovakia | 3.6 | 3.8 | A+ | 24 | | Central and Eastern Europe | 2 out of 25 |
| Slovenia | 5.0 | 5.2 | A | 34 | Frontier | Central and Eastern Europe | 5 out of 25 |
| Solomon Islands | 27.3 | 27.5 | | 168 | | Australasia | 6 out of 7 |
| Somalia | 25.5 | 25.7 | | 166 | | Africa | 46 out of 51 |
| South Africa | 7.7 | 8.1 | BBB- | 60 | Emerging | Africa | 2 out of 51 |
| Spain | 5.9 | 6.0 | BBB+ | 38 | Developed | Western Europe | 16 out of 19 |
| Sri Lanka | 10.0 | 9.9 | B+ | 72 | Frontier | Asia | 14 out of 29 |
| Sudan | 21.3 | 21.5 | | 154 | | Africa | 40 out of 51 |
| Suriname | 13.5 | 13.9 | B+ | 102 | | Latin America | 16 out of 20 |
| Swaziland | 19.6 | 20.8 | | 152 | | Africa | 38 out of 51 |
| Sweden | 0.0 | 0.0 | AAA | 7 | Developed | Western Europe | 6 out of 19 |

§ S&P Credit Rating based on long-term foreign currency issuer rating. See http://www.standardandpoors.com/.

* World rank based on 175 countries covered by Euromoney. Ranking based on ascending order in which '1' equals the smallest country risk premium (CRP) and '175' equals the largest country risk premium (CRP).

† MSCI Market Classification based on MSCI Market Classification Framework. See http://www.msci.com/products/indexes/market_classification.html.

‡ Regional classification based on Euromoney. Regional rankings based on ascending order in which '1' equals the smallest country risk premium (CRP) for each region.

Note: A CRP of 0.0% is assumed in the following cases: (i) when the investor country and the investee country both have an S&P sovereign credit rating of AAA; or (ii) when the investor country has an S&P credit rating of AAA, and the investee country has a sovereign credit rating below AAA, but has a calculated CRP below 0.0% (which would imply lower risk than a country rated AAA); or (iii) when the investor country has an S&P credit rating below AAA, and the investee country has a sovereign credit rating of AAA, but has a calculated CRP above 0.0% (which would imply greater risk than a country rated below AAA). For purposes of this analysis, the U.S. is treated as having a sovereign credit rating equivalent to AAA.

The country risk premium (CRP) is not the cost of equity capital (COE). The CRP is to be added to base COE. See Chapter 6 for proper application.

## Data Updated Through March 2017

| Investee Country | December 2016 Country Risk Premium (CRP) (%) | March 2017 Country Risk Premium (CRP) (%) | S&P Sovereign Credit Rating § | World Rank Out of 175* | MSCI Market Classification † | Euromoney Region ‡ | Regional Rank ‡ |
|---|---|---|---|---|---|---|---|
| Switzerland | 0.0 | 0.0 | AAA | 2 | Developed | Western Europe | 1 out of 19 |
| Syria | 26.3 | 26.7 | | 167 | | Middle East | 13 out of 13 |
| Taiwan | 2.8 | 2.9 | AA- | 18 | Emerging | Asia | 3 out of 29 |
| Tajikistan | 20.9 | 21.5 | | 155 | | Central and Eastern Europe | 25 out of 25 |
| Tanzania | 12.9 | 13.3 | | 95 | | Africa | 13 out of 51 |
| Thailand | 7.1 | 7.1 | BBB+ | 51 | Emerging | Asia | 8 out of 29 |
| Togo | 14.6 | 14.7 | | 113 | | Africa | 20 out of 51 |
| Tonga | 29.8 | 30.0 | | 170 | | Australasia | 7 out of 7 |
| Trinidad & Tobago | 7.5 | 7.6 | A- | 54 | | Caribbean | 2 out of 9 |
| Tunisia | 10.4 | 11.0 | | 79 | Frontier | Africa | 6 out of 51 |
| Turkey | 7.8 | 7.9 | BB | 58 | Emerging | Central and Eastern Europe | 11 out of 25 |
| Turkmenistan | 18.0 | 18.5 | | 140 | | Asia | 24 out of 29 |
| Uganda | 14.0 | 14.5 | B | 110 | | Africa | 18 out of 51 |
| Ukraine | 17.0 | 17.3 | B- | 135 | | Central and Eastern Europe | 20 out of 25 |
| United Arab Emirates | 4.6 | 4.8 | AA | 33 | Emerging | Middle East | 4 out of 13 |
| United Kingdom | 3.0 | 3.3 | AA | 20 | Developed | Western Europe | 11 out of 19 |
| United States | 0.0 | 0.0 | AA+ | 15 | Developed | North America | 2 out of 2 |
| Uruguay | 6.5 | 6.5 | BBB | 45 | | Latin America | 5 out of 20 |
| Uzbekistan | 17.2 | 16.8 | | 132 | | Asia | 21 out of 29 |
| Vanuatu | 18.9 | 19.1 | | 145 | | Australasia | 4 out of 7 |
| Venezuela | 22.8 | 23.4 | CCC | 162 | | Latin America | 20 out of 20 |
| Vietnam | 11.0 | 10.9 | BB- | 78 | Frontier | Asia | 16 out of 29 |
| Yemen | 23.1 | 23.4 | | 161 | | Middle East | 12 out of 13 |
| Zambia | 14.4 | 14.6 | B | 111 | | Africa | 19 out of 51 |
| Zimbabwe | 24.8 | 24.9 | | 164 | | Africa | 44 out of 51 |

## March 2017 Country Risk Premium (CRP) Summary Statistics:

| S&P Rating | Country Count | Average CRP (%) | Median CRP (%) | Min CRP (%) | Max CRP (%) |
|---|---|---|---|---|---|
| AAA ** | 12 | 0.0 | 0.0 | 0.0 | 0.0 |
| AA (AA+, AA, AA-) | 15 | 3.2 | 3.3 | 1.0 | 6.3 |
| A (A+, A, A-) | 14 | 5.3 | 5.4 | 3.8 | 7.6 |
| BBB (BBB+, BBB, BBB-) | 17 | 7.1 | 7.1 | 4.3 | 9.6 |
| BB (BB+, BB, BB-) | 22 | 10.1 | 10.1 | 6.1 | 15.8 |
| B+ − SD | 39 | 15.0 | 14.6 | 9.9 | 23.4 |
| Investment Grade ** | 58 | 4.2 | 4.4 | 0.0 | 9.6 |
| Non-Investment Grade ** | 61 | 13.3 | 13.5 | 6.1 | 23.4 |
| **MSCI Market Classification** | | | | | |
| Developed Markets | 23 | 1.9 | 1.0 | 0.0 | 6.9 |
| Emerging Markets | 23 | 6.8 | 6.3 | 2.5 | 15.0 |
| Frontier Markets | 22 | 9.9 | 9.7 | 4.4 | 15.8 |
| **Euromoney Region ‡** | | | | | |
| Africa | 51 | 17.6 | 15.6 | 6.6 | 38.8 |
| Asia | 29 | 12.1 | 10.7 | 0.0 | 36.1 |
| Australasia | 7 | 16.0 | 19.1 | 0.0 | 30.0 |
| Caribbean | 9 | 13.5 | 13.0 | 6.5 | 23.1 |
| Central and Eastern Europe | 25 | 10.5 | 8.4 | 3.6 | 21.5 |
| Latin America | 20 | 11.1 | 11.8 | 2.5 | 23.4 |
| Middle East | 13 | 11.3 | 8.7 | 3.4 | 26.7 |
| North America | 2 | 0.0 | 0.0 | 0.0 | 0.0 |
| Western Europe | 19 | 3.1 | 2.7 | 0.0 | 14.2 |

## CCR Base Cost of Equity Capital:

| Switzerland | COE (%) |
|---|---|
| March 2017 | 4.9 |
| December 2016 | 5.0 |

CCR base country-level COE for a Switzerland-based investor investing in Switzerland.

§ S&P Credit Rating based on long-term foreign currency issuer rating. See http://www.standardandpoors.com/.

* World rank based on 175 countries covered by Euromoney. Ranking based on ascending order in which '1' equals the smallest country risk premium (CRP) and '175' equals the largest country risk premium (CRP).

† MSCI Market Classification based on MSCI Market Classification Framework. See http://www.msci.com/products/indexes/market_classification.html.

‡ Regional classification based on Euromoney. Regional rankings based on ascending order in which '1' equals the smallest country risk premium (CRP) for each region.

** Investment grade based on S&P sovereign credit rating from AAA to BBB-. Non-Investment grade based on S&P sovereign credit rating from BB+ to SD. For purposes of this analysis, the U.S. is being treated as if it were rated AAA by S&P.

Note: A CRP of 0.0% is assumed in the following cases: (i) when the investor country and the investee country both have an S&P sovereign credit rating of AAA; or (ii) when the investor country has an S&P credit rating of AAA, and the investee country has a sovereign credit rating below AAA, but has a calculated CRP below 0.0% (which would imply lower risk than a country rated AAA); or (iii) when the investor country has an S&P credit rating below AAA, and the investee country has a sovereign credit rating equivalent to AAA, but has a calculated CRP above 0.0% (which would imply greater risk than a country rated below AAA). For purposes of this analysis, the U.S. is treated as having a sovereign credit rating equivalent to AAA.

Investor Perspective: Taiwan
Currency: New Taiwan Dollar (TWD)

Erb-Harvey-Viskanta
Country Credit Rating (CCR) Model

The country risk premium (CRP) is not the cost of equity capital (COE). The CRP is to be added to base COE. See Chapter 6 for proper application.

## Data Updated Through March 2017

| Investee Country | December 2016 Country Risk Premium (CRP) (%) | March 2017 Country Risk Premium (CRP) (%) | S&P Sovereign Credit Rating § | World Rank Out of 175* | MSCI Market Classification † | Euromoney Region ‡ | Regional Rank ‡ |
|---|---|---|---|---|---|---|---|
| Afghanistan | 15.1 | 14.8 | | 139 | | Asia | 23 out of 29 |
| Albania | 9.7 | 9.9 | B+ | 93 | | Central and Eastern Europe | 18 out of 25 |
| Algeria | 9.8 | 9.8 | | 91 | | Africa | 10 out of 51 |
| Angola | 12.1 | 12.2 | B | 121 | | Africa | 26 out of 51 |
| Argentina | 10.3 | 10.0 | B- | 96 | Frontier | Latin America | 13 out of 20 |
| Armenia | 7.3 | 7.5 | | 77 | | Asia | 15 out of 29 |
| Australia | -1.5 | -1.6 | AAA | 12 | Developed | Australasia | 2 out of 7 |
| Austria | -1.4 | -1.4 | AA+ | 13 | Developed | Western Europe | 9 out of 19 |
| Azerbaijan | 8.5 | 8.9 | BB+ | 85 | | Asia | 17 out of 29 |
| Bahamas | 5.9 | 5.6 | BB+ | 65 | | Caribbean | 3 out of 9 |
| Bahrain | 5.8 | 5.6 | BB- | 64 | Frontier | Middle East | 7 out of 13 |
| Bangladesh | 12.6 | 12.4 | BB- | 126 | Frontier | Asia | 20 out of 29 |
| Barbados | 7.5 | 8.6 | CCC+ | 82 | | Caribbean | 4 out of 9 |
| Belarus | 14.8 | 15.2 | B- | 143 | | Central and Eastern Europe | 23 out of 25 |
| Belgium | -0.1 | -0.2 | AA | 17 | Developed | Western Europe | 10 out of 19 |
| Belize | 10.8 | 10.8 | B- | 106 | | Latin America | 17 out of 20 |
| Benin | 16.5 | 16.5 | | 150 | | Africa | 37 out of 51 |
| Bermuda | 3.5 | 3.4 | A+ | 44 | | Caribbean | 1 out of 9 |
| Bhutan | 16.2 | 16.0 | | 148 | | Asia | 25 out of 29 |
| Bolivia | 9.3 | 9.5 | BB | 88 | | Latin America | 12 out of 20 |
| Bosnia & Herzegovina | 15.3 | 15.4 | B | 144 | | Central and Eastern Europe | 24 out of 25 |
| Botswana | 3.5 | 3.5 | A- | 48 | | Africa | 1 out of 51 |
| Brazil | 5.0 | 4.9 | BB | 59 | Emerging | Latin America | 7 out of 20 |
| Bulgaria | 4.9 | 5.0 | BB+ | 61 | | Central and Eastern Europe | 12 out of 25 |
| Burkina Faso | 13.6 | 13.6 | B- | 133 | | Africa | 33 out of 51 |
| Burundi | 25.4 | 25.4 | | 169 | | Africa | 47 out of 51 |
| Cambodia | 17.1 | 16.7 | | 151 | | Asia | 27 out of 29 |
| Cameroon | 12.3 | 12.3 | B | 124 | | Africa | 28 out of 51 |
| Canada | -1.7 | -1.8 | AAA | 9 | Developed | North America | 1 out of 2 |
| Cape Verde | 9.9 | 9.9 | B | 94 | | Africa | 12 out of 51 |
| Central African Republic | 28.9 | 29.0 | | 172 | | Africa | 49 out of 51 |
| Chad | 27.6 | 27.6 | | 171 | | Africa | 48 out of 51 |
| Chile | -0.6 | -0.4 | AA- | 16 | Emerging | Latin America | 1 out of 20 |
| China | 3.3 | 3.3 | AA- | 42 | Emerging | Asia | 7 out of 29 |
| Colombia | 3.3 | 3.3 | BBB | 41 | Emerging | Latin America | 4 out of 20 |
| Congo Republic | 11.9 | 11.7 | B- | 117 | | Africa | 24 out of 51 |
| Congo, DR | 13.1 | 13.1 | B- | 131 | | Africa | 32 out of 51 |
| Costa Rica | 6.3 | 6.5 | BB- | 71 | | Latin America | 8 out of 20 |
| Côte d'Ivoire | 9.8 | 9.8 | | 92 | | Africa | 11 out of 51 |
| Croatia | 5.4 | 5.3 | BB | 63 | Frontier | Central and Eastern Europe | 13 out of 25 |
| Cuba | 19.3 | 19.5 | | 160 | | Caribbean | 9 out of 9 |
| Cyprus | 3.0 | 3.1 | BB+ | 40 | | Central and Eastern Europe | 7 out of 25 |
| Czech Republic | 0.7 | 0.6 | AA- | 23 | Emerging | Central and Eastern Europe | 1 out of 25 |
| Denmark | -2.4 | -2.4 | AAA | 4 | Developed | Western Europe | 3 out of 19 |
| Djibouti | 36.8 | 34.6 | | 175 | | Africa | 51 out of 51 |
| Dominican Republic | 9.6 | 9.7 | BB- | 90 | | Caribbean | 5 out of 9 |
| Ecuador | 11.2 | 11.0 | B | 109 | | Latin America | 18 out of 20 |
| Egypt | 11.6 | 11.6 | B- | 116 | Emerging | Africa | 23 out of 51 |
| El Salvador | 8.7 | 8.5 | B- | 81 | | Latin America | 10 out of 20 |
| Equatorial Guinea | 21.8 | 21.9 | | 165 | | Africa | 45 out of 51 |

§ S&P Credit Rating based on long-term foreign currency issuer rating. See http://www.standardandpoors.com/.
* World rank based on 175 countries covered by Euromoney. Ranking based on ascending order in which '1' equals the smallest country risk premium (CRP) and '175' equals the largest country risk premium (CRP).
† MSCI Market Classification based on MSCI Market Classification Framework. See http://www.msci.com/products/indexes/market_classification.html
‡ Regional classification based on Euromoney. Regional rankings based on ascending order in which '1' equals the smallest country risk premium (CRP) for each region.
Note: A CRP of 0.0% is assumed in the following cases: (i) when the investor country and the investee country both have an S&P sovereign credit rating of AAA; or (ii) when the investor country has an S&P credit rating of AAA, and the investee country has a sovereign credit rating below AAA, but has a calculated CRP below 0.0% (which would imply lower risk than a country rated AAA); or (iii) when the investor country has an S&P credit rating below AAA, and the investee country has a sovereign credit rating of AAA, but has a calculated CRP above 0.0% (which would imply greater risk than a country rated below AAA). For purposes of this analysis, the U.S. is treated as having a sovereign credit rating equivalent to AAA.

2017 Valuation Handbook – International Guide to Cost of Capital | Data Exhibit 4 | Investor Perspective: Taiwan (TWD); Page 1 of 4

The country risk premium (CRP) is not the cost of equity capital (COE). The CRP is to be added to base COE. See Chapter 6 for proper application.

### Data Updated Through March 2017

| Investee Country | December 2016 Country Risk Premium (CRP) (%) | March 2017 Country Risk Premium (CRP) (%) | S&P Sovereign Credit Rating § | World Rank Out of 175* | MSCI Market Classification † | Euromoney Region ‡ | Regional Rank ‡ |
|---|---|---|---|---|---|---|---|
| Eritrea | 33.0 | 31.3 | | 173 | | Africa | 50 out of 51 |
| Estonia | 1.3 | 1.5 | AA- | 32 | Frontier | Central and Eastern Europe | 4 out of 25 |
| Ethiopia | 10.5 | 10.5 | B | 101 | | Africa | 16 out of 51 |
| Fiji | 15.8 | 15.7 | B+ | 147 | | Australasia | 5 out of 7 |
| Finland | -1.6 | -1.7 | AA+ | 11 | Developed | Western Europe | 8 out of 19 |
| France | 0.7 | 0.5 | AA | 22 | Developed | Western Europe | 12 out of 19 |
| Gabon | 8.3 | 8.6 | | 83 | | Africa | 7 out of 51 |
| Gambia | 14.3 | 14.3 | | 138 | | Africa | 34 out of 51 |
| Georgia | 7.0 | 7.3 | BB- | 74 | | Central and Eastern Europe | 15 out of 25 |
| Germany | -1.6 | -1.7 | AAA | 10 | Developed | Western Europe | 7 out of 19 |
| Ghana | 10.0 | 9.6 | B- | 89 | | Africa | 9 out of 51 |
| Greece | 11.1 | 10.9 | B- | 108 | Emerging | Western Europe | 19 out of 19 |
| Grenada | 10.7 | 10.8 | | 105 | | Caribbean | 7 out of 9 |
| Guatemala | 8.7 | 8.7 | BB | 84 | | Latin America | 11 out of 20 |
| Guinea | 18.0 | 18.0 | | 156 | | Africa | 41 out of 51 |
| Guinea-Bissau | 11.6 | 11.6 | | 115 | | Africa | 22 out of 51 |
| Guyana | 10.4 | 10.4 | | 100 | | Latin America | 15 out of 20 |
| Haiti | 20.8 | 18.8 | | 157 | | Caribbean | 8 out of 9 |
| Honduras | 10.1 | 10.1 | B+ | 98 | | Latin America | 14 out of 20 |
| Hong Kong | -1.1 | -1.1 | AAA | 14 | Developed | Asia | 2 out of 29 |
| Hungary | 4.6 | 4.8 | BBB- | 57 | Emerging | Central and Eastern Europe | 10 out of 25 |
| Iceland | 1.7 | 1.4 | A | 30 | | Western Europe | 15 out of 19 |
| India | 4.4 | 4.7 | BBB- | 55 | Emerging | Asia | 10 out of 29 |
| Indonesia | 5.2 | 5.2 | BB+ | 62 | Emerging | Asia | 11 out of 29 |
| Iran | 12.1 | 12.3 | | 125 | | Middle East | 10 out of 13 |
| Iraq | 13.9 | 13.9 | B- | 136 | | Middle East | 11 out of 13 |
| Ireland | 1.2 | 1.1 | A+ | 27 | Developed | Western Europe | 14 out of 19 |
| Israel | 1.1 | 1.1 | A+ | 28 | Developed | Middle East | 2 out of 13 |
| Italy | 4.0 | 3.9 | BBB- | 50 | Developed | Western Europe | 18 out of 19 |
| Jamaica | 10.2 | 10.8 | B | 104 | | Caribbean | 6 out of 9 |
| Japan | 1.0 | 1.0 | A+ | 25 | Developed | Asia | 5 out of 29 |
| Jordan | 7.3 | 7.5 | BB- | 76 | Frontier | Middle East | 8 out of 13 |
| Kazakhstan | 6.8 | 6.4 | BBB- | 70 | Frontier | Asia | 13 out of 29 |
| Kenya | 10.2 | 10.3 | B+ | 99 | Frontier | Africa | 15 out of 51 |
| Korea (North) | 32.4 | 32.0 | | 174 | | Asia | 29 out of 29 |
| Korea (South) | 0.3 | 0.3 | AA | 19 | Emerging | Asia | 4 out of 29 |
| Kuwait | 1.3 | 1.5 | AA | 31 | Frontier | Middle East | 3 out of 13 |
| Kyrgyz Republic | 15.3 | 15.2 | | 142 | | Central and Eastern Europe | 22 out of 25 |
| Laos | 19.6 | 19.0 | | 158 | | Asia | 28 out of 29 |
| Latvia | 3.3 | 3.4 | A- | 43 | | Central and Eastern Europe | 8 out of 25 |
| Lebanon | 12.0 | 11.3 | B- | 112 | Frontier | Middle East | 9 out of 13 |
| Lesotho | 15.5 | 15.6 | | 146 | | Africa | 36 out of 51 |
| Liberia | 10.8 | 10.9 | | 107 | | Africa | 17 out of 51 |
| Libya | 17.0 | 17.4 | | 153 | | Africa | 39 out of 51 |
| Lithuania | 2.5 | 2.6 | A- | 36 | Frontier | Central and Eastern Europe | 6 out of 25 |
| Luxembourg | -2.1 | -2.1 | AAA | 5 | | Western Europe | 4 out of 19 |
| Macedonia | 9.3 | 9.5 | BB- | 87 | | Central and Eastern Europe | 17 out of 25 |
| Madagascar | 11.7 | 12.2 | | 123 | | Africa | 27 out of 51 |
| Malawi | 11.4 | 11.4 | | 114 | | Africa | 21 out of 51 |
| Malaysia | 2.7 | 2.6 | A- | 35 | Emerging | Asia | 6 out of 29 |

§ S&P Credit Rating based on long-term foreign currency issuer rating. See http://www.standardandpoors.com/.

* World rank based on 175 countries covered by Euromoney. Ranking based on ascending order in which '1' equals the smallest country risk premium (CRP) and '175' equals the largest country risk premium (CRP).

† MSCI Market Classification based on MSCI Market Classification Framework. See http://www.msci.com/products/indexes/market_classification.html.

‡ Regional classification based on Euromoney. Regional rankings based on ascending order in which '1' equals the smallest country risk premium (CRP) for each region.

Note: A CRP of 0.0% is assumed in the following cases: (i) when the investor country and the investee country both have an S&P sovereign credit rating of AAA; or (ii) when the investor country has an S&P credit rating of AAA, and the investee country has a sovereign credit rating below AAA, but has a calculated CRP below 0.0% (which would imply lower risk than a country rated AAA); or (iii) when the investor country has an S&P credit rating below AAA, and the investee country has a sovereign credit rating of AAA, but has a calculated CRP above 0.0% (which would imply greater risk than a country rated below AAA). For purposes of this analysis, the U.S. is treated as having a sovereign credit rating equivalent to AAA.

The country risk premium (CRP) is not the cost of equity capital (COE). The CRP is to be added to base COE. See Chapter 6 for proper application.

## Data Updated Through March 2017

| Investee Country | December 2016 Country Risk Premium (CRP) (%) | March 2017 Country Risk Premium (CRP) (%) | S&P Sovereign Credit Rating § | World Rank Out of 175• | MSCI Market Classification † | Euromoney Region ‡ | Regional Rank ‡ |
|---|---|---|---|---|---|---|---|
| Mali | 15.1 | 15.2 | | 141 | | Africa | 35 out of 51 |
| Malta | 1.0 | 1.1 | A- | 26 | | Western Europe | 13 out of 19 |
| Mauritania | 19.2 | 19.2 | | 159 | | Africa | 42 out of 51 |
| Mauritius | 6.1 | 6.1 | | 67 | Frontier | Asia | 12 out of 29 |
| Mexico | 2.6 | 2.7 | BBB+ | 37 | Emerging | Latin America | 2 out of 20 |
| Moldova | 13.6 | 14.0 | | 137 | | Central and Eastern Europe | 21 out of 25 |
| Mongolia | 11.8 | 12.1 | B- | 119 | | Asia | 18 out of 29 |
| Montenegro | 11.0 | 10.8 | B+ | 103 | | Central and Eastern Europe | 19 out of 25 |
| Morocco | 6.1 | 6.3 | BBB- | 69 | Frontier | Africa | 4 out of 51 |
| Mozambique | 12.8 | 12.7 | SD | 128 | | Africa | 29 out of 51 |
| Myanmar | 13.8 | 13.7 | | 134 | | Asia | 22 out of 29 |
| Namibia | 5.8 | 5.9 | | 66 | | Africa | 3 out of 51 |
| Nepal | 16.4 | 16.5 | | 149 | | Asia | 26 out of 29 |
| Netherlands | -2.0 | -2.1 | AAA | 6 | Developed | Western Europe | 5 out of 19 |
| New Zealand | -1.9 | -1.9 | AA | 8 | Developed | Australasia | 1 out of 7 |
| Nicaragua | 12.5 | 12.5 | B+ | 127 | | Latin America | 19 out of 20 |
| Niger | 12.1 | 12.1 | | 120 | | Africa | 25 out of 51 |
| Nigeria | 10.1 | 10.1 | B | 97 | Frontier | Africa | 14 out of 51 |
| Norway | -2.7 | -2.8 | AAA | 3 | Developed | Western Europe | 2 out of 19 |
| Oman | 3.5 | 3.5 | BBB- | 46 | Frontier | Middle East | 5 out of 13 |
| Pakistan | 12.2 | 12.2 | B | 122 | Frontier | Asia | 19 out of 29 |
| Panama | 4.2 | 4.2 | BBB | 52 | | Latin America | 6 out of 20 |
| Papua New Guinea | 11.7 | 11.8 | B+ | 118 | | Australasia | 3 out of 7 |
| Paraguay | 7.7 | 7.9 | BB | 80 | | Latin America | 9 out of 20 |
| Peru | 2.9 | 3.0 | BBB+ | 39 | Emerging | Latin America | 3 out of 20 |
| Philippines | 4.5 | 4.5 | BBB | 53 | Emerging | Asia | 9 out of 29 |
| Poland | 1.5 | 1.4 | BBB+ | 29 | Emerging | Central and Eastern Europe | 3 out of 25 |
| Portugal | 3.9 | 3.7 | BB+ | 49 | Developed | Western Europe | 17 out of 19 |
| Qatar | 0.4 | 0.4 | AA | 21 | Emerging | Middle East | 1 out of 13 |
| Romania | 4.7 | 4.7 | BBB- | 56 | Frontier | Central and Eastern Europe | 9 out of 25 |
| Russia | 6.9 | 6.3 | BB+ | 68 | Emerging | Central and Eastern Europe | 14 out of 25 |
| Rwanda | 12.9 | 12.9 | B | 130 | | Africa | 31 out of 51 |
| São Tomé & Príncipe | 19.3 | 19.8 | | 163 | | Africa | 43 out of 51 |
| Saudi Arabia | 3.8 | 3.5 | A- | 47 | | Middle East | 6 out of 13 |
| Senegal | 9.5 | 9.5 | B+ | 86 | | Africa | 8 out of 51 |
| Serbia | 7.6 | 7.3 | BB- | 75 | Frontier | Central and Eastern Europe | 16 out of 25 |
| Seychelles | 7.1 | 7.1 | | 73 | | Africa | 5 out of 51 |
| Sierra Leone | 12.9 | 12.9 | | 129 | | Africa | 30 out of 51 |
| Singapore | -2.9 | -2.9 | AAA | 1 | Developed | Asia | 1 out of 29 |
| Slovakia | 0.8 | 0.8 | A+ | 24 | | Central and Eastern Europe | 2 out of 25 |
| Slovenia | 2.2 | 2.2 | A | 34 | Frontier | Central and Eastern Europe | 5 out of 25 |
| Solomon Islands | 23.6 | 23.7 | | 168 | | Australasia | 6 out of 7 |
| Somalia | 21.9 | 21.9 | | 166 | | Africa | 46 out of 51 |
| South Africa | 4.7 | 5.0 | BBB- | 60 | Emerging | Africa | 2 out of 51 |
| Spain | 3.0 | 3.0 | BBB+ | 38 | Developed | Western Europe | 16 out of 19 |
| Sri Lanka | 7.0 | 6.7 | B+ | 72 | Frontier | Asia | 14 out of 29 |
| Sudan | 17.9 | 17.9 | | 154 | | Africa | 40 out of 51 |
| Suriname | 10.4 | 10.6 | B+ | 102 | | Latin America | 16 out of 20 |
| Swaziland | 16.2 | 17.2 | | 152 | | Africa | 38 out of 51 |
| Sweden | -2.0 | -2.1 | AAA | 7 | Developed | Western Europe | 6 out of 19 |

§ S&P Credit Rating based on long-term foreign currency issuer rating. See http://www.standardandpoors.com/.

• World rank based on 175 countries covered by Euromoney. Ranking based on ascending order in which '1' equals the smallest country risk premium (CRP) and '175' equals the largest country risk premium (CRP).

† MSCI Market Classification based on MSCI Market Classification Framework. See http://www.msci.com/products/indexes/market_classification.html

‡ Regional classification based on Euromoney. Regional rankings based on ascending order in which '1' equals the smallest country risk premium (CRP) for each region.

Note: A CRP of 0.0% is assumed in the following cases: (i) when the investor country and the investee country both have an S&P sovereign credit rating of AAA; or (ii) when the investor country has an S&P credit rating of AAA, and the investee country has a sovereign credit rating below AAA, but has a calculated CRP below 0.0% (which would imply lower risk than a country rated AAA); or (iii) when the investor country has an S&P credit rating below AAA, and the investee country has a sovereign credit rating of AAA, but has a calculated CRP above 0.0% (which would imply greater risk than a country rated below AAA). For purposes of this analysis, the U.S. is treated as having a sovereign credit rating equivalent to AAA.

The country risk premium (CRP) is not the cost of equity capital (COE). The CRP is to be added to base COE. See Chapter 6 for proper application.

## Data Updated Through March 2017

| Investee Country | December 2016 Country Risk Premium (CRP) (%) | March 2017 Country Risk Premium (CRP) (%) | S&P Sovereign Credit Rating § | World Rank Out of 175* | MSCI Market Classification † | Euromoney Region ‡ | Regional Rank ‡ |
|---|---|---|---|---|---|---|---|
| Switzerland | -2.6 | -2.8 | AAA | 2 | Developed | Western Europe | 1 out of 19 |
| Syria | 22.7 | 22.9 | | 167 | | Middle East | 13 out of 13 |
| Taiwan | 0.0 | 0.0 | AA- | 18 | Emerging | Asia | 3 out of 29 |
| Tajikistan | 17.5 | 17.9 | | 155 | | Central and Eastern Europe | 25 out of 25 |
| Tanzania | 9.8 | 10.0 | | 95 | | Africa | 13 out of 51 |
| Thailand | 4.2 | 4.0 | BBB+ | 51 | Emerging | Asia | 8 out of 29 |
| Togo | 11.4 | 11.4 | | 113 | | Africa | 20 out of 51 |
| Tonga | 26.1 | 26.1 | | 170 | | Australasia | 7 out of 7 |
| Trinidad & Tobago | 4.5 | 4.5 | A- | 54 | | Caribbean | 2 out of 9 |
| Tunisia | 7.4 | 7.7 | | 79 | Frontier | Africa | 6 out of 51 |
| Turkey | 4.9 | 4.8 | BB | 58 | Emerging | Central and Eastern Europe | 11 out of 25 |
| Turkmenistan | 14.7 | 15.0 | | 140 | | Asia | 24 out of 29 |
| Uganda | 10.9 | 11.2 | B | 110 | | Africa | 18 out of 51 |
| Ukraine | 13.7 | 13.8 | B- | 135 | | Central and Eastern Europe | 20 out of 25 |
| United Arab Emirates | 1.8 | 1.8 | AA | 33 | Emerging | Middle East | 4 out of 13 |
| United Kingdom | 0.3 | 0.4 | AA | 20 | Developed | Western Europe | 11 out of 19 |
| United States | -0.8 | -0.8 | AA+ | 15 | Developed | North America | 2 out of 2 |
| Uruguay | 3.6 | 3.4 | BBB | 45 | | Latin America | 5 out of 20 |
| Uzbekistan | 13.9 | 13.3 | | 132 | | Asia | 21 out of 29 |
| Vanuatu | 15.5 | 15.5 | | 145 | | Australasia | 4 out of 7 |
| Venezuela | 19.3 | 19.7 | CCC | 162 | | Latin America | 20 out of 20 |
| Vietnam | 7.9 | 7.7 | BB- | 78 | Frontier | Asia | 16 out of 29 |
| Yemen | 19.6 | 19.7 | | 161 | | Middle East | 12 out of 13 |
| Zambia | 11.2 | 11.3 | B | 111 | | Africa | 19 out of 51 |
| Zimbabwe | 21.2 | 21.2 | | 164 | | Africa | 44 out of 51 |

### March 2017 Country Risk Premium (CRP) Summary Statistics:

| S&P Rating | Country Count | Average CRP (%) | Median CRP (%) | Min CRP (%) | Max CRP (%) |
|---|---|---|---|---|---|
| AAA ** | 12 | -2.0 | -2.1 | -2.9 | -0.8 |
| AA (AA+, AA, AA-) | 15 | 0.3 | 0.4 | -1.9 | 3.3 |
| A (A+, A, A-) | 14 | 2.3 | 2.4 | 0.8 | 4.5 |
| BBB (BBB+, BBB, BBB-) | 17 | 4.0 | 4.0 | 1.4 | 6.4 |
| BB (BB+, BB, BB-) | 22 | 6.9 | 6.9 | 3.1 | 12.4 |
| B+ − SD | 39 | 11.7 | 11.3 | 6.7 | 19.7 |
| Investment Grade ** | 58 | 1.4 | 1.4 | -2.9 | 6.4 |
| Non-Investment Grade ** | 61 | 10.0 | 10.1 | 3.1 | 19.7 |
| **MSCI Market Classification** | | | | | |
| Developed Markets | 23 | -0.5 | -1.4 | -2.9 | 3.9 |
| Emerging Markets | 23 | 3.7 | 3.3 | -0.4 | 11.6 |
| Frontier Markets | 22 | 6.8 | 6.6 | 1.5 | 12.4 |
| **Euromoney Region ‡** | | | | | |
| Africa | 51 | 14.2 | 12.2 | 3.5 | 34.6 |
| Asia | 29 | 8.9 | 7.5 | -2.9 | 32.0 |
| Australasia | 7 | 12.8 | 15.5 | -1.9 | 26.1 |
| Caribbean | 9 | 10.2 | 9.7 | 3.4 | 19.5 |
| Central and Eastern Europe | 25 | 7.3 | 5.3 | 0.6 | 17.9 |
| Latin America | 20 | 7.9 | 8.6 | -0.4 | 19.7 |
| Middle East | 13 | 8.1 | 5.6 | 0.4 | 22.9 |
| North America | 2 | -1.3 | -1.3 | -1.8 | -0.8 |
| Western Europe | 19 | 0.4 | -0.2 | -2.8 | 10.9 |

### CCR Base Cost of Equity Capital:

| Taiwan | COE (%) |
|---|---|
| March 2017 | 8.7 |
| December 2016 | 8.9 |

CCR base country-level COE for a Taiwan-based investor investing in Taiwan.

§ S&P Credit Rating based on long-term foreign currency issuer rating. See http://www.standardandpoors.com/.

* World rank based on 175 countries covered by Euromoney. Ranking based on ascending order in which '1' equals the smallest country risk premium (CRP) and '175' equals the largest country risk premium (CRP).

† MSCI Market Classification based on MSCI Market Classification Framework. See http://www.msci.com/products/indexes/market_classification.html

‡ Regional classification based on Euromoney. Regional rankings based on ascending order in which '1' equals the smallest country risk premium (CRP) for each region.

** Investment grade based on S&P sovereign credit rating from AAA to BBB-. Non-Investment grade based on S&P sovereign credit rating from BB+ to SD. For purposes of this analysis, the U.S. is being treated as if it were rated AAA by S&P.

Note: A CRP of 0.0% is assumed in the following cases: (i) when the investor country and the investee country both have an S&P sovereign credit rating of AAA; or (ii) when the investor country has an S&P credit rating of AAA, and the investee country has a sovereign credit rating below AAA, but has a calculated CRP below 0.0% (which would imply lower risk than a country rated AAA); or (iii) when the investor country has an S&P credit rating below AAA, and the investee country has a sovereign credit rating of AAA, but has a calculated CRP above 0.0% (which would imply greater risk than a country rated below AAA). For purposes of this analysis, the U.S. is treated as having a sovereign credit rating equivalent to AAA.

The country risk premium (CRP) is not the cost of equity capital (COE). The CRP is to be added to base COE. See Chapter 6 for proper application.

## Data Updated Through March 2017

| Investee Country | December 2016 Country Risk Premium (CRP) (%) | March 2017 Country Risk Premium (CRP) (%) | S&P Sovereign Credit Rating § | World Rank Out of 175• | MSCI Market Classification † | Euromoney Region ‡ | Regional Rank ‡ |
|---|---|---|---|---|---|---|---|
| Afghanistan | 10.9 | 10.9 | | 139 | | Asia | 23 out of 29 |
| Albania | 5.5 | 5.9 | B+ | 93 | | Central and Eastern Europe | 18 out of 25 |
| Algeria | 5.5 | 5.8 | | 91 | | Africa | 10 out of 51 |
| Angola | 7.9 | 8.2 | B | 121 | | Africa | 26 out of 51 |
| Argentina | 6.1 | 6.0 | B- | 96 | Frontier | Latin America | 13 out of 20 |
| Armenia | 3.1 | 3.5 | | 77 | | Asia | 15 out of 29 |
| Australia | -5.7 | -5.7 | AAA | 12 | Developed | Australasia | 2 out of 7 |
| Austria | -5.6 | -5.5 | AA+ | 13 | Developed | Western Europe | 9 out of 19 |
| Azerbaijan | 4.3 | 4.8 | BB+ | 85 | | Asia | 17 out of 29 |
| Bahamas | 1.7 | 1.6 | BB+ | 65 | | Caribbean | 3 out of 9 |
| Bahrain | 1.6 | 1.6 | BB- | 64 | Frontier | Middle East | 7 out of 13 |
| Bangladesh | 8.4 | 8.4 | BB- | 126 | Frontier | Asia | 20 out of 29 |
| Barbados | 3.3 | 4.6 | CCC+ | 82 | | Caribbean | 4 out of 9 |
| Belarus | 10.6 | 11.2 | B- | 143 | | Central and Eastern Europe | 23 out of 25 |
| Belgium | -4.3 | -4.3 | AA | 17 | Developed | Western Europe | 10 out of 19 |
| Belize | 6.5 | 6.8 | B- | 106 | | Latin America | 17 out of 20 |
| Benin | 12.2 | 12.5 | | 150 | | Africa | 37 out of 51 |
| Bermuda | -0.7 | -0.6 | A+ | 44 | | Caribbean | 1 out of 9 |
| Bhutan | 11.9 | 12.0 | | 148 | | Asia | 25 out of 29 |
| Bolivia | 5.1 | 5.5 | BB | 88 | | Latin America | 12 out of 20 |
| Bosnia & Herzegovina | 11.0 | 11.4 | B | 144 | | Central and Eastern Europe | 24 out of 25 |
| Botswana | -0.7 | -0.5 | A- | 48 | | Africa | 1 out of 51 |
| Brazil | 0.9 | 0.9 | BB | 59 | Emerging | Latin America | 7 out of 20 |
| Bulgaria | 0.7 | 1.0 | BB+ | 61 | | Central and Eastern Europe | 12 out of 25 |
| Burkina Faso | 9.4 | 9.7 | B- | 133 | | Africa | 33 out of 51 |
| Burundi | 21.2 | 21.5 | | 169 | | Africa | 47 out of 51 |
| Cambodia | 12.8 | 12.8 | | 151 | | Asia | 27 out of 29 |
| Cameroon | 8.1 | 8.3 | B | 124 | | Africa | 28 out of 51 |
| Canada | -5.9 | -5.9 | AAA | 9 | Developed | North America | 1 out of 2 |
| Cape Verde | 5.7 | 5.9 | B | 94 | | Africa | 12 out of 51 |
| Central African Republic | 24.6 | 25.0 | | 172 | | Africa | 49 out of 51 |
| Chad | 23.3 | 23.7 | | 171 | | Africa | 48 out of 51 |
| Chile | -4.7 | -4.4 | AA- | 16 | Emerging | Latin America | 1 out of 20 |
| China | -0.9 | -0.7 | AA- | 42 | Emerging | Asia | 7 out of 29 |
| Colombia | -0.9 | -0.8 | BBB | 41 | Emerging | Latin America | 4 out of 20 |
| Congo Republic | 7.7 | 7.7 | B- | 117 | | Africa | 24 out of 51 |
| Congo, DR | 8.9 | 9.1 | B- | 131 | | Africa | 32 out of 51 |
| Costa Rica | 2.1 | 2.5 | BB- | 71 | | Latin America | 8 out of 20 |
| Côte d'Ivoire | 5.6 | 5.8 | | 92 | | Africa | 11 out of 51 |
| Croatia | 1.2 | 1.2 | BB | 63 | Frontier | Central and Eastern Europe | 13 out of 25 |
| Cuba | 15.1 | 15.5 | | 160 | | Caribbean | 9 out of 9 |
| Cyprus | -1.2 | -0.9 | BB+ | 40 | | Central and Eastern Europe | 7 out of 25 |
| Czech Republic | -3.5 | -3.4 | AA- | 23 | Emerging | Central and Eastern Europe | 1 out of 25 |
| Denmark | -6.5 | -6.5 | AAA | 4 | Developed | Western Europe | 3 out of 19 |
| Djibouti | 32.5 | 30.7 | | 175 | | Africa | 51 out of 51 |
| Dominican Republic | 5.4 | 5.7 | BB- | 90 | | Caribbean | 5 out of 9 |
| Ecuador | 7.0 | 7.0 | B | 109 | | Latin America | 18 out of 20 |
| Egypt | 7.4 | 7.6 | B- | 116 | Emerging | Africa | 23 out of 51 |
| El Salvador | 4.5 | 4.5 | B- | 81 | | Latin America | 10 out of 20 |
| Equatorial Guinea | 17.6 | 17.9 | | 165 | | Africa | 45 out of 51 |

§ S&P Credit Rating based on long-term foreign currency issuer rating. See http://www.standardandpoors.com/.

• World rank based on 175 countries covered by Euromoney. Ranking based on ascending order in which '1' equals the smallest country risk premium (CRP) and '175' equals the largest country risk premium (CRP).

† MSCI Market Classification based on MSCI Market Classification Framework. See http://www.msci.com/products/indexes/market_classification.html

‡ Regional classification based on Euromoney. Regional rankings based on ascending order in which '1' equals the smallest country risk premium (CRP) for each region.

Note: A CRP of 0.0% is assumed in the following cases: (i) when the investor country and the investee country both have an S&P sovereign credit rating of AAA; or (ii) when the investor country has an S&P credit rating of AAA, and the investee country has a sovereign credit rating below AAA, but has a calculated CRP below 0.0% (which would imply lower risk than a country rated AAA); or (iii) when the investor country has an S&P credit rating below AAA, and the investee country has a sovereign credit rating of AAA, but has a calculated CRP above 0.0% (which would imply greater risk than a country rated below AAA). For purposes of this analysis, the U.S. is treated as having a sovereign credit rating equivalent to AAA.

The country risk premium (CRP) is not the cost of equity capital (COE). The CRP is to be added to base COE. See Chapter 6 for proper application.

## Data Updated Through March 2017

| Investee Country | December 2016 Country Risk Premium (CRP) (%) | March 2017 Country Risk Premium (CRP) (%) | S&P Sovereign Credit Rating § | World Rank Out of 175* | MSCI Market Classification † | Euromoney Region ‡ | Regional Rank ‡ |
|---|---|---|---|---|---|---|---|
| Eritrea | 28.8 | 27.4 | | 173 | | Africa | 50 out of 51 |
| Estonia | -2.9 | -2.5 | AA- | 32 | Frontier | Central and Eastern Europe | 4 out of 25 |
| Ethiopia | 6.3 | 6.5 | B | 101 | | Africa | 16 out of 51 |
| Fiji | 11.6 | 11.7 | B+ | 147 | | Australasia | 5 out of 7 |
| Finland | -5.8 | -5.7 | AA+ | 11 | Developed | Western Europe | 8 out of 19 |
| France | -3.5 | -3.5 | AA | 22 | Developed | Western Europe | 12 out of 19 |
| Gabon | 4.1 | 4.6 | | 83 | | Africa | 7 out of 51 |
| Gambia | 10.1 | 10.3 | | 138 | | Africa | 34 out of 51 |
| Georgia | 2.8 | 3.3 | BB- | 74 | | Central and Eastern Europe | 15 out of 25 |
| Germany | -5.8 | -5.8 | AAA | 10 | Developed | Western Europe | 7 out of 19 |
| Ghana | 5.8 | 5.6 | B- | 89 | | Africa | 9 out of 51 |
| Greece | 6.9 | 6.9 | B- | 108 | Emerging | Western Europe | 19 out of 19 |
| Grenada | 6.5 | 6.8 | | 105 | | Caribbean | 7 out of 9 |
| Guatemala | 4.5 | 4.7 | BB | 84 | | Latin America | 11 out of 20 |
| Guinea | 13.7 | 14.0 | | 156 | | Africa | 41 out of 51 |
| Guinea-Bissau | 7.4 | 7.6 | | 115 | | Africa | 22 out of 51 |
| Guyana | 6.2 | 6.4 | | 100 | | Latin America | 15 out of 20 |
| Haiti | 16.6 | 14.8 | | 157 | | Caribbean | 8 out of 9 |
| Honduras | 5.9 | 6.1 | B+ | 98 | | Latin America | 14 out of 20 |
| Hong Kong | -5.2 | -5.1 | AAA | 14 | Developed | Asia | 2 out of 29 |
| Hungary | 0.5 | 0.8 | BBB- | 57 | Emerging | Central and Eastern Europe | 10 out of 25 |
| Iceland | -2.5 | -2.6 | A | 30 | | Western Europe | 15 out of 19 |
| India | 0.2 | 0.7 | BBB- | 55 | Emerging | Asia | 10 out of 29 |
| Indonesia | 1.0 | 1.2 | BB+ | 62 | Emerging | Asia | 11 out of 29 |
| Iran | 7.9 | 8.3 | | 125 | | Middle East | 10 out of 13 |
| Iraq | 9.7 | 9.9 | B- | 136 | | Middle East | 11 out of 13 |
| Ireland | -3.0 | -2.9 | A+ | 27 | Developed | Western Europe | 14 out of 19 |
| Israel | -3.0 | -2.9 | A+ | 28 | Developed | Middle East | 2 out of 13 |
| Italy | -0.2 | -0.2 | BBB- | 50 | Developed | Western Europe | 18 out of 19 |
| Jamaica | 6.0 | 6.8 | B | 104 | | Caribbean | 6 out of 9 |
| Japan | -3.2 | -3.0 | A+ | 25 | Developed | Asia | 5 out of 29 |
| Jordan | 3.1 | 3.5 | BB- | 76 | Frontier | Middle East | 8 out of 13 |
| Kazakhstan | 2.6 | 2.4 | BBB- | 70 | Frontier | Asia | 13 out of 29 |
| Kenya | 6.0 | 6.3 | B+ | 99 | Frontier | Africa | 15 out of 51 |
| Korea (North) | 28.1 | 28.0 | | 174 | | Asia | 29 out of 29 |
| Korea (South) | -3.9 | -3.8 | AA | 19 | Emerging | Asia | 4 out of 29 |
| Kuwait | -2.9 | -2.6 | AA | 31 | Frontier | Middle East | 3 out of 13 |
| Kyrgyz Republic | 11.1 | 11.2 | | 142 | | Central and Eastern Europe | 22 out of 25 |
| Laos | 15.3 | 15.1 | | 158 | | Asia | 28 out of 29 |
| Latvia | -0.9 | -0.6 | A- | 43 | | Central and Eastern Europe | 8 out of 25 |
| Lebanon | 7.7 | 7.3 | B- | 112 | Frontier | Middle East | 9 out of 13 |
| Lesotho | 11.3 | 11.6 | | 146 | | Africa | 36 out of 51 |
| Liberia | 6.6 | 6.9 | | 107 | | Africa | 17 out of 51 |
| Libya | 12.8 | 13.4 | | 153 | | Africa | 39 out of 51 |
| Lithuania | -1.6 | -1.4 | A- | 36 | Frontier | Central and Eastern Europe | 6 out of 25 |
| Luxembourg | -6.2 | -6.2 | AAA | 5 | | Western Europe | 4 out of 19 |
| Macedonia | 5.1 | 5.5 | BB- | 87 | | Central and Eastern Europe | 17 out of 25 |
| Madagascar | 7.5 | 8.2 | | 123 | | Africa | 27 out of 51 |
| Malawi | 7.2 | 7.4 | | 114 | | Africa | 21 out of 51 |
| Malaysia | -1.5 | -1.5 | A- | 35 | Emerging | Asia | 6 out of 29 |

§ S&P Credit Rating based on long-term foreign currency issuer rating. See http://www.standardandpoors.com/.

∗ World rank based on 175 countries covered by Euromoney. Ranking based on ascending order in which '1' equals the smallest country risk premium (CRP) and '175' equals the largest country risk premium (CRP).

† MSCI Market Classification based on MSCI Market Classification Framework. See http://www.msci.com/products/indexes/market_classification.html

‡ Regional classification based on Euromoney. Regional rankings based on ascending order in which '1' equals the smallest country risk premium (CRP) for each region.

Note: A CRP of 0.0% is assumed in the following cases: (i) when the investor country and the investee country both have an S&P sovereign credit rating of AAA; or (ii) when the investor country has an S&P credit rating of AAA, and the investee country has a sovereign credit rating below AAA, but has a calculated CRP below 0.0% (which would imply lower risk than a country rated AAA); or (iii) when the investor country has an S&P credit rating below AAA, and the investee country has a sovereign credit rating of AAA, but has a calculated CRP above 0.0% (which would imply greater risk than a country rated below AAA). For purposes of this analysis, the U.S. is treated as having a sovereign credit rating equivalent to AAA.

The country risk premium (CRP) is not the cost of equity capital (COE). The CRP is to be added to base COE. See Chapter 6 for proper application.

## Data Updated Through March 2017

| Investee Country | December 2016 Country Risk Premium (CRP) (%) | March 2017 Country Risk Premium (CRP) (%) | S&P Sovereign Credit Rating § | World Rank Out of 175* | MSCI Market Classification † | Euromoney Region ‡ | Regional Rank ‡ |
|---|---|---|---|---|---|---|---|
| Mali | 10.9 | 11.2 | | 141 | | Africa | 35 out of 51 |
| Malta | -3.2 | -3.0 | A- | 26 | | Western Europe | 13 out of 19 |
| Mauritania | 14.9 | 15.2 | | 159 | | Africa | 42 out of 51 |
| Mauritius | 1.9 | 2.1 | | 67 | Frontier | Asia | 12 out of 29 |
| Mexico | -1.6 | -1.3 | BBB+ | 37 | Emerging | Latin America | 2 out of 20 |
| Moldova | 9.3 | 10.0 | | 137 | | Central and Eastern Europe | 21 out of 25 |
| Mongolia | 7.5 | 8.1 | B- | 119 | | Asia | 18 out of 29 |
| Montenegro | 6.8 | 6.8 | B+ | 103 | | Central and Eastern Europe | 19 out of 25 |
| Morocco | 1.9 | 2.3 | BBB- | 69 | Frontier | Africa | 4 out of 51 |
| Mozambique | 8.6 | 8.7 | SD | 128 | | Africa | 29 out of 51 |
| Myanmar | 9.5 | 9.7 | | 134 | | Asia | 22 out of 29 |
| Namibia | 1.6 | 1.9 | | 66 | | Africa | 3 out of 51 |
| Nepal | 12.2 | 12.5 | | 149 | | Asia | 26 out of 29 |
| Netherlands | -6.2 | -6.1 | AAA | 6 | Developed | Western Europe | 5 out of 19 |
| New Zealand | -6.0 | -5.9 | AA | 8 | Developed | Australasia | 1 out of 7 |
| Nicaragua | 8.3 | 8.6 | B+ | 127 | | Latin America | 19 out of 20 |
| Niger | 7.9 | 8.1 | | 120 | | Africa | 25 out of 51 |
| Nigeria | 5.9 | 6.1 | B | 97 | Frontier | Africa | 14 out of 51 |
| Norway | -6.8 | -6.8 | AAA | 3 | Developed | Western Europe | 2 out of 19 |
| Oman | -0.7 | -0.5 | BBB- | 46 | Frontier | Middle East | 5 out of 13 |
| Pakistan | 8.0 | 8.2 | B | 122 | Frontier | Asia | 19 out of 29 |
| Panama | 0.0 | 0.2 | BBB | 52 | | Latin America | 6 out of 20 |
| Papua New Guinea | 7.5 | 7.8 | B+ | 118 | | Australasia | 3 out of 7 |
| Paraguay | 3.5 | 3.9 | BB | 80 | | Latin America | 9 out of 20 |
| Peru | -1.3 | -1.0 | BBB+ | 39 | Emerging | Latin America | 3 out of 20 |
| Philippines | 0.4 | 0.5 | BBB | 53 | Emerging | Asia | 9 out of 29 |
| Poland | -2.7 | -2.7 | BBB+ | 29 | Emerging | Central and Eastern Europe | 3 out of 25 |
| Portugal | -0.3 | -0.3 | BB+ | 49 | Developed | Western Europe | 17 out of 19 |
| Qatar | -3.8 | -3.6 | AA | 21 | Emerging | Middle East | 1 out of 13 |
| Romania | 0.5 | 0.7 | BBB- | 56 | Frontier | Central and Eastern Europe | 9 out of 25 |
| Russia | 2.7 | 2.3 | BB+ | 68 | Emerging | Central and Eastern Europe | 14 out of 25 |
| Rwanda | 8.7 | 8.9 | B | 130 | | Africa | 31 out of 51 |
| São Tomé & Príncipe | 15.0 | 15.8 | | 163 | | Africa | 43 out of 51 |
| Saudi Arabia | -0.4 | -0.5 | A- | 47 | | Middle East | 6 out of 13 |
| Senegal | 5.3 | 5.5 | B+ | 86 | | Africa | 8 out of 51 |
| Serbia | 3.4 | 3.3 | BB- | 75 | Frontier | Central and Eastern Europe | 16 out of 25 |
| Seychelles | 2.9 | 3.1 | | 73 | | Africa | 5 out of 51 |
| Sierra Leone | 8.7 | 8.9 | | 129 | | Africa | 30 out of 51 |
| Singapore | -7.0 | -7.0 | AAA | 1 | Developed | Asia | 1 out of 29 |
| Slovakia | -3.4 | -3.2 | A+ | 24 | | Central and Eastern Europe | 2 out of 25 |
| Slovenia | -2.0 | -1.8 | A | 34 | Frontier | Central and Eastern Europe | 5 out of 25 |
| Solomon Islands | 19.4 | 19.7 | | 168 | | Australasia | 6 out of 7 |
| Somalia | 17.6 | 18.0 | | 166 | | Africa | 46 out of 51 |
| South Africa | 0.5 | 0.9 | BBB- | 60 | Emerging | Africa | 2 out of 51 |
| Spain | -1.2 | -1.0 | BBB+ | 38 | Developed | Western Europe | 16 out of 19 |
| Sri Lanka | 2.8 | 2.7 | B+ | 72 | Frontier | Asia | 14 out of 29 |
| Sudan | 13.7 | 13.9 | | 154 | | Africa | 40 out of 51 |
| Suriname | 6.2 | 6.6 | B+ | 102 | | Latin America | 16 out of 20 |
| Swaziland | 12.0 | 13.2 | | 152 | | Africa | 38 out of 51 |
| Sweden | -6.1 | -6.1 | AAA | 7 | Developed | Western Europe | 6 out of 19 |

§ S&P Credit Rating based on long-term foreign currency issuer rating. See http://www.standardandpoors.com/.

* World rank based on 175 countries covered by Euromoney. Ranking based on ascending order in which '1' equals the smallest country risk premium (CRP) and '175' equals the largest country risk premium (CRP).

† MSCI Market Classification based on MSCI Market Classification Framework. See http://www.msci.com/products/indexes/market_classification.html.

‡ Regional classification based on Euromoney. Regional rankings based on ascending order in which '1' equals the smallest country risk premium (CRP) for each region.

Note: A CRP of 0.0% is assumed in the following cases: (i) when the investor country and the investee country both have an S&P sovereign credit rating of AAA; or (ii) when the investor country has an S&P credit rating of AAA, and the investee country has a sovereign credit rating below AAA, but has a calculated CRP below 0.0% (which would imply lower risk than a country rated AAA); or (iii) when the investor country has an S&P credit rating below AAA, and the investee country has a sovereign credit rating of AAA, but has a calculated CRP above 0.0% (which would imply greater risk than a country rated below AAA). For purposes of this analysis, the U.S. is treated as having a sovereign credit rating equivalent to AAA.

The country risk premium (CRP) is not the cost of equity capital (COE). The CRP is to be added to base COE. See Chapter 6 for proper application.

### Data Updated Through March 2017

| Investee Country | December 2016 Country Risk Premium (CRP) (%) | March 2017 Country Risk Premium (CRP) (%) | S&P Sovereign Credit Rating § | World Rank Out of 175* | MSCI Market Classification † | Euromoney Region ‡ | Regional Rank ‡ |
|---|---|---|---|---|---|---|---|
| Switzerland | -6.8 | -6.8 | AAA | 2 | Developed | Western Europe | 1 out of 19 |
| Syria | 18.4 | 19.0 | | 167 | | Middle East | 13 out of 13 |
| Taiwan | -4.2 | -4.0 | AA- | 18 | Emerging | Asia | 3 out of 29 |
| Tajikistan | 13.3 | 13.9 | | 155 | | Central and Eastern Europe | 25 out of 25 |
| Tanzania | 5.6 | 6.0 | | 95 | | Africa | 13 out of 51 |
| Thailand | 0.0 | 0.0 | BBB+ | 51 | Emerging | Asia | 8 out of 29 |
| Togo | 7.2 | 7.4 | | 113 | | Africa | 20 out of 51 |
| Tonga | 21.8 | 22.2 | | 170 | | Australasia | 7 out of 7 |
| Trinidad & Tobago | 0.4 | 0.5 | A- | 54 | | Caribbean | 2 out of 9 |
| Tunisia | 3.2 | 3.7 | | 79 | Frontier | Africa | 6 out of 51 |
| Turkey | 0.7 | 0.8 | BB | 58 | Emerging | Central and Eastern Europe | 11 out of 25 |
| Turkmenistan | 10.4 | 11.0 | | 140 | | Asia | 24 out of 29 |
| Uganda | 6.7 | 7.2 | B | 110 | | Africa | 18 out of 51 |
| Ukraine | 9.5 | 9.8 | B- | 135 | | Central and Eastern Europe | 20 out of 25 |
| United Arab Emirates | -2.4 | -2.2 | AA | 33 | Emerging | Middle East | 4 out of 13 |
| United Kingdom | -3.9 | -3.7 | AA | 20 | Developed | Western Europe | 11 out of 19 |
| United States | -4.9 | -4.8 | AA+ | 15 | Developed | North America | 2 out of 2 |
| Uruguay | -0.6 | -0.6 | BBB | 45 | | Latin America | 5 out of 20 |
| Uzbekistan | 9.6 | 9.3 | | 132 | | Asia | 21 out of 29 |
| Vanuatu | 11.3 | 11.6 | | 145 | | Australasia | 4 out of 7 |
| Venezuela | 15.0 | 15.8 | CCC | 162 | | Latin America | 20 out of 20 |
| Vietnam | 3.7 | 3.7 | BB- | 78 | Frontier | Asia | 16 out of 29 |
| Yemen | 15.3 | 15.7 | | 161 | | Middle East | 12 out of 13 |
| Zambia | 7.0 | 7.3 | B | 111 | | Africa | 19 out of 51 |
| Zimbabwe | 16.9 | 17.2 | | 164 | | Africa | 44 out of 51 |

### March 2017 Country Risk Premium (CRP) Summary Statistics:

| S&P Rating | Country Count | Average CRP (%) | Median CRP (%) | Min CRP (%) | Max CRP (%) |
|---|---|---|---|---|---|
| AAA ** | 12 | -6.1 | -6.1 | -7.0 | -4.8 |
| AA (AA+, AA, AA-) | 15 | -3.7 | -3.7 | -5.9 | -0.7 |
| A (A+, A, A-) | 14 | -1.7 | -1.7 | -3.2 | 0.5 |
| BBB (BBB+, BBB, BBB-) | 17 | 0.0 | 0.0 | -2.7 | 2.4 |
| BB (BB+, BB, BB-) | 22 | 2.9 | 2.9 | -0.9 | 8.4 |
| B+ − SD | 39 | 7.7 | 7.3 | 2.7 | 15.8 |
| Investment Grade ** | 58 | -2.6 | -2.6 | -7.0 | 2.4 |
| Non-Investment Grade ** | 61 | 6.0 | 6.1 | -0.9 | 15.8 |
| **MSCI Market Classification** | | | | | |
| Developed Markets | 23 | -4.6 | -5.5 | -7.0 | -0.2 |
| Emerging Markets | 23 | -0.3 | -0.7 | -4.4 | 7.6 |
| Frontier Markets | 22 | 2.8 | 2.6 | -2.6 | 8.4 |
| **Euromoney Region ‡** | | | | | |
| Africa | 51 | 10.2 | 8.2 | -0.5 | 30.7 |
| Asia | 29 | 4.9 | 3.5 | -7.0 | 28.0 |
| Australasia | 7 | 8.8 | 11.6 | -5.9 | 22.2 |
| Caribbean | 9 | 6.2 | 5.7 | -0.6 | 15.5 |
| Central and Eastern Europe | 25 | 3.3 | 1.2 | -3.4 | 13.9 |
| Latin America | 20 | 3.9 | 4.6 | -4.4 | 15.8 |
| Middle East | 13 | 4.1 | 1.6 | -3.6 | 19.0 |
| North America | 2 | -5.4 | -5.4 | -5.9 | -4.8 |
| Western Europe | 19 | -3.7 | -4.3 | -6.8 | 6.9 |

### CCR Base Cost of Equity Capital:

| Thailand | COE (%) |
|---|---|
| March 2017 | 13.7 |
| December 2016 | 14.0 |

CCR base country-level COE for a Thailand-based investor investing in Thailand.

§ S&P Credit Rating based on long-term foreign currency issuer rating. See http://www.standardandpoors.com/

* World rank based on 175 countries covered by Euromoney. Ranking based on ascending order in which '1' equals the smallest country risk premium (CRP) and '175' equals the largest country risk premium (CRP).

† MSCI Market Classification based on MSCI Market Classification Framework. See http://www.msci.com/products/indexes/market_classification.html.

‡ Regional classification based on Euromoney. Regional rankings based on ascending order in which '1' equals the smallest country risk premium (CRP) for each region.

** Investment grade based on S&P sovereign credit rating from AAA to BBB-. Non-Investment grade based on S&P sovereign credit rating from BB+ to SD. For purposes of this analysis, the U.S. is being treated as if it were rated AAA by S&P.

Note: A CRP of 0.0% is assumed in the following cases: (i) when the investor country and the investee country both have an S&P sovereign credit rating of AAA; or (ii) when the investor country has an S&P credit rating of AAA, and the investee country has a sovereign credit rating below AAA, but has a calculated CRP below 0.0% (which would imply lower risk than a country rated AAA); or (iii) when the investor country has an S&P credit rating below AAA, and the investee country has a sovereign credit rating of AAA, but has a calculated CRP above 0.0% (which would imply greater risk than a country rated below AAA). For purposes of this analysis, the U.S. is treated as having a sovereign credit rating equivalent to AAA.

The country risk premium (CRP) is not the cost of equity capital (COE). The CRP is to be added to base COE. See Chapter 6 for proper application.

### Data Updated Through March 2017

| Investee Country | December 2016 Country Risk Premium (CRP) (%) | March 2017 Country Risk Premium (CRP) (%) | S&P Sovereign Credit Rating § | World Rank Out of 175∗ | MSCI Market Classification † | Euromoney Region ‡ | Regional Rank ‡ |
|---|---|---|---|---|---|---|---|
| Afghanistan | 10.7 | 10.4 | | 139 | | Asia | 23 out of 29 |
| Albania | 6.4 | 6.4 | B+ | 93 | | Central and Eastern Europe | 18 out of 25 |
| Algeria | 6.4 | 6.4 | | 91 | | Africa | 10 out of 51 |
| Angola | 8.3 | 8.2 | B | 121 | | Africa | 26 out of 51 |
| Argentina | 6.8 | 6.5 | B- | 96 | Frontier | Latin America | 13 out of 20 |
| Armenia | 4.4 | 4.5 | | 77 | | Asia | 15 out of 29 |
| Australia | -2.6 | -2.8 | AAA | 12 | Developed | Australasia | 2 out of 7 |
| Austria | -2.5 | -2.6 | AA+ | 13 | Developed | Western Europe | 9 out of 19 |
| Azerbaijan | 5.4 | 5.6 | BB+ | 85 | | Asia | 17 out of 29 |
| Bahamas | 3.3 | 3.0 | BB+ | 65 | | Caribbean | 3 out of 9 |
| Bahrain | 3.2 | 3.0 | BB- | 64 | Frontier | Middle East | 7 out of 13 |
| Bangladesh | 8.6 | 8.4 | BB- | 126 | Frontier | Asia | 20 out of 29 |
| Barbados | 4.6 | 5.4 | CCC+ | 82 | | Caribbean | 4 out of 9 |
| Belarus | 10.4 | 10.7 | B- | 143 | | Central and Eastern Europe | 23 out of 25 |
| Belgium | -1.5 | -1.6 | AA | 17 | Developed | Western Europe | 10 out of 19 |
| Belize | 7.2 | 7.2 | B- | 106 | | Latin America | 17 out of 20 |
| Benin | 11.8 | 11.7 | | 150 | | Africa | 37 out of 51 |
| Bermuda | 1.4 | 1.3 | A+ | 44 | | Caribbean | 1 out of 9 |
| Bhutan | 11.5 | 11.3 | | 148 | | Asia | 25 out of 29 |
| Bolivia | 6.0 | 6.1 | BB | 88 | | Latin America | 12 out of 20 |
| Bosnia & Herzegovina | 10.8 | 10.8 | B | 144 | | Central and Eastern Europe | 24 out of 25 |
| Botswana | 1.4 | 1.3 | A- | 48 | | Africa | 1 out of 51 |
| Brazil | 2.6 | 2.5 | BB | 59 | Emerging | Latin America | 7 out of 20 |
| Bulgaria | 2.5 | 2.6 | BB+ | 61 | | Central and Eastern Europe | 12 out of 25 |
| Burkina Faso | 9.5 | 9.4 | B- | 133 | | Africa | 33 out of 51 |
| Burundi | 18.9 | 18.8 | | 169 | | Africa | 47 out of 51 |
| Cambodia | 12.2 | 11.9 | | 151 | | Asia | 27 out of 29 |
| Cameroon | 8.4 | 8.3 | B | 124 | | Africa | 28 out of 51 |
| Canada | -2.8 | -2.9 | AAA | 9 | Developed | North America | 1 out of 2 |
| Cape Verde | 6.5 | 6.5 | B | 94 | | Africa | 12 out of 51 |
| Central African Republic | 21.7 | 21.6 | | 172 | | Africa | 49 out of 51 |
| Chad | 20.6 | 20.6 | | 171 | | Africa | 48 out of 51 |
| Chile | -1.9 | -1.8 | AA- | 16 | Emerging | Latin America | 1 out of 20 |
| China | 1.2 | 1.2 | AA- | 42 | Emerging | Asia | 7 out of 29 |
| Colombia | 1.2 | 1.1 | BBB | 41 | Emerging | Latin America | 4 out of 20 |
| Congo Republic | 8.1 | 7.9 | B- | 117 | | Africa | 24 out of 51 |
| Congo, DR | 9.1 | 8.9 | B- | 131 | | Africa | 32 out of 51 |
| Costa Rica | 3.6 | 3.7 | BB- | 71 | | Latin America | 8 out of 20 |
| Côte d'Ivoire | 6.4 | 6.4 | | 92 | | Africa | 11 out of 51 |
| Croatia | 2.9 | 2.7 | BB | 63 | Frontier | Central and Eastern Europe | 13 out of 25 |
| Cuba | 14.0 | 14.0 | | 160 | | Caribbean | 9 out of 9 |
| Cyprus | 1.0 | 1.0 | BB+ | 40 | | Central and Eastern Europe | 7 out of 25 |
| Czech Republic | -0.9 | -0.9 | AA- | 23 | Emerging | Central and Eastern Europe | 1 out of 25 |
| Denmark | -3.3 | -3.4 | AAA | 4 | Developed | Western Europe | 3 out of 19 |
| Djibouti | 28.0 | 26.1 | | 175 | | Africa | 51 out of 51 |
| Dominican Republic | 6.3 | 6.3 | BB- | 90 | | Caribbean | 5 out of 9 |
| Ecuador | 7.5 | 7.3 | B | 109 | | Latin America | 18 out of 20 |
| Egypt | 7.9 | 7.8 | B- | 116 | Emerging | Africa | 23 out of 51 |
| El Salvador | 5.5 | 5.3 | B- | 81 | | Latin America | 10 out of 20 |
| Equatorial Guinea | 16.0 | 16.0 | | 165 | | Africa | 45 out of 51 |

§ S&P Credit Rating based on long-term foreign currency issuer rating. See http://www.standardandpoors.com/.
∗ World rank based on 175 countries covered by Euromoney. Ranking based on ascending order in which '1' equals the smallest country risk premium (CRP) and '175' equals the largest country risk premium (CRP).
† MSCI Market Classification based on MSCI Market Classification Framework. See http://www.msci.com/products/indexes/market_classification.html
‡ Regional classification based on Euromoney. Regional rankings based on ascending order in which '1' equals the smallest country risk premium (CRP) for each region.
Note: A CRP of 0.0% is assumed in the following cases: (i) when the investor country and the investee country both have an S&P sovereign credit rating of AAA; or (ii) when the investor country has an S&P credit rating of AAA, and the investee country has a sovereign credit rating below AAA, but has a calculated CRP below 0.0% (which would imply lower risk than a country rated AAA); or (iii) when the investor country has an S&P credit rating below AAA, and the investee country has a sovereign credit rating of AAA, but has a calculated CRP above 0.0% (which would imply greater risk than a country rated below AAA). For purposes of this analysis, the U.S. is treated as having a sovereign credit rating equivalent to AAA.

The country risk premium (CRP) is not the cost of equity capital (COE). The CRP is to be added to base COE. See Chapter 6 for proper application.

## Data Updated Through March 2017

| Investee Country | December 2016 Country Risk Premium (CRP) (%) | March 2017 Country Risk Premium (CRP) (%) | S&P Sovereign Credit Rating § | World Rank Out of 175∗ | MSCI Market Classification † | Euromoney Region ‡ | Regional Rank ‡ |
|---|---|---|---|---|---|---|---|
| Eritrea | 25.0 | 23.4 | | 173 | | Africa | 50 out of 51 |
| Estonia | -0.4 | -0.3 | AA- | 32 | Frontier | Central and Eastern Europe | 4 out of 25 |
| Ethiopia | 7.0 | 6.9 | B | 101 | | Africa | 16 out of 51 |
| Fiji | 11.2 | 11.0 | B+ | 147 | | Australasia | 5 out of 7 |
| Finland | -2.7 | -2.8 | AA+ | 11 | Developed | Western Europe | 8 out of 19 |
| France | -0.8 | -1.0 | AA | 22 | Developed | Western Europe | 12 out of 19 |
| Gabon | 5.2 | 5.4 | | 83 | | Africa | 7 out of 51 |
| Gambia | 10.0 | 9.9 | | 138 | | Africa | 34 out of 51 |
| Georgia | 4.2 | 4.3 | BB- | 74 | | Central and Eastern Europe | 15 out of 25 |
| Germany | -2.7 | -2.8 | AAA | 10 | Developed | Western Europe | 7 out of 19 |
| Ghana | 6.6 | 6.2 | B- | 89 | | Africa | 9 out of 51 |
| Greece | 7.5 | 7.2 | B- | 108 | Emerging | Western Europe | 19 out of 19 |
| Grenada | 7.2 | 7.2 | | 105 | | Caribbean | 7 out of 9 |
| Guatemala | 5.5 | 5.5 | BB | 84 | | Latin America | 11 out of 20 |
| Guinea | 12.9 | 12.9 | | 156 | | Africa | 41 out of 51 |
| Guinea-Bissau | 7.8 | 7.8 | | 115 | | Africa | 22 out of 51 |
| Guyana | 6.9 | 6.8 | | 100 | | Latin America | 15 out of 20 |
| Haiti | 15.2 | 13.5 | | 157 | | Caribbean | 8 out of 9 |
| Honduras | 6.7 | 6.6 | B+ | 98 | | Latin America | 14 out of 20 |
| Hong Kong | -2.3 | -2.3 | AAA | 14 | Developed | Asia | 2 out of 29 |
| Hungary | 2.3 | 2.3 | BBB- | 57 | Emerging | Central and Eastern Europe | 10 out of 25 |
| Iceland | -0.1 | -0.3 | A | 30 | | Western Europe | 15 out of 19 |
| India | 2.1 | 2.3 | BBB- | 55 | Emerging | Asia | 10 out of 29 |
| Indonesia | 2.7 | 2.7 | BB+ | 62 | Emerging | Asia | 11 out of 29 |
| Iran | 8.2 | 8.3 | | 125 | | Middle East | 10 out of 13 |
| Iraq | 9.7 | 9.6 | B- | 136 | | Middle East | 11 out of 13 |
| Ireland | -0.5 | -0.6 | A+ | 27 | Developed | Western Europe | 14 out of 19 |
| Israel | -0.5 | -0.6 | A+ | 28 | Developed | Middle East | 2 out of 13 |
| Italy | 1.8 | 1.6 | BBB- | 50 | Developed | Western Europe | 18 out of 19 |
| Jamaica | 6.7 | 7.1 | B | 104 | | Caribbean | 6 out of 9 |
| Japan | -0.6 | -0.6 | A+ | 25 | Developed | Asia | 5 out of 29 |
| Jordan | 4.4 | 4.5 | BB- | 76 | Frontier | Middle East | 8 out of 13 |
| Kazakhstan | 4.0 | 3.7 | BBB- | 70 | Frontier | Asia | 13 out of 29 |
| Kenya | 6.7 | 6.7 | B+ | 99 | Frontier | Africa | 15 out of 51 |
| Korea (North) | 24.5 | 24.0 | | 174 | | Asia | 29 out of 29 |
| Korea (South) | -1.2 | -1.2 | AA | 19 | Emerging | Asia | 4 out of 29 |
| Kuwait | -0.3 | -0.3 | AA | 31 | Frontier | Middle East | 3 out of 13 |
| Kyrgyz Republic | 10.8 | 10.6 | | 142 | | Central and Eastern Europe | 22 out of 25 |
| Laos | 14.2 | 13.7 | | 158 | | Asia | 28 out of 29 |
| Latvia | 1.2 | 1.3 | A- | 43 | | Central and Eastern Europe | 8 out of 25 |
| Lebanon | 8.1 | 7.6 | B- | 112 | Frontier | Middle East | 9 out of 13 |
| Lesotho | 11.0 | 10.9 | | 146 | | Africa | 36 out of 51 |
| Liberia | 7.3 | 7.2 | | 107 | | Africa | 17 out of 51 |
| Libya | 12.2 | 12.4 | | 153 | | Africa | 39 out of 51 |
| Lithuania | 0.6 | 0.6 | A- | 36 | Frontier | Central and Eastern Europe | 6 out of 25 |
| Luxembourg | -3.1 | -3.2 | AAA | 5 | | Western Europe | 4 out of 19 |
| Macedonia | 6.0 | 6.1 | BB- | 87 | | Central and Eastern Europe | 17 out of 25 |
| Madagascar | 7.9 | 8.3 | | 123 | | Africa | 27 out of 51 |
| Malawi | 7.7 | 7.6 | | 114 | | Africa | 21 out of 51 |
| Malaysia | 0.8 | 0.6 | A- | 35 | Emerging | Asia | 6 out of 29 |

§ S&P Credit Rating based on long-term foreign currency issuer rating. See http://www.standardandpoors.com/.

∗ World rank based on 175 countries covered by Euromoney. Ranking based on ascending order in which '1' equals the smallest country risk premium (CRP) and '175' equals the largest country risk premium (CRP).

† MSCI Market Classification based on MSCI Market Classification Framework. See http://www.msci.com/products/indexes/market_classification.html.

‡ Regional classification based on Euromoney. Regional rankings based on ascending order in which '1' equals the smallest country risk premium (CRP) for each region.

Note: A CRP of 0.0% is assumed in the following cases: (i) when the investor country and the investee country both have an S&P sovereign credit rating of AAA; or (ii) when the investor country has an S&P credit rating of AAA, and the investee country has a sovereign credit rating below AAA, but has a calculated CRP below 0.0% (which would imply lower risk than a country rated AAA); or (iii) when the investor country has an S&P credit rating below AAA, and the investee country has a sovereign credit rating of AAA, but has a calculated CRP above 0.0% (which would imply greater risk than a country rated below AAA). For purposes of this analysis, the U.S. is treated as having a sovereign credit rating equivalent to AAA.

The country risk premium (CRP) is not the cost of equity capital (COE). The CRP is to be added to base COE. See Chapter 6 for proper application.

## Data Updated Through March 2017

| Investee Country | December 2016 Country Risk Premium (CRP) (%) | March 2017 Country Risk Premium (CRP) (%) | S&P Sovereign Credit Rating § | World Rank Out of 175∗ | MSCI Market Classification † | Euromoney Region ‡ | Regional Rank ‡ |
|---|---|---|---|---|---|---|---|
| Mali | 10.7 | 10.6 | | 141 | | Africa | 35 out of 51 |
| Malta | -0.6 | -0.6 | A- | 26 | | Western Europe | 13 out of 19 |
| Mauritania | 13.9 | 13.8 | | 159 | | Africa | 42 out of 51 |
| Mauritius | 3.5 | 3.4 | | 67 | Frontier | Asia | 12 out of 29 |
| Mexico | 0.7 | 0.7 | BBB+ | 37 | Emerging | Latin America | 2 out of 20 |
| Moldova | 9.4 | 9.7 | | 137 | | Central and Eastern Europe | 21 out of 25 |
| Mongolia | 8.0 | 8.2 | B- | 119 | | Asia | 18 out of 29 |
| Montenegro | 7.4 | 7.1 | B+ | 103 | | Central and Eastern Europe | 19 out of 25 |
| Morocco | 3.5 | 3.6 | BBB- | 69 | Frontier | Africa | 4 out of 51 |
| Mozambique | 8.8 | 8.7 | SD | 128 | | Africa | 29 out of 51 |
| Myanmar | 9.6 | 9.4 | | 134 | | Asia | 22 out of 29 |
| Namibia | 3.2 | 3.3 | | 66 | | Africa | 3 out of 51 |
| Nepal | 11.7 | 11.6 | | 149 | | Asia | 26 out of 29 |
| Netherlands | -3.0 | -3.1 | AAA | 6 | Developed | Western Europe | 5 out of 19 |
| New Zealand | -2.9 | -2.9 | AA | 8 | Developed | Australasia | 1 out of 7 |
| Nicaragua | 8.6 | 8.5 | B+ | 127 | | Latin America | 19 out of 20 |
| Niger | 8.3 | 8.2 | | 120 | | Africa | 25 out of 51 |
| Nigeria | 6.7 | 6.6 | B | 97 | Frontier | Africa | 14 out of 51 |
| Norway | -3.6 | -3.7 | AAA | 3 | Developed | Western Europe | 2 out of 19 |
| Oman | 1.4 | 1.3 | BBB- | 46 | Frontier | Middle East | 5 out of 13 |
| Pakistan | 8.3 | 8.2 | B | 122 | Frontier | Asia | 19 out of 29 |
| Panama | 1.9 | 1.9 | BBB | 52 | | Latin America | 6 out of 20 |
| Papua New Guinea | 8.0 | 8.0 | B+ | 118 | | Australasia | 3 out of 7 |
| Paraguay | 4.7 | 4.8 | BB | 80 | | Latin America | 9 out of 20 |
| Peru | 0.9 | 0.9 | BBB+ | 39 | Emerging | Latin America | 3 out of 20 |
| Philippines | 2.2 | 2.1 | BBB | 53 | Emerging | Asia | 9 out of 29 |
| Poland | -0.2 | -0.4 | BBB+ | 29 | Emerging | Central and Eastern Europe | 3 out of 25 |
| Portugal | 1.7 | 1.5 | BB+ | 49 | Developed | Western Europe | 17 out of 19 |
| Qatar | -1.1 | -1.1 | AA | 21 | Emerging | Middle East | 1 out of 13 |
| Romania | 2.3 | 2.3 | BBB- | 56 | Frontier | Central and Eastern Europe | 9 out of 25 |
| Russia | 4.1 | 3.6 | BB+ | 68 | Emerging | Central and Eastern Europe | 14 out of 25 |
| Rwanda | 8.9 | 8.8 | B | 130 | | Africa | 31 out of 51 |
| São Tomé & Príncipe | 14.0 | 14.3 | | 163 | | Africa | 43 out of 51 |
| Saudi Arabia | 1.6 | 1.3 | A- | 47 | | Middle East | 6 out of 13 |
| Senegal | 6.1 | 6.1 | B+ | 86 | | Africa | 8 out of 51 |
| Serbia | 4.7 | 4.4 | BB- | 75 | Frontier | Central and Eastern Europe | 16 out of 25 |
| Seychelles | 4.2 | 4.2 | | 73 | | Africa | 5 out of 51 |
| Sierra Leone | 8.9 | 8.8 | | 129 | | Africa | 30 out of 51 |
| Singapore | -3.7 | -3.8 | AAA | 1 | Developed | Asia | 1 out of 29 |
| Slovakia | -0.8 | -0.8 | A+ | 24 | | Central and Eastern Europe | 2 out of 25 |
| Slovenia | 0.3 | 0.3 | A | 34 | Frontier | Central and Eastern Europe | 5 out of 25 |
| Solomon Islands | 17.5 | 17.4 | | 168 | | Australasia | 6 out of 7 |
| Somalia | 16.1 | 16.0 | | 166 | | Africa | 46 out of 51 |
| South Africa | 2.4 | 2.5 | BBB- | 60 | Emerging | Africa | 2 out of 51 |
| Spain | 1.0 | 0.9 | BBB+ | 38 | Developed | Western Europe | 16 out of 19 |
| Sri Lanka | 4.2 | 3.9 | B+ | 72 | Frontier | Asia | 14 out of 29 |
| Sudan | 12.9 | 12.8 | | 154 | | Africa | 40 out of 51 |
| Suriname | 6.9 | 7.0 | B+ | 102 | | Latin America | 16 out of 20 |
| Swaziland | 11.6 | 12.2 | | 152 | | Africa | 38 out of 51 |
| Sweden | -3.0 | -3.1 | AAA | 7 | Developed | Western Europe | 6 out of 19 |

§ S&P Credit Rating based on long-term foreign currency issuer rating. See http://www.standardandpoors.com/.

∗ World rank based on 175 countries covered by Euromoney. Ranking based on ascending order in which '1' equals the smallest country risk premium (CRP) and '175' equals the largest country risk premium (CRP).

† MSCI Market Classification based on MSCI Market Classification Framework. See http://www.msci.com/products/indexes/market_classification.html.

‡ Regional classification based on Euromoney. Regional rankings based on ascending order in which '1' equals the smallest country risk premium (CRP) for each region.

Note: A CRP of 0.0% is assumed in the following cases: (i) when the investor country and the investee country both have an S&P sovereign credit rating of AAA; or (ii) when the investor country has an S&P credit rating of AAA, and the investee country has a sovereign credit rating below AAA, but has a calculated CRP below 0.0% (which would imply lower risk than a country rated AAA); or (iii) when the investor country has an S&P credit rating below AAA, and the investee country has a sovereign credit rating of AAA, but has a calculated CRP above 0.0% (which would imply greater risk than a country rated AAA). For purposes of this analysis, the U.S. is treated as having a sovereign credit rating equivalent to AAA.

The country risk premium (CRP) is not the cost of equity capital (COE). The CRP is to be added to base COE. See Chapter 6 for proper application.

## Data Updated Through March 2017

| Investee Country | December 2016 Country Risk Premium (CRP) (%) | March 2017 Country Risk Premium (CRP) (%) | S&P Sovereign Credit Rating § | World Rank Out of 175* | MSCI Market Classification † | Euromoney Region ‡ | Regional Rank ‡ |
|---|---|---|---|---|---|---|---|
| Switzerland | -3.5 | -3.7 | AAA | 2 | Developed | Western Europe | 1 out of 19 |
| Syria | 16.7 | 16.8 | | 167 | | Middle East | 13 out of 13 |
| Taiwan | -1.4 | -1.5 | AA- | 18 | Emerging | Asia | 3 out of 29 |
| Tajikistan | 12.6 | 12.8 | | 155 | | Central and Eastern Europe | 25 out of 25 |
| Tanzania | 6.4 | 6.5 | | 95 | | Africa | 13 out of 51 |
| Thailand | 1.9 | 1.7 | BBB+ | 51 | Emerging | Asia | 8 out of 29 |
| Togo | 7.7 | 7.6 | | 113 | | Africa | 20 out of 51 |
| Tonga | 19.4 | 19.3 | | 170 | | Australasia | 7 out of 7 |
| Trinidad & Tobago | 2.2 | 2.1 | A- | 54 | | Caribbean | 2 out of 9 |
| Tunisia | 4.5 | 4.7 | | 79 | Frontier | Africa | 6 out of 51 |
| Turkey | 2.5 | 2.4 | BB | 58 | Emerging | Central and Eastern Europe | 11 out of 25 |
| Turkmenistan | 10.3 | 10.5 | | 140 | | Asia | 24 out of 29 |
| Uganda | 7.3 | 7.5 | B | 110 | | Africa | 18 out of 51 |
| Ukraine | 9.5 | 9.5 | B- | 135 | | Central and Eastern Europe | 20 out of 25 |
| United Arab Emirates | 0.0 | 0.0 | AA | 33 | Emerging | Middle East | 4 out of 13 |
| United Kingdom | -1.2 | -1.2 | AA | 20 | Developed | Western Europe | 11 out of 19 |
| United States | -2.0 | -2.1 | AA+ | 15 | Developed | North America | 2 out of 2 |
| Uruguay | 1.4 | 1.3 | BBB | 45 | | Latin America | 5 out of 20 |
| Uzbekistan | 9.7 | 9.2 | | 132 | | Asia | 21 out of 29 |
| Vanuatu | 11.0 | 10.9 | | 145 | | Australasia | 4 out of 7 |
| Venezuela | 14.0 | 14.3 | CCC | 162 | | Latin America | 20 out of 20 |
| Vietnam | 4.9 | 4.6 | BB- | 78 | Frontier | Asia | 16 out of 29 |
| Yemen | 14.2 | 14.2 | | 161 | | Middle East | 12 out of 13 |
| Zambia | 7.6 | 7.5 | B | 111 | | Africa | 19 out of 51 |
| Zimbabwe | 15.5 | 15.4 | | 164 | | Africa | 44 out of 51 |

## March 2017 Country Risk Premium (CRP) Summary Statistics:

| S&P Rating | Country Count | Average CRP (%) | Median CRP (%) | Min CRP (%) | Max CRP (%) |
|---|---|---|---|---|---|
| AAA ** | 12 | -3.1 | -3.1 | -3.8 | -2.1 |
| AA (AA+, AA, AA-) | 15 | -1.2 | -1.2 | -2.9 | 1.2 |
| A (A+, A, A-) | 14 | 0.4 | 0.4 | -0.8 | 2.1 |
| BBB (BBB+, BBB, BBB-) | 17 | 1.8 | 1.7 | -0.4 | 3.7 |
| BB (BB+, BB, BB-) | 22 | 4.1 | 4.0 | 1.0 | 8.4 |
| B+ − SD | 39 | 7.8 | 7.5 | 3.9 | 14.3 |
| Investment Grade ** | 58 | -0.3 | -0.3 | -3.8 | 3.7 |
| Non-Investment Grade ** | 61 | 6.5 | 6.6 | 1.0 | 14.3 |
| **MSCI Market Classification** | | | | | |
| Developed Markets | 23 | -1.9 | -2.6 | -3.8 | 1.6 |
| Emerging Markets | 23 | 1.5 | 1.2 | -1.8 | 7.8 |
| Frontier Markets | 22 | 3.9 | 3.8 | -0.3 | 8.4 |
| **Euromoney Region ‡** | | | | | |
| Africa | 51 | 9.8 | 8.2 | 1.3 | 26.1 |
| Asia | 29 | 5.6 | 4.5 | -3.8 | 24.0 |
| Australasia | 7 | 8.7 | 10.9 | -2.9 | 19.3 |
| Caribbean | 9 | 6.7 | 6.3 | 1.3 | 14.0 |
| Central and Eastern Europe | 25 | 4.4 | 2.7 | -0.9 | 12.8 |
| Latin America | 20 | 4.8 | 5.4 | -1.8 | 14.3 |
| Middle East | 13 | 5.0 | 3.0 | -1.1 | 16.8 |
| North America | 2 | -2.5 | -2.5 | -2.9 | -2.1 |
| Western Europe | 19 | -1.2 | -1.6 | -3.7 | 7.2 |

## CCR Base Cost of Equity Capital:

| United Arab Emirates | COE (%) |
|---|---|
| March 2017 | 9.4 |
| December 2016 | 9.0 |

CCR base country-level COE for an United Arab Emirate based investor investing in the United Arab Emirates.

§ S&P Credit Rating based on long-term foreign currency issuer rating. See http://www.standardandpoors.com/.

* World rank based on 175 countries covered by Euromoney. Ranking based on ascending order in which '1' equals the smallest country risk premium (CRP) and '175' equals the largest country risk premium (CRP).

† MSCI Market Classification based on MSCI Market Classification Framework. See http://www.msci.com/products/indexes/market_classification.html

‡ Regional classification based on Euromoney. Regional rankings based on ascending order in which '1' equals the smallest country risk premium (CRP) for each region.

** Investment grade based on S&P sovereign credit rating from AAA to BBB-. Non-Investment grade based on S&P sovereign credit rating from BB+ to SD. For purposes of this analysis, the U.S. is being treated as if it were rated AAA by S&P.

Note: A CRP of 0.0% is assumed in the following cases: (i) when the investor country and the investee country both have an S&P sovereign credit rating of AAA; or (ii) when the investor country has an S&P credit rating of AAA, and the investee country has a sovereign credit rating below AAA, but has a calculated CRP below 0.0% (which would imply lower risk than a country rated AAA); or (iii) when the investor country has an S&P credit rating below AAA, and the investee country has a sovereign credit rating of AAA, but has a calculated CRP above 0.0% (which would imply greater risk than a country rated below AAA). For purposes of this analysis, the U.S. is treated as having a sovereign credit rating equivalent to AAA.

The country risk premium (CRP) is not the cost of equity capital (COE). The CRP is to be added to base COE. See Chapter 6 for proper application.

## Data Updated Through March 2017

| Investee Country | December 2016 Country Risk Premium (CRP) (%) | March 2017 Country Risk Premium (CRP) (%) | S&P Sovereign Credit Rating § | World Rank Out of 175∗ | MSCI Market Classification † | Euromoney Region ‡ | Regional Rank ‡ |
|---|---|---|---|---|---|---|---|
| Afghanistan | 13.9 | 13.5 | | 139 | | Asia | 23 out of 29 |
| Albania | 8.8 | 8.9 | B+ | 93 | | Central and Eastern Europe | 18 out of 25 |
| Algeria | 8.9 | 8.8 | | 91 | | Africa | 10 out of 51 |
| Angola | 11.1 | 11.0 | B | 121 | | Africa | 26 out of 51 |
| Argentina | 9.4 | 9.0 | B- | 96 | Frontier | Latin America | 13 out of 20 |
| Armenia | 6.6 | 6.7 | | 77 | | Asia | 15 out of 29 |
| Australia | -1.7 | -1.9 | AAA | 12 | Developed | Australasia | 2 out of 7 |
| Austria | -1.5 | -1.7 | AA+ | 13 | Developed | Western Europe | 9 out of 19 |
| Azerbaijan | 7.7 | 7.9 | BB+ | 85 | | Asia | 17 out of 29 |
| Bahamas | 5.3 | 4.9 | BB+ | 65 | | Caribbean | 3 out of 9 |
| Bahrain | 5.2 | 4.9 | BB- | 64 | Frontier | Middle East | 7 out of 13 |
| Bangladesh | 11.5 | 11.2 | BB- | 126 | Frontier | Asia | 20 out of 29 |
| Barbados | 6.8 | 7.7 | CCC+ | 82 | | Caribbean | 4 out of 9 |
| Belarus | 13.6 | 13.9 | B- | 143 | | Central and Eastern Europe | 23 out of 25 |
| Belgium | -0.4 | -0.6 | AA | 17 | Developed | Western Europe | 10 out of 19 |
| Belize | 9.8 | 9.8 | B- | 106 | | Latin America | 17 out of 20 |
| Benin | 15.2 | 15.1 | | 150 | | Africa | 37 out of 51 |
| Bermuda | 3.1 | 2.8 | A+ | 44 | | Caribbean | 1 out of 9 |
| Bhutan | 14.9 | 14.6 | | 148 | | Asia | 25 out of 29 |
| Bolivia | 8.4 | 8.6 | BB | 88 | | Latin America | 12 out of 20 |
| Bosnia & Herzegovina | 14.0 | 14.0 | B | 144 | | Central and Eastern Europe | 24 out of 25 |
| Botswana | 3.1 | 2.9 | A- | 48 | | Africa | 1 out of 51 |
| Brazil | 4.5 | 4.2 | BB | 59 | Emerging | Latin America | 7 out of 20 |
| Bulgaria | 4.3 | 4.4 | BB+ | 61 | | Central and Eastern Europe | 12 out of 25 |
| Burkina Faso | 12.5 | 12.4 | B- | 133 | | Africa | 33 out of 51 |
| Burundi | 23.5 | 23.4 | | 169 | | Africa | 47 out of 51 |
| Cambodia | 15.7 | 15.3 | | 151 | | Asia | 27 out of 29 |
| Cameroon | 11.3 | 11.1 | B | 124 | | Africa | 28 out of 51 |
| Canada | -1.9 | -2.1 | AAA | 9 | Developed | North America | 1 out of 2 |
| Cape Verde | 9.0 | 8.9 | B | 94 | | Africa | 12 out of 51 |
| Central African Republic | 26.8 | 26.7 | | 172 | | Africa | 49 out of 51 |
| Chad | 25.6 | 25.5 | | 171 | | Africa | 48 out of 51 |
| Chile | -0.8 | -0.7 | AA- | 16 | Emerging | Latin America | 1 out of 20 |
| China | 2.9 | 2.7 | AA- | 42 | Emerging | Asia | 7 out of 29 |
| Colombia | 2.8 | 2.7 | BBB | 41 | Emerging | Latin America | 4 out of 20 |
| Congo Republic | 10.9 | 10.6 | B- | 117 | | Africa | 24 out of 51 |
| Congo, DR | 12.1 | 11.9 | B- | 131 | | Africa | 32 out of 51 |
| Costa Rica | 5.7 | 5.7 | BB- | 71 | | Latin America | 8 out of 20 |
| Côte d'Ivoire | 8.9 | 8.8 | | 92 | | Africa | 11 out of 51 |
| Croatia | 4.8 | 4.6 | BB | 63 | Frontier | Central and Eastern Europe | 13 out of 25 |
| Cuba | 17.8 | 17.8 | | 160 | | Caribbean | 9 out of 9 |
| Cyprus | 2.6 | 2.6 | BB+ | 40 | | Central and Eastern Europe | 7 out of 25 |
| Czech Republic | 0.4 | 0.2 | AA- | 23 | Emerging | Central and Eastern Europe | 1 out of 25 |
| Denmark | -2.5 | -2.6 | AAA | 4 | Developed | Western Europe | 3 out of 19 |
| Djibouti | 34.2 | 31.9 | | 175 | | Africa | 51 out of 51 |
| Dominican Republic | 8.8 | 8.7 | BB- | 90 | | Caribbean | 5 out of 9 |
| Ecuador | 10.2 | 10.0 | B | 109 | | Latin America | 18 out of 20 |
| Egypt | 10.6 | 10.5 | B- | 116 | Emerging | Africa | 23 out of 51 |
| El Salvador | 7.9 | 7.6 | B- | 81 | | Latin America | 10 out of 20 |
| Equatorial Guinea | 20.2 | 20.1 | | 165 | | Africa | 45 out of 51 |

§ S&P Credit Rating based on long-term foreign currency issuer rating. See http://www.standardandpoors.com/.
∗ World rank based on 175 countries covered by Euromoney. Ranking based on ascending order in which '1' equals the smallest country risk premium (CRP) and '175' equals the largest country risk premium (CRP).
† MSCI Market Classification based on MSCI Market Classification Framework. See http://www.msci.com/products/indexes/market_classification.html
‡ Regional classification based on Euromoney. Regional rankings based on ascending order in which '1' equals the smallest country risk premium (CRP) for each region.
Note: A CRP of 0.0% is assumed in the following cases: (i) when the investor country and the investee country both have an S&P sovereign credit rating of AAA; or (ii) when the investor country has an S&P credit rating of AAA, and the investee country has a sovereign credit rating below AAA, but has a calculated CRP below 0.0% (which would imply lower risk than a country rated AAA); or (iii) when the investor country has an S&P credit rating below AAA, and the investee country has a sovereign credit rating of AAA, but has a calculated CRP above 0.0% (which would imply greater risk than a country rated below AAA). For purposes of this analysis, the U.S. is treated as having a sovereign credit rating equivalent to AAA.

The country risk premium (CRP) is not the cost of equity capital (COE). The CRP is to be added to base COE. See Chapter 6 for proper application.

## Data Updated Through March 2017

| Investee Country | December 2016 Country Risk Premium (CRP) (%) | March 2017 Country Risk Premium (CRP) (%) | S&P Sovereign Credit Rating § | World Rank Out of 175* | MSCI Market Classification † | Euromoney Region ‡ | Regional Rank ‡ |
|---|---|---|---|---|---|---|---|
| Eritrea | 30.7 | 28.8 | | 173 | | Africa | 50 out of 51 |
| Estonia | 0.9 | 1.0 | AA- | 32 | Frontier | Central and Eastern Europe | 4 out of 25 |
| Ethiopia | 9.6 | 9.5 | B | 101 | | Africa | 16 out of 51 |
| Fiji | 14.6 | 14.3 | B+ | 147 | | Australasia | 5 out of 7 |
| Finland | -1.8 | -1.9 | AA+ | 11 | Developed | Western Europe | 8 out of 19 |
| France | 0.4 | 0.1 | AA | 22 | Developed | Western Europe | 12 out of 19 |
| Gabon | 7.5 | 7.7 | | 83 | | Africa | 7 out of 51 |
| Gambia | 13.1 | 13.0 | | 138 | | Africa | 34 out of 51 |
| Georgia | 6.3 | 6.4 | BB- | 74 | | Central and Eastern Europe | 15 out of 25 |
| Germany | -1.8 | -2.0 | AAA | 10 | Developed | Western Europe | 7 out of 19 |
| Ghana | 9.1 | 8.6 | B- | 89 | | Africa | 9 out of 51 |
| Greece | 10.2 | 9.8 | B- | 108 | Emerging | Western Europe | 19 out of 19 |
| Grenada | 9.8 | 9.7 | | 105 | | Caribbean | 7 out of 9 |
| Guatemala | 7.9 | 7.8 | BB | 84 | | Latin America | 11 out of 20 |
| Guinea | 16.6 | 16.4 | | 156 | | Africa | 41 out of 51 |
| Guinea-Bissau | 10.6 | 10.5 | | 115 | | Africa | 22 out of 51 |
| Guyana | 9.5 | 9.4 | | 100 | | Latin America | 15 out of 20 |
| Haiti | 19.2 | 17.2 | | 157 | | Caribbean | 8 out of 9 |
| Honduras | 9.2 | 9.1 | B+ | 98 | | Latin America | 14 out of 20 |
| Hong Kong | -1.2 | -1.4 | AAA | 14 | Developed | Asia | 2 out of 29 |
| Hungary | 4.1 | 4.1 | BBB- | 57 | Emerging | Central and Eastern Europe | 10 out of 25 |
| Iceland | 1.3 | 1.0 | A | 30 | | Western Europe | 15 out of 19 |
| India | 3.9 | 4.0 | BBB- | 55 | Emerging | Asia | 10 out of 29 |
| Indonesia | 4.6 | 4.5 | BB+ | 62 | Emerging | Asia | 11 out of 29 |
| Iran | 11.0 | 11.1 | | 125 | | Middle East | 10 out of 13 |
| Iraq | 12.8 | 12.7 | B- | 136 | | Middle East | 11 out of 13 |
| Ireland | 0.9 | 0.7 | A+ | 27 | Developed | Western Europe | 14 out of 19 |
| Israel | 0.8 | 0.7 | A+ | 28 | Developed | Middle East | 2 out of 13 |
| Italy | 3.5 | 3.2 | BBB- | 50 | Developed | Western Europe | 18 out of 19 |
| Jamaica | 9.3 | 9.7 | B | 104 | | Caribbean | 6 out of 9 |
| Japan | 0.7 | 0.6 | A+ | 25 | Developed | Asia | 5 out of 29 |
| Jordan | 6.6 | 6.6 | BB- | 76 | Frontier | Middle East | 8 out of 13 |
| Kazakhstan | 6.1 | 5.6 | BBB- | 70 | Frontier | Asia | 13 out of 29 |
| Kenya | 9.3 | 9.2 | B+ | 99 | Frontier | Africa | 15 out of 51 |
| Korea (North) | 30.1 | 29.5 | | 174 | | Asia | 29 out of 29 |
| Korea (South) | 0.0 | -0.1 | AA | 19 | Emerging | Asia | 4 out of 29 |
| Kuwait | 1.0 | 1.0 | AA | 31 | Frontier | Middle East | 3 out of 13 |
| Kyrgyz Republic | 14.1 | 13.8 | | 142 | | Central and Eastern Europe | 22 out of 25 |
| Laos | 18.0 | 17.4 | | 158 | | Asia | 28 out of 29 |
| Latvia | 2.9 | 2.8 | A- | 43 | | Central and Eastern Europe | 8 out of 25 |
| Lebanon | 10.9 | 10.2 | B- | 112 | Frontier | Middle East | 9 out of 13 |
| Lesotho | 14.3 | 14.2 | | 146 | | Africa | 36 out of 51 |
| Liberia | 9.9 | 9.8 | | 107 | | Africa | 17 out of 51 |
| Libya | 15.7 | 15.9 | | 153 | | Africa | 39 out of 51 |
| Lithuania | 2.1 | 2.1 | A- | 36 | Frontier | Central and Eastern Europe | 6 out of 25 |
| Luxembourg | -2.2 | -2.4 | AAA | 5 | | Western Europe | 4 out of 19 |
| Macedonia | 8.4 | 8.5 | BB- | 87 | | Central and Eastern Europe | 17 out of 25 |
| Madagascar | 10.7 | 11.1 | | 123 | | Africa | 27 out of 51 |
| Malawi | 10.4 | 10.3 | | 114 | | Africa | 21 out of 51 |
| Malaysia | 2.3 | 2.0 | A- | 35 | Emerging | Asia | 6 out of 29 |

§ S&P Credit Rating based on long-term foreign currency issuer rating. See http://www.standardandpoors.com/.
∗ World rank based on 175 countries covered by Euromoney. Ranking based on ascending order in which '1' equals the smallest country risk premium (CRP) and '175' equals the largest country risk premium (CRP).
† MSCI Market Classification based on MSCI Market Classification Framework. See http://www.msci.com/products/indexes/market_classification.html
‡ Regional classification based on Euromoney. Regional rankings based on ascending order in which '1' equals the smallest country risk premium (CRP) for each region.
Note: A CRP of 0.0% is assumed in the following cases: (i) when the investor country and the investee country both have an S&P sovereign credit rating of AAA; or (ii) when the investor country has an S&P credit rating of AAA, and the investee country has a sovereign credit rating below AAA, but has a calculated CRP below 0.0% (which would imply lower risk than a country rated AAA); or (iii) when the investor country has an S&P credit rating below AAA, and the investee country has a sovereign credit rating of AAA, but has a calculated CRP above 0.0% (which would imply greater risk than a country rated below AAA). For purposes of this analysis, the U.S. is treated as having a sovereign credit rating equivalent to AAA.

The country risk premium (CRP) is not the cost of equity capital (COE). The CRP is to be added to base COE. See Chapter 6 for proper application.

### Data Updated Through March 2017

| Investee Country | December 2016 Country Risk Premium (CRP) (%) | March 2017 Country Risk Premium (CRP) (%) | S&P Sovereign Credit Rating § | World Rank Out of 175∗ | MSCI Market Classification † | Euromoney Region ‡ | Regional Rank ‡ |
|---|---|---|---|---|---|---|---|
| Mali | 13.9 | 13.8 | | 141 | | Africa | 35 out of 51 |
| Malta | 0.7 | 0.6 | A- | 26 | | Western Europe | 13 out of 19 |
| Mauritania | 17.7 | 17.6 | | 159 | | Africa | 42 out of 51 |
| Mauritius | 5.5 | 5.3 | | 67 | Frontier | Asia | 12 out of 29 |
| Mexico | 2.2 | 2.2 | BBB+ | 37 | Emerging | Latin America | 2 out of 20 |
| Moldova | 12.4 | 12.7 | | 137 | | Central and Eastern Europe | 21 out of 25 |
| Mongolia | 10.8 | 11.0 | B- | 119 | | Asia | 18 out of 29 |
| Montenegro | 10.0 | 9.7 | B+ | 103 | | Central and Eastern Europe | 19 out of 25 |
| Morocco | 5.5 | 5.6 | BBB- | 69 | Frontier | Africa | 4 out of 51 |
| Mozambique | 11.8 | 11.5 | SD | 128 | | Africa | 29 out of 51 |
| Myanmar | 12.6 | 12.4 | | 134 | | Asia | 22 out of 29 |
| Namibia | 5.1 | 5.2 | | 66 | | Africa | 3 out of 51 |
| Nepal | 15.1 | 15.0 | | 149 | | Asia | 26 out of 29 |
| Netherlands | -2.1 | -2.3 | AAA | 6 | Developed | Western Europe | 5 out of 19 |
| New Zealand | -2.0 | -2.1 | AA | 8 | Developed | Australasia | 1 out of 7 |
| Nicaragua | 11.5 | 11.4 | B+ | 127 | | Latin America | 19 out of 20 |
| Niger | 11.1 | 11.0 | | 120 | | Africa | 25 out of 51 |
| Nigeria | 9.2 | 9.1 | B | 97 | Frontier | Africa | 14 out of 51 |
| Norway | -2.8 | -2.9 | AAA | 3 | Developed | Western Europe | 2 out of 19 |
| Oman | 3.0 | 2.9 | BBB- | 46 | Frontier | Middle East | 5 out of 13 |
| Pakistan | 11.2 | 11.0 | B | 122 | Frontier | Asia | 19 out of 29 |
| Panama | 3.7 | 3.6 | BBB | 52 | | Latin America | 6 out of 20 |
| Papua New Guinea | 10.7 | 10.7 | B+ | 118 | | Australasia | 3 out of 7 |
| Paraguay | 6.9 | 7.0 | BB | 80 | | Latin America | 9 out of 20 |
| Peru | 2.5 | 2.5 | BBB+ | 39 | Emerging | Latin America | 3 out of 20 |
| Philippines | 4.0 | 3.8 | BBB | 53 | Emerging | Asia | 9 out of 29 |
| Poland | 1.2 | 0.9 | BBB+ | 29 | Emerging | Central and Eastern Europe | 3 out of 25 |
| Portugal | 3.4 | 3.1 | BB+ | 49 | Developed | Western Europe | 17 out of 19 |
| Qatar | 0.1 | 0.1 | AA | 21 | Emerging | Middle East | 1 out of 13 |
| Romania | 4.1 | 4.1 | BBB- | 56 | Frontier | Central and Eastern Europe | 9 out of 25 |
| Russia | 6.2 | 5.5 | BB+ | 68 | Emerging | Central and Eastern Europe | 14 out of 25 |
| Rwanda | 11.8 | 11.7 | B | 130 | | Africa | 31 out of 51 |
| São Tomé & Príncipe | 17.8 | 18.1 | | 163 | | Africa | 43 out of 51 |
| Saudi Arabia | 3.3 | 2.9 | A- | 47 | | Middle East | 6 out of 13 |
| Senegal | 8.6 | 8.5 | B+ | 86 | | Africa | 8 out of 51 |
| Serbia | 6.9 | 6.5 | BB- | 75 | Frontier | Central and Eastern Europe | 16 out of 25 |
| Seychelles | 6.4 | 6.2 | | 73 | | Africa | 5 out of 51 |
| Sierra Leone | 11.8 | 11.7 | | 129 | | Africa | 30 out of 51 |
| Singapore | -2.9 | -3.1 | AAA | 1 | Developed | Asia | 1 out of 29 |
| Slovakia | 0.5 | 0.4 | A+ | 24 | | Central and Eastern Europe | 2 out of 25 |
| Slovenia | 1.8 | 1.7 | A | 34 | Frontier | Central and Eastern Europe | 5 out of 25 |
| Solomon Islands | 21.9 | 21.7 | | 168 | | Australasia | 6 out of 7 |
| Somalia | 20.2 | 20.1 | | 166 | | Africa | 46 out of 51 |
| South Africa | 4.2 | 4.3 | BBB- | 60 | Emerging | Africa | 2 out of 51 |
| Spain | 2.6 | 2.4 | BBB+ | 38 | Developed | Western Europe | 16 out of 19 |
| Sri Lanka | 6.3 | 5.9 | B+ | 72 | Frontier | Asia | 14 out of 29 |
| Sudan | 16.5 | 16.3 | | 154 | | Africa | 40 out of 51 |
| Suriname | 9.5 | 9.5 | B+ | 102 | | Latin America | 16 out of 20 |
| Swaziland | 14.9 | 15.7 | | 152 | | Africa | 38 out of 51 |
| Sweden | -2.1 | -2.3 | AAA | 7 | Developed | Western Europe | 6 out of 19 |

§ S&P Credit Rating based on long-term foreign currency issuer rating. See http://www.standardandpoors.com/.

∗ World rank based on 175 countries covered by Euromoney. Ranking based on ascending order in which '1' equals the smallest country risk premium (CRP) and '175' equals the largest country risk premium (CRP).

† MSCI Market Classification based on MSCI Market Classification Framework. See http://www.msci.com/products/indexes/market_classification.html.

‡ Regional classification based on Euromoney. Regional rankings based on ascending order in which '1' equals the smallest country risk premium (CRP) for each region.

Note: A CRP of 0.0% is assumed in the following cases: (i) when the investor country and the investee country both have an S&P sovereign credit rating of AAA; or (ii) when the investor country has an S&P credit rating of AAA, and the investee country has a sovereign credit rating below AAA, but has a calculated CRP below 0.0% (which would imply lower risk than a country rated AAA); or (iii) when the investor country has an S&P credit rating below AAA, and the investee country has a sovereign credit rating of AAA, but has a calculated CRP above 0.0% (which would imply greater risk than a country rated below AAA). For purposes of this analysis, the U.S. is treated as having a sovereign credit rating equivalent to AAA.

The country risk premium (CRP) is not the cost of equity capital (COE).  The CRP is to be added to base COE. See Chapter 6 for proper application.

## Data Updated Through March 2017

| Investee Country | December 2016 Country Risk Premium (CRP) (%) | March 2017 Country Risk Premium (CRP) (%) | S&P Sovereign Credit Rating § | World Rank Out of 175* | MSCI Market Classification † | Euromoney Region ‡ | Regional Rank ‡ |
|---|---|---|---|---|---|---|---|
| Switzerland | -2.7 | -3.0 | AAA | 2 | Developed | Western Europe | 1 out of 19 |
| Syria | 20.9 | 21.0 | | 167 | | Middle East | 13 out of 13 |
| Taiwan | -0.2 | -0.4 | AA- | 18 | Emerging | Asia | 3 out of 29 |
| Tajikistan | 16.1 | 16.3 | | 155 | | Central and Eastern Europe | 25 out of 25 |
| Tanzania | 8.9 | 9.0 | | 95 | | Africa | 13 out of 51 |
| Thailand | 3.7 | 3.4 | BBB+ | 51 | Emerging | Asia | 8 out of 29 |
| Togo | 10.4 | 10.3 | | 113 | | Africa | 20 out of 51 |
| Tonga | 24.1 | 24.0 | | 170 | | Australasia | 7 out of 7 |
| Trinidad & Tobago | 4.0 | 3.9 | A- | 54 | | Caribbean | 2 out of 9 |
| Tunisia | 6.7 | 6.9 | | 79 | Frontier | Africa | 6 out of 51 |
| Turkey | 4.3 | 4.1 | BB | 58 | Emerging | Central and Eastern Europe | 11 out of 25 |
| Turkmenistan | 13.5 | 13.6 | | 140 | | Asia | 24 out of 29 |
| Uganda | 9.9 | 10.1 | B | 110 | | Africa | 18 out of 51 |
| Ukraine | 12.6 | 12.5 | B- | 135 | | Central and Eastern Europe | 20 out of 25 |
| United Arab Emirates | 1.4 | 1.4 | AA | 33 | Emerging | Middle East | 4 out of 13 |
| United Kingdom | 0.0 | 0.0 | AA | 20 | Developed | Western Europe | 11 out of 19 |
| United States | -1.0 | -1.1 | AA+ | 15 | Developed | North America | 2 out of 2 |
| Uruguay | 3.1 | 2.9 | BBB | 45 | | Latin America | 5 out of 20 |
| Uzbekistan | 12.7 | 12.1 | | 132 | | Asia | 21 out of 29 |
| Vanuatu | 14.3 | 14.2 | | 145 | | Australasia | 4 out of 7 |
| Venezuela | 17.8 | 18.1 | CCC | 162 | | Latin America | 20 out of 20 |
| Vietnam | 7.2 | 6.8 | BB- | 78 | Frontier | Asia | 16 out of 29 |
| Yemen | 18.1 | 18.0 | | 161 | | Middle East | 12 out of 13 |
| Zambia | 10.3 | 10.2 | B | 111 | | Africa | 19 out of 51 |
| Zimbabwe | 19.6 | 19.4 | | 164 | | Africa | 44 out of 51 |

## March 2017 Country Risk Premium (CRP) Summary Statistics:

| S&P Rating | Country Count | Average CRP (%) | Median CRP (%) | Min CRP (%) | Max CRP (%) |
|---|---|---|---|---|---|
| AAA ** | 12 | -2.2 | -2.3 | -3.1 | -1.1 |
| AA (AA+, AA, AA-) | 15 | -0.1 | 0.0 | -2.1 | 2.7 |
| A (A+, A, A-) | 14 | 1.8 | 1.9 | 0.4 | 3.9 |
| BBB (BBB+, BBB, BBB-) | 17 | 3.4 | 3.4 | 0.9 | 5.6 |
| BB (BB+, BB, BB-) | 22 | 6.1 | 6.1 | 2.6 | 11.2 |
| B+ − SD | 39 | 10.5 | 10.2 | 5.9 | 18.1 |
| Investment Grade ** | 58 | 1.0 | 1.0 | -3.1 | 5.6 |
| Non-Investment Grade ** | 61 | 8.9 | 9.1 | 2.6 | 18.1 |
| **MSCI Market Classification** | | | | | |
| Developed Markets | 23 | -0.9 | -1.7 | -3.1 | 3.2 |
| Emerging Markets | 23 | 3.1 | 2.7 | -0.7 | 10.5 |
| Frontier Markets | 22 | 6.0 | 5.8 | 1.0 | 11.2 |
| **Euromoney Region ‡** | | | | | |
| Africa | 51 | 12.9 | 11.0 | 2.9 | 31.9 |
| Asia | 29 | 8.0 | 6.7 | -3.1 | 29.5 |
| Australasia | 7 | 11.6 | 14.2 | -2.1 | 24.0 |
| Caribbean | 9 | 9.2 | 8.7 | 2.8 | 17.8 |
| Central and Eastern Europe | 25 | 6.5 | 4.6 | 0.2 | 16.3 |
| Latin America | 20 | 7.0 | 7.7 | -0.7 | 18.1 |
| Middle East | 13 | 7.2 | 4.9 | 0.1 | 21.0 |
| North America | 2 | -1.6 | -1.6 | -2.1 | -1.1 |
| Western Europe | 19 | 0.0 | -0.6 | -3.0 | 9.8 |

## CCR Base Cost of Equity Capital:

| United Kingdom | COE (%) |
|---|---|
| March 2017 | 10.8 |
| December 2016 | 10.6 |

CCR base country-level COE for an United Kingdom-based investor investing in the United Kingdom.

§ S&P Credit Rating based on long-term foreign currency issuer rating. See http://www.standardandpoors.com/.

* World rank based on 175 countries covered by Euromoney. Ranking based on ascending order in which '1' equals the smallest country risk premium (CRP) and '175' equals the largest country risk premium (CRP).

† MSCI Market Classification based on MSCI Market Classification Framework.  See http://www.msci.com/products/indexes/market_classification.html

‡ Regional classification based on Euromoney. Regional rankings based on ascending order in which '1' equals the smallest country risk premium (CRP) for each region.

** Investment grade based on S&P sovereign credit rating from AAA to BBB-. Non-Investment grade based on S&P sovereign credit rating from BB+ to SD. For purposes of this analysis, the U.S. is being treated as if it were rated AAA by S&P.

Note: A CRP of 0.0% is assumed in the following cases: (i) when the investor country and the investee country both have an S&P sovereign credit rating of AAA; or (ii) when the investor country has an S&P credit rating of AAA, and the investee country has a sovereign credit rating below AAA, but has a calculated CRP below 0.0% (which would imply lower risk than a country rated AAA); or (iii) when the investor country has an S&P credit rating below AAA, and the investee country has a sovereign credit rating of AAA, but has a calculated CRP above 0.0% (which would imply greater risk than a country rated below AAA). For purposes of this analysis, the U.S. is treated as having a sovereign credit rating equivalent to AAA.

The country risk premium (CRP) is not the cost of equity capital (COE). The CRP is to be added to base COE. See Chapter 6 for proper application.

## Data Updated Through March 2017

| Investee Country | December 2016 Country Risk Premium (CRP) (%) | March 2017 Country Risk Premium (CRP) (%) | S&P Sovereign Credit Rating § | World Rank Out of 175∗ | MSCI Market Classification † | Euromoney Region ‡ | Regional Rank ‡ |
|---|---|---|---|---|---|---|---|
| Afghanistan | 15.0 | 15.0 | | 139 | | Asia | 23 out of 29 |
| Albania | 9.9 | 10.2 | B+ | 93 | | Central and Eastern Europe | 18 out of 25 |
| Algeria | 10.0 | 10.2 | | 91 | | Africa | 10 out of 51 |
| Angola | 12.2 | 12.4 | B | 121 | | Africa | 26 out of 51 |
| Argentina | 10.5 | 10.4 | B- | 96 | Frontier | Latin America | 13 out of 20 |
| Armenia | 7.7 | 8.0 | | 77 | | Asia | 15 out of 29 |
| Australia | 0.0 | 0.0 | AAA | 12 | Developed | Australasia | 2 out of 7 |
| Austria | 0.0 | 0.0 | AA+ | 13 | Developed | Western Europe | 9 out of 19 |
| Azerbaijan | 8.8 | 9.3 | BB+ | 85 | | Asia | 17 out of 29 |
| Bahamas | 6.3 | 6.1 | BB+ | 65 | | Caribbean | 3 out of 9 |
| Bahrain | 6.2 | 6.1 | BB- | 64 | Frontier | Middle East | 7 out of 13 |
| Bangladesh | 12.7 | 12.6 | BB- | 126 | Frontier | Asia | 20 out of 29 |
| Barbados | 7.9 | 9.0 | CCC+ | 82 | | Caribbean | 4 out of 9 |
| Belarus | 14.7 | 15.4 | B- | 143 | | Central and Eastern Europe | 23 out of 25 |
| Belgium | 0.6 | 0.5 | AA | 17 | Developed | Western Europe | 10 out of 19 |
| Belize | 10.9 | 11.2 | B- | 106 | | Latin America | 17 out of 20 |
| Benin | 16.3 | 16.6 | | 150 | | Africa | 37 out of 51 |
| Bermuda | 4.1 | 4.0 | A+ | 44 | | Caribbean | 1 out of 9 |
| Bhutan | 16.0 | 16.2 | | 148 | | Asia | 25 out of 29 |
| Bolivia | 9.5 | 9.9 | BB | 88 | | Latin America | 12 out of 20 |
| Bosnia & Herzegovina | 15.2 | 15.5 | B | 144 | | Central and Eastern Europe | 24 out of 25 |
| Botswana | 4.1 | 4.1 | A- | 48 | | Africa | 1 out of 51 |
| Brazil | 5.5 | 5.5 | BB | 59 | Emerging | Latin America | 7 out of 20 |
| Bulgaria | 5.4 | 5.6 | BB+ | 61 | | Central and Eastern Europe | 12 out of 25 |
| Burkina Faso | 13.6 | 13.9 | B- | 133 | | Africa | 33 out of 51 |
| Burundi | 24.8 | 25.2 | | 169 | | Africa | 47 out of 51 |
| Cambodia | 16.9 | 16.8 | | 151 | | Asia | 27 out of 29 |
| Cameroon | 12.4 | 12.5 | B | 124 | | Africa | 28 out of 51 |
| Canada | 0.0 | 0.0 | AAA | 9 | Developed | North America | 1 out of 2 |
| Cape Verde | 10.1 | 10.3 | B | 94 | | Africa | 12 out of 51 |
| Central African Republic | 28.1 | 28.6 | | 172 | | Africa | 49 out of 51 |
| Chad | 26.9 | 27.3 | | 171 | | Africa | 48 out of 51 |
| Chile | 0.2 | 0.4 | AA- | 16 | Emerging | Latin America | 1 out of 20 |
| China | 3.9 | 3.9 | AA- | 42 | Emerging | Asia | 7 out of 29 |
| Colombia | 3.8 | 3.9 | BBB | 41 | Emerging | Latin America | 4 out of 20 |
| Congo Republic | 12.0 | 12.0 | B- | 117 | | Africa | 24 out of 51 |
| Congo, DR | 13.2 | 13.3 | B- | 131 | | Africa | 32 out of 51 |
| Costa Rica | 6.7 | 7.0 | BB- | 71 | | Latin America | 8 out of 20 |
| Côte d'Ivoire | 10.0 | 10.2 | | 92 | | Africa | 11 out of 51 |
| Croatia | 5.9 | 5.8 | BB | 63 | Frontier | Central and Eastern Europe | 13 out of 25 |
| Cuba | 19.1 | 19.5 | | 160 | | Caribbean | 9 out of 9 |
| Cyprus | 3.6 | 3.7 | BB+ | 40 | | Central and Eastern Europe | 7 out of 25 |
| Czech Republic | 1.4 | 1.4 | AA- | 23 | Emerging | Central and Eastern Europe | 1 out of 25 |
| Denmark | 0.0 | 0.0 | AAA | 4 | Developed | Western Europe | 3 out of 19 |
| Djibouti | 35.6 | 34.0 | | 175 | | Africa | 51 out of 51 |
| Dominican Republic | 9.8 | 10.1 | BB- | 90 | | Caribbean | 5 out of 9 |
| Ecuador | 11.3 | 11.4 | B | 109 | | Latin America | 18 out of 20 |
| Egypt | 11.8 | 11.9 | B- | 116 | Emerging | Africa | 23 out of 51 |
| El Salvador | 8.9 | 8.9 | B- | 81 | | Latin America | 10 out of 20 |
| Equatorial Guinea | 21.4 | 21.8 | | 165 | | Africa | 45 out of 51 |

§ S&P Credit Rating based on long-term foreign currency issuer rating. See http://www.standardandpoors.com/.
∗ World rank based on 175 countries covered by Euromoney. Ranking based on ascending order in which '1' equals the smallest country risk premium (CRP) and '175' equals the largest country risk premium (CRP).
† MSCI Market Classification based on MSCI Market Classification Framework. See http://www.msci.com/products/indexes/market_classification.html
‡ Regional classification based on Euromoney. Regional rankings based on ascending order in which '1' equals the smallest country risk premium (CRP) for each region.
Note: A CRP of 0.0% is assumed in the following cases: (i) when the investor country and the investee country both have an S&P sovereign credit rating of AAA; or (ii) when the investor country has an S&P credit rating of AAA, and the investee country has a sovereign credit rating below AAA, but has a calculated CRP below 0.0% (which would imply lower risk than a country rated AAA); or (iii) when the investor country has an S&P credit rating below AAA, and the investee country has a sovereign credit rating of AAA, but has a calculated CRP above 0.0% (which would imply greater risk than a country rated below AAA). For purposes of this analysis, the U.S. is treated as having a sovereign credit rating equivalent to AAA.

2017 Valuation Handbook – International Guide to Cost of Capital          Data Exhibit 4          Investor Perspective: United States (USD); Page 1 of 4

The country risk premium (CRP) is not the cost of equity capital (COE).  The CRP is to be added to base COE. See Chapter 6 for proper application.

## Data Updated Through March 2017

| Investee Country | December 2016 Country Risk Premium (CRP) (%) | March 2017 Country Risk Premium (CRP) (%) | S&P Sovereign Credit Rating § | World Rank Out of 175* | MSCI Market Classification † | Euromoney Region ‡ | Regional Rank ‡ |
|---|---|---|---|---|---|---|---|
| Eritrea | 32.0 | 30.8 | | 173 | | Africa | 50 out of 51 |
| Estonia | 1.9 | 2.2 | AA- | 32 | Frontier | Central and Eastern Europe | 4 out of 25 |
| Ethiopia | 10.7 | 10.9 | B | 101 | | Africa | 16 out of 51 |
| Fiji | 15.7 | 15.8 | B+ | 147 | | Australasia | 5 out of 7 |
| Finland | 0.0 | 0.0 | AA+ | 11 | Developed | Western Europe | 8 out of 19 |
| France | 1.4 | 1.2 | AA | 22 | Developed | Western Europe | 12 out of 19 |
| Gabon | 8.6 | 9.0 | | 83 | | Africa | 7 out of 51 |
| Gambia | 14.3 | 14.5 | | 138 | | Africa | 34 out of 51 |
| Georgia | 7.4 | 7.8 | BB- | 74 | | Central and Eastern Europe | 15 out of 25 |
| Germany | 0.0 | 0.0 | AAA | 10 | Developed | Western Europe | 7 out of 19 |
| Ghana | 10.2 | 10.0 | B- | 89 | | Africa | 9 out of 51 |
| Greece | 11.3 | 11.2 | B- | 108 | Emerging | Western Europe | 19 out of 19 |
| Grenada | 10.9 | 11.1 | | 105 | | Caribbean | 7 out of 9 |
| Guatemala | 9.0 | 9.1 | BB | 84 | | Latin America | 11 out of 20 |
| Guinea | 17.7 | 18.0 | | 156 | | Africa | 41 out of 51 |
| Guinea-Bissau | 11.7 | 11.9 | | 115 | | Africa | 22 out of 51 |
| Guyana | 10.6 | 10.8 | | 100 | | Latin America | 15 out of 20 |
| Haiti | 20.4 | 18.8 | | 157 | | Caribbean | 8 out of 9 |
| Honduras | 10.3 | 10.5 | B+ | 98 | | Latin America | 14 out of 20 |
| Hong Kong | 0.0 | 0.0 | AAA | 14 | Developed | Asia | 2 out of 29 |
| Hungary | 5.1 | 5.3 | BBB- | 57 | Emerging | Central and Eastern Europe | 10 out of 25 |
| Iceland | 2.3 | 2.1 | A | 30 | | Western Europe | 15 out of 19 |
| India | 4.9 | 5.3 | BBB- | 55 | Emerging | Asia | 10 out of 29 |
| Indonesia | 5.6 | 5.7 | BB+ | 62 | Emerging | Asia | 11 out of 29 |
| Iran | 12.2 | 12.6 | | 125 | | Middle East | 10 out of 13 |
| Iraq | 13.9 | 14.1 | B- | 136 | | Middle East | 11 out of 13 |
| Ireland | 1.8 | 1.8 | A+ | 27 | Developed | Western Europe | 14 out of 19 |
| Israel | 1.8 | 1.8 | A+ | 28 | Developed | Middle East | 2 out of 13 |
| Italy | 4.6 | 4.5 | BBB- | 50 | Developed | Western Europe | 18 out of 19 |
| Jamaica | 10.4 | 11.1 | B | 104 | | Caribbean | 6 out of 9 |
| Japan | 1.7 | 1.7 | A+ | 25 | Developed | Asia | 5 out of 29 |
| Jordan | 7.6 | 7.9 | BB- | 76 | Frontier | Middle East | 8 out of 13 |
| Kazakhstan | 7.1 | 6.9 | BBB- | 70 | Frontier | Asia | 13 out of 29 |
| Kenya | 10.4 | 10.6 | B+ | 99 | Frontier | Africa | 15 out of 51 |
| Korea (North) | 31.4 | 31.5 | | 174 | | Asia | 29 out of 29 |
| Korea (South) | 1.0 | 1.0 | AA | 19 | Emerging | Asia | 4 out of 29 |
| Kuwait | 2.0 | 2.2 | AA | 31 | Frontier | Middle East | 3 out of 13 |
| Kyrgyz Republic | 15.2 | 15.3 | | 142 | | Central and Eastern Europe | 22 out of 25 |
| Laos | 19.3 | 19.0 | | 158 | | Asia | 28 out of 29 |
| Latvia | 3.9 | 4.0 | A- | 43 | | Central and Eastern Europe | 8 out of 25 |
| Lebanon | 12.1 | 11.6 | B- | 112 | Frontier | Middle East | 9 out of 13 |
| Lesotho | 15.4 | 15.7 | | 146 | | Africa | 36 out of 51 |
| Liberia | 11.0 | 11.2 | | 107 | | Africa | 17 out of 51 |
| Libya | 16.9 | 17.5 | | 153 | | Africa | 39 out of 51 |
| Lithuania | 3.1 | 3.3 | A- | 36 | Frontier | Central and Eastern Europe | 6 out of 25 |
| Luxembourg | 0.0 | 0.0 | AAA | 5 | | Western Europe | 4 out of 19 |
| Macedonia | 9.5 | 9.9 | BB- | 87 | | Central and Eastern Europe | 17 out of 25 |
| Madagascar | 11.8 | 12.5 | | 123 | | Africa | 27 out of 51 |
| Malawi | 11.6 | 11.7 | | 114 | | Africa | 21 out of 51 |
| Malaysia | 3.3 | 3.2 | A- | 35 | Emerging | Asia | 6 out of 29 |

§ S&P Credit Rating based on long-term foreign currency issuer rating. See http://www.standardandpoors.com/.

* World rank based on 175 countries covered by Euromoney. Ranking based on ascending order in which '1' equals the smallest country risk premium (CRP) and '175' equals the largest country risk premium (CRP).

† MSCI Market Classification based on MSCI Market Classification Framework.  See http://www.msci.com/products/indexes/market_classification.html

‡ Regional classification based on Euromoney. Regional rankings based on ascending order in which '1' equals the smallest country risk premium (CRP) for each region.

Note: A CRP of 0.0% is assumed in the following cases: (i) when the investor country and the investee country both have an S&P sovereign credit rating of AAA; or (ii) when the investor country has an S&P credit rating of AAA, and the investee country has a sovereign credit rating below AAA, but has a calculated CRP below 0.0% (which would imply lower risk than a country rated AAA); or (iii) when the investor country has an S&P credit rating below AAA, and the investee country has a sovereign credit rating of AAA, but has a calculated CRP above 0.0% (which would imply greater risk than a country rated below AAA). For purposes of this analysis, the U.S. is treated as having a sovereign credit rating equivalent to AAA.

Investor Perspective: United States
Currency: United States Dollar (USD)
The country risk premium (CRP) is not the cost of equity capital (COE). The CRP is to be added to base COE. See Chapter 6 for proper application.

Erb-Harvey-Viskanta
Country Credit Rating (CCR) Model

### Data Updated Through March 2017

| Investee Country | December 2016 Country Risk Premium (CRP) (%) | March 2017 Country Risk Premium (CRP) (%) | S&P Sovereign Credit Rating § | World Rank Out of 175∗ | MSCI Market Classification † | Euromoney Region ‡ | Regional Rank ‡ |
|---|---|---|---|---|---|---|---|
| Mali | 15.1 | 15.3 | | 141 | | Africa | 35 out of 51 |
| Malta | 1.7 | 1.8 | A- | 26 | | Western Europe | 13 out of 19 |
| Mauritania | 18.9 | 19.2 | | 159 | | Africa | 42 out of 51 |
| Mauritius | 6.5 | 6.6 | | 67 | Frontier | Asia | 12 out of 29 |
| Mexico | 3.2 | 3.3 | BBB+ | 37 | Emerging | Latin America | 2 out of 20 |
| Moldova | 13.6 | 14.2 | | 137 | | Central and Eastern Europe | 21 out of 25 |
| Mongolia | 11.9 | 12.4 | B- | 119 | | Asia | 18 out of 29 |
| Montenegro | 11.1 | 11.1 | B+ | 103 | | Central and Eastern Europe | 19 out of 25 |
| Morocco | 6.6 | 6.8 | BBB- | 69 | Frontier | Africa | 4 out of 51 |
| Mozambique | 12.9 | 13.0 | SD | 128 | | Africa | 29 out of 51 |
| Myanmar | 13.8 | 13.9 | | 134 | | Asia | 22 out of 29 |
| Namibia | 6.2 | 6.4 | | 66 | | Africa | 3 out of 51 |
| Nepal | 16.3 | 16.6 | | 149 | | Asia | 26 out of 29 |
| Netherlands | 0.0 | 0.0 | AAA | 6 | Developed | Western Europe | 5 out of 19 |
| New Zealand | 0.0 | 0.0 | AA | 8 | Developed | Australasia | 1 out of 7 |
| Nicaragua | 12.6 | 12.8 | B+ | 127 | | Latin America | 19 out of 20 |
| Niger | 12.2 | 12.4 | | 120 | | Africa | 25 out of 51 |
| Nigeria | 10.3 | 10.5 | B | 97 | Frontier | Africa | 14 out of 51 |
| Norway | 0.0 | 0.0 | AAA | 3 | Developed | Western Europe | 2 out of 19 |
| Oman | 4.0 | 4.1 | BBB- | 46 | Frontier | Middle East | 5 out of 13 |
| Pakistan | 12.3 | 12.4 | B | 122 | Frontier | Asia | 19 out of 29 |
| Panama | 4.7 | 4.8 | BBB | 52 | | Latin America | 6 out of 20 |
| Papua New Guinea | 11.8 | 12.1 | B+ | 118 | | Australasia | 3 out of 7 |
| Paraguay | 8.0 | 8.3 | BB | 80 | | Latin America | 9 out of 20 |
| Peru | 3.5 | 3.6 | BBB+ | 39 | Emerging | Latin America | 3 out of 20 |
| Philippines | 5.0 | 5.1 | BBB | 53 | Emerging | Asia | 9 out of 29 |
| Poland | 2.2 | 2.1 | BBB+ | 29 | Emerging | Central and Eastern Europe | 3 out of 25 |
| Portugal | 4.4 | 4.3 | BB+ | 49 | Developed | Western Europe | 17 out of 19 |
| Qatar | 1.1 | 1.2 | AA | 21 | Emerging | Middle East | 1 out of 13 |
| Romania | 5.2 | 5.3 | BBB- | 56 | Frontier | Central and Eastern Europe | 9 out of 25 |
| Russia | 7.3 | 6.8 | BB+ | 68 | Emerging | Central and Eastern Europe | 14 out of 25 |
| Rwanda | 13.0 | 13.2 | B | 130 | | Africa | 31 out of 51 |
| São Tomé & Príncipe | 19.0 | 19.8 | | 163 | | Africa | 43 out of 51 |
| Saudi Arabia | 4.4 | 4.1 | A- | 47 | | Middle East | 6 out of 13 |
| Senegal | 9.7 | 9.8 | B+ | 86 | | Africa | 8 out of 51 |
| Serbia | 7.9 | 7.8 | BB- | 75 | Frontier | Central and Eastern Europe | 16 out of 25 |
| Seychelles | 7.4 | 7.5 | | 73 | | Africa | 5 out of 51 |
| Sierra Leone | 13.0 | 13.2 | | 129 | | Africa | 30 out of 51 |
| Singapore | 0.0 | 0.0 | AAA | 1 | Developed | Asia | 1 out of 29 |
| Slovakia | 1.5 | 1.5 | A+ | 24 | | Central and Eastern Europe | 2 out of 25 |
| Slovenia | 2.8 | 2.9 | A | 34 | Frontier | Central and Eastern Europe | 5 out of 25 |
| Solomon Islands | 23.1 | 23.5 | | 168 | | Australasia | 6 out of 7 |
| Somalia | 21.5 | 21.8 | | 166 | | Africa | 46 out of 51 |
| South Africa | 5.2 | 5.5 | BBB- | 60 | Emerging | Africa | 2 out of 51 |
| Spain | 3.6 | 3.6 | BBB+ | 38 | Developed | Western Europe | 16 out of 19 |
| Sri Lanka | 7.4 | 7.2 | B+ | 72 | Frontier | Asia | 14 out of 29 |
| Sudan | 17.7 | 17.9 | | 154 | | Africa | 40 out of 51 |
| Suriname | 10.6 | 10.9 | B+ | 102 | | Latin America | 16 out of 20 |
| Swaziland | 16.1 | 17.3 | | 152 | | Africa | 38 out of 51 |
| Sweden | 0.0 | 0.0 | AAA | 7 | Developed | Western Europe | 6 out of 19 |

§ S&P Credit Rating based on long-term foreign currency issuer rating. See http://www.standardandpoors.com/.
∗ World rank based on 175 countries covered by Euromoney. Ranking based on ascending order in which '1' equals the smallest country risk premium (CRP) and '175' equals the largest country risk premium (CRP).
† MSCI Market Classification based on MSCI Market Classification Framework. See http://www.msci.com/products/indexes/market_classification.html.
‡ Regional classification based on Euromoney. Regional rankings based on ascending order in which '1' equals the smallest country risk premium (CRP) for each region.
Note: A CRP of 0.0% is assumed in the following cases: (i) when the investor country and the investee country both have an S&P sovereign credit rating of AAA; or (ii) when the investor country has an S&P credit rating of AAA, and the investee country has a sovereign credit rating below AAA, but has a calculated CRP below 0.0% (which would imply lower risk than a country rated AAA); or (iii) when the investor country has an S&P credit rating below AAA, and the investee country has a sovereign credit rating of AAA, but has a calculated CRP above 0.0% (which would imply greater risk than a country rated below AAA). For purposes of this analysis, the U.S. is treated as having a sovereign credit rating equivalent to AAA.

The country risk premium (CRP) is not the cost of equity capital (COE). The CRP is to be added to base COE. See Chapter 6 for proper application.

## Data Updated Through March 2017

| Investee Country | December 2016 Country Risk Premium (CRP) (%) | March 2017 Country Risk Premium (CRP) (%) | S&P Sovereign Credit Rating § | World Rank Out of 175* | MSCI Market Classification † | Euromoney Region ‡ | Regional Rank ‡ |
|---|---|---|---|---|---|---|---|
| Switzerland | 0.0 | 0.0 | AAA | 2 | Developed | Western Europe | 1 out of 19 |
| Syria | 22.2 | 22.8 | | 167 | | Middle East | 13 out of 13 |
| Taiwan | 0.7 | 0.7 | AA- | 18 | Emerging | Asia | 3 out of 29 |
| Tajikistan | 17.3 | 17.9 | | 155 | | Central and Eastern Europe | 25 out of 25 |
| Tanzania | 10.0 | 10.4 | | 95 | | Africa | 13 out of 51 |
| Thailand | 4.7 | 4.6 | BBB+ | 51 | Emerging | Asia | 8 out of 29 |
| Togo | 11.5 | 11.7 | | 113 | | Africa | 20 out of 51 |
| Tonga | 25.4 | 25.8 | | 170 | | Australasia | 7 out of 7 |
| Trinidad & Tobago | 5.0 | 5.1 | A- | 54 | | Caribbean | 2 out of 9 |
| Tunisia | 7.7 | 8.2 | | 79 | Frontier | Africa | 6 out of 51 |
| Turkey | 5.4 | 5.4 | BB | 58 | Emerging | Central and Eastern Europe | 11 out of 25 |
| Turkmenistan | 14.6 | 15.1 | | 140 | | Asia | 24 out of 29 |
| Uganda | 11.0 | 11.5 | B | 110 | | Africa | 18 out of 51 |
| Ukraine | 13.7 | 14.0 | B- | 135 | | Central and Eastern Europe | 20 out of 25 |
| United Arab Emirates | 2.4 | 2.5 | AA | 33 | Emerging | Middle East | 4 out of 13 |
| United Kingdom | 1.0 | 1.1 | AA | 20 | Developed | Western Europe | 11 out of 19 |
| United States | 0.0 | 0.0 | AA+ | 15 | Developed | North America | 2 out of 2 |
| Uruguay | 4.1 | 4.1 | BBB | 45 | | Latin America | 5 out of 20 |
| Uzbekistan | 13.9 | 13.6 | | 132 | | Asia | 21 out of 29 |
| Vanuatu | 15.4 | 15.7 | | 145 | | Australasia | 4 out of 7 |
| Venezuela | 19.0 | 19.7 | CCC | 162 | | Latin America | 20 out of 20 |
| Vietnam | 8.2 | 8.1 | BB- | 78 | Frontier | Asia | 16 out of 29 |
| Yemen | 19.3 | 19.7 | | 161 | | Middle East | 12 out of 13 |
| Zambia | 11.4 | 11.6 | B | 111 | | Africa | 19 out of 51 |
| Zimbabwe | 20.8 | 21.1 | | 164 | | Africa | 44 out of 51 |

## March 2017 Country Risk Premium (CRP) Summary Statistics:

| S&P Rating | Country Count | Average CRP (%) | Median CRP (%) | Min CRP (%) | Max CRP (%) |
|---|---|---|---|---|---|
| AAA ** | 12 | 0.0 | 0.0 | 0.0 | 0.0 |
| AA (AA+, AA, AA-) | 15 | 1.2 | 1.1 | 0.0 | 3.9 |
| A (A+, A, A-) | 14 | 3.0 | 3.0 | 1.5 | 5.1 |
| BBB (BBB+, BBB, BBB-) | 17 | 4.6 | 4.6 | 2.1 | 6.9 |
| BB (BB+, BB, BB-) | 22 | 7.4 | 7.4 | 3.7 | 12.6 |
| B+ − SD | 39 | 12.0 | 11.6 | 7.2 | 19.7 |
| Investment Grade ** | 58 | 2.4 | 2.1 | 0.0 | 6.9 |
| Non-Investment Grade ** | 61 | 10.3 | 10.5 | 3.7 | 19.7 |
| **MSCI Market Classification** | | | | | |
| Developed Markets | 23 | 0.9 | 0.0 | 0.0 | 4.5 |
| Emerging Markets | 23 | 4.3 | 3.9 | 0.4 | 11.9 |
| Frontier Markets | 22 | 7.3 | 7.1 | 2.2 | 12.6 |
| **Euromoney Region ‡** | | | | | |
| Africa | 51 | 14.4 | 12.4 | 4.1 | 34.0 |
| Asia | 29 | 9.4 | 8.0 | 0.0 | 31.5 |
| Australasia | 7 | 13.3 | 15.7 | 0.0 | 25.8 |
| Caribbean | 9 | 10.5 | 10.1 | 4.0 | 19.5 |
| Central and Eastern Europe | 25 | 7.8 | 5.8 | 1.4 | 17.9 |
| Latin America | 20 | 8.3 | 9.0 | 0.4 | 19.7 |
| Middle East | 13 | 8.5 | 6.1 | 1.2 | 22.8 |
| North America | 2 | 0.0 | 0.0 | 0.0 | 0.0 |
| Western Europe | 19 | 1.7 | 0.5 | 0.0 | 11.2 |

## CCR Base Cost of Equity Capital:

| United States | COE (%) |
|---|---|
| March 2017 | 8.4 |
| December 2016 | 8.4 |

CCR base country-level COE for an United States-based investor investing in the United States.

§ S&P Credit Rating based on long-term foreign currency issuer rating. See http://www.standardandpoors.com/.

* World rank based on 175 countries covered by Euromoney. Ranking based on ascending order in which '1' equals the smallest country risk premium (CRP) and '175' equals the largest country risk premium (CRP).

† MSCI Market Classification based on MSCI Market Classification Framework. See http://www.msci.com/products/indexes/market_classification.html.

‡ Regional classification based on Euromoney. Regional rankings based on ascending order in which '1' equals the smallest country risk premium (CRP) for each region.

** Investment grade based on S&P sovereign credit rating from AAA to BBB-. Non-Investment grade based on S&P sovereign credit rating from BB+ to SD. For purposes of this analysis, the U.S. is being treated as if it were rated AAA by S&P.

Note: A CRP of 0.0% is assumed in the following cases: (i) when the investor country and the investee country both have an S&P sovereign credit rating of AAA; or (ii) when the investor country has an S&P credit rating of AAA, and the investee country has a sovereign credit rating below AAA, but has a calculated CRP below 0.0% (which would imply lower risk than a country rated AAA); or (iii) when the investor country has an S&P credit rating below AAA, and the investee country has a sovereign credit rating of AAA, but has a calculated CRP above 0.0% (which would imply greater risk than a country rated below AAA). For purposes of this analysis, the U.S. is treated as having a sovereign credit rating equivalent to AAA.

The country risk premium (CRP) is not the cost of equity capital (COE). The CRP is to be added to base COE. See Chapter 6 for proper application.

## Data Updated Through March 2017

| Investee Country | December 2016 Country Risk Premium (CRP) (%) | March 2017 Country Risk Premium (CRP) (%) | S&P Sovereign Credit Rating § | World Rank Out of 175∗ | MSCI Market Classification † | Euromoney Region ‡ | Regional Rank ‡ |
|---|---|---|---|---|---|---|---|
| Afghanistan | 11.0 | 10.7 | | 139 | | Asia | 23 out of 29 |
| Albania | 5.8 | 6.0 | B+ | 93 | | Central and Eastern Europe | 18 out of 25 |
| Algeria | 5.9 | 6.0 | | 91 | | Africa | 10 out of 51 |
| Angola | 8.1 | 8.2 | B | 121 | | Africa | 26 out of 51 |
| Argentina | 6.4 | 6.2 | B- | 96 | Frontier | Latin America | 13 out of 20 |
| Armenia | 3.6 | 3.8 | | 77 | | Asia | 15 out of 29 |
| Australia | -4.9 | -4.7 | AAA | 12 | Developed | Australasia | 2 out of 7 |
| Austria | -4.7 | -4.5 | AA+ | 13 | Developed | Western Europe | 9 out of 19 |
| Azerbaijan | 4.7 | 5.1 | BB+ | 85 | | Asia | 17 out of 29 |
| Bahamas | 2.2 | 2.0 | BB+ | 65 | | Caribbean | 3 out of 9 |
| Bahrain | 2.1 | 2.0 | BB- | 64 | Frontier | Middle East | 7 out of 13 |
| Bangladesh | 8.6 | 8.3 | BB- | 126 | Frontier | Asia | 20 out of 29 |
| Barbados | 3.8 | 4.8 | CCC+ | 82 | | Caribbean | 4 out of 9 |
| Belarus | 10.7 | 11.0 | B- | 143 | | Central and Eastern Europe | 23 out of 25 |
| Belgium | -3.5 | -3.4 | AA | 17 | Developed | Western Europe | 10 out of 19 |
| Belize | 6.8 | 6.9 | B- | 106 | | Latin America | 17 out of 20 |
| Benin | 12.3 | 12.2 | | 150 | | Africa | 37 out of 51 |
| Bermuda | 0.0 | 0.0 | A+ | 44 | | Caribbean | 1 out of 9 |
| Bhutan | 11.9 | 11.8 | | 148 | | Asia | 25 out of 29 |
| Bolivia | 5.4 | 5.7 | BB | 88 | | Latin America | 12 out of 20 |
| Bosnia & Herzegovina | 11.1 | 11.2 | B | 144 | | Central and Eastern Europe | 24 out of 25 |
| Botswana | 0.0 | 0.1 | A- | 48 | | Africa | 1 out of 51 |
| Brazil | 1.4 | 1.4 | BB | 59 | Emerging | Latin America | 7 out of 20 |
| Bulgaria | 1.3 | 1.5 | BB+ | 61 | | Central and Eastern Europe | 12 out of 25 |
| Burkina Faso | 9.6 | 9.5 | B- | 133 | | Africa | 33 out of 51 |
| Burundi | 20.7 | 20.6 | | 169 | | Africa | 47 out of 51 |
| Cambodia | 12.8 | 12.4 | | 151 | | Asia | 27 out of 29 |
| Cameroon | 8.3 | 8.3 | B | 124 | | Africa | 28 out of 51 |
| Canada | -5.0 | -4.9 | AAA | 9 | Developed | North America | 1 out of 2 |
| Cape Verde | 6.0 | 6.1 | B | 94 | | Africa | 12 out of 51 |
| Central African Republic | 24.1 | 23.9 | | 172 | | Africa | 49 out of 51 |
| Chad | 22.8 | 22.6 | | 171 | | Africa | 48 out of 51 |
| Chile | -3.9 | -3.6 | AA- | 16 | Emerging | Latin America | 1 out of 20 |
| China | -0.2 | -0.1 | AA- | 42 | Emerging | Asia | 7 out of 29 |
| Colombia | -0.3 | -0.2 | BBB | 41 | Emerging | Latin America | 4 out of 20 |
| Congo Republic | 7.9 | 7.7 | B- | 117 | | Africa | 24 out of 51 |
| Congo, DR | 9.1 | 9.0 | B- | 131 | | Africa | 32 out of 51 |
| Costa Rica | 2.6 | 2.9 | BB- | 71 | | Latin America | 8 out of 20 |
| Côte d'Ivoire | 5.9 | 6.0 | | 92 | | Africa | 11 out of 51 |
| Croatia | 1.8 | 1.7 | BB | 63 | Frontier | Central and Eastern Europe | 13 out of 25 |
| Cuba | 15.0 | 15.0 | | 160 | | Caribbean | 9 out of 9 |
| Cyprus | -0.5 | -0.3 | BB+ | 40 | | Central and Eastern Europe | 7 out of 25 |
| Czech Republic | -2.8 | -2.6 | AA- | 23 | Emerging | Central and Eastern Europe | 1 out of 25 |
| Denmark | -5.6 | -5.5 | AAA | 4 | Developed | Western Europe | 3 out of 19 |
| Djibouti | 31.6 | 29.1 | | 175 | | Africa | 51 out of 51 |
| Dominican Republic | 5.7 | 5.9 | BB- | 90 | | Caribbean | 5 out of 9 |
| Ecuador | 7.3 | 7.1 | B | 109 | | Latin America | 18 out of 20 |
| Egypt | 7.7 | 7.6 | B- | 116 | Emerging | Africa | 23 out of 51 |
| El Salvador | 4.8 | 4.7 | B- | 81 | | Latin America | 10 out of 20 |
| Equatorial Guinea | 17.3 | 17.2 | | 165 | | Africa | 45 out of 51 |

§ S&P Credit Rating based on long-term foreign currency issuer rating. See http://www.standardandpoors.com/.

∗ World rank based on 175 countries covered by Euromoney. Ranking based on ascending order in which '1' equals the smallest country risk premium (CRP) and '175' equals the largest country risk premium (CRP).

† MSCI Market Classification based on MSCI Market Classification Framework. See http://www.msci.com/products/indexes/market_classification.html.

‡ Regional classification based on Euromoney. Regional rankings based on ascending order in which '1' equals the smallest country risk premium (CRP) for each region.

Note: A CRP of 0.0% is assumed in the following cases: (i) when the investor country and the investee country both have an S&P sovereign credit rating of AAA; or (ii) when the investor country has an S&P credit rating of AAA, and the investee country has a sovereign credit rating below AAA, but has a calculated CRP 0.0% (which would imply lower risk than a country rated AAA); or (iii) when the investor country has an S&P credit rating below AAA, and the investee country has a sovereign credit rating of AAA, but has a calculated CRP above 0.0% (which would imply greater risk than a country rated below AAA). For purposes of this analysis, the U.S. is treated as having a sovereign credit rating equivalent to AAA.

The country risk premium (CRP) is not the cost of equity capital (COE). The CRP is to be added to base COE. See Chapter 6 for proper application.

## Data Updated Through March 2017

| Investee Country | December 2016 Country Risk Premium (CRP) (%) | March 2017 Country Risk Premium (CRP) (%) | S&P Sovereign Credit Rating § | World Rank Out of 175∗ | MSCI Market Classification † | Euromoney Region ‡ | Regional Rank ‡ |
|---|---|---|---|---|---|---|---|
| Eritrea | 28.0 | 26.0 | | 173 | | Africa | 50 out of 51 |
| Estonia | -2.2 | -1.8 | AA- | 32 | Frontier | Central and Eastern Europe | 4 out of 25 |
| Ethiopia | 6.6 | 6.6 | B | 101 | | Africa | 16 out of 51 |
| Fiji | 11.6 | 11.5 | B+ | 147 | | Australasia | 5 out of 7 |
| Finland | -4.9 | -4.8 | AA+ | 11 | Developed | Western Europe | 8 out of 19 |
| France | -2.7 | -2.7 | AA | 22 | Developed | Western Europe | 12 out of 19 |
| Gabon | 4.5 | 4.8 | | 83 | | Africa | 7 out of 51 |
| Gambia | 10.2 | 10.2 | | 138 | | Africa | 34 out of 51 |
| Georgia | 3.3 | 3.6 | BB- | 74 | | Central and Eastern Europe | 15 out of 25 |
| Germany | -4.9 | -4.8 | AAA | 10 | Developed | Western Europe | 7 out of 19 |
| Ghana | 6.1 | 5.8 | B- | 89 | | Africa | 9 out of 51 |
| Greece | 7.2 | 7.0 | B- | 108 | Emerging | Western Europe | 19 out of 19 |
| Grenada | 6.8 | 6.9 | | 105 | | Caribbean | 7 out of 9 |
| Guatemala | 4.9 | 4.9 | BB | 84 | | Latin America | 11 out of 20 |
| Guinea | 13.7 | 13.6 | | 156 | | Africa | 41 out of 51 |
| Guinea-Bissau | 7.6 | 7.6 | | 115 | | Africa | 22 out of 51 |
| Guyana | 6.5 | 6.5 | | 100 | | Latin America | 15 out of 20 |
| Haiti | 16.4 | 14.4 | | 157 | | Caribbean | 8 out of 9 |
| Honduras | 6.2 | 6.3 | B+ | 98 | | Latin America | 14 out of 20 |
| Hong Kong | -4.4 | -4.2 | AAA | 14 | Developed | Asia | 2 out of 29 |
| Hungary | 1.0 | 1.3 | BBB- | 57 | Emerging | Central and Eastern Europe | 10 out of 25 |
| Iceland | -1.8 | -1.9 | A | 30 | | Western Europe | 15 out of 19 |
| India | 0.8 | 1.2 | BBB- | 55 | Emerging | Asia | 10 out of 29 |
| Indonesia | 1.5 | 1.6 | BB+ | 62 | Emerging | Asia | 11 out of 29 |
| Iran | 8.1 | 8.3 | | 125 | | Middle East | 10 out of 13 |
| Iraq | 9.8 | 9.8 | B- | 136 | | Middle East | 11 out of 13 |
| Ireland | -2.3 | -2.2 | A+ | 27 | Developed | Western Europe | 14 out of 19 |
| Israel | -2.3 | -2.2 | A+ | 28 | Developed | Middle East | 2 out of 13 |
| Italy | 0.4 | 0.4 | BBB- | 50 | Developed | Western Europe | 18 out of 19 |
| Jamaica | 6.3 | 6.8 | B | 104 | | Caribbean | 6 out of 9 |
| Japan | -2.4 | -2.3 | A+ | 25 | Developed | Asia | 5 out of 29 |
| Jordan | 3.5 | 3.8 | BB- | 76 | Frontier | Middle East | 8 out of 13 |
| Kazakhstan | 3.0 | 2.8 | BBB- | 70 | Frontier | Asia | 13 out of 29 |
| Kenya | 6.3 | 6.4 | B+ | 99 | Frontier | Africa | 15 out of 51 |
| Korea (North) | 27.4 | 26.7 | | 174 | | Asia | 29 out of 29 |
| Korea (South) | -3.1 | -3.0 | AA | 19 | Emerging | Asia | 4 out of 29 |
| Kuwait | -2.1 | -1.8 | AA | 31 | Frontier | Middle East | 3 out of 13 |
| Kyrgyz Republic | 11.1 | 11.0 | | 142 | | Central and Eastern Europe | 22 out of 25 |
| Laos | 15.2 | 14.6 | | 158 | | Asia | 28 out of 29 |
| Latvia | -0.2 | 0.0 | A- | 43 | | Central and Eastern Europe | 8 out of 25 |
| Lebanon | 8.0 | 7.4 | B- | 112 | Frontier | Middle East | 9 out of 13 |
| Lesotho | 11.3 | 11.3 | | 146 | | Africa | 36 out of 51 |
| Liberia | 6.9 | 6.9 | | 107 | | Africa | 17 out of 51 |
| Libya | 12.8 | 13.1 | | 153 | | Africa | 39 out of 51 |
| Lithuania | -1.0 | -0.8 | A- | 36 | Frontier | Central and Eastern Europe | 6 out of 25 |
| Luxembourg | -5.3 | -5.2 | AAA | 5 | | Western Europe | 4 out of 19 |
| Macedonia | 5.4 | 5.7 | BB- | 87 | | Central and Eastern Europe | 17 out of 25 |
| Madagascar | 7.7 | 8.2 | | 123 | | Africa | 27 out of 51 |
| Malawi | 7.5 | 7.5 | | 114 | | Africa | 21 out of 51 |
| Malaysia | -0.8 | -0.8 | A- | 35 | Emerging | Asia | 6 out of 29 |

§ S&P Credit Rating based on long-term foreign currency issuer rating. See http://www.standardandpoors.com/.

∗ World rank based on 175 countries covered by Euromoney. Ranking based on ascending order in which '1' equals the smallest country risk premium (CRP) and '175' equals the largest country risk premium (CRP).

† MSCI Market Classification based on MSCI Market Classification Framework. See http://www.msci.com/products/indexes/market_classification.html.

‡ Regional classification based on Euromoney. Regional rankings based on ascending order in which '1' equals the smallest country risk premium (CRP) for each region.

Note: A CRP of 0.0% is assumed in the following cases: (i) when the investor country and the investee country both have an S&P sovereign credit rating of AAA; or (ii) when the investor country has an S&P credit rating of AAA, and the investee country has a sovereign credit rating below AAA, but has a calculated CRP below 0.0% (which would imply lower risk than a country rated AAA); or (iii) when the investor country has an S&P credit rating below AAA, and the investee country has a sovereign credit rating of AAA, but has a calculated CRP above 0.0% (which would imply greater risk than a country rated below AAA). For purposes of this analysis, the U.S. is treated as having a sovereign credit rating equivalent to AAA.

The country risk premium (CRP) is not the cost of equity capital (COE). The CRP is to be added to base COE. See Chapter 6 for proper application.

## Data Updated Through March 2017

| Investee Country | December 2016 Country Risk Premium (CRP) (%) | March 2017 Country Risk Premium (CRP) (%) | S&P Sovereign Credit Rating § | World Rank Out of 175∗ | MSCI Market Classification † | Euromoney Region ‡ | Regional Rank ‡ |
|---|---|---|---|---|---|---|---|
| Mali | 11.0 | 11.0 | | 141 | | Africa | 35 out of 51 |
| Malta | -2.4 | -2.2 | A- | 26 | | Western Europe | 13 out of 19 |
| Mauritania | 14.8 | 14.7 | | 159 | | Africa | 42 out of 51 |
| Mauritius | 2.4 | 2.5 | | 67 | Frontier | Asia | 12 out of 29 |
| Mexico | -0.9 | -0.7 | BBB+ | 37 | Emerging | Latin America | 2 out of 20 |
| Moldova | 9.5 | 9.9 | | 137 | | Central and Eastern Europe | 21 out of 25 |
| Mongolia | 7.8 | 8.1 | B- | 119 | | Asia | 18 out of 29 |
| Montenegro | 7.0 | 6.8 | B+ | 103 | | Central and Eastern Europe | 19 out of 25 |
| Morocco | 2.4 | 2.7 | BBB- | 69 | Frontier | Africa | 4 out of 51 |
| Mozambique | 8.8 | 8.7 | SD | 128 | | Africa | 29 out of 51 |
| Myanmar | 9.7 | 9.6 | | 134 | | Asia | 22 out of 29 |
| Namibia | 2.1 | 2.3 | | 66 | | Africa | 3 out of 51 |
| Nepal | 12.2 | 12.2 | | 149 | | Asia | 26 out of 29 |
| Netherlands | -5.3 | -5.2 | AAA | 6 | Developed | Western Europe | 5 out of 19 |
| New Zealand | -5.2 | -5.0 | AA | 8 | Developed | Australasia | 1 out of 7 |
| Nicaragua | 8.5 | 8.5 | B+ | 127 | | Latin America | 19 out of 20 |
| Niger | 8.1 | 8.1 | | 120 | | Africa | 25 out of 51 |
| Nigeria | 6.2 | 6.3 | B | 97 | Frontier | Africa | 14 out of 51 |
| Norway | -5.9 | -5.8 | AAA | 3 | Developed | Western Europe | 2 out of 19 |
| Oman | -0.1 | 0.1 | BBB- | 46 | Frontier | Middle East | 5 out of 13 |
| Pakistan | 8.2 | 8.2 | B | 122 | Frontier | Asia | 19 out of 29 |
| Panama | 0.6 | 0.7 | BBB | 52 | | Latin America | 6 out of 20 |
| Papua New Guinea | 7.7 | 7.8 | B+ | 118 | | Australasia | 3 out of 7 |
| Paraguay | 3.9 | 4.2 | BB | 80 | | Latin America | 9 out of 20 |
| Peru | -0.6 | -0.4 | BBB+ | 39 | Emerging | Latin America | 3 out of 20 |
| Philippines | 0.9 | 1.0 | BBB | 53 | Emerging | Asia | 9 out of 29 |
| Poland | -2.0 | -1.9 | BBB+ | 29 | Emerging | Central and Eastern Europe | 3 out of 25 |
| Portugal | 0.3 | 0.2 | BB+ | 49 | Developed | Western Europe | 17 out of 19 |
| Qatar | -3.0 | -2.8 | AA | 21 | Emerging | Middle East | 1 out of 13 |
| Romania | 1.1 | 1.2 | BBB- | 56 | Frontier | Central and Eastern Europe | 9 out of 25 |
| Russia | 3.2 | 2.7 | BB+ | 68 | Emerging | Central and Eastern Europe | 14 out of 25 |
| Rwanda | 8.9 | 8.9 | B | 130 | | Africa | 31 out of 51 |
| São Tomé & Príncipe | 14.9 | 15.3 | | 163 | | Africa | 43 out of 51 |
| Saudi Arabia | 0.2 | 0.1 | A- | 47 | | Middle East | 6 out of 13 |
| Senegal | 5.6 | 5.6 | B+ | 86 | | Africa | 8 out of 51 |
| Serbia | 3.8 | 3.6 | BB- | 75 | Frontier | Central and Eastern Europe | 16 out of 25 |
| Seychelles | 3.3 | 3.4 | | 73 | | Africa | 5 out of 51 |
| Sierra Leone | 8.9 | 8.9 | | 129 | | Africa | 30 out of 51 |
| Singapore | -6.1 | -5.9 | AAA | 1 | Developed | Asia | 1 out of 29 |
| Slovakia | -2.7 | -2.4 | A+ | 24 | | Central and Eastern Europe | 2 out of 25 |
| Slovenia | -1.3 | -1.2 | A | 34 | Frontier | Central and Eastern Europe | 5 out of 25 |
| Solomon Islands | 19.0 | 18.9 | | 168 | | Australasia | 6 out of 7 |
| Somalia | 17.4 | 17.3 | | 166 | | Africa | 46 out of 51 |
| South Africa | 1.1 | 1.4 | BBB- | 60 | Emerging | Africa | 2 out of 51 |
| Spain | -0.5 | -0.4 | BBB+ | 38 | Developed | Western Europe | 16 out of 19 |
| Sri Lanka | 3.3 | 3.1 | B+ | 72 | Frontier | Asia | 14 out of 29 |
| Sudan | 13.6 | 13.5 | | 154 | | Africa | 40 out of 51 |
| Suriname | 6.5 | 6.7 | B+ | 102 | | Latin America | 16 out of 20 |
| Swaziland | 12.0 | 12.9 | | 152 | | Africa | 38 out of 51 |
| Sweden | -5.3 | -5.1 | AAA | 7 | Developed | Western Europe | 6 out of 19 |

§ S&P Credit Rating based on long-term foreign currency issuer rating. See http://www.standardandpoors.com/.

∗ World rank based on 175 countries covered by Euromoney. Ranking based on ascending order in which '1' equals the smallest country risk premium (CRP) and '175' equals the largest country risk premium (CRP).

† MSCI Market Classification based on MSCI Market Classification Framework. See http://www.msci.com/products/indexes/market_classification.html

‡ Regional classification based on Euromoney. Regional rankings based on ascending order in which '1' equals the smallest country risk premium (CRP) for each region.

Note: A CRP of 0.0% is assumed in the following cases: (i) when the investor country and the investee country both have an S&P sovereign credit rating of AAA; or (ii) when the investor country has an S&P credit rating of AAA, and the investee country has a sovereign credit rating below AAA, but has a calculated CRP below 0.0% (which would imply lower risk than a country rated AAA); or (iii) when the investor country has an S&P credit rating below AAA, and the investee country has a sovereign credit rating of AAA, but has a calculated CRP above 0.0% (which would imply greater risk than a country rated below AAA). For purposes of this analysis, the U.S. is treated as having a sovereign credit rating equivalent to AAA.

The country risk premium (CRP) is not the cost of equity capital (COE). The CRP is to be added to base COE. See Chapter 6 for proper application.

## Data Updated Through March 2017

| Investee Country | December 2016 Country Risk Premium (CRP) (%) | March 2017 Country Risk Premium (CRP) (%) | S&P Sovereign Credit Rating § | World Rank Out of 175* | MSCI Market Classification † | Euromoney Region ‡ | Regional Rank ‡ |
|---|---|---|---|---|---|---|---|
| Switzerland | -5.9 | -5.8 | AAA | 2 | Developed | Western Europe | 1 out of 19 |
| Syria | 18.1 | 18.2 | | 167 | | Middle East | 13 out of 13 |
| Taiwan | -3.4 | -3.2 | AA- | 18 | Emerging | Asia | 3 out of 29 |
| Tajikistan | 13.2 | 13.5 | | 155 | | Central and Eastern Europe | 25 out of 25 |
| Tanzania | 5.9 | 6.1 | | 95 | | Africa | 13 out of 51 |
| Thailand | 0.6 | 0.5 | BBB+ | 51 | Emerging | Asia | 8 out of 29 |
| Togo | 7.4 | 7.4 | | 113 | | Africa | 20 out of 51 |
| Tonga | 21.3 | 21.2 | | 170 | | Australasia | 7 out of 7 |
| Trinidad & Tobago | 0.9 | 1.0 | A- | 54 | | Caribbean | 2 out of 9 |
| Tunisia | 3.6 | 4.0 | | 79 | Frontier | Africa | 6 out of 51 |
| Turkey | 1.3 | 1.3 | BB | 58 | Emerging | Central and Eastern Europe | 11 out of 25 |
| Turkmenistan | 10.5 | 10.8 | | 140 | | Asia | 24 out of 29 |
| Uganda | 6.9 | 7.2 | B | 110 | | Africa | 18 out of 51 |
| Ukraine | 9.6 | 9.7 | B- | 135 | | Central and Eastern Europe | 20 out of 25 |
| United Arab Emirates | -1.7 | -1.5 | AA | 33 | Emerging | Middle East | 4 out of 13 |
| United Kingdom | -3.1 | -2.9 | AA | 20 | Developed | Western Europe | 11 out of 19 |
| United States | -4.1 | -3.9 | AA+ | 15 | Developed | North America | 2 out of 2 |
| Uruguay | 0.0 | 0.0 | BBB | 45 | | Latin America | 5 out of 20 |
| Uzbekistan | 9.8 | 9.2 | | 132 | | Asia | 21 out of 29 |
| Vanuatu | 11.3 | 11.3 | | 145 | | Australasia | 4 out of 7 |
| Venezuela | 14.9 | 15.2 | CCC | 162 | | Latin America | 20 out of 20 |
| Vietnam | 4.1 | 4.0 | BB- | 78 | Frontier | Asia | 16 out of 29 |
| Yemen | 15.2 | 15.2 | | 161 | | Middle East | 12 out of 13 |
| Zambia | 7.3 | 7.3 | B | 111 | | Africa | 19 out of 51 |
| Zimbabwe | 16.7 | 16.6 | | 164 | | Africa | 44 out of 51 |

## March 2017 Country Risk Premium (CRP) Summary Statistics:

| S&P Rating | Country Count | Average CRP (%) | Median CRP (%) | Min CRP (%) | Max CRP (%) |
|---|---|---|---|---|---|
| AAA ** | 12 | -5.1 | -5.2 | -5.9 | -3.9 |
| AA (AA+, AA, AA-) | 15 | -2.9 | -2.9 | -5.0 | -0.1 |
| A (A+, A, A-) | 14 | -1.1 | -1.0 | -2.4 | 1.0 |
| BBB (BBB+, BBB, BBB-) | 17 | 0.6 | 0.5 | -1.9 | 2.8 |
| BB (BB+, BB, BB-) | 22 | 3.3 | 3.2 | -0.3 | 8.3 |
| B+ − SD | 39 | 7.7 | 7.3 | 3.1 | 15.2 |
| Investment Grade ** | 58 | -1.9 | -1.9 | -5.9 | 2.8 |
| Non-Investment Grade ** | 61 | 6.1 | 6.3 | -0.3 | 15.2 |
| **MSCI Market Classification** | | | | | |
| Developed Markets | 23 | -3.7 | -4.5 | -5.9 | 0.4 |
| Emerging Markets | 23 | 0.3 | -0.1 | -3.6 | 7.6 |
| Frontier Markets | 22 | 3.1 | 2.9 | -1.8 | 8.3 |
| **Euromoney Region ‡** | | | | | |
| Africa | 51 | 10.0 | 8.2 | 0.1 | 29.1 |
| Asia | 29 | 5.1 | 3.8 | -5.9 | 26.7 |
| Australasia | 7 | 8.7 | 11.3 | -5.0 | 21.2 |
| Caribbean | 9 | 6.3 | 5.9 | 0.0 | 15.0 |
| Central and Eastern Europe | 25 | 3.6 | 1.7 | -2.6 | 13.5 |
| Latin America | 20 | 4.2 | 4.8 | -3.6 | 15.2 |
| Middle East | 13 | 4.3 | 2.0 | -2.8 | 18.2 |
| North America | 2 | -4.4 | -4.4 | -4.9 | -3.9 |
| Western Europe | 19 | -2.9 | -3.4 | -5.8 | 7.0 |

## CCR Base Cost of Equity Capital:

| Uruguay | COE (%) |
|---|---|
| March 2017 | 18.2 |
| December 2016 | 18.3 |

CCR base country-level COE for an Uruguay-based investor investing in Uruguay.

§ S&P Credit Rating based on long-term foreign currency issuer rating. See http://www.standardandpoors.com/.

* World rank based on 175 countries covered by Euromoney. Ranking based on ascending order in which '1' equals the smallest country risk premium (CRP) and '175' equals the largest country risk premium (CRP).

† MSCI Market Classification based on MSCI Market Classification Framework. See http://www.msci.com/products/indexes/market_classification.html

‡ Regional classification based on Euromoney. Regional rankings based on ascending order in which '1' equals the smallest country risk premium (CRP) for each region.

** Investment grade based on S&P sovereign credit rating from AAA to BBB-. Non-Investment grade based on S&P sovereign credit rating from BB+ to SD. For purposes of this analysis, the U.S. is being treated as if it were rated AAA by S&P.

Note: A CRP of 0.0% is assumed in the following cases: (i) when the investor country and the investee country both have an S&P sovereign credit rating of AAA; or (ii) when the investor country has an S&P credit rating of AAA, and the investee country has a sovereign credit rating below AAA, but has a calculated CRP below 0.0% (which would imply lower risk than a country rated AAA); or (iii) when the investor country has an S&P credit rating below AAA, and the investee country has a sovereign credit rating of AAA, but has a calculated CRP above 0.0% (which would imply greater risk than a country rated below AAA). For purposes of this analysis, the U.S. is treated as having a sovereign credit rating equivalent to AAA.

# Data Exhibit 5:
# Study of Differences in Returns Between Large and Small Companies in Europe

The data exhibits in Professor Peek's Research Note summarize (and may aid in the examination of) the relationships between firm size and the cost of equity capital in European equity markets. These exhibits presented different types of size-related risk premia data, including (i) "risk premia over the risk-free rate", (ii) "risk premia over CAPM", and (iii) "comparative risk characteristics".[D5.1]

The information presented in Data Exhibits 5A, 5B, and 5C are a summary of the information from a Research Note authored by Professor Erik Peek of the Rotterdam School of Management, Erasmus University (RSM), updated through December 2016. The Research Note examines the relationships between firm size and the cost of equity capital in European equity markets. For more information, please refer to Chapter 7, "Firm Size and the Cost of Equity Capital in Europe".

The data exhibits in Professor Peek's Research Note summarize (and may aid in the examination of) the relationships between firm size and the cost of equity capital in European equity markets. These exhibits present different types of size-related risk premia data, including:

- Premia Over the Risk-Free Rate (Data Exhibit 5A)

- Premia Over CAPM, or Size Premia (Data Exhibit 5B)

- Comparative Risk Characteristics (Data Exhibit 5C)

---

[D5.1]  The full Research Note "Differences in Returns Between Large and Small Companies in Europe", is available at http://ssrn.com/abstract=2499205. The Research Note was published as part of the ongoing research that Duff & Phelps performs and sponsors in the area of cost of capital and other valuation issues. Professor Peek is at Rotterdam School of Management, Erasmus University (RSM), Netherlands.

# Data Exhibit 5A: Exhibits A-1 through A-7 Premia Over the Risk-Free Rate ($RP_{m+s}$)

The "risk premia over the risk-free rate" and other statistics presented in Data Exhibit 5A are a summary of the information from a Research Note authored by Professor Erik Peek of the Rotterdam School of Management, Erasmus University (RSM), updated through December 2016. The Research Note examines the relationships between firm size and the cost of equity capital in European equity markets. For more information, please refer to Chapter 7, "Firm Size and the Cost of Equity Capital in Europe".[D5A.1]

The "risk premia over the risk-free rate" presented in Data Exhibit 5A were developed using six different measures of firm size, plus a seventh size measure that is a combination of the six different measures of size, as follows:

> A-1: Market value of equity
>
> A-2: Book value of equity
>
> A-3: Market value of invested capital (MVIC)
>
> A-4: Total assets
>
> A-5: Sales
>
> A-6: Number of employees
>
> A-7: Size factor

---

[D5A.1] The full Research Note "Differences in Returns Between Large and Small Companies in Europe", is available at http://ssrn.com/abstract=2499205. The Research Note was published as part of the ongoing research that Duff & Phelps performs and sponsors in the area of cost of capital and other valuation issues. Professor Peek is at Rotterdam School of Management, Erasmus University (RSM), Netherlands.

## Companies Ranked by Market Capitalization

## Premia Over the Risk-Free Rate ($RP_{m+s}$)

### Exhibit A-1

Historical Equity Risk Premium: Average Since 1990
Data for Year Ending December 31, 2016

Equity Risk Premium Study: Data through December 31, 2016
Data Smoothing with Regression Analysis
Dependent Variable: Average Premium
Independent Variable: Log of Average Market Capitalization

Regression Output:

| | |
|---|---|
| Intercept | 33.576% |
| Log(Size) | -11.606% |
| Log(Size)$^2$ | 1.676% |
| Log(Size)$^3$ | -0.079% |
| Adj. R$^2$ | 86.0% |

Smoothed Premium = 33.576% -11.606% * Log(Market Capitalization) + 1.676% * Log(Market Capitalization)$^2$ -0.079% * Log(Market Capitalization)$^3$

Smoothed Risk Premium vs. Arithmetic Average Risk Premium

| Portfolio Rank by Size | Avg. Mkt Cap (in € millions) | Log of Avg. Mkt Cap | Number as of 2016 | Beta (Sum Beta) Since '90 | StdDev of Returns | Geometric Avg. Return | Arithmetic Avg. Return | Arithmetic Avg. Risk Premium | t-Value of Arithmetic Avg. Risk Premium | Smoothed Avg. Risk Premium |
|---|---|---|---|---|---|---|---|---|---|---|
| 1 (big) | 40,283 | 10.60 | 139 | 0.92 | 18.20% | 9.49% | 11.55% | 5.05% | — | 4.28% |
| 2 | 7,646 | 8.94 | 137 | 0.98 | 19.51% | 9.66% | 11.98% | 5.48% | 0.321 | 7.02% |
| 3 | 3,391 | 8.13 | 135 | 1.03 | 21.09% | 11.36% | 14.16% | 7.68% | 1.418 | 7.32% |
| 4 | 1,839 | 7.52 | 130 | 1.07 | 21.12% | 10.05% | 12.73% | 6.24% | 0.609 | 7.30% |
| 5 | 1,046 | 6.95 | 121 | 1.09 | 22.57% | 10.66% | 13.65% | 7.16% | 0.975 | 7.21% |
| 6 | 642 | 6.46 | 121 | 1.02 | 22.13% | 10.87% | 13.77% | 7.29% | 1.013 | 7.13% |
| 7 | 392 | 5.97 | 122 | 1.03 | 20.28% | 11.66% | 14.33% | 7.84% | 1.403 | 7.12% |
| 8 | 253 | 5.53 | 114 | 1.01 | 20.96% | 11.43% | 14.24% | 7.75% | 1.231 | 7.22% |
| 9 | 173 | 5.15 | 112 | 0.99 | 20.34% | 11.57% | 14.24% | 7.72% | 1.218 | 7.41% |
| 10 | 116 | 4.76 | 104 | 0.97 | 20.94% | 12.82% | 15.71% | 9.23% | 1.829 | 7.75% |
| 11 | 78 | 4.36 | 102 | 0.94 | 20.67% | 13.06% | 15.88% | 9.43% | 1.907 | 8.25% |
| 12 | 53 | 3.96 | 94 | 0.99 | 20.92% | 12.94% | 15.79% | 9.34% | 1.863 | 8.96% |
| 13 | 34 | 3.52 | 86 | 0.97 | 21.58% | 12.07% | 14.91% | 8.44% | 1.402 | 10.03% |
| 14 | 19 | 2.94 | 67 | 1.02 | 22.22% | 13.52% | 16.56% | 10.11% | 1.875 | 11.91% |
| 15 | 11 | 2.41 | 54 | 1.04 | 21.16% | 15.40% | 18.63% | 12.14% | 2.917 | 14.23% |
| 16 (small) | 5 | 1.58 | 31 | 1.44 | 30.23% | 21.80% | 27.88% | 21.38% | 3.247 | 19.12% |
| Pooled | 4,598 | 8.43 | 1,669 | 1.02 | 20.20% | 12.01% | 14.68% | 8.20% | — | — |

Note: "Log" reflects natural logarithm (base e = 2.71828)
Source of underlying data: Thomson Reuters Datastream and Worldscope.

A Study of Return Differences Between Large and Small Companies in Europe (2017 update)

# Companies Ranked by Book Equity

## Premia Over the Risk-Free Rate ($RP_{m+s}$)

### Exhibit A-2

Historical Equity Risk Premium: Average Since 1990
Data for Year Ending December 31, 2016

| Portfolio Rank by Size | Avg. Book Equity (in € millions) | Log of Avg. Book Equity | Number as of 2016 | Beta (Sum Beta) Since '90 | StdDev of Returns | Geometric Avg. Return | Arithmetic Avg. Return | Arithmetic Avg. Risk Premium | t-Value of Arithmetic Avg. Risk Premium | Smoothed Avg. Risk Premium |
|---|---|---|---|---|---|---|---|---|---|---|
| 1 (big) | 18,747 | 9.84 | 133 | 0.96 | 18.88% | 10.29% | 12.54% | 6.03% | – | 5.63% |
| 2 | 2,936 | 7.98 | 132 | 1.02 | 19.74% | 10.77% | 13.22% | 6.72% | 0.528 | 7.43% |
| 3 | 1,435 | 7.27 | 121 | 1.03 | 20.04% | 10.55% | 13.06% | 6.56% | 0.342 | 7.48% |
| 4 | 798 | 6.68 | 128 | 1.03 | 21.49% | 11.04% | 13.83% | 7.35% | 0.644 | 7.41% |
| 5 | 477 | 6.17 | 123 | 1.07 | 21.51% | 11.92% | 14.82% | 8.35% | 1.353 | 7.33% |
| 6 | 310 | 5.74 | 109 | 1.05 | 21.74% | 10.82% | 13.69% | 7.21% | 0.618 | 7.29% |
| 7 | 205 | 5.32 | 123 | 1.03 | 22.07% | 11.49% | 14.47% | 7.96% | 0.866 | 7.37% |
| 8 | 142 | 4.96 | 113 | 0.99 | 18.94% | 11.90% | 14.35% | 7.86% | 0.986 | 7.39% |
| 9 | 101 | 4.62 | 116 | 0.98 | 20.59% | 10.80% | 13.44% | 6.95% | 0.473 | 7.53% |
| 10 | 70 | 4.24 | 108 | 0.97 | 20.37% | 10.99% | 13.58% | 7.14% | 0.673 | 7.79% |
| 11 | 48 | 3.87 | 101 | 0.95 | 22.18% | 13.14% | 16.26% | 9.79% | 1.769 | 8.17% |
| 12 | 32 | 3.47 | 103 | 0.96 | 21.05% | 13.16% | 15.97% | 9.48% | 1.592 | 8.73% |
| 13 | 22 | 3.08 | 88 | 0.96 | 20.78% | 12.61% | 15.46% | 8.99% | 1.632 | 9.46% |
| 14 | 15 | 2.68 | 76 | 1.03 | 21.72% | 12.65% | 15.64% | 9.14% | 1.304 | 10.41% |
| 15 | 8 | 2.08 | 56 | 1.05 | 22.21% | 14.28% | 17.49% | 11.02% | 2.353 | 12.29% |
| 16 (small) | 3 | 1.13 | 39 | 1.32 | 29.26% | 18.98% | 24.17% | 17.68% | 2.747 | 16.59% |
| Pooled | 1,990 | 7.60 | 1,669 | 1.02 | 20.20% | 12.01% | 14.68% | 8.20% | – | – |

Equity Risk Premium Study: Data through December 31, 2016
Data Smoothing with Regression Analysis
Dependent Variable: Average Premium
Independent Variable: Log of Average Book Equity

Regression Output:

| | |
|---|---|
| Intercept | 24.118% |
| Log(Size) | -8.004% |
| Log(Size)$^2$ | 1.250% |
| Log(Size)$^3$ | -0.064% |
| Adj. R$^2$ | 87.0% |

Smoothed Premium = 24.118% –8.004% * Log(Book Equity) + 1.250% * Log(Book Equity)$^2$ –0.064% * Log(Book Equity)$^3$

Smoothed Risk Premium vs.
Arithmetic Average Risk Premium

(Chart: y-axis "Equity Premium" 0% to 20%; x-axis "Log of Book Equity" 0.0 to 12.0)

Note: "Log" reflects natural logarithm (base $e$ = 2.71828)

A Study of Return Differences Between Large and Small Companies in Europe (2017 update)

## Companies Ranked by MV of Invested Capital | Premia Over the Risk-Free Rate ($RP_{m+s}$) | Exhibit A-3

Historical Equity Risk Premium: Average Since 1990
Data for Year Ending December 31, 2016

Equity Risk Premium Study: Data through December 31, 2016
Data Smoothing with Regression Analysis
Dependent Variable: Average Premium
Independent Variable: Log of Average MV of Invested Capital

| Portfolio Rank by Size | Avg. MVIC (in € millions) | Log of Avg. Avg. MVIC | Number as of 2016 | Beta (Sum Beta) Since '90 | StdDev of Returns | Geometric Avg. Return | Arithmetic Avg. Return | Arithmetic Avg. Risk Premium | t-Value of Arithmetic Avg. Risk Premium | Smoothed Avg. Risk Premium |
|---|---|---|---|---|---|---|---|---|---|---|
| 1 (big) | 55,773 | 10.93 | 136 | 0.94 | 18.80% | 9.27% | 11.41% | 4.90% | — | 4.56% |
| 2 | 10,587 | 9.27 | 133 | 1.01 | 19.61% | 9.38% | 11.68% | 5.18% | 0.213 | 6.49% |
| 3 | 4,581 | 8.43 | 123 | 1.05 | 21.55% | 11.50% | 14.41% | 7.91% | 1.661 | 6.80% |
| 4 | 2,537 | 7.84 | 127 | 1.07 | 21.71% | 10.66% | 13.49% | 7.02% | 1.124 | 6.90% |
| 5 | 1,521 | 7.33 | 121 | 1.06 | 20.04% | 10.59% | 13.09% | 6.63% | 0.927 | 6.97% |
| 6 | 889 | 6.79 | 120 | 1.06 | 22.92% | 10.38% | 13.44% | 6.94% | 0.933 | 7.06% |
| 7 | 561 | 6.33 | 117 | 1.01 | 20.58% | 10.46% | 13.01% | 6.53% | 0.775 | 7.20% |
| 8 | 368 | 5.91 | 117 | 1.01 | 20.00% | 11.18% | 13.76% | 7.26% | 1.105 | 7.40% |
| 9 | 243 | 5.49 | 106 | 0.97 | 20.83% | 12.64% | 15.52% | 9.02% | 1.995 | 7.70% |
| 10 | 173 | 5.15 | 102 | 1.00 | 20.33% | 11.47% | 14.22% | 7.73% | 1.443 | 8.03% |
| 11 | 117 | 4.76 | 101 | 0.95 | 21.70% | 13.01% | 16.02% | 9.55% | 2.062 | 8.53% |
| 12 | 80 | 4.38 | 96 | 0.94 | 20.25% | 13.51% | 16.33% | 9.88% | 2.745 | 9.15% |
| 13 | 51 | 3.93 | 94 | 0.95 | 20.70% | 13.20% | 15.98% | 9.53% | 2.115 | 10.08% |
| 14 | 31 | 3.44 | 77 | 0.99 | 21.53% | 13.37% | 16.32% | 9.83% | 2.184 | 11.36% |
| 15 | 18 | 2.87 | 58 | 1.01 | 23.26% | 15.70% | 19.26% | 12.79% | 3.163 | 13.29% |
| 16 (small) | 8 | 2.04 | 41 | 1.38 | 26.73% | 19.43% | 24.30% | 17.82% | 3.114 | 16.98% |
| Pooled | 6,201 | 8.73 | 1,669 | 1.02 | 20.20% | 12.01% | 14.68% | 8.20% | — | — |

**Regression Output:**

| | |
|---|---|
| Intercept | 31.776% |
| Log(Size) | -9.555% |
| Log(Size)$^2$ | 1.240% |
| Log(Size)$^3$ | -0.054% |
| Adj. R$^2$ | 91.0% |

Smoothed Premium = 31.776% -9.555% * Log(MV of Invested Capital) + 1.240% * Log(MV of Invested Capital)^2 -0.054% * Log(MV of Invested Capital)^3

Smoothed Risk Premium vs. Arithmetic Average Risk Premium

Note: "Log" reflects natural logarithm (base $e$ = 2.71828)

*A Study of Return Differences Between Large and Small Companies in Europe (2017 update)*

# Companies Ranked by Total Assets

## Premia Over the Risk-Free Rate ($RP_{m+s}$)

### Exhibit A-4

Historical Equity Risk Premium: Average Since 1990
Data for Year Ending December 31, 2016

| Portfolio Rank by Size | Avg. Total Assets (in € millions) | Log of Avg. Total Assets | Number as of 2016 | Beta (Sum Beta) Since '90 | StdDev of Returns | Geometric Avg. Return | Arithmetic Avg. Return | Arithmetic Avg. Risk Premium | t-Value of Arithmetic Avg. Risk Premium | Smoothed Avg. Risk Premium |
|---|---|---|---|---|---|---|---|---|---|---|
| 1 (big) | 57,852 | 10.97 | 125 | 0.98 | 19.26% | 9.92% | 12.21% | 5.70% | — | 5.42% |
| 2 | 8,551 | 9.05 | 127 | 1.03 | 19.76% | 10.15% | 12.56% | 6.06% | 0.278 | 7.25% |
| 3 | 3,970 | 8.29 | 121 | 1.04 | 20.91% | 11.22% | 13.93% | 7.43% | 1.182 | 7.34% |
| 4 | 2,127 | 7.66 | 118 | 1.03 | 20.70% | 12.17% | 14.94% | 8.47% | 1.594 | 7.29% |
| 5 | 1,257 | 7.14 | 123 | 1.03 | 21.14% | 11.14% | 13.92% | 7.43% | 0.942 | 7.24% |
| 6 | 774 | 6.65 | 120 | 1.05 | 21.09% | 11.28% | 14.11% | 7.63% | 1.094 | 7.22% |
| 7 | 487 | 6.19 | 107 | 1.06 | 20.96% | 9.88% | 12.47% | 5.96% | 0.126 | 7.26% |
| 8 | 336 | 5.82 | 108 | 1.02 | 20.55% | 11.03% | 13.68% | 7.19% | 0.759 | 7.37% |
| 9 | 236 | 5.47 | 111 | 0.99 | 19.84% | 11.14% | 13.66% | 7.16% | 0.768 | 7.53% |
| 10 | 166 | 5.11 | 107 | 1.00 | 21.61% | 12.19% | 15.18% | 8.71% | 1.800 | 7.79% |
| 11 | 118 | 4.77 | 104 | 0.91 | 20.11% | 11.74% | 14.34% | 7.90% | 1.121 | 8.12% |
| 12 | 80 | 4.38 | 106 | 0.97 | 21.90% | 13.82% | 16.92% | 10.47% | 2.306 | 8.65% |
| 13 | 53 | 3.97 | 90 | 0.95 | 21.08% | 11.81% | 14.58% | 8.10% | 1.182 | 9.36% |
| 14 | 34 | 3.52 | 84 | 1.02 | 21.55% | 13.69% | 16.78% | 10.29% | 2.265 | 10.39% |
| 15 | 20 | 3.00 | 68 | 0.99 | 21.28% | 14.54% | 17.54% | 11.07% | 2.159 | 11.89% |
| 16 (small) | 8 | 2.08 | 50 | 1.24 | 27.38% | 17.92% | 22.61% | 16.11% | 2.931 | 15.57% |
| Pooled | 5,667 | 8.64 | 1,669 | 1.02 | 20.20% | 12.01% | 14.68% | 8.20% | — | — |

Note: "Log" reflects natural logarithm (base e = 2.71828)
Source of underlying data: Thomson Reuters *Datastream* and *Worldscope*.

Equity Risk Premium Study: Data through December 31, 2016
Data Smoothing with Regression Analysis
Dependent Variable: Average Premium
Independent Variable: Log of Average Total Assets

Regression Output:

| | |
|---|---|
| Intercept | 29.890% |
| Log(Size) | -9.225% |
| Log(Size)$^2$ | 1.239% |
| Log(Size)$^3$ | -0.055% |
| Adj. R$^2$ | 85.0% |

Smoothed Premium = 29.890% -9.225% * Log(Total Assets) + 1.239% * Log(Total Assets)^2 -0.055% * Log(Total Assets)^3

Smoothed Risk Premium vs.
Arithmetic Average Risk Premium

*A Study of Return Differences Between Large and Small Companies in Europe (2017 update)*

2017 Valuation Handbook - International Guide to Cost of Capital

Data Exhibit 5A-4

## Companies Ranked by Sales

## Premia Over the Risk-Free Rate ($RP_{m+s}$)

**Exhibit A-5**

Historical Equity Risk Premium: Average Since 1990
Data for Year Ending December 31, 2016

Equity Risk Premium Study: Data through December 31, 2016
Data Smoothing with Regression Analysis
Dependent Variable: Average Premium
Independent Variable: Log of Average Sales

Regression Output:

| | |
|---|---|
| Intercept | 28.483% |
| Log(Size) | -9.601% |
| Log(Size)$^2$ | 1.430% |
| Log(Size)$^3$ | -0.069% |
| Adj. R$^2$ | 81.0% |

Smoothed Premium = 28.483% -9.601% * Log(Sales) + 1.430% * Log(Sales)^2 -0.069% * Log(Sales)^3

Smoothed Risk Premium vs. Arithmetic Average Risk Premium

| Portfolio Rank by Size | Avg. Sales (in € millions) | Log of Avg. Sales | Number as of 2016 | Beta (Sum Beta) Since '90 | StdDev of Returns | Geometric Avg. Return | Arithmetic Avg. Return | Arithmetic Avg. Risk Premium | t-Value of Arithmetic Avg. Risk Premium | Smoothed Avg. Risk Premium |
|---|---|---|---|---|---|---|---|---|---|---|
| 1 (big) | 37,344 | 10.53 | 126 | 0.97 | 18.80% | 10.30% | 12.55% | 6.04% | – | 5.75% |
| 2 | 7,000 | 8.85 | 121 | 1.03 | 19.72% | 11.08% | 13.56% | 7.08% | 0.920 | 7.90% |
| 3 | 3,136 | 8.05 | 132 | 1.05 | 21.16% | 11.80% | 14.63% | 8.14% | 1.273 | 8.03% |
| 4 | 1,815 | 7.50 | 123 | 1.03 | 21.50% | 12.34% | 15.30% | 8.80% | 1.729 | 7.93% |
| 5 | 1,123 | 7.02 | 126 | 1.04 | 19.71% | 10.13% | 12.56% | 6.07% | 0.019 | 7.79% |
| 6 | 722 | 6.58 | 112 | 1.03 | 22.37% | 12.02% | 15.09% | 8.58% | 1.370 | 7.65% |
| 7 | 470 | 6.15 | 122 | 1.07 | 21.98% | 11.06% | 13.98% | 7.51% | 0.780 | 7.54% |
| 8 | 311 | 5.74 | 110 | 1.03 | 20.60% | 11.71% | 14.47% | 7.98% | 1.036 | 7.49% |
| 9 | 214 | 5.36 | 114 | 0.99 | 20.94% | 11.84% | 14.63% | 8.16% | 1.151 | 7.52% |
| 10 | 150 | 5.01 | 108 | 0.98 | 19.34% | 11.63% | 14.14% | 7.68% | 0.888 | 7.63% |
| 11 | 107 | 4.68 | 101 | 0.96 | 19.45% | 10.86% | 13.23% | 6.77% | 0.463 | 7.83% |
| 12 | 75 | 4.32 | 100 | 0.95 | 21.37% | 12.71% | 15.66% | 9.18% | 1.956 | 8.15% |
| 13 | 50 | 3.92 | 94 | 0.95 | 21.61% | 12.35% | 15.26% | 8.79% | 1.551 | 8.68% |
| 14 | 30 | 3.41 | 84 | 0.97 | 20.05% | 12.81% | 15.57% | 9.08% | 1.622 | 9.64% |
| 15 | 17 | 2.83 | 53 | 0.98 | 24.10% | 13.28% | 16.50% | 10.04% | 1.598 | 11.21% |
| 16 (small) | 7 | 1.98 | 43 | 1.29 | 29.70% | 17.02% | 21.87% | 15.37% | 2.025 | 14.54% |
| Pooled | 3,937 | 8.28 | 1,669 | 1.02 | 20.20% | 12.01% | 14.68% | 8.20% | – | – |

Note: "Log" reflects natural logarithm (base e = 2.71828)
Source of underlying data: Thomson Reuters Datastream and Worldscope.
Used with permission. All rights reserved.

*A Study of Return Differences Between Large and Small Companies in Europe (2017 update)*

# Companies Ranked by Number of Employees

## Premia Over the Risk-Free Rate ($RP_{m+s}$)

Historical Equity Risk Premium: Average Since 1990
Data for Year Ending December 31, 2016

Equity Risk Premium Study: Data through December 31, 2016
Data Smoothing with Regression Analysis
Dependent Variable: Average Premium
Independent Variable: Log of Average Number of Employees

| Portfolio Rank by Size | Avg. # of Employees (in € millions)† of Employee | Log of Avg. # of Employee | Number as of 2016 | Beta (Sum Beta) Since '90 | StdDev of Returns | Geometric Avg. Return | Arithmetic Avg. Return | Arithmetic Avg. Risk Premium | t-Value of Arithmetic Avg. Risk Premium | Smoothed Avg. Risk Premium |
|---|---|---|---|---|---|---|---|---|---|---|
| 1 (big) | 127,164 | 11.75 | 129 | 1.03 | 19.83% | 10.02% | 12.43% | 5.90% | — | 5.99% |
| 2 | 25,495 | 10.15 | 118 | 1.06 | 20.70% | 10.87% | 13.55% | 7.04% | 1.087 | 7.51% |
| 3 | 12,140 | 9.40 | 130 | 1.05 | 20.75% | 12.28% | 15.07% | 8.59% | 1.772 | 7.72% |
| 4 | 6,991 | 8.85 | 118 | 1.08 | 21.65% | 11.73% | 14.65% | 8.16% | 1.454 | 7.77% |
| 5 | 4,311 | 8.37 | 125 | 0.99 | 20.28% | 12.00% | 14.75% | 8.27% | 1.368 | 7.78% |
| 6 | 2,901 | 7.97 | 123 | 1.03 | 22.08% | 11.47% | 14.47% | 7.97% | 1.277 | 7.78% |
| 7 | 1,964 | 7.58 | 112 | 1.02 | 19.71% | 10.73% | 13.19% | 6.71% | 0.513 | 7.79% |
| 8 | 1,371 | 7.22 | 107 | 1.00 | 20.25% | 11.62% | 14.29% | 7.83% | 1.041 | 7.82% |
| 9 | 962 | 6.87 | 111 | 0.99 | 20.02% | 10.32% | 12.76% | 6.29% | 0.236 | 7.88% |
| 10 | 683 | 6.53 | 99 | 0.99 | 19.59% | 11.60% | 14.12% | 7.63% | 1.117 | 7.99% |
| 11 | 471 | 6.15 | 111 | 0.98 | 20.08% | 12.01% | 14.69% | 8.23% | 1.183 | 8.16% |
| 12 | 325 | 5.78 | 101 | 0.96 | 21.50% | 13.16% | 16.08% | 9.64% | 2.207 | 8.40% |
| 13 | 219 | 5.39 | 91 | 0.96 | 22.70% | 12.76% | 15.93% | 9.45% | 2.105 | 8.76% |
| 14 | 143 | 4.96 | 71 | 0.96 | 21.02% | 12.65% | 15.44% | 8.94% | 1.915 | 9.27% |
| 15 | 83 | 4.42 | 68 | 1.11 | 20.35% | 14.02% | 16.95% | 10.48% | 1.830 | 10.14% |
| 16 (small) | 32 | 3.48 | 55 | 0.96 | 27.55% | 14.53% | 18.50% | 11.99% | 1.748 | 12.38% |
| Pooled | 14,005 | 9.55 | 1,669 | 1.02 | 20.20% | 12.01% | 14.68% | 8.20% | — | — |

Regression Output:

| | |
|---|---|
| Intercept | 31.661% |
| Log(Size) | -8.695% |
| Log(Size)$^2$ | 1.054% |
| Log(Size)$^3$ | -0.043% |
| Adj. R$^2$ | 74.0% |

Smoothed Premium = 31.661% - 8.695% * Log(Number of Employees) + 1.054% * Log(Number of Employees)^2 - 0.043% * Log(Number of Employees)^3

Smoothed Risk Premium vs. Arithmetic Average Risk Premium

Note: "Log" reflects natural logarithm (base e = 2.71828)
Source of underlying data: Thomson Reuters Datastream and Worldscope.

*A Study of Return Differences Between Large and Small Companies in Europe (2017 update)*

Data Exhibit 5A- 7

## Premia Over the Risk-Free Rate ($RP_{m+s}$)

Exhibit A-7

## Companies Ranked by Size Factor

Historical Equity Risk Premium: Average Since 1990
Data for Year Ending December 31, 2016

Equity Risk Premium Study: Data through December 31, 2016
Data Smoothing with Regression Analysis
Dependent Variable: Average Premium
Independent Variable: Average Size Factor

Regression Output:

| | |
|---|---|
| Intercept | 7.266% |
| Size | -0.642% |
| $Size^2$ | 1.734% |
| $Size^3$ | -0.776% |
| Adj. $R^2$ | 84.0% |

Smoothed Premium = 7.266% − 0.642% * (Size Factor) + 1.734% * (Size Factor)^2 − 0.776% * (Size Factor)^3

Smoothed Risk Premium vs. Arithmetic Average Risk Premium

| Portfolio Rank by Size | Avg. Size Factor | Log of Avg. Size Factor | Number as of 2016 | Beta (Sum Beta) Since '90 | StdDev of Returns | Geometric Avg. Return | Arithmetic Avg. Return | Arithmetic Avg. Risk Premium | t-Value of Arithmetic Avg. Risk Premium | Smoothed Avg.Risk Premium |
|---|---|---|---|---|---|---|---|---|---|---|
| 1 (big) | 2.4 | – | 132 | 0.96 | 18.77% | 9.93% | 12.13% | 5.61% | – | 5.02% |
| 2 | 1.7 | – | 130 | 1.03 | 19.59% | 9.91% | 12.26% | 5.77% | 0.135 | 7.41% |
| 3 | 1.3 | – | 127 | 1.04 | 21.20% | 11.37% | 14.19% | 7.69% | 1.338 | 7.65% |
| 4 | 1.0 | – | 124 | 1.05 | 20.83% | 12.34% | 15.16% | 8.68% | 1.757 | 7.59% |
| 5 | 0.8 | – | 123 | 1.05 | 21.76% | 10.66% | 13.54% | 7.07% | 0.770 | 7.45% |
| 6 | 0.5 | – | 116 | 1.03 | 20.94% | 11.18% | 13.93% | 7.44% | 0.903 | 7.31% |
| 7 | 0.3 | – | 127 | 1.04 | 22.04% | 11.16% | 14.06% | 7.56% | 0.961 | 7.23% |
| 8 | 0.1 | – | 115 | 1.00 | 18.99% | 10.04% | 12.29% | 5.81% | 0.104 | 7.23% |
| 9 | -0.1 | – | 106 | 1.01 | 21.39% | 12.16% | 15.12% | 8.62% | 1.585 | 7.34% |
| 10 | -0.3 | – | 103 | 0.95 | 20.08% | 11.89% | 14.62% | 8.16% | 1.372 | 7.57% |
| 11 | -0.5 | – | 109 | 1.02 | 21.12% | 11.91% | 14.65% | 8.19% | 1.319 | 7.96% |
| 12 | -0.6 | – | 100 | 0.87 | 20.06% | 13.80% | 16.58% | 10.13% | 2.199 | 8.50% |
| 13 | -0.8 | – | 84 | 0.95 | 22.08% | 12.01% | 15.00% | 8.53% | 1.468 | 9.38% |
| 14 | -1.0 | – | 75 | 0.98 | 20.44% | 12.17% | 14.81% | 8.31% | 1.397 | 10.52% |
| 15 | -1.3 | – | 56 | 1.05 | 22.16% | 15.35% | 18.63% | 12.17% | 2.550 | 12.60% |
| 16 (small) | -1.7 | – | 42 | 1.29 | 29.04% | 19.43% | 24.71% | 18.21% | 2.964 | 17.19% |
| Pooled | 0.3 | – | 1,669 | 1.02 | 20.20% | 12.01% | 14.68% | 8.20% | – | – |

Note: "Log" reflects natural logarithm (base e = 2.71828)
Source of underlying data: Thomson Reuters Datastream and Worldscope.
Used with permission. All rights reserved.

A Study of Return Differences Between Large and Small Companies in Europe (2017 update)

# Data Exhibit 5B: Exhibits B-1 through B-7 Premia Over CAPM ($RP_s$)

The "risk premia over CAPM" (i.e., size premia) and other statistics presented in Data Exhibit 5B are a summary of the information from a Research Note authored by Professor Erik Peek of the Rotterdam School of Management, Erasmus University (RSM), updated through December 2016. The Research Note examines the relationships between firm size and the cost of equity capital in European equity markets. For more information, please refer to Chapter 7, "Firm Size and the Cost of Equity Capital in Europe".[D5B.1]

The size premia in Data Exhibit 5B have been adjusted to remove the portion of excess return that is attributable to beta, leaving the residual as the size effect's contribution to excess return. These "beta-adjusted" size premia could be added as a "size adjustment" within the context of the capital asset pricing model (CAPM).

The "risk premia over CAPM" (i.e., size premia) presented in Data Exhibit 5B were developed using six different measures of firm size, plus a seventh size measure that is a combination of the six different measures of size, as follows:

> B-1: Market value of equity
>
> B-2: Book value of equity
>
> B-3: Market value of invested capital (MVIC)
>
> B-4: Total assets
>
> B-5: Sales
>
> B-6: Number of employees
>
> B-7: Size factor

---

[D5B.1] The full Research Note "Differences in Returns Between Large and Small Companies in Europe", is available at http://ssrn.com/abstract=2499205. The Research Note was published as part of the ongoing research that Duff & Phelps performs and sponsors in the area of cost of capital and other valuation issues. Professor Peek is at Rotterdam School of Management, Erasmus University (RSM), Netherlands.

## Companies Ranked by Market Capitalization

## Premia over CAPM (Size Premia, $RP_s$)

**Exhibit B-1**

Historical Equity Risk Premium: Average Since 1990
Data for Year Ending December 31, 2016

Equity Risk Premium Study: Data through December 31, 2016
Data Smoothing with Regression Analysis
Dependent Variable: Premium over CAPM
Independent Variable: Log of Average Market Capitalization

Regression Output:

| | |
|---|---|
| Intercept | 22.465% |
| Log(Size) | -8.501% |
| Log(Size)$^2$ | 1.154% |
| Log(Size)$^3$ | -0.053% |
| Adj. R$^2$ | 86% |

Smoothed Premium = 22.465% -8.501% * Log(Market Capitalization) + 1.154% * Log(Market Capitalization)^2 -0.053% * Log(Market Capitalization)^3

Smoothed Premium over CAPM vs. Unadjusted Premium over CAPM

| Portfolio Rank by Size | Avg. Mkt Cap (in € millions) | Log of Avg. Mkt Cap | Beta (Sum Beta) Since '90 | Arithmetic Avg. Risk Premium | Indicated CAPM Premium | Premium over CAPM | t-Value Premium over CAPM | Smoothed Premium over CAPM |
|---|---|---|---|---|---|---|---|---|
| 1 (big) | 40,282.50 | 10.60 | 0.92 | 5.05% | 5.05% | 0.00% | – | -0.53% |
| 2 | 7,645.80 | 8.94 | 0.98 | 5.48% | 5.38% | 0.10% | 0.082 | 1.18% |
| 3 | 3,390.60 | 8.13 | 1.03 | 7.68% | 5.65% | 2.03% | 1.104 | 1.41% |
| 4 | 1,839.10 | 7.52 | 1.07 | 6.24% | 5.87% | 0.37% | 0.216 | 1.47% |
| 5 | 1,046.20 | 6.95 | 1.09 | 7.16% | 5.98% | 1.18% | 0.557 | 1.50% |
| 6 | 642.10 | 6.46 | 1.02 | 7.29% | 5.60% | 1.69% | 0.763 | 1.55% |
| 7 | 391.60 | 5.97 | 1.03 | 7.84% | 5.65% | 2.19% | 1.110 | 1.67% |
| 8 | 252.80 | 5.53 | 1.01 | 7.75% | 5.54% | 2.21% | 1.022 | 1.87% |
| 9 | 172.70 | 5.15 | 0.99 | 7.72% | 5.43% | 2.29% | 1.039 | 2.12% |
| 10 | 116.20 | 4.76 | 0.97 | 9.23% | 5.32% | 3.91% | 1.715 | 2.48% |
| 11 | 78.30 | 4.36 | 0.94 | 9.43% | 5.16% | 4.27% | 1.859 | 2.99% |
| 12 | 52.50 | 3.96 | 0.99 | 9.34% | 5.43% | 3.91% | 1.698 | 3.64% |
| 13 | 33.80 | 3.52 | 0.97 | 8.44% | 5.32% | 3.12% | 1.292 | 4.55% |
| 14 | 19.00 | 2.94 | 1.02 | 10.11% | 5.60% | 4.51% | 1.689 | 6.11% |
| 15 | 11.10 | 2.41 | 1.04 | 12.14% | 5.71% | 6.43% | 2.655 | 7.95% |
| 16 (small) | 4.80 | 1.58 | 1.44 | 21.38% | 7.90% | 13.48% | 2.714 | 11.71% |

Note: "Log" reflects natural logarithm (base e = 2.71828)

A Study of Return Differences Between Large and Small Companies in Europe (2017 update)

# Companies Ranked by Book Equity

## Premia over CAPM (Size Premia, $RP_s$)

**Exhibit B-2**

Historical Equity Risk Premium: Average Since 1990
Data for Year Ending December 31, 2016

Equity Risk Premium Study: Data through December 31, 2016
Data Smoothing with Regression Analysis
Dependent Variable: Premium over CAPM
Independent Variable: Log of Average Book Equity

Regression Output:

| | |
|---|---|
| Intercept | 15.058% |
| Log(Size) | -5.773% |
| Log(Size)$^2$ | 0.834% |
| Log(Size)$^3$ | -0.040% |
| Adj. R$^2$ | 86% |

Smoothed Premium = 15.058% -5.773% * Log(Book Equity) + 0.834% * Log(Book Equity)$^2$ -0.040% * Log(Book Equity)$^3$

Smoothed Premium over CAPM vs. Unadjusted Premium over CAPM

| Portfolio Rank by Size | Avg. Book Equity (in € millions) | Log of Avg. Book Equity | Beta (Sum Beta) Since '90 | Arithmetic Avg. Risk Premium | Indicated CAPM Premium | Premium over CAPM | t-Value Premium over CAPM | Smoothed Premium over CAPM |
|---|---|---|---|---|---|---|---|---|
| 1 (big) | 18,746.90 | 9.84 | 0.96 | 6.03% | 5.27% | 0.76% | – | 0.49% |
| 2 | 2,936.20 | 7.98 | 1.02 | 6.72% | 5.60% | 1.12% | 0.262 | 1.55% |
| 3 | 1,435.40 | 7.27 | 1.03 | 6.56% | 5.65% | 0.91% | 0.077 | 1.63% |
| 4 | 797.90 | 6.68 | 1.03 | 7.35% | 5.65% | 1.70% | 0.441 | 1.66% |
| 5 | 477.10 | 6.17 | 1.07 | 8.35% | 5.87% | 2.48% | 0.959 | 1.69% |
| 6 | 309.70 | 5.74 | 1.05 | 7.21% | 5.76% | 1.45% | 0.323 | 1.75% |
| 7 | 204.80 | 5.32 | 1.03 | 7.96% | 5.65% | 2.31% | 0.665 | 1.86% |
| 8 | 142.20 | 4.96 | 0.99 | 7.86% | 5.43% | 2.43% | 0.894 | 2.01% |
| 9 | 101.00 | 4.62 | 0.98 | 6.95% | 5.38% | 1.57% | 0.407 | 2.20% |
| 10 | 69.70 | 4.24 | 0.97 | 7.14% | 5.32% | 1.82% | 0.617 | 2.49% |
| 11 | 47.90 | 3.87 | 0.95 | 9.79% | 5.21% | 4.58% | 1.780 | 2.86% |
| 12 | 32.30 | 3.47 | 0.96 | 9.48% | 5.27% | 4.21% | 1.588 | 3.38% |
| 13 | 21.80 | 3.08 | 0.96 | 8.99% | 5.27% | 3.72% | 1.639 | 4.01% |
| 14 | 14.60 | 2.68 | 1.03 | 9.14% | 5.65% | 3.49% | 1.114 | 4.80% |
| 15 | 8.00 | 2.08 | 1.05 | 11.02% | 5.76% | 5.26% | 2.085 | 6.29% |
| 16 (small) | 3.10 | 1.13 | 1.32 | 17.68% | 7.25% | 10.43% | 2.247 | 9.54% |

Note: "Log" reflects natural logarithm (base e = 2.71828)

## Companies Ranked by MV of Invested Capital

## Premia over CAPM (Size Premia, $RP_s$)

### Exhibit B-3

Historical Equity Risk Premium: Average Since 1990
Data for Year Ending December 31, 2016

| Portfolio Rank by Size | Avg. MVIC (in € millions) | Log of Avg. MVIC | Sum Beta — Beta (Sum Beta) Since '90 | Arithmetic Avg. Risk Premium | Indicated CAPM Premium | Premium over CAPM | t-Value Premium over CAPM | Smoothed Premium over CAPM |
|---|---|---|---|---|---|---|---|---|
| 1 (big) | 55,772.50 | 10.93 | 0.94 | 4.90% | 5.16% | -0.26% | — | -0.40% |
| 2 | 10,586.60 | 9.27 | 1.01 | 5.18% | 5.54% | -0.36% | -0.038 | 0.55% |
| 3 | 4,580.50 | 8.43 | 1.05 | 7.91% | 5.76% | 2.15% | 1.352 | 0.83% |
| 4 | 2,536.80 | 7.84 | 1.07 | 7.02% | 5.87% | 1.15% | 0.774 | 1.03% |
| 5 | 1,521.40 | 7.33 | 1.06 | 6.63% | 5.82% | 0.81% | 0.615 | 1.22% |
| 6 | 889.20 | 6.79 | 1.06 | 6.94% | 5.82% | 1.12% | 0.658 | 1.47% |
| 7 | 560.90 | 6.33 | 1.01 | 6.53% | 5.54% | 0.99% | 0.618 | 1.74% |
| 8 | 367.90 | 5.91 | 1.01 | 7.26% | 5.54% | 1.72% | 0.937 | 2.06% |
| 9 | 242.90 | 5.49 | 0.97 | 9.02% | 5.32% | 3.70% | 1.936 | 2.44% |
| 10 | 173.30 | 5.15 | 1.00 | 7.73% | 5.49% | 2.24% | 1.287 | 2.81% |
| 11 | 116.70 | 4.76 | 0.95 | 9.55% | 5.21% | 4.34% | 2.058 | 3.32% |
| 12 | 80.00 | 4.38 | 0.94 | 9.88% | 5.16% | 4.72% | 2.765 | 3.89% |
| 13 | 50.90 | 3.93 | 0.95 | 9.53% | 5.21% | 4.32% | 2.109 | 4.70% |
| 14 | 31.30 | 3.44 | 0.99 | 9.83% | 5.43% | 4.40% | 2.070 | 5.75% |
| 15 | 17.70 | 2.87 | 1.01 | 12.79% | 5.54% | 7.25% | 3.036 | 7.21% |
| 16 (small) | 7.70 | 2.04 | 1.38 | 17.82% | 7.58% | 10.25% | 2.578 | 9.88% |

Equity Risk Premium Study: Data through December 31, 2016
Data Smoothing with Regression Analysis
Dependent Variable: Premium over CAPM
Independent Variable: Log of Average MV of Invested Capital

Regression Output:

| | |
|---|---|
| Intercept | 19.665% |
| Log(Size) | -6.085% |
| $Log(Size)^2$ | 0.686% |
| $Log(Size)^3$ | -0.027% |
| Adj, $R^2$ | 90% |

Smoothed Premium = 19.665% -6.085% * Log(MV of Invested Capital) + 0.686% * Log(MV of Invested Capital)^2 -0.027% * Log(MV of Invested Capital)^3

Smoothed Premium over CAPM vs. Unadjusted Premium over CAPM

(y-axis: Premium over CAPM; x-axis: Log of MV of Invested Capital)

Note: "Log" reflects natural logarithm (base e = 2.71828)
Source of underlying data: Thomson Reuters Datastream and Worldscope. *A Study of Return Differences Between Large and Small Companies in Europe (2017 update)*

# Companies Ranked by Total Assets

## Premia over CAPM (Size Premia, $RP_s$)

Exhibit B-4

Historical Equity Risk Premium: Average Since 1990
Data for Year Ending December 31, 2016

Equity Risk Premium Study: Data through December 31, 2016
Data Smoothing with Regression Analysis
Dependent Variable: Premium over CAPM
Independent Variable: Log of Average Total Assets

| Portfolio Rank by Size | Avg. Total Assets (in € millions) | Log of Avg. Total Assets | Beta (Sum Beta) Since '90 | Arithmetic Avg. Risk Premium | Indicated CAPM Premium | Premium over CAPM | t-Value Premium over CAPM | Smoothed Premium over CAPM |
|---|---|---|---|---|---|---|---|---|
| | | | Sum Beta | | | | | |
| 1 (big) | 57,851.70 | 10.97 | 0.98 | 5.70% | 5.38% | 0.32% | – | 0.17% |
| 2 | 8,551.30 | 9.05 | 1.03 | 6.06% | 5.65% | 0.41% | 0.081 | 1.36% |
| 3 | 3,970.20 | 8.29 | 1.04 | 7.43% | 5.71% | 1.72% | 0.932 | 1.47% |
| 4 | 2,127.10 | 7.66 | 1.03 | 8.47% | 5.65% | 2.82% | 1.440 | 1.52% |
| 5 | 1,257.00 | 7.14 | 1.03 | 7.43% | 5.65% | 1.78% | 0.801 | 1.57% |
| 6 | 773.70 | 6.65 | 1.05 | 7.63% | 5.76% | 1.87% | 0.863 | 1.65% |
| 7 | 486.90 | 6.19 | 1.06 | 5.96% | 5.82% | 0.14% | -0.079 | 1.79% |
| 8 | 336.00 | 5.82 | 1.02 | 7.19% | 5.60% | 1.59% | 0.653 | 1.96% |
| 9 | 236.30 | 5.47 | 0.99 | 7.16% | 5.43% | 1.73% | 0.748 | 2.17% |
| 10 | 166.20 | 5.11 | 1.00 | 8.71% | 5.49% | 3.22% | 1.721 | 2.46% |
| 11 | 118.40 | 4.77 | 0.91 | 7.90% | 5.00% | 2.90% | 1.328 | 2.81% |
| 12 | 79.80 | 4.38 | 0.97 | 10.47% | 5.32% | 5.15% | 2.318 | 3.30% |
| 13 | 53.20 | 3.97 | 0.95 | 8.10% | 5.21% | 2.89% | 1.259 | 3.95% |
| 14 | 33.70 | 3.52 | 1.02 | 10.29% | 5.60% | 4.69% | 2.146 | 4.83% |
| 15 | 20.10 | 3.00 | 0.99 | 11.07% | 5.43% | 5.64% | 2.141 | 6.09% |
| 16 (small) | 8.00 | 2.08 | 1.24 | 16.11% | 6.81% | 9.30% | 2.521 | 9.05% |

Regression Output:

| | |
|---|---|
| Intercept | 20.038% |
| Log(Size) | -6.940% |
| $\text{Log(Size)}^2$ | 0.875% |
| $\text{Log(Size)}^3$ | -0.037% |
| Adj. $R^2$ | 83% |

Smoothed Premium = 20.038% -6.940% * Log(Total Assets) + 0.875%
* Log(Total Assets)^2 -0.037% * Log(Total Assets)^3

Smoothed Premium over CAPM vs.
Unadjusted Premium over CAPM

Note: "Log" reflects natural logarithm (base e = 2.71828)
Source of underlying data: Thomson Reuters Datastream and Worldscope.
Used with permission. All rights reserved.

A Study of Return Differences Between Large and Small Companies in Europe (2017 update)

## Companies Ranked by Sales

## Premia over CAPM (Size Premia, $RP_s$)

**Exhibit B-5**

Historical Equity Risk Premium: Average Since 1990
Data for Year Ending December 31, 2016

| Portfolio Rank by Size | Avg. Sales (in € millions) | Log of Avg. Sales | Beta (Sum Beta) Since '90 | Arithmetic Avg. Risk Premium | Indicated CAPM Premium | Premium over CAPM | t-Value Premium over CAPM | Smoothed Premium over CAPM |
|---|---|---|---|---|---|---|---|---|
| 1 (big) | 37,343.70 | 10.53 | 0.97 | 6.04% | 5.32% | 0.72% | — | 0.58% |
| 2 | 7,000.10 | 8.85 | 1.03 | 7.08% | 5.65% | 1.43% | 0.599 | 1.98% |
| 3 | 3,136.20 | 8.05 | 1.05 | 8.14% | 5.76% | 2.38% | 0.976 | 2.11% |
| 4 | 1,815.10 | 7.50 | 1.03 | 8.80% | 5.65% | 3.15% | 1.487 | 2.10% |
| 5 | 1,122.50 | 7.02 | 1.04 | 6.07% | 5.71% | 0.36% | -0.218 | 2.07% |
| 6 | 721.70 | 6.58 | 1.03 | 8.58% | 5.65% | 2.93% | 1.160 | 2.04% |
| 7 | 469.60 | 6.15 | 1.07 | 7.51% | 5.87% | 1.64% | 0.451 | 2.05% |
| 8 | 311.40 | 5.74 | 1.03 | 7.98% | 5.65% | 2.33% | 0.843 | 2.09% |
| 9 | 213.60 | 5.36 | 0.99 | 8.16% | 5.43% | 2.73% | 1.084 | 2.19% |
| 10 | 149.80 | 5.01 | 0.98 | 7.68% | 5.38% | 2.30% | 0.858 | 2.35% |
| 11 | 107.30 | 4.68 | 0.96 | 6.77% | 5.27% | 1.50% | 0.490 | 2.56% |
| 12 | 75.10 | 4.32 | 0.95 | 9.18% | 5.21% | 3.97% | 2.027 | 2.87% |
| 13 | 50.40 | 3.92 | 0.95 | 8.79% | 5.21% | 3.58% | 1.618 | 3.33% |
| 14 | 30.20 | 3.41 | 0.97 | 9.08% | 5.32% | 3.76% | 1.620 | 4.13% |
| 15 | 16.90 | 2.83 | 0.98 | 10.04% | 5.38% | 4.66% | 1.566 | 5.35% |
| 16 (small) | 7.20 | 1.98 | 1.29 | 15.37% | 7.08% | 8.29% | 1.609 | 7.87% |

Equity Risk Premium Study: Data through December 31, 2016
Data Smoothing with Regression Analysis
Dependent Variable: Premium over CAPM
Independent Variable: Log of Average Sales

Regression Output:

| | |
|---|---|
| Intercept | 17.933% |
| Log(Size) | -6.818% |
| Log(Size)$^2$ | 0.966% |
| Log(Size)$^3$ | -0.045% |
| Adj. R$^2$ | 79% |

Smoothed Premium = 17.933% - 6.818% * Log(Sales) + 0.966% * Log(Sales)^2 -0.045% * Log(Sales)^3

Smoothed Premium over CAPM vs.
Unadjusted Premium over CAPM

Note: "Log" reflects natural logarithm (base e = 2.71828)

A Study of Return Differences Between Large and Small Companies in Europe (2017 update)

# Companies Ranked by Number of Employees

## Premia over CAPM (Size Premia, $RP_s$ )

**Exhibit B-6**

Historical Equity Risk Premium: Average Since 1990
Data for Year Ending December 31, 2016

Equity Risk Premium Study: Data through December 31, 2016
Data Smoothing with Regression Analysis
Dependent Variable: Premium over CAPM
Independent Variable: Log of Average Number of Employees

Regression Output:

| | |
|---|---|
| Intercept | 24.284% |
| Log(Size) | -7.775% |
| Log(Size)$^2$ | 0.921% |
| Log(Size)$^3$ | -0.037% |
| Adj. R$^2$ | 75% |

Smoothed Premium = 24.284% -7.775% * Log(Number of Employees) + 0.921% * Log(Number of Employees)^2 -0.037% * Log(Number of Employees)^3

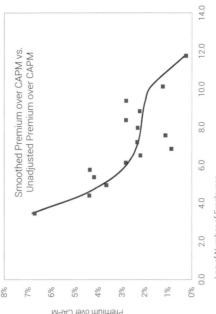

Smoothed Premium over CAPM vs. Unadjusted Premium over CAPM

(Premium over CAPM vs. Log of Number of Employees)

| Portfolio Rank by Size | Avg. # of Employees (in € millions) | Log of Avg. # of Employees | Sum Beta — Beta (Sum Beta) Since '90 | Arithmetic Avg. Risk Premium | Indicated CAPM Premium | Premium over CAPM | t-Value Premium over CAPM | Smoothed Premium over CAPM |
|---|---|---|---|---|---|---|---|---|
| 1 (big) | 127,164.20 | 11.75 | 1.03 | 5.90% | 5.65% | 0.25% | — | 0.30% |
| 2 | 25,495.10 | 10.15 | 1.06 | 7.04% | 5.82% | 1.22% | 0.924 | 1.72% |
| 3 | 12,139.50 | 9.40 | 1.05 | 8.59% | 5.76% | 2.83% | 1.709 | 1.97% |
| 4 | 6,990.70 | 8.85 | 1.08 | 8.16% | 5.93% | 2.23% | 1.284 | 2.07% |
| 5 | 4,310.80 | 8.37 | 0.99 | 8.27% | 5.43% | 2.84% | 1.494 | 2.13% |
| 6 | 2,900.50 | 7.97 | 1.03 | 7.97% | 5.65% | 2.32% | 1.281 | 2.17% |
| 7 | 1,964.10 | 7.58 | 1.02 | 6.71% | 5.60% | 1.11% | 0.546 | 2.22% |
| 8 | 1,370.70 | 7.22 | 1.00 | 7.83% | 5.49% | 2.34% | 1.121 | 2.30% |
| 9 | 961.90 | 6.87 | 0.99 | 6.29% | 5.43% | 0.86% | 0.368 | 2.40% |
| 10 | 682.50 | 6.53 | 0.99 | 7.63% | 5.43% | 2.20% | 1.270 | 2.53% |
| 11 | 470.80 | 6.15 | 0.98 | 8.23% | 5.38% | 2.85% | 1.331 | 2.74% |
| 12 | 324.50 | 5.78 | 0.96 | 9.64% | 5.27% | 4.37% | 2.423 | 3.00% |
| 13 | 218.50 | 5.39 | 0.96 | 9.45% | 5.27% | 4.18% | 2.325 | 3.37% |
| 14 | 142.90 | 4.96 | 0.96 | 8.94% | 5.27% | 3.67% | 2.169 | 3.89% |
| 15 | 83.20 | 4.42 | 1.11 | 10.48% | 6.09% | 4.39% | 1.661 | 4.73% |
| 16 (small) | 32.30 | 3.48 | 0.96 | 11.99% | 5.27% | 6.72% | 1.862 | 6.83% |

Note: "Log" reflects natural logarithm (base e = 2.71828)
Source of underlying data: Thomson Reuters Datastream and Worldscope. A Study of Return Differences Between Large and Small Companies in Europe (2017 update)

## Companies Ranked by Size Factor

## Premia over CAPM (Size Premia, $RP_s$)

**Exhibit B-7**

Historical Equity Risk Premium: Average Since 1990
Data for Year Ending December 31, 2016

Equity Risk Premium Study: Data through December 31, 2016
Data Smoothing with Regression Analysis
Dependent Variable: Premium over CAPM
Independent Variable: Average Size Factor

Regression Output:

| | |
|---|---|
| Intercept | 1.943% |
| Size | -1.019% |
| Size$^2$ | 1.379% |
| Size$^3$ | -0.548% |
| Adj. R$^2$ | 81% |

Smoothed Premium = 1.943% − 1.019% * (Size Factor) + 1.379% * (Size Factor)^2 − 0.548% * (Size Factor)^3

Smoothed Premium over CAPM vs. Unadjusted Premium over CAPM

| Portfolio Rank by Size | Avg. Size Factor | Log of Avg. Size Factor | Beta (Sum Beta) Since '90 | Arithmetic Avg. Risk Premium | Indicated CAPM Premium | Premium over CAPM | t-Value Premium over CAPM | Smoothed Premium over CAPM |
|---|---|---|---|---|---|---|---|---|
| 1 (big) | 2.4 | – | 0.96 | 5.61% | 5.27% | 0.34% | – | -0.13% |
| 2 | 1.7 | – | 1.03 | 5.77% | 5.65% | 0.12% | -0.203 | 1.51% |
| 3 | 1.3 | – | 1.04 | 7.69% | 5.71% | 1.98% | 1.049 | 1.75% |
| 4 | 1.0 | – | 1.05 | 8.68% | 5.76% | 2.92% | 1.475 | 1.76% |
| 5 | 0.8 | – | 1.05 | 7.07% | 5.76% | 1.31% | 0.500 | 1.73% |
| 6 | 0.5 | – | 1.03 | 7.44% | 5.65% | 1.79% | 0.703 | 1.71% |
| 7 | 0.3 | – | 1.04 | 7.56% | 5.71% | 1.85% | 0.735 | 1.75% |
| 8 | 0.1 | – | 1.00 | 5.81% | 5.49% | 0.32% | -0.030 | 1.85% |
| 9 | -0.1 | – | 1.01 | 8.62% | 5.54% | 3.08% | 1.450 | 2.06% |
| 10 | -0.3 | – | 0.95 | 8.16% | 5.21% | 2.95% | 1.391 | 2.39% |
| 11 | -0.5 | – | 1.02 | 8.19% | 5.60% | 2.59% | 1.162 | 2.87% |
| 12 | -0.6 | – | 0.87 | 10.13% | 4.78% | 5.35% | 2.432 | 3.17% |
| 13 | -0.8 | – | 0.95 | 8.53% | 5.21% | 3.32% | 1.482 | 3.92% |
| 14 | -1.0 | – | 0.98 | 8.31% | 5.38% | 2.93% | 1.335 | 4.89% |
| 15 | -1.3 | – | 1.05 | 12.17% | 5.76% | 6.41% | 2.354 | 6.80% |
| 16 (small) | -1.7 | – | 1.29 | 18.21% | 7.08% | 11.13% | 2.543 | 10.35% |

Note: "Log" reflects natural logarithm (base e = 2.71828)

A Study of Return Differences Between Large and Small Companies in Europe (2017 update)

# Data Exhibit 5C: Exhibits C-1 through C-7 Comparative Risk Characteristics

The "comparative risk characteristics" presented in Data Exhibit 5C are a summary of the information from a Research Note authored by Professor Erik Peek of the Rotterdam School of Management, Erasmus University (RSM), updated through December 2016. The Research Note examines the relationships between firm size and the cost of equity capital in European equity markets. For more information, please refer to Chapter 7, "Firm Size and the Cost of Equity Capital in Europe".[D5C.1]

Data Exhibit 5C provides information about the companies that comprise the 16 size-ranked portfolios for *each* of the six different measures of firm size (plus a seventh size measure that is a combination of the six different measures of size) that are used to create the "risk premia over the risk-free rate" and the "risk premia over CAPM" (i.e., size premia) presented in Data Exhibit 5A and Data Exhibit 5B, respectively. The information in Data Exhibit 5C can be useful in assessing how "alike or different" the subject company is to the companies that make up the respective guideline size-ranked portfolios in Data Exhibits 5A and 5B.

The "comparative risk characteristics" presented in Data Exhibit 5C were developed using six different measures of firm size, plus a seventh size measure that is a combination of the six different measures of size, as follows:

  C-1: Market value of equity

  C-2: Book value of equity

  C-3: Market value of invested capital (MVIC)

  C-4: Total assets

  C-5: Sales

  C-6: Number of employees

  C-7: Size factor

---

[D5C.1] The full Research Note "Differences in Returns Between Large and Small Companies in Europe", is available at http://ssrn.com/abstract=2499205. The Research Note was published as part of the ongoing research that Duff & Phelps performs and sponsors in the area of cost of capital and other valuation issues. Professor Peek is at Rotterdam School of Management, Erasmus University (RSM), Netherlands.

## Companies Ranked by Market Capitalization | Comparative Risk Characteristics | Exhibit C-1

Data for Year Ending December 31, 2016

Data Smoothing with Regression Analysis
Dependent Variable: Average Premium
Independent Variable: Log of Average Market Capitalization

| Portfolio Rank by Size | Portfolio Statistics for 2016 | | | Portfolio Statistics for 1990-2016 | | | | | | | | |
| --- | --- | --- | --- | --- | --- | --- | --- | --- | --- | --- | --- | --- |
| | Avg. Mkt Cap (in € millions) | Log of Avg. Mkt Cap | Number as of 2016 | Beta (Sum Beta) Since '90 | Unlevered Beta (Sum Beta) Since '90 | Arithmetic Avg. Risk Premium | Avg. Debt to MVIC | Avg. Debt to Market Value of Equity | Avg. Operating Margin | StdDev Operating Margin | Avg. Z-score | Avg. % Zero-return Days |
| 1 (big) | 40,283 | 10.60 | 139 | 0.92 | 0.76 | 5.05% | 22.53% | 29.08% | 15.25% | 2.20% | 3.92 | 3.98% |
| 2 | 7,646 | 8.94 | 137 | 0.98 | 0.81 | 5.48% | 21.40% | 27.23% | 13.51% | 2.52% | 4.42 | 4.26% |
| 3 | 3,391 | 8.13 | 135 | 1.03 | 0.89 | 7.68% | 17.02% | 20.51% | 9.81% | 2.93% | 4.74 | 6.22% |
| 4 | 1,839 | 7.52 | 130 | 1.07 | 0.92 | 6.24% | 17.04% | 20.54% | 11.14% | 2.48% | 4.19 | 6.23% |
| 5 | 1,046 | 6.95 | 121 | 1.09 | 0.91 | 7.16% | 19.87% | 24.80% | 9.02% | 2.34% | 4.48 | 8.64% |
| 6 | 642 | 6.46 | 121 | 1.02 | 0.88 | 7.29% | 17.55% | 21.29% | 9.02% | 2.36% | 4.38 | 11.20% |
| 7 | 392 | 5.97 | 122 | 1.03 | 0.88 | 7.84% | 18.48% | 22.67% | 8.88% | 3.67% | 4.71 | 13.68% |
| 8 | 253 | 5.53 | 114 | 1.01 | 0.85 | 7.75% | 19.43% | 24.12% | 9.07% | 3.83% | 4.52 | 18.00% |
| 9 | 173 | 5.15 | 112 | 0.99 | 0.85 | 7.72% | 17.78% | 21.62% | 7.47% | 3.51% | 4.08 | 19.28% |
| 10 | 116 | 4.76 | 104 | 0.97 | 0.80 | 9.23% | 22.05% | 28.29% | 7.52% | 2.99% | 4.32 | 25.87% |
| 11 | 78 | 4.36 | 102 | 0.94 | 0.78 | 9.43% | 21.54% | 27.45% | 7.59% | 3.37% | 4.19 | 33.21% |
| 12 | 53 | 3.96 | 94 | 0.99 | 0.83 | 9.34% | 19.66% | 24.47% | 6.16% | 4.31% | 3.94 | 37.37% |
| 13 | 34 | 3.52 | 86 | 0.97 | 0.81 | 8.44% | 21.08% | 26.71% | 3.50% | 5.01% | 3.87 | 40.73% |
| 14 | 19 | 2.94 | 67 | 1.02 | 0.82 | 10.11% | 24.81% | 33.00% | 4.87% | 3.42% | 3.32 | 40.52% |
| 15 | 11 | 2.41 | 54 | 1.04 | 0.81 | 12.14% | 27.52% | 37.97% | 4.36% | 3.88% | 3.37 | 48.95% |
| 16 (small) | 5 | 1.58 | 31 | 1.44 | 1.07 | 21.38% | 29.74% | 42.33% | 3.60% | 4.40% | 3.37 | 64.79% |

Note: "Log" reflects natural logarithm (base e = 2.71828)
Source of underlying data: Thomson Reuters Datastream and Worldscope. *A Study of Return Differences Between Large and Small Companies in Europe (2017 update)*

# Companies Ranked by Book Equity

## Comparative Risk Characteristics

Exhibit C-2

Data for Year Ending December 31, 2016

Data Smoothing with Regression Analysis
Dependent Variable: Average Premium
Independent Variable: Log of Average Book Equity

| Portfolio Rank by Size | Portfolio Statistics for 2016 | | | Portfolio Statistics for 1990-2016 | | | | | | | | |
| | Average Book Equity (in € millions) | Log of Average Book Equity | Number as of 2016 | Beta (Sum Beta) Since '90 | Unlevered Beta (Sum Beta) Since '90 | Arithmetic Average Risk Premium | Average Debt to MVIC | Average Debt to Market Value of Equity | Average Operating Margin | StdDev Operating Margin | Average Z-score | Average % return Days |
|---|---|---|---|---|---|---|---|---|---|---|---|---|
| 1 (big) | 18,747 | 9.84 | 133 | 0.96 | 0.75 | 6.03% | 28.12% | 39.12% | 13.47% | 2.27% | 3.19 | 4.31% |
| 2 | 2,936 | 7.98 | 132 | 1.02 | 0.82 | 6.72% | 24.13% | 31.80% | 12.51% | 2.50% | 3.66 | 4.79% |
| 3 | 1,435 | 7.27 | 121 | 1.03 | 0.84 | 6.56% | 22.88% | 29.67% | 11.75% | 2.68% | 4.11 | 5.66% |
| 4 | 798 | 6.68 | 128 | 1.03 | 0.86 | 7.35% | 20.35% | 25.55% | 10.69% | 2.13% | 4.24 | 8.35% |
| 5 | 477 | 6.17 | 123 | 1.07 | 0.91 | 8.35% | 18.33% | 22.44% | 9.98% | 2.81% | 4.18 | 8.49% |
| 6 | 310 | 5.74 | 109 | 1.05 | 0.87 | 7.21% | 21.69% | 27.70% | 9.24% | 2.51% | 4.15 | 12.35% |
| 7 | 205 | 5.32 | 123 | 1.03 | 0.85 | 7.96% | 21.25% | 26.98% | 9.09% | 3.35% | 4.94 | 15.34% |
| 8 | 142 | 4.96 | 113 | 0.99 | 0.85 | 7.86% | 17.43% | 21.11% | 8.24% | 3.71% | 4.45 | 13.70% |
| 9 | 101 | 4.62 | 116 | 0.98 | 0.83 | 6.95% | 19.33% | 23.96% | 6.76% | 2.40% | 4.36 | 21.44% |
| 10 | 70 | 4.24 | 108 | 0.97 | 0.83 | 7.14% | 17.62% | 21.39% | 8.68% | 2.62% | 4.38 | 23.05% |
| 11 | 48 | 3.87 | 101 | 0.95 | 0.81 | 9.79% | 18.72% | 23.03% | 7.62% | 3.34% | 4.47 | 32.27% |
| 12 | 32 | 3.47 | 103 | 0.96 | 0.81 | 9.48% | 20.13% | 25.20% | 4.75% | 4.64% | 5.27 | 35.30% |
| 13 | 22 | 3.08 | 88 | 0.96 | 0.82 | 8.99% | 18.72% | 23.03% | 6.75% | 4.00% | 4.51 | 34.77% |
| 14 | 15 | 2.68 | 76 | 1.03 | 0.87 | 9.14% | 19.20% | 23.76% | 4.87% | 5.31% | 5.80 | 42.82% |
| 15 | 8 | 2.08 | 56 | 1.05 | 0.95 | 11.02% | 11.60% | 13.12% | 6.53% | 4.44% | 4.93 | 47.11% |
| 16 (small) | 3 | 1.13 | 39 | 1.32 | 1.20 | 17.68% | 10.74% | 12.03% | 4.16% | 5.62% | 4.93 | 49.16% |

Note: "Log" reflects natural logarithm (base e = 2.71828)

A Study of Return Differences Between Large and Small Companies in Europe (2017 update)

## Companies Ranked by MV of Invested Capital

Data for Year Ending December 31, 2016

## Comparative Risk Characteristics

### Exhibit C-3

Data Smoothing with Regression Analysis
Dependent Variable: Average Premium
Independent Variable: Log of Average MV of Invested Capital

| Portfolio Rank by Size | Portfolio Statistics for 2016 | | | Portfolio Statistics for 1990-2016 | | | Comparative Risk Characteristics | | | | | |
| --- | --- | --- | --- | --- | --- | --- | --- | --- | --- | --- | --- | --- |
| | Average MVIC (in € millions) | Log of Average MVIC | Number as of 2016 | Beta (Sum Beta) Since '90 | Unlevered Beta (Sum Beta) Since '90 | Arithmetic Average Risk Premium | Average Debt to MVIC | Average Debt to Market Value of Equity | Average Operating Margin | StdDev Operating Margin | Average Z-score | Average % return Days |
| 1 (big) | 55,773 | 10.93 | 136 | 0.94 | 0.74 | 4.90% | 27.07% | 37.12% | 15.09% | 2.14% | 3.73 | 3.85% |
| 2 | 10,587 | 9.27 | 133 | 1.01 | 0.83 | 5.18% | 21.76% | 27.81% | 13.10% | 2.53% | 4.21 | 5.09% |
| 3 | 4,581 | 8.43 | 123 | 1.05 | 0.88 | 7.91% | 20.34% | 25.53% | 10.78% | 3.23% | 4.54 | 5.02% |
| 4 | 2,537 | 7.84 | 127 | 1.07 | 0.90 | 7.02% | 19.75% | 24.61% | 10.36% | 2.54% | 4.47 | 7.13% |
| 5 | 1,521 | 7.33 | 121 | 1.06 | 0.90 | 6.63% | 19.17% | 23.72% | 9.86% | 2.28% | 4.63 | 8.12% |
| 6 | 889 | 6.79 | 120 | 1.06 | 0.90 | 6.94% | 18.31% | 22.41% | 9.60% | 2.35% | 4.17 | 10.52% |
| 7 | 561 | 6.33 | 117 | 1.01 | 0.84 | 6.53% | 20.84% | 26.33% | 8.19% | 3.25% | 4.18 | 13.35% |
| 8 | 368 | 5.91 | 117 | 1.01 | 0.85 | 7.26% | 20.25% | 25.39% | 8.54% | 4.60% | 4.65 | 15.37% |
| 9 | 243 | 5.49 | 106 | 0.97 | 0.82 | 9.02% | 18.90% | 23.30% | 9.16% | 2.70% | 4.40 | 20.06% |
| 10 | 173 | 5.15 | 102 | 1.00 | 0.85 | 7.73% | 19.35% | 23.99% | 6.77% | 3.42% | 4.36 | 25.13% |
| 11 | 117 | 4.76 | 101 | 0.95 | 0.80 | 9.55% | 19.52% | 24.25% | 7.07% | 3.24% | 4.54 | 29.28% |
| 12 | 80 | 4.38 | 96 | 0.94 | 0.79 | 9.88% | 19.95% | 24.92% | 6.20% | 3.26% | 4.16 | 39.89% |
| 13 | 51 | 3.93 | 94 | 0.95 | 0.80 | 9.53% | 19.64% | 24.44% | 6.03% | 3.58% | 4.22 | 36.27% |
| 14 | 31 | 3.44 | 77 | 0.99 | 0.83 | 9.83% | 20.88% | 26.39% | 3.39% | 5.62% | 4.02 | 41.15% |
| 15 | 18 | 2.87 | 58 | 1.01 | 0.86 | 12.79% | 18.53% | 22.74% | 5.44% | 3.92% | 4.11 | 46.77% |
| 16 (small) | 8 | 2.04 | 41 | 1.38 | 1.24 | 17.82% | 11.77% | 13.34% | 3.38% | 4.48% | 4.11 | 59.30% |

Note: "Log" reflects natural logarithm (base e = 2.71828)
Source of underlying data: Thomson Reuters Datastream and Worldscope.        *A Study of Return Differences Between Large and Small Companies in Europe (2017 update)*

# Companies Ranked by Total Assets

Data for Year Ending December 31, 2016

# Comparative Risk Characteristics

Data Smoothing with Regression Analysis
Dependent Variable: Average Premium
Independent Variable: Log of Average Total Assets

Exhibit C-4

| Portfolio Rank by Size | Average Total Assets (in € millions) | Log of Average Total Assets | Number as of 2016 | Beta (Sum Beta) Since '90 | Unlevered Beta (Sum Beta) Since '90 | Arithmetic Average Risk Premium | Average Debt to MVIC | Average Debt to Market Value of Equity | Average Operating Margin | StdDev Operating Margin | Average Z-score | Average % return Days |
|---|---|---|---|---|---|---|---|---|---|---|---|---|
| 1 (big) | 57,852 | 10.97 | 125 | 0.98 | 0.73 | 5.70% | 32.07% | 47.21% | 13.37% | 2.03% | 3.07 | 4.29% |
| 2 | 8,551 | 9.05 | 127 | 1.03 | 0.82 | 6.06% | 25.68% | 34.55% | 12.64% | 2.63% | 3.21 | 4.62% |
| 3 | 3,970 | 8.29 | 121 | 1.04 | 0.83 | 7.43% | 25.54% | 34.30% | 10.72% | 2.50% | 3.91 | 6.30% |
| 4 | 2,127 | 7.66 | 118 | 1.03 | 0.86 | 8.47% | 20.90% | 26.42% | 9.41% | 2.05% | 3.89 | 7.45% |
| 5 | 1,257 | 7.14 | 123 | 1.03 | 0.87 | 7.43% | 18.79% | 23.14% | 10.93% | 2.85% | 4.07 | 9.39% |
| 6 | 774 | 6.65 | 120 | 1.05 | 0.86 | 7.63% | 22.14% | 28.44% | 8.68% | 2.20% | 4.40 | 11.64% |
| 7 | 487 | 6.19 | 107 | 1.06 | 0.88 | 5.96% | 21.25% | 26.98% | 9.42% | 3.77% | 4.64 | 12.67% |
| 8 | 336 | 5.82 | 108 | 1.02 | 0.86 | 7.19% | 19.44% | 24.13% | 9.01% | 2.83% | 4.37 | 15.04% |
| 9 | 236 | 5.47 | 111 | 0.99 | 0.85 | 7.16% | 17.82% | 21.68% | 6.82% | 3.27% | 4.61 | 18.02% |
| 10 | 166 | 5.11 | 107 | 1.00 | 0.85 | 8.71% | 19.09% | 23.59% | 7.80% | 2.88% | 4.61 | 26.04% |
| 11 | 118 | 4.77 | 104 | 0.91 | 0.77 | 7.90% | 20.18% | 25.28% | 7.88% | 3.01% | 4.48 | 26.66% |
| 12 | 80 | 4.38 | 106 | 0.97 | 0.83 | 10.47% | 18.21% | 22.26% | 7.86% | 2.63% | 4.67 | 32.54% |
| 13 | 53 | 3.97 | 90 | 0.95 | 0.82 | 8.10% | 17.08% | 20.60% | 5.63% | 4.66% | 5.30 | 35.82% |
| 14 | 34 | 3.52 | 84 | 1.02 | 0.92 | 10.29% | 12.54% | 14.34% | 5.31% | 5.09% | 6.38 | 41.85% |
| 15 | 20 | 3.00 | 68 | 0.99 | 0.91 | 11.07% | 10.43% | 11.64% | 7.47% | 5.32% | 6.60 | 46.83% |
| 16 (small) | 8 | 2.08 | 50 | 1.24 | 1.18 | 16.11% | 5.35% | 5.65% | 4.70% | 7.03% | 6.60 | 45.99% |

**Portfolio Statistics for 2016** spans Average Total Assets, Log of Average Total Assets, Number as of 2016. **Portfolio Statistics for 1990-2016** spans the remaining columns.

Note: "Log" reflects natural logarithm (base e = 2.71828)
Source of underlying data: Thomson Reuters Datastream and Worldscope.
Used with permission. All rights reserved.

*A Study of Return Differences Between Large and Small Companies in Europe (2017 update)*

2017 Valuation Handbook – International Guide to Cost of Capital          Data Exhibit 5C-4

# Companies Ranked by Sales

Data for Year Ending December 31, 2016

# Comparative Risk Characteristics

Exhibit C-5

Data Smoothing with Regression Analysis
Dependent Variable: Average Premium
Independent Variable: Log of Average Sales

| Portfolio Rank by Size | Portfolio Statistics for 2016 | | | | | Portfolio Statistics for 1990-2016 | | | | | | |
|---|---|---|---|---|---|---|---|---|---|---|---|---|
| | Average Sales (in € millions) | Log of Average Sales | Number as of 2016 | Beta (Sum Beta) Since '90 | Unlevered Beta (Sum Beta) Since '90 | Arithmetic Average Risk Premium | Average Debt to MVIC | Average Debt to Market Value of Equity | Average Operating Margin | StdDev Operating Margin | Average Z-score | Average % return Days |
| 1 (big) | 37,344 | 10.53 | 126 | 0.97 | 0.75 | 6.04% | 28.96% | 40.77% | 11.09% | 1.77% | 3.36 | 4.24% |
| 2 | 7,000 | 8.85 | 121 | 1.03 | 0.85 | 7.08% | 21.70% | 27.71% | 8.97% | 2.12% | 3.08 | 5.38% |
| 3 | 3,136 | 8.05 | 132 | 1.05 | 0.84 | 8.14% | 24.38% | 32.24% | 10.82% | 2.20% | 4.01 | 6.73% |
| 4 | 1,815 | 7.50 | 123 | 1.03 | 0.85 | 8.80% | 21.96% | 28.14% | 11.40% | 2.02% | 4.15 | 6.45% |
| 5 | 1,123 | 7.02 | 126 | 1.04 | 0.87 | 6.07% | 20.83% | 26.31% | 10.09% | 2.15% | 4.31 | 8.72% |
| 6 | 722 | 6.58 | 112 | 1.03 | 0.86 | 8.58% | 20.76% | 26.20% | 9.32% | 2.38% | 4.33 | 11.77% |
| 7 | 470 | 6.15 | 122 | 1.07 | 0.89 | 7.51% | 20.89% | 26.41% | 8.09% | 2.33% | 4.65 | 13.14% |
| 8 | 311 | 5.74 | 110 | 1.03 | 0.90 | 7.98% | 16.12% | 19.22% | 8.89% | 2.93% | 4.14 | 15.28% |
| 9 | 214 | 5.36 | 114 | 0.99 | 0.83 | 8.16% | 19.95% | 24.92% | 8.32% | 3.09% | 4.57 | 19.16% |
| 10 | 150 | 5.01 | 108 | 0.98 | 0.81 | 7.68% | 21.25% | 26.98% | 8.20% | 3.94% | 3.99 | 22.50% |
| 11 | 107 | 4.68 | 101 | 0.96 | 0.81 | 6.77% | 20.24% | 25.38% | 8.19% | 3.44% | 4.58 | 29.36% |
| 12 | 75 | 4.32 | 100 | 0.95 | 0.82 | 9.18% | 17.16% | 20.71% | 8.64% | 3.24% | 4.70 | 34.47% |
| 13 | 50 | 3.92 | 94 | 0.95 | 0.80 | 8.79% | 19.76% | 24.63% | 7.41% | 4.12% | 5.76 | 37.92% |
| 14 | 30 | 3.41 | 84 | 0.97 | 0.88 | 9.08% | 11.69% | 13.24% | 5.49% | 6.96% | 5.83 | 47.77% |
| 15 | 17 | 2.83 | 53 | 0.98 | 0.88 | 10.04% | 12.95% | 14.88% | 7.93% | 6.10% | 5.95 | 42.23% |
| 16 (small) | 7 | 1.98 | 43 | 1.29 | 1.17 | 15.37% | 10.82% | 12.13% | 6.84% | 8.71% | 5.95 | 49.24% |

Note: "Log" reflects natural logarithm (base e = 2.71828)

A Study of Return Differences Between Large and Small Companies in Europe (2017 update)

# Companies Ranked by Number of Employees

Data for Year Ending December 31, 2016

# Comparative Risk Characteristics

Data Smoothing with Regression Analysis
Dependent Variable: Average Premium
Independent Variable: Log of Average Number of Employees

Exhibit C-6

| Portfolio Rank by Size | Portfolio Statistics for 2016 | | | Portfolio Statistics for 1990-2016 | | | | | | | | | |
|---|---|---|---|---|---|---|---|---|---|---|---|---|---|
| | Average # of Employees | Log of Average # of Employees | Number as of 2016 | Beta (Sum Beta) Since '90 | Unlevered Beta (Sum Beta) Since '90 | Arithmetic Average Risk Premium | Average Debt to MVIC | Average Debt to Market Value of Equity | Average Operating Margin | StdDev Operating Margin | Average Z-score | Average % return Days |
| 1 (big) | 127,164 | 11.75 | 129 | 1.03 | 0.80 | 5.90% | 28.07% | 39.02% | 10.03% | 1.52% | 3.13 | 4.48% |
| 2 | 25,495 | 10.15 | 118 | 1.06 | 0.84 | 7.04% | 25.51% | 34.25% | 10.34% | 2.05% | 3.88 | 5.38% |
| 3 | 12,140 | 9.40 | 130 | 1.05 | 0.89 | 8.59% | 19.36% | 24.01% | 10.76% | 2.50% | 3.47 | 6.95% |
| 4 | 6,991 | 8.85 | 118 | 1.08 | 0.88 | 8.16% | 23.14% | 30.11% | 10.40% | 2.10% | 3.90 | 6.38% |
| 5 | 4,311 | 8.37 | 125 | 0.99 | 0.82 | 8.27% | 20.93% | 26.47% | 10.22% | 2.19% | 4.07 | 9.94% |
| 6 | 2,901 | 7.97 | 123 | 1.03 | 0.85 | 7.97% | 21.66% | 27.65% | 7.88% | 1.84% | 4.15 | 12.32% |
| 7 | 1,964 | 7.58 | 112 | 1.02 | 0.86 | 6.71% | 19.15% | 23.69% | 9.51% | 2.21% | 4.59 | 12.08% |
| 8 | 1,371 | 7.22 | 107 | 1.00 | 0.86 | 7.83% | 17.73% | 21.55% | 9.06% | 2.44% | 4.33 | 15.53% |
| 9 | 962 | 6.87 | 111 | 0.99 | 0.83 | 6.29% | 19.86% | 24.78% | 8.20% | 2.76% | 4.39 | 20.90% |
| 10 | 683 | 6.53 | 99 | 0.99 | 0.84 | 7.63% | 18.83% | 23.20% | 10.14% | 3.19% | 4.88 | 21.76% |
| 11 | 471 | 6.15 | 111 | 0.98 | 0.84 | 8.23% | 18.47% | 22.65% | 8.43% | 3.16% | 4.56 | 29.68% |
| 12 | 325 | 5.78 | 101 | 0.96 | 0.82 | 9.64% | 18.36% | 22.49% | 7.52% | 3.46% | 5.10 | 37.90% |
| 13 | 219 | 5.39 | 91 | 0.96 | 0.82 | 9.45% | 19.01% | 23.47% | 6.42% | 6.33% | 4.99 | 37.20% |
| 14 | 143 | 4.96 | 71 | 0.96 | 0.82 | 8.94% | 17.77% | 21.61% | 7.68% | 5.88% | 5.04 | 35.77% |
| 15 | 83 | 4.42 | 68 | 1.11 | 0.97 | 10.48% | 15.64% | 18.54% | 7.34% | 6.61% | 6.65 | 45.37% |
| 16 (small) | 32 | 3.48 | 55 | 0.96 | 0.88 | 11.99% | 10.09% | 11.22% | 6.02% | 8.99% | 6.65 | 41.41% |

Note: "Log" reflects natural logarithm (base e = 2.71828)

*A Study of Return Differences Between Large and Small Companies in Europe (2017 update)*

## Companies Ranked by Size Factor

Data for Year Ending December 31, 2016

## Comparative Risk Characteristics

Exhibit C-7

Data Smoothing with Regression Analysis
Dependent Variable: Average Premium
Independent Variable: Log of Average Size Factor

| Portfolio Rank by Size | Portfolio Statistics for 2016 | | Portfolio Statistics for 1990-2016 | | | | | | | | | |
|---|---|---|---|---|---|---|---|---|---|---|---|---|
| | Average Size Factor | Log of Average Size Factor | Number as of 2016 | Beta (Sum Beta) Since '90 | Unlevered Beta (Sum Beta) Since '90 | Arithmetic Average Risk Premium | Average Debt to MVIC | Average Debt to Market Value of Equity | Average Operating Margin | StdDev Operating Margin | Average Z-score | Average % return Days |
| 1 (big) | 2.4 | – | 132 | 0.96 | 0.74 | 5.61% | 28.97% | 40.79% | 12.60% | 1.89% | 3.40 | 4.26% |
| 2 | 1.7 | – | 130 | 1.03 | 0.85 | 5.77% | 21.48% | 27.36% | 12.38% | 2.30% | 3.74 | 4.61% |
| 3 | 1.3 | – | 127 | 1.04 | 0.86 | 7.69% | 21.77% | 27.83% | 11.66% | 2.15% | 4.09 | 6.02% |
| 4 | 1.0 | – | 124 | 1.05 | 0.88 | 8.68% | 20.47% | 25.74% | 9.96% | 1.99% | 4.01 | 7.09% |
| 5 | 0.8 | – | 123 | 1.05 | 0.88 | 7.07% | 20.45% | 25.71% | 10.31% | 3.05% | 4.67 | 7.85% |
| 6 | 0.5 | – | 116 | 1.03 | 0.87 | 7.44% | 19.53% | 24.27% | 8.84% | 2.62% | 4.43 | 11.67% |
| 7 | 0.3 | – | 127 | 1.04 | 0.87 | 7.56% | 20.05% | 25.08% | 8.93% | 3.69% | 4.77 | 12.09% |
| 8 | 0.1 | – | 115 | 1.00 | 0.85 | 5.81% | 18.69% | 22.99% | 8.45% | 2.58% | 4.47 | 15.07% |
| 9 | -0.1 | – | 106 | 1.01 | 0.86 | 8.62% | 18.03% | 22.00% | 8.84% | 3.49% | 3.86 | 19.07% |
| 10 | -0.3 | – | 103 | 0.95 | 0.79 | 8.16% | 20.78% | 26.23% | 7.31% | 2.70% | 4.48 | 27.56% |
| 11 | -0.5 | – | 109 | 1.02 | 0.85 | 8.19% | 20.35% | 25.55% | 7.75% | 3.32% | 4.31 | 28.65% |
| 12 | -0.6 | – | 100 | 0.87 | 0.74 | 10.13% | 20.12% | 25.19% | 6.10% | 4.09% | 5.23 | 39.03% |
| 13 | -0.8 | – | 84 | 0.95 | 0.81 | 8.53% | 18.28% | 22.37% | 6.85% | 3.84% | 4.93 | 34.07% |
| 14 | -1.0 | – | 75 | 0.98 | 0.85 | 8.31% | 16.69% | 20.03% | 5.09% | 6.04% | 4.85 | 46.14% |
| 15 | -1.3 | – | 56 | 1.05 | 0.91 | 12.17% | 16.94% | 20.39% | 5.36% | 5.60% | 5.17 | 48.58% |
| 16 (small) | -1.7 | – | 42 | 1.29 | 1.19 | 18.21% | 8.82% | 9.67% | 4.78% | 6.16% | 5.17 | 52.54% |

Note: "Log" reflects natural logarithm (base e = 2.71828)
Source of underlying data: Thomson Reuters Datastream and Worldscope.     *A Study of Return Differences Between Large and Small Companies in Europe (2017 update)*